Great Dutch Paintings from America

For Barbara,
Thank you for the
wonderful story in
your beautiful home.

September 22, 97

Winnie

Love

Evoy

Mauritshuis, The Hague
28 September 1990 – 13 January 1991

The Fine Arts Museums of San Francisco
16 February 1991 – 5 May 1991

Great Dutch Paintings from America

Catalogue by
Ben Broos

With contributions by
Edwin Buijsen
Susan Donahue Kuretsky
Walter Liedtke
Lynn Federle Orr
Juliette Roding
Peter C. Sutton

Final editing by
Rieke van Leeuwen

Exhibition organized by
Hans R. Hoetink

Mauritshuis, The Hague
Waanders Publishers, Zwolle

The exhibition has been organized by the Mauritshuis, The Hague,
and sponsored by Royal Dutch Petroleum Company,
the Dutch parent company of the Royal Dutch / Shell Group,
to mark the centenary of the company.

Production of the Exhibition

Project Group

Hans R. Hoetink *Chairman*
Wim Bloemberg *External coordinator*
Marjolein de Boer *Contributor to the catalogue*
Ben Broos *Main contributor to the catalogue*
Edwin Buijsen *Education and public guidance*
H. Jack Horn & Annètje Horn-Huibregtse *Dutch-English translation*
Rik van Koetsveld *Overall coordination*
Rieke van Leeuwen *Final editing and coordination of the catalogue*
Juliette Roding *Contributor to the catalogue*
Luuk Rutgers van der Loeff *Restoration and conservation*
Albert Verhaar *Finances*
Louise Vermeer *Secretariat*
Lieke Vervoorn *Press and publicity*

Selection Advisers

Beatrijs Brenninkmeyer-de Rooij, The Hague
Ben Broos, The Hague
Susan Donahue Kuretsky, Poughkeepsie
Lynn Federle Orr, San Francisco
Egbert Haverkamp-Begemann, New York
Walter Liedtke, New York
Otto Naumann, New York
Peter C. Sutton, Boston
Arthur Wheelock, Washington

Design of Exhibition, The Hague

Hans Bockting / Henk Hoebé (UNA), Amsterdam
Bureau Van Stapele, Amsterdam

Lenders to the Exhibition

Arlington, Va. *Private collection*
Boston, Mass. *Museum of Fine Arts*
Cambridge, Mass. *Fogg Art Museum, Harvard University Art Museums*
Champaign, Ill. *Krannert Art Museum, University of Illinois*
Chicago, Ill. *The Art Institute of Chicago*
Cincinnati, Ohio *The Taft Museum*
Cleveland, Ohio *The Cleveland Museum of Art*
Coral Gables, Fla. *Private collection*
Dayton, Ohio *The Dayton Art Institute*
Detroit, Mich. *The Detroit Institute of Arts*
Fort Worth, Tex. *Kimbell Art Museum*
Greenville, S.C. *Bob Jones University Collection*
Hartford, Conn. *Wadsworth Atheneum*
Houston, Tex. *Sarah Campbell Blaffer Foundation*
Kansas City, Mo. *The Nelson-Atkins Museum of Art*
Los Angeles, Calif. *Los Angeles County Museum of Art*
Los Angeles, Calif. *Collection Mr. and Mrs. Edward W. Carter*
Malibu, Calif. *The J. Paul Getty Museum*
Manchester, N.H. *The Currier Gallery of Art*
Minneapolis, Minn. *The Minneapolis Institute of Arts*
New Haven, Conn. *Yale University Art Gallery*

New York, N.Y. *The Metropolitan Museum of Art*
New York, N.Y. *Collection Richard L. Feigen*
New York, N.Y. *Private collection*
New York, N.Y. *Private collection*
Norfolk, Va. *Collection Mr. and Mrs. George M. Kaufman*
Northampton, Mass. *Smith College Museum of Art*
Oberlin, Ohio *Allen Memorial Art Museum, Oberlin College*
Philadelphia, Pa. *Philadelphia Museum of Art*
Poughkeepsie, N.Y. *Vassar College Art Gallery*
Providence, R.I. *Museum of Art, Rhode Island School of Design*
Raleigh, N.C. *North Carolina Museum of Art*
Richmond, Va. *Virginia Museum of Fine Arts*
Saint Louis, Mo. *The Saint Louis Art Museum*
San Diego, Calif. *Timken Art Gallery*
San Francisco, Calif. *The Fine Arts Museums of San Francisco*
San Francisco, Calif. *Sarah Ferris Cowles 1941 Trust*
Sarasota, Fla. *The John and Mable Ringling Museum of Art*
Toledo, Ohio *The Toledo Museum of Art*
Washington, D.C. *The Corcoran Gallery of Art*
Washington, D.C. *National Gallery of Art*
Worcester, Mass. *Worcester Art Museum*

Contents

In love of liberty and in the defense of it,
Holland has been our example.

Benjamin Franklin

Foreword

This exhibition of Dutch paintings from American collections presents a broad picture of the incredible richness of American art holdings in the domain of seventeenth-century painting of the United Provinces. Works have been gathered from more than forty museums and private collections in the United States. Many of these will be new to the European public, and some of them are inaccessible even to the American public.

Great Dutch Paintings in America may be viewed as the American counterpart of the exhibition of some forty paintings from the Mauritshuis that traveled through the United States between 1982 and 1984. This exhibition, which was on view in Washington, Fort Worth, Chicago, Los Angeles, and New York, was organized at the time in the context of the celebrations for the bicentennial of Dutch-American diplomatic relations.

Of course, the quality of the works chosen played an important role in the assembly of the present exhibition. From the very beginning, however, it was the intention to do more in this exhibition than show a number of handsome masterpieces. This display is a representation of the fruits of two centuries of collecting in America. During this period there was assembled in the United States a quantity of seventeenth-century Dutch masters almost unequaled in richness and diversity. When we further consider that not quite two centuries ago, in 1794, Holland was the first nation to lend the still young American republic twelve million dollars – as much as the entire American foreign debt at the time – then we realize what changes have taken place in the world.

At the end of the eighteenth century, John Adams, the later Emissary of the North American States to the United Netherlands, still wondered if the Fine Arts indeed served truth, virtue, compassion, or honor. 'From the dawn of history they have been prostituted to the service of superstition and despotism,' he wrote. It was nevertheless around this time that the first modest collectors emerged in New York, Boston, and Baltimore, and, judging from the evidence of a letter of 1780 to his wife, Adams was aware that an interest in art and the humanities would be granted to his progeny. It is the collecting activity of the generations of Adams's grandchildren and their offspring that occupies our attention in this exhibition.

I look back with pleasure at the first discussions that I carried on in 1986 with my colleagues Arthur Wheelock in Washington and Peter Sutton in Boston, both of whom at once reacted positively to the plans. I am also deeply grateful to the other consulting scholars: Egbert Haverkamp-Begemann, New York; Susan Donahue Kuretsky, Poughkeepsie; Walter Liedtke, New York; and Otto Naumann, New York, for their advice with the choice of works. Gratitude also extends to Beatrijs Brenninkmeyer-de Rooij, who, in the early stages, carried on research with respect to the origins of the American collections.

Naturally we were not able to realize the ideal list of art works that we had envisaged. On one hand, many collections have restrictive policies concerning lending, and on the other, the condition of several requested works precluded loan. How gladly would we have shown Rembrandt's *Aristotle* in the museum where his *Homer* may be admired, or Vermeer's *Allegory on the Catholic Faith*! Abraham Bredius, the former director of the Mauritshuis, once sold the latter painting, which was his own property, to the American collector Friedsam, who in turn left the work to the Metropolitan Museum of Art in New York. This same museum houses the legacy of Benjamin Altman, once one of the most important American collectors of Dutch art. It is established, however, that works from this legacy may never leave the museum. Similar restrictive regulations also apply to the works in the Frick Collection in New York, as well as to the paintings in the Isabella Stewart Gardner Museum in Boston. We are all the more grateful to the lenders who did agree to part with their precious works. In addition to the private lenders, I want especially to mention the National Gallery of Art in Washington, which has added luster to this exhibition with a generous contribution of no fewer than six paintings.

The exhibition makes clear how important a role the American private collectors have played, and continue to play, in the formation of the public collections of the United States. It is lamentable that so many important collections have left the Netherlands over the years. Famous collections of the nineteenth century, such as those of Verstolk Van Soelen (1846), King

William II (1850), and Vis Blokhuizen (1870), have largely disappeared, and in our century such collections as Steengracht (1913), Six (1908 and 1928), Ten Cate (after 1940), Van Aalst (1960), Dreesmann (1960), De Geus van den Heuvel (1976), Wetzlar (1977), and Sidney van den Bergh (after 1977) have been lost to our country forever. As the Dutch masters of the seventeenth century were in demand very early on, this exodus of Dutch cultural heritage has a long history.

Moreover, the Dutch paintings had political implications for Americans (just as they did for the French in the nineteenth century). Americans saw a parallel between our Republic's revolt against absolutism and their own struggle for freedom and democratic beginnings. The early capitalism of the free trade of the seventeenth century had affinities with their own culture, with the supposed realism and everyday subjects of Dutch paintings inspiring the American citizens to 'truth' and 'virtue.' The numerous art dealers of European background, such as Duveen, Seligmann, Sedelmeyer, Kleinberger, Rosenberg, and Stiebel & Shickmann, together with scholars who emigrated from Europe, such as Valentiner, Rosenberg, Stechow, Held, and Haverkamp-Begemann, created a climate in which many private and public collections, as well as college and university museums, could flourish successfully.

It was our intention from the beginning that this exhibition would also be shown in America. The choice fell on The Fine Arts Museums of San Francisco. I owe many thanks to the director of this institution, Harry S. Parker III, and his staff members, not only for the important contribution from their museum collection, including Rembrandt's *Portrait of Joris de Caulerij*, but also for the great support that they gave us. We have the best of memories of the meetings that we had with the staff of this museum. The Mauritshuis has greatly benefited from the help and advice of this institution with the compilation of the catalogue and in the realms of transport, insurance, and general organization. Besides Director Harry S. Parker III, I would especially like to thank Lynn Federle Orr, Curator of European Paintings; Ann Heath Karlstrom, Publications Manager; Kittu Gates, former Chief Registrar; and Therese Chen, Registrar.

This exhibition came about thanks to the staff members of the Mauritshuis and of The Fine Arts Museums of San Francisco. It was a privilege to be able to work in both museums with such an inspired and motivated team. The project group did a great deal of work during the lengthy preparations. Rik van Koetsveld was responsible for the organization and the administrative supervision of the exhibition, ably seconded by Wim Bloemberg, who was attached to the exhibition as project manager, and from whom we received valuable managerial advice. Edwin Buijsen served with enthusiasm as secretary of the selection procedure and has taken intelligent charge of the educational program. Lieke Vervoorn, Public Relations Manager, was responsible for the publicity and contacts with the press, supported by the Bureau Burson-Marsteller. Albert Verhaar looked after the financial administration, and Luuk Rutgers van der Loeff, as restorer, took upon herself the care of the works on loan.

Finally, a special word of thanks is in order to the staff of the Mauritshuis, which, under the direction of Messrs. Van der Spek, Zech, and Dutour Geerling, prepared the Mauritshuis for the exhibition. The contribution of the Friends of the Mauritshuis Foundation and the enthusiastic and valued participation of the many volunteers deserve our gratitude as well.

Especially close attention has been paid in the catalogue to the provenance of paintings, as will appear from the scholarly and insightful texts written by Ben Broos, Curator at the Mauritshuis. It is precisely through the study and description of provenances, or at times supposed provenances, that the fascinating peregrinations of art works are revealed to us, and, in addition, a new understanding of the changing taste, perspective, and interests of the American collectors is formed. Because of this approach, the catalogue will become a reference work for the history of collecting and the development of taste in the old and new West, clearly differentiating it from other exhibition catalogues.

To lend greater depth to the exhibition, several detailed essays precede the catalogue section. We are exceptionally beholden to the authors of these essays. In his article, Walter Liedtke discusses the origins of the collecting of seventeenth-century Dutch paintings in the United States, the history of taste and the interest in diverse genres, and the birth of the great museums in this century.

To balance the view, Edwin Buijsen sketches a picture of the reactions caused in the Netherlands by the American collecting activities. Susan Donahue Kuretsky describes the typically American phenomenon of the college or university teaching museum, in which, within the framework of the humanities, works of art occupy a different place than in most European museums. Peter Sutton then presents the development of the

American art market during the last decades, with emphasis on recent private collectors. These essays place the exhibition in a broader historical perspective, which we hope will allow this publication to make a lasting contribution to the field of the history of collecting, a topic that has gained considerable interest in recent years.

In addition to Ben Broos, who wrote most of the voluminous text of this catalogue, I thank Rieke van Leeuwen for her intensive coordinating and editorial activities. Also thanks to the sleuth work of Marjolein de Boer, numerous previously unknown facts and provenances have been revealed during the research for this exhibition. Lynn Orr wrote several of the texts for the catalogue section and, together with Elise Breall, carried out supplementary research for the biographies and literature. In addition to her texts for this catalogue, Juliette Roding supplied the translations of the majority of the American contributions. With great dedication, Hendrik Horn of the University of Guelph in Canada undertook the extensive task of translating the Dutch texts into English. Ann Karlstrom and Fronia Simpson supplied editorial assistance with the preparation of the American edition. We are also grateful to the following people for their selfless help and the information they supplied: Huub van Baarle, Juliusz A. Chrościcki, Hans C. Cramer, Frits J. Duparc, Hans C. Haar, Georges Keyes, Wouter Kloek, Thomas B. Parker, Peter van der Ploeg, Michael Robinson, Otto Schutte, Sam Segal, Jaap van der Veen, Edward van Voolen, Sally Wages, Dennis Weller, and the members of the Rembrandt Research Project. We further wish to express our thanks for the help and contributions received from the Rijksbureau voor Kunsthistorische Documentatie. In addition, we are indebted to the photographic service of the Rijksmuseum in Amsterdam for their cooperation, as well as to the photographer Daniël van der Ven.

Hans Bockting was once again in charge of the design of this catalogue. The printer Waanders has, with great dedication and sense of quality, managed to deliver the catalogue on time.

That an exhibition as precious and extensive as this one could take place at all, we owe to the Royal Dutch Petroleum Company. It chose to add luster to its centennial celebrations with this exhibition organized by the Mauritshuis, which not only represents a highpoint of artistic sensibility but also shows an international character due to the origins of the exhibited works. I particularly wish to commemorate the friendly ties with Mr.

J.G. Hoogland, ex-director Public Affairs of Shell Nederland b.v., who, from the first exchange of ideas, followed the preparations for the exhibition with never-flagging interest. I am greatly beholden to him for his advice. I suspect that he did much within Shell to promote the idea of including an exhibition in this celebration. I am also most grateful to Mr. P.W.H. van der Laan, who showed great understanding of the museological problems and who stood by us in word and deed.

With feelings of deep gratitude, we make mention of the fact that the Ministry of Welfare, Public Health, and Culture has shown itself prepared, within the framework of the indemnity settlement, to grant us an important governmental guarantee.

May this exhibition not only create a picture of the American collections and their collectors, but also make it clear how important a contribution the Netherlands have made to the formation of a new culture.

Hans R. Hoetink, *Director Mauritshuis*

Essays

Walter Liedtke
Curator of Dutch and Flemish Paintings
The Metropolitan Museum of Art, New York

Dutch Paintings in America
The Collectors and Their Ideals

Once in a London bookstore an American living abroad overheard the conversation of a couple who had wandered briefly from their transatlantic shore. '*French Paintings in Soviet Museums*: what will they think of next?' wondered the woman loudly, as if the title of the large book before her were little different from 'Polish Paintings in Peru.'

The reader will think of several reasons why French, and Dutch, and Flemish paintings are among the greatest treasures of Soviet museums, as well as those of other countries such as England. In the case of America, however, it would be appropriate to compare the country's collections of Dutch paintings rather than those of any other Continental school, and to concede at the outset that the history of collecting in the United States and Canada is very different from that of any land in which Americans may trace their ancestors. Why should hundreds of outstanding Dutch pictures be preserved in this much younger country? The scholar has no ready explanation, rather like the lady in the bookstore; knowledge of seventeenth- and eighteenth-century culture will not help bring together the stories of two widely separate lands.

In the 1660s, when Charles II was enjoying the magnificent 'Dutch Gift' of pictures, and when the French nobleman De Monconys and other traveling connoisseurs were visiting the studios of Dutch artists such as Vermeer and Rembrandt, and still in 1696 and 1718, when Peter the Great attended auctions in Holland and consulted with his agents about what paintings should be sent to Saint Petersburg, there were possibly more works by Dutch artists in Bali than in New York. The settlers of New Amsterdam, as the town was known between 1626 and its loss to the English in 1664, had fewer opportunities, and probably less interest, in acquiring Dutch drawings, prints, and paintings than did the officials of the East India Company.

The status of America as a latecomer to the collecting of Dutch art does not make this story simpler. On the contrary, the reader who is passingly familiar with the acquisitions of Catherine the Great, with her French and German sources (Crozat, Cobentzl, Brühl, and other eminent *amateurs*), and with the origins of the galleries in cities such as Berlin, Brunswick, Copenhagen, Kassel, London, Munich, Stockholm, and Vienna will have some idea of the political and social circumstances that gave rise to great collections of Dutch and Flemish art. The history of American collecting has no comparable framework of historical events. A broad outline would include vague associations with the Netherlands in the name of democracy, religious freedom, the rising middle class, the 'Protestant work ethic,' the importance of home and family, or the concept of realism in art and literature. The concrete details, by contrast, turn the student's attention immediately to distractingly local personalities such as the Codmans of Boston, Robert Gilmor in Baltimore, and the Messrs. Johnston and Blodgett who in 1871 bought *en bloc* about 175 paintings, most of them Dutch and Flemish, on behalf of the previously pictureless Metropolitan Museum of Art. It is true that with the turn of the century one encounters names of greater resonance: Frick, Morgan, Mellon, Widener, and Altman, to cite some of the grand acquisitors discussed below. However, most readers will have little idea what these men did apart from collect.

Our subject, then, is at once narrow and exceedingly broad, for the larger theme is the relationship of the arts in America to European culture. To merely chronicle the collectors of Dutch art from the beginning, which may be placed about 1830, would be a painfully parochial approach. Americans adore pioneers, and some American scholars would make much of Gilmor and other early accumulators (they were not collectors in the discriminating sense) of paintings by seventeenth-century Dutch artists. It would take many Gilmors to equal the importance of Sir Robert Peel, whose collection of fifty-five Dutch, twelve Flemish, and ten English pictures was bought by the National Gallery, London, in 1871. However, the comparison does not give the European scholar license to indulge in his own kind of ethnocentrism by dismissing Gilmor, Richard Codman, and their contemporaries as provincial arrivistes. This patronizing view would fail to recognize that the American acquisitions (which were usually made abroad) were part of an international tendency, as the precisely contemporary purchases of the London and New York collections suggest. Furthermore, the foreign critic should concede, if only to make up for a certain Englishwoman's estimate of life in Cincinnati (Frances Trollope,

Domestic Manners of the Americans, 1832), that collectors such as Gilmor, William Walters, and his son Henry (who gave the family treasures to Baltimore) were far more beneficial to the aesthetic well-being of their native cities than collectors of equal magnitude ever could have been in the major cities of the Old World. The 'drawing rooms' of Baltimore, Philadelphia, New York, and a few other cities offered native artists and *amateurs* small vignettes of Europe, which for many educated Americans represented the history of civilization, the embodiment of culture, and the source of finer things.

Gilmor himself sounds a familiar American refrain in the following assessment of his activities: '[My collection] is no doubt equal if not superior to most in the country, yet one good picture of a London cabinet would be worth the whole [...]. I have however seen much worse collections abroad, and if mine only stimulates my countrymen to cultivate a taste for the Fine Arts I shall be well compensated for my expense in making it even such as it is.'[1] The realism and especially the idealism of these lines were echoed by many American collectors later in the nineteenth century.

Gilmor's hopes for the fine arts in America were not fulfilled overnight. When Henry James wrote his early novel *Roderick Hudson* (1875), American collectors frequently resembled his character Mr. Leavenworth who owned large mines of borax in Pennsylvania. He seeks out Roderick Hudson, the momentary sensation of American society in Rome, and commissions him to carve in marble 'an allegorical representation of Culture'; it will be set to striking effect against the leather bindings in the library of Leavenworth's mansion 'on the banks of the Ohio' (Cincinnati again).[2] Leavenworth and Hudson are aesthetic opposites in their equally American responses to European art. For the patron it is a concept – or rather, an attribute – that the self-made man should grasp. For the artist it is Eden, a world of sensations complete with the Temptation and the Fall. Americans had very mixed emotions about Europe in the second half of the nineteenth century, emotions that were complexly rooted in the Puritan heritage, independence, provincialism, pride. 'Culture' was clothed in revealing garments of French or Italian style.

Three decades after Roderick Hudson lost his soul and his life, Chad Newsome, of the fictional but familiar Woollett, Massachusetts, is in Paris, from which he may never return (Henry James, *The Ambassadors*, 1903). Mr. Strether, the mild-mannered 'ambassador' who is sent by Chad's wealthy mother to fetch him home, decides that more time in Europe would be just the right thing for the remarkably refined young man. The next ambassadors from Woollett are led by Chad's hopelessly proper sister, who chaperones her thick-skinned husband and a shy, lovely young woman to whom Chad presents a copy of *Les maîtres d'autrefois*.[3]

Nearly ninety years later, one can no longer discuss America and Europe in terms of Mr. Leavenworth and Chad. American culture has changed greatly (and had already changed greatly by 1903) since the middle of the nineteenth century, when Nathaniel Hawthorne wrote of 'no antiquity, no mystery, no picturesque and gloomy wrong, nor anything but a common-place prosperity.'[4] Students of American taste have much to learn from Hawthorne, in part because he was, as James described him, one of the last innocents abroad.[5] There is even more to learn from James, who was most at home in Europe, but who understood and loved, as he would a difficult parent (or his brother William), his native land. Americans of the nineteenth century, not to mention Thomas Jefferson's time, did not inherit, never grew up with, rich legacies from the past. Culture was imported or made out of whatever materials lay at hand. The proper approach to this subject, then, is neither American nor European but something in between, and something like that of Henry James.

Hawthorne's reference to 'no antiquity' is repeated patiently by tour guides at Versailles, who remind their New World visitors that everything in sight is older than their country. Tourists have disproportionately served as ambassadors of American culture at least since the time when one of them, Mark Twain, wrote *Innocents Abroad* (1869). Travelers in the other direction usually came to stay, but one remarkable exception, Alexis de Tocqueville, toured the country (in so far as it was settled) to study the effects of democratic government (*De la démocratie en Amérique*, 1835). The liberal politician concentrated on questions of intellect and sensibility, categories he was better prepared to evaluate than was Mrs. Trollope. American literature had barely begun, according to the Frenchman, because of the slim supply of books from England, lack of leisure time (in a democracy), and a generally negative attitude towards the arts and letters (and their traditional patrons) on the part of America's settlers. As for art and architecture, 'they will habitually prefer the useful to the beautiful, and they will require that the beautiful be useful.'[6] Earlier and later expressions of this predisposition abound, from Jefferson's handsomely useful home, Monticello (built between 1789 and 1809), and countless more modest dwellings (for example, those in the Shaker style) to the arguments of our own aesthete, James, in his comparison of Jan van der Heyden's trustworthy architectural transcriptions with the fanciful manner of Guardi ('debauched, as it were, by the grace of his daily visions').[7] The history of American architecture, and of painting (portraiture is the only category worth considering in the period before Jefferson's time), is one of clear concepts underscored by temperate embellishment. Similarly, the taste for Dutch and Flemish art has been highly selective, favoring the no-nonsense genres of landscape, still life, and portraiture. Teniers was the only popular Flemish artist (although he was often described as Dutch); Van Dyck was widely regarded as an English painter, and Rubens as a degenerate.[8]

In American art and architecture, and in a study of American society, one frequently senses affinities with qualities that are Dutch, or that an American might be inclined to consider Dutch. Surely De Tocqueville had the Netherlands as well as America in mind when he observed that 'in aristocracies, a few great pictures are produced; in democratic countries, a vast number of insignificant ones.'[9] And De Tocqueville's reader, especially one looking for reminders of Holland, will find them in the most sweeping observations and in the most anecdotal remarks. Americans focus on the family, on work, on physical objects, on independent observation, on the effort to survive ('The whole life of an American is passed like a game of chance, a revolutionary crisis, or a battle').[10] They have 'but little faith for whatever is extraordinary, and an almost insurmountable distaste for whatever is supernatural'; their Catholics do not pay much attention to the saints.[11] 'Americans of all ages, all conditions, and all dispositions, constantly form associations [...] religious, moral, serious, futile, general or restricted, enormous or diminutive.'[12] One recalls the *rederijkers*, the civic guards, the painters' guild, and different kinds of Calvinists, but also Courbet ('Show me an angel and I'll paint one') and the Japanese.

We find what we are looking for and in the end can only speak of parallels and affinities, one of which is the American or Dutch capacity to assimilate foreign influence on native terms. Americans are as insular as the English when it comes to comprehending foreign qualities from a domestic point of view. Monticello is French architecture made suitable to Virginia, quite as American still lifes [11] and other American paintings dating from before the mid-nineteenth century have Continental compositions but hardly a trace of their models' surface effects.

However, one should be wary of this Malrauxian sort of aperçu. The Peales may have had different sensibilities than their European predecessors, but it is important to add that they knew Dutch and Flemish still-life painting mostly through cheap decorative pieces that themselves were merely patterned on the sophisticated pictures of the seventeenth and eighteenth centuries. In this light, one could interpret the literalism of American still-life painting as a return of Dutch values to compositions in which they had become lost. The question of what was available in the United States is central to discussions of Dutch influence on American art, and of collecting in America. Broadly speaking, very few good Dutch paintings crossed the Atlantic before the end of the Civil War (1865).

The following period, from about 1870 to the First World War, was the first and the greatest age of collecting Dutch art (and much else) in America. The 'Gilded Age' that takes its two-edged name (for Gilded is not Golden) from Twain's novel of 1873 was a period of extraordinary economic development, of exploiting natural resources, of building industry and railroads, of banking and financial speculation, and, in Twain's opinion, of ruthless individualism and rampant materialism. The 'embarrassment of riches' was felt mostly in Boston;[13] Twain's less inhibited targets lived in New York and Philadelphia. His subject was not the civic-mindedness that gave rise to America's great libraries and museums, but the new spirit that led to the construction of the country's 'French' châteaux. The palace on Fifth Avenue built for William Vanderbilt in 1881, the Breakers in Newport constructed for Cornelius Vanderbilt 11 in 1893, and the extravagant Biltmore near Asheville, North Carolina, erected for George Vanderbilt in 1895, are among the many mansions (these three by the Paris-trained American, Richard Morris Hunt) that rarely contained good Dutch pictures or any other kind chosen with an appreciation of their intrinsic qualities. The great age of collecting Dutch art in America was not a period in which Dutch ancestry, direct ties with the Netherlands, or even an endorsement of values that were perceived to be Dutch had much to do with the formation of major private collections.

However, this thesis is more positive than it sounds. In the same period there was a widespread admiration of Dutch culture, and of seventeenth- and nineteenth-century Dutch art. Public collections were comparatively rich in Dutch pictures, to which American artists were as responsive as their French counterparts. Even the grand collectors, who were inclined (and encouraged by dealers) to concentrate on the big names, included among them Hobbema, Ruisdael, Wouwermans, Cuyp,

1

Johannes Vermeer
Woman with a Water Jug
Canvas, 45.7 x 40.6 cm (18 x 16 in.)
Neither signed nor dated (ca. 1664)
New York, The Metropolitan Museum of Art,
Marquand Collection, inv. no. 89.15.21

The painting was purchased in Paris by Henry
Marquand in 1887, and given by him to the museum
two years later. This was the first of ten Vermeers to
enter American collections before 1920 (there are
now fourteen).

and Vermeer as well as Hals and Rembrandt. Of course, these were lessons learned from England and France,[14] but Frick, Mellon, Morgan, Widener, and Altman learned them readily. Or they needed no lesson at all: the moment in 1907 when Morgan first heard of Vermeer was reportedly the moment after a painting by the artist was set in front of him and a moment before he bought it (cat. no. 67).[15] This was the fifth of eight Vermeers to enter American collections between 1887 (when Henry Marquand bought the *Woman with a Water Jug* [1] as a De Hooch) and the beginning of the First World War.

In this introductory section our lines have circled around a central point, which is that, with all due respect to New Amsterdam, to America's old Dutch families, and to Dutch support for the United States during the Revolutionary War,[16] the taste for Dutch art in America has been mostly a matter of 'elective affinities,' to borrow Goethe's term (1809) of about the time that Dutch paintings may first be traced in America. There were occasions when affinity became analogy – as in the American writer Motley's epic history (1852) of the Dutch republic – to the American ideals of democracy and religious freedom (which for Motley meant Protestantism).[17] But American sympathy for Dutch culture and American taste for

Dutch pictures have often been spontaneous, and more deeply rooted than even Motley's enthusiasm would suggest. Therefore it would be worthwhile to consider the nature of American culture during the two centuries before any Americans collected Dutch art.

From the Puritans to the Revolutionary War

The seventeenth-century American town was on or near the East Coast and was home to a provincial English society. Still in 1700, about seventy percent of the immigrant population was English, and another twenty percent was Irish, Scotch, or Welsh. There were Dutch in New York (which became increasingly Anglicized), Germans in Pennsylvania, and other communities of non-British immigrants who taken as a whole did not alter the pattern of American culture.

What made this predominantly English society American was that the settlers had left home, often as families (unlike the Spanish), for economic or religious reasons, and in either case with a display of determined independence. Jamestown was settled in 1607 by the Virginia Company, a private enterprise modeled on the Dutch East India Company and intended to exploit the mineral and other natural resources of the New World. Over the next few decades the settlers died like flies, mostly from diseases such as malaria, although the 'Indians,' who were themselves scattered in small, independent tribes (in contrast to natives of South America), massacred over three hundred Virginians on a single day in 1662. The moment was not yet ripe for dabbling in the fine arts.

The English government and the Church of England differed from their Spanish counterparts in that they paid little attention to the American settlers, whose self-sufficiency became an attitude as well as an absolute necessity. They adhered to various faiths which often were radical or fundamentalist versions of Protestantism. The Pilgrims, for example, were extreme Separatists (every congregation should, in their view, be completely separate from the national church) who went by way of Holland to Massachusetts in 1620. Far more numerous were the Puritans, whose various groups wished to cleanse the Church of England from within, purifying it of every remnant of Catholicism. Thousands of Puritans settled in eastern Massachusetts, founded Boston, and in 1639 formed a separate colony in Connecticut. The Puritans imposed their own orthodox doctrines which caused the formation of other independent groups such as the colony of Rhode Island.

By the end of the seventeenth century there were settlements in all the coastal states from Massachusetts to the Carolinas, with a total population of about 250,000. The colonists endured severe hardships but flourished sufficiently to attract closer attention from the English government. By the mid-eighteenth century, all the colonies but four had English governors and an increasing number of officials, whose main interests were in taxes and maritime trade. Different economic levels of society developed through the 1700s, although they never came close to resembling the class distinctions of England and the Continent. The wealthiest families of Virginia and New York lived more modestly than almost any English landowner. On the other hand, most American farmers owned their own land. With few poor and no nobility, Americans of the eighteenth century were already more uniformly middle-class than the Dutch, let alone the English and others, had ever been.

The American economy was very different from that of Holland in the Golden Age; this alone would have discouraged an interest in the arts comparable to the circumstances of seventeenth-century Haarlem and Amsterdam, or for that matter Zwolle and Leeuwarden. There were no cities in America, there was abundant land, and either too little wealth or too many possibilities for investment to consider any income disposable. Furthermore, one or two generations and a great ocean separated American society from the example of people who appreciated the fine arts.

Surveys of American colonial art say the same thing differently. The adherents of Puritanism abhorred 'frivolity and show [...] yet its ideals were as important for the arts as for other aspects of American culture.'[18] Puritanism encouraged skill in the crafts since they were practical, and a 'plain style' of speech, writing, and representation. 'Plain' styles do not lack a strong aesthetic viewpoint, as admirers of Calvinist or Colonial churches, early American furniture, conservative Dutch portraits, or early American portraits will realize. Nor did the Puritan disposition preclude, in its search for simplicity, attention to realistic detail. The conviction that each individual was a separate soul with a fate foreseen in Heaven, and that every event and each object in nature was a part of God's great plan, encouraged an approach to portraiture, and later (and less directly) to landscape and still life, that recalls that of Dutch drawings *naer 't leven* (from life). This New England heritage partially explains why, for Henry James, the principal virtues of a Dutch painter such as Jan van der Heyden were 'fidelity and sincerity.'[19]

The similarities between American and Dutch culture are,

however broad, more important for the 'Dutch' qualities of American art than are any actual cases of Dutch art influencing American painting. To be sure, there are isolated exceptions, and even a few general exceptions in the late and comparatively sophisticated period around 1880 to 1910. But the statement holds true for every epoch of American art and may serve as a word of caution to those particular Americanists for whom seventeenth-century Dutch painting is simply a byword for straightforward realism. The point is important for this essay because indisputably Dutch qualities – meaning stylistic conventions – in the tradition of American painting were insufficient for the purpose of fostering an appreciation of Dutch art. For the most part, American collectors admired Dutch pictures as typical Americans, not as *amateurs*.

The distinction is also emphasized here because historians of American painting cite numerous instances of Dutch influence where the present writer sees none whatsoever, or rather, discerns a *basso continuo* of conservative Dutch forms coming in almost every instance by way of middling artists in England. A prominent scholar of American art, by contrast, maintains in a standard survey that 'the crisp rendering of the skull and the sympathetic treatment' of the face in the *Portrait of Dr. John Clark* [2] 'recall the strength of Dutch realism. In fact, the general portrait format and presentation of the skull and instruments as still-life elements bring to mind Rembrandt's portraits of individuals as well as group pictures such as *Dr. Tulp's Anatomy Lesson*.'[20] Similarly, in that icon of colonial American portraiture, *Portrait of Mrs. Freake and Baby Mary* [3], dated 1674, the 'emphasis on material belongings and the directness of

3
American
Portrait of Mrs. Freake and Baby Mary
Canvas, 108 x 93.4 cm (42 ¹/₂ x 36 ³/₄ in.)
Neither signed nor dated (ca. 1671-1674)
Worcester, Mass., Worcester Art Museum, Gift of Mr. and Mrs. Albert W. Rice, inv. no. 1963.134

Radiographs recently revealed that the costume was modified and the baby was added to the composition around 1674.

2
Attributed to Augustine Clement
Portrait of Dr. John Clark
Canvas, 87.6 x 68.9 cm (34¹/₂ x 27 ¹/₈ in.)
Left center: *1664*
Boston Medical Library in the Francis A. Countway Library of Medicine

observation doubtless reflect Dutch sources.' Dutch readers will find these pictures intriguing, but would they agree that in a child's portrait similar to the one reproduced here [4] 'the floor of black and white tiles [...] seems taken directly from Dutch examples, such as the portraits of children by Paulus Moreelse or interior scenes by Vermeer and others'? Why 'directly' (and why Vermeer), one might ask, when the same tiles may be obtained from anonymous painters in seventeenth-century Cambridge (or Copenhagen)? Finally, in Thomas Smith's *Self-Portrait* [5] of about 1690 the American tradition departs from the 'manner of provincial English portraiture towards the fuller modelling, richer gradations of lighting, and more convincing spatial ambiance of seventeenth-century Dutch and Flemish art.' Specifically, 'the decisive change that has taken place is the imprint of Rubens' and van Dyck's style.'

In reading these lines the scholar of Dutch art feels like a Chinese wondering what is Chinese about a Chinese Chippendale chair. There is no need to press on further eastward than Norfolk or Suffolk to find sources for these various examples of early American portraiture,[21] although they remind one of conservative Dutch portraits in a more general and perhaps more significant way. In each case where the American painter has succeeded on his own terms the individual is impressively particularized; the facial features, the pose, and a restricted repertoire of objects and backgrounds are adjusted to suggest personality. Simple, not sophisticated, conventions limit the portraitist, which is almost the inverse of what happened in London during the generations of Lely and Kneller, and in America during the first half of the eighteenth century [6]. 'The imprint of [...] van Dyck's style' was not what supported but what impeded the progress of a distinctly American style of portraiture between 1700 and 1750.[22]

The increasing importance of European models for American art and architecture in the eighteenth century was one aspect of a changing society. The population grew rapidly with improved living conditions and continued immigration, which came less from England and more from Ireland, Scotland, and Germany. Religious beliefs and family backgrounds became remarkably diverse by 1775, when the non-native population numbered about one-and-a-half million whites and half a million blacks. This cultural complexity and territorial expansion (which was amplified by the British victory in the Seven Years' or French and Indian War) put a tremendous strain on the British budget and administration; the latter attempted to reverse fifty years of 'salutary neglect' (in Edmond Burke's phrase) by means of

4
Dutch artist active in America
Portrait of Sarra Depeyster
Canvas, 97.2 x 61.3 cm (38 ¼ x 24 ⅛ in.)
Upper left: *Sarra·Depeyster AEtatis / 30 · Maenden· 23 Mey·1631*
New York, The Metropolitan Museum of Art, Gift of Livingston L. Short and Anna Livingston Jones, 1961, inv. no. 61.154

5
Thomas Smith
Self-Portrait
Canvas, 62.2 x 60.4 cm (24 ½ x 23 ¾ in.)
Lower left, on paper: *TS* (in ligature) (ca. 1690)
Worcester, Mass., Worcester Art Museum, inv. no. 1948.19

direct taxation, restricted settlement (no whites west of the Appalachian Mountains), and a military occupation. The conflict between this attempt at centralized government from afar and the tradition of local rights and privileges deserves comparison with that of the Netherlands and Spain.[23]

The Revolutionary War of 1775 to 1783 resulted in American independence and a new sense of social identity. The absence of organization into established classes and religions, even the lack of refinement and luxury, came to be seen – by many Europeans as well as Americans – as republican virtues consistent with Enlightenment ideals. In the nineteenth century this image of the American as independent of inherited values ('no antiquity'), and especially of aristocratic decadence, was often linked to the concept of nature as the only trustworthy guide for art. It was precisely when this concept became a reactionary conviction – for example, in the pronouncements of the Society for the Advancement of the Truth in Art (founded, with its journal, *New Path*, in 1863) – that artists revealed paradoxical debts to Europe (in this case as embodied in the early writings of Ruskin).[24] The broader development of nineteenth-century American painting and the eventual abundance of Dutch pictures in American collections (in some cases side by side with American art) demonstrate in a less articulate but more profound way the close relationship between American self-perception and the premium placed on independent observation in the pictorial arts.

Between the Revolution and the Civil War (1783-1860)

John Smibert's instant success in Boston during the 1730s represents the principal means by which an American collector could purchase a European picture in the eighteenth century, which was to have a foreign artist arrive on his doorstep.[25] The Scot's copy of the head of Cardinal Bentivoglio by 'Vandyke' became the local equivalent of Michelangelo's *Cascina* cartoon for young artists in New England.[26] Any closer contact with the Masters required a trip abroad.

The best American artist of the eighteenth century, John Singleton Copley, came to this realization on the slim evidence of Smibert, the visiting portraitist Joseph Blackburn, the prints they had, and the tales they told. In Copley's famous portrait of his friend Paul Revere [7] and others of the late 1760s he was literally painting pictures better than any he had ever seen. The work is intensely American in its forthright description of appearances (the head and hands reveal how Copley was both

6
John Smibert
Portrait of Hannah Pemberton, Wife of the Boston Clergyman Benjamin Colman 11
Canvas, 76.2 x 63.5 cm (30 x 25 in.)
Neither signed nor dated (ca. 1736)
New York, The Metropolitan Museum of Art, inv. no. 43.51

7
John Singleton Copley
Portrait of Paul Revere
Canvas, 88.9 x 72.3 cm (35 x 28 ½ in.)
Neither signed nor dated (ca. 1768-1770)
Boston, Museum of Fine Arts, Gift of Joseph W., William B., and Edward H.R. Revere, inv. no. 30.781

disciplined and untrained) and of the sitter's station in society. As an 'occupational portrait' the painting is reminiscent of Rembrandt in the 1630s and other Dutch precedents of which Copley was apparently unaware.

It is worth noting that Copley's portraits and such modern history paintings as his *Watson and the Shark* (1778) and Benjamin West's *The Death of General Wolfe* (1770) were the most advanced and the most American pictures at the time when, in the 1790s, American collectors first bought paintings abroad. Copley and West, of course, moved permanently to England (West in 1763, after three years in Italy; Copley in 1775, after some months on the Continent). The subsequent story of American art cannot be repeated here, but it is important to recall that after Copley and West many American painters studied and traveled abroad (West's pupils in England included John Trumbull, Washington Allston, John Vanderlyn, Gilbert Stuart, Charles Willson Peale, Thomas Sully, Samuel F. B. Morse, and others – most of the major American artists active between 1780 and about 1840). This was 'the road to eminence which a painter ought to follow,' according to the artist William Dunlap in 1834.[27]

The same route was taken by the first American collectors of Dutch painting (and of European art in general), such as Richard Codman of Boston and Lincoln, Massachusetts. Codman ran a shipping firm with his brother John, and sailed to England as its representative in 1793. He sat to Copley in London and then went on to Paris where he lived lavishly for three years. His *hôtel* and two *châteaux* were filled with the kind of things that John Trumbull, in his later letter (1826) to President John Quincy Adams, described as reprehensible alternatives to American history pictures (of the sober sort he supplied to the Rotunda of the Capitol): 'expensive mirrors and all the frivolous and perishable finery of fashionable upholstery.'[28] Codman sent three shipments of European paintings, totaling over a hundred, to his brother before speculation in France's chaotic economy ruined Richard in 1799. The group of about eighty pictures ('some of them very pretty and done by the finest Masters') that was sent in 1794 apparently included the *Coast Scene* attributed to Willem van de Velde, the *Nymphs Bathing* ascribed to Van Poelenburch, and the small gouache assigned to Willem van Mieris that remain in the Lincoln house.[29] Codman also bought recent Dutch and Flemish genre scenes that in composition look right back to painters like Adriaen van Ostade (a pair by Jacques-Albert Senave) and Salomon Rombouts (the *Cattle Fair* by Jean-Louis Demarne) and forward to American genre scenes of the mid-nineteenth century. The canvas signed *De MARNE* was purchased in 1796 from the principal supplier of old masters in Paris, J.B.P. Lebrun, who gave Codman certificates of authenticity for at least twenty-four pictures. These included paintings by Schalcken, Teniers, 'Paterre,' and Greuze.

The consistency of taste evident even in the fragmentary records of the Codman family may be characterized by quoting Charles Russell Codman (son of John), who wrote that the Demarne 'bears the closest examination [...] each figure is exquisitely finished, as to give the whole [the] appearance of enamel... .'[30] The majority of Parisian *amateurs*, as well as artists such as Watteau, Lancret, Pater, and Greuze, admired the most finished Dutch and Flemish genre pictures; works by Dou, Metsu, Van Mieris, Schalcken, and such broadly comparable painters as Poelenburch, Van Ostade, Teniers, and Wouwermans would have come highly recommended by Lebrun and did come pouring out of French collections right after the Revolution. Thus the Codman house was a kind of mini-Mauritshuis or Cabinet of Willem v, to pay it an extravagant compliment.

The comparison is more excusable when considering the collecting efforts of Charles Russell Codman, who inherited some of his uncle's pictures from his father John. He toured Europe from 1808 until 1812, visiting Copley, West, and numerous museums and private collections. His Boston house, purchased in 1819, had a drawing room hung with pictures, including the Demarne, the 'Poelenburch,' a landscape attributed to Ruisdael, and a banquet still life bearing a Heda signature. In 1829 and 1830 Codman and his wife were in France, Germany, and the Netherlands visiting collections and probably buying some of the forty or fifty paintings he added to the family collection. Some of them were French or Italian, but it appears that most of the European pictures owned by Codman and his brothers were northern. He died in 1852, leaving his collection to his five children.

Charles Russell Codman was a supporter and regular lender to the Boston Atheneum, which in the mid-1820s built a three-story lecture and exhibition hall with a 'Gallery of Paintings' on the top floor. A closer look at the Codman and other Boston collections is now facilitated by the *Art Exhibition Index 1827-1874*, published by the Boston Atheneum in 1980.[31] The owner and artist indices (the latter, of course, give the owners' attributions) provide a fairly representative picture of Boston collections in the middle fifty years of the century. A number of prominent lenders had collections of mostly Italian and French paintings, with Dutch and Flemish pictures accounting for one-quarter or one-third of the loans. British artists made a comparatively modest showing compared with French, Italian, and Spanish (much Murillo), and seventeenth-century Dutch and Flemish (the latter favoring Van Dyck as well as Teniers and other genre and landscape painters). This strongly suggests that a 'supply-side' explanation is in order since the distribution among schools corresponds to that of the collections which were dispersed recently in France.

The American painters Trumbull and Allston were represented in the Atheneum exhibitions by several history pictures; perhaps the former artist would have explained the prevalence of Italian and French pictures (which were more Poussinist than rococo) as an expression of proper taste. However, most of the Trumbull paintings are listed in the catalogues as for sale, and pictures like his *Priam Receiving the Dead Body of Hector* are completely outnumbered by Copley and Stuart portraits (almost none of them for sale) and American landscape, still-life, and genre scenes.

In contrast to Robert Gilmor in Baltimore, Boston patrons of American art were usually not important collectors of European pictures (Dutch and Flemish included) at the same time. The Codman family lent the Atheneum works attributed to Berchem, Both, Cuyp, De Heem, Willem van Mieris, Aert van der Neer, Adriaen van Ostade (three), Poelenburch, Ruisdael (two or three), Schalcken (a *Diana*), Teniers (three), and Wouwermans (two), mostly in the exhibitions dating from 1827 to 1832. Other collectors, such as Benjamin Crowninshield and the insignificant Harrison Gray Otis (who thought he owned a Both, two Pijnackers, two Rembrandts, and a Steen),[32] were represented by dozens of Dutch landscapes and marines, plus a few still lifes, a number of late Leiden genre scenes, and paintings by Van Ostade and the inevitable Teniers. Two of the Atheneum lenders who had both northern and southern European pictures were actually dealers from out of town: the English visitor John Brett, who between 1833 and 1837 offered the usual variety of European paintings in Boston, New York, and Philadelphia; and William Hayward, a New York dealer whose stock of about a hundred European paintings in 1837 was half Dutch and Flemish. One of them was the *Portrait of a Shipbuilder and His Wife* 'by Rembrandt,' which was described by a friendly critic in the *New-York Mirror* as the finest picture in America, but as an old copy of the Queen of England's canvas (cat. no. 51, fig. 5) in a letter from Robert Gilmor to his friend in Philadelphia, Charles Graff.[33]

The effect of the French Revolution on the international art market was of considerable interest not only to Richard Codman but also to John Trumbull, despite his *vanitas* description of fashionable finery referred to earlier. With the advice of his friend Lebrun, Trumbull did a big business sending old masters out of France; about a hundred newly purchased pictures were shipped to London by Trumbull in 1795.[34] He was very much the gentleman dealer: son of Connecticut's governor, and secretary in London to Washington's envoy, John Jay. The painter was still dealing in 1825, when he was dickering with Gilmor (who did not trust him),[35] and ungracefully concluding two decades of dictatorial service as president of the American Academy of Fine Arts in New York. The founding of the National Academy of Design by Samuel F.B. Morse in 1825, Trumbull's resignation in 1836, and the final closing of the enfeebled American Academy in 1841 marked important moments in the period of social change known as the Jacksonian Democracy. Practicing artists were replacing patrician arbiters of taste in the running of academies and as the advisors, or at least the colleagues, of collectors and patrons of art.

More important than any other collector or patron in Boston was the Baltimore *amateur* Robert Gilmor, Jr. This is no discredit to Boston, which had many collectors in a smaller, older, and less mercantile society than those of New York, Philadelphia, and Baltimore. The Puritan heritage and the New England tradition of self-sufficiency may explain why the Museum of Fine Arts in Boston today has only a minor pair of Rembrandt portraits (donated in 1893), his early *Artist in the Studio* (a 1938 gift), the Elison pendant portraits by the same artist (purchased in 1956), and not a single genuine Van Dyck. Rembrandt and Van Dyck are two of the cornerstones of the great collections formed in the late nineteenth and early twentieth centuries, when American merchant princes sought out big names and an aura of venerable ancestry. The latter was never a problem in Boston, which not coincidentally is home to an extraordinary collection of American art.

Baltimore grew rapidly in the nineteenth century, as did Philadelphia and New York:

Population	in 1820	in 1860
Baltimore	63,000	212,000
Boston	43,000	178,000
New York	124,000	1,080,000
Philadelphia	113,000	566,000

The statistics also show that while Boston's population increased over four times between 1820 and 1860 it remained one-third the size of Philadelphia's and shrank from one-third to less than one-sixth the population of New York. These numbers are even more illuminating in that they document the growing size and economic strength of the country as a whole. In 1790 there were about 3,200,000 citizens and nearly 700,000 slaves. The total population was nearly 10,000,000 in 1820, 17,000,000 in 1840, and nearly 32,000,000 (ten percent of them slaves) in 1860. In the last year there were 9,000 miles of roads, more than in all of Europe. American ships were second only to Britain's in tonnage (but not in condition), and second to none in their reach around the globe.[36]

Robert Gilmor, Sr., was a Scottish shipper who traded with the American colonies before he settled in Baltimore around 1770.[37] His business flourished sufficiently to open American trade with Russia and India and to provide Robert, Jr. (1774-1848), with a fortune and the education of a European nobleman. After private tutoring he studied in Amsterdam, where he confided to his journal in 1800, 'I am become so great a Connoisseur, that I can instantly on entering a room point out even from the door all the principal pictures.'[38] Gilmor learned enough about European art over the next thirty years to give a considerably more modest estimate of his achievement (see p. 15) and to know when Trumbull, Pierre Flandin, or New York's most prominent dealer, the devious Michael Paff, were overrating their pictures.[39] He bought hundreds of paintings (holding 300 to 400 but constantly upgrading) from numerous American and English dealers and from private parties, including the Dutch consul

in Baltimore and Cornelis Apostool, the longtime director of the Koninklijk Museum (later Rijksmuseum) in Amsterdam.[40] Gilmor's inventories record about 150 Dutch and Flemish paintings, with all the usual names (as in Boston) but also landscape, genre, and architectural pictures that probably depend upon his Dutch contacts. Along with Berchem, Both, Metsu, Van Mieris, Schalcken, Teniers, and Wouwermans there is Backer, Bakhuizen, Ter Borch, Brouwer, Cuyp, Everdingen, Flinck, Van Goyen, Hals, De Heem, Van der Heyden, Hobbema, Molenaer, Molijn, Maes, Mierevelt, Aert van der Neer, Netscher, Van Ostade, Van der Poel, Ruysch, Van Ruisdael, Van Ruysdael, Savery, Seghers, Sorgh, Steen, Willem van de Velde, Wijnants, De Witte, and the large Hendrick van Vliet now in the Baltimore Museum (cat. no. 69, fig. 1).[41]

Unfortunately, few of these paintings can be traced. Gilmor's hope of leaving them to a public institution was frustrated by financial reverses in the 1830s, and no copy of his 'catalogue raisonné,' as he called it, is known today. However, it is clear that the roster of Dutch names in his collection is consistent not so much with the 'appearance of enamel' praised by Charles Russell Codman as with Gilmor's advice to Thomas Cole about English landscape as a source of inspiration ('too much artificial effect') and about Cole's own poetic inclinations: 'I prefer *real American* Scenes and compositions [...]. Nature, *nature*, after all is the great *Master* in landscape painting.'[42] Gilmor was a great supporter of Cole and other landscape painters of the Hudson River School and of the genre painter William Sidney Mount [8], all of whom had Dutch sources of their own (meaning paintings and engravings, not the director of the Koninklijk Museum).[43]

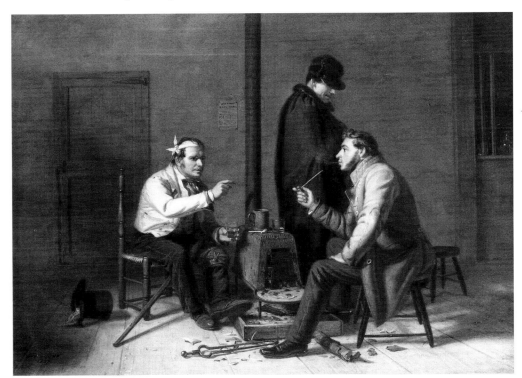

8
William Sidney Mount
The Long Story
Panel, 43.2 x 56 cm (17 x 22 in.)
Lower right: W. M S. MOUNT · / 1837.
Washington, Corcoran Gallery of Art, inv. no. 74.69

Apart from the brief appearance of the Belgian Baron de Stiers and his collection in Maryland between 1794 and 1803, the only other introduction to old master pictures in the area of Baltimore and Washington until the late nineteenth century was provided by the short-lived Baltimore Museum and Gallery of Paintings. It was opened by Rembrandt Peale in 1814 as an alternative, in his words, to the city's 'counting-houses' (such as Gilmor's?) where art and science were sacrificed to 'shortsighted commercial avarice.' American portraits and history pictures shared space with natural and ethnographic curiosities. Rubens Peale, taking over Rembrandt's curatorship in 1822, offered five annual exhibitions of various works of art found in the Peale family and other local collections. Catalogues survive for the years 1823 and 1825 and list works by Bakhuizen, Wouwermans, and Teniers as well as a few more celebrated names (Leonardo, 'Canaletti,' and 'Corregio'). The institution closed in 1830, as did several similar cloisters of culture during the next twenty years.[44]

The importance of the Peales, however, went far beyond their museum, or rather, museums. The father of Rembrandt, Rubens and so on, Charles Willson Peale (1741-1827), is well known for his realistic portraits and his own museum of artistic and natural creations. He studied with West in London (1766-1768) and then settled in Maryland. The portrait of his sons, Raphaelle (with the palette) and Titian Peale [9], dating from 1795, reveals an affinity for Dutch painting similar to that of Peale's colleague, Copley, and may have had a stronger connection, since some of the comparable murals by Samuel van Hoogstraten remained in London when Peale was there. The famous self-portrait of Peale in his own museum [10] is even

9
Charles Willson Peale
The Staircase Group (Titian and Raphaelle Peale)
Canvas, 226.2 x 100.3 cm (89 x 39 ½ in.)
Formerly signed and dated 1795 (below, on the card; now completely effaced)
Philadelphia Museum of Art, George W. Elkins Collection, inv. no. E '45-1-1

10
Charles Willson Peale
The Artist in His Museum
Canvas, 262.9 x 203 cm (103 ½ x 80 in.)
Neither signed nor dated (1822)
Left center, inscribed on the fish: *With this article the / Museum commenced / June 1784. / Presented by Mr. R. Patterson*
Philadelphia, The Pennsylvania Academy of the Fine Arts, Gift of Mrs. Sarah Harrison (The Joseph Harrison, Jr. Collection), inv. no. 1878.1.2

more reminiscent of Van Hoogstraten's perspective views and of Dutch portraits of collectors such as Daniel Mijtens's picture of the earl of Arundel before his hall of antique sculpture (Arundel Castle). Both of Peale's paintings employ illusionistic space (the earlier one with the help of an actual door frame and a real wooden step) to emphasize the artist's powers of realistic description, while the late work documents the artist's career as an amateur naturalist. Peale first planned his museum forty years earlier as 'a great school of nature,' and with public contributions established one in Philadelphia during the 1790s. A sister institution, the American Academy of Fine Arts, was the predecessor of the Pennsylvania Academy of Fine Arts. In 1802 the museum was moved to the top floor of Independence Hall. In the portrait, which was commissioned by the museum's trustees, stuffed birds and mastodon bones compete for attention and seem equally likely to activate the palette and brushes on the table (assuming they are Peale's and not those of his younger contemporary, John James Audubon).

Peale's sons and daughters addressed his central concerns in their portraits and still lifes [11], while contemporary painters such as Charles Bird King turned the trompe-l'oeil still life into an American specialty [12]. King studied with West in London from 1805 to 1812, where he surely admired examples of illusionistic still life by Dutch artists.[45] His sophisticated technique, the use of a niche as a shallow setting, and motifs such as reflecting glassware and tacked-up inscriptions on paper all derive from Dutch pictures, although King's paintings are original compositions with a complex and personal iconography. The illusionistic 'shelf' and 'rack' still lifes by John Frederick Peto

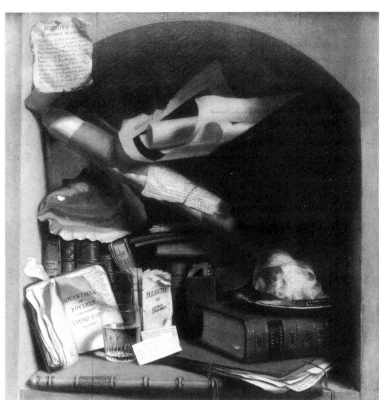

and William Harnett were painted at the end of the century and continued a widespread European tradition that ultimately may be traced back to Dutch artists such as Van Hoogstraten and Edwaert Collier. The inspiration of seventeenth-century Dutch art is also evident in King's genre paintings such as *The Itinerant Artist* [13], which dates from about 1830. By this point in his career King was acquainted with Gilmor.

Societies such as the Pennsylvania Academy of Fine Arts were important for the general interest in Dutch paintings as well as for living American artists. The annual exhibitions in Philadelphia from 1811 to 1836, for example, reveal an increase in Dutch and similar Flemish paintings (nothing Rubensian or Van Dyck-like) from twenty to forty percent.[46] The 1856 sale of the collection of Charles Graff, Gilmor's friend and frequent

correspondent, included fifty Dutch, twenty-six Flemish, and nineteen American paintings among the 143 works sold.[47]

In general, however, the trend in Philadelphia and other cities (especially Washington) was toward American art and also, in the more cosmopolitan centers, toward modern European pictures. The latter were strongly favored in the New-York Crystal Palace Exposition of 1853. Thus, a decade before the Civil War, the idea of patronage, of 'fostering' the arts, and also the desire to be fashionable, were to some extent replacing an interest in collecting old masters and the traditional notion that it was a patrician activity. This did not mean that the appeal of Dutch paintings was on the decline. On the contrary, the styles and subjects of seventeenth-century Dutch artists were generally sympathetic to the development of American painting and of the realistic movement in England and France (not to forget Holland and Belgium, whose artists were soon to be well represented in East Coast homes). The 'little masters' flourished while the Great Masters waned; Italian and French pictures were less popular until the beginning of the twentieth century.

This broad pattern is discernible in nineteenth-century New York despite the comparative complexity of its art market. In 1801 the Society of Fine Arts in New York hired the American painter John Vanderlyn to go to Paris to obtain casts of antique statues and copies of old masters: Raphael, Correggio, Titian, Caravaggio, Poussin, Rubens, and Rembrandt were on the list (four of these names were borne by the brothers Peale). Vanderlyn added Paulus Potter as a likely crowd-pleaser.[48] Seventy years later William Blodgett went off to Paris and Brussels on behalf of the Metropolitan Museum and bought

paintings as if Vanderlyn's opinion of Potter were ringing in his ears: 'These pictures, one hundred and seventy-five in number, are, as we may remind our readers, with some dozen exceptions, of the Dutch and Flemish schools.'[49] Numerous other instances, such as the Augustus Thorndike sale of 1860 in Boston (seventy-six of 104 paintings were Dutch or Flemish; twenty-seven were genre scenes) indicate that Blodgett was following the grain of American taste.[50]

Dealers such as Flandin and Paff were active on Broadway from about 1812, when Paff's catalogue included fifty Dutch and Flemish paintings, 111 other 'European,' and fifty-nine 'old masters.' Paff's sale of dubious pictures to Luman Reed (including two blatantly fake Teniers) encouraged the wholesale grocer to stick with modern American art, of which he was one of the leading patrons until his death in 1836.[51] The landscapes and genre scenes that Reed bought directly from William Sidney Mount and Asher B. Durand are reminiscent of Dutch genre interiors and of landscapes by Teniers; Reed also kept a dozen Dutch and Flemish paintings including Jan Fyt's large *Dogs and Game* in the New-York Historical Society.[52] The top floor of Reed's house served as The New-York Gallery of Fine Arts between 1836 and 1844; the collection's later exhibition at the National Academy of Design and its eventual transferral (in 1857) to the New York Historical Society partially fulfilled Reed's hope of founding a public art museum in New York. Other prominent New Yorkers – mayor Philip Hone a bit before Reed, and the latter's business partner, Jonathan Sturges, after him – shared both his public spirit and the practice of collecting American plus a small amount of Dutch and Flemish art.[53] By

13
Charles Bird King
The Itinerant Artist
Canvas, 113.7 x 146.7 cm (44 ³/₄ x 57 in.)
Neither signed nor dated (ca. 1830)
Cooperstown, New York State Historical Association, inv. no. N-537.67

contrast, the collection of Gideon Nye, when exhibited in 1848 at the National Academy of Design, consisted of sixty European paintings, with Italian, Dutch, Flemish, and other pictures each comprising about one-quarter of the whole.[54] Nye encouraged artists to study and connoisseurs to reattribute the works on view, which he hoped would form 'the nucleus of a Gallery worthy of the position held in New York.'[55]

Certainly the most important predecessor of the Metropolitan Museum's collection of European paintings was The Bryan Gallery of Christian Art. Thomas Jefferson Bryan (1802-1870) of Philadelphia was a Harvard graduate and for twenty-two years a resident of Paris before he settled in New York during the early 1850s. He promptly opened his gallery, which despite its name was concerned with art not Christianity (western civilization was evidently implied), and published a catalogue by Richard Grant White in 1853. One writer remembers his visit to Bryan, who lived next to his collection, as an experience 'like visiting a venerable burgomaster of Holland, or a merchant-prince of Florence in her palmy days [...] he seemed to belong to another sphere, and we have wandered from Babel to Elysium in thus entering his gallery from bustling and garish Broadway.'[56]

Of the 233 paintings exhibited, fifty-eight were Italian, and 101 were Dutch or Flemish. Bryan finally found the role of missionary curator an impossible demand on his time; after attempting other arrangements he gave the collection to the New-York Historical Society in 1867 [**14**]. At his death in 1870 the Historical Society received Bryan's bequest which raised the number of pictures given to 380, of which 146 were Dutch or Flemish. Like all collections of the time Bryan's was filled with

faulty attributions, but its standard was comparatively high. Two representative pictures are Adriaen van Ostade's sensitive *Mother and Child* (now in a private collection),[57] and the *Portrait of Moses ter Borch* by Gerard and Gesina ter Borch (on loan from the Historical Society to the Metropolitan Museum of Art). Unfortunately, most of the Bryan Collection was sold off by the Historical Society in 1971 and 1980.[58] It is generally maintained now that the Bryan Collection had little to do with the institution's purpose of preserving and presenting the history of New York State. Bryan, Nye, Reed, Gilmor, the Peales and other founders of American public art galleries surely would have considered such an opinion wrong.[59]

This formative and at the same time transitional period in the collecting of European art is not easily summarized, but Clark's dissertation and published material makes it easier to focus on the area of Dutch and Flemish painting.[60] He reviews the American expressions of sympathy for seventeenth-century Dutch culture during the first half of the nineteenth century. In 1814, George Murray, reviewing the Pennsylvania Academy's exhibition for *The Portfolio* magazine, compared patronage during the Golden Age in Holland to what could be in America: 'Who were the patrons of the artists? Merchants and other wealthy citizens – men of plain and simple manners, possessing taste without affectation.'[61] The combination of 'wealthy citizens' and 'plain and simple manners' may seem as American to Dutch readers as it seemed Dutch to Murray.

The familiar comparison between the United States and the United Netherlands as republics was made in George Bancroft's *History of the United States* (1834) twenty years before it became

14
Part of the Bryan Collection in the Inner Rooms of the Art Gallery, New-York Historical Society, Second Avenue Building (ca. 1900).
Photo: The New-York Historical Society, New York

Motley's theme.[62] Another important analogy, one more directly related to the interest in nature (both as a scientific and a literary subject), was the appreciation of the Dutch as a society based on simple, essential virtues, such as those of family life, religion, and living close to nature.[63] Americans became increasingly conscious of these values as they seemed to be slipping away: the economy, immigration, urban poverty and decay, the severe labor conditions that accompanied increasing industrialization, and the social tensions that built to the savage conclusion of the Civil War were addressed by artists and writers of about 1800 to 1860 largely by celebrating their opposites. When the popular American writer Washington Irving (alias Diedrich Knickerbocker, author of the satiric *History of New York*) was in Rotterdam on a Sunday in 1805, he observed 'many people were sitting at their doors [...] much as the good folks used to do in New York and Albany in good old simple times.'[64] Ralph Waldo Emerson more emphatically expressed the romantic yearning for a simpler life in his first book, *Nature*, of 1836, and in *The American Scholar*, an address delivered at Harvard in the following year. 'The literature of the poor, the feelings of the child, the philosophy of the street, the meaning of household life, are the topics of the time [...] I embrace the common, I explore and sit at the feet of the familiar, the low.'[65] Similar

◀ **15**
John Gadsby Chapman
The Triumphal Return of Stoffel Brinkerhoff, on His Return from His Conquests in the East
Panel, 22.3 x 30.8 cm (8 ¾ x 12 ⅛ in.)
Lower right: *J.C. 1835*
Washington, National Museum of American Art, Smithsonian Institution, Museum Purchase, inv. no. 1978.69

▶ **16**
Asher B. Durand
The Beeches
Canvas, 153.4 x 122.2 cm (60 ⅜ x 48 ⅛ in.)
Lower left: *A.B. Durand / 1845*
New York, The Metropolitan Museum of Art, Bequest of Maria DeWitt Jesup, from the collection of her husband, Morris K. Jesup, 1914, inv. no. 15.30.59

thoughts, strongly linked to moral codes and a spiritual interpretation of reality, were advanced by Emerson's Concord colleagues, Nathaniel Hawthorne, Henry David Thoreau, and Louisa May Alcott, and by Nathaniel Hawthorne's admirer, Herman Melville, the author of *Moby-Dick* (1851). Melville was especially proud of his Dutch New York ancestors and was one of America's many enthusiasts of Teniers.[66]

Paintings derived from Irving stories [**15**], and more meaningful pictorial parallels to the subjects of writers such as Emerson and Thoreau, were drawn by artists such as Audubon, the Peales, Thomas Cole, Asher B. Durand (the composition of *The Beeches* [**16**] is usually related to Constable but is closer to Jan Both),[67] the 'Hudson River' painters Frederic Church and Albert Bierstadt, the 'Luminist' landscapists John F. Kensett and Martin J. Heade, and painters of everyday life such as William Sidney Mount, Eastman Johnson, George Caleb Bingham, and Winslow

Homer, who might strike the European viewer as America's answer to Courbet and the early Monet. Mount, King, Chapman, and Francis Edmonds [8, 13, 15, 17] provide examples of the inspiration of Dutch art, which was also important for American still-life and landscape painting.[68] Comparisons between Dutch and American landscapes are interesting not only for their stylistic similarities (which must be placed in the broader context of nineteenth-century European developments) but also for the evocations of God and country that many of them convey. Van Goyen's views of the Haarlemmer Meer represent Nature in a guise distinctive of the Northern Netherlands, quite as Frederic Church's *Rocky Mountains* of 1863 (Metropolitan Museum of Art) stands for the new homeland of America as well as for 'forms of Nature as yet spared from the pollutions of civilization.'[69]

In addition to the exhibitions, the collections, the dealers, and the public galleries that are reviewed by Clark, we should finally mention his emphasis upon the books, prints, and especially the drawing manuals that made seventeenth-century Dutch painters familiar. In the latter, the study of nature goes hand in hand with Dutch examples. John Gadsby Chapman (see also fig. 15), in *The American Drawing-Book* (New York, 1858),[70] illustrates several Dutch pictures, and praises Flemish artists for refining their scenes of peasant life through skillful composition. Compositional patterns were the most accessible and perhaps the most beneficial information available in John Burnet's *A Treatise on Painting* (London, 1827); one of the pamphlets that made up part of the final edition (London, 1850), *Practical Hints on Composition*, was awarded to the winner of the 'Antique' class at the National Academy of Design in 1832. Burnet reproduced

104 paintings, of which sixty-two are Dutch or Flemish [18a-b]. He also engraved the genre scenes of David Wilkie, who was the principal intermediary between Dutch antecedents and Mount's paintings of the simple pleasures of everyday life. For Burnet, and apparently for Edmonds [17], it was De Hooch who 'carried the highest principle of the art into the humblest walks, and thereby gave a consequence [...] to the most trifling circumstance; stamping the whole with the firmness and truth of nature.'[71]

One might wonder whether Burnet's book and others like it are interesting for the history of collecting as opposed to emulating Dutch art. Even if our subject were American art it would have to be admitted that the middling (Mount) and mediocre (Edmonds) painters are the ones for whom Dutch lessons meant the most, whereas Cole's interest in Dutch landscape and Thomas Eakins's response to Rembrandt are relationships obscured by those artists' exceptional abilities. However, the issue is not influence but taste, which appears, to judge from the ideals of American painters, writers, and average citizens during the middle decades of the nineteenth century, to have been strongly conducive – perhaps more so than in England, Germany, and France – to an appreciation of seventeenth-century Dutch art.[72] This is essentially true even for those painters and patrons of the mid-nineteenth century who really knew less about Dutch art than did collectors such as Gilmor and Bryan.

And that is important for the 'Gilded Age' of collecting Dutch paintings, from about 1865 to 1915. The captains of industry, banking, stock speculation, railroads, mining, and other lucrative ventures who formed great collections in the late nineteenth century were not, on the whole, gentlemen like Gilmor and Bryan, devoting years of their lives to the study of pictures and to travel abroad. With a few conspicuous exceptions, the great collectors between the Civil War and the First World War had their minds on business, social position, and luxurious homes. Nonetheless, apart from the pantheon of great artists and the portraitists of surrogate ancestors such as Reynolds, Gainsborough, and above all Van Dyck, these wealthy men admired Hobbema, Ruisdael, Cuyp, Hals, Ter Borch, and even (in a private room) Van Ostade. What accounts for this inclination among collectors who lacked Gilmor's knowledge of Hobbema and his experience of Hobbema-like landscapes in the Netherlands;[73] or Burnet's understanding of composition in De Hooch, Van Ostade, and Rembrandt;[74] or Durand and Morse's exposure to the Rijksmuseum?[75]

The hypothesis put forward here is that a taste for Dutch art

17
Francis W. Edmonds
The Bashful Cousin
Canvas, 63.5 x 76.2 cm (25 x 30 in.)
Neither signed nor dated (ca. 1842)
Washington, National Gallery of Art, Gift of
Frederick Sturges, Jr., inv. no. 1978.6.4

18a-b
John Burnet
A Treatise in Four Parts ... , London 1850, vol. IV, pl. 8,
figs. 1 and 2 (both inscribed *P. De Hooge*)
The engraving on the left reproduces in reverse De
Hooch's canvas dated 1658 in the Louvre, while that
on the right reverses Pieter Janssens Elinga's painting
in the Alte Pinakothek, Munich (first assigned to
Elinga by Hofstede de Groot in 1891).

was virtually intuitive for the generation of American collectors that flourished after the Civil War. For decades, American artists and patrons had been sympathetic to seventeenth-century Dutch art. A national school, to some extent inspired by Dutch models, and to a great extent devoted to nature and to everyday life, had become firmly established and had already produced memorable images. Dutch pictures were the almost inevitable foundation of the collection of European paintings in the Metropolitan Museum and of other galleries opened in the 1870s. At the same time, younger American artists, or at least those in the vanguard of modern taste, were painting pictures that required some sophisticated knowledge of the arts. Whistler, Sargent, and the American Impressionists, not to mention William Glackens, Robert Henri, and the rest of the Eight, were making the fine arts into a cosmopolitan adventure when parvenu patrons wanted the cachet of resonant name plates, venerable varnish, and heavy gold frames. As in Europe, only a small part of proper society would cultivate the culture of the time rather than the Culture of the Ages, as embodied by Chinese porcelain, Persian rugs, Renaissance sculpture, English paneling, and old master paintings.

The new collectors of the 1880s and 1890s would have given a respectful reading to Vanderlyn's list: Raphael, Correggio, Titian, Caravaggio, Poussin, Rubens, and Rembrandt. However, most of the new *amateurs*, to judge from their privately printed, gilt-edged, gold-tooled morocco-covered catalogues, would have begun with the last-named artist and added the names of Hobbema, Ruisdael, Cuyp, Van de Neer, Ter Borch, Metsu, De Hooch, Van Ostade, and, yes, Vanderlyn's own suggestion, Potter.

The Gilded Age

The United States was and seemed to be a different kind of country after the Civil War. Henry James, reflecting on Hawthorne, observed in 1879 that the guides of Nature and homespun moral truth were no longer capable of solving every problem: the war 'introduced into the national consciousness a certain sense of proportion and relation, of the world being a more complicated place than it had hitherto seemed, the future more treacherous, success more difficult.' The American, 'in days to come, will be a more critical person than his complacent and confident grandfather. He has eaten of the tree of knowledge.'[76]

The last lines seem appropriate to the great collectors of the late nineteenth and early twentieth centuries. Gilmor, Codman, Bryan, and other serious collectors active before the Civil War were gentlemen of independent means who gave most of their time to travel, the pursuit of pictures, and the idea that Americans would benefit from exposure to the fine arts. The major collectors after the war represented 'a roaring and money-getting democracy, inevitably but almost exclusively occupied with "business success".'[77] John D. Rockefeller's obsessive control of the oil industry, Andrew Carnegie's ruthless forging of an empire built on steel, the mines of Frick, the banks of Morgan and Mellon, the railroads of Morgan, Vanderbilt, and Huntington were preoccupations that would have made these immensely rich men poor company for Gilmor, Bryan, and Reed. However, the 'tree of knowledge' gave post-war collectors powers of vision, organization, and wealth that allowed them to form great collections in the course of a decade, and to endow institutions that would exhibit and in many cases receive their recently imported treasure troves.

Perhaps the most discriminating collectors benefited from and came at the end of this period. A few of them were professional men more concerned with managing money than with amassing it. John G. Johnson, the lawyer of Morgan and Frick, was the first in a line of 'more critical' minds who formed collections that were not the largest or the most valuable but the most instructive for an understanding of Dutch and Flemish art. Michael Friedsam, who was Benjamin Altman's business successor, is seen in a similar light below.

The great collections were concentrated even more than before in New York and Philadelphia, with Pittsburgh, Cincinnati, and Chicago marking the westward progress of the railroads. Economically the railroads ran to the east, bringing raw materials, meat, and grain to the growing cities and industries of the 'North.' It was the North, meaning New York, Pennsylvania, Ohio, and Maryland, that had benefited as well as suffered from the effort of the war. The South was condemned to agrarian isolation by the war and by the ill-conceived Reconstruction, while the West was made subservient to the markets of the East. There were no major businesses or railroads in America before the mid-nineteenth century, but in the 1860s railroads, ships, systems of communication, networks of supply, factories, hospitals, and government bureaucracies were rushed into being, and left for the northeastern states to further expand. Millions of new immigrants, first German and Irish, then Italian, Greek, and Eastern European, supplied labor for the cities and the industries of the East and secondly the Midwest. It seems symbolic that almost all these ingredients – steel, oil, railroads, banking, and thousands of workers – went into the making of America's richest non-collector, Henry Ford.[78]

Analogies to the Netherlands were reinvigorated by the new sense of nationalism that resulted from the war, and were probably encouraged by the Centennial celebrations of 1876. Certainly the waves of immigration inspired Motley-like comparisons between the 'real' America and a democracy composed of old Protestant families. But money was the key

factor in collecting Dutch art during this period, as it was in founding museums, libraries, universities, opera houses, and symphony halls.

The rise of the American art museum goes beyond our subject but has a special relevance to the collecting of Dutch art. Peale's appreciation of the museum as an educational institution took on a moral dimension in the course of the nineteenth century. Exposure to the fine arts had a refining effect, as Gilmor and other cosmopolitan collectors had perceived. Some kinds of art, it was supposed, embodied ethical values, such as the virtues of labor, worship, and family life. European paintings also depicted the customs of different countries and ages and, perhaps more important, reflected truths that did not change. The school of nature received higher accreditation in an increasingly urban and industrial world. The masses could be lured away from the vices of the city 'by alternative entertainment of an innocent and improving character,' according to the poet William Cullen Bryant in his 1869 speech calling for the foundation of a 'metropolitan' museum.[79]

Nature and morality: James's later exasperation with the Ruskinian notion of art ('instead of a garden of delight, he finds a sort of assize court in perpetual session')[80] was the complaint of someone who had heard enough of it. At Harvard, where the Professor of Fine Arts, Charles Eliot Norton, became his elder friend and inspiration,[81] James could never resign himself to the conviction that culture was an obligation: in the Bostonian view it seemed a difficult duty, with the same potential for pleasure that women found in marital sex. Norton was Ruskin's friend and frequent correspondent; his lectures revealed a like disposition, which he had actually inherited from his family of Massachusetts ministers. 'The New England air [...] was no natural conductor of any appeal to an aesthetic aim'; Norton, 'a son of the Puritans,' even though he was 'the most liberally emancipated and initiated possible, could still plead most for substance when proposing to plead for style.'[82]

It has been observed that the founders of the Metropolitan Museum of Art – J.T. Johnston, William Blodgett, A.T. Stewart, Henry Marquand, James Lenox, James Colgate, and the rest of society's 'Fifty' – included one Dutch (Rutherford Stuyvesant), no Jewish, and no nouveau-riche names; they were old money, club men (the Union League and the Century Association), many of them from New England, almost all of them 'WASPS.'[83] The founders of the Museum of Fine Arts in Boston were even more exclusive in their family backgrounds and in their considerable accomplishments (several of them were eminent educators).[84]

Thus the trustees of these two great East Coast institutions shared Norton's social – one might almost say ethical – roots, and their pronouncements suggest that they also shared his approach to 'the illustration of European artistic endeavor.'[85] This task, as James remembered, always tended to involve 'the question of manners, character, conscience, tone, to bristle with questions addressed to the actual and possible American scene.' Perhaps this deeply ingrained American attitude to art partially explains the early predominance of Dutch pictures in the collections of European paintings formed by the New York and Boston museums.

James's essay on the '1871 Purchase' of the Metropolitan Museum remains the best index to its contemporary appreciation.[86] As one might expect of the future critic of Fromentin, who in James's view cared too much 'for the mysteries of the process by which the picture was made,'[87] James deals briskly with Rubens, Van Dyck, Jordaens, and De Crayer, in each case by his usual means of closely describing their subjects. Jordaens, a 'plebian genius,' renders more strongly than Rubens the 'immediate detail of nature.' By contrast, 'the physiognomy' in Van Dyck's *Portrait of a Young Lady* 'is excessively, almost morbidly refined.'[88]

'Close beside this elegant work hangs a masterpiece of inelegant vigour, 'Hille Bobbe of Haarlem,' by Franz Hals' [19]. In the 1860s, as Petra ten Doesschate Chu has found, 'the works of Hals were admired primarily for their typically bourgeois subject matter and their hearty, vigorous mood.'[89] In the following two decades, however, Hals's group portraits (and paintings such as this one) were admired 'for their masterful use of color and their dynamic, *alla prima* facture.'[90] This describes in a nutshell the evolution of American painters active in Europe from the time of Eastman Johnson (1849-1855 in Düsseldorf, The Hague, and Paris) to that of William Merritt Chase (in Munich during the early 1870s). Copies of Hals's civic guard and genre pictures were painted during the 1870s by Chase [20], Mary Cassatt, and J. Alden Weir.[91] James kept up with the times in his description of 'Hille Bobbe' as 'dashed upon the canvas by a brush superbly confident.' Of course the painting not only raises the question of America's long-standing affection for Frans Hals but also that of the copies and fakes that were imported (and 'rediscovered' by Valentiner) as by the master himself.[92]

'We know what it is to have turned with a sort of moral relief, in the galleries of Italy, to some small stray specimen of Dutch patience and conscience.'[93] James delights in paying deprecating compliments. Van der Helst's so-called *Burgomaster* is 'the perfect prose of portraiture': Nature would lay her hand on the artist's 'sturdy shoulder' and say, 'one must choose for the long run: this man I can *trust*.' It would be interesting to know if James enjoyed the same American readership as did Taine, whose Dutch painter lays his hand on Nature, 'with all her irregularities, minutiae, and omissions,' and 'through sympathy [...] renders her beautiful.'[94] With one exception, Taine in 1871 (the date of his New York

19
Follower of Frans Hals
Malle Babbe
Canvas, 74.9 x 61 cm (29 1/2 x 24 in.)
Right center: *FH* (in ligature) (second quarter of the seventeenth century?)
New York, The Metropolitan Museum of Art, inv. no. 71.76

20
William Merritt Chase in his Tenth Street Studio, New York, with the artist's copy of Frans Hals's *Women Regents of the Old Men's Home* on the wall (ca. 1890).
Photo: Parrish Art Museum, William Merritt Chase Archives, Southampton, N.Y.

33

edition) and James in 1872 cite the same artists: Ter Borch, Metsu, Dou, Steen, Frans van Mieris, Wouwerman, 'the two Ostades, Wynants, Cuyp, Van der Neer, Ruysdael, Hobbema, Paul Potter, Backhuysen, the two Vanderveldes, Philip of Koenig, Van der Heyden, and how many more!' Taine's one addition, 'Van der Meer of Delft,' was for his transatlantic audience an appreciation so early as to be obscure.

'Several excellent specimens of eminent names' are singled out for simple praise by James: 'a good example of each of the Van Ostades, a fine Jan Steen, three capital Solomon Ruysdaels [21], a lovely Berghem, an interesting Hobbema.'[95] The latter ranks 'second only to Jacob Ruysdael' as a landscapist. James is exceptional in his admiration for Berchem and 'the great 'Italian Landscape' by Cornelis Huysmans'; the only Dutch Italianate landscapist consistently favored by American collectors from Gilmor's time and almost to the present has been Jan Both.

The account concludes with a comparison of Guardi and Van der Heyden. Here James is Norton's disciple. The *Quay in Leyden* 'tells more of Dutch conscience than all of its neighbors,' while Guardi's 'sceptical reflections of Venetian splendor' illustrate 'the demoralizing influence of lavish opportunity.' The Italian 'dispenses with effort and insight, and trusts to mere artifice and manner,' whereas Van der Heyden's picture demonstrates a 'glowing fidelity and sincerity.' The Dutchman 'feels that, unless he is faithful, he is nothing'; Guardi, by contrast, 'has some shallow faith that the charm of his subjects' will suffice. Van der Heyden cannot depend on his country's 'meaner and duskier' environment: 'He must confer a charm as well as borrow one; he must bring his grist to the mill and grind it with his own strength.'

Thus those inevitable companions, the 'Protestant work ethic' and the 'embarrassment of riches,' brought Dutch paintings home to New Yorkers in the 1870s.

The man who actually did so was William Blodgett, a prominent publisher, opponent of slavery, and collector of nineteenth-century American and European art. In 1870 he retired to Europe, where he exercised his new authority as vice-president of the Metropolitan Museum by purchasing three private collections comprising 174 pictures. His friend John Taylor Johnston, president of the museum from 1870 to 1889, overcame the reservations of others (in good part through his own donations) and bought the 1871 Purchase from Blodgett at cost. Almost all of America's early public collections were formed in a similar manner, which calls into question the extent to which they reflect the taste of the times as opposed to that of a few individuals. In the case of Luigi Cesnola, who sold the Metropolitan Museum (Johnston) hundreds of provincial Cyprian sculptures before he became director in 1879, one can speak of personal preference striking the institution like Zeus's thunderbolt. Blodgett's taste, however, was entirely consistent with that of genteel Americans in the period 1850-1875, and on the whole this may be said for the major benefactors of the museums in Boston, New York, and Philadelphia during the late nineteenth century.

The broader subject of American museums may be explored in an extensive (if not profound) body of literature.[96] Brief accounts of how the important public collections of Dutch paintings were formed are available in Peter Sutton's guidebook, *Dutch Art in America*.[97] The unusual importance of American university and

21
Salomon van Ruysdael
Drawing the Eel
Panel, 74.9 x 106 cm (29 1/2 x 41 3/4 in.)
Lower center: *SvR / 165[?]*
New York, The Metropolitan Museum of Art, inv. no. 71.75

This is one of the finest Dutch paintings acquired by the museum in its founding purchase of 1871.

college art museums is discussed in this volume by Susan Kuretsky. In the future these histories might be given some statistical foundation by the use of computerized inventories, specifically those of the Getty Provenance Project. It would be interesting to see a 'print-out' of when paintings by individual Dutch artists entered the country, different regions, and various museums. However, a great amount of subjective interpretation and connoisseurship (one thinks of Luman Reed's 'Teniers') would need to color in these outlines, which may provide a less reliable image than the catalogues of private collections and the pronouncements of critics such as James.

In the 'Gilded Age' (which in this survey ends with the arrival of income tax in 1916, and with America's later entry into World War I), the founding, maintenance, and acquisitions of museums were entirely dependent upon private patronage. At the Museum of Fine Arts, Boston, which opened on the Centennial day of 4 July 1876, the galleries of paintings were hung with loans from private collectors and from the Atheneum. By 1880, pictures by Corot, Millet, Doré, and a few earlier European artists had been given to the museum. European paintings were not likely to be purchased at market prices, since funds were painfully restricted and the collections were meant to be broad; casts of exemplary sculpture, decorative arts worthy as models for industrial design, and works by Boston artists were high on the list of desiderata. Thus a loan of Dutch paintings in 1881 was an important complement to the American, Italian, and French pictures already on view. The lender was Stanton Blake ('Harvard '57'), a banker who had business in London and Amsterdam. A number of his Dutch paintings had just been purchased at the 1880 Demidoff sale in Florence,[98] which was one of the first complete collections in Europe to come up for sale in this period of prodigious American acquisition. The San Donato gallery was especially strong in Dutch pictures, which included Metsu's *Usurer* and still lifes by Van Huysum and Verelst that are now in the Boston museum. At his death in 1889 Blake left the museum 5,000 dollars plus an option to buy his collection for 22,500 dollars, almost half of which was put up by a Harvard classmate and the rest by friends.

Other northern paintings trickled in, with Rogier van der Weyden's *Saint Luke Painting the Virgin* and a pair of portraits dated 1634 by Rembrandt (*pace* the opinion of the Rembrandt team)[99] coming from different donors in 1893. A decade later, in an effort to use up threatened funds, the museum bought a late Hals *Portrait of a Man*,[100] two 'Rembrandts' and an alleged Van Dyck, a Goya, a Crivelli, an important Velázquez, and paintings

by other artists which document a drift away from didactic collecting and toward the beacon of big names.[101]

Although the Philadelphia Museum of Art now has the largest number of seventeenth-century Dutch paintings in America, there were comparatively few before the Johnson bequest of 1917 and the Elkins bequest of the 1920s (discussed below). Mrs. William P. Wilstach left about 150 American and nineteenth-century French paintings to the eighteen-year-old museum in 1893. John G. Johnson and later Joseph E. Widener used the Wilstach bequest of funds to broaden the collection with paintings by Ruisdael, Snyders, Zurbarán, and others. Large canvases were favored, which redoubled the need for the great 'Greek' temple built between 1919 and 1928.

Two other museums that acquired Dutch pictures before the turn of the century were the Art Institute of Chicago and the Detroit Institute of Arts. The former's first important purchase in the area of European paintings (1892) was Jan Steen's *Family Concert*, a large canvas dated 1666. The museum's president, Charles Hutchinson, returned from Italy in 1890 with a number of paintings from the Demidoff sale. Thirteen of them, including a Hobbema, a late Van Ostade, the *Young Woman at a Dutch Door* attributed to Rembrandt, and a few other Dutch pictures were acquired with the help of individuals approached by Hutchinson and Martin Ryerson (1856-1932). The latter, heir to a lumber fortune and from 1925 director of the museum, was with his friend Hutchinson at the Demidoff sale. These two civic leaders and sensitive collectors pioneered Chicago's collection of old master paintings before the Potter Palmers and their Impressionists came along.[102]

The Palmer fund was used to buy Ruisdael's *Ruins of Egmond Castle* in 1947. Other individual donors, including Hutchinson himself, gave Dutch paintings, such as Rembrandt's *Old Man in a Gorget and Black Cap* of about 1631 (Kimball bequest, 1922).[103] Later purchases such as Ter Brugghen's *Denial of Peter* have given Chicago a couple of rewarding Dutch rooms, if nothing like those in New York and Philadelphia.

The Detroit Institute of Arts was in good part inspired by a newspaper publisher, William Brearley, who organized and financed the Detroit Art Loan Exhibition of 1883. One-fifth of the nearly five thousand objects on view were oil paintings, most of them Salon pictures. Exploiting the interest aroused by the show, Brearley next raised thirty contributions of 1,000 dollars each, which combined with Senator Palmer's offer of 10,000 dollars and another 60,000 dollars from more modest donors allowed a new museum building to open in 1888. Brearley thus encouraged his rival, James E. Scripps, whose family created the nation's first newspaper chain, to give the museum seventy old master paintings in 1889. Scripps was fifty-four at the time and had seventeen years to live, but he had been a collector of rare books and prints as well as paintings, and despite being born in England had dreams for Detroit. 'Why might not Detroit aspire to the honor and become the Florence or Munich of this continent?'[104] Scripps apparently had this goal in mind during the years between the 1883 exhibition and the gift of 1889, which is the period in which he bought most of his paintings in England and on the Continent. Consciously avoiding the likes of Bouguereau, he acquired Van Dyck and Rubens (*The Meeting of David and Abigail*), lesser Flemish artists, and a majority of Dutch. One senses in the immigrant's collecting an American flair for 'one-upmanship'; his rivalry with Brearley is one of the many from which American museums have gained. Detroit's second great period of Dutch and Flemish acquisitions, the directorship of William Valentiner (1924-1944), deserves special mention below.

The Dutch pictures in the Metropolitan Museum are one of the few old master painting collections in America to bear comparison with the same area in any European museum. There are about 260 seventeenth-century Dutch paintings, not a great number by old-world standards, but there is remarkable depth in the landscapes, portraits, and genre scenes, and an immodest emphasis on the masterpiece. True, the five Vermeers comprise only sixty-two percent of those on Fifth Avenue, but there are about twenty Rembrandts (and twenty Rembrandt-like pictures), eleven paintings by Frans Hals, seven Ter Borchs, six Salomon van Ruysdaels, five Jacob van Ruisdaels, five Cuyps, and, significantly, nothing by either Van Ostade.[105]

Almost all of the Rembrandts and ex-Rembrandts are portraits or single historical figures (*Aristotle*, *Flora*, and so on); New Yorkers have had less time for stories than for imposing characters. There is more to it, of course. Portraits suggested some association with old European families, and with actual history (history pictures, by contrast, are often some other culture's mythology). Biblical pictures, even by Rembrandt, were inconsistent with Puritan sentiment and with the inflexible nature of American ethical thought. There is also the mundane matter of supply: family portraits were sold off by European families that had no other good paintings to sell. We should also consider the influential model of the English country house, where portraits hung high around the rooms. There are a great number of fine English portraits in America, many of them by 'Vandyke.'

'Corridor pictures,' like Berchems and Asselijns, hung in English hallways, and cabinet pictures were found in little rooms. What one wanted over the mantel in the Frick or Morgan mansion was a great dark portrait which through dress alone demanded veneration and meant whatever one liked.

Except for Van der Helst's *Musician* (purchased in 1872), not one seventeenth-century Dutch painting was acquired by the Metropolitan Museum after the 1871 Purchase and until the Marquand gift of 1889. It must be added, however, that effectively nothing at all came in during the periods 1876-1879 and 1882-1886, and if it were not for the Catherine Lorillard Wolfe bequest of over fifty works by then fashionable Continental painters in 1887 and several early Italian pictures given by Coudert Brothers in 1888, the collection of European paintings would have been nearly dormant for a quarter-century after the founding without Marquand. New York's great collectors acquired pictures for themselves in the 1880s, and there were many other ways to be socially conspicuous and to benefit mankind.[106]

Henry B. Marquand (1819-1902) was a railroad financier and a supporter of the Metropolitan Museum from its founding year. He had wide but conventional interests: oriental porcelain, Persian carpets and ceramics, Renaissance ironwork, and landscapes by Troyon, Decamps, Rousseau, and so on. Marquand bought old master paintings with the museum in mind, although his apparent goal of a broad collection was strongly slanted to the north. The Lippi and the 'Velázquez' that Marquand, as president, presented to the museum in 1889 were lost in the crowd of Dutch and Flemish pictures [**22**]: a fake but famous Rembrandt, Hals's *Smoker*, the museum's first and best Vermeer [**1**], a major Ruisdael, Van Dyck's superb *Portrait of the Duke of Lennox and Richmond*, and lesser works by Van Dyck, Ter Borch, Netscher, Sorgh, Hanneman, Teniers, and others.[107] These pictures give a representative impression of the hit-or-miss hazards of collecting in Marquand's time, when questions of condition and attribution were given far less thought than those of the artist's reputation and price. When Marquand bought the Vermeer in 1887 from the dealer Charles Pillet in Paris, the name – Pieter de Hooch – was even bigger, and the price was 800 dollars.

Marquand also gave isolated gifts, such as the fine early landscape by Pieter de Molijn (95.7), and an alleged van der Helst (00.17.1; '00' indicates the year 1900). The important windfall of '00,' however, was the bequest of Collis P. Huntington, which was not accessioned (as 25.100.1-188) until one year after Hunting-

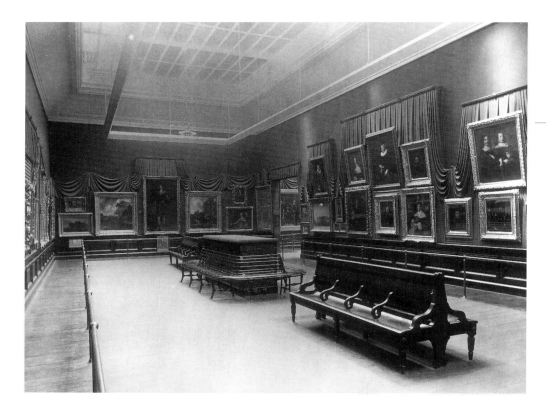

ton's widow died in 1924. His nephew, Henry E. Huntington
(who built the Library and Art Gallery in San Marino, California), married Huntington's widow in 1913. Collis Huntington
was another great railroad man, while Henry's money came from
streetcars and real estate.

The Collis Huntington bequest would have been a rather
routine gift to the museum were it not for Vermeer's *Woman with
a Lute*. However, 'routine' in this opulent period allows for works
of such quality as Cuyp's early *Piping Shepherds*, Van den
Eeckhout's *Isaac Blessing Jacob* (cat. no. 19), Flinck's *Bearded Man*,
and minor works by Mierevelt, Netscher, and Ruisdael. These
Dutch paintings were outnumbered two-to-one by Corot,
Rousseau, Troyon, Daubigny, etc. In 1926, Archer M. Huntington, Collis's son, gave Hals's *Portrait of Paulus Verschuur* and
Rembrandt's *Flora* and *Hendrickje Stoffels* in honor of his father's
memory.

The museum used the unexpected Rogers Fund (five million
dollars left in 1901) to fill in various blanks throughout the
building. Jacob Rogers, locomotive manufacturer, would not
have cared much about the Maes, the Ruysdael, and the fine De
Vlieger that were bought in 1906 with his money, but he cared

even less about his relatives. While Rogers was content with
occasional visits to the museum, Charles T. Yerkes (1837-1905)
was filling his homes with paintings. As a stock broker in
Philadelphia, Yerkes embezzled city funds, spent time in jail, and
worst of all (in this age) got divorced because of a sexual scandal.
He fled to Chicago where he monopolized streetcars with the
backing of two other 'Trolley Car Kings,' Peter Widener and his
partner, William Elkins.

Most of the paintings in the Yerkes collection are reproduced
in the *De Luxe* catalogue of his sale in 1910.[108] Two-thirds of the
122 old masters are by Dutch artists or by Flemish genre painters,
and the names that predominate confirm one's expectations of
conventional taste: Both, Dou (two), Flinck, Van Goyen (three),
Hals (three, and one reject), Van der Heyden, Hobbema (only
one of six autograph), De Hooch (three), Steen (four), Van
Ostade (four or five), Potter (four supposed), and Teniers
(three). However, there are many pictures of exceptional quality,
not only here but in the modern section and especially among the
eighteenth-century French, English, and Italian paintings. A
respectable effort was also made to illustrate early Northern and
Italian Renaissance art. The diversity and overall importance of

the collection lend credibility to the comments of a critic who knew Yerkes personally: 'The fact is, he was not buying for his own taste or aesthetic pleasure, of which he had not much, and that not necessarily catholic; his aim was to acquire good, if possible superlative, examples of all schools, with the ultimate object of making them the nucleus, or else the reinforcement, of the American national gallery... .'[109]

The same writer recalls seeing 'a good deal of him in Paris when he was engaged upon the quest, in a great measure under the tutelage of M. Jan de Beers.' Yerkes was always cheerful and quickly decisive in those days (the early 1890s). But further misfortunes followed; even in Chicago, that 'huge city which almost as by magic has risen on the southern shore of Lake Michigan,'[110] Yerkes was considered impossibly corrupt. He withdrew to London where he tried to electrify the Underground; an old acquaintance described him as 'a broken and dying man.'[111]

Among the most important Dutch paintings in the posthumous sale were Hals's *Portrait of a Woman*, 1635, in the Frick Collection,[112] a Hobbema panel bought for 48,000 dollars by Scott and Fowles for the Tafts in Cincinnati,[113] the De Hooch of 1674 now in Honolulu,[114] Rembrandt's *Philemon and Baucis* in Washington, the '*Rabbi*' by Flinck later in the Guterman collection,[115] Rembrandt's *Raising of Lazarus* in the Los Angeles County Museum, Rembrandt's *Portrait of Joris de Caulerij* in San Francisco (cat. no. 50), and too many good genre paintings and landscapes to mention here.

J. P. Morgan's lawyer, John G. Johnson, was at the Yerkes sale and sent an account of it to Bernard Berenson: 'The Yerkes sale has placed America in the very front rank of art-understanding countries, so far at least as an understanding of art does not extend beyond the ability to pay extraordinary prices [...]. A genuine Hobbema went at a reasonable price, and a lot of fake ones followed at figures not very much less [...] a Hals, attributed to Frans, but [which] his son Herman had obligingly painted for him, went for $33,000 ... .'[116]

Berenson is known principally for his enormous influence in the area of Italian pictures (he sold some to Johnson), but he also recommended a few great Dutch paintings to Isabella Stewart Gardner. Her interest in Italian works of art had begun not with Berenson in the 1890s but with Norton's lectures in 1878. Ten years later, John Singer Sargent painted his famous portrait of 'Mrs. Jack'; it was through him that she met his dear friend Paul Helleu. The stylish artist was with her at Drouot's in Paris on 5 December 1892 and encouraged her to buy *The Concert*, Thoré-

Bürger's own Vermeer (cat. no. 5, fig. 1). Berenson advised Mrs. Gardner to buy three Rembrandts from Colnaghi's in London. Her cable of 1896, 'Yes Rembrandt, Yes Tintoretto,' secured a portrait from Tintoretto's workshop and (for 22,000 dollars) Rembrandt's *Self-Portrait* of 1629 [23]. Two years later Mrs. Gardner purchased *A Lady and Gentleman in an Interior* and *The Storm on the Sea of Galilee*, both signed and dated 1633 and formerly in the Hope Collection (Berenson made five percent from the buyer's side alone). Finally, in 1900, she bought the *Landscape with an Obelisk* [23] from Colnaghi's; the picture is now convincingly assigned to Flinck. Philip Hendy records that Mrs.

23
A view of the Dutch Room in Fenway Court, Isabella Stewart Gardner's home in Boston, during her lifetime (early 1920s).
On the table to the left is Flinck's *Landscape with an Obelisk*, formerly considered a Rembrandt; to the right of the door is Rembrandt's *Self-Portrait*, 1629, next to Dürer's *Man in a Fur Coat*.
Photo: Isabella Stewart Gardner Museum, Boston

Three of the galleries in the Dutch section of the
Hudson-Fulton Exhibition at The Metropolitan
Museum of Art, 20 September to 30 November 1909.
Public attendance was reported as 288,103, with
Boston, Philadelphia, and more distant cities well
represented by visitors. To the left are the 'Bodolphe'
portraits by Hals (cat. nos. 25-26) then owned by
J.P. Morgan.

Gardner had earlier gone right to Lord Lansdowne in quest of
The Mill (p. 122, fig. 1).[117]

The Yerkes sale could not have been timed better since it
immediately followed the great exhibition of Dutch and
American paintings at the Metropolitan Museum, which was part
of the *Hudson-Fulton Celebration* of 1909 [**24**]. The twin pretexts
for the extravaganza were rather tenuously related: Henry
Hudson's sail up the Hudson River in 1609; the same trip (to
Albany) made by Robert Fulton's steamboat, the *Clermont*, in
August 1807. Since the Englishman Hudson sailed for Holland
(Manhattan was claimed in 1612 on this basis), the Metropolitan
Museum let its curator of decorative arts, William Valentiner,
select about 150 Dutch paintings from the New-York Historical
Society, the Art Institute of Chicago, and a number of private
collections, including those of Benjamin Altman, William
Blodgett, William Clark, the Elkins Estate of Philadelphia, Henry
Clay Frick, Mrs. Henry Havemeyer, Sir William van Horne, Mrs.
Collis P. Huntington, John G. Johnson, J.P. Morgan, William K.
Vanderbilt, and Peter Widener. Fulton was commemorated by
fifty-three American paintings as well as furniture, silver, and
other objects.

The Hudson-Fulton exhibition reaffirmed that the most
desirable Dutch paintings were by Rembrandt (thirty-four
pictures bear his name), Frans Hals (twenty by or attributed to
him), Jacob van Ruisdael (eleven), Hobbema (seven), Cuyp
(eleven, at least half of them right), De Hooch (five, one of them
by Van der Burch), Steen (five fine examples), and Vermeer. Of
the five Vermeers one (Johnson's) is an old copy of the Kenwood

Guitar Player; the other four are Frick's *Music Lesson*, Morgan's *Girl Writing a Letter* (cat. no. 67), Huntington's *Woman with a Lute* (Metropolitan Museum of Art), and the *Woman with a Water Jug* from the Marquand Collection [1].

The cornucopia of Rembrandts cannot spill out completely on this page. It should suffice to mention the *Man in Oriental Costume (The Noble Slav)*, 1632 (p. 60, fig. 1), lent by Mrs. Lincoln Ellsworth; *Portrait of Herman Doomer*, 1640, from Mrs. Havemeyer; *Aristotle with a Bust of Homer*, 1653, owned by Mrs. Collis P. Huntington; *The Standard Bearer*, 1654, lent by George Gould (later bought by Jules Bache); and *Hendrickje Stoffels*, 1660, also from Mrs. Huntington. All of these paintings were later given to the Metropolitan Museum with the exception of *Aristotle*, which was purchased at auction in 1961. Some of the other Rembrandts exhibited in 1909 were the *Portrait of a Young Man*, 1631, lent by Edward Drummond Libbey of Toledo, Ohio (given to the Toledo Museum of Art in 1925); *Portrait of Nicolaes Ruts*, 1631, lent by Morgan and bought by the Frick Collection in 1943; Widener's *Self-Portrait*, 1650, by Rembrandt, now in Washington; Rembrandt's great *Self-Portrait* [31], 1658, lent by Frick; and *Lucretia*, 1664 (p. 69, fig. 12), a Demidoff picture lent by Mr. M.C.D. Borden of New York and later given by Andrew Mellon to the National Gallery.[118]

J.P. Morgan [26] was general chairman of the Art Exhibits. He is a major figure in the history of American finance;[119] one of the most important founders, patrons, and (from 1904) presidents of the Metropolitan Museum; a legendary collector of books, manuscripts, paintings, porcelain, and many other kinds of artistic treasure; and the purchaser of great pictures by Rembrandt, Hals, and Vermeer. All that said, he was not an important collector of Dutch art, but a collector of major European paintings, some of which were by celebrated Dutch names. Almost all of Morgan's Dutch pictures appear in the Hudson-Fulton catalogue: a Cuyp, Hals's *Portrait of Andries van der Horn* and the pendant (both now in São Paulo), the pendant portraits ('Bodolphe', cat. nos. 25-26) by Hals in New Haven,[120] two good Hobbemas, Metsu's *Visit to the Nursery* (The Metropolitan Museum of Art), Rembrandt's *Nicolaes Ruts*, and Vermeer's *Girl Writing a Letter* (cat. no. 67), plus a few minor or dubious works. Morgan was much more serious about eighteenth-century French and especially English pictures (almost all of them portraits), and except for the Vermeer his Dutch paintings could equally well illustrate English taste.[121]

And why should this not be? By the centennial of Fulton's steamboat, much bigger versions of it were regularly crossing between New York and England or France. The journey was safe, comfortable (especially in Morgan's staterooms), comparatively inexpensive, and required only a week. Morgan first arrived in London alone and on a steamship at the age of fifteen (1852), and spent vacations there with his family while studying at Vevey and Göttingen during the next few years. In 1871 the thirty-four-year-old financier, having just founded Drexel, Morgan and Co., sailed with his wife and children for London and Paris where, with frequent excursions, they lived for over a year. In 1877 the Morgans spent another year abroad, living mostly in the Morgan townhouse at Prince's Gate, but also steaming up the Nile with an entourage of eighteen. This period saw Americans traveling all over Europe, in varieties ranging

25
Henry Clay Frick (left) and his fellow Pittsburghers Andrew W. Mellon (seated), A.A. Hutchinson, and Frank Cowan, on their first trip abroad during the spring and summer of 1880. The party toured the major museums of Europe and visited private collections.
Photo: Frick Art Museum, Pittsburgh

26
Carlos Baca-Flor
Portrait of J. Pierpont Morgan
Canvas, 114.3 x 101.6 cm (45 x 40 in.)
Neither signed nor dated (ca. 1914, based on a version of 1910)
New York, The Metropolitan Museum of Art, inv. no. 39.119

from Yerkes to James and Sargent (who were literally at home abroad), and including Frick and Mellon [25], Mrs. Gardner (who traveled in the manner of Lady Arundel), and almost every collector worth mentioning here. This was, for better or worse, a very different age from that of the Hawthorne when Americans were fawning over marbles in Florence for months on end. Now they ran into Agnew's, Colnaghi's, Knoedler's, Sedelmeyer's, Kleinberger's [27], Wildenstein's, and Duveen's with funds sufficient to entice those firms to open branches in New York. 'This is a fine place and I think we will do good business here,' wrote Henry Duveen in a letter home to Hull in 1877. The five-story Duveen building designed in 1911 [28] lends substance to 'Uncle Henry's' remark.[122]

The railways controlled by the Vanderbilts and other collectors made it unnecessary to open branches in Boston and Phila-delphia. Not only were the customers there widely traveled, but they were also not in the same class. This is true of William Elkins, for example, despite the large sums that he spent and the fact that his Hobbema, Van Beyeren, and Potter were among the most attractive paintings in the Hudson-Fulton show. His privately printed catalogue of 'early English' (eighteenth century) and old master paintings collected (as the title page discreetly allows) in the brief period between 1887 and 1900 includes ten Italian pictures (mostly Venetian views), a few Spanish paintings and a few 'Van Dycks,' and an extraordinary number of Dutch bargains, many of them duds. The four 'Cuyps' are not even close, the little Hals is a copy, and almost every portrait (Mierevelt, Ravesteyn, Rembrandt, Rubens, and a ridiculous 'Lely') is something less than the catalogue claims. Genuine but minor pictures represent Ruisdael, Van Goyen, Van der Neer, and the inevitable Hobbema.[123] The best Dutch painting in the collection is Ter Borch's *Waiting Orders* now in the Philadelphia Museum of Art (Elkins's son George and his son William left their collections to the museum in the early 1920s). The number of 'low' genre paintings in the Elkins collection was exceptional for this period: Duck, Dirck Hals, Kick, Van Ostade, a Teniers copy, and an imitation Steen.

In fairness to Elkins, it should be conceded that at the same time Valentiner, for one reason or another, was misattributing pictures in at least one case out of three.[124] The sense of public obligation in men such as the Wideners and the Elkinses also counts for a great deal in a decade when William Vanderbilt (whose civic spirit had been questioned by a reporter) said 'the public be damned.' What if his hundred million dollars had been at the disposal of Edwin Crocker, the Sacramento lawyer who in

27
Galerie F. Kleinberger at 9 rue de l'Echelle, Paris (ca. 1913?)
The sign above advertises 'Ancient Paintings'; pendant portraits by a Dutch artist, ca. 1625, are displayed in the windows. The proprietors are presumably Kleinberger and his son-in-law, Harry Sperling.

28
'The Marine,' the Duveen Brothers building at 720 Fifth Avenue, New York, in 1927 (designed in 1911).

the 1870s resolved that his California city would have the finest art collection in the United States? With limited means and the haste of a dying man he sent 750 paintings and over 1,000 drawings from the Continent to the California coast. Some of them were copies of old masters in the Dresden gallery and elsewhere; contemporary labels identify the copyists. Perhaps didactic interest took the place of quality, which was expectable given that small-time dealers were selling Crocker an average of two paintings per day. Minor or dubious Dutch and Flemish pictures, and many good Dutch drawings and prints, are now in the Crocker Art Museum; the 'Art Gallery' and its collections were given to Sacramento by Mrs. Crocker in 1885.[125]

When Peter Widener [29] was not expected in New York, vans from Duveen's would jolt across New Jersey loaded with paintings and decorative arts. A week later, the vans would arrive again at Lynnewood [30], the Widener home outside Philadelphia, and take away the rejects from the week before.[126]

29
John Singer Sargent
Portrait of Peter A.B. Widener
Canvas, 148.9 x 98.4 cm (58 5/8 x 38 3/4 in.)
Upper right: *John S. Sargent 1902*
Washington, D.C., National Gallery of Art, Widener Collection, inv. no. 1942.9.101

Widener also bought many things from Knoedler's, often on the advice of consultants such as Valentiner, Hofstede de Groot, and Berenson. Joe Duveen sent Berenson to the Widener floor at the Bristol in Paris on 26 June 1908. Widener wanted his Italian paintings catalogued; Berenson accepted hesitantly because, according to his wife, Mary, Fairfax Murray, Agnew's partner in London, had dumped 'worthless school things [...] for vast sums' on the old man.[127] Widener's earlier catalogue and fakes that may be connected with Murray (for example, the Tafts' 'Van Dyck,' see fig. 33) tend to substantiate Mary Berenson's claim.

In December 1908 the Berensons went to Lynnewood, having just visited the Morgan mansion ('I hear you are going to Philadelphia to bust up Widener's collection').[128] Hofstede de Groot had warned Berenson about Widener's paintings, since the Dutchman had already 'busted' about 150 of the Dutch and Flemish works. This must have made the young Valentiner's task easier when he prepared the Hudson-Fulton exhibition, to which Widener lent Rembrandt's *Self-Portrait* of 1650 and the *Portrait of Saskia* now in Washington, a copy of Hals's *Portrait of Isabella Coymans* now in the Rothschild collection, Hals's half-length *Portrait of a Man*, two De Hoochs, an Adriaen and an Isack van Ostade, and two outstanding Steens (the *Dancing Couple at an Inn* [cat. no. 59] in Washington and the *Merry Company on a Terrace* in the Metropolitan Museum).[129]

The *Catalogue of Paintings Forming the Private Collection of P.A.B. Widener, Part 11* (*Early English and Ancient Paintings*) is dated 1885-1900 and is identical in design to that of Widener's partner in 'traction' (streetcars), William Elkins. Most of the old masters are Dutch, quite varied, and extremely uneven: Cuyp's superb *Departure for the Chase* and some very good genre paintings are balanced by implausible attributions to Cuyp, Van Dyck, Hals, Potter, Rembrandt, Ter Borch, and Vermeer.[130]

The three 'Vermeers' fall out completely from later literature, but they testify to the extraordinary appeal of the painter to East Coast collectors and artists from about 1890 onward. Between Marquand's acquisition of 1887 [1] and Frick's third Vermeer in 1919, about one-third of the known oeuvre was shipped to America. Valentiner's praise of Vermeer in the Hudson-Fulton catalogue and, in the same year (1909), Charles Caffin's description of him as the greatest of all genre painters were merely expressions of a widely held view among American art lovers. This enthusiasm went well beyond the interest demonstrated in England and France, despite Thoré-Bürger's efforts on the artist's behalf. *The Outcry*, a 1909 play involving the discovery of Vermeer's authorship in a canvas attributed to a

lesser hand, may have been staged in London but it was written by Henry James.[131]

Peter Widener's son Joseph inherited the collection in 1915. He is generally considered to have been more methodical and conservative than his father (who also bought Impressionists), and one supposes that the pronouncements of specialists had a sobering effect. Perhaps it was Joseph's collaboration that led to such spectacular acquisitions before 1915 as *The Mill* attributed to Rembrandt [30] (p. 122, fig. 1) and Vermeer's *Woman Weighing Gold*. Joseph Widener cut the collection down from about five hundred to the hundred that were given to the National Gallery of Art in 1942, and he added a Mantegna, Bellini's *Feast of the Gods*, the great Genoese Van Dycks, Rembrandt's *Philemon and Baucis* from the Yerkes sale, the *Descent from the Cross*, and in the early 1920s the exceptional pair of Rembrandt portraits of about 1660 from the collection of Prince Yusupov.[132] Many of the Italian pictures in the National Gallery's Widener Collection, and also the *Young Girl with a Flute* (in my view certainly) by Vermeer were acquired by Joseph Widener. For social reasons that only ancient residents of Philadelphia could now understand, Widener gave his collection to Washington just before he died.

Maurice Brockwell wrote in 1918 that Philadelphia not only had the Johnson Collection in hand (shortly to open at the late donor's residence), but that it had Widener's collection in view.[133] Had that expectation been fulfilled, Philadelphia would now have a collection of Dutch pictures second only to New York's; Brockwell says so, with a nod to the Altman bequest of 1913. John Graver Johnson (1841-1917) went to the same high school as had Peter Widener, who was seven years older, and then made himself the best corporate lawyer in America (according to his clients, Morgan, Frick, Widener, and Havemeyer). He had no use for society; his only serious interests were his family, his profession, and the paintings that he stuffed into his unpretentious house. Chardins in the closet, Barbizons in the bathroom, Dutch and Italian paintings all over the place spilled into the house next door when Johnson bought it near the end of his life. He left his collection not to the museum where it has been housed as an autonomous collection since the mid-1930s, but to the people of Philadelphia. Johnson not only formed his own collection but also chaired the committee that in the 1890s used the Wilstach fund for purchases (Joseph Widener succeeded him).[134]

Like Elkins, Widener, Henry Walters, and many others, Johnson began with fashionable nineteenth-century painters (as well as Courbet, Manet, Eakins, Sargent, and the leading Impressionists) and then moved on to old masters with the intention of illustrating the history of European art. He consulted Berenson, Bode, Hofstede de Groot, Max Friedländer, and Valentiner, whose catalogues of the Dutch, Flemish, German, and other non-Italian pictures were published in 1913-1914. About 150 paintings entered the collection in the next three years. Johnson bought comprehensively and avoided big names; he knew that many of them were wildly overpriced and each one would have decreased his ability to represent a school. As a result, the Johnson Collection includes a lot of paintings that one would find in storage at the Rijksmuseum, but also a remarkably broad and various selection of seventeenth-century Dutch pictures.[135]

It was partly the goal of comprehensiveness that led Johnson to purchase 'primitives' by Italian and Northern artists. Most authors describe this as pioneering but it was not unprecedented. Early German and Flemish paintings bearing familiar names had been collected since Gilmor's generation; they slumped in the middle of the century and came back in the 1880s in response to European interest. Johnson was hardly the only client for whom Kleinberger advertised 'Primitives of All Schools a Specialty.'[136] However, Johnson bought important Early Netherlandish pictures, his greatest coup being Rogier van der Weyden's large diptych, the *Virgin and Saint John* and *Christ on the Cross* (bought from Kleinberger, Paris, in 1906).[137]

Most readers of this essay will know the Johnson Collection and may review the catalogue themselves. Johnson bought all the usual masters except the big three (his token gestures to Hals, Rembrandt, and Vermeer were all wrong and seem half-hearted), and pictures by Dutch artists who only became more widely appreciated in the 1930s or after World War II (for

example, Christoffel van den Berghe and Pieter Saenredam). While Elkins and Peter Widener were merely grand acquisitors, Johnson was one of the first true collectors of Dutch and Flemish art in America. Like later lawyers — one thinks of collecting couples in Boston and on New York's upper west side — Johnson made Dutch and Flemish art his avocation, to which he devoted years of study, travel, and a passion of the mind.

One is tempted to consider Johnson's complete opposite to be Henry Clay Frick (1849-1919) [32]. It is true that he was predominantly a masterpiece collector whose interest in Dutch art was restricted to about ten well-known names. Frick differed from Morgan, however, in that his main interest was painting (more so than business during the last decade of his life) and that Rembrandt [31] was not only his favorite artist but one for whom Frick had profound respect. In many ways (for example, his relationship with workers) Frick was not a likeable man, but in other respects he was admirable. He was friendly with Johnson and with a number of scholars, but cool to Joseph Duveen. His taste in pictures was outstanding, compared with Widener's and that of others who merely had money to spend. Frick's interest in art began when he was about twenty, to judge from a credit report ('maybe a little too enthusiastic about pictures') submitted by an investigator to the Pittsburgh bank of Thomas Mellon and Sons.[138] One of the sons, Andrew, went to Europe with Frick for some months in 1880 [25]. Frick became a collector only around 1895, starting with Barbizon landscapes, which he never disavowed. Perhaps the most appealing aspect of Frick as a collector was his choice of favorite paintings: the Rembrandt *Self-Portrait* of 1658 [31]; Velázquez's *Portrait of Philip IV*; Holbein's *Portrait of Thomas More*; Bellini's *Saint Francis in Ecstasy*; and the only painting that Frick purchased in the last year of his life, Vermeer's *Mistress and Maid*.

Frick had always intended to leave his collection to the public, an idea evidently inspired by an early visit to the Wallace Collection. This must be considered when one describes Frick as a collector of masterpieces, for they represent all the major European schools. Here we can only mention the Dutch paintings. The first 'old master' acquired was the *Young Artist* signed 'Rembrandt' and close to his style of the 1640s.[139] It was purchased in 1889, a year otherwise devoted to Troyon, Corot, and Millet. In 1901 Frick bought Vermeer's *Music Lesson*, a Wouwermans, a Ruisdael no longer in the collection, and landscapes by Israels, Maris, and Mauve. The years 1902-1904 brought in Cuyp's *Cows and Herdsman*, the Ter Borch portrait, and Hobbema's *Village among Trees*, plus a Constable and portraits by Lawrence, Reynolds, and Gainsborough. The period 1905-1907 was more than half Dutch: Cuyp's *Dordrecht: Sunrise*, the Metsu, the Salomon van Ruysdael, Hals's *Portrait of a Painter*, the 'Van de Cappelle' *View of the Maas*, Isack van Ostade's *Halt at an Inn*, a De Vlieger later deaccessioned, and the great Rembrandt *Self-Portrait*. The other artists represented were El Greco, Van Dyck, Titian, Reynolds, Raeburn, Corot, and Millet. In 1908 and 1909 Frick favored British pictures: Romney, Constable, Turner, the Snyders pendants by Van Dyck, and another Cuyp. Except for a Reynolds, 1910 was devoted to two exceptional portraits by Hals, Jacob Van Ruisdael's *View of the Damrak in Amsterdam*, and Rembrandt's *Polish Rider* (p. 123, fig. 2), for which Roger Fry went to Poland on Frick's behalf. In 1911 Frick bought three English portraits and one each by Velázquez and Goya, plus another Hobbema and Vermeer's *Soldier and Laughing Girl*. The next two years were reserved for a few major acquisitions: Holbein's *Portrait of Thomas More*, El Greco's *Portrait of Vincenzo Anastagi*, two large Veroneses, two Guardis, and Van Dyck's monumental *Portrait of the Earl of Derby with His Wife and Child*. Another Van Dyck (*Portrait of Paola Adorno*), two Goyas, two Turners, a Gainsborough, and three Whistlers came in during 1914; in the next year the great Bellini and the murals by Fragonard; in 1916 Titian's *Man in a Red Cap*; and from then on some eighteenth-century English and French pictures, more of Goya and Van Dyck, plus Hals (the so-called *Portrait of Admiral de Ruyter* in 1917), 'De Hooch' (Van der Burch), a Ruisdael that was later sold, and the third Vermeer in Frick's final year. He never bought a Rubens worth keeping, nor Jordaens, nor anything 'baroque'; but he owned dozens of great Dutch paintings, and many English and French landscapes that are sympathetic to the Dutch school.

Frick was a very different 'masterpiece' collector from Morgan or Henry Havemeyer. Though the latter ran the American Sugar Refining Company he was not a sweet man, according to

31
Rembrandt
Self-Portrait
Canvas, 133.7 x 103.8 cm (52 ⅝ x 40 ⅞ in.)
Lower right: *Rembrandt / f. 1658*
New York, The Frick Collection, inv. no. 06.1.97

32
John C. Johansen
Portrait of Henry Clay Frick (posthumous)
Canvas, 142.2 x 91.2 cm (56 x 35 ⅞ in.)
Lower right: *J.C. Johansen – 1943*
New York, The Frick Collection, Gift of Miss Helen C. Frick, 1943, inv. no. 43.1.165

Marquand's letter to Cesnola in 1891.[140] In the long run this did not spoil Havemeyer's friendly intentions toward the Metropolitan Museum; nearly two thousand objects were eventually given to almost every department of the museum by Havemeyer's widow, Louisine, and by her son, Horace, and his sisters. It is not surprising, then, that in a bequest including celebrated Chinese porcelains and bronzes, Renaissance sculpture, and the many paintings by Courbet, Manet, Monet, Degas, and Cézanne for which the Havemeyers are best known, the Dutch pictures are restricted almost exclusively to Rembrandt, with artists such as Goya, El Greco, and Bronzino for company. The Havemeyer old masters were mostly acquired between about 1900 and Henry Havemeyer's death in 1907 (Louisine, with the help of Mary Cassatt, was the real collector of the Impressionists and the El Grecos). The Rembrandts comprise the 'Van Beresteyn' pendants dated 1632 and *Portrait of Herman Doomer* of 1640; the so-called *Admiral* and the portrait of his wife (the latter inscribed *Rembrandt f / 1643*) and the *Old Woman* similarly signed and dated 1640 would have been considered authentic by any scholar of the period. The Havemeyers also gave Hals's very small portraits of Petrus Scriverius and his wife (1626) and De Hooch's prototypical picture, *The Visit*, of about 1657.[141]

The great collectors of the age made an impression on countless contemporary amateurs who can be discussed here only briefly if at all. For example, William Clark, the copper king and senator from Montana, was a self-made man and self-trained connoisseur whose voracious collecting was inspired by the cultural atmosphere of New York City. From about 1900 onward old masters of uneven quality were crowded into the galleries of Clark's extravagant palace on Fifth Avenue at 77th Street (demolished in 1927). They included the Ter Borch and the five Dutch landscapes that Clark lent to the Hudson-Fulton Exhibition, and other Dutch pictures now in the Corcoran Gallery of Art in Washington.[142] Clark collected with almost indiscriminately catholic (and not at all Catholic) taste, although in general his paintings fall into the following four categories, which are frequently encountered in the collections of the time: seventeenth-century Dutch, eighteenth-century English, nineteenth-century American, and Barbizon. A step inside one of the dusky mansions of the Gilded Age would make one realize that this taste was more consistent than it appears in museums today.

A collection similar but superior to Clark's was formed by Charles and Annie Taft of Cincinnati. Anna Sinton became the richest woman in Ohio when her father died in 1900; his fortune, made in iron ore and real estate, left his daughter about fifteen million dollars. This was more than enough to bring great paintings by Rembrandt and by Hals to Cincinnati and to put Charles's half-brother, William Howard Taft, into the White House. Charles had gone to Yale and to law school at Columbia before earning a doctorate in Heidelberg in 1870. In that year Annie and her father had their busts carved by Hiram Powers in Florence. Thus it was two students of Culture who married 'on the banks of the Ohio' in 1873.

The couple first went to Europe together in 1901; they toured Italy and stayed in Paris after visiting Cairo, Constantinople, Athens, and Jerusalem. In Paris they saw the collection of Baron Gustave de Rothschild which must have increased their interest in old masters as well as in Limoges. Nonetheless, it was Chinese porcelain and Barbizon pictures that the Tafts bought in New York (the paintings at Arthur Tooth and Sons) on two trips in 1902. Over the next five or six years the Tafts bought porcelain and enamels from Duveen's, but resisted the firm's considerable efforts to interest the Tafts in Italian art. English and Barbizon paintings were purchased from Scott and Fowles. In 1905 the Tafts (who had visited Holland two years earlier) bought a group of Hague School pictures and their large 'Van Dyck' [**33**] which also dates from the late nineteenth century.[143]

Hals's extraordinary *Portrait of a Man ('Michiel de Wael')* and a fine Hobbema were acquired in the following year. After obtaining two pictures each by Turner, Gainsborough, Raeburn, Daubigny, and Ziem, the Tafts concentrated on getting William elected president. Within the year after his inauguration in 1909 they bought pendant portraits by Hals, and Rembrandt's *Portrait of a Man Rising from His Chair* [**33**] (cat. no. 51), the pendant (cat. no. 52) which was given to the Metropolitan Museum in 1943.[144] The pictures by Rembrandt, Hals, Hobbema, and the English portraits were exhibited at Scott and Fowles, New York, while the Hudson-Fulton show was still in progress. A writer in *The International Studio* applauded the Tafts' ability 'at this late date to amass such admirable paintings.'[145]

A dozen other Dutch or Dutch-like pictures were purchased in the same years; small works by Ruisdael, Steen, and Van Ostade (the *Toper*) were bought in 1910. The large landscape by Van der Neer was acquired in 1911, the beautiful Ter Borch in 1916, the De Hooch in 1924. Occasionally a spectacular price was paid for a dubious picture, but for the most part the Tafts were well advised by their friend Charles Fowles.[146]

Sir Martin Conway's understated style of putting down a

34
A corner of the reception room in the home of Sir
William van Horne, Montreal (ca. 1905).
According to Van Horne, the paintings were (left to
right) by Maes, Cuyp, Vermeer, and Rembrandt.
From: *The Connoisseur*, July 1905

collector is more memorable than the pictures he mentions: 'I do
not clearly remember the Rembrandt or the Vermeer, but there
is a portrait of an old lady reading, by Nicolas Maes, which it is
impossible to forget' [**34**].[117] He is speaking of the Dutch, Barbizon,
and fake pictures in the Montreal collection of Sir William van
Horne, who was the builder of the Canadian Pacific Railroad
and of railways in Cuba and Central America. His connoisseurship skills were honed on fossils and applied to a house full of
'furniture, bronzes, pottery, and what not. It is impossible to
write of these things at length.' Nonetheless, Conway cites a still
life on which traces of Carel Fabritius's signature were to be
discerned, and a Ruisdael *'Haerlempje'* with later figures. A few
very fine Dutch paintings made their way past the ship models
dangling in Van Horne's hall, including Rembrandt's (?) *Young
Jew* of 1661 (now in the Kimbell Art Museum, Fort Worth), Hals's
pendant portraits of 1637, and his small portrait of Samuel
Ampzing (the latter now in a New York collection).[148] The writer
can vouch for the early De Witte (National Gallery of Canada),[149]
but not for the 'examples of Albert Cuyp, Van der Helst, William
van de Velde, and others.'[150]

It would be difficult, looking back from this point in our

survey, to suggest who the greatest collector of Dutch paintings in the Gilded Age may have been. It would also be hard to imagine, from the foregoing, what kind of person he was. He did not have a railroad, a bank, a mine, or a prominent place in society. He was shy, a bachelor, a merchant, an immigrant, a Jew, and a frugal collector who in 1882 walked up three flights of stairs to the gallery of Henry Duveen. He left with two Chinese cloisonné vases that are now in the Metropolitan Museum, 'Bequest of Benjamin Altman, 1913.'

Altman [35] continued to buy from Duveen's, and from a few other dealers such as Seligman. He was one of those new collectors who '*know*, especially since Mr. Joseph Duveen has confirmed the fact, that Rembrandt is a great artist and they are insatiable in gluttony of his portraits. Mr. Altman feels, very properly, that he cannot get too much of a good thing. He now has eight' [36]. These waspish opinions were offered by Johnson to, ironically, Berenson, in the fall of 1909.[151] Earlier in the year Berenson had been summoned to Altman's 'enormous shop' on Fifth Avenue where he was asked to form a collection. Unfortunately, Altman seemed barely familiar with the names that Berenson mentioned (except Rembrandt's), since he had previously pursued 'Dutch pictures and pictures of the Barbizon school.'[152] The next encounter took place in London on

6 September. Berenson and Henry Duveen showed Altman two paintings by Velázquez. 'Altman and his train simply jeered and sneered at them,' Berenson wrote to Mary, adding that he caught a cold from Altman in the Victoria and Albert Museum. 'I truly believe that is all I positively shall have got out of that old sheenie.'[153]

To make matters worse for his 'advisor,' Altman went back on his own to Duveen's and bought three Rembrandts and 'the great Ruysdael' (*The Wheatfields* by Jacob van Ruisdael) which the firm had just acquired along with the rest of the collection of Maurice Kann.[154] Despite such sweeping gestures, Altman was 'the despair of dealers,' a slow, careful collector who read books, consulted experts, and ignored opinions when they failed to dovetail with the evidence of his very good eye.[155] This approach, the opposite of Morgan's spontaneous decisions, cost Altman the *Aristotles* which Duveen sold instead to Mrs. Collis P. Huntington. However, Altman's Rembrandts include the *Self-Portrait* of 1660, a great pair of late portraits (*Man with a Magnifying Glass* and *Woman with a Pink*), the small *Bathsheba*, two single portraits and the doubtful *Auctioneer*, plus such once-impressive works signed 'Rembrandt' as the *Titus* and the *Old Woman Cutting Her Nails* [37].[156]

Johnson's view of Altman is brushed aside by the evidence of Hals's *Merry Company* and the '*Jonker Ramp*,' two famous early genre pictures that stand quite apart from the Halses bought by Frick, Morgan, Widener, Huntington, and the Tafts. The same is true of Altman's early Vermeer, *The Sleeping Maid* (Rodolphe Kann to Duveen to Altman in 1907-1908), which looks more at home next to Altman's Maes than it would next to any other Vermeer in America. Altman's Cuyp, Hobbema, and Ruisdael are outstanding, while the *Self-Portrait* by Dou and the genre scene by Ter Borch are very good. When one considers that Altman's portraits by Rembrandt once hung with Van Dyck's '*Marchesa Durazzo*' and the commanding *Portrait of Lucas van Uffele* [36]; that the Dou and the Ter Borch shared space with three portraits by Memling, his *Marriage of Saint Catherine*, and an exceptional portrait by Bouts; that Christian subjects by Gerard David, Dürer, Bernaert van Orley, and Velázquez (*The Supper at Emmaus*) were purchased largely for reasons of sheer quality; then Johnson's remarks and even his approach to collecting seem like the products of a comparatively petty mind. In a contest with Johnson, Altman could have sent in the second string, his cousin and successor at B. Altman's, Michael Friedsam [39]. Altman not only left one of the finest collections of northern paintings to be formed in his generation, but he also inspired one of the finest formed in the next.[157]

35
Ellen Emmet Rand
Portrait of Benjamin Altman
Canvas, 112.4 x 84.5 cm (44 ¼ x 33 ¼ in.)
Upper right: *Ellen Emmet Rand / 1914*
New York, The Metropolitan Museum of Art, Estate of Benjamin Altman, inv. no. 14.122

36

An interior view of Benjamin Altman's art gallery, which was built in 1909 behind his house at 626 Fifth Avenue, New York (ca. 1915?).
The paintings on the left wall are: Rembrandt, *Man with a Magnifying Glass*; Style of Rembrandt, *Pilate Washing His Hands*; Rembrandt, *Lady with a Pink*; Cuyp, *Young Herdsmen with Cows*; Rembrandt (?), *Portrait of a Man Holding Gloves*; Vermeer, *A Girl Asleep*; Rembrandt, *Portrait of a Woman*, 1633; Hals (recently attributed to Leyster), *Boy with a Lute*; Rembrandt (?), *Portrait of a Young Man (The Auctioneer)*; possibly the Rembrandt School *Man with a Steel Gorget*; two small paintings, perhaps the Dou *Self-Portrait* and Gerard ter Borch's *Woman Playing the Theorbo*. On the end wall are Van Dyck's *Portrait of Lucas van Uffele*, Velázquez's *Philip IV*, and Van Dyck's *Portrait of the Marchesa Durazzo*.

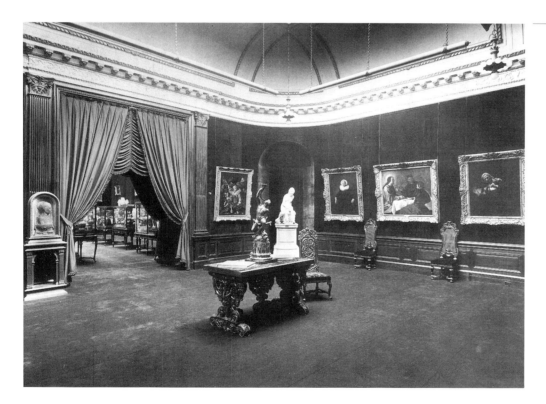

37

An interior view of Benjamin Altman's art gallery behind his house at 626 Fifth Avenue (ca. 1915?).
The paintings are Hals's early *Merrymakers at Shrovetide*; the Dutch (Jacob Backer?) *Old Woman in an Armchair* signed and dated *Rembrand: f. / 1635*; Velázquez's *Supper at Emmaus*; the Rembrandt School *Old Woman Cutting Her Nails*, from the Rodolphe Kann Collection, which was a famous Rembrandt of the time.

Johnson and Altman were two of the best and least typical collectors of the Gilded Age, which should discourage any short synopsis of the period. Taste, social background, artistic and even ethical ideals remained decisive undercurrents in the sea of money and ambition that gave America its public museums and its major collections of Dutch painting. Sheer volume and quality are part of our story; nearly one-third of Vermeer's oeuvre and substantial parts of the oeuvres of Rembrandt, Ruisdael, Hobbema, Hals, and other important Dutch painters entered America during this first great period of prosperity and involvement in world affairs. It will never happen again in this country, probably for reasons of demand and certainly for those of supply. Both sides of the market, it should be remembered, were parts of the equation, which was calculated daily by dealers such as Agnew, Colnaghi, Dowdeswell and Dowdeswell, Duveen, Kleinberger and his son-in-law Sperling, Knoedler, Scott and Fowles, Seligman, and Wildenstein. A great number of America's Dutch paintings came out of England (thus The Outcry, James's play of 1909), France, Belgium, Poland, and later Russia, as well as the Netherlands. The American government's repeal of import duties on works of art over one hundred years old, which was adopted on 5 August 1909, allowed Morgan's paintings to be sent from Paris and from London, two cities in which the Kann collections were available from Duveen's. Rodolphe and Maurice Kann were themselves masterpiece collectors; Duveen, for whom the only great Dutch painters were Hals and Rembrandt, bought both Kann collections for 4.5 million dollars in 1907 (R. Kann) and 2.5 million dollars in 1909 (M. Kann). An astonishing number of America's Dutch paintings came from the Kanns, including the Aristotle and other great Rembrandts once owned by Morgan, Altman, Mrs. Huntington, and, to his credit, William van Horne. The historian who speaks of what Americans 'want' in the way of Rembrandt, Hals, Ruisdael, Hobbema, Cuyp, Ter Borch, Metsu, Vermeer (Altman's), Potter, Wouwermans, and so on had better consider what Americans got out of Rodolphe Kann.[158]

In the same year that Duveen struck a deal for the second Kann collection, 1909, Kleinberger bought en bloc the old masters belonging to King Leopold of Belgium.[159] This was 'slim pickin's' by comparison, about forty Dutch and Flemish pictures of uneven quality. A closer study of American collecting during the Gilded Age could begin with the sales of many similar collections in Europe, perhaps starting with that of Prince Demidoff in 1880. The same study would dig deeper into the scholarly middlemen. Few critics who have raised an eyebrow at Berenson seem to be

familiar with the hundreds of certificates, let alone the more confidential correspondence, written by Bode, Bredius, Hofstede de Groot, Valentiner, and other authorities on Dutch art. Their big publications, which were usually translated into English and often published in New York, were supported by one foot in the profession and the other in the trade.

It would be narrow, however, to complain about Dutch and German certificates or the 'really big Yankee cheque' (borne by Breckenridge Bender, the dealer in James's The Outcry).[160] The end of American isolation thrust the Last Innocents onto an international stage where no one, it turned out, was innocent. How does one answer Duveen's declaration that a Qing blue and white pot (which brought 4,300 dollars at auction in 1974) was 'simply put, the finest extant piece of Chinese porcelain'?[161] Perhaps with a compliment Altman once paid to Berenson – that he had at least the 'makings of one of the best merchants he ever saw.'[162]

Between the World Wars

Advertisements for the evocatively named Metropolitan Galleries (New York) in the April 1929 issues of the Art News list 'English XVIII Century, Dutch XVI and XVII Century, Spanish XVII Century, Venetian XVI Century, Also Early American and Contemporary Art' as the firm's specialties. Similar announcements in journals such as The Arts, The Art Digest, Art News, and Arts and Decoration provide an entertaining index to upscale American taste and reflect a gradual change in the art market from 'The Brown Decades' of Dutch, American, and Barbizon painting to the bright and colorful epoch of the Impressionists and modernism.[163] Some dealers hedged their bets, while others, such as Duveen and Wildenstein, showed American clients what they ought to have: French and Italian paintings. A decorator of the 1920s and 1930s would be better qualified than the art historian is now to describe the common denominator between Duveen's Botticellis, Wildenstein's Bouchers, and any dealers' pictures by Degas. Windows were larger, spaces uncluttered, furniture cream and gold, walls nearly bare by nineteenth-century standards and discreetly embellished by 'classical' details. The definitive designers were Ogden Codman and Elsie de Wolfe who were all wrong by Wright's standards but perfectly well suited to Knoedler and Gimpel et fils.[164] Mrs. Kate Shaeffer remembers the market for Dutch paintings during the 1930s as struggling (especially for a dealer accustomed to Bode's Berlin). Money was tight and Monet was everywhere.

The major collectors of Dutch paintings during the Gilded Age were working within the mainstream of American taste. Dutch art never went out of favor but it was no longer fashionable after the First World War. The most important purchasers of seventeenth-century Dutch paintings were, in a very broad view, of two kinds: the masterpiece collector, such as Andrew Mellon, whose list of desirable Dutch painters was just slightly longer than Duveen's; and the specialized collector, such as Michael Friedsam, whose collection was left in 1931 to the Metropolitan Museum.

Friedsam was strongly influenced by Altman; his interests, like those of Mellon and Joseph Widener, developed in the decades of Johnson and Frick. Thus, Friedsam and Mellon, although important collectors after the war, were the old guard when the new guard was represented by Louisine Havemeyer (whatever the lady's age) and the avant-garde by the Cone sisters in Baltimore, and by their friends Leo and Gertrude Stein.[165] With this perspective, a survey of the Metropolitan Museum's accessions from 1915 to as late as 1970 (bequests often come from collections formed at least a generation earlier) reveals comparatively little interest in Dutch art.[166] Perhaps a dozen Dutch pictures (which in some cases were stragglers from decades before) came in between the Altman bequest of 1913 and the Bache bequest of 1949, apart from those collected and usually promised much earlier: Morgan (17.190), Vanderbilt (20.155), Collis P. Huntington (25.110), Havemeyer (29.100), Theodore Davis (30.95), and Friedsam (32.100). In the same period there was a constant flow of French and Italian art; nineteenth-century French painting is by no means confined to the Havemeyer collection, nor is early Italian limited to the gifts of George Blumenthal (41.100 and 41.190). Indeed, Friedsam's own collection and, secondly, that of Jules Bache recall the Johnson Collection in their concentration on early Italian and early Northern art. This is not to say that the Friedsam and Bache collections were old-fashioned, but that, on the contrary, they followed Johnson's in defining a trend of the twentieth century. Both in old masters and in moderns, the tendency was toward more specialized and (in this sense, at least) more sophisticated collections. Mellon's collection, however, was the last great American effort to reach the level of European museums.

This point provides one more symbol that can be read into Van Eyck's *Annunciation*, since Mellon bought it in 1930, for 503,000 dollars, from the walls of the Hermitage. Four of the Rembrandts, two of the Halses, a Rubens and four Van Dycks, Raphael's *Alba Madonna*, Botticelli's *Adoration*, and five other great paintings were also sold by the Soviets through Knoedler's to Mellon in 1930 and 1931.[167] Duveen supposedly applauded the transaction with the words 'He's ready for me' [**38**].[168] On behalf of the National Gallery, Mellon was eventually prepared to buy some very important Italian pictures from Duveen.[169] The Dutch paintings, consisting of nine Rembrandts (among them *Portrait of a Young Man*, cat. no. 53), six portraits by Hals, three by Hobbema, and one picture each by Cuyp, De Hooch, Maes, and Vermeer (the *Girl with a Red Hat*) had for the most part already been acquired by 1931. Mellon had little knowledge but genuine appreciation of these works of art, as is evident from their

38
Joseph Duveen and Andrew Mellon at the Mellon tax hearing in Washington, 9 May 1935.
Photo: UPI / Bettman Archive, New York

consistently high quality. He was a late bloomer, but in hindsight the worthy companion of his old friend Frick.

'Some of us regret that the Woolworth building, which could have been taller than the Eiffel Tower, is merely more beautiful': this is how the painter and writer Guy Pène du Bois placed the possessions of Michael Friedsam [**39**] among 'Famous American Collections' as of 1917.[170] 'Its predominating note is made by Italian, Flemish, French and German Primitives,' and some 'simpler Dutchmen.' There were also English portraits in the 'Adam Room.' Scholars primarily interested in Dutch art may not realize the extent to which early Italian and early Netherlandish paintings figured in Friedsam's collection, which was generally grouped by nationality in his rooms. The Dutch section [**40**], like the rest, 'harbors a number of great names [...] quite incidentally.' Friedsam gave to the Metropolitan Museum its fourth Vermeer, the now remarkably underrated *Allegory of Faith*, Rembrandt's *Bellona*, Ruisdael's *Grainfields*, Brouwer's famous *Smokers*, Cuyp's superb *Starting for the Hunt*, Maes's small *Lacemaker*, Brekelenkam's *Sentimental Conversation*, and a few other Dutch pictures that are exceptional in the artists' oeuvres and in American collections of the period. Equal or greater discrimination is seen in Friedsam's early Flemish paintings, such as Rogier van der Weyden's *Portrait of Francesco d'Este*, *The Annunciation*

39
Photograph of Michael Friedsam (ca. 1910)

attributed to Van Eyck, and the panels by Gerard David, Massys, Memling, Gossaert, and others. To conclude that Friedsam was not precisely a collector of Dutch art would fail to appreciate that he was precisely that as well as an unusually careful collector in other categories.

More than Johnson, although with similar interests and public goals, Friedsam was a collector whose aim was to represent certain schools. The increasing importance of art museums and specialized scholars and literature must have determined his progress, although it is unclear to what extent. However, one of the remarkable aspects of the Friedsam Collection is the relatively low number of misattributions, especially of the kind that betray (as do Valentiner's) the enthusiasms of the period.

The quality, historical interest, and for the most part condition found in the Friedsam pictures may be contrasted to the results of John Ringling's approach in the late 1920s. In about five years the circus impresario acquired over six hundred paintings, most of them Dutch or Flemish, the latter with an unprecedented emphasis, for an American, on theatrical baroque designs. Ringling employed the Munich dealer Julius Boehler and his own eye, with consequences similar, if superior, to those of Crocker in the 1870s. One of several outstanding Dutch paintings in Sarasota is Hals's *Portrait of Pieter Olycan*.[171]

A different kind of outdated approach was taken by the Wall Street investor Jules Bache. Although born in 1861 Bache did not attempt until the 1920s to build his 'Collection of Masterpieces.'[172] Inspired by Philip Lehman and George Blumenthal, Bache began in 1919 with a little 'Rembrandt' (*Young Man in a Red Cloak*), a ruined imitation for which he paid a fortune (40,000 dollars) to Wildenstein. By 1924 Bache was firmly sheltered under Duveen's wing: Van Dyck's *Self-Portrait*, bought in that year, was followed in the next by the same master's *Portrait of the Earl of Warwick*. In 1926 Duveen sold Bache Rembrandt's *Standard-Bearer (Portrait of Floris Soop)* of 1654 and a supposed Velázquez 'self-portrait'; at the same time a Boucher, a Drouais, and three Fragonards were acquired from Wildenstein. Paintings by Titian, Bellini, Goya, Romney, and other diverse but familiar names came in during 1927, when Bache also bought Ter Borch's exquisite *Curiosity* and the *Christ with a Pilgrim's Staff* which is still attributed by some scholars to Rembrandt. In 1928 Bache obtained Hals's *Portrait of Claes van Voorhout* from Duveen, and his second fake Vermeer, the *Young Woman Reading*, from Wildenstein (135,000 dollars; worth 5,000 dollars today). During 1928 and 1929 Duveen sold Bache a number of Italian and Northern Renaissance pictures, and Watteau's *French Comedians*.

His house full, Bache was finished, just before the Wall Street
Crash.

Bache adored Joseph Duveen, who treated the old man fairly
and affectionately. Many of the late acquisitions from Duveen
were paid for years after the Crash. In the mid-1930s Duveen
persuaded 'Julie' to establish a public foundation, which opened
in 1937; Bache himself, ten years after Duveen's death in 1939,
decided to leave his collection to the Metropolitan Museum.
The whole story – the dependence on Duveen, the great paintings,
the duplication (later dismantled) of Bache's private rooms in
the museum, and the purchase of a 'Vermeer' that would have
embarrassed Hannema – tempts one to repeat the familiar
refrain 'only in America.'

Dutch paintings form a comparatively small part of the
collection named for Samuel Kress, the department store
entrepreneur who bought Italian pictures by the hundreds
during the 1920s and 1930s. Boredom and his lady friend led
Kress to Count Contini-Bonacossi, the Florentine *marchand-
amateur*, stamp collector, and Fascist senator. The rest is history
beyond our topic here, and one written well enough by John
Walker, the man who secured the Kress Collection for the
National Gallery of Art.[173] It is less well known that the Northern
paintings in the Kress Collection, which have been catalogued by
Colin Eisler,[174] were purchased for the Kress Foundation mostly
by Sam's modest younger brother Rush. Both of the Saenredams
in Washington were bought by Rush Kress in 1954, eight years
after Samuel Kress had a debilitating stroke. Other Dutch paintings now in the Kress Collection at many American museums
have nothing to do with Dutch art collecting *per se*, but a great
deal to do with the American tradition of private support for
public institutions.

The role of curators and directors (Walker was both), and of
museums in general, became increasingly important for the
collecting of Dutch and Flemish art in America from about 1920
onward. The most conspicuous example, of course, is William
Valentiner's directorship of the Detroit Institute of Arts (from
1924 to 1944). Whatever reservations scholars may have about his
'almost absurd expansionist approach' to defining the oeuvres of
Hals and Rembrandt,[175] Valentiner's books and exhibitions,[176]
his constant contact with private collectors,[177] his solicitation of
donors, and truly last but not least his purchases of Dutch and
Flemish paintings for the Detroit museum made him one of the

most influential figures in America. This was during a period when Dutch pictures, apart from masterpieces by certain artists, were less in demand than they were during Valentiner's earlier tenure as curator of decorative arts at the Metropolitan Museum. Valentiner bought Rembrandt's affecting *Visitation* of 1640 but also such academic acquisitions as the perspective box attributed to Van Hoogstraten. His role at Raleigh in the 1950s and other aspects of Valentiner's career are discussed in Sterne's biography.[178]

It was between the two world wars that museums first began to surpass private collectors as purchasers of European art. From all of the above it will be clear that private and institutional collecting were virtually inseparable throughout most of American history. However, the anti-trust and other reform movements of around 1900-1915, the introduction of income tax, and the Great Depression of the 1930s were among the factors that discouraged the making of outrageous fortunes like those of the Gilded Age. At the same time, the growth of American cities (which accounted for over half the country's population from 1920 onward) and more widespread civic-mindedness encouraged the founding and flourishing of cultural institutions in many of the states. The Baltimore Museum of Art opened in 1929, the same city's Walters Art Gallery in 1931 (Dutch pictures are minor parts of these collections).[179] The Cincinnati Art Museum is older, but its Dutch paintings come mostly from the bequest of Mary Emery in 1927 and from that of Mary Hanna in 1946.[180] Both collectors purchased pictures with the city's museum in mind. Cleveland's acquisitions were advised by Wolfgang Stechow,[181] who with Julius Held and other eminent European scholars of Northern art came to America in the 1930s. Among the museums that were founded or expanded in the 1920s and 1930s are those in Hartford, Kansas City, Indianapolis, and San Francisco, each of which has a small but distinguished collection of Dutch art.[182]

Many of the donations made in this transitional period were of collections formed in or by the fortunes of the Gilded Age. New collectors looked at European pictures without the same background in traditional American taste. The rise of the Impressionist market and the influence of even more modern art (Altman died in the year of the Armory Show) were developments likely to dampen interest in artists such as the Van Ostades, if not Hals. Saenredam's reputation dates from the 1920s and 1930s, a Dutch cause soon to be celebrated by the Boston, Washington, and Worcester acquisitions of 1948, 1954, and 1955, respectively.

In a very broad view, American collecting of Dutch art appears to have been an exercise in nineteenth-century taste from about 1830 to 1945. More recent collections have benefited from the influence of museums and universities. The educational function of museums as envisioned by their founders was aimed at the masses not *amateurs*, and in any case was to some extent perverted during the age of affluence. Collectors like Bache were enlightened by dealers such as Duveen and by a small circle of experts who were not always disinterested. From the 1940s onward, collectors turned increasingly to museum curators and directors for advice. A more specialized or historically-minded approach was also fostered by the increasing rarity of unlimited, untaxable, unconscionable wealth; dealers as well as scholars came around to the notion that a collection could be great on relative, not absolute, grounds.

These general tendencies did not turn collectors of Dutch paintings into one group among equals. There is no comparable circle of 'Flemish' collectors, and none of English, French, Italian, or other, except of American art. For several obvious reasons baroque painting has until very recently been unfashionable in America. Even Rubens is an entirely twentieth-century story on this side of the Atlantic; the only seventeenth-century pictures long in favor have been Dutch, or have been thought to be by David Teniers.[183]

After the Second World War

The subject of American collectors active from the 1930s onward raises the question of who is American: Einstein, Panofsky, Thomas Mann? One could replace these names with those of numerous collectors from abroad. They are all American, with the possible exception (that is, objection) of Mann. Like many modern questions, this one is more complicated than it would have been for James.

Late and living collectors of Dutch art will be barely mentioned here; they will be discussed in Peter Sutton's contribution to this catalogue. Attention should shift in this section to museums and to universities, which will be more thoroughly treated in the essay by Susan Kuretsky. Private (and lately, corporate) benefactors remain indispensable to American museums, but in contrast to earlier periods many paintings have been purchased or pursued individually, with close consideration of what a collection lacked. The Dutch collections that have developed since the war – for example, Hartford, Los Angeles, Minneapolis, Raleigh, Saint Louis, Toledo, Worcester, and of course Malibu (The J. Paul

Getty Museum) – are respected not for the rate but for the intelligence of their acquisitions.

Some of the pictures that have been purchased by the Metropolitan Museum since the war are the early and extraordinary still life by Claesz (Rogers Fund, 1949), the large *Falconer's Bag* by Jan Weenix (1950), Ter Brugghen's *Crucifixion* (1956), the *Merry Company on a Terrace* by Jan Steen (1958), Rembrandt's *Aristotle* (1961), and the 1603 *Vanitas* by Jacques de Gheyn (1974). One will notice a certain variety of style and subject, especially if all the other acquisitions are added in and compared with the collections of Frick and Mellon. Perhaps the finest private collection of Dutch pictures formed in the United States since the war is now occasionally criticized for its narrow conception of what is Dutch.[184]

And that is pedantry: taste is not a textbook. The most remarkable aspect of Dutch art collections today is that they are almost all specialized, as scholars describe them, since Americans are still shy of the word 'sophisticated.' The reasons for this are only partly economic or academic; the collectors themselves are an exceedingly diverse crowd. Abrams, Bader, Carter, Goldschmidt, Guterman, Heinz, Kaufman, Lowenthal, Steinberg, Weldon, and Wolf – one can only delight in what different people these individuals are.[185] The present market for Dutch art in America would drive Duveen crazy, and few of these collectors would visit him. Most of them prefer the company of dealers and scholars who know the material better than they do and are willing to give time.

To explain the rejuvenation of American interest in Dutch painting since the second World War, one would not compare the collectors' professions or trace their family trees. They are not mostly Dutch or English, nor mostly Protestant, or 'typically' Protestant when they are. To compare the United States and the United Netherlands as democracies would seem to them a quaint idea. In other ways, however, Americans of the present resemble those of the past. They esteem independent observation, in themselves and in others, and in the pictures they collect. They are wary of institutions, doctrines, conformity (their own non-conformity is conventional), and of those who represent powerful patronage. They enshrine the Unknown Soldier and discover the unknown artist; they root for the little guy. They love nature, family, the home, privacy, and work that is self-assigned. Craftsmanship is valued, and more so individuality.

Since 1945 major collections that are partly Dutch have been formed and given away: the Blaffer Foundation in Houston; the Chrysler Museum in Norfolk; the Lehman and Linsky collections in the Metropolitan Museum; the Bob Jones University Museum of Sacred Art in Greenville, South Carolina; and the Norton Simon Museum in Pasadena, California. In the future, donations will be smaller and probably more specialized; surely collections like those in New York and Washington will never be formed again. New collectors will flourish, but the nation as a whole may rest content in this area, and in many others too. It is time to appreciate what we have, 'much as the good folks used to do in New York and Albany in good old simple times.'[186]

Postscript: America and Europe

One does not reach a conclusion in an essay such as this. 'Notes for further study' would be a better way to end, and the endnotes partly provide them. For the broader perspective we might, for the last time, clutch at the sleeve of James. How does this story read from the opposite shore?

James's relevance to the subject is that he was devoted to European culture but retained an American point of view. It might be objected, however, that our collectors were not critics, but enthusiasts like Hawthorne at the famous Manchester exhibition of 1857: 'such life-like representations of cabbages, turnips, cauliflowers, and peas.'[187] After two weeks Hawthorne declared himself to be 'making some progress as a connoisseur,' and was 'able to distinguish the broader differences of *style*, as, for example, between Rubens and Rembrandt.'[188]

It may have been better to tip the balance of our essay toward the other side of James, that is, to Ruskin, Thoré-Bürger, and nineteenth-century European painting and politics. After all, the many American critics of Rubens were right in line with Ruskin, for whom the artist was 'a healthy, worthy, kind-hearted, courtly-phrased animal.'[189] Similarly, Motley, in the *Rise of the Dutch Republic*, recalls Thoré's interpretation of seventeenth-century Holland as 'a new, strange society [...] as is today the young, Protestant and Democratic society of America.'[190] Thoré is also of interest for his support of the Barbizon painters, not to mention his devotion to Vermeer.[191]

We might also widen our horizon by reviewing the stature of Dutch art in England and France. In 1828 the Scottish dealer James Irvine wrote of London dealers that 'their taste is chiefly formed on that of England where they are so particular about Dutch and Flemish pictures.'[192] The idea of collecting paintings of specific schools as historical specimens was well-established in England by the mid-nineteenth century.[193] The collection of the prime minister, Sir Robert Peel, was dedicated exclusively to

Dutch and Flemish pictures and was formed with the help of dealers such as John Smith and C.J. Nieuwenhuys, and the painter David Wilkie.[194] In our introductory pages we compare the National Gallery's '1871 purchase' of the Peel collection with that of the Metropolitan Museum. On the subject of public collections, the American reader who considers bequests to be a native tradition should read the history of English museums (for example, the Wallace Collection, which was left to the nation in 1897), and the recent exhibition catalogue, *Les donateurs du Louvre*.[195]

The appreciation of Dutch art in nineteenth-century England and France has been studied with respect to the painters by Petra ten Doesschate Chu,[196] and with regard to 'taste, fashion and collecting' by Francis Haskell.[197] The same rediscovery was made in the Netherlands itself during the first half of the nineteenth century, as we were reminded by two exhibitions, *Het Vaderlandsch Gevoel* (The Patriotic Sentiment), and *Op zoek naar de Gouden Eeuw* (In Search of the Golden Age).[198] The close relationship between American artists active during the Gilded Age and Dutch and Flemish painters of the same period (The Hague School, and others) is documented emphatically by the 1883 'Pedestal Fund Art Loan Exhibition' (on behalf of the Statue of Liberty), and is analyzed in Annette Stott's excellent dissertation on the many *American Painters who worked in the Netherlands, 1880-1914*.[199]

It is left for the reader to further fill in the background of Dutch art in America. The more complicated social and psychological questions go beyond our sphere. On this subject one of the most well-informed, if not subtle, discussions from a European perspective is William Valentiner's article 'Amerikanische Privatsammlungen,' written in enemy territory during 1918.[200] Valentiner knew that this essay would not be read in America; his blunt remarks about Morgan, Frick, Widener, and other (in his view) typically American collectors make fascinating reading but do not bear repeating here.[201] We are better off with the elliptical prose of James.

1 *Rutledge 1949*, p. 34, quoting a letter of 1837.
2 *James 1875 / 1986*, p. 173
3 *James 1903 / 1960*, p. 259, referring to *Fromentin 1876*.
4 Quoted by Tony Tanner in the 1985 Penguin edition of *James 1878 / 1985*, p. 13, with no reference, but James is quoting Hawthorne (in *James 1879?*).
5 *Edel 1956*, pp. 4-5
6 *Tocqueville / Heffner 1956*, p. 18
7 *James 1872 / 1956*, p. 65
8 See my introductory essay in *Bauman / Liedtke et al. 1990*.
9 *Tocqueville / Heffner 1956*, 172
10 *Tocqueville / Heffner 1956*, p. 18
11 *Tocqueville / Heffner 1956*, pp. 144, 155

12 *Tocqueville / Heffner 1956*, p. 19
13 The phrase is taken from *Schama 1987*.
14 See my 'Postscript' below, pp. 55-56.
15 According to *Allen 1965*, p. 160
16 *Sutton 1986*, p. xiii, and in lectures, has recalled that the Netherlands was first to recognize the United States, in April 1782. The political, let alone the cultural, significance of this is unclear. Throughout the Revolutionary War the Dutch were generally sympathetic to the Americans but behaved with consistent self-interest. J.D. van der Capellen's pamphlets and speeches in support of America, and especially his argument against lending Britain Dutch troops to fight overseas (1775), earned him the Stadholder's enmity and expulsion from the States of Overijssel. The Dutch supplied gunpowder to the Americans but at seven times the Amsterdam price. Formal recognition of the United States was long debated and was achieved in good part through the efforts of an eccentric Dutchman, Charles Dumas, and the diplomacy of John Adams, then envoy to the Netherlands. 'Not even the foundation of the Roman Empire had cost such exertions,' Dumas wrote (in Latin) to Benjamin Franklin when recognition was finally announced. Relations with England and France were central to the Dutch decision. On these questions see *Schulte Nordholt 1982*, pp. 25-26, 34-36, 47-56, and chaps. 14-16. Adams himself praised Dutch 'Learning and Arts' but lamented their 'general Littleness arising from the incessant Contemplation of Stivers and Doits' (letters of 1780 and 1781 quoted in *Schulte Nordholt 1982*, p. 5).
17 *Motley 1852*
18 *McLanathan 1968*, p. 15
19 *James 1872 / 1956*, p. 65
20 *Wilmerding 1976*, pp. 17-20, for this and the following quotes.
21 *Green 1971*; *Mooz 1973*, pp. 27-28
22 Compare *Wilmerding 1976*, chap. 4 on Smibert. My concern here is not Smibert's importance but the antagonism between an international style and a native tradition.
23 Gordon S. Wood in *Schlesinger 1983*, p. 21, quoting Burke.
24 *Taylor 1979*, pp. 96-99
25 Two other British visitors were Joseph Blackburn (in America 1753-1763) and John Wollaston (in America 1749-1758), both of whom painted overdressed sitters with vapid expressions.
26 *Perkins / Gavin 1980*, pl. VII; *Bauman / Liedtke et al. 1990*, introduction, fig. 3
27 *Dunlap 1834*, vol. I, p. 243
28 Quoted by *Dunlap 1834*, vol. I, p. 384
29 *Redmond 1981*, p. 105. Peter Sutton knows the collection and doubts all of the attributions with the possible exception of the Heda. He mentions a good Jan Miense Molenaer and a seascape by Pieter Mulier in the Lincoln house.
30 *Redmond 1981*, p. 106
31 *Perkins / Gavin 1980*
32 Otis has been emphasized in a colleague's lectures (see note 16), but the politician appears to have relied on Washington Allston (see *Clark 1982-B*, pp. 54, 115), and his loans to the Atheneum comprise eight dubiously attributed Dutch pictures (*Perkins / Gavin 1980*, p. 213).
33 *Clark 1982-B*, pp. 104 (on Brett), 109-111 (on Hayward), and 138, note 36, for Gilmor's letter of 1837. Brett had a gallery in the American Academy of Fine Arts building (which suggests a close relationship between Brett and Trumbull in New York); he was wiped out in the fire of 1837.
34 *Jaffe 1975*, pp. 172-175
35 *Rutledge 1949*, p. 31
36 For these statistics, see *Schlesinger 1983*, pp. 148-150.
37 *Rutledge 1949*; see also *Baltimore 1984*, pp. v, 1-8
38 *Rutledge 1949*, p. 19. In 1800 Gilmor wrote that a Mr. de Schmedt in Amsterdam 'has the choicest collection of works of Wouwermans, Rubens, Ruysdael, Dow, Tenier, Berghem, and Van de Velde. You can scarcely name a greater treat to me than such a sight' (*Clark 1982-B*, p. 78).
39 *Rutledge 1949*, pp. 31-32
40 In a letter to Trumbull dated 1825, Gilmor records his delight in having just

received from Apostool 'five very good pictures,' including a De Witte church interior and 'the best specimen of Adriaen van Ostade in the Country' (*Clark 1982-B*, pp. 80-81). On Apostool, see *Jonker 1977*.

41 *Liedtke 1982*, fig. 47

42 *Rutledge 1949*, pp. 26, 31, quoting Gilmor's letters of 1830 (on English landscape painting) and 1826.

43 On the Dutch sources of these artists, see *Engelson 1966*; *Hoover 1981*; *Clark 1982-B*, chap. 5.

44 *Baltimore 1984*, p. v, for the information and quotes in this paragraph.

45 See *Cosentino 1974*, pp. 55-56, 61-62, proposing Dutch models for King's still lifes and genre scenes. Cosentino has trouble finding the right Netherlandish 'prototype' (for example, 'a small Flemish panel of about 1470,' cited on p. 58, for fig. 12 here), but King's Dutch interests are obvious. See also *Cosentino 1977*.

46 *Clark 1982-B*, p. 108

47 *Clark 1982-B*, p. 120, citing *Auction Philadelphia 1856*.

48 *Clark 1982-B*, p. 105, citing *Miller 1966*, p. 92.

49 *James 1872 / 1956*, p. 52

50 *Clark 1982-B*, pp. 115-116, 142, note 66

51 *Craven 1980*; one of the 'Teniers' is reproduced in *Clark 1982-A*, fig. 5.

52 *Craven 1980*, p. 46; *Clark 1982-B*, pp. 63-64

53 *Craven 1980*, pp. 40, 59; *Clark 1982-B*, pp. 66-70

54 *Clark 1982-B*, pp. 70-71, 96, notes 108, 109 (recording approximately the same distribution when Nye exhibited 101 paintings in the Lyceum Building on Broadway in 1849).

55 *Clark 1982-B*, p. 71, quoting from the 1848 exhibition catalogue.

56 *Clark 1982-B*, p. 73, quoting *Tuckerman 1867*, p. 13.

57 *Haverkamp-Begemann / Adams 1988*, no. 33

58 Sotheby Parke-Bernet, New York, 2 December 1971, and 9 October 1980

59 As does Julius Held, whose view was expressed in a letter to *The New York Times*, 15 August 1988. He writes of the Bryan and Louis Durr (1882) bequests that 'as historical documents, demonstrating the taste and range of interest of cultural New Yorkers in the middle of the 19th century, they had this historical value only as long as they remained intact.'

60 See especially Clark's publications of 1982 and the exhibition catalogue of 1988.

61 *Clark 1982-B*, pp. 25-26, citing Murray in *The Portfolio*, n.s. 6, vol. III (June 1814), p. 569

62 *Clark 1982-B*, pp. 7-8, 14-16. Bancroft's ten-volume history was published in Boston between 1834 and 1874.

63 See especially *Edwards 1986* (reviewed, along with *Clark 1988*, by Sally Webster in the *Art Journal* 48 [1989], pp. 99-101).

64 *Clark 1982-B*, p. 27, citing a secondary source.

65 *Clark 1982-A*, p. 24

66 *Clark 1982-B*, pp. 30-31. Another Anglo-Dutch descendant, Walt Whitman, adopted the manner of the common man (and the rebel) in the early 1850s. Emerson, Millet, and Courbet were among his inspirations (the painters were discussed by Laura Meixner and by Albert Boime at the symposium on 'Whitman and the Visual Arts,' Rutgers University, Camden, New Jersey, 28 April 1989).

67 *New York 1987*, pp. 104-106, citing Claude and Constable, but no Dutch artists. Compare Both's *Landscape with Resting Travelers and an Oxcart* in the Centraal Museum, Utrecht (*Blankert 1965*, no. 52, fig. 52). The etched version of this composition may have been known to Durand, but *The Beeches* and similar compositions by the artist bring many Dutch landscape paintings to mind (the accent on the trees in the foreground recalls Pijnacker). Durand visited the Rijksmuseum in August 1840 (*Clark 1982-B*, p. 172).

68 *Gerdts / Burke 1971*; *Gerdts 1981*; *Engelson 1966*

69 Asher B. Durand, 'Letters on Landscape Painting,' *The Crayon*, 1855, quoted by *McLanathan 1968*, p. 248

70 *Chapman 1858*; see *Clark 1982-A*, pp. 30-31

71 From Part Four, 'Practical Hints on Colour,' p. 60, in *Burnet 1850*; see *Clark 1982-A*, p. 32, figs. 14, 15, and *Clark 1988*, pp. 46-49

72 Of the kind that is celebrated by Thoré-Bürger (see *Blankert 1978-A*, pp. 67-69) and in *Taine 1871*, *Valentiner 1914*, and *Rosenberg / Slive / Ter Kuile 1966*

73 In a letter of 17 July 1800, Gilmor wrote, 'The road was lined with beautiful cottages, all enclosed in trees, and providing in actions and instances the originals of those sweet pictures of Hobbema whose charming works were ten times more pleasing to me since I have taken this ride' (quoted in *Clark 1982-B*, p. 79).

74 *Burnet 1859* for his monograph on Rembrandt

75 Durand visited the Rijksmuseum in 1840, Morse in 1845 (*Clark 1982-B*, pp. 29, 172).

76 *James 1879*, p. 144

77 *Edel 1956*, p. 121 (from *James 1909 / 1956*)

78 See *Behrman 1952*, pp. 139-141

79 Quoted in *Burt 1977*, p. 91

80 H. James, 'Recent Florence,' *Atlantic Monthly* (May 1878), quoted in *Sweeney 1956*, p. 21. On James as critic, see *Edel 1974*.

81 *Edel 1985*, pp. 63-69. On Norton, see *Vanderbilt 1959*.

82 *Edel 1956*, pp. 121, 127 (from *James 1909 / 1956*)

83 *Burt 1977*, pp. 86-91. WASP = White Anglo-Saxon Protestant. Somewhat less 'old money' were Stewart, who owned a big department store, and Johnston, whose fortune came from railroads and coal.

84 *Whitehill 1970*, pp. 9-14

85 *Edel 1956*, p. 126 (from *James 1909 / 1956*), for this and the following quote.

86 *James 1872 / 1956*. Pictures from the 1871 Purchase still in the museum's collection as of 1980 are listed in *Baetjer 1980*, vol. I, pp. 201-202, under accession numbers 71.1 to 71.174. See also *Decamps 1872* and *Harck 1888*.

87 From James's review of Fromentin's book, in *The Nation* (1876), quoted by *Sweeney 1956*, p. 19 (see also p. 16).

88 *James 1872 / 1956*, p. 55, for this and the following quote. The 'Van Dyck' is by Cornelis de Vos, see *Liedtke 1984*, pp. 273-274, pl. 106. My remark that the painting was purchased in 1871 as a De Vos seems to have been misled by an absence of relevant records.

89 *Ten Doesschate Chu 1987-A*, p. 112

90 *Ten Doesschate Chu 1987-A*, p. 112 (see also p. 115)

91 *Ten Doesschate Chu 1987-A*, figs. 7.8 and 7.10, for copies after Hals's *Saint Hadrian Civic Guard Company* by Mary Cassatt (1873) and by J. Alden Weir (1875). A partial copy of the *Women Regents of the Old Men's Home* by Sargent is in the Birmingham Museum of Art, Birmingham, Alabama (*Thompson 1989*, pl. IV), and is seen in a photo of Sargent's studio (*Ormond 1970*, fig. 17; *Olson 1986*, pl. XI; *Thompson 1989*, fig. 1).

92 The Hals quote is from *James 1872 / 1956*, p. 55. See *Valentiner 1935-B* for two of his rediscoveries, and for the genre painting in the Taft Museum (*Slive 1970-1974*, vol. III, no. D 29, fig. 148) by a nineteenth-century imitator of Hals.

93 *James 1872 / 1956*, p. 58; p. 56 for the lines on Van der Helst.

94 *Taine 1871*, pp. 178-179, for this and the following list. James much admired Taine after meeting him in Paris in 1889 (*Edel 1985*, p. 357).

95 *James 1872 / 1956*, p. 59

96 For example, *Burt 1977* and *Tomkins 1973*

97 *Sutton 1986*

98 *Galichon 1868*; *Auction Florence 1880*

99 *Bruyn et al. 1986*, nos. C 72 and C 73

100 *Slive 1970-1974*, vol. III, no. 220

101 *Whitehill 1970*, pp. 51, 68-70, 77-78, 86-87, 189-193. On the Dutch pictures, see *Sutton 1986*, pp. 18-30, and *Walsh / Schneider 1979*.

102 *Burt 1977*, pp. 178-181; *Saarinen 1968*, pp. 3-24 on Mrs. Palmer.

103 *Bruyn et al. 1982*, no. A 42

104 *Burt 1977*, p. 182

105 Autograph but mediocre works by each of the Van Ostades have been deaccessioned: 71.74 (1871 Purchase) by Adriaen; 93.22.1 (1893 gift of George Hearn) by Isack.

106 Near to the museum on 14th Street in the 1880s were the Academy of Music in

Union Square, the New-York Historical Society, the Astor Library, the New Society Library, and New York University. Elsewhere in the city were the Metropolitan Opera, the New York Symphony at Carnegie Hall, the National Academy of Design, the American Museum of Natural History, the Association for Improving the Condition of the Poor, the Charity Organization Society, the Children's Aid Society, various hospitals and schools, and several departments other than European Paintings in the Metropolitan Museum (on these institutions, see *Bender 1987*, pp. 169-171, 217, etc.). There were also dozens of civic-minded clubs, such as the all-male Rembrandt Club in Brooklyn Heights, founded in 1880 and dedicated to the 'promotion and encouragement of the arts' (*MacKay 1989*, p. 47).

107 *Baetjer 1980*, vol. I, p. 203, for Marquand paintings, which bear accession numbers 89.15.3 to 89.15.37. Also given by Marquand, in 1891, are 91.26.1 through 91.26.12, which include Rembrandt's ruined *Portrait of a Man*, the 'Cuyp' *Landscape with Cattle* recently reassigned to Jacob van Strij, Hals's three-quarter-length *Portrait of a Man* and his portrait of a seated woman (with a later background), Metsu's *Musical Party* of 1659, and the *Lamentation* by Petrus Christus.

108 *Auction New York 1910-A*

109 *Spielmann 1910*, p. 111

110 *Stephens 1895*, p. 96

111 *Spielmann 1910*, p. 111

112 *Slive 1970-1974*, vol. III, no. 107, bought by Yerkes in Paris, 1893, and by Frick at the 1910 Yerkes sale. For Yerkes's small pendant genre paintings by Hals, see *Slive et al. 1989*, nos. 25-26 (now in a private collection, Montreal).

113 *Auction New York 1910-A*, no. 43; *Broulhiet 1938*, no.179; not in the Taft Museum, Cincinnati. The Yerkes Hobbemas are catalogued indiscriminately by Broulhiet as nos. 7, 64, 96, 125, 131, 179, 205.

114 *Sutton 1980*, no. 108, fig. 110

115 *Auction New York 1988*, no. 15, from the Demidoff sale, 1880.

116 *Saarinen 1968*, p. 110, who was shown Johnson's letters by Berenson (see p. xv).

117 On the *Landscape with an Obelisk*, see p. 127, note 2; *Hendy 1974*, p. 206, and p. 284 on the Vermeer purchase; see also *Saarinen 1968*, p. 38, and, on the Rembrandts, *Samuels 1979*, pp. 244, 302, 337-338.

118 *Valentiner 1909* is an essential index to the taste for Dutch art during the Gilded Age. The other painters represented were Berchem, Van Beyeren, Bol, Van de Cappelle, Van Goyen (three), Dirck Hals, Van der Helst, Van der Heyden, Kalf, Koninck, Leyster, Maes, Metsu, Aert van der Neer, Adriaen van Ostade, Potter, Salomon van Ruysdael (four), Ter Borch, Adriaen and Willem van de Velde, Verspronck, Simon de Vlieger, and Wouwermans, which altogether make up a remarkably selective list of names, with the most familiar favored heavily.

119 *Allen 1965*

120 *Slive 1970-1974*, vol. III, nos. 117-118 and 149-150

121 *Roberts 1907*

122 *Behrman 1952*, pp. 32-33 on Henry Duveen, and p. 10 on the 'Marine,' where the letter of 1877 was framed on the wall.

123 *Elkins 1887-1900*. For Hobbemas in Gilded Age collections, see *Broulhiet 1938*, nos. 10, 19, 41-47, 64, 65, 71, 87, 94, 113, 128, 134, 139, 171, 181, 236, 255, 262. The New York galleries of Duveen, Kleinberger, and Scott and Fowles are cited frequently.

124 As will be evident from *Valentiner 1923* and *Valentiner 1936*.

125 *West 1979*; *Sutton 1986*, pp. 258-260. Crocker had close political and business connections with Collis P. Huntington.

126 *Constable 1964*, pp. 115-116. In 1989 Edith Standen, the tapestry expert who worked for Joseph Widener, confirmed the Duveen anecdote.

127 *Samuels 1987*, p. 62, quoting Mary Berenson's letter of 28 June 1908.

128 *Samuels 1987*, pp. 73-74. Mary Berenson is quoting Morgan.

129 *Valentiner 1909*. The Washington pictures are National Gallery of Art inv. nos. 666, 667, 624, 629, 630, 644, 645, and 677. On the copy of the Rothschild Hals see *Slive 1970-1974*, vol. III, p. 98, under no. 189. The New York Steen was purchased in 1958.

130 *Ashbourne 1885-1900*

131 *Tintner 1986*, pp. 228-230, on *The Outcry*; *Caffin 1909*, p. 133 (cited by *Stott 1986*, p. 39, note 42). *Leader 1980* associates Vermeer's influence on Boston painters such as Philip Leslie Hale (author of a thick monograph on Vermeer: *Hale 1913*) with the 1904 Boston publication of a *Masters of Art* book, but the Marquand and Gardner acquisitions and Widener attributions indicate that the artist's reputation in America had (as Caffin claimed) been ascending since the late 1880s.

132 *Williams 1980*, pp. 22-26, for the Yusupov Rembrandts (National Gallery inv. nos. 663, 664), which involved a famous lawsuit and competition from Gulbenkian and Duveen. The *Descent from the Cross* is catalogued as by an anonymous Rembrandt pupil in *Sumowski 1983-C*, vol. IV, no. 1972.

133 *Brockwell 1918*, p. 143

134 *Burt 1977*, pp. 273-275; *Constable 1964*, pp. 55-59; on Johnson, see *Saarinen 1968*, pp. 92-117.

135 See *Van Puyvelde 1941*, *Valentiner 1913-1914 / 1972*, and *Sutton 1986*, pp. 222-225

136 Kleinberger's full-page advertisement in *Arts and Decoration* 3 (January 1913), p. 77, which announces the firm's move from 12 West 40th Street to the upscale address of 709 Fifth Avenue.

137 *Valentiner 1913-1914 / 1972*, p. 94; see also my introductory essay in *Bauman / Liedtke et al. 1990*.

138 *New York 1968*, p. xxx; see also *Harvey 1928*, pp. 331-343, and the essays by Kahren J. Hellerstedt (on collecting) and Joanne B. Moore (on the Frick family) in *Hellerstedt 1988*.

139 *New York 1968*, pp. 270-273

140 *Tomkins 1973*, p. 207

141 On the Van Beresteyn Rembrandts, see *Liedtke 1989*, rebutting the Rembrandt team. Havemeyer paintings are reproduced in *Baetjer 1980*, vol. III, and are listed under nos. 29.100.1 and following in vol. I, pp. 208-209.

142 *Haverkamp-Begemann 1978-A*, with various essays (three on Dutch paintings); *Sutton 1986*, pp. 298-301.

143 *Larsen 1988*, vol. II, p. 133, no. 325, as one of Van Dyck's 'more important realizations.' As realized by the Metropolitan Museum's conservation department in 1988 and as discussed in my forthcoming contribution to the Taft Museum catalogue, this Genoese portrait is a modern imitation, probably Italian ca. 1900.

144 *Slive et al. 1989*, nos. 63, 64, for the Halses, and *Bruyn et al. 1986*, nos. A 78, A 79, for the Taft and the New York Rembrandts.

145 *Hoeber 1909-1910*, p. lxxi

146 Fowles went down with the *Lusitania* in 1915. On the Taft Museum, see the December 1988 issue of *Apollo*; my entries on the Dutch pictures will appear in the museum's complete catalogue, to be published in 1992.

147 *Conway 1905*, pp. 137, 140

148 *Slive 1970-1974*, vol. III, nos. 109-110, 76

149 *Manke 1963*, no. 11, fig. 13

150 *Conway 1905*, p. 141

151 *Saarinen 1968*, p. 108

152 *Samuels 1987*, p. 76, quoting Mary Berenson

153 *Samuels 1987*, pp. 90, 91, quoting Berenson's letters to his wife. The term 'sheenie' is derisive slang for 'Jew', and is wickedly funny coming from B B.

154 *Samuels 1987*, p. 91. The 'great Ruysdael' (the misspelling was common in America) is Jacob van Ruisdael's *Wheatfields* in the Metropolitan Museum of Art (14.40.623). On the Maurice Kann collection, see *Les Arts 1909* and *American Art News 1909*.

155 *Tomkins 1973*, p. 90, quoting the critic Gustav Kobbe in 1914.

156 The *Titus* is a later imitation; *Sumowski 1983-C*, vol. IV, no. 1595, plausibly assigns the *Old Woman Cutting Her Nails* to Karel van der Pluym.

157 For the Altman Collection as originally installed in seven rooms of the museum, see *New York 1928-A*. The best appreciation of Altman as collector is *Haskell 1970*. See also *Monod 1923* and *Burke 1968*.

158 On Rodolphe Kann's collection, see *Bode 1900*, *Michel 1901*, *Holmes 1907-1908*, and *Nicolle 1908*.

159 *Roberts 1909*

160 See *Edel 1985*, pp. 641-642, and *Tintner 1986*, p. 227. Tintner sees the name as a play on 'Bernard Berenson,' and the character as a reference to Morgan, who advanced Duveen $2 million toward the purchase of the Rodolphe Kann collection.

161 *Derham 1988*, pp. 406-407, quoting a Duveen letter (the article is on Chinese porcelain in the Taft Museum).

162 *Samuels 1987*, p. 77, quoting Mary Berenson's letter to her mother dated 6 February 1909.

163 The quote is borrowed from *Mumford 1931*, who coined this apt description of late nineteenth-century American taste.

164 On these designers, see *Smith 1982-B* and *Metcalf 1988*.

165 On the Cones, see *Baltimore 1984*, p. 48; for the Havemeyers, see *New York 1958-A* and *Weitzenhoffer 1986*.

166 *Baetjer 1980*, vol. I, pp. 206-218

167 *Williams 1980*, p. 173, with prices

168 *Behrman 1952*, p. 153

169 *Walker 1969*, pp. 127-132; *Koskoff 1978*, pp. 330-339

170 *Du Bois 1916-1917*, p. 397, for this and the following quotes; see also *Burroughs / Wehle 1932*.

171 *Slive 1970-1974*, vol. III, no. 128. For Ringling's Dutch and Flemish pictures, see *Robinson et al. 1980*.

172 Bache, quoted by *Levey*; see *Brandus 1928*, *New York 1929*, and *New York 1937*.

173 *Walker 1969*, chap. 7

174 *Eisler 1977*

175 *Bruyn et al. 1982*, p. x, referring to *Valentiner 1921*; see also *Valentiner 1936*.

176 For example, *Valentiner 1909*, *Valentiner 1914*, *Valentiner 1936*, and the exhibitions *Valentiner 1935*, *New York 1937*.

177 An example not discussed in the text is the Hydes of Glen Falls, New York, who obtained their ruined Rembrandt (?) through Valentiner from the Soviet government in 1933; see *Kettlewell 1981*, pp. x-xi and no. 51.

178 *Sterne 1980*

179 On Walters and other Maryland collectors, see *Baltimore 1984* and *Sutton 1986*, pp. 4-11.

180 *Scott 1987*

181 *Sutton 1986*, pp. 63-71. The Dutch gallery was recently rehung and is now one of the most attractive cabinets of Dutch pictures in America. Of the four 'Rembrandts' on view, only one is by him, the 1635 *Portrait of a Woman* rejected by the Rembrandt team (*Bruyn et al. 1989*, no. C 105).

182 *Sutton 1986*; on the collection in San Francisco, see *Haverkamp-Begemann 1980*.

183 On Flemish collecting, see *Bauman / Liedtke et al. 1990*; *Rosenberg 1982* to compare the collecting of seventeenth-century French art.

184 On this collection, see *Walsh / Schneider 1981-1982*.

185 Several of these collections have been exhibited in part. See, for example, *Gilbert 1966* (Wolf collection), *Wright 1979*, *Varriano 1979*, *Robinson 1982*, *Walsh / Schneider 1981-1982*, *Auction New York 1988*, *Washington 1989*.

186 Washington Irving (see note 64)

187 *Haskell 1976*, p. 160, quoting from *Hawthorne 1941*.

188 See note 187, and my introductory essay in *Bauman / Liedtke et al. 1990*, on Rubens and the question of *style* in American art.

189 Ruskin, quoted by Goris in *Goris / Held 1947*, p. 16, citing J. Hamerton, *Art Essays*, New York, 1880, p. 66.

190 *Haskell 1976*, p. 147, quoting *Thoré-Bürger 1858-1860*, vol. I, p. ix.

191 *Haskell 1976*, pp. 147-149

192 *Brigstocke 1982*, p. 28, quoting Irvine's letter to Sir William Forbes, dated 9 February 1828.

193 *Brigstocke 1982*, pp. 35-37

194 *Brown 1981*, p. 9

195 *Paris 1989*

196 *Ten Doesschate Chu 1974*. On the Hals revival, see also *Jowell 1974*, *Ten Doesschate Chu 1987*, and Jowell's essay in *Slive et al. 1989*.

197 *Haskell 1976*, in the subtitle

198 *Amsterdam 1978* and *Haarlem 1986*

199 *O'Brien 1986* and *Stott 1986*

200 *Valentiner 1918-1919*

201 Editor's note: the essay that follows, by Edwin Buijsen, deals with the European reaction to the phenomenon of American collecting in the heyday of the 'Gilded Age.'

Edwin Buijsen
Project Collaborator Mauritshuis

The Battle against the Dollar
The Dutch Reaction to American Collecting in the Period from 1900 to 1914

In the years before World War I, the Netherlands witnessed a cultural struggle that stirred up strong feelings, and a battle was waged for the preservation of the national artistic heritage. The danger came from America. Millionaire collectors were after the Dutch masters of the Golden Age. Many paintings had already been sold abroad during the preceding centuries, and it was feared that rich Americans would further thin out the national art possessions. Worried Dutchmen made every effort to keep irreplaceable art treasures within the frontiers. Among these were prominent art historians such as Abraham Bredius, Cornelis Hofstede de Groot, and Willem Martin, and the art critic Jan Veth.[1]

The fight against the dollar could be followed blow by blow in newspapers and magazines. Whenever famous masterpieces threatened to depart for America, feelings of concern and displeasure were expressed in articles and letters. Sometimes a heated discussion would arise about how a work of art might be saved for the Netherlands. It was a time when people readily reached for the pen to settle in public their differences of opinion in matters concerning art, a practice that has since largely fallen into disuse.

Sale

Even before 1900, old masters had been on sale in the Netherlands. Paintings had already begun to be sold abroad in the seventeenth century, but around the middle of the eighteenth century a true exodus got under way.[2] Dutch masters were much in demand with English, German, and French buyers. At that time there was still no question of any national striving to preserve the cultural heritage for the fatherland. Around 1785, acting for the duke of Rutland, the English painter Sir Joshua Reynolds simply bought 'all the pictures which were worth bringing home.'[3]

Many art collections were auctioned and thus converted to hard cash. When the Amsterdam collector Gerret Braamcamp died in 1771, his friend Cornelis Ploos van Amstel, himself a passionate collector, wrote that the Braamcamp cabinet should be preserved for Amsterdam to 'thus be kept in honor of the Founder himself, and to be saved from oblivion.'[4] Nothing came of it, however. The Dutch merchant mentality left little room for a quest for eternal fame. Like so many other collections, the Braamcamp cabinet was to be auctioned and dispersed forever.

This trend continued into the nineteenth century, its low point being the auction of 1850 of the collection of King William II. This collection, which was princely in every way, had to be auctioned to pay for the private debts of the deceased monarch. The government made no attempt whatsoever to preserve these important works for the country. Thus, for example, Rembrandt's *Portrait of Nicolaes Ruts* and *Man in Oriental Costume* [1] disappeared to England.[5]

The predicament of Dutch art treasures was accurately characterized in 1871 by the German art historian Wilhelm von Bode [2]: 'But for a small fraction, anything that was not nailed down has been squandered abroad, along with countless Dutch

1
Rembrandt
Man in Oriental Costume
Canvas, 152.7 x 111.1 cm (60 1/8 x 43 3/4 in.)
Lower right: *RHL van Rijn / 1632* (RHL combined)
New York, The Metropolitan Museum of Art,
inv. no. 20.155.2

private collections.'[6] Not until the last quarter of the nineteenth century were any serious steps taken to call an end to this exodus.

Until then there had been no sound public policy with respect to the arts, and the government kept itself at a distance as much as possible. After all, in the words of the Dutch statesman Thorbecke, art was 'no business of government.'[7] It was on private initiative that, in 1860, the Commissie voor Oude Vaderlandsche Kunst (Commission for Old Fatherlandish Art) was founded, which tried to stimulate concern for the cultural heritage.[8] This commission could do little without any method of enforcement or support from the government, and it ceased to exist in 1873. Nevertheless, the way to better policies had been cleared. This took form in 1875, when Victor de Stuers was appointed Department Head for Arts and Sciences at the Ministry of the Interior.[9] He continued to fill this post until 1901.

De Stuers fought in his publications against the short-sightedness and profit-hunting of his contemporaries. With his article 'Holland op zijn smalst' (Holland at Its Meanest), which appeared in *De Gids* of 1873, he exposed the lamentable condition of the Dutch art treasures. Concerning the exodus of art works he noted, 'In the meantime untold quantities have left the Netherlands for abroad. It is known that annually whole ship cargoes leave for Paris, Brussels, or London, in order to be sold there.'[10]

De Stuers managed to convince the government that a better art and museum policy was essential, and, from 1875 on, he himself shaped these policies to an important degree [3]. In 1881, after a visit to the Netherlands, Bode wrote that the situation of Dutch art treasures had improved significantly over the past years: 'My own eyes [...] have convinced me how thoroughly those old, bad traditions have been broken with, how by the example and actions of the government, the municipalities, communities, and corporations do their duty for the preservation, installation, and cataloguing of their art works.'[11]

Although the care for the art possessions had undergone an improvement, their preservation for the Netherlands was still a major problem. Bode observed that whereas the public collections of Holland did possess a number of top pieces, these constituted but 'a rapidly disappearing remnant of the work of its great school of art.'[12] For instance, there were no more than ten Rembrandts to be found in the Dutch public domain.

De Stuers, too, had to look on helplessly as many art treasures

2
Wilhelm von Bode (1845-1929)
From: I. Beth, *Verzeichnis der Schriften von Wilhelm v. Bode*, Berlin / Leipzig 1915

3
'The St.... Demonstration'
Satirical print on the autocratic behavior of De Stuers as Department Head.
From: *De Nederlandsche Spectator*, 14 January 1899

continued to leave the country. He was well informed about the extravagance of the foreign collectors. He knew, for instance, that of the 298 works that he had seen in 1867 at an exhibition of old art in the club premises of *Arti et Amicitiae* society in Amsterdam, 54 had already been sold abroad by 1881.[13] Accordingly, De Stuers wrote on the occasion of the *Tentoonstelling van schilderijen van oude meesters te 's Gravenhage ten behoeve van de watersnoodlijdenden* (Exhibition of Old Master Paintings for the Benefit of the Victims of Flooding), which was held in 1881, 'May, at the end of the exhibition, all these paintings find their way back to the nails on which they hung only yesterday, despite the foreign merchants who are already roaming about like snorting lions, searching for what they shall pirate.'[14]

Although the official policy with respect to art had taken firmer shape with the appointment of De Stuers, the most important impulse behind the preservation of the national patrimony was an initiative on the part of private individuals.[15] In 1883 the collection of Jacob de Vos Jbzn, which contained many important seventeenth-century drawings, was auctioned. To prevent the departure of these drawings, the members of the *Arte et Amicitia* society decided to establish, by means of loans, a fund that would allow them to buy the most important works at this auction.[16] The initiators asked the counsel of Victor de

Stuers, who advised them to found a society of a permanent nature. He also thought up the name for this body: *Vereeniging Rembrandt* (Rembrandt Society).[17] On 10 July 1883, shortly after important acquisitions had been made using the fund at the De Vos auction, the Rembrandt Society was officially founded. The society set as its goal to 'act as buyer wherever the danger should lurk that important works of art might otherwise leave the country.'[18] The purchased works were to be offered to museums at cost. Later the society also proceeded with donations.

In the beginning, the Rembrandt Society had only limited financial means and could hardly compete with the foreign buyers. Occasionally a success could be registered, as in the case of the acquisition of Vermeer's *Love Letter* from the Messchert van Vollenhoven cabinet in 1892,[19] but many old masters continued to disappear across the borders. When a statue in honor of Frans Hals was erected in 1895, *De Kroniek* published a satirical print by Marius Bauer [4] with the inscription 'Here beautiful paintings depart by sea, / And ugly statues are put up instead. / A good Dutchman mutters – is it any wonder: / Well, blast and thunder.'

The American Menace

The paintings that departed by sea around the turn of the century did not go exclusively to other European countries. Ever more Americans were active as art collectors. Thus, in 1890, Charles Yerkes of Chicago bought Rembrandt's *Portrait of Joris de Caulerij* (cat. no. 50) from the Amsterdam dealer Preyer. Abraham Bredius [5], Director of the Mauritshuis from 1889 to 1909, had tried in vain to buy the portrait. His offer looked like a mere pittance compared to what the American millionaire was able to pay.

Several years later, around 1900, Bredius witnessed increasing numbers of works of art being sold from Europe to the New World. In those days he regularly went to London, where Dutch masters were constantly coming under the hammer.[20] At these auctions he saw American millionaires bidding against the Rothschilds, and among the new buyers he discovered the 'king of steel,' Pierpont Morgan. 'It was the time when the Americans began to buy and the English began to sell,' later observed Willem Martin [6], who in 1901 became Assistant Director of the Mauritshuis.[21] Both Rembrandts from the collection of William II, which had gone to England in 1850, also fell into American hands.[22]

4
Rusticus (Marius Bauer)
'A Statue for Frans Hals'
Satirical print on the exodus of seventeenth-century works of art.
From: *De Kroniek*, 21 July 1895
Lithograph, 395 x 295 mm (15 1/2 x 11 5/8 in.)
Amsterdam, Rijksprentenkabinet

5
Antoon van Welie
Portrait of Dr. Abraham Bredius (1855-1946)
Canvas, 100 x 70 cm (39 5/8 x 27 1/2 in.)
Upper left: *Antoon van Welie / Ft 1918*
The Hague, Museum Bredius, inv. no. 216-1946

6
Willem Martin (1876-1954)
Photo: documentation archives Mauritshuis, The Hague

Although the Americans had already bought works of art in Europe before 1900, their influence on the European art market increased sharply during the first decade of the twentieth century.[23] This development is clear from a series of articles dedicated to the phenomenon of the American collector written by Wilhelm von Bode in the period between 1895 to 1910. As Director of the Kaiser-Friedrich-Museum in Berlin, he was in competition with the Americans where important masterpieces were concerned.

In 1895, on the occasion of a visit to the United States, Bode wrote that the American collectors did not yet constitute a danger to the European market because no one in America as yet collected old art systematically.[24] But at the same time he observed that this could change any day. In addition, according to Bode, the Americans had very good taste and did not go after famous names, but after quality. Art historical knowledge they possessed only in limited measure, however, and Bode encountered numerous incorrect attributions during his visits to museums in New York, Boston, and Chicago.[25]

Seven years later Bode once again paid attention to American collecting in an article with the pregnant title 'Die Amerikanische Konkurrenz im Kunsthandel und Ihre Gefahr für Europa' (The American Competition in the Art Trade and Its Danger for Europe).[26] In it he observed that a new kind of American collector had come to the fore. The nineteenth-century collectors had picked up some understanding of art during their European travels and bought what they thought beautiful, having the good fortune to be able to pay more than the Europeans. The new collectors, who had now turned out to be the terror of the European museums and collectors, were quite another kettle of fish: 'Just as they seek by means of strenuous and coercive operations to merge the separate branches of trade and industry into one syndicate and to subject it to their dominion, so they also wish to dominate the art market.'[27] They had virtually no understanding of art, but they did have a great deal of money, with which they had agents and dealers buy up whole collections.

Through the arrival of these new collectors the art trade had overnight gained a new character, and the dealers now thought about nothing but rich Americans. There were also newcomers among the dealers, who sometimes went about their work ruthlessly to please their American customers. Because they knew almost nothing about art, the American millionaires were easy prey for unscrupulous sorts who passed off worthless works as masterpieces.

As an example Bode named Henry Walters. For five million francs this 'cautious' collector had, on the advice of 'good

7
'Pierpont Morgan before God's Throne'
Inscription: *Morgan: – Deze stoel is very nice. What moet ze kosten* (This chair is very nice. How much do you want for it?)
Satirical print on the occasion of the death of J. Pierpont Morgan.
From: *De Amsterdammer, Weekblad voor Nederland*, 4 May 1913

8
Johannes Vermeer
The Kitchenmaid
Canvas, 45.5 x 41 cm (17 3/8 x 16 5/8 in.)
Neither signed nor dated (ca. 1660)
Amsterdam, Rijksmuseum, inv. no. A 2344

friends,' bought the entire collection of Don Marcello Mazzarenti Ordelaffi, Chaplain to the Pope. Although this collection had been announced in the press as a top one, with works by Rembrandt, Rubens, and Raphael, according to Bode it consisted of but a half-dozen mediocre works and countless very poor and forged pieces.[28]

Certainly not all American collectors allowed themselves to be gulled like Walters, but according to Bode, too many mediocre works had been carried across the Atlantic Ocean for inflated prices. Only rarely was a work included that constituted a serious loss for Europe. In 1902 Bode was therefore not afraid of the future. 'The spending mania of the Americans is at the moment precisely in its dog days; it will certainly recede, and probably even recede rapidly and sharply.'[29] According to him the Americans would soon arrive at the insight that art collections could not be stamped out of the ground, but could only be assembled gradually, with love and insight.

Only two years later Bode had to revise his optimistic picture of the future. Although he did not yet see the Americans as a threat to European museums, he did think them a menace to private collectors.[30] By 1906 his optimism had totally evaporated: 'The exodus of good, old works of art to America is now so strong that these days the collections over there require mention in connection with diverse genres and artists, and are in part even of the first rank.'[31]

With their 'contempt for money bordering on indifference,' the Americans bought virtually every important work of art that came on the market.[32] It was above all J. Pierpont Morgan [7] who left the European buyers almost no chance. Years later, in his memoirs, Bode was to describe this uncrowned king of the collectors as follows: 'Without knowledge in any field of art, without any particular taste or natural talent, even without good advisors, but only through his financial means and the generosity with which he dispensed these, and through his shrewdness and perseverence, this remarkable man assembled in a few years a collection that in part approaches, and in some respects even surpasses, the major, old museums.'[33] In addition to the private collectors, the American museums, which had become financially strong by way of great donations, had attained an important place in the European art market.[34]

In his article of 1906 Bode still expressed the hope that the American competition and the enormous rise in prices would soon abate.[35] Three years later, however, he had to observe that the Americans' hunger for art and their willingness to pay excessive prices were greater than ever.[36] Even works of art in the public domain were no longer safe. Thus a swindler, who passed himself off as Count of San Gallo, had bought the precious church treasury of the German city of Cranenburg. Ostensibly out of charity, he gave the needy church a measly amount for what he claimed were worthless articles, which he then sold to Pierpont Morgan for a great deal of money.[37]

In 1910 Bode came to the conclusion that it had become very difficult for the European museums to still acquire top works: 'Only as a matter of exception will chance or national sense of honor save such outstanding works for this or that European collection.'[38] Only the crumbs that the Americans left behind remained in the art market, such as works by lesser-known masters or objects that were thought unattractive.

Holland on Guard

The storm by which the Americans took the art market was also noted in the Netherlands. Whereas it had always been difficult to keep the old masters within the frontiers, people now saw themselves confronted by buyers who knew almost no financial limits. There was even talk of 'the yellow menace, by which the American gold steadily threatens the old Dutch masters!'[39] Only a few could withstand the call of the big money. Around 1903 Bredius, himself a man of means, had set a good example. The American millionaire Charles Schwab offered 100,000 pounds sterling (about 1.2 to 1.5 million guilders) for Rembrandt's *Saul and David*.[40] Bredius rejected this offer for one of the stars of his own collection. He gave as reason for his refusal 'because I believe that with the Saul, which I intended for my fatherland, I have captured an especially beautiful work by Rembrandt and deem this piece too good for American billionaires.'[41] Years later this deed was still hailed as a striking example of patriotism.[42]

Fear of the American collectors played a considerable role in 1907, when a part of the renowned Six collection was to be sold.[43] This was one of the most important private collections remaining in the Netherlands.[44] The showpiece was, and still is, the portrait that Rembrandt painted in 1654 of his good friend Jan Six, the ancestor of the present owners. In addition there were no fewer than two works by Vermeer: *The Little Street* and *A Maid Pouring out Milk*, better known as *The Kitchenmaid* [8]. The collection did not belong to just one person, but to several family members. In 1905 one of these, Jonkheer Pieter Hendrik Six van Vromade, died. His heirs decided to sell about sixty paintings from his legacy, among which was *The Kitchenmaid*.

At first the firm of Frederik Muller & Cie was asked to bring the works to auction. However, the Rembrandt Society approached the heirs in an attempt to retain the Vermeer for the Netherlands. It was agreed that the Society would acquire the work along with thirty-eight other paintings for 750,000 guilders. It was all or nothing; acquisition of *The Kitchenmaid* alone was impossible. The remaining paintings in the legacy would – for the time being – remain in the family.

The Rembrandt Society itself could contribute no more than 200,000 guilders. They therefore appealed to the government to put the remaining amount at their disposal. Even before the purchase of the Six collection came to be discussed in the parliament, there was a fierce reaction to the proposed transaction. The young art historian Frits Lugt published a brochure with the provocative title *Is de aankoop door het Rijk van een deel der Six-collectie aan te bevelen?* (Is the Acquisition by the State of a Part of the Six Collection to be Recommended?).[45] His answer to this question was in the negative. After all, the majority of the thirty-nine paintings offered were of mediocre quality. Only a few of the works were worthwhile and, with the exception of *The Kitchenmaid*, the best pieces were to remain in the hands of the family. Lugt was therefore strongly of the impression that 'those few handsome works are to fulfill the function of allowing the whole "to sail under false colors," i.e., as if they must also serve to help fetch the highest possible prices for inferior paintings.'[46] At the same time Lugt believed that the qualities of *The Kitchenmaid* had been overestimated.[47] He did not consider it by any means to be Vermeer's masterpiece. He believed *The Little Street*, which was to remain in the Six collection, to be of much greater importance.

Lugt thought that the amount that was being asked for the thirty-nine works was much too high. He estimated the value of the Vermeer by itself to be at most 350,000 guilders. He further noted, 'One ought not to forget that the number of art lovers who are prepared to pay more than 200,000 guilders for an old Dutch painting is extremely limited. On the basis of experience, we can inform the reader that in all of America, on which purchasing power we are after all primarily relying, their number amounts to no more than six.' In a footnote he added 'that there is question here only of "America's constant buyers," who are the only ones that one needs to take into consideration. The others, who out of "snobbism" buy a famous painting at a fancy price on one occasion, exert no influence on the art market; their interventions are much too sporadic and capricious for art buyers to count on. Furthermore, this intimately Dutch

Vermeer does not have the appearance and the dimensions that are needed to entice such buyers to part with an excessive amount.'[48]

In his brochure Lugt proposed two possible solutions. The government could break off negotiations and hope for a better offer from the Six heirs. Should this not materialize, then the government could always attempt to buy the work at public auction with the support of the Rembrandt Society. If this failed, then the 'national honor' would still be saved, and the available money could be reserved for the moment when *The Little Street* would be sold.[49] A second solution, one that Lugt preferred, was that the government attempt to persuade the heirs to sell the Vermeer separately. It would then be possible to offer a very high sum, but one that would still be considerably lower than the 750,000 guilders for the thirty-nine works.[50]

Lugt's brochure unleashed a heated discussion in the newspaper *Het Vaderland*. Bredius, who had advised the government in the matter of the acquisition of the Six collection, rejected Lugt's point of view in a letter to the editor. He accused Lugt of being biased because he was associated with the firm of Muller & Cie, which was originally to have auctioned the collection, and rejected his solutions. Because the Six family had made 'all or nothing' the condition of sale, there remained nothing for the government but to take all: 'Let us instead rejoice over an act of the Government, which rightly realizes that Holland has already allowed too much of value to move abroad to allow more of the little that still remains in private hands to depart for the other side of the ocean.' Bredius emphasized these words with the addition: 'Just now I hear that one of the greatest American collectors has requested the Six family for an option should the negotiations with our Government fail!'[51]

Several days later Anton Mensing, who directed the affairs of Muller & Cie, backed his colleague Lugt. He dismissed all accusations of partiality. Lugt had not written in self-interest, 'but in the realization that the country's interests in matters of art could be seriously damaged.' Aside from the Vermeer, the transaction included only the 'least attractive pieces. [...] Now look, Mr. Bredius, this is not a worthy proposal to the Government.' According to Mensing, the proposal of 'all or nothing' was putting 'the knife to the throat of the Government.'[52]

It goes without saying that Bredius, who was known as a 'pugnacious sort,' did not let things go at that. In an open letter to Mensing he wrote, among other things, that, as Director of the Mauritshuis, he was prepared on the spot to trade *The Bull* by

9
Georg Rueter
Portrait of Jan Veth (1864-1925)
Drawing in black chalk, dimensions and location
unknown
Lower right: *Georg Rueter 1922*
Photo: Iconographisch Bureau, The Hague

Potter for the Vermeer. In addition, he again emphasized the American threat to *The Kitchenmaid*: 'If the Government does not accept the offer: these 39 paintings or nothing – then Vermeer's kitchenmaid will most probably go to America. I know that one of these Americans, who is no more concerned about spending a few hundred thousand more or less than any other man might a dime, has his fowling net poised.'[53]

Once again Mensing picked up the gauntlet. In a letter to the editor he wrote, 'They now repeatedly brandish an American buyer, who serves as bogeyman. This man who is said to be a bird catcher is nothing but a scarecrow.' Mensing revealed the name of the American: Pierpont Morgan (p. 40, fig. 26). According to him, however, the interest of 'this rich merchant' in *The Kitchenmaid* was no more than a rumor: 'Mr. Morgan buys only "la crême de la crême," to which Vermeer's "Kitchenmaid" really does not belong [...]. Although in exceptional cases some Americans spend one hundred thousand as others might spend a dime, one does them an injustice to pass them off as fools. They are quite able to make distinctions in matters of art.' As an example he offered the renowned collector John G. Johnson,

who had written to him 'that in his opinion the offer of the Six van Vromade family to the Government constituted an insult to the artistic sense of the Dutch intelligentsia.'[54]

Bredius, however, had an entirely different opinion of Pierpont Morgan. In a reply to Mensing he revealed that Morgan regularly allowed himself to be duped with bad works and fakes. Thus he had submitted to an exhibition in the Royal Academy in London a so-called Titian which so little resembled the work of the Venetian painter 'that the visitors to the exhibition thought it to be an error in the catalogue.' For good measure Bredius added, 'To this same exhibition he had sent show cases filled with Renaissance bronzes, among which there were so many obvious fakes that the connoisseurs walked by filled with pity and shrugging their shoulders.'[55]

Mensing closed the discussion with the comment 'Mr. Bredius's observations regarding P.M. are quite correct: is it any wonder, therefore, that this collector has become more choosey due to his acquired experience.'[56] Whether Pierpont Morgan indeed intended to buy *The Kitchenmaid* is now difficult to ascertain, but is not improbable because when in 1907 he first saw a painting by Vermeer, he bought it without hesitation (cat. no. 67). Prior to that, however, he had never heard of the painter from Delft.

In addition to Lugt, Bredius, and Mensing, others voiced their opinion on the matter. Some agreed with Bredius and thought that, regardless of the stated conditions, this painting should be preserved for the Netherlands. The artist and critic Jan Veth [9] observed, 'That this country's Government, which has often displayed a lamentable indifference in these matters, is prepared to make an important offer in this instance, seems to me glad-dening.'[57] According to the painter Jozef Israëls the acquisition would not be 'wasted money [...] for if ever, which is not to be hoped, the State should come to be financially embarrassed, then the millions could be extracted from the Rijksmuseum, and this Vermeer would be one of the first works to fetch a colossal sum.'[58]

Others took Lugt's side and thought it irresponsible that the government was forced, as it were, to come up with an extremely high amount for the preservation of one important work of art.[59] In the *Middelburgsche Courant* a columnist using the pen name of 'de Torenwachter' (the Lighthouse Keeper) made a number of critical observations about the transaction at hand.[60] He asked himself, 'where are things going when, under the slogan "keep the national art treasures," we continue to treat barrels of gold from the national treasury as if they were so many dimes?'[61] He saw more to be gained from a law that would forbid the export of art treasures.[62]

Bredius was unable to resist reacting to this opponent as well. In a letter to the editor he snapped at the columnist, 'But through all your writing [...] it may well come to a pass that the Vermeer goes to America, and then people will later lament the cheapness and small-mindedness of our people in matters concerning our artistic interest.'[63]

There was also extensive debate in parliament about the proposal to acquire the thirty-nine paintings from the Six collection. A political commentator of the *Middelburgsche Courant* reported 'that various members would join the government in regret if "the Kitchenmaid" were to fall into the hands of foreigners.'[64] The discussion in the Second Chamber (House of Representatives) was largely between the socialist Troelstra and De Stuers.[65] Since 1901, the former Department Head for Arts and Sciences represented the district of Weert in the House. Naturally he was a great supporter of the proposal to buy. Troelstra, however, was of the opinion that the Netherlands already had enough 'art products of the old Dutch Masters of the seventeenth century.' It would therefore be insane to compete with the 'American financial princes, among which Pierpont Morgan has been named.'[66] The government could better employ the money by supporting young, contemporary artists.

De Stuers pointed out that too many old art treasures had already disappeared abroad. He did not consider the danger of modern art disappearing all that great. After all, the artists were still alive and continued to produce new works: 'If, however, Ruysdaels, Vermeers, Metsus leave for America, then these are forever lost to our nation.' He added to this: 'As for this competing of the Minister with Pierpont Morgan, this is hardly to be feared if one considers that the latter has just bought a Raphael for f. 1,200,000 –.'[67]

10a-b
Jan Rinke
'The Minister P. Rink and the Milkmaid from the Six Collection'
Inscriptions: *Raakt Holland op de beurs aan Sam zijn goeie geld kwijt, / Hij dingt er mee, brutaal, naar Hollands knapste melkmeid; Maar – zegt zij – Hollands kunst volg' Hollands duiten niet, / Toe, laat me in Holland blijven bij mijn Piet!* (Does Holland lose its good money to [Uncle] Sam on the stock-market, / He uses it to court, what nerve, Holland's best-looking milkmaid; But – says she – Dutch art, don't follow Dutch lucre, / come, let me remain in Holland with my Piet!)
Satirical print on the occasion of a bill of Minister of the Interior P. Rink to make government funds available for the acquisition from the Six collection of *The Kitchenmaid* by Vermeer.
From: *Het Vaderland*, 9 November 1907, 'Avondblad', p. B

The proposal to make 550,000 guilders of government money available for the acquisition was in the end passed by parliament with a large majority. 'Holland's best-looking milk maid' was kept out of American hands [10a-b] and could henceforth be seen in the Rijksmuseum.[68] With the acquisition of a part of the Six collection, the Dutch government had for the first time made an important contribution to the battle to preserve the Dutch art possessions for the fatherland. Jan Veth called it an act of progressive policy to 'no longer denude the already so destitute Netherlands of its best art objects.'[69] He observed with elation that 'Holland at its meanest is behind us. And many questions of art that are under too much pressure will as a consequence come to a better resolution.'[70]

However, there remained much to criticize about the art policies of the government. Thus Cornelis Hofstede de Groot [11], one of Holland's most renowned art historians, deplored the fact that the museums were forced to spend their entire acquisitions budgets every year. If they failed to do this, then the remaining amount went back to the treasury. The annual budgets did not suffice for the acquisition of important works and were generally spent on paintings of lesser quality. Hofstede de Groot proposed that the museums be allowed to save up their annual budgets so that every once in a while a work of art could be bought that would truly enrich the collection and not simply to use up the money.[71] As member of parliament, De Stuers also insisted on the formation of a so-called museum or acquisition fund.[72] Although subsequently people have pleaded repeatedly for the establishment of such a fund, nothing has yet come of it.[73]

Because of their limited financial means, Dutch museums could not possibly compete with the rich American collectors. If an important masterpiece was discovered, such as the *The Woman Weighing Gold* by Vermeer in 1910, then it was assumed to be inevitable that it would soon depart for the other side of the ocean.[74]

When Veth visited the exhibition of old Dutch paintings from Parisian collections held in Paris in 1911, the extent to which the Americans dominated the European art market became clear to him. He had to conclude that Rembrandt in particular was rather poorly represented at the exhibition.[75] According to him this was because of the sale of the famous collection of Rodolphe Kann, which had included a large number of works from Rembrandt's late period.[76] After the death of the owner in 1905, the dealer Duveen had in a rather devious way come into possession of the collection. The majority of the works were sold to American collectors.[77] The departure of this collection brought Veth to a somewhat somber vision of the future: 'This is perhaps the first time that it has become publicly apparent: America is the winning element in the world of collectors. [...] There is no resisting it. [...] The Old World will gradually have to hand over to the New everything that it has not yet placed in safekeeping in public museums.'[78]

Only sporadically did an important Dutch painting return from America to the land of its origins. This occurred in 1913, when the Amsterdam collector August Janssen bought a *Lucretia* by Rembrandt from the dealer Frederik Muller & Cie [12].[79] The work had come from the collection of M.C. Borden of New York. After his death, the painting was acquired by Knoedler's, who sold it to A.W. Mensing of the Muller firm. The return of

▲ 11
Dr. Cornelis Hofstede de Groot at the E. Simon auction in Berlin, 7 October 1929
From: H.E. van Gelder, *Levensbericht van Dr. C. Hofstede de Groot*, Leyden 1931

▶ 12
Rembrandt
Lucretia
Canvas, 120 x 101 cm (47¼ x 39¾ in.)
Center left: *Rembrandt / 1664*
Washington, National Gallery of Art, Andrew W. Mellon Collection, inv. no. 1937.1.76 (76)

the Rembrandt was greeted with enthusiasm in the Netherlands. Under the heading of 'A Rembrandt Recaptured,' *Het Nieuws van den Dag* wrote, 'Next to the Nightwatch, the Syndics of the Cloth Guild, the Jewish Bride, the Portrait of the Burgomaster Six, and the Homer, the Lucretia may henceforth be named as one of the sublime works owned by the land of Rembrandt. One may therefore speak in this connection of a truly patriotic deed.'[80]

Bredius, who was in the United States at the time, was able to explain how the *Lucretia* could return to the Netherlands: 'Knoedler could not sell the Lucretia in America. Frick found the subject so unpleasant that he was simply not interested. The same was true of Mrs. Evans, a great collector in Boston. Altman, too, had turned it down, so that the piece had become unsaleable here!!'[81] The joy over the repatriation of the *Lucretia* was in any case to be short-lived. After the death of August Janssen in 1918, his collection was sold, and the painting came once more, and this time permanently, into American possession.[82]

Despite the increasing competition from American collectors, several successes in the battle to retain the Dutch art patrimony were recorded after 1910, in part because the heirs of important collectors were granted exemption from death taxes for works of art that they donated to the State.[83] The most important feat of arms was the acquisition by the State and the Rembrandt Society of five paintings from the Steengracht collection.

Like the Six collection, the Steengracht was a Dutch collection with a long history and an illustrious reputation.[84] Jonkheer Johan Steengracht van Oostcapelle, who from 1816 to 1841 was Director of the Royal Cabinet of Paintings (which had been housed in the Mauritshuis since 1822), had inherited several paintings from his mother. He supplemented this modest collection with numerous important works by Dutch masters, including paintings by Rembrandt, Steen, and Ter Borch. In 1875 Jonkheer Hendrik Adolf Steengracht van Duivenvoorde inherited the collection, which had in the meantime been enlarged by his father, Jonkheer Hendrik Steengracht van Oosterland, with nineteenth-century masters. The public could view the paintings in his house on the Lange Vijverberg in The Hague, near the Mauritshuis. After his death in 1912, following the terms of his will, the collection had to be sold.

Once again it was the Rembrandt Society that initiated a rescue attempt.[85] Shortly after it became known that the Steengracht collection was to be sold, Martin, who had become Director of the Mauritshuis in 1909, conferred with Hofstede de Groot, the secretary of the society. They discussed how the most important works of the collection could be preserved for the Netherlands.

In the board meeting of 16 July 1912, Hofstede de Groot raised the matter. According to him there was the possibility that the collection would be sold 'direct and as a whole' to America. He stressed the importance of the Steengracht collection: 'If "Rembrandt" were not yet to exist, this sale would be a reason for founding the Society.' It was established, however, that it was not essential that the entire collection be saved for the Netherlands and that the acquisition of the most important pieces would suffice.[86]

Early in 1913 it became known that on 9 June of that year the Steengracht collection would come under the hammer at the Galerie Georges Petit in Paris. The Rembrandt Society decided to make an important part of its own capital available for the purchase of several top pieces at this auction. Private parties were asked for a financial contribution. Queen Wilhelmina was one of the many who responded to this call. The government turned out to be willing to help as well. Presuming the society would buy at the auction for no more than half a million guilders, the Minister of the Interior would submit a proposal to have the State pay three-quarters of the amount.[87]

The press received the news of the pending sale of the Steengracht collection with great disappointment. On the eve of the sale, the Paris correspondent of the *Nieuwe Rotterdamse Courant* wrote, 'The very assumption is heartbreaking that the dollars will once more win tomorrow afternoon, and that an insanely rich American will carry off across the ocean these pieces of delight and happiness, which belong to all of humanity, and will lock them away somewhere on such-and-such "Avenue".'[88] The correspondent took it for granted that the most important

13
Jan Steen
'The Way You Hear It, Is the Way you Sing It'
Canvas, 134 x 163 cm (52 ¾ x 64 ⅝ in.)
Neither signed nor dated (ca. 1663)
The Hague, Mauritshuis, inv. no. 742

14
Rembrandt
Bathseba
Panel, 57.2 x 76.2 cm (22 ½ x 30 in.)
Lower left: *Rembrandt f/ 1643*
New York, The Metropolitan Museum of Art,
inv. no. 14.40.651

works at the auction would go to America. After all, the European museums had too little money 'to triumph over the railway, tin can, or other trust kings of the new world.' As a defense against the 'dollar-attacks' he suggested a cooperative union among the large European museums. If they were to unite their funds, the most important state museums would be able to compete with the American collectors. 'The pieces thus rescued by the International European Museum Trust would be placed in turn, that is to say each time during, for instance, 3 or 5 years, in a member museum of the trust. In this way an exceptionally large number of people would be able to enjoy them.'[89]

The Rembrandt Society's Steengracht campaign came to a successful conclusion. Five paintings were acquired at the auction.[90] The most important acquisition was '*The Way You Hear It, Is the Way you Sing It*' by Jan Steen [**13**], which fetched 375,000 French francs (about 198,000 guilders, including premium).[91] The other works were *The Lice Hunt* by Gerard ter Borch, *The Water Mills of Singraven near Denekamp* by Meindert Hobbema (cat. no. 32, fig. 4), *Farmer with Pig* by Isack van Ostade, and *The Old Canal in Haarlem* (then known as *Canal in Delft*) by Job Berckheyde. Other paintings that had been on the wish list, *The*

Smokers by Adriaen Brouwer and *The Sick Child* by Gabriël Metsu, went for too much money.[92]

The top piece of the auction was the *Bathseba* by Rembrandt [**14**]. The Rembrandt Society had decided not to bid on this painting because it was expected that its price would be driven up too high.[93] This assumption turned out to be correct. The estimated amount of 800,000 French francs was soon reached. At a quarter to three, forty-five minutes after the beginning of the auction, the auctioneer called out one million. A deathly silence ensued, followed by loud applause. Never before had a painting been sold for such an amount at a public auction [**15**].[94] Following the third and final gavel blow, everyone asked who the buyer was. It turned out to be Duveen, the famous dealer with almost exclusively American customers. Everyone then knew that the painting would go to America.

The work came into the possession of the great Rembrandt collector Benjamin Altman in New York. The prediction of the

15
'Auction Downstairs'
Inscription: *Tevreden Rembrandt?... Je bent nu millionnair..!* (Satisfied Rembrandt?...You are now a millionaire..!)
Satirical print on the occasion of the sale of Rembrandt's *Bathseba* for the record price of one million francs at the Steengracht auction.
From: *De Amsterdammer, Weekblad voor Nederland*, 29 June 1913

Paris correspondent that the painting would be locked up in 'such-and-such Avenue' seemed initially to come true. Only a small elect were allowed to view Altman's collection in his house on Fifth Avenue. Hofstede de Groot wrote, 'One had to have exceptional letters of recommendation indeed to obtain permission to see his collections, and as member of the female sex one did not get it even then.'[95] It did not take long, however, before the *Bathseba* could again be shown to the public. Altman died in that same year (1913), and his collection was donated to The Metropolitan Museum of Art in New York.[96]

On the occasion of the spectacular sale of the Rembrandt, C. Harms Tiepen wrote in *Holland*, 'Compared to the American gold, our currency is but small change.'[97] Nevertheless there was every reason for the Dutch to be satisfied with the way the auction had turned out. In addition to the five works that had been purchased by the Rembrandt Society, diverse Dutch collectors had bid with success on important pieces. Mrs. C.A. Rose-Molwater bought the *Portrait of a Boy* by Jacob Backer, which she subsequently donated to the Mauritshuis.[98] From the chairman of the Rembrandt Society, M.P. Voûte, the Rijksmuseum got *King David* by Aert de Gelder, which he had acquired with his own money.[99] About one-third of the entire collection remained in Dutch hands. 'Holland on guard!', a triumphant Harms Tiepen accordingly wrote above his article.[100]

The acquisition of the five works by the Rembrandt Society had cost about 550,000 guilders. The State subsequently bought them for 400,000 guilders. From August to September of 1913, the acquisitions from the Steengracht collection were exhibited in the Stedelijk Museum in Amsterdam.[101] Now that the paintings had been preserved for the Netherlands, a new problem presented itself. It had to be decided where the works would go, although it was naturally established that they were destined for a state museum. Both the citizens of Amsterdam and those of The Hague believed that their city was the appropriate one.[102] The argument from The Hague was that the Steengracht collection had come from their city and therefore belonged there. Moreover, the Rijksmuseum in Amsterdam had already profited several years earlier from the acquisitions from the Six collection. Of course, the Amsterdammers had different ideas. They pointed out that a considerable part of the money contributed by the Rembrandt Society had come from Amsterdam.[103] Had the citizens of The Hague wanted so badly to retain the works for their city, they should have reached deeper into their pockets.

The managing board of the Rembrandt Society also debated vehemently about the placing of the paintings.[104] The Amsterdam members believed that at least one important work, the Steen, should end up in their Rijksmuseum. August Allebé, former director of the State Academy for Visual Arts in Amsterdam, was of the opinion that 'the national honor demands that the most important work go to the most important museum.' Bredius, also a member of the board and an advocate for placement in The Hague, accused the Amsterdammers of small-mindedness.[105]

The Hague won out in the end. Despite the advice of the Rembrandt Society to house the Steen in the Rijksmuseum, the minister decided in 1914 to place all five works in the Maurits-huis, the state museum in The Hague.[106] Hobbema's *The Water Mills of Singraven near Denekamp* (cat. no. 32, fig. 4) was later to leave the fatherland after all. It was given to Canada in 1950, in gratitude for the contribution of that country to the liberation of the Netherlands in 1945.

The year 1913 was a great success for those who fought for the preservation of the Dutch art patronage. Beside the Steengracht auction, success was also achieved at the Heseltine auction, held in Amsterdam on 27 May.[107] With the support of the Rembrandt Society, the drawing *Sleeping Woman* by Rembrandt was acquired for the Rijksprentenkabinet in Amsterdam.[108] In total no fewer than fifteen of the thirty-two drawings at the Heseltine auction were bought by Dutchmen.[109] On the subject of both auctions, the German art historian Max J. Friedländer spoke of a 'movement activitated by national pride to save for Holland whatever can be saved.'[110]

The acquisitions from the Steengracht collection marked the end of the first phase of the battle against the dollar. The preservation of Dutch cultural heritage was relegated to the background by the outbreak of World War I. On account of the poor financial situation, the acquisition budgets of the museums were entirely eliminated from the national budget.[111] The acquisitions of 1913 had substantially shrunk the reserves of the

16
Karel du Jardin
Saint Paul Healing the Lame Man in Lystra
Canvas, 179 x 139 cm (70 ¹/₂ x 54 ³/₄ in.)
Upper left: *K. DU / IARDIN / fe / (16)63*
Princeton, Jasna Polana, collection Mrs. Piasecka Johnson

Rembrandt Society.[112] The membership also fell sharply because of the financial crisis. In the period from 1913 to 1919, the number of contributing members declined from 512 to 398.

The battle for the preservation of Dutch art possessions was to flare up once more in the years after World War I. There were both successes and reversals. In 1921 *The Little Street* by Vermeer from the Six collection was preserved for the Netherlands.[113] On the other hand, in 1938 Rembrandt's *Portrait of Marten Looten* went from the Mensing collection to America. Although the conflict has lost its edge with the years, Dutchmen and Americans still fight over the old masters. Usually the dollar wins out over the guilder. Thus, in 1982, an excellent landscape by Jacob van Ruisdael, *Two Water Mills and Open Locks*, was offered for sale to the Mauritshuis. However, the museum could not pay the asked price of 750,000 guilders, and the painting was sold for more than twice that amount to The J. Paul Getty Museum in Malibu.[114] Only recently the Mauritshuis and another Dutch museum had to look on while, at a London auction, *Saint Paul Healing the Lame Man in Lystra* by Karel du Jardin [16] was sold to America.[115]

With the benefit of hindsight one may observe that the emergence of the American collectors had more of a positive than a negative effect on the Netherlands. The American threat

Vijfhonderd Gulden belooning!

Afbeelding van een schilderij van
FRANS HALS,
GESTOLEN zonder de lijst uit het Mauritshuis te 's Gravenhage den zevenden **Juli 1905.**
Het is op paneel geschilderd, 24½ centimeter hoog en 19½ centimeter breed,
De Minister van Binnenlandsche Zaken looft een
Belooning van vijfhonderd Gulden
uit aan hem, die het ontvreemde terugbezorgt of zoodanige aanwijzingen doet welke tot vinding en terugbezorging der schilderij leiden.
De Directie van het Mauritshuis verzoekt onmiddellijk bericht.

certainly contributed to the general realization that too many art treasures had already left the country. It was feared that if nothing were done, the Americans of means would carry off forever everything that still remained in private Dutch hands. In order to prevent that, people united in a major effort. Even the government, which had long stood aside, turned out to be prepared to make financial sacrifices. Had the American collectors not taken front stage so obviously, the danger to the national heritage would probably have been realized less quickly and, just as before 1900, numerous art treasures would have continued to be sold abroad without much ado.

Envy and Admiration

When *The Kitchenmaid* by Vermeer had been saved for the Netherlands, Jan Veth wrote, 'it is, in the name of a deeper sense of art itself, reasonable and desirable that every country apply itself in the first instance to keeping the select products of its own art within its frontiers.'[116] According to him it was 'improper' to take important paintings 'far away from the atmosphere in which they were born.'[117] Dutch paintings ought therefore to be kept as much as possible within the 'boundary markers.'[118]

National pride was an important motive force behind the battle against the dollar. There was, however, another aspect of importance, namely the negative image that people had of the American collectors.[119] They were reputed to be interested primarily in the financial value of a painting, and not in its beauty. For them a work of art was mainly a status symbol. More Rembrandts brought more status. True love of art they were assumed not to possess.

The Americans were the target of the reproach that they took the Dutch masters out of their original context and placed them in a foreign, loveless environment. They presumably 'locked away' the acquired works in their dwellings, thus withdrawing them from the admiration of the public. One other prejudice was that they had no understanding of art whatsoever, and were therefore easily cheated. They therefore preferred to buy paintings from renowned collections, thus guaranteeing their authenticity.

The negative image of the American collector is clearly projected in a satirical article that appeared in 1905 in the *Rotterdamsch Nieuwsblad* on the occasion of an art theft.[120] On 7 July a *Portrait of a Man* by Frans Hals was stolen from the Mauritshuis [17].[121] The article has the form of a short play, with

17
'Five Hundred Guilders Reward'
Pamphlet on the occasion of the theft of a *Portrait of a Man* by Frans Hals from the Mauritshuis on 7 July 1905.
The Hague, documentation archives Mauritshuis

an American multi-millionaire and an art thief as principal actors. The scene is the study of the multi-millionaire. A pale young man enters and says, 'You are a famous art lover... and an excellent connoisseur... .' He subsequently offers to sell the millionaire a painting. The American answers that he already has enough paintings by well-known masters: 'Even Pierpont Morgan envies me on account of them.' When the man shows him the stolen Hals, he says he does not like it. When he hears, however, that the work was purloined from the Mauritshuis, he becomes wildly enthusiastic. 'But man, why did you not say that at once? That is splendid! And did you filch it yourself?'

The man admits he has stolen the portrait himself and adds, 'If I had remained in Europe with it, and had offered it to a dealer or a museum director, I might just as well have walked straight to prison. [...] No, thank God there is still an art-loving America, and that's why I came here.' The multi-millionaire buys the painting and gives the thief an extra hundred dollars for the 'unforgettably bold, masterful, safe manner' in which he came by the painting. The new acquisition is hung in the drawing room. The frame is adorned with a gold sign with the inscription 'Stolen on 7 July 1905 from the Mauritshuis in The Hague.'

The play was not based on fact. In late July the painting turned up in Antwerp and was returned to the Mauritshuis shortly thereafter.[122] However, the article gives a good indication of what people of the time thought about American collectors. It is hardly surprising that many Dutchmen preferred to see national treasures go to another European country than have them disappear to America. The Atlantic Ocean was considered to be 'a river Styx for works of art.'[123]

The Dutch also wrote about American collectors in more positive terms. Thus, in 1907, Lugt drew a distinction between serious collectors and occasional buyers.[124] In 1909 Martin wrote 'On American Collections of Paintings.'[125] He admitted that the negative view of American collectors was understandable. They had, after all, driven up the prices for old art and seen to it that the number of works of art in private possession had shrunk noticeably. 'For us the American art collector is moreover the one who has forced us to cease our museum acquisitions, to limit ourselves to works by second-rate masters, or to have to put up with almost irresponsible financial sacrifices.'[126]

Nevertheless, according to Martin, there was also cause for admiration. Alongside the worthless collections, there were ever more collections of high quality in America: 'Thus it would appear that the time has now come for America to progress in knowledge and taste in the domain of art collecting: they no longer allow themselves to be fooled just like that!'[127] The collectors compensated for their lack of art historical knowledge by calling in European experts. Moreover, with much private energy and money, numerous museums were being founded, which raised the American cultural standards to a higher level. 'Thus they do much, very much in America for art education, in the certain conviction that by those means, as well, the taste of the American, including that of the American art collector, will steadily improve and become more refined.'[128]

According to Martin the negative image of the American collectors could be substantially corrected if people in the Netherlands were better informed about their collections. He was therefore gratified by the appearance in 1907 of the book *Noteworthy Paintings in American Private Collections* by J. La Farge and A.F. Jacacci.[129] In it, several important collections were illuminated in detail. This book showed that 'in addition to much that is mediocre and inferior, nevertheless wonderfully much of splendor has been assembled' in America.[130]

Martin concluded his article with the observation that though it is painful for the Europeans when art treasures go from the Old World to the New, that is still no reason to have an aversion to American collectors who spend their dollars 'to savor enjoyment of art in their own home [...]. It would be an aversion born of envy.'[131]

Veth, too, pleaded for a more positive attitude towards American collectors. In 1909 he visited the New York exhibition of old Dutch paintings in American possession.[132] This was held on the occasion of the Hudson-Fulton celebrations. Veth was very much impressed by the quality of the exhibited works. The exhibition proved beyond a doubt 'that the convenient fairytale that in America one encounters primarily fake old masters and trash ought once and for all to be relegated to the land of fables.'[133]

As has already been observed, Veth believed that Dutch works of art were best located in their own country. But when sale was inevitable, it in fact made no difference if they ended up in Moscow or New York: 'the opinion that the relationship between the work of art and its owner is so much cooler in the New World than it is customarily in the Old World should emphatically be revised.'[134] Veth did not deny that there were Americans who bought a painting only because it was worth a lot. However, such folks were also in good supply in Europe. There was, therefore, not a single reason for the Dutch to presuppose 'that it is exclusively the Yankee who buys up our art treasures because they are expensive, and that the beautiful paintings end up over there hanging not in a cozy little corner but in the draft of cool speculative lust.'[135]

Many collectors in the Old World could learn a lesson from someone such as John G. Johnson of Philadelphia, a collector of the 'virtuous and amiable kind.'[136] The most important difference between European and American collectors was that the latter could dispose of more money. There was nothing to it but to accept that, henceforth, a crossing by sea would be required if one was to get to know the Dutch masters better. 'A trip to America is not at all a journey to hell. We ought not to consider the blossomed New Amsterdam as an enemy.'[137]

The Hudson-Fulton exhibition got the full attention of the Dutch press. Exhaustive discussions appeared in the periodicals *Onze Kunst* (Our Art) and *Kunstkroniek*.[138] The *Nieuwe Rotterdamsche Courant* printed a letter to the editor by a Dutch visitor of the exhibition who had been amazed by the behavior of the American public.[139] Many visitors were more interested in the name of the owner than in the maker of a painting. Comments such as 'Look, there are the Altmans' and 'Come along, there are three more Morgans in the next room' were rife. However, the anonymous letter-writer had to admit that the sensibilities of the average Dutchmen were not much finer: 'What percentage of the people of The Hague, for instance, visits the Mauritshuis once every five years?'

Hofstede de Groot was also staying in America at the time of the Hudson-Fulton exhibition. He was there at the request of Peter A.B. Widener of Philadelphia. This collector had become the victim of a swindler who had sold him fakes and inferior works.[140] However, the millionaire was not to be deterred by this. The matter did not come to court. After all, as Hofstede de Groot observed, 'a rich American does not make a fool of himself over a few millions.'[141]

Widener asked Hofstede de Groot to scrutinize his collection.[142] The Dutch expert approved of only a few paintings. Everything that had not withstood critical examination Widener disposed of and replaced with famous work of assured authenticity. Of the eighty-three Dutch and Flemish works in the collection catalogue of 1900, only twenty-three remained in the new catalogue of 1913.[143] The methods of Widener, who was much praised in the Netherlands, indicated to what extent Americans strove to improve the quality of their collections.[144]

Hofstede de Groot is said to have observed to an American reporter, 'I came here to see your masterpieces, but I return in despair.' Once returned to the Netherlands, however, he denied having said anything of the kind. He had instead seen much of beauty in America. That there were so many good paintings in America, he claimed, had little to do with the 'artistic sense of detection' of the Americans: 'The system is simple enough; one buys familiar paintings from long-renowned collections. The price does not matter.' It seemed as if the American collectors wished to buy a painting only if it was expensive. A cheap work was mistrusted.[145] The Americans also had a preference for large dimensions: 'The bigger, the better.'[146] There were plenty of fakes in America, but one ought not to exaggerate: 'In Europe, too, hang many works with the signature of, for instance, Rembrandt, which were brought into the world by the hands of daubers.'[147]

What disappointed Hofstede de Groot was the arrangement of the museums. The works of art were often used for purposes of art education. Although this was in itself praiseworthy, it was often accomplished at the expense of viewing pleasure. That is why an American museum was not what it ought in the first place to be, 'a house of prayer for those who believe devoutly in the holiness and glory of art.'[148]

If Hofstede de Groot was rather critical of the Americans and their collections, Bredius, on the other hand, was unusually enthusiastic when he visited the New World. In 1913 he ventured the crossing. He had previously let it be known on several occasions that he did not have a high opinion of the American collectors. Thus he thought the *Saul and David* by Rembrandt too good for the Americans.[149] He further spoke rather derisively of the many fakes that were presumably to be found in America: 'Numerous copies pass for genuine there... brand new Ruysdaels are there... .'[150] In his polemical exchange with Mensing on the occasion of the Six controversy, he had summed up Pierpont Morgan's bad buys with thinly disguised gloating.[151]

During his journey through America, which took place late in 1913 and during the first months of 1914, he gained greater sympathy for the American collectors. This was already apparent from the letters that he sent regularly to the editors of the *Nieuwe Rotterdamsche Courant*, in which he reported on his experiences in the New World.[152] He visited many collectors and museums,[153] and was warmly received almost everywhere. A disappointment awaited him only with Isabella Stewart Gardner in Boston. Despite letters, telephone conversations, and numerous introductions, she refused to receive the renowned connoisseur by himself. He could come on the days that her collection was open to one and all, at one dollar admission.[154]

Bredius saw many old acquaintances, such as *The Polish Rider* by Rembrandt. This work, which he had himself discovered, was now located in the Frick collection in New York (p. 123, fig. 2).[155] In the collection of the 'copper king' William A. Clark, he discovered *The Rape of the Sabine Women* by Jan Steen, 'once sold at the de Gruyter auction for f. 800 – our Government let it go for that – and now it has become the property of this art collector for many thousands!'[156] Bredius was very much impressed by the arrangement of Clark's house: 'It is enough to make one heady. But the whole is of a refined taste, and a pleasure for the eyes.' Accordingly, he had great admiration for 'this man, who had risen from being a miner to become the owner of this palace, of an *hôtel* in Paris, of a similar residence in Montana etc. etc..'[157]

A subsequent high point of his journey was a visit to the collection of John G. Johnson in Philadelphia, 'probably the largest, the best rounded, and, from an artistic point of view, the most important to have been assembled for a long time by an artistically minded collector.' Every piece from this collection betrayed 'the artistic sensitivity, the refined taste, and the sense of beauty of this remarkable collector.'[158]

It became clear to Bredius that the American collectors were not as self-centered as was believed in Holland. Various private collections were open to the public on specified days. It was also the intention of many to leave their own art possessions to the community. Mrs. Emery of Cincinnati told him 'that she would not think it responsible of herself to spend so much money on paintings were it not that she did so with the plan of leaving her entire collection to the city, and it should have nothing but the best!'[159] Bredius was later to follow the American example in leaving a part of his collection to the Mauritshuis, and the remainder to the municipality of The Hague. Such a grand gesture was less customary in the Netherlands. Over the years countless old masters have disappeared from the fatherland because important private collections, such as those of Sidney van den Bergh, C.J.K. van Aalst, and B. de Geus van den Heuvel, were sold by the owners or their surviving relatives.

Bredius was unusually positive about the quality of American collections: 'Yes... America is rich in divine artworks!'[160] Nevertheless there were still collectors, such as Mr. Walker of Minneapolis, who owned primarily fakes and copies. This 'self-made man' had a great many bad pieces, 'so that all that junk leaves one nauseous in the end.' Bredius made haste to observe that Walker was only an exception: 'In recent times the collections have been much purged, and I have almost never encountered bad or dubious works in the good collections.'[161]

In one of his last letters, he summed up his altered opinion of the American collectors: 'I must here observe once more with emphasis that most art collectors that I have met here love their paintings and possess a warm feeling for art. It is not true that all these wealthy people collect out of "bluff" and "snobbism." Almost all of them have every bit as much heart for art, and the longing to surround themselves with masterpieces on account of their beauty, as do the European collectors. I have had the privilege to get to know many very intelligent and charming owners of art treasures of all sorts, and almost all of them are engrossed in their collections, which they love like their children.'[162] With these words Bredius resolutely put an end to the negative image of the American collectors that he had formed before his journey, though it continued to live on in many others in Holland.

I thank those who have helped me with the realization of this essay, especially Marjolein de Boer, Beatrijs Brenninkmeyer-de Rooij, J.F. Heijbroek, and Josefine Leistra.
Editor's note: With one exception (Sir Joshua Reynolds), all quotations are translated from the Dutch or German.

1 Abraham Bredius (1855-1946) was director of the Mauritshuis from 1889 to 1909. He published many articles and books on old Dutch painting. He was also highly active on various committees and boards (see *Ekkart 1979*). After a brief career in the museum world, notably as Assistant Director of the Mauritshuis from 1891 to 1896, Cornelis Hofstede de Groot (1863-1930) established himself as an independent art historian in The Hague. He earned his livelihood writing books and catalogues and giving appraisals (see *Ekkart 1979-A*). Willem Martin (1876-1954) was Director of the Mauritshuis (1909-1941) and Adjunct Professor in the History of Art at the University of Leyden (1907-1943). In addition, he was an important author of books and articles about Dutch painting of the seventeenth century (see *Ekkart 1985*). Jan Veth (1864-1925) wrote many articles and books about old and contemporary art from his point of view as an artist (see *Ekkart 1989*).
2 *Martin 1925*, pp. 477-478
3 *Martin 1925*, p. 480; on the interest in, and the movement in prices of, the Dutch masters, see *Reitlinger 1982*, vol. I, pp. 11-15, 136-142, 203-206.
4 *Ploos van Amstel 1771*, p. 140; see also *Bille 1961*, vol. I, p. 67
5 For a detailed discussion of the collection of William II and the auction of 1850, see *Hinterding / Horsch 1989*. The *Portrait of Nicolaes Ruts* (Auction The Hague 1850, no. 86) came to the collection of Adrian Hope in London by way of the dealer Weimar in The Hague; *Bruyn et al. 1986*, no. A 43, p. 121; *New York 1968*, p. 256; *Hinterding / Horsch 1989*, no. 86, p. 84. The *Man in Oriental Costume* (Auction The Hague 1850, no. 91) came to the collection George Tomline, Orwell Park, Ipswich, by way of the dealer Nieuwenhuys in London; *Bruyn et al. 1986*, no. A 48, p. 157; *Hinterding / Horsch 1989*, no. 91, p. 86. See also note 22.
6 Cited in *De Gou 1922*, p. 240
7 *The Hague 1985*, p. 42. On the opportunities missed by the Dutch government to preserve important collections for the Netherlands, see *De Stuers 1873 / 1975*, p. 23, and *Hecht / Luijten 1986*, pp. 190-191.
8 *The Hague 1985*, pp. 43, 45
9 *The Hague 1985*, pp. 61, 63; see also *Duparc 1975*, pp. 1-16.
10 *De Stuers 1873 / 1975*, p. 78. 'Holland op zijn smalst' appeared as an article in *De*

Gids, year 37, 3rd series, year 11, vol. III, November 1873, pp. 320-403.

11 *Bode 1881-A*, p. 298 (Dutch translation of *Bode 1881*, p. 293)

12 *Bode 1881-A*, p. 298 (Dutch translation of *Bode 1881*, p. 294)

13 *De Gou 1922*, pp. 238-239

14 *De Stuers 1881*, p. 94

15 For De Stuers's efforts to preserve the Dutch artistic heritage, see *Duparc 1975*, pp. 14-16, 80-81, 89-90, 111-112, 119-120.

16 *Heijbroek 1983*, pp. 155-160; *Hijmersma 1983*, pp. 24-26

17 *Heijbroek 1983*, pp. 156-157

18 *Kyzer 1883*, p. 3

19 Rijksmuseum, Amsterdam, inv. no. A 1595; for information on the acquisition, see *Van Thiel 1983*.

20 *Bredius 1901*, p. 143

21 *Martin 1946*, p. 72

22 The *Portrait of Nicolaes Ruts* was acquired by J. Pierpont Morgan before 1903, and later ended up in The Frick Collection in New York (inv. no. 43.1.150; *New York 1968*, p. 256). The *Man in Oriental Costume* arrived in the McKay Twombly collection in New York in 1897, and was acquired around 1909 by W.K. Vanderbilt, New York. In 1920 the painting was bequeathed to The Metropolitan Museum of Art in New York (inv. no. 20.155.2; *Baetjer 1980*, vol. I, p. 148).

23 *Reitlinger 1982*, vol. I, p. 177: 'In the "eighties" and "nineties" the drift was not yet mainly towards the U.S.A.'; 'It was not till after 1900, when Duveen Brothers had established a strong American market, that London again became the centre for old-master sales.'

24 *Bode 1895*, p. 13

25 *Bode 1895*, pp. 14-19

26 *Bode 1902*

27 *Bode 1902*, p. 7

28 *Bode 1902*, pp. 10-11. According to *Simpson 1988*, p. 97, the Mazzarenti collection was sold to John T. Walters of Baltimore.

29 *Bode 1902*, p. 11

30 *Bode 1904*, p. 388

31 *Bode 1906-A*, p. 3

32 *Bode 1906-A*, p. 3

33 *Bode 1930*, vol. II, p. 144

34 *Bode 1906-A*, p. 4

35 *Bode 1906-A*, p. 5

36 *Bode 1909*, p. 441

37 *Bode 1909*, pp. 443, 525

38 *Bode 1910-A*, p. 83

39 *NRC 26-10-1909*

40 See *De Boer / Leistra 1991*, cat. no. 11. Bredius had given the *Saul and David* on loan to the Mauritshuis, and in 1946 the painting was bequeathed to this museum (inv. no. 621).

41 *Utrechtsche Courant 1903*

42 *Residentie Bode 1910*; *Hofstede de Groot 4-17-1925*

43 For a detailed report on this matter, see *Heijbroek 1983*, pp. 164-170; *Duparc 1975*, pp. 160-162.

44 For the history of the Six collection, see *Amsterdam 1900*; *Freise 1908*, p. 48, and H. van de Waal in *Fromentin 1876 / 1976*, pp. 304-305.

45 *Lugt 1907*. This brochure appeared in September 1907.

46 *Lugt 1907*, p. 8

47 *Lugt 1907*, p. 11

48 *Lugt 1907*, p. 13

49 *Lugt 1907*, p. 21

50 *Lugt 1907*, p. 21

51 *Bredius 9-18-1907*

52 *Mensing 9-21-1907*. For biographical data on Mensing, see cat. no. 29.

53 *Bredius 9-23-1907*

54 *Mensing 9-30-1907*

55 *Bredius 10-2-1907*

56 *Mensing 10-3-1907*. In the meantime Lugt himself had also reacted to the pieces submitted by Bredius (*Lugt 10-2-1907*). A second edition of Lugt's brochure appeared in October, supplemented by a foreword (dated 4 October) in which he gave consideration to the commentary of Bredius (*Lugt 1907-A*).

57 *Avondpost 1907*

58 *Avondpost 1907*

59 Lugt was supported by: *Roland Holst 1907*; *Nijland 10-6-1907* (reaction to this in *Marius 1907* and answer in *Nijland 10-11-1907*).

60 *Middelburgsche Courant 9-23-1907*; *Middelburgsche Courant 9-30-1907*; *Middelburgsche Courant 10-5-1907*

61 *Middelburgsche Courant 9-23-1907*

62 For reactions to this see *NRC 9-26-1907* and *NRC 9-27-1907*. Legal regulations with respect to the export of the cultural heritage were not to come into being in the Netherlands until after World War II; see P.W.L. Russell 'Wet tot behoud van cultuurbezit,' in *Russell 1989*, pp. 49-105.

63 *Bredius 10-1-1907*

64 *Middelburgsche Courant 11-9-1907*

65 For a detailed report of the discussion, see *Tillema 1982*, pp. 178-182.

66 *Tillema 1982*, p. 179

67 *Tillema 1982*, p. 180

68 For reflections on the acquisition of the Six collection, see *Steenhoff 1908*; *Veth 1908*, and *Martin 1908*. In addition to *The Kitchenmaid* by Vermeer (inv. no. A 2344), the remaining works from the Six collection also ended up in the Rijksmuseum, see *Van Thiel et al. 1976*, pp. 35-36.

69 *Veth 1908*, p. 190

70 *Veth 1908*, p. 192

71 *Hofstede de Groot 1910*

72 *Duparc 1975*, p. 156

73 For a proposal to establish an acquisitions fund, see *Frederiks 1913*.

74 *Delftsche Courant 1910*

75 *Veth 1911*

76 Bode had catalogued the Kann collection in 1900 (*Bode 1900*). The importance of the collection is discussed in *Bredius 1902*; *Bode 1905*; and *Schmidt-Degener 1908*. On the sale of the collection, see *Mesnil 1908*; *Bode 1907-1908*; *Bode 1930*, vol. II, pp. 187-188.

77 *Simpson 1988*, pp. 106-114

78 *Veth 1911*

79 On August Janssen as collector, see *Lugt 1918*.

80 *Nieuws van den Dag 1913*; see also *Veth 1914*.

81 *Bredius 12-8-1913*

82 Around 1920 the *Lucretia* was located in the H. Heilbluth collection in Copenhagen, and then came into the possession of Andrew W. Mellon. In 1937 the work was absorbed into the collection of the National Gallery of Art in Washington (inv. no. 1937.1.76 [76]; *Washington 1969*, p. 33, no. 23).

83 Thus works from the collection of Mr. [Master of Jurisprudence] C. Hoogendijk came to the Rijksmuseum in Amsterdam, see *Duparc 1975*, p. 162.

84 On the history of the Steengracht collection, see *Auction Paris 1913*, p. 7, and *Lilienfeld 1913*.

85 *Martin 1914*; *Duparc 1975*, pp. 166-169. *Notulenboek Rembrandt*, 16 July 1912; 14 October 1912; 6 January 1913; 29 January 1913; 22 February 1913; 30 May 1913; 21 June 1913; 25 August 1913. I thank Mrs. A.M. Renaud-Deurvorst for her help with the study of these notebooks.

86 *Notulenboek Rembrandt*, 16 July 1912

87 *Duparc 1975*, p. 167

88 *NRC 6-9-1913*. On the pending sale of the Steengracht collection, see also *Schmidt Degener 1913* and *Frederiks 1913*.

89 *NRC 6-9-1913*

90 *Auction Paris 1913*. For a report on the auction, see *NRC 10-6-1913*; *Mesnil 1913*, and *Harms Tiepen 1913*. For reflections on the acquisitions, see *Steenhoff 1913*; *Martin*

1914; Vermeulen 1914.

91 *Duparc 1975*, p. 188, note 80

92 *The Smokers* by Adriaen Brouwer was acquired by the dealer F. Kleinberger & Co., Paris / New York. In 1919 the work came into the possession of Michael Friedsam of New York, and in 1931 it was bequeathed to The Metropolitan Museum of Art, New York (inv. no. 32.100.21; *Liedtke 1984*, vol. I, pp. 5-10). *The Sick Child* by Metsu returned to the Netherlands finally when, with the aid of the Rembrandt Society, it was purchased at the Huldschinsky auction in Berlin (5-10-1928) for the Rijksmuseum in Amsterdam (inv. no. A 3059; *Van Thiel et al. 1976*, pp. 379-380).

93 *Martin 1914*, p. 9

94 *NRC 6-10-1913*

95 *Hofstede de Groot 1913*

96 Inv. no. 14.40.651; *Baetjer 1980*, vol. I, p. 149

97 *Harms Tiepen 1913*, p. 121

98 Inv. no. 747; *Hoetink et al. 1985*, p. 333

99 Inv. no. A 2695; *Van Thiel et al. 1976*, p. 239

100 *Harms Tiepen 1913*, p. 121

101 *Amsterdam 1913*

102 *Duparc 1975*, pp. 168-169

103 *Vermeulen 1914*, pp. 443-444

104 *Notulenboek Rembrandt*, 21 June 1913 and 25 August 1913

105 *Notulenboek Rembrandt*, 3 September 1913

106 *Jaarverslag Rembrandt 1913*, pp. 4-5. On the placing of the works in the Mauritshuis, see also *Algemeen Handelsblad 1914* and *Nieuwe Courant 1914*. The works were included under the following inventory numbers: J. Steen, inv. no. 742; G. ter Borch, inv. no. 744; M. Hobbema, inv. no. 743; I. van Ostade, inv. no. 745; J. Berckheyde, inv. no. 746.

107 For reflections on the Heseltine auction, see *De Boer 1913* and *Friedländer 1913*.

108 *Jaarverslag Rembrandt 1913*, pp. 6 and 17

109 *Harms Tiepen 1913*, p. 121

110 *Friedländer 1913-A*

111 *Duparc 1975*, p. 156

112 *Jaarverslag Rembrandt 1912*, p. 7

113 In 1921 Sir Henry Deterding bought *The Little Street* from the Six collection and donated it to the Rijksmuseum (inv. no. A 2860; *Van Thiel et al. 1976*, pp. 571-572); on the acquisition, see *Van Kleffens 1980*, pp. 169-173.

114 Inv. no. 82.PA.18; *Fredericksen 1988*, p. 24

115 From 1894 to 1912 the painting by Du Jardin hung in the Mauritshuis on loan from J.C. van Hattum van Ellewoutsdijk. In 1987 the painting was sold at the auction of the Van Hattum collection in London for 341,000 pounds to Mrs. Piasecka Johnson, Jasna Polana, Princeton. For further information on the painting, see *Brochhagen 1958*, pp. 66-69 and notes 241 and 248.

116 *Veth 1908*, p. 189

117 *Veth 1908*, p. 189

118 *Veth 1908*, p. 190

119 For a summary of the negative notions about American collectors, see *Veth 1910*, pp. 88-89, and *Brusse 1926*, p. 49. On the Dutch image of America in general, see *Lammers 1989*.

120 *Rotterdamsch Nieuwsblad 1905*

121 Inv. no. 618; *Hoetink et al. 1985*, p. 371. For information on the theft, see *NRC 7-8-1905*.

122 *NRC 7-30-1905*

123 *Van Stuwe 1913*, p. 532

124 See note 48

125 *Martin 1909*

126 *Martin 1909*, p. 75

127 *Martin 1909*, p. 77

128 *Martin 1909*, p. 80

129 *Martin 1909*, p. 80; *La Farge / Jacacci 1907*

130 *Martin 1909*, p. 87

131 *Martin 1909*, p. 87

132 *Valentiner 1909*

133 *Veth 1910*, pp. 83-84

134 *Veth 1910*, p. 88

135 *Veth 1910*, p. 89

136 *Veth 1910*, p. 89

137 *Veth 1910*, p. 90

138 *Breck 1910*; *Waldmann 1910*

139 *NRC 10-21-1909*

140 *Martin 1918*, pp. 17-19; *Brusse 1926*, pp. 42-43, 98

141 *NRC 11-4-1909*

142 *Van Gelder / Gerson 1931*, p. 17, note 1; *NRC 11-4-1909*. In America, Hofstede de Groot also judged (and condemned) the collection of J.J. van Alen, see *Hofstede de Groot 12-21-1925*.

143 *Hofstede de Groot / Valentiner 1913-1916*

144 See the literature mentioned in note 139.

145 Hofstede de Groot was later to observe that Widener decided not to buy a painting by Rembrandt (*Pilate Washing His Hands*, now as 'style of Rembrandt' in The Metropolitan Museum of Art in New York, inv. no. 14.40.610; *Baetjer 1980*, vol. I, p. 150), because he thought it so inexpensive that there had to be something wrong with it; see *Hofstede de Groot 1928*.

146 On Widener's preference for large works, see *NRC 1915*.

147 *NRC 11-4-1909*

148 *NRC 11-4-1909*

149 See note 40

150 *Harms Tiepen 1913-A*, p. 40

151 See note 55

152 *Bredius 11-12-1913*; *Bredius 12-8-1913*; *Bredius 12-9-1913*; *Bredius 12-19-1913*; *Bredius 12-20-1913*; *Bredius 1-5-1914*; *Bredius 1-21-1914*; *Bredius 2-18-1914*; *Bredius 2-19-1914*; *Bredius 2-20-14*

153 During his journey Bredius visited the following cities: New York, Montreal, Boston, Worcester, Providence, New Haven, Philadelphia, Cincinnati, Minneapolis, Toledo, Detroit, Chicago, and Buffalo.

154 *Bredius 12-20-1913*

155 *Bredius 11-12-1913*

156 *Bredius 12-9-1913*. The painting by Steen is now in the John and Mable Ringling Museum of Art, Sarasota (*Robinson et al. 1980*, no. 120).

157 *Bredius 12-9-1913*

158 *Bredius 12-19-1913*

159 *Bredius 1-5-1914*

160 *Bredius 1-5-1914*

161 *Bredius 1-21-1914*

162 *Bredius 1-21-1914*

Susan Donahue Kuretsky
Sarah Gibson Blanding Professor of Art
Vassar College, Poughkeepsie, New York

Dutch Art in Academia
Observations on College and University Collecting

'I must study Politicks and War, that my sons may have the liberty to study Mathematicks and Philosophy. My sons ought to study Mathematicks and Philosophy, Geography, Natural History and Naval Architecture, Navigation, Commerce and Agriculture, in order to give their children a right to study Painting, Poetry, Musick, Architecture, Statuary, Tapestry and Porcelaine.'[1]

When John Adams wrote these words to his wife Abigail on 12 May 1780, he was implying that the place of the fine arts in a new nation was more a matter of luxury than of practical necessity. Yet, he also saw the opportunity to study art as a hard-won human right that every generation owes to its descendants. This way of thinking helps explain the early appearance and phenomenal growth of college and university art museums, distinctively American institutions that began to develop around the beginning of the nineteenth century.[2] Beginning with Dartmouth College (Hanover, New Hampshire) in 1785 and Bowdoin College (Brunswick, Maine) in 1811, campus collections have proliferated so widely that they now comprise roughly one-third of all the art museums in the United States.[3] It is startling to realize that they actually predate, by more than a generation, not only the introduction of art history to the American college curriculum, but also the major public museums that began to be founded in American cities during the 1870s.

Diverse, wide-ranging, and unpredictable in their areas of emphasis, college museums have played a vital role in the collecting of Dutch art in America. The examples in this exhibition (cat. nos. 7, 15, 16, 21, 25-26, 62, and 64), all of superlative quality, represent only a limited sampling of the fine Dutch pictures to be found in these special collections, many of which, because of their out-of-the-way locations, may be unfamiliar to European (or even American) art historians. Investigation of these collections, many still uncatalogued, yields important and unexpected finds.[4]

Any generalizations about museums in academia should begin, however, with the recognition that limited or sporadically available resources have done much to condition their special character. Unlike civic museums, college art collections compete for attention and support with other sectors of their own institutions – a situation that is hardly new, as indicated by this irascible comment from a Bowdoin College publication of 1883: 'If these pictures are worth as much as claimed, they ought to be exchanged for a decent telescope and observatory [...] there are lots of things we need, and we don't need the fossilized, antiquated collection of brown paint.'[5]

With internal funding in short supply, college collections develop primarily through gifts and bequests. Yet, however loyal and generous a college's alumni and friends may be – and this generosity has been very great – the biggest American philanthropists have most often been attracted to public collections with their larger and more diverse audiences. One exception is the Samuel H. Kress Foundation's gift in 1961 of study collections (primarily Italian Renaissance painting and sculpture) to nineteen American colleges and universities – although, again, the most important Kress paintings had been earmarked earlier for the National Gallery and other public museums.[6]

As has often been pointed out, examples given to the 'teaching collection' of a college or university may pose problems of authenticity, condition, quality, or sheer obscurity of authorship or subject matter. Problem pictures, however, can be of unusual interest to scholars and specialists and can provide exciting research projects for students, assuming that works of impeccable quality and condition are available for comparison. Moreover, the inquisitive, open-minded environment of an academic institution fosters appreciation of material that might not interest a more general audience. A discerning director will therefore make a point of seeking such donations or will muster available funds and collect against the market, buying works by artists not currently in style. These factors explain the impressive Dutch mannerist, Caravaggesque, and pre-Rembrandtist holdings in American college collections, for these artists (still largely unknown by the general public) often choose the kinds of arcane narrative themes that appeal to scholars and students [1-3], but may frighten away the non-specialist buyer. Their prices can be reasonable.

Similarly, drawings and prints have become a special strength in such museums. Until recently, examples by even major artists have been affordable. Gifts of works on paper have also been generous and frequent, perhaps because the graphic media are so appropriate for teaching students about artists' thinking and working processes. Impressive holdings of Dutch prints and drawings exist in many of the older college and university collections, such as Harvard, Yale, Princeton, Oberlin, Bowdoin, Vassar, Smith, and Williams. Even colleges that have not collected Dutch paintings may have important graphic examples. Two cases in point are the Davison Art Center at Wesleyan University (Middletown, Connecticut) and the Grunwald Center for the Graphic Arts at the University of California in Los Angeles, whose fine and comprehensive print collections, including major Rembrandt etchings, bear comparison with those in large public museums. Sometimes even a modest academic collection will own an important work on paper, such as Rembrandt's drawing of the thirties of *Christ on the Mount of Olives* (Ben. 173), a gift to Queen's College (Flushing, New York) from Mr. and Mrs. Norbert Schimmel.

Beyond their role as collectors, American campus museums have been involved with Dutch art through the small, scholarly shows such museums occasionally generate as a way of temporarily enlarging their holdings, while offering students direct experience with cataloging and exhibition procedures. These exhibitions have frequently broken scholarly ground in important areas, as did the ones designed by the late Wolfgang Stechow to clarify areas of Dutch art history in need of research or reappraisal. Thus, *Italy through Dutch Eyes* (The University of Michigan Museum of Art, Ann Arbor, Michigan, 1964) was put on in conjunction with a graduate seminar in Dutch landscape. A few years later, in 1969, Stechow came to Vassar College (Poughkeepsie, New York) to work with an undergraduate seminar on *Dutch Mannerism: Apogée and Epilogue* (Vassar College Art Gallery, 1970). Even though both shows were restricted entirely to loans from American collections, both catalogues are still worth consulting. Some recent exhibitions have gone far beyond the scope of the usual 'teaching show,' such as Seymour Slive's comprehensive *Jacob van Ruisdael*, 1982, Fogg Art Museum, Harvard University (Cambridge, Massachusetts) or Frima Fox Hofrichter's *Haarlem: The Seventeenth Century*, 1983, Jane Voorhees Zimmerli Art Museum, Rutgers, the State University of New Jersey (New Brunswick, New Jersey).[7] Indeed, the growth of modern museum facilities in American universities during the last decade now makes possible increasingly sophisticated exhibitions, including foreign loans. College museums have come a long way since their beginnings.

1
Joachim Wtewael
The Marriage of Peleus and Thetis
Panel, 109 x 165 cm (43 x 65 in.)
Lower left: *Joachim wte wael fecit Anno 1610*
Providence, R.I., Museum of Art, Rhode Island
School of Design, Mary B. Jackson Fund,
inv. no. 62.058

2
Gerard van Honthorst
Artemesia Drinking Her Husband's Ashes to Make Herself
a Living Tomb
Canvas, 170 x 150 cm (67 x 59 ⅛ in.)
Lower left: *G. Honthorst* (ca. 1630-1635)
Princeton, N.J., The Art Museum, Princeton
University, Mr. and Mrs. George L. Craig Purchase
Fund, inv. no. 1968-117

The earliest collegiate collections in America were molded by the character and intentions of their institutions – denominationally inspired Christian colleges, nearly always located in small towns or remote rural settings, in keeping with the American ideal of education as a residential enterprise best undertaken in cloistered surroundings. The motto of Dartmouth College (Hanover, New Hampshire), *vox clamantis in deserto* or 'a voice crying in the wilderness' (John 1:23), movingly expresses the mission of the college to convert and civilize, as a remote outpost within a new nation, itself far removed from European centers of culture.

Indeed, the civilizing potential of art, particularly as it applies to the development of young minds, has been recognized in this country from the beginning, for Thomas Jefferson's original goals for the University of Virginia included the fine arts as an integral part of the curriculum.[8] In the course of this study it will become apparent that educators from the nineteenth century onward have used art for various purposes: to develop taste and aesthetic discrimination (ultimately for the public good), to promote spiritual and ethical standards, and to encourage deeper understanding of the past and greater tolerance toward foreign cultures. A statement made in 1934 by Princeton's great medievalist Charles Rufus Morey (inventor of the Index for Christian Art) summarizes well the role art still plays in the American college curriculum 'as an integrating factor in the liberal education of the student, furnishing the armature of historical categories into which he can fit the disjointed information acquired in other disciplines, and a means whereby he can vitally appropriate the points of view of various races and epochs.'[9]

Accordingly, the earliest of these collections tended to be cabinets of curiosities, featuring ethnographic artifacts and trophies of natural history – modest descendants of the old European *Wunderkammers* – whose intention was to convey empirical knowledge about the wonders of the world and the diversity of Creation. Stuffed alligators (University of Michigan), Zulu eating spoons (Mount Holyoke), Samoan war clubs (Yale), and the like were commonly given by faculty or alumni, especially those who had become field missionaries.[10] A typical museum donation of the period is described in a letter to the president of Dartmouth College, written in 1785 by David McClure, one of the college tutors: 'I have collected a few curious Elephants Bones found about six hundred miles down the Ohio River for the young Museum of Dartmouth which I shall forward to Philadelphia the first conveyance.'[11] In 1796

3
Claes Cornelisz Moeyaert
The Meeting of Jacob and Joseph in Egypt
Canvas, 137 x 164 cm (54 x 64 ¾ in.)
Neither signed nor dated (ca. 1636)
Brunswick, Maine, Bowdoin College Museum of Art,
Florence C. Quinby Fund in memory of Henry Cole
Quinby, inv. no. 1970.41

other curiosities were given to the museum by Elias Hasket Derby of Salem – most notably the famous stuffed zebra of Dartmouth Hall which mischievous undergraduates were in the habit of spiriting away and joyfully unveiling in unexpected locations, such as the chapel roof. It is fair to say that of the diverse hazards (fires were common) that put the earliest college collections at risk, one of the greatest was the youthful high spirits of the students themselves. In 1811, frustrated by the fact that their library-museum room blocked circulation between student rooms, an enterprising band of Dartmouth undergraduates borrowed a cannon and blew out the museum walls.[12]

Another important emphasis in early collections was archeological material. Especially prized were objects that could give students direct evidence of the ancient biblical world. During the mid-1850s, when the English archaeologist Sir Austin Henry Layard was excavating the palace of King Ashurnasirpal II (884-859 B.C.) at Ninevah, alumni-missionaries sent back fragments of these major Assyrian reliefs to a number of American colleges, including Dartmouth, Middlebury, Bowdoin, Williams, Mount Holyoke, Yale, the University of Vermont, and Amherst College. Amherst even attempted to recreate the original setting of the reliefs by adding to its scientific building (The Octagon) a small cubicle paved with imitation Assyrian brickwork [4].

The first paintings acquired by educational institutions were usually portraits by American or British artists representing individuals considered historically significant to the country or to the college itself. Such paintings were valued primarily as likenesses, for their historical and patriotic interest, and because they helped give the new colleges a reassuring atmosphere of stability and tradition [5]. The acquisition of objects for their aesthetic value was more gradual, for the earliest college collections often included more copies than original works of art, and made little distinction between the two.

Copies after old masters or reproductions of famous works, either prints or plaster casts, were eagerly sought and widely used well into the twentieth century.[13] A late-nineteenth-century photograph [6] of Vassar art students working beside a human skeleton amid ghostly reminders of the classical past might have been taken at any number of American colleges of the period. Reproductions after Dürer and Rembrandt hang on the wall at the right, while the painting of a cow's head standing on the floor at the left brings to mind seventeenth-century Dutch animal portraits by such artists as Jacques de Gheyn II and Nicolaes Berchem.[14]

4
Relief from the Palace of King Ashurnasirpal II, Ninevah (883-859 B.C.), as installed in 'The Octagon' (ca. 1878)
Photograph: Amherst College Archives; object: Mead Art Museum, Amherst College, Amherst, Mass.

Considering this heterogeneous and aesthetically uncritical background, the quality of the first college picture collection in America – at Bowdoin College (Brunswick, Maine) – was nothing less than extraordinary. Morever, a large part of it consisted of Netherlandish art. The benefactor, James Bowdoin III, son of the governor of Massachusetts for whom the college was named, served from 1805 to 1808 as United States minister plenipotentiary to Spain. During his European travels (his residence was Paris), this intelligent and curious man, possibly under the influence of his friend Thomas Jefferson, acquired an extensive art collection, which he bequeathed to the college at his death in 1811. Two portfolios of drawings (142 sheets with an additional ten *versi*), valued by the estate appraisers at seven dollars and seventy-five cents, were locked in the college library and left undisturbed until 1881, when they were first inventoried. What emerged, among other treasures, was Pieter Bruegel the Elder's incomparable *View of 'Waltensspurg'* [7]. The thirty-one seventeenth-century Dutch drawings included landscapes by Koninck, Breenbergh, J.B. Weenix, and four Moeyaerts.[15] The painting collection, typically for the time, numbered many copies after old masters. Several, including a copy after Titian's *Danaë*, were destined for quiet deaccessioning on the grounds that 'they were unsuitable for public exhibition, and still more for the private inspection of the youth of either sex.'[16] Most of the

5
Interior view of the Dartmouth Gallery of Paintings in
Wilson Hall (late nineteenth century)
Hanover, N.H., Dartmouth College

6
Art students at work at Vassar College, Poughkeepsie,
N.Y. (ca. 1890)
Photograph: Vassar College Library, Special
Collections, Poughkeepsie, N.Y.

7
Pieter Bruegel the Elder
View of 'Waltensspurg'
Pen and brown ink, 311 x 270 mm (12 ⅝ x 10 ⅝ in.)
Neither signed nor dated (ca. 1552-1553)
Brunswick, Maine, Bowdoin College Museum of Art,
Bequest of James Bowdoin III, inv. no. 1811.142

bequest remains intact, however, with landscapes by Berchem and Breenbergh, a seascape by Abraham Willaerts, and several works in the style of Dutch and Flemish still-life and genre painters (Adriaen van Ostade, Melchior d'Hondecoeter, Jan Fyt). Thanks to a bequest from the Quinby family in 1967, the museum has added further Dutch purchases in more recent years: a fine church interior by Hendrick van Vliet (*The Choir of Saint Jacob's Church in The Hague with the Tomb of Admiral Jacob van Wassenaer*) of the late 1660s and Nicolaes Moeyaert's *The Meeting of Jacob and Joseph in Egypt* of 1636 [**3**].

The fact that James Bowdoin bequeathed his collection to the college at a time when neither college art instruction nor college museums existed seems an act of either foreknowledge or faith, for the museum itself, designed by Charles McKim, was not dedicated until 1894. Indeed, in the period before the Civil War (1860) only one academic institution actually built its own art gallery, and only because of special circumstances. The Trumbull Gallery at Yale University (New Haven, Connecticut), which opened in 1832, had the distinction of being the oldest university art museum, versus art collection, in the western hemisphere. It was designed to house the works of Colonel John Trumbull, artist-patriot of the American Revolution (and canny art dealer), who agreed to sell a large collection of his own paintings to Yale in return for a life annuity for himself and his wife. He made several further stipulations: that the college build premises to house the pictures, that the paintings never be loaned, and that when he and his wife died, they be interred under the floor of the gallery beneath his famous painting of *George Washington at the Battle of Delaware*.[17]

In 1858, an exhibition of paintings and sculptures that the Yale librarian had borrowed from nearby private collections was put on in Alumni Hall and was so enthusiastically received that the idea of actively collecting art was sparked, along with initial discussions about forming an art school. The Yale School of Fine Arts, established in 1866 in a new building on Chapel Street, had second-floor exhibition rooms that displayed classical and Renaissance casts, as well as four of the ubiquitous reliefs from the palace of Ashurnasirpal II. Extensive classical, medieval, and oriental holdings developed subsequently, along with an exceptionally fine collection of decorative arts, unusual in a college museum. The present gallery at Street Hall, built in 1928 with modern additions by Louis Kahn, also includes a major collection of European and American painting.

Yale's most important acquisitions of the nineteenth century were to lie not with Northern art, but with the collection of 119

Italian paintings (thirteenth- through seventeenth-century) amassed by James Jackson Jarves (1818-1887), a Boston businessman turned influential art educator. Jarves, who had built his collection in Florence during the 1850s, lamented the low aesthetic standards and uncertain taste of his countrymen and hoped to make his paintings – the first collection of Italian art formed by an American – the core of a National Gallery in Boston or New York, along the lines of the National Gallery in London.[18] When the collection was auctioned in 1871, however, the sole bidder was Yale, which had been holding the pictures since 1868 as security for a loan. This major acquisition, made possible through a gift from Augustus Russell Street (Class of 1812), made Yale the leading university art gallery in the 1870s, and did much to encourage the founding of other such museums during this period.

At the time of Yale's bicentennial in 1901, extensive exhibits were on view including European drawings (seventeenth- through nineteenth-century) from the estate of Robert Weir and, most significant for our purposes, a group of about one hundred Dutch and Flemish paintings known as the Ehrich Collection, belonging to Louis F. Ehrich (Class of 1869).[19] None of these paintings, however, remained at Yale, whose Dutch and Flemish collection, acquired through both gift and purchase, was built during the 1950s and sixties. Although not large, it includes significant examples by Joachim Wtewael (*The Deluge*), Jacques de Gheyn II (*Vanitas Still Life*), Karel du Jardin (*Story of a Soldier*), and landscapes by Jan van Goyen, J.B. Weenix, and Joos de Momper. The two superb pendant portraits by Frans Hals in this exhibition (cat. nos. 25-26) were a bequest of Stephen Clark in 1951. Indeed, Haarlem painting is especially well represented at Yale with a fine late-fifteenth-century Haarlem School *Virgin and Child with Saint Anne* and grisaille panels by Maerten van Heemskerck. A rare Bosch fragment (*The Allegory of Intemperance*) should also be mentioned, as well as Elsheimer's *Coronis and Apollo* and an early Rubens *Hero and Leander*. Most of the substantial Northern drawing collection, which includes fine examples by Abraham Bloemaert, Jan Muller, Jacques de Gheyn II, and the earliest known dated drawing by Pieter Lastman (*Hagar in the Wilderness* of 1600), came to the university in a series of six albums (543 sheets) known as the Egmont Albums, assembled by an Irish peer, John Percival, first earl of Egmont (1683-1748), and presented by an anonymous donor to Yale in 1957.[20]

Another of the rare collegiate collections begun before the Civil War dates from 1842, the founding date of the University of Notre Dame (South Bend, Indiana), whose first president, Father Edward F. Sorin of the French Order of the Congregation of the Holy Cross, believed that a university should own works of art. This pioneering collection in the wilderness of the Midwest numbered 150 paintings by 1853, but was destroyed by a fire of 1879 except for one especially prized painting 'erroneously and euphemistically attributed to van Dyck.'[21]

Notre Dame's collection, since 1980 housed in the modern Snite Museum of Art, contains substantial baroque holdings (mostly Italian, French, and Flemish), which began with the large purchase in 1917 of 136 paintings from the Braschi Collection in Rome, featuring optimistic attributions to Rubens, Caravaggio, Bernini, Tintoretto, and others. The first Dutch acquisition (a Jacobus Storck port scene) was given in 1924, but nearly all of the Dutch collection was acquired, like Yale's, during the fifties and sixties. Gifts from diverse donors have brought in several striking classical subjects: Jan Lievens's *Virgil*, Pieter Mulier's *Mercury and Argus*, and a fine Lairesse tondo, *The Daughters of Cecrops Find the Infant Erichthonius*. A *Bathsheba* by Willem van Mieris was given in 1977 and an *Arcadian Landscape* by Jan van Huysum, in 1986. Purchases include a Ruisdael *Watermill*, a Jan Wynants *Landscape with Figures*, and Thomas de Keyser's *Portrait of Heer van Romunde*. Most distinctive in this collection are the baroque portraits given by various donors, with examples by Isaac Luttichuys (dated 1657), Jan van Ravesteyn (dated 1619), Nicolaes Maes (dated 1664), Abraham van den Tempel, and Gonzales Cocques, as well as portraits attributed to Mytens, Lely, and Aelbert Cuyp. Two full-length pendants after Paulus Moreelse arrived in 1961 with the Kress Study Collection.[22]

As is already apparent, academic collections tend to be built in fits and starts over prolonged periods, and seventeenth-century acquisitions often appear very late in the game. Nonetheless, the early nineteenth-century context is of interest because it illustrates not only when and how colleges began to collect, but also the beginnings of a relationship between collecting and teaching. Surprisingly, these two activities were quite unconnected at the start, for before the 1870s virtually no correlation can be defined between colleges offering art courses (either studio or art history) and those possessing galleries.[23] During this period lectures on art were still given primarily in conjunction with other subjects or departments, such as Classics, History, or 'Intellectual and Moral Philosophy.'

Information is scarce about the content of early art courses, but it appears that one of the first to use objects specifically collected for art historical instruction was offered at the University of Michigan (Ann Arbor). In 1855, Henry Simmons Frieze, classical scholar and acting president, raised appropriations from his Board of Regents to tour Europe in order to purchase copies of antique sculpture, engravings, photographs, and architectural models which he used to illustrate his lectures on classical art, taught in the Department of Latin.[24] These acquisitions became the core of a large and diverse collection which in 1928 would split into separate museums of art and classical archaeology.

Michigan's Dutch holdings are modest but have begun to grow in recent years. The earliest acquisitions came through a bequest in 1895 of three portraits: after Thomas de Keyser, after Mierevelt, and after Rubens. In the late 1950s two Northern Renaissance works were purchased (Joos van Cleve's *Saint John on Patmos* and Jan van Hemessen's *Parable of the Unmerciful Servant*), followed in 1965 by a Teniers guardroom interior and a *vanitas* still life with globe attributed to Pieter Claesz. A large lunette attributed to Baburen (*Christ on the Mount of Olives*) was also acquired by purchase in 1979, while in 1985 there were gifts of a much-restored Carel van Mander (*The Deluge*) and a Bartholomeus Molenaer peasant interior. Michigan also deserves mention here for distinguished exhibitions. In 1960 Jacob Rosenberg, curator of prints at Harvard's Fogg Art Museum, worked with Michigan students on a show of the best Rembrandt prints from midwestern collections. The Museum Practice Program, initiated in 1963 to train graduate students for museum careers, put on the previously mentioned *Italy through Dutch Eyes* in 1964 and *Dürer's Cities: Nuremberg and Venice* in 1971.

As Walter Liedtke's essay demonstrates, the great or 'gilded' age of American collecting developed during the time of expansion, surplus capital, and national optimism between the Civil War and World War I (around 1865 to 1915). This period also witnessed a revolution in American higher education made possible by the same wealth and philanthropy that created the public museums of the later nineteenth century. New colleges were established, and others grew or expanded into universities intended to rival those of Europe. While the older colleges had been founded on piety, the newer institutions had different aims: training in practical public service, the development of resources for advanced research in diverse fields, and the creation of new standards of taste.[25] The connection between the new prosperity and instruction in art was amusingly spelled out by James Jackson Jarves who commented in *Art Thoughts* of 1869, 'Actually it is a grave social problem to know what to do with the

8
Unknown American artist
The Apartment of the Art Gallery, Vassar College
Canvas, 45.6 x 55.6 cm (18 x 21 7/8 in.)
Neither signed nor dated (ca. 1870)
Poughkeepsie, Vassar College Art Gallery, Gift of
Gladys Jane Orcutt Blatter, inv. no. 82.37

increasing numbers of young men born to great incomes; rather for them to know what to do with themselves after leaving college [...]. Rich idlers do well, therefore, to become collectors as a corrective to ennui, and to benefit the public.'[26]

Significantly, two major colleges founded during this period to offer women an education equal to that of men saw both the collecting and the teaching of art as fundamental to their educational mission from the very beginning. When Hudson River brewer, Matthew Vassar, opened a pioneering college for women in 1865 (Poughkeepsie, New York), an art gallery was included on the top floor of the new James Renwick building [8].[27] From 1867 on, Professor Henry van Ingen delivered lectures to juniors and seniors on the theory and history of art. The art collection, purchased from Reverend Elias L. Magoon of Albany for 20,000 dollars – an extraordinary commitment to art in the mid-1860s – was exceptional for its focus on small-scale landscapes, both English and Hudson River School. Magoon believed passionately in the power of original works of art rather than 'sterile copies, or a mass of dead engravings,' and he argued with feverish evangelical rhetoric for the importance of a college

gallery: 'Cumulate languages, science and art, in as huge an aggregate as possible; but in God's name, sent to the center – fire! From at least one chair let positive electricity neutralize the prostrating influence of all the rest. For that purpose collect an ample and diversified gallery of actualities in artistic elegance [...] which shall at once illustrate the loftiest principles and refine the most delighted hearts.'[28]

In the quest to elevate Taste in the late nineteenth century (Europeans accused Americans of having none), contemplation of nature was thought to improve aesthetic sensitivity. Indeed, in early college collections like Vassar's, this was the purpose of American landscape paintings, which could also foster patriotic appreciation of native scenes, while encouraging higher thoughts on nature as divine creation.[29] Although Magoon had also recommended collecting old masters, substantial acquisitions in this area would not come about until the twentieth century, beginning with a collection of early Italian panel paintings given by Charles M. Pratt in 1917. In 1941, Vassar received from Mrs. Felix M. Warburg and her children a major gift of more than one hundred prints by Dürer and Rembrandt. The Warburg family later donated funds for a print room which opened in April of 1964.

Instruction in Netherlandish art began early at Vassar. In 1911 Oliver Tonks arrived from Princeton and began teaching a course entitled 'Northern Painting,' which covered Flemish and Dutch painting from the fifteenth through the seventeenth century. During the 1930s, courses in Italian baroque art taught by Professor Agnes Rindge Claflin seem to have stimulated the acquisition of seventeenth-century paintings (primarily French and Italian examples by Salvator Rosa, Guercino, Valentin de Boulogne, and others). Dutch acquisitions began in 1939 with the gift of a full-length *Portrait of a Young Man* (dated 1641) by the Frisian painter Harmen Wieringa, followed in the next year by the fine Pieter Claesz breakfast piece exhibited here (cat. no. 16). Aside from a Daniel Mytens full-length *Portrait of James Hamilton*, given in 1967, the most significant acquisitions of this decade were all purchases: Cornelis van Poelenburch's *Rest on the Flight*, Daniel Vosmaer's *View of a Dutch Village*, and a little *Bacchus* attributed to Jan van Bijlert (possibly by Poelenburch). During the 1980s there were further purchases: Nicolaes Moeyaert's *Sacrifice of Noah*, Adriaen van de Venne's *Battle over the Pants*, pendant portraits by Paulus Lesire, as well as gifts of a large Rubens schoolpiece (*Adoration of the Magi*) and a fragment (*Saint Peter [?] Asleep*) attributed to Honthorst. Northern Renaissance acquisitions include the purchase in 1956 of a Ludger Tom Ring still life (*The Open Missal*) and gifts of Joos van Cleve's *Portrait of a Man* (1967) and Pieter Bruegel the Younger's *Spring* (1973).[30]

Similarly, Smith College (Northampton, Massachusetts), founded in 1871, began with a powerful commitment to art, already singled out ('the useful and the fine arts') in the last testament of the founding benefactor, Miss Sophia Smith, and in the inaugural address of the first president, L. Clarke Seelye: 'Too many of the grandest creations of the human intellect are embodied in the fine arts to remain unnoticed by an institution which seeks the highest mental culture [...] it [the college] should have its gallery of art, where the student may be made directly familiar with the famous masterpieces.'[31] Smith's collection, begun in 1877 with the usual casts of famous sculptures and reproductive prints, also included contemporary American art. The earliest Dutch acquisition, a fine impression of the fourth state of Rembrandt's *Three Crosses* (B. 78), was purchased in 1911 by students in the enthusiastic Studio Club who in that year were introduced to prints by famous artists in the college's first exhibition of borrowed works. The Rembrandt formed the

9
Dieric Bouts
Portrait of a Young Man
Silverpoint on prepared paper, 140 x 107 mm
(5½ x 4 ⅜ in.)
Neither signed nor dated (ca. 1467)
Northampton, Mass., Smith College Museum of Art,
Purchase, Drayton Hillyer Fund, inv. no. 1939:3

beginning of what was to become an exceptional print and drawing collection, which includes a Rembrandt sketch of a woman kneeling (Ben. 481), the only Grunewald drawing in America (a drapery study), and perhaps the most precious northern drawing in any American college collection: Dieric Bouts's little silverpoint *Portrait of a Young Man* [9], purchased in 1939.

The large painting collection is best known today for nineteenth- and twentieth-century American and French art, but Smith also owns some thirty Dutch pictures, including one of the best Dutch Caravaggesque examples in America: Ter Brugghen's *Old Man Writing by Candlelight* (cat. no. 15), purchased in 1957. Dutch acquisitions have been made more frequently at Smith than at many colleges, thanks to a combination of generous alumnae, interested directors and the presence in the Art Department of such Dutch scholars as A.P.A. Vorenkamp (between 1926 and 1948) and J. Richard Judson (between 1956 and 1974). In 1942 Jan van Goyen's fine *View of Rijnland*, dated

1647, was purchased, followed a year later by Jacob van Ruisdael's *Landscape with the Church of Beverwijk*. Purchases of the fifties and sixties include Jan Steen's *The Drinkers*, Esaias van den Velde's *Bridge over a Waterfall* (dated 1625), and works by Lieve Verschuier and Philips Wouwermans. Among the gifts of this period were Gerard van Honthorst's *Portrait of a Woman* dated 1633, Cornelis van Poelenburch's *The Good Samaritan*, pendant portraits by Daniel Mytens, genre scenes by Pieter van Slingelant and Claes Molenaer, and a landscape by Adriaen van de Velde. Still life is also an area of unusual strength in this collection, thanks to the gift of a painting by Maria van Oosterwijk and purchases of fine examples by Ambrosius Bosschaert the Elder, Jacob Foppens van Es (earlier attributed to Willem van Aelst), and Abraham Mignon (the latter in honor of Vorenkamp).

During America's era of industrial prosperity after the Civil War, art education not only focused on the cultivation of taste in colleges like Smith and Vassar, but also expanded its role to address the practical need for establishing standards for industrial designers and manufacturers. Following the great Philadelphia Centennial Exposition of 1876 with its displays of the useful and the fine arts, Mrs. Helen Adelia Rowe Metcalfe, leader of the Women's Centennial Commission of Rhode Island, found herself with leftover contributions of 1,675 dollars on her hands. With this sum the Rhode Island School of Design (known as RISD) was founded in Providence in 1877, Mrs. Metcalfe serving as its first director.[32] The school's purposes, spelled out in the original bylaws were, first, to instruct artisans 'so that they may successfully apply the principles of art to the requirements of trade and manufacture'; second, to train students to become artists and art teachers; and, third, to advance public art education by collecting and exhibiting works of art.[33] RISD's museum, an integral part of the art school from its founding in 1880, began with casts and reproductions, but went on to build comprehensive collections from Egyptian to modern, including furniture, costumes, wallpaper, and textiles, thus making this the leading art museum in the state.

Dutch acquisitions began slowly with a suite of Anthonie Waterlo etchings, given in 1894. A fine print department was later built in the 1940s by Dr. Heinrich Schwarz, former curator of the Austrian State Gallery in Vienna. The large drawings collection (with important examples by Maerten van Heemskerck, Jan Gossaert, Esaias van den Velde, Pieter Molijn, and Rembrandt) was fully catalogued in 1983.[34] Dutch paintings began to be added first in 1904 with gifts of two portraits attributed to Schalcken, and genre paintings by Wouwermans

and Drooghsloot. The splendid Aert de Gelder *Esther and Mordecai Writing the Second Purim Letter* in this exhibition (cat. no. 21), was purchased in 1917, followed in 1933 by Salomon van Ruysdael's *River Scene with Ferryboat*, dated 1645. Many of RISD's major Dutch paintings were purchases of the late fifties and early sixties during the directorships of John Maxon and David Carter – beginning with Matthias Stomer's *Christ on the Column*, added in 1956. Three years later, Adriaen van der Werff's *Dismissal of Hagar* was purchased, followed almost immediately by Lastman's *Saint Matthew and the Angel* of 1613. In 1961 the museum bought Goltzius's *Christ on the Cold Stone* dated 1602 and the next year, Wtewael's exceptional *Marriage of Peleus and Thetis* dated 1610 [1]. A fifteenth-century Utrecht *Crucifixion with Two Thieves* was also purchased in 1961.

Within the last decade, under the directorship of Franklin Robinson (a specialist in Dutch art) there have been additional Dutch gifts: Willem Drost's *Portrait of a Young Man*, a *Portrait of a Woman* by Nicolaes Maes, Frans van Mieris's *Self-Portrait as a Drinker* (dated 1670), a Willem van Mieris *Portrait of a Lady*, Isaac de Jouderville's *Young Woman in a Kitchen*, Jacob Torenvliet's *Old Woman with Glass*, a landscape by Jacobus Mancadan, and a harbor scene by Lieve Verschuier.

Considering the number of substantial campus museums founded by 1880, it seems surprising that Princeton (New Jersey) and Harvard (Cambridge, Massachusetts), two of the oldest and largest universities in the country, waited so long – especially because both had already begun to collect and to give instruction in art. Indeed, lectures at Princeton on Roman antiquities, first offered in 1831, and on the history of architecture, begun the following year, mark the earliest substantial college art instruction in this country.[35] Unlike earlier collegiate collecting, much of which had happened willy-nilly, that of the late nineteenth century came to be increasingly identified with a burgeoning interest in the teaching of fine arts, which only began to emerge as a distinct academic discipline during the last quarter of the century. Princeton's prime mover was Allan Marquand of the Class of 1874 and son of the collector Henry G. Marquand (one of the founders, and later director, of the Metropolitan Museum of Art in New York). In 1882, the year the Princeton Art Museum was founded, young Marquand began to give lectures in the history of art at the urging of the university president. His account of his first efforts will sound familiar to anyone who has suffered through the beginnings of a teaching career: 'It was a new field for me, but I put up a good bluff and stumbled along lecturing on Early Christian and

Byzantine architecture, as if I understood it well, and as if I knew beforehand all there was to follow in the unexplored fields of Romanesque and Gothic.'[36]

Instruction at Princeton, strongest at the start in the classical and medieval fields, came to include some of the earliest courses in America on Dutch and Flemish art. Just after the turn of the century, Marquand gave a senior course described as 'Renaissance painting, a study of technique, subjects, composition and historical relations (among) Italian, German, French and Dutch painting.' In 1907-1908, Oliver Tonks, who had arrived from Harvard in 1905, offered a senior elective course entitled 'Flemish and Dutch painting [...] from their origins to modern time.'[37] Frank Jewett Mather, Jr., who joined the department in 1910 from Johns Hopkins University, taught mostly Italian painting (from Cavallini to Michelangelo), but he also gave a seminar in Northern painting and, after 1913, a course in Early Netherlandish art. Marquand and his colleagues put strong emphasis on connoisseurship and on students' need for direct and frequent contact with original works of art. As a result, when the museum building was erected (1886-1889), classrooms and study areas were combined with the Marquand Library of Art and Architecture, and the museum itself was made the central focus – an arrangement that still prevails in the most recent expansion and renovation, designed by the firm of Mitchell / Giurgola Associates and completed in 1988.

Princeton's Dutch paintings, although not a major focus of this large and varied collection, feature a number of important mannerist and Caravaggesque purchases, beginning in 1954 with Paulus Moreelse's *Shepherdess*, dated 1633, and Gerard van Honthorst's spectacular *Artemesia Drinking Her Husband's Ashes* [2], which entered the collection in 1968. Cornelis van Haarlem's pendants of *Jacob and Esau* and *The Israelites Crossing the Red Sea* followed in 1973, Wtewael's fine *Judith with the Head of Holofernes* in 1975, and Goltzius's *Christ as Redeemer* in 1985.[38]

Interestingly, the earliest gifts of Northern paintings came directly from Allan Marquand's private collection: *Portrait of a Man* by Michiel van Mierevelt, given before 1911, and *Christ before Pilate*, attributed to Bosch, which entered the collection between 1922 and 1924. In 1928 Frank Jewett Mather gave a *Circumcision* attributed to Salomon Koninck. An interesting Pieter Quast (*The Doctor's Shop*) and a Dirck Hals *Couples around a Table* were also given in the 1920s, but nearly all of Princeton's Netherlandish gifts and bequests are more recent: a Daniel Seghers garland with a memorial bust of Rubens, given by the friends of the museum in 1956; two outdoor scenes by David Vinckboons, given in the early 1970s; as well as landscapes by Aert van der Neer (1959), Pieter de Neyn (1969), Jacob van Ruisdael (1979), Salomon van Ruysdael (1980), and Gillis Claesz d'Hondecoeter (1985). A Cornelis Jonson van Ceulen *Portrait of a Woman* was given in 1984. The important print and drawing collections at Princeton (again, exceptionally strong in mannerist examples) have always benefitted from the involvement of faculty members, even as early as the time of Mather, who collected with a discerning eye, both for his own pleasure and for teaching purposes.

The giant of America's university art museums – known to generations of students simply as 'the Fogg' – was founded not long after Princeton's, in 1895 at Harvard University. The present building, constructed in 1927, also houses classrooms, lecture halls, and one of the largest art libraries in the world.[39] The 1931 museum handbook, which noted that a 'trained chemist' was attached to the museum staff and that x-ray equipment was available on the premises, offered what still seems the quintessential definition of a university museum: 'It should be an Art Laboratory, where students may come into actual contact with works of art, study technical methods and do research work themselves.'[40]

Harvard's extensive collection of Dutch art began with an important bequest of 1857, left by the nation's first great print connoisseur, Francis Calley Gray (1790-1856). A man of quiet taste and reticent personality, Gray honed his skills at collection, description, and classification on another visual discipline – conchology.[41] His collection. which consisted of fine engraved reproductions of paintings (fifteenth- through eighteenth-century) as well as original prints, is especially strong in Dutch and German examples. Some four thousand sheets were left to Harvard, but because there was not yet a safe place to store or display them, the prints (exhibited temporarily in the library in Gore Hall) were sent to the brand new Boston Museum of Fine Arts between 1875 and 1897. Nine cases of Gray's Rembrandt etchings were exhibited there in 1881 (the collection has a total of seventy-two).[42] Gray's agent and buyer, Louis Thies, who became curator of the Gray collection, offered Harvard's first art instruction in 1863: lectures on the history of design, from which undergraduates were excluded. Not until 1901 did the Department of Fine Arts introduce a specific print course (History and Principles of Engraving).[43]

The figure most identified with the beginnings of fine arts instruction at Harvard is Charles Eliot Norton (1827-1908), who had graduated in 1846. Businessman, journalist, social and aesthetic commentator, Norton returned to America in 1874 after five years in Europe and took up a twenty-three-year teaching career at Harvard. Before 1896 he lectured without illustrations or slides, but his richly expressive voice, powerful descriptions, and caustic wit eventually attracted classes of more than five hundred.[44]

Norton's approach to art (and his biases) bear significantly on our subject, because his presence at Harvard was both long and influential. Partly under the influence of his friend Ruskin, he saw art as an expression of the moral and intellectual conditions of earlier times and used it to make students aware of the aesthetic barrenness of their own (his son dubbed them 'Lectures on Modern Morals as Illustrated by the Art of the Ancients').[45] Ancient Athens and late medieval Florence and Venice were the civilizations he most admired; his lectures focused on the decline of stylistic and moral purity in post-Periclean Athens and early Renaissance Italy. For Norton the history of art virtually ended by the year 1600. The last question in his final examination of June 1875, speaks volumes: 'Why is the history of the arts since the beginning of the seventeenth century of less importance than their preceding history?'[46]

While Norton did much to advance the development of art instruction in this country, he was hardly a booster for seventeenth-century Dutch art. Indeed, one wonders if his influence did not in some measure retard early Dutch gifts and bequests to the Fogg, particularly as so many alumni / collectors would have taken his courses (at Norton's retirement in 1897, one of his colleagues estimated that he had taught some ten thousand students).[47] In any case, the first Dutch painting given to Harvard came with the bequest of 1895 from Mrs. William Hayes Fogg that established the new museum: a nineteenth-century *Street Scene* by Jan Weissenbruch. The second was not received until twenty-seven years later: Jacob Ochtervelt's *Family Portrait*, given in 1922 by Frederic Fairchild Sherman.

Harvard today has exceptionally rich Dutch holdings in all media, a development that has paralleled the presence of scholars with strong interests in this area (Seymour Slive, who has taught at Harvard since 1954, also directed the museum between 1974 and 1982). Interestingly, a profile of the Fogg's painting collection diverges significantly from the museums surveyed thus far – not only in quantity but also in the absence of the mannerist, Caravaggesque, and pre-Rembrandtist pictures that have been standard purchases in other college museums. In fact, the Fogg rarely buys paintings (more than ninety-five percent of acquisitions come from gifts and bequests) and the collection features the kinds of artists most often found in large public museums: Rembrandt, Hals, Ter Borch, Aelbert Cuyp, Jan van Goyen, Jacob van Ruisdael, and Jan Weenix, among others.[48]

The growth of the Fogg's collection is closely associated with the names of particular donors, beginning with Nettie Naumberg, whose bequest of 1930 included Frans Hals's *Portrait of a Man* and a *Portrait of an Old Man* by Rembrandt, in collaboration with Jan Lievens. Grenville L. Winthrop, who donated two Salomon van Ruysdael landscapes in 1935 and an Antonio Moro portrait in 1942, also bequeathed an Aert van der Neer landscape in 1943, along with important examples of American and European furniture and nineteenth-century painting. A number of important Dutch paintings came in two major bequests of the sixties: in 1966 from Edwin A. Abbot, who bequeathed pendant portraits by Nicolaes Maes, three Aert van der Neer landscapes, and two by Jacob van Ruisdael. The 1969 bequest from James P. Warburg added two Van Goyen landscapes, and portraits by Bartholomeus van der Helst, Dirck van Santvoort (pendants), and Rembrandt (a *Self-Portrait* and a *Portrait of a Man*, both monogrammed and dated 1629).[49] Two more Rembrandts have been gifts of William Coolidge (*Head of Christ* in 1964 and *Portrait of an Old Man* in 1985). Significant purchases in Dutch paintings have included Michael Sweerts's *Portrait of a Boy* (1941), Simon de Vlieger's *The Wreckers* (1954), Nicolaes Maes's *Portrait of a Family* (1957), Benjamin Cuyp's *Nativity* (1961), Cornelis van Poelenburch's *Rest on the Flight* (1965), and Jan Lievens's *Portrait of a Man* (purchased in 1972 in honor of Jacob Rosenberg).

Probably the most important of the Fogg's benefactors – in the impact of his presence and influence as much as his tangible gifts – was Paul J. Sachs (1878-1965), who in 1915 was persuaded by Director Edward W. Forbes to leave the family banking business of Goldman Sachs in New York and become the Fogg's assistant director. Sachs (Class of 1900) had already presented an impression of Rembrandt's *Great Jewish Bride* (B. 340) to Harvard in 1910; he was to give altogether more than two thousand prints of diverse schools and periods, as well as three of the ten Rembrandt drawings in the collection.[50] Sachs taught a print course first, but around 1923 he instituted his famous museum course [10] which trained the future directors of America's largest museums (along with students who would become enthusiastic amateur collectors) and which became a blueprint for other such courses throughout the country. Sachs was clearly a crucial influence, both directly and indirectly, on the uncommon size and quality of the Fogg's

gifts and bequests. Moreover, it was Sachs who in 1937 helped bring Jacob Rosenberg from Berlin (Kupferstichkabinett, Kaiser-Friedrich Museum) to Harvard, where he began his own deeply influential twenty-five-year career as professor of fine arts and as curator of prints.[51]

Although Paul Sachs was the Fogg's most important benefactor for seventeenth-century Dutch drawings, there have been others, beginning with Charles Alexander Loeser whose bequest of 1932 included two well-known Rembrandt drawings: *Winter Landscape* (Ben. 845) and *Copy of an Indian Miniature* (Ben. 1198).[52] The bequest of Frances L. Hofer in 1979 included fine examples by Esaias van den Velde, Nicolaes Maes, and Willem

10
Paul J. Sachs with the Harvard Museum Seminar in the Naumberg Room, Fogg Art Museum, Cambridge, Mass. (ca. 1943)
Photograph: Harvard University Art Museums, Cambridge, Mass.

van de Velde the Elder.[53] Within the last decade Maida and George Abrams have added substantially to the drawing collection, with significant examples ranging throughout the century. Harvard's graphic collections also, of course, encompass the holdings of the Houghton Library, just down the street from

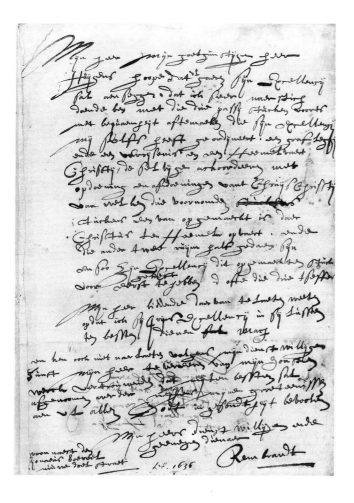

11
Rembrandt
Letter to Constantijn Huygens, ca. February 1636
Cambridge, Mass., Harvard University, The
Houghton Library, Gift of Mr. and Mrs. Samuel
B. Grimson, 1960

institutions of higher learning were teaching art history (only sixty-eight 'adequately' in his opinion), and that the great majority of courses were in ancient art and archaeology and medieval art. Harvard, not surprisingly, was offering both ancient and Italian art (even Japanese art) – but none of the 'Northern art' courses that had begun to appear at Dartmouth, Princeton, Cornell, Bates, Pennsylvania State, Mount Holyoke, Vassar, and Wells. Oberlin College listed a Rembrandt seminar, while courses specifically designated 'Dutch and Flemish painting' were reported at the universities of Chicago, Nebraska, and Rochester (New York).[56] Indeed, Rochester, whose museum was founded in the year of Marquand's survey, would go on to develop a substantial collection of Dutch art.

The Memorial Art Gallery at Rochester opened in 1913 with a collection consisting of 'two paintings, four plaster casts and a lappet of lace,' but the ground had already been well prepared for the kind of local interest that promises future growth.[57] As early as 1872 the university president, Dr. Martin B. Anderson, Professor of Intellectual and Moral Philosophy, had given lectures on art that were reportedly so popular with both the university students and the ladies of Rochester 'that one had to be early to get in at all to hear them.'[58] This unusual melding of town and gown was also to characterize the new museum, whose founder, Mrs. Emily Sibley Watson, specified that it serve the general public (many of whom were Rochester graduates) as well as the university. Modest Dutch acquisitions began with gifts in 1929 and 1930 of paintings attributed to Berchem and Ter Borch. A *Doctor's Visit* by Hendrik Heerschop was purchased in 1946 and a Jan Davidsz de Heem *Still Life with Oysters* in 1949. The Bertha Buswell Bequest of 1955 included ten Dutch paintings, among them Jan Steen's *Pancake Maker*, Salomon de Bray's *Girl with Cherries*, and portraits attributed to Thomas de Keyser (pendants), Nicolaes Maes, and Dirck van Santvoort. In 1966 a Jan van Ravesteyn portrait dated 1632 was given, and in 1968 a second major bequest came from George Eastman, inventor of the Kodak camera and founder of the Eastman Kodak Company. The Eastman bequest added a Jan van de Cappelle seascape, a Van Dyck *Portrait of a Nobleman*, and late portraits (in poor condition) by Rembrandt and Hals. Eastman,

the Fogg. Houghton owns not only an extensive collection of seventeenth-century Dutch emblem books, but also a unique and special treasure: one of the seven extant letters by Rembrandt [**11**], written around February 1636, in which Rembrandt reports to Constantijn Huygens on his progress toward completion of the Passion Cycle for Prince Frederick Henry.[54]

In 1912 Allan Marquand of Princeton sent out a questionnaire about the study of art history in American colleges and universities; the results were presented in Rome at the Tenth International Congress of the History of Art.[55] Marquand's survey, which was sent to four hundred institutions and which also inquired about campus art museums and their collections, reveals much about the level of college and university interest in Dutch art shortly after the turn of the century: still limited, but clearly beginning to grow. Marquand discovered that ninety-five

whose liking for portraits probably relates to his involvement in portrait photography, apparently had a special affection for the Rembrandt because it reminded him of his own early, under-exposed negatives.[59] Recently, two important additions to this collection have been made: in 1982, the purchase of a Rachel Ruysch *Flower Still Life with Snake and Lizard*, dated 1686, and in 1983 a gift of Govaert Flinck's fine *Vertumnus and Pomona*.

The factors that build a major college art collection may be somewhat unpredictable, but the presence of a scholar who relishes the art market and likes to teach directly 'from the object' is always a powerful influence. No museum illustrates this relationship more vividly than the Allen Memorial Art Museum (Oberlin, Ohio), which was conceived specifically as a teaching museum at its founding in 1917 and which became Wolfgang Stechow's (1896-1974) base of operations after his emigration from Nazi Germany.

When Stechow began at Oberlin College in 1940, he was entering an institution that had long understood the instructional value of art. Indeed, a required course – Lectures on Art – had been instituted there as early as 1874.[60] By 1899 Oberlin undergraduates could elect courses not only in ancient art, Greek sculpture, and medieval architecture, but also in Italian and Dutch painting. In 1860, the students began trying to raise funds for an art gallery by allocating the proceeds of their own commencement concert for that purpose.[61] Not surprisingly, it was an alumnus, Dr. Dudley Peter Allen (Class of 1875) who spearheaded the fundraising campaign and worked closely with the architect, Cass Gilbert. His widow made the building his memorial.

Twenty-three years after its opening, the museum as Stechow found it was still largely devoted to plaster casts and miscellaneous bric-a-brac, although a Ming vase had been the first donation in 1894. Prophetically, there was one Dutch picture (given in 1919): an Italianate *Landscape with Ruins of a Castle* by Abraham Begeyn, dated 1665. By Stechow's retirement in 1963, the museum had been transformed, largely through his efforts and involvement, into one of the best college collections in the country. A substantial catalogue of the paintings was published in 1967 and one devoted to the drawings in 1976 – both by Stechow.[62]

Stechow's approach to building Oberlin's collection, which closely followed his scholarly predilections, stressed unostentatious pictures of uncommon quality – 'Lugt pictures,' he liked to call them (having arranged for Frits Lugt to spend the war years in Oberlin).[63] The museum's first purchases in

1941 were exemplary: a Michael Sweerts *Self-Portrait as a Painter* (cat. no. 64) and a Jan van Goyen *Dune Landscape* dated 1647. The money was supplied by another devoted alumnus, R.T. Miller (Class of 1891), who gave some 25,000 dollars annually between 1940 and his death in 1958, with the wise stipulation that it always be spent in the year it was given. The Miller fund made possible Stechow's (and director Charles Parkhurst's) proudest coup: the majestic Ter Brugghen *Saint Sebastian Attended by Saint Irene* of 1625 [**12**], acquired in 1943, as well as Emanuel de Witte's *Interior of the Old Church in Delft* (1943),

Rubens's *The Finding of Erichthonius* (1944), Job Berckheyde's *Bakery Shop* (1956), and Esaias van den Velde's *Landscape with the Road to Emmaus* (1958). In 1944 Mrs. F.F. Prentiss (widow of Dudley Peter Allen) bequeathed a number of paintings, including a major Hobbema landscape, *Pond in a Forest* dated 1668. Prentiss funds also stood behind the 1954 purchase of the J.D. de Heem *Banquet Piece* (formerly owned by the Hermitage), as well as paintings by Adriaen van de Venne (1960) and Nicolaes Berchem (1962), and Adriaen van der Werff's *Jacob Blessing the Sons of Joseph* (1963). The museum also purchased, from other sources, a *Landscape with Nymphs* by Paulus Bril dated 1623 (1953) and Jan Steen's *Merry Company* (1956), while two Dutch paintings have been presented in Stechow's honor: in 1963 an Adriaen Bloemaert landscape dated 1657 and in 1972 Quiringh van Brekelenkam's *Interior with Mother and Child*. Since Stechow's time, Oberlin has concentrated on building other areas of the collection, but at the end of 1989 yet another fine Dutch picture was purchased, a seascape by Bonaventura Peeters.

As one would expect, the periods of greatest development and expansion for American art museums were the decades before World War I and after World War II. Yet even during the unstable and financially precarious years between, college and university art instruction developed substantially. After the First World War, the role of art in America came to be understood more broadly and democratically, not merely as polishing for a cultural elite, but as an expression of permanence and creative ordering that could help produce peace of mind for everyone. As one writer noted in 1933, 'the problem of art, like that of religion and recreation, turns today on its service to man in his inner adjustment to an environment which shifts and changes with unexampled rapidity. Art appears to be one of the great forces which stands between maladjusted man and mental breakdown, bringing him comfort, serenity and joy.'[64] Studies about the place of art in post-secondary education (and it is significant that these were done repeatedly during the twenties and thirties) commonly stress the 'need' for college graduates to enter the world armed with knowledge about art.[65] Accordingly, a survey conducted in 1934 by the Association of American Colleges discovered that 425 colleges and universities were then teaching art and that art history was being offered in 283.[66] A second analysis done in the same year by the Carnegie Corporation noted an increasing interest in 'baroque art' (nationality unspecified) over the past decade.[67]

A direct connection between teaching and the need to establish an art museum can be seen at Williams College (Williamstown, Massachusetts), which dates from the late eighteenth century, but whose museum was founded only in 1926. Professor Karl E. Weston (1874-1956), then the sole instructor in art history, attracted so many enthusiastic students to his courses that he brought the trustees around to his own deeply held conviction that teaching art without original examples is a form of self-delusion.[68] Weston found space for the museum in a nineteenth-century building, scoured attics and college storerooms (where he unearthed three long-forgotten reliefs from the palace of Ashurnasirpal II), installed displays and pursued gifts. When he retired as director in 1948, his museum had become a vital part of the college.

Williams's small Dutch collection, which includes good prints and drawings, has come primarily through gifts, beginning in 1958 with a *Peasant Interior with Figures* by Isack van Ostade, followed the next year by a Pieter Wouwerman landscape. Most examples were given in the 1960s: an *Adoration of the Shepherds*, dated 1602, attributed to Wtewael; pendant portraits by Wybrand de Geest of *The Grand Pensionary de Witt and His Wife*, dated 1630; Jan Weenix's *Dead Game and Fruit*; and a *Harbor Scene* by Willem van Drielenburgh. A landscape attributed to Aert van der Neer was purchased in 1979.

More Dutch works can be found in Williamstown's second art museum, the Sterling and Francine Clark Art Institute, founded in 1955 to display the large and varied collections of Robert Sterling Clark.[69] Although independently incorporated, the Clark Institute is the site of the Williams graduate program in art history (in which Julius Held has frequently participated), and houses an art library and faculty offices. It therefore functions much like a university museum. Best known for its outstanding nineteenth-century paintings, this museum also owns a charming pair of Dirck Hals pendants dated 1631 (*Children with a Cat* and *Children Playing Cards*), a Gerard Dou *Girl in a Niche with a Pitcher*, a David Teniers *Cardplayers* dated 1646, and two landscapes by Jacob van Ruisdael. Two paintings once attributed to Rembrandt (*Man Reading* and *Crucifixion*) are no longer accepted, but the collection does include two fine Rembrandt drawings of the mid-1650s: *Christ Finding the Apostles Sleeping* (Ben. 941) and *Houses among Trees* (Ben. 1326), along with top impressions of a number of his etchings. Recently two architectural paintings have been added: Dirck van Delen's *Church Interior with the Parable of the Pharisee and the Publican*, dated 1653, and Gerrit Berckheyde's *Church of Saint Cecelia in Cologne*.

To function effectively, a campus collection need not be large or studded with famous names. Works illustrating a variety of

significantly, had also been one of the earliest institutions in the country to offer art instruction, for by 1853 Reverend Joseph Torrey, Professor of Intellectual and Moral Philosophy, was giving lectures entitled 'Principles of the Fine Arts.'[71]

The museum's first Netherlandish acquisition, a *Portrait of Dr. Buchanan*, attributed to Van Dyck, was given in 1942. The Dutch paintings were all gifts of the late 1950s, among them Lambert Doomer's *Couple Looking at a Globe* [**13**], signed and dated 168[4?]. An exemplary instructional picture, this unusual work not only invites stylistic comparison with paintings of the Rembrandt School, but also poses interpretive questions ideal for student research.[72] The other Dutch paintings include a signed *Landscape with Sheep by a Brook* by Adriaen van de Velde; *Scandinavian Landscape with Waterfall* by Allaert van Everdingen; Egbert van der Poel's *Beach Scene at Night*, signed and dated 1661; Aert van der Neer's *Fire in Amsterdam by Moonlight*; and a *Portrait of a Boy with Plumed Hat*, attributed to Govaert Flinck. Among the works on paper are an interesting sepia drawing of a drunken artist, attributed to Abraham Bloemaert, watercolor insect studies of the eighteenth century, and four Rembrandt etchings (B. 30, 97, 192, and 276).

As the Fleming Museum illustrates, American college and university museums often have such a prolonged and gradual development that it may be difficult to define exactly when they were 'founded' – when reproductions were acquired, when original objects were first given or purchased, when space was first set aside to display them, or when a separate building was erected. The fact that these phases have often been widely separated says much about the stately pace of educational institutions in which nothing happens quickly – yet in which individual initiative and tenacity can have great repercussions. Thus, at the University of Illinois (Champaign-Urbana, Illinois) the acquisition and exhibition of original works of art did not actually begin until 1931 with the founding of a College of Fine and Applied Arts. Nonetheless, the history of this important collection (since 1961 housed in the modern Krannert Art Museum) belongs equally to the periods before and after this

styles and media (as well as a few striking or unusual subjects) can provide rich opportunities for student research. Such is the small but useful Dutch collection at the Robert Hull Fleming Museum at the University of Vermont (Burlington). Designed in 1932 by McKim, Mead and White, the new museum featured yet another of the monumental reliefs from the palace of Ashurnasirpal II, given to the university in the mid-nineteenth century. Having begun with a cabinet of curiosities in the 1820s, Vermont decided to form an art gallery, to be called the Park Gallery of Fine Arts, in 1872 by constructing an appropriate space on the top floor of the ethnographic and natural history museum. This was a brave venture, because the art collection did not yet exist (the trustees' announcement of construction plans included a plea for donations to fill the new gallery).[70] Vermont,

date. In 1876, eight years after the university was founded, President John Milton Gregory returned from a summer in Europe with some 250 plaster casts, photographs, and prints. In a mighty show of presidential fundraising, he had collected the acquisition money himself by giving art history lectures throughout the state.[73]

Illinois began to collect works by contemporary American artists during the Depression (twentieth century art remains a major focus, for the university hosts the oldest and most respected biennial survey of contemporary American art). In 1937 Mr. and Mrs. Merle J. Trees of Chicago began making annual presentations to the university of paintings from their collection, including important Netherlandish examples. Beginning in 1938 with a Jan Gossaert portrait, these gifts eventually brought in a late Pieter de Hooch *Night Scene with a Woman Paying a Maidservant* (1942), David Teniers's *Steen Castle* (1948), a portrait attributed to Rembrandt (1949), a courtyard scene by Hendrick van der Burch (1951), and in 1953 the two best paintings of all, a late landscape (*Ford in the Woods*) by Jacob van Ruisdael and one of the finest works by Frans Hals in this country, the small *Portrait of Cornelis Guldewagen* [**14**]. Other donors have added portraits by Bartholomeus van der Helst (*Portrait of Mevrouw van Daems*) and Cornelis Jonson van Ceulen (*Portrait of Lady Godolfin*, dated 1635), as well as the major Abraham van Beyeren banquet piece that is in this exhibition (cat. no. 7). The Van Beyeren was given in 1972 by Mrs. Herman Krannert who, with her husband (Class of 1912), had founded the museum in 1961.

As already indicated, the vast majority of Dutch paintings in

14
Frans Hals
Portrait of Cornelis Guldewagen
Panel, 41.6 x 31.4 cm (16 ⅜ x 12 ⅜ in.)
Neither signed nor dated (ca. 1660)
Champaign-Urbana, Ill., Krannert Art Museum, University of Illinois, Gift of Merle J. and Emily N. Trees, 1953, inv. no. 53-1-1

academic institutions have been acquired since World War II. The influx of European scholars to the United States, following the Nazis' dismissal of Jewish officials in the spring of 1933, clearly had a profound influence on the subsequent development of art history in the United States, particularly in the fields of Renaissance and baroque art.[74] Yet educational surveys also reveal that interest in the discipline had begun to develop even before the arrival of scholars from abroad. A study prepared in 1966 for the College Art Association of America concluded that academic course offerings in art history had been approximately doubling every twenty years since 1900 and that by the 1960s almost as many graduate courses were being offered in seventeenth- and eighteenth-century art as in ancient art.[75] Did gifts of seventeenth-century Dutch paintings during this period encourage increased instruction, or did the course offerings themselves generate Dutch acquisitions? Probably both. In any case, after 1945 increasing numbers of students flocked to colleges and universities whose more specialized programs began producing a new generation of professionally trained art historians. At the same time, old master paintings were reaching the dealers and auction houses in new quantities as scores of European and British collections were broken up and dispersed. The post-war art market, particularly during the fifties and sixties, offered exciting opportunities, even for collectors with modest sums to spend. Dr. Bob Jones, Jr., Chancellor of Bob Jones University (Greenville, South Carolina), seized the day.

The museum at Bob Jones opened on Thanksgiving Day 1951, with some thirty paintings and a few pieces of sculpture. Today the collection has grown to more than four hundred paintings (thirteenth- through nineteenth-century, and all biblical subjects), along with textiles, stained-glass windows, a Byzantine baptistery, at least one hundred sculptures, and more than one thousand biblical artifacts. At Bob Jones, unlike America's other campus museums, religious art is the only focus of the collection, and it serves a purpose closely akin to its original function: to teach, inspire, and intensify the faith of members of this fundamentalist Christian community.[76] Indeed, these dramatic religious narratives, many large in scale, have an even more powerful effect when viewed together in their colorfully decorated galleries, which are further enlivened with background music [**15**]. As one visitor observed, 'The spirit of these paintings is more that of the Counter-Reformation than of Martin Luther.'[77]

Son of the university's founder and an ordained Baptist minister himself, Dr. Bob Jones, Jr., formed the collection at a

time when baroque history paintings with religious subjects could be purchased from New York and London dealers for three- and four-figure prices. An extraordinary personality in the history of collecting, Dr. Jones – through energy, determination, and the intelligence to seek advice in the right quarters – managed to build one of the largest and most interesting collections of European painting in this country, all the while running the university, maintaining a heavy schedule of evangelical preaching, and making missionary trips to the Holy Land and the Far East.[78] As the museum pamphlet given to visitors points out, 'As phenomenal as has been this growth, it comes as no surprise to anyone who is familiar with Bob Jones University, every aspect of which is a witness to the miraculous power and blessing of God upon the "World's Most Unusual University".'[79]

Although the main emphasis of the Bob Jones museum is Italian Renaissance and baroque art, there are approximately forty Netherlandish paintings, more than half of which are by seventeenth-century Dutch artists. Most fall within one of three categories: mannerists, Utrecht Caravaggisti, and the Rembrandt School. Among the mannerist examples are Carel van Mander's *Saint John Preaching in the Wilderness* and Cornelis van Haarlem's *Christ Healing the Blind Man* of 1619. The larger group of paintings by Dutch followers of Caravaggio includes the dramatic Matthias Stomer *Lot Leaving Sodom* exhibited here (cat. no. 62), Jan van Bijlert's signed *Mary Magdalen Turning from the World to Christ*, Jan Gerritsz van Bronchorst's *Idolatry of Solomon* dated 1642, and works attributed to Ter Brugghen, Baburen, and Honthorst. The Rembrandt School is represented by a number of good examples, including Willem de Poorter's *Jerobeam's Apostasy Rebuked*, Govaert Flinck's representation of *Solomon's Prayer for Wisdom* (an oil sketch for his chimney piece of 1658 in the Amsterdam Town Hall), Gerbrand van den Eeckhout's *Joseph Interpreting Dreams*, and Jan Victors's *Esther Accusing Haman* of 1651. Other significant Dutch paintings in the collection are the early Aert van der Neer *Arrival at Emmaus*, Benjamin Gerritsz Cuyp's *Saint Peter Delivered from Prison*, and Gerard Hoet's *Decapitation of John the Baptist*. Haarlem classicism (only recently beginning to be appreciated) is represented by a fine Pieter de Grebber *Adoration of the Shepherds*.[80]

Only a few years after the Bob Jones museum was founded, another university museum was established in a neighboring southern state: the Ackland Memorial Art Center, which opened in 1958 at the University of North Carolina (Chapel Hill, North Carolina). Ackland, an amateur poet, novelist, and inveterate traveler (he logged more than thirty trips to Europe), decided to promote the development of the arts in the South by endowing a major southern university with a gallery.[81] Chapel Hill was ready for such a gift, for in 1937 the university's little eighteenth-century chapel had been renovated as a place for teaching and exhibiting art.[82] At the same time, a program for fostering art appreciation and raising acquisition funds had been initiated through the rental of framed reproductions of famous paintings to students and faculty for twenty-five cents per month. The new museum opened with only a handful of works of art, a print room, and a suite of eighteenth-century English furniture. Appropriately, the first exhibition to fill the empty galleries consisted of masterpieces borrowed from university museums.

Dutch art has never been a major priority at the Ackland, for the nearby North Carolina Museum of Art at Raleigh, which opened in 1956, has many good Dutch pictures. Fortunately, there were already two useful examples in the university's possession: a late *Portrait of a Man* by Nicolaes Maes and Horatius Paulijn's *Idolatry of Solomon* (which has also been attributed to Pot). Subsequent acquisitions included the gift of Salomon Koninck's *Mocking of Ceres* in 1963 and three major purchases: Emanuel de Witte's *Interior of the Old Church in Amsterdam* (1973), Matthias Stomer's *Christ before Caiphas* (1979), and a fine Jan Weenix game piece (1984). Other Dutch paintings in the museum are of less certain authorship (works in the style of Philips Wouwermans, Jan Davidsz de Heem, Jan van Goyen, Godfried Schalcken, and Cornelis van Poelenburch), but the drawings collection includes fine examples by Bramer, Molijn, and Jan Baptist Weenix.

'How do you go about building a university art collection when you have no funds, no storage space, and almost no administrative recognition?'[83] Henry Hope posed this question in 1971 on the occasion of his retirement as the first director of the Indiana University Art Museum (Bloomington, Indiana). Among the newer university museums, Indiana's illustrates most dramatically how individual commitment and ingenuity can create much, in a relatively short time, out of virtually nothing. The history of this museum therefore forms an encouraging conclusion to this survey.[84]

When the GIs returned home from the war in 1946, the sudden expansion of Indiana's art department (both studio and art history) created a pressing need for exhibition space. The earliest facilities consisted of several abandoned army barracks and a cement block gallery, whose closet became museum storage. When a generous alumnus gave a large Maillol terracotta in 1955, Professor Hope, then chairman of the Art Department, felt the time was right to attempt forming a permanent collection. Hope's reminiscences (which ought to be required reading for anyone involved with a college or university museum) record the first careful approaches to the university administration, the gradual cultivation of donors, the seeking of advice from experts in various fields, and finally the purchases (more often than not at prices under $500) of objects in non-fashionable areas. Within a decade, a substantial collection had come into being, with an emphasis on Egyptian, Greek, Roman, Oriental, and African objects, as well as prints and drawings. A Kress Foundation gift of ten paintings was gratefully received in 1961, and in 1962 a new Fine Arts Building was dedicated. The subsequent growth of the collection, by both gift and purchase, has been extraordinary both in quality and in scope.[85] In 1981 the museum reopened in elegant new premises designed by I.M. Pei.

Indiana's picture collection includes a dozen seventeenth-century Dutch paintings, the most important of which were purchased during the seventies and eighties, under the directorship of Thomas T. Solley. Their variety of subjects and styles reveals a conscious and deliberate intention to build a truly representative Dutch collection. Thus, there is a fine Pieter de Ring *Still Life with Lobster*; a tavern interior by Cornelis Bega, dated 1661; a church interior by Emanuel de Witte; a portrait by Jacob Backer; history paintings representing *The Young Daniel* by Pieter de Grebber and *The Mocking of Christ* by Matthias Stomer; and landscapes by Jan Wyck and Jan Hackaert. The museum's proudest Dutch acquisition came about in 1977 when Registrar Adelheid Gealt noticed in a French dealer's catalogue a superb Ter Borch portrait of a woman and called it to the attention of her director. Mr. Solley immediately bought the picture in Paris, unaware that he had purchased it only hours before the arrival on the scene of his fellow director from the Indianapolis Museum of Art, who came in vain to buy the companion piece of the portrait by Ter Borch in his museum [**16-17**].[86]

In investigating the collecting of Dutch art, or for that matter any kind of art, in academia, one encounters what appears a fairly hit-or-miss situation, as gifts, bequests, and purchase funds trickle in from diverse individuals (most often the faithful alumni) at various unpredictable intervals. Although the

◄ 16
Gerard ter Borch
Portrait of a Man
Canvas, 28 x 23 cm (11 x 9 in.)
Lower right: G T B (in ligature) (ca. 1658)
Indianapolis, Ind., Indianapolis Museum of Art,
Gift of the Friends of Art, inv. no. 49.86

► 17
Gerard ter Borch
Portrait of a Woman
Canvas, 28 x 23 cm (11 x 9 in.)
Lower right: G T B (in ligature) (ca. 1658)
Bloomington, Ind., Indiana University Art Museum,
Purchase 1977, inv. no. 77.78

planning of the participants (when one can discover it) has been of crucial overall importance, the details of this story often seem to happen by chance. Nonetheless, a few general observations rise to the surface.

First, in the broadest sense, the impetus for collecting relates closely to the distinctively residential character of American colleges and universities, many in locations remote from cultural centers. Because undergraduates actually live on these campuses (and during four of the liveliest and most formative years of their lives), they often come to feel a deep and lasting connection to the place, its setting, and its resources. Works of art studied in a context that encourages prolonged and repeated contemplation are often viewed by students in a highly personal, even proprietary way. When a painting or etching serves as the topic of a term paper or a seminar report, it becomes the writer's permanent possession, remembered even more vividly than the course itself. It is therefore not surprising that alumni and alumnae have shown such sustained interest in the development of these collections, for if people give to public museums to be remembered by the world at large or to benefit society, they often give to their colleges and universities, so to speak, for the good of the family (alma mater).

The question of how seventeenth-century Dutch art fits into this development yields some surprises: first, of course, the number and diversity of the paintings themselves, which are often of unusual interest and at times of superlative quality as well. At the same time, however, it is remarkable that so few of these works were acquired before World War II, especially considering the great popularity of Dutch art, from the nineteenth century on, with generations of American collectors and with the public museums. Thus, the Rhode Island School of Design's acquisition in 1917 of the Aert de Gelder Old Testament scene exhibited here (cat. no. 21) was a far more exceptional event than one might think, not only because of the subject of the painting, but also because it was acquired deliberately, through purchase.[87]

By 1917 the relatively few Dutch paintings that had made their way into collegiate collections consisted almost entirely of gifts and bequests, and were nearly always portraits, with the exception of the odd genre scene, Italianate landscape, or still life, often of dubious attribution. By the 1940s a few museums (primarily Oberlin and Smith) had begun to make significant purchases; Dutch gifts had began to increase as well (mostly landscapes, portraits, and a few genre scenes and works by artists of the Rembrandt School). Nonetheless, this level of interest and involvement contrasts dramatically with the virtual explosion of Dutch acquisitions in academia during the post-war era. The same period also witnessed a new interest on the part of academic institutions in Dutch history painting (mannerists, pre-Rembrandtists, and followers of Caravaggio), not only because the prices were right, but also because the development of scholarship in baroque art in general, beginning in the 1930s, seems to have fostered interest in complex narrative and allegorical subjects.

This relationship between patterns of scholarship and collegiate art collecting, difficult to assess with any precision, may also help explain the curious lack of emphasis on Dutch art earlier in the century. As already noted, the teaching of art in America began in the nineteenth century with the classical world (classics and archeology). Classical art was seen as the highest standard of aesthetic and intellectual merit, and this was reflected in the earliest collegiate art collections with their photographs and engravings of antiquities and their forests of plaster casts. Indeed, the enthusiastic appreciation for Dutch painting throughout the nineteenth century was largely a popular taste, and quite at variance with the pronouncements of art educators of the period. James Jackson Jarves, outspoken as always in 1869, had this to say about Dutch art: 'Those whose aesthetics are in sympathy with its mental mediocrity will not desert it for anything I may say. Nor would I have them until they are prepared to appreciate a higher standard. That of Holland [...] gives honest work for hard-earned dollars. But as an agent of intellectual progress it is of doubtful worth. The tendency is rather to materialize the understanding and sensualize the taste, without yielding any sustenance to the imagination.'[88] (It should also be noted here that Jarves, who recommended the pure style of Greek sculpture, reacted to Michelangelo's *Pietà* as 'an impossible event.')

A close analysis (well worth doing) of publications on Dutch painting used by early art history students in this country is clearly beyond our scope. Yet, even preliminary examination of this material reveals that although Dutch art was highly praised for its craftsmanship and 'honesty,' even its admirers found much of it either lacking in intellectual content or inferior in beauty and imagination to works in a classical style (whether Greek sculpture or Italian painting). Thus, Henry Havard's popular treatise on Dutch art, published in English translation in 1885, found Rembrandt more profound in thought and invention than Titian, but 'in common with many Dutch painters, Rembrandt appears to have been quite unable to appreciate the regularity of feature, the elegance and grace of form, which for us constitute the beautiful [...]. He ignores the delicacy and perception which constitute taste.'[89] Much of the literature used by American students during the early decades of the twentieth century further implies that the aspect of empirical observation in Dutch art (however delightful in effect) limits either the formal or intellectual seriousness of these works, if not both.[90] Thus, it is perhaps not surprising that acquisitions made by educational institutions in the European 'old master' category

have not emphasized Dutch art until relatively lately.

In any case, Dutch painting is valued today – as never before – by American scholars, graduate students and undergraduates, for whom the study of this material is pursued at a level of intellectual intensity and seriousness that would have astounded Mr. Jarves. What this boom in scholarship promises for the future of college art collections remains to be seen, but the prospects seem bright. After all, the most satisfying aspect of the academic world is the fact that one's professorial enthusiasms, whatever they are, can be handed along so easily, and that when students move on, they carry this shared involvement with them. Sometimes, even decades later, they give it back.

1 Quoted in *Backlin-Landeman 1967*, p. 670. The full text of this important letter is reproduced in *Butterfield et al. 1762-1784*, p. 260. Adams, writing from Paris and deeply impressed by his exposure to European art and architecture, was both admiring and mistrustful of what he saw. Earlier in the same letter he noted, 'It is not indeed the fine Arts which our country requires. The Usefull, the mechanic Arts, are those which we have occasion for in a young country, as yet simple and not far advanced in Luxury, altho perhaps much too far for her Age and Character.'
2 A scattering of university museums also exists in England, the oldest of which must have inspired the earliest American collections. The Ashmolean Museum at Oxford was founded as a primarily scientific collection in 1683 by Elias Ashmole (1617-1692). Not until 1855, however, were the scientific specimens and art collections separated. In 1894 the archeological and artistic works were at last displayed together in a new building known as the University Galleries (*Oxford 1920*, pp. 5-12). The Fitzwilliam Museum at Cambridge University, begun in 1816 with a handsome bequest of paintings, prints, books, and money from Viscount Fitzwilliam of Merrion, first opened (in a still uncompleted building) in 1848 (*Winter 1958*, pp. 1-6; *Cambridge 1989*). The Barber Institute of Fine Arts at the University of Birmingham was founded in 1932 by Dame Margaret Constance Hattie Barber in memory of her husband Sir William Henry Barber. The Barber Trust, which also provides professorships and prizes for students, supported the building, which opened in 1939, as well as the impressive art collection (*Birmingham 1952*, pp. ix-x). Around the same time, Samuel Courtauld endowed, in 1931 at the University of London, the first specialized center in Britain for study of the history of art. Co-founded by Lord Lee of Fareham and Sir Robert Witt, the Courtauld Institute has always emphasized students' close contact with original works of art, a mission well served by the recent combination of exhibition and educational functions at Somerset House (*Chilvers / Farr 1988*, p. 123). The Whitworth Art Gallery, since 1958 part of the University of Manchester, was originally founded by Royal Charter in 1892 as the Whitworth Institute. Today it works closely with Manchester's Department of Art History (*Hawcroft 1967*, p. ii).
3 *Spencer 1971*, p. 84
4 Special thanks are extended to the following individuals who responded generously to requests for detailed information about their collections: Hilliard Goldfarb and Joy Kenseth (Dartmouth College); Donald A. Rosenthal and Hetty Tye (Bowdoin College); Richard S. Field and John Klein (Yale University); Stephen Spiro (University of Notre Dame); Hilarie Faberman and Charles H. Sawyer (University of Michigan); Pamela Askew, Rebecca Lawton, Joann Potter, James Palmer (Vassar College); Michael Goodison (Smith College); Franklin Robinson, Louann Skoroupa, Ann Slimmon (Rhode Island School of Design); Barbara T. Ross and Betsy Rosasco (Princeton University); Seymour Slive, Judith Neiswander, William Robinson, David Becker, Marjorie Cohn (Harvard University); Bernard Barryte (University of Rochester); William Chiego and Larry Feinberg (Oberlin

College); Vivian Patterson (Williams College); Ann Porter and Judy Hurd (University of Vermont); Kathleen Jones (University of Illinois); Joan C. Davis (Bob Jones University); Dean Walker and Charles Millard (University of North Carolina); Adelheid M. Gealt (Indiana University). Although up-to-date catalogues and guidebooks of these collections are not always available, one can consult Peter Sutton's useful handbook (*Sutton 1986*), which includes discussions of seventeen college and university museums.

5 *Burke 1981*, p. xix

6 *Maser 1962*, pp. 177-178; *Eisler 1977*

7 The following recent Dutch exhibitions with catalogues from American college and university museums should also be cited: *Held 1981-A*; *Simons 1982*; *Stone-Ferrier 1983-1984*; *Barnes 1988*; and *Perlove 1989*.

8 On Jefferson's proposals about the fine arts for both the College of William and Mary and the University of Virginia, see *Hiss / Fansler 1934*, pp. 3-6.

9 *Palmer / Holton 1934*, p. 39

10 On the formation and character of early college collections, see *Harris 1976*, pp. 7-19.

11 *Baas 1985*, p. 10. The full text of the letter is reproduced as the frontispiece to *Bowen 1958*.

12 *Baas 1985*, p. 13. The new Dartmouth museum, known as the Hopkins Art Center and designed by Charles Moore, opened in 1985. Dartmouth has a good (and growing) collection of Dutch prints, all of which were acquired after 1948. The most important of the few Dutch paintings in the collection are a Pieter van Laer street scene, given in 1962, and Cornelis Saftleven's *Barn Interior*, purchased in 1983.

13 By the later nineteenth century dozens of reproductive processes had come into use, as shown by the catalogue of an exhibition of 1892 at the Boston Museum of Fine Arts, significantly entitled *Exhibition illustrating the Technical Means of the Reproductive Arts from the XV. Century to the Present Time with special Reference to the Photo-Mechanical Processes* (*Boston 1892*). Especially popular with American college museums were the reproductions produced by A. Braun of Dornach, for the Autotype Printing and Publishing Company, London. 'Braun's Autotypes,' which would be hung on screens in a gallery, were billed as 'most exact fac-similes of the originals, as reproducing not only every line and dot, but the very pigment and material employed by the Masters themselves' (*London 1871*, n.p.). I am indebted to Marjorie Cohn, curator of prints at the Fogg Art Museum, Harvard University, for these references.

14 *Janssen et al. 1988*, nos. 4 and 17

15 The comprehensive drawings catalogue (*Becker 1985*), now listing some three hundred sheets, gives eloquent testimony to the profound effect a college art collection can have on undergraduates. The author, David Becker (Bowdoin '70) notes (p. xi) that he was first introduced to the drawings collection as a student assistant doing rematting chores.

16 *Burke 1981*, p. 35

17 *Harris 1976*, p. 40. The gallery built to house the Trumbull Collection remained standing until 1901. The paintings, which had been transferred to Street Hall in 1866, were later moved to the Trumbull Room of the present museum in February 1929. Yale has always meticulously followed the terms of the original agreement, refusing all loan requests and carefully moving Trumbull's and his wife's remains each time the paintings have shifted location.

18 Jarves was very clear about his preference for what he considered the 'idealisms' and more lofty motives of Italian art. His comments on Dutch are less sympathetic: 'There never was a more purely mechanical, commonplace school of painting combined with so much minute finish and fidelity to the ordinary aspect of things, heedless of idealisms of any sort. If it labored for any special end it was that of ocular deception. In this respect, therefore, its notion of art was like that of a child or savage' (*Jarves 1869*, p. 181).

19 *New Haven 1931*, p. 6. The catalogue of the Ehrich Collection exhibition (*Chicago 1888*) sponsored by the American Fine Arts Society, lists artists from Berckheyde to 'Zorg' (Sorgh). The focus of the collection was on finely finished landscapes, still lifes, and genre paintings. One Hals portrait is listed and a Rubens 'Peasant Dance.'

Ehrich gave only one painting to Yale, a Venetian School *Rape of Europa* that entered the collection in 1909.

20 Other Northern drawings entered the collection in 1945, as gifts to the Yale library from Mrs. Cornelius Vanderbilt, whose husband had been in the Class of 1895. A 1956 bequest from Everett V. Meeks (Class of 1901 and director of the museum between 1929 and 1940) has allowed further purchases of seventeenth-century drawings (*Haverkamp-Begemann / Logan 1970*).

21 *Notre Dame 1967*, p. x

22 An exhibition of Notre Dame's Dutch portraits was held in 1961 at the University of Chicago (*Chicago 1961-A*). In the following year a selection of the seventeenth- and eighteenth-century paintings from this collection was shown at the University of Illinois (*Miller 1962*).

23 *Harris 1976*, p. 16

24 A complete account of the history of Michigan's museum and the development of its art instruction is contained in *Faberman / Wight 1988*, pp. 1-13.

25 *Veysey 1965*, p. 12. For a survey of the nineteenth-century development of American colleges and universities, see *Thwing 1906*.

26 *Jarves 1869*, pp. 340-341

27 The physical layout and location of the gallery anticipated the recommendations of George Fisk Comfort who, in 1867, developed a plan for an ideal museum of art history proposed for Allegheny College in Meadville, Pennsylvania (*Harris 1976*, p. 13). Comfort's full theory is set forth in *Comfort 1867*, pp. 21-23.

28 From 'Report of the Committee on the Art Gallery of Vassar Female College,' made to the Board of Trustees on 23 February 1864. The full text of this extraordinary document is reproduced in *Tonks / Rindge 1939*, pp. 19-24.

29 *Foshay / Mills 1983*, pp. 13-15

30 Much of Vassar's Northern painting collection is reproduced in *Poughkeepsie 1983*.

31 *Northampton 1986*, p. 16

32 This energetic woman, the mother of five, also hired the teachers, managed the finances, and even, when necessary, swept and dusted the classrooms. The Metcalfe family also endowed the museum's collections (Eliza Metcalfe Radeke) and donated funds for a building in 1893 (Jesse Metcalfe). A full account of RISD's history is given in *Woodward 1985*, pp. 11-60.

33 *Woodward 1985*, p. 11

34 *Johnson 1983*

35 To celebrate the centenary of Princeton's Department of Art and Archaeology, a booklet recounting the department's founding and development was published by Marilyn Aronberg Lavin in 1983 (*Lavin 1983*).

36 *Lavin 1983*, p. 9

37 *Lavin 1983*, pp. 19-20. The bibliography for Tonks's course consisted of three books: A.L. Wauters, *The Flemish School of Painting* (*Wauters 1885*); W.M. Conway, *Early Flemish Artists* (*Conway 1887*); and H. Havard, *The Dutch School of Painting* (*Havard 1885*). In 1911, Tonks left Princeton to become Chairman of the Department of Art at Vassar College, where he remained until his retirement in 1944.

38 The earliest purchases of Dutch paintings were a *Farmhouse on a Canal* by Egbert van der Poel (1929) and a *Forest Landscape*, attributed to Jacob van Ruisdael (1930). There is not yet a catalogue of Princeton's collection, but a number of the major works are illustrated in the handbook published in 1986 (*Princeton 1986*).

39 The first location of Harvard's art museum, from 1895 to 1927, was at Hunt Hall. In 1985 the collections were divided between the Fogg, which retained the painting collections and was given substantial renovation, and the new Sackler Museum, designed by Charles Stirling, which displays the university's vast ancient, oriental, and Islamic holdings. The Germanic collections of the Busch-Reisinger Museum will be displayed in a new wing of the Fogg, designed by Gwathmey, Siegel and Associates, which is now under construction.

40 *Cambridge 1931*, p. x

41 This methodological connection between art and science is made in Marjorie B. Cohn's biography of Gray, which also explores the cultural context of the time

(*Cohn 1986*, p. 58). Other nineteenth-century American art collectors were amateur naturalists, such as Luman Reed and Robert Gilmor (collectors of shells and minerals).

42 Also sent on loan to the Boston Museum were approximately 15,000 prints and drawings (including another forty Rembrandt etchings) bequeathed in 1892 by John Witt Randall (Class of 1834). There have also been major twentieth-century additions to the print room, including bequests of Arnold H. Knapp in 1956 and Edwin deT. Bechtel in 1957. In 1987 one of the albums from the Spencer Collection was added (which includes almost complete collections of Adriaen van Ostade and Moses van Uyttenbroek).

43 *Cohn 1986*, pp. 252, 260. Louis J. Thies carefully catalogued the engravings in 1869 (*Thies 1869*).

44 Norton's course enrollment shows impressive growth: from 34 students in 1875 to 446 in 1895 (*Vanderbilt 1959*, pp. 125-126, p. 132). According to *Hiss / Fansler 1934*, p. 23, Norton's course in ancient art in 1895-1896 had an enrollment of 551. Norton's distaste for lantern slides may reflect not only a common prejudice against photographing works of art (or using reproductions), but perhaps also the discomfort of working in a dark room filled with oily fumes. In 1872 the oil lamp in projection lanterns was replaced with less smoky and odoriferous kerosene, but it was not until the 1890s that electrically powered projectors were introduced. The Zeiss arc lamp 'epidiascope' (a major breakthrough, yielding accurate vertical projection) was invented in 1898 (*Lavin 1983*, pp. 12-13).

45 *Hiss / Fansler 1934*, p. 23

46 The entire examination is reproduced in *Hiss / Fansler 1934*, pp. 179-180.

47 *Vanderbilt 1959*, p. 140

48 There is no up-to-date catalogue or handbook of the Fogg's holdings, but William Robinson is now preparing a catalogue of the drawings. Both the May and June 1978 issues of *Apollo* were devoted to the Fogg, the latter including an essay by Seymour Slive on the Rembrandt holdings at Harvard (*Apollo 1978*, pp. 453-463). The following alphabetical list of seventeenth-century Dutch paintings is taken from the computer printout kindly prepared by Judith Neiswander (it excludes works designated as anonymous, copy, 'school of,' and 'attributed to' and includes the date the painting entered the collection): Claes Berchem, *Shepherds and Sheep* (1958); Gerrit Berckheyde, *View of the Dam* (1968) (Van der Heyden, cat. no. 30 in this volume); Ferdinand Bol, *Girl with a Fan* (1961); Adam Colonia, *Annunciation to the Shepherds* (1939); two paintings of horses by Aelbert Cuyp (1960); Aelbert Cuyp, *Portrait of a Child* (1970); Benjamin Cuyp, *Nativity* (1961); two Jan van Goyen landscapes (1969); Frans Hals, *Portrait of a Preacher* (1930); Bartholomeus van der Helst, *Portrait of a Woman* (1969); Jacob de Heusch, *Roman Landscape* (1958); Hans de Jode, *Landscape* (1955); Jan Lievens, *Portrait of a Man* (1972); C. Luycks, *Still Life with Lobster* (1960); Nicolaes Maes, *Family Group* (1957) and pendant portraits of a man and woman (1966); Claes Molenaer, *Winter Sports* (1924); Pieter Mulier, *Classical Landscape* (1961); three landscapes by Aert van der Neer (1966); Jacob Ochtervelt, *Family Portrait* (1922); Cornelis van Poelenburch, *Apollo Starting for the Chase* (1938) and *Rest on the Flight* (1965); Rembrandt and Lievens, *Portrait of an Old Man* (1930); Rembrandt, *Head of an Old Man* (1943), *Head of Christ* (1964), *Self-Portrait* (1969), *Portrait of a Man* (1969), *Portrait of an Old Man* (1985); Pieter de Ring, *Still Life* (1934); Jacob van Ruisdael, *Waterfall* (1953); *Wooded Landscape with an Old Oak* (1966); *Road Lined with Trees* (1966); two Salomon van Ruysdael seacoast scenes (1935); Dirck van Santvoort, pendant portraits (1969); Michael Sweerts, *Man with Pipe* (1941); Gerard ter Borch, *Portrait of a Young Lady* and *Portrait of Neeltje van der Cruysse* (1962); Adriaen van de Venne, *Men and Horse* (1962); Simon de Vlieger, *The Wreckers* (1954); Jan Vonck, *Still Life with Birds* (1957); Jan Weenix, *Still Life with Dead Game* (1957); Philips Wouwermans, *The Army Kitchen* (1957).

49 James Warburg (son of Paul M. Warburg, who masterminded the U.S. federal banking system) had already given Ter Borch's *Portrait of a Lady* and a portrait of Rembrandt's mother (now called a copy) in 1962.

50 In her foreword to the Fogg exhibition of 1965 in memory of Paul Sachs, Agnes Mongan mentions that he was in the habit of scouting out purchases in the company of his close friend, the esteemed Boston print connoisseur W.G. Russell Allen.

Mongan evokes an endearing image of the two collectors in action together at home and abroad: Sachs was 5 feet tall; Allen was 6 feet 4 inches (*Mongan 1965-1966*, p. 9).

51 Sachs also brought Otto Benesch in 1940. Benesch did much of the research for his vast corpus on Rembrandt drawings at the Fogg before returning to Vienna in 1948 (*Apollo 1978*, p. 452). Another significant figure already on the premises when Rosenberg and Benesch arrived was Charles Kuhn, then curator (later director) of the Museum of Germanic Art (later called the Busch-Reisinger Museum), who had a career of more than thirty years at Harvard. In a survey of art instruction in the United States made in 1934, Kuhn appears under Harvard's listing as the instructor of 'Flemish and Dutch Painting in the Middle Ages and the Renaissance' and 'Flemish and Dutch Painting of the Renaissance' (*Hiss / Fansler 1934*, p. 88).

52 An exhibition of selections from this bequest was put on at the Fogg Art Museum in 1979 (*Oberhuber 1979*).

53 Drawings and watercolors from Philip Hofer's collection were exhibited at the Fogg Museum in 1984 (*Oberhuber / Robinson 1984*).

54 *Apollo 1978*, p. 459. The Rembrandt letter belongs to an album assembled by Frederick Locker-Lampson (1821-1895), in which there are also documents by Michelangelo, Veronese, Rubens, Poussin, Hogarth, Reynolds, and Blake. It was given to Harvard in 1960 by Mr. and Mrs. Samuel B. Grimson, the daughter and son-in-law of Paul M. Warburg.

55 The results of Marquand's survey were published in pamphlet form (*Smith 1912*).

56 As noted earlier, there is evidence that both Princeton and Vassar were teaching specific courses in Dutch and Flemish art by 1912.

57 *Sutton 1977*, p. 1

58 The quotation (from the *University Record* of December 1874) is cited in *Hiss / Fansler 1934*, pp. 18-19.

59 An unusually deliberate collector, Eastman liked to live with each painting for intervals ranging from six months to three years before making a decision and sending payment. His purchases from M. Knoedler and Co. consisted not only of paintings, but also of frames used in his home for after-dinner tableaux in which guests were asked to impersonate the portraits. 'Do you have any old frames about the size of the Rembrandt and the Reynolds [...] that it will not do any harm to handle but just something that will do to frame the tableaux [...]. If so, send them along anytime next week' (*Brayer 1979*, p. 4).

60 *Hiss / Fansler 1934*, p. 18

61 The history of art instruction at Oberlin and the development of the museum are discussed in *Apollo 1976-A*, pp. 90-93. This issue of *Apollo*, which was devoted to Oberlin, also contains an article on landscape by Wolfgang Stechow and one on baroque painting by Richard E. Spear (*Apollo 1976-A*, pp. 106-111 [Spear], 112-117 [Stechow]).

62 *Stechow 1967* and *Stechow 1976*

63 *Walsh 1976*, pp. 855-856. Seymour Slive also gave a moving tribute on the occasion of the posthumous award from the Art Dealers Association of America to Stechow for excellence in art history (*Slive 1974-1975*, pp. 87-93).

64 Quoted in *Palmer / Holton 1934*, p. 6 (from *New York 1933*, p. liii).

65 A number of publications of this type are cited in *Palmer / Holton 1934*, p. 13, note 6, such as *Nimmons 1923*.

66 *Palmer / Holton 1934*, p. 19

67 *Hiss / Fansler 1934*, p. 49. The authors note that baroque courses were then being offered at Harvard by Leonard Opdyck and Arthur McComb (whose *Baroque Painters of Italy*, Cambridge, 1934, was the first study in English on Italian baroque art), at New York University by A. Philip McMahon and Erwin Panofsky, and at Bryn Mawr by Ernest Dietz. A list of M.A. papers and doctoral dissertations produced in American universities between 1875 and 1932 includes only one in Dutch art. In 1928 Grace D. Willis received an M.A. degree at the University of Chicago for a paper entitled 'Holland and the Dutch Genre Painters of the XVII Century' (*Hiss / Fansler 1934*, p. 184).

68 S. Laine Faison, one of Weston's students, who went on to become Director of the Williams College Museum, described him as a 'magician' who could evoke for students Titian's most vivid colors, even though the only color slides he possessed

were hand-tinted views (circa the 1890s) of the River Nile (*Faison 1979*, p. vii).

69 Not to be confused with his estranged brother Stephen Clark (a major donor to both the Metropolitan Museum and Yale University), Sterling Clark was a man of extreme privacy who began collecting as early as 1912 and continued until his death in 1956. Since his collection had been so little known to the art world, the severe white marble museum (somewhat incongruous in its picturesque New England environment) soon came to be known as 'the Tomb of the Unknown Collector' (*Sutton 1986*, p. 316).

70 *Harris 1976*, p. 46

71 *Hiss / Fansler 1934*, p. 7

72 A gallery brochure from the Robert Hull Fleming Museum (no author or date specified) suggests that the painting be interpreted not as a wedding portrait, but as an allegory of Holland's economic success (represented by the pearls from the Far East) and scientific progress (represented by the calipers and the globe).

73 *New York etc. 1973-1975*, p. 9

74 Erwin Panofsky wrote about this period, and specifically about his own experiences as a transplanted European scholar, in 'Three Decades of Art History in the United States,' published first in *Crawford 1953*, pp. 82-111, and reprinted in *Panofsky 1955*, pp. 321-346. An extensive account of the migration of European art historians to America was compiled in *Eisler 1969*.

75 *Ritchie 1966*, pp. 19-23

76 *Steel 1984*, p. 13

77 *Hope 1965-1966*, p. 162

78 *Hope 1965-1966*, pp. 154-162

79 *Greenville*, p. 1

80 *Sutton 1986*, pp. 96-102, offers useful comments on the attributions at Bob Jones. Northern paintings in the collection were catalogued in 1962, with a supplement published in 1968 (*Greenville 1962*, vol. II; *Greenville 1968*). The museum is now in the process of preparing a new catalogue.

81 At the time of Ackland's unexpected death in 1940, his beneficiary was still in doubt; only after nine years of litigation did the courts finally award the Ackland Bequest to the University of North Carolina. Further delays were caused by the imposition of a freeze on heavy construction during the Korean War. Thus, the dedication of the new museum on 20 September 1958 was a moment of considerable triumph. Mr. Ackland's remains were laid to rest in a memorial area within it (*Turner 1983*, pp. xiv-xvi).

82 At the rededication ceremony, President Frank Porter Graham made a stirring address, which captured the emotion of the occasion: 'This little hall has a story which it could tell of a University's decision in slender times to make an investment in art, with no assurances of a roof for many months to keep out the rain which beat upon its inner walls; faith and failure, aspiration and frustration, but always dreams and struggle, have been in this little pile since the first bricks of the red clay of Orange County were laid for Person Hall in the last decade of the eighteenth century' (*Turner 1983*, p. xx).

83 *Hope 1970-1971*, p. 170

84 It is not possible to give a complete survey here of all collegiate museums that own Dutch art, but a few additional collections should be mentioned. The University Art Museum at Berkeley (Berkeley, California), best known for modern art, also has good Dutch prints and drawings, as well as Pieter de Grebber's *Moses and the Daughters of Jethro* and Rubens's oil sketch *The Road to Calvary*. The Spencer Museum of Art at the University of Kansas (Lawrence, Kansas), with comprehensive collections from ancient to modern, owns a pair of Nicolaes Maes pendant portraits given by the Kress Foundation, a Dirck Hals *Merry Company*, Gillis van Tilborch's *Interior of a Picture Gallery with the Artist and His Patrons*, and an interesting series of Allaert van Everdingen drawings of *The Twelve Months*, whose provenance can be traced back to the estate of Valerius Röver. The Syracuse University Art Collection (Syracuse, New York), an old collection begun before 1876 (when George Fisk Comfort was dean of the new Art School), owns a *Portrait of Maurice of Nassau* by Jan van Ravesteyn, Jan Steen's *Girl Frying Cakes*, and a Rubens oil sketch of *Briseis Restored to Achilles* (all gifts since the mid-1950s).

85 An extensively illustrated guide to the collection was published in 1980 (*Bloomington 1980*).

86 Correspondence (7 September 1989) from Adelheid Gealt, now Interim Director of the Indiana University Art Museum.

87 Exactly why RISD chose a De Gelder as the first painting bought with its Museum Appropriations Fund remains obscure, although the publication of Karl Lilienfeld's monograph on the artist (*Lilienfeld 1914*) may have provided some incentive. Interestingly, the acquisition announcement in the museum bulletin (*Rowe 1921*, pp. 38-40) not only applauded the color and technique of the work, but also noted the importance of such biblical subjects in the Netherlands during the seventeenth century (a point that has not always been emphasized in much of the later scholarship on Dutch art).

88 *Jarves 1869*, p. 182

89 *Havard 1885*, p. 87

90 R.H. Wilenski, whose widely read survey first appeared in 1929, divided Dutch art into popular vs. serious forms ('serious' meaning Rembrandt, Vermeer, and many of the Italianate and narrative painters). His remarks about both types of artists are illuminating: 'Bloemaert taught his own pernicious system of eye-and-hand painting to a large number of pupils, including Terbrugghen, Sandrart and Gerard Honthorst' (*Wilenski 1929*, p. 49), or 'Terborch's use of this craftsmanship to achieve illusionistic imitation of textures was bound to appeal to spectators who ask nothing more from art than the confirmation of their own everyday experience of life' (*Wilenski 1929*, p. 241).

Peter C. Sutton
Baker Curator of European Paintings
Museum of Fine Arts, Boston

Recent Patterns of Public and Private Collecting of Dutch Art

The history of public collecting of Dutch art in the United States following the Second World War and prior to the change in the tax laws in 1986 is one of gradual but gratifying growth.[1] In traditional fashion the permanent collections of most major museums have benefited both from gifts and purchases, the latter financed from endowed funds or the support of private benefactors. Corporate support for purchases are rare, and public expenditures – be they federal, state or municipal – are virtually unknown; the decision by the North Carolina legislature in 1952 to allocate funds for the purchase of old master paintings for the state museum in Raleigh offers an exceptional, indeed unique case.[2] Most larger established museums have added consistently to their holdings of Dutch art, expanding and upgrading the collections. However, in recent years the rate has slackened as endowed purchase funds have failed to keep pace with the soaring art market. Gifts too have become scarcer; indeed they virtually disappeared when, four years ago, the tax-deductible percentage of the value of a donation of appreciated property was lowered and the 'alternative minimum income tax' was initiated – changes that in most cases have made it more profitable to sell works of art than to give them to museums.

Although it is regarded as an article of faith among leaders of American museums that acquisitions and operating budgets must be held strictly separate, this decline in purchasing power has ironically come at a time of rapid physical expansion of museums and their programs and a shift in most major museums' operating economies from a significant dependence on endowed incomes and public subsidies (mostly in the form of tax exemptions) to ever greater reliance on earned income (attendance, membership, and, of course, merchandising).[3] After several breathless decades of post-war growth, American art museums are now regularly running deficits. Many analysts believe they are embarking on something akin to middle age, a period of more measured growth and more modest goals. Simultaneously the great era of old master collecting is winding down, mostly from sheer want of supply, while the engines driving the art market are individuals not institutions. The trends in museum collecting of Dutch art are outlined below, with private collectors' interests to follow.

Among the diverse institutions that share their Dutch paintings with the public in the United States there are no 'typical' museums of art, but Boston's Museum of Fine Arts offers a fairly representative case study in collecting. Of the thirty-three Dutch paintings that have entered the collection since 1945 more than two-thirds were purchases.[4] Quite naturally the commitment to Dutch art varied with different administrations and curators. Under Perry Rathbone's directorship (1955-1972) the endowed monies were still competitive in the market and enabled him to make such remarkable acquisitions as Rembrandt's *Portrait of Reverend Johannes Elison* and its pendant *Portrait of Maria Bockenolle* (1956), Jacob van Ruisdael's *Rough Sea* (1957), and excellent works by Aert de Gelder (1957) and Pieter Lastman (1962). During these years the museum also received the gift of an unusually evocative late Frans Hals (1966).[5] By the time John Walsh became curator in the late seventies the funds had to be spent more sparingly. He still was able to acquire a fine Salomon van Ruysdael landscape but turned increasingly to less expensive purchases of an excellent but unconventional or uncharacteristic nature, such as Pieter Cornelisz van Slingeland's tightly painted little double *Portrait of Jan van Musschenbroek and His Wife* of 1688 and Philips Wouwermans's so-called *Knight Vanquishing Time, Death, and Demons* [1], which was part of the famous Braamcamp collection in the eighteenth century (see cat. no. 54, fig. 1). More recently Boston has stretched purchase funds by acquiring works by artists who are still relatively modestly priced, such as Roelandt Savery (inv. no. 1988.14), Cornelis van Poelenburch (inv. no. 1987.56), and the little-known Daniel Jansz Thievaert (inv. no. 1988.15).

The Dutch collections of the Metropolitan Museum of Art, on the other hand, have benefited more from donations. Since the famous purchase of Rembrandt's *Aristotle Contemplating the Bust of Homer* in 1961, Dutch paintings have been bought only intermittently; Jacques de Gheyn's *Still Life* (the earliest dated *vanitas*) of 1603 and Abraham Bloemaert's great *Moses Striking Water from the Rock (Aqua)* of 1596 (cat. no. 8) came during John Walsh's curatorship there in the early 1970s. It comes as no surprise that under Sir John Pope-Hennessy's leadership of the European Paintings Department, Italian painting flourished more than

1

Philips Wouwermans
Knight Vanquishing Time, Death, and Demons
Panel, 65.7 x 48 cm (25 ⅞ x 18 ⅞ in.)
Lower left: *PHILS: W/ 1662* (PHILS in ligature)
Boston, Museum of Fine Arts, inv. no. 1981.78

Dutch; nonetheless, a Philips Koninck panorama and a fine Frans Post were added in the 1980s.[6] More significant were gifts like that of Robert Lehman in 1975, a vast collection housed separately at the Metropolitan which is strongest in early Italian and French nineteenth-century art but includes Rembrandt's *Portrait of Gerard de Lairesse* and excellent works works by Pieter de Hooch and Gerard ter Borch.[7] The Linsky collection followed in 1982, bringing with it an excellent Jan Steen genre scene of the 'Dissolute Household' theme, a Metsu, and Ter Borch's *Van Moerkerken Family Portrait*,[8] while Mrs. Wrightsman donated her haunting *Head of a Girl* by Vermeer in 1979. Often overlooked are a group of anonymous but exceedingly generous gifts made by a collector in 1964 (but who retained life interest) which brought to the museum, among other excellent Dutch paintings, Thomas de Keyser's *Musician and His Daughter* and the large Jan van Goyen of 1647. The Metropolitan's enviable ability to continue to attract the gifts of collections thus has partly offset their virtually insignificant acquisitions budget.

Other museums with limited purchase funds have sought to fill lacunae in their collections selectively. The gifts early in this century of substantial collections (Johnson, Elkins, and others) brought to the Philadelphia Museum of Art holdings that now constitute the largest gathering of Dutch paintings in this country. However, these early benefactors shared the tastes of their time in assembling mostly naturalistic landscapes, still lifes, portraits, and genre scenes, while largely ignoring history and Dutch Italianate paintings, then regarded as 'un-Dutch.' These omissions have been filled only in the last decade by the acquisition of Gerbrand van den Eeckhout's *Continence of Scipio* and Jan Baptist Weenix's *Rest on the Flight into Egypt* (cat. no. 70, fig. 5), and through the gift of Gerard de Lairesse's *Bacchus and Ariadne*.[9] In this same period, still other museums made a conscious effort to expand their Dutch collections relative to other strengths. Following the build-up of the Italian collections under the directorship of Anthony Clark at the Minneapolis Institute of Arts, his successor, Samuel Sachs, consciously sought to add to the representation of Northern paintings. Minneapolis's curator, George Keyes, has subsequently purchased an excellent group of Dutch landscapes (Jan van Goyen's *Riverscape with the Pellecussen Gate* of 1648 [cat. no. 24] and Esaias van den Velde's *Landscape with Courtly Procession* of 1619; Philips Wouwermans's *Merry and Rowdy Peasants at an Inn* of 1653 [cat. no. 72] was a gift from the Sweatt Collection) and marines (Abraham Storck's *The Four Days Battle* of 1666 and Ludolf Backhuizen's *Fishing Vessels in a Heavy Sea* of 1684).[10]

Better endowed institutions, on the other hand, were less likely to concentrate their acquisitions policy. The Cleveland Museum of Art's paintings collection has benefited exceptionally from the Hanna, Severance, and Marlatt purchase funds, enabling Sherman Lee in his salad days to acquire superb old masters of all schools, but including important Dutch history paintings (such as Jan Steen's *Wrath of Ahasuerus* [cat. no. 61] and Gerard van Honthorst's *Samson and Delilah*), landscapes (Simon de Vlieger, Jacob van Ruisdael, Jan van Goyen) and still lifes (Willem Kalf and Abraham van Beyeren).[11] His able successor, Evan Turner, has recently added a glowing *Still Life of Gooseberries* of 1701 by Adriaen Coorte, an excellent Melchior d'Hondecoeter, and the *Portrait of Machteld Suijs* by Maerten van Heemskerk – three works that might not have been first among the tastes of Dutch collectors early in this century but which now seem particularly astute, even shrewd, purchases. The popularity of Coorte's poetically understated art has grown enormously in recent decades. And early mannerist art of the quality of the Heemskerk is now exceedingly rare, while the present market has yet to fully embrace game pieces or bird paintings despite the fact that they originally were the prized possessions of noblemen and the aristocracy.

Ohio's great industrial fortunes also benefited the Dutch reserves of Toledo, another city where endowed funds (principally that of the glass manufacturer, Edward Drummond Libbey) were ample enough to sustain a purchasing program that has remained very active until quite recently. Toledo's long-time director, Otto Wittmann, tripled the holdings of the collections during the thirty years of his association with the museum prior to retirement in 1976.[12] He gave special priority to the European baroque and rococo, while acquiring a particularly impressive group of Dutch paintings. Except perhaps for history painting, no major genre of Dutch painting was stinted; Wittmann bought portraits (Thomas de Keyser, Bartholomeus van der Helst [cat. no. 29], and, of course, Rembrandt), high- and low-life genre (De Hooch [from the J.P. Morgan collection and Wittmann's first purchase], Ter Borch [cat. no. 10; from the Hermitage], Molenaer, and Van Ostade), native Dutch as well as Dutch Italianate landscapes (Avercamp, Van Ruysdael, Hobbema [from Ten Cate], Van Goyen, Van Poelenburch, Berchem, Both, and Aelbert Cuyp's *Riding Lesson* [again from the Hermitage]), still lifes (Van der Ast, Van Beyeren, Jan Davidsz de Heem), marines (Van de Cappelle), and town views (Isaac Ouwater). Splendid examples of the Dutch decorative arts were also acquired to complement the paintings collection. Wittmann's successor, Roger Mandle, carried on this distinguished tradition, acquiring the great *Ships in a Stormy Sea* (inv. no. 77.62, formerly in collection of Lord Ellesmere), by Willem van de Velde the Younger. Other distinguished directors have left their marks on the collections of museums in America's medium-sized cities; 'Chick' Austin and Charles C. Cunningham at the Wadsworth Atheneum in Hartford, for example, built up their baroque and Dutch collections.[13] James Welu, first as

curator and now as director, has also personally informed the excellent little collection of Dutch art at the Worcester Museum, acquiring paintings like Jacob Duck's *Merry Company* (yet again, formerly in the Hermitage) and fine examples by Cornelis van Haarlem and the *Bamboccianti*, while simultaneously garnering promised gifts from local collectors.[14] However, there is scarcely another museum person whose personal stamp will be as enduring as Otto Wittmann's in Toledo. I hasten to add that throughout the Dutch collections of the museums in Toledo and Cleveland, one also detects the benign advisory presence of Wolfgang Stechow, who ended his distinguished academic career at nearby Oberlin.

Whether for want of funds or of champions, collecting in the Dutch field has been relatively dormant at several of America's great midwestern museums in recent decades. Among them we include the Detroit Institute of Arts, long ironically the preserve of W.R. Valentiner (p. 126, fig. 4; cat. no. 70, fig. 1) and as recently as 1965 the glad recipient of Ter Borch's *Woman at Her Toilet* (Gift of Mrs. Edsel Ford and the Founders' Society), though Samuel Sachs's assumption of the directorship may signal a change, and the Art Institute of Chicago which has added several Flemish baroque paintings to the collection in recent years but seems to have set its priorities in nineteenth- and twentieth-century art. On the other hand, the Saint Louis Art Museum (under the directorship of James Burke, the author of a dissertation on Jan Both) has acquired landscapes by Hobbema and Pijnacker, and the Nelson-Atkins Museum of Art in Kansas City has purchased two indisputable masterpieces in the last decade: Dirck van Baburen's *Christ Crowned with Thorns* and Joachim Anthonisz Wtewael's *Saint Sebastian* of 1600 (cat. no. 73). Much to the credit of the curator, Roger Ward, these acquisitions also attest to Kansas City's uncommonly generous benefactors, not to say deep pockets.[15]

Deep pockets have always been handy for collecting good Dutch art and remain so today. In the 1980s the museums with the largest purchase funds generally have been the most successful acquisitors of Dutch art. While Edmund P. Pillsbury shows a greater interest in Italian, Spanish, and French painting, he has had money enough at the wealthy Kimbell Art Museum in Fort Worth to acquire in recent years Pieter Saenredam's *Interior of the Buurkerk, Utrecht* of 1645,[16] and a handsome Jacob van Ruisdael seascape (cat. no. 54). Similarly bolstered by the substantial funds of the Ahmanson Foundation, Scott Schaefer purchased a splendid trio of Dutch history paintings for Los Angeles – Hendrick Golzius's *Danaë* of 1603 (cat. no. 22), Jan Steen's

Samson and Delilah, and Pieter Lastman's *Hagar and the Angel* — as well as an important collaborative landscape by Philips Koninck and Adriaen van de Velde (who painted the staffage), and a Jan Davidsz de Heem still life of 1653.[17] Just this year, Schaefer's successor, Philip Conisbee, has also added the *Mercury and Argus* by Carel Fabritius, which came to light only in 1985 in a sale in Monaco.[18] The picture's discovery has facilitated additional attributions to the small oeuvre of this exceedingly rare Rembrandt pupil.

Certainly, during the last decade the institution that has been more active in the acquisition of Dutch art than any other museum either here or abroad has been the incomparably wealthy J. Paul Getty Museum in Malibu.[19] Indeed, under John Walsh's directorship, the Getty not only has purchased a dazzling array of paintings but, at least during the mid- and late eighties, has also bought more Dutch pictures than those of any other school save the French. There are large and impressive works such as Hendrick ter Brugghen's genial *Bacchante with a Monkey* of 1627, Jacob van Ruisdael's *Two Watermills and an Open Sluice* of 1653, Philips Koninck's *Panoramic Landscape* of 1665 (cat. no. 38), a monumental Berchem, two outstanding Van Huysums, and Dou's unexpectedly life-size *Portrait of Prince Rupert of the Palatinate and a Tutor as Eli and Samuel* (the pendant to Jan

Lievens's *Portrait of Prince Charles Louis of the Palatinate with His Tutor Wolrad von Plessen*, which was already owned by the museum [inv. no. 71.PA.53]). But more exquisite are the small-scale, cabinet-sized pictures, including ravishing genre scenes like Jan Steen's *Drawing Lesson* [2], two stable subjects by Ter Borch, De Hooch's *Schoolboy*, Dou's *Astronomer*, Van Mieris's *Doctor's Visit* and Cornelis Bega's *Alchemist*. Notable too are the intimately scaled history (Joachim Wtewael's sexy *Mars and Venus*, Van Mieris's *The Art of Painting* of 1661 [cat. no. 44], and Godfried Schalcken's *Annunciation*) and architectural paintings (Saenredam's *Interior of Saint Bavo* of 1628), landscapes (a spritely pair by Adriaen van de Venne of 1614), still lifes (an Ambrosius Bosschaert the Elder, also of 1614), and portraits (be it the double portrait of mysterious, beturbaned 'orientals' by Michael Sweerts or Paulus Potter's wonderfully vital 'portrait' of a *Dappled Stallion*). So great and numerous are the new Dutch pictures at the Getty that it would seem to belie the market's waning supply, but there is only one Croesus among America's museums. And even the Getty's riches have had to be budgeted and its depots gleaned for deaccessioning funds following such major purchases as the glorious Pontormo acquired last year.

The clearest trend that emerges from a review of recent patterns of institutional collecting is that purchases greatly outnumber gifts. Further, museums' acquisitions obviously signal that the era of masterpiece collecting has ended, giving way out of necessity to an appreciation of the merits of lesser-known masters. In this regard the famous depths of seventeenth-century Dutch artistic ranks and the Dutch painter's legendary concern about craft — a commendable fastidiousness that has surely been a factor in the survival of so many paintings today — has probably favored Dutch art over other schools. The last decade also reveals an ever closer relationship between collecting and new scholarship. For example, immediately preceding and following the appearance of Anne Lowenthal's welcome monograph on Wtewael (1986), examples of the artist's work were acquired by not only Kansas City and the Getty, but also Chicago, Cleveland, and Los Angeles.[20] Once spurned, mannerism, like Dutch Italianate painting, has entered the mainstream of modern taste. Similarly, following the publication of Otto Naumann's book on Van Mieris (1981) and preceding the recent exhibitions in Leiden and Amsterdam of *fijnschilder* painting, a renewed enthusiasm — most vividly demonstrated at the Getty but also detectable elsewhere — arose for the highly refined, polished manner first popularized by Dou and his followers, a taste not witnessed since the late nineteenth

2
Jan Steen
The Drawing Lesson
Panel, 49.3 x 41 cm (19³/₈ x 16¼ in.)
Lower left: *JSteen* (JS in ligature) (about 1665)
Malibu, The J. Paul Getty Museum,
inv. no. 83.PB.388

century.[21] On the other hand, there is little evidence of any special appetite for symbolically charged Dutch paintings, despite the recent fashion for iconographic studies.

If one accepts the prospect of ever-diminishing supply and the constancy of human nature, the short-term future of institutional collecting of Dutch art, indeed of all museum acquisitions, probably depends primarily on the tax laws. If greater incentives are provided for donations, America's museums will continue their recent patterns of modest but steady growth; without them the collecting will soon stop. Few institutions in these lean philanthropic times are able to follow the example of the National Gallery of Art in Washington, which recently raised fifty million dollars of endowment for purchase funds – money that has enabled their curator, Arthur Wheelock, to acquire an excellent large marine by Ludolf Backhuizen and a dramatically conceived night scene by Aert van der Neer, the first Dutch purchases in many years.

Though we live in an era of personal promotion and advertisement, modern life ironically often imposes anonymity and self-effacement. The greatest single exhibition of Dutch art ever mounted in this country was the *Hudson-Fulton Celebration* organized by W.R. Valentiner and held at the Metropolitan Museum of Art in New York in 1909.[22] It is a measure of the magnitude of change in the last eighty years that the vast majority of works in the show were privately owned (131 paintings out of a total of 149), but only one painting was lent anonymously. In today's more complicated world, pride of ownership is usually outweighed by legitimate concerns about security and privacy. There also may be reticence about disclosing one's assets, since the rising value of art and declining scale of individual fortunes in the last century has meant that an art collection often represents a much larger portion of a collector's personal wealth. Whatever the individual motivations, the trend toward ever greater anonymity is clear. Where nineteenth-century spectatorial writers like Gustav Waagen (p. 126, fig. 3) in Europe and Strahan and Durand-Gréville in this country were granted not only access to collectors' homes but also leave to discuss and even inventory their collections, modern reviewers no longer enjoy such candor.[23]

Nonetheless, most of the leading private collections of Dutch art on this continent have already been exhibited and published at least in part. Even many secretive collectors regularly share their paintings with the public through publications or loans to shows. Thus with a certain amount of calculated circumspection, one may adumbrate their range and content. Folio-sized, tooled

moroccan leather catalogues of private collections have become as scarce as the Rembrandts and Halses that once inspired them, but the collections have often become more interesting and consistent at their own level of quality. Moreover, the expertise of private collectors has probably improved significantly.

In the latter half of the twentieth century in America, the single most successful private collector of old masters, indeed of European paintings generally, is arguably Norton Simon, whose achievement is displayed at the Norton Simon Museum in Pasadena, California. Although Simon has not restricted himself to a single school of painting, he has acquired an extensive group of Dutch paintings by many of the greatest masters, including not only Rembrandt and Hals, but also Van Ruisdael, Steen, Metsu [**3**], Aert van der Neer, Aelbert Cuyp, the Van Ostades, and many others. His tastes, moreover, often break with the traditional conventions and patterns of American collectors of Dutch art, extending, for example, to religious paintings by Jan Steen (*The Marriage at Cana*) and Karel du Jardin (*The Denial of Saint Peter*) and outstanding works by lesser-known artists such as Jan van Bijlert's so-called *Officer in Armor*, as well as unusual pictures by more famous masters, such as Salomon van Ruysdael's daringly composed early *Landscape with a Sandy Road* of 1628.[24] Simon is famous for buying at auction, driving a hard

3
Gabriël Metsu
Woman at Her Toilette
Panel, 61 x 54.6 cm (24 x 21½ in.)
Lower right, on the book: *G.Metsu* (GM in ligature)
(ca. 1658-1660)
Pasadena, Norton Simon Museum, The Norton
Simon Foundation, inv. no. F.72.15

bargain, and canvasing scholars' opinions extensively (some would say intrusively) before acting. By the same token, he stubbornly keeps his own counsel in making final decisions. The success of these decisions can be gauged by comparing his accomplishment to that of Dr. Armand Hammer. While Hammer concentrated chiefly on French art, in the same years he also bought Dutch paintings, notably Rembrandt's *Juno*, together with works from other schools, but with far more uneven results overall.[25]

Both Simon and Hammer have installed their collections in the vicinity of Los Angeles. In recent decades, Southern California has probably been the single most active region for the collecting of Dutch painting in the world. To no small extent, of course, this reflects the activities of the Getty Museum. However if the Getty collected the best Dutch art in the 1980s, in the preceding decade, the institution's achievement was anticipated by Edward (cat. no. 68, fig. 1) and Hanna Carter.[26] Financed by the success of Carter Hawley Hale Stores Inc., and formed chiefly in the 1970s, the Carter collection is composed exclusively of Dutch landscapes, seascapes, architectural and town views, and still lifes. There are no portraits, genre scenes, or history paintings, indeed no paintings in which the human form has a conspicuous presence. But the collection makes no claim to surveying the variety of Dutch art; rather it celebrates specific aspects of Dutch painting, notably its intimacy, naturalism, and technical brilliance. An assembly of superbly well-preserved, mostly cabinet-sized works of art, the Carter paintings sustain an extraordinarily high level of quality. Moreover, within individual genres, they offer a representative sampling of the history and diversity of the painting type; for example, the landscapes include not only their famous Hendrick Avercamp *Winter Scene on a Frozen Canal* and an early Esaias van den Velde, but also an outstanding Van Goyen of 1646 [**4**] and Jacob van Ruisdael of 1652 [**5**] – both relatively recent acquisitions, river landscapes by Van Goyen and Salomon van Ruysdael, a first-rate marine by Van de Cappelle, a winter scene by Aert van der Neer, panoramas by Philips Koninck and Anthonie van Borssom, beach scenes by Simon de Vlieger (cat. no. 68), Adriaen van de Velde, and Willem van de Velde the Younger, as well as Dutch Italianate landscapes by Jan Both and Aelbert Cuyp, and even a Brazilian view by Frans Post. Similarly, the flower still lifes range from an early Ambrosius Bosschaert the Elder on copper to a late Jan van Huysum of 1724, and include such pleasing curiosities as the *Flowers in a Glass Vase* (cat. no. 12) by the little-known Dirck de Bray. The architectural

4
Jan van Goyen
View of Arnhem
Panel, 44 x 54 cm (17¼ x 21¼ in.)
Lower left: *VGOYEN 1646* (VG in ligature)
Los Angeles, collection Mr. and Mrs. Edward William Carter

5
Jacob van Ruisdael (the figures by Nicolaes Berchem)
Landscape with a Great Oak
Canvas, 86.4 x 107.6 cm (34 x 42 in.)
Bottom center: *JVRuisdael / 1652* (JVR in ligature)
Los Angeles, collection Mr. and Mrs. Edward William Carter

paintings by Saenredam and de Witte and the town views by Gerrit Berckheyde and Jan van der Heyden characteristically are excellent examples, while Adam Pijnacker's *Harbor View* is an unusual painting that reveals an unforeseen aspect of the Italianate master's art. Like other Dutch painting collectors, the Carters benefited from advisers (including Wolfgang Stechow, Egbert Haverkamp-Begemann, A. B. de Vries, and John Walsh) and typically enjoy living with their pictures in the handsomely reserved surroundings of their home.

The domestic appeal of the Dutch paintings continues to be a strong lure for collectors. It surely is not coincidental that at least two other major American collectors of Dutch seventeenth-century paintings came to these enthusiasms after years of collecting outstanding early American furniture. As interior designers have discovered, the felicitous combination of Dutch paintings and American decorative arts can create a stately but understated effect of ensemble. Linda and George Kaufman own Dutch landscapes [**6**], city views (cat. no. 31), marines, and even figure studies (cat. no. 39) that beautifully complement one of the nation's outstanding collections of colonial, neoclassical, federal, and empire-style American furniture.[27] Also noted for the strength of its American decorative arts, the Peter Eliot collection in New York recently added an excellent Jan Miense Molenaer [**7**] to its collection of Dutch landscapes and genre scenes. These persistent trends seem to acknowledge an intrinsic stylistic sympathy between the excellence of early American design and Dutch painting.

Senator John and Theresa Heinz also enjoy living with their pictures and likewise came to the collecting of Dutch and

7
Jan Miense Molenaer
The Duet
Canvas, 44.5 x 52 cm (17½ x 20½ in.)
Lower left: M. MOLENAER
New York, collection Peter Eliot

6
Jacob van Ruisdael
Wooded Landscape with a Bridge
Panel, 70.5 x 92.8 cm (27 ³/₄ x 36½ in.)
Lower left: JVRuisdael (JVR in ligature) (ca. 1650-1655)
Norfolk, Va., collection Linda and George M. Kaufman

Flemish still lifes only after collecting American paintings (portraits, landscapes, still lifes, and genre scenes). A United States senator from Pennsylvania, John Heinz III took advantage of a family fortune made in processed foods to assemble the largest private collection (more than eighty paintings) of Northern European still lifes in this country.[28] More narrowly focused than even the Carter collection, the Heinz collection is exceptional for its high degree of specialization.[29] The Flemish paintings (Osias Beert, Jacob van Hulsdonck, Jan van Kessel, Kerstiaen Luyckx, among others) are perhaps more distinguished than the Dutch, but the collection boasts special depth in the early 'additive' table-top still lifes, *vanitas* still lifes, and the later *pronk* banquet piece. Of special note among the Dutch paintings are Balthasar van der Ast's *Still Life with Fruit, Flower, and Shells*, Willem Claesz Heda's *Still Life with Ham and Drinking Vessels*, Hubert van Ravesteyn's *Tobacco Still Life*, and the German-born Abraham Mignon's *Cavern Scene*. A virtue of the Heinz collection is its devotion to excellent examples of the work of painters to whom the nineteenth century referred without condescension as 'minor masters' – painters like Maerten Boelema ('De Stomme'), Nicolaes Lachtropius, Harmen van Steenwyck, and Simon Luttichuys, whose *Allegory of the Arts* is one of the most intriguing works in the collection. Here too are unusual paintings such as Franciscus Gysbrechts's *Trompe-l'Oeil Window* [8], an illusionistic piece painted on both sides and actually hinged to enhance its deception. Despite its numbers, the Heinz collection is still young and in active formation; a half dozen paintings have been added since its exhibition in 1989. Thus we can expect its overall quality, variety, and historical representativeness to continue to improve.

Still another specialized collection, but one that has taken shape gradually over four decades, is the Milwaukee collection of Dr. and Mrs. Alfred Bader (cat. no. 15, fig. 3; cat no. 64, fig. 3).[30] Dr. Bader has assembled an extensive and wide-ranging collection of Dutch art but concentrated primarily in paintings of the

9
Nicolaes Maes
The Sacrifice of Isaac
Canvas, 113 x 91.5 cm (44½ x 36 in.)
Neither signed nor dated (ca. 1655)
Kingston, Ont., Queen's University (on loan from
Dr. Alfred Bader)

School of Rembrandt, above all biblical subjects. A chemist who unabashedly uses his company's newsletter to publish his own collection, Dr. Bader takes special interest in biblical iconography, especially Old Testament subjects. As a collector, he is drawn to unattributed paintings of high quality and delights in the sleuthing and squabbles of connoisseurs seeking names for his pictures: 'I will die with many such puzzles in my estate – things of beauty that challenge and tantalize.'[31] Typical of the collection is the fascinating painting of *Joseph and the Baker* which, despite its many assignments to, among others, Rembrandt himself, Carel Fabritius, and Johann Ulrich Mayr, is still without a certain attribution. The painting has also perplexed iconographers because of its unusual treatment of the story of Joseph explaining the prisoners' dreams (Genesis 40:16-19), which omits the butler entirely to concentrate on the unfortunate baker. Some of Dr. Bader's puzzles have happily been solved; William Robinson has persuasively shown through preliminary drawings that the lovely *Sacrifice of Isaac* [9], formerly assigned to Barent Fabritius and Jan Victors, is an early work by Nicolas

8
Franciscus Gysbrechts
Trompe-l'Oeil Window
Canvas, wood and metal, 136.5 x 102.3 cm
(53¾ x 40¼ in.)
On the back: *F. Gysbrechts* (ca. 1675)
Pennsylvania, Heinz Family Collection

◀ 10
Jan Lievens
Portrait of Rembrandt's Mother
Panel, 43.2 x 35 cm (17 x 13 ³/₄ in.)
Upper right: *JL* (ca. 1629)
Milwaukee, Wis., collection Dr. Alfred Bader

▶ 11
Rembrandt (?)
Head of an Old Man (Portrait of Rembrandt's Father?)
Panel, 24.2 x 20.3 cm (9½ x 8 in.)
Upper right: *RHL* (in ligature)
Kingston, Ont., Queen's University (on loan from
Dr. Alfred Bader)

Maes.[32] Still other paintings in the Bader collection are above
dispute, such as the splendidly memorable *Portrait of Rembrandt's
Mother* by Jan Lievens [**10**] that was acquired recently at the
Guterman sale. The haunting quality of this work is typical
of the collection, which also includes paintings like Michael
Sweerts's bizarre *Self-Portrait with a Skull* (cat. no. 64, fig. 3) and
the ruminative image of *Two Boys with a Skull and Striped Tulip*
attributed variously, but probably by Jan de Bray.

Given the cheerfully contentious nature of the Bader
collection, it is little wonder that it includes two works assigned to
Rembrandt but rejected by the Rembrandt Research Project. It
is a measure of the interest of the collection, however, that the
painterly little *tronie* known as the *Portrait of Rembrandt's Father (?)*
[**11**] split the vote of the 'Team,' who in a rare case admit of a
minority opinion in favor of the picture's assignment to the
master.[33] Despite popular misconceptions in Holland, there still
are autograph Rembrandts fully vetted by the 'Team' in private
hands in the United States. Most, like the wonderfully animated
Rape of Europa – virtually the last multi-figured history painting
left in private hands – on loan to The Metropolitan Museum
of Art, were inherited by their present owners; but a handful,
including the powerful little *Saint Peter in Prayer* [**12**], now owned
by a Florida collector, were purchased recently. All collectors
lament today's speedy decline in the supply of works by the
greatest Dutch masters, but it is worth recollecting that one

distinguished Washington official has owned no less than one-
half dozen Rembrandts (including Hammer's *Juno*) in his
lifetime, still possesses one of the last pairs of pendant portraits
by Frans Hals, and manages to collect avidly, though increasingly
in the highly specialized Early Netherlandish market where
prices are still relatively depressed.

A portion of America's Dutch collectors regularly turn over
their collections, returning them to the market either to upgrade
their collections, to collect in new areas, or merely to take
advantage of appreciated assets. We have always had and surely
will always encounter overextended, spendthrift collectors,
like the early-twentieth-century Chicagoan Yerkes, who rise
majestically only to immolate and disperse like so many sulphur
flares. Two recent examples were the late Oklahoma collector,
Tom Fee, whose collection was auctioned by Christie's in 1987,
and Gerald Guterman (briefly the owner of the Stanhope Hotel,
and famous for throwing a vast party on the luxury liner *QE2*),
who sold his collection at Sotheby's in New York on 14 January
1988. The latter collection included an exceptionally fine group
of Dutch paintings (landscapes, genre scenes, still lifes, and, to
his credit, history paintings and portraits – all recently purchased), many of which have found their way into other
distinguished American collections. Still other collectors choose
alternately to sell and donate their collections piecemeal; several
years ago, for example, the New York collector Emile Wolf left

perhaps the finest Jan Victors in existence, *The Expulsion of Hagar*, to the Israel Museum in Jerusalem, but chose to sell the best paintings in his collection – an outstanding Bartholomeus Breenbergh *Landscape with Stoning of Saint Stephen* and Nicolaes Knupfer's *Solon before Croesus* – to the Getty Museum.[34] Still another important Washington area collector with an extensive Dutch collection (including, among other works, a lovely Hals, Berchem, Van der Neer [cat. no. 46], Van Goyen, Clara Peeters, Cornelis Bega, Jan van Walscapelle, Jan Davidsz de Heem, and Adriaen van de Venne) has cropped his collection in recent years (the Saenredam went to Fort Worth, the De Keyser to West Berlin, and a Van der Heyden is now on the market) only to move in new directions, such as Venetian art.

The shift from Dutch to Italian paintings is hardly unparalleled; Saul P. Steinberg, the immensely successful financier and corporate raider who owns one of the finest collections of Dutch and Flemish art in New York (including both Hals and Rembrandt), has been attracted increasingly to Italian painting, a predisposition that might have been anticipated by his acquisition of Sweerts's grand and haunting *Plague in an Ancient City*.[35] On the other hand, Barbara Piasecka Johnson's ownership of Karel du Jardin's *Saint Paul Healing the Lame Man in Lystra* (p. 72, fig. 16) and the *Saint Praxedis* attributed improbably to Johannes Vermeer demonstrates that Italian old master collectors can also be drawn to Northern history painters working in a Southern vein. Despite the present overheated art market, it is a rare collector who is in it only for the money. Even commercial institutional buyers of Dutch paintings, like the ill-fated David Paul of Florida-banking-fiasco-fame and Citibank's eminently

respectable Patrick Cooney, express a personal enthusiasm for the art. Indeed Paul's undoing was partly precipitated by his impetuous decision to hang the bank's paintings in his own apartments. At the very least, Paul acquiesced to the purchase of the right pictures, but having entered at the top of the market he was forced to sell too early.

Extensive knowledge of art history has never been a prerequisite for a successful collector; it is enough to have absorbed a large body of visual material and be able to read the surface of a picture and discern its state to develop a discriminating eye. Nevertheless, there have long been U.S. collectors (one thinks of Thomas Jefferson Bryan and John G. Johnson) with a strong historical sense as well as a connoisseur's skills. Moreover, today's private collectors are probably better informed about the history of art and connoisseurship than any previous generation. Typical of this species of seasoned and well-educated collector are George and Maida Abrams, who over a period of more than three decades have quietly assembled the foremost private collection of Dutch drawings in this country and probably the world (to be exhibited at The Pierpont Morgan Library, New York; the Rijksmuseum, Amsterdam; and the Albertina, Vienna, in 1991 and 1992).[36] Although the Abramses profess drawings to be their first love, they have simultaneously assembled a collection of paintings that can scarcely be considered adjunctive. The collection is particularly strong in landscapes and genre scenes. Among the highlights are an excellent Jacob van Ruisdael *Hilly Landscape with Rushing Stream* [**13**], a merry company by Jan Steen and a guardroom scene by Gerbrand van den Eeckhout, the well-known *Hunter in a*

12
Rembrandt
Saint Peter in Prayer
Panel, 59.1 x 47.8 cm (23¼ x 18 ⅞ in.)
Lower right: RHL 1631. (RHL in ligature)
Florida, private collection

13
Jacob van Ruisdael
Hilly Landscape with Rushing Stream
Canvas, 78.8 x 96.5 cm (31 x 38 in.)
Right, on the rock: JVRuisdael (JVR in ligature)
(ca. 1670)
Collection George and Maida Abrams

Landscape which is a collaborative effort between Cornelis and Herman Saftleven,[37] and one of Dirck Hals's finest high-life scenes [14]. Seeking out quality before famous names, the Abramses have been drawn to a fine Gillis d'Hondecoeter, a splendid early Cornelis Bega, and an important large *brunaille* by Adriaen van de Venne. Their searches have also been rewarded with discoveries, including a rare early Adriaen Bouwer which revealed its autograph monogram only after cleaning.

America has never claimed scholar-collectors of Dutch art of the importance (or, for that matter, wealth) of Abraham Bredius (1885-1946) and Frits Lugt (1884-1970), whose personal collections are preserved respectively in institutions in The Hague and Paris. However, at least one highly regarded Dutch art historian and spouse have assembled an impressive group of smaller cabinet-sized paintings, including excellent still lifes like the Balthasar van der Ast in this show (cat. no. 3), a superb Christoffel van den Berghe, a Jan Jansz den Uyl, and, among other subjects, a fine small-scale *Portrait of Samuel Ampzing* by Frans Hals, a tiny Wtewael *Supper at Emmaus* on copper, and a lovely domestic genre scene by Jan Baptist Weenix.[38] Other academics and curators treasure a few odd but often distinguished Dutch pictures in their studies. The economist who has revealed so much about the seventeenth-century art market through his studies of the Delft archives, John Michael Montias, has built up a very respectable collection, acquiring several important Dutch religious paintings, including two images of Mary Magdalen by the Haarlem artists Hendrick Goltzius [15] and Jan de Bray, well before the prices for such paintings rose so prohibitively in recent years.

15
Hendrick Goltzius
Mary Magdalen with an Angel
Panel, 125.8 x 95.2 cm (49½ x 37½ in.)
Lower right: HG / *1610* (HG in ligature)
Collection Prof. and Mrs. John Michael Montias

14
Dirck Hals
Merry Company
Panel, 38.7 x 51.5 cm (15¼ x 20¼ in.)
Right, on the colomn: DHALS. *an 1625*
Collection George and Maida Abrams

16
Caesar van Everdingen
Violinist (Self-Portrait?) with a Woman Singing
Canvas, 106 x 83.5 cm (41 ³/₄ x 32 ⁷/₈ in.)
Neither signed nor dated (ca. 1630)
New York, collection Malcolm Wiener

One need only be open-minded, not prescient, to buy ahead of the market. The New York collector Malcolm Wiener, for example, has discovered the quality of pre-Rembrandtist and Haarlem classicist paintings, recently acquiring a Jacob Pynas,[39] and an unpublished Caesar van Everdingen [16] – the type of paintings that are still probably undervalued. With the prospect of finding an outstanding Ter Borch or Metsu genre scene becoming ever more remote, private collectors have discovered the charms of the guardroom painters, like Jacob Duck (in the Peter Eliot collection),[40] Simon Kick (in an extensive collection of several dozen Dutch paintings in Burlingame, California),[41] and Willem Duyster [17]. Proof that even well-financed collectors now seek quality before names, the last mentioned (an important and, I believe, again unpublished work by this gifted but short-lived painter) is the property of the Florida collector who owns

Rembrandt's *Saint Peter in Prayer* [12]. Similarly, with exceptional marines of any scale by the likes of Willem van de Velde and Jan van de Cappelle becoming increasingly scarce, American collectors have turned to masterpieces by lesser-known specialists like Lieve Verschuier [18]. Still other collectors, like Dr. and Mrs. Richard W. Levy in New Orleans, have been drawn to Dutch Italianate artists like Bartholomeus Breenbergh and Cornelis van Poelenburch (including a collaboration with Jan Both), who, though patronized by the stadholder and well-priced in their own times, have yet to be resuscitated by the modern market.

America's private collectors of Dutch art are broadcast and reveal few regional characteristics apart from the fact that New York collectors tend to be richer and benefit from closer proximity to the supply of art, claiming the major auction houses and dealers. Ann Jensen Adams and Egbert Haverkamp-

19
Willem Claesz Heda
Still Life with Tankard and Oyster
Panel, 50.2 x 83.5 cm (19 ³/₄ x 32 ⁷/₈ in.)
Center, on the knife: HEDA / *1636*
West Coast, private collection

Begemann assembled a handsome selection of paintings owned privately in New York at the exhibition held at the National Academy of Design in New York in 1988.[42] Some of the finest pictures in that show, including Steen's lovely little *Bathsheba* illustrated on the cover and two of the charmingly naive Jacob Vrels, are from a collection that also includes stunning nineteenth-century and impressionist paintings – proof that many of the finest collections still resist parochialism or confinement to any single school. Another West Coast collector has set a breathtaking standard of quality in recent acquisitions, purchasing the Willem Claesz Heda of 1636 that sold last year in Paris [19], a fine Van Goyen, and the Verschuier mentioned above [18]. Only a few months ago they bought an outstanding pair of Salomon van Ruysdaels. In 1979 James Welu exhibited a group of Dutch paintings from greater New England private collections at the Worcester Art Museum that sampled the variety of art in the region, revealing much modest charm.[43] Some of the paintings (for example, the Hondius and the Van der Poel) have since been given to Worcester, but others, like Steen's important *Tavern Scene* and the frisky works by Hendrick Pot and Pieter Quast, remain in private hands. The Boston area also has several relatively new and very promising collectors who have assembled a variety of Dutch paintings including some fine genre scenes and landscapes; notable among the latter is a well-preserved early Salomon van Ruysdael with a tumbled-down farmhouse [20].[44] The Ruisdael exhibition held in Cambridge in 1982 and the survey show of Dutch landscape mounted in Boston in 1988 probably helped foster these interests.

Today's American collectors buy at auction more regularly than their forebears but also, as with past generations, rely on dealers for information, expertise, and guidance. A few form special relations with individual merchants; for example, Senator Heinz works closely with Peter Tillou, a dealer in both American and Netherlandish art. Others make the rounds of the galleries in New York, London, and the Netherlands, forming many contacts and ties. In addition to the venerable triumvirate of Sam Nijstad, Hans Cramer, and John Hoogsteder in The Hague, a somewhat younger generation of dealers, including Charles Roelofsz in Amsterdam, Otto Naumann, Bob Haboldt, and Adam Williams (Newhouse Galleries) in New York, Johnny van Haeften and Rob Noortman in London, and Roman Herzig in Galerie St. Lucas in Vienna, has fostered and supplied these new collectors. Curators like Arthur Wheelock at the National Gallery of Art, Walter Liedtke at the Metropolitan Museum of Art, and until recently Frits Duparc in Montreal, and scholars like Egbert Haverkamp-Begemann and Seymour Slive have also successfully cultivated collectors, serving in the traditional roles of consultants and advisors.

Just as the collection of Van Horne, R.B. Angus, Sir George A. Drummond, and Frank Wood should be mentioned in any thorough history of twentieth-century North American collecting of Dutch art, so too at least two other contemporary

20
Salomon van Ruysdael
Landscape with Farmhouse
Panel, 30.6 x 42.5 cm (12 x 16 ³/₄ in.)
Lower right: *S.v. RUYESDAEL 1629*
Boston, private collection

collectors in Canada today deserve recognition. One of these resides in Vancouver and has acquired an attractive little group of works by Aelbert Cuyp, Gerrit Heda, Brekelenkam, and others. Of far greater importance is a Montreal collector who has assembled more than 120 old masters with a special emphasis on Dutch and Flemish artists. The collection is not only extensive and unusually discerning, with outstanding examples by many lesser-known painters, but rivals in sheer quality any that has been assembled on this continent in the last score of years. As befits the cosmopolitan city where the collection resides, it has something of a European flavor in its broad and unconventional representation of the individual genre. There are not only two lovely little lozenge-shaped panels of heads by Frans Hals and an equally diverting pair by Salomon de Bray, but also excellent genre scenes by Dou, Brekelenkam, and Codde, as well as Cornelis de Man.[45] The landscapes claim a superb Salomon van Ruysdael *View of Nijmegen* from the Guterman sale, a rare winter

scene by Jacob van Ruisdael, works by Cornelis Vroom, and first-rate paintings by Simon de Vlieger and Aert van der Neer, as well as outstanding Dutch Italianate paintings by Van Poelenburch, Breenbergh, Both, Berchem (from the Girardet collection), and Pijnacker, as well as a dazzling Wouwermans with horses and bathers [**21**].[46] The still lifes include an excellent late Pieter Claesz as well as fine examples by Coorte, Van Aelst, and Van Beyeren. A recent acquisition is a Jan Davidsz de Heem *Flower Still Life* [**22**], a painting of great resolution and pristine clarity. This is the type of brilliant masterpiece that would be welcome in virtually any Dutch collection. It is testament,

▲ **22**
Jan Davidsz de Heem
Flower Still Life
Copper, 49.2 x 38.4 cm (19 ³/₈ x 15 ¹/₈ in.)
On the edge of the table: *J.D. De Heem f.* (ca. 1660–1665)
Montreal, private collection

◀ **21**
Philips Wouwermans
River Landscape with Bathers
Canvas, 68 x 104 cm (26 ³/₄ x 41 in.)
Lower right: *PHILS. W* (PHILS in ligature) (ca. 1650–1655)
Montreal, private collection

23
Johannes Verspronck
Portrait of Andries Stilte
Canvas, 101.6 x 76.2 cm (40 x 30 in.)
Not signed, lower left: : *1640* :
Montreal, private collection

however, to this particular collector's independence of mind, and certainly of taste, that it hangs near the *Portrait of Andries Stilte* [**23**] by Johannes Verspronck, an artist who rarely rises above the conventional but who has here masterfully captured all the swagger and self-confidence of the age.

Surveying the continent's diversity of private collectors leaves little doubt that the traditional American love affair with Dutch art continues unabated, indeed with ardor. I have touched here only on the most distinguished and successful; just as in Europe and elsewhere, there are many more mediocre or poorer agglomerations of paintings, assembled by the merely ambitious, credulous, or ill-informed, than truly great collections. Yet even without a full census and statistical study, several trends emerge. American collectors are still more readily drawn to domestically scaled landscape, still life, and genre scene than to portraits or history paintings and tend to be more specialized in these tastes. There is, of course, no seventeenth-century precedent for such specialization, and indeed few parallels in later centuries.

Perhaps for the same reasons, the best larger North American collectors tend to be less concerned than their European counterparts about the historical comprehensiveness of their collections; it is a rare collector on this side of the Atlantic who will buy a painting simply because the artist is considered worthy historically. Americans' proverbial disregard for history, noted already by De Tocqueville, thus still has its healthy manifestations. On the other hand, American collectors have often been in the vanguard of stylistic revivals; in this century they preceded European collectors, for example, in acquiring Dutch Italianate art. Whether the achievements of today's collectors will be remembered as those of their forebears may again ironically hinge on the tax laws, which now tend to encourage the dispersal of estates. Civic largesse could conceivably make a comeback, but its return would surely be hastened if individuals could expect to donate their collections to public museums and still provide for their descendants. Dr. Bader's recent gift of thirty-seven paintings to Queen's University is an exceptional case of beneficence that ensures at least one collector's memory will survive in perpetuity.

1 The history of individual American museums' collections of Dutch art is briefly recounted in the entries to *Sutton 1986*.
2 See the introduction to *Bowron 1983*.
3 These trends were noted by all the attending museum directors but most clearly outlined by Neil Rubenstine of the Andrew W. Mellon Foundation, at the conference 'The Economics of Art Museums,' organized by Martin Feldstein's National Bureau of Economic Research, Inc., in Boston, Mass., 30 November-2 December 1989.
4 *Murphy 1985*. More recent acquisitions are published in the museum's annual reports.
5 *Boston 1972*
6 For all of the above, see *Baetjer 1980*. The Frans Post is inv. no. 1981.318.
7 *Szabo 1975*, figs. 72-82
8 *Pope-Hennessy 1984*
9 *Sutton 1990*, pp. 79-83, no. 28 and fig. (Van den Eeckhout), pp. 158-161, no. 57 and fig. (De Lairesse), and p. 353, no. 130 and fig. (Weenix)
10 *Minneapolis 1986*, pp. 56-63
11 *Cleveland 1982*, nos. 121, 106, 126, 117, 118, 102, 109, and 93
12 *Toledo 1976*
13 *Haverkamp-Begemann 1978-A*
14 See *Worcester 1974* and more recent issues of the museum's bulletin, like *Welu 1975*.
15 See *Ward 1987*, nos. 57 and 63; *Goheen 1988*, nos. 20 and 22
16 *Fort Worth 1987*, p. 213
17 *Schaefer / Fusco / Wiens 1987*, pp. 46, 49, 54, and 55
18 *Brown 1986-A*
19 For selected examples, see *Malibu 1986* and *Fredericksen 1988*. The Getty's acquisitions are listed in their entirety at the back of *The J. Paul Getty Museum Journal*.
20 *Lowenthal 1986*
21 *Naumann 1981*; *Sluijter et al. 1988*; *Hecht 1989-1990*

22 *Valentiner 1909*

23 *Waagen 1837-1839*; *Waagen 1843-1845*; *Waagen 1854*; *Strahan 1879*; *Durand-Gréville 1887*, pp. 65-75, 220-255. Unfortunately for our purposes, Strahan reviewed only contemporary (nineteenth-century) art, and Durand-Gréville confined his remarks to French painting in U.S. private collections. No comparable nineteenth-century survey exists for Dutch art.

24 *Herrmann 1980*

25 *Walker 1980*

26 *Walsh / Schneider 1981-1982*

27 *Flanigan 1986*

28 *Bergström / Wheelock 1989*

29 A rare case of similar specialization is the collection of T.W.H. Ward at Oxford, see *Van Gelder 1950*.

30 See the various publications and catalogues of the exhibitions of the Bader Collection: *Kalamazoo 1967*; *Bader 1968*; *Stechow 1974*; *Bader 1976*; *Varriano 1979*; *Parrish 1980*; *McTavish 1984*.

31 *McTavish 1984*, p. viii

32 *Robinson 1984*

33 *Bruyn et al. 1982*, pp. 576-580, no. C 22 and fig.

34 For selections from the Wolf collection, see *Robinson 1982*; for the Victors, see *Zafran 1976*, pp. 92-120.

35 *Haverkamp-Begemann / Adams 1988*, no. 29

36 *Robinson 1969-A* and *Williamstown 1973*

37 *Sutton et al. 1987-1988*

38 For the Van den Berghe, Hals, Weenix, and Wtewael, see *Haverkamp-Begemann / Adams 1988*, nos. 3, 24, 58, and 62.

39 *Sutton et al. 1987-1988*, pp. 423-424, no. 75 and fig.

40 *Philadelphia / Berlin / London 1984*, pp. 192-193, no. 38, fig. and pl. 40

41 *Philadelphia / Berlin / London 1984*, pp. 227-228, no. 58, fig. and pl. 41

42 *Haverkamp-Begemann / Adams 1988*

43 *Welu 1979*

44 *Sutton et al. 1987-1988*, pp. 323-324, no. 34 and fig. (Van Goyen), pp. 336-337, no. 40 and fig. (Joris van der Haagen), and pp. 497-499, no. 105 and fig. (Esaias van den Velde). The owner of the latter two also owns an excellent Asselijn (*Steland-Stief 1971*, no. 66).

45 *Philadelphia / Berlin / London 1984*, pp. 178-179, no. 29, fig. and pl. 15 (Codde), pp. 181-182, no. 31, fig. and pl. 52 (Dou), pp. 245-247, no. 69, fig. and pl. 118 (De Man)

46 *Sutton et al. 1967-1988*, pp. 288-287, no. 18 and fig. (Van de Cappelle), p. 381-383, no. 59 and fig. (Van der Neer), pp. 514-516, no. 113 and fig. (De Vlieger)

Catalogue

Introduction to the Catalogue
In Search of the History of Paintings: 1591-1991

The acquisition of *The Mill* by 'Rembrandt' (Washington, National Gallery of Art) [1] from the collection of Lord Lansdowne was for a long time considered to be the sensation of the century in the American art world. The impact of this somewhat inflated transaction is still felt today, when completely contradictory opinions on the painting are being voiced. Even after a recent cleaning of the canvas, John Walker, Director Emeritus of the National Gallery, is prepared to take back little of his claim that '*The Mill* is Rembrandt's supreme achievement in landscape painting.'[1] This statement is only an echo of the enormous fame that this painting once enjoyed. The opinion of the experts of the Rembrandt Research Project stands diametrically opposed. According to them, it has no place in Rembrandt's oeuvre – something that had in any case been observed earlier by other connoisseurs. At present, they attribute it to Ferdinand Bol on stylistic grounds, and appear to be not in the least impressed by the provenance from a famous English collection.[2]

In 1911 Lord Lansdowne, who was a trustee of the National Gallery in London, asked 100,000 pounds for his 'Rembrandt.' He was prepared to let the English State have it for 5,000 less, but Isabella Stewart Gardner of Boston and Peter A.B. Widener of Philadelphia vied for the honor of being allowed to pay the full amount. The railroad baron won. In the general excitement of the moment several critical comments, in which the attribution to Rembrandt was questioned, were ignored.[3] Only a very few were astonished by the extremely high price that was demanded for a painting that an ancestor of the marquess had bought for only 800 guineas.[4] The popularity of the piece had taken on legendary dimensions. That the work depicts a mill apparently had a fruitful effect on the nineteenth-century spirit, with its predilection for the romantic. It was believed that this was the mill of Rembrandt's father, where the young artist was to have discovered chiaroscuro in the grinding loft. Light-dark was after all the theme of his life's story. The archetypal Dutch mill is still one of the most popular folkloristic themes of the Rembrandt mythology.[5]

The legend may also take form within the somewhat more limited framework of the arthistorical literature. During a journey through Poland in 1897, Abraham Bredius, Director of the Mauritshuis, discovered a previously unknown 'Rembrandt' at Dzikóv Castle, a work that later acquired fame as *The Polish Rider* (New York, Frick Collection) [2].[6] He was able to get the painting on loan for the great Rembrandt exhibition of 1898 – the year of Queen Wilhelmina's coronation – in Amsterdam, where it drew the attention of the rich foreign collectors who

1
Ferdinand Bol (formerly attributed to Rembrandt)
The Mill
Canvas, 87.5 x 105.5 cm (34 1/2 x 41 1/2 in.)
Neither signed nor dated (ca. 1650)
Washington, National Gallery of Art,
inv. no. 1942.9.62

had come there to window-shop. In 1910 the coal and steel magnate Henry C. Frick (p. 45, fig. 32) finally succeeded in buying it from the Polish Count Tarnowski for 60,000 pounds. In 1944, in a lengthy exegesis, the art historian Julius Held elevated this portrait to an iconological monument, which he interpreted as a history piece, a *Miles Christianus*, an almost visionary painting. With respect to this point of view, a discussion later arose in which Held continued to participate enthusiastically until 1983.[7] It turned out to be of crucial importance whether the painting came from old Eastern European property, thus probably being 'only' an ancestral portrait. The battle of the pens would probably never have occasioned such strong feelings if the equestrian piece had from the first been attributed to

Willem Drost, who, according to a recent opinion, may possibly have been the painter.[8] In both the case of *The Mill* and that of *The Polish Rider* the provenance turned out to be in part responsible for the appreciation and even the explanation of the meaning of the work of art. In view of their interesting early history, neither painting would have been at all out of place in the present exhibition, because in the accompanying catalogue the history of the provenance runs like a red thread through the descriptions of the works of art. Alas, due to all sorts of restrictions imposed by the owners, the ideal exhibition may be realized only on paper.

Although in most catalogues the provenance of a painting is summed up only as a list, there is in many cases a whole story to be told. This catalogue deals with four centuries of the history of collecting, from the earliest mention of a Dutch collection in 1591 (cat. no. 8, note 15) to the presentation of this exhibition in Holland and America in 1990-1991. The best paintings often have a dramatic or triumphant past before they come to lead the quiet life of the museum piece. In the process of research, this history generally turned out to have been poorly investigated or to have large gaps. Particularly the earliest vicissitudes of each painting remain a mystery for numerous current owners, who often take satisfaction with vague claims that it came from old (preferably English) family property (cat. nos. 36, 40, 51, 52, and 65). Typical are the works with a provenance from the Hope collection (cat. nos. 47, 49, and 59), of which it was emphatically claimed around 1900 that they had been bought in the seventeenth century by the ancestors of this banking family 'from the easels of the artists.' It was totally forgotten that the core of the Hope collection had once been assembled by the Bisschop brothers (cat. no. 59, fig. 1), in Rotterdam, who, in the middle of the eighteenth century had set up one of the first museums of the Netherlands on the Leuvehaven of that city. In several texts the coll[ectie] Bisschop was even turned into 'colonel Bisschop.'

Also striking was the fate of the *Danaë* by Hendrick Goltzius (cat. no. 22), which became famous through the description by his friend Van Mander. Until 1777 this masterpiece hung in several well-known Amsterdam collections, after which it suddenly disappeared to remote places in Eastern Europe. It emerged around 1900 in the Parisian art market, but before a sensible museum director was able to react it was lost once more: five years ago the painting was encountered in a neglected state in a warehouse in Los Angeles. Once again the art world experienced a sensation when in 1984 the canvas was auctioned for three quarters of a million dollars.

The history of a painting's provenance is subject to the vagaries of fate, but it is naturally also determined by changes in taste. *Rediscoveries in Art* by Francis Haskell offers a fascinating examination of 'Some Aspects of Taste, Fashion & Collecting in England & France.'[9] Pursuing this line of thinking, the present catalogue attempts to sketch a picture of the past and present situations in these fields in Holland and America. During the selection of paintings for this exhibition, it soon became apparent that the behavior of collectors was indeed determined by fashion: the *fijnschilders*, long beloved in the fatherland, have only recently gathered a following in the United States (cat. no. 44). That is equally true of the Mannerists (cat. nos. 8 and 73), the Italianizing landscape painters (cat. nos. 6, 11, and 14), the

flower still life (cat. nos. 1, 3, 12, and 66), and history painters (cat. nos. 13, 14, 22, 61, 62, and 73). Recent exhibitions, primarily in the Netherlands, have stimulated renewed interest in these genres.[10]

At the same time, the account of the provenance of the works in this exhibition illustrates the wealth of small, often qualitatively eminent, collections of ordinary bourgeois amateurs to be found in all the large cities of the Netherlands of the eighteenth century. These private cabinets, which were then still a matter of course, had a century later turned into a rarity. Today, only a handful of private collections of old art remain in the Netherlands, whereas, in contrast, the number constantly increases in the United States. Rarely before 1800 did anyone give thought to the preservation of the national art patrimony, as, for instance, when the Braamcamp collection was to be auctioned in 1771 (cat. no. 54, fig. 1): this 'Cabinet [...] deserved to be transferred to a Princely Palace, and thus to be preserved in honor of its Founder, and to be withdrawn from oblivion' (in translation), Ploos van Amstel wrote with concern.[11] Long before this thought was to be realized by the foundation of public museums or of a Rembrandt Society (for the preservation of art in the Netherlands), numerous renowned cabinets had been dispersed over foreign collections. In the confusion of the French Revolution, many Dutch masters ended up in the great collections in and outside London. When around 1900 the Americans became active on the art market, they initially modeled their collections closely on what was then still assembled in the English country residences. Thus, for instance, Andrew Mellon (cat. no. 53, fig. 5) wanted a collection like that of Lord Hertford, which is now known as the Wallace Collection in London. The result was that paintings of the Dutch golden century came to be placed at the top of the American wish lists. How the collectors in the United States refined their initially conservative taste (Rembrandt, Ruisdael, Hobbema, Vermeer) into a much broader range of interests is elucidated in the essay by Walter Liedtke in the present publication.

Such observations of a general nature are the result of the research that has been carried out here on the history of the provenance of each work of art. It was an exciting business to find out how a portrait by Rembrandt of a militiaman of The Hague could end up in San Francisco (cat. no. 50), or why *The Art of Painting* by Frans van Mieris (cat. no. 44) was not preserved for the Netherlands (it proved impossible for the Mauritshuis to gather three quarters of a million guilders for a painting the size of a substantial postage stamp). Though the Dutch past of whole collections had sometimes been long forgotten by American owners, it turned out even more often that over the years a painting had come to be estranged from the Dutch themselves: 'out of sight, out of mind' is a repeatedly applicable saying. That is why rediscoveries could be made in a field that had seemed so familiar to us. For example, the recently cleaned *Flower Still Life with Watch* by Willem van Aelst (cat. no. 1) established that an alternate version, which was presumed to be the original, is nothing more than a copy. Thus a splendid, authentic, and newly discovered Van Aelst may be seen at this exhibition. Long ago Jan Lingelbach's *Italian Harbor* (cat. no. 40) was in the possession of Anthony Bierens, the organizer of the once-renowned but since completely forgotten *physisch kabinet* in Amsterdam. Such once-famous collections, when dispersed, are easily forgotten. Who still recalls the Van Loon collection of the year 1850 (cat. no. 34), the 'Gallerie Six' of the year 1900 (cat. no. 6), or the Dreesmann Museum of the year 1950 (cat. no. 61)? Paulus Potter's *Horse Stable with Figures* (cat. no. 49) may also be called a rediscovery, as even some insiders did not know that it had ended up in Philadelphia. Much the same is true for Ruisdael's *Spruce Trees at a Waterfall* (cat. no. 55) in Raleigh. The provenance of Vermeer's *Girl Writing a Letter* (cat. no. 67), which we initially assumed to be well known, had to be partly rewritten.

Our investigations also yielded other surprises. Altogether spectacular is the trompe-l'oeil by Van der Spelt, one half of which turns out to have been painted by Frans van Mieris (cat. no. 57). It speaks volumes that we did not notice this any earlier. Also shown here are divers paintings that remained obscure because they have for a long time been in private hands, including those of the relatively inaccessible Rothschilds (cat. no. 32, 34, and 45) or of the even more reclusive owners such as Ernest Cook of Bath (cat. no. 36). The dealer Richard Feigen has continuously had in his collection two paintings by Breenbergh (cat. no. 14) that have only rarely been shown to the public. Jan Asselijn's *Frozen Canal* (cat. no. 2; earlier in the Verkolje collection in Amsterdam) is newly discovered here. Several paintings that have become public property only recently were selected for precisely that reason: Jan van Goyen's *Riverscape with the Pellecussen Gate* (cat. no. 24) and Ruisdael's *Rough Sea at a Jetty* (cat. no. 54), which (just like Potter's *Horse Stable*) came from the Braamcamp cabinet. A work of art that is described here for the first time is the key piece in the oeuvre of the aging Willem van de Velde the Younger and his closest collaborators (cat. no. 65). Also highly satisfying, finally, is that the portraits of two married couples by Frans Hals (cat. nos. 27-28) and Rembrandt (cat. nos.

51-52) could temporarily be reunited. Finally, the method of research applied deserves some explanation because we employed several new points of departure.

Facts without context did not seem of interest to us. Accordingly, the unadorned announcement that *The Art of Painting* by Frans van Mieris (cat. no. 44) was bought in 1765 by Johan van der Marck is recounted here as part of a story about the acquisition by that culturally oriented ex-burgomaster of Leyden of a work, renowned in the arthistorical literature, by the much lauded painter of that city. Another example: it was not known until now that, for a considerable time, the name of Creejans van Winter hid behind the more anonymous term 'Van Winter collection' (cat. no. 6). Along with Catherine the Great, she was one of the few women collectors active before 1900. More relevant than the simple fact that Pierpont Morgan bought a Vermeer in 1907 (cat. no. 67) seemed to be the revelation that he had never heard of the painter until then. Admittedly of an anecdotal nature, but no less significant, we consider the information that the man who acquired Rembrandt's *Portrait of Joris de Caulerij* (cat. no. 50) in 1891 had tried to buy the Column of Trajan for 250,000 dollars.

To the standard research, such as the ordering and analysis of the index cards of Hofstede de Groot in the unsurpassed Rijks-bureau voor Kunsthistorische Documentatie in The Hague, we here added research into the personal history of the collector or donor. We concentrated on the Dutch and American collectors who, whenever possible, have been placed in their time by their dates of birth and death, and by a biographical note. This required detective work in archives and specialized libraries, and sometimes inquiries to insiders as well. An index of the names of collectors, dealers, and museums has been compiled for the user of this catalogue. The results of this too brief period of research confirmed what Haskell pointed to in his *Rediscoveries in Art*: a broad and fallow field for research.[12]

We have attempted to go a step beyond what has thus far been customary in such studies.[13] The nature and size of the collection from which a painting came were sometimes the occasion for an essential atmospheric description. When necessary, intermediaries – dealers, heirs, brokers – were also assigned individual features.[14] Thus Pieter Fouquet, Jr. (cat. no. 2, fig. 2, and cat. no. 6, fig. 1), became a familiar figure to us, turning out to have been the dealer who supplied many French and English collectors of the late eighteenth century with Dutch paintings. Thus it could be established that in 1777 Ploos van Amstel, who had earlier pleaded for the preservation of the Braamcamp

3
Ludwig Knaus
Portrait of Gustav Waagen
Canvas, 56.5 x 42 cm (22 ¼ x 16 ½ in.)
Upper right: *L. Knaus. 1855.*
Berlin, Nationalgalerie, inv. no. A I 1094

no. 70, fig. 1). He was incessantly active in the promotion of old Dutch art in the New West. As organizer of exhibitions and author of numerous publications, he gave the American nation a 'crash course' in becoming a worthy guardian of this somewhat orphaned Dutch art. That his book *Rembrandt Paintings in America* of 1931 describes many paintings that would no longer appear to be by the great master (such as *The Mill* and *The Polish Rider*) is above all symbolic of the enthusiasm with which Dutch art of the seventeenth century was collected in America.[16] His big-hearted approach has in the meantime given way to the much more cautious modern arthistorical methods. Now American scholars also make discoveries in Dutch archives, as Michael Montias demonstrated when, among other things, he revealed the name of Vermeer's true Maecenas (cat. no. 67).

In conclusion, one could say that the historical setting has become the most important subject of the research on the works of art in this catalogue. With hindsight it appears that comparisons of such marginal phenomena yield an insight into the sometimes bizarre capriciousness of taste. Here the reader may learn how the spirit of the times decreed that Cuyp's *Ships on the Maas River at Dordrecht* (cat. no. 17) was called world famous at the same moment that the *Self-Portrait at Age Fifty* by Dou (cat. no. 18) was rejected from a German museum collection on

collection, sold Goltzius's *Danaë Receiving Zeus as a Shower of Gold* (cat. no. 22) from this collection, which is how it ended up in Latvia and later in South Silesia. In addition, both past and recent eyewitnesses who have visited and described collections have been cited: from Carel van Mander to Peter Sutton. The letters of museum director Gustav Waagen [3], who, in 1837, saw the Van der Spelt (cat. no. 57) hanging next to *The Box Bed* by Pieter de Hooch (cat. no. 35) in Stafford House in London, remain a rich source from which to draw. Waagen's writings (and many other nineteenth-century publications) are too often neglected as an aid in the establishment of a provenance.[15]

The bibliographical research centered on collection and exhibition catalogues, and on articles in American periodicals, because they helped form an idea of the public reception of a painting in the United States. We have therefore added an overview of the exhibitions in America in which the works of the Dutch masters of the golden century were on view. Of the authors in the list of biographical abbreviations, the name of one art historian stands out: Wilhelm (William) Valentiner [4] (cat.

4
Wilhelm Valentiner
Self-Portrait
Colored pen drawing, 127 x 105 mm (5 x 4 ¼ in.)
On the shoulder: WRV *1901* (WRV in ligature)
Collection heirs Valentiner

the grounds that it was uninteresting or redundant. This fate was later to befall Jan de Bray's splendid *Banquet of Antony and Cleopatra* (cat. no. 13). Research into the history of paintings further makes it understandable why some canvases, such as the 'Wachtmeister Rembrandt' (cat. no. 53), have been handed down to us in lamentable condition, while it remains incomprehensible that, despite the intervention of incompetent restorers (cat. no. 32), other works have somehow retained their original freshness. It also provides the somewhat sobering observation that the fame of a work of art is closely tied to that of its owner. After all, at the Hudson-Fulton exhibition in 1909 (p. 39, fig. 24), the Americans goggled not so much at the paintings by Rembrandt as at the Rembrandts of Frick and Widener.[17] The selection of the paintings for this exhibition is a contribution to the fame of each of these masterpieces. We hope that the approach chosen here will add extra luster to this 'reunion with the masters.'[18]

1 Inv. no. 658; *Walker 1985*, p. 74, no. 358 and fig.

2 *Bruyn et al. 1989*, p. 49, no. 52 and fig. (with more literature in note 133)

3 *Von Seidlitz 1911*, pp. 550-552

4 *Connoisseur 1911*, p. 268

5 *Wheelock 1977-A*, pp. 27-29

6 Inv. no. 10.1.98; *New York 1968*, pp. 258-265 and fig.

7 *Held 1983*, pp. 37-69

8 *Bruyn 1984*, p. 158

9 *Haskell 1976*

10 *Blankert 1965*; *Amsterdam / Detroit / Washington 1980-1981*; *Segal 1982*; *Sluijter et al. 1988*; *Hecht 1989-1990*

11 *Ploos van Amstel 1771*, p. 149

12 *Haskell 1976*, pp. 3-8 pointed to the complexity of the material, which compelled him to limit himself to the mention of 'case-histories.'

13 Exemplar publications in this field were *Maclaren 1960*, which, however, supplied the annotations but no context, and *Hecht 1989-1990*, which did mention a (simplified) context, but gave no annotations.

14 Because of the dearth of time, we limited the research mainly to biographical reference works, making grateful use of the research in American sources that was carried out by Lynn Federle Orr, with the aid of Elise Breall.

15 *Waagen 1837-1839*; *Waagen 1854*

16 *Valentiner 1931*

17 See also the essay by Edwin Buijsen, p. 75

18 I wrote 'we' because the research for the material presented here was carried out together with Marjolein de Boer and Rieke van Leeuwen. I wish to thank as well the innumerable people who contributed in any manner whatsoever to the realization of this book.

List of Exhibited Paintings

1 Willem van Aelst *Flower Still Life with Watch*
2 Jan Asselijn *A Frozen Canal*
3 Balthasar van der Ast *Flowers in a Wan Li Vase*
4 Hendrick Avercamp *Winter Landscape*
5 Dirck van Baburen *The Procuress*
6 Nicolaes Berchem *A Moor Offering a Parrot to a Lady*
7 Abraham van Beyeren *Banquet Still Life*
8 Abraham Bloemaert *Moses Striking Water from the Rock (Aqua)*
9 Ferdinand Bol *'Portrait' of a Young Man with a Sword*
10 Gerard ter Borch *A Lady and Gentleman Making Music*
11 Jan Both *A Ford between Trees*
12 Dirck de Bray *Flowers in a Glass Vase*
13 Jan de Bray *The Banquet of Antony and Cleopatra*
14 Bartholomeus Breenbergh *The Preaching of Saint John the Baptist*
15 Hendrick ter Brugghen *Old Man Writing by Candlelight*
16 Pieter Claesz *Little Banquet*
17 Aelbert Cuyp *Ships on the Maas River at Dordrecht*
18 Gerard Dou *Self-Portrait at Age Fifty*
19 Gerbrand van den Eeckhout *Isaac Blessing Jacob*
20 Aert de Gelder *Allegory on Peace*
21 Aert de Gelder
    Esther and Mordecai Writing the Second Purim Letter
22 Hendrick Goltzius *Danaë Receiving Zeus as a Shower of Gold*
23 Jan van Goyen *View of Rhenen*
24 Jan van Goyen *Riverscape with the Pellecussen Gate*
25-26 Frans Hals *Portraits of a Seventy-Three-Year-Old Man and
    His Seventy-Two-Year-Old Wife*
27 Frans Hals *Portrait of a Man*
28 Frans Hals *Portrait of a Woman*
29 Bartholomeus van der Helst *Self-Portrait in 1655*
30 Jan van der Heyden
    View of the Dam and the Damrak in Amsterdam
31 Jan van der Heyden *An 'Amsterdam' Canal*
32 Meindert Hobbema *The Water Mills of Singraven near Denekamp*
33 Gerard van Honthorst *Young Woman Holding a Medallion*
34 Pieter de Hooch *A Mother with an Infant*
35 Pieter de Hooch *The Box Bed*
36 Pieter de Hooch *A Music-Making Family (the Del Court Family?)*
37 Willem Kalf *Still Life with Goblets and Lemon*

38 Philips Koninck *Panoramic Landscape*
39 Jan Lievens *A Bearded Man with a Beret*
40 Johannes Lingelbach *An Italian Harbor*
41 Nicolaes Maes *A Girl Plucking a Duck*
42 Gabriël Metsu *A Girl Receiving a Letter*
43 Gabriël Metsu *A Young Woman with a Cello*
44 Frans van Mieris *The Art of Painting*
45 Jan Miense Molenaer *Allegorical Engagement Portrait*
46 Aert van der Neer *'Kolf' Players on the Ice*
47 Adriaen van Ostade *Courtyard with a Woman Cleaning Mussels*
48 Adam Pijnacker *A Forest View with Hunters*
49 Paulus Potter *A Horse Stable with Figures*
50 Rembrandt *Portrait of Joris de Caulerij*
51 Rembrandt *Portrait of a Man Rising from His Chair*
52 Rembrandt *Portrait of a Sitting Woman*
53 Rembrandt *Portrait of a Young Man*
54 Jacob van Ruisdael *A Rough Sea at a Jetty*
55 Jacob van Ruisdael *Spruce Trees at a Waterfall*
56 Salomon van Ruysdael *River Landscape with a Ferry*
57 Adriaen van der Spelt and Frans van Mieris
    A Trompe-l'Oeil with a Flower Piece and a Curtain
58 Jan Steen *Fantasy Interior with Jan Steen and Jan van Goyen*
59 Jan Steen *Dancing Couple at an Inn*
60 Jan Steen *Doctor's Visit*
61 Jan Steen *The Wrath of Ahasuerus*
62 Matthias Stomer *Lot Leaving Sodom*
63 Michael Sweerts *A Boy with a Hat*
64 Michael Sweerts *Self-Portrait as a Painter*
65 Willem van de Velde the Younger and Cornelis van de
    Velde(?) *An English Man-of-War at Anchor*
66 Simon Verelst *Full Daffodils in a Vase*
67 Johannes Vermeer *A Girl Writing a Letter*
68 Simon de Vlieger *View of a Beach*
69 Hendrick van Vliet *Interior of the Old Church in Delft*
70 Jan Baptist Weenix *Mother and Child in an Italian Landscape*
71 Emanuel de Witte
    Interior of the Old Church in Amsterdam during a Service
72 Philips Wouwermans *Merry and Rowdy Peasants at an Inn*
73 Joachim Wtewael *Saint Sebastian*

Ben Broos
with contributions by Lynn Federle Orr and Juliette Roding;
research by Marjolein de Boer

Catalogue numbers 31, 36, 61, 64, and 72 are not on view in
San Francisco.
Catalogue numbers 4, 23, 37, 42, and 73 are not on view in
The Hague.

Catalogue numbers 1-3, 6-14, 16-22, 24-29, 31-32, 34-36, 38-41,
43-62, 64-68, 70, and 72 are by Ben Broos [BB].
Catalogue numbers 4, 5, 15, 23, 33, 37, 42, and 73 are by
Lynn Federle Orr [LFO].
Catalogue numbers 30, 63, 64, 69, and 71 are by Juliette Roding
[JR].

Willem van Aelst

Delft 1627 – Amsterdam after 1683

Canvas, 67.6 x 54.5 cm (26 5/8 x 21 1/2 in.)
Lower left: *Guill.mo van Aelst. 1663*
San Francisco, Calif., The Fine Arts Museums of San Francisco, inv. no. (D) 51.21

Willem van Aelst was a pupil of his uncle Evert van Aelst in Delft, where he joined the guild in 1643. Around 1645 he undertook a journey to France and subsequently went to Italy, where he entered the service of the Grand Duke of Tuscany in Florence. In 1656 he was back in Holland. After 1657 he was active in Amsterdam as a painter of flower and game still lifes, of which the last dated work is from 1683. His style is that of the *fijnschilders*, and his compositions are always cunning and avoid repetition. Van Aelst introduced asymmetrical arrangements of bouquets, which he rendered with exceptionally handsome light effects and subtly interrelated colors.

Provenance
Auction Hawkins, London, 1936
Hermann Schuelein Collection, New York, 1936(?)-1951
The Fine Arts Museums of San Francisco, 1951 (gift of Mr. & Mrs. Hermann Schuelein)

Bibliography
Auction London 1936, p. 13, no. 85
San Francisco 1966, p. 140 and fig.
Haverkamp-Begemann 1980, pp. 210, 211 and note 35
Sutton 1986, p. 277 and fig. 417

One heart-warming effect of exhibitions such as the present one is that sometimes paintings that have previously lived in undeserved obscurity are placed in the limelight. This is such a painting. Thanks to a recent cleaning, it again sparkles as only the best still lifes of Willem van Aelst can. The recent exhibition in Delft, Cambridge, and Fort Worth, *A Prosperous Past*, proved that Van Aelst was a consummate master of his genre, one who could even render a herring so as to make one's mouth water.[1] When the Mauritshuis was reinstalled in 1987, two of his brilliant still lifes were chosen to flank the *View of Delft* by Jan Vermeer.[2] However, the subtlety of his brushwork is still so little understood that a copy after the still life in San Francisco has until now passed for an authentic Van Aelst (Oxford, Ashmolean Museum) [**1**].[3]

A meticulous comparison shows that in his superimposed layers of paint, the copyist was not able to achieve that sweetly flowing and softly melting quality to which the true *fijnschilder* owed his fame. For example, the reflections of light in the silver vase seem to be harsher in the copy in Oxford than in the original in San Francisco. An apparently authentic still life, which even has the signature of Willem van Aelst, has recently been characterized as a copy on account of the drier handling of the paint and the less fluid rendering of the lines (Rotterdam, Museum Boymans-van Beuningen).[4] Possibly in these instances the copyist or atelier assistant was Hendrick de Fromantiou, whose work was possibly signed by the master himself.[5]

1
Attributed to Hendrick de Fromantiou, after Willem van Aelst
Flower Still Life with Watch
Canvas, 66 x 53 cm (26 x 207/8 in.)
Neither signed nor dated (ca. 1663)
Oxford, Ashmolean Museum, inv. no. A 527

Willem van Aelst Flower Still Life with Watch

In the far from meager literature on the (floral) still life there is no mention of the painting in San Francisco. It was auctioned in 1936 from the estate of C.H.T. Hawkins, who, after the death of his spouse, Mrs. J.E. Hawkins, resided at 10 Portland Place in London.[6] The canvas was then (or later) bought by the beer brewer Hermann Schuelein (1884-1970), who went to the United States from Munich in 1936 and was nationalized there in 1944. He was the director of Liebmann-Rheingold Brewers in Brooklyn. In 1951, a year after the death of his wife, he donated the flower piece by Van Aelst to the museum in San Francisco.[7]

The flower still life by Willem van Aelst in the Mauritshuis [2] shows striking resemblances to that in San Francisco. Both works are signed *Guill[er]mo van Aelst* and dated 1663. With this signature the painter naturally alluded to his stay in Italy, where, until 1656, he worked for the Grand Duke of Tuscany. In the following year the painter was back in Amsterdam, and he apparently intended to refer emphatically to this residence by arranging his flower pieces in vases that can be recognized as works by the famous Amsterdam silversmith Johannes Lutma the Elder, whose portrait was etched by Rembrandt in 1656.[8] In paintings with dates from 1659 to 1663 we repeatedly encounter these vases in the relatively rigorous, symmetrical auricle (or lobe, cartilage, or *knörpel*) style (see also cat. no. 19, fig. 1).

Typical of both bouquets is the diagonal line that runs from the red roses at the lower left to the red poppy at the upper right [3]. This structure is one of the innovations that Van Aelst introduced to the flower still life of his time, the earlier compositions being characterized by greater stiffness (see cat. no. 3).[9] He achieved chiaroscuro effects through concentrated

3
Scheme of cat. no. 1 (drawing and research by Sam Segal)
1 Provins Rose *Rosa x provincialis* Mill.
2 French Marigold *Tagetes erecta* L.
3 Snowball *Viburnum opulus* L. cv. *Roseum*
4 Pale Iris *Iris pallida* Lam.
5 Opium Poppy *Papaver somniferum* L. *rubrum plenum*
6 African Marigold *Tagetes patula* L.
7 Tulip *Tulipa clusiana* Vent. x *T. stellata* Hook.
8 Carnation *Dianthus caryophyllus* L. bicolor subplenus
a Red Admiral *Vanessa atalanta* (L.)
b Painted Lady *Cynthia cardui* (L.)
c Dragonfly *Aeschna juncea* (L.)
d Wood Snail *Cepaea nemoralis* (L.)

lighting and the deliberate choice of light flowers (the white viburnum and the purple-white tulip) against a dark background of leaves. The color composition is artfully arranged with a harmonious division of cool and warm tints, while the metal of the vase and the surface of the gray-and-pink veined marble glow softly. A third flower piece of 1663, in the Ashmolean Museum in Oxford [4], is, probably incorrectly, believed to be a pendant of the copy [1]. There is no Lutma vase in this depiction, which is dominated by a diagonal piling up of flowers.[10] These three paintings of 1663 all feature blue leaves to a greater or lesser degree, which may be discolored by a too abrasive cleaning in the past, in which the yellow glaze was removed. It is nevertheless not out of the question that the painter may have intended such a green with a hint of blue. Bluish leaves are in any case highly characteristic for Van Aelst.[11]

2
Willem van Aelst
Flower Still Life with Watch
Canvas, 62.5 x 49 cm (24⅝ x 19¼ in.)
Lower left: *Guill.mo van Aelst. 1663*
The Hague, Mauritshuis, inv. no. 2

4
Willem van Aelst
Flower Still Life with a Slug
Canvas, 67 x 55 cm (26³/₈ x 21⁵/₈ in.)
Lower right: *Guill.mo van Aelst. 1663*
Oxford, Ashmolean Museum, inv. no. A 526

A tulip and an iris in one vase, as in the painting in San Francisco, is an unnatural phenomenon, and the painter knew this perfectly well. He wanted not only to delight the eye but to provoke his spectator into reflecting. To that end he painted an open watch next to the vase. For some time this had been a well-known attribute of *vanitas* still lifes and not easily misconstrued. Naturally it symbolizes the passing of time, and thus the vanity of existence in general.[12] Even more dramatically than in the painting in The Hague, the leaves of the flowers have been attacked by a creeping slug and are withered and rotten. Thus the displayed opulence itself is an image of glory soon to perish: 'the flower is a mirror of life, she blossoms but perishes in the wind' (cat. no. 3, fig. 6). A symbolic balance is provided by the butterflies and the dragonfly, which have been interpreted as signs of the resurrection.[13]

1 *Segal 1988-1989*, p. 250, nos. 58-59
2 Inv. nos. 2 and 3; *Hoetink et al. 1985*, p. 331, nos. 2-3 and fig.; *Broos 1986*, pp. 108-114, nos. 1-2 and fig.
3 *Van Gelder 1950*, pp. 30-31, no. 3
4 Inv. no. 1005; *Rotterdam 1962*, p. 17, no. 1005; *Meijer 1989*, pp. 50-51, no. 1 and fig.
5 *Meijer 1989*, p. 50; *Broos 1987*, pp. 18-19 and fig. 3, still described both works as being by Van Aelst.
6 *Auction London 1936*, title page
7 *WWWA*, vol. v, p. 643
8 B. 276; *Hollstein*, vol. XVIII, p. 129, no. 276, vol. XIX, pp. 224-225, no. 276 and fig.
9 *Bol 1969*, pp. 324-326
10 *Van Gelder 1950*, pp. 28-29, no. 2; *Bol 1969*, p. 325, fig. 295; see also *Broos 1987*, p. 19, note 9
11 *Groen 1987*, pp. 107-108 and figs. 45-46; *Struyck-van der Loeff 1987*, p. 114
12 Numerous examples in *Leyden 1970* and *De Jongh et al. 1982*; see also *Bergström 1947/1956*, pp. 189-190.
13 *Segal 1983*, pp. 40 and 53
BB

Jan Asselijn

Diemen ca. 1615 – Amsterdam 1652

Canvas, 67.4 x 106.1 cm (26½ x 41¾ in.)
Lower right: *J As[sel]y[n]* (ca. 1648)
Worcester, Mass., Worcester Art Museum, inv. no. 1969.24

Jan Asselijn presumably learned the trade of painting in Amsterdam from Jan Martsen the Younger, in whose manner he executed his earliest dated cavalry skirmishes of 1635 and 1636. Around 1639 he went to Rome, where the *schildersbent* (the local club of Netherlandish artists) nicknamed him 'Crabbetje' (Little Crab) on account of his misshapen hand. It is apparent from his predilection for genre-like scenes in the shadow of mighty ruins that Pieter van Laer must have been Asselijn's most important model there. Unfortunately, no dated work from Asselijn's Roman period remains.

In 1644, on his return from Italy, he married in Lyon and worked for some time in Paris, with his brother-in-law Nicolaes de Helt Stockade. By 1647 he was again in Amsterdam and there painted mainly landscapes in which the Dutch and southern elements are interwoven, such as a flat countryside ornamented with Roman monuments.

The number of Dutch private collections of paintings in the first half of the eighteenth century has neither been properly counted nor assessed for their quality. There must have been a great many of them. Although the names of many collectors are not known to us, it was definitely not just members of the upper strata of society who owned representative art collections.[1] This handsome winter landscape by Jan Asselijn used to be in such a middle-class Amsterdam collection, one that was composed primarily of paintings by masters of the Golden Age. The collector is known as Johannes (Jan) Verkolje, who, according to the title page of the catalogue of his collection, was the 'Son of the Painter JOHANNES VERKOLJE' (in translation).[2]

The genre and portrait painter Johannes Verkolje the Elder (1650-1693) was born in Amsterdam, but he worked in Delft, where he married in 1672. His three daughters later lived in Warmond (near Leyden), but his two sons established themselves in Amsterdam around 1700. Nicolaas Verkolje (1673-1746) became a portrait and history painter, engraver, and draftsman, whereas his ten-year-younger brother Johannes (Jan) Verkolje the Younger (1683-1755) chose the trade of (art) broker. In 1705 his name was entered in the register of brokers in Amsterdam,

Provenance

Collection Jan Jansz Verkolje, Amsterdam, before 1755
Collection Gerard Verkolje, Amsterdam, 1755-1762
Auction Verkolje, Amsterdam, 1763 (*f*305 to Pieter Fouquet)
Auction London, 1935
Auction London, 1937 (£20)
Collection Lady Frances Vyvyan, London, before 1950
Auction Vyvyan, London, 1950 (£25.4 to Bloch)
Dealer Duits, London
Private collection, England, 1964
Dealer Gooden & Fox, London, 1969
Worcester Art Museum, Worcester, 1969 (Eliza S. Paine Fund in memory of William R. and Frances T.C. Paine)

Bibliography

Auction Amsterdam 1763, p. 7, no. 34
Auction London 1935, p. 27, no. 190
Auction London 1937, p. 21, no. 92
Auction London 1950, p. 1, no. 1
Steland-Stief 1962-1963, vol. I, pp. 128, 174-175, vol. II, no. 237
Steland-Stief 1964, pp. 101-102 and 105 and fig. 1
Stechow 1966, p. 203, note 37
Art Quarterly 1969, pp. 439 and 445 and fig.
Catton Rich 1969, pp. x and XII
Steland-Stief 1970, pp. 62-63 and fig. 5
Steland-Stief 1971, pp. 77-78, 103-104, 107 and 164, no. 237 and pl. LI, p. 179, no. 335
Slive 1974, vol. I, pp. 77-79, vol. II, p. 552 and fig.
Nihom-Nijstad 1983, pp. 5-6 and note 5
Sutton 1986, p. 323 and fig. 479
Sutton et al. 1987-1988, pp. 250-251, no. 3 and fig.

Jan Asselijn A Frozen Canal

and, to give an example of his activity, on 18 April 1746 he auctioned the estate of his brother Nicolaas in the hall called the Keyserskroon (Emperor's Crown).[3] However, in the auction catalogue of his own collection there is mention of five mezzotints rendered by Johannes himself. One of these prints, *A Lady with a Parrot*, is now in the Rijksprentenkabinet (Amsterdam).[4] Further there exists a genre scene, *The Soldier and the Girl*, signed and dated 1707 (Mount Stuart, Scotland, collection the Marquess of Bute) [**1**], so that he may also be called an artist.[5]

Jan Verkolje the Younger left eighty-two paintings, largely by Dutch masters. Until now it has been assumed that he died in the year in which his estate was auctioned (1763), but that is a misunderstanding. The artist-broker had died a widower as early as 1755, and the collection then came to his only son, Gerard Verkolje, who was born in 1708. Gerard practiced the same trade as his father and was entered in the register of brokers in 1748.[6] He had married a year before the death of his father and was himself a widower when he died in 1763. He had no children, so that the collection of paintings and graphic arts that he had inherited from his father – which included the complete print oeuvre of his grandfather Johannes and uncle Nicolaas – had to be auctioned.[7] The painting by Jan Asselijn, 'A City View, depicting a Winter, the Ice, richly provided in the foreground with loaded Mules, Figures, and other Animals, in the background a burning Lime Kiln, all painted very handsomely and naturally on Canvas' (in translation), fell into the hands of Fouquet for the considerable amount of 305 guilders.[8]

Pieter Fouquet, Jr. (1729-1800) [**2**], became known as the man who personally arranged the sale of numerous Dutch paintings to foreign customers (see also cat. nos. 14, 44, 54, and 60). In 1753 he was registered in the guild of Saint Luke in Amsterdam as a painter and buyer of art but not as an art broker. In the period from 1750 to 1800 his name repeatedly crops up in the margins of annotated auction catalogues. For instance, at the Lormier auction, which also took place in 1763, he paid out no less than 20,000 guilders. At the Verkolje auction he spent 2,000 guilders.[9] If one encounters the name of Fouquet at a Dutch auction of the eighteenth century, the painting in question is almost certainly soon to be found in a French or English collection. There was even an auction held in London in 1773 of 150 paintings supplied by 'that celebrated collector De Heer Fouquet' and described as 'consigned from Amsterdam.'[10]

After the Verkolje auction, Fouquet presumably sold the painting by Jan Asselijn that is now in the Worcester Art Museum to a foreign buyer. For almost two centuries it dropped out of sight. In 1935 and 1937 it was offered for sale by auction houses in London as being from a private collection, a situation that repeated itself in 1950. At this latter auction, Lady Frances Vyvyan, residing at 9a Albany, Piccadilly, in London, is mentioned as the owner. She was presumably the widow of Captain William Geoffrey Vyvyan (1876-1914), who died in World War I. She herself passed away in 1964.[11] The painting remained in private hands until 1969. Much to her regret, Anne Charlotte Steland-Stief, the writer of a dissertation, articles, and, finally, a monograph on the artist, was not able to examine the painting itself.[12] In 1969 the Worcester Art Museum in Massachusetts became the owner of this remarkable painting, which was at last again to be seen in the Netherlands in 1987, at the great landscape exhibition in the Rijksmuseum.[13]

Of course it was observed on this occasion that a winter scene is actually a very unusual subject for a painter of mainly Italian or Italianizing landscapes. Most comparable with this subject is a canvas by Jan Asselijn, *Snowball Throwers by a Frozen Canal* (Schwerin, Staatliches Museum) [**3**], which was unfortunately lost during World War II.[14] Particularly noticeable in both works is the grim atmosphere of a severe, freezing day with ice-covered city walls under a slate-gray sky. In the painting in Worcester one sees that it has been below the freezing point for so long that the water level has gone down, so that the ice has broken and is sagging down. It is nevertheless thick enough to carry a host of people and animals. In the foreground one sees, among other things, how two men and a boy attempt to hoist several calves on a donkey.

It is plausible that Jan Asselijn made both these winter views in

1
Johannes Verkolje the Younger
The Soldier and the Girl
Canvas, measurements unknown
Lower left: *I. VERKOLY* / 1707
Mount Stuart, Scotland, collection the Marquess of Bute

1647 or 1648, when he had returned to Holland after his long stay in the sunny south.[15] After Asselijn's return, Rembrandt made a portrait etching of 'Crabbetje,' which is dated around 1648 [4].[16] In the first state of this etching, Asselijn poses with his palette and brushes, standing before a canvas on an easel. At the left of this painting we see a towering bulwark of the kind seen in his two winter views. In other words, he had himself portrayed as a painter who made such landscapes at the time. He had this trademark removed from the second state. It is but another argument for dating his wintry city views around 1648, that is, after Asselijn had returned from Italy and France.[17]

Steland-Stief pointed to the connection with the winter views of Nicolaes Berchem and Willem Schellinks. A painting by Schellinks (Amsterdam, Rijksmuseum)[18] used to be attributed to Jan Asselijn when it was in the famous collections of Herman ten Kate and Van Loon-Van Winter in Amsterdam. However, Steland-Stief spotted the monogram *W.S.* on this painting, which, with its sharp recession of the city wall, bright hole in the dark clouds, and burning lime kiln, certainly looks like an Asselijn.[19] The composition is comparable to that of a winter landscape signed *W. schellinks Ft* (The Netherlands, private collection),[20] with, at the right, mooring posts and ice floes looking like small white skirts that have been taken over directly from the painting by Asselijn. It seems likely that, at least in this latter painting, Schellinks borrowed the details directly from Asselijn, and that, in this monogrammed work, he allowed himself to be inspired by him to such a degree that it could be mistaken for an authentic Asselijn.[21]

A View of the City Wall of Haarlem in the Winter by Nicolaes Ber-

chem (Amsterdam, Rijksmuseum) [**5**][22] is dated 1647. Steland-Stief believed it, too, to be a variant on Asselijn's winter view, which, she argued, must therefore have been made in or before 1647.[23] It is more probable, however, that Asselijn instead worked after Berchem and other landscape painters active in Holland after he had returned from the south.[24] On the basis of this and similar examples, he formulated his composition with the diagonally receding city walls, still using the large stone blocks of his Roman ruins. This means that the winter view in Worcester must have been painted after, not before, 1647.

Although the city walls feature arches and details comparable to many of Jan Asselijn's drawings and paintings with Italian ruins or monuments, here he nevertheless sought to give an impression of a Dutch city in the grip of Jack Frost. Unlike most Italianizing painters, he took the trouble after returning from the south to paint something other than sun-drenched landscapes. In this celebration of the rigors of winter, the lime kiln does not need to be a derivation from Pieter van Laer's Italian depictions, and consequently a foreign element, as has sometimes been assumed.[25] It is a true Dutch motif, as is shown, for instance, by a drawing of the subject from 1653 by Jan van Goyen (Rotterdam, Museum Boymans-van Beuningen) [**6**].[26]

5
Nicolaes Berchem
A View of the City Wall of Haarlem in the Winter
Panel, 39.5 x 48.5 cm (15½ x 19 in.)
Left, on the wall: *CBerchem 1647*
Amsterdam, Rijksmuseum, inv. no. A 27

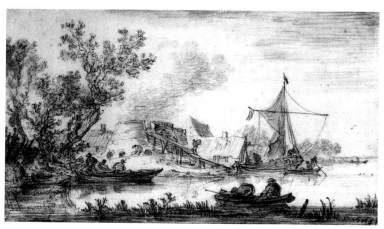

6
Jan van Goyen
A Lime Kiln
Chalk drawing, 120 x 199 mm (4¾ x 7⅞ in.)
Lower right: *vG 1653*
Rotterdam, Museum Boymans-van Beuningen,
inv. no. J.v.Goyen.8

1 See the many anonymous auctions in *Hoet 1752-1770*, *Dudok van Heel 1975*, and *Dudok van Heel 1977*

2 *Auction Amsterdam 1763*, title page

3 *Auction Amsterdam 1746*; *Burman Becker 1869*, p. 19; *Bille 1961*, vol. I, p. 184; his name in the capacity of auctioneer crops up between 1743 and 1749 (L. 576-711).

4 *Auction Amsterdam 1763*, p. 17, nos. 52-57; *Kramm 1857-1864*, vol. VI, p. 1724

5 *Waagen 1854*, vol. III, p. 477: 'Jan Verkolie ... a capital specimen of this otherwise secondary master. Inscribed 1707.'

6 *Bille 1961*, vol. I, p. 184

7 In an appendix *Burman Becker 1869* gave a genealogical tree of the Verkolje family; documentation Centraal Bureau voor Genealogie, The Hague.

8 *Auction Amsterdam 1763*, p. 7, no. 3

9 *Bille 1961*, vol. I, p. 197; *Auction Amsterdam 1763*, pp. 5-13, nos. 24, 29, 34, 38, 46, 65, 76

10 *Auction London 1773*, title page

11 *Auction London 1950*, title page; *Debrett's 1980*, p. 818

12 *Steland-Stief 1970*, p. 62 and *Steland-Stief 1971*, pp. 77 and 164, no. 237, believed that the painting was not signed; according to *Slive 1974*, p. 78, note 3, this was not based on personal observation.

13 *Sutton et al. 1987-1988*, pp. 250-251, no. 3 and fig.

14 Inv. no. 2638; *Schlie 1882*, p. 21, no. 33

15 The other winter scenes that Asselijn made around 1645 are mentioned by *Steland-Stief 1970*, p. 61, figs. 2 and 4.

16 B. 277; *Hollstein*, vol. XVIII, pp. 129-130, no. 277; vol. XIX, pp. 226-227 and fig.

17 *Steland-Stief 1971*, p. 113: in a document of 11 July 1647 Asselijn is said to be in Amsterdam.

18 Inv. no. A 2112; *Van Thiel et al. 1976*, p. 503, no. A 2112 and fig.

19 *Steland-Stief 1971*, pp. 102 and 179, no. 335

20 *Swillens 1949*, pp. 19-21 and fig. 1

21 *Steland-Stief 1964*, p. 101

22 HdG 802; *Van Thiel et al. 1976*, p. 109, no. A 27 and fig.

23 *Steland-Stief 1964*, p. 102 and *Steland-Stief 1970*, p. 62

24 See also *Slive 1974*, pp. 77-78 (who also pointed to examples by Jan van Goyen and Salomon van Ruysdael) and Chong in *Sutton et al. 1987-1988*, p. 251.

25 Chong in *Sutton et al. 1987-1988*, pp. 250-251, note 1, in which he mentions a painting by Asselijn that does feature such a borrowing (*Steland-Stief 1971*, p. 165, no. 243 and pl. XVIII).

26 *Beck 1972-1973*, vol. I, p. 166, no. 495 and fig.

BB

Middelburg 1593 / 1594 – Delft 1657

Panel, 36.6 x 27.7 cm (14⅜ x 11 in.)
Lower left: *B. vandeR. ast.* (ca. 1623)
New York, private collection

After the death of his father in 1609, Balthasar van der Ast lived in Bergen op Zoom as part of the family of his sister Maria and her husband, Ambrosius Bosschaert the Elder, who was his teacher until 1615. In 1619 Van der Ast became a master in the guild in Utrecht, and in 1632 in that of Delft, where he worked from then on. He painted still lifes with flowers, fruit, and shells in a detailed style, initially with symmetrical compositions in the manner of Bosschaert. From about 1620 on, the addition of all sorts of small creatures (favorites were lizards and grasshoppers) betray the influence of Roelant Savery. In the twenties his compositions came to consist of flower vases and fruit baskets with many elements set against a light background. In the Delft period he developed new types of still lifes, such as scattered flowers with shells, simple 'portraits' of exotic shells, and freestanding, loosely composed bouquets.

Provenance
(?) Auction London, 1803
(?) Dealer Victor D. Spark, New York
(?) Dealer Eugene Slatter, London, 1945
Collection Sidney J. van den Bergh, Wassenaar, 1955-1972
Dealer G. Cramer, The Hague, 1972
Private collection, New York, 1972

Bibliography
Van Gelder 1950, p. 37, no. 6
Bol 1955, p. 139 and fig. 1, p. 141, note 20b and p. 143
Laren 1959, no. 21 and fig. 14
Bol 1960, pp. 37-38 and 70, no. 6 and pl. 33
Ghent 1960, p. 106, no. 7 and fig. 72
Delft 1962, pp. 12-13, no. 9
Pavière 1962, p. 9
De Vries 1964, pp. 353-354 and fig. 3
Spriggs 1964-1965, p. 76 and pl. 62c
Leyden 1965, p. 3, no. 2
De Vries 1968, pp. 9 and 14-15 and fig.
Segal 1988-1989, p. 103 and fig., pp. 105 and 234, no. 20 and fig.

Sidney J. van den Bergh (1898-1977) [1] experienced the development of the family business into the international corporation called Unilever (since 1929), but as a collector he kept within the Dutch borders and the pleasant limitations of the Golden Century. Only after the conclusion of World War II did he begin to collect paintings.[1] His first acquisition was perhaps a little obvious: *A View of Leyden* of 1653 by Jan van Goyen (The Netherlands, private collection),[2] which he bought in 1947. Twenty years later he had assembled a modest collection of about fifty masterpieces, especially landscapes and still lifes.[3] Conspicuous was his preference for unusual works by minor masters (such as Pieter van Anraadt and Dirck de Bray), to which group Balthasar van der Ast was then thought to belong. Symptomatic of the more recent reevaluation of this still-life painter is, for instance, the acquisition of his *Fruit Still Life with Shells* by the Mauritshuis in 1983.[4] A quarter of a century earlier, this purchase would have been unthinkable.

Van den Bergh usually followed his own taste. He bought the *Flowers in a Wan Li Vase* by Balthasar van der Ast in the early fifties in London, where he made most of his purchases. In 1945 the panel was exhibited there in the Eugene Slatter gallery.[5] The history of the provenance before 1945 is wrapped in obscurity.

1
Sidney J. van den Bergh (1898-1977)
Photograph: Unilever NV, Rotterdam (1962)

We do know that in 1803 in London there was brought to auction 'A Flower piece with Insects, very fine' by Balthasar van der Ast, the dimensions of which correspond somewhat with those of Van den Bergh's still life.[6] But this description could naturally apply equally well to the panel differing in only minor details that was formerly in Aachen (Suermondt-Museum).[7] Unfortunately this work was lost in World War II, so that it is difficult to judge if it was an autograph replica of the work presently under discussion.[8]

In 1964 the director of the Mauritshuis, A.B. de Vries, published the Van den Bergh collection in the international art periodical *Apollo*. He then professed to be more charmed by the loose brushwork of Jan Brueghel than by the handling of the somewhat drier Van der Ast, who struck him as stiffer in his compositions, though still refined in his color combinations.[9] One year later the Stedelijk Museum De Lakenhal in Leyden for the first time showed the entire collection of fifty paintings owned by Mr. and Mrs. Van den Bergh-Bendix.[10] In 1968 De Vries himself compiled a catalogue of the Wassenaar collection, in which forty-three works were described. His conviction, expressed indirectly in the foreword, that the pieces of the Van den Bergh collection ought to be reserved for the Netherlands (and the Mauritshuis), turned out to be largely wishful thinking.[11]

From 1970 on Sidney van den Bergh systematically disposed of the most handsome paintings from his collection. He had earlier traded or sold less important works, but all of a sudden he was being offered improbably high sums for his top pieces. Within a couple of years Edward William Carter of Los Angeles came into possession of Van den Bergh's Avercamp, Dirck de Bray (cat. no. 12), Van der Heyden, and Hobbema.[12] After the death of the Dutch collector in 1977, the remainder of his collection was dispersed all over the globe. The flower piece by Van der Ast had been sold back in 1972. By way of the agent H. Cramer, who had also mediated for Carter and others, the painting ended up in a private collection in New York.

Following the customary practice of his generation, Van der Ast assembled a bouquet with spring and summer flowers. The painter can hardly have seen a tulip and rose standing together in full bloom in one vase, and it is therefore highly probable that he worked after preparatory drawings. His vision differed substantially from that of Dirck de Bray (cat. no. 12), who painted exclusively summer flowers in 'realistic' bouquets almost fifty years later. A present-day flower lover will recognize various still-popular ornamental flowers in the work of Van der Ast [**2**]:

a large red-yellow flamed tulip crowning the bouquet, with, to the left and right, light purple and blue columbines and sweet-brier; below these, to the left and right, anemones, pink roses (both budding and in full bloom), the lily-of-the-valley, a white-and-vermilion-striped carnation, and blue forget-me-nots. A cyclamen leaf is inserted into the vase at the bottom.

This vase is decorated with a so-called Wan Li design, so named after the last emperor of the Ming dynasty, who ruled from 1573 to 1619. Characteristic of this design are flowers, animals, and simple landscapes, often with ornamental borders of emblems and good-luck signs in medallions, painted in

2
Scheme of cat. no. 3 (drawing and research by Sam Segal)
1 Tuberose Cranesbill *Geranium tuberosum* L.
2 Batavian Rose *Rosa gallica* L. cv. *Batava*
3 Yellow Rose *Rosa foetida* Herrm.
4 Columbine *Aquilegia vulgaris* L. *bicolor duplex*
5 Feverfew *Chrysanthemum parthenium* (L.) Bernh. *subplenum*
6 Tulip *Tulipa praecox* Ten. x *T. chrysantha* hort.
7 Columbine *Aquilegia vulgaris* L. *pallida*
8 Pride Anemone *Anemone pavonina* Lam. *purpurea*
9 Carnation *Dianthus caryophyllus* L. *bicolor plenus*
10 African Marigold *Tagetes patula* L.
11 Lily-of-the-Valley *Convallaria majalis* L.
12 Cyclamen *Cyclamen hederifolium* Ait.
13 Forget-me-not *Myosotis scorpioides* L.
14 Grapes *Vitis vinifera* L.
15 Red Currants *Ribes rubrum* L.
16 Cherries *Prunus cerasus* L.
a Sand Lizard *Lacerta agilis* L.
b Painted Lady *Cynthia cardui* L.
c Damselfly *Coenagrion puellum* (L.)
d Dragonfly *Aeschna juncea* (L.)
e Clusterfly *Pollenia rudis* (Fabr.)

Balthasar van der Ast Flowers in a Wan Li Vase

monochrome blue. Even before 1620 the majolica painters of Delft imitated these decorations, which is why blue became the most commonly used color and has remained so over the centuries. The Dutch market was in any case inundated with the Chinese product: in 1612 the ship *Vlissingen* imported 38,641 pieces of porcelain, and in 1615 the ship *Gelderland* arrived with 69,075 pieces.[13] Balthasar van der Ast was especially fond of the Wan Li design, which he interpreted in his own way in the vases, dishes, and bowls in his still lifes. In the painting under discussion he drew a grasshopper on the vase, which may have been taken from a Chinese model. Along with the salamander, the grasshopper was a kind of trademark of Van der Ast.[14] Both may be seen in the recent acquisition of the Mauritshuis, *Flowers in a Wan Li Vase* [3].[15]

Repetitions occur repeatedly with the painters of the Bosschaert dynasty, who worked in the studio after drawn models or each other's compositions. For instance, the cyclamen leaf in the lower right of the vase is a motif that also occurs in the flower piece in Oxford (Ashmolean Museum) [4], which Van der Ast dated 1623.[16] One is also inclined to date the painting in the private collection in New York in or around that year. A similar cyclamen leaf lies at the lower right in a bouquet that Ambrosius Bosschaert painted in 1619 (Amsterdam, Rijksmuseum) [5].[17] L.J. Bol came close to calling this a pendant of the undated painting by Van der Ast. There are indeed major and minor correspondences, such as the use of the Wan Li vase, the symmetrical structure, and the frontal placing of the bouquet, with the large tulip on top, next to a couple of water drops on a leaf and the butterfly, a Painted Lady. But Balthasar van der Ast was

no mere follower of his brother-in-law and master, for he also experimented.[18] The younger painter contributed a sense of liveliness, which is above all achieved by means of the whimsical flower leaves, the shadows on the wall, and the approaching insects: a dragonfly on the right and a fly at the upper left. The large dragonfly on the bunch of grapes, the red currants, and the cherries, the curves of whose stems are repeated in the lizard's tail, provide the foreground especially with greater flair than what is found in Bosschaert.

The earliest known flower piece by Bosschaert originated in 1605, remarkably enough almost exactly contemporaneously

▲ 4
Balthasar van der Ast
Flowers in a Wan Li Vase
Panel, 30 x 24 cm (11¾ x 9½ in.)
Lower center: *B. vander. ast. fe. / 1623*
Oxford, Ashmolean Museum, inv. no. A 530

3
Balthasar van der Ast
Flowers in a Wan Li Vase
Panel, 41 x 32 cm (16⅛ x 12⅝ in.)
Lower right: *.B. vandeR. ast. fé.* (ca. 1623)
The Hague, Mauritshuis, inv. no. 1073

▶ 5
Ambrosius Bosschaert
Flowers in a Wan Li Vase
Copper, 31 x 22.5 cm (12¼ x 8⅞ in.)
Lower left: *AB 1619*
Amsterdam, Rijksmuseum, inv. no. A 1522

143

with the first works in the same genre by Roelandt Savery (1603), Jan Brueghel the Elder (1605), and Jacques de Gheyn (before 1604).[19] In 1604 the painter-theoretician Carel van Mander published his *Schilder-Boeck*, in which he specifically disapproved of such specialities because history painting was the highest branch of art: 'If the perfection is not [found] in figures and Histories / then it may be [in] Animals / Kitchens / Fruits / Flowers / Landscapes' (in translation).[20] Nevertheless, specialization was to become one of the characteristics of Dutch painting of the seventeenth century. The popularity of the flower piece in some cities of Holland has been rightly related to the growing interest in botany among scholars and laymen and to the growing trade in tulips and other bulbous plants, which was fanned by the fanaticism of some collectors. The prominent role of the tulip high in the bouquet by Van der Ast is certainly an indication of the great decorative value that was attached to this flower. It reminds us of the national rage that has become known as 'tulip mania.' The trade in bulbs reached such levels in Holland that, as an investment, thousands (now hundreds of thousands) of guilders were paid for one single tulip bulb. This 'tulip madness' came to an abrupt end in 1637, when people came to realize that they were engaged in pure speculation.[21]

Although Van der Ast was less inclined than his brother-in-law Ambrosius Bosschaert to include *vanitas* elements, such as chewed leaves and withered flowers, the mere sight of flowers in a vase could give contemporaries of these artists occasion to reflect. In 1604 a print by Jan Theodoor de Bry after a flower piece by Jacob Kempener – also with full-blown tulips, anemones, and columbines, and complete with approaching insects –

received the inscription: 'Flos speculum vitae modo vernat et interit aura' (The flower is a mirror of life, she blossoms but perishes in the wind) [6].[22] Van der Ast was never to know that his flamed and fancifully shaped tulip, which aroused the collector's mania of tulip lovers, was in fact the result of a fatal viral desease.[23] For us that information evokes reflections on mortality that the painter cannot have intended.

1 *De Vries 1968*, p. 7
2 HdG 138; *Beck 1972-1973*, vol. II, p. 165, no. 334 and fig.; *Beck 1987*, p. 181, no. 334
3 In 1965 he had twenty landscapes / cityscapes and eleven still lifes; see *Leyden 1965*, pp. 3-14, nos. 1-50.
4 Inv. no. 1066; *Broos 1987*, pp. 24-28, no. 3 and fig.; on this acquisition, see *Hecht / Luijten 1986*, p. 202.
5 According to *Van Gelder 1950*, p. 37, no. 6 (it proved impossible to obtain the catalogue for this exhibition); it was also impossible to establish the authority for the provenance from the dealer Victor D. Spark, which has been mentioned since *De Vries 1968*, p. 14.
6 *Auction London 1803*, p. 12, no. 118 (14 x 10 in.)
7 *Aachen 1932*, p. 6, no. 19
8 *De Vries 1968*, p. 14; *Bol 1960*, p. 70, no. 7; *Segal 1988-1989*, p. 234, no. 20
9 *De Vries 1964*, pp. 353-354
10 See note 3; selections had earlier been on view in Laren and Delft (*Laren 1959* and *Delft 1962*).
11 *De Vries 1968*, p. 8
12 *Walsh / Schneider 1981-1982*, pp. 3-7, nos. 1, 24-27, no. 6, pp. 54-57, no. 13 and pp. 58-61, no. 14 A
13 *Korf 1981*, pp. 180-181
14 *Bol 1981*, p. 578
15 *Bol 1960*, p. 70, no. 9 and pl. 34
16 *Van Gelder 1950*, pp. 36-37, no. 6 and fig.; *Bol 1960*, p. 69, no. 3
17 *Van Thiel et al. 1976*, p. 136, no. A 1522 and fig.; *Bol 1960*, pp. 31 and 68-69, no. 47 and pl. 29b
18 *Bol 1960*, pp. 37-38
19 *Segal 1987*, p. 96
20 *Van Mander 1604*, 'Voor-reden'
21 An exhibition on 'tulip mania' was held in Haarlem (*Haarlem 1974*); *Janse 1966* gives a good historical overview, pp. 30-38
22 *Hollstein*, vol. IV, p. 43, nos. 451-456 and fig.
23 *Segal 1987*, p. 94
    BB

6
Jan Theodoor de Bry after Jacob Kempener
Vase with Flowers
Engraving, 302 x 228 mm (11⅞ x 9 in.)
Lower left: *Jacobus kempener pinxit*; lower right:
Io Theodor de bry sculpsit (1604)
Amsterdam, Rijksprentenkabinet

Hendrick Avercamp 4 | Winter Landscape

Amsterdam 1585 – Kampen 1634

Panel, 31 x 46.5 cm (12¼ x 18¼ in.)
On tree trunk lower left: *HA* (in ligature) (ca. 1615-1620)
San Francisco, Calif., Sarah Ferris Cowles 1941 Trust, no inv. no.

Contemporary documents report the baptism of Hendrick Avercamp in Amsterdam on 27 January 1585. The following year his parents moved to the provincial town of Kampen on the IJssel River, where his well-educated family figured as prominent citizens. It is believed that Avercamp studied in Amsterdam with the Dutch-Danish artist Pieter Isackz, who remained in Amsterdam until his return to Denmark in 1607. That year at the sale of the estate of Gillis van Coninxloo, several drawings by Isackz were purchased by 'De Stom tot Pieter Isacqs.' This reference is generally thought to be to Hendrick Avercamp himself, because we know from the will of Avercamp's mother, Beatrix Vekemans, drawn up in 1633, that the artist was 'stom en miserabel' (mute and miserable). The artist seems to have lived the rest of his life in Kampen, where he was buried on 15 May 1634.

Avercamp's paintings and drawings, both sketches and highly finished watercolors, have always been extremely popular and commanded strong prices, even in the seventeenth century. Avercamp's works were also collected by other artists: for example, the estate of landscape artist Jan van de Cappelle included approximately 900 Avercamp drawings. His compositional motifs were continued by direct imitators, including his nephew, Barent Avercamp, and Arent Arentsz, called Cabel, as well as by other more independent masters, such as Adriaen van de Venne.

Unfortunately, in part owing to the similarity of his numerous winter scenes, it is sometimes difficult to track the early history of individual Avercamp paintings. The present panel can first be identified in a mention by Hofstede de Groot, who saw it around 1919 in the Vischer Boelger collection in Basel, Switzerland.[1] The painting then appeared in the family collection of André A. Bourcart of nearby Montbéliard, France, with whom it remained until going to auction in Monaco in 1985.[2] One of several Dutch paintings recently added to the Cowles family collection, presently being built under the direction of Mrs. Phoebe Cowles of San Francisco, the Avercamp came to America in 1988.

Perceived first as a backdrop for the dramatic action of biblical or historical events or for the routine human activities

Provenance
Collection Vischer Boelger, Basel, ca. 1880
Collection André A. Bourcart, Montbéliard, by 1929
Collection Bourcart heirs, until 1985
Auction Bourcart, Monaco, 1985 (Frf. 3,500,000)
Dealer Richard Green, London, 1985
Cowles Family Collection, San Francisco, 1988

Bibliography
Welcker 1933, p. 206, no. S 36
Welcker / Hensbroek-van der Poel 1979, p. 209, no. S 36
Auction Monaco 1985, no. 137 and fig.
Mayer, vol. XX (1986), p. 710

representing the seasons or the months of the year, landscape only became an artistic subject in its own right during the sixteenth century. Although the genre of the independent winter landscape was codified in Flanders, it was in the early seventeenth-century works of the Dutchman Hendrick Avercamp that the painted winter scene achieved its perfected form.

The Flemish tradition, which had its genesis in the winter scenes of Pieter Bruegel the Elder, was surely known to Avercamp through the works of Hans Bol, Gillis van Coninxloo, and David Vinckboons. These artists had emigrated from the Southern Netherlands and established themselves in Amsterdam, where Avercamp resided during the early years of the new century.[3] The example set in compositions by Vinckboons and others provided a pictorial vocabulary on which Avercamp both drew and elaborated [1].[4] Borrowing the formal elements of the Flemish landscape composition, he frequently utilized an elevated vantage point and a high placement of the horizon line, as a tondo from about 1609 in the National Gallery (London) [2] demonstrates.[5] Silhouetted *repoussoir* elements frame the scene and provide an introduction for the viewer into the pictorial space. These devices, coupled with the scattering of strong local color accents across the surface of the painting, characterize

2
Hendrick Avercamp
Winter Scene with Skaters near a Castle
Panel, 40.7 cm diam. (16 in. diam.)
Neither signed nor dated (ca. 1609)
London, National Gallery, inv. no. 1346

1
Hessel Gerritsz after David Vinckboons
Winter Scene with Slot Zuylen (Hyems)
Etching, 200 x 269.8 mm (7⅞ x 10⅝ in.)
Neither signed nor dated (ca. 1605-1610)
Hanover, N.H., Hood Museum of Art, Dartmouth
College, inv. no. Pr.972.150

Avercamp's earliest works and give them a distinctly mannered quality.

A more convincing illusion of space is achieved in a group of paintings, including the *Winter Scene on a Frozen Canal* (Los Angeles, collection of Mr. and Mrs. Edward William Carter) [3], which is generally dated about 1620.[6] In these works the prominent coulisse is discarded, the ground line recedes much more rapidly – deep into the pictorial space, not up the picture plane – and the composition is united through subtlety of color and atmospheric perspective. Avercamp, however, employed these two modes of spatial construction (one *retardataire*, the other progressive) interchangeably throughout his career. This varying practice, coupled with the scarcity of dated paintings, makes the chronology of his oeuvre problematic.[7]

3
Hendrick Avercamp
Winter Scene with a Frozen Canal
Panel, 36.8 x 65 cm (14½ x 25⅝ in.)
On sled at right: *HA* (in ligature) (ca. 1620)
Los Angeles, collection Mr. and Mrs. Edward William
Carter

Hendrick Avercamp Winter Landscape (not in The Hague)

In the present *Winter Scene* the artist has maintained the *repoussoir* tree, whose bare, lacy branches create a flat, decorative pattern across the top of the composition. However, here too we find the lowered horizon and subtlety of color and atmospheric effects working together to suggest the depth of the frosty winter landscape. The combination of archaic and more progressive compositional elements, in conjunction with the costumes, suggests a date of about 1615-1620 for this painting.[8] Another version of the present work, utilizing in reverse the major compositional elements and (on the basis of a reproduction) seemingly by another, later hand, was with the dealer Goudstikker in Amsterdam in 1928.[9]

As in all of his most delightful works, Avercamp here describes the daily activities and diversions of the Dutch townsmen as they go about their lives in winter, around and on the frozen rivers and canals.[10] A profusion of anecdotal motifs clutters the pictorial space: people skate,[11] converse, fish, play *kolf* (a type of ice hockey which eventually gave rise to our golf; see cat. no. 46), watch each other, and watch us watching them. The artist's acuity of observation, capturing the many nuances of human interaction, must surely have been heightened by his reliance on his eyesight to compensate for whatever deficiency he may have had in his hearing. It can be no accident that the artist dubbed 'De Stomme van Kampen' (the mute of Kampen) had such a keen awareness of and predilection for visual detail.

1 *Welcker / Hensbroek-van der Poel 1979*, p. 209. Along with the winter scenes by Avercamp recorded by Hofstede de Groot, there were other Dutch paintings in the Vischer Boelger collection. Those that can be identified include two works by Van Goyen (*Beck 1972-1973*, vol. II, p. 427, no. 955 and p. 488, no. 1110 A) and an old copy of *A Boy Blowing Bubbles* by Frans van Mieris (The Hague, Mauritshuis, inv. no. 106; *Naumann 1981*, vol. II, p. 73, no. 58p).
2 *Auction Monaco 1985*, no. 137 and fig.
3 Avercamp could have been introduced to this circle of immigrant Flemish artists through fellow students of the Isackz studio, the Antwerp artists Adriaen and Willem van Nieulandt. On the influence of the Flemish school on Avercamp, see *Welcker / Hensbroek-van der Poel 1979*, pp. 88-91; *Blankert et al. 1982*, pp. 19-26; *Keyes 1982*, pp. 37-45.
4 *Hollstein*, vol. VII, p. 107, no. 20 and fig.; from a series of the four seasons with views of castles near Amsterdam (*Hollstein*, vol. VII, p. 107, nos. 17-20 and figs.).
5 *Maclaren 1960*, p. 4, no. 1346; *London 1973*, p. 9, no. 1346; *Welcker / Hensbroek-van der Poel 1979*, p. 213, no. S 54
6 *Walsh / Schneider 1981-1982*, pp. 3-7, no. 1 and fig.; *Sutton et al. 1987-1988*, pp. 259-261. For a discussion of the dating, see *Walsh / Schneider 1981-1982*, p. 6.
7 Dated works exist for 1608, 1609, 1626, and 1632.
8 I would like to thank George Keyes for discussing with me the dating of this work.
9 *Amsterdam 1928*, no. 2
10 Usually creating a festive mood (with unpleasant details, such as skaters fallen through the ice, kept to the background), Avercamp's scenes do not suggest the severity of the winters during this period. They were part of a little ice age, which lasted from the early fifteenth through the eighteenth century. For an economy reliant on a system of rivers and canals to move people and commerce, the implications of such cold were very serious; not simply a diversion, mastery of the ice became a necessity (*Van Straaten 1977*, p. 13).
11 For the history of skating as depicted in European art, see *Van Straaten 1977* and *Dixon 1987*.
LFO

Wijk bij Duurstede ca. 1595 – Utrecht 1624

Canvas 101 x 107.3 cm (39¾ x 42¼ in.)
On the lute: *TBaburen fe 1622* (TB in ligature)
Boston, Mass., Museum of Fine Arts, inv. no. 50.2721

Records regarding the family of Dirck (or Theodoor) van Baburen suggest that his birthplace was Wijk bij Duurstede in about 1595. The earliest mention of the artist himself, in the records of the Utrecht guild for 1611, names Baburen as a student of Paulus Moreelse. Baburen then traveled to Italy, there to experience firsthand the artistic revolution that the great Roman paintings of Caravaggio had helped to initiate. Documented first in Parma in 1615, Baburen next worked with his fellow Dutchman David de Haen (died Rome 1622) on the important public commission for the decoration of the Pietà Chapel in San Pietro in Montorio in Rome. Important private patronage was also forthcoming, particularly from Cardinal Scipione Borghese and the Marchese Vincenzo Giustiniani. Both men were ardent collectors, each owning a number of paintings by Caravaggio. Through such contacts Baburen would also have become familiar with the works of other artists influential to his own development, particularly Bartolomeo Manfredi, an Italian follower of Caravaggio, who also worked for the Giustiniani family.

Baburen used the Caravaggesque vocabulary, immediately discernible in the *Entombment* executed for the San Pietro in Montorio altarpiece, throughout his career. The style emphasized the human figure as the primary artistic vehicle, with the fully three-dimensional forms pushed close to the pictorial surface. Baburen also relied on sharp light-dark contrasts to heighten the corporeality of his coarse players, who act out the scenes represented with a theatricality of gesture, expression, and pose.

Returning to Holland in the early 1620s, Baburen, along with Hendrick ter Brugghen and Gerard van Honthorst, helped to popularize the Caravaggesque mode. Together they became known as the Utrecht Caravaggisti. In Utrecht, as in Rome, Baburen attracted the notice of influential patrons, including possibly Prince Frederik Hendrik and his secretary Constantijn Huygens. However, Baburen's very personal interpretation of Caravaggio's style, with coarse figures blocked out with broad brushstrokes, attracted no important followers. He resided in Utrecht until his death in 1624.

Provenance

(?) Collection Maria Thins, Gouda / Delft, before 1641-1680
(?) Collection Catharina Bolnes, Delft, 1680-1688
(?) Collection Johannes Johannesz Vermeer, Delft, 1688-1713
(?) Collection Sir Hans Sloane, Chelsea
Collection Lt. Col. Ronald Francis Assheton Sloane-Stanley, Cowes, Isle of Wight
Auction Sloane-Stanley, London, 1949 (£105 to Colnaghi)
Dealer Colnaghi, London, 1949
Dealer Roger Thesiger, Buckinghamshire
Museum of Fine Arts, Boston, 1950

Bibliography

Auction London 1949, p. 7, no. 52
Constable 1950, pp. 35-36
Gowing 1951, pp. 169-170 and fig. 29
Gowing 1952, pp. 123, 126 and fig. 28
Nicolson 1952, p. 248
Utrecht 1952, p. 9, no. 9 and fig. 9
Nicolson 1958-A, p. 63
Judson 1959, pp. 75-76 and fig. 79
Maclaren 1960, pp. 438-439
Stechow 1960, pp. 177-178
Nicolson 1962-A, p. 540
Slatkes 1965, pp. 74-78, no. A 12, pp. 116-118 and fig. 17
Van Peer 1968, pp. 220-221
Spear 1971, p. 40, no. 1 and fig.
London 1973, p. 774
Walsh 1973, p. 3 and fig. 43
Hendy 1974, p. 282
Robinson 1974, p. 61
Blankert 1978-A, pp. 27, 146-147, 162, 170 and fig. 22
Kahr 1978, pp. 42, 284, 296-297 and fig. 27
Snow 1979, p. 82 and fig. 35
Slatkes 1981, pp. 20, 66 and 91
Moreno 1982, pp. 53, 57 and fig. 2
Brown 1984, p. 182 and fig.
Gowing 1984, p. 60 and fig. 7
Philadelphia / Berlin / London 1984, p. XXXII, no. 1, pp. 130-131
Murphy 1985-A, p. 10 and fig.
Mayer-Meintschel 1986, p. 11 and fig. 5
Stebbins / Sutton 1986, p. 46 and fig.
Sutton 1986, p. 26 and fig. 29
Blankert / Slatkes 1986-1987-A, pp. 39-40, 174 and fig. 38
Schama 1987, p. 431 and fig. 208
Blankert et al. 1988, pp. 51, 87-90, 183, 193, 201, 222 and fig. 72
Wheelock 1988, pp. 14, 54, 94 and fig. 9
Montias 1989, pp. 57, 122, 146-147, 188, 192, 195 and fig. 21

The Boston *Procuress*, which has been frequently published, is among the most significant paintings of the Utrecht Caravaggisti in America. One of the most interesting aspects of the picture is its provenance. Early in the literature its appearance in the background of two paintings by Vermeer was noticed, namely *The Concert* (Boston, Isabella Stewart Gardner Museum) [1][1] and the *Lady Seated at a Virginal* (London, National Gallery) [2].[2] It was theorized that Vermeer had actually owned the Baburen. This hypothesis gained credibility with the publication of the 27 November 1641 divorce settlement of Vermeer's future mother-in-law, Maria Thins (1593-1680), recorded in Gouda at the time of the dissolution of her marriage to Reinier Bolnes.[3] One of the items listed in the document under lot C[4] was 'Een schilderije daer een coppelerste die in de hant wijst' (A painting of a procuress pointing in the hand).[5] Given that Baburen's *Procuress* is indeed included as a motif in two separate paintings by Vermeer (who would take up residence in the house of Maria Thins in Delft after his marriage in 1653 to her daughter Catharina Bolnes [ca. 1631-1688]),[6] this painting, or a copy of it, must surely be the picture described in the document.[7]

At the time of Vermeer's death, the noted Dutch scientist Anthony van Leeuwenhoek, widely known for his work in optics, was appointed to administer the artist's estate on behalf of Vermeer's widow. Based on Van Leeuwenhoek's contacts among the wider scientific community, particularly the Royal Society in England, it has been suggested that through his agency the Baburen *Procuress* passed into an English collection.[8] In fact the subsequent history of the painting is not known until it appears in the 1949 sale of the collection of the late Lt. Col. R.F.A. Sloane-Stanley of the Isle of Wight and Bay House, Alverstoke, Hampshire.[9]

Bought at the 1949 sale by Colnaghi's, *The Procuress* then passed into the possession of Mr. Roger Thesiger of Buckinghamshire. A noted art consultant, he would become director of Colnaghi's from 1955 to 1971. In 1950 the Baburen entered the collection of the Museum of Fine Arts, Boston. After the acquisition Mr. Thesiger wrote to curator William G. Constable regarding the provenance of the painting.[10] This letter states that at the time of sale the picture was in an eighteenth-century English frame. In addition, Thesiger claimed that an inscription on the frame dated from the early eighteenth century and attributed the work to Honthorst. This evidence suggests that *The Procuress* had actually been in England since the eighteenth century.

Lt. Col. Sloane-Stanley (1867-1949) was, in addition to being a noted sportsman, a descendant of the esteemed physician and voracious collector Sir Hans Sloane (1660-1753). The evidence of the frame and its inscription has led to the theory that the Boston *Procuress* may have been part of the Sloane collection.[11] The residence of Sir Hans at Chelsea housed vast holdings of over 200,000 objects, including natural artifacts and specimens, paintings, drawings, sculpture, manuscripts, cameos, and medals; on his death most of the collection formed the founding core of the British Museum. The rest of the estate, including the manor at Chelsea, was divided between his two daughters, one of whom, Sarah, had married George Stanley of Hampshire. Thus the two families merged, with subsequent descendants adopting the name Sloane-Stanley. The Stanleys were also a family of stature

1
Johannes Vermeer
The Concert
Canvas, 69 x 63 cm (27¼ x 24¾ in.)
Neither signed nor dated (ca. 1660-1665)
Boston, Isabella Stewart Gardner Museum,
inv. no. P21W27

2
Johannes Vermeer
Lady Seated at a Virginal
Canvas, 51.5 x 45.5 cm (20¼ x 18 in.)
At the right of the head of the lady: *IMeer* (IM in
ligature) (ca. 1670-1675)
London, National Gallery, inv. no. 2568

Dirck van Baburen The Procuress

with a country estate: Paultons, an eighteenth-century manor, was remodeled by Kent of Southampton, with a park laid out by Capability Brown.[12] Therefore, although it would seem more likely that the Baburen did indeed come from the Sloane family, it is possible that Lt. Col. Sloane-Stanley could have inherited the painting from either one of these notable families.[13]

Signed and dated 1622, the Boston *Procuress* is a work of uncompromising vitality. The three bawdy figures press against the picture plane; as their truncated forms invade our space, we become, perhaps unwillingly, participants in the scene. Here a young, full-breasted woman playing a lute exchanges glances with a man; he draws her to him with one hand around her bared shoulder, while offering a coin with the other hand. The third figure is an old woman, turbaned and wrapped in a heavy cloak, who points to her hand as if demanding payment for favors yet to be rendered. The subject has been variously interpreted as a brothel scene, which in Northern art could also be understood to portray the biblical theme of the prodigal son (Luke 15:13),[14] or, most recently, as a depiction of the theme of the gypsy fortune teller.[15] Although the interpretation is open to debate, scholarly consensus is that Baburen rendered the scene of mercenary love, which had been treated frequently in the Northern tradition,[16] in a distinctly novel Caravaggesque, that is, Italian, style.

The fine collection of paintings is also mentioned in various guidebooks, such as *London 1888*, p. 341.
13 For a listing of old master paintings exhibited by the Sloane-Stanley family during the nineteenth century, see *Graves 1913-1915*, vol. v, p. 2582.
14 *Philadelphia / Berlin / London 1984*, pp. 130-131
15 *Stebbins / Sutton 1986*, p. 46. Peter Sutton will discuss the Baburen *Procuress* in a forthcoming article, examining the depiction of the gypsy in Northern art, to appear in the *Museum of Fine Arts Bulletin*.
16 *Brown 1984*, pp. 182-187; *Brunswick 1987*, pp. 59-65
     LFO

---

1 *Hendy 1974*, pp. 282-284, fig. xxxiii; *Blankert / Montias et al. 1987*, pp. 121, 187-188, no. 17 and pl. 17; the painting was among those stolen from the Gardner Museum 18 March 1990.
2 *Maclaren 1960*, pp. 438-439, no. 2568; *London 1973*, p. 773, no. 2568 and fig.; *Blankert / Montias et al. 1987*, pp. 145, 202, no. 31 and pl. 30
3 *Blankert 1978-A*, doc. 7, pp. 145-146
4 At the time of the divorce, some properties belonging to the Thins family were returned to them. Lot C was awarded to Maria's brother Johan. Maria herself later inherited these items.
5 I use Blankert's translation.
6 *Montias 1989*, p. 146
7 Although Vermeer would not have legally owned the painting, after Maria Thins's death, it may have passed by descent to her daughter, Catharina Bolnes, his wife, and then to their son, Johannes Johannesz Vermeer (ca. 1664-1713). A seventeenth-century copy of *The Procuress* is in the Rijksmuseum, Amsterdam (inv. no. C 612). Another copy was bought in at Christie's, London, 29 November 1968, lot 10. There is also a modern forgery by Han van Meegeren at the Courtauld Institute of Art, London (*London 1961*, no. 37).
8 *Gowing 1984*, p. 60
9 *Auction London 1949*, p. 7, no. 52
10 Ms. letter in curatorial file, Museum of Fine Arts, Boston. I would like to thank Marcy Rockoff for bringing this letter to my attention. Both Gowing and Slatkes mention having seen *The Procuress* while it belonged to Mr. Thesiger (*Gowing 1951*, p. 169; *Slatkes 1965*, p. 116).
11 *Slatkes 1965*, p. 116. On Sir Hans Sloane, see *St. John Brooks 1954*.
12 On Paultons, the seat of the Stanleys and Sloane-Stanleys, see *Oswald 1938*.

Nicolaes Berchem   6 | A Moor Offering a Parrot to a Lady

Haarlem 1620 – Amsterdam 1683

Canvas, 93.7 x 89 cm (36⅞ x 35 in.)
Lower right: *N Berchem / F* (ca. 1665)
Hartford, Conn., Wadsworth Atheneum, inv. no. 1961.29

Nicolaes Berchem was the son and pupil of the still life painter
Pieter Claesz, but he was also trained (or at the very least influenced) by painters from Amsterdam and Haarlem, such as Jan
van Goyen, Nicolaes Moeyaert, Pieter de Grebber, and Jan Baptist
Weenix. In 1642 he became master in the guild of Haarlem,
where he worked most of the time. At the end of his life he is also
recorded in Amsterdam, where he took up residence in 1677.
Berchem's oeuvre consists almost exclusively of landscapes,
which have long been recognized as important examples of the
Dutch Italianate style of painting. From the start his work showed
the influence of Pieter van Laer, who was the best-known artist to
have visited Rome; he was living in Haarlem when Berchem was
learning the trade. Only recently was it established that Berchem,
too, went to Italy; presumably he was there from 1651 to 1653.
His most mature works, which were influenced by Jan Asselijn
and Jan Both, and which are alternately grand or simple in
concept, with very lively figures, were made after 1660.

In 1807 Lucretia Johanna (Creejans) van Winter (1785-1845)
and her sister Anna Louisa Agatha (Annewies) van Winter
(1793-1877) each inherited half of the famous art collection of
their father, Pieter van Winter (1745-1807) [1] (see cat. no. 34).

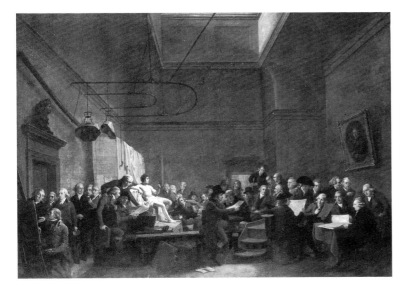

1
Adriaan de Lelie
*The Drawing Room of the Felix Meritis Society in
Amsterdam with Portraits of Painters, Collectors, and
Dealers.* Pieter van Winter is the figure at the far left;
seated at the easel next to him is Pieter de Smeth van
Alphen; Pieter Fouquet, Jr., with outstretched arm, is
to be seen at the lower right of the model.
Canvas, 100 x 131 cm (39⅜ x 51⅝ in.)
On a portfolio: *A. de Lelie* (1801)
Amsterdam, Rijksmuseum, inv. no. C 538

Provenance

Collection César Gabriel(?) and Renaud de Choiseul-
Chévigny, Dukes of Praslin
Auction Choiseul-Praslin, Paris, 1793 (Frf. 2,001)
Collection Pieter Baron de Smeth van Alphen,
Amsterdam / De Bilt, 1793(?)-1810
Auction De Smeth van Alphen, Amsterdam, 1810
(ƒ1,625 to Jeronimo de Vries)
Collection Lucretia van Winter (from 1822, Six-van
Winter), Amsterdam 1810-1845
Collection Jonkheer Hendrik Six van Hillegom,
Amsterdam, 1845-1847
Collection Jonkheer Jan Pieter Six van Hillegom and
Jonkheer Pieter Six van Vromade, Amsterdam, 1847-
1899 / 1905
Collection Jonkheer Jan Six, Amsterdam, 1905-1926
(from 1922, Six Foundation)
Auction Six, Amsterdam, 1928 (ƒ3,400 to P. de Boer)
Dealer P. de Boer, Amsterdam, 1928
Collection Dr. Schäffer, Berlin, after 1932(?)
Dealer Hans Schäffer Galleries, New York, 1961
Wadsworth Atheneum, Hartford, 1961 (The Ella
Gallup Sumner and Mary Catlin Sumner Collection)

Bibliography

Auction Paris 1793, pp. 38-39, no. 79
Auction Amsterdam 1810, p. 5, no. 11
Smith 1829-1842, vol. v (1834), pp. 38-39, no. 103
Blanc 1857-1858, vol. II, p. 162
Steenhoff 1899-1901, p. 23
Amsterdam 1900, p. 6, no. 6
t Hooft 1900, p. 251
Mireur 1901-1912, vol. I, p. 195
Six 1919, p. 83 and fig. 1
HdG 71 (vol. IX [1926], p. 70, no. 71)
Auction Amsterdam 1928, p. 1, no. 2
Onze Kunst 1928, p. 232
Wilenski 1929, p. 156
Von Sick 1930, pp. 25-26
Plietzsch 1960, p. 152
Art Quarterly 1961, p. 200 and fig. p. 202
Bille 1961, vol. I, p. 72
New York 1961, no. 23 and fig.
Chronique des arts 1962, p. 30, no. 120 and fig.
WAB 1962, pp. 12, 23 and pl. II
Stechow 1966, pp. 159 and 217, note 70
San Francisco / Toledo / Boston 1966-1967, p. 115, no.
73 and fig.
Faison 1968, pp. 470-471 and pl. VIII
Paris 1970-1971, pp. 14-15, no. 13 and fig.
Schulz 1974, p. 8, no. 17
Chronique des arts 1978, p. 17 and fig. 28
Haverkamp-Begemann 1978, pp. 13, 65 and 116-118,
no. 13 and fig.
Zafran 1978, p. 245 and fig. 8
Dresden 1979, p. 106, no. 1479
Schloss 1982, pp. 12, 19-20, 49, 63-64 and 156, notes
3, 6 and 7 and fig. 34
Hofrichter 1983, p. 57, no. 5 and fig.
Hofrichter 1983-A, pp. 270, 273 and fig. 4
Berlin / London / Philadelphia 1984, pp. 90-91, no. 5
and fig.
Sutton 1986, pp. 105-106
Ten Doesschate Chu 1987, p. 76

In the spirit of her father Pieter, Creejans expanded her share of the inheritance by making acquisitions of her own from important collections (Brentano, Coclers, Muilman) that were auctioned in Amsterdam at the beginning of the nineteenth century.[1] In 1810 she bought diverse works at the auction of De Smeth van Alphen, and it was probably at this time that Creejans also acquired this intriguing masterpiece, *A Moor Offering a Parrot to a Lady*, which is now the pride and joy of the Dutch collection of the Wadsworth Atheneum in Hartford. Through her marriage of 1822 to Jonkheer Hendrik Six (1790-1847), a Master of Jurisprudence, two interesting collections of paintings from the Golden Age were united at 509-511 Herengracht in Amsterdam, the most important work naturally being the *Portrait of Jan Six* painted by Rembrandt (Amsterdam, collection Six Foundation).[2]

Rembrandt's portrait lent the name of Six an international reputation, but few people know that, along with the state collection in the Trippenhuis, the family collection was for a long time one of the chief attractions for foreigners visiting the capital.[3] After the deaths of Hendrik and Creejans in 1845 and 1847, their two sons, Jan Pieter Six van Hillegom (1824-1899) and Pieter Hendrik Six van Vromade (1827-1905), continued to live in the paternal home: 'At the age of twenty-three Jan is already the absent-minded professor and the three-year-younger Piet is a man of procrastination' (in translation), a remote relative later wrote.[4] After they both married (in 1856 and 1860), they decided that Jan should live in the house on the Herengracht, which had in the meantime been arranged as a museum and 'where a spiral staircase of oak has carried half of Europe to the "Galerie Six"' (in translation).[5] In 1900 B.W.F. van Riemsdijk gave a striking description of this unusual collection. 'The interior courtyard of this dwelling was covered with glass and that space was turned into a museum hall in which a part of the collection found an outstanding accommodation. In addition the room facing the street, as well as the adjoining dining room, continued to be reserved for exposition, and there one found, surrounded by the most refined luxury, the most splendid paintings hanging on the walls' (in translation).[6]

After the death in 1899 of Jan Pieter Six, who had made his name as numismatist and archaeologist, his son Jan Six (1857-1926) [2] governed the family collection. He was a classicist and art historian and became a professor at the State Academy and later also at the University of Amsterdam. He was furthermore the moving force behind the (Dutch) Royal Archaeological Society. He had the misfortune to live to see how, owing to the widening of the Vijzelstraat, the property at 509-511 Herengracht had to be torn down, after which he found a good home at number 218 Amstel. It is there that the Six Foundation, which was founded in 1922, is presently accommodated.[7] This foundation still has Rembrandt's *Portrait of Jan Six* in its care, but the Six collection has been substantially thinned out over the years. In 1907 Frits Lugt wrote a brochure with the pregnant title 'Is the Acquisition by the State of a Part of the Six Collection to be Recommended?' (in translation). His answer to this question was negative because, in his opinion, the best pieces would remain in the collection.[8] Again a number of Six paintings were sold in 1920, but the lion's share came under the hammer in 1928, after the death of Professor Jan Six. Thus the last great private collection of Amsterdam came to be dispersed.[9]

The Six auction of 1928 was a double sensation. In the first place the sixty-six paintings fetched more than two million guilders, and in the second, it was quite unexpectedly the Dutch buyers who reached deep into their pockets. Stranger yet: to their own amazement, the Anglo-American buyers came off second best, at least where the most coveted pieces were concerned.[10] For example, Sir Henry Deterding acquired *A Woman Writing a Letter* by Gerard ter Borch (The Hague, Mauritshuis)[11] (cat. no. 67, fig. 3) for the unheard-of amount of 290,000 guilders. He wanted to buy the painting at any price to be able to offer it to the Mauritshuis. Deterding also bought the smallest painting by Jan Steen, *A Girl Eating Oysters* (The Hague, Mauritshuis)[12] for 190,000 guilders, even though it had been estimated at 60,000 guilders.[13] In 1936 he donated it to the Hague museum as well. These prices were in enormous contrast

2
Georg Rueter
Portrait of Jan Six (1857-1926)
Upper left: *Georg Rueter.*; upper right: AET.64 / 1921.
Canvas, measurements unknown
Location unknown

Nicolaes Berchem A Moor Offering a Parrot to a Lady

to those of paintings that appealed less to Dutch nationalist sentiment, such as the works by the Italianate painters. With hindsight it is incomprehensible that Berchem's masterpiece in Hartford then fetched only 3,400 guilders.[14] This evident lack of appreciation was apparently also a consequence of the rather time-bound aversion to his technical precision. It seems like an echo of what Steenhoff – who later became director of the Hendrik Willem Mesdag Museum in The Hague – observed in 1900 on the occasion of an exhibition of the Six collection in the Stedelijk Museum in Amsterdam. He thought the painting was made 'of a unity which is so cold and hard [that it is] as if the work were of a glass-like substance' (in translation).[15]

In 1793, when the art of the *fijnschilder* had not yet been relegated to the background by the more impressionistic, broader painters, this painting was auctioned in Paris as an atypical but very handsome work by Berchem, in which one could enjoy 'all the beauty of detail and touch that usually characterize him [Berchem]' (in translation).[16] It came from the collection of Renaud de Choiseul-Chévigny (1735-1791), whose father, César de Choiseul-Chévigny (1712-1785, since 1762 Duke of Praslin), had assembled the greater part of the collection.[17] It is not clear if *A Moor Offering a Parrot to a Lady* also belonged to the oldest core of this collection. At the same time of or shortly after this auction in Paris it was bought by Pieter Baron de Smeth van Alphen (1753-1810) [1], who was, according to a no longer verifiable notation, abroad on a trip.[18] De Smeth was an Amsterdam banker and regent, whose collection at 554 Herengracht presumably would have been admired more than once by the young Creejans van Winter.[19] That she purchased the gallant scene from the De Smeth collection indicates that it must have exerted an unusually strong attraction on her.

After the Six auction of 1928 the painting remained out of sight for thirty years, until it appeared in the art trade in New York, to be acquired in 1961 by the Wadsworth Atheneum in Hartford, which was renowned for its acquisition policy.[20] Officially the canvas is said to belong to the Ella Gallup Sumner and Mary Catlin Sumner collection, though this was never a collection in the true sense of the word. In 1927 the museum of Hartford came into a considerable legacy from the rich businessman Frank C. Sumner (1850-1924), who had in turn been heir to the fortune of his brother George C. Sumner (1841-1906), one-time mayor of Hartford. The fund formed from this legacy was named after the wives of Frank and George, Ella Gallup Sumner, who had died in childbirth, and Mary Catlin Sumner, who remained childless. From then on the fund was used to finance important acquisitions for the Wadsworth Atheneum.[21] The painting by Berchem was purchased by the remarkable Charles C. Cunningham, director of the Atheneum beginning in 1946. He enriched the collection with the work of several Italianate landscape painters, and this even before they enjoyed their renaissance thanks to the well-known Utrecht exhibition of 1965.[22]

In 1919 Professor Jan Six [2] devoted a short dissertation to his Berchem, identifying the subject as 'the king of Egypt [who] sends a Negro for SARAH' (in translation).[23] He further believed that it must be a pendant to Berchem's *Abraham Receiving Sarah from King Abimelech* (Geneva, Musée d'Art et d'Histoire) [3].[24] Hofstede de Groot rightly dismissed this because the dimensions differ too much.[25] Furthermore, the piece in Geneva has another scene as pendant, namely *The Prodigal Son* (Geneva, Musée d'Art et d'Histoire).[26] During the exhibition of the Six collection in the Stedelijk Museum in 1900, Jan Six had named the painting *Othello and Desdemona*.[27] Both titles are unsatisfactory, as Haverkamp-Begemann now concludes in the catalogue of the Hartford collection.[28]

It must nevertheless be admitted that there are correspondences between the ostensible pendant in Geneva and the work in Hartford. In 1930 Ilse von Sick pointed out that the compositional schemes are identical, that both paintings show diagonal dark bands of clouds, and that the Moors wear the same attire (some details of his clothing indeed correspond).[29] But one also encounters comparable details in the clothing, the composition, and the sky of other paintings with a vertical format, which do not depict a specific historical subject. The small orchestra and

3
Nicolaes Berchem
Abraham Receiving Sarah from King Abimelech
Canvas, 105 x 98 cm (41 3/8 x 38 5/8 in.)
Lower left: *NBerchem f* (NB in ligature) (ca. 1665-1670)
Geneva, Musée d'Art et d'Histoire, inv. no. 1826-18

4
Nicolaes Berchem
The Arrival of an Oriental Prince
Canvas, 94 x 98.5 cm (37 x 38¾ in.)
Lower left: *C Berchem f.* (ca. 1665)
Dresden, Staatliche Kunstsammlungen,
Gemäldegalerie, inv. no. 1479

Below this statue we see a glass of wine with an orange and a lemon: this signifies sweet and sour, as love can sometimes be.[33] The music-making duo nearby makes it clear that this painting is about the pleasant things of life: Wine, Women, and Song.

In these surroundings, pregnant with love, the young Negro wants something from the lady, and this is underlined by the black dog that barks at the light blonde yapping lapdog of the young lady. The lady is offered a parrot, and that makes us think of a series of paintings made in the seventeenth century of ladies with parrots. Around 1660 Berchem must have observed the popularity of this theme in scenes with amorous overtones, especially those by *fijnschilders*. An early example of this is *The Duet* by Frans van Mieris (Schwerin, Staatliches Museum) [5] of 1658,[34] which shows drink, love, and music in Dutch surroundings under the observant eye of a parrot. In 1663 Van Mieris painted *A Woman Feeding a Parrot* (London, National Gallery).[35] After him followed a whole series of such depictions, by Gabriël Metsu, Caspar Netscher, Godfried Schalcken, Pieter van Slingelandt, and Arie de Vois.[36]

Although the correct interpretation of the meaning of the parrot is not always easy, the animal is in many cases more than merely a decorative element. In sixteenth-century paintings the bird was sometimes the symbol of the Virgin Mary, but in the seventeenth century, the exotic bird is on the one hand an example of immoderation and eloquence and on the other – especially in the works of Van Mieris and his emulators – clearly an amorous and even an erotic symbol.[37] The bird must also carry this latter meaning in the case of Berchem, which is confirmed by the inclusion of a Negro, who in the mentality of

the man in old-fashioned costume looking on the scene also appear in *Music in a City Square* (Rouen, Musée des Beaux-Arts).[30] We again see the young Moor, the amused spectator, the jolly orchestra, and the frolicking dogs in *The Arrival of an Oriental Prince* (Dresden, Staatliche Kunstsammlungen, Gemälde-galerie) [4].[31]

All the above works are signed but not dated. It is almost unanimously believed that they were painted in the mid-sixties.[32] By then Berchem had long returned from Italy, back to which he seems to be looking with some nostalgia in these harbor scenes. Typically Dutch, however, is the hidden symbolism, which even appears to have been borrowed from the genre pieces of his colleagues. In the case of Berchem, the towering statue of Venus – which imitates the pose of the lady in blue – with Amor and a few turtledoves at her feet, is naturally telling.

5
Frans van Mieris
The Duet
Panel, 31.5 x 24.6 cm (12⅜ x 9⅝ in.)
On the back of the chair: *F. van Mieris 1658*
Schwerin, Staatliches Museum, inv. no. G 82

the seventeenth century still stands as the prototype of everything uncouth, heathenish, and lascivious.[38] At best, the Negro was depicted merely as an exotic phenomenon, as did the Swedish court painter David Klöcker Ehrenstrahl in 1670 (Stockholm, Nationalmuseum) [6].[39] The voluptuous role of the black man seems clear enough, but what escapes us for the time being is why the onlooker at the right is dressed in clothing known to be old-fashioned. He looks like a member of the Swiss Guard at the Vatican. Does he perhaps stand guard for common decency? This scene by Nicolaes Berchem, in which the (heathen) East meets the (Christian) West, in any case stands unmistakably under the sign of Venus, the universally recognized goddess of love. This must still have been understood in the time of Creejans van Winter.

6
David Klöcker Ehrenstrahl
A Negro with Monkeys and Parrots
Canvas, 144 x 120 cm (56³/₄ x 47¹/₄ in.)
On the rail at the right: *David Klöker fecit / Ao 1670*
Stockholm, Nationalmuseum, inv. no. NM 1407

1 *Van Riemsdijk 1900*, p. 442
2 *Gerson / Bredius 1969*, pp. 211 and 570-571, no. 276 and fig.
3 *Van Eeghen 1958*, p. 226
4 *Van Lennep 1959*, p. 140
5 Ibidem
6 *Van Riemsdijk 1900*, p. 442
7 *Wijnman et al. 1974*, pp. 388 and 393
8 *Lugt 1907*; see also pp. 65-67
9 *Van Eeghen 1958*, p. 228 and *Auction Amsterdam 1928*
10 *Huebner 1928*, pp. 713-714
11 Inv. no. 797; *Hoetink et al. 1985*, pp. 146-147, no. 14 and fig., p. 342, no. 797 and fig.
12 Inv. no. 818; *Broos 1987*, pp. 345-349, no. 57 and fig.
13 *H. 1928*, pp. 354-355
14 *Onze Kunst 1928*, p. 232: in most reviews of this auction, this painting was not even mentioned.
15 *Steenhoff 1899-1901*, p. 23
16 *Auction Paris 1793*, p. 39, no. 79
17 *Auction Paris 1793*, p. iii; *Larousse*, vol. VIII, p. 264 (NB: This was not the famous Choiseul auction of the collection of Etienne François de Choiseul, which took place in 1772, see cat. no. 30 and *Levallet 1925*).
18 *Auction Amsterdam 1810*, p. 4, no. 11: 'door de heer de Smeth zelfs gekogt op reis' (copy from the Lugt collection, RKD).
19 *NNBW*, vol. VII, cols. 1149-1150; *Wijnman et al. 1974*, p. 385
20 *Sutton 1986*, p. 103; the sources adduced for the period from 1928 to 1961 in *Haverkamp-Begemann 1978*, p. 116, notes 5 and 6 only raise questions.
21 *Haverkamp-Begemann 1978*, p. 12
22 *Haverkamp-Begemann 1978*, p. 13; *Blankert 1965 / 1978*
23 *Six 1919*, p. 83
24 HdG 3; *Ten Doesschate Chu 1987*, pp. 76-77, no. 11 and fig.
25 HdG 71 (vol. IX [1926], p. 70, no. 71)
26 Inv. no. 1826-17; HdG 25; *Ten Doesschate Chu 1987*, pp. 78-79, no. 12 and fig.
27 *Amsterdam 1900*, p. 6, no. 6
28 *Haverkamp-Begemann 1978*, p. 116, note 7
29 *Von Sick 1930*, p. 26
30 Inv. no. 847-1; HdG 83 and 96; *Popovitch 1967*, p. 8; *Paris 1970-1971*, pp. 14-15, no. 13 and fig.
31 HdG 74; *Dresden 1979*, pp. 106-107, no. 1479 and fig.
32 *Schaar 1958*, p. 86; *Haverkamp-Begemann 1978*, p. 116; *Schloss 1982*, p. 20; Brown in *Berlin / London / Philadelphia 1984*, p. 90; *Ten Doesschate Chu 1987*, p. 87
33 See cat. no. 58, note 26
34 *Jürss 1982*, p. 109, no. 237 and fig. 1; *Naumann 1981*, vol. II, pp. 24-26, no. 22 and fig.
35 Inv. no. 840; *Maclaren 1960*, pp. 249-251, no. 840; *Naumann 1981*, vol. II, pp. 65-69, no. II 54 and fig.
36 *Sluijter et al. 1988*, pp. 253-255, no. 90 and fig.
37 *Snoep-Reitsma 1973*, pp. 215-216; *Naumann 1981*, vol. II, p. 69; *Schloss 1982*, p. 19; *Broos 1987*, p. 359, note 23
38 *Otte 1987*, p. 8; on the earliest image of the Negro from a Dutch perspective, see *Van den Boogaart 1982*, pp. 15, 19 and 25, note 68.
39 *Stockholm 1952*, p. 35 and fig.; on the Negro in art, see *Debrunner 1979*, pp. 57-63 and 91-96.
BB

The Hague 1620 / 1621 – Overschie 1690

Canvas, 119.4 x 101.5 cm (47 x 40 in.)
To the left, on the edge of the table: *A V B F* (*A V B* in ligature) (ca. 1660-1665)
Champaign, Ill., Krannert Art Museum, inv. no. 1972.2.2

Abraham van Beyeren was presumably a pupil of the Hague painter Pieter de Putter, after whose manner he initially made fish still lifes that show a sure touch and great skill in the rendering of materials. In 1640 he was a member of the guild in The Hague. There in 1647 he married (for the second time) the daugher of the society portraitist Crispiaen van den Queborn and received more mention as a dubious debtor than as a successful painter. In 1657 he became a member of the Delft guild, but he returned to The Hague in 1663, after which he settled in Amsterdam in 1669. Five years later he left for Alkmaar, and finally ended up living in Overschie in 1678.

From 1650 on he painted, besides fish still lifes, flower and banquet still lifes and, as a surprising sideline, sea pieces. Because of the dearth of dated work it is difficult to arrive at a chronology. His oeuvre is nevertheless characterized by the admirable representation of materials, from silver goblets and mirroring glasswork to moistly gleaming cut ham. Obviously he was able to give full expression to his technical virtuosity in his *pronk* (banquet) still lifes.

Provenance
Dealer P. de Boer, Amsterdam, 1963
Collection Mr. and Mrs. David W. Steadman, Berkeley, Calif., 1966
Collection Herman Charles Krannert, Indianapolis, before 1972 (bought from Newhouse Galleries, New York)
Krannert Art Museum, Champaign, 1972 (bequest from Krannert)

Bibliography
Amsterdam 1963, no. 2 and fig.
San Francisco / Toledo / Boston 1966-1967, p. 152, no. 104
Christison 1972, p. 487
Hope 1973-1974, p. 266
New York etc. 1973-1975, pp. 34-35, no. 8 and fig.
Sullivan 1974, p. 278
Johnson 1975, pp. 10-26
Gerdts 1981, p. 32 and fig. 2.1
Cleveland 1982, p. 221
Sutton 1986, pp. 44-45, fig. 58

In 1977 the Mauritshuis acquired the *Banquet Still Life* [1] by Abraham van Beyeren as a virtually unknown work.[1] Exactly the

1
Abraham van Beyeren
Banquet Still Life
Canvas, 99.5 x 120.5 cm (39¼ x 47⅜ in.)
At the right, on the edge of the table: *A V B f* (*A V B* in ligature) (ca. 1660-1665)
The Hague, Mauritshuis, inv. no. 1056

2
Abraham van Beyeren
Banquet Still Life
Canvas, 99.7 x 82 cm (39¼ x 32¼ in.)
Lower left, on the tabletop: *AVBf.* (AVB in ligature)
(ca. 1660-1665)
Cleveland, Ohio, The Cleveland Museum of Art,
Mr. & Mrs. William H. Marlatt Fund, inv. no. 60.80

3
Abraham van Beyeren
Banquet Still Life
Canvas, 102 x 85 cm (40⅛ x 33½ in.)
Neither signed nor dated (ca. 1660-1665)
Oxford, The Ashmolean Museum, inv. no. 534

same may be said of the *Banquet Still Life* shown here, which the Krannert Art Museum in Champaign, Illinois, had acquired from the Krannert estate only five years earlier. In 1961 Herman Charles Krannert (1888-1972), a manufacturer from Indianapolis, made a substantial contribution to the financing of the museum and art center at Champaign, which were both named after him. Upon his death in 1972, he left his art collection of paintings and sculptures to the museum.[2] The Krannert Art Museum has a small collection of Dutch masters of which this still life is a little gem.[3] These two banquet still lifes in Champaign and The Hague by Van Beyeren have not only their recent discovery in common but, as we shall see, also their outstanding quality and even numerous details.[4]

David Wilton Steadman had bought the painting in Amsterdam before 1966. It is not by accident that it was the dealer P. de Boer of Amsterdam who, in 1963, showed the painting, now in the collection in Champaign, for the first time.[5] This firm has always made every effort to convert the ever-decreasing interest in still lifes, which began at the beginning of our century, into admiration. In 1935 the dealership had organized the exhibition *Bloemstukken van Oude Meesters* (Flower Pieces by Old Masters), and in 1982 it celebrated its sixtieth anniversary with the exhibition *A Flowery Past*, at which many paintings were shown that had at one time been sold or displayed by the De Boer firm.[6] The latter exhibition was the first of a series of successful overviews of Dutch still life to feature scholarly contributions by Sam Segal.[7]

The most recent exhibition in this series, entitled *A Prosperous Past* (shown in Delft, Cambridge, Massachusetts, and Fort Worth, Texas) was dedicated to the banquet still life in the seventeenth century in Holland. There were two canvases by Van Beyeren on view that are closely related to the acquisitions in The Hague and Champaign: one coming from Cleveland, Ohio (The Cleveland Museum of Art) [2],[8] the other from Oxford (The Ashmolean Museum) [3].[9] Segal explained why all these still lifes must have originated between 1660 and 1665.[10]

Typical – and a kind of hallmark of the master – is the reflection in a shiny pitcher of the artist at his easel, which also occurs in a number of other banquet still lifes.[11] This old motif had been used in 1612 by Clara Peeters in a *Still Life with Goblets and a Bouquet* (Karlsruhe, Staatliche Kunsthalle) [4].[12] Clara is repeatedly mirrored in the gleaming lobes of the silver goblet in the right rear, which appears to be of the same type as those in the Van Beyeren still life in Champaign. The lid shows a harnessed figure, a so-called *Miles Christianus* (Christian

Abraham van Beyeren Banquet Still Life

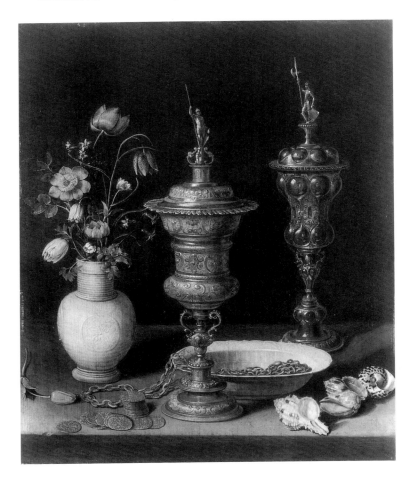

4
Clara Peeters
Still Life with Goblets and a Bouquet
Panel, 59.5 x 49 cm (23⅜ x 19¼ in.)
On the plinth: *CLARA. P. ANNO 1612*
Karlsruhe, Staatliche Kunsthalle, inv. no. 2222

motif is also clearly the same every time, but in the variant in Champaign it has not merely been copied from another example. The often repeated Chinese bowl is a product of the early seventeenth century known as a *klapmuts*.[15] The form and decoration are not always identical and usually look like a product of the painter's imagination. The watch with its open lid and the lemon with the curling peel are also recurring motifs. The cut melon, however, is a detail that appears in just this fashion only in a banquet still life in Rotterdam (Museum Boymans-van Beuningen).[16] In the niche in the left rear an ornamental glass 'à la façon de Venise' stands on a well-thumbed book, and that would appear to be a minor innovation of the painter.

Despite the meager proceeds that he got from his craft, Van Beyeren painted his banquet still lifes with love and pleasure. It is perhaps a somewhat bitter thought that the displayed abundance does not give a picture of his daily table. But that was not his intent. It would appear that, like a true man of the seventeenth century, the painter almost casually reminded his public that this splendor was nothing but vanity. It is presumably not without reason that a watch lies next to the bunch of juicy grapes. After all, the regularity of the clockwork alludes to moderation in general, which is not a vain admonition in the context of this excess.[17] A tipped-over glass like the one that lies at the right is included in many *vanitas* still lifes as a reminder of the brevity of earthly pleasures.[18] The figure of the *Miles Christianus* on the lid of the goblet was known from prints as the popular image of the fighter against the seven deadly sins.[19] It is a frequent symbol in *vanitas* still lifes (cat. no. 16, fig. 2), which is

5
Illustration from Roemer Visscher, *Sinnepoppen*
(1614), no. LIII

Knight).[13] The same goblet occurs in the earliest dated still life by Van Beyeren, one of 1651 (Düsseldorf, Kunstmuseum, collection Bentinck-Thyssen).[14] Possibly it was an atelier prop; possibly he knew it from other paintings, for this sort of beaker was popular with the earlier generation of still life painters.

Repetition of details is common with Van Beyeren, and he could, so to speak, paint the silver pitcher with the handle in the shape of a caryatid with his eyes closed. Nevertheless, the reflection of the arrangement on the table appears to have been freshly observed with each version. This is also true for the tray with hams that rests on a woven breadbasket. This pictorial

not to say that Van Beyeren's *Banquet Still Life* is a pronounced *vanitas* piece. At the most we are given subtle hints.

Such a piled-up table gives an image of the luxury that one did have to learn to resist.[20] Had Van Beyeren read Roemer Visscher's *Sinnepoppen*? In it we find a print with the title: 'Ad Tragoedias' [5].[21] The correspondence with the composition by Clara Peeters [4] is striking. The commentary presented with the print states that 'Great silver gilded Bowls, cups, Basins [and] Pitchers' do not serve 'the daily necessities' (in translation) but are instead cause for discord and strife.

1 *Broos 1987*, pp. 64-67, no. 10 and fig.
2 *Christison 1972*, p. 487; NCAB, pp. 342-343 (documentation The Fine Arts Museums of San Francisco)
3 *Sutton 1986*, p. 44
4 *Johnson 1975*, passim
5 *Amsterdam 1963*, no. 2 and fig.
6 *Amsterdam 1935-A*; *Segal 1982*, pp. 1-2
7 *Segal 1983*; *Segal 1984*; *Segal 1988-1989*
8 *Sullivan 1974*, passim; *Cleveland 1982*, pp. 220-221, no. 93 and fig.; *Segal 1988-1989*, p. 247, no. 51 and fig.
9 *Van Gelder 1950*, pp. 44-45, no. 10 and fig.; *Segal 1988-1989*, p. 246, no. 50 and fig.
10 *Segal 1988-1989*, p. 176
11 *Cleveland 1982*, p. 221, gave a summary (see also *Sullivan 1974*); *Van Gelder n.d.*, pp. 34-37, gave an overview of repeated motifs in the work of Van Beyeren.
12 *Lauts 1966*, vol. I, p. 236, no. 2222, vol. II, pp. 397, 462 and fig.; *Vorenkamp 1933*, p. 59, note 1, summarized this painterly topos; see also p. 211 (cat. no. 16).
13 *Bergström 1983*, pp. 440-443 and fig. 1
14 Inv. no. D 37 / 1974; *Segal 1988-1989*, p. 173, fig. 9.2
15 *Jörg 1983*, p. 70, no. 4 and fig.
16 Inv. no. VdV 2; *Meijer 1989*, p. 123, no. 38 and fig.
17 *Bergström 1947 / 1956*, pp. 189-190
18 *Leyden 1970* gave two examples; *Sullivan 1974*, pp. 278-281, presented an extensive account of the *vanitas* in the work of Van Beyeren; see also *Bergström 1983*, pp. 443-444.
19 *Bergström 1983*, p. 442 and figs. 4-6; *Ter Kuile 1985*, pp. 72-73, fig. VI-5; on the tradition of the *Miles Christianus* in word and image, see *Wang 1975*.
20 For the most extensive treatment of the symbolism of Van Beyeren's painting, see *Johnson 1975*.
21 *De Jongh 1967-A*, pp. 59-60, pointed out that a banquet still life can be a call for moderation; *De Jongh et al. 1982*, pp. 80-83.
22 *Roemer Visscher / Brummel 1614 / 1949*, p. 53, no. 53; on banquet still lifes in an allegorical context (transitoriness), see *Klessmann et al. 1978*, pp. 174-177, no. 41; see cat. no. 19, p. 227

BB

Abraham Bloemaert Moses Striking Water from the Rock (Aqua)

Gorinchem 1564 – Utrecht 1651

Canvas, 79.7 x 107.9 cm (31⅛ x 42½ in.)
Lower right: *A. Blomaert. fe / aº. 1596*
New York, The Metropolitan Museum of Art, inv. no. 1972.171

Bloemaert was a student of Joos de Beer in Utrecht and in 1580 went to Paris and Fontainebleau for about three years. With the exception of a short stay in Amsterdam (1591-1593), where his father Cornelis Bloemaert was city builder, he continued to live and work in Utrecht. Between 1590 and 1600 his style was strongly mannerist, in the mode of Bartholomeus Spranger. In addition to portraits, he depicted biblical and mythological scenes and allegories; he was also a competent draftsman.

After 1610 he began to paint more broadly, and when his pupil Gerard van Honthorst returned from Italy in 1620, Bloemaert belatedly underwent the influence of Caravaggio, which manifested itself especially in strong chiaroscuro. Still, the Caravaggesque realism never supplanted Bloemaert's bent for the decorative. His landscapes show the painter renewing himself even in advanced age: around 1600 he painted somewhat restless compositions with manneristically animated figures, which, after 1630, became less overloaded, more reserved, and less brightly colored, with the emphasis shifting to an idyllic atmosphere of bucolic life. Bloemaert had many pupils (four of his sons, Andries and Jan Both, Jan van Bijlert, and Gerard van Honthorst), and he may therefore be called the father of the seventeenth-century Utrecht school of painting.

In 1965 or 1966 Professor J.G. van Gelder and Mrs. I. van Gelder-Jost saw this important signed and dated (1596) scene by Abraham Bloemaert, *Moses Striking Water from the Rock*, at the dealer A. Stein on the Boulevard de LaTour-Maubourg in Paris.[1] The painting was then known only from black-and-white illustrations in several auction catalogues and in an out-of-date monograph of 1928 by Gustav Delbanco.[2] Naturally these images did not do justice to the splendid coloration of this mannerist masterpiece by the father of the Utrecht school of painting. The woman with the water pitcher in the middle is especially dazzling in her turquoise-and-enamel-pink striped dress and her crimson-red cloak, which wafts up in a voluptuous whirl. In the photograph that the Van Gelders received from Stein in 1966, the standing man at the right still has his hips modestly covered [1].[3] The sensual realism characteristic of mannerism was apparently not always appreciated.

Provenance

(?) Collection Jan Vincent, Amsterdam, 1622
Collection Isidor Sachs, Paris, 1871
Auction Sachs, Vienna, 1872
Auction Schönlank, Franze et al., Berlin, 1916
Collection Curt Glaser, Berlin, before 1928-1933
Auction Glaser, Berlin, 1933 (bought by Gurlitt)
Dealer Wolfgang Gurlitt, Munich, 1933-1962
Dealer A. Stein, Paris, 1965-1966
Dealer Kleinberger & Co., New York
Collection Bagley Reid, New York, ca. 1967-1970
Collection Mary V.T. Eberstadt, New York, 1972
The Metropolitan Museum of Art, New York, 1972
(gift of Mary V.T. Eberstadt by exchange)

Bibliography

Auction Vienna 1872, p. 17, no. 97
Auction Berlin 1916, p. 8, no. 63 and pl. 18
Delbanco 1928, pp. 24-25 and 74, no. 8 and fig. VIII
Lindeman 1928, p. 233
Lindeman 1929, pp. 120 and 233 and note 1
Lugt 1929, vol. I, p. 13
Auction Berlin 1933, p. 15, no. 241 and pl. 4
Munich 1962, no. 8 and fig.
Röthlisberger 1967, pp. 20-21
Minneapolis etc. 1968, no. 5
Stechow 1970, pp. 18-19, no. 3 and pl. 38
Slatkes 1970, p. 432, no. 3
New York 1973, no. 1
Lowenthal 1974, pp. 127-129 and fig. 5, p. 130, note 13, pp. 131 and 133
Walsh 1974, pp. 340-341 and fig. 1, p. 349, notes 1-2
Lowenthal 1975, vol. I, pp. 69 and 74, vol. III, fig. 11
New York 1975, p. 92 and fig.
Baetjer 1980, vol. I, p. 12, vol. III, p. 395 and fig.
Hibbard 1980, pp. 276 and 278 and fig. 498
Lowenthal 1986, p. 69 and fig. 34
Sutton 1986, pp. 179-180 and fig. 254

1
Detail of cat. no. 8, before the restoration of about
1970

studio apparatus.[6] It is known that Bloemaert kept old drawings for consultation.[7]

Until 1972 the painting remained in private hands; most recently it was with Mary V.T. Eberstadt, widow of the banker Ferdinand Eberstadt. The next year The Metropolitan Museum of Art organized a small exhibition of prints and drawings by Bloemaert from the museum's collection to honor the new acquisition, *Moses Striking Water from the Rock*.[8] It was the first painting by a Dutch mannerist to be acquired by the Metropolitan.[9] Before the canvas came to the dealer Stein in Paris, it had apparently spent almost thirty years with the dealer Gurlitt in Munich. In 1962 Bloemaert's painting was still part of an exhibition there entitled *Meister der Manierismus* (Masters of mannerism), and, according to the catalogue, the dealer had acquired the work from the Glaser collection.[10] The library and paintings of the Berlin professor Curt Glaser had come under the hammer in 1933.[11] At that auction Glaser was identified only as an anonymous 'Berlin Art Lover' (in translation), but his name was divulged by Lindeman and Lugt.[12] Before that the painting had been auctioned in Berlin in 1916 from the otherwise un-familiar collection of Carl Franze in Tetschen a. E., and, still earlier, sold in Vienna in 1872 from the collection of one Isidor Sachs. This collector was said to have 'died in Paris during the

In 1970 Wolfgang Stechow, then Mary Conover Mellon Professor of Art at Vassar College in Poughkeepsie, and his students organized an exhibition, held in the Vassar College Art Gallery, with the intriguing title: *Dutch Mannerism: Apogee and Epilogue*. The painting by Bloemaert, which had in the years since 1966 been sold to an owner in the United States, was included in this exhibit, and the overpainting on the male figure had in the meantime been removed.[4] Since then it is again more readily apparent that a drawing by Abraham Bloemaert of a male nude with one leg drawn up (Vienna, Graphische Sammlung Albertina) [**2**][5] shows correspondences (in reverse) with the lower portion of the figure in the painting and is therefore to be considered as a kind of preparatory study. The drawing was made around 1590 and apparently belonged to the

2
Abraham Bloemaert
Study of a Standing Man
Drawing, 315 x 199 mm (12⅜ x 7⅞ in.)
Lower right (scratched out): *A Bloemaert* (ca. 1595)
Vienna, Graphische Sammlung Albertina,
inv. no. 8102

terror of 1871' (in translation), that is, during the bloody struggle between the Communards and the government troops.[13] Here the trail ends.

There is a small chance that the canvas is identical with 'a piece in which Moses strikes water from the rocks' (in translation) that is mentioned in the inventory of 1622 of Jan Vincent of Amsterdam.[14] But that is far from certain, as Bloemaert depicted the subject more than once (although the painting in New York is the only version in oil that may now be identified). We know the earliest painted version only from a citation. In 1591 the Utrecht lawyer and historian Arnoldus Buchelius listed in his diary the works by Bloemaert known to him, among which was a 'Moisen Israelitis aquam ex rupe producentem' (Moses strikes water from the rock for the Israelites).[15] We know of no painted Moses scene from this early period. We do, however, have a drawing of a slightly later date (Weimar, Schlossmuseum) [3],[16] of which there may possibly once have existed a painted version. John Walsh related this sheet to the painting of 1596.[17] Although some connection certainly exists between the painting and drawing, as with the drawing of the nude [2], it is not a question of a direct preparatory study; the arrangement is generally the same.

The departure point for both compositions is the biblical story of Exodus, in which we are told how the chosen people arrived in Rephidim, where there was no water: 'and the people murmured against Moses, and said, Wherefore is this that thou hast brought us up out of Egypt, to kill us and our children and our cattle with thirst?' (Exodus 17:3). At the Lord's command, Moses then struck the rock at Horeb with his staff, and water came forth so that the people could drink. In both versions Moses is a small figure in the background, before the rock face from which gushes a stream of water. The Israelites and their flocks are gathered around a deep, dry well which, in the painting, is suggested more than actually shown. There are corresponding details between the two works, such as the animals to the left and the dishes in the foreground, and above all the man who, with his back turned to us, bends over the filling basin. A stooping man seen from behind is a recurring motif with Bloemaert. He appears in a drawing (Paris, Musée du Louvre) [4] which is considered to be either a copy after the preparatory study by Bloemaert or the preparatory study itself for the 1596 painting in The Metropolitan Museum of Art.[18] In the drawing the man lifts a large jug. Behind him is a broadly gesturing woman, who, in the painting, is located a little more to the right. The animals at the left stand with their tails facing us, as in the drawing in Weimar. The right half of the sheet in Paris

3
Abraham Bloemaert
Moses Striking Water from the Rock
Drawing, 340 x 487 mm (13⅜ x 19⅛ in.)
Lower right (not autograph?): *A. Bloemart* (ca. 1590-1595)
Weimar, Schlossmuseum, inv. no. KK 4481

4
Abraham Bloemaert (copy after)
Moses Striking Water from the Rock
Drawing, 312 x 409 mm (12¼ x 16⅛ in.)
Neither signed nor dated (ca. 1596)
Paris, Musée du Louvre, inv. no. 20.483

shows so many correspondences with the painting that here we may certainly speak of a preparatory study, even though it has not survived in an autograph version.[19] It is yet more proof that Bloemaert used drawings to prepare his compositions in many different ways.

In this (probably copy after the) preliminary study and in the final version, the emphasis is on the woman in the middle with the jug. Her prominent place in the painting is further underscored by the lighting and the unusual coloration. Obviously she symbolizes the water that saved the people of the Old Testament. In the miracle of the water, people saw a parallel with baptism as a Christian sacrament. Saint Paul already saw this correspondence, as his first letter to the Corinthians demonstrates: 'And did [our fathers] all drink the same spiritual drink: for they drank of that spiritual Rock that followed them: and that Rock was Christ' (1 Corinthians 10:4).[20] The many earlier and later depictions of the miracle performed by Moses rarely show so much of an ode to water as does Bloemaert, who quite literally banishes the events from Exodus to the background.[21] By contrast, though in the painting of his fellow townsman Joachim Wtewael, *Moses Striking Water from the Rock* of 1624 (Washington, D.C., National Gallery of Art),[22] there is a crowd of drinking people and animals to be seen, and Moses is clearly the principal actor.

One may therefore ask if Bloemaert actually rendered the same subject as did his many colleagues. A print of 1586 after Hendrick Goltzius depicting *Aqua* (Water) [5] gives occasion for such a reassessment.[23] Here a graceful female figure with a water jug is the personification of Water: in the background, we see Christ baptized by Saint John. The attention paid to the biblical subject matter is little greater than with Bloemaert. On the basis of these correspondences, we get the distinct impression that Abraham Bloemaert, too, depicted *Aqua* rather than a story from the Old Testament.

1 According to the caption with the photograph (KHI-U).
2 *Delbanco 1928*, pp. 24-25, 74, no. 8 and fig. VIII.
3 This loincloth is also seen in *Delbanco 1928*, fig. VIII.
4 *Stechow 1970*, pp. 18-19, no. 3 and pl. 38
5 *Benesch 1928*, p. 36, no. 368 (Cornelis Cornelisz) and pl. 95
6 *Reznicek-Buriks 1956*, pp. 165-166, figs. 1-2; for an autograph variant, see *Dittrich 1976-1977*, pp. 89-90, fig. 1.
7 *Broos 1988-A*, pp. 62-72
8 *New York 1973*, no. 1; on Eberstadt, see *WWW*, vol. XXX, p. 206.
9 *Walsh 1974*, p. 341
10 *Munich 1962*, no. 9: 'Erworben aus Slg. Glaser, Berlin.'
11 *Auction Berlin 1933*, p. 15, no. 241 and pl. 4
12 *Lindeman 1928*, p. 233; *Lugt 1929*, vol. I, p. 13, no. 86
13 *Auction Vienna 1872*, title page; from the mention in *Auction Berlin 1916*, p. 8, no. 63, it appears that the painting did not come from the Schönlank collection, as is sometimes thought, but from the collection Car. Franze, Tetschen a. E.
14 Notations of A. Bredius (RKD), 'Abraham / Lowijs Blommaert,' p. 4
15 *Hoogewerff / Van Regteren Altena 1928*, p. 31, note 3. Ineke Wansink (research collaborator at the RKD) assured me that it has become apparent from examination of the diary that this notation truly dates from 1591. I hereby thank her for allowing me to peruse her text on Bloemaert's painting.
16 *Barth 1981*, p. 82, no. 64
17 *Walsh 1974*, pp. 340-341, fig. 2; Mrs. I. van Gelder-Jost wrote next to the photograph of this drawing (KHI-U): 'Eerste schets voor schilderij 1965/66 bij A. Stein, Parijs ... gedat. 1596.'
18 *Lugt 1929*, vol. I, p. 13, no. 86 and pl. XII: 'nous ne sérions pas étonné de rencontrer ailleurs un meilleur exemplaire de ce dessin.'
19 *Slatkes 1970*, p. 432, no. 3 and *Walsh 1974*, p. 349, note 2
20 *Stechow 1970*, p. 19; *Réau 1955-1959*, vol. II, p. 201
21 *Réau 1955-1959*, vol. II, pp. 201-202, gave an overview of the theme in art; see also *DIAL* 71 E 19.2 and *Lowenthal 1974*, pp. 134-135, note 21.
22 Inv. no. 1972.11.1; *Washington 1985*, p. 440 and fig.; *Lowenthal 1986*, pp. 151-152, no. A-88 and pls. 122 and XXII
23 B. 21; *Hollstein*, vol. VIII, p. 138, no. 498
    BB

5
Anonymous after Hendrick Goltzius
Aqua
Engraving, 214 x 158 mm (8⅜ x 6¼ in.)
On another print from the series: *H Goltzius excudebat*
Ao. 1586
Amsterdam, Rijksprentenkabinet

Ferdinand Bol

9 | 'Portrait' of a Young Man with a Sword

Dordrecht 1616 – Amsterdam 1680

Canvas, 205.7 x 130.8 cm (81 x 51½ in.)
Neither signed nor dated (ca. 1645-1650)
Dayton, Ohio, The Dayton Art Institute, inv. no. 62.18

Son of a barber-surgeon in Dordrecht, Bol received his first instruction in painting from Jacob Gerritz Cuyp. Around **1635** he qualified himself as a history painter in Amsterdam with Rembrandt, who traded in the work of his pupil. Bol was never able to free himself from the example of his master, not even after **1650**, when his style became looser and his palette – especially in his portraits – clearer. This fashionable change in style brought him, like some of his fellow pupils, official commissions that passed Rembrandt by. A figure borrowed from Rembrandt's renowned *Hundred-Guilder Print* (**B. 74**) in Bol's painting *Pyrrhus and Fabricius* (**1656**) was to be the only contribution of the old master to the decoration of the new city hall in Amsterdam, the palace on the Dam. On 8 October **1669**, the day on which Rembrandt was carried to his grave, Bol was joined in matrimony to a rich widow, after which he hardly touched his brushes again.

This handsomely painted portrait with its theatrical pose was for a long time one of the showpieces of the collection Van Aalst in Hoevelaken. C.J.K. van Aalst (1866-1939) [**1**], who held an honorary doctorate, was president of the Dutch Trading Company in Amsterdam. In 1925 he settled at Huis-te-Hoevelaken in the Province of Gelderland, after allowing his splendid Huis

Provenance

Collection of the seventh Duke of Richmond, Goodwood House, Sussex, 1877, Gordon Castle, 1879-1928
Collection of the eighth Duke of Richmond, Goodwood House, 1928-1935
Collection C.J.K. van Aalst, Hoevelaken, before 1939
Collection N.J. van Aalst, Hoevelaken, 1939-1960
Auction Van Aalst, London, 1960 (£840)
Dealer Central Picture Gallery, New York
Collection Mr. and Mrs. Elton F. Macdonald, Grosse Pointe Park, Michigan
The Dayton Art Institute, Dayton, Ohio, 1962 (gift of Mr. & Mrs. Elton F. Macdonald)

Bibliography

Goodwood House 1877, p. 15, no. 23
Von Moltke 1939, pp. 78-79 and fig. XVIII
Valentiner 1939, p. XII
Auction London 1960, p. 7, no. 7 and pl. IV
WCA, vol. XII (1960), p. 498, no. 5572
McCoy 1962, p. 2 and fig.
Van Hall 1963, p. 32, no. 31
Sumowski 1965, p. 124, no. 20
Evans 1969, pp. 98-99 and 143, no. 35 and fig.
Sumowski 1973, p. 100, note 70
Blankert 1976, pp. 86 and 207-208, no. A 73
Dayton 1976, p. 6
Sumowski 1979-1985, vol. I, p. 300, no. 138
Wilson 1980-1981, no. 6 and fig.
Blankert 1982, pp. 58-59, 67 and 122-123, nos. 72 and 74 and pl. 79
Sumowski 1983, pp. 301 and 358, no. 119 and fig.
Sutton 1986, pp. 76-77 and fig. 109
Vasseur 1987, p. 279 and fig. on cover
Giltay et al. 1988, p. 26, no. 3

1
Antoon van Welie
The Board of the Dutch Overseas Trust. The standing man in the center is C.J.K. van Aalst (1866-1939). Medium, measurements, and location unknown

met de kolommen (House with the Columns) to be turned into the official residence of the mayor of Amsterdam.[1] After Van Aalst's death in 1939 this collection was catalogued by J.W. von Moltke, with the Rembrandt connoisseur Wilhelm Valentiner contributing the foreword.[2] Valentiner outlined how Van Aalst brought together at Huis-te-Hoevelaken works of the Golden Age, with paintings by Rembrandt and his pupils at the core of the collection as well as work by the Leyden *fijnschilders*, marine paintings, and portraits. He compared collecting in the old world and in the new and stated candidly that American collectors were primarily characterized by their unlimited means and the Dutch ones, by contrast, by their thorough connoisseurship and sharp insight. In the case of Van Aalst this observation was presumably justified because he also collected Rembrandt's early work, whereas in America there was interest only in the more commercially viable later Rembrandt. These early Rembrandt paintings of Van Aalst (such as the 'Braamcamp Tobit') are no longer believed to be by the great master's hand.[3] When N.J. van Aalst had the collection of his father auctioned in London in 1960, the chief attraction was the *Juno* by Rembrandt, then still controversial (Los Angeles, The Armand Hammer Collection).[4] It caused a stir in the press that this canvas did not fetch the estimated million guilders but was held back when the bidding went no higher than 500,000 guilders.[5] With the benefit of hindsight, one could observe that there was a great deal of chaff amid the wheat of the Van Aalst collection. The *Juno* and the monumental painting by Ferdinand Bol belonged to the best works at Huis-te-Hoevelaken. By way of a New York dealer, the *'Portrait' of a Young Man with a Sword* was acquired by Elton F. MacDonald (1901-1978) from Michigan, who was a trustee of the Dayton Art Institute from 1960 to 1967. He gave the painting to the museum in 1962.[6]

Upon the death of the eighth Duke of Richmond (1860-1935), the painting was sold. In 1936 Valentiner supplied a certificate with the portrait in which he attributed it to Bol.[7] Its nineteenth-century owner, the seventh Duke of Richmond, in Sussex, cherished it as a *Portrait of a Flemish Nobleman* by Rembrandt, but this attribution (and title) were not taken seriously in a single publication.[8] Naturally there exists a strong affinity with the work of Bol's master. In virtually all discussions of the work, one is directed to Rembrandt's *'Self-Portrait'* of 1635 (formerly Vaduz, collection of the Prince of Liechtenstein), which is said to have served as the most important model.[9] However, the autograph status of this work is by no means secure, so that the most one can say is that during Bol's student years in Rembrandt's

atelier such 'portraits' were rendered after models – sometimes the master himself – in picturesque garb. A clear example of this is Rembrandt's etching of 1634, 'Self-Portrait' with Beret and Sword [2].[10] This is not a portrait but a study of a pose, a gesture, and a costume. Pupils made copies of such figures, which we might call travesty portraits. Depictions of heads only were called 'mugs.' Rembrandt himself studied Eastern types to be able to insert them into biblical scenes, as may be seen in a work like *Samson Threatening His Father-in-Law* of 163[5?] (Berlin, Staatliche Museen, Gemäldegalerie).[11]

Already before Bol became his pupil, Rembrandt rendered standing figures in ostensibly Eastern costumes, ones showing a marked resemblance to the portrait under discussion. Compare, for instance, his etching *The Persian* of 1632 [3],[12] in which a pose found in his 'Self-Portrait' with a Poodle of 1631 is repeated (Paris, Petit Palais).[13] It has recently been shown that in 1633 or after Rembrandt himself most likely added the poodle.[14] By then a collaborator in Rembrandt's atelier, possibly Isaac Jouderville, had made a copy of the earlier state of the painting (present location unknown) [4].[15] It would appear that Bol knew this very version.

Although in the work by Bol the velvet mantle is draped over the shoulders somewhat differently than in the copy after Rembrandt, and though Bol chose a feathered beret instead of a turban, the similarity of costume and presentation of the figure is striking. Moreover, the table with the coat of arms above it may be seen as a decorative element inspired by this prototype. A paraphrase of the composition by Rembrandt is seen in the drawing *Standing Oriental with a Sword* (Windsor Castle, collection

4
Pupil of Rembrandt (Isaac Jouderville?)
Copy (minus poodle) after the 'Self-Portrait' with a Poodle
Panel, 70.4 x 50.2 cm (27³⁄₄ x 19³⁄₄ in.)
Neither signed nor dated (ca. 1631-1633)
Location unknown

5
Ferdinand Bol
Standing Oriental with a Sword
Pen drawing with wash, 318 x 202 mm (12¹⁄₂ x 8 in.)
Neither signed nor dated (ca. 1635-1640)
Windsor Castle, collection Her Majesty the Queen,
inv. no. 6515

6
Ferdinand Bol
'Self-Portrait'
Canvas, 90 x 72 cm (35½ x 28⅜ in.)
Left, at shoulder height: *Bol [fe] 1646*
Dordrecht, Dordrechts Museum, inv. no. 887/372

Her Majesty the Queen) [5],[16] which used to be ascribed to Barent Fabritius, but which has for some time been rightly attributed to Ferdinand Bol. It is well possible that Bol used this drawing as a modello and that, as a young man wanting to be immortalized in exotic dress, he submitted the sheet to him as a concept for the composition of the portrait (see cat. no. 52, fig. 3).[17]

In 1939 Valentiner proposed that Bol painted himself in this life-size portrait.[18] Bredius and Hofstede de Groot had earlier carried on a somewhat emotional dispute about the self-portraits of Bol (occasioned by Valentiner's book *Wiedergefundene Rembrandtbilder*), which debouched into a polemic in *The Burlington Magazine* in 1923.[19] Not until the monograph on Bol by Albert Blankert appeared in 1982 was this discussion finally laid to rest. According to him there was but one fairly well-documented *Self-Portrait* (Amsterdam, Rijksmuseum), which Bol presumably made after the death of his first wife in 1660 and before his second marriage in 1669.[20] The so-called self-portraits of the second half of the forties may show some relationship to the way Bol looked, but are to be construed as mugs. These paintings,

such as the *'Self-Portrait' with Beret* of 1646 (Dordrecht, Dordrechts Museum) [6],[21] depict the concept of an artist more than the artist himself.[22] It is apparent that the Dayton painting of the young man with the long chin is not a portrait of Ferdinand Bol, as American scholars have been fond of claiming. The premature conclusion that it is a self-portrait has generally led to a too early dating of the painting, to the period between 1635 and 1640.[23] Reassuringly, recent monographs on the painter propose a later date of origin, namely between 1645 and 1650.[24]

For an interpretation of this depiction we must once again transport ourselves to the atelier of Rembrandt. In contemporary inventories there are descriptions of portraits in disguise of the kind he marketed. Applicable to the copy (by Jouderville?) [4] may well be a notice in the inventory of Lambert Jacobsz, dated 1637: 'A beautiful young Turkish prince after Rembrandt' (in translation), in which instance it should be clear that a true Turk was not depicted.[25] As becomes apparent from other references in the same inventory, any suitable model could pose: 'a small oriental female's mug [being] a depiction of H. Ulenburg's wife' (in translation).[26] In emulation of the painters themselves and of their models, the burghers also began to present themselves as gods of antiquity, as biblical types, as shepherds or shepherdesses, or as literary figures. The term *portrait historié* has been coined for this genre.[27] Bol painted a beautiful example of this kind of picture in 1647, the *Portrait of a Man in the Guise of Aeneas* (London [Blackheath], Ranger's House) [7].[28] The pendant represents the wife as Dido hunting (Stockholm, collection Bergsten).[29] This role playing was probably intended as a

7
Ferdinand Bol
Portrait of a Man in the Guise of Aeneas
Canvas, 130.2 x 101.9 cm (51¼ x 40⅛ in.)
Upper right: *f. Bol fecit. 1647*
London (Blackheath), Ranger's House, no inv. no.

Ferdinand Bol 'Portrait' of a Young Man with a Sword

metaphor for love, but there are also pictures of costume parties for which no good explanation can be offered.[30]

The dress of the personage in the painting by Bol shows striking similarities to the drawings that Rembrandt made of costumed actors at the Amsterdam theater.[31] One of these could well depict Gijsbrecht van Aemstel (London, Victoria and Albert Museum) [8],[32] the hero of one of Joost van den Vondel's tragedies. Another represents Capitano from the commedia dell'arte (Amsterdam, Rijksprentenkabinet).[33] In *Gebruik èn misbruik des toneels* (Uses and abuses of the stage) the poet Pels dismissed such theatrical getup as unclassical bric-a-brac: 'Harnesses, helmets, Japanese daggers, fur, / And frayed collars, which he [Rembrandt] thought picturesque' (in translation).[34] At the expense of Rembrandt, the poet here meted out criticism of the theater costumes of his time and, indirectly, of Bol's model.

Is the young man in the painting in Dayton also intended as a Gijsbrecht or a Capitano? For us he must remain an unknown man who had himself depicted life size in the theatrical trappings used by Rembrandt and his pupils as an alternative to an everyday presentation.

1 *Brugmans / Japikse 1938*, pp. 22-24; GPW, vol. I, p. 15; *Wijnman et al. 1974*, p. 382
2 *Von Moltke 1939*
3 *Valentiner 1939*, p. IX; relevant here are the numbers B 1, B 2, and C 4 in *Bruyn et al. 1982*, pp. 399-409 and 467-477.
4 *Gerson / Bredius 1969*, pp. 396 and 617, no. 639 and fig.
5 See the newspaper clipping in the copy of *Auction London 1960*, RKD.
6 WWA-A, vol. XXXIV
7 *Auction London 1960*, p. 7, no. 7; see also *Valentiner 1939*, p. XII
8 *Von Moltke 1939*, p. 78 (with mention of a catalogue of Gordon Castle of 1879) and *Auction London 1960*, p. 7, no. 7; *Goodwood House 1877*, p. 15, no. 23
9 *Gerson / Bredius 1969*, pp. 21 and 548, no. 25 and fig.
10 B. 23; *Hollstein*, vol. XVIII, p. 11, no. B. 23, vol. XIX, pp. 14-15, no. B. 23 / I and B. 23 / II
11 Inv. no. 802; *Gerson / Bredius 1969*, pp. 412 and 598, no. 499 and fig.
12 B. 152; *Hollstein*, vol. XVIII, p. 76, no. B. 152, vol. XIX, p. 128, no. B. 152
13 Inv. no. Dut. 925; *Gerson / Bredius 1969*, p. 12 and 548, no. 16 and fig.
14 *Bruyn et al. 1982*, pp. 373-382, no. A 40 and fig.
15 *Wright 1982*, p. 22, no. 38 and fig.; *Bruyn et al. 1982*, p. 381, no. 7.1 and fig. 7; *Van de Wetering 1983*, pp. 64, 66 and fig. 9; *Sumowski 1983-A*, pp. 1438 and 1447, no. 94 and fig.
16 *Van Puyvelde 1944*, p. 60, no. 659 and pl. 73; *Sumowski 1979-1985*, vol. I, pp. 300-301, no. 138 and fig.
17 *Sumowski 1973*, p. 100, note 70, pointed to the connection with the painting in Dayton.
18 *Valentiner 1939*, p. XII; this was not first assumed in *Auction London 1960*, p. 7, no. 7, as *Blankert 1982*, p. 123, no. 72 believed.
19 *Bredius 1923*, *Hofstede de Groot 1923*; see also *Mellaart 1923* and *Van Hall 1963*, pp. 30-33, nos. 1-45
20 Inv. no. A 42; *Van Thiel et al. 1976*, p. 123, no. A 42 and fig.; *Blankert 1982*, pp. 131-133, no. 103 and pl. 112
21 *Blankert 1982*, p. 118, no. 60 and pl. 60
22 *Blankert 1982*, p. 58
23 Especially *McCoy 1962*, p. 2, *Evans 1969*, p. 143, and *Wilson 1980-1981*, no. 6
24 *Sumowski 1983*, p. 301, no. 119 and *Blankert 1982*, p. 122, no. 72
25 *Strauss / Van der Meulen 1979*, p. 144, no. 1637/4 (present transcription improved)
26 Ibidem
27 *Wishnevsky 1967*, especially pp. 13-15: 'Zur Terminologie'
28 *Blankert 1982*, p. 99, no. 22 and pl. 9
29 *Blankert 1982*, pp. 99-100, no. 23 and pl. 10
30 According to *Wilson 1980-1981*, no. 6 and *Giltay et al. 1988*, pp. 26-27, no. 3, cat. no. 9 is in Polish dress, but this is not the case (compare also *Broos 1974*, p. 200).
31 *Van de Waal 1969* and *Albach 1979*
32 *Benesch 1973*, vol. II, p. 79, no. 312 and fig. 379; this drawing could have been made by Bol.
33 Inv. no. 1961:76; *Benesch 1973*, vol. II, p. 75, no. 293 and fig. 354; *Schatborn 1985*, pp. 20-21, no. 8 and fig.
34 *Pels 1681*, p. 36; *Slive 1953*, pp. 102-103
BB

8
Rembrandt (attributed to)
Actor as Gijsbrecht van Aemstel
Drawing, 160 x 105 mm (6¼ x 4⅛ in.)
Neither signed nor dated (ca. 1638)
London, Victoria and Albert Museum, inv. no. 50580

Zwolle 1617 – Deventer 1681

Canvas, 86.4 x 72 cm (34 x 28 in.)
Lower left, on the chair: *GTB 166[?]* (GTB in ligature)
Toledo, Ohio, The Toledo Museum of Art, inv. no. 52.9

He was the son of Gerard ter Borch the Elder, an artistically inclined tax collector of the city of Zwolle, who urged his children (including the artist's sister Gesina and brother Moses) to practice art. Gerard was trained in 1633 in Amsterdam by Pieter Molijn, and in 1635 became master in the guild in Haarlem. In that year he undertook a journey to England. In 1637 he also went to Italy, and in 1639 to Spain; from there he returned to Holland (Haarlem and Amsterdam) by way of France in 1640. The stay in Italy had no discernible influence on his style. He made his name as a portraitist, above all of burghers, whom he painted full-length but in small format. In 1646 he accompanied the Dutch delegation to the peace conference in Münster, where he painted portraits of the diplomats as well as depicting the moment of the closing of the Treaty of Münster in 1648.

After having worked in Amsterdam, Zwolle, The Hague, and Kampen, he married in 1654 in Deventer, and continued to live and work there. The portraits of the propertied bourgeoisie and the genre scenes that he later painted form the most admired part of his oeuvre because of their matchless rendering of fabrics, the subtle light effects, and the delicate handling. The interior scenes of about 1660 form a high point. Caspar Netscher was his most important pupil, but Ter Borch's influence extended to a broader circle of emulators, including ones of later generations.

Around 1930 *A Lady and Gentleman Making Music* by Gerard ter Borch was sold from the collection of the Hermitage in Leningrad. That is about all the information concerning the provenance that is given in the literature.[1] The complicated story of how, at the end of the twenties, the Russian government sold the art treasures that had been assembled by Catherine the Great has never been completely told. Well known are the massive auctions of decorative arts and paintings held in Berlin in 1928, and of prints and drawings held in Leipzig in 1930, 1931, and 1932.[2] But much less has been publicized concerning sales to private individuals. In 1979, however, José de Azeredo Perdigão, secretary to the Armenian oil magnate Calouste Gulbenkian (1869-1955) [1], used the personal papers of his former employer to compile a fascinating biography in which, among other things,

Provenance

(?) Collection Catherine the Great, Saint Petersburg, before 1796
Hermitage, Saint Petersburg, before 1864
Antikvariat, Leningrad, 1930; sold to Calouste Gulbenkian, Paris, 1930; sold to Georges Wildenstein, Paris and New York, 1930
Dealer Wildenstein & Co., New York, 1930-1951
The Toledo Museum of Art, Toledo, 1952 (bought with the aid of the Edward Drummond Libbey Fund)

Bibliography

Waagen 1864, p. 193, no. 874
Waagen 1870, p. 193, no. 874
Leningrad 1885, p. 156, no. 874
Somof 1895, p. 385, no. 874
Rosenberg 1897, p. 33, fig. 28 and p. 49
Somof 1901, pp. 430-431, no. 874
Wrangel 1909, p. 159 and fig.
Wurzbach, vol. II (1910), p. 701
Hellens 1911, p. 126 and fig. opp. p. 96
EdG ad 140 (vol. V [1912], p. 53, no. 140)
Von Weiner 1923, p. 179 and fig.
Los Angeles 1933, no. 15 and fig.
Chicago 1934, p. 20, no. 112
Cleveland 1936, p. 97, no. 247 and pl. LIV
Milliken 1936, pp. 12-13 and fig.
Milliken 1936-A, p. 438 and fig.
Toronto 1936, p. 5, no. 10 and fig.
Stechow 1938-B, no. 54 and fig.
Buffalo 1942, p. 16 and fig.
McCall / Barnouw 1942, p. 84, no. 64 and fig.
Hannema 1943, pp. 104-105 and 191 and fig.
Montreal 1944, p. 49, no. 90
Plietzsch 1944, pp. 24 and 53, no. 92 and fig.
Hartford 1950-1951, p. 19, no. 44 and pl. IX
Ohl Godwin 1953, pp. 22-23 and fig.
Museum News 1954, fig. on cover
Blake-More Godwin 1955, pp. 136 and 139, fig. 11
Gudlaugsson 1959, pp. 159-160
White 1959, pp. 71-72
Gudlaugsson 1960, p. 232, no. 271-II and pl. 92
Wittmann 1966, n.p., fig.
Waterhouse 1967, p. 170
Wittmann 1967, pp. 473-474 and fig. 14
The Hague 1974, pp. 196-197, no. 61 and fig.
Toledo 1976, pp. 26, 265 and fig. 129
Toledo 1976-A, p. 58, no. 17 and fig.
De Azeredo Perdigão 1979, p. 109
Sutton 1986, p. 294

Gerard ter Borch A Lady and Gentleman Making Music

1
Calouste Gulbenkian (1869-1955), oil magnate and collector
From: *De Azeredo Perdigão 1979*, frontispiece

Gulbenkian's transactions with the Russians are discussed in great detail. It is clear from his correspondence that on 28 May 1930 Gulbenkian sent Leningrad confirmation that, for 140,000 pounds sterling, he would buy a statue, the *Diana* by Houdon (Lisbon, Museu Calouste Gulbenkian),[3] and five paintings. One of these five was *A Lady and Gentleman Making Music* by Gerard ter Borch.[4]

As late as 1924 the Russian authorities had firmly denied that they intended to 'clean out' the former imperial collections. This denial had the opposite effect, because just then great collectors everywhere began to wave with fistfuls of dollars.[5] Armand Hammer was the first to attempt to acquire paintings from the Hermitage, but it was in effect Gulbenkian who made the break-through. We have been informed of the background to this story by John Walker, who for years was friends with the oil magnate, but who did not succeed in acquiring his collection for the National Gallery of Art in Washington. Walker wrote how Gulbenkian advised the Russians to dump their oil on the Western market, by which maneuver he managed to do the Royal Dutch Petroleum Company a bad turn. Out of gratitude, the Bolshevists agreed to sell art treasures from the Hermitage.

They thus granted a favor which also happened to yield them hard Western currency.[6]

On four occasions between 1928 and 1930, Calouste Gulbenkian carried on discussions in Paris with the chief of the Russian Department for the Purchase and Sale of Antiquities, the Antikvariat in Leningrad, concerning the acquisition of artworks. Detailed contracts were soon sealed, and thus the first consignments of French silver and Flemish paintings passed through the Berlin customs, to be followed in 1930 by the already mentioned five paintings, among which were two Rembrandts and *A Lady and Gentleman Making Music* by Ter Borch. The *Diana* by Houdon had gone by ship. The trusted agent whom Gulbenkian had sent to Leningrad to be present at the packing wrote back that it had been done at night by sparse candlelight. This report clearly indicates that the operation could not stand the light of day.[7] Gulbenkian's last coup was Rembrandt's *Portrait of an Old Man* (Lisbon, Museu Calouste Gulbenkian), which he was able to buy in October 1930 for 30,000 pounds.[8]

To keep the competition at bay, Gulbenkian had earlier made arrangements with the New York dealer Georges Wildenstein. In exchange for the promise that Wildenstein would not get involved with the Russians, Gulbenkian sold him four of the five paintings that he had acquired by the middle of 1930. With the sculpture by Houdon having been valued at 20,000 pounds, Gulbenkian had paid a total of 120,000 pounds. Wildenstein gave him just over 100,000 pounds for the four paintings, with Gulbenkian retaining one work that had therefore cost him not quite 20,000 pounds. This was Rembrandt's *Alexander the Great*,

2
Rembrandt
Alexander the Great
Canvas, 118 x 91 cm (46½ x 35⅞ in.)
Neither signed nor dated (ca. 1660)
Lisbon, Museu Calouste Gulbenkian, inv. no. 1488

now the pride of the Museu Calouste Gulbenkian in Lisbon [2].[9] Gulbenkian brought an abrupt end to his business with the Russians when the art dealer Zatsenstein (Matthiesen Galerie of Berlin) insinuated himself between them on behalf of American customers, notably Andrew Mellon.[10]

Wildenstein exhibited Gerard ter Borch's *A Lady and Gentleman Making Music* around the United States and Canada: in Los Angeles (1933), Chicago (1934), Cleveland (1936), Toronto (1936), Providence (1938), Buffalo (1942), New York (1942), Montreal (1944), and Hartford (1950-1951), usually referring to the impressive provenance of the painting.[11] It was said to have been auctioned from the collections of De Julienne (1767), of the Duke of Choiseul (1772), and of the Prince of Conti (1777). It was believed that Catherine the Great had acquired it at the latter auction. A. Somof had published this reconstruction in 1895, in the catalogue of the Hermitage.[12] Only in 1960 did Sturla Gudlaugsson divulge that there was a possible confusion with a painting in the National Gallery (London) [3], which also has a music-making lady and gentleman as its subject.[13] Even Somof's emphatic claim that the painting came from the collection of Catherine the Great is now difficult to verify. When the empress died, she left no fewer than 3,926 paintings: this figure is all we know about them.[14] The 1838 catalogue of the Hermitage in Saint Petersburg does mention a painting by Ter Borch that is said to have been acquired by Catherine and that is described as depicting a lady and gentleman making music, but it has much smaller dimensions (18 x 16 inches).[15]

However, Somof was certainly right when, in 1895, he postulated the similarity of the present work to a fully signed

and dated Gerard ter Borch of 1675 (Waddesdon Manor, The National Trust) [4].[16] This painting was bought by Gustave Baron de Rothschild from the Six collection in Amsterdam (see cat. no. 34) and later ended up in the collection of Ferdinand de Rothschild. In the eighteenth century it had been highly rated at several renowned auctions.[17] Somof considered the Saint Petersburg version to be a replica of the signed work, whereas Hofstede de Groot judged it to be 'an apparently old copy' (in translation). But, he added, it was difficult to give a definitive opinion because it was kept behind glass.[18] It is striking how these two works resemble each other like two drops of water. Though the painting in Waddesdon Manor is around three to four centimeters smaller than that in Toledo, it is apparent from the composition of the latter work that it must have been cut down on all sides. Originally these two canvases must have been identical.[19]

The existence of this second painting may have been the reason why, for more than twenty years, Wildenstein was obliged to harbor the version under discussion. In 1952 he sold the canvas to Otto Wittmann, director of The Toledo Museum of Art.[20] The museum in Toledo, Ohio, was founded in 1901 by a group of citizens under the ardent leadership of the successful glass manufacturer Edward Drummond Libbey (1854-1925). At his death in 1925, Libbey bequeathed the paintings that he had been collecting since 1900 (Rembrandt, Holbein, Turner, Constable) to the museum. When his widow died childless in 1938, the estate of the Libbeys came to the museum as well. Out of its proceeds a fund was formed for art acquisitions.[21] The Libbey fund has done much to enrich the collection of the Toledo museum. *A Lady and Gentleman Making Music* by Gerard ter Borch is also an Edward Drummond Libbey fund acquisition. Wittmann's most important goal was to strengthen the collection of seventeenth-century Dutch masters.[22]

The acquisition of the Ter Borch indicates the appreciation of the unmistakable qualities of this painting. Already in 1960

3
Gerard ter Borch
A Lady and Gentleman Making Music
Canvas, 67.6 x 57.8 cm (26⅝ x 22¾ in.)
Neither signed nor dated (ca. 1670)
London, National Gallery, inv. no. 864

▶ 4
Gerard ter Borch
A Lady and Gentleman Making Music
Canvas, 82.5 x 66.7 cm (32½ x 26¼ in.)
On the foot heater: *GT Borch / 1675* (GT in ligature)
Waddesdon Manor, The National Trust,
inv. no. W 1/63/1

Gudlaugsson considered it an autograph work in which there are at most two overpainted passages, in the door and in the hair of the seated man.[23] Accordingly, the Toledo painting was included in the exhibition dedicated to Gerard ter Borch held in the Mauritshuis in 1974, which was organized in memory of Sturla Gudlaugsson.[24] A year after this exhibition, the monogram *GTB* was seen on the canvas. The surprise was all the greater because of the date that had emerged, *166[6?].*[25] The date meant that the painting in Toledo was made a considerable time before the replica in Waddesdon Manor. Until that time it had been assumed that the version dated 1675 was the first to be painted. Repetitions in the work of Ter Borch were, actually, nothing new. Thus it was possible to ascertain at the 1974 exhibition in The Hague that *A Lady and Gentleman Making Music* in Cincinnati (Cincinnati Art Museum) [**5**][26] is a precise repetition of the painting in Toledo with the girl about to turn a page of her music book.[27] That a painter should repeat himself right down to the exact brushstrokes remains an intriguing phenomenon. Perhaps in 1675 Ter Borch had not yet been willing or able to dispose of the earlier painting.

The existence of such autograph replicas further suggests that there was a ready market for them. Presumably the matchless rendering of fabrics and the patient detailing of the costumes in Ter Borch's paintings were their biggest selling point, and not so much the messages that may be hidden in them. In the case of this depiction, the painter did not go out of his way to clarify his subject, as he did in *A Lady and Gentleman Making Music* in London [**3**]. The expressions of the eyes of the music makers in the Toledo work – he, hopeful; she, demure – remain a bit mysterious.[28] The couple is apparently oblivious to a third person, who gives no indication of what he is thinking. Just like us, he looks on with interest. We can at most posit that this work may be about Wine, Women, and Song. But there is no greater contrast imaginable than with Steen's *Interior with Jan Steen and Jan van Goyen* (cat. no. 58), where the same theme is represented.

Jan Steen makes his point with clamour, whereas Gerard ter Borch does so with restraint.

1 *Toledo 1976*, p. 26; see also *Gudlaugsson 1960*, p. 232, no. 271-II: 'Eremitage, St. Petersburg [...] verkauft ca. 1920.'
2 *Descargues 1967*, pp. 71-73
3 Inv. no. 1390; *Lisbon 1982*, pp. 105 and 292, no. 609 and fig.
4 *De Azeredo Perdigão 1979*, p. 109
5 *De Azeredo Perdigão 1979*, p. 106
6 *Walker 1973*, pp. 108-109 and 242-243
7 *De Azeredo Perdigão 1979*, pp. 102-113
8 Inv. no. 1489; *Gerson / Bredius 1969*, pp. 191-192 and 567, no. 239 and fig.; *Lisbon 1982*, pp. 151 and 371, no. 967 and fig.
9 *Gerson / Bredius 1969*, pp. 387-388 and 594, no. 479 and fig.; *Lisbon 1982*, pp. 151 and 371, no. 966 and fig.
10 *Walker 1973*, p. 243
11 See Bibliography
12 *Somof 1895*, p. 385, no. 874
13 *Maclaren 1960*, pp. 33-35, no. 864; *Gudlaugsson 1960*, pp. 201-202 and 354, no. 220 and fig.
14 *Descargues 1967*, p. 51
15 *Leningrad 1838*, p. 267, no. 80: 'T. – Haut. 18 pouces. Larg. 16 pouces. Une dame, vêtue de satin blanc, et assise près d'un jeune homme qui accorde son violon, tient à la main un cahier de musique. S.M.C. 11.'
16 HdG 140; *Waterhouse 1967*, pp. 170-171, no. 72 and fig.; *Gudlaugsson 1960*, pp. 231-232 and 394, no. 271-I and fig.
17 *Gudlaugsson 1960*, p. 231
18 *Somof 1895*, p. 385, no. 874 and HdG 140 (vol. V [1912], p. 53, no. 140)
19 *Gudlaugsson 1960*, p. 231, gave the dimensions as 78.5 x 66 cm, which ought to be 82.5 x 66.7 cm; *Somof 1895*, p. 385, no. 874, specified the dimensions as 86 x 70 cm, and also that the painting had been transferred from panel to canvas.
20 *Museum News 1954*, fig. on cover
21 *DAB*, vol. XI, p. 233; *Wittmann 1976-A*, pp. 9-11; *Schulze 1977*, pp. 64-65
22 *Wittmann 1976-A*, pp. 9-11
23 *Gudlaugsson 1960*, p. 232
24 *The Hague 1974*, pp. 196-197, no. 61 and fig.
25 *Toledo 1976*, p. 26
26 *Gudlaugsson 1960*, pp. 230-231 and 393, no. 270 and fig.; *Scott 1987*, pp. 24-27, no. 6 and fig. (and fig. on cover)
27 *The Hague 1974*, pp. 194-197, nos. 60 and 61 and fig.
28 A couple playing the lute and singing is easily explained as an image of Harmony (see also cat. no. 43), but in fact this scene appears to be open to numerous interpretations; see *Amsterdam 1976*, pp. 24-25, figs. 5-7, conversely also pp. 58-61, no. 8, pp. 104-107, no. 21, pp. 210-211, no. 53.
B B

5
Gerard ter Borch
A Lady and Gentleman Making Music
Panel, 55 x 44 cm (21⁵⁄₈ x 17³⁄₈ in.)
Neither signed nor dated (ca. 1675)
Cincinnati, Cincinnati Art Museum, inv. no. 1927.421

Utrecht ca. 1618 – Utrecht 1652

Canvas, 105.7 x 132.1 cm (41⅝ x 52 in.)
At the left, on a rock: *JBoth* (JB in ligature) (ca. 1648-1650)
Detroit, Mich., The Detroit Institute of Arts, inv. no. 54.441

Jan Both first learned the rudiments of his trade from his father, who was a glass engraver, and he was further trained as a painter by the Nestor of the Utrecht school of painting, Abraham Bloemaert. In 1638 he joined his brother Andries in Rome. When Andries drowned in Venice three years later, Jan returned to the Netherlands. Subsequently, in Utrecht, he created his best works, which are ranked among the 'classic' Italianizing landscapes. He dated only one painting, in 1650. Both died in 1652, at the height of his artistic career, when he was not yet thirty-five years old. He was then making monumental, sun-drenched landscapes with large copses of trees and a lively staffage, in the manner of the 'Bamboccianti.' The southern sunlight in his scenes made a profound impression on Nicolaes Berchem, Aelbert Cuyp, Adam Pijnacker, and other painters.

This monumental landscape by Jan Both was once intended for a national museum that the Polish King Stanislaw II (1732-1798) wanted to found in Warsaw. The Frenchman Noël Joseph Desenfans (1745-1807) [1] had acquired it around 1780, possibly during one of his forays into Holland, where he sought work by Aelbert Cuyp or, if need be, recently made copies after Cuyp.[1] In 1925, however, it was claimed that the painting had been part of

Provenance

(?) Auction John Astley, London, 1777 (£187.6 to [illegible])
Collection Noël Joseph Desenfans, London, before 1786-1795
Collection Joseph Martin, Ham Court, Worchestershire, 1802(?)-after 1854
(?) Collection G. Martin, Ham Court, after 1854-1860
Auction E. Bromley Martin et al., London, 1925
Collection Ralph Harman Booth, Detroit, before 1929-1931
Collection Mrs. William Dickerman Vogel, Detroit, 1931-1954
The Detroit Institute of Arts, Detroit, 1954 (gift of Mrs. William D. Vogel in memory of her father, Ralph Harman Booth)

Bibliography

Desenfans 1786, p. 5. no. 81
Auction London 1795, p. 11, no. 77
Smith 1829-1842, vol. VI, pp. 182-183, no. 29
London 1850-A, p. 9, no. 43
Waagen 1854, vol. III, p. 224
Auction London 1925-A, p. 4, no. 9
HdG 78 (vol. IX [1926], p. 444, no. 78)
Detroit 1929, p. xii. no. 8
Washburn Freund 1929, p. 705
Bulletin Detroit 1954-1955, pp. 10-11 and fig.
Bulletin Detroit 1954-1955-A, p. 54
Detroit 1967, p. 17
Burke 1976, p. 193, no. 19, p. 227, no. 78, pp. 245-246, no. 108, p. 318 and fig. 19
Sutton 1986, p. 86

1
James Northcote
Portrait of Noël Joseph Desenfans (1745-1807)
Canvas, 73.3 x 60.9 cm (28⅞ x 24 in.) (oval)
Neither signed nor dated (ca. 1790)
London, Dulwich Picture Gallery, inv. no. 28

Jan Both A Ford between Trees

the Astley collection, which was auctioned in 1777 in London.[2] This was a collection assembled by the society figure and amateur painter John Astley (1730?-1787), of whom it was sometimes said that his best works were the copies he made after Italian paintings.[3] In any event, the description in the 1777 auction catalogue of 'a most capital and perfect picture, very highly finished' applies to the Detroit painting, but to other landscapes by Both as well.[4] It is still a question whether Desenfans acquired the painting in the Netherlands or in England.

Desenfans must have been a colorful individual, who was both loved and hated. He had studied literature at the University of Paris and moved to England around 1770, where he married the wealthy Margaret Morris, to whom he had given language lessons when she was still a young girl. While on his honeymoon, Desenfans bought a work by Claude Lorrain, which he sold at a profit to King George III. This gave him the idea of getting into the art trade. He was friends with the painter-dealer Jean-Baptiste Pierre Lebrun (1748-1813) and moved in the circles of painters and collectors around Sir Joshua Reynolds (1723-1792).[5]

Reynolds, however, did not hold him in high esteem as a connoisseur. Desenfans himself preferred not to be called a dealer, but he did have pretensions to being a connoisseur. On 21 March 1796 Joseph Farington noted irritably in his famous diary: 'Desenfans knew nothing of pictures.'[6] An English critic of the time gave an acid assessment in a newspaper article: 'A certain foreign gentleman who is said to be a great encourager of the arts, has discovered that of dealing in pictures without posing *as a dealer*, of exhibiting them without being an *exhibitor*, and of heaping money without passing as a monied man. When he buys pictures it is *out of love for the art*; when he sells them he *only parts with them to oblige his friends*; and when he exhibits them in Pall Mall he puts them on view at one shilling entrance, to be sure, but this is *only to keep out the mob*.'[7]

Desenfans popularized the concept of the sale-exhibition in London. The title page of the catalogue of 1785, which he wrote himself, claimed that the collection was being sold because of Desenfans's departure for the Continent.[8] In 1786, apparently on account of the success of this event, there followed a second sale of 420 paintings 'At the Great Rooms, late the Royal Academy, No. 125, *Pall Mall*.' On this occasion he once again wrote a catalogue, with a foreword replete with flattery directed to King George III as the founder of the Royal Academy. The paintings were sold 'by private contract,' which meant that one could take out an option up to the last day of the exhibition. In this catalogue, the painting by Jan Both was published for the

first time as 'Landscape and figures 4 ft.4 by 3 ft.6, on canvas.'[9] Despite all this, few buyers showed up, but this was said to be because Vincent Lunardi had staged an air show at the same time, 'which drew almost everybody to the Artillery Ground.'[10] As a consequence, the painting by Jan Both remained in the possession of Desenfans.

Thanks to his good connections, after 1790 the Frenchman was permitted to call himself the Consul General of Poland in England, and he was given the task of assembling a large collection of paintings at the expense of King Stanislaw II for a national museum in Warsaw. The paintings that he had not been able to sell in 1785 and 1786 were therefore earmarked for this purpose. But politics dealt him bad cards, for the Polish king was deposed in 1795, and the Russian Tzar Paul I bluntly denied the existence of any obligations to the art dealer.[11] In 1795, without waiting for the conclusion of this affair, Desenfans sold some of the paintings that he had in the meantime gathered at some expense and difficulty at the auctioneers Skinner & Dyke. Presumably the piece that was introduced as 'Both, A landscape and figures' was identical to the painting now in Detroit.[12] In 1799 Desenfans offered an unsold portion and the remainder of his collection to the British government to form the core of a national British museum. This offer was turned down.[13] Subsequently, in 1802, the gentleman-dealer, who now labeled himself 'late Consul General of Poland, in Great Britain,' organized a sale-exhibition of the paintings that he had bought for the late King of Poland. This, too, was not a commercial success, so his house in Charlotte Street near Portland Place continued to hold a collection of paintings that might well have stocked two national collections.[14]

Upon his death in 1807, it turned out that Desenfans had left the paintings to his wife and (in the eventuality of her death) to his bosom friend Sir Peter Francis Bourgeois (1756-1811). Though Margaret was to outlive them both (until 1814), she earlier renounced her rights to support the plans of Sir Peter.[15] Bourgeois wished to turn Desenfans's residence into a museum. However, this proposal met with objections from the owner of the land, the Duke of Portland. After this lack of cooperation, Sir Peter bequeathed the collection to the Dulwich College in London instead of to the British Museum or the Royal Academy. Sir John Soane (1753-1837) designed a mausoleum for the three benefactors and, with it, the gallery for the paintings, which opened in 1812.[16] Until 1824, when the National Gallery in London was opened, this was the most important picture gallery in England. There are still many Dutch paintings on view that

were originally intended for the national museum in Warsaw.

The landscape by Jan Both in Detroit did not end up in Dulwich because it was among the paintings that were sold by Skinner & Dyke in 1795. A monumental landscape by Aelbert Cuyp, acquired in 1965 by the Rijksmuseum (Amsterdam) [2], also changed owners at the time, for only 350 guineas.[17] One half century later Smith believed that this same Cuyp would be worth at least 1,500 to 2,000 guineas, and that giveaway prices were paid for such works back in Desenfans's time.[18] It is not known if the buyer of the Cuyp in 1795 bought the Both at the same time, but that is certainly more than probable. This buyer was the Honourable Joseph Martin of Ham Court in Worcestershire, who, around 1800, was the presiding Canon of Exeter Cathedral.[19] Not much is known about his collection other than that the paintings by Both and Cuyp from the former Desenfans collection were lent in 1850 to an exhibition at the British Institution.[20] On this occasion, Gustav Waagen visited the owner

at Ham Court in Worcestershire, which he described as a simple house in a park with beautiful trees.[21] It was, therefore, an appropriate environment for Jan Both's landscape.

For more than a century the painting remained in the collection at Ham Court before it was acquired by the American collector Booth.[22] Ralph Harman Booth (1873-1931) was a publisher and newspaper magnate. He was also director of The Detroit Institute of Arts, which grew from the museum of Detroit, founded in 1888.[23] He made several donations to this museum and established a fund that later allowed both the museum in Detroit and the National Gallery in Washington to make important acquisitions. Two years after the new building of the Institute was opened in 1927, an exhibition of Dutch genre and landscape paintings was held there, to which Booth lent his landscape by Both.[24] Finally, in 1954, his daughter, Mrs. William Dickerman Vogel (Victoria Kingswood Booth), donated the painting to the Detroit Institute of Arts in memory of her father.[25]

Thus this *Ford between Trees* was shown in London in 1850 and in Detroit in 1929, but it has never before been exhibited in the Netherlands. It is a splendid and representative work from the last years of the short-lived Jan Both, that is, from just before 1650. In the 1972 catalogue of Both's oeuvre, James D. Burke established that it is a later and richer version of a painting in Munich (Bayerische Staatsgemäldesammlungen) [3].[26] The central motif of the travelers crossing a river is already in evidence here. Both repeated the compositional structure of the whole, with the large tree in the right foreground serving as a *repoussoir*, and the copse of trees just to the left of center as an eye-catcher, in a painting in Dulwich that comes from the Bourgeois legacy (and may therefore also have belonged to Desenfans).[27] The artist apparently thought this was such a successful composition that he recorded it in a drawing (Leyden, Prentenkabinet) [4].[28]

One of the attractive aspects of the works by Jan Both is the staffage, which, in his later works (between 1641 and 1652), he definitely painted himself. This is apparent from the drawing in Leyden and also, for instance, from one of his prints with a mounted lady at a ford, the *View along the Tiber* (Amsterdam, Rijksprentenkabinet) [5].[29] The staffage of this etching is quite close to that in the painting in Detroit. Both was a witty raconteur, who had an eye for amusing details such as the recalcitrant donkey being hit with a stick, the old woman on the back of a man who is crossing the river on the wobbly stones, and the gentleman putting his shoes back on. Moreover, the landscape is a feast for the eye, as John Smith had already established in 1835: 'This is a superlative production of art.'[30]

In 1854 Waagen noted: 'finely and poetically composed, rich in details, of singular power, transparency, and freshness of coloring, and of admirable touch.'[31]

1 To the by-now familiar story of the fake Cuyps (see *De Bruyn Kops 1965-A*, pp. 168-174; *Dordrecht 1977-1978*, pp. 56-57; *Broos 1986*, pp. 183-184 and 187, notes 2-5) can be added the fact that Desenfans admitted in 1797 having been mixed up with works by the forger-copyist (Jacob van Strij?) (*Farington 1922-1928*, vol. I, p. 197).
2 *Auction London 1925-A*, p. 4, no. 9
3 *DNB*, vol. II (1885), p. 207
4 *Auction London 1777*, p. 6, no. 55
5 *Whitley 1973*, vol. I, pp. 30-34 and *Murray 1980*, pp. 18-20, gave the best

4
Jan Both
A Ford between Trees
Pen and wash drawing, 255 x 380 mm (10 x 15 in.)
Neither signed nor dated (ca. 1645-1650)
Leyden, Prentenkabinet der Rijksuniversiteit,
inv. no. AW 1159

3
Jan Both
A Ford
Panel, 50 x 60 cm (19¾ x 23⅝ in.)
Neither signed nor dated (ca. 1645-1650)
Munich, Bayerische Staatsgemäldesammlungen,
inv. no. 192

5
Jan Both
View along the Tiber
Etching, 195 x 274 mm (7⅝ x 10¾ in.)
Neither signed nor dated (ca. 1641-1645)
Amsterdam, Rijksprentenkabinet

characterization of the career of Desenfans; see also *Redford 1888*, vol. I, pp. 42-45; *Farington 1922-1928*, vol. I, p. 144, vol. II, p. 226; *De Bruyn Kops 1965-A*, pp. 168-171.

6 *Farington 1922-1928*, vol. I, p. 144

7 *Whitley 1973*, vol. I, p. 31

8 L. 3814; *Murray 1980*, p. 18

9 *Desenfans 1786*, p. 5, no. 81; *Redford 1888*, vol. I, pp. 42-43; *Murray 1980*, p. 18, believed incorrectly that this second auction never took place.

10 *Redford 1888*, vol. I, p. 45

11 *Farington 1922-1928*. vol. I, p. 144; *Murray 1980*, p. 19; *Brunswick etc. 1988-1990*, pp. 11-12

12 *Auction London 1795*, p. 11, no. 71

13 *Redford 1888*, vol. I, p. 43

14 *Desenfans 1802*; *Smith 1829-1842*, vol. VI, p. 183, no. 29, mistakenly thought that Both's painting was sold at this auction; see also *Whitley 1973*, vol. I, pp. 31-32.

15 *Redford 1888*, vol. I, p. 44

16 *Murray 1980*, pp. 19-20

17 HdG 458; *Van Thiel et al. 1976*, p. 183, no. A 4118 and fig.; *De Bruyn Kops 1965-A*, p. 168

18 *Smith 1829-1842*, supplement, pp. 659-660, no. 35

19 *Boase 1965*, vol. II, col. 765

20 *London 1850-A*, p. 9, no. 43

21 *Waagen 1854*, vol. III, p. 224

22 *Bulletin Detroit 1954-1955*, p. 11

23 *WWWA*, vol. I, p. 117; *Art Digest 1931-A*, p. 6; *Art News 1931-A*, p. 12; *Comstock 1942*, p. 40; *Frankfurter 1948*, pp. 15 and 52-53

24 *Detroit 1929*, p. xii, no. 8

25 *Bulletin Detroit 1954-1955-A*, p. 54

26 *Burke 1976*, pp. 193, no. 19 and 227, no. 78 and fig. 73

27 Inv. no. 208; HdG 235; *Burke 1976*, p. 220, no. 64 and fig. 59; *Murray 1980*, pp. 30-31, no. 208 and fig.

28 *Burke 1976*, p. 266, no. D 18

29 *Hollstein*, vol. III, pp. 160-161, no. 7 and fig.

30 *Smith 1829-1842*, vol. VI, pp. 182-183, no. 29

31 *Waagen 1854*, vol. III, p. 224

B B

Haarlem ca. 1635 – Goch 1694

Panel, 49.1 x 36.6 cm (19³/₈ x 14³/₈ in.)
Lower left: *1671 DDBraij f.* (DDB in ligature)
Los Angeles, Calif., collection Mr. and Mrs. Edward W. Carter

In 1656 Dirck de Bray, a younger brother of Jan de Bray, became a bookbinder's apprentice with Passchier van Westbusch in Haarlem. He was there for a considerable time as secretary of the Guild of Saint Luke (at least until 1675). We know of prints by him with dates from 1658 on: etchings and fine woodcuts with largely religious subjects. Along with Jan, he survived the Haarlem plague epidemic of 1663, which took the lives of six of his closest family members. His limited painted oeuvre has dates ranging from 1671 to 1680 and consists mainly of still lifes. With advancing age Dirck de Bray became a lay brother in the Gaesdonck cloister near Goch, and he died there as a bookbinder in 1694.

This attractive little bouquet of 1671 by Dirck de Bray could have belonged to the collection of the Mauritshuis instead of to that of Edward W. Carter in Los Angeles, where it is presently found. Around 1972 the owner at the time, Sidney J. van den Bergh (1898-1977) (cat. no. 3, fig. 1) of Wassenaar, was prepared to sell the American a number of works from his collection, among which was the unique *Still Life with Stone Jug and Pipes* of 1658 by Pieter van Anraadt (The Hague, Mauritshuis) [1].[1] However, the Van Anraadt, which in 1966 had shone at the

Provenance

Auction London, 1948 (£2,100 to P.E. Kroyer)
Auction London, 1954 (£997.10 to Jones)
Dealer Duits Ltd., London
Collection Sidney J. van den Bergh, Wassenaar, before 1959-1973
Dealer G. Cramer, The Hague, 1973
Collection Mr. and Mrs. Edward W. Carter, Los Angeles, 1973

Bibliography

Auction London 1948, p. 12, no. 92 and fig.
WCA, vol. 1 (1948), p. 81, no. 1085 and fig. opp. p. 201
Bernt 1948-1962, vol. IV, no. 38 and fig.
Auction London 1954, p. 3, no. 2
Laren 1959, no. 31 and fig. 18
Pavière 1962, p. 17
De Vries 1964, pp. 353-355 and fig. 3 and pl. II
Leyden 1965, p. 4, no. 6 and fig. 3
San Francisco / Toledo / Boston 1966-1967, pp. 148-149, no. 102 and fig.
De Vries 1968, pp. 30-31 and fig.
Bol 1969, pp. 333-334 and fig. 302
Bernt 1970, vol. 1, p. 18, no. 178 and fig.
Mitchell 1973, p. 61
Bernt 1979-1980, vol. 1, no. 178 and fig.
Walsh 1981, p. 389 and note 20 and fig.
Walsh / Schneider 1981-1982, pp. xxiii and 24-27, no. 6 and fig.
Segal 1982, pp. 51 and 53, note 11

1
Pieter van Anraadt
Still Life with Stone Jug and Pipes
Canvas, 67 x 59 cm (26³/₈ x 23¹/₄ in.)
Lower left: *Pieter van/ Anraadt. An. 1658*
The Hague, Mauritshuis, inv. no. 1045

exhibition *In the Light of Vermeer* in The Hague, was thought to be promised to the Mauritshuis.[2] Van den Bergh's generous proposal that the museum accept the equally rare flower piece by De Bray in trade for the desired piece by Van Anraadt was nevertheless considered a disappointing alternative. After much (legal) tug-of-war, it was agreed that the Mauritshuis would buy the Van Anraadt in installments for a reduced price.[3] Nevertheless, it was rumored at the time that the price paid was astronomically high for such a virtually unknown artist. The transaction was later even called a painful one 'because a Dutch private individual, who as a collector had profited extraordinarily from the knowledgeable advice of the director of the Mauritshuis of that time, in fact had that institution pay heavily in return' (in translation).[4] The decision of the museum was subsequently rewarded with the public acknowledgment that a minor master had here created a grand work, one that is well able to hold its own next to Vermeer, and that it is sometimes even viewed as a work by the Delft painter himself.[5] However, as with other choice works from the Van den Bergh collection, it was not possible to keep the painting by Dirck de Bray for the Netherlands. Carter benefited from the altercations, although he (and especially his wife) would have preferred to acquire the Van Anraadt as well.[6]

With 'knowledgeable advice' the writers of the quotation above alluded to, among other things, the catalogue of the collection of Sidney van den Bergh (see cat. no. 3) that the director of the Mauritshuis, A.B. de Vries, published in 1968. In an article in the periodical *Apollo* in 1964 he had already fixed the international spotlight on this collection.[7] The collection of Van den Bergh took shape in Wassenaar (near The Hague) after 1945, during the time that De Vries was director of the Mauritshuis. It is probably illustrative of the relationship between Van den Bergh and De Vries that in 1964 Van den Bergh was able to acquire from the museum collection a *Flower Still Life* (The Netherlands, private collection) by Rachel Ruysch, which was considered to be a duplicate.[8] Sidney van den Bergh had a special predilection for still lifes, in which the museums were then only slightly interested.[9] De Vries tried in vain to interest the collector in French painting. Over the course of twenty years, Van den Bergh founded a modest collection of Dutch masters with unusual works such as the two still lifes by Van Anraadt and Dirck de Bray.

In his catalogue of 1968 De Vries recalled how, during the past two decades, although much art from the private domain had crossed the Dutch borders, that export had in some instances been prevented (perhaps permanently?) by Van den Bergh's activities as a collector.[10] However, this hint fell on deaf ears, for, after 1970, the collector sold one after another of his important paintings to non-Dutch buyers, first disposing of works of lesser quality.[11] Americans usually offered for his top pieces ten times the amount that the collector had himself paid for them.[12] One of the first to depart was the splendid *Winter Scene* by Hendrick Avercamp (cat. no. 4, fig. 3).[13] In 1972 the Los Angeles collector Edward Carter bought it, which meant a great loss to art treasures in Holland. In 1971 Carter had already purchased Jan van der Heyden's *View on the Herengracht* from the Wassenaar collection, to be joined in 1973 by a landscape by Meindert Hobbema.[14]

Edward Carter (born 1911; cat. no. 68, fig. 1) shares some traits with Sidney van den Bergh. He, too, is a businessman with broad cultural interests, and he, too, only began to collect paintings in his late forties. As with Van den Bergh, his first painting was a Van Goyen (whose works are always in ready supply). Later followed works by Willem van de Velde and Jacob van Ruisdael. After his marriage in 1963 to Hannah Locke Caldwell, Flemish, Italian, and French masters were also added. Seymour Slive praised the collection and spoke of 'miraculously well-preserved, cabinet-size Dutch pictures of the highest quality that fit perfectly in the intimacy of a home.'[15] Around 1970 the Carters decided to leave their collection to the Los Angeles County Museum of Art, and they subsequently made it their aim to acquire 'the most representative collection of the finest quality seventeenth-century Dutch landscapes, seascapes, architectural interiors, town views, and still lifes in this country.'[16] In addition to the still life by De Bray, it was also possible to select Simon de Vlieger's *View of a Beach* (cat. no. 68) from this remarkable small collection for the present exhibition.

Since the flower piece by Dirck de Bray was offered at auction in London in 1948, the date at the lower left has always been read as 1673, though De Vries and Bol established in 1968 and 1969 that this should be 1671.[17] Graphic works by Dirck de Bray exist from before that year, but no paintings. A second flower still life, *A Bouquet with Tulips and Daffodils* (The Netherlands, private collection) [2] has a date which has been deciphered alternately as 1671 or 1674.[18] The date is even more difficult to read because by preference De Bray wrapped the lower left corner, in which he placed his signatures, in deep shadow. We also see this phenomenon in a third flower piece dated 1674 (formerly Zwolle, Van Voorst tot Voorst collection) [3].[19] The poppy in the right rear of this bouquet has the same form as the

Dirck de Bray Flowers in a Glass Vase

flower located in the similar position in the painting under discussion.

Other characteristics shared by these flower pieces are the bright passages next to the shaded areas, as if the bouquet stands in a shaft of concentrated light. There is always an insect on the border between light and shadow, and in Carter's painting there is also a fly walking behind the glass vase. Beside the artificial but very beautiful lighting, the structure of these bouquets is loose and nonchalant, as if to suggest naturalness. According to Bol that is a 'modern touch' of De Bray, who furthermore had the courage to paint overblown flowers on limp stems, which heightens the verisimilitude.[20]

Flowers subject to decay are generally to be interpreted as a *vanitas* element (see cat. no. 1). In the painting *A Bouquet with Tulips and Daffodils* by De Bray [2], Segal distinguished hidden symbolism in the choice of insects. Two butterflies are depicted, as well as the caterpillar of a moth, the hairy Garden Tiger Moth. The ruddy glow of the painting presumably refers to the frontier between day and night, twilight.[21] This same day-and-night symbolism determined the composition of the flower piece in Los Angeles.

In contrast with many old-fashioned bouquets (see cat. no. 3) it is in fact possible to make such a summer-like arrangement, for the depicted flowers all bloom in the same season. The Small Morning Glory (a tri-colored bindweed), and the Morning Glory – white with a red heart – belonging to the same family, which here determine the center of the composition, are rarely encountered in seventeenth-century bouquets. Later Rachel Ruysch and Jan van Huysum often painted these flowers.[22] The various kinds

▲ 2
Dirck de Bray
Bouquet with Tulips and Daffodils
Panel, 40.6 x 34.3 cm (16 x 13½ in.)
Lower left: *1674[1?] DDBray* (DDB in ligature)
The Netherlands, private collection

◄ 3
Dirck de Bray
A Bowl of Flowers
Panel, 49 x 36 cm (19¼ x 14¼ in.)
Lower left: *DDBray 1674*
Formerly Zwolle, collection Van Voorst tot Voorst

of poppies were recently discovered as decorative flowers by Jan Davidsz de Heem and Willem van Aelst. De Bray was apparently well informed about the very latest developments.[23]

The bindweed and the Rose of Sharon at the right are diurnal flowers. The poppy is sometimes called opium poppy and, according to Segal, is here intended as a contrast to these day flowers, as they were generally associated with sleep and the night.[24] It is probably also significant that the flowers depicted here bloom at the same time of year, but open and close at different times of the day.[25] Thus the Morning Glory opens shortly after dawn but closes toward dusk, whereas the poppies remain open. Dirck de Bray must have had some botanical expertise if he intended this symbolism of night and day.

1 *Broos 1987*, pp. 20-23, no. 2 and fig.

2 *The Hague 1966*, no. 25 and fig.; *De Vries 1968*, p. 9

3 It is not apparent from *Hoetink 1974*, pp. 213-215 and *Hoetink 1979*, pp. 192 and 215 and fig., that the payments were to be divided over a few years and that Van den Bergh would keep the painting on loan until his death (documentation archives Mauritshuis).

4 *Hecht / Luijten 1986*, p. 202: the cited price ('meer dan een half miljoen') is an incorrect estimate.

5 *Broos 1988*, pp. 110-111 and fig. 1

6 I thank Hans C. Cramer for his communications concerning the Carters and Sidney van den Bergh.

7 *De Vries 1964*; *De Vries 1968*

8 Inv. no. 152; HdG 23; *the Hague 1954*, p. 75, no. 152 (as on long-term loan); *De Vries 1968*, pp. 90-91 and fig.; the still life was sold in 1964 to buy *A Dead Rooster* by Melchior d'Hondecoeter (inv. no. 968).

9 *De Vries 1964*, pp. 352-354

10 *De Vries 1968*, p. 8

11 Of the fifty paintings in 1965, Van den Bergh still had forty-three left in 1968, see *Leyden 1965*, pp. 3-14, nos. 1-50 and *De Vries 1968*, pp. 12-111.

12 According to Hans C. Cramer, Van den Bergh bought the Van Anraadt from the dealer Duits for about ƒ22,000; Carter offered ƒ850,000 for the Van Anraadt, De Bray, and Hobbema together (oral communication).

13 *Walsh / Schneider 1981-1982*, pp. 3-7, no. 1 and fig.

14 *Walsh / Schneider 1981-1982*, pp. 54-57, no. 13 and fig., pp. 58-61, no. 14 A and fig.

15 *Walsh / Schneider 1981-1982*, p. xiii

16 *Walsh / Schneider 1981-1982*, p. xiv; see also *Walsh 1981*, p. 380

17 *De Vries 1968*, p. 30; *Bol 1969*, p. 334

18 '1671' according to *Auction London 1948*, p. 47, no. 91 and *Walsh / Schneider 1981-1982*, p. 26, fig. 2; '1674' according to *The Hague 1982*, pp. 72-73, no. 17 and fig. and *Segal 1982*, p. 102, no. 58

19 *Walsh / Schneider 1981-1982*, p. 26, fig. 3; the year 1672 occurs on a *Still Life with a Sword and a Bird of Paradise* (London, dealer R. Valls, 1987) (photo RKD).

20 *Bol 1969*, p. 334

21 *Segal 1982*, p. 51

22 *Van Boven / Segal 1980*, p. 87

23 *Van Boven / Segal 1980*, p. 85

24 *Segal 1982*, p. 51

25 *Walsh / Schneider 1981-1982*, pp. 26-27: Sam Segal identified the flowers.

BB

Haarlem ca. 1627 – Haarlem 1697

Canvas, 247,5 x 191 cm (97½ x 75¼ in.)
On the dish at the left: *1669 JDBray* (JDB in ligature)
Manchester, N.H., The Currier Gallery of Art, inv. no. 1969.8

Jan de Bray was the oldest son of the painter, poet, and architect Salomon de Bray (1597-1664), who was also his teacher. His younger brothers Dirck and Josephus were artists as well, but brother Jacob was not. On the authority of the biographer Houbraken, the work signed *J[an]DBraij* was for a long time wrongly attributed to Jacob. With the one exception of a short stay in Amsterdam (from 1686 to 1688), Jan de Bray worked all his life in Haarlem. He joined the guild in 1664, and was later many times officer and dean. The plague that scourged Haarlem in 1663 took away his parents, two of his brothers, and both his sisters. Disaster was always close on his heels: his first wife, whom he married in 1668, died a year later in childbirth, and both his subsequent spouses died, in 1673 and 1680, again shortly after their wedding. In 1689, following conflicts about their legacies, De Bray was declared bankrupt. He left an important painted oeuvre of portraits and monumental historical pieces in a classical style. Further, he was a prolific draftsman who practiced all genres, but he made especially fine portraits.

'The Höch collection in Munich, of which the sale has been announced for the 19th of September and the following days,' wrote Cornelis Hofstede de Groot (in translation) in 1892 in *De Nederlandsche Spectator*, 'is more the shop of an art dealer than the cabinet of an art lover. The handsomely produced catalogue is nevertheless of lasting value.' He called Jan de Bray's large history piece with the story of Antony and Cleopatra the portrayal of a Dutch family: 'eleven life-sized figures, his most important work outside of Haarlem.'[1] Heinrich Theodor Höch was a developer (and the builder of the famous Café Luitpold), who, around 1888, opened a sales room for dealers in art and antiques at 8 Briennerstrasse, Munich, above his Café Luitpold. This, however, was a business failure, so he decided to auction the old and modern art that he had assembled.[2] The Germanisches Nationalmuseum in Nuremberg bought the masterpiece by Jan de Bray for 1,750 German marks. In his copy of the auction catalogue, Hofstede de Groot noted cryptically: 'duplicate, I believe copy in Hampton Court' (in translation).[3] Indeed, there is a smaller version of the scene in the British royal

Provenance

Dealer A. Rupprecht, Munich, 1889
Auction Höch, Munich, 1892 (DM1,750 to Baye:dorfer)
Germanisches Nationalmuseum, Nuremberg, 1892-1966
Auction London, 1966 ($5,880)
Dealer Julius Böhler, Munich, 1966
Dealer S. Nijstad, The Hague, 1968-1969
The Currier Gallery of Art, Manchester, N.H., 1969

Bibliography

Munich 1889, p. 35, no. 215
Auction Munich 1892, p. 12, no. 28
Auction Munich 1892-A, p. 12, no. 28 and fig.
Hofstede de Groot 1892-A, pp. 296 and 304
Nuremberg 1893, p. 50, no. 328
Wurzbach, vol. I (1906), p. 175
Nuremberg 1909, p. 122, no. 400 (328)
Von Moltke 1938-1939, pp. 445, 447-448 and 484, no. 184
London 1946-1947, p. 121, no. 368
Bénézit 1948-1955, vol. II, p. 112
Bernt 1948-1962, vol. I, no. 135 and fig.
Pigler 1955, pp. 178-180 and fig. 10
Pigler 1956, vol. II, p. 381
Gudlaugsson 1964, p. 519
Apollo 1966, p. 345 and fig. 2
Auction London 1966, p. 52, no. 88 and fig.
Connoisseur 1966, p. XCII and fig.
Munich 1966, p. 41 and fig.
WCA, vol. XVIII (1966), p. 55, no. 601
Mayer, vol. I (1967), p. 287
Wishnevsky 1967, p. 96, note 4
De Pauw-de Veen 1969, fig. 5
Robinson 1969, n.p. and fig. 1 and cover
Robinson 1970, pp. 284-285 and fig.
Pigler 1974, vol. II, p. 397
Brown 1976, p. 29
Manchester 1979, p. 15, no. 17 and fig.
Amsterdam / Detroit / Washington 1980-1981, pp. 22-23 and fig. 8, p. 224 and note 1
Wilson 1980-1981, no. 13
White 1982, pp. 28-29
Haak 1984, p. 380 and fig. 805
Sutton 1986, pp. 147-148 and fig. 216
Haverkamp-Begemann / Adams 1988, p. 38

Jan de Bray The Banquet of Antony and Cleopatra

collection (Hampton Court, collection Her Majesty the Queen) [1].[4] King Charles II is said to have acquired the painting; below his ownership will appear to be an important fact for the interpretation of the subject.

In 1966 the large history piece was quite unexpectedly auctioned at Christie's in London.[5] Why the Nuremberg museum decided to dispose of the masterpiece was not divulged. Through the art trade, it ended up in Manchester, New Hampshire,[6] and is now the star of the small collection of Dutch art in The Currier Gallery of Art. This exclusive museum was opened in 1929 in memory of Moody Currier (1806-1898), former governor of the State of New Hampshire.[7] In 1969 the museum bulletin featured an article by F.W. Robinson on the new acquisition. Regrettably, he did not do justice to the connection with the work in Hampton Court, and he repeated the conventional but by that time outdated idea that the figures of Antony and Cleopatra are portraits of Jan de Bray and his wife.[8]

In 1946 the look-alike in England was exhibited at the Royal Academy in London. The text of the catalogue announced that Professor I.Q. van Regteren Altena was of the opinion that the main actors of this scene portrayed not Jan and his wife but his parents, Salomon de Bray (1597-1664) and Anna Westerbaen (ca. 1605-1663).[9] The painting is dated 1652; thus Jan and his first wife cannot be depicted here, as they were married only in 1668. However, thorough genealogical research was carried out in 1964 by J. van der Marel,[10] and he recognized the facial features of Anna and Salomon in a curious double portrait that Jan painted of his parents (Princeton, N.J., The Art Museum, Princeton University) [2].[11] We know who the sitters are because in the testament of Jan de Bray this painting was mentioned as a 'portrayal of his before-[mentioned] deceased father and mother standing in one piece, and painted from the side' (in translation).[12] The couple is clothed entirely in black and is placed in profile against a dark background, as if on a medallion. Anna and Salomon had died of the plague in 1663 and 1664, respectively, so it is highly probable that their portraits were rendered posthumously. It even looks as if the Cleopatra of the painting of 1652 served as model for the portrait of the mother. Jan had laid down his father's features in a drawing of 1657 (Berlin, Staatliche Museen, Kupferstichkabinett).[13] Brother Dirck made a woodcut after it, again posthumously [3].[14] There is little doubt that in 1652 Salomon de Bray, with his long, bony nose – then about fifty-five years old – posed for Antony, who wears the laurel wreath behind the table. The forty-seven-year-old Anna Westerbaen was the model for Cleopatra, who takes off her earring.

In 1955 Pigler concluded that the version of 1669 (then still in Nuremberg) also presented the remaining De Bray family members, in memory of the parents, brothers, and sisters who had died of the plague in 1663 and 1664. He further believed this to be at the heart of the meaning of the scene: beauty also perishes.[15] This interpretation seems plausible but can be only partly true. Indeed, the first version was done in 1652, when there was no question of a family drama. Robinson and, later, Blankert wondered about this, because they, too, were convinced the picture was painted at a later date or even as a memorial. According to them, the portraits must have been painted posthumously, and thus they doubted the correctness of the 1652 date. After the painting was restored, White determined that 1652 is indeed the original dating.[16] Moreover, another date has emerged a little farther down that may be read as [16]56 or [16]58. According to White, this must mean that the painter later completed or touched up the first version.[17] The earlier scene in any case originated when the family was still able to pose for it. In short, the coupling of the tragic family history with the origins of this group portrait is superseded.

At first sight the painting in Manchester looks like no more than a repetition of the one in Hampton Court, with enlargements of the top and bottom sections. At the bottom a balustrade was added, with a Persian carpet and a large golden bowl, and a dog looks back to lead us into the scene. However, the least conspicuous changes turn out to be the most important. At the right, for instance, an additional woman is to be seen, directly behind Cleopatra. In a letter to the museum in Manchester, F.G.L.O. van Kretschmar explained her presence and

identified the remainder of the company around the table.[18] The added woman is Maria van Hees, whom Jan de Bray married in 1668, a year before he signed the painting. Maria looks at the man with the halberd opposite her, in whom we may see a self-portrait of the artist. According to Van Kretschmar, this brand-new marital couple had been immortalized earlier in their wedding year in a *portrait historié* by Jan himself: *Odysseus and Penelope* (Louisville, The J.B. Speed Art Museum) [4].[19]

To the comparisons with existing portraits, we can add another one. The boy behind Cleopatra has the same oval face as Dirck de Bray's in an etched *Self-Portrait* [5].[20] In 1652 he was not yet twenty.[21] The woman in the orange dress with the tray of glasses and the girl in front of Antony are, respectively, Juliana and Margaret de Bray, who both died in 1663. The boy at the left, looking back, is apparently the approximately fourteen-year-old Jacob: at the right stands the slightly older Josephus with a pitcher on a tray. The two remaining figures are the untimely deceased children, in fact the only ones who had already been portrayed posthumously in the version of 1652.[22]

Although all the children carry a dish or bowl and thus appear to have a function in the whole, most of them look a little lost. They do not really belong in the story from Roman antiquity. In brief, the story, which Pliny relates (*Naturalis Historiae*, 9:120-122), goes as follows. Cleopatra, Queen of Egypt, had the world's largest pearls as earrings. Antony, who went out of his way to let her bathe in luxury, asked what was her heart's desire. She wagered with him that she could spend ten million sestertii on a single banquet. Antony did not believe her, whereupon she called for an everyday meal that made Antony laugh derisively. But then a biting acid was placed on the table, in which she dissolved one of her eardrops. She then drank the concoction and thus won the wager. She even had to be restrained from wasting the second earring.

The story offered material for seventeenth-century playwrights and poets, and Jacob Cats repeated the contents in his *Trou-Ringh* (Wedding Ring) of 1637, with the title: 'The splendid and wanton Caresses of Marc Antony, Field Marshal of the Romans, and Cleopatra, Queen of Egypt' (in translation).[23] The Dutch and Flemish rhetoricians liked to stage the *Spel van [Play of] Cleopatra* (published in 1624 with the title *Aegyptica ofte Aegyptische tragoedie* [Egypt or the Egyptian tragedy]) by the painter-poet Willem van Nieulant.[24] Inspired by such performances, Jan Steen repeatedly painted the banquet of Antony and Cleopatra.[25] The fact that Salomon de Bray was a member of the Haarlem chamber of rhetoric, De Wijngaardranken (The

3
Dirck de Bray
Portrait of Salomon de Bray
Woodcut, 180 x 128 mm (7 x 5 in.)
Left center: *1664*; lower right: *DBraij f B* (DB in ligature)
Amsterdam, Rijksprentenkabinet

Vineyard creepers), undoubtedly contributed to his choosing this subject. The laurel crown on the head of Salomon de Bray, alias Antony, may well refer to his achievements as a poet. Salomon was a close friend of the Haarlem composer Cornelis Padbrué (ca. 1592-1670) and of the poet Jacob Westerbaen (1599-1670) and his brother, the painter Jan Westerbaen (ca. 1600-after 1677). He married their sister Anna, who must also have been much interested in poetry and the popular theater.[26]

The depiction is a piece of domestic theater rather than a dramatic stage performance of the *Aegyptica*. It depicts the De Bray parents, posing as Antony and Cleopatra and surrounded by their children, who function as addenda in this historiated portrait. As was customary in such portraits, the poses and likenesses appear to be more important than the details of the story.[27] In retrospect, it is perhaps more understandable that Jan de Bray introduced his spouse in 1668 as the virtuous Penelope [4], than that his mother was prepared to pose as the seductive and wasteful Cleopatra. Fatal love could be the true subject, but at the same time there may also be a *vanitas* idea hidden behind this little bit of theater.[28]

In addition, the depiction appears to have also been appreciated on another level, namely as a history piece. It is striking that in the inventory of the English king James II, the version of 1652 /1658 [1] is not referred to as a portrait or an allegory but as the unadulterated depiction of ancient history:

'John Thebray. The history of Mark Anthony and Cleopatra.'[29] His predecessor Charles II is said to have acquired the painting, which presumably means that he purchased it, or had it bought, from the painter himself.[30] Thus we have an unexpected explanation for the origins of the replica of 1669. Jan de Bray did not want the memory of his family, of which only his brother Dirck was still alive in 1664, to be lost. Before he delivered the piece, he painted a copy with embellishments, in which his loved ones were depicted as they looked in 1652. He incorporated his

first wife in this company that was not known to her. Possibly her portrait is also posthumous, for the group portrait is signed in the year in which Maria van Hees died, probably while giving birth to her son Salomon.[31]

A no more obvious addition in the definitive version was a gigantic peacock pie in the left rear (where a man stands in the other version), a familiar *vanitas* symbol. The peacock tail referred to the well-known saying: 'Man know thyself.'[32] Such a peacock pie is a correspondingly admonitory element in the famous *Double Portrait of Rembrandt and Saskia* (Dresden, Staatliche Kunstsammlungen, Gemäldegalerie) [**6**] of around 1636.[33] Rembrandt here showed himself with his wife at one of the happiest moments of his life, and nevertheless as the prodigal son with a whore. Jan de Bray must have intended a similar content in 1652 as well as in 1669. Finally, for him there remained only memories of the happier decade of the fifties.

6
Rembrandt
Self-Portrait as the Prodigal Son, with Saskia
Canvas, 161 x 131 cm (63⅜ x 51½ in.)
At the left, next to the peacock head: *Rembrandt f*
(ca. 1636)
Dresden, Staatliche Kunstsammlungen,
Gemäldegalerie, inv. no. 1559

1 *Hofstede de Groot 1892-A*, p. 296
2 *Auction Munich 1892-A*, p. XI; see also a press cutting in *Munich 1889* (copy RKD).
3 *Auction Munich 1892*, p. 12, no. 28 (copy RKD); see also *Munich 1889*, p. 35, no. 215 (copy RKD with annotations by Hofstede de Groot).
4 *White 1982*, pp. 28-29, no. 31 and pl. 24
5 *Auction London 1966*, p. 52, no. 88 and fig.; *Munich 1966*, p. 41 and fig.; *Apollo 1966*, p. 345 and fig. 2
6 *Auction London 1966*, p. 52, no. 88 and fig.; *Apollo 1966*, p. 345 and fig. 2
7 *Sutton 1986*, p. 147
8 *Robinson 1969*; see also *Robinson 1970*, p. 284: 'possibly the artist and his first wife.'
9 *London 1946-1947*, p. 121, no. 368
10 *Van der Marel 1964*, col. 19
11 *Haverkamp-Begemann / Adams 1988*, pp. 22 and 38, no. 6 and fig.; *Von Moltke 1938-1939*, pp. 426 and 483-484, no. 177a
12 *Van der Marel 1964*, cols. 13-14
13 Inv. no. 707; *Bock / Rosenberg 1930*, vol. I, p. 95, no. 707, vol. II, pl. 73; *Von Moltke 1938-1939*, p. 501, no. Z 66
14 *Hollstein*, vol. III, p. 189, no. 122 and fig.; the inscription of the drawing '1657 ouwt [old] 60 Jaar' was brought up to date in the print '1664 Oud 67.'
15 *Pigler 1955*, pp. 178-180
16 *Robinson 1969*, n.p. (Appendix) and Blankert in *Amsterdam / Detroit / Washington 1980-1981*, p. 224, note 1; *White 1982*, p. 28
17 *White 1982*, pp. 28-29, no. 31
18 Transcription of this missive dated 29 April 1971 (RKD).
19 *Von Moltke 1938-1939*, pp. 447 and 484, no. 178 and fig.; *Amsterdam / Detroit / Washington 1980-1981*, pp. 226-227, no. 62 and fig.
20 *Hollstein*, vol. III, p. 186, no. 25
21 The brothers Jan and Dirck may also be seen in *The Deans of the Haarlem Guild of Saint Luke* of 1675 (Amsterdam, Rijksmuseum, inv. no. A 58; *Von Moltke 1938-1939*, pp. 485-486, no. 189; *Van Thiel et al. 1976*, p. 142, no. A 58 and fig.)
22 See also *Brown 1976*, p. 29 and *White 1982*, p. 29
23 *Cats 1712*, vol. II, pp. 170-176; see also *Kirschenbaum 1977*, p. 86
24 *Van Nieulant 1624*; *Keersmaekers 1957*, pp. 85-87; see also *Heppner 1939-1940*, p. 36
25 *Kirschenbaum 1977*, pp. 70-71 and 144-146, nos. 85-86c
26 *Van der Marel 1964*, cols. 11 and 16-17
27 Thus, for instance, Caesar Augustus, the third principal character to the story, is missing; on the *portrait historié*, see *Wishnevsky 1967*, p. 96; *De Jongh 1986*, pp. 312-331.
28 *Pigler 1955*, p. 180
29 *Bathoe 1758*, p. 68, no. 769
30 *White 1982*, p. 28; there is only an (unpublished) inventory of Charles's collection from 1666-1667, see *Brenninkmeyer-de Rooij / Broos et al. 1988*, p. 61.
31 *Van der Marel 1964*, col. 19
32 *Henkel / Schöne 1967*, col. 809; I thank Frederieke Trouw for drawing my attention to this detail.
33 *Gerson / Bredius 1969*, pp. 26 and 549, no. 30 and fig.; the interpretation of this scene was recently described by *Tümpel 1986*, pp. 115-116: 'Overvloedige rijkdom associeerde hij [Rembrandt] met de vergankelijkheid ervan, Christus met de schuld en het huwelijk met de lusten van de mens.'
BB

Deventer 1598 / 1600 – Amsterdam 1657

Panel, 54.5 x 75 cm (21 ½ x 29⅝ in.)
Lower right: *B.B. f. A 1634*
New York, collection Richard L. Feigen

After the death of his father, who was the municipal apothecary in Deventer, Bartholomeus Breenbergh accompanied his family to the western part of the country, where, presumably in Amsterdam, he received instruction in painting. In 1619 he was in Rome, where he was to remain for over ten years. In the *schildersbent* (the club of northern artists staying in Rome) he was nicknamed 'Het Fret' (The Ferret). Though he did not paint much in Italy, he did make many handsome drawings, especially of the ruins and monuments in and around Rome.

When he married in Amsterdam in 1633, he had presumably been back from Italy for several years. His landscapes show the influence of Paul Bril and Cornelis van Poelenburch, and after 1630 he fell under the influence of the figure pieces of Pieter Lastman and his circle, which continued the tradition of Adam Elsheimer. In his historical works the landscape is at least as important as the story.

In the first two decades of the eighteenth century two versions of *The Preaching of Saint John the Baptist* by Bartholomeus Breenbergh were repeatedly auctioned in Amsterdam. This has led to a never-ending confusion concerning the correct provenance of these paintings, which remarkably enough are both now the property of the New York dealer and collector Richard L. Feigen. On the basis of two important auctions that were held in the later eighteenth century, we call the first piece the Van der Marck Breenbergh – the work here under discussion – and the other the Braamcamp Breenbergh [1].[1] The famous collector Gerret Braamcamp (1699-1771) (cat. no. 54, fig. 1) bought

1
Bartholomeus Breenbergh
The Preaching of Saint John the Baptist
Panel, 103.5 x 146.05 cm (40¾ x 57½ in.)
Lower right: *BBreenbergh. / faciebat. Anno. / 1643*
New York, collection Richard L. Feigen

Provenance

Auction Amsterdam, 1708 (*f*450)
Auction Amsterdam, 1709 (*f*430)
Collection Johan van der Marck, Leyden, before 1770
Auction Van der Marck, Amsterdam, 1773 (*f*800 to Fouquet)
Auction Randon de Boisset, Paris, 1777 (Frf. 5,020)
Collection Joseph-François Count of Vaudreuil, Paris, 1777-1784
Auction Vaudreuil, Paris, 1784 (Frf. 4,990 to Lenglier)
Auction Paris, 1802 (Frf. 4,581 to Paillet)
Collection Charles Scarisbrick, Scarisbrick Hall or Wrightington Hall, Lancashire, before 1860
Auction Scarisbrick, London, 1861 (£28.10 to Bohn)
Collection Henry George Bohn, Twickenham, 1861-1884
Auction Bohn, London, 1885
Private collection, Essex, 1885-1902
Auction London, 1902
Collection Karl Baron Kuffner, Diosek (Czechoslovakia), until 1940
Collection Raoul Baron Kuffner, New York, 1940-1948
Auction Baron Kuffner de Dioszegh, New York, 1948
Dealer Paul Drey, New York, 1948-1951(?)
Collection Walter P. Chrysler, Jr., New York, 1951(?)-after 1958
Dealer M.R. Schweitzer, New York, 1969
The Metropolitan Museum of Art, New York, 1969-1973 (on loan from Schweitzer)
Collection Richard L. Feigen, New York, 1977 (bought from Schweitzer)

Bibliography

Auction Amsterdam 1708, no. 18
Hoet 1752-1770, vol. 1, p. 125, no. 12 and p. 135, no. 15
Auction Amsterdam 1773, pp. 11-12, no. 30
Auction Paris 1777, p. 51, no. 96
Auction Paris 1784, p. 60, no. 49
Auction Paris 1802, p. 8, no. 13
Auction London 1861, p. 100, no. 675
Auction London 1885, p. 32, no. 200
Mireur 1901, vol. 1, pp. 448-449 (1708, 1709, 1773, 1777, 1784, 1802)
Auction London 1902-A, p. 10, no. 60
Wurzbach, vol. 1 (1906), p. 179
Auction New York 1948, p. 18, no. 29 and fig.
Hartford 1948, p. 10, no. 54
Bénézit 1948-1955, vol. 11, p. 117
Feinblatt 1949, pp. 268 and 270, fig. 3
Coral Gables 1951, no. 11
Birmingham etc. 1957-1958, p. 9 and fig.
Bille 1961, vol. 11, pp. 90-91, no. 26
Art Journal 1969, p. 361 and fig.
Burlington Magazine 1969, p. 416 and pl. XXIX
Paris 1970-1971, p. 29
Fuchs 1973, pp. 80-81, note 11 and pl. 10, no. 33
Salerno 1977-1978, vol. I, pp. 239-241, vol. III, p. 1000, note 25
Roethlisberger 1981, pp. 17 and 68, no. 165 and fig., p. 80, no. 203
Haak 1984, p. 144 and fig. 298
New York 1985, pp. 85, 88-89, no. 11 and fig.
Vergara 1985, pp. 405-406 and 408 and fig. 82
Haverkamp-Begemann / Adams 1988, pp. 24-25 and fig. p. 39, no. 7

Bartholomeus Breenbergh The Preaching of Saint John the Baptist

his version in 1748, after it had been auctioned in 1720 in Amsterdam for 310 guilders.[2] The history of the provenance of this piece from 1748 to its arrival in the present collection can be reconstructed without any gaps whatsoever. Its longest stay was with the Hope family in Amsterdam and London (see cat. nos. 47, 49, and 59).[3] The Braamcamp version is dated 1643, and, despite this impressive provenance, must surely be the least-known, -illustrated, and -discussed masterpiece by Breenbergh.[4]

The Van der Marck Breenbergh of 1634 may pride itself on a somewhat bigger reputation, albeit one of relatively recent vintage. The peregrinations of this panel are much more difficult to reconstruct than those of the Braamcamp Breenbergh.[5] Although we are here able to reveal several previously unknown locations, its history is still not uninterrupted. The painting traveled by a route that may be called traditional for Dutch masterpieces now in American possession: from prominent collections in the Netherlands to France, then during the French Revolution to England, after which it ended up in the United States.

This painting was auctioned in Amsterdam in close succession, in 1708 and 1709. In the former year the depiction was described as 'vol Beelden [en] Ruinen' (full of Figures [and] Ruins), which means that it referred in any case not to the Braamcamp variant, because it features no ruins.[6] In the catalogue of the anonymous auction of 1709 it was warmly recommended as 'The Preaching of Saint John, full of Figures, in a Landscape, being a capital Piece by Bartholomeus Breenberg, most delightfully painted' (in translation) and, in the advertisement for this auction, placed in the *Amsterdamsche Courant*, the name of the painter was honorably mentioned in the company of those of the great Italian masters and of Rubens and Van Dyck.[7]

In 1708 and 1709 the painting fetched 450 guilders and 430 guilders respectively, and by 1773 the proceeds had almost doubled. It was then auctioned from the estate of Johan van der Marck (1695-1770), after 1751 four times burgomaster of Leyden and in addition governor of the West Indies Company in Amsterdam.[8] He had assembled a renowned collection of paintings (including portraits of artists), and he also possessed a large collection of prints, drawings, and auction catalogues (now in the Bibliothèque Nationale in Paris). He himself wrote the catalogue of his painting collection, which in 1773 served as the basis for the auction catalogue.[9] About his Breenbergh he wrote: 'This Piece is as handsome in its drawing and Imagination of the Passions, variety of clothing, and elaborateness of Painting, as is to be seen by this master' (in translation).[10] The buyer of the

biblical piece was the dealer Pieter Fouquet, Jr. (1729-1800), who primarily acted for foreign customers (see cat. nos. 2, 44, 54, and 60). Hence the Van der Marck Breenbergh has not been seen in the Netherlands since 1773.

Randon de Boisset, Receiver General of France, was the owner of the painting when he suddenly died in 1777. The painter Pierre Rémy, who wrote the auction catalogue, had been Boisset's artistic advisor. Rémy was able to report that De Boisset acquired his love for Dutch and Flemish art during the numerous visits that he paid to cabinets of paintings while on the journeys he undertook to the North from 1766 on, of which he kept journals.[11] *The Preaching of Saint John the Baptist* ended up in the collection of Joseph-François Count of Vaudreuil (1740-1817), who had earned his spurs during the Seven Years War and who later became Grand Falconer of France.[12] In 1784 he decided to sell his collection of Italian, Flemish, and Dutch masters, but, reported the auction catalogue, he was not able to part with his French paintings. After the Restoration, this proof of his patriotism helped secure him the position of Governor of the Louvre.[13] Breenbergh's painting was again auctioned in Paris in 1802, this time as part of an anonymous collection.[14]

In the professional literature, the history of the Van der Marck Breenbergh version ends with this last auction, and picks up again only around 1948, when the painting was auctioned in New York. It has not been known until now that during the nineteenth century it was in several estimable collections in England. In view of the subject from the New Testament, it is not surprising that it was at one time acquired by Charles Scarisbrick (1801/1802-1860), who came from an old Catholic family in Lancashire.[15] The collection of this eccentric recluse also included *The Box Bed* by Pieter de Hooch (cat. no. 35). At the Scarisbrick auction of 1861 the painting was sold for very little money (twenty-eight pounds and ten shillings) to the collector Bohn. Henry George Bohn (1796-1884) was a renowned bookseller and publisher, who wrote scholarly catalogues about the antiquarian books in his holdings, and who was responsible for inexpensive editions of works of world literature. For more than half a century he attended the major auctions in London and assembled such an extensive art collection in his residence at Twickenham that a great part of it had to be sold between 1875 and 1878, as he was running out of space. However, he did keep the paintings, and from 1882 on he worked with his daughter on a catalogue raisonné of his collection, which had in the meantime grown substantially. Two days before his death, he introduced the last corrections into his foreword to the

2
Rembrandt
The Preaching of Saint John the Baptist
Canvas on panel, 62 x 80 cm (24⅜ x 31½ in.)
Neither signed nor dated (ca. 1634-1636)
Berlin, Staatliche Museen, Gemäldegalerie,
inv. no. 828 K

catalogue. The auction of the Bohn collection was the sensation of the 1885 London season.[16] Where *The Preaching of Saint John the Baptist* subsequently ended up is only vaguely known: until 1902 it hung in a 'mansion in Essex.'[17]

In 1940 the painting was moved to America, where Breenbergh was then virtually unknown. In 1941 The Detroit Institute of Arts was the first museum in the United States to acquire a work by the Italianate painter: *The Cave of Egeria*.[18] In 1948 the Los Angeles Museum of Art followed suit with the *Rain of Manna*.[19] The Van der Marck Breenbergh came to America with the collection of the Czech Baron Raoul Kuffner of Dioszegh (died 1962). In 1908 a wing was added to the family castle in Diosek (to the east of Bratislava) for the collection of paintings, which was open to the public. After the death of his wife in 1933, the Baron married his mistress, the Polish painter Tamara de Lempicka (1898-1980). She managed to convince him that the advance of Nazi Germany represented a threat to the family possessions, and he consequently sold his estate and took a part of his art collection to Switzerland for safekeeping. In 1939 the couple took refuge in the United States, where, in 1940, the paintings were shipped as well.[20] The public auction of the Kuffner collection took place in New York in 1948. It was then said to have been assembled almost exclusively by Raoul's father, Karl Baron Kuffner.[21]

Presumably the painting was subsequently acquired by the dealer Paul Drey (1885-1953), who, around 1951, sold it to Walter Percy Chrysler, Jr. (1909-1988), the son of the founder of the Chrysler Corporation.[22] Quite unlike his father, Chrysler, Jr., was very interested in art. He acquired his first painting (a *Nude* by Renoir) at age fourteen.[23] In 1958 he housed his collection of old and modern masters in the Chrysler Museum in Provincetown, Massachusetts, but in 1971 he donated the greater part to the museum in Norfolk, Virginia, which, in gratitude, has since carried the name of Chrysler Museum.[24] In 1957 and 1958 the painting by Breenbergh was on view all over America: in Birmingham, Alabama; Washington, D.C.; Atlanta, Georgia; Columbus, Ohio; Dallas, Texas; Columbus, Georgia; New Orleans, Louisiana; West Palm Beach, Florida; Columbia, South Carolina; and Chattanooga, Tennessee.[25]

After 1958 the collector parted with his *Preaching of Saint John the Baptist*, which is now in the private collection of the dealer Richard L. Feigen (born 1930) in New York. This collection is built around a core of early-twentieth-century classics: Max Beckmann, Georg Grosz, Wassily Kandinsky.[26] Thus the journey of the Van der Marck Breenbergh has not come to an end in a museum. Though for some years the painting hung on loan in The Metropolitan Museum of Art in New York (1969-1973), this did not lead to an acquisition.

The painting is dated 1634 and was therefore done in Amsterdam, where Breenbergh had married in 1633.[27] By this marriage he became remotely related to the Sweelinck family, of which the best-known members were the composer Jan Pietersz and the painter Gerrit Pietersz, who was the teacher of Pieter Lastman. It is apparent from numerous formal debts that Breenbergh was much interested in the works of Pieter Lastman, who was the Nestor of the Amsterdam history painters.[28] *The Preaching of Saint John the Baptist* of 1634 is a multifigured history piece of the kind that Lastman's followers (the so-called pre-Rembrandtists) loved to paint. After the death of Lastman in 1633, it was above all his former pupil Rembrandt who displayed a pronounced interest in such compositions. This is clear from a series of drawn copies after his crowd scenes with historical subjects.[29] Almost simultaneously with Breenbergh, Rembrandt also painted a *Preaching of Saint John the Baptist* (Berlin, Staatliche Museen, Gemäldegalerie) [2].[30] In it many reminiscences of Lastman can be identified.[31] For instance, the obelisk points by way of Lastman back to Rome.

Just as Lastman was fond of incorporating his remembrances of Italy into his biblical scenes, so Breenbergh repeatedly made use of the drawings from his Roman period in his later paintings. In his case the Holy Land is invariably provided with Italian scenery.[32] The ruins in the background of this biblical piece resemble those of the Colosseum. Breenbergh often drew this amphitheater; it appears in a sketch in the British Museum (London) [3].[33] He thought the gigantic block of rubble in the middle of the encircling remains of the walls to be an especially nice motif, which he repeated in the background of his paintings. In the foreground he gave himself free rein in the 'multitude and diversity' of the figures (*copia* and *varietas*, to use Carel van Mander's words). Just like Rembrandt, Breenbergh kept to the guidelines recommended in theory books for a good history piece. 'But unusually merry / to regard / [are] Fresh Youths / and beautiful Damsels / Old Men / Matrons / all sorts / Of children / older and newly born ones' (in translation), Van Mander had observed on this topic in his *Schilder-Boeck* of 1604.[34] Thus Breenbergh has placed a mother with a child 'newly born' in the foreground. This was a popular motif for this kind of history, as Rembrandt informed us in an inscription on his copy after Pieter Lastman's *Saints Paul and Barnabas Preaching at Lystra* (Bayonne, Musée Bonnat): 'en voor uyt is een jonck kint' (and in front is a young child).[35]

We know of numerous preparatory studies for the figures in Rembrandt's *Preaching of Saint John the Baptist*, but in the case of Breenbergh, none of these have survived. He nevertheless scoured his shop apparatus for material that he could use for the picturesque Eastern types with which he wished to populate his

3
Bartholomeus Breenbergh
The Colosseum
Pen drawing with wash, 90 x 147 mm (3½ x 5¾ in.)
Lower left: *BB f.* (ca. 1627)
London, British Museum, inv. no. 1836.8.11.90

4
Jacques Callot
The Sermon of Saint Amandus
Etching, 221 x 281 mm (8³/₄ x 11 in.)
Lower left: *Iac. Callot f* (ca. 1622)
Amsterdam, Rijksprentenkabinet

5
Hans Schäufelein and Josse de Negker
The Ensign Bearer
Woodcut, 207 x 135 mm (8¹/₈ x 5³/₈ in.)
Lower left: *de [maker's mark of Josse de Negker]* n and on
a tablet: *HS* (in ligature) (ca. 1512-1515)
Vienna, Graphische Sammlung Albertina

composition. For the *repoussoir* group at the right he reached for a print by Jacques Callot, *The Sermon of Saint Amandus* [**4**].³⁶ He took the standing soldier with the lance, engaged in conversation with several spectators, verbatim from this model.³⁷ The old man who leans on a cane and listens attentively to Saint John may have been borrowed from this print as well. Behind him poses a dashingly accoutered soldier with a flamboyant hat with ostrich feathers. He looks like an escapee from an old German print, such as *An Ensign Bearer* by Hans Schäufelein, which was cut by Josse de Negker [**5**].³⁸ In truth he looks a little lost amid all these Orientals.

1 *Roethlisberger 1981*, p. 80, no. 203 and figs. IV and 203
2 *Bille 1961*, vol. II, pp. 90-91, no. 26
3 *Bille 1961*, vol. II, pp. 7-7a, no. 26
4 *Roethlisberger 1981*, p. 80, no. 203
5 *Feinblatt 1949*, p. 268; *Roethlisberger 1981*, p. 68, no. 165, first opposed the presumed provenance from the Braamcamp collection.
6 *Roethlisberger 1981*, p. 68, no. 165, believed incorrectly that the mention could apply to both paintings; at the Ietswaart auction in 1749 a *Prediking van Johannes* by Breenbergh was still offered for sale, but in view of the price (*f* 17) this must have been of lesser quality than the two pieces owned by Feigen (*Hoet 1752-1770*, vol. II, p. 255, no. 279).
7 *Hoet 1752-1770*, vol. I, p. 135, no. 15; *Dudok van Heel 1975*, p. 171, no. 132
8 *Van der Aa 1852 / 1969*, vol. V, p. 58; *Goudappel / Snapper 1979*, p. 58
9 *Lugt 1921*, p. 564
10 *Auction Amsterdam 1773*, pp. 11-12, no. 30
11 *Auction Paris 1777*, pp. VIII-XII
12 *Larousse 1865-1878*, vol. XV, p. 812; *Auction Paris 1784*, title page
13 *Auction Paris 1784*, pp. 5-6; *Larousse 1865-1878*, vol. XV, p. 812
14 *Auction Paris 1802*, title page: according to an annotation in the copy in the RKD the paintings came from the collections Montaleau, Langeac, and Senet.
15 Cat. no. 35, note 15
16 *DNB*, vol. V, pp. 304-306
17 *Auction London 1902-A*, title page
18 Inv. no. 41.61; *Feinblatt 1949*, pp. 266 and 271, note 1; *Roethlisberger 1981*, pp. 76-77, no. 193 and fig.
19 Inv. no. 48.26; *Feinblatt 1949*, p. 266; *Roethlisberger 1981*, pp. 59-60, no. 136 and fig.
20 *De Lempicka-Foxhall / Phillips 1987*, pp. 115-116 and 127
21 *Auction New York 1948*, p. V
22 *Art Digest 1941-A*, p. 10; *Art News 1953*, p. 7
23 *DAB*, vol. XI (supplement I), pp. 103-105; *WWA*, vol. I, p. 553; *WWWA*, vol. IX, p. 69
24 *Carter 1976*, pp. 56-62; *Sutton 1986*, p. 204
25 *Birmingham etc. 1957-1958*, p. 9 and fig.
26 *Arts Magazine 1971*, p. 61
27 *Roethlisberger 1981*, p. 3, note 4
28 *Roethlisberger 1981*, cat. nos. 122, 123, 138, 141, 145, 146, 166, 170, 205, 215, and 217, gave numerous examples of the artistic relation between Breenbergh and Lastman.
29 *Broos 1975-1976*, pp. 199-228 (especially p. 210, note 21)
30 *Gerson / Bredius 1969*, pp. 469 and 606, no. 555 and fig.; *Berlin 1975*, pp. 350-351, no. 828 K and fig.
31 *Broos 1977*, p. 59, no. Br. 555

32 *Sutton et al. 1987-1988*, p. 285, note 4

33 *Hind 1915-1931*, vol. III, p. 58, no. 15 and pl. XXXI; *Roethlisberger 1969*, p. 35, no. 82 and fig.

34 *Van Mander 1604*, fol. 17 recto; *Broos 1975-1976*, pp. 202-203

35 Inv. no. D 1470; *Benesch 1973*, vol. II, p. 1c7, no. 449 and fig. 536; *Broos 1975-1976*, pp. 214-215, fig. 17

36 *Schröder 1971*, vol. II, p. 1457 and fig. (Lieure 406)

37 *Roethlisberger 1981*, p. 68, no. 165

38 B. 100 (vol. VII, pp. 266-267, no. 100); *Dodgson 1903-1911*, vol. II, p. 34, no. 91 and fig.; *Illustrated Bartsch*, vol. XI, p. 280, no. 100 (266)

B B

The Hague(?) 1588 – Utrecht 1629

Canvas, 65.8 x 52.7 cm (25⅝ x 20¾ in.). On the paper lower left: *HTBrugghen fecit 16[..]*
(last two digits illegible; нтв in ligature) (ca. 1623-1627)
Northampton, Mass., Smith College Museum of Art, inv. no. 1957:10

New documentary evidence regarding the family of Hendrick ter Brugghen suggests that the artist was born in either The Hague or Utrecht in 1588. Because his father, a tax collector, is regularly named in the archives of The Hague between 1585 and 1602, it may be assumed that Hendrick spent most of his childhood there, before being apprenticed to Abraham Bloemaert in Utrecht. Around 1604 the young Ter Brugghen journeyed to Italy, the first of the major Dutch Caravaggesque painters to reach Rome, and the only one who could have actually met Caravaggio, who would leave Rome permanently in 1606. Although we are told by near-contemporary sources that Ter Brugghen lived in Rome for ten years, and documents place him in Rome, Naples, and Milan, no works of his Italian period are known.

By late 1614 Ter Brugghen was again in Utrecht, having traveled back to Holland via Milan. In 1616 he entered the Utrecht guild; the same year he married Jacoba Verbeeck. Securely dated works exist from 1620 on, and from mid-1621 until his death in 1629 Ter Brugghen is noted regularly in the Utrecht civil archives. The artist died 1 November 1629, four months before the birth of his eighth child.

As enumerated by Nicolson, the Smith College *Old Man Writing by Candlelight* passed through several private collections early in the twentieth century. In 1956, when Nicolson first published the painting, it was owned by Mejuffrouw ter Brugghen of Baarn.[1] Two years later Nicolson remarked that 'this lady was not a descendant of the painter, but his name weighed heavily in his favour when she acquired it.'[2] In his catalogue raisonné of Ter Brugghen's works, Nicolson goes on to note that until 1956 the painting hung in the house of Ir. Mindert Peekema, of Bussum, the head engineer of the Telegrafie and Telefonie; however, it was subsequently given by Mej. ter Brugghen to Mr. J. Oomkens at Huizen.[3] The painting was then turned over to the dealer Cramer, in The Hague.

The *Old Man Writing by Candlelight* entered the collection of the Smith College Museum of Art in 1957, thanks to the efforts of Robert O. Parks, who was director from 1955 to 1961. Smith's first president, L. Clarke Seelye, had established the tradition of

Provenance

Collection Johan Rabo Baron van Keppel, Apeldoorn
Auction Van Keppel, Amsterdam, 1925
Dealer D. Komter, Amsterdam
Auction Komter, Amsterdam, 1926
Collection Mejuffrouw E.L.A.C. ter Brugghen, Baarn, by 1956
Collection J. Oomkens, Huizen
Dealer G. Cramer, The Hague, by 1957
Smith College Museum of Art, Northampton, Mass., 1957 (purchased with the Gift of Adeline F. Wing ['98] and Caroline R. Wing ['96])

Bibliography

Auction Amsterdam 1925, p. 11, no. 10
Auction Amsterdam 1926, p. 14, no. 26
Czobor 1956, p. 230 and fig.
Nicolson 1956, pp. 109, 110 and fig. 11
Parks 1957, p. 75 and fig.
Faison 1958, pp. 140-141 and fig. 15
Indianapolis / San Diego 1958, no. 81 and fig.
Nicolson 1958-A, pp. 9, 19, 72, 74, 89, no. A 53, pp. 85-86 and pl. 74
Nicolson 1958-B, pp. 52-57 and fig. 48
Nicolson 1960, p. 470, note 24
Judson 1961, pp. 347-348
Hartford 1964, no. 205
Slatkes 1965, p. 138
Dayton / Baltimore 1965-1966, pp. 9, 10, no. 14, pp. 40-41 and fig.
Chetham 1969, p. 775
Chetham 1970, n.p., fig. 22
Nicolson 1979, p. 101
Miami 1984, pp. 158-159, no. 47 and fig.
Chetham et al. 1986, p. 86 and fig. 36
Sutton 1986, p. 208 and fig. 301
Blankert / Slatkes 1986-1987-A, pp. 50, 146 and fig. 45
Brunswick 1987, pp. 20-21 and fig. 13

1
Hendrick ter Brugghen
Weeping Heraclitus
Canvas, 125 x 101.6 cm (49¼ x 40 in.)
On open book: *H TBrugghen 1621*
Cleveland, The Cleveland Museum of Art, purchase,
Mr. and Mrs. William H. Marlatt Fund, inv. no. 77.2

2
Attributed to Aertgen van Leiden
Saint Jerome Studying by Candlelight
Panel, 48 x 38 cm (18⅞ x 15 in.)
On cartouche on wall at left: *G1* (almost illegible)
(ca. 1525-1530)
Amsterdam, Rijksmuseum, inv. no. 1433

collecting original works of art for study purposes. In 1879 he purchased twenty-seven paintings by contemporary American artists, including Albert Bierstadt, Thomas Eakins, and Winslow Homer. Because of this program of collecting works of art, Smith can boast the oldest and most important collection of any women's college in America, with particular strength in nineteenth- and twentieth-century French and American paintings. Two students who benefited from this curriculum were the sisters Caroline R. (class of 1896) and Adeline F. (class of 1898) Wing. When in 1957 the funds anticipated to purchase the *Old Man Writing by Candlelight* were redirected to buy another work of art, the Wing sisters provided the money to secure the acquisition of the painting.

Ter Brugghen, Gerrit van Honthorst, and Dirck van Baburen were the leading figures among the Utrecht Caravaggisti. However, each devised a personal interpretation of the Caravaggesque idiom. Ter Brugghen in particular developed a soft luminosity and palette peculiar to him. In addition to the half-length genre figures that were the stock in trade of these Utrecht artists – and seen also in the works of the older Abraham Bloemaert, who had not gone to Italy – Ter Brugghen repeatedly depicted traditional religious subjects, which continued to be in demand in Catholic Utrecht. Two marvelous examples of Ter Brugghen's handling of religious subject matter are in American collections: the *Crucifixion with Mary and Saint John the Baptist* (New York, The Metropolitan Museum of Art)[1] and the *Saint Sebastian Tended by Saint Irene* (Oberlin, Ohio, Allen Memorial Art Museum, Oberlin College) (p. 93, fig. 12).[5] These two works represent opposite poles of interpretation: the *Crucifixion* is iconic and almost medieval in its imagery and hieratic figural arrangement; the *Saint Sebastian* is very baroque in its realism, in the compression of the large forms into the pictorial space, and in the internalized emotional intensity. The secular nature of the Smith College painting contrasts with the religious content of these paintings.

The *Old Man Writing by Candlelight* is the secular counterpart to the traditional portrayals of church scholars and ancient philosophers, including Ter Brugghen's own *Weeping Heraclitus* (The Cleveland Museum of Art) [1].[6] The pictorial sources for the Smith College painting are, not unexpectedly, to be found in Northern representations of the scholarly Jerome and other men of letters, such as Erasmus of Rotterdam. Of particular relevance is a type of *Saint Jerome Studying by Candlelight* attributed to Aertgen van Leiden (Amsterdam, Rijksmuseum) [2].[7] As noted in Justus Müller Hofstede's recent discussion of 'Artificial Light

Hendrick ter Brugghen Old Man Writing by Candlelight

in Honthorst and Terbrugghen: Form and Iconography,' this panel was probably known in Utrecht, especially as it seems to have inspired a *Saint Jerome Studying by Night* by Ter Brugghen's master Abraham Bloemaert (Milwaukee, collection Dr. Alfred Bader) [3].[8] Müller Hofstede also suggests that 'Aertgen's small panel might have been attractive for Terbrugghen in several respects: quite apart from some motifs (old man; candle-light), which he planned for his own composition, the extremely delicate and subtle solution of the color and chiaroscuro problems of a nocturne might have fascinated him. Moreover he found in Aertgen's painting the same soft amalgamation of artificial light, colours and material surfaces, which he cultivated himself with the greatest skill.'[9]

Ter Brugghen has severely limited the number of objects in his *Old Man Writing by Candlelight*; only the essentials to create the scene are included. The artistic interest is not on accoutrements or setting but on the effects of the light from the bare flame as it flickers across the various materials, qualifying form and color. The description of the man's environment is confined to the very limited area which the light of the candle can illuminate. And this area is itself restricted, as the form of the man crowds in on the light, blocking its further penetration into the darkness. Within this concentrated area are gathered all of the pictorial elements. The result is an intensity of form and light, which echoes the intensity of the man's concentration.[10] Most remarkable are the lush color combinations – contrasting shades of yellow ocher, violet, reddish brown, and pink – creating an opalescent luminosity unique to Ter Brugghen.

4
Hendrick ter Brugghen
Melancholy
Canvas, 67 x 56.5 cm (26³⁄₈ x 22¹⁄₄ in.)
Neither signed nor dated (ca. 1626-1627)
Toronto, Art Gallery of Ontario (long-term loan)

1 *Nicolson 1956*, pp. 109, 110
2 *Nicolson 1958-B*, p. 53, note 3
3 *Nicolson 1958-A*, p. 85, no. A 53
4 Inv. no. 56.228; *Nicolson 1958-A*, pp. 79-82, no. A 49, pls. 53, 54, 55c, 56, 57
5 Inv. no. 53.256; *Nicolson 1958-A*, pp. 86-87, no. A 54, pls. 58, 59, 60, 61
6 *Cleveland 1982*, pp. 278-280, no. 123 and fig.; *Tzeutschler-Lurie 1979*, pp. 279-287 and fig. The dating of the *Old Man Writing by Candlelight* is problematic; for a review of the dates proposed by various scholars, see *Blankert / Slatkes 1986-1987-A*, p. 50 ('1626-28') and *Brunswick 1987*, pp. 35-36, note 14.
7 *Van Thiel et al. 1976*, p. 345, no. A 3903 and fig.; *Dayton / Baltimore 1965-1966*, p. 42; *Brunswick 1987*, pp. 19-20 and fig. 14
8 *Nicolson 1979*, p. 23, pl. 108; engraved in reverse by his son Cornelis Bloemaert, see *Brunswick 1987*, p. 20 and fig. 15.
9 *Brunswick 1987*, p. 20
10 Utilizing essentially the same pictorial elements, Ter Brugghen created a similar composition featuring a female subject: the *Melancholy* (Toronto, Art Gallery of Ontario, long-term loan from a private collection) [4]. However, the addition of the human skull and hourglass, coupled with the intensification of the dramatic lighting effects, imbues that work with a greater emotional intensity. This has led to the interpretation of the subject as the penitent Magdalene (*Nicolson 1958*, pp. 89-90, no. A 58 and pl. 75; *Blankert / Slatkes 1986-1987-A*, pp. 146-148, no. 25 and fig.).

LFO

3
Abraham Bloemaert
Saint Jerome Studying by Night
Canvas, 64.4 x 53 cm (25³⁄₈ x 20⁷⁄₈ in.)
Lower right: *A Bloemaert. fe.* (ca. 1622)
Milwaukee, collection Dr. Alfred Bader

Burgsteinfurt 1597/1598 – Haarlem 1661

Panel, 60.5 x 101.5 cm (23⅞ x 40 in.)
At the left, on the rim of the pewter plate: *PC' 1641* (PC in ligature)
Poughkeepsie, N.Y., Vassar College Art Gallery, inv. no. 40.1.5

Born in Westphalia, Pieter Claesz married Geertjen Hendriks in Haarlem in 1617. In 1620 their son Claes was born, who was later to become a famous painter as Nicolaes Berchem. Pieter applied himself to the painting of still lifes, a great many of which have been preserved. His characteristic monogram *PC'* occurs on dated paintings from 1621 to 1660. Initially he painted *vanitas* still lifes. Later he more often applied himself to meticulously composed *ontbijtgens* (breakfasts), *banketgens* (banquets), and *toebackjes* (tobacco pieces), in which the emphasis is on the rendering of materials and the content is of secondary importance. In the thirties he used a monochrome palette of the kind also in fashion in landscape painting at the time. His initially precise brush strokes then became ever freer.

Houbraken's biography of Pieter Claesz was brief and more in the nature of a footnote to the life of his son Nicolaes Berchem. He summarized the father's oeuvre as follows: '[paintings] in which usually appeared a small table with all sorts of sugar confectionary, in a silver bowl or porcelain dish, etc.' (in translation).[1] One of the many 'small tables' is this *Little Banquet*, monogrammed and dated 1641 by the artist himself, from the Vassar College Art Gallery in Poughkeepsie. Since the book by N.R.A. Vroom, such depictions have been called 'monochrome little banquets' (in translation), but this was one of the works with which Pieter Claesz announced the end of his monochrome period.[2] Striking is the red of the wine in the tall glass, of the berries and cherries in the bowl, and of the plaited sheath of the knife. Subtle nuances of color make it possible to recognize the pewter of the plates, the gold of the watch, and the gold and silver of the saltshaker.

The Haarlem painter Pieter Claesz painted only still lifes. It is noteworthy that in that very city, in 1604, high-flown standards were set for the ideal artist. According to Van Mander, the artist had to be a universal spirit and the opposite of a specialist. The theoretician added with a sigh that 'it does not daily occur / that a [painter] may be capable of everything / to learn / to understand / or to become outstanding in everything.' For him the true artist remained the history painter and only the painter of lesser talent

Bibliography

AMAM Bulletin 1953, pp. 49 and 66, no. 16 and fig.
Faison 1964, p. 231 and fig. 357
Bloomington 1966, no. 1
Poughkeepsie 1967, pp. 13-14 and fig.
Poughkeepsie 1983, p. 110 and fig.
Sutton 1986, p. 240 and fig. 355

1
Pieter Claesz
Little Banquet
Panel, 64 x 82 cm (25¼ x 32¼ in.)
Lower right: *PC'. / . A' 1647* (PC in ligature)
Amsterdam, Rijksmuseum, inv. no. A 1857

Pieter Claesz Little Banquet

limited himself to 'Animals / Kitchens / Fruits / Flowers / Landscapes [or] Portraits after life' (in translation).[3]

Three-quarters of a century later, theory had still not given way to practice, although the high quality of some specialists (Frans Hals, for instance) was by then largely beyond dispute. At that time Samuel van Hoogstraten wrote in his chapter 'On the three levels in the art of Painting' that the still life should be considered to belong to the first or lowest rank. 'This, however, is certain, that no matter how nicely some flowers, fruit, or other still lifes, as we call them, have been painted, these Paintings may nevertheless not be rated higher than in the first grade of works of art' (in translation), be they as deceptively real as those by Zeuxis and Parrhasios (see cat. no. 57).[4] Pieter Claesz himself was so modest about his trade that, when the most important court commission of the seventeenth century presented itself – the decoration of the Oranjezaal in the Huis ten Bosch in The Hague – he offered his services as a gilder. On the list compiled by Constantijn Huygens in 1649 of the applicants for the work to be executed, Pieter Claesz figured as a painter of the 'silver en gout [gold].'[5] His more ambitious son Nicolaes, on the other hand, was one of the candidates qualified as a history painter.[6]

By being highly productive, the specialist of the seventeenth century could still hope for a reasonable income. One such prolific painter was the portraitist Michiel van Mierevelt, whom Van Mander introduced as some kind of narrow-minded specialist.[7] The famous landscape painter Jan van Goyen was also exceptionally prolific (but nevertheless went bankrupt), as was Pieter Claesz in his own field, the still life. His diligence is reflected in the size of his oeuvre. His paintings have become dispersed throughout the world in numerous private and public collections, from the Museum for Fine Arts in Voronezh, in the Soviet Union,[8] to the Vassar College Art Gallery in Poughkeepsie in the United States.

The *Little Banquet* by Pieter Claesz is now the treasure of the collection in Poughkeepsie.[9] This study collection is able to present a handful of Dutch masters with justified pride: 'One of the strongest areas in the Collection – that of the XVII Century paintings and drawings – is a tribute to the imagination and perspicacity of Agnes Rindge Claflin, Professor of Art at Vassar College from 1923 to 1965, who concentrated on building up the Baroque at a time when it was still ignored by most museums. The Gallery has continued to strengthen its holdings by gifts and purchases so that the Collection now includes examples from all the major European countries.'[10] In 1940 the College Museum was enriched with the still life by Pieter Claesz. Mrs. Lloyd

Williams donated it to the museum in memory of her father, Daniël Cottier (1838-1891). Cottier had been an art dealer in London and maintained close contacts with the Dutch dealer E.J. van Wisselingh, who, in 1876, persuaded the Hague School painter Matthijs Maris to go to work for Cottier in London.[11] The dealer opened a branch in New York, where his daughter Margaret married and continued to live. Even as a child, she had regularly received paintings from her father, so that collecting had become second nature to her. The decision to bequeath her collection to a public institution was suggested by a good friend, the painter Mary Turley Robinson, whose grandfather was a trustee of the Vassar College Art Gallery. Mrs. Williams recounted in 1940 that the still life by Claesz used to hang in the dining room of Daniël Cottier's home in London.[12]

Insofar as can be determined, this *Little Banquet* has never been exhibited in the Netherlands. It nevertheless looks familiar. This is natural because Pieter Claesz composed according to a few rules of thumb and had a fixed repertoire of pictorial means. In his paintings one usually looks down on a tabletop with round dishes in a triangular arrangement, beside which a saltshaker and a glass or pitcher provide some vertical relief within the horizontal image. A plate balancing on the edge of the table is always present as well.[13] Familiar ingredients in the piece in Poughkeepsie are the pewter plate with the bun, the obligatory diagonally placed knife in a sheath, the walnuts and hazelnuts, and the vines around the dish at the left. Sometimes the main course is a fish, a crab, a pie, a ham, or, as here, a roasted fowl with the head and legs still attached. Everything is set out on a white tablecloth, with a half complexly draped contrasting with a half that is neatly ironed into folds. We know the artifices of the painter well from his *Little Banquet* of 1647 in the Rijksmuseum (Amsterdam) [1].[14]

Claesz nevertheless liked to add a new prop to his customary stock. In this case, it is the curious cross-shaped watch in the left foreground, which has been taken out of its case and opened, with the key on a ribbon lying at its side. He presumably painted it after an actual specimen. This type of watch had a lid of rock crystal and, on account of its shape, was somewhat misleadingly called a *montre d'abbesse* (abbess's watch).[15] The saltshaker appears instead to be an invention. The miniature sculpture on this piece of table silver has little to do with its function. This is the so-called *Miles Christianus*, known to us as the crowning touch on the lids of the tall goblets that were quite popular with still life painters (see cat. no. 7).[16] Pieter Claesz himself repeatedly painted such beakers, such as in a *Vanitas Still Life* of 1624

(Dresden, Staatliche Kunstsammlungen, Gemäldegalerie) [2].[17] In this painting the sculpture on the goblet functions in a context that unmistakably refers to the transience of existence and the sinfulness of man. The *Miles Christianus* is the fighter against the seven deadly sins.[18] As Bergström demonstrated, the painter portrayed another such beaker in 1640, in a depiction with an emblematic character (New York, private collection, in 1983).[19]

In this latter, symbolic piece, the watch and cracked nut are to be interpreted as references to the finiteness of existence. That is not to say that these objects in the still life in Poughkeepsie are to be interpreted in the same way – although we are free to think so. As there are no explicit references to secondary connotations, the scene appears to have been intended only as a feast for the eye. If one looks carefully at the smooth surface of the bulbous pitcher, one sees the painter mirrored between the reflections of an open window and the table linen with the bun on the pewter dish. This trick was often employed, especially in still lifes. Clara Peeters had used it 1612, and Abraham van Beyeren later elevated it to a kind of trademark (cat. no. 7, figs. 1-4).[20]

An older example is a *Vanitas Still Life* of 1634 (London, dealer H. Terry-Engel, in 1970), in which we see Pieter Claesz painting at his easel in the reflective surface of a sphere.[21] An undated *Vanitas Still Life* (Nuremberg, Germanisches Nationalmuseum) [3][22] also features the watch and the cracked nut, and, in addition, a fallen glass and a skull that point to the vanity of human pursuits. Here Pieter Claesz clearly portrayed himself in mirror image, painting with his left hand, in order to heighten the impression of realism. He is apparently telling us that he felt involved with the meaning of the *vanitas* scene, just as people used to have themselves portrayed with a skull. Compared to this, what we see on the belly of the pitcher in the *Little Banquet* in Poughkeepsie is no more than a glimpse of the self-portrait, while the depiction as a whole is more pleasant than disturbing. The idea of the transience of things seems literally to have been relegated to the background.

3
Pieter Claesz, *Vanitas Still Life*
Panel, 36 x 59 cm (14⅛ x 23¼ in.)
Neither signed nor dated (ca. 1635)
Nuremberg, Germanisches Nationalmuseum,
inv. no. Gm 1409

1 *Houbraken 1718-1721*, vol. II, pp. 110-111
2 *Vroom 1945*
3 *Van Mander 1604*, n.p., 'Voor-reden'
4 *Van Hoogstraten 1678*, p. 87: just like Van Mander, he rated the still life painter on the same, low level as the portraitist.
5 *Van Gelder 1948-1949*, p. 126
6 Nicolaes did not work on the Oranjezaal, but went to Italy instead; see *Broos 1987*, pp. 44-45.
7 *Van Mander 1604*, fol. 281 recto and verso
8 Inv. no. 461; *Kuznetsov / Linnik 1982*, no. 253 and fig.
9 *Sutton 1986*, p. 240; the painting was illustrated on the cover of the collection catalogue (*Poughkeepsie 1983*).
10 *Poughkeepsie 1967*, p. 13
11 *De Leeuw / Sillevis / Dumas 1983*, p. 131
12 According to a document compiled by Ruth Benedict on 20 February 1940 (Vassar College Art Gallery archives).
13 *Vroom 1945*, pp. 21-54 and 198-203, nos. 17-82, gave a since superseded overview of his oeuvre.
14 *Van Thiel et al. 1976*, p. 168, no. A 1857 and fig.
15 *Spierdijk 1973*, p. 65 and figs. 30 and 39; *Meis 1981*, pp. 44-45 and 72-74, figs. 44-49
16 *Bergström 1983*, pp. 440 and 443; see also *Segal 1988-1989*, pp. 68-69, 129 and 132
17 *Dresden 1979*, p. 133, no. 1370 and fig.; *Segal 1988-1989*, p. 237, no. 29
18 *Segal 1988-1989*, p. 70; on the *Miles Christianus* in prints (and in other media), see *Wang 1975*.
19 *Bergström 1983*, p. 440, fig. 1
20 *Vorenkamp 1933*, p. 59, note 1 listed these; see also *Münster / Baden Baden 1979-1980*, pp. 458-462
21 *Leyden 1970*, p. 5, no. 6 and fig.
22 *Münster / Baden Baden 1979-1980*, pp. 458-459, no. 236 and fig.
    B B

2
Pieter Claesz, *Vanitas Still Life*
Panel, 65 x 55.5 cm (25⅝ x 21⅞ in.)
At the left, on the plinth: PC A°1624 (PC in ligature)
Dresden, Staatliche Kunstsammlungen,
Gemäldegalerie, inv. no. 1370

Aelbert Cuyp Ships on the Maas River at Dordrecht

Dordrecht 1620 – Dordrecht 1691

Canvas, 115 x 170 cm (45¼ x 67 in.)
On the lee board of the boat at the right: *A. cuijp* (ca. 1650-1655)
Washington, D.C., National Gallery of Art, Andrew W. Mellon Collection, inv. no. 1940.2.1

Aelbert Cuyp was the pupil and closest collaborator of his father, Jacob Gerritsz Cuyp, until the latter's death in 1651/1652. Although his father painted historical works and portraits, he himself specialized in landscapes inhabited by animals that served as more than pure staffage. His earliest works date to the early forties: the near monochrome tints show an affinity with the landscapes of Jan van Goyen. His palette subsequently changed thanks to the influence of such Italianate landscape painters as Jan Both and Adam Pijnacker. He drew the landscape of Utrecht and Gelderland and later used these sketches for the compositions of his paintings. After 1650 the landscapes are drenched in a southern sunlight that he himself never actually experienced. Striking in his compositions are the lofty sky and the low horizon, which form the setting for the horsemen or large animals dominating the front plane. He generally depicted his equestrian portraits in imaginary costumes and in entirely invented surroundings. Although his figures are at times somewhat awkwardly proportioned, his most beautiful landscapes feature a shimmering fall of light that illuminates the contours of animals and human beings against prospects that dissolve into mist.

In the eighteenth and early nineteenth century the world watched in amazement as the Dutch engaged in a massive sale of the works of Aelbert Cuyp, which found eager buyers and viewers elsewhere, especially in England. One admirer was Joseph Mallord William Turner, who, in 1818 in Holland, painted his *Ships on the River Maas at Dordrecht* (New Haven, Yale Center for British Art) [1]¹ in homage to Cuyp. While rendering

1
Joseph Mallord William Turner
Ships on the River Maas at Dordrecht
Canvas, 157.5 x 233 cm (62 x 91¾ in.)
Lower right: *J M W Turner RA 1818 Dordt*
New Haven, Yale Center for British Art, Paul Mellon Collection, inv. no. B 1977.14.77

Provenance
Collection Johan van der Linden van Slingelandt, Dordrecht, before 1752-1782
Auction Van Slingelandt, Dordrecht, 1785 (f1,825 to Rens)
Dealer Alexis Delahante, London 1804(?)-1814
Collection Sir Abraham Hume, Bart., Wormley (Hertfordshire), 1814-1838 (bought for 1,300 guineas from Delahante)
Collection John Hume Cust Viscount Alford, Ashridge Park (Hertfordshire), 1838-1851 (inherited from Sir Abraham Hume)
Collection John William Spencer second Earl Brownlow, Ashridge Park, 1851-1867
Collection Adelbert Wellington third Earl Brownlow, Ashridge Park and London, 1867-1923
Auction Brownlow, London, 1923 (17,500 guineas to Joseph Duveen)
Collection Joseph Duveen / Duveen Brothers, New York, 1923-1940
National Gallery of Art, Washington, 1940 (bought with the Mellon Fund)

Bibliography
Hoet 1752-1770, vol. II, p. 490
Descamps 1753-1765, vol. II, p. 80
Auction Dordrecht 1785, pp. 20-21, no. 70
London 1815, p. 17, no. 67
Van Eijnden / Van der Willigen 1816-1820 / 1976, vol. III, p. 403
Buchanan 1824, vol. II, p. 192, no. 10
London 1824, pp. 166-167, no. 5
Smith 1829-1842, vol. V, p. 311, no. 98
Waagen 1837-1839, vol. II, p. 21
London 1838, p. 9, no. 37
Waagen 1854, vol. II, p. 316
London 1867, n.p., no. 21
Veth 1884, p. 284, no. 70
London 1892, no. 85
Wurzbach, vol. II (1906), p. 367
HdG 28 (vol. II [1908], p. 16, no. 28)
Graves 1913-1915, vol. II, p. 240, no. 67 (1815), p. 243, no. 37 (1838), p. 245, no. 21 (1867), p. 250, no. 85 (1892)
Graves 1918-1921, vol. V, p. 2245, no. 78 (1878)
Auction London 1923, p. 21, no. 75
Cannons 1923, p. 207, no. 4447
Valentiner 1925, no. 3 and fig.
Washburn Freund 1925, p. 460
Toronto 1926, p. 36, no. 143
Art News 1928, p. 1
London 1928, p. 167, no. 1424 and fig.
Borenius 1929, p. 64
Gibson 1929, p. 84 and fig.
London 1929, p. 129, no. 267
London 1929-A, p. 21, no. 17 and fig.
Martin 1929, p. 302
Martin 1929-A, p. 137
Zwartendijk 1929, p. 391 and fig. LXXXVII
Bauch 1929-1930, p. 15
Brussels 1935, p. 162, no. 714
Amsterdam 1936, p. 9, no. 37
Hennus 1936, pp. 229-230 and fig.
Detroit 1939, no. 7 and fig.
Liège 1939, p. 37, no. 54
Apollo 1941, p. 112 and fig.
Berenson / Valentiner 1941, no. 209 and fig.

this work, he apparently thought of the masterpiece by Cuyp under discussion, which he may have seen in 1815 at an exhibition at the British Institution in London.[2] The owner at the time was Sir Abraham Hume (1749-1838), a passionate collector and director of the British Institution.[3]

Hume bought the painting around 1814 for 1,300 guineas from the Frenchman Alexis Delahante, who was described as 'a gentleman of refined taste and correct judgement in works of art.'[4] He was one of those dealers who operated on an international scale and knew how to take clever advantage of the abundance of private property that became available following the French Revolution. He was a (miniature) painter by training. Delahante came from a prominent family and was a royalist. During the Napoleonic period he lived in exile in England.[5] Upon his return to Paris in 1814, his collection of Italian, Flemish, and Dutch paintings was auctioned in London.[6] Shortly before the auction, he had sold the Cuyp to Sir Abraham Hume. Delahante himself rated Cuyp's riverscape among the finest pieces he had brought to England.[7]

Sir Abraham was very proud of his Cuyp and, shortly before his death, told Dr. Waagen, director of the museum in Berlin, that he had been offered as much as 3,000 pounds for it.[8] He and his descendants parted with it several times for exhibitions in London.[9] When he died in 1838, his grandson John Hume Cust Viscount Alford (1812-1851; since 1839 Home-Cust), inherited his collection. Viscount Alford died in 1851 in Ashridge Park in Berkhamsted, after which his grandfather's paintings became the property of his son, John William Spencer, the second Earl Brownlow (1842-1869). In 1867 the latter's

Washington 1941, p. 51, no. 101
Finley / Walker 1949, p. xiii and p. 97, no. 501 and fig.
Baird 1960, p. 20 and fig. p. 21
Walker 1963, p. 196, no. 501 and fig.
Kindlers, vol. II (1964), p. 863
Washington 1965, p. 35, no. 501
Stechow 1966, p. 119 and fig. 237
Bol 1973, pp. 268-269 and fig. 271
Reiss 1975, p. 143, no. 104 and fig., pp. 204, 212 and fig. VIII
Walker 1976, no. 399 and fig.
Butlin / Joll 1977, vol. II, p. 92
Reiss 1978, p. 88 and note 12
Reitlinger 1982, vol. II, p. 204
Wheelock 1984, p. 22 and fig.
Sutton 1986, p. 306 and fig. 457

2
Aelbert Cuyp
Ships on the River Maas at Dordrecht
Canvas, 114 x 167 cm (44⅞ x 65¾ in.)
Lower left: *A. Cuijp* (ca. 1650-1655)
Waddesdon Manor, The National Trust, inv. no. WI/61/3

brother, Adelbert Wellington (1844-1921), the third Earl Brownlow, inherited the collection, including Cuyp's riverscape.[10] With the death of Adelbert, the earldom became extinct; in 1923 the Brownlow collection was put up for public auction in London. Before the eyes of Frits Lugt and Cornelis Hofstede de Groot, *Ships on the River Maas at Dordrecht* was started at 17,000 guineas and went for no less than 17,500 guineas to Joseph Duveen, the well-known art dealer. Thanks to this and several other top works, the total yield of this auction broke all records.[11]

It looked like a repeat of the Van Slingelandt auction of 1785. At that auction, too, the riverscape had been one of the highlights. According to the foreword to the catalogue, for years international attention had been greedily fixed on the collection of Johan van der Linden van Slingelandt (1701-1782), a bachelor living in Dordrecht. He was a master minter, trader in iron, and a great collector.[12] In 1754 J.B. Descamps (1706-1791), the French painter and professor at the Academy of Rouen, indicated the fame the collection had achieved beyond the frontiers of the Netherlands. We can deduce from his description that he had seen the painting by Cuyp firsthand: 'The view of Dordt is nearly the same as the first Painting above; an infinite number of Sloops & Boats that follow the one in which the Prince [Maurits] is found' (in translation).[13] In his spacious residence on the Walenvest, Johan van der Linden van Slingelandt had housed more than seven hundred paintings, which he cherished lovingly: 'the Lord Collector has been [...] most careful not to let the Unqualified handle and disadvantage the Works' (in translation).[14] He had an astonishing thirty-eight works by, or attributed to, his one-time fellow townsman Cuyp. Very few or none of these paintings are presently to be seen in the Netherlands.[15]

The Van Slingelandt collection was catalogued by Gerard Hoet in 1752. He described this painting as the companion piece of a second work, *Ships on the River Maas at Dordrecht* (Waddesdon Manor, The National Trust) [2].[16] The Van Slingelandt auction was the international turning point for the appreciation of Cuyp's work and a gauge for its later popularity. The biographers Van Eijnden and Van der Willigen called the rise in price of the pendant typical for the ruling rage for Cuyps. Several years after the auction of 1785 – where it was a little cheaper than the painting in Washington – it 'passed hands for a price more than four times higher' (in translation).[17] In 1834 an analysis of the old auction prices led the art dealer John Smith to observe with a sigh that until 1750 paintings by Cuyp never fetched more than three pounds, and that, with hindsight, the

amounts of the Slingelandt auction were still on the moderate side.[18] He pointed to Bryan's encyclopedia, which stated in 1816 that prices had risen a hundredfold in half a century.[19] The Cuyp craze naturally had its ramifications. For instance, to meet the great demand the Rotterdam artist and dealer Arie Lamme scoured the villages around Dordrecht with English clients, looking for Cuyps, which he traded for his own works. The painter Jacob van Strij so admired Cuyp that, around 1800, he made numerous copies after the earlier artist's work, which were later marketed as originals.[20] For many years a *Cows in a Landscape* hung in The Metropolitan Museum of Art in New York as a work by Cuyp until, in 1980, it was recognized as a Van Strij.[21] The highpoint of the Cuyp renaissance occurred around 1870: in 1868 Lord Hertford bought the *Lane at Meerdervoort* (London, Wallace Collection)[22] for 140,000 francs, the highest amount paid until then for a landscape. By that time more than seventy-five percent of Cuyp's painted oeuvre was in English possession. Then the American collectors got their turn.

For more than fifteen years after the Brownlow auction in London, *Ships on the River Maas at Dordrecht* remained the property of the dealer Joseph Duveen (1869-1939), later Lord Duveen of Millbank, in New York. He regularly parted with it for exhibitions, but he never sold it (see p. 41, fig. 28). It was on view in Detroit in 1925, where it left an impression in part because of the fabulous price that Duveen had paid for it in 1923.[23] The globe-trotter Duveen, who commuted between France, England, and America, showed his Dordrecht riverscape all over the world: in 1926 in Toronto, in 1928 and 1929 in London, in 1935 in Brussels, and in 1936 in Amsterdam.[24] As a consequence the painting got 'a well-deserved reputation' and it was even called 'world famous' (in translation).[25] After Joseph Duveen's death the firm Duveen Brothers still lent it to an exhibition in Detroit and Liège in 1939.[26] One year later it had apparently become part of the Mellon collection. Andrew Mellon (cat. no. 53, fig. 5) had died in 1937 but had given his collection to the nation for the benefit of the National Gallery of Art, which opened in Washington in 1941. In addition, Mellon had placed a considerable amount of money in a fund out of which salaries for employees could be paid, and works of art, such as this magisterial painting by Cuyp, could be bought.[27]

When still in the Van Slingelandt collection, the two riverscapes by Cuyp now at Washington and Waddesdon Manor [2] had been considered to belong together and had apparently been framed and hung as such. Gerard Hoet had described the latter painting as a depiction in which Prince Maurits was being

▲ 3
Aelbert Cuyp
Ships on the River Maas at Dordrecht
Canvas, 98 x 138 cm (38⅝ x 54⅜ in.)
On the oar at the right: *A. cuyp* (ca. 1648-1650)
London (Kenwood), The Iveagh Bequest, inv. no. 46

▼ 4
Aelbert Cuyp
View of the River Maas at Dordrecht
Chalk and wash drawing, 185 x 458 mm (7¼ x 18 in.)
Lower left (not autograph): *A: Cuijp fecit.* (ca. 1648-1650)
Amsterdam, Rijksprentenkabinet, inv. no. A 4376

conveyed in a rowboat to a yacht, whereas the painting under consideration was said to depict how 'Oldebarnevelt, standing up, looks at Prince Maurits, [done] after Life' (in translation).[28] In the auction catalogue of 1785 this romantic interpretation was no longer taken seriously. Now and then an (unsuccessful) attempt was made to interpret the Washington painting as a history piece. It was said to depict the moment on 24 May 1660 when King Charles II anchored in Dordrecht on his journey from Breda to The Hague, before returning to England.[29] It has been proposed that the painting shows an episode from the life of Jan van de Corput, the first husband of Cuyp's wife, who had been the director of diverse admiralties.[30] Here, too, solid evidence is lacking.

Cuyp used the profile of the city of Dordrecht as background for a scene showing the departure of a substantial company, while the rattle of drums and blare of trumpets sound over the flat expanse of water beneath the damp morning mist. Dordrecht is seen from the north, and the sun still stands low to the east. We have two other grand compositions by Cuyp with ships on the same body of water, one in The Iveagh Bequest (London, Kenwood) [3][31] and one in The National Trust at Ascott (Buckinghamshire).[32] It is highly probable that in making each of these three paintings Cuyp employed a drawing that he had made of this part of Dordrecht (Amsterdam, Rijksprentenkabinet) [4].[33] This chalk sketch is seen from the Papendrecht shore, where the rivers Merwede, Noord and Old Maas come together. At the left we see the Groothoofdspoort and, more to the right, behind ships lying before the Damiatenbolwerk, the blunt tower of the Great Church. These are also the two prominent points of the city visible in the painting in Washington. In the drawing Cuyp indicated the appearance of the profile of the houses behind the ships next to the Groothoofdspoort,[34] yet in the painting he was not so topographically accurate. Most of the city is hidden behind a tangle of masts and raised sails. At the left and in the center background we see a transom yacht. Before the city and at the right lie broad ships; next to the city gate a small sprit-sailed ship with a white sail is seen. Details of the drawing demonstrate that the city is shown after restoration work had been commenced on this site in 1647. The three riverscapes are therefore almost unanimously dated after 1647 / 1648, but before 1655.[35] Thus Charles II cannot be the figure depicted in the scene in Washington.

1 *Butlin / Joll 1977*, vol. II, pp. 91-93, no. 137, vol. II, pl. 122 (on the understanding that the example has not been in the Bridgewater collection).
2 *London 1824*, pp. 166-167, no. 5
3 *DNB*, vol. XXVIII, pp. 208-209
4 *Buchanan 1824*, vol. II, p. 190; *Haskell 1976*, p. 26, note 10
5 *Thieme / Becker*, vol. VIII, p. 580; *Whitley 1973*, vol. II, p. 215
6 *Auction London 1814*; in HdG 28 (vol. II [1908], p. 16, no. 28) Hofstede de Groot incorrectly assumed that the Cuyp was also auctioned in London in 1814.
7 *Buchanan 1824*, vol. II, p. 194
8 *Waagen 1837-1838*, vol. II, p. 21
9 See Bibliography
10 *Complete Peerage*, vol. II, pp. 348-550; *Burke's 1963*, p. 348; *Debrett's 1980*, p. 185; *Auction London 1923*, 'Note'
11 *Auction London 1923*, p. 21, no. 75 (see also press cutting in copy HdG, RKD)
12 *NNBW*, vol. VIII, col. 1059
13 *Descamps 1753-1765*, vol. II, p. 80
14 *Auction Dordrecht 1785*, p. VII
15 *Reiss 1975*, p. 212
16 HdG 36; *Waterhouse 1967*, pp. 134-135, no. 55 and fig.
17 *Van Eijnden / Van der Willigen 1816-1820 / 1976*, vol. II, p. 388, see also vol. III, p. 403
18 *Smith 1829-1842*, vol. V, pp. 284-285
19 *Bryan 1816 / 1964*, vol. II, p. 863
20 *De Bruyn Kops 1965-A*, pp. 172-176; *Broos 1977-B*, p. 45
21 Inv. no. 91.26.8; HdG 211; *Baetjer 1980*, vol. II, p. 39, vol. III, p. 432 and fig.; *Broos 1986*, pp. 183-184 and fig. 1
22 Inv. no. P 51; HdG 168; *London 1968*, pp. 75-76, no. P 51 and fig.; *Reiss 1975*, p. 159, no. 119 and fig.
23 *Valentiner 1925*, no. 3 and fig.; *Washburn Freund 1925*, p. 460
24 See Bibliography
25 *Hennus 1936*, p. 230; *Borenius 1929*, p. 97
26 *Detroit 1939*, no. 7 and fig.; *Liège 1939*, p. 37, no. 54
27 *Burlington Magazine 1937*, p. 143
28 *Hoet 1752-1770*, vol. II, p. 490
29 *Berenson / Valentiner 1941*, no. 209
30 *Reiss 1978*, p. 88, note 12
31 HdG 165; *London 1965*, p. 11, no. 46 and fig.; *Reiss 1975*, p. 136, no. 97 and fig.
32 Inv. no. (collection A. de Rothschild); HdG 164; *Ascott 1963*, pp. 9-10, no. 10; *Reiss 1975*, p. 137, no. 98 and fig.
33 *Schapelhouman / Schatborn 1987*, p. 40 and fig.
34 The details of the buildings were identified in *Dordrecht 1977-1978*, pp. 88-89, no. 30.
35 For the dating, see *Van Gelder / Jost 1972*, p. 236, note 5.
BB

Leyden 1613 – Leyden 1675

Panel, 53.3 x 39.4 cm (21 x 15½ in.). On the corner of the table: *GDOV* (GD in ligature); at the right, on the base of the column: *GDOV 1663 AEt 50* (GD in ligature) (?)
Kansas City, Mo., The Nelson-Atkins Museum of Art, inv. no. 32-77

The biography of 'Gerrit' Dou, published in 1641 by I.I. Orlers, city chronicler of Leyden, has turned out to be so accurate that much of it must have been recorded straight from the mouth of the painter. He was the son of the glazier Douwe Jansz, who, when Dou was only eleven, placed him under the tutelage of Bartholomeus Dolendo to learn the rudiments of drawing. He then learned to engrave glass and actually practiced this trade with his father.

In 1628 (on 14 February, Dou tells us), he entered the atelier of Rembrandt because he wanted to become a painter. He became an 'outstanding Master / particularly in small / subtle / and curious things,' wrote Orlers, who observed that Dou's work was much sought after and very expensive. His fame brought him a request from Charles II to become painter to the English court, which he turned down. Further indicative of Dou's reputation is the fact that, during his lifetime, the rich collector Johan de Bye had assembled no fewer than twenty-seven paintings by the master. Dou is considered to be the Nestor of the Leyden *fijnschilders* (painters of minute refinement), and he called Frans van Mieris 'the prince of his pupils.' Beside Mieris, Gabriël Metsu and Godfried Schalcken are the best known of his numerous students and emulators.

At the German courts there existed, as of old, a keen interest in the work of the Leyden *fijnschilders*. In the nineteenth-century configuration of the Alte Pinakothek in Munich, next to the renowned Passion series by Rembrandt in room XI, hung no fewer than twelve panels by Gerard Dou, among them the *Self-*

Provenance
Collection of the Elector of the Palatinate, Schleißheim, near Munich, before 1788
Hofgarten-Galerie, Munich, 1799
(Alte) Pinakothek, Munich, 1836-1932
Dealer Hoogendijk, Amsterdam, 1932
Gallery of Western Art, Kansas City, 1932
The Nelson-Atkins Museum of Art, Kansas City, 1933 (Nelson Fund)

Bibliography
Bryan 1816 / 1964, vol. II, p. 85
Smith 1829-1942, vol. I, pp. 37-38, no. 109, supplement, p. 20, no. 65
Munich 1836, p. 209, no. 272
Nagler, vol. III (1836), p. 469
Dillis 1839, p. 225, no. 272
Kramm 1857-1863, vol. I, p. 360
Hirth / Muther 1888, p. 164 and fig.
Moes 1897-1905, vol. I, p. 241, no. 9
Martin 1901, pp. 17, 58, 69, 82 and 198, no. 100
Martin 1902, pp. 34 and 130, no. 135
Munich 1904, p. 95, no. 397
Voll 1905, p. XXII and fig. on p. 219
Wurzbach, vol. I (1906), p. 418
HdG 274 (vol. I [1907], p. 428, no. 274)
Madsen 1907, p. 228
Martin 1913, p. 20 and fig., p. 180
Munich 1913, p. 37, no. 397
Munich 1920, p. 38, no. 416 (397)
Munich 1925, p. 40, no. 416 (397)
Munich 1930, p. 42 no. 416 (397)
Frankfurter 1933, p. 30 and fig. on p. 40
Kansas City 1933, p. 31 with fig. and p. 136
San Francisco 1939, no. 74 and fig.
Kansas City 1959, p. 259
Maclaren 1960, p. 104, note 2
Plietzsch 1960, p. 37
Van Hall 1963, p. 81, no. 527-5
Eckardt 1971, pp. 39 and 177, fig. 26
Jaffé 1972, pp. 509 and 511 and fig.
Kansas City 1973, p. 117 and fig.
Gaskell 1982, pp. 21-22 and fig. 7
Sumowski 1983, pp. 501, 537 and 601, no. 304 and fig.
Raupp 1984, p. 265
Hunnewell 1986, pp. 85, 120-130 and 131, note 1, p. 149, note 76, pp. 149-150, note 81 and pp. 280-281, no. 7
Sutton 1986, pp. 122 and 124
Sluijter et al. 1988, p. 60, fig. 30, pp. 115 and 208-210, no. 67 and note 1

1
Adriaen van der Werff
Portrait of Elector Johann Wilhelm of the Palatinate
Canvas, 76 x 53.8 cm (30 x 21⅛ in.)
Left center, on the base of the column: *Adr^n v^r werff fec / an° 1700*
Munich, Bayerische Staatsgemäldesammlungen, inv. no. 210

2
Gerard Dou
The Quack
Panel, 112 x 83 cm (44 x 32⅝ in.)
At the right, on a stone: *GDov 1652* (GD in ligature);
on the proclamation: *GDov* (GD in ligature)
Rotterdam, Museum Boymans-van Beuningen,
inv. no. St. 4

Portrait at Age Fifty that is now in Kansas City.[1] Most of these twelve had already been assembled in the gallery of the Elector Johann Wilhelm in Düsseldorf [1].[2] One of these works was the renowned *Quack* (Rotterdam, Museum Boymans-van Beuningen) [2].[3] Before 1788, the Kansas City self-portrait had been added to the collection of the electors, which was moved to Munich in 1799.[4] There, in 1836, the Royal Picture Gallery opened and received its present name with the founding of the Neue Pinakothek in 1853.[5] In the official paintings catalogue of 1904, sixteen works by Dou are mentioned and were on exhibit in rooms VIII to XI of the Alte Pinakothek.[6] However, the majority of these works have since been transferred elsewhere or deaccessioned. Of the four pieces still listed in the 1930 catalogue of exhibited works, two were sold shortly thereafter: *The Quack*, now in Rotterdam, and the *Self-Portrait*, now in Kansas City.[7] In the Alte Pinakothek itself, only one work by Dou is now permanently on view.[8]

The vicissitudes of Dou's paintings in Munich seem to reflect a decline in the appreciation of his work. In 1972 the Dutch art historian Jan Emmens wrote: 'Since the second half of the nineteenth century, Dou has ceased to belong to the great masters' (in translation). He explained: 'His oppressive detail, his deadly lead-blue effects [...] his *petit bourgeois* morality – these are hardly characteristics attuned to what is at present deemed to be especially artistic.'[9] This negative assessment differs substantially from Emmens's earlier enthusiastic comments on the realistic depictions by Dou.

Just which pictures filled Emmens with revulsion is not known. The Kansas City self-portrait is not likely to have numbered among his favorite paintings. Nevertheless, the work has met with only incidental criticism, at least if an observation of 1829 by the English art dealer Smith is to be interpreted as such. Smith thought that though the painter depicted himself as a fifty-year-old, 'the strong marks of application and study, in his countenance, give him the air of a man of sixty.'[10] Yet Dou painted this work precisely when he had reached the height of his fame. The portrait demonstrates his self-awareness and social standing, although, looking through Emmens's eyes, one might also speak of a measure of self-satisfaction and ostentation.

How the work was viewed in the seventeenth century is apparent from an eyewitness account at the time the portrait was painted. On 9 November 1662 the Danish scholar Ole Borch (1620-1690) traveled to Leyden, where he called on the famous painter. In his diary he described a portrait on which Dou was at work: 'We have just paid a visit to the most excellent Leyden painter Daw, who in the making of miniatures has yet to meet his equal in the Low Countries or even any other country in the world. We saw at his place a self-portrait that, with the aid of a mirror, he had made with the greatest of delicacy' (in translation).[11] Considering that the Kansas City portrait was signed in 1663, it must be the picture Ole Borch saw late in 1662.

Just like Rembrandt, Dou made anecdotal self-portraits. In 1647, for instance, he posed in an allegory of science (Dresden, Gemäldegalerie).[12] Several years later, he depicted himself as a painter with brushes and palette, leaning against a stone windowsill (Paris, Musée du Louvre).[13] Around 1650 he painted himself as a bourgeois, holding for the viewer's inspection a group portrait of his parents and brother that serves as a memorial (Brunswick, Herzog Anton Ulrich-Museum) [3].[14] In 1658 he posed with a skull (Florence, Galleria degli Uffizi).[15] Finally, in 1663 – in the painting under discussion – he presented himself as a *grand seigneur*.

Dou's appearance is impeccable, with a silk cravat knotted

3
Gerard Dou
Self-Portrait
Panel, 27 x 23 cm (10⅝ x 9 in.)
On the edge of the table: *GDov* (GD in ligature)
(ca. 1650)
Brunswick, Herzog Anton Ulrich-Museum,
inv. no. 303

4
Godfried Schalcken
Portrait of Gerard Dou
Etching, 163 x 123 mm (6⅜ x 4⅞ in.)
Neither signed nor dated (ca. 1665)
Amsterdam, Rijksprentenkabinet

above his satin waistcoat. He wears a fur-trimmed velvet mantle and a fur cap placed jauntily on his long locks. In his left hand he dangles a walking cane with a silver knob, while leaning on a table draped with a precious Persian carpet. There is no clue to the identity of the wrinkled book next to his elbow. Finally, the stone portico serves as a baldachin. The nonchalant but gallant manner of posing was probably inspired by a well-known prototype, Rembrandt's *Self-Portrait* of 1640 (London, National Gallery).[16] Rembrandt in turn drew his inspiration from Raphael's portrait of the courtier, scholar, and diplomat Baldassare Castiglione and Titian's portrait of the epic poet Ariosto (as a reminder that the prestige of painting fully matched that of poetry).[17] The *Portrait of Gerard Dou*, etched around 1665 by Godfried Schalcken [4],[18] demonstrates that the Leyden painter liked to see himself as a second Rembrandt.

In addition to Dou's name on the edge of the table, the Kansas City painting has a second signature, found on the base of the column, with the explicit addition: *1663 AEt 50*.[19] We see, then, that Dou was proud to be both a celebrated artist and a prosperous man who had reached a blessed age. Werner Sumowski calls it a *Jubiläumsselbstporträt*.[20] There was reason for jubilation. A painting by the Leyden artist, *The Young Mother* (The Hague, Mauritshuis),[21] had been selected in 1660 as a diplomatic gift for the king of England. Ole Borch's expressions of praise in 1662 were therefore not an isolated incident. Charles II's high esteem for Gerard Dou is also apparent from the monarch's attempt to attach the Leyden painter to his court.[22] In 1662, the year in which Dou was working on his *Self-Portrait*, Dirck Traudenius wrote a poem on the occasion of King Charles's prestigious request:

To Gerard Dou, Esq.
When you were, at the charge of the King,
requested to come paint in England
How now, Dou! Is Stewart to drag you,
the crucible of brushes
To Whitehall? Nay! Go not to Charles's Court
Sell not thy freedom for smoke, for wind, for dust.
He who would seek the favor of princes,
must play the part of slave and sycophant (in translation).[23]

But Dou did not succumb to the temptation and remained in Leyden, under the care of his niece Antonia van Tol, who ran the household of the fifty-year-old bachelor.[24] His Kansas City self-portrait is, so to speak, an answer to Traudenius's petition. For Dou depicted himself in front of a then universally recognizable landmark of Leyden, the Blue Gate. This gate was

Gerard Dou Self-Portrait at Age Fifty

symbolic of the prosperity of the city in the first half of the seventeenth century. Built between 1601 and 1610, it was one of the most important gates of Leyden. The rustication of the blue stone from Namur, to which the building owed its name, is clearly visible in the painting. In 1611 a new extension to the city was begun, so that the Blue Gate came to lie within the walls and thereby lost its original function. This may be seen on the plan of Leyden by Joan Blaeu, published in 1649 [5].[25] The handsome building subsequently became a strikingly picturesque site of the city.

In part on the basis of the *Self-Portrait at Age Fifty*, Willem Martin, who was later to become the director of the Mauritshuis, believed he could locate the residence of Dou on the Galgewater (the Gallows Water), just below the word *Ryn* on this fragment of Blaeu's map. According to Martin, Dou's atelier looked out on the Blue Gate, which the artist depicted in the background of at least six of his paintings, including *The Quack* [1].[26] As is apparent from a comparison with a print by an unknown artist [6],[27] made shortly after 1667, Dou was indeed most accurate in his rendering of the details of the gate.

Finally, the presence of the monumental gate in the self-portrait led the German art historian Raupp to think that Dou depicted himself here as painter-poet ('Der Maler als "Rhetor" ').[28] The Blue Gate was the meeting place of the Leyden *rederijkers* (rhetoricians or amateur actors), and notably of the Chamber of the Witte Akelei (White Columbine), which had as its motto *Liefde est Fondement* (Love is Fundamental).[29] Raupp's theory sounds plausible and it may well help to explain Dou's painting *The Quack*. But such a context is wanting in connection with the Kansas City *Self-Portrait*, and it seems improbable that Dou would have depicted himself as a rhetorician in this instance.

By the middle of the seventeenth century, the rhetoricians were already in precipitous decline, and in 1664 they were even compelled to yield their space to the guild of apothecaries. By then citizens of standing had long ceased to show themselves in the Witte Akelei.[30] Moreover, the gate is also found in works by Dou that can have nothing to do with the rhetoricians, such as the *Portrait of a Young Lady on a Balcony* (Prague, Národní Galeri) [7].[31] The 'crucible of the brushes' therefore appears to have intended nothing other than to indicate pride in the city of his birth, which he was not prepared to abandon in exchange for 'the favor of princes.'

▼ 6
Anonymous
View of the Blue Gate of Leyden
Engraving, 145 x 190 mm (5¾ x 7½ in.)
Neither signed nor dated (ca. 1670)
Leyden, Gemeentearchief, inv. no. PV 3203. 9

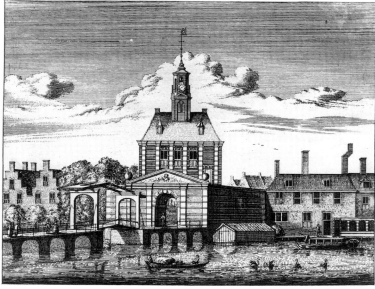

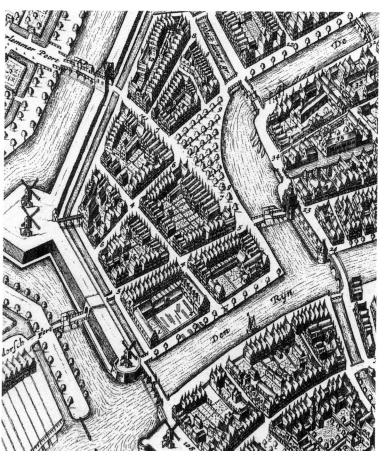

◄ 5
Joan Blaeu
City Plan of Leyden (detail)
Engraving, 450 x 530 mm (17¾ x 207/8 in.)
(the entire map)
From: J. Blaeu, *Tooneel der Steden van de Vereenigde Nederlanden*, 1649
Leyden, Gemeentearchief, inv. no. PV 350-1

7
Gerard Dou
Portrait of a Young Lady on a Balcony
Panel, 38 x 29.5 cm (15 x 11⅝ in.)
Neither signed nor dated (ca. 1660)
Prague, Národní Galeri, inv. no. O 650

1 *Munich 1836*, pp. 206-213
2 *Van Gool 1750-1751*, vol. II, pp. 529-567, published the catalogue of the Düsseldorf collection after the first printed catalogue of 1716; see also *Munich 1930*, p. XXXI.
3 HdG 68; *Rotterdam 1972*, pp. 97 and 208, no. St. 4 and fig.; *Sumowski 1983*, pp. 532 and 577, no. 280 and fig.
4 Stated in a description of 1788 of the city of Munich, cited in *San Francisco 1939*, no. 74; *Munich 1983*, p. 26.
5 *Munich 1983*, p. 27
6 *Munich 1904*, pp. 94-97, nos. 393-408
7 *Munich 1930*, p. 42, nos. 585 and 416
8 *Munich 1983*, p. 162, no. 588
9 *Emmens 1981*, vol. II, p. 181; *Eckardt 1971*, p. 34: 'Seine pedantische Feinmalerei fand bei den Zeitgenossen höchste Bewunderung.'
10 *Smith 1829-1842*, vol. I, p. 38
11 *Madsen 1907*, p. 228 (after a manuscript in the Royal Library in Copenhagen).
12 Inv. no. 1704; HdG 269; *Sumowski 1983*, pp. 531 and 571, no. 274 and fig.
13 Inv. no. 1222; HdG 275; *Bréjon de Lavergnée et al. 1979*, p. 48, no. 1222 and fig.
14 HdG 268; *Klessmann 1983*, pp. 55-56, no. 303 and fig.; *Sumowski 1983*, pp. 537 and 598, no. 301 and fig.
15 Inv. no. A 311; HdG 270; *Florence 1980*, p. 861, no. A 311 and fig.
16 Inv. no. 672; HdG 550; *Gerson / Bredius 1969*, p. 29 and 549, no. 34 and fig.
17 *De Jongh 1969*; *Raupp 1984*, pp. 168-181
18 *Hollstein*, vol. XXIV, p. 154, no. 4 and fig.
19 Now illegible; there is a transcription in *Munich 1904*, p. 95, no. 397.
20 *Sumowski 1983*, p. 537, no. 304
21 Inv. no. 32; HdG 110; *Broos 1987*, pp. 111-118, no. 20 and fig.; *Sumowski 1983*, pp. 533 and 581, no. 284 and fig.
22 *Broos 1987*, p. 112 and 117, notes 1-6
23 *Traudenius 1662*, 'Rym-bundel.' p. 25; quoted in *Houbraken 1718-1721*, vol. III, p. 33.
24 *Martin 1901*, p. 81
25 *Van Oerle 1975*, vol. I, pp. 344-347, vol. II, map no. 49
26 *Martin 1901*, pp. 56-59
27 *Van Oerle 1975*, vol. I, p. 382, fig. 407
28 *Raupp 1984*, pp. 264-265; also reported by *Hunnewell 1986*, pp. 149-150, note 81 (this author argued for an elaborate emblematic exegesis of the self-portrait; see pp. 120-130).
29 *Van Mieris / Van Alphen 1762-1784*, vol. I, p. 14, vol. II, pp. 452-453
30 *Van Mieris / Van Alphen 1762-1784*, vol. I, p. 14, vol. II, p. 453; *Schotel 1871*, vol. II, pp. 148-168
31 HdG 366; *Prague 1971*, p. 50, no. 324 and fig. 49

BB

Gerbrand van den Eeckhout Isaac Blessing Jacob

Amsterdam 1621 – Amsterdam 1674

Canvas, 100.6 x 128.3 cm (39⅝ x 50½ in.)
Below the chair: *G.V. eeckhout/A° 1642*
New York, The Metropolitan Museum of Art, inv. no. 25.110.16

He was the son of Jan Pietersz van den Eeckhout (1584-1652), who was a goldsmith, a highly prestigious trade at the time. The biographer Houbraken later called him 'a great friend of Rembrandt van Rhijn' and his pupil as well. Possibly he had first been a pupil of a follower of Lastman, someone like Nicolaes Moeyaert or Salomon Koninck. Houbraken remarked that right up to his death, Van den Eeckhout was painting in Rembrandt's style. This applies more to his (biblical) history pieces than to his portraits, which gradually came to show a more Flemish elegance. After 1650 his genre pieces began to conform to a type that, thanks to Pieter de Hooch, became particularly popular about that time. He knew very well how to adapt his style to his subject matter.

Van den Eeckhout was not only a versatile and gifted artist, superior in handling of color and powers of imagination to such well-known Rembrandt pupils as Ferdinand Bol and Nicolaes Maes, but he was highly productive as well. At least one dated painting can be identified from almost every year of his career from 1641 to 1674. In addition he created a large drawn oeuvre with historical subjects, figures, landscapes, and genre scenes in varied techniques, including watercolor. He died a bachelor in 1674.

'[The] Passions are natural and to the point, the Coloring strong, and with a masterful handling of the brush, as if made by Rembrandt' ran the description (in translation) of the painting *Isaac Blessing Jacob* by Gerbrand van den Eeckhout when it was auctioned in Amsterdam in 1796.[1] It came from the estate of Elisabeth Hooft (1712-1796), who died childless. She was the widow of the alderman and regent Wouter Valckenier (1705-1784). This scion of the well-known Amsterdam patrician dynasty lived in the family home on the Kloveniersburgwal (now no. 23) and was the owner of the country estate Valk-en-Heining on the Amstel. As a matter of course he had a collection of quality Dutch paintings from the Golden Age,[2] which, even before 1784, may possibly have included the work under discussion.

The biblical piece by Rembrandt's pupil Van den Eeckhout was said to have been auctioned sixty years earlier, in The

Provenance

(?) Auction The Hague 1737 (ƒ25.15)
Auction Elisabeth Valckenier-Hooft, Amsterdam, 1796 (ƒ630 to Agtienhoven)
Dealer Lesser, London, 1914
Auction Mary Lady Carbery, London, 1921
Auction London, 1925
Collection Archer M. Huntington, 1925
The Metropolitan Museum of Art, New York, 1925
(added to the bequest of Collis P. Huntington, 1900)

Bibliography

Hoet 1752-1770, vol. III, p. 13, no. 34
Auction Amsterdam 1796, p. 6, no. 10
Bangel 1914, p. 355
Auction London 1921, p. 4, no. 11
Auction London 1925, p. 10, no. 70
Burroughs 1925-A, pp. 142 and 146 and fig.
Wehle 1925, p. 180
Burroughs 1926, p. 101, no. Ee1-2
Burroughs 1931, p. 111, no. Ee1-2
Chicago 1935-1936, p. 24, no. 16
Iserlov 1936, p. 34
Worcester 1936, p. 30, no. 17
Ailen / Gardner 1954, p. 34
Brion / Heimann 1956, p. 212 and fig. 55
Sumowski 1957-1958, pp. 239 and 278, fig. 127
Sumowski 1961, p. 10, no. 507
Sumowski 1962, p. 11
Duyvené de Wit-Klinkhamer 1966, p. 91, note 20, p. 93, fig. 13
Haak 1968, p. 183 and fig. 294
Chicago / Minneapolis / Detroit 1969-1970, pp. 57-58 and 129, no. 45 and fig.
Roy 1972, pp. 7-9 and 212, no. 11
Pigler 1974, vol. I, p. 60
Bader 1976, pp. 36-37, no. 13 and fig.
Milnes Gaskell 1977, p. 170
Sumowski 1979-1985, vol. III, pp. 1311 and 1320
Baetjer 1980, vol. I, p. 53, vol. III, p. 435 and fig.
Amsterdam / Detroit / Washington 1980-1981, p. 162
Broos 1981, p. 110
Sumowski 1983-A, pp. 719, 720, 725, no. 392, pp. 726 and 760, no. 397 and fig.
Haak 1984, p. 298 and fig. 631
Sutton 1986, p. 183

Hague, from the estate of the mayor Samuel van Huls, who died in 1737. However, it does not appear in the auction catalogue.[3] The misunderstanding is based on the fact that on 24 April 1737, the day on which the first part of the Van Huls collection was auctioned at the home of the deceased mayor, a second auction of an anonymous, smaller collection took place in The Hague 'in the Fraternity-Room of the Society of Painters.' A painting was sold there that went for twenty-five guilders and fifteen five-cent pieces and that was described as 'An equally handsome Little Piece, showing Isaac, who is blessing his Son Jacob, by *Gerbrand van den Eekhout*.'[4] Presumably this was the biblical piece now in The Metropolitan Museum of Art in New York.

The whereabouts of the painting in the nineteenth century are entirely unknown. In 1914 it was sighted in the art trade in London, and since then it was twice auctioned there, in 1921 and in 1925.[5] In the latter year it was bequeathed to The Metropolitan Museum in New York, as part of the Collis P. Huntington bequest of 188 paintings. C.P. Huntington (1821-1890) was a Californian railroad baron who was described as one of the first American millionaires to be interested in collecting art.[6] When he died in 1900, the will he had drawn up three years earlier revealed that he had left his collection to the Metropolitan, but that his wife, Arabella, and his adopted son, Archer, would retain life interest in the paintings. Arabella – who had been the moving force behind the Huntingtons' collecting activities – continued to make acquisitions after 1900. After her death in 1924, Archer M. Huntington (1870-1955) decided to forgo his rights and to transfer all the paintings to the museum. However, upon reflection, he preferred to keep a few Rembrandts and

a Vermeer in his possession.[7] The work by Van den Eeckhout must have been added to the collection at the very last moment, in 1925, shortly before he made his generous decision.[8]

The provenance of this painting was only first researched for the occasion of this exhibition. It turned out that the painting that was so praised in 1796 got short shrift in the literature until 1966, when a great deal of attention focused on one detail. This was the pitcher on the table to the right, which portrays a silver goblet that was renowned in the seventeenth century.[9] The model was a pitcher with lid that was manufactured in 1614 by the Utrecht silversmith Adam van Vianen in remembrance of his brother Paulus, who had died recently in Prague (Amsterdam, Rijksmuseum) [1].[10]

It is an irregularly shaped object in the so-called auricle (or lobe, cartilage, or *knörpel*) style, which was chased from one piece of silver without seams or joints. The object features all sorts of bizarre details. A squatting monkey carries a swirl of shapes from which emerges a sea monster with coiled beard; from his nose grows the handle which, at the lid, changes into the body of a woman. The unattached lid resembles a wave frozen in its upward movement, but it is also reminiscent of a strange swan sailing by. This jug was a showpiece of the Amsterdam silversmith guild, about which Joachim von Sandrart remarked in 1675: 'The city of Amsterdam ordered a jug [...] to be made in his [Paulus van Vianen's] memory / on which everything is depicted as Grotesques or jocundities / as they call such a thing; [this] was considered to be a wondrously rare piece' (in translation).[11]

This 'wondrously rare piece' enjoyed great esteem, especially in the artistic circles surrounding Rembrandt. His teacher, Pieter Lastman, the Nestor of the Amsterdam history painters, depicted the vase in paintings of 1615, 1617, 1618, 1619, 1622, and 1630.[12] For the painting of 1618 Lastman made a preparatory study in black chalk, *The Angel Leaving Tobias and His Family* (Amsterdam, Rembrandthuis) [2].[13] In the center fore-

ground lies Adam van Vianen's jug, with the lid next to it. At one time the drawing had been in the possession of Rembrandt, who added the landscape in the background. It is apparent from all these paintings by Lastman, as well as from this preparatory study, that he was able to study the famous jug from all sides. Possibly there were casts available for the use of painters and silversmiths. The 1656 inventory of Rembrandt's property shows that such copies after works by silver- or goldsmiths did indeed belong to the studio's props: in the 'Antechamber of the Room of Preciosities' there were to be found 'A plaster bath of Diana by Adam van Viane' and a 'basin covered with nude figures, by Adam van Vianen' (in translation).[14]

In 1966 Duyvené de Wit-Klinkhamer listed nineteen paintings in which the jug is depicted, not only works by Van den Eeckhout and Lastman but also by Jacob Backer, Nicolaes Moeyaert, Adriaen van Nieulant, and Jan Tengnagel. Like Lastman, Salomon Koninck used this showpiece at least six times in his history pieces.[15] In his case the depiction of the famous jug is sometimes more important than the story that is being told, as, for example, in *Sophonisba Receiving the Cup of Poison* (Los Angeles, University of Southern California, Elisabeth Holmes Fisher Gallery).[16] This was one of the almost ten examples that Ter Molen was able to add to the aforementioned list, all works by history painters from the Lastman school.[17] Finally, Rüdiger Klessmann wondered what these depictions had in common and concluded that the pitcher was always the center of negative examples drawn from Jewish or ancient history. In addition, the emblematic literature warns about shining objects.[18] Klessmann adduced Roemer Visscher's *Sinnepoppen*, in which on a picture of precious dinnerware with the inscription *Ad Tragoedias* (About Tragedy) one is cautioned that the coveted gold and silver may lead to 'dispute, discord and mistrust' (in translation) (see cat. no. 7, fig. 5). That is why the Greeks and Romans displayed precious vases as a warning in their tragedies.[19]

The biblical scene rendered by Gerbrand van den Eeckhout deals with human deceit. Depicted here is the moment at which Jacob cozens from his father Isaac the blessing that was meant for his brother Esau. His mother Rebecca had goaded him into posing as the hairy Esau by putting a goatskin over his arms and neck. The disguised Jacob here kneels before his blind father while Rebecca coaches him, and Esau, seen in the background, returns from the hunt. 'So he blessed him. And he said, art thou my very son Esau? And he said, I am' (Genesis 27:23-24).

Though Adam van Vianen's beaker may therefore constitute an admonition, for our painter it was first and foremost a

3
Gerbrand van den Eeckhout
Design for a Vase
Chalk drawing, 227 x 183 mm (9 x 7¼ in.)
Neither signed nor dated (ca. 1652)
Schwerin, Staatliches Museum, inv. no. 1307 Hz

precious object. His father, Jan Pietersz van den Eeckhout, was a goldsmith, who apparently nurtured in his son a lasting love for his craft. That is evident not only from the son's paintings. As it happens, Gerbrand also made designs for ornaments and pottery for the benefit of other artists, mostly in the form of drawings that were published in series of prints.[20] The title of the series of prints that Cornelis Danckerts published around 1652 is significant: 'Several Skilful Inventions To be worked out in Gold, Silver, Wood, and Stone Useful for Silversmiths Sculptors and Painters after the invention of Gerbrand van den Eeckenhout [and others]' (in translation).[21] The first page of this series shows a variant of the famous jug by Adam van Vianen, with different options for the base. The preparatory drawing for this, done in black chalk by Gerbrand van den Eeckhout, has been preserved (Schwerin, Staatliches Museum) [**3**].[22] This is a fairly rare example of a different aspect of his artistic activity. Von Graevenitz concluded from this and other preserved studies that Van den Eeckhout made his designs in the first instance as a painter or as a draftsman and not so much from the viewpoint of the silversmith, who had to try to give shape to such a drawing in an object of silver or gold.[23] Thus, the drawing and the painting in New York are an overt homage to the art of the gold- and silversmith and to Adam van Vianen in particular – a tribute that by no accident came from the twenty-one-year-old son of a gold-smith, who himself preferred to become a painter.

1 *Auction Amsterdam 1796*, p. 6, no. 10
2 *Elias 1903-1905 / 1963*, vol. II, p. 658
3 According to *Chicago / Minneapolis / Detroit 1969-1970*, p. 57, no. 45, but not in *Auction The Hague 1737*.
4 *Hoet 1752-1770*, vol. III, p. 13, no. 34
5 *Bangel 1914*, p. 355: 'Das früheste datierte Bild E.s von 1641 [should be 1642] ist die Segnung Jakobs durch Isaak (Lesser, London)'; *Auction London 1921*, p. 4, no. 11; *Auction London 1925*, p. 10, no. 70 (in both cases with the dimensions 39½ x 49½ in.).
6 *Tomkins 1973*, p. 190; *Simpson 1988*, pp. 22-23; NCA, vol. V, pp. 15-17
7 *Burroughs 1925*, pp. 134-135 and *Burroughs 1925-A*, pp. 142-143; *Tomkins 1973*, p. 191
8 The auction in London took place on 27 April 1925 (see note 5) and the painting was mentioned in the June issue of the museum bulletin (*Burroughs 1925-A*, pp. 142, 146 and fig.). The year of acquisition mentioned by *Baetjer 1980*, vol. I, p. 53 (1900) is therefore incorrect.
9 *Duyvené de Wit-Klinkhamer 1966*
10 *Ter Molen 1984*, vol. I, p. 137, fig. 23, vol. II, pp. 81-82, no. 409
11 *Sandrart 1675*, vol. I, p. 342
12 *Duyvené de Wit-Klinkhamer 1966*, pp. 86-89 and fig. 9; *Ter Molen 1979*, pp. 485-487, fig. 5; *Ter Molen 1984*, vol. II, pp. 81-82
13 *Filedt Kok 1972*, pp. 27-28, no. X and fig.; *Benesch 1973*, vol. II, p. 113, no. 474 and fig. 565
14 *Strauss / Van der Meulen 1979*, pp. 378-381, nos. 1656/12-296 and -308; see also *Ter Molen 1984*, vol. I, p. 31
15 *Sumowski 1983-B*, p. 1642, nos. 1084-1086, p. 1644, no. 1097, p. 1645, nos. 1101-1102 and fig. pp. 1658-1660, 1671, 1675-1676
16 *Sumowski 1983-B*, pp. 1645 and 1675, no. 1101 and fig.
17 *Ter Molen 1984*, vol. II, pp. 81-82
18 *Klessmann 1981*, p. 370
19 *Roemer Visscher / Brummel 1614 / 1949*, p. 53, no. LIII; *Broos 1987*, p. 67, note 11
20 *Von Graevenitz 1973*, pp. 227-231
21 *Hollstein*, vol. V, p. 126, nos. 127-133, vol. VI, p. 135, nos. 10-47; *Ter Molen 1984*, vol. II, p. 78, no. 397
22 *Sumowski 1979-1985*, vol. III, pp. 1376-1377, no. 633 and fig.
23 *Von Graevenitz 1973*, p. 231; see also *Broos 1981*, pp. 110-112, no. 29

BB

Dordrecht 1645 – Dordrecht 1727

Canvas, 177.8 x 114.3 cm (70 x 45 in.)
Lower right: *ADe Gelder f.* (ca. 1685)
Houston, Tex., Sarah Campbell Blaffer Foundation, no inv. no.

Around 1660 he was a student of his fellow townsman Samuel van Hoogstraten, who must have urged him to further qualify himself with Rembrandt in Amsterdam. Thus De Gelder became Rembrandt's last pupil (until ca. 1663) and continued to work in the latter's late, broad style after his return to Dordrecht, even though this manner was by then deemed to be old-fashioned. Surrounded by the pervasively smooth and polished classicists, De Gelder obstinately continued to work in warm dark brown and red tints, and with an almost exaggeratedly rough, Rembrandtesque application of paint, in which he liked to use the palette knife and the wooden end of the brush. The result was a highly individual and readily recognizable style. His subjects were the same as those of his teacher and great example: besides portraits, above all he depicted biblical and historical scenes. The formal conventions, too, are borrowed from Rembrandt: large (half-) figures, or small, multifigured depictions.

Until the present time it was not known where this autograph, signed work by Aert de Gelder had been before it was auctioned in London in 1911 as a *Portrait of a Lady*, probably from a Scottish collection.[1] On the basis of the dimensions it can now be established that the painting came under the hammer in Rotterdam in 1817, as a depiction of Peace.[2] This is doubly surprising because, as we shall see, the subject has thus far usually been considered to be an *Allegory of Abundance*. The execution of the scene was aptly described in 1817 as 'altogether in the manner of Rembrandt' (in translation).[3] Clearly the reference was to the broad, plastic application of paint that was derived from Rembrandt's technique of the sixties.

In 1914 Lilienfeld introduced the painting in his monograph on Rembrandt's last pupil. He employed the title *Allegory of Abundance* for the first time and further mentioned that the work had just then been acquired for the Van Gelder collection in Ukkel.[4] This collection had been assembled by Michel van Gelder in a newly constructed castle-like villa in this suburb of Brussels.[5] His dining room was decorated with works by Flemish masters of the seventeenth century; there were two Italian rooms with fifteenth- and sixteenth-century masterpieces, another Flemish

Provenance
Auction Rotterdam, 1817
Collection Pierce, Glasgow, before 1911, or 1911-1914
Auction ('The Property of a Gentleman'), London, 1911
Dealer H.M. Clark, London, 1914
Collection Michel van Gelder, and subsequently of the widow Van Gelder, Castle Zeecrabbe, Ukkel, 1914-1938 / 1940(?)
Dealer Dr. Hans Schaeffer, New York, 1956
Auction ('The Property of a Gentleman'), London, 1965 (£3,200 to Mathews)
Dealer Shickman, New York, 1967, 1969
Sarah Campbell Blaffer Foundation, Houston, 1978

Bibliography
Auction Rotterdam 1817, p. 27, no. 94
Auction London 1911, p. 6, no. 17
Lilienfeld 1914, p. 177, no. 129
London 1929, p. 130, no. 269
Bauch 1929-1930, p. 20
Dumont-Wilden, p. 20, no. 158
Isarlov 1936, p. 46 and fig.
Rotterdam 1938, vol. 1, p. 20, no. 74, vol. 11, fig. 148
Stechow 1938-B, no. 14 and fig.
Veth 1938, p. 198
Vorenkamp 1938, p. 10 and fig.
Valentiner 1956, p. 119, no. 43 and fig.
Auction London 1965, p. 36, no. 61 and fig.
WCA, vol. XVII (1965), p. 170, no. 1619
Montreal / Toronto 1969, p. 93, no. 71
Haverkamp-Begemann 1969, p. 283
Foucart-Borville 1970, p. 214, note 28
Wright 1981, pp. 10, 16 and 112-113 and fig.
Sumowski 1983-A, pp. 1175 and 1249, no. 789 and fig.

Aert de Gelder Allegory on Peace

room with works by the so-called primitives, and a Dutch room. Among other things there was a copy on a smaller scale after Vermeer's *View of Delft* (the original is located in the Mauritshuis in The Hague),[6] which was attributed to the Delft painter himself in the catalogue of the collection.[7] Though the painting by De Gelder was there entitled *Peace*, at exhibitions (in London in 1929 and in Rotterdam and Providence in 1938), it was nevertheless presented as *Abundantia* (Abundance or Plenty).[8]

Already before 1940, the widow Van Gelder sold works from the collection, and thus this allegorical depiction came into the international art trade. It was finally acquired in 1978 by the Sarah Campbell Blaffer Foundation. Founded in Houston in 1964, this is a collection from which traveling exhibitions are formed. Sarah Campbell Blaffer, who was born in Waxahachie, Texas, intended her foundation to bring the citizens of small places such as Wichita Falls, Waco, Lufkin, and Panhandle in contact with works of art that are usually kept only in the great museums.[9] Accordingly, the painting by De Gelder came to be seen throughout the state of Texas in the early eighties, but only after it had undergone a true metamorphosis during a restoration in 1978. Behind the figure of a woman there used to be a baldachin with draperies and, in the distance, a hilly landscape with a city [**1**]. According to Wright's catalogue of 1981, these were later additions that contrasted in style with the loose handling of the brush in the main subject and were therefore removed. 'It is possible that the artist's original sketched intention suffered damage in its later overpainting and cleaning. In its present state, however, the painting could well be as the artist intended rather than being unfinished.'[10]

The entire background did not disappear during this restoration. At the lower left a sheep and a wolf were happily spared because they apparently belonged to the original painting and are finished to the same degree as the figure of the woman. Although the animals are not singled out for description in any discussion of the work, they are in fact of genuine importance to an understanding of the depiction. They refer to the biblical text in which Isaiah speaks of the Messiah and the kingdom of peace: 'The wolf also shall dwell with the lamb' (Isaiah 11:6). The customary image of the Creation before the Fall of Adam indeed shows peacefully cohabiting animals of all sorts, with predators next to their prey. In her bundle of Christian emblems of 1571, under the title *Foedere perfecto* (In perfect unity), Georgette de Montenay depicted a paradisiacal scene with the lamb, who together with the wolf and the lion, eats from a bale of hay [**2**].[11] In the often-consulted work by Cesare Ripa, published in 1644 by Dirck Pietersz Pers as *Iconologia of uytbeeldingen des Verstands* (Iconology or depictions of the Intellect), diverse options were given for the representation of Peace (*Pace*): 'A Woman [...] and at her side a Lion with a little Lamb, which lie next to each other' or 'A young sitting Woman, holding with the right hand a small Lamb and a Wolf bound together by the same yoke, carrying an olive branch in the left hand.'[12] There can be no doubt that De Gelder intended to depict Peace, and not Abundance.

According to Ripa, we must interpret the somewhat curious vegetation in the left hand of this woman as an olive branch. The horn of plenty (*Cornucopia*), here filled with precious vessels, fruits, and ears of corn, is one of the attributes of Peace. For 'Peace bears Plenty,' Pers would have us know in his *Bellerophon, of Lust tot Wysheyt* (Bellerophon, or Desire for Wisdom; Amsterdam 1662).[13] De Gelder appears to have been thoroughly familiar with the texts published by Pers. In one of his publications the depiction of *Pace* on Roman coins is described: 'Peace after the Medal of *Augustus*: A Woman, who in her left hand holds a horn of Plenty, with many fruits, flowers, leaves, also an Olive branch'

2

From: G. de Montenay, *Emblemes, ov devises chrestiennes*, Lyon 1571, no. 48

1

Cat. no. 20 before the restoration in 1978

and 'Peace, after the Medal of *Trajan*: A Woman, who in her right hand holds an Olive branch, and in the left a horn of Plenty.'[14] De Gelder's depiction of Peace is therefore ultimately based on ancient models.

In the visual arts of the sixteenth and seventeenth centuries, an olive branch or cornucopia may sometimes suffice to identify Peace, as in the handsome woodcut of 1627 by Bartolomeo Coriolano after Guido Reni, which depicts *The Concord between Peace and Abundance* with two female figures [**3**].[16] Sometimes Peace is surrounded by scenes that depict the situation before and after peace, in which instances the references are generally to violence as opposed to abundance. Often Peace also tramples on, or burns, a pile of weapons.[17] Clearly one remnant of this manner of depiction is the object next to the right foot of the female figure, which has again become visible after the recent restoration. This looks like a sabotaged weapon: a pike with a bent point. It now appears that the American art historian Peter Sutton was right in suspecting that the painting contains a greater wealth of allegorical details than had thus far been assumed.[18]

1 *Auction London 1911*, p. 6, no. 17
2 *Auction Rotterdam 1817*, p. 27, no. 94: 'Sur toile, haut 66¼, large 42¾ pouce. Une figure de femme, réprésentant la paix, richement costumée'.
3 *Auction Rotterdam 1817*, p. 27, no. 94
4 *Lilienfeld 1914*, p. 177, no. 129
5 *Dumont-Wilden*, p. 1
6 Inv. no. 92; *Broos 1987*, pp. 382-389, no. 65 and fig.
7 *Dumont-Wilden*, p. 20, no. 143
8 *Dumont-Wilden*, p. 20, no. 158; *London 1929*, p. 130, no. 269; *Rotterdam 1938*, vol. I, p. 20, no. 74; *Stechow 1938-B*
9 *Sutton 1986*, p. 110
10 *Wright 1981*, p. 112; communication from the Sarah Campbell Blaffer Foundation; in all earlier publications up to and including *Sumowski 1983-A*, p. 1249, fig. 789, the old state is reproduced.
11 *De Montenay 1571 / 1973*, p. 48
12 *Ripa / Pers 1644*, pp. 569-570
13 *Pers 1662*, no. 7 (a lion leads a horse with a triumphant Peace with a Cornucopia).
14 *Ripa / Pers 1644*, pp. 568 and 570
15 *Pauly 1964-1975*, vol. IV, col. 576
16 B. 10; I thank Jochen Becker for alerting me to this print.
17 *Pigler 1974*, vol. II, pp. 481-482; DIAL 45 A 23.0
18 *Sutton 1986*, p. 113: 'perhaps Peace and Prosperity or a reference to the Dutch State.'
BB

3
Bartolomeo Coriolano after Guido Reni
The Concord between Peace and Plenty
Woodcut, 213 x 154 mm (8⅜ x 6 in.)
Lower left: *Saulo Guidotto Patritio Bonon. Illustris Bart.⁵ Coriolanus Eq. D.* and lower right: *G.R. In. B.C. sc. Romae* and lower center: *1642*
London, British Museum

Dordrecht 1645 – Dordrecht 1727

Canvas, 59.7 x 143.5 cm (23½ x 56½ in.)
Neither signed nor dated (ca. 1690)
Providence, R.I., Museum of Art, Rhode Island School of Design, inv. no. 17.138

The Museum of Art in Providence acquired this biblical piece in 1917. It had earlier been in the collection of Mrs. H.S. Sanford of Derby, Connecticut, and between 1901 and 1915 it was exhibited in The Metropolitan Museum of Art in New York as *The Misers* by Ferdinand Bol.[1] Since 1917, however, no one has questioned the correctness of the attribution to Aert de Gelder. Since then it has also been clear that the work depicts a scene from the Book of Esther, of which several other versions by De Gelder were then known. It was one of the first paintings by Rembrandt's most intriguing pupil to arrive in an American public collection.[2]

Though the museum in Providence had been set up as a study collection for the Rhode Island School of Design and Brown University, it also serves the city as its most important artistic institution. After the death of Miss Lyra Brown Nickerson, the museum was able to start a Museum Appropriation Fund, which is used for acquisitions. Because the work by De Gelder was the very first acquisition that was made possible by this fund, it has occupied a unique place in the collection in Providence.[3] The painting was lent for the most important Rembrandt retrospectives to be held in the New World: in Chicago in 1935-1936, in Raleigh in 1956, in Montreal and Toronto in 1969, and in Chicago, Minneapolis, and Detroit, also in 1969.[4] In the Netherlands, the work has never before been shown in this century.

At these exhibitions the subject was usually identified as an illustration of the biblical passage that mentions the establishment of the Purim feast (Esther 9). The Old Testament story of Esther is about the victory of the Jews over the Persian king Ahasuerus. It was popular in the literature and on the stage of the seventeenth century and, as a consequence, in the visual arts as well (see cat. no. 61). It reminded the Dutch of their own successful struggle for independence waged against the Spaniards. The identification with the chosen people was appealing.[5] On Purim the Jews still commemorate how, with the aid of her uncle Mordecai, Esther, wife of Ahasuerus, was able to prevent the eradication of her people. Esther is the radiant focal point of this biblical love story, and she was therefore sometimes called a Protestant alter ego of Venus.[6] The very popular play *Hester, oft verlossing der Jooden* (Esther, or the liberation of the

Provenance
Collection Mrs. H.S. Sanford, Derby. Conn., before 1894
The Metropolitan Museum of Art, New York, 1901-1915
(?) Dealer Meyer Reifstahl, New York, 1917
Museum of Art, Rhode Island School of Design, Providence, 1917

Bibliography
Rowe 1921, pp. 38-40 and fig.
Art Digest 1935, p. 7
Chicago 1935-1936, pp. 25-26, no. 18
Magazine of Art 1936, p. 50
Worcester 1936, pp. 31-32, no. 19
Banks 1937, p. 24
Gilman 1937, p. 19 and fig.
Pigler 1956, vol. I, p. 203
Providence 1956, n.p. and fig.
Valentiner 1956, pp. 39 and 119, no. 46 and fig.
Cohen 1963, no. 114
Pigler 1968, vol. I, p. 255
Czobor 1969, no. 46
Von Fossen 1969, pp. 157 and 224-245, no. 34
Heverkamp-Begemann 1969, p. 283
Montreal / Toronto 1969, p. 93, no. 70 and fig.
Chicago / Minneapolis / Detroit 1969-1970, pp. 70-71 and 152, no. 65 and fig.
Garas 1973, p. 168
Pigler 1974, vol. I, p. 204
Bader 1976, pp. 130-131, no. 60 and fig.
Dresden 1979, p. 185
Lettieri 1980, pp. 72, 76, 79-81, fig. 17, p. 82, note 30, pp. 84 and 86
Sumowski 1983-A, pp. 1162, 1166 and 1208, no. 748 and fig.
Sutton 1986, p. 245

Aert de Gelder Esther and Mordecai Writing the Second Purim Letter

Jews) by Jan Serwouters, which, from 1659 on, drew full halls in Amsterdam, ended with the last sentence of Mordecai: 'Thus the Jewish lineage was saved by a woman' (in translation).[7] People visualized Esther as a bride dressed in fantastic garments, as may be seen in a print after Maarten van Heemskerck [1].[8]

The book of Esther was particularly popular in Rembrandt's circle. With his *Haman Begging Esther for Mercy* (Warsaw, Muzeum Narodowe)[9] and *The Triumph of Mordecai* of 1617 (Amsterdam, Rembrandthuis),[10] Rembrandt's teacher, Pieter Lastman, created a pair of prototypes that inspired the so-called pre-Rembrandtists and the School of Rembrandt. From the hand of Rembrandt himself have survived drawings, etchings, and paintings with scenes from the story of Esther, of which *Ahasuerus, Haman, and Esther* of 1660 formed the apotheosis (Moscow, Pushkin Museum).[11] In this work everything concentrates on the dramatis personae. Possibly De Gelder knew this painting. In general he built on the type of history piece with large half-figures that Rembrandt had developed toward the end of the fifties, such as *Ahasuerus, Haman, and Harbonah* (Leningrad, Hermitage),[12] *David Playing the Harp for Saul* (The Hague, Mauritshuis),[13] or *'The Jewish Bride'* (Amsterdam, Rijksmuseum).[14] While these masterpieces were being created, De Gelder was learning the trade in Rembrandt's atelier. He imitated Rembrandt not only in his subjects and way of painting, but, in emulation of his master, he also began a collection that the biographer Houbraken described as a 'junk stall of all sorts of clothing, draperies, firearms and other weapons, harnesses, etc.' (in translation).[15] In his depictions of the story of Esther, which called for much Eastern pomp and splendor, De Gelder, like Rembrandt, used such atelier props.

Without ever denying to whom he owed his definition of forms and handling of the brush, Aert de Gelder also made his own contribution, one that made him a distinct personality among Rembrandt's pupils and emulators. Especially marked was his predilection for a category of half-figure compositions made up of biblical couples: *Lot and His Daughter*, *Ruth and Boas*, *Juda and Tamar*, and *Esther and Mordecai*. What is striking is that he identified closely with these dramatic biblical histories, which he studied thoroughly before staging his interpretation. Just as he read Ripa for his *Allegory on Peace* (see cat. no. 20), so he read the Bible with care before he thrice painted *Juda and Tamar* with details derived from Scripture.[16]

On the occasion of the acquisition by The J. Paul Getty Museum of a canvas by De Gelder depicting a scene from the beginning of the book of Esther, *The Feast of Ahasuerus* (Malibu,

HESTER PROPIETATE TVA TIBI REGIA SCEPTRA,
HOSTI PRO SCELERE EST FVRCA PARATA SVO.

1
Anonymous after Maarten van Heemskerck
Esther
Engraving, 197 x 284 mm (7½ x 11¼ in.)
Lower right: *Martini Petri excu* (ca. 1560-1565)
Amsterdam, Rijksprentenkabinet, inv. no. 65:429

The J. Paul Getty Museum),[17] Daniel Lettieri analyzed – in *The J. Paul Getty Museum Journal* – all the then known Esther scenes by De Gelder. His claim that these eleven paintings belong to one series done as part of one commission, is too neat to be true, especially because the formats are rather varied.[18] Nonetheless, he rightly concluded that each and every one of these scenes depicts a different episode from the story of Esther. Earlier it was thought that the subject of the painting in Providence was the same as both that of a canvas in Dresden (Staatliche Kunstsammlungen, Gemäldegalerie) [2][19] and of a version, dated 1685, in Budapest (Szépmüvészeti Múzeum) [3].[20] This turns out to have been a superficial judgment. The scene in Dresden shows Esther sitting at the table in all her Oriental splendor as if dictating to her uncle Mordecai what he should write: 'And Mordecai wrote these things, and sent a letter unto all the Jews, that were in the provinces of the king Ahasuerus, both nigh and far, to establish this among them, that they should keep the fourteenth day of the month Adar, and the fifteenth day of the same, yearly' (Esther 9:20-21). The work of 1685 in Budapest, apparently so closely related, depicts a much earlier episode from the story of Esther and Mordecai, namely the moment at which Esther's uncle tells her about an intended assassination attempt on Ahasuerus (Esther 2:22).[21]

In the painting in Providence the pair sits at a table, both with papers in front of them. Mordecai has his pen poised, and the effort and excitement can be read on his face. Esther points to a document, perhaps the hated decree that describes the destruction of the Jews. Next to the inkwell lies a second pen. Lettieri concluded that they are writing the second Purim letter: 'Then Esther the queen, the daughter of Abigail, and Mordecai the Jew, wrote with all authority, to confirm this second letter of Purim'

(Esther 9:29).[22] Never before had this biblical passage been depicted in a painting.[23] We do know, however, of illustrations of one of the five megillah (biblical books on parchment scrolls), namely the Easter scroll, which is read in the synagogue at the celebration of the Purim (New York, The Library of the Jewish Theological Seminary of America) [4].[24] Assuming De Gelder had a patron, he must have been familiar with Jewish rituals and the concomitant depictions.

2
Aert de Gelder
Esther and Mordecai Writing the First Purim Letter
Canvas, 102 x 152 cm (40⅛ x 59⅞ in.)
Neither signed nor dated (ca. 1685)
Dresden, Staatliche Kunstsammlungen,
Gemäldegalerie, inv. no. 1792-A

3
Aert de Gelder
Esther and Mordecai
Canvas, 93 x 148.5 cm (36⅝ x 58½ in.)
Upper right: *ADe Gelder f. 1685* (AD in ligature)
Budapest, Szépmüvészeti Múzeum, inv. no. 1342

1 According to *Rowe 1921*, p. 38, and the documentation archives of The Metropolitan Museum of Art; not in *Blankert 1982*, pp. 162-192: 'Rejected Attributions.'

2 *Lilienfeld 1914*, pp. 247-270; the author of the first monograph on De Gelder did not know this work.

3 *Banks 1937*, p. 24; *Sutton 1986*, p. 244

4 See Bibliography

5 *Kahr 1966*, p. 228; *Van de Waal 1952*, vol. I, pp. 22-23

6 *Kahr 1966*, pp. 235-236, note 26, pointed to the similarity of this name to Astarte or Ishtar (Venus).

7 *Serwouters 1659 / 1698*, p. 55

8 *Hollstein*, vol. VIII, p. 247, nos. 476-481/5

9 Inv. no. M. Ob. 558; *Brunswick etc. 1988-1990*, pp. 24-27, no. 1 and fig.

10 Inv. no. S 1 (on loan from the Rijksdienst Beeldende Kunst, The Hague, inv. no. 706); *Tümpel 1974*, p. 53, fig. 72

11 Inv. no. 297; *Gerson / Bredius 1969*, pp. 441 and 602, no. 530 and fig.; *Kahr 1966*, p. 229, among others, enumerated the Esther scenes by Rembrandt.

12 Inv. no. 795; *Gerson / Bredius 1969*, pp. 442 and 602-603, no. 531 and fig.; for an interpretation, see *Schwartz 1984*, p. 276, no. 312.

13 Inv. no. 621; *Gerson / Bredius 1969*, pp. 435 and 602, no. 526 and fig.

14 Inv. no. C 216; *Gerson / Bredius 1969*, pp. 330 and 586, no. 416 and fig.; for an interpretation, see *Schwartz 1984*, p. 328.

15 *Houbraken 1718-1721*, vol. III, p. 207; see also *Pels 1681*, pp. 35-37; *Slive 1953*, pp. 91 and 102-103

16 *Broos 1987*, pp. 147-148

17 Inv. no. 78.PA.219; *Sumowski 1983-A*, pp. 1162 and 1192, no. 732 and fig.

18 *Lettieri 1980*, pp. 70-83, figs. 1, 7-10, 12, 15-19; *Sumowski 1983-A*, pp. 1161-1166, nos. 727, 732, 739, 740, 742, 743, 745-748 (NB: no. 744 was unknown to Lettieri, and his fig. 10 is not found in Sumowski).

19 *Dresden 1979*, p. 185, no. 1792-A and fig.; *Sumowski 1983-A*, pp. 1165 and 1207, no. 747 and fig.

20 *Pigler 1968*, vol. I, p. 255, no. 1342, vol. II, fig. 260; *Sumowski 1983-A*, pp. 1165 and 1206, no. 746 and fig.

21 *Lettieri 1980*, p. 81 (with the possibility that it may also be Esther 2:10 that is intended); *Sumowski 1983-A*, p. 1165, no. 746, believed both interpretations possible.

22 *Lettieri 1980*, pp. 79-80

23 *DIAL* 71 U 83-71 U 85, does not distinguish a separate class for the writing of Purim letters; *Pigler 1974*, vol. I, p. 204, adduced the wrong biblical text.

24 *Lettieri 1980*, pp. 83-85, note 31 and fig. 22

BB

4
Anonymous
Esther and Mordecai Writing the Second Purim Letter
Detail of a megillah
New York, The Library of the Jewish Theological
Seminary of America, inv. no. L 229

Mühlbracht (near Venlo) 1558 – Haarlem 1617

Canvas, 173.4 x 200 cm (68¼ x 78¾ in.)
At the left, on the lid of the box: *HGoltzius ANNO 1603* (HG in ligature)
Los Angeles, Calif., Los Angeles County Museum of Art, inv. no. M.84.191

Hendrick Goltzius learned the trade of glass painting from his father, Jan Goltz, in Duisburg, and received instruction in the technique of engraving from Dirck Volkertsz Coornhert in Xanten (1574-1576). In emulation of Coornhert he settled in Haarlem, where, among other things, he made a large number of engravings for the Antwerp publisher Philips Galle. In 1582 Goltzius had a flourishing atelier in Haarlem, in which prints were made and published, and at the age of thirty he was the engraver most in demand in Holland. One of his numerous collaborators was his son-in-law Jacob Matham. When the Flemish painter-theoretician Carel van Mander and the painter Cornelis Cornelisz returned from Italy in 1583, they and Goltzius founded a so-called academy in Haarlem, which probably meant that they studied as a threesome and exchanged ideas on art. Thanks to Van Mander, Goltzius learned about the work of the mannerist Bartholomeus Spranger, whose style he sometimes imitated a little too enthusiastically. In 1590-1591 he left for Italy himself, in part to seek a cure for his tuberculosis. While there he studied contemporary and antique art in Venice, Bologna, Florence, Naples, and Rome.

His most famous prints, the so-called *Meisterstiche*, were made after his return in 1591. These were six illustrations from the Life of the Virgin, done in the manner of old masters such as Dürer, in which the exaggerations of mannerism had given way to the classic forms of the Renaissance. He further engraved a Passion series in the manner of Lucas van Leyden and made chiaroscuro woodcuts after Italian models. Toward 1600 he exchanged the burin for the brush, probably in the realization that painting enjoyed greater prestige than the graphic arts, as his friend Van Mander certainly believed. The painted compositions by Goltzius show the strong influence of Correggio, Raphael, Titian, and Veronese. By preference he chose mythological subjects. His drawings contributed greatly to the development of the art of his time, especially in the rendering of the landscape and nude.

In 1604 Carel van Mander described this painting as the most recent work by his friend Hendrick Goltzius: 'Finally / in the Year 1603, he made on a canvas large as life / a sleeping, nude

Provenance

Collection Bartholomeus Ferreris, Leyden, 1603, 1605
(?) Collection Hendrick Ferreris, Leyden, after 1622
Collection Jeronimus Tonneman, Amsterdam, before 1750
Collection Maria van Breusegom, Amsterdam, 1750-1752
Auction Tonneman, Amsterdam, 1754 (*f*300 to Braamcamp)
Collection Gerret Braamcamp, Amsterdam, 1754-1771
Auction Braamcamp, Amsterdam, 1766 (*f*500 bought in by De Bosch)
Auction Braamcamp, Amsterdam, 1771 (*f*410 to Van der Dussen)
Collection Jan Lucas van der Dussen, Amsterdam, 1771-1774
Auction Van der Dussen, Amsterdam, 1774 (*f*630 to Ploos van Amstel)
Collection Cornelis Ploos van Amstel, Amsterdam, 1774-1776(?)
Collection Peter Duke of Courland, Latvia, before 1777, Duke of Sagan, South Silesia, 1785-1800
Collection Catharina of Courland, Sagan Castle, 1800-1839
Collection Dorothea of Courland, Sagan Castle, 1845-1862
Collection Edmund of Talleyrand-Périgord Duke of Dino, Sagan Castle, 1862-1872
Collection Louis third Duke of Talleyrand-Périgord and Sagan, Sagan Castle, 1872-1898
Auction Talleyrand-Périgord-Sagan, Paris, 1899 (Frf. 950)
Museum voor Schone Kunsten, Antwerp, 1912
Collection Viscount Chabert de Vatolla, Paris, 1912-1916
Collection Claës Adolf Tamm, Stockholm, 1928
Auction Stockholm, 1933 (kr. 4,100 to Runnquist)
Collection Runnquist, Stockholm, 1933-1935
Auction Stockholm, 1935 (kr. 2,300 to Nordgren)
Dealer M. Nordgren, Stockholm, from 1935
Collection Suzanne's Studio Inc., New York
Collection Eugene Allen, Los Angeles, 1974-1984
Auction San Francisco, 1984 ($732,500 to the Los Angeles County Museum of Art)
Los Angeles County Museum of Art, Los Angeles, 1984 (bought with the aid of The Ahmanson Foundation)

Bibliography

Van Mander 1604, fol. 286 recto
Hoet 1752-1770, vol. III, p. 97, no. 6
Auction Amsterdam 1754, pp. 1-2, no. 6
De Jongh 1764, vol. II, p. 112
Auction Amsterdam 1766, p. 1, no. 1
Auction Amsterdam 1771, p. 27, no. 66
Ploos van Amstel 1771, p. 141
Auction Amsterdam 1774, p. 2, no. 4
Kramm 1857-1864, vol. I, p. 585
Parthey 1863-1864, vol. I, p. 503, no. 26
Hymans 1884-1885, vol. II, p. 196 and note 1
Auction Paris 1899-A, p. 10, no. 31
Floerke 1906, vol. II, pp. 254 and 442, note 428
Dezarrois 1912, pp. 219-222 and fig.
Bredius 1914, p. 146
Hirschmann 1915, pp. 130-131 and fig.

Hendrick Goltzius Danaë Receiving Zeus as a Shower of Gold

Danaë, reclining in a very beautiful fashion: this nude is wonderfully voluptuously and upliftingly painted / and of great understanding in outline and interior modeling' (in translation).[1] The vicissitudes of this highly acclaimed canvas have been rather marvelous. It circulated in several renowned Amsterdam art cabinets in the eighteenth century but then disappeared for more than a century to a remote Polish castle, the contents of which were unexpectedly put up for auction in Paris in 1899. The art historians were overjoyed, but the museums showed no interest in the painting, which was once again lost from sight in 1935. In 1984 it was found in a slum of Los Angeles in the effects of a bankrupt businessman who had no notion of its value. The museum in Los Angeles finally bought it for a princely sum. The history of this masterpiece proves that rediscoveries in art are still possible (see also pp. 122-127).[2]

In 1604 Goltzius's *Danaë* was owned by Bartholomeus Ferreris (ca. 1557-after 1618), who was then *tafelhouder* (record keeper) of a pawnshop, collector, and amateur painter in Leyden. Van Mander dedicated a part of his *Schilder-Boeck* to him, the lives of the Italian painters, which he published in 1603: 'To the Honorable, most estimable Gentleman, Bartholomeus Ferreris, Painter, and lover of the Art of Painting, my particularly good friend' (in translation).[3] This amateur had a preference for traditional and contemporary art from the Netherlands and Germany: in addition to the recently acquired canvas by Goltzius, Van Mander named paintings by Cornelis Cornelisz, Hans Holbein, Lucas van Leyden, Quinten Matsijs, and Michiel van Mierevelt.[4] The travel-mad Arnoldus Buchelius from Utrecht admired Ferreris's collection in 1605. Among other things he saw a Bruegel and a Van Scorel, and he noted in his diary: 'GOLTZII Danaë annum habebat 1603' (Goltzius's Danaë with the date 1603).[5] Possibly Bartholomeus's painter son Hendrick Ferreris (ca. 1589-after 1625) came into the possession of the collection. In 1622 Hendrick still lived as a *frutagie-schilder* (fruit painter) at the address of his father on the Pieterskerkhof.[6]

More than a century later the *Danaë* had a new owner in Amsterdam, Jeronimus Tonneman (1687-1750). Tonneman had a small cabinet of paintings, but above all he assembled one of the most handsome collections of Dutch drawings that ever existed, parts of which were to form the core of many later collections.[7] He was a Maecenas of Cornelis Troost, whose pastel drawings he collected (now in the Mauritshuis, The Hague, and elsewhere).[8] In 1736 Troost painted the *Portrait of Jeronimus Tonneman and His Son* (Dublin, National Gallery of Ireland) [1].[9] On the table at which father and son are seated lies *Het Schilder-*

Hirschmann 1916, pp. 42-46 and 73-74, no. 5 and fig. 7
Hirschmann 1921, p. 353
Hoogewerff / Van Regteren Altena 1928, p. 78 and note 7
Van Rijckevorsel 1932, p. 131
Panofsky 1933, pp. 210-211, note 1 and fig. 22
Auction Stockholm 1935, p. 16, no. 80 and pl. 14
Van de Wall 1936, p. 498, note 32
Von Holst 1939, p. 123
Gerson 1942, p. 497
Bénézit 1948-1955, vol. IV, p. 334
Noë 1954, p. 230, note 2
Pigler 1956, vol. II, p. 60
Bille 1961, vol. I, pp. 34 and 36 and fig. 66, vol. II, pp. 16-16a and 96, no. 66
Pigler 1974, vol. II, p. 64
Broos 1977, p. 47, no. Br. 474
Foucart 1981, pp. 117 and 122, note 10
Waterschoot 1983, p. 196 and fig., pp. 209 and 224, note 483
Auction San Francisco 1984, no. 2072 and fig.
Artis 1985, p. 20 and fig.
Brooks 1985, p. 19 and fig.
Nichols 1985, pp. 158 and 161 and fig. 15 (reversed)
Erftemeijer 1986, p. 292
Schaefer 1986, pp. 412-413 and fig. 2
Sluijter 1986, pp. 42, 98 and 380, note 43-1
Sutton 1986, pp. 129-130 and fig. 186
Moormann / Uitterhoeve 1987, pp. 71-72
Schaefer / Fusco / Wiens 1987, p. 46 and fig.

1

Cornelis Troost
Portrait of Jeronimus Tonneman and His Son
Panel, 68 x 58 cm (26³/₄ x 22⁷/₈ in.)
On the plinth, under the statue: *C. Troost 1736*
Dublin, National Gallery of Ireland, inv. no. 497

Boeck by Carel van Mander. When the painting came into his hands, Jeronimus undoubtedly read the just-cited passage on the *Danaë* of Goltzius. When the collector died in 1750, his mother Maria van Breusegom turned out to have been named executrix of his will. At her death in 1752 an inventory of Tonneman's collection was drawn up, after which it was auctioned in 1754.[10]

The *Danaë* was praised in the catalogue of this sale as a capital piece and one 'of the most beautiful' that 'has ever been seen' (in translation).[11] The wealthiest collector in Amsterdam, Gerret Braamcamp (1699-1771) (cat. no. 54, fig. 1), was personally present at the Tonneman auction and in the end bought the painting by Goltzius for 300 guilders. Despite the celebrated past of the canvas, it was not included in the 1766 laudatory poem on this Amsterdam collection, *Le Temple des arts ou le cabinet de M. Braamcamp*, but was instead sold publicly. The writer of the auction catalogue of 1766 probably used Van Mander's text when he called the arrangement and execution powerful and glowing, but above all 'handsome in outline.' Despite the fact that the work was the first one listed in the catalogue and praised as 'the best by that Master known to us,' not enough was offered for it, and the auctioneer De Bosch held it back.[12] After the death of the collector, the second and most famous Braamcamp auction took place, which drew buyers from around the world to Amsterdam. The auction became renowned in part because the works bought for Catherine the Great were lost in a shipwreck on the way to Saint Petersburg.[13]

Until 1777 the painting remained in the hands of a small circle of Amsterdam collectors who knew each other well or were even related to each other. Braamcamp, for instance, had been the Maecenas of Cornelis Troost. At Braamcamp's auction – the catalogue of which was written by Cornelis Ploos van Amstel – Van der Dussen was mentioned as the buyer.[14] In 1763 Jan Lucas van der Dussen (1723-1773) married Johanna Maria Chalon, who was eighteen years younger and a niece of the wife of Cornelis Troost. Jan Lucas was a rich and distinguished man, who, by 1755, had been Heer of Groeneveld, and later also of Gooiland.[15] Van der Dussen had but two years to enjoy his acquisition, for he died in 1773, after which his collection came to be auctioned as well.[16] At this sale of 1774, Goltzius's *Danaë* was bought for 630 guilders by his cousin by marriage, Cornelis Ploos van Amstel (1726-1798), with whom Van der Dussen had maintained the best of relations during his lifetime, both men being passionate collectors.[17]

Ploos probably had not purchased the painting for himself, as he quite quickly found a foreign buyer for it. This was Peter

Duke of Courland in Latvia (1724-1800), to whom he must have passed on the *Danaë* even before 1777.[18] The duke was so pleased with his agent in Holland that in 1778 he gave him a gold medal for his services. Ploos van Amstel made a drawing of this honorary medallion, which shows the portrait of his Latvian patron on the front. The obverse depicts the museum that the duke had opened in 1775, of which the Goltzius was the showpiece (Oldenburg, Landesbibliothek) [2].[19] Peter of Courland had come into the Duchy of Latvia in 1769, after his father had abdicated his rights, and in 1785 he bought the Duchy of Sagan in South Silesia (now Poland). Ten years later Courland was annexed by Russia. His oldest daughter, Catharina (1781-1839), got Sagan by inheritance, after which her youngest sister, Dorothea Princess Biron of Courland (1793-1862), inherited the duchy in 1845. Dorothea, the last living scion of the Courland-Sagan family, was married in 1809 to Edmund Count of Talleyrand-Périgord (1787-1872), Duke of Dino, Duke of Valençay, and, from 1838, Duke of Talleyrand. Thus the castle and its paintings fell into the hands of the Talleyrand-Périgord dynasty. After the death of Dorothea's son Louis, the third Duke of Talleyrand-Périgord and Duke of Sagan (1811-1898), the old family possessions were finally auctioned.[20]

In the nineteenth century, therefore, the *Danaë* hung in the

2
Cornelis Ploos van Amstel
The Golden Medal of the Duke of Courland
Pen and wash drawing, diam. 40 mm (1⅝ in.) each
Neither signed nor dated (after 1778)
Oldenburg, Landesbibliothek, inv. no. Te IIIa 117,
fol. 158

241

Sagan Castle in remote South Silesia. When in 1884-1885 Hymans published a new edition of Van Mander's *Schilder-Boeck*, he stated: 'Nobody has been able to tell us where she [Danaë] is to be found today' (in translation).[21] But he had overlooked one snippet of information. It so happens that twenty years earlier Parthey had made mention of the painting as being in Sagan Castle. Though he had not actually seen the piece, he based his knowledge on a catalogue of the collection of Dorothea of Courland that had been made in 1855.[22] In 1899 the *Danaë* was freed from her isolation. Between 29 May and 1 June the property of the Duke of Talleyrand-Périgord from Valençay Castle came under the hammer in Paris, to be followed on 2 December by the collection from Sagan Castle. However, Goltzius's painting hardly attracted attention, probably because in the catalogue it was attributed to Goltzius with reservations, in spite of the obvious signature. It was started at 1,200 francs, but sold for only 950 francs.[23]

It was to take still another ten-odd years before the once famous painting was more or less rediscovered. In the summer of 1912 it was offered to the Antwerp museum, and the director of the Museum Boymans in Rotterdam, F. Schmidt Degener, got to see it as well. The latter tipped off Otto Hirschmann, who was preparing a monograph of the paintings by Goltzius.[24] Apparently neither museum felt like making an acquisition. A French art periodical was subsequently able to mention in September 1912 that the Parisian Viscount Chabert de Vatolla had by accident gotten his hands on a splendid work by Goltzius 'in the provinces.'[25] The new owner made photographs of his painting available for publication, which occurred most importantly in an article of 1915 by Hirschmann in *Oud-Holland*.[26] Only a year earlier, in this same periodical, Abraham Bredius had incorrectly linked rumors about a rediscovered Goltzius to the *Jupiter and Antiope* of 1616, which had just then been donated to the Louvre in Paris.[27]

Not long after the painting had been fully vindicated as the work once described by Van Mander, Viscount Chabert sold it. It ended up in a private collection in Stockholm, and then in the art trade in that city.[28] It was auctioned there in 1933 and 1935 and subsequently again passed for a missing work of art.[29] It had to be rediscovered for the last time. That occurred in 1984. A Los Angeles businessman, Eugene Allen, was then in financial difficulties, so that the Internal Revenue Service had to confiscate his property. Among the goods stored in a drafty warehouse was a painting that attracted attention, but Allen had no notion of its possible value (a few hundred dollars, he thought).

In 1974 he had taken over a few odds and ends from his sister and paid her 14,000 dollars for them. An expert from an auction house was called in, and to his astonishment he recognized the signed and dated canvas by Goltzius that had been thought lost. All's well that ends well. Shortly after that Butterfield and Butterfield of San Francisco brought the painting to auction and sold it for no less than 732,500 dollars: this was the second-highest amount that had ever been paid for a work of art on the West Coast of America. Many collectors and museum directors looked on with envious eyes. Eugene Allen was able to settle his problems with the tax inspector, and the Los Angeles County Museum of Art had (with the aid of The Ahmanson Foundation) captured a work of art that had repeatedly been praised to the skies but had also been maligned and forgotten.[30]

Carel van Mander described the depiction concisely: 'It includes a nice[ly executed] old Woman with a glowing mug / with further a cunning *Mercury*, and I don't know how many friendly little children / coming flying in with a *Stock-beurs* [a purse with handle] and other [things] / so that it is also not to be improved on in beauty of ordination' (in translation).[31] Van Mander simply assumed that his readers knew the story of Danaë, but we will nevertheless summarize it here. An oracle had told Acrisius, King of Argos, that his daughter Danaë would give birth to his murderer. He shut her up in a tower (or an underground chamber), in the charge of an old nurse. But, taking the form of shower of gold, Zeus was able to force his way in through the cracks of the roof, and thus she became pregnant and bore Perseus, who later indeed – albeit by accident – killed his grandfather with a discus.

Danaë became the personification in art of chastity and virtue.[32] At the same time the story offered scope for erotic fantasies that have tempted numerous artists to depict diverse interpretations. Titian's *Danaë* of about 1553-1554 (Madrid, Museo del Prado) [3][33] was famous, and it inspired many versions. Goltzius probably borrowed the old maid from it.[34] The figure of his Danaë, however, comes from an entirely different source. For her he took the *Aurora* (Dawn) from one of Michelangelo's Medici tombs in the New Sacristy of San Lorenzo in Florence as a model. As is shown in a drawing from a private collection (Paris, collection Stephan Higgons) [4],[35] Goltzius had a plaster replica of this statue, which he used as study material.

Finally, the painter intended this painting to state a moral. The golden bolts of lightning that are being sent to the sleeping maid by the symbol of Zeus, the eagle, are transformed into coins when they touch the ground. With this Goltzius wished to

3
Titian
Danaë
Canvas, 129 x 180 cm (50³/₄ x 70⁷/₈ in.)
Neither signed nor dated (ca. 1553-1554)
Madrid, Museo del Prado, inv. no. 425

4
Hendrick Goltzius after Michelangelo
Aurora
Chalk drawing with wash, 204 x 293 mm (8 x 11½ in.)
Neither signed nor dated (ca. 1600-1603)
Paris, collection Stephan Higgons

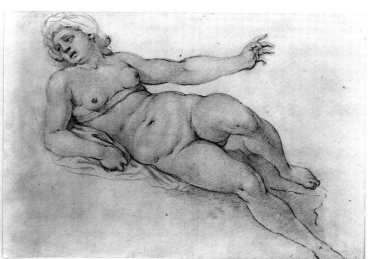

point to the temptations of money. This explanation of the story is also found in Van Mander. He explained, after all, that Zeus 'his girlfriend / and her Nurse / with great gifts of gold has charmed / and deceived: so that one may well say / that the ubiquitously beloved and desired gold subdues all / and triumphs' (in translation).[36] In this scene Goltzius (who wrote his name on the money chest for good reason) has cast his personal motto ('Honor above Gold') in painted form. We know the motto from a drawing in an *album amicorum* with the inscription *Eer boven Golt.^{ius}* (Honor above Golt.^{ius}) (The Hague, Koninklijke Bibliotheek) [**5**],[37] from which it is evident that he also applied the saying to himself. His biographer and friend Van Mander explained that Goltzius was deeply concerned to be known as honorable and virtuous, and certainly not as avaricious.[38]

In the painting we encounter several important pictorial elements of the drawing: the staff purse, the coins, and the golden vessels which together represent the concept *Golt*. Mercury's caduceus is present as a reference to Goltzius's profession (painters are, after all, children of Mercury), while the laureate putto head has been replaced by the chaste Danaë as an exemplar of virtue. Rembrandt possibly also intended 'Honor above Gold' with his *Danaë* (Leningrad, Hermitage) [**6**].[39] He probably

5
Hendrick Goltzius
Honor above Gold
Pen drawing, 150 x 100 mm (5⁷/₈ x 4 in.)
In the caption: *Golt.^{ius}* (ca. 1610)
The Hague, Koninklijke Bibliotheek, inv. no. 133
M 86 fol. 245

6
Rembrandt
Danaë Receiving Zeus as a Shower of Gold
Canvas, 185 x 203 cm (72⅞ x 80 in.)
Lower left: *Rembrandt. f. 1[63]6*
Leningrad, Hermitage, inv. no. 723

got to see the actual painting by Goltzius. Long before 1636
(when he painted his own *Danaë*) he could have studied it at the
Leyden home of the art lover Bartholomeus Ferreris or his son
Hendrick.

1 *Van Mander 1604*, fol. 286 recto
2 In honorem *Haskell 1976*
3 *Van Mander 1604*, fol. 92 (72) recto and verso, written on 31 August 1603: he
called Ferreris 'selfs constigh oeffenaer by lust' and a pupil of Antonio Moro and
Pieter and Frans Pourbus; see also *Noë 1954*, pp. 229-230, note 2.
4 *Van Mander 1604*, fols. 214 recto, 216 recto, 223 verso, 281 verso, 293 recto
5 *Van Ryn 1887*, p. 149
6 *Wurfbain 1976-1977*, pp. 79 and 113
7 *Niemeijer 1973*, p. 205
8 Inv. nos. 180-182; *Hoetink et al. 1985*, p. 450, nos. 180-182 and fig.
9 *Potterton 1986*, pp. 155-156, no. 497 and fig. 161
10 Gemeentearchief Amsterdam (notary public S. Dorper, N.A. 10747, 520-521);
Lugt 1921, supplement, p. 408
11 *Auction Amsterdam 1754*, pp. 1-2, no. 6
12 *Auction Amsterdam 1766*, p. 1, no. 1
13 Cat. no. 54, note 6
14 *Ploos van Amstel 1771*, pp. 139-147; *Auction Amsterdam 1771*, p. 27, no. 66: an
annotated copy (RKD) states 'ƒ410 van der dussen ingekogt voor ƒ300'; concerning
the relations between Braamcamp and Troost, see *Bille 1961*, vol. I, pp. 41-42 and
Niemeijer 1973, p. 109
15 *Niemeijer 1973*, pp. 7-8 and 417
16 *Auction Amsterdam 1774*, p. 2, no. 4
17 Ibidem, p. 2, no. 4 (copy RKD); *Niemeijer 1973*, p. 7
18 *Von Holst 1939*, p. 123 (without mention of source); *Gerson 1942*, p. 497:
'Goltzius' Danaë von 1603 war das Hauptstück in der Sammlung des Herzogs von
Kurland.'
19 *Laurentius / Niemeijer / Ploos van Amstel 1980*, pp. 82, 149, no. A 14, pp. 168 and
383 and fig.
20 *Blarek 1887*, p. 20; supplemental genealogical data were supplied by O. Schutte
(Hoge Raad van Adel, The Hague).
21 *Hymans 1884-1885*, vol. II, p. 196, note 1
22 *Parthey 1863-1864*, vol. I, p. 503, no. 26, vol. II, p. 863; it proved impossible to
locate this catalogue.
23 *Auction Paris 1899* and *Auction Paris 1899-A*, p. 10, no. 31 (reference copy RKD)
24 *Hirschmann 1915*, p. 131
25 *Dezarrois 1912*, p. 220
26 *Hirschmann 1915*, fig. and *Hirschmann 1916*, fig. 7
27 Inv. no. RF 2125; *Brejon de Lavergnée et al. 1979*, p. 63 and fig.; *Bredius 1914*,
p. 146; *Panofsky 1933*, p. 211, fig. 22, was confused by this communication.
28 The information (see Provenance) on this Swedish episode is based on research
by Larry Nichols, reported to the Los Angeles County Museum of Art.
29 *Auction Stockholm 1935*, p. 16, no. 80; *Bille 1961*, vol. II, p. 96, no. 66: 'The
painting has not been seen since 1935.'
30 *Brooks 1985*, p. 19
31 *Van Mander 1604*, fol. 286 recto
32 *Panofsky 1933*; *Pigler 1974*, vol. II, pp. 62-66; *Erftemeijer 1986*, pp. 290-293
33 *Madrid 1980*, pp. 156-157, no. 425 and fig.
34 According to *Panofsky 1933*, pp. 210-211
35 *Reznicek 1961*, vol. I, pp. 456-457, no. 442, vol. II, fig. 336; see also idem, vol. I,
pp. 448-449, no. 424, vol. II, fig. 332 and *Hirschmann 1916*, p. 44, note 1
36 *Van Mander 1604-A*, fol. 39 recto and verso; see also *Nichols 1985*, p. 158 and
Moormann / Uitterhoeve 1987, p. 72, with references to alternate versions of this
explanation.
37 *Reznicek 1961*, vol. I, pp. 315-316, no. 195, vol. II, fig. 355
38 *Van Mander 1604*, fol. 286 recto and verso
39 *Bruyn et al. 1989*, pp. 209-223, no. A 119 and fig.
BB

Leyden 1596 – The Hague 1656

Canvas, 101.5 x 136 cm (40 x 53½ in.)
Lower right: *VGoyen 1646* (vg in ligature)
Washington, D.C., The Corcoran Gallery of Art, inv. no. 26.95

The only teacher who truly influenced Van Goyen was Esaias van den Velde, in Haarlem (ca. 1617), from whom he inherited a clear eye for the specifically Dutch characteristics in landscape. He worked in Leyden from 1619 to 1631, and finally in The Hague from 1634 on, where he eventually became head of the guild. Thanks to his sketchbooks it is known that he liked to draw while traveling: in North and South Holland (ca. 1647), in Brabant (1648), and on the banks of the river Rhine (1650-1651). Ill-advised speculations ruined him, and he died destitute. His pupil Jan Steen was his son-in-law as well.

Van Goyen was one of the most important of the Dutch landscape painters. His earliest works show a variegated coloring and many figures. After 1627 his palette became more monochrome and he simplified his compositions through a consistent outline of elongated triangles with alternating light and dark planes. Topographic elements are often found in his landscapes because of their decorative effect and not so much to render a specific place. Late in life he reached his artistic zenith. His landscapes became characterized by a very low horizon line, dark figures in the foreground that provide depth, and a high, cloud-covered sky that together create a threatening, cheerful, or gloomy, but always grand, atmosphere. He was at the same time a brilliant draftsman, who knew how to capture in a few lines the essence of what he saw. As a rule his sketches served as the foundation for the compositions that he painted in the studio, or for the finished drawings that were intended to be sold.

BB

Provenance

(?) Collection H. Smith Wright, Nottingham, 1878
(?) Collection Thomas Wright, Upton Hall (commonly cited as Apton Hall), Nottinghamshire
Dealer Sir George Donaldson, London, by 1906
Collection William A. Clark, New York, 1906
The Corcoran Gallery of Art, Washington, D.C., 1926 (gift of William A. Clark)

Bibliography

Valentiner 1909-B, p. 19, no. 18
Breck 1910-A, p. 59
Valentiner 1910-A, p. 85, no. 18
HdG 210 (vol. VIII [1923], p. 55, no. 210)
Washington 1932, p. 47, no. 2095 and fig.
Breckenridge 1955, p. 21 and fig.
New York 1959, p. 11 and fig.
Richmond 1961, p. 63 and fig.
Dobrzycka 1966, p. 111, no. 164
Stechow 1966, p. 41 and fig. 71
Beck 1972-1973, vol. II, p. 188-189, no. 387 and fig.
Haverkamp-Begemann 1978-A, pp. 51-55 and fig. 40
Deys 1981, p. 30 and fig. 68
Sutton 1986, p. 298 and fig. 450
Beck 1987, p. 187, no. 387
Sutton et al. 1987-1988, pp. 329-330, no. 37 and fig.

The View of Rhenen came to The Corcoran Gallery of Art in 1926. The gift of Senator William A. Clark, the Montana copper king, the painting had been purchased in 1906 from the London dealer Sir George Donaldson (1845-1925).[1] The earlier provenance of the Corcoran picture, since its publication by Hofstede de Groot in 1923, has been recited as listed above.[2] However, on reviewing the supporting documents, it would seem that the pre-Donaldson history of the *View of Rhenen* is somewhat muddled, because the documents in fact do not substantiate the provenance traditionally given for the painting.

Jan van Goyen View of Rhenen (not in The Hague)

What we do know is the following: Thomas Wright of Upton Hall, near Newark (Newark-on-Trent is close to Nottingham), is recorded as having lent one or more paintings to exhibitions in Birmingham and London in the years 1833 and 1843.[3] None of these paintings are given to Van Goyen. 'The More Important Part of the Collection' of Thomas Wright, Esq., of Upton Hall, Newark, 'Author of the "Life of R. Wilson," and an Amateur Painter of elegant Taste' was sold at Christie's, London, on 7 June 1845 (L. 17822). A copy of the Wright sale catalogue, annotated by Lord Northwick,[4] notes three paintings acquired by one Smith Wright. However, among the several Dutch paintings in the sale, there is no picture attributed to Van Goyen nor any under a different attribution that could describe the *View of Rhenen*.

Another entry of the provenance provided by the Corcoran for their *View of Rhenen* is the sale of 'A Gentleman of Nottingham,' Christie's, London, 1846. Unfortunately Christie's archival department has been unable to verify this citation.[5] Hofstede de Groot also wrote that the present Van Goyen was probably cat. no. 48 in the Nottingham exhibition of 1878, which was lent by H. Smith Wright. However, Graves lists the title and date of that painting as 'Dordrecht. 1647.'[6] Thus it would seem that firm documentation linking the Corcoran *View of Rhenen* with either Thomas Wright or H. Smith Wright eludes us.

Van Goyen's stylistic development can be divided into several distinct phases. The early works show the pronounced influence of Esaias van den Velde and, to a lesser degree, the decorative Flemish tradition. The pictorial innovations of the Haarlem landscape artists Pieter de Molijn and Salomon van Ruysdael parallel changes discernible in the paintings of Van Goyen in the late 1620s as he moved toward a more unified portrayal of the landscape subject matter. In the tonal phase of the 1630s Van Goyen's works are characterized by a severely restricted color scheme in which gradations of tone, coupled with the rapid recession of the ground plane, create a novel sense of pictorial space and atmosphere. By the mid-1640s Van Goyen's style had evolved further, and he produced the many great panoramic landscapes and townscapes for which he is known. The Corcoran *View of Rhenen*, with its typical dark green and brown tones, dates from this period. In these compositions the almost uninterrupted horizontals eloquently suggest the flat expanse of the Dutch countryside. In the landscape and marines of his late period Van Goyen achieved an effect of classical monumentality and grandeur.

As Stechow noted, in landscapes such as the 1646 *View of Rhenen* Van Goyen brought to full realization the pictorial possibilities of the 'wingless' oblong panoramic views of Hendrick Goltzius and Hercules Segers.[7] In several instances in their landscape compositions, these two Haarlem artists discarded the *repoussoir* elements and mannerist tripartite division of the landscape in favor of a more unified spatial construction and realistic treatment of the Dutch countryside. Although isolated, these innovative images would have been known to the next generation of landscape painters, particularly those compositions executed in prints [**1**].[8]

The city of Rhenen was a favored subject of Dutch artists of the seventeenth and eighteenth centuries. It was (before its near destruction during World War II) a walled city, picturesque in its site, and rich with historical associations.[9] Deys, in his book *Achter Berg en Rijn, Over boeren, burgers en buitenlui in Rhenen*, describes at length the character of the old city as captured in the works of many artists, including those of such diverse nature as Rembrandt and Saenredam [**2, 3**].[10] The city also figures repeatedly in the works of Van Goyen, either as the focal point of a composition or simply as a recognizable skyline in the distance. The twenty-six paintings recorded by Beck span two decades, from 1636 to 1655.[11] However, no drawings of Rhenen by Van Goyen have been identified.

By selecting the city of Rhenen, Van Goyen began with a subject boasting a number of striking architectural and topo-

1
Hercules Segers
Large View of Rhenen
Etching, 86 x 303 mm (3³⁄₈ x 12 in.)
Neither signed nor dated (ca. 1630)
Amsterdam, Rijksprentenkabinet

graphical features. The tower of the Church of Saint Cunera, notable for its height and elaborate late Gothic design, the twin-towered Rijnpoort, and the palace of the king of Bohemia, combine with the elevated position of Rhenen above the Rhine to create a silhouette of variety and markedly contrasting horizontals and verticals. By manipulating these elements, modifying the actual layout of the city, exaggerating or omitting details as his composition required, Van Goyen strategically located accents of light and dark across the pictorial surface.[12] The whole scene is then placed beneath a heavily clouded sky that creates lines of movement both deep into the space as well as diagonally up the surface of the canvas. The result is a painting imbued with a great sense of animation which belies the realities of the scene portrayed.

1 On the collection of Senator Clark, see Walter Liedtke's essay, p. 46

2 HdG 210 (vol. VIII [1923], p. 55, no. 210)

3 *Graves 1913-1915*, vol. III, p. 1009, no. 121 (1833): a *Storm* by Rembrandt [HdG 965a]; p. 1180, no. 115 (1833): a *Landscape* by Ruysdaal [*sic*]; p. 1305, no. 151 (1843); vol. IV, p. 1800, no. 34 (1833)

4 The catalogue is part of the Northwick Park Library, housed at Yale University.

5 The lots attributed to Van Goyen do not immediately strike one as describing the Corcoran *View of Rhenen*. However, no. 19 on 14 March 1846 is described as by Van Goyen: 'A grand landscape, with figures near a river – *capitally painted*.' No dimensions are given. The seller was Rutley; the buyer Capt. Cunningham. Whether or not this is related to the present work is open to speculation.

6 *Graves 1913-1915*, p. 2300, no. 48 (1878). In 1942 Smith College professor Dr. A.P.A. Vorenkamp questioned the identity of the city represented in the Corcoran picture, but it was proposed that the sight was Amersfoort, not Dordrecht (*Breckenridge 1955*, p. 21). Beck records five paintings of Dordrecht from 1647 (*Beck 1972-1973*, vol. II, pp. 148-150, nos. 302-306), none of them immediately identifiable with the work listed in Graves. Of course it is possible, although unlikely, that

the skyline of Rhenen could be mistaken for that of Dordrecht. This would not, however, explain the misreading of the date. There is a *View of Dordrecht* by Van Goyen in the Corcoran collection, which also came from Senator Clark; it is signed in monogram and dated 1651. Its provenance goes via France and Holland, not England.

7 *Springer 1910-1912*, no. 34; *Stechow 1966*, p. 39

8 It should also be noted that Goltzius and Segers would have been living in Haarlem when Van Goyen was there as the student of Esaias van den Velde. Segers is also recorded as living in The Hague in 1633, just at the time when Van Goyen was establishing residency there. Several panoramic drawings by Goltzius survive, including those in Paris (Lugt Collection, Institut Néerlandais, inv. no. 2628; *Reznicek 1961*, vol. I, pp. 428-429, no. 400; signed and dated 1603; see also cat. no. 38, note 16) and Rotterdam (Museum Boymans-van Beuningen, inv. no. H 253; *Reznicek 1961*, vol. II, pp. 430, no. 404; signed and dated 1603; inv. no. DN 199 / 96: *Reznicek 1961*, vol. II, p. 431, no. 405). There is also a painted *View of Rhenen* by Segers in West Berlin (Staatliche Museen Preussischer Kulturbesitz, Gemälde-galerie, inv. no. 808 A; *Berlin 1975*, p. 399, no. 808 A). This painting was originally the same oblong format as the print; the upper edge of the panel has been markedly extended, nearly doubling the area of sky.

9 The city of Rhenen had in medieval times been the major line of defense for the bishopric of Utrecht against approach from the southeast.

10 *Benesch 1973*, vol. IV, p. 212-213, no. 825 and fig. 1026; *Swillens 1935*, pp. 35, 115, no. 161 and fig. 119; *Utrecht 1961*, pp. 106, 156-157, no. 104; *Schwartz / Bok 1989*, p. 194, fig. 203 and p. 271, no. 104

11 *Beck 1972-1973*, vol. II, nos. 374-400a

12 For the adjustments made by Van Goyen to the actual plan of the city, see *Sutton et al. 1987-1988*, pp. 329-330.

LFO

▼ 2
Rembrandt
View of Rhenen
Pen and brown ink and wash, 212 x 326 mm
(8³/₈ x 12⁷/₈ in.)
Lower center (not autograph): *Rembrandt 1632*
(ca. 1647-1648)
The Hague, Museum Bredius, inv. no. T87-1946

▶ 3
Pieter Saenredam
Exterior of the Church of Saint Cunera and of the Kings Palace, Seen from the Southwest
Pen and watercolor, 353 x 464 mm (13⁷/₈ x 18¹/₄ in.)
Inscription on wall at right: *Pieter Saenredam dese gemaeckt den 27 ende 28 Junij int Jaer 1644*
Haarlem, Teylers Museum, inv. no. O 81

Leyden 1596 – The Hague 1656

Panel, 64.1 x 94 cm (25¼ x 37 in.)
On the boat at the left: *VGOYEN 1648*
Minneapolis, Minn., The Minneapolis Institute of Arts, inv. no. 83.84

It is virtually impossible to identify the numerous works of Jan van Goyen that are vaguely described in old auction catalogues as a *watertje* (small water scene), a *wintertje* (small winter scene), or a *zomertje* (small summer scene). Only rarely can the whereabouts before 1800 of a specific Van Goyen be determined, as is the case with the *Riverscape with Thunderstorm* (The Fine Arts Museums of San Francisco) of 1641.[1] This painting used to be in the famous picture gallery of Gerret Braamcamp and was described at the auction in 1771 as 'better colored than those one usually sees from the Master' (in translation).[2] The monochrome landscapes that are so beloved today were apparently judged differently back then.

The *Riverscape with the Pellecussen Gate* of 1648, with its predominantly brown and gray hues, is a recent, capital acquisition of the Minneapolis museum. It has rightly been praised as 'one of the most important and best preserved Dutch landscape paintings in North America.'[3] In this instance, too, the provenance is wrapped in obscurity. Tradition has it that it was in the property of an old English family. In 1866, and again in 1937, it was auctioned in London. After that it was for some time in the J. Walter collection in The Hague before it at last moved permanently to the United States.[4]

The Pellecussen gate on the outskirts of Utrecht owes its present reputation mainly to the fact that this picturesque topographic motif apparently struck Van Goyen's eye around 1640. At that time he made a number of drawings of the gate, which he later used over and over in his paintings. Only one of these sheets appears to have been preserved, providing one agrees with the attribution to Jan van Goyen of a small sketch that is preserved in the Rijksprentenkabinet under the name of Antoni Waterlo [1].[5] This rapid impression served as a preliminary study for, among others, a painting of 1645, *Skaters at the Pellecussen Gate* (Lille, Musée des Beaux-Arts) [2].[6] In 1938 Wolfgang Stechow published an absorbing article about the many guises of this small piece of old Utrecht in the paintings of

Provenance
Collection John Shaw Phillips, Culham House, Oxon
Auction John Shaw Phillips, London, 1866 (£52.10 to Holloway)
Auction Edward N.F. Lloyd, London, 1937 (£860 to Katz)
Dealer D. Katz, Dieren, 1937
Collection J. Walter, The Hague
Dealer K. & V. Waterman, Amsterdam, 1981
The Minneapolis Institute of Arts, Minneapolis, 1983 (gift of Bruce B. Dayton)

Bibliography
Auction London 1866, p. 7, no. 31
Auction London 1937-A, p. 28, no. 102 and fig.
Dieren 1937, p. 9, no. 24
Stechow 1938, p. 207
Beck 1972-1973, vol. II, pp. 316-317, no. 693 and fig.
Amsterdam 1981, pp. 126-127 and fig.
Keyes 1984, pp. 67 and 396, fig. 40 (List of Comparative Figures)
Keyes 1986, p. 59 and fig., pp. 61 and 66
Sutton 1986, p. 157 and fig. 224
Beck 1987, p. 226, no. 693
Lipschultz 1988, p. 96

▲ 2
Jan van Goyen
Skaters at the Pellecussen Gate
Panel, 65 x 97 cm (25⅝ x 38¼ in.)
Lower left: *IVGoyen 1645*
Lille, Musée des Beaux-Arts, inv. no. 267

◀ 1
Jan van Goyen
The Pellecussen Gate
Drawing, 94 x 144 mm (3¾ x 5⅝ in.)
Neither signed nor dated (ca. 1640)
Amsterdam, Rijksprentenkabinet, inv. no. A 2947

Jan van Goyen Riverscape with the Pellecussen Gate

Jan van Goyen and, in his wake, Salomon van Ruysdael; Stechow illustrated both the drawing, which he did not recognize as a preliminary study, and the painting in Lille. Of more recent vintage is the somewhat more copiously illustrated overview by Jos de Meyere in his book *Utrecht op schilderijen* (Utrecht in paintings). Somewhat earlier, in the Van Goyen monograph by Beck, twelve paintings, with dates ranging from 1640 to 1655, in which the Pellecussen gate appears in one form or another, were catalogued.[8] Not one of these scenes shows the gate situated in an identical, let alone a recognizable, landscape. Usually they feature to the left or right of the building a wide body of water that is quite invented.

The Pellecussen gate used to stand next to the river Vecht, north of Utrecht, where a small brook joined the river. Around 1600 an anonymous draftsman recorded this spot, at which the traveler quit Utrecht territory going in the direction of Amsterdam (Utrecht, Gemeentearchief) [3].[9] This was neither a gate intended for defense nor an outer gate of Utrecht but private property. It was built in 1371 as a municipal castle outside the walls, the only one of its kind so close to the town itself.[10] The gate derived its name from the medieval Pellecussen family, which owned the Lauwerecht estate in that area. It was later also the residence of the lords of Lauwerecht.[11] In 1625 Hendrick Jansz Verstralen engraved a town prospect that, to the extreme left, next to the name *Lauwenrecht*, shows the building rising above the trees alongside the Vecht [4].[12] On a drawn map of 1629 or 1630 by the same Verstralen of the cultivated fields and pastures around the city of Utrecht, the location of this Pellecussen gate alongside the river has been clearly indicated (Utrecht, Gemeentearchief) [5].[13] This is one of a very few plans of the town in which the gate is depicted with topographical accuracy.

In the seventeenth century the house retained the form in which Van Goyen still encountered it, with the step gables, the characteristic little stair tower, and the bricked-in cannon balls.

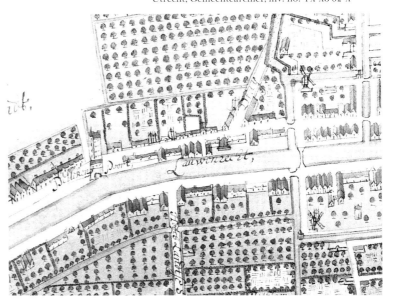

5
Hendrick Jansz Verstralen
'*VTRECHT*' (detail with Pellecussen gate)
Colored pen drawing, 1215 x 920 mm
(47⅞ x 36¼ in.) (the whole map)
Neither signed nor dated (ca. 1629-1630)
Utrecht, Gemeentearchief, inv. no. TA Ab 62 A

◄ 3
Anonymous
The Pellecussen Gate
Drawing, 234 x 174 mm (9¼ x 6⅞ in.)
Neither signed nor dated (ca. 1600)
Utrecht, Gemeentearchief, no inv. no.

► 4
Hendrick Jansz Verstralen after Cornelis Drooghsloot
Profile of Utrecht (detail with Pellecussen gate and Lauwerecht)
Engraving, 217 x 400 mm (8½ x 15¾ in.) (the whole map)
Inscription at upper left: *H. VERSTRALEN* (first edition 1625)
Utrecht, Gemeentearchief, inv. no. TA Ba 32 (A)

Different draftsmen later depicted the glory and speedy demise of the Pellecussen gate.[14] Around 1660 Antoni Waterlo drew the residence subsequent to a renovation; the wooden bay window had been demolished and a new wing, facing the Vecht, had been erected next to it (whereabouts unknown).[15] In the disastrous year of 1672 the French troops wreaked great havoc in and around Utrecht, and Herman Saftleven recorded how, according to his own inscription, the *Pellecuespoort a° 1674* had been transformed into a ruin (Haarlem, Teylers Museum).[16] Less than ten years later he made another drawing of the spot, where all that was left was the vaulting over the little brook and some remains of the walls (Utrecht, Gemeentearchief) [6].[17] This is our last image of the once-so-picturesque castle. Abraham Rademaker's *Kabinet van Nederlandsche outheden en gezichten* (Cabinet of Dutch antiquities and prospects) of 1725 included two pictures, made after drawings of 1620, which reproduce the gate as Van Goyen saw it, from the opposite shore of the Vecht. A short comment proclaims that this 'Pelkus Gate has today come to be totally leveled' (in translation).[18]

The painting in Lille [2] demonstrates how Jan van Goyen manipulated reality. Behind the Pellecussen gate he painted the church of Saint Mary, which in fact used to be situated a few kilometers to the south, within the city ramparts of Utrecht. The only part of the painting in Minneapolis that bears a resemblance to the Amsterdam drawing [1] done 'after real life' is the four-story central section with the hexagonal stair tower and the side wings with the stepped gables and wooden bay window. The vaulting over the brook leading to the Vecht is here a gate, from which a set of stairs leads down to a broad expanse of water. Both these stairs, in addition to all the other encrustations, bridges, and the well installation to the right, are fantastical. The composition as a whole is invented and, according to George Keyes, goes back to the sketches by Esaias van den Velde, who had also introduced the small boat or ferry as a *repoussoir* element in the expanse of water.[19]

In contrast with our conception of reality, determined by the invention of photography, Van Goyen's working methods may strike us as somewhat curious. This must be why various art historians have sought to explain the painter's approach. Henri van de Waal rightly saw in these fantasized riverscapes a parallel with the typical seventeenth-century historical consciousness, which did not aim at truth.[20] Bruyn made an unfortunate attempt to differentiate the contents of such scenes. According to him, buildings in ruin meant transitoriness: the Hoogland Church was to be understood as the heavenly Jerusalem, and the river signified the brevity of life.[21] Christopher Brown refuted this and held that painters like Van Goyen did not envisage a continuation of a medieval pictorial tradition but simply painted what sold well.[22] Van Goyen did not record reality as a cartographer would, but instead addressed himself to a public that was apparently taken with the 'romanticized images,' as Stechow called them.[23]

1 Inv. no. 48.7; HdG 1054; *Beck 1972-1973*, vol. II, pp. 359-361, no. 803 and fig.
2 *Auction Amsterdam 1771*, p. 27, no. 67; on the Van Goyens in Dutch collections, see *Van de Watering 1981*, pp. 29-35.
3 *Keyes 1986*, p. 61
4 See Provenance
5 *Stechow 1938-A*, pp. 202-203, fig. 1; not in *Beck 1972-1973* and *Beck 1987*
6 HdG 1165; *Beck 1972-1973*, vol. II, p. 38, no. 74
7 *Stechow 1938-A*, p. 202, fig. 1 and p. 205, fig. 6
8 *Beck 1972-1973*, vol. II and *Beck 1987*, nos. 74, 639, 640, 690, 693, 711, 721, 760, 762, 765, 788, 1210a (generally with fig.); *De Meyere 1988*, pp. 87-95, figs. 27-34 (NB: De Meyere did not mention the painting in Minneapolis, although, on p. 92, fig. 32, he illustrated a painting incorrectly identified as being of the Pellecussen gate).
9 *Wilmer 1980*, p. 32 and fig.
10 I thank Dr. J.E.A.L. Struick (Gemeentearchief, Utrecht) for information about the Pellecussen gate.
11 *Wilmer 1980*, p. 32
12 *De Meyere 1988*, pp. 44-45, fig. 4; Verstralen was granted a monopoly on the print in 1625, which after 1642 was also reprinted elsewhere.
13 The gate, which lay outside the city walls, is missing in most of the street plans and city views.
14 *Van Hulzen 1981*, p. 2 and *De Meyere 1988*, p. 87, gave (according to Dr. J.E.A.L. Struick, see note 10) unreliable information on the history of the gate; the primary sources (archival documents and depictions) have yet to be carefully analyzed.
15 *Auction Amsterdam 1959*, no. 163 (from the collection of H.E. ten Cate) (photo Gemeentearchief, Utrecht)
16 Inv. no. P 28; *Schulz 1982*, p. 280, no. 571 (photo Gemeentearchief, Utrecht)
17 Not in *Schulz 1982*
18 *Rademaker 1725*, nos. 223-224 and fig.
19 *Keyes 1984*, p. 67
20 *Van de Waal 1952*, vol. I, pp. 50-52
21 *Bruyn 1987-1988*, pp. 96-98
22 *Brown 1988*, p. 79
23 *Stechow 1938-A*, pp. 207
BB

6
Herman Saftleven
Remains of the Pellecussen Gate
Drawing, 234 x 196 mm (9¼ x 7¾ in.)
Lower right: *HSL* (in ligature) (ca. 1675)
Utrecht, Gemeentearchief, inv. no. TA DC 3.20

Frans Hals

Antwerp between 1581 / 1585 – Haarlem 1666

25-26 | Portraits of a Seventy-Three-Year-Old Man and His Seventy-Two-Year-Old Wife

Canvas, both 122.4 x 97.5 cm (48¼ x 38⅜ in.). Right, next to the head of the man: *AETAT SVAE 73/ AN.° 1643 / FH.* (in ligature); left, next to the head of the woman: *AETAT SVAE 72 / AN.° 1643 / FH.* (in ligature).
New Haven, Conn., Yale University Art Gallery, inv. nos. 1961.18.23-1961.18.24

The Hals family came from Mechelen and fled from Flanders to Haarlem, where they are first mentioned in 1591. In a biography from 1618, the theoretician and history painter Carel van Mander referred to Frans Hals as his pupil and specifically as a portrait painter. Nevertheless, there is no detectable influence from Van Mander in his early work. In essence, Hals was never anything but a pure portraitist: even in his genre pieces he painted primarily heads (with some addenda). This degree of specialization was not much esteemed by Van Mander.

The earliest dated portrait is from 1611, and in 1616 Hals painted the first of a series of imposing group portraits (processions and banquets of militia companies) that are still the pride of the Frans Halsmuseum in Haarlem. These official commissions continued to feature traditional poses and compositions; until 1630, he reserved his virtuosic brushstrokes for the treatment of the lace and the multicolored embroidery of the costumes. In his non-commissioned works, primarily portraits of common types, he rendered the hands and faces using the broad brushstrokes that have been so appreciated since the end of the nineteenth century. Between 1630 and 1640 he produced important portraits featuring increasingly monochromatic color schemes. In the last phase of his life (after 1640) he also used his loose way of painting for the portrait heads. His colors became darker and the contrasts with the white passages ever stronger. Van Mander's objections to the trade of portrait painting applied not only to the slight honor to be gained by it but equally to its meager profits. Hals learned that the hard way. He knew continual financial worries, and, from 1662 on, he received a modest annual subsidy from the city council of Haarlem. Nevertheless his last great regent portraits, which he painted when well into his eighties, show an astonishing vitality.

On 9 February 1935 *The Illustrated London News* made mention of the spectacular sale of six works by old masters (Ghirlandaio, Filippino Lippi, Frans Hals, Rubens) from the collection of the American banker John Pierpont Morgan, Jr. (1867-1943), reputedly for an amount of 600,000 pounds. The pendant portraits that Frans Hals painted in 1643 of a seventy-three-year-

Provenance

Auction Mme James Odier, Paris, 1861
Collection André Count Mniszech, Paris, before 1871-1905
Collection John Pierpont Morgan, London, 1906, New York, 1907-1913
The Metropolitan Museum of Art, New York, 1907-1915 (on loan from John Pierpont Morgan)
Collection John Pierpont Morgan, Jr., New York, 1913-1935
Dealer Knoedler & Co., New York, 1935
Collection Edward Stephen Harkness, New York, 1935-1937
Collection Stephen Carlton Clark, New York / Cooperstown, 1938-1961
Yale University Art Gallery, New Haven, 1961 (bequest of Stephen Carlton Clark, B.A. 1903)

Bibliography

Auction Paris 1861, p. 9, no. 18
Bode 1871, p. 23
Rendell Head 1879, p. 110
Bode 1883, pp. 67 and 84, nos. 55-56
London 1906, pp. 8-9, nos. 10 and 12
Wurzbach, vol. 1 (1906), p. 639
Burroughs 1907, p. 23 and figs. pp. 140-141
Roberts 1907, n.p., *sub voce*
Moes 1909, p. 105, nos. 105-106
Preyer 1909, p. 142
Stephenson 1909, p. 170
Valentiner 1909, pp. XV and 34-35, nos. 33-34 and figs.
Cox 1909-1910, pp. 245-246
Breck 1910, p. 6
Friedländer 1910, p. 97
HdG 157-158 (vol. III [1910], p. 49, nos. 157-158)
Bode / Binder 1914, vol. II, p. 61, nos. 208-209 and figs. 132-133
Valentiner / Voll 1923, pp. 204-205 and figs., p. 319
Dülberg 1930, pp. 162, 171-174 and figs.
Illustrated London News 1935, p. 194 and figs.
Pantheon 1935, p. 147 and fig.
T.H.L. 1935, p. 167 and fig.
Valentiner 1936, nos. 72-73 and figs.
Art Digest 1937, p. 7
Comstock 1937, p. 87
Van Dantzig 1937, pp. 111-112, nos. 112-113
Frankfurter 1937, pp. 12 and 24
Frankfurter 1937-A, pp. 10, 25 and fig.
Haarlem 1937, p. 47, nos. 85-86 and figs. 86-87
Singer 1937 / 1967, vol. I, nos. 3435-3436
Siple 1937, p. 90
New York 1938, nos. 3 and 4 and figs.
Lane 1939, p. 157 and fig. and pp. 158 and 160
McCall / Valentiner 1939, pp. 88-89, nos. 184-185
Stechow 1941, p. 114
McCall 1942, pp. 41-43, nos. 23-24 and figs. pp. 115-116
Gratama 1943 / 1946, p. 43 and figs. 82-83
New York 1946, nos. 11-12 and fig.
Gerson 1950, p. 64 and figs. 170-171
Chanin 1954, p. 13
Munro 1954, p. 85
New York 1954, nos. 2-3
New Haven 1956, nos. 8-9 and fig.
Taylor 1957, p. 33
Winchester 1959, p. 170

Frans Hals Portrait of a Seventy-Three-Year-Old Man

Frans Hals Portrait of a Seventy-Two-Year-Old Woman

old man and his wife, younger by a year, were said to have fetched almost 60,000 pounds. The name of the buyer was not communicated. One was further reminded in the announcement that these portraits had earlier been exhibited at the dealer T. Agnew & Sons in London in 1906, shortly after John Pierpont Morgan, Sr. (1837-1913) (p. 40, fig. 26), had acquired them from the extensive collection of the portrait painter Andrzej Count Mniszech (1824-1905) in Paris.[1] In that year the portraits were described enthusiastically in, for instance, the *London Times*, where it was regretfully observed that Morgan had bought them with the intention of lending them to The Metropolitan Museum of Art in New York. This was thought to be a shame because there were then so few works by Hals to be admired in London.[2] In 1904 Pierpont Morgan had accepted the presidency of The Metropolitan Museum, and he wished the museum to rival the greatest temples of art in the world. To this end he concentrated his collections – which had been spread out among houses in London and elsewhere – in New York, after which the museum received various works on loan.[3] In 1907 the museum bulletin wrote proudly about the two portraits by Frans Hals: 'Of all the art treasures brought to America, few are more precious than these magnificent pictures.'[4]

Nevertheless, the portraits of this unknown couple did not in the end remain in The Metropolitan Museum of Art. The multi-millionaire Edward Stephen Harkness (1874-1940) of New York, trustee of The Metropolitan Museum, turned out to be the new owner when, in 1937, the paintings were lent by way of Knoedler & Co. to the first great Frans Hals exhibition in Haarlem.[5] Upon their return to New York, the loaned paintings (and several others from private collections) were exhibited in the Schaeffer Galleries in New York.[6]

But during the World Exposition of 1939 in New York, Stephen C. Clark (1882-1960), who had acquired them in 1938, lent the pendant portraits to the art exhibition at the fair.[7] At the time his collection was described in *Art News Annual* as an example of a remarkably eclectic and sound taste. Clark owned several Dutch old masters but was especially interested in European and American paintings of the last century.[8] He was the younger brother of the collector Robert Sterling Clark (see cat. no. 28), with whom he traveled through Europe in the company of the American sculptor George Grey Bernard, who advised them on their art purchases.[9] The brothers were heirs to the fortune that the Singer Company had amassed with sewing machines. Stephen Clark bought his first painting when seventeen years old. Thanks to his preference for modern

Yale Alumni Magazine 1961, p. 16 and fig.
Chronique des arts 1962, p. 30, fig. 115
Comstock 1962, p. 132 and figs.
Haarlem 1962, p. 63, nos. 49-50 and figs. 51-52
Constable 1964, pp. 111 and 170
Slive 1964, p. 71 and fig.
Slive 1970-1974, vol. I, pp. 158 and 174, vol. II, figs. 231-234, vol. III, pp. 76-77, nos. 149-150 and fig. 59
Grimm 1972, pp. 105 and 204, nos. 115-116
Grimm / Montagni 1974, pp. 103-104, nos. 157-158 and figs., and Taf. IL
Baard 1981, p. 54, fig. 56, pp. 132-135, pls. 35-36
Sutton 1986, p. 163 and fig.

1-2
Frans Hals
Portraits of Jacob Pietersz Olycan and His Wife Aletta Hanemans
Canvas, 124.6 x 97.3 cm and 124.2 x 98.2 cm
(49 x 38¼ in. and 48⅞ x 38⅝ in.)
At the right, next to the head of Jacob: AETAT SVAE 29 / A⁰ 1625; at the left, next to the head of Aletta: AETAT SVAE. 19 / AN.⁰ 1625
The Hague, Mauritshuis, inv. nos. 459-460

masters (Picasso, Miró), he was chosen as one of the first trustees of The Museum of Modern Art in New York.[10] Clark parted with his paintings for several exhibitions, including one in 1956 of works from the collections of alumni of Yale University. He himself had graduated in 1903.[11] Five years later, in 1961, it was learned that he had bequeathed the portraits by Frans Hals to the Yale University Art Gallery in New Haven.[12]

The new acquisitions from New Haven were present at the Frans Hals commemorative exhibition in Haarlem in 1962. They were then catalogued under what had in the meantime come to be accepted as their identity: 'Mr. and Mrs. Bodolphe.'[13] This name first emerged in London in 1906, in the catalogue of the exhibition at the dealer T. Agnew & Sons: *De Heer Bodolphe* and *Me Vrouw Bodolphe*.[14] This can be nothing other than a transcription of a Dutch notation either on the old canvas, on the stretcher, or on the frame. In 1909 Wilhelm Valentiner wrote that the identity of the couple was uncertain, and he repeated this in 1923, but in 1936 he spoke of a record on the back of one or the other painting. Whatever it was, these texts have in the meantime been lost.[15] Yet in 1861 people were not interested in any inscription whatsoever. The sitters were then called Jan Six and his wife: 'Hals (Frank [*sic*], dated 1643). The burgomaster Six and his wife. Natural grandeur. Two pendants' (in translation).[16] It was then quite customary to attach interesting-sounding names to unidentified sitters.

No proper investigation has been undertaken into the identity of this elderly couple, a situation that is true of other couples immortalized by Frans Hals. There have been a few guesses. On the basis of the name Bodolphe, it was sometimes thought that the pair must have belonged to a Huguenot family that had fled France for religious reasons.[17] In his standard work on Frans Hals, Slive asserted that, in view of the age of the sitters, the portraits could have been done on the occasion of their fiftieth wedding anniversary.[18] In the seventeenth century very few people reached the age of seventy-two or seventy-three, and

certainly not together. It is therefore no vain hope that the Haarlem archives will one day yield the names of this 'golden couple.'

The quality of these portraits has been praised from the beginning. Wilhelm von Bode had already seen them before 1871 with Count Mniszech in Paris and later called them works of the first rank.[19] They are still considered to be two of the most impressive portraits that Hals rendered during his mature period.[20] Horst Gerson compared the 'Bodolphe' portraits with the 'serious effigies' by Rembrandt and the 'colorful show portraits' of the same time by Bartholomeus van der Helst. He concluded that Hals maintained his own style: 'The portrait painter Frans Hals is not as fashionably modern as the brilliant Van der Helst' (in translation).[21] To this should be added that the execution of Hals's portraits was apparently closely bound to the wishes of his patrons. For instance, Stephanus Geraerdts and his wife, Isabella Coymans, married for only six years, had themselves depicted around 1650 as anything but worn-out oldsters but rather as dashing hedonists (Antwerp, Museum voor Schone Kunsten)[22] (Paris, collection Édouard Baron de Rothschild).[23] By contrast, the older couple in New Haven deliberately had themselves immortalized in 1643 in extremely conservative dress and in a composition that shies away from any kind of fashionableness.

The liberties that Hals permitted himself in his compositions were dependent on the nature of the commission. In single, male portraits he was often able to suggest action, whereas the pendant portraits feature more static poses. The rather early *Portraits of Jacob Pietersz Olycan and His Wife Aletta Hanemans* (The Hague, Mauritshuis) [**1-2**][24] are based on a highly traditional formula. Frans Hals has reinforced the symmetry of these pendants by having the position of Jacob's arms mirror that of Aletta's.[25] The 'Bodolphe' portraits still feature such mirror-image rendering, with the shaft of light behind the wife constituting the only mildly asymmetric element. It is as if Hals wished to let us know for an instant that he knew well how, in the twenties and thirties, Anthony van Dyck had painted his portraits with an Italian flourish.

These compositions are dominated by a stylized simplicity. It is striking that in the series of portraits that Hals made for the Olycan family, it was the ladies who preferred a standard formula. In 1631 Cornelia Vooght Claesdr had herself portrayed sitting in a chair (Haarlem, Frans Halsmuseum) [**3**],[26] with one hand on the armrest. Eight years later her sister Maritge Vooght Claesdr had herself immortalized in precisely the same way (Amsterdam, Rijksmuseum) [**4**].[27] It certainly looks as if 'Mrs. Bodolphe' knew these portraits. In any case, in 1643 she wanted to be painted in a corresponding pose, albeit with gloves instead of a book in her hand.

One ought not to expect seventy-two- and seventy-three-year-olds to dress frivolously and according to the latest fashion. The couple here wears the dress of the regent class in its most sober manifestation. For instance, the woman wears the so-called *brede vleugelmuts* (broad-winged cap), which was already being worn in the beginning of the seventeenth century. It was precisely in the forties that its wings came to be narrower or bent downward. She thus shows herself to be absolutely old-fashioned. This is also true of her *molensteenkraag* (millstone collar), which around 1640 had come to be a rarity and which ceased to be worn after 1650.[28] The large collar goes with her classic *vliegerkostuum* (kite-shaped dress), which, with its trim of brown fur and its high shoulder wheels, was a favorite attire of the elderly. According to one interpretation, the old woman took into account her approaching end through her choice of this 'stilled dress, which carefully avoids the clamorous mobility of fashion' (in translation).[29] Her seventy-three-year-old husband does not yield to her in sobriety. He wears a gray suit with a darker cloak and all the little buttons done up tightly. He, too, wears an old-fashioned millstone collar and avoids the fashionable show of bows, braid trimmings, or metal decorations.[30] Not even the smallest edge of shirt cuff protrudes from his sleeves. In closing, Gerson observed in connection with these pendants: 'Despite all the inventive liveliness, [Hals's] portrait style remains one of old-fashioned respectability' (in translation).[31] To which one might add that this old-fashioned style goes wonderfully well with the indisputably conservative taste of the patrons.

The true-to-life characterization of the two elderly but still vital citizens of Haarlem speaks to the imagination. When the portraits arrived in America in 1907, Burroughs wrote: 'The man is a staid and rather clerical-looking gentleman, who, despite his seventy-three years, has about the corners of his mouth and in his eyes an expression that might betoken joviality of a seemly sort at times. Vrouw Bodolphe, however, lacks any sense of humour.'[32] Preyer wrote two years later: 'They are typical characters of the Dutch bourgeoisie, the man staid, firm, and yet good-natured; the woman serious, virtuous, and self-satisfied.'[33] Only recently, H.P. Baard, former director of the Frans Halsmuseum, described the portrait of the woman as a monument for the class-conscious burgher [**5**]: 'When we approach this self-possessed woman, we feel we must be duly on

3
Frans Hals
Portrait of Cornelia Vooght Claesdr
Panel, 126.5 x 101 cm (49¾ x 39¾ in.)
Upper left: AETAT SVAE 53 / Ao 1631
Haarlem, Frans Halsmuseum, inv. no. 132

4
Frans Hals
Portrait of Maritge Vooght Claesdr
Canvas, 128 x 94.5 cm (50⅜ x 37¼ in.)
Upper right: AETAT SVAE 62 / ANo 1639
Amsterdam, Rijksmuseum, inv. no. C 139

5
Detail of cat. no. 26

our guard, for with her strong will and domineering personality she will obviously not suffer anything that conflicts with her rigid principles.'[34]

1 *Illustrated London News 1935*, p. 194; see also *T.L.H. 1935*, pp. 166-167 and fig.; *Genealogisches Taschenbuch*, vol. x, p. 574

2 The newspaper report was cited in detail in *Roberts 1907*, n.p., *sub voce*

3 *Taylor 1957*, pp. 28 and 34

4 *Burroughs 1907*, p. 23

5 According to a notation on the photograph in the RKD; *Haarlem 1937*, p. 47, nos. 85-86: 'Particuliere verzameling'; about Harkness: *WWA-A*, vol. xx, p. 1126; *WWWA*, vol. I, p. 520; *Block 1940*, p. 364

6 *Frankfurter 1937*, pp. 12 and 24

7 *New York 1938*, nos. 3-4 and fig.

8 *Lane 1939*, p. 131; about Clark: *WWWA*, vol. IV, p. 177

9 *Durden-Smith / Desimone 1984*, p. 89

10 *Winchester 1959*, p. 170

11 *New Haven 1956*, nos. 8-9

12 *Comstock 1962*, p. 132

13 *Haarlem 1962*, p. 63, nos. 49-50

14 *London 1906*, pp. 8-9, nos. 10 and 12

15 *Valentiner 1909*, p. 34, no. 33 (see also p. xx, fig. 24); *Valentiner / Voll 1923*, p. 319; *Valentiner 1936*, nos. 72-73; *Haarlem 1962*, p. 63, no. 49

16 *Auction Paris 1861*, p. 9, no. 18

17 *Lane 1939*, p. 158; the name 'Bodolphe' does not occur in Dutch genealogical compendia.

18 *Slive 1970-1974*, vol. I, p. 158

19 *Bode 1871*, p. 23; *Bode 1883*, p. 67

20 *Haarlem 1962*, p. 63, no. 49; we here ignore the preposterous descriptions of *Van Dantzig 1937*, pp. 111-112, nos. 112-113.

21 *Gerson 1950*, p. 64

22 Inv. no. 674; *Slive 1970-1974*, vol. II, fig. 290, vol. III, pp. 97-98, no. 188

23 *Slive 1970-1974*, vol. II, fig. 291, vol. III, pp. 98-99, no. 189

24 *Slive 1970-1974*, vol. II, figs. 58-59, vol. III, pp. 21-22, nos. 32-33

25 *Smith 1982*, pp. 96-100; *Broos 1987*, p. 183

26 *Slive 1970-1974*, vol. II, fig. 124, vol. III, p. 47, no. 78

27 *Slive 1970-1974*, vol. II, fig. 207, vol. III, pp. 69-70, no. 129

28 *Der Kinderen-Besier 1950*, pp. 147-150

29 *Der Kinderen-Besier 1950*, p. 144

30 *Der Kinderen-Besier 1950*, pp. 133-134

31 *Gerson 1950*, p. 64

32 *Burroughs 1907*, p. 23

33 *Preyer 1909*, p. 142

34 *Baard 1981*, p. 132; on p. 134, he described how a film fragment made during the Frans Hals exhibition of 1962 zoomed in on her face and right eye, which, as 'a window of the soul,' provided a disquieting insight into the character of the woman.

BB

Frans Hals Portrait of a Man

Antwerp between 1581 / 1585 – Haarlem 1666

Canvas, 106.7 x 91.5 cm (42 x 36 in.)
Neither signed nor dated (ca. 1650)
Kansas City, Mo., The Nelson-Atkins Museum of Art, inv. no. 31-90

1
Cat. no. 28

Provenance
Collection Maurycy Count Zamoyski, Warsaw / Paris,
before 1897-1921 (bought for $150,000)
Collection John McCormack, New York, 1921-1931
Bachstitz Galleries, The Hague / New York, 1931
Gallery of Western Art, Kansas City, 1931
The Nelson-Atkins Museum of Art, Kansas City,
1933 (Nelson Fund)

Bibliography
Bredius 1897, p. 197
Moes 1909, p. 105, no. 117
HdG 320 (vol. III [1910], p. 89, no. 320)
Haarlem 1911, p. 5
Kronig 1911, pp. 137-138 and fig.
Bode / Binder 1914, vol. II, p. 67, no. 261 and fig. 170
Art News 1921, p. 1 and fig.
Hofstede de Groot 1922, p. 534
Valentiner / Voll 1923, p. 240 and fig., p. 321
Art News 1928, pp. 1 and 14, fig. p. 13
London 1929, p. 65, no. 123
London 1929-A, p. 35, fig. 34
Steeman 1929, p. 149 and fig. XXXIV
Dülberg 1930, p. 194
London 1930, pp. 51-52, no. 123 and pl. XXII
Antiquarian 1931, p. 41 and fig., p. 54
Art News 1931, p. 4 and fig.
Frankfurter 1933, p. 30 and fig. p. 33
Kansas City 1933, p. 29 and fig., p. 137
Art Digest 1935-A, pp. 5 and 13
Valentiner 1935, 'Introduction', n.p., no. 46 and fig.
Valentiner 1935-A, p. 4 and fig. cover
Valentiner 1936, no. 95 and fig.
Art Digest 1937, p. 7
Comstock 1937, p. 87
Haarlem 1937, p. 50, no. 100 and fig.
Indianapolis 1937, no. 21 and fig.
New York 1937, no. 24
Richardson 1937, pp. 5-7 and fig. p. 6
Siple 1937, p. 90
Grand Rapids 1940, p. 6, no. 26
Kansas City 1941, pp. 56-57, p. 64 and fig.
Gratama 1943 / 1946, p. 58, no. 102 and fig.
NYT *1945*, p. 23
Art Quarterly 1955, p. 417
Kansas City 1955, p. 78 and fig.
Comstock 1956, pp. 278-279 and fig.
Kansas City 1959, p. 98 and fig., p. 259
Raleigh 1959, pp. 116-117, no. 65 and fig.
Slive 1970-1974, vol. I, p. 184, vol. II, fig. 284,
vol. III, p. 95, no. 182
Grimm 1971, p. 163, no. 20
Grimm 1972, p. 215, no. 182
Jaffé 1972, pp. 508-509 and fig. 13
Kansas City 1973, p. 118 and fig.
Grimm / Montagni 1974, pp. 113-114, no. 274 and fig.
Baard 1981, p. 62 and fig. 67
Sutton 1986, pp. 122 and 124 and fig. 178, p. 265

The honor belongs to Abraham Bredius for unlocking
numerous East European private collections for the Western
public – and therefore also for the art market. On 3 June 1897
he wrote a report from Moscow for *De Nederlandsche Spectator*
about his exploratory expedition through Poland, Galicia, and
Russia, where he was primarily on the lookout for still unknown
Rembrandts. In his account he announced his 'discovery' of the
'*Polish Rider*' (p. 123, fig. 2) at Dzikóv castle, 'one of Rembrandt's
greatest masterpieces' (in translation).[1] Earlier on, in Berlin, he
had spoken to Wilhelm von Bode, who had alerted him to this
then already controversial painting and who had told him about
the owner, Johann-Zdzislaw Count Tarnowski (1862-1937). In

Warsaw ('where there is little of significance,' he had heard in Holland) Bredius was not able to speak to the appropriate party, and therefore used his time with visiting diverse collections. As a consequence he ended up in a private collection, standing eye to eye with the *Portrait of a Man*, now in Kansas City, which was then still united with its pendant (cat. no. 28) [1]: 'two divine three-quarter-length portraits by Frans Hals with Count Zamoyski' (in translation).[2]

The nephew of Count Tarnowski, Count Mycielski, had accompanied Bredius to Dzikóv. Fourteen years later it was this same Georg Mycielski (1856-1928), who had in the meantime become Professor in the History of Art at the University of Cracow, who arranged for Count Zamoyski to lend the two portraits by Frans Hals for several months to the Municipal Museum in Haarlem. The director, Joseph O. Kronig, proudly announced this fact: 'Both portraits, which, judging from the way they are painted, originated in the fifties, form the missing link between the regents of the Saint Elisabeth Hospital of 1641 and the male and female regents of the Old Men's Home of 1664, so that, in this museum, as in no other museum in the world, we are now able to follow the development of HALS as a portraitist in all its phases' (in translation).[3] Kronig was Abraham Bredius's friend, and it came to pass that the former was appointed in 1910, for a period of merely one year, as director of the Haarlem museum. When, in 1911, Bredius tried to secure a permanent appointment for him, he was met with objections from the city council. Kronig took the honorable way out and withdrew his candidature.[4] The loan of the pair of portraits, which had been extended on a personal basis, was naturally terminated as well.[5]

Maurycy Count Zamoyski (1871-1939), who became Polish ambassador in Paris in 1919, was Minister of Foreign Affairs from 1924 to 1926.[6] During the twenties, he sold his Frans Hals portraits separately to American collectors. The portrait of a man was the first to cross the ocean. In 1921 the transaction was made public in the American periodical *Art News*: for 150,000 dollars John McCormack (1884-1945) of New York became the new owner. This Irish opera tenor had become a naturalized American in 1919. 'The painting was one of the gems of the historic Zamoyski art collection,' read the weekly, 'and formerly hung in the "Blue Palace" in Warsaw, which Count Zamoyski had turned over to the American government and which is now being used as the American legation.'[7] There was no mention of a pendant. According to Valentiner, the portrait of a woman had stayed behind in Warsaw, in the collection of Countess Zamoyska.[8]

McCormack's portrait once more made the front pages of newspapers in the United States when it was announced that – along with other old master paintings in American private hands – it was to be lent to the great exhibition of Dutch art in the Royal Academy in London in 1929. The dealer Joseph Duveen had assembled sixteen works (by Rembrandt, Hals, Vermeer, and others) in New York for transport and insured them for six million dollars. Schmidt Degener, director of the Rijksmuseum in Amsterdam and advisor for the exhibition, saw to it that the painting by Hals hung in a place of honor in London.[9] The divorce from its pendant appears to have been effected so quietly that there was no mention of a female companion piece, who 'still dwells with Countess Zamoyska,' as Dülberg knew in 1930. Dülberg further supplied a nice characterization of the dynamism of the man's pose: 'The old man, with his straight, fine nose, clear shining eyes, and merrily protruding lower lip, seems to be making his way through a crowd in which he has just spotted an acquaintance' (in translation).[10] One contemporary critic of the exhibition was less pleased by the highly personal features that Hals generally bestowed on his models: 'He gives a mocking goatshead-smirk, in the Man of the Mc. Cormack Collection' (in translation).[11]

After the exhibition in London, the portrait was bought by Bachstitz Galleries in The Hague, which had been established in New York since 1922.[12] The dealer let it be known that experts such as Schmidt Degener and Bredius esteemed it as one of the most beautiful masterpieces by Frans Hals, surpassed only by the *Portrait of Willem van Heythuyzen* owned by the Prince of Liechtenstein (which in 1969 was sold for twelve million marks to the Alte

2
Cornelis Ketel
Costume Study
Drawing in black chalk, 247 x 175 mm (9³/₄ x 6⁷/₈ in.)
Neither signed nor dated (ca. 1590-1600)
Amsterdam, collection Van Regteren Altena,
inv. no. 9802

Pinakothek in Munich).[13] In 1931 it became the property of the William Rockhill Nelson Collection, which since 1933 has been housed in the museum in Kansas City.[14] William Rockhill Nelson (1841-1915) was the celebrated journalist and publisher of the *Kansas City Star*. To raise the cultural niveau of his hometown, he collected full-size replicas of works such as Rembrandt's '*Nightwatch.*' During the Depression years, important authentic paintings were bought with the proceeds of his legacy, including the *Self-Portrait at Age Fifty* by Gerard Dou (cat. no. 18).[15]

The couple by Frans Hals were only reunited on paper in 1955, when the pendant that had lived such a long, closeted existence was acquired by the Saint Louis Art Museum (cat. no. 28), by chance also in the state of Missouri.[16] In the present exhibition they are seen next to each other for the first time since 1921. In recent publications it has sometimes been doubted whether these paintings are indeed pendants of each other, though in view of their common provenance and dimensions this is highly plausible.[17] This doubt is caused largely by the unconventional frontal pose of the man, which is directed more to the spectator than to his spouse, so that the work could very well pass for an independent portrait. But what we have here is surely an experiment on the part of the artist. It is a good example of one of the new formulas for the portrait that the painter would try out if he got the chance. Naturally, when called upon to do so, he immortalized his patrons in traditional portraits (see cat. nos. 25-26, figs. 3 and 4) of the kind rendered by numerous colleague-portraitists from Cornelis Ketel to Caspar Netscher.[18] With Ketel one could choose from standard poses and costumes, which he was able to show in drawings (Amsterdam, collection Van Regteren Altena) [2].[19] But Hals was surely aware of the objections to this kind of factory-like production, which was utilized 'without taking into account if the build corresponds to that of the sitter, and the clothing with his status, and the nature of his face; yea, whether the head even fits on that body' (in translation), as Gerard de Lairesse observed disapprovingly in 1707.[20]

It looks as if Hals painted the somewhat amused-looking man spontaneously, as he posed for him. Some later commentators have been amazed at the far from classical – or cliché-like – expressions of his models.[21] His broad brushstrokes have been called both old-fashioned and well ahead of their time.[22] In any case, even early on there were already admirers of his methods and technique. When he portrayed this unknown man, the ink had hardly dried on *Harlemias* by T. Schrevelius, in which Hals's way of working was commented on with enthusiasm: 'for there is in his painting such force and life / that he appears to be defying nature itself with his Brush / thus say all his Portraits / that he has made / unbelievably many / that are so colored / that they appear to breathe' (in translation).[23]

---

1 *Bredius 1897*
2 Ibidem
3 *Kronig 1911*, p. 137
4 *Barnouw-de Ranitz 1978*, p. 15
5 Because the private corresponcence of Bredius and Kronig is not yet accessible for study, there remain unanswered questions as to the facts of the matter.
6 *Larousse*, vol. x, p. 11000
7 *Art News 1921*, p. 1; *NYT 1945*, pp. 21 and 23; about McCormack, see *WWWA*, vol. II, p. 357
8 *Valentiner / Voll 1923*, pp. 240-241 and 321
9 *Art News 1928*, pp. 1 and 14; *Art News 1931*, p. 4
10 *Dülberg 1930*, p. 194
11 *Stheeman 1929*, p. 149
12 *Art News 1931*, p. 4; *Art Digest 1931*, p. 17
13 Inv. no. 14101; *Munich 1983*, pp. 238-239, no. 14101 and fig. x; *Slive 1970-1974*, vol. II, figs. 56-57, vol. III, pp. 20-21, no. 31
14 *Frankfurter 1933*, p. 29
15 *Sutton 1986*, p. 122; *WWWA*, vol. I, p. 890
16 *Art Quarterly 1955*, p. 417; *Comstock 1956*, p. 278 and fig.
17 *Sutton 1986*, p. 124: 'The presumed pendant to the Hals.'
18 *Judson 1963*, pp. 38-41 and figs. 26-27; *Blankert 1966*, pp. 263-269 and figs. 1-8 (Netscher and other examples)
19 *Judson 1963*, p. 39 and pl. 27
20 *De Lairesse 1707*, vol. II, p. 19
21 *Vinken / De Jongh 1963*
22 *Broos 1978-1979*, pp. 121-123
23 *Schrevelius 1648*, p. 383
BB

Antwerp between 1581 / 1585 – Haarlem 1666

Canvas, 102.5 x 89 cm (40⅜ x 35 in.)
Neither signed nor dated (ca. 1650)
Saint Louis, Mo., The Saint Louis Art Museum, inv. no. 272:1955

Before the Saint Louis Museum acquired this portrait of a woman, the picture had for a quarter of a century been in the collection of Robert Sterling Clark (1877?-1956). He had bought it in the late twenties from Count Zamoyski, formerly Minister of Foreign Affairs for Poland (see cat. no. 27). Clark was described as a somewhat shy and mysterious collector, who kept his collection mainly in Paris. 'No museum man or art historian, so far as is known, ever saw it as a whole,' Constable determined in his handbook on collecting in America.[1] Robert S. Clark and his brother Stephen C. Clark (1882-1960), who was also a collector (see cat. nos. 25-26), were grandsons of Edward Clark, who was the business partner of Isaac Singer, the inventor of the sewing machine. In 1912 Robert had gone to Paris, where he bought his first painting. He had a preference for Dutch, Flemish, and Italian art, but after his marriage to a Frenchwoman, he primarily specialized in the French Impressionists. Because he was afraid of the nuclear destruction that might threaten a huge city like New York in a third world war, he left his collection to Williamstown, a small town in Massachusetts. A year prior to his death, the Sterling and Francine Clark Art Institute was opened there.[2] In that year Clark sold the *Portrait of a Woman* by Frans Hals to the Saint Louis Art Museum by way of Knoedlers for 150,000 dollars.

Provenance

Collection Maurycy Count Zamoyski, Warsaw / Paris, before 1897-1930(?)
Collection Robert Sterling Clark, Paris / New York, 1930(?)-1955
The Saint Louis Art Museum, 1955 (bought for $150,000 from Clark via Knoedler & Co., with Museum Funds and funds given by The John M. Olin Charitable Trust, Friends Fund, Mr. and Mrs. Sydney M. Shoenberg, Sr., and the Misses Stella and Effie C. Kuhn, Mrs. Clifford W. Gaylord, Joseph L. Werner)

Bibliography

Bredius 1897, p. 197
Moes 1909, p. 105, no. 118
HdG 396 (vol. III [1910], p. 113, no. 396)
Haarlem 1911, p. 5
Kronig 1911, pp. 137-138 and fig.
Bode / Binder 1914, p. 67, no. 262 and fig. p. 171
Valentiner / Voll 1923, p. 241 and fig., p. 321
New York 1925, no. 5 and fig.
Dülberg 1930, p. 194
Valentiner 1936, no. 95
Indianapolis 1937, no. 21
Art Quarterly 1955, pp. 416-417 and fig.
Comstock 1956, pp. 278-279 and fig.
Eisendrath 1956, pp. 18-21
Hoffmann 1958, p. 453
New York 1958, p. 9, no. 9 and fig. p. 27
Kansas City 1959, p. 98
Seattle 1962, pp. 70-71, no. 28 and fig.
San Francisco / Toledo / Boston 1966-1967, pp. 53-54, no. 20 and fig.
Slive 1970-1974, vol. I, p. 184, vol. II, fig. 285, vol. III, p. 95, no. 183
Grimm 1971, p. 160, fig. 15, p. 163, no. 20, p. 166
Boston 1972, p. 196, no. 171 and fig.
Grimm 1972, p. 215, no. 183
Jaffé 1972, pp. 508-509, no. 13
Grimm / Montagni 1974, pp. 113-114, no. 275 and fig.
Burke 1980, p. 12 and fig. p. 13 and cover
Sutton 1986, pp. 124 and 265

1
Cat. no. 27

Frans Hals Portrait of a Woman

Upon its acquisition by the museum, the portrait by Frans Hals was greeted like a long-lost daughter. The painting had been separated from its pendant, the *Portrait of a Man* (cat. no. 27) [1] for thirty-five years, since 1921. Both paintings are now in the possession of museums in the state of Missouri, one in Kansas City and the other in Saint Louis. It is only at this exhibition that the paintings can again be seen next to each other, if only temporarily. Before 1955 the male half of the pair had made an impression at diverse exhibitions with its powerful brushwork and unusual composition. The broad, direct way of painting is also characteristic for its counterpart. 'The *Portrait of a Lady* [...] has not been known to students here, although long in America in the collection of Robert Sterling Clark,' claimed Comstock in 1956.[3] It is more probable that the portrait of a woman had only recently been brought over from Paris.

When, in 1897, Abraham Bredius saw this portrait and its pendant hanging in the Warsaw residence of Count Zamoyski, he wrote in his notebook: '2 *splendid* three-quarter portraits by Frans Hals – the woman is *very ugly*' (in translation).[4] Hofstede de Groot took over this qualification in his catalogue of Hals's oeuvre, even though he had yet to see the paintings: 'Hässlich.'[5] Bredius – who had little use for women – clearly meant the appearance of the lady, not the way in which the portrait is painted. It was he who in 1911 arranged for the pair to be lent for several months to the Municipal Museum in Haarlem (see cat. no. 27). Hofstede de Groot observed on this occasion: 'though not of the very best, nevertheless of very good quality' (in translation).[6] He no longer expressed an opinion on the physical beauty of the unknown lady. Much later Slive reminded his readers of Bredius's emotional pronouncement and reparteed: 'I find the woman attractive.'[7]

The correctness of the attribution to Frans Hals was not questioned until 1971, when Grimm included the two works, and especially the unsigned portrait of a woman, in a group of works that, according to him, must have been painted by Frans Hals the Younger in view of the nervous brushwork.[8] Grimm's methodology has been fiercely contested, and in this case, too, his conclusion seems somewhat premature and based on an all too hasty examination.[9] The portrait of a woman does indeed reveal characteristics that we have especially come to appreciate in the oeuvre of Frans Hals. It is a typical example of *alla prima* painting in a broad, direct way, without making preliminary drawings. This method was known as the most difficult manner, reserved for only the most experienced masters. 'To paint at once almost without drawing, is not suited to everyone' (in

translation), Van Mander already believed, referring to Vasari's description of Titian's virtuosic style of painting.[10] Precisely because Hals registered so directly what he saw, several details seem to us to have lost their clarity. Thus the light passage under the left hand of the woman came to be described as a hand-kerchief, and the accessory in her right hand as a purse.[11] However, like most women in portraits, she holds her gloves and rests her left hand on the point at the bottom her *lijfje* (a kind of bodice).

The components of her dress become easier to recognize when we compare her costume with that of the mother in a family

2
Frans Hals
Family Group in a Landscape
Canvas, 202 x 285 cm (79½ x 112¼ in.)
Neither signed nor dated (ca. 1648)
Lugano, collection Baron Thyssen-Bornemisza, inv. no. 124

2a
Detail of fig. 2

portrait of the same period (Lugano, collection Baron Thyssen-Bornemisza) [2-2a].[12] The eye-catching element of the costume is the *lijfje* or *borst*, here in a horizontally striped pattern. To suggest a narrow waist, it terminates in a point. Beneath her skirt, which is split open at the front, an olive brown petticoat may be seen. Because the fashion of about 1650 prescribed a sloping shoulder line, the shoulder flaps are missing, and a folded shawl accentuates the conical profile.[13] This unstarched shawl is held together at the front of the bodice by a small black-and-gold bow. The light red sleeve under the translucent cuffs constitutes the sole color accent in the costume. The woman wears a double gold chain around her neck and earrings that protrude from under her bonnet. Following the fashion of the day, its points have been bent flat against the head.[14]

Like her husband, she is painted *naar het leven* (after life), in a shaft of light coming from the left that casts a shadow on the wall. This detail indicates that her portrait, no matter how casual it may seem, is nevertheless not free of conventions. It was the tradition in portraiture to depict married couples according to the conventions of heraldry, that is (for the spectator) with the man to the left and the woman to the right. The man therefore occupied the place of honor with respect to the woman, on her right side. The figures had been arranged this way in the Middle Ages for the donor portraits of altarpieces, and thus they remained in the seventeenth century.[15] This placement had turned into a practice every bit as fixed as it was the rule to have the light in a painting come from the left. This resulted in a constant lighting for portraits of women, for which a theoretician like Gerard de Lairesse even came up with an explanation: 'for as the female sex usually possesses greater tenderness and grace, thus the same also requires [...] the most beautiful and pleasant light' (in translation).[16] In his pendant portraits, Hals never deviated from this rule.

1 *Constable 1964*, pp. 81-82; R.S. Clark is not mentioned in the biographical dictionaries, such as DAB, WWA, and WWWA.
2 *Durden-Smith / Desimone 1984*, pp. 89-90; *Sutton 1986*, p. 316
3 *Comstock 1956*, p. 279; see also *Art Quarterly 1955*, p. 417
4 Bredius notebooks (Polish journey 1897) (RKD)
5 HdG 396
6 Index cards Hofstede de Groot (RKD)
7 *Slive 1970-1974*, vol. III, p. 95, no. 183
8 *Grimm 1971*, p. 166
9 *Gerson 1973*, p. 173 and *De Jongh 1975*, p. 584
10 *Van Mander 1604*, fol. 47 recto; see also *Broos 1978-1979*, p. 122
11 *Art Quarterly 1955*, p. 417; *Comstock 1956*, p. 278
12 *Slive 1970-1974*, vol. II, figs. 276-281, vol. III, pp. 92-93, no. 177
13 *Der Kinderen-Besier 1950*, p. 143

14 *Der Kinderen-Besier 1950*, p. 150
15 *Slive 1970-1974*, vol. I, p. 51
16 *De Lairesse 1707*, vol. II, pp. 6-7; *De Jongh 1975*, p. 585, draws attention to this passage.

BB

Bartholomeus van der Helst Self-Portrait in 1655

Bartholomeus van der Helst   29 | Self-Portrait in 1655

Haarlem 1613 – Amsterdam 1670

Canvas, 96.5 x 99 cm (38 x 39 in.)
Lower center: *B. van der Helst. 1655*
Toledo, Ohio, The Toledo Museum of Art, inv. no. 76.12

Van der Helst apparently apprenticed himself in Amsterdam to the portraitist Nicolaes Eliasz before 1636, as may be deduced from his earlier works, which initially also showed the influence of Rembrandt. After 1640 he developed a style characterized by elegance, quite invisible brushstrokes, and an even lighting. His smooth technique, his minutely rendered fabrics, and his mastery of a faithful likeness eminently satisfied the craving of the ever richer bourgeoisie for open display. Thus, toward the middle of the seventeenth century, he became the celebrated and sought-after portrait painter of the Amsterdam patrician class. His imposing *Banquet of the Civic Guard* of 1648, now in the Rijksmuseum in Amsterdam, met with greater approbation than Rembrandt's so-called *Nightwatch*.

When in 1921 an exhibition of Dutch art was held in Madrid, the firm of Frederik Muller & Co. lent this signed and dated portrait of a man by Bartholomeus van der Helst. Abraham Bredius, the retired director of the Mauritshuis, had been consulted beforehand, and his opinion was published in the catalogue: 'Doctor A. Bredius believes that it is a self-portrait by the painter and is of the opinion that it is one of the most outstanding portraits known to him by the master' (in translation).[1] That same year the monograph on Van der Helst by J.J. de Gelder appeared, in which the painting was still described as a portrait of an unknown gentleman.[2] Up to the present, The Toledo Museum of Art has not exhibited it as a self-portrait but as the portrait of an unknown man. The museum was recently supported in this practice by Peter Sutton, whose firm opinion was premature considering that a serious investigation of the correctness of Bredius's identification had not been undertaken.[3]

The firm Frederik Muller & Co. purchased the painting at auction in Paris in 1919. De Gelder pointed out that the subject was identical to that of a portrait that had been auctioned earlier, in both Amsterdam (1799 and 1802) and Rome (1845). However, that canvas was fifteen centimeters wider. Moreover, its sitter was described in 1799 as an 'aged gentleman,' and in 1845 the date was read as 1657.[4] In short, it must have been either an autograph variation of a later date or an inauthentic old copy in a slightly larger format.

Provenance

Auction Lebeuf de Montgermont, Paris, 1919 (Frf. 12,000 to Frederik Muller)
Firm F. Muller & Co., Amsterdam, 1919-1921
Collection A.W.M. Mensing, Amsterdam / Aerdenhout / Lausanne, after 1921-1938
Auction Mensing, Amsterdam, 1938 (ƒ2,500 to De Geus van den Heuvel)
Collection B. de Geus van den Heuvel, Amsterdam / Nieuwersluis, 1938-1976 (from 1949 to 1952 on loan to the Stedelijk Van Abbe Museum, Eindhoven)
Auction De Geus van den Heuvel, Amsterdam, 1976 (ƒ42,000)
The Toledo Museum of Art, Toledo, Ohio, 1976 (gift of Edward Drummond Libbey)

Bibliography

Auction Paris 1919, p. 131, no. 192 and fig.
Auction Paris 1919-A, p. 78, no. 192
Chronique des arts 1919, p. 220, no. 192
De Gelder 1921, p. 178, no. 176, pp. 190-191, nos. 285 and 290, p. 194, no. 347 and p. 206, no. 527
Madrid 1921, pp. 26-27, no. 49
Art News 1938, p. 19
Auction Amsterdam 1938, p. 12, no. 45 and fig.
Weltkunst 1938, p. 2
Schiedam 1952-1953, p. 9, no. 30
Rome 1956-1957, p. 145, no. 130
Arnhem 1960-1961, p. 14, no. 22 and fig. 39
Van Hall 1963, p. 134, no. 881-5
Eckardt 1971, p. 189
Auction Amsterdam 1976, p. 23, no. 22
Nienhuis 1976, vol. I, p. 24, no. 22, vol. II, fig. 22
Toledo 1976, p. 75 and pl. 101
WCA 1976, vol. XXVIII (1976), p. 140
Wittmann 1976, p. 64 and fig.
Chronique des arts 1977, p. 49, no. 195 and fig.
Mayer, vol. XI (1977), p. 784
Schulze 1977, p. 67
Sutton 1986, pp. 291-292

At some unknown time the partner of Frederik Muller, Anton Mensing, became the owner of the original portrait by Van der Helst. Quite a few masterpieces passed through his hands. The fame of Amsterdam in the international art world was largely due to the firm Frederik Muller and its director, Mensing. Muller & Co. auctioned renowned collections, from those of Heseltine and Steengracht in 1913 to Van Stolk and Six in 1928.[5] Mensing was continually praised for his grasp of art-historical facts and his extensive experience. He had assembled for himself a choice collection of paintings by Dutch old masters. The Mensing auction of 1938 was a major event for Amsterdam, Rembrandt's *Portrait of Marten Looten* (Los Angeles County Museum of Art)[6] being the pièce de résistance. It fetched 102,000 guilders, while the no less handsome portrait by Bartholomeus van der Helst went under the hammer for a mere 2,500 guilders.[7]

De Geus van den Heuvel became the new owner of the portrait from 1655 (his merits as a collector are elucidated in cat. no. 31). He lent the painting to the Van Abbe Museum in Eindhoven from 1949 to 1952 and parted with it for several exhibitions during the fifties and sixties.[8] At the De Geus van den Heuvel auction in 1976, it was purchased by the museum in Toledo, Ohio, for the not altogether exorbitant amount of 42,000 florins.[9]

Sutton has recently claimed that this cannot be a self-portrait because 'the costume and the park-like surroundings point to a gentleman of standing with ample free time – a position that artists only acquired later in the century,' and because nothing points to the sitter's profession as a painter.[10] The latter argu-

ment carries little weight, as may be demonstrated by the case of Rembrandt, who – in comparison with his Dutch colleagues – depicted himself relatively often, but rarely as a painter.[11] Nor did Van der Helst explicitly depict himself as such in his *Self-Portrait in 1662* (Hamburger Kunsthalle) [**1**].[12] Sutton's first argument does no justice to the fact that in 1655 the artist could indeed lay claim to status and prestige. The elegant pose and the backdrop of a park with a country residence featured in the painting in Hamburg are strongly reminiscent of the setting of the piece in Toledo. Van der Helst had every reason to present himself as a successful citizen. Around 1660 he was a much sought-after and well-paid painter. We know from documents that he could command twice as much as his fellow portraitists. For a (lost) group portrait he received about three times the amount Rembrandt did for his '*Nightwatch*.'[13] The dashing presentation therefore in no way excludes the possibility that Van der Helst here portrayed himself – quite the contrary (see also cat. no. 18).

Since 1683 an indisputable self-portrait of Bartholomeus van der Helst has been in the self-portrait collection of the Galleria degli Uffizi in Florence.[14] The painter signed it with *Dit is B. vander helst fecit 1667*. Abraham Blooteling made a mezzotint after this portrait [**2**].[15] The illustration to the biography of Van der Helst in Houbraken's *Groote Schouburgh* is based on this portrait of 1667 (or on the print or an alternate painted version).[16] Not long ago another portrait of the painter was published, one that shows him at a considerably younger age.[17] He is depicted at the far left of a militia piece of 1639, *The Militia Company of Captain Roelof Bicker* (Amsterdam, Rijksmuseum) [**3**].[18] Hence we have a good picture of the steady aging of the painter's blushing, bulbous face from 1639 to 1667. The portrait of 1655 fits perfectly into this sequence; it depicts the artist in the prime of his life, at age forty-two. The work was identified as such in 1971, in Götz Eckardt's book on the self-portraits by Dutch masters of the seventeenth century.[19]

Bartholomeus van der Helst is dressed in a black velvet coat with open sleeves that reveal a doublet trimmed with gold braid, from which the shirt pops out at the sleeves in lavish pleats, all closely following the latest fashion. It was chic to leave the collar of the shirt open and to have the cords with the tags hanging loose. The black hat with the cord is part of his outfit as a *grand seigneur*.[20] The fashionable painter points to a dog that has laid its head on the balustrade against which he leans. The gesture is strongly reminiscent of that of the man in the *Family Group*, painted in 1654 (London, Wallace Collection) [**4**].[21] In this

1
Bartholomeus van der Helst
Self-Portrait in 1662
Canvas, 132.5 x 112 cm (52⅛ x 44 in.)
Left, at the height of the hand: *B. van der Helst 1662*
Hamburg, Hamburger Kunsthalle, inv. no. 297

2
Abraham Blooteling
Portrait of Bartholomeus van der Helst
Mezzotint, 555 x 422 mm (21⅞ x 16⅝ in.)
Lower right: *A. Blooteling fecit* (ca. 1670)
Amsterdam, Rijksprentenkabinet

3
Bartholomeus van der Helst
The Militia Company of Captain Roelof Bicker (detail)
Canvas, 235 x 750 cm (92½ in. x 24 ft. 7¼ in.)
(the whole painting)
Lower left: *B. van der Helst f. 163[9]*
Amsterdam, Rijksmuseum, inv. no. C 375

instance a family poses with hounds and with a hare as catch, even though hunting was in fact a prerogative of the nobility. The work is one of the depictions of status-seeking burghers who, even before 1655, had themselves painted with the paraphernalia of a pastime still reserved for an elite,[22] an early and well-known example being Rembrandt's *Self-Portrait with a Bittern* (Dresden, Gemäldegalerie) of 1639.[23] There is no reason to suppose that Rembrandt ever took part in a hunt.

The comparison with the above-mentioned *Family Group* is additionally useful because it creates the impression that the *Self-Portrait* of 1655 had a pendant. This counterpart would have had the same dimensions and would have portrayed Anna du Pire, the wife of the painter, with another attribute of the hunt. Alas, we know of no such painting.[24] If the Van der Helst couple were indeed depicted together, greater significance could be attached to several details of the *Self-Portrait*. The ivy or grapevine (of the kind we see on the wall behind the painter) occurs repeatedly in portraits of married couples.[25] Ivy clinging to a wall or a grapevine winding itself around a tree is the standard image of marital fidelity, love, or friendship. This convention is formulated in an emblem by Andrea Alciatus (*Emblematum Libellus*, 1542) of a grapevine around a tree trunk [**5**].[26] The Latin inscription proclaims *Amicitia etiam post mortem durans* (Love outlives even

4
Bartholomeus van der Helst
Family Group
Canvas, 167.6 x 196.2 cm (66 x 77¼ in.)
Lower right: *van der Helst. f. 1654*
London, Wallace Collection, inv. no. 110

AND. ALCI. EMBLE. LIB.

Amicitia etiam post mortem
durans.

Arentem senio, nudam quoq; frondibus ulmum,
Complexa est uiridi uitis opaca coma.
Agnoscitq; uices naturæ, & grata parenti
Officij reddit mutua iura suo.
Exemploq; monet, tales nos quærere amicos,
Quos ne que disiungat fœdere summa dies,

death). Such a pendant would establish the painter's intention to express love symbolism. It would then also become apparent whether the dog was intended to be a hound, then an established symbol of (marital) fidelity (see also cat. no. 43).

1 *Madrid 1921*, p. 27, no. 49
2 *De Gelder 1921*, p. 178, no. 176
3 *Toledo 1976*, p. 75; *Sutton 1986*, pp. 291-292
4 *Auction Amsterdam 1799*, p. 14, no. 43; *Auction Amsterdam 1802*, p. 67, no. 19; *Auction Rome 1845*, pp. 82-83, no. 100-65; *De Gelder 1921*, pp. 190-191, nos. 285 and 290 and p. 194, no. 347
5 *Amstelodamum 1935*, p. 105
6 Inv. no. M 53.50.3; *Bruyn et al. 1986*, pp. 190-198, no. A 52 and fig.
7 See the newspaper clippings in the annotated copy of *Auction Amsterdam 1938* (RKD); see also *Art News 1938* and *Weltkunst 1938*.
8 See Bibliography; according to an unverifiable annotation with the photo (RKD), the dealer Douwes Bros. in Amsterdam had it on sale around 1945.
9 A list of prices with *Auction Amsterdam 1976*.
10 *Sutton 1986*, pp. 291-292
11 *Wright 1982*; Rembrandt had a predilection for 'poetic' self-portraits; see *Raupp 1984*, pp. 168-181 (see as well the same, pp. 36-40, for the fairly rare subject of the artist at work in self-portraits).
12 *De Gelder 1921*, p. 161, no. 30 and frontispiece; *Hamburg 1966*, p. 79, no. 297 and fig.; *Raupp 1984*, p. 264: 'Vornehme Zurückhaltung in der Tracht und Verzicht auf Attribut kennzeichnen das Selbstbildnis [in Hamburg].'
13 *De Gelder 1921*, pp. 25-26
14 Inv. no. A 969; *De Gelder 1921*, p. 161, no. 29 and fig. XXXV; *Florence 1980*, p. 1026, no. A 969 and fig.
15 *Hollstein*, vol. II, p. 233, no. 166 and fig.; because of a misunderstanding, this print is sometimes described as being after the portrait in Toledo (for example, in *Auction Amsterdam 1976*, p. 23, no. 22).
16 *Houbraken 1718-1721*, vol. II, pl. A
17 *De Bruyn Kops 1965*, pp. 20-25
18 *De Gelder 1921*, pp. 46 and 230, no. 835 and pls. VI-VII; *Van Thiel et al. 1976*, p. 267, no. C 375 and fig.
19 *Eckardt 1971*, p. 189
20 *Der Kinderen-Besier 1950*, pp. 136-138, 170-171, 176
21 *De Gelder 1921*, p. 241, no. 864 and pl. XXII; *London 1968*, p. 147, no. P 110
22 *Sullivan 1984*, pp. 33-45; *Broos 1986*, pp. 113-114; *Broos 1987*, pp. 398-399
23 Inv. no. 1561; *Gerson / Bredius 1969*, pp. 27 and 549, no. 31 and fig.; *Sullivan 1980*, passim
24 For the portraits of Anna du Pire, see *De Gelder 1921*, p. 162, nos. 47-48, p. 208, no. 541, p. 244, no. 888
25 *De Jongh 1986*, pp. 126-127; see also *De Jongh / Vinken 1961*, pp. 118-129 and figs. 1-8
26 *Alciatus 1542 / 1967*, pp. 40-41, no. XII

BB

Gorkum 1637 – Amsterdam 1712

Canvas, 62.8 x 71.7 cm (24¾ x 28¼ in.)
Neither signed nor dated (ca. 1669)
Cambridge, Mass., Fogg Art Museum, Harvard University Art Museums, inv. no. 1968.65

The beginnings of the artistic career of Van der Heyden are rather obscure. By the time of his marriage in 1661, he referred to himself as a painter, whereas the earliest known date on any of his paintings is 1664. He was above all an inventor. In 1668 he designed a new plan for the city lighting of Amsterdam (which, with 2,556 street lamps, remained in use until 1840). In 1672 he constructed the first fire engine with hoses, which he brought into production in 1681 and later described in his personally illustrated 'fire engine book' (1690). Nevertheless he is primarily known for his topographic and invented cityscapes and for his landscapes with country estates.

Characteristic of Van der Heyden is his minute detail, with every brick of the walls depicted individually. The unmatched rendering of materials and the intimate light effects remind us so much of photographic realism that it comes as a surprise to discover that some cityscapes sprang entirely from the painter's imagination. He had the figures in his works painted by others – until 1672 by Adriaen van de Velde – even though, on the evidence of preparatory studies for his 'fire engine book,' he was himself competent at figure drawing. At the end of his life he also painted some interiors with bizarre still lifes.

BB

This painting was once part of the famous collection of Etienne François Duke of Choiseul (1719-1785) [1]. After having been ambassador of the French king in Rome and Vienna, he became Minister of War and Foreign Affairs of France. Between 1750 and 1770 he bought a large number of paintings at well-known

Provenance
(?) Collection Willem Lormier, The Hague, 1754
(?) Auction Willem Lormier, The Hague, 1763 (ƒ400 to Balden)
Collection Etienne François Choiseul-Stainville Duke of Choiseul and Amboise, Paris, 1763(?)-1772
Auction Choiseul, Paris, 1772 (Frf. 791 to Boileau)
Gallery Alexander Prince Bezborodko, Saint Petersburg, 1783 (?)-1800
Collection Georg Count Kushelev-Bezborodko
Auction Kushelev-Bezborodko, Paris, 1869 (Frf. 20,000)
Collection Edwards, Paris
Auction Edwards, Paris, 1905 (Frf. 11,800 to Féral)
Dealer Julius Böhler, Munich
Collection Paul M. Warburg (from Julius Böhler by way of James Loeb), October 1909
Collection Mr. and Mrs. Samuel B. Grimson (Bettina Warburg, sister of James P. Warburg)
Fogg Art Museum, Harvard University Art Museums, Cambridge, Mass., 1968 (gift of Mr. and Mrs. Samuel B. Grimson)

Bibliography
d'Ailly, fig. p. 29 (as Job Berckheyde)
Hoet 1752-1770, vol. III, p. 322, no. 138
The Hague 1754, p. 14, no. 146
Auction The Hague 1763, p. 17, no. 137
Recueil Choiseul 1771, no. 116 and fig.
Auction Paris 1772, pp. 25-26, no. 74
Auction Paris 1869, pp. 7-8, no. 4 and fig.
Paris 1892, p. 51, no. 47
Gabeau 1904, p. 266
Auction Paris 1905, p. 4, no. 2 and fig.
Auction Paris 1905-A, p. 4, no. 2
't Hooft 1912, fig. (2)
HdG 37 (vol. VIII [1927], p. 369, no. 37)
Wagner 1971, p. 116, no. 37
Mortimer 1985, p. 169, no. 193
Sutton 1986, p. 40, fig. 52

1
Anonymous
Portrait of Etienne François Duke of Choiseul (1719-1785)
Engraving, 134 x 98 mm (5¼ x 3⅞ in.)
Not signed (1771)
The Hague, Rijksbureau voor Kunsthistorische Documentatie

Jan van der Heyden View of the Dam and the Damrak in Amsterdam

auctions such as those of Vence (Paris 1760), Gaillard de Gagny (Paris 1762), Lormier (The Hague 1763), Julienne (Paris 1767), and Gaignat (Paris 1768). By his marriage in 1750 to Louise-Honorine Crozat de Châtel he came into the possession of the splendid Hôtel Crozat on the rue de Richelieu, where he housed most of the paintings in a rococo interior especially designed for the purpose. This interior, which we know only from miniature depictions on a snuffbox, on which the *View of the Dam* can unfortunately not be made out, formed a source of inspiration for other collectors.[1] Thus Gustaf Adolf Sparre (1746-1794), who stayed in Paris from 1768 to 1771 and was well acquainted with the Duke of Choiseul, probably had the Hôtel Crozat in mind when he housed his collection in his residence in Göteborg (see cat. no. 53).[2]

In 1771 and 1772 the duke had engravings made after the most important paintings in his collection, which were assembled into a catalogue. At that time he owned ten paintings by Wouwermans, eight by Rembrandt, seven by Teniers, six by Berchem, five by Ter Borch, and five by Metsu, as well as works by Steen, Ruisdael, Dou, Van Mieris, and Van der Werff. In this catalogue we also find, in mirror image, the *View of the Dam*, with the inscription: 'Painted [by] Berkheyden and the figures [are] by V. Velde' (in translation) [**2**].[3] Possibly the Duke of Choiseul had bought this painting in 1763, shortly after the auction of Willem Lormier in The Hague. The catalogue of this auction mentions 'A View of the Dam in Amsterdam full of houses and figures' (in translation), which corresponds precisely in its dimensions with this painting.[4] However, the catalogue attributed it to Jan van der Heyden and Adriaen van de Velde.

Shortly after the appearance of the catalogue of his collection, the duke fell into disfavor with King Louis XV. In 1772 the greater part of his collection was auctioned in his own home. The auctioneer was J.F. Boileau, who was court painter to the Duke of Orléans and who dealt in art on the side. Boileau, who also compiled the auction catalogue, once more gave the painting to Jan van der Heyden and Adriaen van de Velde. At the auction he bought the painting in.[5]

Later it came into the possession of the Russian Prince Alexander Bezborodko, State Chancellor and Minister of Foreign Affairs under Catherine II and Paul I. He had a private museum in Saint Petersburg. When Alexander Bezborodko died in 1800, first his brother inherited the collection, and then his eldest daughter, who was married to Count Kushelev. They had two sons, who each got half of the collection. The one donated his share to the Academy of Saint Petersburg, the other, Georg

2
Lienard after Jan van der Heyden
View of the Dam and the Damrak in Amsterdam
Engraving, 141 x 162 mm (5½ x 6⅜ in.)
Lower left: *Lienard sculps* (1771)
The Hague, Rijksbureau voor Kunsthistorische Documentatie

Count Kushelev Bezborodko, had his share auctioned in Paris in 1869 by the well-known Parisian auction house Drouot. The painting once more went as a work of Gerrit Berckheyde. Someone (presumably Hofstede de Groot) noted in this auction catalogue: 'true Jan v.d. Heyden first quality' (in translation), apparently after having seen the piece in 1892 at the exhibition *Cent chefs-d'oeuvre des écoles françaises et étrangères* in the Galerie Georges Petit in Paris.[6]

In the catalogue of the Edwards auction of 1905 in Paris, which includes an extensive description of the painting, the attribution to Gerrit Berckheyde was openly questioned: 'It has been [...] attributed to Berckheyden, although it is not signed and it is in fact worthy of Van der Heyden' (in translation).[7]

In 1909 the piece entered the collection of Paul Moritz Warburg (1868-1932), a scion of an old Hamburg banking dynasty. In 1895 he had married Nina J. Loeb, daughter of

Salomon Loeb, who was co-owner of the firm Kuhn Loeb & Company in New York. In 1902 Paul Warburg and his wife settled in New York, where he began to work for his father-in-law. In 1911 he became an American citizen. Warburg bought the Van der Heyden from the Munich dealer Julius Böhler by way of a James Loeb, a relative of his wife.[8]

The uncertainty about the correct attribution continued. In 1912, without qualification, C.G. 't Hooft, director of the Museum Fodor in Amsterdam and a Jan van der Heyden connoisseur, incorporated an illustration of the painting into a commemorative booklet of the Amstelodamum Society published on the occasion of the bicentennial of the painter's death.[9] In 1927 Hofstede de Groot published it with the comment: 'The painting always counted as a G. Berckheyde, but it is an outstanding Jan van der Heyden' (in translation).[10] In a few folds of one of the bags lying on a horse sleigh at the left, he thought he recognized the initials of Adriaen van de Velde. More recently, in her monograph on Van der Heyden, Helga Wagner again attributed the work to Berckheyde without further explanation, a viewpoint endorsed by Cynthia Lawrence, whose monograph on this artist is about to appear.[11] However, in this catalogue entry the painting is considered to be a Van der Heyden, for reasons discussed below.

Hofstede de Groot was the first to specify the location depicted, which at the Edwards auction was still simply called *Quai à Amsterdam*. It is a view of the Dam and the Damrak, seen from the southwest, from the Gasthuissteeg (now Paleisstraat), in the direction of the Vismarkt. The fish market, which had been held in this location since 1492, and which was subdivided into River and Ocean Fish Markets, was almost totally separated from the Dam by the so-called Huis onder 't Zeil. This consisted of a block of seven row houses, built in 1559 in the Dutch Renaissance style, possibly after the design of Hendrick de Keyser. Initially the city rented them out as stores, but they later primarily housed *tapperijen* (taverns) or public houses. For the benefit of the customers, the benches in front of the door were covered with canvas. Thus originated the name Huizen onder 't Zeil (Houses under the Sail), called Huis onder 't Zeil (House under the Sail) for short, which, due to its poor state of repair, was renovated in 1774 and 1775, and demolished in 1912.[12] From the sixteenth century on people began to consider the presence of fish and meat markets on an important square like the Damrak a nuisance, especially because of their customary business, such as the cleaning of fish and the slaughter of cattle, with all the associated blood, waste, and stench. The measures imposed by the authorities were not always appreciated by the guilds involved. Thus the Meat Hall by Lieven de Key on the Great Market of Haarlem (1602-1603) may be seen as a compromise solution, whereby the guild retained its prominent position in the city, but the dirty work was henceforth hidden behind a richly ornamented facade which was intended to block out its memory altogether. The River and Ocean Fish Markets, for their part, were able to remain on the Dam until 1841.

To the left of the Huis onder 't Zeil, we see the so-called small lock of the Damrak, which then still had the character of an inner harbor. A painting by Jacob van Ruisdael (The Hague, Mauritshuis) [3] shows us this part of the Dam in close-up, with a little bit of the Huis onder 't Zeil still visible at the right.[13] In the far background we see the houses of the Zeedijk quarter, surmounted by the tower of the Old Church.

The right section of the Huis onder 't Zeil is hidden from our eyes by several buildings combining shops and residences built *op vlucht* (for flight), which is to say that they had deliberately been constructed with facades leaning slightly forward. At the very front we see part of a house built of bricks alternating with bands of natural stone, called De Engelsche Dog (The English Mastiff). According to its signboard and the inscription on the awning, it housed the office of a notary public. Next to it we see a much older type of house with a richly decorated wooden facade, in which the inn De Roode Leeuw (The Red Lion) was located. In the open door a man sells a woman some eggs, which he places in her apron. A bakery is located in the cellar (cellars were often rented out separately). Behind this house, painted in green, debouches an alley that used to be named Rooleeuwsteegje after the just-mentioned inn and that ran in an arc from the Rokin to the Dam. With the next house the building line jumps back about twenty-five feet, and we look at the side facade of a property housing a shoemaker's workplace and store. This is one of two houses built in 1612 at the initiative of the city in the style of Hendrick de Keyser on the corner of the Rokin and Dam.[14]

3
Jacob van Ruisdael
The Damrak in Amsterdam
Canvas, 46.8 x 43 cm (18 3/8 x 16 7/8 in.)
Lower left: *JvRuisdael* (ca. 1675)
The Hague, Mauritshuis, inv. no. 803

This facade creates a section of deep shadow in the entire right foreground, which receives additional emphasis due to the white horse just beyond, on which the full sun just happens to shine. The painter has here depicted a situation which, along general lines, corresponds to reality.

The Dam basks under a sparsely clouded sky in a late afternoon sun, which causes the small figures occupying the square to cast clear but not too heavy shadows on the pavement. It is a kind of light that has been used in our own century by artists who work in the style called photo-realism. Although the anonymous party who annotated the catalogue of the 1869 Bezborodko auction in French could have known little about photography and nothing about photo-realism, he too observed the unusual light: 'Overall greenish in tone and as if lit by an artificial light,' after which he further noted: 'Summing up, a beautiful painting. The figures are charming' (in translation).[15] Among the many figures on the Dam, of which some stand out due to the cheerful, orange color of their clothing, are a few distinguished men and women who walk or talk together. Other women carry baskets on their arms or on their heads. We see hawkers, vendors, fishwives, and beasts of burden. In the foreground a man attempts to separate four fighting dogs. At the left a man guides a horse pulling a heavily loaded sledge. Naturally the intriguing but unanswered question remains, Did Adriaen van de Velde, who until his death in 1672 painted the figures in the paintings of Jan van der Heyden, also supply the figures in this instance? Or did Jan van der Heyden render them himself, now that they made up such an important part of his whole composition? If Van de Velde did paint the figures, one may ask whether he also rendered the cast shadows or whether he left this to the 'inventor.'

As a view of the Dam this painting may be called unique because of the vantage point occupied by the painter. Nothing of the otherwise so obligatory buildings on the Dam, the new City Hall by Jacob van Campen, which was built between 1648 and 1665, the New Church, which was restored in its original Gothic style after the fire of 1645, and the Weighing House, built between 1563 and 1566 (and torn down in 1808 at the command of king Louis Napoleon (ruled Holland from 1806 to 1810; not to be confused with emperor Louis Napoleon), is to be seen. The only building that is completely visible is also the oldest one within the chosen composition, namely the inn De Roode Leeuw.

It appears, therefore, that the painter was less concerned with architecture than with the square, which he must have wanted to show as expansively as possible. In order to realize such a

4
Anonymous
The Cloth Market in Den Bosch
Panel, 126 x 67 cm (49⅝ x 26⅜ in.)
Neither signed nor dated (ca. 1500-1550)
Den Bosch, Noordbrabants Museum, inv. no. 1596

panorama, the painter must have chosen a vantage point that was higher than that of the pedestrian in the square. He therefore turned back to a type of cityscape that had long since passed its prime and that could pride itself on a long tradition.[16] An early sixteenth-century panel by an anonymous master (Den Bosch, Noordbrabants Museum) [4] shows us the Great Market of this city.[17] Here, too, the houses around the square only form a frame for the activities in the marketplace. The market here serves first and foremost as the setting for a biblical scene, which is depicted in the foreground. During the entire sixteenth century, depictions of squares and markets, which could be invented, were very popular as locations for historical events, such as scenes of combat or joyous entries.[18]

The painter of the *View of the Dam and the Damrak* must have been aware of this tradition. He invented very subtle variations on the theme. Instead of taking a traditional vantage point in the center front (from which the Weighing House would have been in the way), he opted for a position from the side. To be precise, we see the Dam from one of the windows of the second story of the new City Hall. Besides, there is no question of a true market or square scene. Nothing of consequence is taking place, and even the market is coming to an end. It is, after all, late in the day. Moreover, as we have already observed, the monumental buildings that usually dominate are left out and the square is portrayed from, as it were, the opposite direction.

The question still remains, Who was the painter, Gerrit Berckheyde or Jan van der Heyden? Of the latter, Houbraken wrote: 'for he painted every little brick of the buildings, both those that stood in the foreground, and those he showed at a distance, even so that one could see the lime between the courses; and in such a way that it was neither detrimental to the work nor caused any hardness, when one viewed the works with a general eye from some distance' (in translation).[19] We also encounter these working methods, which are indeed characteristic of Jan van der Heyden, in this painting. The fall of light and the ensuing shadows, which are long and clear but never too heavy, are also typical for Van der Heyden, who, in the words of Lyckle de Vries, shows us Amsterdam as 'a beautiful city at her Sunday's best,' without 'references to heavy, boring, or dangerous work, to noise, stench, or commotion' (in translation).[20]

The Dam must have had a special meaning for Van der Heyden. He was present when the old City Hall went up in flames and made drawings of it.[21] In 1699 he was privileged to demonstrate his fire engine in front of the new City Hall, to which, as a functionary in the service of the civic authorities, he must certainly have had free admission and in which he may even have had a small office.[22] Van der Heyden rendered the square from the most impossible angles. In a painting that he made in 1667 for the Grand Duke of Tuscany, he chose a position from which the facade of the City Hall receded so radically that he ran into trouble when he wanted to render the dome in perspective (Florence, Galleria degli Uffizi).[23] He later sent the Grand Duke a device, probably a lens, with which the error could be optically corrected.[24] In the *View of the Dam* (Amsterdam, Rijksmuseum) [5] he shows the corner between the City Hall and the New Church, with a tiny piece of the Weighing House.[25] Not one building is included in its entirety. As far as we know, he is also the only one who painted the Dam from the City

5
Jan van der Heyden
View of the Dam in Amsterdam with the City Hall, New Church, and Weighing House
Panel, 68 x 55 cm (26¾ x 21⅝ in.)
Right: *VHeyde* (ca. 1670)
Amsterdam, Rijksmuseum (long-term loan from the city of Amsterdam), inv. no. C 571

6
Claesz Jansz Visscher
Profile of Amsterdam with Description: The Fish Market (detail)
Engraving, etching, and letterpress, four sheets, together ca. 260 x 1,125 mm (10¼ x 44 in.)
Left sheet, lower left on the edge: *HA CJV 1611* (HA and CJV in ligature)
Rotterdam, Historisch Museum, Stichting Atlas van Stolk

Hall; Houbraken also seems to suggest this when he says: 'He has made diverse drawings of the Amsterdam City Hall, which he later painted, some seen from the Water, others again from the Kalverstraat, including the Weighing House and the New Church; further the bustling of the people on the Dam, as these usually teem together to carry on trade. But to this [end] he used the services of Adriaen van den Velde' (in translation).[26]

In this *View of the Dam and the Damrak*, Jan van der Heyden chose the oldest section of this square as his subject, where, as appears from prints of that time [**6**], the fish market gave Vitruvian expression to the prosperity of Amsterdam.[27] The fish market, and above all the sturdy, radiantly healthy fishwives, were in these years also a beloved subject of Van der Heyden's contemporary Emanuel de Witte.[28] The Dam itself was the stage for joyous entries, official funerals, uprisings, and popular festivities.[29]

The wooden house probably both fascinated Jan van der Heyden and filled him with concern. Fascinated because it is the most flexibly constructed facade that one can imagine; concern because, in view of the danger of fire to the surrounding buildings, including the new City Hall, the presence of a wooden facade was decidedly undesirable. Accordingly, the city authorities forbade the building of wooden facades in Amsterdam in 1669.[30] It is most tempting to date this *View of the Dam and the Damrak* around that year.

1 See *Watson 1963*, from whom all biographical data have also been taken; see also *Gabeau 1904* and *Levallet 1924*.

2 *Hasselgren 1988*, p. 144

3 *Recueil Choiseul 1771*, no. 116 (engraving by Lienard)

4 In *The Hague 1754*, p. 14, no. 146 and *Auction The Hague 1763*, p. 14, no. 146, however, there is mention of a panel, which could be a mistake (RKD); according to an annotation in *The Hague 1754*, p. 14, no. 146 (copy RKD), Lormier bought the painting for ƒ250, whereas, according to a notation in *The Hague 1763*, opp. p. 17, no. 147 (copy RKD), it was sold for ƒ400 to 'de heer Balden.'

5 *Auction Paris 1772*, pp. 25-26, no. 74, where it states: '791 fr., Boileau' (copy RKD).

6 *Auction Paris 1869*, no. 4, no. 2; the engraving is by Léon Gauchenel (RKD); the biographical data are taken from the introduction to *Auction Paris 1869*.

7 *Auction Paris 1905*, p. 4 (copy RKD); according to *Auction Paris 1905-A*, p. 4, no. 2 (copy RKD), the painting went to 'feral' for 11,800 francs.

8 *DAB*, vol. XIX (1936), pp. 412-413

9 *'t Hooft 1912*, fig. (2)

10 HdG 37 (vol. VIII [1927], p. 369, no. 37)

11 *Wagner 1971*, p. 116, no. 37; Cynthia Lawrence kindly allowed us to examine her manuscript.

12 *d'Ailly*, pp. 21-23

13 *Hoetink et al. 1985*, p. 436, no. 803 and fig.

14 *Wijnman et al. 1974*, pp. 88-89

15 *Auction Paris 1869*, p. 7, no. 4 (copy RKD)

16 For this material, see *Peeters / Fleurbaay 1989*

17 *Amsterdam / Toronto 1977*, p. 78 and fig. p. 79

18 *Peeters / Fleurbaay 1989*, pp. 34-36

19 *Houbraken 1718-1721*, vol. III, p. 80

20 *De Vries 1984*, p. 106

21 See the third print in the *Brandspuitenboek* of 1690; reproduced in *De Vries 1984*, p. 75, fig. 40

22 See the advertising print of this demonstration, made by J. van Vianen after J. van der Heyden, in *De Vries 1984*, p. 77, no. 41.

23 Inv. no. 1211; *Florence 1980*, p. 561, no. P 1773 and fig.

24 *Wagner 1971*, p. 67, no. 1 and fig. and *De Vries 1984*, pp. 60, 62 and p. 61, fig. 35

25 *Wagner 1971*, p. 67, no. 4 and fig. and *De Vries 1984*, p. 19 and p. 18, fig. 8

26 *Houbraken 1718-1721*, vol. III, p. 81

27 *Amsterdam / Toronto 1977*, p. 116 and fig. p. 117

28 See *Manke 1963*, pp. 53-54, 124-127 and fig.

29 *d'Ailly*, pp. 33-38

30 *Zantkuijl 1975*, section 8, p. 66

JR

Gorkum 1637 – Amsterdam 1712

Panel, 32.5 x 39 cm (12³/₄ x 15³/₈ in.)
To the right, on the boat: *IVH* (in ligature) (ca. 1670)
Norfolk, Va., collection Mr. and Mrs. George M. Kaufman

It is not known how long this painting by Jan van der Heyden had been in the collection of the dukes of Norfolk when, in 1880, the fifteenth duke (1847-1919) lent it to the exhibition at the Royal Academy in London as *A Landscape and Buildings*.[1] At the auction of this collection in London in 1938, B. de Geus van Heuvel (1886-1976) made the highest bid on the painting. The Amsterdam businessman retired around his fiftieth year and began to collect paintings because, as he himself put it, he was bored to death. *An 'Amsterdam' Canal* by Van der Heyden was one of the first acquisitions for his rapidly growing collection. After his death in 1976, he was praised as one of the last great Dutch collectors. As early as 1963 he asked H.S. Nienhuis of the auction house S.J. Mak van Waay to compile a catalogue of his collection, which he wanted auctioned in Amsterdam after his death: 'I have lived and worked here, therefore let as much as possible [of the collection] remain here' (in translation).[2] With respect to Van der Heyden's cityscape, this wish was not to be granted. At the De Geus van den Heuvel auction there was much interest in the painting, which had been appraised at 40,000 guilders and went for more than seven times that amount to the Swiss art dealer David Koetser.[3] After a spell in a private collection in West Berlin, it is presently the property of Mr. and Mrs. George M. Kaufman of Norfolk, Virginia. 'I wasn't making the first move on a new way of life; I was merely getting out of the rain,' Kaufman explained his first visit to an art dealer.[4]

The Dutch public has been able to enjoy the painting fairly often, for De Geus van Heuvel repeatedly parted with it for exhibitions. It is said that the collection in his country estate Rupelmonde, located on the River Vecht near Nieuwersluis, was never complete, because there were always some pieces out on loan. At the Christmas exposition of 1950-1951 in Schiedam, Rupelmonde paintings of all periods were on view, and, ten years later, in the Gemeentemuseum of Arnhem, a selection of the seventeenth-century masters could be seen.[5]

According to Helga Wagner, who in 1971 published a monograph on Van der Heyden, the majority of his Amsterdam cityscapes originated in a relatively short time span, namely between 1667 and 1672. The earliest date is 1667, on a *View of the Dam* (Florence, Galleria degli Uffizi).[6] This painting, which had been

Provenance
Collection dukes of Norfolk, London, before 1880
Auction Duke of Norfolk, London, 1938 (£1,050 to De Geus van den Heuvel)
Collection B. de Geus van den Heuvel, Amsterdam / Nieuwersluis, 1938-1976
Auction De Geus van den Heuvel, Amsterdam, 1976 (ƒ316,000 to Koetser)
Dealer D. Koetser, Zürich, 1976
Private collection, Berlin, 1976(?)-1984
Dealer Hoogsteder-Naumann, Ltd., New York, 1986
Collection Mr. and Mrs. Kaufman, Norfolk, Va., 1986

Bibliography
London 1880, p. 18, no. 76
HdG 305 (vol. VIII [1923], p. 445, no. 305)
Auction London 1938, p. 19, no. 99
Rotterdam 1938-1939, p. 8, no. 15 and fig. XXII
Delft 1952-1953, p. 20, no. 35
Rotterdam 1955, p. 40, no. 74 and fig. 144
Delft 1956, p. 39, no. 164
Laren 1958, p. 26. no. 102 and fig.
Arnhem 1960-1961, p. 15, no. 23 and fig. 69
Wagner 1971, pp. 83 and 87-88, no. 91, p. 146 and fig.
Auction Amsterdam 1976, pp. 24-25, no. 23 and fig.
Nienhuis 1976, vol. I. p. 25, no. 23, vol. II, fig. 23
WCA, vol. XXVIII (1976), p. 143
Kelch / Becker 1984, pp. 54-55, no. 24 and fig.

provided with figures by Adriaen van de Velde, was bought in 1669 by Cosimo de' Medici, Grand Duke of Tuscany. A few years later, Cosimo's secretary commissioned an Amsterdam agent to look for a comparable painting by Van der Heyden, provided this work was furnished with figures.[7] Nothing came of this because, after 1672, the painter applied himself exclusively to his inventions and because, in that same year, his collaborator Van de Velde died.

From the description of the estate of Van der Heyden's widow, one can deduce that a painting without figures was deemed to be incomplete.[8] According to the biographer Houbraken, the painter had primarily made use of the services of Adriaen van de Velde,[9] but occasionally Jan van der Heyden painted the figures himself, or else he had Johannes Lingelbach do them. There are numerous examples from 1668 and 1669 of figures that can indeed be attributed to Van de Velde, and in old inventories mention is almost automatically – perhaps too automatically – made of his contribution.[10] In the Kaufman cityscape the staffage is rather modest and consists of a man with a long, dark coat at the left, who looks in the direction of two women who are cleaning dishes at the waterside, and, farther away, pedestrians on the bridge. According to Wagner, these figures are definitely by Van de Velde, which would mean that the painting should be dated before 1672, the year of Adriaen's death.

Not merely the staffage but also the whole composition of the work appears to have clear correspondences with the *View of the Oudezijds Voorburgwal in Amsterdam* (The Hague, Mauritshuis) [**1**], painted around 1670.[11] Identical are the low viewpoint from the opposite side of a canal and the perspectival recession of the row of houses behind the treetops to a vanishing point at the right. The bridge that provides depth and the church that lends monumentality to the whole were painted from the same spot. From a topographical study for the Mauritshuis painting (Amsterdam, Koninklijk Oudheidkundig Genootschap) [**2**][12] we may deduce that Van der Heyden drew the Oudezijds Voorburgwal on the spot. In view of such major similarities between the two paintings, it is all the more striking that there remains one important difference, namely that the view in the work at The Hague is (virtually) topographically correct, whereas that in the Kaufman collection turns out to be entirely imaginary.

Any attempt to identify this 'Amsterdam' cityscape were doomed to be fruitless. Wagner pointed out that this work depicts a pastiche of motifs. The bridge looks like those over the Heren- and Keizersgracht (with five arches), and, according to her, the houses at the left correspond to house numbers 180 and up of the Keizersgracht. In fact, however, we have here imaginary architecture, with facades that at most resemble those of the first half of the seventeenth century by Hendrick de Keyser. In reality, these houses would be uninhabitable. The placement of the windows and doors is highly improbable, and the indispensable hoisting hooks are missing. The third house from the left has a church window (such as those of the Westerkerk) high up in the facade, and a bell cage on the roof![13] More than anything else, it is striking that behind the row of houses there rises a church tower with pointed Gothic arches that has no place in the Amsterdam townscape, but that does look like the curiously blunt tower of the Great Church of Veere.[14]

1
Jan van der Heyden
View of the Oudezijds Voorburgwal in Amsterdam
Panel, 41.2 x 52.5 cm (16¼ x 20 ⅝ in.)
Lower left: *VHeiden* (ca. 1670)
The Hague, Mauritshuis, inv. no. 868

2
Jan van der Heyden
The Oudezijds Voorburgwal with the Old Church
Drawing (counter proof), 289 x 405 mm (11⅜ x 16 in.)
Neither signed nor dated (ca. 1670 or 1680-1690)
Amsterdam, Koninklijk Oudheidkundig
Genootschap, Atlas Amsterdam, Portfolio 14-B

Jan van der Heyden An 'Amsterdam' Canal (not in San Francisco)

This church shows up in at least five works by Van der Heyden, with the tower that, around 1500, saw only its lower section completed and capped with a small spire.[15] One of these views of Veere is in the Mauritshuis [3].[16] In this instance the church has been correctly represented, but, just as in the other versions of 'Veere,' the surroundings are invented. The manipulation of existing features is highly characteristic of Van der Heyden. He preferred to mix the old with the new and to place Gothic buildings between contemporary ones in a kind of confrontation. A handsome example of this juxtaposition is a cityscape in the Wellington Museum (London, Apsley House) [4].[17] In the left foreground we see a corner of the old City Hall of Amsterdam, which burned down in 1652, and in the distance the new City Hall that rose from its ashes. In 1838 Waagen was moved to tender transports by this kind of scene: 'One feels altogether transplanted to Holland' (in translation).[18] 'Just like real' is indeed the correct reaction to the cityscapes by Van der Heyden, which reproduced the atmosphere of Amsterdam rather than the city itself.

The picturesque combination of the old and the new in Amsterdam early on earned the city the immortal name of the 'Venice of the North.' Both cities appear to have exerted a great attraction on landscape painters and draftsmen who were looking for romantic spots. The Amsterdam cityscapes by Van der Heyden have often been compared to the Venetian *vedute* of Canaletto.[19] In the case of the latter painter, three kinds of cityscapes may be differentiated: the *vedute del naturale* (scenes after reality), the *vedute ideate* (imaginary views), and the *capriccio* (images composed from topographic features). In his review of Wagner's monograph, Haverkamp-Begemann labeled Van der Heyden as the pioneer of the latter type. He called him not only the forerunner of Canaletto but also the model for the Venetian artist and the true inventor of the *capriccio*, which had presumably not been made at an earlier date.[20] This is probably somewhat exaggerated, as Van der Heyden naturally also elaborated on a strong tradition. In the first half of the seventeenth century, there already existed a rich gamut of genres within that of architectural painting. These varied from purely imaginary views (Hendrick van Steenwijk) to depictions of reality (Pieter Saenredam), with the work of Jan van Goyen (see cat. no. 24), as it were, holding the center ground. Jan van der Heyden married fact and fiction much as, among others, Gerrit Berckheyde did, but he did so entirely in his own way.

What is fascinating about Van der Heyden's work is that in his case, as with none of his predecessors, one is inclined to assume

3
Jan van der Heyden
The Great Church in Veere
Canvas, 31.5 x 36 cm (12⅜ x 14⅛ in.)
Lower right: *J. V. DH.* (ca. 1672)
The Hague, Mauritshuis, inv. no. 815

4
Jan van der Heyden
An 'Amsterdam' Cityscape
Panel, 48 x 58 cm (18⅞ x 22⅞ in.)
Lower center: *VHeyde f*, traces of a date (ca. 1670)
London, Wellington Museum, inv. no. 1500

that his precious way of painting must reflect topographic exactitude. This is precisely what gives his illusionism its great impact. By depicting the tower of Veere on an Amsterdam canal, he consciously strove for an alienating effect, one that his contemporaries must have recognized as an anachronism. This is surrealism *avant la lettre*.

1 *London 1880*, p. 18, no. 76
2 *Nienhuis 1976*, p. 5
3 According to handwritten annotations and newspaper clippings in the copy of *Auction Amsterdam 1976* (RKD).
4 *Art & Antiques 1987*, p. 58
5 *Arnhem 1960-1961*
6 Inv. no. 1211; HdG 12; *Wagner 1971*, p. 67, no. 1 and fig.
7 *Wagner 1971*, pp. 17-18
8 *Bredius 1912*, pp. 136, note 2 and p. 137
9 *Houbraken 1718-1721*, vol. III, p. 81
10 *Wagner 1971*, p. 34, note 80 and *Van Eeghen 1973*, p. 130
11 HdG 25; *Wagner 1971*, p. 68, no. 6; *Broos 1987*, pp. 203-207, no. 35
12 *Broos 1987*, pp. 206-207, fig. 3
13 *Wagner 1971*, p. 128, figs. 9 and 11; I thank Boudewijn Bakker for his analysis of the architectural style of the houses.
14 *Wagner 1971*, p. 87, no. 91
15 *Wagner 1971*, pp. 82-83, nos. 72-76 and fig.
16 HdG 189; *Wagner 1971*, p. 83, no. 75; *Hoetink et al. 1985*, p. 376, no. 815 and fig.
17 HdG 207; *Wagner 1971*, p. 85, no. 79 and fig.; *Kauffmann 1982*, pp. 71-72, no. 70 and fig.
18 *Waagen 1837-1839*, vol. II, p. 112
19 *Wagner 1971*, pp. 41-43
20 *Haverkamp-Begemann 1973*, p. 402

BB

Amsterdam 1638 – Amsterdam 1709

Canvas, 102.2 x 134.6 cm (40¼ x 53 in.)
Lower right: *m. hobbema*. (ca. 1668)
Minneapolis, Minn., The Minneapolis Institute of Arts, inv. no. 41.2

As an orphan Meindert Hobbema apprenticed himself to Jacob van Ruisdael, whose compositional schemes and motifs he sometimes followed very closely, especially in the landscapes done until around 1662. Ruisdael served as witness at Hobbema's wedding in 1668. Shortly thereafter Hobbema became gauger of the wine buyer's guild of Amsterdam, and his production subsequently decreased. However, he did not stop working, as has sometimes been assumed. Even though Hobbema's landscapes are at first less varied than those of his teacher, they still excel by their playfulness and clarity of tone. The compositions of his later works are much less cliché-ridden, as, for instance, his surprising *Lane at Middelharnis* (London, National Gallery) of 1689 shows. Characteristic of most of his works is the brightly lit background, against which several trees are sharply silhouetted.

Joseph Farington (1747-1821) had more talent as a chronicler than as a painter. He therefore owes his fame primarily to the diaries that he kept between 1793 and 1821, which are a gold mine of information concerning the art trade and artists of that period.[1] On Friday, 5 May 1809 he visited the vintner and collector Charles Offley, who just happened to be varnishing paintings for their pending sale at the Phillips auction house in Bond Street, London. One of the pieces he was working on was 'a fine Hobbima,' undoubtedly the painting called *The Water Mills of Singraven near Denekamp*, which is now in Minneapolis.[2] Four days later Farington discussed a possible purchase of this Hobbema with Sir George Beaumont, who thought, however, that 'it had been rubbed very much, but had been, he believed, a fine picture.'[3] At the Offley auction on 12 May 1809, 280 guineas were offered for the painting and, for the sake of appearances, the bidding continued to 462 guineas because the reserve was not met. Farington wrote: 'Elwin & another person were the persons employed by Phi[l]lips to buy in the pictures which were marked not to go below a certain price.'[4] Apparently the unknown accomplice was Michael Zachary, to whom the painting was after all officially sold. As we shall see, he later owned the painting for some time.[5] It is clear from the diary that the buyers

Provenance

Auction Caauw, Leyden, 1768 (*f*300 to Van Spijk)
Collection Paulus van Spijk, Leyden, 1768-1781
Auction Van Spijk, Leyden, 1781 (*f*580)
Collection Crawford, Rotterdam / London, before 1806
Auction Crawford, London, 1806 (£210 to Barnet)
Collection Charles Offley, London, 1809
Auction Offley, London, 1809 (£462 to Zachary, bought in)
Dealer Eycoot, London
Collection Michael Zachary, London, before 1828-after 1835 (bought from Eycoot)
Auction Zachary, London, 1828 (bought back for £1,500)
(?) Collection James Baron de Rothschild, before 1868
Collection Betty Baroness de Rothschild, Paris, before 1886
Collection Alphonse Baron de Rothschild, Paris, 1886-1905
Collection Leonora Baroness de Rothschild, Paris, 1905-1911
Collection Gustave Baron de Rothschild, Paris, 1911
Collection Zoe Lucie Betty Baroness Lambert, born Baroness de Rothschild, Brussels, 1911-1916
Collection heirs of Baroness Lambert, Brussels and New York, 1916-1941
Auction Schaeffer et al., New York, 1941 ($13,500 to Finakos Inc.)
Dealer Knoedler & Co., 1941
The Minneapolis Institute of Arts, Minneapolis, 1941 (The William Hood Dunwoody Fund)

Bibliography

Hoet 1752-1770, vol. III, pp. 667-668, no. 15
Auction Leyden 1768, p. 6, no. 15
Auction Leyden 1781, p. 17, no. 41
Auction London 1806, p. 4, no. 7
Auction London 1809, p. 9, no. 59
Buchanan 1824, vol. II, p. 182, no. 7
Auction London 1828, p. 17, no. 58
Smith 1829-1842, vol. VI, pp. 123-124, no. 31
Michel 1890, p. 48
Bode 1906, pp. 147 and 149
HdG 98 (vol. IV [1911], p. 403, no. 92 and p. 405, no. 98)
Graves 1913-1915, vol. II, p. 30, no. 58 (1828)
Farington 1922-1928, vol. V, pp. 157, 159 and note
Martin 1936, p. 516, note 427
Auction New York 1941, pp. 18-19, no. 35 and fig.
Art Quarterly 1942, pp. 344-347 and fig.
McCall / Barnouw 1942, pp. 46-47, 120, 765, no. 28 and fig.
Boston 1945, p. 10
Dayton 1948, no. 6 and fig.
Myers 1955, pp. 231-232, no. 95 and fig.
Minneapolis 1955, p. 5, no. 9
New York / Palm Beach 1957, n.p. and fig.
Minneapolis 1963, n.p. and fig., *sub voce*
Minneapolis 1970-A, pp. 104-105, no. 53 and fig.
Cave 1978-1984, vol. IX, pp. 3347-3462
Keyes 1983, pp. 199-200, fig. 8
Miami 1984, pp. 114-115, no. 55 and fig.
Sutton 1986, pp. 157-158 and fig. 227

Meindert Hobbema The Water Mills of Singraven near Denekamp

had reason for suspicion. Farington noted that Offley came to tell him on 20 May that he had tried to remove the painted-in sky of the Hobbema, 'which Walker the picture cleaner put upon it, & which was the objection urged against it at the sale.'[6] One does not often get such an intimate glance behind the scenes of the art trade.

The landscape by Hobbema, like so many old masters, wandered through diverse Dutch, English, and French collections before it finally arrived in America. The very first mention of the painting dates from 1768, when it was auctioned from the estate of the former councillor and ex-burgomaster of the city of Leyden, Pieter Caauw.[7] Paulus van Spijk (1727-1779), a Leyden beer brewer, bought it for 300 guilders. Early in the 1770's this brewer, a member of the poetry society Kunst Wordt Door Arbeid Verkregen (Art Is Achieved Through Labor), had himself portrayed as an art collector by Johannes Janson (Leyden, private collection) [1].[8] In 1781, one and a half years after his death, Van Spijk's collection was sold in public: for 580 guilders an unknown party came into the possession of the landscape by Hobbema.[9] In a short span of time ending with this sale, several important Leyden collections had been dispersed, those of Pieter Caauw (1768), Jan Palthe (1770), Pieter de la Court (1772), Johan van der Marck (see cat. no. 14), and that of Paulus van Spijk.[10] In 1806 we reencounter the painting by Hobbema in London, at the same auction at which *The Doctor's Visit* by Jan Steen was offered for sale (cat. no. 60). The collector was named as a 'Mr. Crawford of Rotterdam,' who, during his business sojourn in Holland, had gathered more than thirty, primarily seventeenth-century, masterpieces.[11]

1
Johannes Janson
Portrait of the Leyden Art Collector Paulus van Spijk (1727-1779) and His Wife
Panel, 76.5 x 56 cm (30⅛ x 22 in.)
Neither signed nor dated (ca. 1770-1775)
Leyden, private collection

After its false success at the Offley auction, the Hobbema ended up in the 'Gallery of Mr. Eycoot,' who sold it to Michael Zachary 'of the Adelphi Terrace,' who had apparently turned to dealing in paintings himself.[12] In 1828 Zachary had his entire collection auctioned at Phillips's as well, where the highest praises were sung about the qualities of 'The Water Mill': 'for beauty of composition, faithful delineation of nature, and elaborate finish, it cannot be surpassed.'[13] But even so, it appears no buyer was found, as Zachary bought the painting back for 1,500 guineas. In 1835 John Smith was able to report that it was still in the Zachary collection.[14]

In 1911 Hofstede de Groot took over the information in Smith's catalogue verbatim without realizing he was actually describing the same painting that he knew to be in the collection of Alphonse de Rothschild in Paris. This mistake has never before been noted.[15] A pair of casual references appears to be of importance for the reconstruction of the history of the Hobbema while it was owned by the Rothschild family. First, the connoisseur Emile Michel spotted the painting in 1890 with Alphonse Baron de Rothschild in Paris, at which time he learned that it had previously belonged to Baroness James de Rothschild.[16] Michel was the very first to recognize that the water mill is the same one as is featured in the much more often described painting in the Louvre (Paris) [2].[17] Secondly, Wilhelm von Bode divulged in 1906 that the owner had in the meantime become Baroness Alphonse de Rothschild.[18] The German scholar proposed in turn that the water mills are to be seen in many more paintings by Hobbema, such as in the version in the National Gallery, London [3].[19]

From all this we may conclude the following. James de Rothschild (1792-1868), the founder of the Parisian branch of the famous firm of bankers, had been married since 1824 to his thirteen-year-younger cousin Betty von Rothschild (1805-1886) of the Viennese branch, who survived him by twenty years.[20] Thus at some time either James or Betty bought *The Water Mills of Singraven near Denekamp* by Meindert Hobbema, now in Minneapolis. In 1890 it was found that her son Alphonse (1827-1905), who was married to Leonora de Rothschild (1837-1911) of the London branch, had inherited the painting. Leonora was Alphonse's widow in 1906, when Bode saw the painting, perhaps at her residence. Leonora died in January of 1911, after which time her brother-in-law Gustave de Rothschild (1829-1911) may have become the owner. If so, it can only have been for a short while, for he died in the fall of that year. Thus the landscape went to his daughter Zoe Lucie Betty de Rothschild (1863-1916) in Brussels. She had been married since 1882 to Baron Léon Lambert (1851-1919), the Brussels branch manager of the banking houses of Rothschild in Paris, London, Vienna, and Frankfurt.[21] When, by order of the heirs of Baroness Lambert, the painting was auctioned in New York in 1941, the collection of Gustave de Rothschild was given as its provenance. Naturally he was remembered as the link between the two families and presumably not really as the owner of the painting, which he had been for no more than half a year in 1911.[22] The last mentioned auction took place in May of 1941, and, by way of Knoedler's, the painting was sold two months later to the museum in Minneapolis.[23]

In his pending publication on the painting, George Keyes, curator at the museum, notes with amazement that 'the picture was not cited by Broulhiet in his monograph on Hobbema and has been overlooked in specialized literature on Dutch landscape painting ever since.'[24] That is entirely correct, although naturally its stay until 1941 with the Rothschilds must have contributed to this. It is generally true that, with the exception of a few high points, Hobbema's oeuvre remains little known. Thus, in 1980, the Mauritshuis was able to make a surprisingly advantageous purchase with the acquisition of a virtually unknown masterwork, *Half-Timber Houses beneath Trees*, which, furthermore, turned out to be in outstanding condition.[25] This acquisition made up for the loss of the painting *The Water Mills of Singraven near Denekamp* (Ottawa, National Gallery of Canada) [4],[26] which Queen Juliana gave to the Canadian people in 1950 in appreciation of the support and hospitality they extended to Holland during World War II. It had been purchased for the Mauritshuis

in 1913 by the Rembrandt Society from the famous Steengracht collection (see pp. 70-72). Although it is not nearly as well preserved as the current Hobbema in the Mauritshuis, the doubts recently expressed in Ottawa as to the authenticity of the painting are not justified.[27]

The topographical motif shown in the paintings in Minneapolis and Ottawa is the same as that of versions in London and Paris, but that fact appears to be unknown or almost unknown in connection with the former two works.[28] Here we see the water mills of Singraven, a country residence near Denekamp, in the province of Overijssel. From 1652 on, Gerhard Sloet, land agent of Twente, Diepenheim, and Haaksbergen, had Singraven drastically renovated and therefore needed a sawmill. For some time, an oil mill had been located near the house, on the left bank of the Dinkel, and a grain mill on the right bank. These mills were an important source of income for Singraven. In addition Sloet had a sawmill built on the Omdinkel. It was torn down in the early eighteenth century, while brick versions of the grain and oil mills were erected that still stand today.[29] In a drawing of 1729 by the amateur Andries Schoemaker, only the two remaining mills are to be seen (Zwolle, Rijksarchief in Overijssel) [5].[30] In 1934 this drawing was a great help to the archaeologists Döhmann and Dingeldein in the task of identifying the site in the paintings in London and Paris [6].[31]

These researchers spoke of an 'almost photographic correctness' pursued by Hobbema,[32] but that was naturally not the case. After all, the paintings were made in the studio, and liberties were taken in the process. In the scene in Minneapolis the temporary sawmill is the central subject. Behind it to the left lies

2
Meindert Hobbema
The Water Mills of Singraven near Denekamp
Canvas, 80 x 66 cm (31½ x 26 in.)
Lower right, on the gate: *m. hobbema* (ca. 1668)
Paris, Musée du Louvre, inv. no. M.I. 270

3
Meindert Hobbema
The Water Mills of Singraven near Denekamp
Panel, 60 x 84.5 cm (23⅝ x 33¼ in.)
Lower right: *m. hobbema* (ca. 1668)
London, National Gallery, inv. no. 832

4
Meindert Hobbema
The Water Mills of Singraven near Denekamp
Canvas, 90.1 x 128.3 cm (35½ x 50½ in.)
Lower right: *m. hobbema* (ca. 1668)
Ottawa, National Gallery of Canada, no inv. no.

the oil mill with the house of the oil-crusher half-way in front of it. In the version in Ottawa, Hobbema omitted this latter small building [4]. He added a house in the London variant [3], probably sticking to the facts only in the version in Paris [2]. It is possible to ascertain that he always had the overall disposition of the land and the existing buildings in mind, and that he therefore must have had a good visual memory or have worked after drawings (which have not come down to us). But it is improbable that, looking from all directions of the compass, he would again and again have had a great tree in the middle of his view. This is a theatrical intervention, thought up in the atelier, as well as being a motif that he borrowed from Ruisdael.[33]

Nor is it the case that the great open spaces between the trees were due to the chopping done by Gerhard Sloet. Hobbema liked to create vistas in his forests. This may be seen in the *Forest Prospect with a Pool* (Oberlin, Ohio, Allen Memorial Art Museum) of 1668,[34] which is once again dominated by a gnarled woodland giant. The same goes for a *Forest Landscape with Travelers*, also dated 1668 (Buckingham Palace, collection Her Majesty the Queen).[35] These related compositions indicate that *The Water Mills of Singraven near Denekamp* in Minneapolis was painted around 1668.

Finally, the consultation of old auction catalogues has its uses beyond establishing the provenance of a painting. For instance,

5
Andries Schoemaker
The Water Mills of Singraven near Denekamp
Pen and wash drawing, 124 x 200 mm (4⁷⁄₈ x 7⁷⁄₈ in.)
Lower left: AS; lower right: *Anno 1729*
Zwolle, Rijksarchief in de Provincie Overijssel, inv. no. O.R.G. 862-863

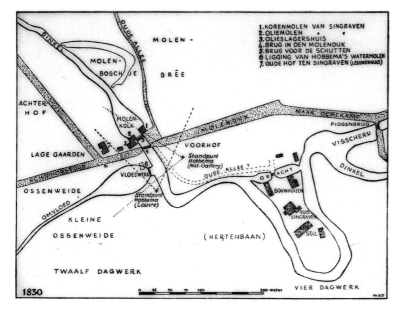

6
W.H. Dingeldein
Surroundings of the Water Mills and House Singraven
Site plan from: *Dingeldein / Döhmann 1934*, vol. III,
fig. p. 139

at two Leyden auctions of 1768 and 1781 it was mentioned that the cattle in this painting were added by 'D[irck] van [den] Berg[en].'[36] At the auctions in London, this name was corrupted to that of the more familiar Nicolaes Berchem.[37] Subsequently both Philips Wouwermans and Johannes Lingelbach have been incorrectly identified as the painters of the staffage.[38] It would appear that the specialized painter of cows, Dirck van den Bergen, was indeed responsible for the flock of sheep and for the herd of cows, which is being driven by a farmer. No doubt he also painted the hunter with the bright red coat in the center.[39]

1 *Cave 1978-1984*; the diaries are the property of Her Majesty the Queen (Windsor Castle); I thank George Keyes (The Minneapolis Institute of Arts) for allowing me to examine his manuscript on the Hobbema, which employs Farington's diaries.
2 *Farington 1922-1928*, vol. I, p. 8: Farington had been friends with Offley since 1793; *Cave 1978-1984*, p. 3447
3 *Farington 1922-1928*, vol. V, p. 157; *Cave 1978-1984*, p. 3452
4 *Cave 1978-1984*, p. 3454: 'The real bidding for the Hobbima was 280 guineas.'
5 *Auction London 1809*, p. 9, no. 59 (annotated copy RKD).
6 *Cave 1978-1984*, p. 3462
7 *Auction Leyden 1768*, p. 6, no. 15
8 *Staring 1953*, fig. opp. p. 114; *Pelinck 1953*, pp. 120-121; *Fock 1976*, p. 122, fig. 8 and p. 128
9 *Auction Leyden 1781*, p. 17, no. 41
10 *Bille 1961*, vol. I, p. 115
11 Cat. no. 60, note 3
12 *Auction London 1828*, title page
13 Ibidem, p. 17, no. 58
14 *Smith 1829-1842*, vol. VI (1835), p. 124, no. 31; in 1834 Zachary bought an Ochtervelt at the Berry auction, see *Whitley 1973*, vol. II, p. 273.
15 HdG 92 and 98
16 *Michel 1890*, p. 48
17 HdG 89; *Broulhiet 1938*, pp. 322 and 436, no. 441 and fig.; *Brejon de Lavergnée et al. 1979*, p. 70, no. M.I. 270 and fig.
18 *Bode 1906*, p. 147
19 HdG 76; *Broulhiet 1938*, pp. 212 and 406, no. 220 and fig.; *Maclaren 1960*, p. 169, no. 832
20 All the following information concerning the Rothschilds was taken from *Morton 1961*, which includes a complete genealogical tree.
21 BNB, vol. XLII, cols. 427-461
22 *Auction New York 1941*, p. 18, no. 35
23 See note 1; purchased with the William Hood Dunwoody Fund (see cat. no. 56).
24 See note 1
25 Inv. no. 1061; *Broos 1987*, pp. 208-211, no. 36 and fig.
26 *Martin 1936*, p. 312 and fig. 169
27 *Laskin / Pantazzi 1987*, pp. 134-135 and 158, fig. 157 and fig.; Frits Duparc communicated that the elaborate staffage in the foreground was rather roughly removed.
28 *Hagens 1979*, p. 86 and *Enschede 1980*, p. 62, instead claimed that Hobbema had depicted these mills in dozens of paintings (not allowing for nonautograph works).
29 *Hijszeler / Wassenbergh-Clarijs 1972 / 1984*, pp. 8-11 and 26; *Dingeldein 1969*, pp. 93-107; *Enschede 1980*, pp. 62 and 77, note 77
30 *Hagens 1979*, p. 88 and fig.
31 *Dingeldein / Döhmann 1934*, vol. III, pp. 137-140
32 *Dingeldein / Döhmann 1934*, vol. III, p. 141
33 In this context Keyes (see note 1) pointed to the influence of the etching by Ruisdael (B. 4), which Hobbema copied in paint in 1662 (*Slive / Hoetink 1981-1982*, fig. 108).
34 Inv. no. 44.52; HdG 218; *Oberlin 1967*, pp. 74-75 and 256 and fig. 69
35 Inv. no. 680; HdG 78; *White 1982*, p. 50, no. 67 and fig. 55
36 *Auction Leyden 1768*, p. 6, no. 15 and *Auction Leyden 1781*, p. 17, no. 41
37 *Auction London 1809*, title page: 'a matchless *Landscape* by Hobbima, with *Figures and Cattle* by BERCHEM.'
38 *Michel 1890*, p. 48; *Art Quarterly 1942*, p. 345
39 *Martin 1936*, p. 516, note 427
BB

Utrecht 1590 – Utrecht 1656

Canvas, 81.2 x 64.3 cm (32 x 25⅜ in.)
Upper left: *G. Honthorst fesit 1625*; on the medallion: *Wie kent mijn naers / Van afteren*
Saint Louis, Mo., The Saint Louis Art Museum, inv. no. 63.1954

Born in Utrecht on 4 November 1590, Gerard van Honthorst first trained with the Utrecht history painter Abraham Bloemaert before traveling to Italy. By the middle of the second decade of the century he had established his reputation in Rome. There, because he painted many nocturnal scenes, he became known as 'Gherardo della Notte.' Honthorst worked for the Marchese Vincenzo Giustiniani, the prominent collector-amateur and patron of Caravaggio. While enjoying the support of leading private collectors, Honthorst also received the official patronage of the Counter-Reformation Church.

The paintings of Caravaggio, both in their style and subject matter, greatly influenced Honthorst, as they did Hendrick ter Brugghen and Dirck van Baburen. Together these three artists, the most prominent exponents of the Dutch Caravaggesque style, became known as the Utrecht Caravaggisti. Their works, although differing from one to another in palette and technique, share stylistic elements which differentiate them from the French and Italian followers of Caravaggio.

Back in Utrecht by 1620, Honthorst married there in October and entered the guild in 1622. Having established himself in Utrecht, the artist attracted the attention of important patrons in Holland and abroad. Beginning in 1628, when called to work for Charles I of England, he carried out numerous commissions for European heads of state, including the Danish crown and the Stadholder in The Hague. He also worked on the decorations for the Oranjezaal at the Huis ten Bosch. The Caravaggesque manner, so pronounced on his return from Italy, was greatly tempered in this later phase as Honthorst adopted a stylistic vocabulary more suited to portraiture and to the stature of his patrons. This more formal style was derived in part from the courtly idiom of Van Dyck and the Dutch court portraitists, such as Michiel van Mierevelt.

Although Judson suggests that the Saint Louis painting is the work by Honthorst sold at the auction Gerard van Oostrum (and others), The Hague, in 1765,[1] the whereabouts of the *Young Woman Holding a Medallion* cannot be verified until it appeared in the twentieth century. Notes regarding the collection of W.J.

Provenance
(?) Auction Van Oostrum et al., The Hague, 1765
Collection Scott, London
Collection Charles Roots, Hereford, by 1922
Collection W.J. Davies, Hereford, 1922
Collection Mrs. Greville Phillips, Friar House, Hereford, by 1929
Dealer Adolph Loewi, Los Angeles, by 1954
The Saint Louis Art Museum, 1954 (purchase, Friends Fund)

Bibliography
London 1929, p. 170, no. 363
London 1929-A, p. 60, no. 363
New York 1958, p. 9, no. 11 and fig.
Judson 1959, pp. 221-222, no. 149
Maclaren 1960, pp. 438-439
Braun 1966, pp. 98-99, no. 61 and pp. 198-200
Slive 1970-1974, vol. I, p. 93 and fig. 83
De Jongh 1975, p. 586
Nicolson 1979, p. 61 and pl. 146
Burke 1980, p. 17 and fig.
Connaissance des arts 1984, p. 30 and fig.
Apollo 1985, p. 393 and pl. VI
Foucart 1985, pp. 62-63
Antiques 1986, p. 380 and fig.
Sutton 1986, p. 264, fig. 397 and pl. 4
Auction London 1989, p. 136

1
Detail of cat. no. 33

Gerard van Honthorst Young Woman Holding a Medallion

Davies from the personal papers of the London dealer Frank Simpson, dating from the period of about 1922 to 1929, give a provenance for the painting that reappears in Judson's monograph of 1959.[2] The painting, owned jointly by Colnaghi and Scott, was inherited by Mr. Scott's widow, who in turn left the painting to a Mr. Charles Roots of Hereford. On the death of Mr. Roots, the executors of his estate sold the Honthorst in 1922.[3] The painting was bought by Mr. W.J. Davies, also of Hereford. Several works from the Davies collection were exhibited in 1912.[4] However, based on descriptions of the paintings given in the catalogue when the collection was sold in 1948, it may be surmised that, except for the Honthorst, this collection was undistinguished.

From the annotated sales catalogues of Sir Ellis Waterhouse, we learn that a number of the paintings from the Davies collection were inherited by Mrs. Greville Phillips of Friar's House, Hereford.[5] Although not mentioned in the family sales, the Honthorst must also have followed this path. Upon the death of Mr. Davies his collection of pictures was sold by the executor of his estate, Mrs. Greville Phillips, at Robinson & Foster's, London, on 6 May 1948. One week later, on 13 May, approximately forty paintings, 'the property of Mrs. Grevile [sic] Phillips and [...] removed from Friar's House, Hereford,' were sold at Christie's, London.[6] The Honthorst does not appear in either sale. However, by 1954 the painting was in Los Angeles with the dealer Adolph Loewi, from whom it was purchased that year by The Saint Louis Art Museum.

The *Young Woman Holding a Medallion*, signed and dated 1625, comes from Honthorst's first years after returning from Italy. This is a work of immediate appeal, as the vivacious, fulsome young woman confronts us good-naturedly, pointing to the motto on the medallion she holds. In translation it reads: 'Who knows my ass / from the rear' [1].[7] Our smiling friend must surely be a courtesan. This is confirmed by the appearance of the same model, wearing almost the identical costume, as a courtesan in *The Procuress* [2], also signed and dated 1625, in the Centraal Museum, Utrecht.[8]

Slive referred to the Saint Louis painting in conjunction with contemporary literary sources, such as the 1631 *Miroir des Plus belles Courtisanes de ce temps* by Crispijn de Passe [3] and Jean François Regnard's *Voyage en Flandre, en Hollande, en Danemark et en Suède* of 1681, in which the etiquette of Dutch brothels is discussed.[9] Both texts refer to the practice of displaying portraits of the 'ladies of the house' to help their clientele select a companion. Braun also cited the *Miroir*, suggesting parallels between

the Honthorst and one of De Passe's illustrations, in which a procuress holds a portrait of a courtesan [4].[10]

The gesture of the figure depicted on the medallion in the Saint Louis painting, peering through spread fingers at the viewer, also has pictorial precedents. The Fool makes the same

2
Gerard van Honthorst
The Procuress
Canvas, 71 x 104 cm (28 x 41 in.)
Upper right: *GHonthorst fecit 1625*
Utrecht, Centraal Museum, inv. no. 10786

3
Crispijn de Passe the Younger
Frontispiece from: *Miroir des Plus belles Courtisanes de ce temps*, 1631
Santa Monica, The Resource Collections of The Getty Center for the History of Art and the Humanities

4
Crispijn de Passe the Younger
Margo la Macrelle and *La belle* DANS
Engraving from: *Miroir des Plus belles Courtisanes de ce temps*, 1631
Santa Monica, The Resource Collections of The Getty Center for the History of Art and the Humanities

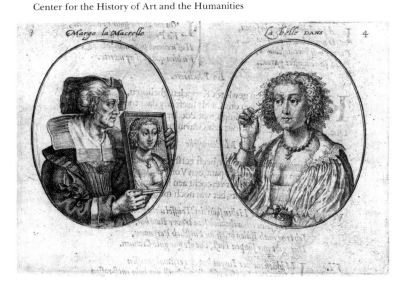

gesture in the illustration of *The Adulteress* [**5**] in Sebastian Brant's *Das Narrenschiff* (The Ship of Fools).[11] There the accompanying verse refers to the folly of the husband who pretends not to see the moral disarray of his household, as his wife defiles the sacrament of marriage.[12] These illustrations from contemporary sources give us the flavor of the message Honthorst wished to present. Similar popular literature might produce a single, closer pictorial source for Honthorst's *Young Woman Holding a Medallion*, and the source of its crude motto might also be found.

1 *Auction The Hague 1765*, no. 241: 'Een Laggende Vrouw met een naakt Pourtraitje in de Hand, waar onder een divisje staat' (A laughing woman holding a small picture of a nude in her hand, under which is a motto); cited by *Judson 1959*, p. 221. It should be noted that Judson also cites numerous copies.
2 Part of the Resource Collections of the Getty Provenance Index, The Getty Art History Information Program, Santa Monica, California. This information was culled from the archives by the Getty staff.
3 The Honthorst was illustrated in the advertisements of *The Burlington Magazine* in October 1922. The caption read: 'From an important Collection now being offered for sale by Private Treaty. 31 x 25. By Gerard Van Honthorst. Originally from the Coombe Abbey Collection.' The advertisement was placed by Wilbey Wilbery of 4 King Street, London. Although Mr. Simpson also notes: 'Purchased from Coombe Abbey by Colnaghi & Scott,' the Coombe Abbey provenance cannot be confirmed. The following information was also provided by the Getty staff: 'Coombe Abbey was the residence of the Earl of Craven. The Craven collection came primarily from the estate of Elizabeth of Bohemia and included many pictures by Honthorst, who worked for her and her husband from 1628 onwards. There is an excellent thesis on the collection by Willem-Jan Hoogsteder done for the Utrecht University (1984-1986), but he also failed to find a picture of this description in any of the inventories' (Ms. letter in curatorial file, The Saint Louis Art Museum).
4 *Graves 1913-1915*, vol. I, p. 33, no. 100 (1912), p. 1017, no. 53 (1912), p. 1323, no. 111 (1912)
5 *Auction London 1948-A*, p. 10 (Resource Collections of The Getty Center for the History of Art and the Humanities). The Honthorst was lent by Mrs. Greville Phillips to an exhibition of Dutch art at the Royal Academy in 1929; see *London 1929*, p. 170, no. 363 and *London 1929-A*, p. 60 no. 363.
6 *Auction London 1948-A*, p. 6
7 I use the translation in *Sutton 1986*, p. 264. The translation of *naers* as 'nose' suggested by *De Jongh 1975*, p. 586, seems unlikely.
8 *Blankert / Slatkes et al. 1986-1987-A*, pp. 297-298, no. 66 and fig. The same model and costume appear also in *An Allegory of Lust* by Honthorst recently on the art market (*Auction London 1989*, no. 73).
9 *Slive 1970-1974*, vol. I, pp. 91-93. On the depiction of Dutch brothels, see *Brown 1984*, pp. 182-184.
10 *Braun 1966*, pp. 98-99 and 199-200. The portrait of a young woman that the older 'Margo' holds is actually created by the reflection of 'La belle DANS,' who faces her, in a mirror.
11 *Brant 1494* is one of the most important German books of the fifteenth century; it was widely translated. The woodcut illustrations are by Dürer and other German printmakers.
12 *Braun 1966*, p. 98, note 2. Paraphrasing an English translation which appeared in 1570, the verse runs: 'A fool blind forsooth and witless is that man / which though his wife openly defiled be / Before his own face, yet such a craft he can, / to feign him asleep, not willing it to see / Or else he layeth his hand before his eye, / And though he hear and see how the matter goes / He snorting sleepth, and will it not disclose' (*Brant 1570*, p. 64 and fig.).
 LFO

5
Meister des Haintz Narr
The Adulteress
Woodcut from: Sebastian Brant, *Das Narrenschiff*, Basel 1494
Santa Monica, The Resource Collections of The Getty Center for the History of Art and the Humanities

Rotterdam 1629 – Amsterdam 1684

Canvas, 67.8 x 55.6 cm (26⅝ x 21⅞ in.)
On the footwarmer (barely visible): *P. d Hooch* (ca. 1658-1660)
San Francisco, Calif., The Fine Arts Museums of San Francisco, inv. no. 61.44.37

According to the biographer Houbraken, Pieter de Hooch (who after 1660 also spelled his name De Hoogh) was a pupil of Nicolaes Berchem in Haarlem. In 1654 he was married in Delft to the sister of the painter Pieter van der Burch. A year later he was mentioned for the first time as a painter, and he appears to have then entered the service of a cloth merchant who continually provided him with commissions. Perhaps as a consequence of this, we encounter from the very beginning autograph repetitions in his work of whole compositions or parts thereof. Since the nineteenth-century commentary by Théophile Thoré (who published under the pseudonym William Bürger), the oeuvre of De Hooch has been compared to that of Vermeer. The atmospheric effect and fall of light of his Delft interior pieces with mothers and children are often entrancing, but his figures are sometimes executed astonishingly weakly. In 1661 he appears to have moved to Amsterdam, where the prosperity of his clientele was reflected in the richer interiors he subsequently painted. One might imagine that his heart was not in the reproduction of this opulence. In the year in which he dated his last painting (1684), he died in an insane asylum.

From the catalogue raisonné of the work of 'Peter de Hooge' made in 1833 by the London dealer John Smith, it appears that he had seen the painting *A Mother with an Infant* in 1825 in Amsterdam in the 'Collection of M. van Loone.'[1] He mistakenly believed that it was the counterpart of *A Woman with a Rummer in a Garden*, also by Pieter de Hooch (Paris, collection of the heirs of Edmond Baron de Rothschild) [1].[2] However, this train of thought is quite understandable, for the paintings in the Van Loon collection used to be displayed in identical black frames.[3] The two De Hoochs had apparently been made to conform to the same format and hung next to each other. The Van Loon collection in Amsterdam was formed from the splendid collection of Pieter van Winter (1745-1807) (see cat. no. 6, fig. 1),

Provenance
Collection Pieter van Winter, Amsterdam, before 1807
Collection Anna Louisa Agatha van Loon-van Winter, Amsterdam, 1807-1877
Collection Gustave Baron de Rothschild, Paris, 1877-ca. 1900(?)
Collection Robert Brakespeare, Henley-on-Thames, Oxon (England), before 1916
Dealer Knoedler & Co., New York, 1916
Private collection, New York, 1925
Collection Katherine Mary Deere Butterworth, Moline, Ill., 1925(?)-1954
Auction Butterworth, New York, 1954 ($34,000)
Dealer Frederick Mont, New York, 1955
Samuel H. Kress Foundation, New York, 1955-1961
M.H. de Young Memorial Museum, San Francisco, 1961 (gift of the Samuel H. Kress Foundation)

Bibliography
Smith 1829-1842, vol. IV, pp. 232 and 318, no. 43
Thoré-Bürger 1858-1860, vol. I, p. 99
Havard 1879-1881, vol. III, pp. 91-92
Hofstede de Groot 1892, p. 186, no. 73
HdG 11 (vol. I [1907], p. 477, no. 11)
De Rudder 1914, p. 97
New York 1925, no. 6 and fig.
Brière-Misme 1927, pp. 70 and 72 and fig.
Valentiner 1927, p. 61 and fig. 6, p. 76, no. 15
Valentiner 1929, p. xviii, pp. 71 and 276 and fig.
Van Thienen 1945, pp. 40 and 46 and fig.
WCA, vols. V-VIII (1953-1956), pp. 414-415, no. 4030
Auction New York 1954, title page, pp. 26-27, no. 29 and fig.
Art News 1955, p. 14 and fig.
Neumeyer 1955, pp. 279 and 281 and fig. 5
Suida 1955, pp. 26-27 and fig. (and cover)
Emerson 1961, pp. 832 and 853 and fig.
Seymour et al. 1961, pp. 154-155 and 212 and fig.
Washington 1961-1962, no. 45
San Francisco 1966, p. 133 and fig.
Kansas City 1967-1968, pp. 11 and 22, no. 6 and fig.
London 1968, p. 153
Eisler 1977, p. 153, no. K 2120 and fig. 139
Durantini 1979 / 1983, pp. 27-28, 38 and fig. 11
Haverkamp-Begemann 1980, pp. 207-208 and pl. XVII, p. 211, note 20
Sutton 1980, pp. 21, 83-84, no. 32, p. 95, no. 61 and pls. VII and 30-31
Reitlinger 1982, vol. I, p. 344 (1954), vol. III, p. 201 (1954)
Berlin / London / Philadelphia 1984, pp. 194-195, no. 54 and fig., p. 365, no. 54, notes 1-6
Sutton 1986, pp. 276-277, fig. 415
Franits 1989, pp. IX, 211 and fig. 104

1
Pieter de Hooch
A Woman with a Rummer in a Garden
Canvas, 62 x 58 cm (24⅜ x 22⅞ in.)
At the left, on the window frame: *P. D hooch* (ca. 1658-1660)
Paris, collection of the heirs of Edmond Baron de Rothschild

a trader in indigo and a man of letters. Van Winter lived in Saxenburg House at 224 Keizersgracht (now part of the Pulitzer Hotel). Upon his death in 1807, his daughters Lucretia Johanna (Creejans) (1785-1847) and Anna Louisa Agatha (Annewies) van Winter (1793-1877) inherited his art collection, which they divided between them (see cat. no. 6).[4] Creejans married Jonkheer (a title roughly equivalent to Sir or Squire) Hendrik Six (1794-1847), and Annewies wed Jonkheer Willem van Loon (1790-1847). As a result of these alliances, a number of important works from the art collection that were inherited by the elder daughter were preserved for the Netherlands, but the remainder disappeared across the borders. By way of the Six collection, for instance, *The Street* by Vermeer has ended up in the Rijksmuseum.[5]

Jonkheer Willem van Loon lived at 499 Herengracht, in the renowned Golden Bend, where, in 1666, his grandfather Adriaen van Loon (1631-1722) had a residence built, one that his father Willem van Loon (1707-1783) renovated thoroughly from 1752 to 1753.[6] It was there that the paintings from Saxenburg House were moved and there that the English merchant John Smith saw them in 1825.[7] Precisely fifty years later, in 1875, Lord Ronald Gower described the handsome collection of the eighty-two-year-old dowager Van Loon. Gower got to see only one room and noted down several facts that point to the makings of legend. According to the old lady, the paintings had been commissioned by the founder of the collection (Van Winter), had never been removed from the walls, and, further, had never been in the hands of incompetent restorers: in short, they were ostensibly all authentic and of excellent quality.[8]

Willem van Loon had died in 1847 and the dowager in 1877. Her ten children hastily disposed of the paintings. Apparently the cash portion of the inheritance had not amounted to much. Gustave Baron de Rothschild of Paris offered the heirs one and one half million guilders for the lion's share of the collection. 'The brothers and sisters are ecstatic,' a family member wrote later (in translation).[9] Thus, among other works, Rembrandt's *Portraits of Maerten Soolmans and Oopjen Coppit* (cat. no. 51, figs. 3-4) were lost to the Netherlands. It was only in 1883 that the Rembrandt Society was founded with the purpose of preventing such bleeding away of the Dutch national heritage (see p. 62).[10]

Rumors circulated that the Rothschilds intended to divide the paintings among various branches of the family, with the Rembrandt portraits together forming a batch worth 360,000 guilders.[11] In 1881 Henry Havard encountered the paintings by Pieter de Hooch in the collection (or collections; how many there

were remains unclear) of the Rothschilds in Paris. He did not understand that these were the two 'pendants' that Smith had seen with Van Loon, even though he must have heard from the owner(s) at the time that the works had come from that collection.[12] The French branch of the family, which then consisted of the families of the sons of James de Rothschild (1792-1868) – Alphonse (1827-1905), Gustave (1829-1911) and Edmond (1845-1934) – lived in various residences in and around Paris.[13] In 1892 Hofstede de Groot expressed his astonishment over the fact that *A Mother with an Infant* was not in the collection that he got to see: 'I nonetheless did not see it at the home of Mr. Rothschild' (in translation).[14] Perhaps it had already been disposed of by then. Around 1900 the Rothschilds bought other works by De Hooch.[15] In any case, by 1916 the painting was in New York with the dealer Knoedler, and it was to remain in American hands from then on.[16]

It is astonishing to have to conclude that this entire previous history appears to have been forgotten. Sutton believed a provenance from the Van Loon legacy to be no more than a possibility and thought that the Rothschilds had acquired that collection around 1880.[17] Suida and Eisler started the story of the provenance only in this century, with Ronald Brakespeare, in Henley-on-Thames in Oxon (England).[18] He was the owner from whom the dealer Knoedler, according to his own information, had bought it in 1916.[19] In 1925 the painting was again exhibited by Knoedler as belonging to a private owner in New York.[20] It was included in an article of 1927 by Clothilde Brière-Misme, in which she discussed previously unpublished and little-known works by De Hooch.[21] Only in the fifties did the public life commence of the painting that Sutton recently called 'one of Pieter de Hooch's most beautiful interior genre scenes in the United States.'[22]

In 1954 it was auctioned in New York from the estate of Katherine Deere Butterworth for 34,000 dollars, which later turned out to be the highest price, in all categories, to be paid at Parke-Bernet in the 1954-1955 season.[23] Katherine Mary Deere Butterworth (187?-1954) was the daughter of Charles Henry Deere (1837-1907), president of Deere & Co. (inventors of the steel plow), and the wife of William Butterworth (1864-1936), who succeeded his father-in-law as president of the company in 1907.[24] Katherine and William had no offspring when he died in 1936, and upon her death, the collection was auctioned. It consisted primarily of English portraits of the eighteenth century and French impressionists, and included only a few Flemish and Dutch masters.[25]

Pieter de Hooch A Mother with an Infant

The Kress Foundation became the new owner of the canvas by De Hooch. After Samuel H. Kress had donated his collection to the National Gallery in Washington in 1939, the Kress Foundation was founded with the aim of collecting for the benefit of the National Gallery and a series of American museums from Miami to Honolulu.[26] The director of the M.H. de Young Memorial Museum in San Francisco, Walter Heil, was an old friend of Samuel Kress. De Hooch's painting *A Mother with an Infant* was Heil's personal favorite, because for him it perfectly represented the Dutch Golden Century.[27] The Kress Foundation bought the painting for Heil, exhibited it in San Francisco in 1955, and finally donated it to the museum in 1961, along with a total of thirty-nine Kress paintings, which were then put on view in a specially built wing.[28]

A cleaning of the painting around 1960 removed a small branch on the bird cage and a handle on the jug on the cupboard at the right, which had appeared in all reproductions up to 1955. At the same time the signature *P. d Hooch* again became somewhat legible.[29] For a long time people spoke about the painting in lyrical terms such as 'the sensitive handling of effects of light in which De Hooch was second only to his one-time rival in Delft, Vermeer.'[30] Ever since Bode wrote in 1911, the theme of De Hooch and Vermeer as competitors has remained popular.[31] It was Blankert who formulated most clearly how, between 1658 and 1660, Vermeer refined the examples set by De Hooch.[32] On the content of De Hooch's paintings, however, the commentators rarely had anything to say.

For instance, very few observed that in perfecting the work of De Hooch, Vermeer invariably omitted the children from his quieted compositions. Moreover, Vermeer concentrated on a single figure, a man or a woman. His women are never engaged in daily tasks but read or write (love) letters (see cat. nos. 42 and 67), or make music. With De Hooch the children are instead a fixed part of the scene, and the mothers do domestic work, as can be seen in *A Woman Peeling Apples* (London, Wallace

Collection) [2],[33] a somewhat simplified version of the painting in San Francisco. In this approach, De Hooch did not look forward but back. It was Sutton who, in 1980, pointed emphatically to the fact that such subjects originated in the oeuvre of Nicolaes Maes, for instance in the compositionally related painting *The Seamstress* (London, Wallace Collection) [3].[34] In and around 1655 Maes painted a whole series of housewives at work, often accompanied by a child.[35] Sometimes these paintings have light erotic undertones (see cat. no. 41), but otherwise they usually appear to depict no more than 'The praise of the virtuous housewife,' who, thanks to Solomon's song in the Bible (Proverbs 31:10-31) has become proverbial. De Hooch appears to have taken this sentiment as his point of departure.

Durantini has recently indicated that there are significant messages hidden in many details of this depiction, namely erotic references to counter the symbols of virtue. The dog eating from the lap of the toddler (while looking at us roguishly) should presumably be viewed in the light of sexuality, which is also embodied by the cupid in the carving of the hearth. In the painting in the Wallace Collection [2], on the contrary, this same

cupid seems to be divested of any double meaning. In contrast to the dog in the San Francisco piece, again according to Durantini, the nursing mother (Mary and the Christ Child) with the bird cage over her head (joy through slavery) is the image of virtue.[36] With the scene with the dog, the painter naturally intended something like: 'As mother, so daughter.' Sutton demonstrated that the negative side of the imitation of parents by children was unambiguously expressed by Jan Steen in the painting '*The Way You Hear It Is the Way You Sing It*' (p. 70, fig. 13). Pieter de Hooch instead presented a largely positive image.[37]

1 *Smith 1829-1842*, vol. IV, p. 232, no. 43

2 *Sutton 1980*, p. 86, no. 38 and fig. 41

3 *Van Eeghen 1958*, p. 226

4 *NNBW*, vol. IV, col. 1468; *Elias 1903-1905 / 1963*, vol. II, pp. 1040-1041; *Wijnman et al. 1974*, pp. 393 and 405

5 Inv. no. A 2860; *Van Thiel et al. 1976*, pp. 571-572, no. A 2860 and fig.; *Blankert 1975*, p. 144, believed incorrectly that Lucretia inherited the entire Van Winter collection.

6 *Wijnman et al. 1974*, p. 394

7 See note 1

8 *Gower 1875-A*, p. 131 (he added to this that they were exhibited only once, but paintings owned by Van Loon were on view at the exhibitions in Arti in 1867 and 1872). Thoré-Bürger also visited the Van Loon collection, witness his repeated descriptions of the garden scene (note 2), of which he admired 'l'effet de plein-air': *Thoré-Bürger 1858-1860*, vol. II, p. 61, note 1 and *Thoré-Bürger 1865*, p. 318.

9 *Van Lennep 1959*, p. 137; *Spectator 1877*, p. 265; in 1878 still another twelve paintings from the Van Loon-Van Winter collections were auctioned (L. 38060), see *Spectator 1878*, p. 65.

10 *Hijmersma 1983*, p. 20

11 *Spectator 1877-A*, p. 354

12 *Havard 1879-1881*, vol. III, pp. 91-92 and 117: he thought that with 'the Companion' Smith meant the title of the painting.

13 *Morton 1961*, p. 170 (with an appendix with the family tree).

14 *Hofstede de Groot 1892*, p. 186, no. 73; HdG 11: 'Vermutlich bei einem der Pariser Rothschilds.'

15 *Sutton 1980*, p. 79, no. 21 and pl. v, p. 81, no. 26 and pl. 23

16 *Eisler 1977*, p. 153; no Dutch library has the 1916 Knoedler catalogue.

17 *Sutton 1980*, p. 83, no. 32: '(Prob.) Van Loon Collection'; Sutton in *Berlin / London / Philadelphia 1984*, p. 194, no. 54; see also *Valentiner 1929*, p. 276: 'Aus der Sammlung van Laon, Amsterdam(?).'

18 *Suida 1955*, p. 26; *Eisler 1977*, p. 153, no. K 2120 and note 6

19 *Brière-Misme 1927*, p. 72

20 *Brière-Misme 1927*, p. 72, note 1; see also *Valentiner 1927*, p. 76, no. 15

21 *Brière-Misme 1927*, pp. 70-72 and fig.

22 *Sutton 1986*, p. 276

23 *Art News 1955*, p. 14

24 *NCAB*, vol. XXVIII, pp. 252-253

25 *Auction New York 1954*

26 *Emerson 1961*; *Washington 1961-1962*, n.p., gave an overview of the geographic spread of the paintings of the Kress Foundation; *Constable 1964*, pp. 133-137.

27 *Suida 1955*, p. 26; *Emerson 1961*, p. 832

28 *Neumeyer 1955*, pp. 272-273; *Emerson 1961*, pp. 829-832

29 *Emerson 1961*, p. 853, was the first to illustrate the painting in its restored state; *Eisler 1977*, p. 153, note 2.

30 *Seymour et al. 1961*, p. 154

31 *Bode 1911*, pp. 1-2 and fig.

32 *Blankert 1975*, pp. 44-46 and 54-55

33 *London 1968*, p. 153, no. P 23 and fig.; *Sutton 1980*, p. 95, no. 61 and fig. 65; *Suida 1955*, p. 26, believed that the painting was dated 1663.

34 *Sutton 1980*, p. 21; *London 1968*, p. 190, no. P 239 and fig.; *Sumowski 1983-B*, pp. 2018 and 2082, no. 1356 and fig.

35 *Sumowski 1983-B*, pp. 2013-2016 and 2059-2074, nos. 1333, 1342, 1343, 1345, 1347 and 1348 and figs.

36 *Durantini 1979 / 1983*, p. 27

37 Sutton in *Berlin / London / Philadelphia 1984*, pp. 194 and 365, no. 54, note 2
BB

Pieter de Hooch The Box Bed

Rotterdam 1629 – Amsterdam 1684

Canvas, 50.5 x 59.7 cm (20 x 23½ in.)
Neither signed nor dated (ca. 1658-1660)
Washington, D.C., National Gallery of Art, Widener Collection, inv. no. 1942.9.33

In 1822, at the order of King William I, *The View of Delft* by Jan Vermeer was bought at the Stinstra auction for the Royal Picture Gallery Mauritshuis in The Hague.[1] It went for 2,900 guilders, which is an enormous amount compared to the 25 guilders for which a painting by Pieter de Hooch, *The Box Bed*, was then auctioned. Precisely which work this was can no longer be established, as there are three versions of this composition, with only slight differences between them. There is a monogrammed version in Karlsruhe (Staatliche Kunsthalle) [**1**].[2] A slightly weaker version is now at an unknown location (auction Lloyd, London, 1937).[3] A third version, neither signed nor dated, now in the National Gallery of Art in Washington, is the work here under discussion. Only after 1822 did these three canvases gain their separate identities.[4] The first of these works went permanently to Karlsruhe in 1831. The lost work was in the Lloyd collection in Manchester from 1842 to 1937. But it was the version in Washington that led the most adventurous existence of the three.

In 1826 this painting was auctioned in London as part of the estate of baron Radstock. William Waldegrave, the first Baron Radstock (1753-1825), was a naval commander and, after 1802, an admiral. In 1785 he was married in Smyrna to the Dutch woman Cornelia van Lennep, daughter of David van Lennep, who had settled there as a manufacturer.[5] Probably thanks to his spouse, the baron had a preference for Dutch painting. At the auction of the Radstock collection, the Marquess of Stafford bought the painting by Pieter de Hooch.[6] Upon his father's death in 1803, George G. Leveson-Gower (1785-1833) inherited the title of Marquess, to be elevated six months before his death to first Duke of Sutherland. He inherited and owned immense riches, among which were many estates and art collections, including the Bridgewater paintings. He was one of the first private owners to admit visitors to his collections.

In 1827 he purchased Stafford House (now Lancaster House), located near Buckingham Palace in London, for his son of the same name, the second Duke of Sutherland.[7] This house had been built by the Duke of York and, between 1833 and 1841, was considerably enlarged by the second Duke of Sutherland. In 1833, when he saw *The Bed Box* by Pieter de Hooch hanging

Provenance
(?) Auction S.J. Stinstra, Amsterdam, 1822
Auction Radstock, London, 1826 (70 guineas to the Marquess of Stafford)
Collection Marquess of Stafford, from 1833 on, the Duke of Sutherland, Stafford House, London, 1826-1846
Dealer Emery Rutley, London, 1846 (from the Duchess of Sutherland by way of Morant)
Collection Robert Field, Pyrgo Park, Essex, before 1856
Auction Field, London, 1856 (£43.1)
Collection Charles Scarisbrick, Scarisbrick Hall or Wrightington Hall, Lancashire, before 1861
Auction Scarisbrick, London, 1861 (£441 to F. Nieuwenhuys)
Collection Adrian Hope, London, before 1894
Auction Hope, London, 1894 (£2,150 to Ch. Wertheimer)
(?) Dealer Ch. Sedelmeyer, Paris, 1894
Collection Peter A.B. Widener, Lynnewood Hall, Philadelphia, 1894-1915 (bought for $13,000)
Collection Joseph E. Widener, Lynnewood Hall, Philadelphia, 1915-1942
National Gallery of Art, Washington, D.C., 1942 (gift of Widener)

Bibliography
Auction London 1826, p. 16, no. 14
Smith 1829-1942, vol. IV, p. 227, no. 29
Passavant 1833, p. 63
Waagen 1837-1839, vol. II, p. 67
Jameson 1844, p. 205, no. 124
Jervis 1854, p. 328
Waagen 1854, vol. II, p. 71
Auction London 1856, p. 32, no. 520
Thoré-Bürger 1857, p. 319
Blanc 1860-1863, vol. II, 'Pierre de Hooch,' p. 8
Auction London 1861, p. 22, no. 119
Thoré-Bürger 1865, p. 319
Havard 1879-1881, vol. III, p. 107
Ashbourne 1885-1900, vol. II, p. 215 and fig.
Auction London 1894, p. 65, no. 32 and fig.
Richter 1894, p. 332
Roberts 1897, vol. I, p. 193
Paris 1898, p. 86, no. 70 and fig.
Mireur 1901-1912, vol. III, p. 482
Bode 1906, p. 58
Wurzbach, vol. I (1906), p. 717
HdG 78 (vol. I [1907], p. 496, no. 78)
HdG-MS 78
Valentiner 1909, pp. XXVI, 56, no. 55 and fig.
Breck 1910, p. 42
Valentiner 1910, p. 9
Hofstede de Groot / Valentiner 1913-1916, n.p.: 'Pieter de Hooch'
De Rudder 1914, p. 105
Graves 1918-1921, vol. I, p. 210, no. 14 (1826), p. 211, no. 32 (1894)
Elkins Park 1923 / 1931, n.p., 'Pieter de Hooch' and fig.
Collins Baker 1925, p. 6
Brière-Misme 1927, p. 58
Valentiner 1927, pp. 61 and 76, no. 2 and note 2 and fig. 3
Valentiner 1929, pp. XVII, 59 and 275 and fig.
Waldmann 1938, p. 336

there, the painter and connoisseur Johann David Passavant (cat. no. 57, fig. 1) called it 'this most beautiful of all the palaces of London' (in translation).[8] 'I have come from my house to your palace,' Queen Victoria is to have said to the Duchess of Sutherland.[9] The public and foreign art lovers (among whom numbered Waagen and Thoré) were thoroughly familiar with the collection at Stafford House.[10] On one of his visits, Théophile Thoré, who published under the pseudonym of William Bürger, noted the similarity between the painting owned by the Duke of Sutherland and the one then in the Lloyd collection.[11] Only in 1907 did Hofstede de Groot observe that the canvas in Washington is practically identical to that in Karlsruhe. In his opinion the only difference was in the execution of the frame of the mirror next to the bed.[12] The other differences (in the decorations of the small tiles, for instance) are indeed minimal.

The version in Stafford House was sold in 1846 by the Duchess of Sutherland and, by way of the art dealer Emery Rutley, ended up in English private hands again.[13] It happened that it remained in the collection of Robert Field in Pyrgo Park, Essex, until 1856, after which time it was acquired by Charles Scarisbrick.[14] The Scarisbricks were an old Catholic family in Lancashire. In 1837 Charles Scarisbrick (1801/1802-1860), Sheriff of Lancashire, had Augustus W.N. Pugin rebuild the family residence, Scarisbrick Hall, in Neo-Gothic style. Scarisbrick's life-style as an eccentric recluse inspired the novelist Nathaniel Hawthorne (who, from 1853 to 1857, was the American consul in Liverpool).[15] After Scarisbrick's death, the Scarisbrick auction took place in installments in 1860 and 1861. First the furniture went, then the library, and finally the paintings. The latter were sold in three separate sessions, in between which prints, drawings, curiosities, and cigars were sold. The total yield was 42,347 pounds sterling.[16]

The Box Bed by Pieter de Hooch fell into the hands of Adrian Hope. The literature stated that the painting was still in the Sutherland collection, even though it had in the meantime changed owners three times.[17] In 1894 the Hope auction was *the* event of the season because the owner had died under suspicious circumstances (see also cat. no. 41). The auction house Christie's made skillful use of this information, as is reported in the *Nieuwe Rotterdamsche Courant* of 3 July 1894: 'The outcome of the Hope auction is fresh proof of how, in London, a cleverly marketed collection of older art, with the name of a celebrity on the title page, may be a great success even in these days of depression' (in translation). The painting by De Hooch caused a sensation; in 1861 it had been sold for 441 pounds and now fetched more

Blake-More Godwin 1939, p. 106 and fig.
Art Digest 1940, p. 11
Washington 1948, no. 629 and fig.
Washington 1959, p. 63 and fig.
Karlsruhe 1960, no. 25 and fig. on cover
Polesden Lacey 1964, p. 24
Washington 1965, p. 69, no. 629
Lauts 1966, vol. 1, p. 152, no. 259, vol. 11, p. 360 and fig. 259
Toledo 1976, p. 81
Sutton 1980, pp. 26, 72, note 28, p. 87, no. 40B, p. 88 and fig. 44
Wheelock 1981, pp. 34-35 and fig. 34
Clark 1982, p. 92 and fig. 22
Reitlinger 1982, vol. 1, p. 344 (1861, 1894)
Berlin / London / Philadelphia 1984, p. 196, fig. 1
Walker 1984, p. 291, no. 382 and fig.
Washington 1985, p. 206 and fig.
Sutton 1986, p. 311

1
Pieter de Hooch
The Box Bed
Canvas, 51.8 x 60.6 cm (20³/₈ x 23⁷/₈ in.)
Lower left, on the table leg: PH (in ligature)
(ca. 1658-1660)
Karlsruhe, Staatliche Kunsthalle, inv. no. 259

than five times that amount. Abraham Bredius, who naturally was present at the auction, noted: 'The ugly woman ruins a great deal, but the central section is superb in its sun and correctly balanced light effect' and added 'sweet child' (in translation).[18] Bredius apparently was quick to think women ugly (see also cat. no. 28).

In 1894, via the dealer Ch. Wertheimer, the painting ended up in the Widener collection in Philadelphia (see cat. no. 59). Peter A.B. Widener (1834-1915) (p. 42, fig. 29), who had come up in life from butcher's helper to multimillionaire, began collecting around 1890, showing a preference for the Grand Manner: the Italian High Renaissance, the Dutch Golden Century, and the English eighteenth century. He emulated the collections of the great English country estates and therefore preferred to collect what had come from there (p. 42, fig. 30). The Rembrandts and Vermeers were the pride of his collection, but he also owned landscapes, still lifes, and genre paintings by the minor masters. For his De Hooch he paid 13,000 dollars.[19] Peter Widener died in 1915 and in his will empowered his son and heir Joseph E. Widener (1860-1943) to donate his paintings in due time to a museum in Washington (or Philadelphia, or New York). When, at the initiative of Andrew W. Mellon, the National Gallery of Art rose on the Mall in Washington, Joseph Widener parted with much of his collection and that of his father. Naturally the Philadelphia museum made attempts to acquire the collection from Lynnewood Hall. But in August of 1942 President Roosevelt was able to announce that the Widener collection had become national property.[20]

'Sweet child,' wrote Abraham Bredius when he saw *The Box Bed* at the Hope auction. Bode added to this that such comfortable rooms must depict the house of the artist and that the figures must be his wife and children.[21] Possibly he noticed that repetitions are a common phenomenon in the work of De Hooch. In Bode's time recurring models or settings were all too readily thought to represent the family of the artist or his surroundings. The same spatial arrangement (although the window is shown at the right) with a view into a sun-drenched back room, and with the same painting is featured in *The Lice Hunt* (Amsterdam, Rijksmuseum) [2].[22] The motif of a child with its hand on the door latch apparently appealed so much to the painter that he repeated it in a somewhat unusual composition, *A Child with a 'Kolf' Stick* (Polesden Lacey, National Trust) [3].[23] The individual features of this curly-haired child make us suspect that this painting was intended to be a portrait. This suspicion is supported by the fact that the *kolf* stick and ball were

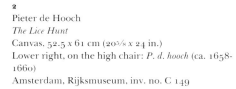

2
Pieter de Hooch
The Lice Hunt
Canvas, 52.5 x 61 cm (20⅝ x 24 in.)
Lower right, on the high chair: *P. d. hooch* (ca. 1658-1660)
Amsterdam, Rijksmuseum, inv. no. C 149

not at all unusual attributes in portraits of children.[24] If the work dates from the artist's last Delft years, between 1658 and 1660, it could indeed be a portrait of Pieter de Hooch's elder son, Pieter Jr., who was baptized on 2 February 1655.[25]

The young Pieter, presumably with his mother, Jannetje van der Burch, may well be depicted in the Washington painting, but this can hardly have mattered much to De Hooch's clients. Nicolaes Maes and Gerard ter Borch had popularized the genre with the theme of the virtuous housewife in the fifties, and De

3
Pieter de Hooch
A Child with a 'Kolf' Stick
Panel, 63.5 x 45.7 cm (25 x 18 in.)
Above the door, at the left: *P d hooch* (ca. 1658-1660)
Polesden Lacey, National Trust, inv. no. (cat. 1964, no. 44)

Hooch embroidered on it with success (see cat. no. 34). The repetition of compositions was tolerated, for the scene expressed a widely familiar idea, as would a saying or a proverb. The title that has invariably been used for this painting until now, *The Bedroom*, is somewhat misleading. The typical seventeenth-century home had no separate bedrooms on the ground level. One slept in the room in which daily life was carried on, and there one ate, played cards, or made music. The bed was usually a portable wooden construction with curtains (see cat. no. 36) and sometimes, as is here the case, a built-in box bed.[26] The most important attribute of the nightly ritual was the chamber pot, which has for now been placed in the center of the room. In the version from the Lloyd collection, this bit of sanitary ware was once thought to be unseemly and hence painted over.[27]

Pieter de Hooch here shows a (or his) housewife engaged in one of her daily activities, the making of the bed. It is striking that, with the exception of a tiny piece of straw that has fallen out of the mattress and onto the floor, the room is impeccably clean. From the sixteenth century on, Dutch domestic cleanliness found expression in a nearly unhealthy scrubbing and polishing that dumbfounded foreigners.[28] This mania had little to do with true hygiene, as the cleanliness of the home stood in marked distinction to the unwashed condition of the body.[29] In depictions of the housecleaning or, for example, of the delousing of children, people were also wont to see an edifying reference to the purity of the soul.[30] Order and neatness were discussed in countless publications, proverbs, and sayings as indicative of the virtuous housewife.[31] To emphasize the point of her virtue, a child playing was often added to paintings as a contrasting image of frivolity.[32] Consequently it is the 'Praise of the virtuous housewife' that is here being sung, in emulation of the Proverbs of Solomon (31:10-31). In no period in the history of art other than the Dutch Golden Century have women been so excessively often depicted as housewives.

1 Inv. no 92; *Broos 1987*, pp. 382-389, no. 65 and fig.
2 *Lauts 1966*, vol. I, p. 152, no. 259, vol. II, p. 360 and fig.; *Sutton 1980*, pp. 86-87, no. 40A and fig. 43
3 *Sutton 1980*, p. 87, no. 40C (photo RKD)
4 *Sutton 1980*, p. 87, no. 40D, believed that the identification with the painting in Washington (see HdG 78) cannot be made to stick; there is also a (later?) version in The Toledo Museum of Art (inv. no. 26.79; *Toledo 1976*, p. 81, fig. 132).
5 *DNB*, vol. LIX, pp. 23-24
6 According to a note in *Auction London 1826*, p. 26, no. 14 (copy RKD) and *Graves 1918-1921*, vol. I, p. 210; *Sutton 1980*, p. 87, no. 40B, missed this fact, which is why he wrongly identified the Smith auction of 1828 in a possible provenance.
7 *DNB*, vol. XXXIII, pp. 146-147; *Whitley 1973*, vol. I, pp. 108-109
8 *Passavant 1833*, p. 59, therefore correctly called Stafford House 'York oder Gower House'; *Sutton 1980*, p. 87, no. 40B, notes 3 and 4, thought that this phrase referred to different houses.
9 *Beresford Chancellor 1908*, p. 347
10 *Waagen 1837-1839*, vol. II, p. 67
11 *Thoré-Bürger 1857*, p. 319
12 HdG 78
13 According to a note by John Smith (HdG-MS, ad no. 78, RKD).
14 *Auction London 1856*, p. 32, no. 520: 'From the Sutherland Collection.'
15 *Boase 1965*, vol. III, col. 432; *Pevsner 1969*, p. 218
16 *Roberts 1897*, vol. I, pp. 192-193
17 *Blanc 1860-1863*, vol. II, 'Pierre de Hooch,' p. 8; *Havard 1879-1881*, vol. III, p. 107
18 Newspaper clippings (*The Observer*, 1 July 1894 and NRC [?], n.d.) with *Auction London 1894*, reference copy of Bredius (RKD).
19 *Comstock 1946*, pp. 129-135; *Walker 1948*, pp. VII-IX; 'Inventory of Paintings. P.A.B. Widener' (Ms. National Gallery of Art, Washington).
20 *Finley 1973*, pp. 93-102 and 105-107; a list of Widener's paintings was published in *Art Digest 1940*, p. 11.
21 *Bode 1906*, p. 58
22 *Van Thiel et al. 1976*, p. 288, no. C 149 and fig.
23 *Polesden Lacey 1964*, p. 24, no. 44; *Sutton 1980*, p. 88, no. 41 and fig. 45
24 *Bergen op Zoom etc. 1982*, pp. 18, 25, 51 and 78 and fig.; on the game of *kolf*, see cat. no. 46.
25 *Sutton 1980*, p. 146, no. 22; his sister Anna was baptized on 14 November 1656, ibidem, no. 29.
26 *Schotel / Rogge*, p. 14; *Catalani 1968*, pp. 16-17
27 See note 3
28 *Sutton 1980*, pp. 47 and 69, notes 58-62
29 *Roding 1986*, p. 24
30 *Amsterdam 1976*, pp. 196-199, no. 49; *Broos 1987*, pp. 74-77, no. 12
31 For one source of examples, see *Sutton 1980*, pp. 46-47 and 69, notes 47-54.
32 *Amsterdam 1976*, pp. 98-99, no. 19
BB

Rotterdam 1629 – Amsterdam 1684

Canvas, 100.3 x 119.4 cm (39½ x 47 in.)
At the left, under the seat of the chair: *P D HOOCH [16]63*
Cleveland, Ohio, The Cleveland Museum of Art, inv. no. 51.355

In 1818, at an auction in Bordeaux, a work by Pieter de Hooch came up for sale which, according to the description in the catalogue, corresponded in detail with what we see in this *Music-Making Family* of The Cleveland Museum of Art. After a characterization of the group at the table, mention is made of the view into the back room in which 'a very bright daylight from the garden sets a [...] lady with a child on her arm all aglow, just as it does a little girl who precedes her with a plate of peaches, while they are both making their way to the main room' (in translation).[1] Although the specified dimensions (36 x 43 inches) are a little smaller than those of the painting under discussion, the description and the addition that it is without doubt one of the master's most beautiful paintings, nevertheless appear to refer to it. Until now the provenance of the painting before 1829 was wrapped in obscurity. For that matter, many musical parties by De Hooch mentioned in eighteenth-century auction catalogues cannot be identified because their descriptions are too concise.[2]

In 1829 this *Music-Making Family* turned up at an exhibition at the British Institution in London, together with paintings by De Hooch belonging to King George IV and the Duke of Wellington.[3] The painter – who was later to achieve popularity as the competitor of Vermeer (see cat. no. 34) – was then known only in the circles of a few collectors. The dealer C.J. Nieuwenhuys described how the prices for works by De Hooch suddenly rose steeply between 1810 and 1825.[4] One result of this upturn was the compilation of the first catalogue of his paintings by another dealer, John Smith, which was published in 1833.[5] Smith enthusiastically described the genius of the painter and made eager mention of the qualities of this musical party, such as 'the enchanting half-tone and reflections, accompanied by brilliant transparency and masterly execution.'[6]

In 1833 the owner was Lord Wharncliffe, who had parted with it in 1829 for the exhibition in London. James Archibald Stuart-Wortley-Mackenzie (1776-1845) had sat for Yorkshire in the House of Commons starting in 1818 and in 1826 became Baron Wharncliffe of Wortley.[7] In his supplement of 1842 to the catalogue of De Hooch's works, Smith announced that he had managed to obtain this *Music-Making Family* and other paintings

Provenance
(?) Auction Bordeaux, 1818
Collection Lord Wharncliffe, Wharncliffe House, London, or Wortley Hall, Yorkshire, before 1829-after 1833
Dealer John Smith, London, after 1833-1842
Collection William Theobald, London / Calcutta, 1842-1851
Auction Theobald, London, 1851 (£115.10 to Mullason)
Collection Ernest Cook, Bath, between 1930 / 1940-1951
Dealer Scott & Fowles, New York, 1951
The Cleveland Museum of Art, Cleveland, 1951 (gift of the Hanna Fund)

Bibliography
Smith 1829-1842, vol. IV, p. 239, no. 63, supplement, p. 571, no. 27
Auction London 1851, p. 14, no. 76
Havard 1879-1881, vol. III, p. 122
HdG 157 (vol. I [1907], p. 517, no. 157)
HdG-MS 157
Graves 1913-1915, vol. I, p. 268, no. 165 (1829)
De Rudder 1914, p. 101
Art News 1952, pp. 32-33 and fig.
Burchfield 1952, pp. 118, 121-123 and fig.
Cleveland 1952, p. 28 and fig.
Staring 1956, pp. 86-87, no. x and fig.
Cleveland 1958, no. 58
Cleveland 1958-A, no. 447 and fig.
Cleveland 1966, p. 126 and fig.
Gerson 1966, p. 310
Kansas City 1967-1968, p. 22, no. 5 and fig.
Cleveland 1970, p. 126 and fig.
Praz 1971, pp. 184 and 190, fig. 151
Eikemeier 1974, p. 260, note 6
Sherrill 1976, pp. 163-165 and fig. XXI
Thornton 1978, pp. 42 and 405, note 48 and fig. 48
Sutton 1980, pp. 28-30, 49 and 64, note 5, p. 92, no. 53 and pls. XII and 57
Naumann 1981, vol. I, p. 142 and fig. 206
Cleveland 1982, pp. 246-248, no. 107 and fig.
Sutton 1986, pp. 66-67, fig. 92
Brunswick etc. 1988-1990, pp. 158 and 160, fig. 65

Pieter de Hooch A Music-Making Family (the Del Court Family?) (not in San Francisco)

from the collection of Lord Wharncliffe. He added that he had in the meantime sold 'this splendid picture' to the jurist William Theobald (1798-1870), who left for Calcutta in 1843.[8] In 1851 the Theobald collection came under the hammer, and the painting then disappeared without a trace.[9] The statement in many catalogues that it was located in a private collection in Yorkshire may have been based on a confusion with its stay in the collection of Lord Wharncliffe, as his paintings were presumably divided between Wharncliffe House in London and Wortley Hall in Yorkshire.[10] For exactly a century the description by John Smith remained the only eyewitness testimony to De Hooch's masterpiece. Havard (1879) and Hofstede de Groot (1907) had to make do with his text: only the latter author adopted Smith's earlier quoted expressions of praise.[11]

In 1951 The Cleveland Museum of Art bought *A Music-Making Family* by Pieter de Hooch as a previously unknown painting. The New York dealer Scott & Fowles had acquired it from Ernest Cook of Bath, England, who was then known by only a few as a collector.[12] Ernest Cook (1866-1955) was the grandson of Thomas Cook, the founder of the oldest travel bureau in the world, Thos. Cook & Son on the Haymarket in London. In the twenties, Ernest withdrew from the family business to devote himself to charity work and to the collecting of art and antiques. He carried out his activities in secrecy, showing, according to a well-informed source, an 'almost morbid fear of publicity.' Only a few initiates knew the extent of his collections.[13] The collection of paintings, containing primarily English and Dutch old masters, was mostly assembled between 1929 and 1939, and was kept in the large mansion on Sion Hill Place in Bath, where he died in 1955. He bequeathed his paintings to the National Art-Collections Fund.[14] How Scott & Fowles were able to separate the canvas by De Hooch from the Cook collection in 1951 is not known. In any case it was owing to the mediation of this dealer that the painting ended up in an American public collection.

The acquisition by the Cleveland museum was made possible by the Hanna Fund. Leonard Colton Hanna, Jr. (1889-1957), acted as a Maecenas to The Cleveland Museum of Art in three ways. He made gifts during his lifetime, bequeathed his collection to the museum in 1957, and founded the Hanna Fund in 1941 to make acquisitions possible.[15] The first illustrations of the painting appeared in 1952 in the bulletin of the museum and in a picture book.[16] Only then was it possible to study the depiction more closely.

In 1956 Staring illustrated the painting in his book entitled,

quite tellingly in the present context, *De Hollanders thuis* (The Dutch at home).[17] Staring and others have made sundry attempts to identify details in the depiction, for it so happens that an element or two appear to have been taken from real life. The eye-catcher in this interior is the large Dutch bombé chest on ball feet, which appears to have been made of an exotic species of wood or of pale oak that has not yet been darkened by furniture wax. The blue vases on the corners of the cupboard look like Chinese products of the K'ang Hsi period, according to Stechow.[18] The K'ang Hsi period began in 1662. Thus the family poses with very recently acquired precious objects on a brand-new cupboard: they show themselves as nouveaux riches. The lacquer boxes on the cupboard could have been imported from Japan. Since 1641 the Dutch had been admitted to Deshima, and the Amsterdam market was flooded with all sorts of such curiosities.[19] The knotted rug on the table has been identified as a Transylvanian church carpet, which must have been painted after an actual specimen.[20] A chimneypiece with *The Sacrifice of Abraham* is displayed above the columned fireplace.[21] The tapestry in the background shows a wooded mountain landscape with hunters. Around the time this painting was made, such tapestries went out of fashion because they were not very practical.[22] An identical wall hanging may be seen in the *Fantasy Interior with Jan Steen and Jan van Goyen* (cat. no. 58). The comparison with this painting demonstrates the difference between a symbolic double portrait and a realistically conceived setting.

The musical parties by De Hooch are only rarely group portraits, but, owing to the individual features of these music makers, this is clearly the case here. Sutton, who in 1976 discovered the date of 1663 on the painting, also attempted to identify the family.[23] He thought that this group portrait was listed as part of the estate of Petronella de la Court (1624-1707), wife of Adam Oortmans, as: 'Figures in a Room' (in translation).[24] However, in 1663 Petronella had six children – three girls and three boys – and not the four we see here. On the one hand Sutton cast doubt on the idea that the Oortmans-de la Court family was depicted, but elsewhere he nevertheless assumed this to be true.[25] Perhaps a better candidate appears to be the Del Court family from Amsterdam (the similarity of names being totally accidental). The face of the pontifically posing woman strongly resembles that of Maria de Keerssegieter in the *Portrait of the Del Court Couple* (Rotterdam, Museum Boymans-van Beuningen) [1],[26] painted by Bartholomeus van der Helst in 1654. If it is indeed she who is also portrayed in the

1
Bartholomeus van der Helst
Portrait of the Del Court Couple
Canvas, 172 x 146.5 cm (67³/₄ x 57⁵/₈ in.)
Lower left: *B. vander. helst. / 1654*
Rotterdam, Museum Boymans-van Beuningen,
inv. no. 1296

2
Frans Floris
Family Portrait
Panel, 130 x 225 cm (51¹/₈ x 88¹/₂ in.)
At the right, at the bottom of the frame: *1561*
Lier, Museum Wuyts-Van Campen-Caroly,
inv. no. 52

painting in Cleveland, she had in the meantime aged almost ten years, which may explain why she is a lot heavier here. She still has the somewhat long, pear-shaped nose. Abraham del Court as painted by Van der Helst looks like a younger version of the father of the painting of 1663 by De Hooch. In that year the Del Courts indeed had four children: Juda, the eldest son of about twelve; the slightly younger Catharina; Suzanna, who was then five years old; and the newly born Thomas, precisely the ages of the four children in this painting.[27] But there must have been more families in Amsterdam in 1663 that were thus constituted. Hence our identification is possible but by no means certain.

What is certain, however, is that the group portrait has a double meaning. This family had itself depicted making music to demonstrate that they lived together in harmony. This pictorial language could pride itself on a long tradition, and we have many portraits of music-making families from the seventeenth century that contain this message.[28] One sixteenth-century example of this sentiment is a *Family Portrait* of 1561 by Frans Floris (Lier, Museum Wuyts-Van Campen-Caroly) [**2**].[29] Surrounded by their numerous offspring and a depiction of their deceased forefather, a married couple makes music. The Latin legend on the frame explains: 'Just as there can be nothing happier in life than a harmonious marriage and a bed without strife, so there is nothing more pleasant than, with unsullied heart, to watch one's united descendants enjoying peace' (in translation).[30] Harmony is here described twice over as being at the core of the depiction.

At the left of the group portrait by De Hooch we see a viola da gamba leaning against a chair. The boy blows on an alto recorder, while his sister strums on a small lute and their father plays on a viola in the French style.[31] They accompany the mother, who does not really sing but instead marks the time with her right hand. This gesture is apparently a further reference to moderation (see cat. no. 58), which is a condition for a harmonious society. For instance, this symbolism has been unambiguously incorporated into the *Allegorical Engagement Portrait* of 1633 by Jan Miense Molenaer [**3**] (cat. no. 45). In this context the dog entering the room can represent nothing but (marital) fidelity, as in Metsu's *Young Woman with a Cello* (cat. no. 43). The depiction of *The Sacrifice of Abraham* as a chimneypiece harmonizes completely with this musical family, because this biblical story is an example of family fidelity and obedience.[32] Abraham's reward was prosperity and many children, and it is understandable that someone who was himself called Abraham might have been fond of this story. If it is indeed Abraham del

3
Detail of cat. no. 45

Court with Maria de Keerssegieter and their four children who were depicted here in the year 1663, then the portrait by Van der Helst [1] is not our only evidence that the Del Courts prized simple symbolism in a natural setting.

1 *Auction Bordeaux 1818*, no. 20 (quoted from the index cards of Hofstede de Groot, RKD).

2 See, for instance, *Sutton 1980*, p. 129, no. C 83-97

3 *Graves 1913-1915*, vol. I, pp. 267-268, nos. 108, 165, 181 (1829)

4 *Nieuwenhuys 1834*, p. 154

5 *Smith 1829-1842*, vol. IV, pp. 217-242

6 Idem, p. 239, no. 63; see also *Sutton 1980*, p. 55

7 *DNB*, vol. LV, pp. 110-113; *Complete Peerage*, vol. XII-II, pp. 590-591

8 *Smith 1829-1842*, supplement, p. 571, no. 27; *Boase 1965*, vol. III, col. 920

9 *Auction London 1851*, p. 14, no. 76

10 *Cleveland 1958*, no. 58; *Sutton 1980*, p. 92, no. 53; *Cleveland 1982*, p. 247, no. 107; see also *Complete Peerage*, vol. XII-II, pp. 590-591

11 *Havard 1879-1881*, vol. III, p. 122; HdG 157

12 *Art News 1952*, p. 32 and fig. p. 33; *Cleveland 1958*, no. 58

13 *London 1957*, p. 3

14 Idem, pp. 6-7

15 *Cleveland 1958*, n.p., 'Foreword'; *Constable 1964*, p. 182

16 *Burchfield 1952*, pp. 118, 121-123 and fig.; *Cleveland 1952*, p. 28; see also *Art News 1952*, p. 32 and fig. p. 33

17 *Staring 1956*, pp. 86-87, no. x and fig.

18 Stechow in *Cleveland 1982*, p. 247

19 *Rotterdam 1986-1987*, pp. 79-81 (Stechow differentiated between a Japanese and a Chinese lacquer box, see *Cleveland 1982*, p. 247).

20 *Sherrill 1976*, pp. 164-165 and figs. XXI-XXII

21 Not a *Descent from the Cross* as *Staring 1956*, p. 86, thought; the composition is of the type that we know from Rubens or Rembrandt, see *Broos 1972*, pp. 137-142, figs. 1, 2, 4 and 5.

22 *Staring 1956*, p. 86

23 The signature is illustrated in *Cleveland 1982*, p. 247, fig. 107a.

24 *Hoet 1752-1770*, vol. I, p. 107, no. 57; *Sutton 1980*, p. 29

25 *Sutton 1983*, pp. 64-65, note 5 (with reference to *Van Eeghen 1960*) and p. 47: 'Petronella de la Court, the wife of one of De Hooch's patrons.'

26 *De Gelder 1921*, pp. 243-244, no. 876; *Rotterdam 1962*, p. 64, no. 1296

27 *Vorsterman van Oijen 1885-1890*, vol. I, p. 165

28 *Fischer 1972*, pp. 102-114 and 121; *Amsterdam 1976*, pp. 182-185, no. 45, note 3; *De Jongh 1986*, pp. 40-45, 280-290, nos. 69-71

29 *Van de Velde 1975*, pp. 290-292, no. 150 and fig. 78

30 The translation is from *De Jongh 1986*, p. 45.

31 Compare the illustrations in *Munrow 1976*, pp. 39, 80-81 and 91.

32 *Sutton 1980*, p. 49

BB

Rotterdam 1619 – Amsterdam 1693

Canvas, 69 x 58 cm (27⅛ x 227⅞ in.)
On edge of table: *W. Kalf* (ca. 1660)
New York, private collection

Willem Kalf was born in Rotterdam in 1619, and although details are known about his family, little is known about the artist's early life or artistic training. He worked in Paris from about 1640 until 1645 or 1646, before returning to establish himself permanently in Holland. In 1653 Kalf is recorded in Amsterdam. How the intervening years were spent is not known; however, in 1651 he traveled to Hoorn, North Holland, where he married Cornelia Pluvier, a noted glass etcher.

Working in Amsterdam until his death in 1693, Kalf enjoyed great popularity during his lifetime, and his works were described in poems by Jan Vos and Joost van den Vondel. Kalf's consummate skill made him one of the most respected and sought-after still life painters of the seventeenth century. Owing in part to the great demand for his paintings, numerous copies exist, and some of them were executed by Kalf's students under his direction. These multiples may account for the uneven quality of some works traditionally attributed to the artist. The dating of his works is also problematic, because although the subject matter changes over his long career, few pictures are dated. Kalf had a number of followers, both in Holland and abroad, the most important of whom was Willem van Aelst.

Provenance

Collection Princess Louise-Henriette of Orange-Nassau, Schloss Oranienburg, near Berlin, before 1667
Collection King Frederick I of Prussia, Stadtschloss, Berlin, before 1718
Collection Emperor William II, Huis Doorn, Doorn, 1918
Dealer Griese, London, 1938
Collection Eugene Leopold Garbáty, East Norwalk, Conn.
Auction London, 1956 (£1,120 to Duits & Co.)
Dealer Duits & Co., London, 1956-1958
Private collection, New York, 1958

Bibliography

Rumpf 1794, p. 142, no. 1811 A 120
Pach 1940, no. 104
Corning 1952, p. 25, no. 9 and pl. V
Auction London 1956, p. 15, no. 82
Burlington Magazine 1957, pl. XI
New York 1965, no. 57 and fig.
Gilbert 1966, no. 17 and fig.
Grisebach 1974, pp. 160, 262-263, no. 111 and pl. 117
Norfolk 1982, no. 24
Segal 1988-1989, p. 221, note 40

This *Still Life with Goblets and Lemon* has a distinguished provenance, stretching back to within a few years of its completion around 1660. Two inventory numbers on the verso of the canvas help to establish the history of its ownership. The picture is first mentioned as number 148 in the 1699 inventory of the Schloss Oranienburg near Berlin. This castle was built and largely decorated at the orders of Princess Louise-Henriette of Orange (1627-1667), daughter of the Stadholder Prince Frederick Henry of Orange, after her marriage to Frederick William the (Great) Elector of Brandenburg-Prussia (1620-1688).[1] The *Still Life with Goblets and Lemon* entered the elector's collection before 1667 and bears the inventory number 148. Thus early on it was associated with both the House of Orange and the Hohenzollern family, which ruled Brandenburg-Prussia into modern times.

The Kalf remained in the Schloss Oranienburg until it was

Willem Kalf Still Life with Goblets and Lemon (not in The Hague)

transferred to the Stadtschloss in Berlin during the reign of King Frederick I of Prussia (1657-1718). The second inventory number on the back of the canvas, 1546, dates from this time. The work was also listed as item 1811 A 120 in the 1793 inventory of the Stadtschloss. Later moved to the Marmorpalais in Potsdam, the picture appears as number GK I 2255 in the inventory of 1860.

By descent the painting subsequently belonged to William II, Emperor of Germany (1859-1941). In 1918 it was moved from Potsdam to Huis Doorn, Holland, where William sought asylum after Germany's defeat at the end of World War I. The royal provenance ends in 1938 when the painting passed to the London dealer Griese, from whom Eugene Garbáty purchased it.

Garbáty (1885-1966), born in Berlin, headed one of the leading tobacco firms in pre-World War II Germany. An avid collector, he left much of his collection behind when he fled Schloss Alt-Doebern, Nieder-Lausitz, at the outbreak of the war. Living later in Shorehaven, East Norwalk, Connecticut, Garbáty remained an active collector and supporter of the arts; he donated for example, a number of European decorative arts to the Museum of Fine Arts, Boston. The Kalf appeared among the nineteen paintings sold by Garbáty in 1956,[2] and was purchased by Duits & Co. of London. The picture was subsequently acquired by an American private collector.

Although remaining anonymous, the current owner has shared the collection with the public in a series of handsome exhibitions.[3] From these it is evident that the collection's strength lies in its Dutch seventeenth-century holdings. Of interest to the topic at hand is another still life attributed to Kalf in this New York collection, which depicts the rustic subject matter (a *Kitchen Scene*) typical of Kalf's Paris period.[4]

While in Paris Kalf painted two distinct subject types: rustic farm or stable interiors in which special attention is given to humble still life elements, such as *A Kitchen Corner* (The Detroit Institute of Arts) [1],[5] and pure still lifes featuring heavily wrought silver and gold objects, such as the *Still Life with Ewer, Vessels, and Pomegranate* (Malibu, The J. Paul Getty Museum) [2].[6] After his return to Holland, the low-life interiors disappeared from Kalf's repertoire in favor of the increasingly elegant and haunting still lifes for which he is today so famous.

From this latter period the *Still Life with Goblets and Lemon* can be placed around 1660 with a group of highly sophisticated *pronkstilleven* compositions, such as the *Still Life with Goblets and Nautilus Cup* (Moscow, Pushkin Museum).[7] In the shallow pictorial space the artist clusters his objects at the table's edge,

1
Willem Kalf
A Kitchen Corner
Panel, 21.4 x 19.5 cm (8⅜ x 7⅝ in.)
Neither signed nor dated (ca. 1642-1643)
Detroit, The Detroit Institute of Arts, inv. no. 69.358

2
Willem Kalf
Still Life with Ewer, Vessels, and Pomegranate
Canvas, 103.5 x 81.2 cm (40¾ x 32 in.)
On table at right: *Kalf* (ca. 1646)
Malibu, The J. Paul Getty Musuem, inv. no. A54.P-1

emphasizing their three-dimensionality. Simultaneously he builds the composition out toward the viewer; the agate knife handle, the truncated folds of the Turkish carpet, and the playful spiral of the lemon peel all attempt to break through the barrier between our space and the one the objects inhabit. Kalf is interested in creating the most convincing illusion of the form, contour, and texture of his opulent and exotic objects, which include a *roemer*, *façon-de-Venise* goblet, flute glass, nautilus cup, blue-and-white porcelain dish, and a ripe melon. Here, as in all of Kalf's best works, the rarefied objects emerge as haunting, yet tangible, forms, picked out from the darkened setting by the mysterious light. Falling obliquely into the scene, the light differentiates the various textures, sparkles across the raised decorative patterns, and etches the contours of the exquisite glassware into the darkness.

1 Much of this early provenance was recorded by Dr. H. Börsch-Supan, Director of the Berlin Castles, 8 February 1966. Ms. in the collection of the present owner.
2 *Auction London 1956*, no. 82
3 *Gilbert 1966*; *Norfolk 1982*
4 *Norfolk 1982*, no. 23 and fig. 23
5 *Grisebach 1974*, pp. 222-223, no. 29 and fig. 31
6 *Fredericksen 1972*, p. 83, no. 107 and fig. 107;
Grisebach 1974, pp. 235-236, no. 62 and fig. 671
7 Inv. no. 582; *Moscow 1961*, p. 90; *Grisebach 1974*, pp. 264-265, no. 113 and fig. 119
LFO

Amsterdam 1619 – Amsterdam 1688

Canvas, 138.4 x 166.3 cm (54½ x 65½ in.)
Lower right: *P. koninck 1665*
Malibu, Calif., The J. Paul Getty Museum, inv. no. 85.PA.32

In 1641, after an apprenticeship of about two years with his brother Jacob, Philips Koninck (who also spelled his name Koning) returned to Amsterdam. By that time he was presumably already an independent painter. The paintings that were mentioned in 1639 in the inventory of his father, the goldsmith Aert Conincx, were copies after Rembrandt that Philips may have made even before becoming his brother's pupil. According to the biographer Houbraken, he was more than just a student of Rembrandt, as the two artists maintained close contact with each other over the years. Koninck must certainly have known Rembrandt's landscapes (especially the etchings) of the forties, as well as the fantastic etchings of Hercules Segers. His friend Joost van den Vondel aroused his interest in Catholicism, which helps explain a long series of biblical depictions. These originated quite independently of his painted work; it is primarily his panoramic landscapes that make an individual contribution to the fame of Dutch painting of the seventeenth century.

In 1955 the Swiss collector Emil Georg Bührle bought this painting, signed *P. koninck 1665*, from the dealer Edward Speelman of London. For three generations it had hung in the London residence of a family of bankers. In 1887, a year after he had become Baron Hillingdon, Charles Henry Mills (1830-1898) lent out the painting for an exhibition at the Royal Academy.[1] His son Charles William (1855-1940) succeeded him as a partner of the bank Glyn, Mills & Co., after which his place was taken by the third Baron Hillingdon, Arthur Robert Mills (1891-1952). After the latter's death, the fourth Baron, Charles Hedworth Mills (1922-1978),[2] disposed of the landscape by Koninck, whereupon it ended up with Speelman.

The purchase of Bührle may safely be called unusual. In the first place, the strength of Bührle's collection resided in the great French masters of the nineteenth century, and, secondly, less than a year earlier he had bought another landscape by Koninck, amazingly enough, one also from the year 1665. This was the *Landscape with a Resting Traveler* from the former H.E. ten Cate collection in Almelo, a work that still remains in the Emil G. Bührle Foundation Collection in Zürich.[3] Perhaps the unusual

Provenance

Collection Charles Henry Mills first Baron Hillingdon, London, before 1887-1898
Collection Charles William Mills second Baron Hillingdon, London, 1898-1919
Collection Arthur Robert Mills third Baron Hillingdon, London, 1919-1952
Collection Charles Hedworth Mills fourth Baron Hillingdon, London, 1952-1955
Dealer Edward Speelman, Ltd., London, 1955
Collection Emil Georg Bührle, Zürich, 1955-1956
Heirs Emil Georg Bührle, Zürich, 1956-1984
Dealer Edward Speelman, Ltd., London, 1984-1985
The J. Paul Getty Museum, Malibu, 1985

Bibliography

London 1887, p. 19, no. 72
Graves 1913-1915, vol. I, p. 270, no. 72 (1887)
Gerson 1936, p. 113, no. 97
London 1952-1953, vol. I, fig. 55, vol. II, p. 55, no. 269
Gerson 1953, p. 48
Zürich 1958, p. 68, no. 75 and p. 192, fig. 24
Maclaren 1960, p. 211
Plietzsch 1960, p. 111
Chicago / Minneapolis / Detroit 1969-1970, pp. 76 and 136, no. 74 and fig.
Gerson 1980, p. 113, no. 97
Sumowski 1983-B, pp. 1548 and 1611, nos. 1061-1062 and fig.
Chronique des arts 1986, p. 62
Sutton 1986, p. 145 and fig. 211
Walsh 1986, p. 217-218, no. 123 and fig.
Reinewald 1987, p. 65
Fredricksen 1988, no. 28 and fig.

Philips Koninck Panoramic Landscape

colorfulness and atmospheric effects of Koninck's panoramas made Bührle think of the landscapes of the impressionists. The collector died somewhat unexpectedly in 1956, when the construction of the wing to the Kunsthaus in Zürich that he financed was still in progress. In 1958 his entire collection was shown there, after which it was also to be seen in Edinburgh, London, Berlin, Munich, and Lucerne.[4] In 1960 the Bührle heirs set up the foundation to which they entrusted two-thirds of his collection, which since that time has been accessible to the public for a few hours a week in the house on 172 Zollikerstrasse in Zürich.[5] The landscape by Koninck that Bührle had bought shortly before his death was not selected for the foundation, but remained in the family. Once more by way of Speelman, it was sold in January of 1985 to The J. Paul Getty Museum in Malibu.[6]

In 1953 Horst Gerson perceived important correspondences between this painting and the *Panoramic Landscape with Fishermen* (Glasgow, Hunterian Art Gallery) [1],[7] both of which were then on view at the winter exhibition at the Royal Academy in London.[8] Also relevant is a comparison with the *Panoramic Landscape* of 1666, which was acquired in 1986 by the National Gallery of Scotland (Edinburgh) [2].[9] This recent museum acquisition was all the more remarkable because the painting – which had for some time hung on loan in the Fitzwilliam Museum in Cambridge – had never before been published.[10] The above-mentioned paintings from the years 1665 and 1666 show skies with the fleecy cloud formations that are customary for Koninck, whereas this part of the painting in Malibu shows strong contrasts of light and sharply demarcated edges of clouds. Peter Sutton wrote about this: 'Its unusually dramatic sky may be

by another hand.'[11] It is indeed possible that a seventeenth-century owner had these overpaintings done by another artist. X-ray examination has established that there was originally a cloudy sky in strips to be seen at the left. 'The present sky seems to reflect the influence of the Dutch Italianate landscapists,' wrote John Walsh somewhat vaguely.[12]

The general conception of Philips Koninck's panoramas of the fifties and sixties is simple and, as it were, reproduced schematically in a drawing in the Fondation Custodia (Paris) [3].[13] In the drawing one looks down on a landscape that unrolls from a high foreground. (Bird's-eye perspective is the revealing name for this concept.) In the foreground, copses of trees with houses have been placed without any suggestion of depth in the architecture. The open space of the winding river enabled the painter to take strides in the landscape as if wearing seven-league boots, for which he only needed to depict the remoter elements of the landscape somewhat smaller. In the distance, the forms fade into horizontal strips of light and dark. The illusion of an endless landscape is not disturbed by high mountains or buildings.

Also characteristic of Koninck in the Malibu painting are the inserted figures of somewhat deficient proportions. Maclaren expressed a preference for the decorative staffage of Adriaen van de Velde or Johannes Lingelbach and showed himself insensitive in this to what is unique about Koninck's style.[14] A somewhat naive treatment of the figures – and this is also true of the buildings – should be seen as a sort of trademark of the painter. It gives his work its own charm. In the drawing *A View of the Westerkerk and Its Surroundings* (Amsterdam, Amsterdams Historisch Museum)[15] his bungling of the perspective is so obvious that one has difficulty believing in the autograph status of the sheet. But Koninck rendered atmospheric images and not topographically correct records. With his surprisingly original coloration, the painter usually at once gains the sympathy of his public. Moreover, his grand vision adds an extra dimension to the art of landscape of his time.

Judson, among others, observed that composing panoramic landscapes is a Dutch tradition that began in the seventeenth century with the *Landscape outside Haarlem*, drawn by Hendrick Goltzius in 1603 (Rotterdam, Museum Boymans-van Beuningen).[16] Around 1650 Johannes Ruischer etched the river landscape as it unfolded before his eyes from the Cunera tower of Rhenen [4].[17] The birth of these two topographic records meant a break in the long tradition of largely imaginary landscapes. In both instances

▲ 1
Philips Koninck
Panoramic Landscape with Fishermen
Canvas, 111.8 x 155 cm (44 x 61 in.)
Neither signed nor dated (ca. 1665)
Glasgow, University of Glasgow, Hunterian Art Gallery

▶ 2
Philips Koninck
Panoramic Landscape
Canvas, 90.1 x 111.5 cm (35½ x 43⅞ in.)
At the bottom, to the right of center: *[P. koninck] 166[6]*
Edinburgh, National Gallery of Scotland, inv. no. 2434

the cause was somewhat prosaic. For in taking his walks in the open air, Goltzius was seeking a cure for his illness.[18] And Ruischer was one of many artists who, thanks to the Peace of Westphalia of 1648, were once again able to travel with sketchbook in hand along the Rhine to Germany.[19]

The combination of invention and reality, of tradition and innovation, may be one of the most fascinating characteristics of landscape painting of the seventeenth century. Koninck painted in his studio what Ruischer had seen in reality, and, in so doing, may well have made use of the latter's etchings (or of those by Rembrandt). Recognizable buildings or landscapes are the exception in his paintings.[20] The great example for Koninck was undoubtedly Hercules Segers, who was much admired by the artists of his circle. 'He was [...] as if pregnant with whole Provinces, to which he gave birth with immeasurable spaces' (in translation), Samuel van Hoogstraten wrote lyrically in 1678.[21] In 1656 Rembrandt owned no fewer than eight paintings by Segers and, naturally, numerous prints as well.[22] Hercules invented the combination of flat Dutch panoramas with wild foreign mountain fantasies that was first and foremost an inspiration for Rembrandt, especially in his paintings. Rembrandt must have communicated his enthusiasm to his pupils Samuel van Hoogstraten and Philips Koninck. Rembrandt certainly also had an eye for reality, and it is even probable that he drew out-of-doors with his friend Philips Koninck.[23] In their paintings, however, they continued to build on the innovations of Hercules. Rembrandt primarily took over the atmospheric effect of his landscapes, whereas Koninck carried the subject of the bird's-eye panorama to its greatest heights.

1 *London 1887*, p. 19, no. 72; *Graves 1913-1915*, vol. I, p. 270, no. 72 (1887)
2 *Burke's 1963*, p. 1226; *Debrett's 1980*, p. 604
3 *Vey 1973*, pp. 358-359, no. 156 and fig.; *Sumowski 1983-B*, pp. 1548 and 1611, no. 1061 and fig.
4 *Zürich 1958*
5 *Kauffmann 1973*, pp. 29-30; see also *Luthy 1979*, pp. 324-327
6 *Chronique des arts 1986*, p. 62; *Walsh 1986*, pp. 217-218, no. 123
7 *Glasgow 1973*, no. 16 and fig. (color plate) I; *Sumowski 1983-B*, pp. 1548 and 1612, no. 1062 and fig.
8 *Gerson 1953*, p. 48
9 *Edinburgh 1986*, p. 1 and fig.: 'Purchased by Private Treaty.'
10 *Edinburgh 1986-A*, p. 634, no. 74 and fig.; *Gerson 1936*, p. 109, no. 47, knew only the print after the painting; not in *Sumowski 1983-B*; not mentioned in the catalogues of the Fitzwilliam Museum.
11 *Sutton 1986*, p. 145
12 *Walsh 1986*, p. 218
13 *Van Hasselt 1977-1978*, p. 95, no. 63 and pl. 77; *Sumowski 1979-1985*, vol. VI, pp. 3030-3031, no. 1357 and fig.
14 *Maclaren 1960*, p. 211
15 Inv. no. A 10287; *Broos 1981*, pp. 159-161, no. 44 and fig.; *Sumowski 1979-1985*, vol. VI, pp. 3036-3037, no. 1359a and fig.
16 Inv. no. HG 253; *Reznicek 1961*, vol. I, p. 430, no. 404, vol. II, fig. 381; Judson in *Chicago / Minneapolis / Detroit 1969-1970*, p. 76, no. 74
17 *Hollstein*, vol. XX, pp. 157-158, nos. 16-18; *Deys 1981*, pp. 26-27, fig. 58, presented an assemblage of the three prints without the additions by Antoni Waterlo.
18 *Reznicek 1986*, pp. 61-62 (for the earliest development of the Dutch landscape, see the catalogue in which his article is included).
19 *Broos 1987*, p. 157
20 Regarding the rare topographic elements in the work of Koninck, see *Gerson 1936*, p. 13; *Dattenberg 1967*, pp. 250-251, no. 278; *Sumowski 1983-B*, p. 1532: 'Von Anfang an handelt es sich um Ideallandschaften.' The country residence at the right of the Getty painting is a recurring motif in Koninck's work, see *Gerson 1936*, p. 39.
21 *Van Hoogstraten 1678*, p. 312
22 *Strauss / Van der Meulen 1979*, pp. 348-388, nos. 1656 / 12-17, 40, 70, 93, 104, 124, 292
23 *Broos 1981*, pp. 150-151
    B B

3
Philips Koninck
Panoramic Landscape
Drawing, 194 x 310 mm (7⅝ x 12¼ in.)
On the back: *p. ko.* and *p. koning* (ca. 1650-1653)
Paris, Fondation Custodia, inv. no. 1199

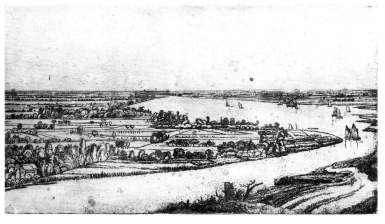

4
Johannes Ruischer
The Rhine near Rhenen (one etching of a set of three)
Etching, 118 x 209 mm (4⅝ x 8¼ in.)
Neither signed nor dated (ca. 1650)
London, British Museum

Jan Lievens

Leyden 1607 – Amsterdam 1674

Panel, 54 x 46.5 cm (21¼ x 18¼ in.)
Neither signed nor dated (ca. 1628)
Norfolk, Va., collection Mr. and Mrs. George M. Kaufman

Jan Lievens's was a precocious talent. As an eight-year-old he was already receiving painting lessons in Leyden, and in his tenth year he went to Amsterdam, where he preceded his fellow towns-man Rembrandt as a pupil of Pieter Lastman. Lievens had been working independently for some time before Rembrandt's debut in 1625. In Leyden, they are said to have shared a studio, or in any case to have arrived at a far-reaching form of collaboration, between 1626 and 1630 / 1631. In 1632 Lievens sought his fortunes in England, where he came under the influence of Anthony van Dyck. Between 1635 and 1644 he worked in Antwerp, and afterward, until his death in 1674, in Amsterdam. In the exhibition in Brunswick (1979) that was dedicated to the painter, Lievens was called 'a painter in the shadow of Rembrandt,' which does not do justice to his individual qualities, especially as a draftsman and etcher.

Provenance
Collection Marion Louise Nichols, Cambridge, Mass.
Private collection, Boston, 1975-1986
Dealer Hoogsteder-Naumann, Ltd., New York, 1986
Collection Mr. and Mrs. George M. Kaufman,
Norfolk, Va., 1986

Bibliography
Sumowski 1983-B, p. 1799, nos. 1252 and 1253,
p. 1892, fig. 1253

This study of a head in the collection of Linda and George M. Kaufman (see cat. no. 31) went totally unmentioned in the scholarly literature before it emerged in the art market in 1986, after which Sumowski published the unsigned and undated panel as an authentic Jan Lievens.[1] Of the numerous depictions of gray-haired old men or bearded men by Lievens that are mentioned in old auction catalogues, not one conforms in format or execution to this powerfully painted *Bearded Man with a Beret*.[2] The attribution by Sumowski is nevertheless convincing if, for instance, one compares this 'portrait' to a painted *Old Man in Profile* of identical size, dated around 1626 (Vienna, Kunst-historisches Museum),[3] in which a similar beret appears. The diagonal placing of the head of the model is most similar to the painting *An Old Man with a Broad Beard* of around 1629 (Brunswick, Herzog Anton Ulrich-Museum) [1],[4] which features Lievens's monogram. The painting under discussion originated in the period in which Lievens collaborated with Rembrandt, and, to be more precise, after the work in Vienna and before the one in Brunswick.

In these three studies of heads, the way in which the structure of the beard is drawn in the wet paint with the end of the brush is typical of how Jan Lievens and Rembrandt worked in their

1
Jan Lievens
An Old Man with a Broad Beard
Panel, 54 x 42 cm (21¼ x 16½ in.)
Upper right, above the shoulder: *IL* (in ligature)
(ca. 1628-1630)
Brunswick, Herzog Anton Ulrich-Museum,
inv. no. 243

Jan Lievens A Bearded Man with a Beret

Leyden period. One encounters a comparable treatment of the hair passages in the sketch *A Bearded Man with a Book* (Darmstadt, Hessisches Landesmuseum) [2].[5] This attractive drawing in red chalk has been attributed to Rembrandt himself, or to one of his pupils from Leyden, but is now considered with growing consent to be a study by Jan Lievens.[6] This opinion, no doubt, relates to the renewed appreciation of the graphic qualities of Lievens's work. These are best expressed in his etchings of character heads dating from the end of the Leyden period, such as *An Old Man Seen from the Side* [3].[7]

A number of the etchings of male heads were published in sets with titles such as *Variae Effigies a Joanne Livio* or, in a Dutch version, *Diverse Tronikens geëtst van I[an] L[ievens]* (Diverse Mugs etched by Jan Lievens).[8] The latter title indicates how we ought to interpret the head in the Kaufman collection, namely as a 'mug.' In the seventeenth century, this term was used to denote distinctive heads, such as 'an old man's mug with a long, broad beard' (in translation). A comparable work by Rembrandt in a 1637 inventory was so named.[9] In the same inventory, a youthful variant of this genre was described as an invention of Lievens: 'A boy's mug with long, curly hair [and] bulging fair cheeks' (in translation).[10] Working after life, Jan Lievens and Rembrandt drew, painted, and etched their family members, each other, or picturesque models, whom they wrapped in Eastern-looking robes and whom they adorned with caps or turbans and gold necklaces, or with the attributes of some saint or apostle. The mug was probably a new genre that was jointly conceived by the two Leyden painters, who found in it an acceptable compromise between the portrait and the history piece. They knew that in the theoretical literature historical painting was more highly esteemed than portraiture. Their teacher Pieter Lastman had undoubtedly directed them to *Het Schilder-Boeck* of Carel van Mander, who had asserted that only the 'road of historical images' could lead to perfection, and that the 'rendering after life' was a dead-end side road.[11]

It is not inconceivable that Lievens and Rembrandt partly derived this new type of painting from the work of the greatest history painter of their time, Peter Paul Rubens. He, after all, also made studies of picturesque male and female heads for later application in history pieces.[12] Paulus Pontius engraved some of these oil studies for a model book. One of its pages shows several heads that could have specifically inspired Jan Lievens [4].[13] But the credit goes to Rembrandt and Jan Lievens for creating with the mug a genre intended for the art trade.

We have a highly astute, contemporary assessment of the way in which the two young Leyden painters expressed their ambition. Before 1630 the critic and connoisseur Constantijn Huygens, who sought out both painters in their studio, passed the judgment 'that in taste and liveliness of feeling Rembrandt excels over Lievens, but the latter overshadows Rembrandt in a certain grandeur of invention and of bold designs and figures' (in translation).[14] Huygens thus acknowledged that each painter had his strong points, and he added that Lievens painted life-size, and by preference, even bigger forms, and thus competed with Rembrandt, who preferred to work in a small format. One can illustrate this mutual competition with various examples, especially among the history pieces of the years 1628 to 1631.[15]

In the painting of mugs, too, the two painters had crossed their brushes, as would appear from the two 'portraits' for which Rembrandt posed with a halberd. Lievens's work is in the Cevat collection (Saint Peter Port, Guernsey),[16] that of Rembrandt in the Mauritshuis.[17] Finally, the comparison presents itself between the Kaufman painting and a history piece that Rembrandt painted in the same period, *Two Disputing Scholars* (Melbourne,

2
Jan Lievens
A Bearded Man with a Book
Chalk drawing, 166 x 134 mm (6½ x 5¼ in.)
Neither signed nor dated (ca. 1626-1627)
Darmstadt, Hessisches Landesmuseum,
inv. no. AE 672

3
Jan Lievens
An Old Man Seen from the Side
Etching, 162 x 144 mm (6⅜ x 5⅝ in.)
Lower left: *I. L* (ca. 1628-1630)
Amsterdam, Rijksprentenkabinet

4
Paulus Pontius after Rubens
Nine Studies of Heads
Engraving, 327 x 220 mm (12⅞ x 8⅝ in.)
On the title page: *Paul Pontius sculpsit* (after 1623)
Amsterdam, Rijksprentenkabinet

5
Rembrandt
Two Disputing Scholars
Panel, 72.3 x 59.5 cm (28½ x 23⅜ in.)
Lower left: *RL* (ca. 1628)
Melbourne, National Gallery of Victoria,
inv. no. (cat. 1961, no. 349/4)

National Gallery of Victoria) [**5**].[18] Thus we may assume that Rembrandt (from whose hand we have a drawn preparatory study for this painting) and Lievens made use of the same model with the splendid white beard. One is once more inclined to concur with Huygens, who found that 'in history pieces, as we usually call them, he [Lievens] is a great and admirable artist, but he is not likely to match the lively powers of imagination of Rembrandt' (in translation). Huygens predicted a great future as portraitist for the former painter.[19] Lievens was indeed to receive commissions from the English court thanks to his fame as a portrait painter.[20] That was much more lucrative than the making of mugs.

1 See Provenance; *Sumowski 1983-B*, pp. 1799 and 1892, no. 1253 and fig.
2 *Schneider / Ekkart 1973*, pp. 131-142, nos. 154-214a
3 Inv. no. 741; *Schneider / Ekkart 1973*, p. 135, no. 170; *Sumowski 1983-B*, pp. 1799 and 1891, no. 1252 and fig.
4 *Sumowski 1983-B*, pp. 1801 and 1902, no. 1263; *Klessmann 1983*, pp. 121-122, no. 243 and fig.; there is another version of this painting in The Hague (Mauritshuis / Schilderijengalerij Prins Willem v, inv. no. 85; *Hoetink et al. 1985*, p. 392, no. 85 and fig.); these two versions could be compared at the Jan Lievens exhibition, *Brunswick 1979*, pp. 74-77, nos. 20-21 and fig.
5 *Sumowski 1979-1985*, vol. VII, pp. 3664-3665, no. 1643 and fig.
6 An overview of the opinions was given by Sumowski (see note 5); see also *Benesch 1973*, vol. I, p. 7, no. 16 and fig. 21; *Schneider / Ekkart 1973*, pp. 384-385, no. SZ. 413
7 B. 22; *Hollstein*, vol. XI, p. 38, no. 40
8 *Schatborn / Ornstein-van Slooten 1988-1989*, pp. 6 and 9, notes 2-6, p. 13, figs. VI-IX, pp. 48-50, nos. 22-27 and fig.
9 *Strauss / Van der Meulen 1979*, p. 144, no. 1637 / 4
10 *Broos 1981-1982*, pp. 252-253 and note 35
11 *Van Mander 1604*, fol. 281 recto; see also *Broos 1978-1979*, pp. 117-118
12 See, for instance, *Braun 1979-1980*, vol. I, p. 122, no. 231 and fig., vol. II, pp. 110-111, no. 643 and fig.
13 *Hollstein*, vol. XVII, p. 200, no. 157; *Van den Wijngaert 1940*, pp. 84-85, no. 557-14 (on this sheet appear reproductions of the studies of heads mentioned in note 12).
14 *Kan 1946*, p. 79; see also *Junius 1644*, p. 72
15 *Broos 1977-A*, proposition 2
16 *Brunswick 1979*, pp. 72-73, no. 19 and fig.; *Schneider / Ekkart 1973*, p. 335, no. 264b
17 Inv. no. 148; *Bruyn et al. 1982*, pp. 225-230, no. A 21 and fig.; *Broos 1986*, pp. 285-290, no. 40 and fig.
18 *Bruyn et al. 1982*, pp. 159-168, no. A 13 and fig.
19 *Kan 1946*, p. 80
20 *Brown 1979*, p. 745 and *Brown 1983*, p. 670
    BB

Johannes Lingelbach An Italian Harbor

Frankfurt 1622 – Amsterdam 1674

Canvas, 85.1 x 114.3 cm (33½ x 45 in.)
Lower right: *I LINGELBACH/ 1667*
Sarasota, Fla., The John and Mable Ringling Museum of Art, inv. no. SN 272

Johannes Lingelbach was born in Frankfurt, but in 1634, when he was twelve, he moved to Amsterdam with his family. In 1644 he traveled to Rome, where he is mentioned until 1649. In the following year he was back in Amsterdam, and in 1653 the painter married Tietje Bussi. Even after he had returned to the Netherlands, he continued to incorporate into his landscapes, market scenes, and harbor views the manifold impressions that he had gathered in Italy. The scenes in the manner of the *Bamboccianti***, especially street scenes with tradesmen, originated before 1650. Subsequently his figures remained more important than their setting, with the latter consisting ever less of recognizable topographic (Roman) elements.**

'Many of his art works depict one or another Italian Seaport,' wrote the biographer Arnold Houbraken (in translation), who knew many of the scenes that were still in Amsterdam.[1] In Houbraken's day this harbor view dated 1667, now in Sarasota, was most probably among those still in Amsterdam, in the collection of Anthony Bierens, both father and son. In 1747 it was auctioned as 'An Italian Seaport, by J. Lingelbagh; as good and capital as is to be seen by him; 46 in. broad, 33 in. high' (in translation).[2] Anthony Bierens, Jr. (1693-1747), lived at 106 Warmoesstraat, in the house called De gekroonde Star (The crowned Star), which had been bought in 1702 by his father, Anthony Bierens, Sr. (ca. 1653-1738), who dealt in silk. Possibly the father had already begun to collect art – the son was in any case a passionate collector. We know exactly what used to be in the rooms of De gekroonde Star in 1741, because in that year an inventory was compiled to facilitate the division of property upon the death of the mother of Anthony, Jr.[3] In addition to a collection of paintings, among which was 'An Italian Seaport by I. Lingelbach' (in translation), there was a well-stocked scholarly library and a then famous 'physisch kabinet,' that is, a collection of instruments for chemistry and physics.[4] Anthony Bierens, Jr., was single when he died intestate in 1747. In May of that year the library and the 'physisch kabinet' were sold in public. In June the house itself was sold, and in July the furnishings and paintings.[5] The harbor view by Lingelbach then went underground for more than one and a half centuries.

Provenance

(?) Collection Anthony Bierens, Amsterdam, before 1738
Collection widow Bierens, Amsterdam, 1738-1741
Collection Anthony Bierens, Jr., Amsterdam, 1741-1747
Auction Anthony Bierens, Jr., Amsterdam, 1747 (ƒ341)
Collection Joshua Charles Vanneck fourth Baron Huntingfield, Heveningham Hall, Yoxford, Suffolk, before 1915
Auction Huntingfield, London, 1915
Auction London, 1920
Auction London, 1929 (£141.15 to Ringling)
Collection John Ringling, Sarasota, Ca' d'Zan, 1929-1936
The John and Mable Ringling Museum of Art, Sarasota, 1936

Bibliography

Hoet 1752-1770, vol. II, p. 199, no. 10
Auction London 1915, p. 21, no. 93
Auction London 1920, p. 3, no. 3
Auction London 1929-A , p. 18, no. 132
Suida 1949, p. 237, no. 272
Bierens de Haan 1957, p. 119, no. 8, pp. 124, 125, no. 10
Burger-Wegener 1976, p. 260, no. 73
Robinson et al. 1980, no. 95 and fig.
Janson 1986, p. 111, no. 44., and fig.

When John Ringling bought Lingelbach's painting in 1929, nothing was known about the earlier history of the piece. Research in the excerpts of auction catalogues in the Rijksbureau voor Kunsthistorische Documentatie (RKD) in The Hague has revealed that it must nevertheless be identical to the painting dated 1667 that was auctioned in London in 1915 and 1920. In 1915 the collection of Lord Huntingfield came under the hammer. Joshua Charles Vanneck fourth Baron Huntingfield (1842-1915) died a bachelor. He had served with the Scotch Guards and took part in the Egyptian expedition of 1882 and the campaign in the Sudan of 1885. His collection (almost seventy pieces, largely by Dutch masters) was auctioned in the ancestral home, Heveningham Hall in Yoxford, Suffolk. Whether (and if so, for how long) Lingelbach's harbor view was in the family remains an unanswered question. In 1796 his great-grandfather, also named Joshua Vanneck (1745-1816), became the first Baron Huntingfield of Heveningham Hall.[6] In 1920 Christie's in London once again auctioned Lingelbach's painting, then said to be 'the property of a nobleman.' Notable is that this 'collection' contained a number of the same paintings as in 1915, so that we may conclude that the unsold portion of the Hunting-field collection came under the hammer more than once.[7]

In 1929 Christie's brought *An Italian Harbor* by Johannes Lingelbach to auction for the third and last time. Present in the hall was the American magnate John Ringling (1860-1936), the co-owner of Bros. Barnum & Bailey Circus, who had emerged since 1925 as a collector of repute.[8] Remarkably, he himself did the bidding at auctions, whereas American collectors normally bought from, or by way of, intermediaries, mainly from the major art dealers. In the summer, it was Ringling's practice to combine the contracting of new circus acts with many visits to dealers and auction houses. He sometimes bought twenty or thirty paintings in one afternoon. On 25 June 1929 he acquired a mere four paintings at Christie's: a *Saint Sebastian* by Francesco Zaganelli da Cotignola, a *Candaules and Gyges*, attributed to

Eustace Le Sueur (now called 'French School'), a *Susanna and the Elders* by Titian (now believed to be a copy after Luca Giordano),[9] and Lingelbach's *Italian Harbor*. In general, he preferred baroque, theatrical representations, and it must have been the Italian atmosphere of Lingelbach's painting that struck his fancy.

On the Sarasota Bay in Florida, between 1924 and 1926, Ringling built a handsome pink-colored country residence in the Venetian Gothic style, which was called the Ca' d'Zan (John's House). Here, and in the subsequently constructed museum nearby, his growing collections were housed [I]. The museum was not yet completed when his fifty-four-year-old wife, Mable, died in 1929. Only after the death of John in 1936, and after much haggling over his inheritance, could the doors to the John and Mable Ringling Museum of Art be opened in 1948. Within the remarkably short period of one decade John Ringling had assembled an unusually attractive collection of more than one

▲
2
Johannes Lingelbach
An Oriental Harbor View
Canvas, 154 x 194 cm (60⅗ x 76⅜ in.)
Lower left, on a small column: *I. LINGELBACH / 1670*
The Hague, Schilderijengalerij Prins Willem V,
inv. no. 86

I
John Ringling (1860-1936) on the grounds of the
John and Mable Ringling Museum of Art.
Photograph from the 1920s

hundred Dutch and Flemish masters, to which another twenty-five works or so were added later to fill in gaps (see cat. no. 48).[10]

The Ringling Museum on the Gulf of Mexico appears to be in such a remote place that the compiler of an oeuvre catalogue of Johannes Lingelbach did not know that this handsome, dated canvas was kept there. Catja Burger-Wegener lost track of this painting after the Huntingfield auctions of 1915 and 1920.[11] It should be mentioned in this context that it had not been lent out for an exhibition and that this is the first time in about 250 years that it can be seen in the Netherlands. It can well stand comparison with similar harbor views by Lingelbach in the Rijksmuseum in Amsterdam and also with an *Oriental Harbor View* of 1670 in the Schilderijengalerij Prins Willem v in The Hague [2].[12] Characteristic of the artist is the large number of figures in the foreground, arranged in small groups between barrels, bales, and other merchandise, and in each case constituted of a few men seated next to a standing Oriental. Because of the dramatic recession of the coastlines, with their ever diminishing buildings and vanishing point at the horizon, the landscape has a strong perspectival effect. Striking is the absence of (sub)tropical vegetation. The colorful costumes, including the odd turban, and the galleys create a sufficiently Eastern atmosphere within the 'Italian' surroundings.

These harbor views painted in Amsterdam depicted the idea of far-away places and not a specific location. While in the Netherlands, Lingelbach did draw on his memories of such things as the buildings and monuments of Rome, but he also liked to use prints to refresh his memory. Specifically, the prints of Stefano della Bella were a continual source of inspiration for him.[13] For instance, diverse compositions feature a Polish rider taken from a print by Della Bella.[14] For the painting in Sarasota he may have consulted a print of *The Harbor of Livorno* from 1654 or 1655 [3].[15] From it he could have taken the form of the boat at the left, with the protruding bunch of oars. However, he painted the somewhat unstable statue of Mercury, which here dominates the quay, after a prototype by Raphael that was rendered in prints by Marcantonio Raimondi and others [4].[16]

All this gave the agreeable sensation of a far-away world, comparable with the 'Chinese' decorations on the porcelain manufactured in Delft in the seventeenth century (cat. no. 41, fig. 1). Houbraken greatly appreciated these scenes: 'The way in which, especially in the depictions of his Seaports [...], he also renders and differentiates the diverse national character of the merchants, at the loading and unloading of Sea ships and Galleys, in their recognizable costume, and further treats these

with a pleasant water view, blue horizon, and thinly clouded sky, giving strength to and bringing out the foreground' (in translation).[17]

1 *Houbraken 1718-1721*, vol. II, p. 146
2 *Hoet 1752-1770*, vol. II, p. 199, no. 10
3 *Bierens de Haan 1957*, pp. 113-123
4 *Bierens de Haan 1957*, pp. 114-120; *Wijnman et al. 1974*, p. 114
5 *Bierens de Haan 1957*, pp. 123-124
6 *Complete Peerage*, vol. VI, p. 674
7 *Auction London 1920*, p. 3, no. 3
8 *WWWA*, vol. I, p. 1036; *NCAB*, vol. XL, pp. 55-56
9 *Suida 1949*, pp. 49-50, no. 48 and fig. (see also *Sarasota 1976*, pp. 70-71, no. 65 and fig.); pp. 140-141, no. 162 (see also *Sarasota 1976*, p. 170, no. 186 and fig.); p. 314, no. 384 and fig.
10 Wilson in *Robinson et al. 1980*, n.p.
11 *Burger-Wegener 1976*, p. 260, no. 73, in which the provenance is still given as the collection of an A.M. Bouwens in The Hague.
12 *Duparc 1980*, pp. 56 and 189, no. 86 and fig.; *Burger-Wegener 1976*, pp. 269-270, no. 90
13 *Burger-Wegener 1976*, pp. 85, 88, 90, 91 and 99; *Schloss 1982*, p. 37
14 *Broos 1977-A*, proposition 3; *Burger-Wegener 1976*, pp. 102-103 and 109, notes 236-237; *Schloss 1982*, pp. 22, 37 and 157, note 30
15 *De Vesme / Massar 1971*, vol. I, no. 847, vol. II, fig. 847
16 B. 343; *Illustrated Bartsch*, vol. XXVII, p. 38, no. 343 and fig.
17 *Houbraken 1718-1721*, vol. II, p. 147
   BB

4
Marcantonio Raimondi after Raphael
Mercury
Engraving, 309 x 205 mm (12⅛ x 8 in.)
Neither signed nor dated (ca. 1517-1520)
London, British Museum

◄ **3**
Stefano della Bella
The Harbor of Livorno
Engraving, 228 x 347 mm (9 x 13⅝ in.)
Lower left: *S. D. Bella In & F.* (ca. 1654-1655)
Vienna, Graphische Sammlung Albertina

Dordrecht 1634 – Amsterdam 1693

Canvas, 60 x 66 cm (23⅝ x 26 in.)
Lower right: .N. MAES (ca. 1655)
Philadelphia, Pa., The Philadelphia Museum of Art, inv. no. 44-9-4

According to the biographer Houbraken, Maes had learned the art of drawing from a 'common Master' (in Dordrecht?) but the art of painting from Rembrandt in Amsterdam. By 1653 he was back in Dordrecht, where he put a date to his first painting and got married a year later. His genre scenes with large figures all date from the period before 1660. After that time he painted only portraits. To quote Houbraken: 'He had a skillful and flattering brush that served him wonderfully well in the painting of portraits' (in translation). Also striking is Houbraken's claim that Maes abandoned Rembrandt's way of painting for the sake of his public, especially 'the young Ladies': Maes's oeuvre clearly shows this shift in style. In 1673 he settled permanently in Amsterdam, where the elegance of his portraits met with great success.

When, in 1911, August de Ridder died at the age of seventy-four, only a few of his intimate friends knew that in his villa at Schönberg near Kronberg in the Taunus area, he had assembled a large collection of paintings by Dutch and Flemish old masters. In 1910 Wilhelm von Bode compiled the collection catalogue, which appeared in a very limited edition and was reprinted in 1913. The present painting by Nicolaes Maes was one of the showpieces of the collection.[1] De Ridder was a successful industrialist. He was born in Antwerp and settled in Frankfurt, where he first collected modern art. After 1890, not liking the impressionism advancing from France, he applied himself mainly to older art, which he usually procured in Paris and New York from the dealer Kleinberger (p. 41, fig. 27).[2] After his death it was rumored that the same Kleinberger put the entire collection up for sale and refused an offer of half a million pounds sterling from a 'dollar king.'[3]

The Städelsches Kunstinstitut at Frankfurt could for a few years show the De Ridder collection to the public as a loan from his heirs, but in 1913 the latter decided to put the old master paintings up for auction in Paris. Then World War I broke out, and the French government confiscated the collection, which was deemed to be German property.[4] Finally, in 1924, the public sale took place, luring art dealers and museum directors from all

Provenance

Auction Count De Turenne, Paris, 1852 (Frf. 4,860 to Nieuwenhuys)
Auction Adrian Hope, London, 1894 (900 guineas to Sedelmeyer)
Dealer Ch. Sedelmeyer, Paris, 1898
Collection Jules Porgès, Paris, 1898
Dealer F. Kleinberger, Paris
Collection August de Ridder, Schönberg (near Kronberg, in the Taunus area), before 1910-1911
Städelsches Kunstinstitut, Frankfurt, 1911-1913 (on loan from the De Ridder heirs)
Heirs De Ridder, Paris, 1913-1924 (sequestered by the French state, stored with Kleinberger)
Auction De Ridder, Paris, 1924 (Frf. 245,000 to Kleinberger)
Dealer F. Kleinberger, New York, 1925
(?) Dealer D.A. Hoogendijk, Amsterdam, 1928
Dealer Duveen Brothers, New York
Collection Roland L. Taylor, Philadelphia, 1929(?)-1943
The Philadelphia Museum of Art, Philadelphia, 1944 (gift of Mrs. Gordon A. Hardwick and Mrs. W. Newbold Ely in memory of Mr. and Mrs. R.L. Taylor)

Bibliography

Auction Paris 1852, p. 15, no. 44
Auction London 1894, p. 79, no. 39 and fig.
Richter 1894, p. 332
Roberts 1897, vol. II, p. 237
Paris 1898, no. 81 and fig.
Bode 1910, pp. 12-13 and 32 and fig.
Wurzbach, vol. II (1910), p. 90
Benkard 1912, pp. 606-608 and fig.
Bode 1913, p. 9, no. 33 and fig.
Van Stuwe 1913, pp. 538-539
HdG 28 (vol. VI [1915], p. 489, no. 28)
Graves 1918-1921, vol. II, p. 196, no. 39 (1894)
Auction Paris 1924, no. 38
Catroux 1924, p. 129
Rouchès 1924, p. 529
Valentiner 1924, p. 49 and pl. 43
Valentiner 1925, no. 14 and fig.
De Jonge 1947, pp. 71-72 and fig. 42
Philadelphia 1965, p. 42
Chicago / Minneapolis / Detroit 1969-1970, pp. 84-85 and 147, no. 88 and fig.
Rifkin 1969, p. 90
Sumowski 1979-1985, vol. VIII, p. 4178
Sumowski 1983-B, pp. 1954, 1956, 2017 and 2077, no. 1351 and fig.
Berlin / London / Philadelphia 1984, pp. 216-217 and 366, no. 65 and fig.
Miller 1985, vol. I, p. 75, vol. II, pp. 497 and 515 and fig. 21
Sutton 1986, pp. 230-231, fig. 337
Sutton 1990, pp. 190-192, no. 66 and fig.

Nicolaes Maes A Girl Plucking a Duck

over the world. In the newspapers the event was compared to the Rudolf Kann auction in 1907 and that of Steengracht in 1913. The auction raised a total of almost twelve million francs, which meant an absolute record for that time.[5] Willem Martin bought Aart van der Neer's *Winterscape* for the Mauritshuis for 61,000 francs.[6] *A Girl Plucking a Duck* by Nicolaes Maes was started at 100,000 and went for 245,000 francs to Kleinberger.[7]

Kleinberger took the painting to his establishment in the United States, where, in 1925, he parted with it for an exhibition in Detroit.[8] What a critic had already feared in 1913 was indeed to come true: 'What once ends up on the other side of the duck's pond rarely returns' (in translation).[9] Around 1929 the American banker and financier Roland Leslie Taylor (1868-1943) bought the painting from the Duveen Brothers. He was a collector of art, antiques, and first editions, and was of a philanthropic disposition. After his death in 1943 his daughters Anita Marjory (Mrs. Gordon A. Hardwick) and Elisabeth Anne (Mrs. W. Newbold Ely) donated the painting in memory of their parents to the museum in Philadelphia, of which Roland Taylor had been a trustee.[10]

Little is known about the former owners of the *Girl Plucking a Duck*. In 1894 it was auctioned in London for 900 guineas as part of the collection of Adrian Hope. This sale, too, caused quite a stir, not because of the high value of the collection but because the owner had gone bankrupt and there was talk of the defrauding of the Bank of England.[11] On this occasion the work of Maes was presented as a highlight of the collection, and in later commentaries on the De Ridder collection one can also detect admiration for the light-dark effect and special coloring of this painting. Bode spoke of a solemn, sometimes even melancholic mood in this scene.[12]

The painting is among the first of a series of interior views from the second half of the fifties in which women play the leading role. Initially, Maes had some difficulty with his spatial constructions, showing a preference for views through adjoining rooms. In the painting in Philadelphia, the tile floor is so steep that the apples cannot help but roll out of the basket, while the entrance to the back room defies the laws of perspective. Although Maes constructed the space not without some inept juggling, he nevertheless derived several details from reality.

Lady De Jonge pointed out that the bowl displayed in the middle of the floor is a typical example of the Northern Netherlandish pottery that was manufactured after the second decade of the seventeenth century.[13] The decoration consists of a heavy, dark edge with good-luck emblems of the kind that were copied from Chinese models by Dutch majolica painters, which were often reproduced with distortions. The center of such a dish could display an edifying inscription, a Dutch landscape, or a simple decoration [1].[14] The jugs on the windowsill and along the wall, and the bowl on the larder, are examples of the utilitarian pottery or decorative Delft blue porcelain that Maes also painted in other interiors.

Until now it has gone unobserved that the girl plucking a duck was also painted after life, or, at least, was rendered after some preparatory work. As it happens, Maes made a drawing with two studies of his mother's maid Aeltje (London, British Museum) [2].[15] He added the inscription: 'this is my aeltien / the good woman of my mother' (in translation). On this sheet he subsequently drew another woman in profile and, finally, in duplicate at the bottom, a girl with a white cap on her bent head. He used these last two studies for the duck-plucking girl.[16]

Nevertheless, the painter was not out to depict daily reality. The game bag hanging from a nail and the gun on the wall indicate that the ducks are a catch. Hunting was no pastime for

◀ 1
Majolica plate
Diameter 34.3 cm (13½ in.)
Delft pottery (ca. 1620-1640)
The Hague, Haags Gemeentemuseum,
inv. no. OCN-1-1924

▶ 2
Nicolaes Maes
Studies of Heads of Women
Drawing, 160 x 93 mm (6¼ x 3⅝ in.)
Neither signed nor dated (ca. 1655)
London, British Museum, inv. no. 1895-9-15-1202

common people (see cat. no. 29), so something out of the ordinary is happening here. That unusualness is emphasized by the half-empty wineglass and the jug on the table in the back room, things that make the hunter's absence intriguing. Obviously present, however, is the stalking cat, who is set to disturb the domestic peace. Maes more than once painted a stalking cat in scenes in which the maid has fallen asleep (London, National Gallery) [**3**][17] or is courting (Dordrecht, Dordrechts Museum).[18] In these paintings of 1655 and 1657 the neglect of the household is unambiguously exposed, but in the painting of the same period in Philadelphia, things seem, for the moment, to be all virtuous. However, one is forewarned.

The cat with its lurking eyes constituted a clear hint to the contemporary spectator, who was familiar with what was said of the stealthy animal in popular parlance. The book of proverbs of 1636 by Johan de Brune includes the expression, 'The lurking cats are a clever lot; they snatch the meat out of the pot' (in translation).[19] 'That is to say, that silent sneaks are treacherous, and that one must be especially on one's guard for them' (in translation), Tuinman explained in 1726.[20] Perhaps applicable here is what Father Poirters had already stated in 1646, in his exposition on the 'Supervision of Parents of their Daughters': 'it would not be for the first time that the creeping cats have stolen the Meat from the pot' (in translation).[21]

Numerous images show the cat as a symbol of voluptuousness, which Maes more than once depicted in the company of kissing couples.[22] Here the animal apparently serves as a symbol for the absent man, who has brought the unsuspecting girl a couple of birds. At the time, a hunter offering fowl was a relatively common metaphorical image for an attempt at seduction. *Vogelen* (birding) is an expression that is still understood today.[23] The double meaning in this scene refers to this figure of speech. A follower of Maes, Reynier Covyn, understood his message very well and translated it after his own fashion. In a variation on the composition, he even had the hunter perform instead of the cat.

The wag embraces the girl who plucks his duck, and he raises his glass in the process (location unknown) [**4**].[24] Part of the possibilities and charms of seventeenth-century painting is that what the one (Bode) takes for melancholy, the other may interpret as erotica.[25]

1 *Bode 1910* and *Bode 1913*
2 *Bode 1910*, *passim*
3 *Van Stuwe 1913*, p. 530
4 *Catroux 1924*, p. 126, and newspaper clippings with *Auction Paris 1924* (RKD).
5 *Hôtel Drouot 1924*, p. 1: 'La vente de la galerie De Ridder bat tous les records'; see also the newspaper clippings with *Auction Paris 1924* (RKD).
6 Inv. no. 787; *Duparc 1980*, pp. 61-62, no. 787 and fig. p. 194
7 *Auction Paris 1924*, no. 38 and accompanying price list with notes by Hofstede de Groot (RKD).
8 *Valentiner 1925*, no. 14 and fig.
9 *Van Stuwe 1913*, pp. 531-532
10 *NCAB*, vol. XXXII, pp. 146-147
11 *Richter 1894*, p. 331
12 *Bode 1910*, pp. 12-13; see also *Van Stuwe 1913*, pp. 538-539
13 *De Jonge 1947*, pp. 71-72
14 Examples in *Korf 1981*, p. 51, fig. 101, pp. 181-182, figs. 476-478, p. 214, fig. 604, p. 226, fig. 651 and opp. p. 227
15 *Sumowski 1979-1985*, vol. VIII, pp. 4008-4009, no. 1781 and fig.
16 According to a communication from W. van de Watering (photo collection RKD); *Miller 1985*, vol. I, p. 75, pointed out that the girl is dressed in West Frisian costume.
17 *Maclaren 1960*, pp. 228-229, no. 207; *Sumowski 1983-B*, pp. 2017 and 2078, no. 1352 and fig.
18 Inv. no. NK 3045; *Sumowski 1983-B*, pp. 2023 and 2096, no. 1370 and fig.
19 *De Brune 1636*, p. 326
20 *Tuinman 1726*, vol. I, p. 185
21 *Poirters 1646/ 1714*, p. 320
22 *De Jongh 1968-1969*, pp. 47-48; *Amsterdam 1976*, pp. 144-149, nos. 33-34; with Maes, see *Sumowski 1983-B*, pp. 2016 and 2075, no. 1349 and fig., pp. 2019 and 2083, no. 1357 and fig., pp. 2023 and 2096, no. 1370 and fig.
23 *De Jongh 1968-1969*, pp. 35-40, figs. 9-12
24 *Auction New York 1981*, p. 108, no. 161 and fig.; the similarity was noted by Robinson in *Berlin / London / Philadelphia 1984*, p. 366, no. 65, note 4; see also *Sumowski 1983-B*, p. 2017, no. 1351.
25 The erotic secondary meaning of the painting in Philadelphia was described for the first time by Judson in *Chicago / Minneapolis / Detroit 1969-1970*, pp. 84-85, no. 88.

BB

◄ 3
Nicolaes Maes
The Sleeping Kitchen Maid
Panel, 70 x 53.5 cm (27¼ x 21 in.)
Lower right: N. MAES. 1655.
London, National Gallery, inv. no. 207

► 4
Reynier Covyn
A Girl Plucking a Duck
Panel, 72.5 x 58.5 cm (28½ x 23 in.)
Fake inscription: N. MAES (ca. 1665-1670)
Location unknown

Leyden 1629 – Amsterdam 1667

Panel, 25.7 x 24.4 cm (10⅛ x 9⅝ in.)
Lower left: *G Metsu* (possibly later addition) (ca. 1658)
San Diego, Calif., Timken Art Gallery, inv. no. 1958.01

The old biographical information about Metsu is incorrect or confusing and offers an incomplete picture of his artistic career. At the age of fifteen (in 1644) he is said to have been one of the founders of the Leyden guild of Saint Luke. He probably lived in Utrecht around 1650, for his earliest work consists of religious and mythological representations in the manner of Nicolaas Knüpfer and Jan Baptist Weenix. His brushwork was then quite broad.

Around 1657 he moved to Amsterdam, where he painted mainly genre scenes with an ever-finer handling of the paint like that of the Leyden *fijnschilders*. These works were mainly interiors with ordinary burghers, in which the daily actions often contain deeper (amorous or erotic) meaning. In his group portraits he also introduced narrative elements that were much imitated in the eighteenth century in the so-called conversation pieces.

B B

The whereabouts of the San Diego painting of *A Girl Receiving a Letter* by Gabriël Metsu can be traced to the early nineteenth century, when it was sold from the collection of the Dowager Boreel in Amsterdam in 1814.[1] The painting and its pendant, *A Man Writing a Letter* (Montpellier, Musée Fabre) [1], were purchased by the Amsterdam dealer Van Iperen.[2] The two panels by Metsu did not stay long with Van Iperen, because the pair was sold again in 1815 at Stanley's in London.[3]

Previously unmentioned in the Metsu literature is the fact that the entry for each painting in the 1815 auction catalogue notes that the works came from the collection of the king of Sardinia. In 1815 Victor Emanuel I (1759-1824) was head of the House of Savoy and King of Sardinia.[4] If in fact the paintings by Metsu had belonged to the king of Sardinia, either this was at some earlier period, or they had been held by him for only a few months before reaching Mr. Stanley; they have not been identified in the inventories of that royal collection.

The two paintings by Metsu did not find buyers at the Stanley sale and were bought in. They next appear at the Paris sale of Madame Le Rouge in 1818, with *A Girl Receiving a Letter* bringing

Provenance
Collection Dowager Boreel, Amsterdam
Auction Boreel, Amsterdam, 1814 (*f* 950 to Van Yperen [*sic*])
Dealer Van Iperen, Amsterdam, 1814
(?) Collection King of Sardinia
Auction London, 1815 (200 guineas, bought in)
Collection Madame Le Rouge, Paris, 1818
Auction Le Rouge, Paris, 1818, (Frf. 5,080 to Le Rouge)
Dealer Nieuwenhuys, Brussels
Collection Auguste-Marie-Raimond Prince of Arenberg, Brussels, before 1829
Collection Duke of Arenberg, Brussels
Dealer Wildenstein & Co., New York, by 1958
Timken Art Gallery, San Diego, 1958 (acquired by The Putnam Foundation)

Bibliography
Auction Amsterdam 1814, pp. 6-7, no. 8
Auction London 1815, p. 13, no. 170
Auction Paris 1818, p. 22, no. 34
Spruyt 1829, p. 10, no. 54 and fig.
Smith 1829-1842, vol. IV, pp. 95-96, no. 70
Brussels 1833, p. 24, no. 57
Thoré-Bürger 1859, pp. 140-141, no. 36
Düsseldorf 1904, p. 143, no. 341
Marguillier 1904, p. 284
HdG 183 (vol. I [1907], pp. 310-311, no. 183)
Plietzsch 1936, p. 5 and fig.
Mongan / Mongan 1969, pp. 72-73, no. 26, pp. 123-124 and fig.
Robinson 1974, pp. 39-41, 60, 81, fig. 76, frontispiece
Robinson 1985, n.p., fig. 3

▶ 1
Gabriël Metsu
A Man Writing a Letter
Panel, 25 x 24 cm (9⅞ x 9½ in.)
On spine of book on shelf at left: *Metsu* (ca. 1658)
Montpellier, Musée Fabre, inv. no. 836-4-38

Gabriël Metsu A Girl Receiving a Letter (not in The Hague)

5,080 francs,[5] *A Man Writing a Letter* bringing 2,450 francs. It is at this point that the pendants were separated.

The San Diego painting was presumably then bought by the dealer Lambert Jean Nieuwenhuys (1777-1862). This we determine from comments in the 1833 catalogue of the paintings in the collection of Auguste-Marie-Raimond Prince of Arenberg and Count de la Marck, of Brussels. The introduction remarks that a number of the works listed in the catalogue entered the collection through the agency of 'M. Nieuwenhuys, père.'[6] The Metsu entry indicates this route and also records that the painting had come from the Boreel collection, Amsterdam, and had most recently been bought from the Le Rouge sale in Paris.

Interestingly, eighteen of the 115 paintings recorded in the catalogue of the Arenberg collection are connected with Nieuwenhuys, all of them Dutch and Flemish works of the seventeenth century. And in addition to the Metsu, the Adriaen van Ostade also has a Boreel provenance. Looking again at the Boreel sale catalogue, it would seem that one of the members of the Nieuwenhuys family had attended that sale, because 'Nieuwenhuys' is noted as the buyer of five lots. Both the Metsu and Ostade, however, were purchased at the Boreel sale not by Nieuwenhuys but by 'Van Yperen,' perhaps as Nieuwenhuys's agent or partner.

The most significant paintings in the Arenberg picture collection were acquired by Auguste-Marie-Raimond Prince of Arenberg (1753-1833). A worldly man, he had been involved in revolutionary politics, both in his native Belgium and in France.[7] By 1815, retiring from political life, he returned permanently to Belgium and began to collect paintings, particularly examples from the Northern schools of the seventeenth century. These works, including the Metsu, were catalogued and then exhibited at the Palais Ducal in Brussels in 1855 and later in Düsseldorf in 1914. At the time of Prince Auguste's death in 1833, his collections were inherited by his nephew, Louise-Prosper Duke of Arenberg (1785-1861). Early in the twentieth century much of the collections were sold. Of particular note is the sale in July 1902 in London, when over several days approximately 40,000 prints in 669 lots were sold by Engelbert-Marie Duke of Arenberg.

The Metsu *Girl Receiving a Letter* reached San Diego in 1958, having been purchased from Wildenstein & Co. of New York. The painting's acquisition was funded by the Putnam Foundation. This foundation, created in 1950, is the beneficiary of the estate of Amy (1874-1958) and Anne R. (1867-1962) Putnam, who inherited five million dollars from their cousin, Willie Putnam, in 1937.[8] With these funds the Putnam sisters continued the tradition of supporting the arts in San Diego established by Amelia C. Bridges. Born a Timken, Mrs. Bridges and her husband, Appleton S. Bridges, had given money to build the Fine Arts Gallery in San Diego's Balboa Park. Mrs. Bridges also provided the funds to pay the salary of the gallery's director. At her death in 1940, the Putnam sisters assumed this responsibility. When a new facility was built to house the collection of art purchased by the Putnam Foundation, it was named the Timken Art Gallery in honor of the Timken Foundation of Canton, Ohio, which had made substantial contributions to the new gallery's construction and endowment. Today the Timken boasts a small but exquisite collection of old master paintings, including such Dutch works as Rembrandt's *Saint Bartholomew*,

Pieter Claesz's *Breakfast Still Life*, and *A Girl Receiving a Letter* by Gabriël Metsu.

A Girl Receiving a Letter is a painting of great charm, dated to the late 1650s, when Metsu had moved from Leyden to Amsterdam. At this moment in his career Metsu began to reveal, both in his technique and choice of subject matter, the influence of the Leyden *fijnschilder* Gerard Dou, with whom he supposedly studied, and Frans van Mieris. However, *A Girl Receiving a Letter* is characterized by what Robinson calls 'Metsu's natural warmth and freshness of touch,'[9] which set his works from this phase apart from both his own later works and those of his contemporaries, Dou, Van Mieris, and Gerard ter Borch.

The San Diego painting represents the very popular theme of a woman receiving a love letter and was conceived as one of a pair of paintings. Its dimensions and early provenance, both of which it shares with the Montpellier *Man Writing a Letter*, confirm this theory. In the Montpellier panel a man composes a letter, which the young woman in the San Diego panel receives from a messenger. The two figures and their environments are cleverly contrasted: he works in the fading light, and a young maid enters the room, bringing a candle; she, seated beneath a stone arcade with an airy view to a Palladian villa beyond, is accompanied by an adolescent boy. If the two paintings were hung together again as a pair, the main figures would be seen to be beautifully related via reciprocal gesture and pose.

It should be noted that the figures represented in *A Girl Receiving a Letter* and *A Man Writing a Letter* might actually portray Metsu and his wife, Isabella de Wolff, whom he married on 12 April 1658. The strong resemblance between these two figures and the several portraits of Metsu and Isabella, such as those at Louisville, Kentucky, has been noticed [**2-3**].[10]

Much has been written about the vogue of letter writing in Holland in the seventeenth century.[11] The fashion gave rise to a number of contemporary tracts on the craft of writing letters. This skill could be learned through the aid of books such as the very popular *Secrétaire à la mode* of 1643 by Jean Puget de la Serre. Translated into Dutch in 1651, this manual provided particular assistance with the writing of love letters. The theme of the love letter written and received is found repeatedly in Dutch art of the time, in the works of artists such as Metsu,[12] Ter Borch, and Johannes Vermeer (cat. no. 67). However, the theme was rarely developed with such tenderness as is observed in the San Diego and Montpellier pendants.

◄ **2-3**
Gabriël Metsu
Self-Portrait and *Portrait of the Artist's Wife*
Panel, both 20 x 16 cm (7⅞ x 6¼ in.)
Neither signed nor dated (ca. 1658-1660)
Louisville, Ky., The J.B. Speed Art Museum, inv. nos. 70.56.1 and 17.56.2

1 *Auction Amsterdam 1814*, pp. 6-7, no. 8. The Dowager Boreel may have been Maria Trip (1750-1813), wife of Willem Boreel (1744-1796) of Amsterdam; see *Genealogie Boreel*, p. 78.
2 *Robinson 1974*, pp. 39-40, fig. 75; Hofstede de Groot noted that the Montpellier painting had been purchased at the Boreel sale by one 'Van Spaan' (HdG 24). An annotated copy of the Dowager Boreel sale catalogue, in the Resource Collection of The Getty Center for the History of Art and the Humanities, clearly notes 'Van Yperen.'
3 *Auction London 1815*, p. 13, nos. 169-170
4 The residence of the kings of Sardinia, as well as their seat of power and wealth, was actually in Piedmont (the kingdom was also known as the Kingdom of Piedmont-Sardinia), as it had been prior to 1718, when the House of Savoy gained control of Sardinia through the Treaty of London.
5 *Auction Paris 1818*, p. 22, no. 34. The annotated copy of this sale catalogue at the Frick Art Reference Library notes that the buyer was also 'Le Rouge,' no doubt a relative, and possibly the M. Le Rouge listed on the catalogue's front page as one of the four sellers of the estate of the deceased Mme Le Rouge.
6 *Brussels 1833*, n.p. The Nieuwenhuys family of dealers included the Dutch-born Lambert Jean Nieuwenhuys, who moved to Brussels in 1805, and his two sons, Chrétien Jean (1799-1883) and François (died 1880), who ran branch offices in London and Paris respectively. On the family, see the introduction in *Auction Paris 1881-A*, n.p.; see also *Hinterding / Horsch 1989*, p. 9, note 17.
7 Arenberg was the friend and correspondent of the Comte de Mirabeau, one of the great figures of the French Revolution. The Mirabeau-Arenberg letters were later published, see *De Bacourt 1851*.
8 For an extensive discussion of the Putnam sisters, see *Moore 1985*.
9 *Robinson 1985*, n.p. It should also be noted that there is a copy of the San Diego painting in the Nasjonalgalleriet, Oslo (*Oslo 1959*, n.p., no. 40 and fig.); recently another copy was auctioned (*Auction New York 1990*, no. 95 and fig.).
10 *Louisville 1973*, p. 106 and fig.; *Robinson 1974*, p. 31 and fig. 43 and *Louisville 1973*, p. 106 and fig.; *Robinson 1974*, p. 31, fig. 44. I would like to thank Gay Michal Nay for her kind assistance and for bringing to my attention the ms. letter from the staff of the Honnef-Archiv, suggesting that the San Diego and Montpellier paintings represent the artist and his wife.
11 *Slatkes 1981*, p. 70; *Brown 1984*, pp. 137-140
12 The celebrated pair by Metsu were, until their recent theft, in the collection of Sir Alfred Beit, Blessington: *A Man Writing a Letter* (*Robinson 1974*, pp. 59-60 and fig. 145) and *A Woman Reading a Letter* (*Robinson 1974*, pp. 59-60 and fig. 146).
 LFO

Gabriël Metsu

Leyden 1629 – Amsterdam 1667

Panel, 43.9 x 36.1 cm (17¹/₄ x 14¹/₄ in.)
On the music book: *G. Metsu A° 1663*
San Francisco, Calif., The Fine Arts Museums of San Francisco, Roscoe and Margaret Oakes Collection, inv. no. 60.30

In 1907, in the addenda to his catalogue of the paintings by Gabriël Metsu, Hofstede de Groot incorporated a description of this painting, which was then located in the collection of Edward Count Raczyński (1847-1926) in Ragolin (near Poznan) in Poland.[1] Raczyński was one of the greatest of Polish collectors, who, in the period from 1910 to 1912, had a pavilion built next to his palace in Ragolin to house his collection of paintings. His son Edward Adam (born in 1891) [1], who presently lives in London as president of the Polish government in exile, inherited the collection together with his brother Roger Adam (1889-1945). In May 1939 the latter transferred the collection, which had been supplemented by new acquisitions, to Warsaw, where it was accommodated partly in the national museum and partly in the Raczyński palace. What subsequently became of the painting by Metsu remains obscure. By 1928 Edward and Roger had sold paintings from the collection, but evidently not this work. Fortunately it was not lost in World War II, when 300 paintings were burnt in (or stolen from) the Raczyński palace.[2] The Red Army returned the paintings that the Germans had confiscated in Poland to the original owners, at least when they could still be located.[3] By some untraceable route, Metsu's *Young Woman with a Cello* emerged in the Moser collection in Wallisellen, Switzerland.[4]

In 1957 the work suddenly turned up with a New York dealer, where it was bought by Margaret and Roscoe Oakes for the museum in San Francisco. Roscoe Oakes (1871-1964) and his wife, Margaret (1880-1957), were among the most important benefactors of the M.H. de Young Memorial Museum. They came from Portland to San Francisco in 1906, several months before the great earthquake and fire that robbed them of all their possessions, save their clothes. Twenty years later Roscoe Oakes was one of the most prominent industrialists of San Francisco, who, from 1950 on, regularly made donations to the de Young Museum. In 1953 a Roscoe and Margaret Oakes wing, containing French furniture, sculpture, and carpets, was opened. Three years later followed an outstanding donation of eight paintings (among which were works by Rembrandt and Frans Hals) and, after Margaret Oakes's death in August 1957, Metsu's *Young Woman with a Cello* was added to the collection.[5]

Provenance
Auction Laurens van der Hem, Amsterdam, 1713 (ƒ82)
Auction Angran Viscount de Fonspertuis, Paris, 1748 (Frf. 855 to Laurent)
Collection Edward Count Raczyński, Ragolin (near Poznan), before 1907-1926
Collection Edward Adam Count Raczyński and Roger Adam Count Raczyński, 1926-1944(?) (until 1939 in Ragolin)
Collection V. Moser, Wallisellen (near Zürich)
Dealer Frederick Mont, New York, 1957
Collection Roscoe and Margaret Oakes, San Francisco, 1957
M.H. de Young Memorial Museum, San Francisco, 1957 (since 1972 The Fine Arts Museums of San Francisco)

Bibliography
Gersaint 1748, pp. 204-206, no. 438
Hoet 1752-1770, vol. I, p. 148, no. 14
HdG 157a (vol. I [1907], p. 297, no. 157a, pp. 332-333, no. 157a)
Errera 1920-1921, vol. I, p. 309
Gerson 1930, p. 440
Art Quarterly 1957, pp. 332-335 and fig.
Leyden 1966, p. 23, no. 18
San Francisco 1966, p. 136 and fig.
San Francisco / Toledo / Boston 1966-1967, p. 127, no. 83 and fig.
Gudlaugsson 1968, pp. 34 and 41, no. HdG 157a
Schneede 1968, p. 47, no. 2
Robinson 1974, pp. 58-59, 85, notes 103-104, p. 188, fig. 143
Raupp 1978, p. 120, note 56
Haverkamp-Begemann 1980, pp. 207-208, pl. XVI
Sutton 1986, pp. 132, 276-277 and fig. 416

1
Edward Raczyński (born 1891), former president of Poland, with his companion Mieczyslawska, in their apartment in London
Photograph: Bert Nienhuis, 1989

Gabriël Metsu A Young Woman with a Cello

At that time the Roscoe and Margaret Oakes Foundation was established with four million dollars for the benefit of charitable, cultural, and scholarly causes. After the death of Oakes in 1964, their gifts to the museum alone were estimated at more than a million dollars.[6]

On the publication of the new acquisition in San Francisco, people praised its excellent condition and its obvious quality. 'The picture itself is immaculately preserved and reveals all the qualities for which the painter is famous: his well-balanced composition; his consummate draftsmanship; and his virtuosity in rendering the nature and texture of things – the satin of the dress, the woolly Persian rug, the fur of the dog, and above all, the harmony of luminous colors and sparkling lights.'[7]

The painting had already attracted praise of this kind in the eighteenth century. Hofstede de Groot associated this *Young Woman with a Cello* with the estimable piece sold at the Van der Hem auction in Amsterdam in 1713.[8] It had escaped him,

however, that the Metsu again came under the hammer as a 'très-beau Tableau' in 1748, at the Angran de Fonspertuis auction in Paris. Ambroise Agran de Fonspertuis was 'conseiller du Roy' and was raised to the peerage in 1716.[9] The connoisseur Edmé François Gersaint wrote the auction catalogue, which is of great interest because he included in it elaborate art criticism. The *Young Woman with a Cello* was for him a pretext for making a critical annotation. He praised the brilliance and clarity of the painting by Metsu but subsequently noted: 'All that remains to be desired is that he might have made a more gratifying selection of female models; but that is a failing of virtually all Dutch masters, who, in their small, carefully finished, and splendidly composed paintings, chose character heads that are not of the finest. This fault also arises from the fact that these masters made portraits after nature, which they necessarily had to reproduce as they saw them before their eyes' (in translation).[10] His objections are an echo of the familiar classicist criticism of Rembrandt, which was directed at his ostensible aversion to the 'rules of art' and which labeled his stubborn imitation of nature as heresy.[11]

Just as Rembrandt used female 'clodhoppers' as models, so Metsu depicted no classical Venus: Gersaint was apparently somewhat put off by the individualized features of the cello player. She does indeed appear to have been painted after life. One is inclined to compare her facial features with the music-making woman in *The Artist Painting a Cello Player* (Los Angeles County Museum of Art) [2], a work that also was made in the early sixties.[12] In this and other genre scenes scholars have recognized the painter and his wife. The portraits of Gabriël Metsu and Isabella de Wolff – they married in 1658 – have survived (Louisville, The J.B. Speed Art Museum; cat. no. 42, fig. 2-3) [3].[13] Gudlaugsson summarized what had struck him about these and similar works by Metsu: 'Portraits lacking the genre-like element form an exception in his oeuvre. It is not rare, on the other hand, for the figures of his genre paintings to

2
Gabriël Metsu
The Artist Painting a Woman Playing a Cello
Canvas, 41.2 x 35 cm (16¼ x 13¾ in.)
On the stage: *G Metsu* (ca. 1663)
Los Angeles County Museum of Art,
inv. no. 1.81.45.5

◀ **3**
Detail of cat. no. 42, fig. 3

▶ **4**
Woodcut from Cesare Ripa (edited by D.P. Pers),
Iconologia, Amsterdam 1644, p. 341

display a portrait-like character' (in translation).[14] Although Isabella de Wolff can be recognized as the cello player depicted in San Francisco, we are not concerned here with an ordinary portrait.

The attention of most commentators has thus far concentrated on the unmatched beauty of the rendering of the satin dress, which Robinson called 'one of Metsu's most remarkable *tours de force*.'[15] Even so, the subject matter of the painting was occasionally touched on. It may be neutrally denoted as a reverie, but Raupp labeled it a personified *Vanitas*. However, his argument that the cello often occurs in seventeenth-century *vanitas* still lifes elucidates little.[16] Peter Sutton proposed that the cello player might personify Harmony, and this is the most attractive interpretation.[17] He referred to a depiction in Ripa's *Iconologia* (which appeared in Dutch in 1644), in which a woman with a cello symbolizes Harmony [4]. The accompanying commentary reads in part: 'A very respectable and beautiful young Lady with a double Viol with fifteen strings, having a crown on the head with seven gems that are all alike' (in translation).[18] Metsu's Harmony has no crown on her head, but just as in Ripa's woodcut, she holds the bow in an underhanded grip and leans her musical instrument on her foot. Metsu would surely not have objected to Sutton's comparison, although he definitely did not copy the woodcut. The six-stringed cello of the painting (which was also called *violone*) may well have been rendered after an actual specimen.[19]

Likewise, the little dog standing on its hind feet seems to be a purely decorative element. In numerous paintings by Metsu such an animal, often a black-and-white spaniel, is the faithful com-panion of a young woman, as is seen in *A Lady Writing Music* (The Hague, Mauritshuis)[20] and *A Lady at the Virginal* (Rotterdam, Museum Boymans-van Beuningen) [5a-c].[21] A young woman with a dog can occasion varying interpretations. The dancing dog in the Rotterdam painting is interpreted as a symbol of the enamored man who succumbs to the temptations of the woman.[22] Its congener in *The Dancing Dog* by Frans van Mieris (Leningrad, Hermitage)[23] is explained as the stupid suitor who dances to the piping of his mistress. Presumably Van Mieris also wished to illustrate the saying 'as the young lady is, so is her dog' (in translation).[24] In these latter instances the context made clear what the young lady wanted, namely, to make love. But in *The Artist Painting a Cello Player* [2] the musician could instead convincingly be interpreted as the inspiring muse of the painter.[25]

However, an explanatory context or indications of an amorous kind are missing in Metsu's depiction in San Francisco (the figure in the wood carving of the bedpost, a chained Andromeda[?], has not as yet supplied a key). In comparison to earlier musical parties by Metsu, such as the piece dated 1659 in New York (The Metropolitan Museum of Art),[26] the formal language of his later works is much more sober. That is a stylistic matter which has been observed before, but it may also apply to the content of his works, which appear to be less loaded with meaning and no longer so much directed to the amorous side of the male-female relationship.[27] Thus in this extinguished candle one need not see a 'forgotten erotic symbol.'[28]

The standing dog must nevertheless be related to the central theme, that of Harmony. It is more likely to play a traditional role than the alter ego of the lover. The dog is naturally an old

5a-c
Details from cat. no. 43 and the paintings mentioned in notes 20 and 21

6
Maerten de Vos
Fidelitas
Drawing, 300 x 200 mm (11⁷/₈ x 7⁷/₈ in.)
Neither signed, nor dated (ca. 1570-1580)
Antwerp, Museum Plantin Moretus en
Prentenkabinet, inv. no. 64

acquaintance of 'portraits of marriage and troth.'[29] Numerous examples of this may be given. For instance, in his 'Depictions of the Figures' Carel van Mander wrote: 'With the Dog is meant fidelity, for the Dog is most faithful / as well as never forgetting a good deed' (in translation).[30] On a drawing by Maerten de Vos with the inscription *FIDELITAS. getrouwicheyt* (Antwerp, Museum Plantin Moretus) [6], a small dog jumps up against a female figure symbolizing Fidelity.[31] Thus, if in this scene Metsu did give more than a demonstration of his fabulous technique by depicting his wife, Isabella, in a *portrait historié*, then he was referring to Harmony (in marriage) and to (marital) Fidelity.

1 HdG 157a (vol. I [1907], p. 332, no. 157a): his description creates the impression that he had seen the piece with his own eyes.
2 Letter from Juliusz A. Chrościcki, Warsaw, dated 8 March 1989 (documentation archives Mauritshuis).
3 *Tomkiewicz 1950*, p. 6
4 Label on the back of the panel: 'Roslistr. 24 Wallisellen.'
5 Newspaper report from the M.H. de Young Memorial Museum, dated 8 January 1960 (documentation archives The Fine Arts Museums of San Francisco).
6 *San Francisco Chronicle 1964*, p. 26
7 *Art Quarterly 1957*, p. 335
8 HdG 157a (vol. I [1907], p. 297, no. 157a); *Hoet 1752-1770*, vol. I, p. 148, no. 14
9 Communication from O. Schutte, Hoge Raad van Adel, The Hague.
10 *Gersaint 1748*, p. 205
11 *Slive 1953*, pp. 83-103 and *Emmens 1968*, pp. 63-95
12 HdG 229; *Moes 1897-1905*, vol. II, p. 95, no. 5005-8; *Robinson 1974*, pp. 31, 122 and fig. 42
13 HdG 229 and 232; *Renckens / Duyvetter 1959*, pp. 179-182; *Robinson 1974*, pp. 31-32, 123 and figs. 43-44
14 *Gudlaugsson 1968*, p. 38
15 *Robinson 1974*, p. 58
16 *San Francisco 1966*, p. 136; *Raupp 1978*, p. 120 and note 56
17 *Sutton 1986*, pp. 132 and 277
18 *Ripa / Pers 1644*, p. 341
19 *Munrow 1976*, p. 88
20 Inv. no. 94; HdG 162; *Broos 1987*, pp. 236-239, no. 41 and fig.
21 Inv. no. vdV 49; HdG 160; *Leyden 1966*, pp. 98-99, no. 33 and fig.
22 *Naumann 1981*, vol. I, pp. 105-106
23 Inv. no. 915; *Naumann 1981*, vol. I, p. 105, vol. II, pp. 35-36, no. 32 and fig.; *Kuznetsov / Linnik 1982*, nos. 103-105 and figs. 104-105
24 *De Jongh 1967-A*, pp. 38-41, figs. 26-27
25 *Raupp 1984*, p. 199
26 Inv. no. 91.26.11; *Baetjer 1980*, vol. I, p. 125, vol. II, p. 443 and fig.
27 *Gudlaugsson 1968*, p. 34; *Robinson 1974*, p. 59
28 *Broos 1971*, p. 25
29 *De Jongh 1986*, pp. 231-235, note 11 (further references to be found there)
30 *Van Mander 1604-A*, fol. 128 verso
31 *De Jongh 1986*, pp. 232, 234 and fig. 52c
BB

Leyden 1635 – Leyden 1681

Copper, 12.5 x 8.5 cm (5 x 3⅜ in.) (arched at the top)
At the right, above the shoulder: *F. v. Mieris f / i66i*
Malibu, Calif., The J. Paul Getty Museum, inv. no. 82.PC.136

Houbraken tells us that Gerard Dou called Frans van Mieris the 'Prince of his Pupils.' With his interior scenes and portraits, painted with meticulous diligence, he was the most important of the Leyden *fijnschilders*; his work was emulated more often by this school than Dou's. From the very start he reaped international fame and had important patrons (Archduke Leopold Wilhelm in Vienna and Grand Duke Cosimo III in Florence), who rewarded him munificently. Despite being offered the position of court painter in Vienna, he continued to live and work in Leyden. Perhaps the strength of his best works is that the minute detail never becomes boring but shimmers under the surface. On closer examination, his ostensibly everyday scenes often appear to have a deeper meaning (amorous or admonishing). In the last decade of his life he sometimes limited himself to the repetition of earlier successes and exaggerated his facility with the brush.

Gerard de Lairesse demonstrated that he had a good visual memory when, in 1707, he described this work of art painted on copper. He had seen a small painting by Frans van Mieris, 'which still amazes me when I only think of it. It was a Figure, down to the knees, of a palm's length, depicting the Art of Painting, with a stage mask in her hand, being in essence, covering, clothing, and accouterment unsurpassably beautiful and purely Antique; of such a kind as I have never again seen by any Modern painters, no matter how skillful they may have been' (in translation).[1] This text concisely but quite accurately describes this minimonument, and it is only right that it has often been adduced.

The theoretician claimed that he had seen the painting. That must have been before 1690, for in that year he went blind.[2] Unfortunately De Lairesse did not specify in which collection the work was then located. The domiciles of this gem form a story apart, one that is not to be told in a few words. The ups and downs of European history often play an exceptionally important role. In 1765 we encounter the painting at an auction in Amsterdam in a collection 'Brought together with great difficulty and at high cost by the Late Heer de N****' (in translation).[3] At the time everyone knew that in place of the asterisks one ought to fill in (N)eufville.

Provenance
Unknown collection, Amsterdam (?), before 1690
Collection Pieter Leendert de Neufville, Amsterdam, before 1759
Collection Leendert Pieter de Neufville, Amsterdam, 1759-1765
Auction De Neufville, Amsterdam, 1765 (ƒ425 to Van der Marck)
Collection Johan van der Marck, Leyden, 1765-1773
Auction Van der Marck, Amsterdam, 1773 (ƒ800 to Fouquet)
Auction Lebrun, Paris, 1773 (Frf. 3,400 to Paillet)
Collection Poullain, Paris, 1773(?)-1780
Auction Poullain, Paris, 1780 (Frf. 3,300 to Langlier)
Collection Duke of Chabot, Paris, 1781-1787
Auction Duke of Chabot, Paris, 1787 (Frf. 3,000 to Lebrun)
Auction Destouches, Paris, 1794 (Frf. 1,601 to Lebrun)
Auction, Paris, 1808 (Frf. 1,550 to Berry)
Collection Duke of Berry, Paris, 1808-1820
Collection Duchess of Berry, Paris, 1820-1837 (in 1834 offered by Christie's, London, £300)
Auction Berry, Paris, 1837 (Frf. 2,047 to Durand-Duclos for Williams Hope)
Collection William Williams Hope, Rushton Hall, Northamptonshire, 1837-1849
Auction Williams Hope, London, 1849 (£108.3 to Farrer for Bredel)
Collection Charles A. Bredel, London, 1849-1851
Collection Miss Bredel, London, 1851-1875
Auction Bredel, London, 1875 (£250 to Colnaghi)
Auction Lord Revelstoke, London, 1929 (to F. Partridge)
Collection C.J.K. van Aalst, Hoevelaken, 1929-1939
Collection N.J. van Aalst, Hoevelaken / Breda, 1939-after 1960
Collection W. van Aalst, Huizen, 1982
Dealer G. Cramer, The Hague, 1982
The J. Paul Getty Museum, Malibu, 1982

Bibliography
De Lairesse 1707 / 1740, vol. I, p. 175
Hoet 1752-1770, vol. III, p. 473, no. 62
Auction Amsterdam 1765-A, p. 10, no. 62
Auction Amsterdam 1773, p. 61, no. 181
Auction Paris 1773, pp. 28-29, no. 60
Auction Paris 1780, pp. 38-39, no. 74
Basan 1781, p. 11, no. 59 and fig.
Auction Paris 1787, p. 22, no. 39
Auction Paris 1794, p. 23, no. 48
Auction Paris 1808, pp. 32-33, no. 48
Smith 1829-1842, vol. I, p. 71, no. 36 and p. 81, no. 77, vol. IX, p. 41, no. 22
London 1834, pp. 29-30, no. 57
Auction Paris 1837, p. 73, no. 68
Auction London 1849, p. 23, no. 84
London 1850, p. 10, no. 70
Blanc 1857-1858, vol. I, p. 226
London 1863, p. 11, no. 90
Auction London 1875, p. 21, no. 118
Redford 1888, vol. II, p. 309 (1875)
Roberts 1897, vol. I, p. 237
Mireur 1901-1912, vol. V (1911), p. 186 (1773, 1780, 1837) and p. 187 (1875)
Graves 1913-1915, vol. II (1913), p. 777, nos. 70 (1850) and 90 (1863)

Frans van Mieris The Art of Painting

The name De Neufville had a very negative ring to it in Amsterdam at the time. Pieter Leendert de Neufville (ca. 1706-1759), who descended from an old Amsterdam family of merchants, dealt in insurance, a risky line of business in those troubled times. Though forced in 1735 to apply for bankruptcy, he was later able to meet his obligations, so that the art collection remained intact. His son Leendert Pieter (1729-after 1774?) was less fortunate. After the death of his father in 1759, he continued the firm of De Neufville Brothers on his own. He turned out to be a poor speculator, who had to recoup his losses with quick deals and by trading with the enemy during the Seven Years' War (1756-1763). In 1763 the son also went bankrupt, dragging down hundreds of others with him in his fall.[4] It was said that the debts of the firm had run up to thirty million guilders. It was not at all appreciated that he nevertheless managed to live on a grand scale. For instance, the fifteen paintings that Leendert had bought on 4 July 1763 at the Lormier auction for more than 9,000 guilders were still not paid for when, a month later, his bankruptcy was final.[5]

Although the collection must almost certainly have been begun by Pieter Leendert ('the Late Heer de N****'), it is in point of fact incorrect to connect his name, instead of that of his son Leendert Pieter, to the auction of 1765.[6] At the end of 1763 the news came from Amsterdam that the firm ('Ces messieurs toujours frauduleux' [These ever fraudulent gentlemen] – read: Leendert Pieter) had attempted to exempt the best paintings from the public sale that was planned for 3 December. The intended auction was therefore postponed and held in 1765 instead.[7] Apparently Leendert de Neufville was still in trouble ten years later, for he was then forced to sell his country estate near Heemstede.[8]

The burgomaster of Leyden, Johan van der Marck (1694-1770), was present at the De Neufville auction of 1765 in person to place a bid on *The Art of Painting* by his famous fellow townsman Frans van Mieris. It went to him for 425 guilders, a considerable sum at that time. *The Milkmaid* by Jan Vermeer (Amsterdam, Rijksmuseum; p. 65, fig. 8),[9] already renowned, was sold at the same auction for 560 guilders.[10] Van der Marck was an art lover who had assembled a large collection of paintings, drawings, and prints (see cat. no. 14). He personally compiled a description of his collection, which served in 1733 as the foundation for the catalogue of his estate. He had noticed that De Lairesse had known his painting. '*See on this piece*, which was painted in the very best period of this Master, *Laresse Schilderboek*, 1st Volume p. 175,' Van der Marck reported (in

Graves 1918-1921, vol. II (1921), p. 220 (1875)
HdG 26 (vol. X [1928], p. 6, no. 26)
Auction London 1929, p. 12, no. 65
Von Moltke 1939, p. 202, no. XLVIII and fig.
Arnhem 1953, p. 16, no. 41
Van Gelder / Emmens 1958, p. 13 and fig. 10
Badt 1961, p. 110
Delft / Antwerpen 1964-1965, pp. 76-77, no. 80 and fig. 36
Wurfbain 1980, p. 55
Naumann 1981, vol. I, pp. 91-92 and 194, vol. II, pp. 48-49, no. 37 and pl. 37
Tableau 1982, p. 387
Van de Watering 1982, pp. 150-151, no. 55 and fig.
Raupp 1984, p. 199
Dolders 1985, pp. 215-216, note 85 and fig. 4
Malibu 1986, p. 100 and fig.
Sutton 1986, p. 144
Hecht 1989-1990, pp. 82-84, no. 14 and fig.

translation).[11] One continues to encounter this comment in the auction catalogues until 1837.

Pieter Fouquet, Jr. (1729-1800), bought the tiny painting at the Van der Marck auction for 800 guilders. Whenever he managed to lay his hands on a work of art, it usually meant that the painting was about to leave Holland (see cat. nos. 2, 14, 54, and 60). Just before Christmas of the same year, 1773, it was indeed offered at an auction in Paris and sold there for 3,400 francs.[12] It ended up in the cabinet of the collector Poullain (died in 1780), Receiver General of the domains of the King. Poullain had his collection reproduced in an album of engravings, which was published a year after his death. He had wanted to give young and beginning artists the chance to make reproductions after his paintings under the direction of the engraver Pierre François Basan (1723-1797). *The Art of Painting* was rendered in print by Eléonore Lingée (ca. 1753-after 1800), the wife of the painter Charles Louis Lingée [1]. Curiously enough, Frans's son Willem ('Mieris [Guillaume] 1662-1747') is mentioned as the painter in the accompanying commentary.[13] This mistake was never repeated: the painting is, after all, signed and dated *F. v. Mieris f 166i*.

The text of the album further mentioned that the piece on copper had in the meantime been acquired by the Duke of

1
Éléonore Lingée after Frans van Mieris
The Art of Painting
Engraving, 166 x 112 mm (6½ x 4⅜ in.)
Lower right: *M[adam]e Lingée* (1781)
The Hague, Rijksbureau voor Kunsthistorische Documentatie

Chabot. We will not linger on the peregrinations of the Van Mieris in French collections: the facts are more or less known. The collection of the Duke of Chabot was auctioned in 1787.[14] Charles-René-Dominique Sochet Chevalier Destouches (1727-1794) was the next owner. He was a French admiral who had, among other things, won great victories in naval engagements against the English at the liberation of Virginia during the American War of Independence (1775-1783). Early in 1794 he escaped from the guillotine but died while fleeing: the collection of 'Citoyen Destouches' was auctioned shortly thereafter.[15] According to an annotation in the catalogue of a sale of 1808 organized by the art dealers Paillet and Delaroche, *The Art of Painting* was bought for 1,550 francs by 'Bellie.'[16] 'Bellie' was none other than Charles Ferdinand Duke of Berry (1778-1820), who was murdered in 1820. Elsewhere (cat. no. 72 and fig. 4) we related the story of how his widow subsequently tried in vain to secure the throne for his posthumously born son.

The campaign waged by the duchess in 1832 had ruined her, and she decided to sell paintings from the family collection. She expected to find the greatest number of buyers at that moment in London, so the collection was transported to Christie's in 1834. An exhibition of the 130 Flemish and Dutch paintings, including *The Art of Painting*, was staged in the auction rooms. In the printed catalogue it was described as a 'Portrait of a Female Artist.'[17] A communication of 1842 by John Smith informs us that Christie's hung a price tag of 300 pounds on it, but that no buyer was found.[18] The painting was returned to Paris, where a public sale was held in 1837 of those paintings belonging to the Duchess of Berry that had come from the old gallery of the Palais de l'Elysée. *The Art of Painting* was described again as the portrait of a woman painter, and as one of the nec plus ultra (extremes) of the art of the *fijnschilder*. It went for a total of 2,047 francs, or 82 pounds.[19]

The jewel by Van Mieris passed into the hands of yet another eccentric owner. The buyer was William Williams Hope (1802-1855), the son of John Williams Hope (1757-1813). The father took care of affairs in Holland for the famous bankers Hope after they left for England in 1794 (see cat. no. 59).[20] William Williams Hope became Sheriff of Northamptonshire and, in 1828, bought Rushton Hall near Kettering. He disposed of the paintings he had assembled there (including *The Art of Painting* by Van Mieris) in 1849, and five years later he sold Rushton Hall. He settled in Paris, where he became a striking figure in its society life, renowned for his eccentric behavior and his collection of diamonds.[21] At the Williams Hope auction, the dealer Farrer bought the painting for the collector Charles Bredel (died 1851) of London, who parted with it in 1850 for an exhibition at the British Institution. In the catalogue it was again called 'A Female Artist.'[22] The notion that the depiction was allegorical in character therefore appears to have been completely lost by then. After 1834 the customary reference to the text by De Lairesse was no longer cited.

Gustav Waagen (p. 125, fig. 3) had visited the small but exquisite collection of Bredel in 1838 and later voiced the vain hope that the collection might not be dispersed.[23] In 1851 Bredel's daughter, who lived on Eaton Square in London, inherited the paintings, which came under the hammer after her death in 1875: the dealer Colnaghi bought the 'portrait' for 250 pounds.[24] The *Brothel Scene* by Frans van Mieris, now in the Mauritshuis (The Hague),[25] appears to have been sold at the same auction for no less than 4,100 pounds.[26] The remarkable difference in price may possibly have been due to the fact that *The Art of Painting* was considered to be 'only' a portrait. The amounts that were paid for the small painting over a period of more than one hundred years suggest that there was only a modest appreciation of its value. Roughly estimated and converted these were: 33 pounds in 1765, 80 pounds in 1773, 132 pounds, also in 1773, 130 pounds in 1787, 65 pounds in 1794, 65 pounds in 1808, 300 pounds (was asked) in 1834, 82 pounds in 1837, 108 pounds in 1849, and 250 pounds in 1875.[27] A greater appreciation for the forgotten subject was still some time off.

It has been thought that Colnaghi acted in 1875 on the orders of Lord Revelstoke. If so, this cannot have been the then twelve-year-old John, the second Baron Revelstoke (1863-1929). Lord Revelstoke was director of the Bank of England and a confirmed bachelor, from whose estate the painting was auctioned yet again in 1929.[28] It is hard to believe that the sitter was identified on this occasion as Anna Maria Schouman, a corruption of the name of Anna Maria [van] Sch[u]urman (1607-1678).[29] Possibly it was thought she resembled the portrait that Jan Lievens painted of this learned woman in 1649 (London, National Gallery).[30] Once again the allegory was not recognized, and the lady in the painting was instead provided with a false identity.

In the thirties *The Art of Painting* returned to Holland after the collector C.J.K. van Aalst (1866-1939) (cat. no. 9, fig. 1) was able to acquire it. In 1960 the painting was kept out of the auction of this collection. It was still in the possession of his grandson W. van Aalst in 1982, when it was on view in an exhibition in the Mauritshuis that was organized by three art dealers in The

Hague.[31] It was also in 1982 that, by way of the dealer G. Cramer of The Hague, the long peregrination of the small painting came to an end. After the exhibition in The Hague, The J. Paul Getty Museum in Malibu bought it for 750,000 guilders. That amount was then beyond the reach of the Mauritshuis.[32] The acquisition demonstrates that there now exists in the United States a serious interest in the art of the *fijnschilder*.

In the meantime, virtually contemporaneously with the Revelstoke auction, the catalogue of C. Hofstede de Groot had appeared, in which, as of old, the text by Gerard de Lairesse was noted, and in which the subject was identified as an allegory on the Art of Painting. In the Van Aalst collection the painting was named 'The muse of the Art of Painting.'[33] Without doubt the beautiful Cunera (Kniertje) van der Cock (1629 / 1630-1700), who married Frans van Mieris in 1657, posed for this allegory. We know a portrait of her by her husband from the wedding year (London, National Gallery) [2],[34] after which Frans continued to paint her often. The Van Mieris couple figured many times in the genre pieces of the master, such as in *Teasing the Dog* (The Hague, Mauritshuis) [3].[35]

On the basis of the stage mask, De Lairesse was able to identify the subject as the Art of Painting. His source – and certainly also that used by Van Mieris – was the influential book *Iconologia of*

2
Frans van Mieris
Portrait of Cunera van der Cock
Parchment, 11.1 x 8.2 cm (4³⁄₈ x 3¹⁄₄ in.)
Neither signed nor dated (ca. 1657)
London, National Gallery, inv. no. 1415

3
Frans van Mieris
Teasing the Dog
Panel, 27 x 20 cm (10⅝ x 7⅞ in.) (arched at the top)
At the right, above the door: *F v Mieris 1660*
The Hague, Mauritshuis, inv. no. 108

4
Title page of Cesare Ripa (published by D.P. Pers),
Iconologia, Amsterdam 1644 (detail)

uytbeeldingen des Verstands (Iconology or representations of the Intellect) by Cesare Ripa, which appeared in the Dutch version in 1644.

'PITTURA. *The Art of Painting*,' wrote Ripa, is 'A beautiful Woman [...] with a gold chain on the neck on which hangs a Stage Mask [...]. She should hold a Brush in the one hand and a Palette in the other, with a shining robe' (here in translation from the Dutch edition). Van Mieris kept to the general picture described by Ripa, without concerning himself with the latter's details, such as the inscription *Imitatio* on the forehead. That would also have been redundant, for the mask was widely known as the symbol of imitation, which is characteristic of the art of painting. Without doing violence to her beauty, Frans gave Kniertje the 'arched eyebrows' described by Ripa (symbol for 'fantastic thoughts') and the 'tightly closed mouth' (symbol for the solitariness that the painter should seek out). He abandoned the 'ribbon tied behind the ears,' as she is depicted on the title page of the Dutch edition of Ripa by Dirck Pietersz Pers [**4**].[36] The antique male nude that *Pictura* presses to her bosom appears to be an invention of the painter himself. It strengthens the image of 'beautiful and pure Antique' that De Lairesse so appreciated in 'essence, covering, clothing, and accouterment' of this small depiction.[37] Finally, an amusing touch added by Frans van Mieris is the palette he applied to *The Art of Painting*, who holds seven brushes in her hand, the seven colors that he used to execute the painting.[38]

1 *De Lairesse 1707 / 1740*, vol. I, p. 175
2 *De Lairesse 1707 / 1740*, vol. I, n.p. (preceding the numbered pages)
3 *Auction Amsterdam 1765-A*, title page and no. 62; the traditional mention of a provenance from the Lubbeling collection does appear to be verifiable (contrary to what *Hecht 1989-1990*, p. 82 believed): the latter happens to be mistaken (see *Hoet 1752-1770*, vol. II, pp. 517-522).
4 *Van Nierop 1936*, pp. 199-200, 223-225 and 228-232
5 *Van Nierop 1936*, p. 228 and note 2, p. 229 and *Bille 1961*, vol. I, pp. 111-112 and 116
6 *Bille 1961*, vol. I, p. 247, knew only of P.L. de Neufville; the same is true of *Van de Watering 1982*, p. 150 and *Hecht 1989-1990*, p. 82.
7 *Bille 1961*, vol. I, pp. 116-117; *Van Nierop 1936*, p. 229, note 4
8 *Van Nierop 1936*, p. 231, note 3
9 Inv. no. A 2344; *Van Thiel et al. 1976*, p. 572, no. A 2344 and fig.
10 *Hoet 1752-1770*, vol. III (1770), p. 473, nos. 62 and 65
11 *Auction Amsterdam 1773*, p. 61, no. 181; *Hecht 1989-1990*, p. 82, was apparently surprised at this comment.
12 *Auction Amsterdam 1773*, 'Prijzen der schilderijen,' p. 10, no. 181; *Auction Paris 1773*, pp. 28-29, no. 60
13 *Basan 1781*, p. 11, no. 59 and fig.; Lingée himself was mistakenly thought to be the engraver (*Van de Watering 1982*, p. 150).
14 *Auction Paris 1787*, p. 22, no. 39
15 *Auction Paris 1794*, p. 23, no. 48; *DBF*, vol. XI (1967), cols. 103-104

16 *Auction Paris 1808*, pp. 32-33, no. 48

17 *London 1834*, pp. 29-30, no. 57 (with thanks to Willem van de Watering, for his reference to this unique copy: RKD, bound with L 13307); *Whitley 1973*, vol. II, p. 272, thought no catalogue was printed; see also cat. no. 72, note 13.

18 *Smith 1829-1842*, vol. IX (1842), p. 41, no. 22

19 *Auction Paris 1837*, p. 73, no. 68

20 *Grijzenhout / Van Tuyll van Serooskerken 1989*, p. 182, nos. 209-210 and p. 185, no. 219

21 *Boase 1965*, vol. I, col. 1532

22 *London 1850*, p. 10, no. 70

23 *Waagen 1854*, vol. II, pp. 289-292

24 *Auction London 1875*, title page, pp. 15 and 21, no. 118

25 Inv. no. 860; HdG 102; *Broos 1987*, pp. 240-243, no. 42 and fig.

26 *Auction London 1875*, p. 21, no. 119

27 The calculations are taken from, or based on, the specifications in *Smith 1829-1842*, vol. I, p. 71, no. 36 and p. 81, no. 77; vol. IX, p. 41, no. 22

28 *Van de Watering 1982*, p. 150; *Burke's 1963*, p. 2051

29 *Auction London 1929-A*, p. 12, no. 65

30 Inv. no. 1095; *Maclaren 1960*, pp. 222-223, no. 1095; *London 1973*, p. 372, no. 1095 and fig.

31 *Van de Watering 1982*, pp. 150-151 and fig.

32 According to a kind communication from H. Cramer, The Hague.

33 HdG 26; *Von Moltke 1939*, p. 202, no. XLVIII; *Arnhem 1953*, p. 16, no. 41; *Hecht 1989-1990*, p. 82, note 1, believed that no one could have missed the meaning of the depiction, which certainly does not hold true for the period from 1834 to 1929.

34 HdG 365; *Maclaren 1960*, pp. 251-253, no. 1415; *Naumann 1981*, vol. II, p. 33, no. 30 and fig.

35 HdG 208; *Naumann 1981*, vol. II, pp. 40-41, no. 35 and fig.; see there pp. 127-128 on the countless portraits of Frans and Kniertje.

36 *Ripa / Pers 1644*, pp. 452-453

37 See note 1; the literature is silent about the meaning of this statue, which has without cause been identified as Hercules (HdG 26; *Delft / Antwerp 1964-1965*, p. 76, no. 80).

38 This has been confirmed after microscopic examination by Wouter Kloek (Rijksmuseum, Amsterdam), for which I thank him.

BB

Jan Miense Molenaer

Haarlem ca. 1610 – Haarlem 1668

Canvas, 99.1 x 140.9 cm (39 x 55½ in.)
Lower left, on the woodblock: *MLE NAE R 1633* (MLE and NAE in ligature)
Richmond, Va., Virginia Museum of Fine Arts, The Williams Collection, inv. no. 49.11.19

Jan Miense Molenaer was born in, or a little before, 1610, in Haarlem. His first painting dates from 1629, but we do not know who his teacher was. In 1636 he was married in Heemstede to the painter Judith Leyster, who was a pupil of Frans Hals. Shortly after their wedding they settled in the Kalverstraat in Amsterdam. After a financially difficult beginning, they bought a residence in Heemstede in 1648 and a house in Amsterdam in 1655, but toward the end of his life they lived once more in Haarlem, where Jan was buried in 1668. With the exception of a few portraits, he mainly made genre scenes with an abundance of symbolic details. His work is sometimes confused with that of Judith Leyster.

In 1902 Cornelis Hofstede de Groot visited the collection of 'A. Rothschild' in Vienna, where he identified this painting as a work of Jan Miense Molenaer. He noted down: 'Eight music-making figures on a terrace. To the right a gentleman in red. Named Dirk Hals. Is a handsome early painting with fairly large figures' (in translation).[1] Apparently the signature, M[O]LE NAE R, and the date 1633, located on the block of wood to which the little monkey is chained, were not clearly visible, for Hofstede de Groot made no mention of them. Albert Baron von Rothschild (1844-1911), financier and Maecenas, was a brother of Nathaniël Baron von Rothschild (1836-1905), who made his name primarily as a writer of travel books and a collector.[2] These scions of the Austrian branch of the mighty banking family were immensely rich and lived in palaces in Vienna: Nathaniël on the Theresianumgasse and Albert on the Prinz Eugenstrasse.[3] Hofstede de Groot must have seen Molenaer's painting in Baron Albert's sumptuous Louis XVI house, which, according to the family biographer Morton, was sometimes jokingly called the 'Albert Memorial.' The later reports that Nathaniël, too, is to have been the owner of this piece,[4] were probably based only on the fact that he was known as the art collector. After the death of Albert in 1911, the painting came into the hands of his son Eugene Baron von Rothschild (1884-1962), who in the end brought it to America. After World War II, the Viennese Rothschilds immigrated to the United States. Eugene lived on an estate on Long Island, where, four years after the death of his first wife in 1948,

Provenance

Collection Albert Baron von Rothschild, Vienna, 1902
Collection Eugene Baron von Rothschild, Vienna / Long Island, 1911-1949
Newhouse Galleries, New York, 1949
Virginia Museum of Fine Arts, Richmond, 1949 (gift of Mrs. A.D. Williams)

Bibliography

Art News 1952-A, pp. 34-35 and fig., pp. 65-66
Richmond 1966, p. 56, no. 88 and fig.
San Francisco / Toledo / Boston 1966-1967, p. 122, no. 79 and fig.
Kindlers, vol. IV (1967), p. 449
Van Thiel 1967-1968, pp. 90-99 and figs. 1, 5, and 7
Robinson 1969, n.p., note 12
Leyden 1970, p. 17
Toledo 1976, p. 113
Daniëls 1976-1977, pp. 331 and 337
Kren 1980, pp. 75-76 and fig. 14
Wilson 1980-1981, no. 52 and fig.
Zafran 1981, p. 329 and fig. 4
Moreno 1982, p. 56 and fig. 5
Smith 1982, pp. 32-35, 64, 127, and 177, note 79 and fig. 13
Hofrichter 1983, pp. 104-105, no. 80 and fig.
Berlin / London / Philadelphia 1984, p. 246
Near 1985, pp. 441-443 and fig. 4
Hecht 1986, pp. 182, 184 and fig. 24
Hellerstedt 1986, pp. 66-67, no. 26 and fig.
De Jongh 1986, pp. 66, 68 and fig. 2a
Smith 1986, p. 21 and fig. 20
Sutton 1986, p. 255 and fig. 382

he married the actress Jeanne Stuart.[5] Around 1949 Newhouse Galleries in New York was able to acquire this genre scene by Molenaer, which had gone unmentioned in the literature until then.[6]

Only in 1952 was the painting published and depicted in color in *Art News*. It was part of the considerable legacy of the Williams family to the museum in Richmond. Adolph Dill Williams was the son of a tobacco baron of Virginia. His wife had assembled a collection of antiques and paintings following the by then traditional pattern – 'Rembrandt,' Hals, Ter Borch, and the English School – which contained several pieces that had come from the Rothschild collection. At his death in 1952, Williams left three and a half million dollars and a collection of forty-two paintings to the art museum of his hometown. In 1949 his wife, Mrs. Wilkins Coons Williams, had already formally donated Molenaer's painting to the Richmond museum.[7] It is a remark-ably fresh work by Hals's fellow townsman, in which 'the racy portrayal of Haarlem's polite society' and 'the incisive obser-vation of life and the earthy Dutch humor' were praised.[8] What appears to be humor turns out to be in deadly earnest as well, but in 1952 it was still not known that the so celebrated realistic scene was chock-full of symbolism.

In fact this is not a *Music Party* (as the painting was initially entitled) but a double portrait in a narrative context. Jan Miense Molenaer was an expert in this sort of symbolic portrait. A very handsome example attributed to him is the *Group Portrait of the Ruychaver-Van der Laen Family* (Amsterdam, Stichting Museum Van Loon) [1].[9] Made around 1630, it shows a family, some of whose members, such as the man to the right with his hand on a skull, had already died by that time. In addition, the four ages of man are depicted here: from left to right, youth, courting age, marriage, and old age. We furthermore recognize the five senses in the same sequence: Taste (children eating), Touch (the scratching cat), Smell (fragrant carnations), Hearing (music), and Sight (grandmother with glasses). The parents make music to

represent marital harmony: they are the leading actors of the group portrait.[10] A so-called *Merry Company* (Amsterdam, Rijks-museum), which is inscribed *Isack Elyas f. 1620*,[11] appears to be a prototype for this painting and for the Richmond work of three years later. It is in fact a double portrait of the couple standing at the right next to a dining company that depicts the five senses [2].[12] We know of no other work by this Isack Elyas, so we can only state that this mayfly discovered, in Haarlem or in Amster-dam, the formula that was later to be repeatedly applied by Molenaer.[13]

The unidentified young man and his lady at the right are an engaged couple.[14] We know that they are not yet married because the woman is located on the right side of the man. In the

Jan Miense Molenaer Allegorical Engagement Portrait

married state he would have been to her right. This exchange of places is clearly depicted on the title page of the often-read *Houwelick* (Marriage) of 1625 by Jacob Cats.[15] In the thirties betrothed couples had themselves portrayed with conspicuous frequency, including in a painting by Pieter Codde in 1634 (The Hague, Mauritshuis) (cat. no. 51, fig. 6).[16] In 1633 Molenaer translated the open door, seen in Codde's double portrait as a symbol of transience, into a much more elaborate program of references to the virtues and vices. Pieter van Thiel analyzed this accurately in 1967, when it was not yet widely known that such an apparently mundane scene must have been intended 'tot lering and vermaak' (to edify and amuse) and could even convey abstract concepts.[17]

Moderation, harmony, and fidelity are here depicted between gluttony, licentiousness, and lewdness. The neat trick performed by the man at the center rear with his water jug was immediately recognizable for people of the seventeenth century as an image of Temperantia (Moderation), one of the cardinal virtues. 'To add water to the wine' is the still well-known saying that an artist such as Jacob de Gheyn II thought fitting for the depiction of the allegorical female figure *Temperantia* [3].[18] The woman with the songbook underscores this message with a gesture of her hand: she indicates the measure and therefore also stands for moderation (see cat. no. 36). She is surrounded by virtuous figures, for the two gentlemen with their stringed instruments symbolize Harmony or Concordia (Concord), a long-established image.[19] The dog naturally refers to Fides (Fidelity) (see cat. no. 43), as does the ivy on the wall surrounding the terrace (see cat. no. 29). The hand that the future bride has placed on her breast is to be understood as a promise of fidelity.[20]

The dangers that threaten the virtues are threefold. The fighting farmers in the background naturally denote Ire (Anger) or disorder as disruption of harmony: this is Ira contra Concordia.[21] Van Thiel recognized the boy behind the lute player, who sees that the wine is all gone, as the so-called *kannekijker* (one who

4
Cornelis Cornelisz van Haarlem
The Fall of Man (detail)
Canvas, 273 x 220 cm (107½ x 86⅝ in.) (the entire painting)
On the boulder at the right: *C.C.H. f. Ao 1592*
Amsterdam, Rijksmuseum, inv. no. A 129

is always peering into jugs, meaning a lush).[22] He wants 'het onderste uit de kan' (what is at the very bottom of the jug) and is therefore a glutton: here we see Gula versus Temperantia. The monkey who presses a cat against its stomach is the representation of lasciviousness, of evil, and of sin in general. In this detail all the forces of darkness conspire against Fides.[23] Cat and monkey as brothers in evil appear in the painting *The Fall of Man* of 1592 by Cornelis van Haarlem (Amsterdam, Rijksmuseum) [4].[24] Molenaer must have known this famous work by his fellow townsman and borrowed the sinister duo from it. They allude to the dispositions of Adam and Eve: just like Adam, the monkey has a sanguine temperament, which succumbs to the temptations of the flesh. Like Eve, the cat is a choleric creature, cruel and devious.[25] However, Jan Miense Molenaer has the monkey chained to a block of wood, across from the agitated dog. With sharp eyes he guards the lecherous duo. Marital fidelity therefore stands diametrically opposed to the temptations of the flesh. Thus the prospective bridal pair allows itself to be lectured to, and we enjoy along with them this sample of marital counseling from the time of 'Father Cats.'

1 Index cards HdG (RKD)
2 *ÖBL*, vol. IX, pp. 288-289
3 *Morton 1961*, p. 184
4 In all museum and exhibition catalogues since 1952.
5 *Morton 1961*, p. 236
6 The photograph (RKD) received in those days from Newhouse Galleries shows overpainting, especially in the two figures at the right.

3
Jacob de Gheyn II
Temperance
Engraving, diameter 147 mm (5¾ in.)
Neither signed nor dated (ca. 1590)
Amsterdam, Rijksprentenkabinet

7 *Art News 1952-A*, pp. 35 and 65-66; *Near 1985*, p. 440

8 *Art News 1952-A*, p. 35

9 *De Jongh 1986*, pp. 215-217, no. 47 and fig.

10 *Van Eeghen 1973-A*, pp. 124-127

11 *Van Thiel et al. 1976*, p. 220, no. A 1754 and fig.

12 *Amsterdam 1976*, pp. 112-115, no. 23 and fig.

13 Examples of Molenaer in *Berlin / London / Philadelphia 1984*, p. 246, no. 79 and fig. 2; *De Jongh 1986*, pp. 68-69, no. 2 and fig., pp. 215-217, no. 47 and fig., pp. 280-284, no. 69 and fig.

14 *Wilson 1980-1981*, no. 52, suggested that members of the Van Loon family might be depicted here.

15 *Cats 1625*, title page; see also *De Jongh 1986*, p. 40 and fig. 35; on pp. 66-95, De Jongh gave diverse examples of engaged couples in paintings; *Smith 1982*, p. 32 and *Smith 1986*, p. 21, spoke consistently of marriage portraits, as was also the case in all the older literature.

16 Inv. no. 857; *Broos 1987*, pp. 101-105, no. 18 and fig.

17 *Van Thiel 1967-1968*, pp. 90-99. It was especially the exhibition *Tot lering en vermaak* (*Amsterdam 1976*) that brought these insights to the public.

18 *Hollstein*, vol. VII, p. 118, no. 46 and fig.; see also, for instance, *De Jongh 1967-A*, pp. 56-59.

19 Examples in, among others, *De Jongh 1986*, pp. 40-47; *Broos 1987*, pp. 198 and 239.

20 *Hellerstedt 1986*, p. 67; *De Jongh 1986*, pp. 54-55, gives examples of this symbol.

21 *Van Thiel 1967-1968*, pp. 92-93 and fig. 5

22 *Van Thiel 1967-1968*, pp. 93-94; the girl with her hand in a glass may possibly be an erotic symbol.

23 *Janson 1952*, p. 133; see also *Van Thiel 1967-1968*, pp. 96-98 and *Broos 1987*, pp. 328-329

24 *Van Thiel et al. 1976*, pp. 174-175, no. A 129 and fig.

25 *Van Thiel 1967-1968*, p. 98

BB

Amsterdam 1603 /1604 – Amsterdam 1677

Panel, 40 x 55 cm (15¾ x 21⅝ in.)
Lower left: A V D N (AV and DN in ligature) (ca. 1655-1660)
Arlington, Va., private collection

Aert van der Neer was born in Amsterdam (he did not know the precise year himself) and probably learned to paint from Raphael Govertsz Camphuysen in Gorkum, while he was a servant to the lords of Arkel. Around 1632 he returned to Amsterdam, where his son Eglon van der Neer, later to become famous as a *fijn-schilder*, was born in 1634. In 1658 he leased a wine bar in the Kalverstraat, but went bankrupt four years later. From 1633 on he painted landscapes, of which the *maneschijntjes* (small moonlight scenes) and *wintertjes* (small winter scenes) apparently found a large public. In 1656 Archduke Leopold William of Austria had an evening landscape by Van der Neer in his collection. Nevertheless, as was often the fate of specialists, Van der Neer's income was not all that large. He appears to have died in dire poverty.

Provenance
Collection Major J.C.T. Mills, Hilborough, Norfolk, 1955
Auction London, 1975 (£110,000)
Dealer, London, 1975-1979
Private collection, Arlington, Va., 1979

Bibliography
London 1955, no. 20
Auction London 1975, no. 71 A and fig.
WCA, vol. XXVII (1975), p. 212

1
Aert van der Neer
Skaters near the Montelbaan Tower
Brush drawing, 92 x 153 mm (3⅝ x 6 in.)
Upper right: A V D N (AV and DN in ligature) (ca. 1660-1665)
The Hague, Koninklijke Bibliotheek, inv. no. Hs. 131, H. 26, p. 133

This winter landscape by Aert van der Neer is described here for the first time. It is mentioned neither in C. Hofstede de Groot's catalogue of 1918 nor in Fredo Bachmann's 1982 monograph on the artist.[1] It seems impossible to associate the work with any description in the auction catalogues up to 1975 that have been entered into the files in The Hague (RKD) under the name of the artist. In that year it was auctioned as a completely unknown painting; yet, in view of the proceeds of 110,000 pounds sterling, its quality must nevertheless have been fully recognized.[2] In 1955 the Courtauld Institute in London compiled a list of the collection of Major J.C.T. Mills in Hilborough, Norfolk. He turned out to be the owner of this painting at the time. The Mills collection was of modest size and contained, among other things, about thirty Dutch paintings, often with overly optimistic attributions.[3]

In this case, however, the attribution to Aert van der Neer is undoubtedly correct. It is marked at the left, under the frost-covered tree, with the remarkable monogram A V D N, which occurs on his paintings and also on several of the ten-odd drawings that are known by him. He made one of these in the *album amicorum* of Jacobus Heyblocq (1623-1690), a teacher of calligraphy at the Latin School in Amsterdam: *Skaters near the Montelbaan Tower* (The Hague, Royal Library) [1].[4] In contrast to this somewhat cluttered but nicely observed scene, most of the characteristic paintings by Van der Neer are composed accor-

Aert van der Neer 'Kolf' Players on the Ice

ding to a fixed scheme. They in fact look to older models. When we compare the painting under discussion with *Diversions on the Ice* by Hendrick Avercamp, a panel in the Mauritshuis (The Hague) [**2**][5] that was composed half a century earlier, it becomes clear that Van der Neer breathed new life into Avercamp's wintry scenes, much as, after 1672, Adriaen van Ostade revived Avercamp's colored drawings (see cat. no. 47). Just as with Avercamp, the public houses and farms have been placed to the left and right, like the wings of a stage set. A large tree in the foreground serves as a *repoussoir*, and, because of the high viewpoint, we see the scene as a stage from above, as if we were sitting in one of the boxes.

It is a clear day. Still another striking correspondence with Avercamp is the choice of details, such as the snow-covered farms under the high, thatched roofs, the mill, the drawbridge, the outhouse built above the water, the frozen-in rowboats, and the skater who has fallen on his behind. At the same time, the differences between the two winter scenes reflect their dates. In the Avercamp, the horizon is still high up, as was customary in compositions of the early seventeenth century, and the skaters wear the millstone collars of that time. In the Van der Neer, on the contrary, we see the lower horizon that was favored at a later date, which allowed space for a higher sky filled with wintry clouds. Judging further from the costumes and the flat lace collars, we are now in the fifties.

Bachmann dated a number of winter views in this period, calling them the 'blue series.' The most important work of this group is the *View of a River in Winter* in Amsterdam (Rijksmuseum) [**3**].[6] Always characteristic is the diagonal direction of

the river, which runs to a mist-wrapped horizon to the left or right. The gray and light blue canopy of clouds is reflected in the ice, which, in the empty foreground, shows blue-green tints. The dominating element is the clear atmosphere that goes so well with a windless, snow-free winter day. The painting in a

▲ **3**
Aert van der Neer
View of a River in Winter
Canvas, 64 x 79 cm (25¼ x 31⅛ in.)
On a tree stump at the left: *A V DN* (AV and DN in ligature) (ca. 1655-1660)
Amsterdam, Rijksmuseum, inv. no. C 191

2
Hendrick Avercamp
Diversions on the Ice
Panel, 36 x 71 cm (14¼ x 28 in.)
At the left, on the tree: *HA* (in ligature) (ca. 1610)
The Hague, Mauritshuis, inv. no. 785

private collection in Arlington undoubtedly belongs to this series, which Bachmann dated between 1655 and 1660.[7] After 1650, Van der Neer no longer (or rarely) dated his paintings.[8]

Typical of this artist is his preference for a lively staffage, although the number of figures is rather limited in this instance. Van der Neer has depicted every kind of pastime on ice, from riding on the horsedrawn sleigh to weaving about on the narrow blades of skates: fun for young and old, rich and poor. The painter clearly knew the rules of the game of *kolf* that is depicted in the front center and right rear. The older couple skating by look at four *kolf* players, one of whom has slipped and fallen. The game was to be played by two or four people and with two or four balls. The point was to cover a fixed distance or to reach a fixed goal, a post for instance, with as few strokes as possible, which is what the four men at the right are doing.[9] Because a smooth surface was necessary, *kolf* was played in Holland only during the winter, on the ice. In 1634 the seventeen-year-old Gerard ter Borch drew *'Kolf' Players on the Ice* (Amsterdam, Rijksprentenkabinet) [4].[10] His father dated this sheet 'Anno 1634 den 23 januarij,' thus indicating that it had been drawn from life that winter. Van der Neer, too, must have often looked at these authentic Dutch winter diversions, of which he gave such a lively account in his paintings.

The 'blue series' is considered to be the high point in the oeuvre of Aert van der Neer and further forms a striking phase in the development of the Dutch winter landscape. The genre of the 'winter view' was introduced to the North by Flemish painters who had fled to Holland after the fall of Antwerp (see cat. no. 4). It had developed out of the painted series of the months of the year or of the seasons, or out of the context of religious depictions. The Flemish tradition continued in the invented (mountain) landscapes. Typically Dutch, by contrast, are the 'realistic' flat, deep prospects, in which the horizon was placed ever lower. Avercamp populated his scenes with skaters, sleigh riders, and other figures who are making a virtue out

of necessity. In the course of the seventeenth century, artists dispensed with this cheerful staffage and emphasized the landscape in the grip of Jack Frost.

The concept of Aert van der Neer's *'Kolf' Players on the Ice* is traditional in the manner of Avercamp. Recently such winter views have even been called an homage to his famous predecessor.[11] The frost-covered trees are nevertheless related to the contemporary desire to represent the atmosphere of winter. However, it was only later that Van der Neer gave full expression to the grimness of the harsh season in scenes showing either fierce storms (Richmond [England], Cook collection)[12] or heavy snows (Vienna, Gemäldegalerie).[13] These remind one of the pure winter landscapes by Jan van de Cappelle, in which the figures are subservient to frigid nature.[14] This painting from the 'blue series' still offers a scene primarily of old-fashioned diversions on the ice.

1 HdG (vol. VII [1918]); *Bachmann 1982*
2 *Auction London 1975*, no. 71 A. In 1960 an *Ice View* with corresponding dimensions was auctioned that, in view of the price paid (£200) is not likely to have been this painting (*Auction London 1960-A*, p. 23, no. 133).
3 *London 1955*; a copy of this list may be found at the RKD, which also keeps photographs of all the Dutch paintings from the Mills collection.
4 *Bachmann 1972*, pp. 26-27, no. VIII and fig.; *De Kruyter 1976*, p. 126, fig. 17
5 *Broos 1987*, pp. 29-33, no. 4 and fig.
6 *Van Thiel et al. 1976*, p. 410, no. C 191 and fig.
7 *Bachmann 1982*, pp. 115-120 and figs. 86-93
8 *Bachmann 1982*, p. 75; see also HdG, vol. VII, pp. 517-518 and *Bachmann 1966*, pp. 61-62
9 *Bergen op Zoom etc. 1982*, pp. 27-28
10 *McNeil Kettering 1988*, vol. I, pp. 110-111, no. GJr 33 and fig.
11 De Bruyn Kops in *Sutton et al. 1987-1988*, p. 385
12 HdG 531; *Bachmann 1982*, p. 117 and fig. 88a
13 HdG 534; *Stechow 1966*, p. 95 and fig. 185
14 *Broos 1987*, pp. 372-373 and fig. 2
   BB

4
Gerard ter Borch
'Kolf' Players on the Ice
Chalk drawing with wash, 165 x 208 mm
(6¹⁄₂ x 8¹⁄₄ in.)
Not signed, dated at upper left (by his father):
Anno 1634 den 23 januarij
Amsterdam, Rijksprentenkabinet, inv. no. A 794

Haarlem 1610 – Haarlem 1684

Canvas, 44 x 39.5 cm (17³⁄₈ x 15⁵⁄₈ in.)
Below, to the left of center: *Av. Ostade. 1673* (Av in ligature)
Washington, D.C., National Gallery of Art, Widener Collection, inv. no. 1942.9.48

According to the biographer Houbraken, Van Ostade was a pupil of Frans Hals together with Adriaen Brouwer, with whom he shared an interest in Brueghelesque themes. They painted a popular genre of works on a small scale that in the seventeenth century were called *grillen* (caprices), these being mainly interiors of country inns and other scenes of common life, which until about 1640 often included fighting, guzzling, or ranting characters. In the forties Adriaen van Ostade's almost monochrome coloring became warmer and he used (after Rembrandt's example?) light-dark effects.

After 1665 his depictions became more serene, and, using clear, transparent shades, he primarily painted minutely detailed exterior scenes, which were often preceded by a series of carefully considered figure studies. His vision of country life became more charitable and, toward the end of his career, almost idyllic. After 1672 he began making his famous watercolors, which have a color intensity comparable to that of his oil paintings. This way of working was most unusual at that time and may have been intended as a revival of similar colored drawings by Hendrick Avercamp.

Auction prices are a good gauge for the appreciation of an artwork. In 1747 this farmyard scene by Adriaen van Ostade came under the hammer twice. On 15 May about forty paintings were sold in Rotterdam from the collection of Adriaan Swalmius (1689-1747), who had been *stadsadvocaat* (pensionary) of Schiedam. A landscape by Jacob van Ruisdael ('of his best period') only fetched twenty guilders. By contrast, an Italian landscape by Berchem (also 'of his best period'), brought more than 400 guilders, and works by the Leyden *fijnschilders* went for an average of about 200 guilders. The top work, however, was this painting of 1673 by Adriaen van Ostade ('one of the best that is known by him'), which was sold for no less than 775 guilders.[1] The new owner was Jacob ('Jaques') de Roore (1686-1747), a painter and art dealer from Antwerp, who, together with Gerard Hoet, executed decorative wall paintings in The Hague.[2] De Roore was not able to enjoy his acquisition for long, as he died a month and two days after the auction, after which his collection

Provenance

Auction Adriaen Swalmius, Rotterdam, 1747 (*f*775)
Auction Jacob de Roore, The Hague, 1747 (*f*680 to Bisschop)
Collection Pieter and Jan Bisschop, Rotterdam, 1747-1771
Collection Adrian and John Hope, Amsterdam, 1771-1781 (bought after the death of Jan Bisschop)
Collection John Hope, Amsterdam, 1781-1784
Heirs Hope (Hoop), Bosbeek, Heemstede, 1784-1794
Collection Henry Hope, London, 1794-1811
Collection Henry Philip Hope, London, 1811-1839 (temporarily collection Thomas Hope of Deepdene, London, 1819-1831)
Collection Henry Thomas Hope, London, 1839-1862
Collection Adèle Bichat, widow of H.T. Hope, London, 1862-1884
Collection Henry Francis Hope Pelham-Clinton-Hope, London, 1884-1898 (from 1891 to 1898 on loan to the South Kensington Museum)
Dealer Asher Wertheimer, London, 1898
Collection Peter A.B. Widener, Lynnewood Hall, Philadelphia, 1899-1915
Collection Joseph Widener, Lynnewood Hall, Philadelphia, 1915-1942
National Gallery of Art, Washington, D.C., 1942 (gift from Widener)

Bibliography

Auction The Hague 1747, p. 9, no. 84
Hoet 1752-1770, vol. II, p. 196, no. 2, p. 206, no. 84 and p. 528
Rotterdam 1771, p. 4
Hope 1785, sub voce
Josi 1821, n.p., 'Adrien van Ostade,' note 1
London 1824, pp. 186-187, no. 7 (1815)
Westmacott 1824, p. 239
Smith 1829-1842, vol. I, p. 158, no. 188
Waagen 1837-1839, vol. II, p. 146
Waagen 1854, vol. II, p. 119, no. 3
Manchester 1857, p. 56, no. 735
Thoré-Bürger 1857, pp. 315-316 and note 1
Thoré-Bürger 1865, pp. 315-316
Gaedertz 1869, pp. 157 and 190, no. 234
London 1881, p. 24, no. 106
Ashbourne 1885-1900, p. 234 and fig.
Wertheimer 1891 / 1898, no. LXXVI and fig.
Valentiner 1909, pp. xxviii and 70-71, no. 69 and fig.
HdG 503 (vol. III [1910], pp. 299-300, no. 503)
Valentiner 1910, pp. 16 and 242 and fig.
Wiersum 1910, p. 167
Wurzbach, vol. II (1910), p. 278
Graves 1913-1915, vol. II, p. 887, no. 142 (1815) and p. 891, no. 106 (1881)
Hind 1915-1931, vol. IV, p. 17
Hofstede de Groot / Valentiner 1913-1916, n.p., 'Adriaen van Ostade' and fig.
Elkins Park 1923 / 1931, p. 218 and fig. p. 219
Waldmann 1938, p. 336
Art Digest 1940, p. 11
Paris 1950, p. 60, no. 143
Washington 1959, p. 55, no. 644 and fig.
Bille 1961, vol. I, p. 105
Washington 1965, p. 98, no. 644
Buist 1974, p. 492
Niemeijer 1981, pp. 192-193, no. 180 and fig. 16
Schnackenburg 1981, vol. I, p. 127

Adam Pijnacker A Forest View with Hunters

also was auctioned. On this occasion, Italian paintings and works by Rembrandt and Rubens brought considerably less than this 'divine Cabinet piece' by Adriaen van Ostade, which was auctioned for 680 guilders to one of the Bisschop brothers (cat. no. 59, fig. 1) of Rotterdam.[3]

The Bisschop collection, which was housed in a private museum at the Leuvehaven in Rotterdam, has been written about extensively elsewhere (see cat. no. 59). In the 1752 catalogue of this gallery, the painting by Van Ostade was described as: 'A country house with sundry figures, in which [we see] a little Woman cleaning Mussels and Children playing with a Dog, by *Adr. van Ostade*' (in translation).[4] From that moment on, the history of the provenance is completely identical to that of Jan Steen's *Dancing Couple at an Inn* in Washington (National Gallery of Art) (cat. no. 59). The Bisschop collection was bought in 1771 by the Amsterdam bankers Hope, who left the country shortly before the French Revolution. In the nineteenth century, the Hope collection in London could compete with the royal collection. Since 1891, eighty-three paintings (primarily Dutch old masters) were housed in the South Kensington Museum there. In 1898 a judge had to intervene to give Lord Henry Francis Hope Pelham-Clinton-Hope permission to sell the collection. The dealer Asher Wertheimer undertook the sale, and he found new owners for every one of the former Hope paintings. On 30 May 1899 in London, the collector Peter A.B. Widener (1834-1915) (p. 42, fig. 29) from Philadelphia bought *A Courtyard with a Woman Cleaning Mussels* from Wertheimer. 'This picture was a favorite of Mr. P.A.B. Widener's, who said it contained every variety of Dutch painting, genre, still-life, landscape etc.,' according to notes on the Widener collection, which became American national property in 1942 (see cat. no. 35).[5]

The popularity of the painting in the eighteenth and nineteenth century was temporarily eclipsed by that of a watercolor with the same composition, which Adriaen van Ostade rendered in the same year that the painting was made (Amsterdams Historisch Museum) [1].[6] This version in body color and watercolor was bought for a large amount by such well-known collectors as Basan, Jacob de Vos, Six, and Fodor, and was then mainly known from the color print made after it in 1778 by Janinet [2].[7] The relationship with the painting, which differs from the watercolor only in small details, was rarely noticed. In 1821 the connoisseur Josi mentioned the print and the colored drawing in admiration, adding in a note that he found it remarkable that the artist had executed his most successful watercolor in oil paints as well.[8] He knew the painting from the Hope

Clark 1982, p. 78
Clark 1982, pp. 25-26 and fig. 2
Berlin / London / Philadelphia 1984, pp. 272-274, no. 93 and fig.
Washington 1985, p. 295 and fig.

▲ 1
Adriaen van Ostade
Courtyard with a Woman Cleaning Mussels
Watercolor drawing, 237 x 211 mm (9³⁄₈ x 8¹⁄₄ in.)
Lower left: *Av. Ostade. 1673*
Amsterdam, Amsterdams Historisch Museum, inv. no. A 10235

▶ 2
Jean François Janinet after Adriaen van Ostade
Courtyard with a Woman Cleaning Mussels
Color print, 230 x 200 mm (9 x 7⁷⁄₈ in.)
Lower right: *Janinet sculp.* (1778)
Paris, Bibliothèque Nationale

collection, which he had probably seen in 1815, at the exhibition at the British Institution to which Henry Philip Hope had then lent it.[9] The painting once more drew attention at an exhibition in Manchester in 1857, where the well-known art critic William Bürger (pseudonym for Théophile Thoré) described it enthusiastically: 'It is both vigorous and clear, very bold in execution and very spiritual in the details' (in translation).[10]

It was typical for Van Ostade not merely to execute the same image in both watercolors and oil paints but especially to repeat faithfully sections of these images in new compositions. For example, the fencing above the archway, with the slanting slat third from the left, is repeated in the watercolor *The Slaughtering of a Pig* (London, British Museum) [**3**],[11] also of 1673. Repeated in this work are the wooden structures in the courtyard and other details, such as the linen on the clothesline at the right, the broom, and the ivy. Van Ostade again used the pump at the left and the wooden fence with the pointed slats in an undated watercolor, *The Scraping of a Pig* (Amsterdams Historisch Museum) [**4**].[12] A more sketch-like preliminary study of this exists as well (Paris, Musée du Louvre).[13] From all this one can conclude that the production of Van Ostade's country scenes was almost factory work, complete with the use of templates.

Houbraken tells us a nice anecdote about the creation of these watercolors. This biographer was not able to tell us much about the painter's life. However, he had studied his 'artfully colored drawings [which he] viewed several times with great pleasure' (in translation).[14] According to him these drawings were to be found in the collection of Jonas Witsen (1676-1715). He had acquired them from the collection of the Amsterdam silk painter and art dealer Constantijn Sennepart (1625-1703).[15] Houbraken claimed that Van Ostade had been fleeing from the French in 1672 and had ended up in Amsterdam with Sennepart, who gave him the idea of making those watercolors: 'but the Art-loving Konstantyn Sennepart knew how to persuade him so beautifully that he remained with him in his house, where he made those skillfully colored drawings for 1300 guilders, which Mister Jonas Witzen subsequently [...] bought' (in translation).[16] How much of this story is true we leave undecided for now. In any case, it is certain that in 1672 large colored drawings suddenly became a specialty of the painter, who was then well over sixty years old. In a recently discovered copy of the auction catalogue of 1704 of Sennepart's estate, Van Ostade's watercolors appear to have been the pride of the collection: 'In the Artbook No. 1: 36 Drawings by Ostade uncommonly strong, drawn with colors; consisting of Companies of Farmers, Inns, and all sorts of other images: his very best manner' (in translation).[17]

In his monograph on Adriaen van Ostade and his brother Isack, Bernard Schnackenburg listed more than fifty works in this genre from the period between 1672 and 1684. He also pointed to the influence of the watercolors by Hendrick Avercamp.[18] In 1680 the contents of Avercamp's atelier, including hundreds of drawings, was to be found in the collection of Jan

4
Adriaen van Ostade
The Scraping of a Pig
Watercolor drawing, 175 x 144 mm (6⅞ x 5⅝ in.)
Lower left: *Av. Ostade* (ca. 1673)
Amsterdam, Amsterdams Historisch Museum,
inv. no. A 10234

3
Adriaen van Ostade
The Slaughtering of a Pig
Watercolor drawing, 260 x 220 mm (10¼ x 8⅝ in.)
Lower left: *Av. Ostade. 1673* (Av in ligature)
London, British Museum, inv. no. 1895.9.15.1239

van de Cappelle in Amsterdam, who kept some of them framed as if they were paintings.[19] Sennepart shared with Jan van de Cappelle his occupation of silk painting and passion for the art of drawing, and the latter's unique Avercamp collection possibly gave Sennepart the idea to have Adriaen van Ostade revive this genre. This may possibly confirm the essence of Houbraken's story. In 1704 Sennepart himself possessed '12 pieces of capital drawings by the Mute of Kampen [Avercamp], as elaborately drawn as ever has been seen by anyone' (in translation).[20] Adriaen van Ostade must have been familiar with these works. He renewed Avercamp's technique not only by coloring his drawings inside the contours but also by painting them with body color and watercolors as if in oils. Now and then, as in the painting in Washington, he repeated a successful composition in bigger format in a painting (or the other way around).

A remarkable turn in Adriaen van Ostade's work is the replacing of the earlier Brueghelesque images of countryfolk in all their ignorance and crudity with a more neutral vision.[21] The watercolors of the years 1672 and after show peaceful scenes of which Houbraken aptly remarked: 'Small inns and small pubs, with all their equipment, he managed to depict as amusingly and naturally as anyone ever did. Including the small figures in their clothing, and all sorts of activities, so naturally rural and inventive that it is astonishing how he was able to invent it all' (in translation). According to him this kind of scene existed mainly in the artist's imagination, and he identified a striking parallel with poetry: 'In one word, he has depicted all of life with the brush as did L. Rotgans with the pen' (in translation). Subsequently he cited the latter's poem, in which a farm girl is described as a 'Field Goddess.'[22] Houbraken obviously already saw that Van Ostade, like Rotgans in his broad epic poem *Boerekermis* (Country fair) of 1708, gave evidence of a mildly mocking but also tender view of the country folks. The painter of the simple life could therefore measure up to the poet who practiced this genre.[23]

1 *Hoet 1752-1770*, vol. II, pp. 196-197, nos. 2, 5, 6, 11, 12; Swalmius's year of birth appears in *Album studiosorum 1875*, col. 808; in 1709 he registered in Leyden as a twenty-year-old law student.
2 *Thieme / Becker*, vol. XXVIII (1934), p. 577
3 *Hoet 1752-1770*, vol. II, p. 206, no. 84
4 *Hoet 1752-1770*, vol. II. p. 528; *Rotterdam 1771*, p. 4: 'Een Buytehuys met verscheyde Beelden daer een Vrouw Mossels zit schoon te maken en twee kinders met een Hond spelen.'
5 Documentation archives of the National Gallery of Art, Washington, D.C.
6 *Schnackenburg 1981*, vol. I, p. 127, no. 237, vol. II, pl. 111
7 *Wurzbach*, vol. II (1910), p. 285, nos. 130-137 (130): one of these prints is dated 1778.

8 *Josi 1821*, n. p., 'Adrien van Ostade'
9 *Graves 1913-1915*, vol. II, p. 887, nos. 142 (1815); *London 1824*, pp. 186-187, no. 7 (1815)
10 *Thoré-Bürger 1857* and *Thoré-Bürger 1865*, pp. 315-316 (not included in the first edition of the catalogue, *Manchester 1857*; in the second edition, p. 56, no. 735).
11 *Hind 1915-1931*, vol. IV, p. 17, no. 62 and pl. IX; *Schnackenburg 1981*, vol. I, p. 127, no. 238, vol. II, pl. 111
12 *Schnackenburg 1981*, vol. I, p. 136, no. 274, vol. II, pl. 130
13 Inv. no. RF 681; *Schnackenburg 1981*, vol. I, p. 136, no. 275, vol. II, pl. 130
14 *Houbraken 1718-1721*, vol. I, p. 347
15 *Broos 1984*, p. 25
16 *Houbraken 1718-1721*, vol. I, p. 347
17 *Auction Amsterdam 1704*, p. 4, no. 1
18 *Schnackenburg 1981*, vol. I, pp. 41 and 73, note 111a
19 *Bredius 1892*, p. 34, no. 73, pp. 37-39, nos. 14, 38, and 73
20 *Auction Amsterdam 1704*, p. 5, no. 8
21 *Broos 1987*, p. 245
22 *Houbraken 1718-1721*, vol. I, pp. 347-348; *Rotgans / Strengholt 1708 / 1968*, p. 11, made a connection with the French classical *poème heroï-comique*.
23 *McNeil Kettering 1983* did not mention Van Ostade's tableaux in her book *Pastoral Art and Its Audience in the Golden Age*.
BB

Adam Pijnacker

Schiedam 1620 / 1621 – Amsterdam 1673

Canvas, 82 x 70.5 cm (32¼ x 27¾ in.)
Lower right: *APynacker* (AP in ligature) (ca. 1665)
Sarasota, Fla., The John and Mable Ringling Museum of Art, inv. no. SN 896

According to the biographer Houbraken, Adam Pijnacker, who came from Schiedam, spent three years in Italy. His earliest dated painting, an Italian harbor view, is from 1650. Between 1649 and 1651 he was active in Delft, possibly for the art dealer Adam Pick, but he continued to live in Schiedam until 1661. Pijnacker then left for Amsterdam, where he carried out many commissions.

His early landscapes are serene and simple in organization. After 1660 (possibly in emulation of Nicolaes Berchem) he introduced a new type of composition, with wild forest groves from which a few gnarled tree trunks protrude. In these works, the dramatic lighting contrasts with the dominant deep blue-green coloration. At the end of his life he lived, as did Rembrandt, on the Rozengracht of Amsterdam.

Provenance

Auction London, 1812 (£105 or £199.10 to Murray)
Collection Sir John Murray, London, 1812-1827
Collection Lady Murray, London, 1827-1848
Heirs Murray, London(?), 1848
Auction London, 1913 (£33.12 to Davis)
Collection J.H. Galloway, Ayr, Scotland, 1925
Auction London, 1970 (£5,200 to B. Cohen)
Dealer Leonard Koetser, London, 1971
Dealer H. Schickman, New York, 1971
The John and Mable Ringling Museum, Sarasota, 1971

Bibliography

Auction London 1812, p. 3, no. 9 or p. 4, no. 13
Redford 1888, vol. II, p. 315 (1812)
Auction London 1913, p. 21, no. 97
HdG 14 (vol. IX [1926], p. 526, no. 14)
Auction London 1970, title page and pp. 36-37, no. 55 and fig.
Apollo 1971, p. 79 and fig.
Connoisseur 1971, p. 35 and fig.
Chronique des arts 1972, p. 85, no. 297 and fig.
Robinson et al. 1980, no. 113 and fig.
Janson 1986, pp. 68-69 and fig.
Sutton 1986, p. 281 and fig. 423
Harwood 1988, p. 96, no. 81 and pls. XVII and 81

It was pure visual pleasure that Houbraken encountered in the landscapes that Pijnacker made in his Amsterdam period: 'Artful, natural, and amusingly painted: here a copse of trees in the blue shadow: there a sunlight coming down, which paints the green foliage with glowing sparkles' (in translation).[1] He quoted extensively from the poet P. Verhoek, who, around 1665, described what is also in evidence in the painting in Sarasota: 'The tree bark coarse with moss here represents the oak, which calmly / perseveres three centuries, and shows itself green and merry, / Just as the Birch tree is known by its bark: / Their tops, brown and dense, loaded with leaves, / Shadow the ground, and repulse Phoebus's [the sun's] rays' (in translation).[2]

Pijnacker often painted the effect of sunlight on the white bark of birch trees, as, for instance, in a related composition in the Schilderijengalerij Prins Willem V (The Hague) [1].[3] During a recent restoration there emerged a somewhat spot-lit figure of a bathing boy, which was apparently painted out at a later date because of his nudity.[4] In this same spot, the canvas in Sarasota (which was painted about the same time, around 1665) features the deep black of a dark ravine. An alternate version of this composition (Nottingham, City Art Museum) [2][5] shows a different staffage, but the landscape is virtually the same. This must be a later replica, for Pijnacker never repeated himself so literally. At the most, his compositions are only generally similar,

1
Adam Pijnacker
A Landscape with Bathers
Canvas, 101 x 91 cm (39¾ x 35⅞ in.)
Neither signed nor dated (ca. 1665)
The Hague, Schilderijengalerij Prins Willem V, inv. no. (Mauritshuis) 132

Adriaen van Ostade Courtyard with a Woman Cleaning Mussels

2
Copy after Pijnacker
A Landscape with Cattle
Canvas, 90 x 76.2 cm (35½ x 30 in.)
Lower right: *A Pynacker* (not autograph) (eighteenth century?)
Nottingham, City Art Museum, inv. no. 26

as shown, for instance, in his *Ships on an Italian Lake* (Amsterdam, Rijksmuseum).[6]

We again see a dominant, crooked tree with large leaves in the center foreground of the drawing *A Hunter with a Deer* (Amsterdams Historisch Museum) [3].[7] This is one of his rare signed sheets. Apparently Pijnacker was attracted to the tree not only as a pictorial aid but also as a botanical phenomenon. In any case, he specialized in drawings of tree studies.[8] This interest in nature is also apparent in his paintings, as the poet P. Verhoek expressed so effectively: 'Just as the Birch tree is known by its bark.'[9]

Owing to the perfect condition of the painting, one can clearly see details such as 'the curvature of the lines [which] is further emphasised [...] by long, razor-thin, white lines superimposed at the top of the surface of the painting.'[10] These white lines occur elsewhere in Pijnacker's work, for instance in the canvas in the Schilderijengalerij Prins Willem v (The Hague) [1]. It also displays the spidery twigs that consist of one thin, white brushstroke. The razor-sharp flickering lines are once more to be seen in *A Barge on a Riverbank* (Amsterdam, Rijksmuseum) [4],[11] serving in this case to graze the contours of the boat with

sunlight. Pijnacker apparently cultivated this artifice in his later works.

An earlier owner of the Sarasota painting was exceptionally attached to such refined details. This previous owner was Sir John Murray (1768-1827), who, when in the Mauritshuis in The Hague, preferred Gerard Dou's 'highly-finished' style and Houckgeest's 'clearness' over Vermeer's *View of Delft*, which he believed had been brushed too broadly.[12] Murray wrote a journal of his journeys through Holland in 1819 and 1822-1823, which was printed in a limited edition. In it he noted all sorts of curiosities about the art works that he saw. He was in his own way a connoisseur, who especially loved the so-called *fijnschilders* of genre pieces and smoothly rendered landscapes and still lifes. He owned two Pijnackers (including the work under discussion) himself, and he therefore paid particular attention to this artist while he was in Holland. In Rotterdam he admired a small landscape about which he sighed: 'The lights are beautifully disposed. It is a perfect gem.'[13] In The Hague, N. Heideloff, who guided foreign visitors through the Mauritshuis, offered to sell him a painting by Pijnacker. At the time Murray thought the price of 5,000 guilders too high.[14] Finally, when in the Six collection in Amsterdam he saw the *Barge on a River Bank* [4], which he also called a jewel.[15] That designation is certainly also applicable to the painting from Sarasota, which was then in his possession. It can here be established that he must have bought it in 1812 at an anonymous auction in London, where he also acquired his second, no longer identifiable, landscape by Pijnacker.[16]

Sir John Murray enjoyed a military career in the Middle East,

3
Adam Pijnacker
A Hunter with a Deer
Chalk drawing, 155 x 237 mm (6⅛ x 9⅜ in.)
Lower right: *APijnacker* (AP in ligature) (ca. 1665)
Amsterdam, Amsterdams Historisch Museum, inv. no. A 10267

4
Adam Pijnacker
A Barge on a Riverbank
Panel, 40 x 43 cm (15³/₄ x 16⁷/₈ in.)
On the rudder: *APijnacker* (AP in ligature) (ca. 1665)
Amsterdam, Rijksmuseum, inv. no. A 2335

which, because of his rather high-handed actions, came to an inglorious end in 1812.[17] Having lost his commission, he spent his time traveling to see art, accompanied by his wife, a daughter of Lord Mulgrave. Sir John (who, at the end of his life, was allowed to call himself General) had a substantial collection when he died in 1827. His childless widow survived him until 1848. She bequeathed a number of paintings to the National Gallery in London, but the legacy was turned down.[18] It is not entirely clear whether the estate was then divided between the heirs or auctioned. Pijnacker's work in Sarasota was in any case not among the small number of paintings from the collection of General Murray that was auctioned at Christie's in London in 1852, as has sometimes been claimed.[19]

In 1913 the landscape came under the hammer as being 'the property of a gentleman,' probably one of the heirs of Lady Murray. The provenance in any case explicitly stated that the painting came from the former collection of Sir John.[20] In 1970 the painting was once more auctioned anonymously in London. By way of the art trade it ended up in Sarasota, where, together with Lingelbach's *Italian Harbor* (cat. no. 40), it is ranked as one

of the high points of Dutch landscape painting of the seventeenth century. Sutton praised Pijnacker's 'brilliant clarity of vision and gift for precise, calligraphic detail.'[21] Sir John Murray would have agreed wholeheartedly.

1 *Houbraken 1718-1721*, vol. II, p. 97
2 *Houbraken 1718-1721*, vol. II, p. 98; the poem was written in response to wall hangings by Pijnacker in the house of magistrate Cornelis Backer, 348 Herengracht, Amsterdam, see *Sutton et al. 1987-1988*, p. 399 and *Harwood 1988*, pp. 31-32.
3 HdG 54; *Duparc 1980*, pp. 68-69 and 201, no. 132 and fig.; *Harwood 1988*, p. 97, no. 82 and pl. 82
4 This is the first time that the painting is published in this restored state.
5 *Harwood 1988*, p. 96, no. 81b
6 Inv. no. A 321; HdG 18; *Van Thiel et al. 1976*, p. 458, no. A 321 and fig.; *Harwood 1988*, pp. 90-91, no. 74 and pls. XV and 74
7 *Amsterdam 1863*, p. 37, no. 156
8 *Van Hasselt 1977-1978*, pp. 122-123, no. 82 and pl. 119
9 *Houbraken 1718-1721*, vol. II, p. 98
10 *Harwood 1988*, p. 96; see also *Robinson et al. 1980*, no. 113
11 HdG 19; *Van Thiel et al. 1976*, p. 458, no. A 2335 and fig.; *Harwood 1988*, p. 72, no. 47 and pl. 47
12 Inv. no. 92; *Broos 1987*, pp. 382-389, no. 65 and fig.; *Murray 1819-1823*, pp. 45 and 50
13 *Murray 1819-1823*, p. 27 (not identified)
14 *Murray 1819-1823*, p. 66; presumably this was the painting in Shrewsbury, Attingham Park, National Trust (inv. no. 6; *Harwood 1988*, p. 80, no. 60 and pl. 60).
15 *Murray 1819-1823*, p. 155
16 *Auction London 1812*, p. 3, no. 9 and p. 4, no. 13
17 *DNB*, vol. XXXIX, pp. 389-390; *Staring 1925*, p. 101
18 *Staring 1925*, p. 107; there exists an inventory of 1828 (unknown to us) of the paintings of Sir John Murray.
19 *Auction London 1852*; *Harwood 1988*, p. 96, no. 81
20 *Auction London 1913*, p. 21, no. 97.
21 *Auction London 1970*, pp. 36-37, no 55 and fig.; *Sutton 1986*, p. 281
 BB

Paulus Potter A Horse Stable with Figures

Enkhuizen 1625 – Amsterdam 1654

Panel, 44.3 x 37.5 cm (17 3/8 x 14 3/4 in.)
Lower left: *paulus potter f. 1647.*
Philadelphia, Pa., Philadelphia Museum of Art, William L. Elkins Collection, inv. no. E' 24-3-17

Paulus Potter was taught in Amsterdam by his father, Pieter Potter, and by Nicolaes Moeyaert. In 1646 he became a member of the painters' guild in Delft. Beginning in 1649 he worked in The Hague (where he was Jan van Goyen's neighbor), and he returned to Amsterdam in 1652. In 1653 he there received the unique commission to paint a life-size equestrian portrait of Dirck Tulp. After its completion he died, only twenty-nine years old.

Potter was a specialist in the depiction of animals, which play a more important role in his landscapes than was customary. He sometimes made animals the principal motif of his scenes, which therefore may also be thought of as portraits of animals. His landscapes are often dominated by an unmistakable atmospheric mood, sometimes somber, sometimes sunny. His renowned *Bull* (The Hague, Mauritshuis) has been both praised and reviled. This varying appreciation also appears to have formed a barrier to the thorough study of his work. There is, in any case, no monograph on his oeuvre, which also includes masterful drawings and etchings.

The collaborating art brokers Gijsbert Hol (ca. 1680-1755) and Philippus van der Land (ca. 1700-1775) arranged auctions in Amsterdam of collections that had been entirely procured outside of Holland.[1] This activity greatly contributed to Amsterdam's reputation as an international center for the art trade. In 1738, in close succession, they brought the collections of the German Count of Plettenberg and Baron Schönborn under the hammer.[2] The painting by Paulus Potter discussed here was mentioned in the catalogue of the Plettenberg auction as 'A stable with Horses and Figures [...] very natural. *high* 1 : 6. *wide* 1 : 3½' (in translation).[3] Ferdinand Adolph Count of Plettenberg and Wittem (1690-1737) had been First Minister to the Archbishop Elector of Cologne. A few of his honorable titles were mentioned on the title page of the catalogue: 'Knight of the Golden Fleece, Secret Council of His Imperial and Catholic Majesty; and the latter's designated Ambassador to Rome. Etc. Etc.' (in translation).[4]

The Plettenberg collection was known above all for its excellent Italian paintings, which were in point of fact not all that

Provenance

Auction Ferdinand Adolph Count of Plettenberg and Wittem, Amsterdam, 1738 (*f*185 to Lormier)
Collection Willem Lormier, The Hague, 1738-1756
Collection J.W. Frank, The Hague, 1756 (bought for *f*600 from Lormier)
Collection John Hope, Amsterdam, 1774-1784 ('bought out of hand' [without intermediary] for *f*3,800)
Heirs Hope (Hoop), Bosbeek, Heemstede, 1784-1794
Collection Henry Hope, London, 1794-1811
Collection Henry Philip Hope, London, 1811-1839 (temporarily collection Thomas Hope of Deepdene, London, 1819-1831)
Collection Henry Thomas Hope, London, 1839-1862
Collection Adèle Bichat, widow of H. T. Hope, London, 1862-1884
Collection Henry Francis Hope Pelham-Clinton-Hope, London, 1884-1898 (on loan from 1891 to 1898 to the South Kensington Museum)
Dealer Colnaghi & Wertheimer, London, 1898
Collection William L. Elkins, Philadelphia, 1898-1903
Collection Mrs. W.L. Elkins and George W. Elkins, Philadelphia, 1903-1919 .
Philadelphia Museum of Art, William L. Elkins Collection, Philadelphia, 1924

Bibliography

Auction Amsterdam 1738, p. 6, no. 66
Hoet 1752-1770, vol. I, p. 500, no. 66, vol. II, p. 435
The Hague 1754, p. 22, no. 221
Hope 1771-1778, fol. 7
Hope 1785, sub voce
London 1824, pp. 174-175, no. 4 (1815)
Smith 1829-1842, vol. v, pp. 153-154, no. 87
Waagen 1837-1839, vol. II, p. 147
Waagen 1854, vol. II, p. 120
Blanc 1857, pp. 181 and 186
Manchester 1857, p. 69, no. 996
Thoré-Bürger 1857, pp. 283-284 and note 1
Van Westrheene 1867, pp. 83 and 156-157, no. 35
London 1881, p. 18, no. 71
Wertheimer 1891 / 1898, fig. 17
Valentiner 1909, p. 73, no. 72 and fig.
HdG 156 (vol. IV [1911]), pp. 636, 679-680, no. 156, p. 690)
Graves 1913-1915, vol. II, p. 946, no. 137 (1815), p. 947, no. 996 (1857) and no. 71 (1881)
Von Arps-Aubert 1932, p. 36, no. 17
Philadelphia 1965, p. 55
Buist 1974, p. 492
Niemeijer 1981, p. 194, no. 191
Sutton 1986, p. 225 and fig. 328
Sutton 1990, pp. 239-240, no. 85 and fig.

popular with the Dutch collectors, probably because they were too large for their cabinets.[5] Nevertheless, a work attributed to Raphael was sold at the Plettenberg auction for the unheard-of large sum of 10,000 guilders. By contrast, *A Horse Stable with Figures* by Potter fetched 185 guilders, including commission.[6] Until now, the facts concerning the further peregrinations of the painting have been only fragmentarily presented, even though that story can be recounted virtually without any gaps.[7] We can announce, for instance, the name of the buyer at the Plettenberg auction: Willem Lormier from The Hague. The name Lormier is still associated above all with the art cabinet from which his nephew Adriaan van Heteren was able to acquire the important pieces that finally ended up in the Rijksmuseum in Amsterdam.

Willem Lormier (1682-1758) was descended from a Walloon family and, like his father, engaged in the profitable profession of *solliciteur militaire*. This official functionary advanced money to officers of the army of the United Provinces so that they could pay their soldiers, and he was allowed to charge a substantial rate of interest for this service. Lormier also supplied goods to the army and described himself as an agent. According to his fellow townsman Jacob Campo Weyerman, he was even the 'Agent of diverse foreign Rulers,' though this was not specified any more exactly.[8] In his house on the Lutherse Burgwal in The Hague, he assembled a large collection of paintings, coins, and medals. The military solicitor apparently traded in these as well, for he appears not only to have bought art works but to have sold them as well, and often at a substantial profit. However, Lormier did not advertise himself as an art dealer. As a consequence of the unstable political situation during the Seven Years' War (1756-1763), it was not possible to auction his cabinet until five years after his death.[9] At that time the painting by Paulus Potter was no longer in the collection, as Lormier had in the meantime been able to dispose of it at a profit.

In 1754 this gentleman-dealer had a catalogue of his collection printed, and he used a copy of it to note down when and where he had done his buying and selling. This is a unique source of information, which is still too little consulted. Next to the painting by Potter, which is described as a 'Landscape, figures, Horses, and a white Horse that stands before a Stable' (in translation), Lormier noted: 'sale amsterdam 2 April 1738' and the price of 170 guilders (without commission).[10] It is clear from this that Lormier was the buyer who is indicated by the code 'R L' in the catalogue of the Plettenberg auction. He also set up a kind of administration for 'sold Paintings,' from which one can deduce, among other things, that he supplied works to important

collectors. However, Mr. J.W. Frank, to whom he sold the Potter, was not known as such. On 4 June 1756 Lormier noted down: 'to J.W. Franc [...] potter. stable white horse [...] 600,-.-' (in translation).[11] Thus, in 1756, at a profit of more than 400 guilders, he managed to sell the painting that he had acquired in 1738 for 170 guilders (185 with commission).

Only twenty years later a much higher amount was to be paid for the Potter. The Hope family was then active in the Dutch art market. In 1771 they had managed to lay hands on the complete Rotterdam Bisschop collection and thus in one blow had become collectors of stature (see cat. no. 59). Subsequently, it was especially John Hope (1737-1784) who expanded the collection with what were often expensive acquisitions.[12] For example, in 1774, he purchased Potter's *Horse Stable with Figures* for no fewer than 3,800 guilders, which meant a sixfold increase in price in less than twenty years. The Hope collection was also described. The collector had a clerk keep perfect track of what he purchased, and for how much, between 1771 and 1778. 'To I.H. [John Hope] for the following paintings bought out of hand [i.e., direct from the owner] in A° 1774. [and] brought to the Cabinet. A painting by P. Potter. A landscape with a stable in the foreground, where a farmer ties up the tail of a dun horse, while they are both strongly lit by the sun through a skylight. high 18 in. wide 14½ in. P[anel] 3800.-.-' (in translation).[13] From whom John Hope bought the painting 'out of hand' we will probably never find out.

The description in the Hope catalogue is, for that matter, unusually accurate. The tying up of the horse's tail with straw was correctly interpreted, whereas all later authors either ignored this barely visible detail or spoke incorrectly of grooming.[14] One copyist either did not see this action or did not recognize this old Dutch custom, and his depiction is consequently exposed as a pastiche (New York, auction Christie's, 1983) [1].[15] This replica can therefore lay no claim to having been painted by the master himself, as Smith and Hofstede de Groot thought.[16] John

1
Copy after Paulus Potter
A Horse Stable with Figures
Panel, 52 x 43 cm (20½ x 17 in.)
Lower left (not autograph): *paulus. potter 1643*
(eighteenth century?)
New York, auction Christie's, 1983

Hope or his clerk saw not only the tying up of the horse's tail but also the handsome lighting of the figures in the stable. Due to the perfect condition of the painting, this is still a striking part of the scene.

We may venture further to speculate as to why John Hope wanted the painting so badly that he paid such a large amount for it. It is in point of fact quite probable that he considered it to be the pendant to another painting by Paulus Potter in his collection, one of virtually the same format and also dated 1647, *Cattle in a Thunderstorm* (London, National Gallery) [**2**].[17] This painting came from the Bisschop collection in Rotterdam, where it had already been mentioned in 1752.[18] Because of its format, the new acquisition was able to serve as a pendant in his collection, even though the depictions are not at all coordinated. Hope probably did not know that Paulus Potter repeatedly painted in this unusual format and that a whole series of paintings dates from the year 1647.[19] In 1834 the two pieces apparently hung in identical frames at the London residence of Henry Philip Hope, when John Smith described them as belonging together.[20] Dr. Gustav Waagen also saw the 'counterparts' in this way when he studied the Hope collection on Duchess Street. 'In impasto, warmth, and force of colouring, the master here appears in all his excellence,' was Waagen's commentary on *A Horse Stable with Figures*.[21] The widow of Henry Thomas Hope left the collection to Lord Henry Francis Hope Pelham-Clinton-Hope, who sold the paintings in 1898, after they had been exhibited for ten years at the South Kensington Museum in London (see cat. no. 59).

Around 1900 William Lukens Elkins (1832-1903) of Philadelphia became the new owner of Potter's *Horse Stable*. Elkins had climbed from grocery boy to oil baron. His biographers call him a capitalist by profession.[22] Together with his fellow townsman Peter A.B. Widener (1834-1915) (p. 42, fig. 29), who began around 1890 to invest his money in an art collection, he bought land on a large scale. Elkins and Widener shared their cultural

2
Paulus Potter
Cattle in a Thunderstorm
Panel, 46.3 x 37.8 cm (18¼ x 14⅞ in.)
Lower left: *Paulus. Potter. f. 1647*
London, National Gallery, inv. no. 2583

3
Paulus Potter
The Bull
Canvas, 235.5 x 339 cm (92¾ x 133½ in.)
At the left, on the horizontal board of the gate:
Paulus Potter. / f. 1647
The Hague, Mauritshuis, inv. no. 136

interests and a pronounced preference for the Dutch Golden Age. Elkins bequeathed his ninety-eight paintings, of which his widow temporarily enjoyed life interest, to the city of Philadelphia. Together with the paintings of Elkins's son George W. (1858-1919), the collection was transferred in 1924 to the newly built museum in Philadelphia.[23] In 1909 Elkins's widow had lent the painting to the Hudson-Fulton celebration in New York (see pp. 39-40). It was then scarcely known that it had come from the English Hope collection.[24] It is just one of many paintings in American possession whose Dutch history appears to have passed into oblivion.

The collection at Philadelphia has a treasure of excellent but at times somewhat obscure Dutch paintings, which have been called 'a connoisseur's dream and a cataloguer's nightmare.'[25] The painting by Paulus Potter is a pronounced example of the surprises that this museum collection may yet yield. In the 1960 catalogue of the National Gallery in London the location of the so-called pendant of *Cattle in a Thunderstorm* [2] was given as unknown.[26] When, in 1981, Niemeijer published his impressive reconstruction of the Hope collection, he did not know that the painting in Philadelphia was the same panel that John Hope had bought in 1774 to serve as a pendant to the piece from the Bisschop collection.[27] Even more amazing, when the copy of the painting [1] was auctioned in New York in 1983, people were apparently unaware of the existence of the original in Phila-delphia.[28] There was, therefore, every reason to ask that this forgotten painting be included in the present exhibition. It is furthermore a good opportunity to show that the young Potter could also paint small, engaging scenes in the same year in which he created his imposing *Bull* (The Hague, Mauritshuis) [3].[29]

1 *Bille 1961*, vol. I, pp. 182-183

2 L. 480 and 482

3 *Auction Amsterdam 1738*, p. 6, no. 66

4 *Auction Amsterdam 1738*, title page; data from the Centraal Bureau voor Genealogie, The Hague.

5 *Bille 1961*, vol. I, pp. 140-141

6 *Auction Amsterdam 1738*, p. 3, no. 1 and p. 6, no. 66

7 The most comprehensive, though incomplete, provenance was given by Hofstede de Groot (HdG 156).

8 *Breesnee 1948-1949*, p. 136; *Weyerman 1729-1769*, vol. IV (II), p. 15

9 *Bille 1961*, vol. I, p. 111; *Auction The Hague 1763*

10 *The Hague 1754*, p. 21, no. 221; this catalogue is reprinted in *Hoet 1752-1770*, vol. II, pp. 415-450.

11 *The Hague 1754* (MS copy RKD)

12 *Niemeijer 1981*, pp. 147-148

13 *Hope 1771-1778*, fol. 7

14 *Manchester 1857*, p. 69, no. 996 and *Blanc 1857*, pp. 181 and 186, spoke of grooming.

15 *Auction New York 1983*, p. 32, no. 44

16 *Smith 1829-1842*, vol. V, p. 154 and HdG 156 (according to Hofstede de Groot, Jan Wubbels, the curator of the Hope collection, bought it at the time of the Philips van der Land auction; Wubbels and Hope must have known it was a copy, as they no doubt knew the original).

17 *Maclaren 1960*, pp. 299-300, no. 2583

18 *Hoet 1752-1770*, vol. II, p. 531

19 *Von Arps-Aubert 1932*, gave a summary of the dated paintings; see p. 36 for the ones dated 1647 (see also HdG, vol. IV, pp. 689-690).

20 *Smith 1829-1842*, vol. V, p. 153, no. 87: 'The Companion.'

21 *Waagen 1854*, vol. II, p. 120: 'the companion picture'; see also *Waagen 1837-1839*, vol. II, p. 147.

22 WWWA, vol. I, p. 365; DAB, vol. VI, pp. 84-85

23 *Philadelphia 1965*, p. V; *Ingersoll 1971*, p. 5

24 *Valentiner 1909*, p. 73, no. 72

25 *Sutton 1986*, p. 221; see, however, *Sutton 1990*

26 *Maclaren 1960*, p. 300, no. 2583 and note 1: 'formerly in the Hope collection.'

27 *Niemeijer 1981*, p. 194, no. 191

28 *Auction New York 1983*, p. 32, no. 44

29 *Broos 1987*, pp. 254-260, no. 45 and fig.

BB

Leyden 1606 – Amsterdam 1669

Canvas transferred to panel, 102.5 x 83.8 cm (40 3/8 x 33 in.)
To the right, below center: *RHL. van Ryn / 1632* (RHL in ligature)
San Francisco, Calif., The Fine Arts Museums of San Francisco, inv. no. 66.31

After an apprenticeship of three years in Leyden, Rembrandt studied history painting with Pieter Lastman in Amsterdam. It is apparent from his earliest works (1625-1626) that he had studied Lastman's multifigured 'Italian' compositions closely and had adopted his bright colors. Back in Leyden, however, Rembrandt painted in somber brown and gray tints and with strong chiaroscuro. Constantijn Huygens admired this concentrated power more than the life-size formats of his artistic competitor and studio companion Jan Lievens. Through Huygens's intervention, Rembrandt received commissions from the court (including a Passion series).

Late in 1631 Rembrandt left Leyden permanently for Amsterdam to make his fortune painting portraits. He had not done these up to that time because he wanted to be a history painter. Through the art dealer Hendrick Uylenburgh (in whose house he lived) he received many commissions for portraits and got to know Uylenburgh's niece Saskia, whom he married in 1633. In 1641, after three children who died in infancy, they had a son named Titus. Saskia died the following year. That same year, 1642, Rembrandt also completed the '*Night Watch*,' his greatest group portrait, which he conceived as a history piece. It was praised for this reason, and not maligned, as has sometimes been thought.

In the forties Rembrandt painted less, applying himself to drawings and etchings. The colors of his history paintings became clearer and his touch broader. A striking new theme, also apparent in etchings and drawings, was the (imagined) landscape. In 1649 Hendrickje Stoffels came to live with Rembrandt, who considered her to be his *huysvrou* (wife). They had a daughter named Cornelia, and Hendrickje continued to share the good and the bad times with Rembrandt and Titus until her death in 1663. Although his broad touch of around 1650 must have seemed a little old-fashioned, it did not reduce the number of his portrait commissions. He made a new type of painting, biblical pieces and historical portraits, consisting of large half-figures, for which he even got commissions from the Sicilian nobleman Antonio Ruffo. Speculation and outstanding debts forced him to declare bankruptcy in 1656, on which occasion his art collection was inventoried. Particularly noticeable among the expansive collection

Bibliography

Amsterdam 1867, p. 25, no. 163
Gorter 1867, p. 480
Vosmaer 1868, p. 427
Van Westrheene 1868, p. 41
The Hague 1881, p. 35, no. 247
De Stuers 1881, pp. 92-93
Brussels 1882, p. 87, no. 215
Bode 1883, p. 559, no. 17
Dutuit 1885, pp. 53, 64, and 66, no. 364
Wurzbach 1886, p. 79, no. 346
Bredius / Veth 1887, p. 51, note 2
Bredius 1893, p. 127
Chicago 1893, no. 48
Michel 1893, pp. 117-118 and fig.
Bode / Hofstede de Groot 1897-1905, vol. II (1897), pp. 49-50, no. 84 and fig.
Moes 1897-1905, vol. I (1897), p. 173, no. 1512
The Hague 1900, p. 116, no. 978
Neumann 1902 / 1905, vol. I, p. 315
New York 1904, no. 84 and fig.
Hofstede de Groot 1906, p. 177, no. 156, p. 289, no. 242
Valentiner 1909-A, pp. 85 and 552 and fig.
Auction New York 1910, n.p., no. 115
Auction New York 1910-A, n.p., no. 84
Wurzbach, vol. II (1910), p. 406
Martin 1911-A, p. 504
Martin 1911-B, pp. 170-171
Paris 1911, p. 23, no. 127
Veth 1911, 'Avondblad', p. B1
HdG 633 (vol. VI [1915], p. 270, no. 633)
Netscher 1918, pp. 328-331 and 390
Valentiner 1931, no. 21 and fig.

are the prints, which allowed him to study the work of famous old masters. He felt a kinship with Leonardo, Raphael, and Titian: like these Italians, for instance, he signed his works, beginning in 1633, with only his first name, Rembrandt.

After the auction of his collection in 1658, Rembrandt continued to work as of old, a situation made possible by the art dealership of Hendrickje and Titus, in which Rembrandt had life interest. His colors became dark and simple, with much red, yellow, and brown, and the application of paint was powerful. He also continued to receive important portrait commissions, painted his loved ones in historical costume, and made self-portraits in which he presented himself as a self-confident and mature artist.

Our Dutch ancestors are to blame that this *Portrait of Joris de Caulerij*, painted by Rembrandt in 1632, now hangs in San Francisco. It is not just an impressive painting but also an important historical document. However, that was only recognized after it had already been in the United States for a long time. It is in fact one of the first works by Rembrandt to be taken to America. For that reason this unusual portrait was the first choice for this exhibition held in The Hague and San Francisco, which has as its theme the history of collecting. An additional argument was that the sitter was a contemporary of the founder of the Mauritshuis. He must have been an eyewitness to the building of the residence of 'Maurits the Brazilian' between 1634 and 1644. Joris de Caulerij was then a lieutenant in the militia in the nearby *Sebastiaansdoelen* (the civic-guard premises dedicated to Saint Sebastian).

Abraham Bredius (1855-1946), the legendary director of the Mauritshuis (1899-1909), must have recognized the importance of the portrait when, in 1890, he tried to buy it for the museum. Bredius was able to offer 10,000 guilders. Sadly, the dealer Preyer had found the American millionaire Yerkes prepared to part with ten times that amount.[1] Abraham Preyer (1862-1927) [**1**] was an art dealer in The Hague (since 1880) and Amsterdam (since 1891), and he made a major contribution to the popularization in America of the painters of the Hague School.[2] His customer, Charles Tyson Yerkes (1837-1905), was an immensely rich financier (including investments in the London Underground) and collector, who once believed that he could buy Trajan's Column in Rome for 250,000 dollars![3]

In 1881 Victor de Stuers, then head of the Department of Arts and Sciences at the Ministry of the Interior of the Netherlands,

Benesch 1935, p. 12
Benesch 1935-A, p. 262
Bredius 1935, p. 8, no. 170 and fig.
Pach 1940, p. 64, no. 86
New York 1950, p. 17, no. 4 and pl. 11
Art Quarterly 1956, pp. 420-421 and fig.
Comstock 1956-A, pp. 73-74
Seligman 1961, pp. 120 and 202
Bauch 1966, p. 19, no. 359 and fig.
San Francisco 1966, p. 121 and fig.
Gerson 1968, pp. 266 and 494, no. 124 and fig.
Gerson / Bredius 1969, p. 145 and 562, no. 170 and fig.
Lecaldano et al. 1969 / 1976, pp. 92-93, no. 75 and fig.
Bolten / Bolten-Rempt 1978, p. 176, no. 96 and fig.
Strauss / Van der Meulen 1979, pp. 313-315, nc. 1654/9 and fig., p. 490, no. 1661/7
Haverkamp-Begemann 1980, pp. 204-205 and fig. 5, p. 211, note 7
Schwartz 1984, p. 69, no. 62
Bruyn et al. 1986, pp. 7, 8, 26, 92, 97, 106 and 199-205, no. A 53 and fig.
Sutton 1986, pp. 274-275 and fig. 412
Tümpel 1986, pp. 99 and 412, no. 196 and fig.
San Francisco 1987, p. 77 and fig.

1
Abraham Preyer (1862-1927)
From: *De Hollandsche Revue* (1918), p. 324

Rembrandt Portrait of Joris de Caulerij

spotted the portrait and pleaded for its acquisition. He knew that it was 'perhaps the only indisputable Rembrandt, aside from those in the cabinets of Six and Steengracht, to remain in private hands in the Netherlands' (in translation).[4] The sale to America in 1890 occasioned several indignant protests in the press, in which it was pointed out that there were then only twenty-one Rembrandts still to be found in the Netherlands.[5] But the story was soon forgotten. It was slight comfort for Bredius that he had in the meantime uncovered the identity of the sitter. In a note of 1887 and a short article of 1893 – both in the then fledgling periodical *Oud-Holland* – he published the document establishing that Captain Joris de Caulerij had himself portrayed by Rembrandt 'with the *roer* [musket] in the hand' (in translation). In the latter publication Bredius announced with resignation that he had seen an announcement in the *Chicago Times* about the American millionaire who was able to call himself the new owner of the work of art.[6]

Five years after the death of Yerkes, the painting went on public sale in New York and fetched 34,000 dollars.[7] As for G. Rasmussen of Chicago, the collector who got hold of the intriguing portrait around 1924, nothing more is known about him than his name and place of residence. However, in April 1937 John Levy Galleries in New York sold the painting to another American collector, Edward David Levinson (1875-1954).[8] Levinson was an American stockbroker who, in that time of the Depression, paid no less than 55,000 dollars for the Rembrandt. After his death in 1954, his daughters Edna and Evelyn sold the portrait through Julius Weitzner via Knoedler's to Roscoe and Margaret Oakes of San Francisco (see cat. no. 43). The peregrinations of Joris came to an end in 1955. The painting was then exhibited in the museum at San Francisco, initially on loan from the Oakes couple, but after 1966, permanently, as a gift from the foundation.[9] Other than in San Francisco, the *Portrait of Joris de Caulerij* has been on view in this century only at exhibitions in Paris (1911) and New York (1940). It was missing from all the major Rembrandt exhibitions.[10]

'Out of sight, out of mind' goes the old adage. Since Bredius's publications, nothing of any real value has been written about the portrait. Who or what Joris de Caulerij (ca. 1606-after 1661) was has never been investigated. His name is invariably written as Caullery (with double el) following Bredius, whereas most of the sources call him Caulerij or Coleri(j). On 1 July 1654 he personally gave his name as *Joris De Caulerij* in the document by which, in his capacity as 'Captain by water of the United Netherlands,' he bequeathed his portrait to his heirs.[11] Misleading are

the recent suggestion that he was never a sea captain (more on that later) and Haverkamp-Begemann's claim that the portrait depicts an Amsterdam militiaman and therefore not a burgher of The Hague. Begemann's hasty conclusion was that 'this painting is the first instance of Rembrandt's relationship with the Amsterdam's civic guard, a body which ten years later would award him the commission for *The Nightwatch*.'[12]

According to Bredius, De Caulerij was a maritime hero who later became a 'respectable wine merchant,' but Hofstede de Groot instead called him 'a wine merchant and innkeeper in The Hague, later a ship captain' (in translation).[13] Only the latter version of occupations can have been true, as De Caulerij died at sea in active service. Which sources said he was a dealer in wine is a mystery. Precisely when De Caulerij was born is also obscure, but he must have been about the same age as Rembrandt. Sometime before 1625 he married Maria de la Samme (or Somme), who died on 4 April 1640, leaving him eight children, Maria (born ca. 1626), Johan (born 1627), Lambert (born ca. 1630), Philip (born 1633), Josina (born 1634), Sara (born 1635), Joris (born ca. 1637), and Catharina (born 1639).[14] We know their names from, among other sources, Joris de Caulerij's testament of 1654, published by Bredius, in which, in addition to a portrait by Rembrandt, he bequeathed several portraits of himself and his wife to their children.[15] Apart from Rembrandt, De Caulerij and his wife had themselves immortalized by Paulus Lesire, Moyses van Uyttenbroeck, Louis Queborn, Anthony van Dyck, and Jan Lievens. The portrait of De Caulerij painted by Van Uyttenbroeck, which was left to Lambert, has been tentatively identified as a work that was once believed to be a self-portrait (Doorn, Collection H.M.W. van der Wijck) [2].[16] The remaining portraits of the couple have never been rediscovered.

In 1661 the sea captain had his last will and testament drawn up once more. In it, the same family heirlooms are listed, but in addition we find mention of a portrait by Rembrandt of the oldest son, Johan, who had died in the interim. It was recently

2
Moyses van Uyttenbroeck
Portrait of Joris de Caulerij(?)
Panel, 65.7 x 48 cm (25⅞ x 18⅞ in.) (oval)
At the left, next to the shoulder: *Mo. v. wb 1633* (wb in ligature)
Doorn, collection H.M.W. van der Wijck

proposed that a *Portrait of a Young Man* (United States, private collection) (cat. no. 53, fig. 1) of 1632 could be this portrait of Johan,[17] but that is out of the question. We know Johan was only five years old in 1632, for in 1647, when twenty years old, he registered as a student of law in Leyden.[18] Also, Rembrandt must have painted this lost 'portrait of his [Joris's] late son Johan de Caullerij' after 1654 and before 1661.[19]

The existence of so many portraits of the De Caulerij couple points to a degree of self-awareness and social status. Joris had himself depicted in 1632 as a militiaman wearing the yellow tunic of the Hague *kloveniersgilde* (harquebusier's guild).[20] He wears an iron-ring-collar – the longest surviving part of the earlier harness – and a ceremonial sword on a shoulder strap. In his right hand he has a *roer* (also called *bus* or *clover*, a small kind of musket).[21] It is identified as such in the testament of 1654: 'an Image of him Present with the *roer* in the hand.'[22] A pointless discussion has ensued in the literature concerning the interpretation of the word *roer*, which can also mean 'rudder.' The latter translation implies that De Caulerij is depicted as a sea captain at the rudder of his ship. Bauch and Gerson asked themselves if Bredius's identification of the portrait was correct, after which Bruyn and the rest of the Rembrandt Research Project of Amsterdam proposed that Joris was not a ship captain. With this they intended to demonstrate that *roer* could not have been intended in the maritime sense of the word.[23]

Joris de Caulerij was both a militiaman and a ship captain. He turns out to have had a brilliant military career with its zenith being his heroic performances as a captain of the Dutch fleet during the first Dutch-English Sea War (1652-1654) and the sea war with Sweden (1658-1659). During the thirties we first encounter him as Lieutenant of the Hague *kloveniers* (harquebusier's civic guard). On the night of 1 May 1635, following an old tradition, he joined his civic guard company in erecting a maypole with five palm wreaths on the Buitenhof (the outer court) in honor of Prince William of Orange. As reward they received one hundred silver ducats. Since the maypole had cost eighty guilders, they used the leftover money to have a medal struck, showing on one side the militiamen in action in the outer court and on the other side the verse: 'In honor of the Prince, Is planted this May, By Joris de Coleri, being our lieutenant' (in translation) [**3**].[24] When he joined the army of the United Provinces is not known. In 1638 Joris received an award from the Stadholder Frederik Hendrik for the contracting and construction of fortifications.[25]

Only in 1652 do we first hear of De Caulerij as a naval officer.

Under the command of Rear Admiral Maarten Harpertz Tromp, he was at the time captain of the ship *De Hoop*, with twenty-eight cannons and a crew of one hundred.[26] A year later, several captains were called before the military tribunal on charges of 'Wandebvoiren / ende disobedientien' (navigational incompetence / and disobedience) during the 'laetste rencontres' (last encounters) with the English. In these proceedings, on 29 September 1653, the 'Manhaften [brave] Capiteyn Ioris de Cavlery' was completely rehabilitated and compensated [**4**]. Though in command of a floating wreck – the *Jonas*, which was described as 'a leaking tub' – he had not turned tail on the guns of the enemy.[27]

Joris was in a risky trade. On 23 February 1654 Jacob van der

4
Pamphlet 'COPIE van't DICTUM,' 1653
Amsterdam, Rijksmuseum Nederlands Scheepvaart
Museum, inv. no. B I, 343-no. 60

3
Anonymous
Commemorative Medal of Joris de Caulerij
Silver, diameter 5 cm (2 in.)
Top and bottom: *Anno 1635*
Haarlem, Teylers Museum, no inv. no.

Poel, Clerk of Finances of Holland and married to Joris de Caulerij's eldest daughter, acted as guarantor for his father-in-law for a sum of 244 guilders.[28] Some months later De Caulerij prepared the aforementioned testament because he had debts and feared confiscation of his property during his absence.[29] He must have repeatedly been away from home for prolonged stretches of time. We know that he was present at the Siege of Danzig and the Battle of the Sont. On 27 July 1656 the Dutch navy, under the command of Vice Admiral De Ruyter, lay at anchor before Danzig. In command of the *Uitrecht* from Amsterdam, with thirty cannons and 120 men on board, was De Caulerij.[30] During the Battle of the Sont in 1658, he rushed to the aid of Rear Admiral Van Wassenaar van Obdam, despite the seventy-five hits taken by his ship (the *Stavoren*) and the fifty dead and wounded on board. Joris himself sustained a head wound in the ear when the rim of his hat was shot off. These facts and trivialities are mentioned in a pamphlet 'tot Respect en Reputatie Van Den Manhafften Capitejn Joris de Caulerii' (on the [vindication of the] Respect [for] and Reputation of the Valiant Captain Joris de Caulerij), which was published in Copenhagen on 5 February 1659 [**5**].[31] He is mentioned among the 'most courageous commanders who gave the best account of themselves' (in translation) in the naval battle.[32] In 1661 Captain Joris de Caulerij had his will drawn up once more, and he died not much later in Denmark, presumably on active service.[33]

The portrait that Rembrandt painted of Joris de Caulerij in 1632 came to his spinster daughter Josina (ca. 1630-1712), who lived with her sister Sara (1635-1722). Sara inherited the portrait in 1712, and in turn left it to her nephew and only living male relative, George van der Poel (1660-1750) (a son of Maria de Caulerij). He died in 1750, ninety years old and childless.[34] The portrait of his grandfather must then have been sold after his death.

It has been suggested that the *Portrait of Joris de Caulerij* was sold as 'A Youth with a Gun' (in translation) in 1770 and auctioned as 'A Knight in Spanish Dress' (in translation) in Frankfurt eight years later.[35] But this is certainly not probable, for in the middle of the nineteenth century the painting was still (or again?) in The Hague. In 1867 an exhibition was held in Amsterdam of works from private collections. The organizers hoped it would match the success of a similar exhibition held in Manchester ten years earlier.[36] The then nameless portrait of 1632 by Rembrandt was lent for the former occasion by 'de Heer Stortenbeker' of The Hague. This must have been one of the artist brothers by that name, Johannes (1821-1899), Pieter (1828-1898), or Cornelis Samuel (1838-1885).[37] When it was displayed in The Hague in 1881 at an exhibition for the benefit of flood victims, Jonkheer Jan Hendrik Jacob Quarles van Ufford (1855-1917) turned out to be the owner.[38]

Quarles van Ufford must have been the one who, by way of Preyer, sold the painting to Yerkes as an ancestral portrait. Presumably as a ploy to drive up the price, the American

◄ **5**
Title page of 'tot Respect en Reputatie Van den Manhafften Capitejn Joris de Caulerii,' 1659
Copenhagen, Det Kongelige Bibliotek,
inv. no. HJ 3377-4°

► **6**
Joachim Ottensz Houckgeest
An Ensign with a Green Banner
Canvas, 199 x 103.5 cm (78³/₈ x 40³/₄ in.)
Unsigned, lower right: *Anno. 1621.*
The Hague, Haags Gemeentemuseum,
inv. no. 5-1862

millionaire was told that the painting had been in the possession of the family for more than a century and that Quarles was a descendant of the sitter.[39] But even after Bredius's discovery of the true identity of 'Joris,' no one bothered to investigate who this captain had been. Thus it was until recently still possible to make an arbitrary statement about this man: 'He was a court hanger-on with more than a small streak of vanity.'[40]

Joris de Caulerij was no prima donna. That he had himself portrayed in 1632 as a militiaman was more a traditional than a radical choice. For in addition to the large group portraits, The Hague and Leyden saw a steady production of portraits of militiamen, such as *An Ensign with a Green Banner* (The Hague, Haags Gemeentemuseum) of 1621 by Joachim Ottensz Houckgeest [6].[41] A well-known example from Amsterdam is *Loef Vredericx as an Ensign* (The Hague, Mauritshuis) of 1626 by Thomas de Keyser.[42] De Caulerij presumably chose Rembrandt not because the naval officer 'had more than a small streak of vanity' but because, precisely in 1632, the artist was active in The Hague, working for, among others, Frederik Hendrik.[43]

Rembrandt's professed preference for a dramatic fall of light is exceptionally well expressed in his *Portrait of Joris de Caulerij*. By placing the profile of the dark body in relief against a light background and by exposing only the face and shoulders to a strong beam of light, he has given the figure a strong plastic quality. He had employed this three-dimensionality much earlier, in his bust-length portraits, but only since 1632 in large half-figures, such as the *Man in Oriental Dress* (New York, The Metropolitan Museum of Art) (p. 60, fig. 1).[44] That an ambitious young man of The Hague had himself painted by a young artist from Amsterdam at least as ambitious as himself led to this most appealing result.

1 *Netscher 1918*, pp. 328-331, wrote in great detail about the first Rembrandt of Preyer, whose business practices were described as 'op z'n Amerikaansch.'

2 *De Leeuw / Sillevis / Dumas 1983*, p. 134

3 NCAB, vol. IX (1907), pp. 462-463; *Simpson 1988*, p. 96

4 *De Stuers 1881*, p. 93

5 *Netscher 1918*, p. 331

6 *Bredius / Veth 1887*, p. 51, note 2; *Bredius 1893*, p. 127

7 *Auction New York 1910-A*, n.p., no. 84

8 NCAB, vol. XLIII (1961), p. 235

9 *Bruyn et al. 1986*, p. 205, gave a wrong sequence for the successive dealers and collectors.

10 *Paris 1911*, p. 23, no. 127 and *Pach 1940*, p. 64, no. 86 (both times as 'Joris de Coulery').

11 The Hague, Gemeentearchief, NA 306, fol. 239; *Strauss / Van der Meulen 1979*, pp. 313-314, no. 1654/9

12 *Haverkamp-Begemann 1980*, p. 205; taken over almost verbatim by *Sutton 1986*, p. 275

13 *Bredius 1893*, pp. 127; HdG 633

14 At the request of The Fine Arts Museums of San Francisco, F.G.L.O. van Kretschmar compiled a genealogical tree of the De Caulerij family on the basis of archival research (manuscript in the Iconographisch Bureau, The Hague).

15 *Bredius 1893*, pp. 127-128

16 *Weisner 1964*, p. 219, no. 3 and fig. 1, p. 197; *Bruyn et al. 1986*, pp. 204-205 and fig. 5

17 *Bruyn et al. 1986*, pp. 243-248, no. A 60 and fig.; see there pp. 205 and 247

18 *Album studiosorum 1875*, col. 381: 'Joannes de Caulery Hagiensis. 20. J[uris].'

19 The Hague, Gemeentearchief, NA 308, fol. 192 verso; *Strauss / Van der Meulen 1979*, p. 490, no. 1661/7

20 About the Sebastiaansdoelen, see *Kulik 1960*, esp. pp. 28-30.

21 On the civic guards in general, see *Carasso-Kok / Levy-Van Halm et al. 1988* and on the arms of the civic guards in particular, ibidem, p. 219, figs. 37a-b (*ringkraag*), pp. 223-224, figs. 41a-e (*doelroers*), p. 228, fig. 45 (*sierdegen*).

22 See note 11

23 *Bauch 1966*, p. 19, no. 359; *Gerson 1968*, p. 494, no. 124, *Haverkamp-Begemann 1980*, p. 205 and *Bruyn et al. 1986*, p. 204

24 *Van Loon 1723-1731*, vol. II, pp. 224-225 and fig.; see also *Carasso-Kok / Levy-Van Halm et al. 1988*, p. 319, no. 144 and fig.

25 *Ten Raa / De Bas 1911-1950*, vol. IV, p. 229, note 1

26 *Ballhausen 1923*, p. 294; *Elias 1916-1930*, vol. III, pp. 111-112

27 With thanks to Robert Vorstman, curator of the Rijksmuseum Nederlands Scheepvaart Museum, Amsterdam. See also *Elias 1916-1930*, vol. V, pp. 202-203.

28 Handwritten notes in the Centraal Bureau voor Genealogie, The Hague (the reference therein to the resolutions of the Court of Holland did not yield additional information).

29 *Hofstede de Groot 1906*, p. 177, no. 156

30 *Quakers mondstoper 1659*, p. E; *Brandt 1687*, p. 99; *Ballhausen 1923*, p. 705

31 *The Hague 1900*, p. 116, no. 979

32 *Quakers mondstopper 1659*, title page; *Brandt 1687*, p. 155; *Ballhausen 1923*, pp. 716 and 743

33 According to the manuscript mentioned in note 14.

34 Ibidem

35 Published by *Bruyn et al. 1986*, p. 205; however, the differing dimensions (113.7 x 80.85 cm and 104.2 x 78.2 cm, respectively) allow for the possibility that this was another painting (perhaps a copy?).

36 *Amsterdam 1867*, p. 25, no. 163; *Manchester 1857*

37 *Scheen 1970*, vol. II, pp. 402-403

38 *The Hague 1881*, p. 35, no. 247

39 *New York 1904*, no. 84: 'It belonged to the Chevaliers Quarles van Ufford, of The Hague, for over a century, who received it into their halls through the marriage of an old and noble family of Dordrecht, who were heirs of the De Coulery family'; *Netscher 1918*, p. 328, spoke of a provenance from a collection in Axel, in Zeeuwsch-Vlaanderen.

40 *Schwartz 1984*, p. 69, fig. 62; without mentioning his source, he cited the short poem on the commemorative medal of 1635 (note 24), a discovery of R.W. Scheller, see *Bruyn et al. 1986*, pp. 204.

41 *Knuttel 1935*, p. 103, no. 227

42 *Hoetink et al. 1985*, pp. 222-223, no. 52 and fig. and p. 387, no. 806 and fig.; see also *Carasso-Kok / Levy-Van Halm et al. 1988*, p. 387, no. 197 and fig.

43 *Schwartz 1984*, pp. 67-77

44 Inv. no. 20.155.2; *Bruyn et al. 1986*, pp. 151-157, no. A48 and fig.; this comparison had already been made by *Veth 1911*.

BB

Leyden 1606 – Amsterdam 1669

Canvas, 124 x 98.5 cm (48⅞ x 38¾ in.)
At the right, under the hand: *Rembrandt. f / 1633*
Cincinnati, Ohio, The Taft Museum, inv. no. 1931.409

Bertram fourth Earl of Ashburnham (1797-1878), was a renowned collector of early and rare books and manuscripts, some of which after his death became national property and others (including the Dante manuscripts) were bought by the Italian government for the Biblioteca Laurenziana in Florence. During his life he sold paintings that had long been in the family to raise money for his hobby.[1] As a consequence, Rembrandt's *Portrait of a Man Rising from His Chair* was auctioned in London on 20 July 1850. It was lauded in the catalogue as 'Full of fine character and admirably painted.' The art dealer Farrer became the new owner for 724 pounds and 10 shillings.[2] The foreword of the catalogue mentioned that the paintings had been collected in the middle of the eighteenth century by John second Earl of Ashburnham (1724-1812), and that around 1819 the collection had been transferred to the family's country house. The condition of the paintings to be auctioned was apparently none too good, for it was announced that they were in urgent need of a coat of varnish, 'but [that] it has been deemed advisable to exhibit them to the Public in their purest state.'[3] Since then the painting by Rembrandt under discussion was relined and so flattened that the paint lost virtually all relief. It has been restored where paint was lost, and varnished. It is presently judged to be in good condition.[4]

    Farrer sold the portrait for 18,000 French francs to the Count of Pourtalès-Gorgier. James-Alexandre Pourtalès-Gorgier (1776-1855) was made a Count by the King of Prussia in 1814.[5] The Hôtel Pourtalès in Paris was described at the time as a city palace in the Italianate style, and it housed a collection much like that of a museum: from antique sculptures, Italian panel paintings, and Eastern antiquities to Dutch masterpieces.[6] The best known of these was *The Laughing Cavalier* by Frans Hals (London, Wallace Collection).[7] Ten years after the death of Pourtalès in 1855 his collection of paintings was sold in public by his heirs. Lord Hertford bought the painting by Hals for 51,000 French francs at the 1865 auction. The painting by Rembrandt also came up for auction, but the family bought it back for 34,500 francs.[8] Edmond Count of Pourtalès (1828-1914) lent the monumental portrait to the great Rembrandt exhibition of 1898 in Amsterdam.[9]

Provenance

Collection John second Earl of Ashburnham, London, mid-eighteenth century
Collection Bertram fourth Earl of Ashburnham, Ashburnham Place near Battle (East Sussex), 1819-1850
Auction Ashburnham, London, 1850 (£724.10 to Farrer)
Collection James-Alexandre Count of Pourtalès-Gorgier, Paris, 1850-1855 (bought from Farrer for Frf. 18,000)
Collection heirs Pourtalès-Gorgier, Paris, 1855-1865
Auction Pourtalès-Gorgier, Paris, 1865
Collection Edmond Count of Pourtalès, 1865-1909 (bought back for Frf. 34,500 in 1865)
Collection Mr. and Mrs. Charles Phelps Taft, Cincinnati, 1909 (bought by way of Knoedler & Co.)
The Taft Museum, Cincinnati, Ohio, 1932 (bequest of Mr. and Mrs. Charles Phelps Taft)

Bibliography

Smith 1829-1842, vol. VII, p. 120, no. 332
Auction London 1850, p. 12, no. 47
Blanc 1859-1864, vol. III, p. 451
Auction Paris 1865, pp. 67-68, no. 181
Mantz 1865, p. 105
Vosmaer 1868, p. 433
Vosmaer 1877, pp. 121 and 500
Bode 1883, p. 597, no. 299
Wurzbach 1886, p. 74, no. 311
Michel 1893, pp. 143 and 564
Bode / Hofstede de Groot 1897-1905, vol. II, pp. 9 and 81-82, no. 100 and fig.
Amsterdam 1898, no. 24 and frontispiece
Von Schleinitz 1898-1899, col. 196
Bell 1899, p. 161
Cook 1899, p. 256
Veth 1906, p. 48
Six 1908, p. 3, note 1
Valentiner 1909-A, p. 96 and fig., p. 552
Hoeber 1909-1910, p. lxxi and fig. p. lxxiii
Walton 1909-1910, p. 368 and pl. II
Cary 1910, pp. 525-526 and fig.
Wurzbach, vol. II (1910), p. 408
HdG 736 (vol. VI [1915], p. 309, no. 736, pp. 364-365, no. 881)
Brockwell 1920, p. XVI, pp. 47-49, no. 13 and fig.
Collins Baker 1920, p. 101
Meldrum 1923, pp. 51, 189 and pl. LXXXVIII
New York 1928, no. 8
Art News 1930, p. 1
Heil 1930, p. 380
Valentiner 1930, p. 7 and no. 16 and fig., no. 17
Valentiner 1930-A, p. 4 and fig.
Valentiner 1930-B, no. 51
Valentiner 1931, no. 34 and fig.
Siple 1933, p. 13
Benesch 1935, p. 14
Bredius 1935, p. 8, no. 172 and fig.
Chicago 1935-1936, p. 17
Cincinnati 1939, p. 59, no. 275 and fig. 17
Coronet 1939, p. 12 and fig.
Veth / Van Regteren Altena 1941, p. 54, fig. 20, p. 73, note 1
Wehle 1944, pp. 177, 180 and fig.
Cincinnati 1945, pp. 91 and 95, no. 275 and fig.
Los Angeles 1947, p. 65

That memorable exhibition served as a showroom in generating a great desire to buy, especially among American collectors. Thus, more than ten years later, the portrait of a man was bought by Charles Phelps Taft (1843-1929), a Cincinnati newspaper magnate and an editor. In 1909, on the occasion of the opening of the new gallery of Scott & Fowles in New York, a selection of ten old master paintings from the Taft collection were shown, among which was the Rembrandt.[10] For their own pleasure, the Tafts collected Chinese pottery, French enamels, Italian crystal, antique furniture, and paintings by older and nineteenth-century masters (p. 47, fig. 33). In 1927 their home and collection were donated to the citizens of Cincinnati and, since 1932, have officially been called The Taft Museum.[11]

The portrait in Cincinnati has a pendant that is now in New York, the *Portrait of a Sitting Woman* (cat. no. 52) [**1-2**]. The portrait of a lady was sold at auction in 1793 without its pendant, but if the compiler of the Ashburnham collection catalogue was right, the portraits had already been separated by the middle of the eighteenth century. Wilhelm von Bode was the first to recognize the correspondence between the dimensions and the compositions and, in his eight-volume catalogue of 1897 of Rembrandt's paintings, presented the man and woman as a married couple.[12] When the portrait of a woman was displayed in London in 1899, one critic regretted that the pendant owned by the Count of Pourtalès was not available for comparison.[13] Only in 1930, at the major Rembrandt exhibition in Detroit organized by Wilhelm Valentiner, were the paintings brought together. Already in 1909 Valentiner had written that the two were probably pendants, and, after seeing the paintings side by side, he concluded that the compositions form a balanced whole.[14] Since then no one has doubted Bode's deduction, which a recent technical examination confirmed once more. The Rembrandt Research Project concluded that 'similarities in thread density and weave structure suggest that the canvases of [cat. nos. 51 and 52] come from the same bolt of cloth.'[15] In 1973 and 1974 the portraits were again united, in New York and Cincinnati; until now, however, they have never been shown together to the Dutch public.[16]

The portrait of the man is signed *Rembrandt. f 1633*, but we do not know the sitter by name. J.Q. van Regteren Altena thought that it may well be Constantijn Huygens, the secretary of Stadholder Frederik Hendrik, who is portrayed here, and that the pendant must therefore depict Huygens's wife, Susanna van Baerle.[17] No one has ever taken that seriously. H.E. van Gelder thought the resemblance far from striking and believed that the

Van Gelder 1957, p. 36
Houston 1958, n.p., no. 42 and fig.
Raleigh 1959, no. 71 and fig. 129
Seattle 1962, pp. 66-67, no. 26 and fig.
Constable 1964, p. 132
Bauch 1966, p. 19, no. 366 and fig.
Gerson 1968, pp. 276-277 and 495, no. 140 and fig.
Tokyo / Kyoto 1968-1969, no. 45
Gerson / Bredius 1969, pp. 147 and 562, no. 172 and fig., p. 576, no. 341
New York 1973-A, no. 6 and fig. on cover
Cincinnati 1973-1974, n.p. and fig. on cover
Bolten / Bolten-Rempt 1978, p. 181, fig. 172
Smith 1978, pp. 271-272 and fig. 102
Braun / Lecaldano 1979, pp. 96-97, nos. 125-126 and fig.
Strauss / Van der Meulen 1979, p. 95
Hibbard 1980, p. 336
Smith 1982, pp. 125-127 and 129
Smith 1982-A, pp. 268-270 and fig. 17, p. 273
Dickey et al. 1983, p. 24
Liedtke 1984, vol. I., p. 60, note 9
Schwartz 1984, p. 165 and fig. 166
Atlanta 1985, p. 105
Bruyn et al. 1986, pp. 10, 27, 38, 69, 127, 373, 378-383, no. A 78 and fig., pp. 386, 391, and 557
Guillaud / Guillaud 1986, p. 304 and fig. 359
Sutton 1986, p. 60, fig. 85
Tümpel 1986, p. 86 and fig., p. 412, no. 200, p. 415, no. 232
Van de Wetering 1986, vol. III, p. 69
Meyer 1988, pp. 388, 392-393 and fig.
Liedtke 1989, pp. 326 and 329 and fig. 5

1-2
Cat. nos. 51 and 52 (details)

Rembrandt Portrait of a Man Rising from His Chair

two portraits by Rembrandt would not have left the family collection in complete silence. Moreover, around 1633 Huygens wrote a poem in which he commented derisively on the poor resemblance of a portrait by Rembrandt, so he is unlikely to qualify as a possible patron.[18]

Given the rather youthful appearance of this couple as they are portrayed in 1633, we may assume that they had only just been married. They could well be close contemporaries of Maerten Soolmans and Oopjen Coppit, who had themselves painted in full-length by Rembrandt a year later (Paris, collection of the heirs of Robert Baron de Rothschild) [3-4].[19] Maerten and Oopjen were joined in matrimony in 1633 and had these pretentious portraits made in commemoration. Both came from wealthy backgrounds and showed this by their clothes. The suit of the unknown man could be by the same tailor as that of the young Soolmans. Maerten chose a striped cloth and the unknown man a fancy pattern, with black ribbon rosettes at the waist instead of white ones. Even more than with the Soolmans pair, Rembrandt has succeeded in bringing about an interaction between his models. The former chose the convention of a state portrait, whereas the unknown couple preferred a less customary pose. The man rises halfway out of his chair and appears to want to

3-4
Rembrandt
Portraits of Maerten Soolmans and Oopjen Coppit
Canvas, 209.8 x 134.8 cm and 209.4 x 134.3 cm
(82⅝ x 53 in. and 82½ x 52⅞ in.)
Lower left of the portrait of Maerten: *Rembrandt ft: 1634*
Paris, collection of the heirs of Robert Baron de Rothschild

5
Rembrandt
The Shipbuilder Jan Rijcksen and His Wife, Griet Jansz
Canvas, 114.3 x 168.6 cm (45 x 66⅜ in.)
On the sheet of drawing paper: *Rembrandt. f: / 1633.*
London, Buckingham Palace, collection Her Majesty
the Queen, inv. no. 1158

draw the spectator's attention to his young bride, who looks serenely straight ahead. Her position suggests that she is getting up while leaning on the table, a device that implements the old-fashioned symmetry of the compositions in a playful fashion.

In 1633 Rembrandt also demonstrated how two people could be portrayed in one dynamic composition: *The Shipbuilder Jan Rijcksen and His Wife, Griet Jansz* (London, Buckingham Palace) [**5**].[20] Clearly Rembrandt thought much more deeply about this manner of depiction than did, for instance, his colleague Pieter Codde, when in 1634 he immortalized an engaged couple (The Hague, Mauritshuis) [**6**].[21] With the pendant portraits in Cincinnati and New York, Rembrandt foreshadowed what he had in

mind for his best-known group portrait, the *'Nightwatch'* (Amsterdam, Rijksmuseum) of 1642.[22] That painting was praised in its time because it was a historical piece full of action instead of a row of men posing for their portraits. The praise that Rembrandt harvested from this work from Samuel van Hoogstraten could apply retroactively to these superb pendant portraits: '[They are] so dashing in movement, and so powerful, that, according to the feelings of some, all the other pieces look like playing cards next to it' (in translation).[23]

1 *Boase 1965*, vol. I, cols. 93-94; *Complete Peerage*, vol. I, p. 274
2 *Auction London 1850*, p. 12, no. 47
3 *Auction London 1850*, 'Notice'; *Complete Peerage*, vol. I, pp. 272-273
4 *Bruyn et al. 1986*, pp. 380-382; see also *Six 1908*, p. 3, note 1
5 *Schweizerisches Geschlechterbuch 1936*, p. 529
6 *Jacquemart 1864*, pp. 377-378; see also *Mantz 1865*, pp. 102-106
7 Inv. no. P 84; *London 1968*, p. 144, no. P. 84 and fig.; *Slive 1970-1974*, vol. II, figs. 52, 53 and 55, vol. III, pp. 19-20, no. 30
8 *Auction Paris 1865*, p. 60, no. 158 and p. 67, no. 181
9 *Amsterdam 1898*, no. 24
10 *Cary 1910*, p. 525; *Hoeber 1909-1910*, p. lxxi; *Walton 1909-1910*, p. 368
11 *WWWA*, vol. I, p. 1213; *Wilson 1930*; *Siple 1933*; Hanna in *Cincinnati 1945*, n.p.; *Meyer 1988*

6

Pieter Codde
Portrait of an Engaged Couple
Panel, 43 x 35 cm (16⅞ x 13¾ in.)
Above the door: *16 PC 34* (PC in ligature)
The Hague, Mauritshuis, inv. no. 857

12 *Bode / Hofstede de Groot 1897-1905*, vol. II, p. 9
13 *Von Schleinitz 1898-1899*, col. 196
14 *Valentiner 1909-A*, pp. 97 and 552; *Valentiner 1930*, no. 16 and 17; *Valentiner 1931*, nos. 34 and 35
15 *Bruyn et al. 1986*, p. 380; see also p. 38
16 *New York 1973* and *Cincinnati 1973-1974*
17 *Veth / Van Regteren Altena 1941*, p. 73, note 1
18 *Van Gelder 1957*, pp. 36-37; on Huygens's satirical poem, see *Schwartz 1984*, pp. 95-97.
19 *Bruyn et al. 1986*, pp. 547-557, nos. A 100-101 and fig.
20 *Bruyn et al. 1986*, pp. 367-377, no. A 77 and fig.
21 *Broos 1987*, pp. 101-105, no. 18 and fig.
22 Inv. no. C 5; *Gerson / Bredius 1969*, pp. 324 and 584-585, no. 410 and fig.
23 *Van Hoogstraten 1678*, p. 176; *Smith 1982-A*, pp. 268-269, also presented an analysis of the unusual aspects of the composition.
     B B

Rembrandt Portrait of a Sitting Woman

Leyden 1606 – Amsterdam 1669

Canvas, 126.2 x 100.5 cm (49¾ x 39½ in.)
Lower left (not autograph): *Rembrand. fv. / 1633*
New York, The Metropolitan Museum of Art, inv. no. 43.125

It was at least two centuries ago that Rembrandt's *Portrait of a Sitting Woman* was last in the Netherlands. In the present exhibition she is shown to the Dutch public together with her husband for the first time. The painting was exhibited in 1899 at the Royal Academy in London, whereas a few months earlier its pendant, the *Portrait of a Man Rising from His Chair* (Cincinnati, The Taft Museum) (cat. no. 51), had been lent to the Stedelijk Museum in Amsterdam for the great Rembrandt commemoration of 1898.[1]

A critical commentator of the time believed that there could be no question of these two works being pendants because the portrait of a lady was dated 1635 (according to the catalogue), whereas that of the man featured the date 1633.[2] According to that critic, the former date had escaped the eye of Wilhelm von Bode, who in 1897 had published the portraits as possible pendants. But Bode had indeed looked carefully and had observed that the portrait of a woman was much neglected and had such an ugly coat of varnish that 'a date, which I cannot discern on it, should certainly be locatable once the varnish is renewed' (in translation).[3] The concomitant reproduction actually shows this lamentable condition. Bode was the first connoisseur to see this painting at Petworth House in Sussex, where three other Rembrandts still hung at the time. He published his descriptions of them in 1883.[4]

It used to be claimed that the portrait of a lady had been at Petworth House in Sussex as long as anyone could remember, and it was also thought that it had never been lent to an exhibition.[5] In fact it had already been shown in 1821 at the British Institution in London, and it can have been acquired for Petworth only after it was auctioned in Paris in 1793.[6] The third Earl of Egremont, George O'Brien Wyndham (1751-1837) [1], is thought to have bought the portrait, after which his son George Wyndham (1787-1869), since 1859 Baron Leconfield, and his successors inherited it. In the last decade of the eighteenth century, the third Earl of Egremont had considerably expanded the collection of old family portraits with paintings by Van Dyck and the young Joseph Mallord William Turner. He then bought a handsome *Self-Portrait* of 1632 by Rembrandt (Glasgow, The Burrell Collection).[7] In 1899 Lord Leconfield parted with his

Provenance
Auction Vincent Donjeux, Paris, 1793 (1,600 livres to Le Brun)
Collection George O'Brien Wyndham third Earl of Egremont, Petworth House, Sussex, before 1822
Collection George Wyndham first Baron Leconfield, Petworth House, Sussex, 1837-1869
Collection Henry Wyndham second Baron Leconfield, Petworth House, Sussex, 1869-1901
Collection Charles Wyndham third Baron Leconfield, Petworth House, Sussex, 1901-1928
Dealer Knoedler & Co., New York, 1928
Dealer Scott & Fowles, New York, 1929
Collection Helen Swift Neilson, Chicago, 1929-1943 (bought from Scott & Fowles)
The Metropolitan Museum of Art, New York, 1943 (gift of Mrs. Neilson, Chicago)

Bibliography
Auction Paris 1793-A, p. 40, no. 147
London 1824, p. 162, no. 40 (1821)
Bode 1883, pp. 459 and 591, no. 253
Dutuit 1885, pp. 46, 62 and 67, no. 285
Wurzbach 1886, p. 64, no. 217
Michel 1893, p. 559
Bode / Hofstede de Groot 1897-1905, vol. 11, pp. 9 and 83-84, no. 101
Von Schleinitz 1898-1899, col. 196
Bell 1899, p. 154
Cook 1899, p. 256
London 1899, p. 21, no. 55
Sharp 1905, p. 69
Valentiner 1909-A, pp. 97 and 552 and fig.
Wurzbach, vol. 11 (1910), p. 403
HdG 881 (vol. VI [1915], p. 309, no. 736 and pp. 364-365, no. 881)
Brockwell 1920, pp. 47-48
Collins Baker 1920, p. 101, no. 105
Meldrum 1923, pp. 51, 72, 189 and pl. LXXXIX
Hussey 1926, p. 40
Borenius 1928, pp. 213-214 and fig.
New York 1928, no. 8 and fig.
Pantheon 1928, pp. 270-271 and fig.
Art News 1930, p. 1 and fig.
Heil 1930, p. 380
Valentiner 1930, nos. 16 and 17 and fig.
Valentiner 1930-A, p. 4 and fig.
Valentiner 1930-B, no. 51 and fig.
Valentiner 1931, nos. 34-35 and fig. 35
Benesch 1935, p. 14
Bredius 1935, p. 8, no. 172, p. 15, no. 341 and fig.
Art Digest 1935-1936, p. 7
Chicago 1935-1936, pp. 16-17, no. 3 and fig.
Magazine of Art 1936, p. 49
Cincinnati 1939, p. 59
Veth / Van Regteren Altena 1941, p. 55, fig. 21 and p. 73
Allen 1943, p. 73
New York 1944, n.p., no. 2 and fig.
Wehle 1944, pp. 177 and 179-180 and fig.
Cincinnati 1945, p. 91, no. 275
Los Angeles 1947, p. 65, no. X and fig.
Van Gelder 1957, p. 36
Raleigh 1959, no. 71
Bauch 1966, p. 19, no. 366, p. 24, no. 469 and fig.
Gerson 1968, pp. 276-277, no. 141 and fig., p. 495, nos. 140-141

Tokyo / Kyoto 1968-1969, no. 45 and fig.
Gerson / Bredius 1969, p. 268, p. 562, no. 172, p. 576, no. 341 and fig.
New York 1973-A , no. 6 and fig. on cover
Cincinnati 1973-1974, n.p. and fig. on cover
Bolten / Bolten-Rempt 1978, p. 180, no. 158 and fig.
Smith 1978, pp. 271-272 and fig. 203
Braun / Lecaldano 1979, pp. 96-97, no. 126 and fig.
Strauss / Van der Meulen 1979, p. 95
Baetjer 1980, vol. 1, p. 149, vol. III, fig. p. 413
Hibbard 1980, p. 336, no. 578
Ainsworth / Brealey et al. 1982, pp. 29, 37-40 and pls. 19-22, p. 46
Smith 1982, pp. 125-127 and 129
Smith 1982-A, pp. 268-270 and fig. 18, p. 273
Dickey et al. 1983, pp. 24-25, no. 7 and fig.
Schwartz 1984, p. 165 and fig. 167
Atlanta 1985, pp. 104-105, no. 46 and fig.
Bruyn et al. 1986, pp. 10, 27, 38, 69 and fig. 11, pp. 71, 373, 380, 382, 384-391, no. A 79 and fig., pp. 420 and 557
Guillaud / Guillaud 1986, no. 360 and fig.
Sutton 1986, p. 60
Tümpel 1986, p. 87 and fig., p. 412, no. 200, p. 415, no. 232
Van de Wetering 1986, pp. 69, 71 and fig. 11
Liedtke 1989, pp. 328-329 and fig. 6

1
Thomas Phillips
Portrait of George O'Brien Third Earl of Egremont
(1751-1837)
Canvas, 186 x 155 cm (73¼ x 61 in.)
Neither signed nor dated (ca. 1825)
Sussex, Petworth House (The National Trust, inv. no. 25.86D)

Rembrandts, of which two were of dubious quality, for the exhibition in London at the Royal Academy.[8] In a 1920 catalogue of the Petworth collection they were all considered to be authentic.[9] However, when in 1925 Petworth House was described in detail in *Country Life*, only one of the five Rembrandts was deemed worthy of an illustration, namely the *Portrait of a Young Man*, now in Kansas City (The Nelson-Atkins Museum of Art).[10] The remaining four, including the *Portrait of a Sitting Woman*, were considered to be of much lesser quality and importance. Probably the poor condition of the paintings observed by Bode contributed to this somewhat cavalier judgment. It is not surprising that Lord Leconfield sold his disputed Rembrandts a few years later. By way of the American dealers Knoedler & Co. and Scott & Fowles, the portrait of a lady came into the collection of Mrs. Francis Neilson in Chicago around 1930. Helen Swift Morris (1869-1943) was known as an author – she published under her maiden name – and wrote articles for the cultural magazine *The Freedom*, which was published by her second husband, Francis Neilson (1967-1961). Her husband was also a playwright and a 'Fellow in perpetuity' of The Metropolitan Museum of Art. In 1943 she gave the painting to the New York museum.[11]

A comparison with the portraits of 1634 of the Soolmans couple (cat. no. 51, figs. 3-4) demonstrates that in this kind of representative wedding portrait Rembrandt endeavored to reproduce the luxurious clothing and the elegant lace work in detail. The customer was always right, and the contents of his purse determined the form of his portrait. If desired, the painter made a half-portrait of reduced format, as the case of *Portrait of a Young Woman* (formerly Santa Barbara, private collection) [2] establishes.[12] This portrait further demonstrates the uniformity of the fashions for young women in 1633; from the rosette under the heart and the precious flat collar with lace, the rows of pearl necklaces, and the fashionably flared hair, to the barely visible arch of lace on the little cap, she is dressed identically to the unknown lady in New York.[13]

2
Rembrandt
Portrait of an Young Woman
Panel, 65.3 x 48.6 cm (25¾ x 19⅛ in.) (oval)
At the left, above the shoulder: *Rembrandt. f / 1633*.
Formerly Santa Barbara, private collection

3
Rembrandt
Study of a Sitting Woman
Drawing in black chalk, 265 x 190 mm (10½ x 7½ in.)
Neither signed nor dated (ca. 1633)
Hamburg, Hamburger Kunsthalle, inv. no. Z 1732

The inscription *Rembrand. fv. / 1633* is not autograph and was probably added after the example of the true signature on the pendant, presumably some time before the two canvases were sold separately. Often only one of two pendant pieces was signed. In the meantime technical examination has established that these canvases came from the same roll of linen, so that the attribution of the portrait of a lady to Rembrandt no longer presents any problem.[14] X-ray photographs and infrared reflectographs have further demonstrated that the painter made diverse alterations during the execution of the portrait.[15] The table at the right is a later addition and took the place of an armrest of the chair. The fan (which, through abrasion, has become an amorphous spot) was painted only after the hand had been given form. There was once a ribbon in the center of the chest. Whereas details of costume were apparently altered at the request of the sitter, the subtle change in the position of the model is an intervention of an artistic nature, one conceived by Rembrandt himself. The preceding text concerning the pendant (cat. no. 51) describes how the painter searched for a less static pose to add dynamism to the composition. This procedure was especially unusual in the case of women's portraits. Even Frans Hals almost always had the man in pendants take the active role (cat. no. 27). It also happened that a woman posed for her portrait only after the costume had been painted according to pattern drawings or a stand-in, a practice that resulted in the so-called fill-in portraits.[16] In this instance one can imagine that Saskia modeled for a study in black chalk (Hamburg, Kunsthalle) [3],[17] which Rembrandt later used as the basis of the portrait of the unknown young lady.

What he began as a standard portrait, Rembrandt thus completed as a subcutaneously shimmering composition. He appears to have already been occupied with its application in a history piece: *Artemisia Receiving the Ashes of Her Husband* (Madrid, Museo del Prado) [4] of 1634.[18] Although in the thirties he had his work cut out for him with portrait commissions, he remained constantly aware of his calling as a history painter. In his dissertation on Dutch marriage portraits, D.R. Smith concluded: 'In these two marriage portraits, Rembrandt reveals both the freedom of his imagination and his restlessness with the conventions and meanings of portrait decorum.'[19] According to Smith that conflict also lay at the heart of the matter with the '*Nightwatch*.' In any case this restlessness had already been observed in the seventeenth century, as is evident from the commentary on the pendant (cat. no. 51).

4
Rembrandt
Artemisia Receiving the Ashes of Her Husband
Canvas, 142 x 153 cm (55⅞ x 60¼ in.)
On the armrest of the chair, to the right:
Rembrant / f:. 1634
Madrid, Museo del Prado, inv. no. 2132

1 *Amsterdam 1898*, no. 24; *London 1899*, p. 21, no. 55

2 *Cook 1899*, p. 256, note 1; *London 1899*, p. 21, no. 55: *Rembrandt f. 1635*, but see *Collins Baker 1920: 16[35?]*.

3 *Bode / Hofstede de Groot 1897-1905*, vol. II, p. 9

4 *Bode 1883*, pp. 408, 421, 459 and 591, nos. 251-254

5 *Von Schleinitz 1898-1899*, col. 196; *Cook 1899*, p. 256; see also the article in *The Times* (31 December 1898), cited in *New York 1928*, no. 8.

6 *London 1824*, p. 162, no. 40 (1821); *Auction Paris 1793*, p. 40, no. 147; *London 1899*, p. 21, no. 55; HdG 881

7 Inv. no. 35 / 600; *Bruyn et al. 1986*, pp. 230-237, no. A 58 and fig. (the 'pendant,' at the time also with Lord Leconfield, is catalogued there as an atelier piece: pp. 686-690, no. C 59 and fig.); *London 1962*, p. 46, no. 124.

8 *London 1899*, p. 17, no. 39, p. 18, no. 41, p. 21, no. 55, p. 29, no. 86 (probably not mentioned by *Bode 1883*, p. 591, because he did not think it a Rembrandt), p. 31, no. 96; *Bell 1899*, p. 154, also gave a summary; illustrations in *Valentiner 1909-A*, pp. 59, 97, 505 and 509.

9 *Collins Baker 1920*, pp. 101-102, nos. 105, 170, 183, 451 and 565

10 Inv. no. 31-75; *Gerson / Bredius 1969*, pp. 249 and 575, no. 322 and fig.; the articles in *Country Life* were collected in *Hussey 1926* (the Rembrandts on pp. 38-40).

11 *New York 1928*, no. 8; *WWWA*, vol. IV, p. 697; documentation Fine Arts Museums of San Francisco (*NCAB*).

12 *Bruyn et al. 1986*, pp. 418-421, no. A 84 and fig.

13 *Der Kinderen-Besier 1950*, pp. 104-118

14 *Bruyn et al. 1986*, p. 386

15 *Ainsworth / Brealey et al. 1982*, pp. 38-40, pls. 20-22

16 Cat. no. 27, note 18

17 *Benesch 1973*, vol. II, p. 101, no. 428 and fig. 515

18 *Bruyn et al. 1986*, pp. 504-510, no. A 94 and fig.; on the interpretation of the depiction, see *Tümpel 1986*, pp. 182-185.

19 *Smith 1982*, p. 126

BB

Leyden 1606 – Amsterdam 1669

Canvas, 109.7 x 89 cm (43⅛ x 35 in.)
Middle right, at chest height: *Rembrandt 166[.]* (last figure illegible)
Washington, D.C., National Gallery of Art, Mellon Collection, inv. no. 1937.1.77

Anyone in the nineteenth century prepared to take the trouble could discover Rembrandts galore, as Bredius experienced in Eastern Europe (see cat. no. 27). On an August day in 1883, the Swedish art historian Olof Granberg had an hour to spare before his train was due to depart, and he used it to visit the Castle Wanås near Kristianstad. It was rumored that a collection of old master paintings was to be found there that had not yet been examined by an expert. Thus he discovered two Rembrandts in the Wachtmeister collection, works that had not previously been described in the oeuvre catalogues.[1] Granberg had someone fetch a long ladder to be able to look at two portraits that were located high up, just under the rafters. What had been thought to be mediocre copies or school works turned out to be genuine Rembrandts. He was justifiably enthusiastic about the quality of a signed *Portrait of a Young Man*, dated 1632 (United States, private collection) [**I**].[2] The second Rembrandt was the work under discussion, which is now owned by the National Gallery of Art in Washington. It was in a much inferior condition to the first. Granberg wrote: 'The painting, like the one just mentioned, is well preserved insofar as it has not been touched up. On the other hand, it is badly cracked, and as it hangs in poor light up there, I sought in vain for a signature. Probably it has none' (in translation).[3]

Apparently after Granberg published his discovery of the Rembrandts in the Wachtmeister collection at Wanås, people there began to look at these paintings with different eyes. The portrait from the National Gallery was made more presentable and drastically cleaned. Presumably it was then that traces of the original signature were discovered, which is now to be read only

Provenance (up to 1837 with reservations)
Collection Gustaf Adolf Count Sparre, ca. 1770, Göteborg and Kulla Gunnarstorp, after 1775-1794
Collection Elisabeth Countess Sparre, born Ramel, 1794-1830
Collection Gustaf Adolf Frederik Count de la Gardie, Kulla Gunnarstorp, 1830-1833
Collection Jacob Count de la Gardie, Kulla Gunnarstorp, 1833-after 1837
Collection Carl Count de Geer of Leufstra, Kulla Gunnarstorp, after 1837
Collection Elisabeth Countess Wachtmeister, Wanås, 1855
Collection Wachtmeister family, Wanås, 1855-1926
Dealer Duveen Brothers, 1926 (bought from Carl Wachtmeister for $410,000)
Collection Andrew Mellon, Washington, 1926-1937
A.W. Mellon Educational and Charitable Fund, Washington, D.C., 1937-1941
National Gallery of Art, Washington, D.C., 1941

Bibliography
Granberg 1884, p. 32
Granberg 1885, p. 3, no. 2
Granberg 1886, p. 27, no. 49
Ny Illustrerad Tidning 1892, p. 311
Michel 1893, p. 568
Stockholm 1893, p. 27, no. 81
Göthe 1895, p. 24, no. 53
Bode / Hofstede de Groot 1897-1905, vol. VII, pp. 4, 41-42, no. 488 and fig.
Bell 1899, p. 183
Valentiner 1909-A, pp. 500 and 564 and fig.
Hahr 1910, p. 83 and fig.
Wurzbach, vol. II (1910), p. 411
Granberg 1911, vol. I, p. 125, no. 536
HdG 784 (vol. VI [1915], pp. 327-328, no. 784)
Meldrum 1923, p. 203 and pl. CCCCXXXI
A. 1926, pp. 207-208
Art News 1928, pp. 1, 12 and fig.
Gibson 1929, p. 7 and fig.
London 1929, p. 47, no. 83
London 1929-A, p. 59, no. 67 and fig.
Van Puyvelde 1929, p. 158
Bauch 1929-1930, p. 19
Valentiner 1930-A, p. 4 and fig.
Valentiner 1931, no. 159 and fig.
Amour de l'art 1935, p. 271 and fig. 77
Amsterdam 1935, pp. 60-61, no. 29 and fig.
Benesch 1935, p. 67
Bredius 1935, p. 14, no. 312 and fig.
Rich 1935, p. 2 and fig., pp. 4-5
Burlington Magazine 1937, pp. 142-143 and fig. c
San Francisco 1939, no. 88a and fig.
Berenson / Valentiner 1941, no. 203 and fig.
Washington 1941, p. 167, no. 77
Finley / Walker 1949, pp. xiii and 88, no. 77 and fig.
Behrman 1952, p. 18
Knuttel 1956, pp. 219 and 273
Bauch 1959, p. 105 and fig. 24
Behrman 1960, p. 16
Porkay 1963, pp. 15, 27 and figs. II and IV
Washington 1965, p. 109, no. 77
Bauch 1966, p. 23, no. 439 and fig.
Gerson 1968, p. 130 and 153 and fig., p. 446 and fig., p. 505, no. 405
Washington 1968, pp. 98 and 166, no. 77 and fig.

I
Rembrandt
Portrait of a Young Man
Panel, 64 x 47 cm (25¼ x 18½ in.) (oval)
Middle right: RHL. *van Ryn* / *1632* (RHL in ligature)
United States, private collection

Gerson / Bredius 1969, pp. 238 and 574, no. 312
and fig.
Washington 1969, pp. 7 and 30, no. 20 and fig.
Hasselgren 1974, pp. 111, 127, 131, 195 and fig. 43,
p. 198, no. G 53
Bolten / Bolten-Rempt 1978, p. 202, no. 549 and fig.
Braun / Lecaldano 1979, pp. 128-129, no. 422 and fig.
Schwartz 1984, p. 339, no. 396 and fig.
Walker 1984, p. 279, no. 363 and fig.
Washington 1985, p. 330 and fig.
Sutton 1986, p. 314
Tümpel 1986, p. 326 and fig., p. 414, no. 217

2
The signature from cat. no. 53: *Rembrandt 166[.]*
Photograph: documentation archives National
Gallery of Art, Washington, D.C. (1990)

3
Copy after Rembrandt
Head of a Man
Canvas, 40.5 x 34.5 cm (16 x 13⅝ in.)
Neither signed nor dated (late nineteenth century?)
Warsaw, collection J. Mlodecki, 1935

with technical aids as *Rembrandt 166[.]* [**2**].[4] The craquelure seems to have been put right by relining, at which time other restoration may also have taken place. This was confirmed in 1989 by an examination undertaken by the conservation department of the National Gallery. On the basis of the two canvases that had been inserted behind the original linen to strengthen it, the conclusion was drawn that the painting had undergone at least one other major restoration after the first. A yellowed coat of varnish makes the entire canvas seem darker than it once was, which is why the repaired cracks are no longer visible and why the autograph overpainting by Rembrandt (in the hands) can only be seen in x-ray photographs. 'However, there are many areas of discolored overpaint which has been glazed or dabbed over the hands, the background, the hair and the facial features, so that there is probably extensive abrasion, if not actual losses,' reads the conservators' report.[5]

Fortunately, the man's face has kept its expression. A copyist who was fascinated by it rendered an impressionistic variant of this most beautiful section of the portrait (Warsaw, collection J. Mlodecki, 1935) [**3**].[6] In 1935 the Polish owner sent a photograph of this copy to the director of the Mauritshuis asking if his painting was indeed a work by Jan Vermeer. Willem Martin answered dryly: 'It is an altered copy after the head of a portrait by Rembrandt' (in translation).[7]

The first restoration of the portrait took place before 1893. It then hung in Stockholm, at an exhibition of art from Swedish private collections, and the catalogue said the inscription read: *Rembrandt f. 1662*. Contradictory reports about the signature circulated later on, which proves that it was then already virtually illegible. In the 1929 Royal Academy exhibition catalogue one reads: 'Signed to the left at top: *Rembrandt f. 1662*.'[8] When, six years later, the painting was on loan to the Rembrandt exhibition at the Rijksmuseum in Amsterdam, the inscription was observed at the right side of the painting. According to the 1935 catalogue, the background of the portrait consisted of a 'bluish black window curtain' and, to its right, a 'vaguely indicated window opening with beveled sill.' It was 'signed on the flat part of the sill: *Rembrandt f. 1663*' (in translation).[9] In 1935 Bredius positively affirmed the reading of the date as 1663 instead of 1662, but in many later reports there was much squabbling about the correct interpretation of the last figure.[10] The most recent catalogue of the National Gallery reported: 'Inscribed at center right: Rembrandt 166[2 or 3].'[11] Gary Schwartz recently sowed confusion with a statement that has since been disproved: 'It used to be said that the painting was dated 1662 or 1663.

Rembrandt Portrait of a Young Man

The museum says it is not so.'[12] When all is said and done, the painting has an autograph signature and date, but unfortunately the last figure cannot be read anymore, whether as a two or as a three.[13]

The interesting Swedish history of the portrait has in the meantime been largely lost. Generally one reads only that a certain Count Wachtmeister from Wanås was the former owner. That the core of this collection was brought together long before 1800 is less well known. Nevertheless, this fact was already explained in 1895, in a catalogue of the Wanås collection, and in 1974, in a book about the collector Sparre by Ingmar Hasselgren.[14] Gustaf Adolf Sparre (1746-1794) [4] was keen on traveling and built up a nice collection of paintings, among other things, on his trips through Holland, France, and England between 1768 and 1772 (see also cat. no. 30). In a diary he described very precisely the collections that he visited, such as in October 1768 the one of Stadholder Prince Willem v in the Oude Hof (Old

Court) in The Hague, where the recent, spectacular acquisitions from the Govert van Slingelandt collection were to be seen. About his own purchases, however, he was silent as the grave. Nevertheless, all those who wrote about the collection at Wanås took it for granted that Sparre acquired the paintings by Rembrandt (perhaps in Holland) in the eighteenth century.[15]

In 1775 Gustaf Adolf Sparre bought the Castle Kulla Gunnarstorp, where he lived after his marriage to Elisabeth Ramel in 1777. However, he kept a house in Göteborg. His collection was divided between this latter abode and the estate near Helsingborg. After his death in 1794, the widow Sparre continued to live in Kulla Gunnarstorp until 1830. Her grandson Gustaf Adolf de la Gardie (1800-1833) inherited the country estate, but following his early death, the castle and the Sparre collection came into the hands of his father, Jacob Count de la Gardie. In 1837 the latter sold the castle and, several years later, also the collection, to Carl Count de Geer of Leufstra. In 1855 De Geer moved the majority of the art treasures of Kulla Gunnarstorp to Castle Wanås as a gift to his granddaughter (his daughter's daughter), Elisabeth Countess Wachtmeister (1834-1918). She was a lady-in-waiting to the queen and in 1852 married the Lord Chamberlain, Axel Frederik Count Wachtmeister. In 1855 Carl de Geer placed the collection of paintings in a family trust, of which Elisabeth Countess Wachtmeister and her offspring were to be members.[16]

In 1926 the Wachtmeister Trust sold the late Rembrandt portrait for three quarters of a million crowns, and, in due time, it came into American hands by way of the art trade. A German art magazine of May 1926 published a protest that was noticed by only a few: 'The collection contains three paintings by Rembrandt, of which the "Portrait of a Young Man," signed and dated 1662, has now been sold by the present owner to the well-known American collector Mr. Joseph Widener of Philadelphia. The price amounts to no less than 410,000 dollars' (in translation). The anonymous writer concluded his article with:

'Perhaps one ought to consider preventing the export of such priceless artworks by legal means.'[17]

The report was only partly true. The *Herald Tribune* of 19 February 1926 mentioned a dashing new exploit by the famous dealer Joseph Duveen (1869-1939). Sir Joseph had bought the 'Wachtmeister Rembrandt' for more than 400,000 dollars, 'one of the highest prices ever paid for a Rembrandt.'[18] As usual when spectacular paintings were sold (see cat. no. 50, note 39), we are further told that the painting had been in the family for centuries. Naturally it was not known that the family had much neglected the portrait until Granberg rediscovered it as a Rembrandt. More than half a year later – on 7 December 1926 to be precise – Duveen Brothers (p. 41, fig. 28) did indeed sell the painting to an American collector. The millionaire in question was not Joseph Widener but Andrew Mellon (1855-1937) [**5**].[19] This remarkable circumstance confirms once again that Duveen Brothers supplied first-rate works to Mellon at an earlier date than some, such as the biographers Sam Behrman and John Walker, have assumed.[20] However, in his book on the intriguing relationship between Joseph Duveen and the connoisseur Bernard Berenson, Simpson has demonstrated that, despite a difficult personal relationship, professional contacts were always maintained between Duveen and Mellon (see also p. 51, fig. 38). After all, before 1927 (when there arose a temporary breach between the gentlemen), Mellon had already spent three million dollars with Duveen Brothers.[21] In 1920 he first bought a Rembrandt there, namely the *Portrait of an Old Woman with a Book* of 1647 (Washington, National Gallery of Art).[22] Mellon had this painting in his house for a year before he decided to buy it.[23] It is not known if, and for how long, he had had the portrait from the Wachtmeister collection on approval in 1926. He never bought at auctions himself, and only rarely from private owners. Unfortunately, we are not told in the memoirs of the Duveen Brothers how Joseph Duveen in turn 'discovered' the Wanås Rembrandt.[24]

Andrew Mellon, like his friend Henry Clay Frick (see p. 40, fig. 25; p. 45, fig. 32), was a collector of great masters, with a special predilection for the Dutch Golden Century (Rembrandt, Vermeer, Hals, Hobbema). The Wallace Collection in London was his cynosure. His criteria for acquiring a painting were that it had to be in good condition and not be too dark.[25] Initially Mellon collected for his own pleasure, but in 1927 he decided to found a national museum, with his own collection as the core. Four years after his death in 1937, the National Gallery of Art

in Washington was opened. Mellon had accumulated nine paintings by Rembrandt.[26]

It is remarkable that the Wachtmeister portrait does not altogether live up to Mellon's requirements of condition and clarity. Nevertheless, he must have recognized the qualities that made Gerson remark: 'One of the most beautiful late, commissioned portraits. Only the hands have suffered' (in translation).[27] Bauch was so impressed by the painting that he used it in 1959 as a bench mark to establish the authenticity of another portrait of a man (Bremen. Kunsthalle).[28] At the time, Bode and Hofstede de Groot held that a comparison was called for between the former portrait and the impressive *Portrait of a Man with a Hat*, also in Washington (National Gallery of Art) [**6**].[29] According to these authors both works were stylistically related to the group portrait painted in 1661 known as *The Syndics of the Cloth Drapers's Guild* (Amsterdam, Rijksmuseum) [**7**].[30] On the basis of this similarity one can date this portrait to the early sixties and not to the forties as was thought in the distant past, before the signature and date were noticed.[31]

The formal pose of the unknown man makes it clear that the painting was an official commission, and it is probable that there was once a pendant that portrayed the man's wife. Valentiner thought he could recognize in him the features of Rembrandt's

6
Rembrandt
Portrait of a Man with a Hat
Canvas, 121 x 94 cm (47⁵/₈ x 37 in.)
Neither signed nor dated (ca. 1660-1665)
Washington, D.C., National Gallery of Art,
inv. no. 1942.665

7
Rembrandt
The Syndics of the Cloth Drapers' Guild
Canvas, 191.5 x 279 cm (75³/₈ x 109⁷/₈ in.)
Upper right: *Rembrandt f. 1661*
Amsterdam, Rijksmuseum, inv. no. C 6

son, Titus, but that identification was based on a superficial resemblance.[32] Rembrandt always portrayed his son very informally, preferably in some disguise.[33] Nevertheless, we here point to the possibility in the hope of helping to provide this young man with an identity.

Closer investigation will have to establish if the portrait did in fact end up in the Wachtmeister collection by way of Sparre, for it is not mentioned in the (admittedly incomplete) inventory of his estate.[34] This lack of information is the reason the provenance up to 1837 has been cited with reservation. It may also have been Carl Count de Geer who brought the painting into the collection, and in that case there is a chance that it might be an old family portrait. Carl de Geer descended from the Dutch De Geers, who, by the seventeenth century, maintained trade with Sweden. He could be a member of the Trip-De Geer family, one of Rembrandt's clients around 1660. In that case Jacob Louysz Trip (1636-1664) is a candidate. He died when only twenty-eight years old, in 1664, and the portrait could have originated several years earlier, on the occasion of his marriage.[35] With even fewer indications than have been adduced here, Miss Van Eeghen wanted to identify this Jacob Trip with another portrait by Rembrandt, one also in the National Gallery of Art in Washington.[36] A more thorough investigation of the provenance of the painting may bring us closer to the identity of the person portrayed.

1 *Granberg 1884*, pp. 30-32 (the third Rembrandt that he discovered was *The Apostle Peter*, now in Stockholm [Nationalmuseum], inv. no. 1349; *Bruyn et al. 1986*, pp. 138-144, no. A 46).
2 *Blankert et al. 1983*, pp. 86-87, no. 11 and fig.; *Bruyn et al. 1986*, pp. 243-248, no. A 60 and fig.
3 *Granberg 1884*, p. 32
4 'Examination Summary,' 2 March 1989 (documentation archives National Gallery of Art, Washington, D.C.), p. 3
5 Ibidem, p. 1
6 Photo RKD
7 Letters of 18 November and 6 December 1935 in the archives of the Mauritshuis.
8 *London 1929*, p. 47, no. 83
9 *Amsterdam 1935*, p. 61, no. 29
10 *Bredius 1935*, p. 14, no. 312; *Gerson / Bredius 1969*, p. 574, no. 312
11 *Washington 1985*, p. 330
12 *Schwartz 1984*, p. 339, no. 396; see also *Tümpel 1986*, p. 414, no. 217
13 In 1969 the museum reported: 'This inscription is not visible' (*Washington 1969*, p. 30, no. 20).
14 *Göthe 1895*, pp. 3-9; *Hasselgren 1974*, pp. 203-207 (an English summary); *Berenson / Valentiner 1941*, no. 203, were the only authors to use the information of *Göthe 1895*, but with the wrong place names and without the dates.
15 Such as *Stockholm 1893*, p. 27, no. 81 and *Hasselgren 1974*, p. 131 and *Hasselgren 1988*, pp. 143-144. Carl Axel Count Wachtmeister, the grandson of the Carl Wachtmeister who sold the painting, informed us that according to him the painting was bought by G.A. Sparre (letter of 27 September 1989).
16 *Göthe 1895*, pp. 6-7; *Hasselgren 1974*, pp. 110-112
17 *A. 1926*, p. 208; Hofstede de Groot, too, noted the price in Swedish crowns in a copy of *Göthe 1895*, p. 24, no. 53 (RKD).
18 *Behrman 1952*, p. 18
19 From the Finley Notebooks (documentation archives National Gallery of Art, Washington, D.C.).
20 *Behrman 1952*, p. 127; *Walker 1973*, p. 104

21 *Simpson 1988*, p. 226

22 Inv. no. 1937.1.73; *Gerson / Bredius 1969*, pp. 283 and 578, no. 362 and fig.

23 *Fowles 1976*, p. 137

24 *Fowles 1976*; see also *Walker 1973*, pp. 102-132; *Berenson / Valentiner 1941*, n.p., 'Index of Collections,' gave an overview of Mellon's purchases from the Duveen Brothers.

25 *Finley / Walker 1949*, p. v

26 *Finley / Walker 1949*, pp. vi and xiii; see also *Finley 1973* and *Washington 1969*, nos. 1, 3, 4, 11, 13, 16, 19, 20, 23

27 *Gerson 1968*, p. 505, no. 405

28 Inv. no. 36-b; *Bauch 1959*, p. 82, fig. 1 and pp. 105-106 and fig. 26; see also *Porkay 1963*, pp. 15, 27 and figs. II and IV

29 *Gerson / Bredius 1969*, pp. 241 and 574, no. 313 and fig.; *Bode / Hofstede de Groot 1897-1905*, vol. VII, p. 4

30 *Gerson / Bredius 1969*, pp. 327, 329 and 585-586, no. 415 and fig.; *Van Thiel et al. 1976*, pp. 471-472, no. C 6 and fig.

31 *Granberg 1886*, p. 27, no. 49; *Michel 1893*, p. 568

32 *Valentiner 1909-A*, p. 564

33 *Gerson / Bredius 1969*, pp. 107-114 and 557-558, nos. 119-127 and fig.

34 *Hasselgren 1974*, pp. 112-118; see note 15

35 *Van Eeghen 1983*, p. 60

36 Inv. no. 1942.9.67; *Gerson / Bredius 1969*, pp. 255 and 575, no. 327 and fig.; *Van Eeghen 1983*, pp. 72-73, fig. 25; see also *Schwartz 1984*, pp. 344-345, nos. 405 and 407 and fig.

BB

Haarlem 1628 / 1629 – Amsterdam 1682

Canvas, 98.1 x 132 cm (38⅝ x 52 in.)
Below, just to the right of center: *JvRuisdaeL* (JvR in ligature) (ca. 1650-1655)
Fort Worth, Tex., The Kimbell Art Museum, inv. no. AP 1989.01

Jacob van Ruisdael was a pupil of his father, Isaack, and possibly also of his uncle Salomon van Ruysdael. His work is demonstrably influenced by all kinds of landscape painters active in Haarlem. For instance, his early works of 1645 and 1646 remind us of Cornelis Vroom. He derived his Scandinavian mountain landscapes from examples by Allaert van Everdingen, who had journeyed to Norway and Sweden in 1645. In 1650 Jacob van Ruisdael himself traveled with sketchbook in hand through the Dutch-German border region, accompanied by his friend Nicolaes Berchem, who later on occasionally added the staffage to Ruisdael's landscapes. Only in 1648 was he first mentioned as a member of the Haarlem guild of painters. In 1657 he moved to Amsterdam, where he continued to live and work until his death.

Landscapes were Ruisdael's speciality: about 700 paintings are now attributed to him. He also etched and drew landscapes; one might add that the drawings undeservedly constitute the least-known part of his oeuvre. Within his speciality, he displayed a great diversity, for he painted dunes and country roads, panoramas, river and forest views, winter and summer landscapes, beach views and seascapes, topographical city views and imaginary landscapes. Despite the programmatic repetition of some light effects and dramatic compositional elements, his depictions of nature are highly varied. The atmosphere of his landscapes was much appreciated in the eighteenth and nineteenth century, especially in England, where Ruisdael's work was then collected and emulated on a large scale.

In 1766 the widely known Amsterdam collector Gerret Braamcamp (1699-1771) [1] auctioned part of his collection. 'The paintings of the Heer Braamkamp are not to be qualified as trash,' stated an announcement (in translation) in the catalogue, trying to put the suspicious buyer at ease; they were being sold 'because the same could find no place for them in his Noble Cabinet.'[1] Braamcamp considered his collection complete in 1766, when he let it be praised by the man of letters Jean François de Bastide (1724-1798) as *Le Temple des Arts ou le Cabinet de M. Braamcamp* (The Temple of the Arts, or the Cabinet of Mr. Braamcamp; Amsterdam 1766).[2] Recently acquired by The Kimbell Art

Provenance

Auction widow Hoogeveen et al., Amsterdam, 1765 (*f*214 to P. Fouquet for Braamcamp)
Collection Gerret Braamcamp, 1765-1771 (auctioned in 1766, bought back for *f*160 by Jeronimo de Bosch for Braamcamp)
Auction Braamcamp, Amsterdam, 1771 (*f*264 to P. Fouquet)
Dealer Paillet, Paris, 1802
Collection John Smith, London, 1824 (bought for £360 from the Merialva family)
Collection Robert Bankes, second Earl of Liverpool, London, before 1828
Auction Earl of Liverpool, London, 1829 (£535 to the Marquess of Lansdowne)
Collection third to seventh Marquess of Lansdowne, Bowood, Calne, Wiltshire, 1829-1944
Collection Baroness Nairne, Bignor Park, Pulborough, Sussex, 1944-1950(?)
Dealer Agnew & Sons, London, 1950(?), 1976
Collection Charles Cunningham, Boston, 1976-after 1982
The Kimbell Art Museum, Fort Worth, 1989

Bibliography

Hoet 1752-1770, vol. III, p. 456, no. 36
Auction Amsterdam 1765, p. 11, no. 45
Auction Amsterdam 1766, p. 3, no. 6
Auction Amsterdam 1771, p. 84, no. 198
Auction Amsterdam 1771-A, p. 8, no. 198
Ploos van Amstel 1771, p. 142
Auction London 1829, p. 8, no. 76
London 1829, p. 16, no. 65
Smith 1829-1842, vol. VI (1835), pp. 7-8, no. 2
Waagen 1837-1839, vol. II, pp. 296-297
Waagen 1854, vol. III, pp. 158-159
London 1884, p. 39, no. 191
HdG 945 (vol. IV [1911], p. 283, no. 945 and p. 288, no. 966)
Graves 1913-1915, vol. III (1914), p. 1177, no. 65 (1829), p. 1183, no. 191 (1884)
Graves 1918-1921, vol. III (1921), p. 127, no. 76 (1829)
Rosenberg 1928, p. 108, no. 579
Bille 1961, vol. I, p. 88, vol. II, pp. 48-48a, no. 198, p. 82, no. 6 and pp. 116-117, no. 198
Stechow 1966, p. 209, note 53
The Hague 1981-1982, no. 27 and fig.
Slive / Hoetink 1981-1982, pp. 88-89, no. 27 and fig.
Potterton 1986, p. 137
Goedde 1989, p. 190, fig. 151, pp. 191-193 and 241-242, notes 52 and 58

Museum in Fort Worth, *A Rough Sea at a Jetty* belonged to the rejected part of the Braamcamp collection, which, naturally, was generally of lesser quality than the pieces that Braamcamp kept.[3] The seascape, called *A Threatening Thunderstorm*, was bought back by the auctioneer Jeronimo de Bosch for 160 guilders. Though clearly signed *JvRuisdael*, the painting was erroneously listed in the catalogue under the name of Hendrick Dubbels. Apparently a printing error caused the name of Jacob van Ruisdael to be placed one number too low. In one copy of the catalogue the correction *Ruijsdael* has been written in at the right place.[4]

Initially Gerret Braamcamp was a wine merchant, but he showed himself to be a gifted businessman, who was able to turn 'wood into gold.' From Amsterdam he primarily carried on trade with Portugal, where two of his brothers lived. Starting in 1736, using the money of several financiers, he made such profitable transactions that, from 1748 on, he was able to continue expanding his fortune as an independent wood dealer. The Catholic businessman invested his money in houses. Thus he bought the monumental canal property Sweedenryck, in the bend of the Herengracht, where he moved with his by then considerable art collection. At his death he was able to call himself a millionaire. In his private life Gerret Braamcamp was less fortunate. Both his children died young, and his wife died in 1742. His godchild and nephew, Geraldo Braamcamp, was the principal beneficiary of his will. The firm continued to exist, but the collection had to be liquidated. Gerret Braamcamp had decided that his cabinet should go under the hammer within eight to ten months after his death.[5] The buyers came from all over Europe. Destined for

a sad fate were the dozens of top pieces bought for Catherine the Great of Russia: they perished in a shipwreck on their way to Saint Petersburg.[6]

The sea view by Ruisdael cannot have been omitted from *Le Temple des Arts* on account of its lack of quality. The reason was presumably that Braamcamp had acquired it only in 1765. It was then auctioned in Amsterdam from a collection that contained, among other things, paintings belonging to the widow Hoogeveen, whose husband had been burgomaster of Leyden.[7] Where the painting was before that time is not known. Pieter Fouquet, Jr. (1729-1800) (see cat. nos. 2, 14, 49 and 60), who had bought the painting for Braamcamp in 1765 for 214 guilders, bought it once more from his estate in 1771 for precisely fifty guilders more.[8] Fouquet spent no less than 46,000 guilders at this auction, largely on behalf of foreign customers.[9] Thus Ruisdael's *Rough Sea at a Jetty* permanently left Dutch ownership at the end of the eighteenth century. There exists a copy in a slightly smaller format that was probably made around this time (Dublin, National Gallery of Ireland) [**2**].[10] Hofstede de Groot and Rosenberg still thought it an autograph work, but Slive resolutely dismissed this on the occasion of the great Ruisdael exhibition of 1981-1982 (The Hague and Cambridge, Mass.) because it 'misses the extraordinary range of grays of the original.'[11]

In 1835 the art dealer and connoisseur John Smith, who compiled the first oeuvre catalogue of the landscape painter, again mentioned this original. He used his description to elaborate on the meager appreciation that, at least according to the auction prices, the Dutch and French had shown for Ruisdael's paintings. Smith converted guilders and francs to pounds and established that the painting had been sold at the Braamcamp auction for twenty-five pounds, at the Sijdervelt auction five years earlier for nineteen pounds (this was an error on his part), and at an auction at Paillet's in Paris in 1802 for fifty-eight pounds (this turns out to be no longer verifiable). He claimed to have himself paid 360 pounds in 1824 to the family

1
Reinier Vinkels after Jacob Xavery
'*GERRIT BRAAMKAMP Konst-minnaer*'
Engraving, 214 x 154 mm (8³/₈ x 6 in.)
Lower right: *R. Vinkeles. Sculp. 1766.*
The Hague, Iconographisch Bureau

2
Copy after Jacob van Ruisdael
A Rough Sea at a Jetty
Canvas, 89.7 x 123.6 cm (35³/₈ x 48⁵/₈ in.)
Neither signed nor dated (late eighteenth century?)
Dublin, The National Gallery of Ireland, inv. no. 916

Jacob van Ruisdael A Rough Sea at a Jetty

of a certain Marquess Merialva. Along with this exposition he presented a hymn of praise on the seascape: 'The awful grandeur of this magnificent picture fills the mind of the beholder with sensations of wonder and delight, and while lost in the contemplation of the powers of art, he will be compelled to exclaim, that the author of such a work must have been both a poet and a painter.' He probably expressed himself in words of this kind before he sold the painting around 1826 to the second Earl of Liverpool for no less than 500 pounds. That meant thirty-five percent pure profit.[12]

Robert Bankes, second Earl of Liverpool (1770-1828), was able to enjoy his painting for only a few years. It was bought in 1829 at the auction of his estate by the Marquess of Lansdowne, who paid 535 pounds for it.[13] The Marquess showed off his new acquisition that very same year in an exhibition at the British Institution.[14] For more than a century it remained in the Lansdowne collection at Bowood, Calne, Wiltshire. Henry Petty-Fitzmaurice, the third Marquess of Lansdowne (1780-1863), gave new brilliance to his family's reputation as collectors, after the paintings of his grandfather, the first marquess, had been sold in public in 1806.[15] Before 1838 and again in 1850 Gustav Waagen visited Bowood, describing the curious structure, the handsome park, and the once again sizable collection. In connection with Ruisdael's painting he noted: 'in point of grandeur of conception and astonishing truth, [it] is one of the finest.'[16] The canvas hung in the drawing room, where a painting attributed to Rembrandt, *The Mill* (Washington, National Gallery of Art) (p. 122, fig. 1),[17] which was to make the Lansdowne collection world-famous, also hung. In 1911 the fifth Marquess of Lansdowne (1845-1927) created a wave of indignation by selling this famous and controversial work to America for 100,000 pounds.[18] The childless seventh Marquess (1917-1944) died in Italy in World War II, after which his older sister Baroness Nairne (born 1912) inherited his titles and, apparently, a part of his collection as well.[19] She sold Ruisdael's *Rough Sea at a Jetty* around 1950. In 1955 Bowood Castle was largely dismantled.[20] In 1976 the painting ended up by way of the art trade in the collection of Charles Cunningham in Boston. It remained in private hands until 1989, when The Kimbell Art Museum in Fort Worth was able to acquire it.

Waagen and Hofstede de Groot were among the very few connoisseurs who had seen the paintings of the marquesses of Lansdowne with their own eyes. In the case of the Ruisdael, Rosenberg was forced to depend on the judgment of Hofstede de Groot.[21] Once, in 1884, the canvas was lent for an exhibition at the Royal Academy in London. Its presentation at the aforementioned Ruisdael exhibition of 1981 was in fact a first for the greater public.[22] At that time the depiction was described less accurately than in the earliest mention of the piece in 1765: 'A *tossing Sea*, in which in the foreground the Water very naturally beats against the head of a Jetty, and a Ship [that] enters the Harbor before the wind with a lowered Sail. In the distance one sees several more Ships' (in translation).[23] Here we do indeed see a beacon at an entrance to a harbor, toward which a row of ships sets sail. The front ship lowers the gib and strikes the mainsail, while it is awaited on the pier by two men with gaffs.

Roemer Visscher used the image of a beacon in his *Sinnepoppen*, published in 1614 [3], with the text: 'In many corners of the Sea signs are set up, that there is a good harbor or anchor ground, so that the Helmsmen should know to where to steer to salvage their Ships: but that is only for those who have understanding of Navigation' (in translation).[24] Under the motto 'Intelligentibus' (for those who understand) this thought applied to life in general. It is doubtful if we should also embark on a general reflection on Ruisdael's beacon at sea. On the basis of this emblem it has nevertheless recently been assumed that this seascape could depict 'salvation in distress,' and specifically in matters of love. In that case we must be prepared to interpret the duo with the gaffs as an amorous couple.[25] However, the 'woman' definitely wears pants. Even in Simon de Vlieger's *View of a Beach* in the Mauritshuis (cat. no. 68, fig. 5), in which we really do see a (married) couple at a beacon, symbolism of this kind does not appear to have been intended.

Jacob van Ruisdael did not date any of his seascapes. With good reason it is thought that they originated between 1650 and 1670, an early example being *Storm at Sea* (Stockholm, Nationalmuseum),[26] and a late one, *Troubled Sea with Sailboats* (Boston, Museum of Fine Arts).[27] The *Storm on the IJ* (Worcester, The Worcester Art Museum) [4] originated around 1660.[28] Apart from a few color accents, this latter work is an almost mono-

3
Illustration from Roemer Visscher, *Sinnepoppen* (Amsterdam 1614), no. 119

chrome painting in gradations of white and gray. A limited palette of white, blue, brown, and dark gray tints also characterizes the canvas in Fort Worth, which was therefore presumably painted in the first half of the fifties. The subject of the painting was apparently derived from Allaert van Everdingen, who also supplied his fellow townsman with themes such as that of the Scandinavian landscape (cat. no. 55). His *Snowstorm at Sea* (Chantilly, Musée Condé) [5],[29] with its prominent beacon and wild waves, unmistakably served as Ruisdael's model, as Stechow had mentioned in passing in 1966.[30] The painting in Fort Worth therefore appears to be a key work in the development of Ruisdael's seascapes, one that has too long been virtually unknown.

4
Jacob van Ruisdael, *Storm on the IJ*
Canvas, 65.8 x 82.7 cm (25⁷⁄₈ x 32¹⁄₂ in.)
Lower right (not autograph): *JvRuysdael* (JvR in ligature) (ca. 1660)
Worcester, The Worcester Art Museum, inv. no. 1940.52

5
Allaert van Everdingen
Snowstorm at Sea
Canvas, 97 x 121 cm (38¹⁄₄ x 47⁵⁄₈ in.)
Neither signed nor dated (ca. 1648-1650)
Chantilly, Musée Condé, inv. no. 136

1 *Auction Amsterdam 1766*, n.p. (flyleaf); *Bille 1961*, vol. II, pp. 82-85, gave a summary of the sixty-eight lots of this auction.
2 *De Bastide 1766*
3 *Bille 1961*, vol. I, pp. 35-36
4 *Auction Amsterdam 1766*, p. 3, no. 6 (copy RKD); it is less plausible that Braamcamp had intended to sell it as a Dubbels, as proposed in *Bille 1961*, vol. II, p. 117, no. 198 and *Slive / Hoetink 1981-1982*, p. 88.
5 *Bille 1961*, vol. I, pp. 11-18
6 *Bille 1961*, vol. I, p. 56, note 30, vol. II, p. 105, no. 130: thus all the acquisitions of A. van den Bogaarde were intended for Catherine (with P. Fouquet and B. Tideman acting for her simultaneously).
7 *Auction Amsterdam 1765*, p. 11, no. 45
8 *Auction Amsterdam 1771*, p. 84, no. 198
9 *Bille 1961*, vol. I, p. 197
10 HdG 960; *Potterton 1986*, pp. 136-137, no. 916 and fig. 145
11 *Rosenberg 1928*, p. 109, no. 595: he made no connection with the copy of Braamcamp; *Slive / Hoetink 1981-1982*, p. 89.
12 *Smith 1829-1842*, vol. VI (1835), pp. 7-8, no. 2
13 *Burke's 1963*, p. 1490; *Auction London 1829*, p. 8, no. 76
14 *London 1829*, p. 16, no. 65
15 *Brigstocke 1982*, p. 470
16 *Waagen 1854*, vol. III, p. 159 (see also *Waagen 1837-1839*, vol. II, pp. 292-293); he further cited Smith (note 12) and his wrong information; he saw the copy in Dublin only later (p. 434).
17 Inv. no. 1942.9.62; HdG 952; *Walker 1984*, pp. 274-275, no. 358 and fig.; *Bruyn et al. 1989*, p. 49, fig. 52 (F. Bol)
18 *Burlington Magazine 1911*, pp. 3-4
19 *Burke's 1963*, pp. 1406 and 1768; *Debrett's 1980*, p. 854
20 *Pevsner 1963*, pp. 109-110
21 *Rosenberg 1928*, p. 108, no. 579 (the paintings marked with an asterisk he had not seen himself).
22 *London 1884*, p. 39, no. 191; *Slive / Hoetink 1981-1982*, pp. 88-89, no. 27 and fig.
23 *Auction Amsterdam 1765*, p. 11, no. 45; *Slive / Hoetink 1981-1982*, p. 89, spoke vaguely of a 'breakwater.'
24 *Roemer Visscher 1614*, no. 119 and fig.
25 *Goedde 1989*, pp. 191-193 and (especially) pp. 241-242, note 58
26 Inv. no. NM 616; HdG 962 and 968h; *Slive / Hoetink 1981-1982*, pp. 48-49, no. 11 and fig.
27 Inv. no. 57.4; HdG 957; *Slive / Hoetink 1981-1982*, pp. 138-139, no. 48 and fig.
28 HdG 959; *Slive / Hoetink 1981-1982*, pp. 98-99, no. 32
29 *Stechow 1966*, p. 121 and fig. 246
30 *Stechow 1966*, p. 209, note 53
BB

Haarlem 1628 / 1629 – Haarlem 1682

Canvas, 104.1 x 143.5 cm (41 x 56½ in.)
Lower right, on a boulder: *JvRuisdaeL* (JvR in ligature) (ca. 1670)
Raleigh, N.C., North Carolina Museum of Art, inv. no. 52.9.56

'He painted domestic and foreign landscapes, but especially such, where one sees the water plunging down from one Rock to another, to finally disperse itself with rustling [*geruis*] (to which his name appears to allude) in and through the dales, or plains: and knew how to depict the sprinkling, or the water foaming because of the enormous splashing on the rocks, so naturally thin and translucent that it appeared to be nothing other than natural water,' wrote Arnold Houbraken (in translation) in 1721.[1] His characterization is certainly applicable to the work under discussion, *Spruce Trees at a Waterfall* from the North Carolina Museum of Art. As far as Houbraken was concerned, Ruisdael and falling water were inseparable. This idea was apparently common currency in his time, as would appear from a poem of 1708 by Jan Luiken, in which the prolific poet has a waterfall clatter down in a *Ruis-dal* (rustling valley), no doubt in memory of the name of the preeminent painter of this subject.[2]

Luiken presented the noisily plunging water as a symbol of the bustle of everyday – 'o Ruis-dal, all the vanity, of the tossing and teeming life' – as opposed to the 'Quiet Abode of the valley of virtue' (in translation). He did so in his collection *Beschouwing der wereld* (Observation of the world), along with an emblem of a waterfall with the device 'Tot verdooving' (meaning, roughly, conducive to deafness) [1].[3] The poet has encompassed all of the visible world in his profundities – beginning with household effects – but we do not know if the painter looked at his environment in the same way. Ruisdael has not in any way indicated that he envisaged the image of the 'World's heavy Waterfall' when he painted a rapid or cascade.[4] In 1971, however, Wiegand emphatically sought to explain Ruisdael's waterfalls in the spirit of Jan Luiken as images (representations) of *vanitas*, and recently received support in this from J. Bruyn.[5] Going by descriptions in contemporary inventories, the painter simply made 'waterfalls' or *Haerlempjes* (small views of Haarlem) – to stay with his best-known motifs – rather than *vanitas* pieces or representations of the heavenly Jerusalem.[6] No more than Jan van Goyen (see cat. no. 24) did Jacob van Ruisdael carry on a medieval symbolic tradition.

This painting, *Spruce Trees at a Waterfall* in the museum in Raleigh, is one of the countless versions of the subject with which

Provenance
Auction De Beurnonville, Paris, 1881 (Frf. 15,000 to Sedelmeyer)
(?) Collection Wesendonck, Bonn
Collection Elsbeth von Risselmann, Görbitsch Castle, Brandenburg, before 1952
Dealer Newhouse Galleries, New York
North Carolina Museum of Art, Raleigh, 1952 (purchased with funds from the State of North Carolina)

Bibliography
Auction Paris 1881, p. 283, no. 458
HdG 409 (vol. IV [1911], p. 121, no. 409)
Rosenberg 1928, p. 80
Valentiner 1956-A, pp. 26 and 52, no. 66 and fig.
Utica / Rochester 1963, p. 39, no. 33 and fig.
Jackson 1978, p. 7, no. 58 and fig. p. 21
Raleigh 1983, p. 109 and fig.
Raleigh 1986-1987, pp. 12 and 18, fig. 13
Sutton 1986, p. 252

I
Illustration from Jan Luiken, *Beschouwing der wereld* (Amsterdam 1708), p. 90

Jacob van Ruisdael Spruce Trees at a Waterfall

Ruisdael achieved fame early on.[7] Most authors state that he did not derive such landscapes from his own observation but from the works of others, especially Allaert van Everdingen. Around 1644 this fellow townsman traveled around Sweden and, from 1647, recorded remembrances of the northern landscape in a series of paintings, drawings, and etchings that Ruisdael must undoubtedly have known.[8] The representation of bodies of water particularly obsessed him, with his preference going to dramatic or imposing images, from water mills in action to boiling seas (cat. no. 54) and foaming mountain brooks. That is why he initially felt attracted to scenes of rugged nature, such as those Van Everdingen rendered. The latter's painting *A Scandinavian River with a Water Mill* of 1650 (Munich, Bayerische Staatsgemäldesammlungen) [2][9] is a good example of the kind of painting that must have fascinated Ruisdael.

But beginning in the early sixties Ruisdael transformed these into creations entirely his own, in which he rose high above the rather old-fashioned stylization of Van Everdingen. In principle the painting in Raleigh features the same pictorial elements as that by Van Everdingen in Munich: a hilly landscape with pointed spruce trees set against the sky and a swirling river with great boulders. Nevertheless, Ruisdael's composition is less stagelike and more natural, the light effects more highly varied, and the water more lively. Stechow wrote enthusiastically about Ruisdael's interpretations of the Scandinavian landscape: 'Looking at what Ruisdael wrought here, one is reminded of the way in which Raphael reacted to Perugino or Rubens to Otto van Veen.'[10] Kurt Simon believed some time ago that the influence of Van Everdingen is generally greatly exaggerated. He pointed out that in his landscapes with waterfalls, Ruisdael in fact placed no emphasis on the Scandinavian elements (for instance, log cabins), but rather incorporated remembrances of his journey to the area around Bentheim (including half-timber houses).[11] Naturally Van Everdingen did not entirely hold the patent for the motif of the waterfall, and he was therefore not Ruisdael's

sole source. It had been painted earlier by others, for instance by Van Everdingen's teacher, Roelant Savery, and by Herman van Swanevelt and other Italianizing landscape painters.[12]

A drawing by Jacob van Ruisdael is of importance in this context because, as far as we know, it is the only sheet by him with a waterfall as its subject (New York, The Pierpont Morgan Library) [3].[13] Like the majority of his large, drawn landscapes, this one could also have been done after real life, after which it served as a preparatory study for one or more paintings. Giltay saw correspondences between this composition and a landscape in Dresden (Gemäldegalerie).[14] But such a kinship is equally present in the lesser-known landscape in Raleigh. The drawing served as a source of inspiration for the painting but not as a study for its details. We see mountainsides rising up to the left and right and spruce trees silhouetted against the sky; a small river tumbles down with splashing water, carrying tree trunks with it; at the right stands a simple mountain hut. We may conclude from this that the theme of the waterfall must have been passed on by Van Everdingen and the tradition, but that Ruisdael was also able to draw from his own observations and imagination. His virtuoso handling of paint did the rest: 'So that in that manner of painting he was already one of the best' (in translation).[15]

▲ **3**
Jacob van Ruisdael
A Landscape with a Waterfall
Chalk drawing with wash, 196 x 232 mm
(7³/₄ x 9¹/₈ in.)
Neither signed nor dated (ca. 1650-1660)
New York, The Pierpont Morgan Library,
inv. no. III, 218

◄ **2**
Allaert van Everdingen
A Scandinavian River with a Water Mill
Canvas, 112 x 88 cm (44 x 34⁵/₈ in.)
Lower right: *A.v.Everdingen / 1650*
Munich, Bayerische Staatsgemäldesammlungen,
inv. no. 387

4
Jacob van Ruisdael
Waterfall with a Hilly Landscape
Canvas, 109 x 143.5 cm (42⅞ x 56½ in.)
Lower left: *JvRuisdaeL* (JvR in ligature) (ca. 1670)
Leningrad, Hermitage, inv. no. 932

In his earliest works, dating from the beginning of the sixties, Ruisdael was mostly dependent on Van Everdingen (see cat. no. 54), which is apparent in part from a series of paintings with mainly vertical formats.[16] Around 1670 his waterfalls were put in a more spacious setting, and the landscapes observed from up close were replaced by more remote prospects with great, cloudy skies, to which only a horizontal format was suited. Handsome examples of this kind are found in Amsterdam (Rijksmuseum),[17] Leningrad (Hermitage) [4],[18] London (Wallace Collection),[19] and in the collection in Balcarres Castle (Collinsburgh, collection Dowager Crawford and Balcarres) [5].[20] The painting under discussion here is still another splendid example of this kind of composed landscape, in which the rugged 'Scandinavian' mountains are combined with the somewhat friendlier-looking hilly landscape of the eastern Netherlands and Germany.

Until about 1950 this painting was in private hands and had never been publicly exhibited, which did little for the popularity that it undoubtedly deserves. Hofstede de Groot knew the work only from a description in an auction catalogue that is related to this painting here for the first time. In Paris, on 13 May 1881, a part of the collection of E. Baron de Beurnonville came under the hammer. A foreword took the measure of the quality and extent of this collection, but there was not a word about the collector himself. Sixteen landscapes by Jacob van Ruisdael were auctioned on that day.[21] The canvas in Raleigh, entitled *Site norvégien*, fetched almost as much (15,000 francs) as did the *Landscape with an Obelisk* – then attributed to Rembrandt, but probably painted by Govaert Flinck – (Boston, Isabella Stewart Gardner Museum) (p. 38, fig. 23),[22] which was auctioned for 16,500 francs.[23]

Even after the museum in Raleigh bought the landscape in 1952, it remained a virtually unknown work. One will search for it in vain in the literature on the painter.[24] It was to be seen only at some lesser exhibitions in America, and it was missing from the great Ruisdael commemoration of 1981 and 1982 in the Mauritshuis in The Hague and the Fogg Art Museum in Cambridge.[25]

According to the museum, the painting was most recently in the possession of Elsbeth von Risselmann in Görbitsch Castle, which now lies in Poland. The Prussian family Von Risselmann inhabited the castle to the east of Frankfurt an der Oder beginning in 1827. In a description of 1913 of the interior, the piece by Ruisdael is not mentioned. Only a small number of paintings of little allure were then to be found in Görbitsch Castle.[26] Elsbeth Vogel von Falckenstein (born 1875) was married in 1905 to Friedrich von Risselmann, who died in 1907.[27]

Apparently relying on the information supplied by Elsbeth von Risselmann, people in Raleigh assume that her painting came from the Wesendonck family in Bonn.[28] It is not clear if the reference was to the well-known (Berlin) Wesendon[c]k collection, which was catalogued in 1888, when it contained six Ruisdaels.[29] Otto Wesendonk died in 1896, after which a large part of his collection went on loan to, and later became the property of, the Provinzialmuseum in Bonn, where it was described in 1914.[30] Neither in the catalogues of 1888 and 1914 nor in that of the collection Wesendonk-Von Bissing, which was auctioned in Cologne in 1935, was there any mention of a

5
Jacob van Ruisdael
Waterfall near a Hill with Huts
Canvas, 106.7 x 150.5 cm (42 x 59¼ in.)
On the large boulder: *JvRuisdaeL* (JvR in ligature) (ca. 1670)
Collinsburgh (Scotland), collection Dowager Crawford and Balcarres

painting that can be identified with *Spruce Trees at a Waterfall*.[31] The provenance from the famous Wesendonk collection appears, therefore, to be incorrect. The information probably goes back to a vague tradition, or perhaps once served as a sales pitch.

1 *Houbraken 1718-1721*, vol. III, pp. 65-66

2 *Brom 1957*, p. 212

3 *Luiken 1708*, pp. 90-92

4 *Luiken 1708*, p. 92; *Wiegand 1971*, pp. 87-91, discussed the possible emblematic meaning of Ruisdael's waterfalls in detail.

5 *Wiegand 1971*, pp. 87-91; Bruyn in *Sutton et al. 1987-1988*, p. 99; the waterfall in the context of a Jewish cemetery could possibly have symbolic meaning (*Wiegand 1971*, p. 59).

6 *Künstler-Inventare*, vol. II, p. 423, no. 40: 'Een Waterval van de Jonge Ruysdalen'; *Broos 1987*, pp. 333-334 (a *Haerlempje*).

7 A (still incomplete) summary is to be found in *Rosenberg 1928*, pp. 79-87, nos. 120-254 (see also HdG 198-439).

8 For example, *Rosenberg 1928*, pp. 43-44; *Schmidt 1981*, pp. 115-119; *Slive / Hoetink 1981-1982*, p. 103

9 *Sutton et al. 1987-1988*, pp. 309-311, no. 28 and fig.

10 *Stechow 1966*, p. 145

11 *Simon 1930*, p. 60

12 *Simon 1930*, p. 61; *Sutton et al. 1987-1988*, p. 310

13 *Giltay 1980*, pp. 162-163, no. 28 and fig. and p. 198, no. 81

14 Inv. no. 1495; HdG 214; *Dresden 1979*, p. 289, no. 1495 and fig.

15 *Houbraken 1718-1721*, vol. III, p. 66

16 *Slive / Hoetink 1981-1982*, pp. 102-105, no. 34 and figs. 44-47

17 Inv. no. C 210; HdG 198; *Van Thiel et al. 1976*, p. 487, no. C 210 and fig.

18 HdG 276; *Somof 1895*, p. 338, no. 1147 and fig. (signature); *Slive / Hoetink 1981-1982*, p. 107, fig. 50

19 Inv. no. P 56; HdG 251; *London 1968*, pp. 298-299, no. P 56 and fig.

20 HdG 252; *Slive / Hoetink 1981-1982*, pp. 106-107, no. 35 and fig.

21 *Auction Paris 1881*, pp. 272-284, nos. 445-460; there were many De Beurnonville auctions between 1872 and 1892 (L., vol. III, p. 709).

22 Inv. no. P 21W24; HdG 941; *Gerson / Bredius 1969*, pp. 353 and 589, no. 443 and fig.; *Hendy 1974*, pp. 204-206 and fig.; *Bruyn et al. 1989*, pp. 737-742, no. C 117 and fig. (Govaert Flinck). This painting was among those stolen from the Gardner Museum on 18 March 1990.

23 *Spectator 1881*, p. 187

24 *Rosenberg 1928*, p. 80, no. 134, wrongly identified its catalogue number as HdG 409.

25 See Bibliography

26 *Göcke / Jung / Spass 1913*, pp. 85-86

27 *GGT*, vol. XXXI (1939), p. 497

28 *Valentiner 1956-A*, p. 52, no. 66: 'Coll.: The Wesendonck family, Bonn.'

29 *Berlin 1888*, vol. I, pp. 82-84, nos. 251-257

30 *Cohen 1910*; *Cohen 1914*

31 *Berlin 1888*, vol. I, pp. 82-84, nos. 251-257; *Cohen 1914*, p. 111, nos. 240-241; *Auction Cologne 1935*

BB

Naarden around 1600/1603 – Haarlem 1670

Canvas, 105.4 x 134.6 cm (41½ x 53 in.)
On the ferry boat: *S. Rvysdael 1656*
Minneapolis, Minn., The Minneapolis Institute of Arts, inv. no. 45.9

Salomon van Ruysdael was the uncle of Jacob van Ruisdael. In 1623 he was registered in the guild in Haarlem, where, in 1626, he signed his first landscape. The influence of Pieter de Molijn, and also that of Esaias van den Velde, is already discernible in his earliest work. In emulation of De Molijn, he painted relatively uncontrived landscapes. The atmospheric effect is always most important. Until 1640 Ruysdael painted monochromatically, in brown, gray, or green tints, but his palette subsequently became more varied and lighter, and the cloud formations are by preference silhouetted against high, radiantly blue skies. Without ever becoming boring, he produced ever more river landscapes with quiet water, with compositions built up of stretched-out triangles, following the simple schemes established by Jan van Goyen. After 1650 he even resorted to bright colors and also began to paint other subjects, such as winter landscapes, and – surprisingly enough – a few still lifes with spoils of the hunt, in the manner of Willem van Aelst.

In 1919 a commemorative album was published dedicated to the collection of the late Edward R. Bacon, whose name one looks for in vain in reference works on American collectors.[1] In the foreword the collector was described as a fastidious person, who, by trading and selling, continuously improved the quality of his collection as a whole. He rarely lent works to exhibitions. His collecting activity had begun with modern art. He then sought out French art and English portraits of the eighteenth century, followed by paintings of the Dutch Golden Century, and, finally, also early Italian Renaissance panels.[2] Edward Rathbone Bacon (1846-1915) had been the president of various railroad companies.[3] He apparently did not feel the need to gain immortality by way of a donation to a museum. In 1919 part of the collection was auctioned in London from the estate of his widow, Mrs. Virginia Purdy Bacon. Four years later her heirs proceeded to auction the last sixteen paintings, which were said to come from the house of the late Edward Bacon on Fifth Avenue in New York and a country residence in Turriff in Scotland.[4]

This perfectly preserved canvas by Salomon van Ruysdael, *River Landscape with a Ferry*, was one of Bacon's last acquisitions.

Provenance

Auction London, 1908 (£504 to Fischhof)
Dealer Sedelmeyer, Paris, 1911
Collection Edward R. Bacon, New York, and Netherdale House, Turriff, Aberdeenshire, before 1915
Collection Mrs. Virginia Purdy Bacon, New York, 1915-1919
Collection Bacon heirs, New York, 1919-1923
Auction Bacon et al., London, 1923 (£714 to Tooth)
Dealer P. Cassirer, Berlin
Collection Paul Kempner, Berlin, before 1925-after 1938
Dealer Knoedler & Co., New York, 1944-1945
The Minneapolis Institute of Arts, Minneapolis, 1945 (The William Hood Dunwoody Fund)

Bibliography

Auction London 1908, p. 28, no. 122
Townsend / Howard 1919, pp. XIV and 117, no. 140
Auction London 1923-A, p. 8, no. 29
Berlin 1925, p. 54, no. 342
Stechow 1938, p. 113, no. 377
Winnipeg 1952, pp. 5, 15 and 27, no. 8 and fig.
Minneapolis 1955, p. 5, no. 10
New York / Palm Beach 1957, n.p. and fig.
Minneapolis 1963, n.p. and fig.
Minneapolis 1970, pp. 104-105, no. 19 and fig.
Minneapolis 1970-A, pp. 120-121, no. 63 and fig.
Stechow 1975, pp. 127-128, no. 375 A (377) and pl. 29, no. 40, p. 162
Keyes 1983, pp. 199-200 and fig. 6
Sutton 1986, p. 157
Lipschultz 1988, p. 99 and fig.

Salomon van Ruysdael River Landscape with a Ferry

After the auction it ended up in the collection of Dr. Paul Kempner in Berlin. In 1925 he parted with it for a major exhibition of art from private Berlin collections, which was organized by Wilhelm von Bode.[5] During World War II the painting returned to American hands and eventually became public property. In 1945 the museum in Minneapolis bought the work from the New York dealer Knoedler & Co. with money from the William Hood Dunwoody Fund. This fund was founded in January 1911. At one of the gatherings of the Minneapolis Society of Fine Arts (founded in 1883), Clinton Morrison made land available for the building of a museum, provided that, in addition to his gift, another half million dollars were raised. William Hood Dunwoody (1841-1914), a local flour miller, spontaneously donated the greater part, first 100,000 dollars, and on 10 January, during a dinner, still another 250,000 dollars. With this money the society, which in 1911 owned only nine paintings, was able to build up a substantial collection, in which the Dutch school naturally had to be represented (see cat. no. 32).[6]

The Minneapolis Institute of Arts has supplied four remarkable landscapes for this exhibition, namely two semi-topographical views, the *Riverscape with the Pellecussen Gate* by Jan van Goyen (cat. no. 24) and *The Water Mills of Singraven near Denekamp* by Meindert Hobbema (cat. no. 32), two anecdotal depictions, *Merry and Rowdy Peasants at an Inn* by Philips Wouwermans (cat. no. 72), and the painting now under discussion. This shows the activity at a ford in a typically Dutch setting, with sailing ships on a lake (or broad river) under a high, cloud-filled sky. At the left we see a village with a church and, far away on the horizon, the contours of a castle. You can't get any more Dutch than that.

Salomon van Ruysdael painted the scene almost without foreground, as if he himself were sitting in a boat. Though he often employed such devices, they always remain effective thanks to the compelling play of lines. In the direction of sight,

the shore and the tops of the trees recede to a vanishing point on the horizon at the right, where the ships are also heading. Striking is the bright blue of the sky, which was applied in broad diagonal stripes before treetops were painted over it. Such a thinly painted sky, with the traces of the broad brush showing, is also the most notable feature of a *River View with a Church* by Ruysdael in the Mauritshuis (The Hague) [1].[7] This landscape is dated to the end of the forties but should probably be placed later. It shows the same anecdotal detail of the ferry jammed with people and cattle, and especially a cow rubbing her head against the edge of the boat.

The German-American art historian Wolfgang Stechow catalogued more than one hundred paintings by Ruysdael in which a small ferry is to be seen.[8] The motif occurs for the first time with Salomon in a river landscape dated 1631 (Sarasota, John and Mable Ringling Museum of Art).[9] One can hardly imagine any work by him after 1635 without the ferry boat. According to Stechow, he borrowed this quintessential Dutch theme from Esaias van den Velde, who had already painted it in 1622, in *The Ferry Boat* (Amsterdam, Rijksmuseum) [2].[10] Perhaps both artists knew the scenes by Jan Brueghel, such as a *River Landscape with a Ferry Boat* of 1603 (Antwerp, Koninklijk Museum voor Schone Kunsten) [3].[11] Sutton referred to this painting and gave still other sources of inspiration.[12] In the fifties the ferry was in any case one of the most beloved, most frequently used narrative elements in the landscapes of Salomon van Ruysdael.[13]

Despite the uniformity of overall design in his compositions, he only rarely repeated himself in details, and that was probably the strength of this specialist. Specialization was a characteristic of Dutch painting of the seventeenth century. Carel van Mander, the writer of *Het Schilder-Boeck* (1604), thought this was actually reprehensible. The true artist ought to be universal, for that is what the ancients had maintained. However, Van Mander concluded his theoretical treatise with the sigh that those not fitted by nature for history painting (the highest attainable art form), had better apply themselves to one or another genre and do that as well as possible: 'thus may it be Animals / Kitchens / Fruits / Flowers / Landscapes' (in translation) and subjects of this kind (see cat. no. 16).[14] In his best works Salomon van Ruysdael remained inspired to the very last brushstroke.

Between 1626 and 1670 he found a ready market for a large series of landscapes in which the Dutch element is emphasized. If, for instance, an imaginary landscape featured the striking profile of the Saint Bavo church, it was called with endearment 'Een Haerlempje van Ruysdael' (a little [view of] Haarlem by

1
Salomon van Ruysdael
River View with a Church
Panel, 75 x 106.5 cm (29½ x 42 in.)
On the boat: *S vRvysDAEL 164[7?]* (almost illegible)
The Hague, Mauritshuis, inv. no. 738

2
Esaias van den Velde
The Ferry Boat
Panel, 75.5 x 113 cm (29¾ x 44½ in.)
Lower right: *E.V. Velde 1622*
Amsterdam, Rijksmuseum, inv. no. A 1293

3
Jan Brueghel the Elder
River Landscape with a Ferry Boat
Panel, 39 x 60 cm (15⅜ x 23⅝ in.)
Lower left: ʙʀᴠᴇɢʜᴇʟ *1603*
Antwerp, Koninklijk Museum voor Schone Kunsten,
inv. no. 910

Ruysdael), even though it was known that a view of the city was not intended.[15] The painting in Minneapolis lacks any explicit topographical points of reference. But the degree of verisimilitude seems established by the figures, which look as if taken from real life. In the foreground jolly couples, waving and kissing, sit in a rowboat. A stately family waits stiffly in a carriage, while the horses are given to drink. In the background two horsemen ride calmly out of the picture. The ferry, which is being both punted and pulled to the shore, carries a farmer with his cows. Salomon van Ruysdael may not have been a great figure painter, but he definitely did not wish to limit himself to predictable and unimaginative scenes. In 1628, two years after Ruysdael had signed his first painting, Samuel Ampzing already sounded the trumpet of praise for this specialist in Dutch landscape: 'How could I here omit *Rustdael* [Ruysdael, or, literally, valley of rest] / Who excels in landscape / and figures with it / and such concerns [pertinent to] landscape painting?' (in translation).[16]

1 *Townsend / Howard 1919; Constable 1964* did not mention Bacon.
2 *Townsend / Howard 1919*, pp. xɪɪɪ-xɪᴠ
3 *wwa*, vol. ɪ, p. 42
4 *Auction London 1919*, title page; *Auction London 1923-A*, title page
5 *Berlin 1925*, p. 54, no. 342
6 *Minneapolis 1970*, p. 7; *wwwa*, vol. ɪ, p. 349
7 *Stechow 1975*, p. 124, no. 361 and fig. 32; *Duparc 1980*, pp. 96-97 and 218, no. 738 and fig.; the signature and date mentioned in this catalogue are virtually illegible.
8 *Stechow 1975*, pp. 116-135, nos. 321-434
9 Inv. no. sɴ 274; *Stechow 1975*, p. 116, no. 321; *Robinson et al. 1980*, no. 117 and fig.
10 *Van Thiel et al. 1976*, p. 558, no. A 1293 and fig.; *Keyes 1984*, p. 148, no. 104 and pl. 116
11 *Antwerp 1959*, p. 40, no. 910; *Ertz 1979*, p. 573, no. 94 and fig. 22 (with mention of autograph replicas and later versions).
12 *Sutton et al. 1987-1988*, p. 472, no. 94, also referred to other examples (Jan van de Velde and Jan van Goyen).
13 *Stechow 1966*, p. 55; *Stechow 1975*, p. 20
14 *Van Mander 1604*, n.p. ('Voor-reden'); on specialization, see *Broos 1978-1979*, pp. 117-118.
15 This label was not intended to refer to the paintings by Jacob van Ruisdael, as has sometimes been thought; see *Broos 1986*, pp. 310 and 312, notes 4-7.
16 *Ampzing 1628*, p. 372
    ʙ ʙ

Adriaen van der Spelt and Frans van Mieris

Leyden 1632 – Gouda 1673 and
Leyden 1635 – Leyden 1681

57 | A Trompe-l'Oeil with a Flower Piece and a Curtain

Panel, 46.5 x 63.9 cm (18¼ x 25⅛ in.)
Lower left, on the flower piece: *A. van der Spelt. 1658*
Chicago, Ill., The Art Institute of Chicago, inv. no. 1949.585

Adriaen van der Spelt was born in Leyden in 1632. His father, Job Adriaensz van der Spelt, was a glass painter and, before his marriage, worked in Gouda. Adriaen's mother came from Leyden, where the family settled. Actually without foundation it has been assumed that Adriaen was trained in Gouda by Wouter Crabeth II to become a glass painter. On 15 May 1658 he became a member of the Leyden guild of painters. He married in 1661 in Gouda, where he subsequently lived. His first wife died in 1662, his second in 1664. He was then probably for some time in the service of the Great Elector in Berlin. His third marriage took place in 1671, and he died two years later. According to the biographer Houbraken, his third wife was a 'vicious bitch' from Groningen, who 'snuffed out not only his joy in painting but, in the year 1673, the light of his life as well' (in translation). We know mainly flower pieces by his hand as well as garlands around portraits by other painters.

A biographic note on Frans van Mieris is given in cat. no. 44.

Provenance
Collection Henric Bugge van Ring, Leyden, 1658(?)-1669
Collection Duke of Sutherland, Stafford House, London, before 1833, after 1837
Dealer Vitale Bloch, Paris, 1949
The Art Institute of Chicago, Chicago, 1949 (Wirt D. Walker Fund)

Bibliography
Passavant 1833, p. 63
Waagen 1837-1839, vol. II, p. 67
Wurzbach, vol. II (1910), p. 645
Paris 1952, p. 68, no. 48
Rich 1953, pp. 31-32 and fig.
New York 1954-A, n.p., no. 76
Reuterswärd 1956, pp. 102 and 104, fig. 8
Chicago 1961, p. 439
Mitchell 1973, p. 242, fig. 348 and p. 244
Fowler / Cornforth 1974, pp. 100-101 and fig. 80
Geelhaar 1978, p. 234, fig. 8 and p. 237
Münster / Baden Baden 1979-1980, p. 545 and fig.
Reuterswärd 1980, pp. 2 and 5, fig. 5
De Jongh et al. 1982, pp. 146 and 148, fig. 25c
Milman 1984, p. 59 and fig. (also on dust jacket)
Sutton 1986, p. 52 and fig. 70
Sluijter et al. 1988, p. 27, fig. 11, pp. 40, 100 and 122
Hecht 1989-1990, p. 42 and note 7
Milwaukee 1989, p. 108 and fig. 2
Schneider 1989, p. 13 and 16 and fig.

For a long time there were only two eyewitness descriptions of this masterwork, albeit not by novices but by Passavant and Waagen, the founders of the German school of connoisseurship. The very first commentary – by Passavant – was not even rooted in the already scarce literature on the painter of this flower piece, Adriaen van der Spelt. In 1833 the German art critic and painter Johann David Passavant (1787-1861) [1] took a journey through Belgium and England, during which he visited the great art collections. In Stafford House near Buckingham Palace – 'This most beautiful of all palaces in London,' Passavant called it – he saw this trompe-l'oeil with amazement: 'Flowers that are partially covered by a blue curtain that is so exceptionally deceptively painted that one believes one could draw it back' (in translation).[1]

Four years later, Dr. Gustav Waagen (1794-1864) (p. 125, fig. 3), director of the Royal Museum in Berlin, made his art journey through the public and private collections of England. His letters contain a precise account of what he saw there, and they still constitute a priceless source of information. On 16 July he reported on an evening reception given by the Duchess of

---

1
Johann David Passavant
Self-Portrait with Beret before a Roman Landscape
Canvas, 45 x 31.6 cm (17¾ x 12½ in.)
Neither signed nor dated (ca. 1820)
Frankfurt, Städelsches Kunstinstitut, inv. no. 1585

Adriaen van der Spelt and Frans van Mieris A Trompe-l'Oeil with a Flower Piece and a Curtain

Sutherland in Stafford House. Harriet Elisabeth Georgina Leveson-Gower (1806-1868) was married to her cousin, one of the richest men in England and, since 1833, the second Duke of Sutherland. Waagen feasted his eyes on the riches of Stafford House but nevertheless did not let himself get too distracted by the luxury. It was his task to record in detail what paintings were on view. Thus he described the flower piece signed by Adriaen van der Spelt, whose name he probably knew only slightly: 'A flower garland in which he comes very close to Pater Seghers. In a blue curtain he achieved that deceptive reality in which many Dutchmen sometimes took pleasure' (in translation).[2] Until The Art Institute of Chicago bought this trompe-l'oeil in 1949, it was inaccessible to the public: the art historians had to make do with Waagen's description. The acquisition was made using the Wirt D. Walker Fund, which was begun with a donation by this former trustee of the museum, who had died in 1899 at the age of thirty-nine.[3]

In Stafford House the flower piece hung right next to *The Box Bed* by Pieter de Hooch (cat. no. 35), which the Duchess of Sutherland sold in 1846. The fate of the Van der Spelt is unknown: it was not mentioned in catalogues or in later descriptions of the Sutherland collection. Shortly before the panel was acquired by the museum in Chicago in 1949, it fell into the hands of Vitale Bloch (1900-1975) in Paris.[4] This art historian and critic of Russian descent had entered the art trade in Berlin in the thirties, but he later found alternative hometowns in The Hague and Paris. He was especially charmed by the so-called minor masters of the Dutch seventeenth century, to which group Van der Spelt belongs. In 1975 Bloch left a small collection of drawings and paintings to the Museum Boymans-van Beuningen in Rotterdam.[5] No doubt through his efforts, the work by Van der Spelt was shown in 1952 at the great still-life exhibition in the Orangerie des Tuileries in Paris.[6] Only then did the painting begin to get the attention it deserves. For instance, it was reproduced on the dust jacket of a book devoted to the theme of the

trompe-l'oeil.[7] Recent research has made it clear that this is a most unusual painting, as we shall see.

The spontaneous commentaries by Passavant and Waagen turn out to contain accurate elements. Passavant wished, as it were, to draw back the curtain from the painting, and this is precisely the effect the curtain was intended to have. We are dealing here with a well-known painter's joke, which finds its origins in antiquity. Tall tales used to make the rounds about artists who wished to outdo each other in the imitation of reality. In his *Schilder-Boeck* of 1604, Carel van Mander repeated one such story, concerning the competition between Zeuxis and Parrhasios, after the writings of Pliny. Zeuxis had painted grapes so deceptively real that birds tried to feast on them, but Parrhasios was able to improve on that. When he showed Zeuxis his piece of work, the latter said 'that it was about time to take off the bedsheet / so that one might see / what kind of painting *Parasius* had brought' (in translation). To Zeuxis's amazement

▲ 3
Willem van Haecht
Apelles Painting Campaspe (detail)
Panel, 105 x 149.5 cm (41³/₈ x 58⁷/₈ in.) (the whole painting)
Neither signed nor dated (ca. 1628)
The Hague, Mauritshuis, inv. no. 266

◄ 2
Gerard Dou
A Painting with a (Self?)-Portrait
Panel, 48 x 37 cm (18⁷/₈ x 14⁵/₈ in.)
Lower center, on the paper: *GDou* (ca. 1645)
Amsterdam, Rijksmuseum, inv. no. A 86

the cloth that covered the painting turned out to have been painted, and he admitted frankly that 'Parasius had done more [outdone him] / having deceived him / who was experienced in the Art of Painting' (in translation).[8] Such feats of deceptively real painting must have made a great impression on Gerard Dou and his followers, the Leyden *fijnschilders*, who strove for the perfect reproduction of nature.[9]

This is why the poet Traudenius called Gerard Dou, who handled his brush like a magic wand, 'the Dutch Parrhasius.'[10] Dou showed himself worthy of this title in *A Painting with a (Self?)-Portrait* (Amsterdam, Rijksmuseum) [2],[11] which shows a framed panel or canvas with a deceptively real curtain suspended from a rod. In the seventeenth century valuable paintings were sometimes actually covered with a hanging, as Willem van Haecht shows us in his *Apelles Painting Campaspe* (The Hague, Mauritshuis).[12] In fact, it gives the impression of a contemporary art cabinet – in this instance that of Cornelis van der Geest in Antwerp. No fewer than eight paintings in the painted cabinet could be covered with a protective curtain [3].[13]

The intention of Dou was therefore to show a painted painting. His trick was often imitated in the seventeenth century. The best-known example is Rembrandt's *Holy Family with the Cat* (Kassel, Gemäldegalerie) of 1646,[14] in which a drawn-back

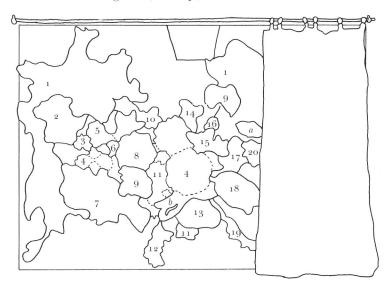

curtain and a sculpted frame are painted. What is conspicuous in this instance is that Rembrandt aimed for the same illusionism with his rough way of painting as Gerard Dou did with his fine style. Painted curtains appear to have been a rage, not only in Leyden and Amsterdam but also in Dordrecht and Delft.[15]

Without doubt Van der Spelt wanted to imitate 'Parrhasios' Dou. Instead of a portrait, he painted a flower festoon, which was, after all, his specialty, suspended in a stone arch. It consists of a bouquet of roses, poppies, borage, scalloped thistle, and even a squill and a tulip. In short, spring and summer flowers are mixed, constituting an invented ensemble [4].[16] He gave this painting a narrow, painted frame, inside which he placed his signature and the year 1658. In front of the main subject hangs a curtain suspended from a copper rod that rests in a hook and a screw eye which, just as in Dou's painting, have been twisted into the black frame.

This curtain of blue silk is especially dazzlingly well executed. In 1658 in Leyden (where Van der Spelt then worked) only Gerard Dou and Frans van Mieris could really paint with such virtuosity – witness two works of about that year in the Mauritshuis: *The Young Mother* by Dou;[17] and the *Brothel Scene* by Van Mieris.[18] And it is Frans van Mieris who was the painter of the curtain in the work of Van der Spelt. The surprising proof for this was recently provided by Eric Jan Sluijter, who identified an interesting statement in the 1667 inventory of the Leyden burgher Henric Bugge van Ring (died 1669) with the panel in Chicago: 'A piece with flowers by Van der Spelt and a curtain standing in it by Mieris' (in translation).[19] Now we can also understand why Van der Spelt provided only the flower piece with his name, and not the whole painting. With the benefit of hindsight it is curious that the obvious stylistic difference between the execution of the flower garland and the curtain has never raised any questions.

We no longer know if the trompe-l'oeil came about on Adriaen's initiative or at the request of a patron (Henric Bugge van Ring?). Adriaen van der Spelt and Frans van Mieris must in any case have known each other well. In the year in which they made their collaborative masterpiece, they registered in the painters' guild in Leyden: Frans on 14 May, and Adriaen the day after.[20] We learn from the will of the physician Johannes van der Spelt, a brother of Adriaen, that in 1664 Frans van Mieris owed

4
Diagram of cat. no. 57 (research and drawing by Sam Segal)

1 Ivy *Hedera helix* L.
2 Honeysuckle *Lonicera periclymenum* L.
3 Squill *Scilla bifolia* L.
4 Provins Rose *Rosa x provincialis* Mill.
5 Pomegranate *Punica granatum* L. *plenum*
6 Yellow Rose *Rosa foetida* Herrm.
7 Scalloped Thistle *Carduus crispus* L.
8 White Rose *Rosa x alba* L.
9 Field Poppy *Papaver rhoeas* L.
10 Stock *Matthiola incana* (L.) R. Br. *spadicea*
11 Borage *Borago officinalis* L. *plena*
12 Stock *Matthiola incana* (L.) R. Br. *bicolor plena*
13 Pot Marigold *Calendula officinalis* L. *plena*
14 Larkspur *Consolida ambigua* (L.) Ball & Heyw.
15 Poppy Anemone *Anemone coronaria* L. *lutea pseudoplena*
16 Forget-me-not *Myosotis scorpioides* L.
17 Hollyhock *Alcea rosea* L.

18 Tulip *Tulipa clusiana* Vent. *x T. agenensis* DC.
19 Almond blossom *Prunus dulcis* (Mill.) Webb.
20 Scarlet Runner *Phaseolus coccineus* L.
a Red Admiral *Vanessa atalanta* (L.)
b Lackey caterpillar *Malocosoma neustria* (L.)

5
Adriaen van der Spelt
Flower Still Life with Peaches
Panel, 64 x 48 cm (25¼ x 187⁄8 in.)
Lower right: *A. van der Spelt. 1658*
Amsterdam / London, dealer Douwes Bros. Fine Art,
1990

200 guilders to the doctor. Johannes's collection then included a portrait of himself by Van Mieris and a flower still life by Adriaen.[21] Van der Spelt continued to work in Leyden for only a short time after the completion of this trompe l'oeil made with the aid of Van Mieris. In this city he painted a second flower still life, which he dated 1658 as well. It was recently on view at the art and antique fair in Maastricht (Dealer Douwes Bros. Fine Art, Amsterdam / London, 1990) [5].[22] In 1661 he left for Gouda, where his father had lived and where he wed a rich young woman.[23]

It was presumably after the death of his second wife in 1662 that he offered his services at the court of the Great Elector in Berlin. His success radiates from a portrait in mezzotint of 'Hadrianus vander Spelt' that Bernard Vaillant made around this time [6].[24] According to the inscription, he was then a 'celebris apud Goudanos Florum Pictor' (celebrated Gouda flower painter).[25] For Louise Henriëtte, the spouse of the elector and daughter of the Stadholder Frederik Hendrik, he painted a cartouche of flowers around the portrait of her son Karl Emil of Brandenburg (Berlin, Jagdschloss Grunewald) [7].[26] The portrait of the prince-elector is attributed to the court painter Johann Gottfried Bartsch (ca. 1640-after 1690). It must have been made around 1665, when the lad was ten years old.[27] Indeed, this practice is how Daniël Seghers also worked as a flower painter together with diverse (portrait) specialists. Waagen therefore observed quite rightly in 1837 that, in the trompe-l'oeil now in Chicago, Van der Spelt 'comes very close to Pater Segers.'[28] This observation could much earlier have given someone the idea that a second painter had a hand in the depiction. ·

► **6**
Bernard Vaillant
Portrait of Adriaen van der Spelt
Mezzotint, 117 x 90 mm (45⁄8 x 3½ in.)
Lower right: *B. Vaillant fecit* (ca. 1665)
Amsterdam, Rijksprentenkabinet

Hadrianus vander Spelt
Celebris apúd Goudanos Florum Pictor
B. Vaillant fecit

▲ **7**
Adriaen van der Spelt and Johann Gottfried Bartsch
Portrait of Karl Emil, Prince Elector of Brandenburg
Canvas, 118.5 x 95 cm (465⁄8 x 373⁄8 in.)
Lower right: *AVSpelt* (AVS in ligature) (ca. 1665)
Berlin, Jagdschloss Grunewald, inv. no. GK I 30063

1 *Passavant 1833*, p. 63; about Passavant: *Thieme / Becker*, vol. XXVI (1932), p. 280; *Waetzoldt 1924*, pp. 14-29

2 *Waagen 1837-1839*, vol. II, p. 67; about Waagen: *Waetzoldt 1924*, pp. 29-45

3 *Bulletin* AIC *1915*, pp. 80-81

4 According to an annotation with the photograph (KHI-U).

5 *Rotterdam 1978*; see the preface by J.C. Ebbinge Wubben on pp. 3-9.

6 *Paris 1952*, p. 68, no. 48

7 *Milman 1984*

8 *Van Mander 1604*, fol. 67 verso; comparable remarkable feats were mentioned by *Kris / Kurz 1934*, pp. 70-71.

9 See especially *Sluijter et al. 1988*, pp. 19-23

10 *Traudenius 1662*, 'Rym-bundel', p. 17: 'hy goochelt met 't pinceel.'

11 *Van Thiel et al. 1976*, pp. 196-197, no. A 86 and fig.; *Sumowski 1983*, pp. 530 and 568, no. 271 and fig.

12 *Broos 1987*, pp. 162-174, no. 29 and fig.

13 Only a few frames have been preserved with the curtain rod still attached to them, see *Van Thiel / De Bruyn Kops 1984*, pp. 302-304, no. 92 and fig. (also mention of curtains in inventories).

14 Inv. no. GK 240; *Gerson / Bredius 1969*, pp. 486 and 608, no. 572 and fig.

15 *Reuterswärd 1956*, pp. 97-112, gave an extensive list of painted curtains (without mention of the story of Zeuxis and Parrhasios); in a dissertation on the theme of the trompe-l'oeil this type of image is not mentioned separately (*Burda 1969*, pp. 28-32).

16 A *vanitas* meaning cannot be ruled out here (see cat. no. 3).

17 Inv. no. 32; HdG 110; *Broos 1987*, pp. 111-117, no. 20 and fig.

18 Inv. no. 860; HdG 102; *Broos 1987*, pp. 240-243, no. 42 and fig. (the painter deliberately left out the last numeral of the year: a kind of trompe-l'oeil effect).

19 Leyden, Gemeentearchief, notarial archives, no. 1005:10, fol. 16 verso; *Sluijter et al. 1988*, pp. 40 and 53, note 212

20 *Geselschap 1970*, p. 187; *Naumann 1981*, vol. I, pp. 164-165

21 *Naumann 1981*, vol. I, p. 170 (22 September): it proved impossible to locate the document; see also *Sluijter et al. 1988*, p. 53, note 213; the portrait of Johannes van der Spelt is located (as a portrait of Adriaen) in Florence, Galleria degli Uffizi (inv. no. 1183; *Florence 1980*, p. 572, no. P 1818 and fig.).

22 *Maastricht 1990*, p. 54 and fig.

23 *Geselschap 1970*, p. 187; *Schneider 1919*, p. 229: in 1661 Van der Spelt, painter in Gouda, still had debts in Leyden.

24 *Hollstein*, vol. XXXI (1987), p. 49, no. 23

25 *Naumann 1981*, vol. I, p. 138, mistook this print for the portrait of Jan van der Spelt.

26 *Börsch-Supan 1964*, pp. 122-123, no. 167 and fig.

27 *Geselschap 1970*, p. 187, assumed incorrectly that Van der Spelt also painted the portrait and that he had already left for Berlin around 1660.

28 See note 2

BB

Leyden 1626 – Leyden 1679

Canvas, 84.4 x 101 cm (33¼ x 39¾ in.)
Neither signed nor dated (ca. 1659-1660)
Kansas City, Mo., The Nelson-Atkins Museum of Art, inv. no. 67.8

According to the biographer Houbraken, Steen was a pupil of Jan van Goyen, whose daughter Margaretha (Grietje) he married in 1649. His earliest work shows the influence of Nicolaus Knüpfer, to whom he may have been apprenticed in Utrecht, but above all it shows that of Adriaen van Ostade, who apparently was his teacher in Haarlem. Until 1654 Steen worked in The Hague, after which for some years he ran a brewery in Delft, but with little success. From 1656 to 1661 the family lived in Warmond (near Leyden) and then, until 1670, in Haarlem. In that year Steen returned to Leyden, where, two years later, he opened an inn, which turned out to be no gold mine either.

The chronology of Steen's work still presents problems because he rarely dated his paintings and worked in different styles within any one period. He quickly adapted himself to his artistic surroundings. In his Warmond period he was able to paint finely in the Leyden manner, and in Haarlem the broad brushstroke à la Hals apparently suited him equally well. In Haarlem he began making the large paintings with interior domestic scenes that frequently come with a moralizing inscription, often a popular saying. It was then, as well, that the well-known works of popular amusements or feasts, such as the *Prinsjesdag* (day of celebration of the Prince Stadholder) and Twelfth Night, originated. Less well known are Steen's religious scenes, in which the Brueghelesque manner of narration yields a mixture of the biblical and the everyday. His anecdotal vision and humor remain the most remarkable characteristics of his work in all its diversity. For his contemporaries Steen always had a moralizing message at the ready, one which for us may serve as a mirror of the mores and customs of the seventeenth century.

Provenance

Collection Ferdinand Count d'Oultremont, Brussels, before 1882-1889
Auction d'Oultremont, Paris, 1889 (bought back for Frf. 13,500)
(?) Collection Tabourier, Paris, before 1898
Collection Henri-Georges Heugel, Paris, 1898-1916
Collection Jacques-Paul Heugel, Paris, 1916-1967
The Nelson Atkins-Museum of Art, Kansas City, 1967 (Nelson Fund)

Bibliography

Bredius 1882, p. 183
Brussels 1882, p. 92, no. 233
Auction Paris 1889, pp. 7 and 18, no. 11 and fig. opp. p. 18
HdG 398 (vol. I [1907], p. 94, no. 398)
HdG-MS, ad no. 398 (413A)
Paris 1921, p. 10, no. 103
Bredius 1927, p. 52 and pl. 39
Trautscholdt 1937, p. 512, nos. 398 and 413 A
De Groot 1952, pp. 129-130
Martin 1954, pp. 14 and 84, note 19
Keyszelitz 1956, pp. 58-61
Staring 1956, pp. 92-93 and fig. XIII
The Hague 1958-1959, no. 41 and fig. 42
Van Hall 1963, p. 315, no. 38
Mirimonde 1967, pp. 331 and 334, fig. 26
Art Quarterly 1968, pp. 93 and 95 and fig. p. 98
Jaffé 1972, pp. 510-511 and pl. IV
Kansas City 1973, p. 116 and fig.
Thornton 1974, p. 100, fig. 4
De Vries 1976-A, p. 19 and fig.
De Vries 1977, pp. 55 and 163, no. 106
Braun 1980, pp. 170-171, no. B-110 and fig.
Sutton 1982-1983, p. 23, note 3
Berlin / Detroit / Philadelphia 1984, p. 370, no. 105, note 8
Sutton 1986, pp. 124-125 and fig. 179
Van Dijck / Koopman 1987, no. 170 and fig.

Before 1967, when the museum in Kansas City came into possession of this painting, which had traditionally but incorrectly been called *The Van Goyen Family*, it was in the Heugel collection in Paris. At the end of the nineteenth century, it was acquired by Henri-Georges Heugel (1844-1916) of the firm Heugel & Co., publishers of music.[1] It is clear that its depiction of a musical party must have attracted him to this painting, and not necessarily that it represents the painter Jan van Goyen and his next of kin. Henri Heugel had success with the publication of works by J. Offenbach, A. Delibes, G. Fauré, and G. Charpentier.[2] His son Jacques-Paul (1890-1979) continued the list with editions of the work of D. Milhaud, F. Poulenc, A. Jolivet, P. Boulez, and many others. He was also a prolific poet and man of letters. After the death of his father, the interior scene by Jan Steen came into his possession.

According to Cornelis Hofstede de Groot, the painting had been in the Tabourier collection in Paris before it became the property of the music publishers Heugel.[3] However, it is not mentioned in the auction catalogue of L. Tabourier, so that the correctness of Hofstede de Groot's communication cannot be verified.[4] The earliest sighting of the colorful scene dates from 1882, when it appeared as an *Intérieur* at a Brussels charitable exhibition.[5] In a review of this exhibition, Abraham Bredius wrote: 'One of the best pieces is that of the Count d'Oultremont. It shows us the painter with his father-in-law Jan van Goyen and the latter's three daughters, among whom is certainly Jan Steen's spouse Margaretha, in a stately room' (in translation).[6] Ferdinand Count d'Oultremont (1840-1902) was then the owner. The d'Oultremont family was of old Southern Netherlandish nobility, originating in Liège and already mentioned there in the fourteenth century.[7] This family name gained prominence in Holland because of Henriëtte d'Oultremont de Wégimont (1792-1864), a lady-in-waiting who, after the death of Queen Wilhelmina, married King William I. The couple became immortal in popular parlance as 'William Cheesehead and Jetje Thundermouth' (in translation). In 1889 the Brussels d'Oultremonts auctioned twelve paintings (among which was the

Jan Steen) from their collection, which was said to be one of the oldest and richest in Belgium.[8] The auction catalogue observed that the painting was traditionally said to depict the house of the painter Jan van Goyen, with Frans Hals in front of the hearth and Jan Steen himself to the left, with a silver tray in his hand.[9] To quote the Dutch proverb, 'they had heard the bell sound, but did not know where the clapper hung' (in translation), meaning that this information conveyed the general idea but lacked any precise facts.

It was Bredius who rang the bell, and this fact has sadly passed into oblivion. In his review from 1882 that we cited above, he published an archival investigation that he had carried out in the baptismal registers of The Hague. Steen's two oldest children, Thaddeus and Eva, appear to have been born in the court capital. From this he drew, among other things, the proof that Jan Steen had lived in The Hague from 1649 to 1654, and he determined that Steen must therefore have lived in one of the houses belonging to his father-in-law, Jan van Goyen, who speculated in real estate.[10] The identification of the seated man with the broad-brimmed hat as the painter Jan van Goyen appears to have been quite correct; there are correspondences with the portrait of the landscape painter that Gerard ter Borch painted around 1652 / 1653 (Vaduz, collection of the Princes of

▲ 1
Carel de Moor
Portrait of Jan van Goyen
Etching, 200 x 150 mm (7⅞ x 5⅞ in.)
Upper left: *C. D. Moor* (ca. 1680)
Amsterdam, Rijksprentenkabinet

◄ 2
Jan Steen
Self-Portrait
Canvas, 73 x 62 cm (28¾ x 24⅜ in.)
Middle right: *JSteen* (js in ligature) (ca. 1666)
Amsterdam, Rijksmuseum, inv. no. A 383

Jan Steen Fantasy Interior with Jan Steen and Jan van Goyen

Liechtenstein).[11] Bredius probably knew the print that Carel de Moor made after this portrait [1].[12] Why the d'Oultremonts thought that Frans Hals was also depicted is not clear, but it probably had something to do with his mounting popularity around that time. We know the head of Jan Steen from numerous figures seen smirking, if not roaring with laugher, in genre scenes, but also from the relatively dignified, official *Self-Portrait* of about 1666 (Amsterdam, Rijksmuseum) [2].[13] We may consider the man next to the hearth, pointing at Jan van Goyen, as an anecdotal self-portrait by Jan Steen.

In general this painting is dated about 1670, almost twenty years later than Bredius placed it. However, Lyckle de Vries believed that the painting could not have been painted after 1661.[14] If it was painted around 1660, and that seems to be the correct dating, it features a posthumous portrait of Steen's father-in-law, who had died in 1656. In the copy of the catalogue annotated by Hofstede de Groot himself, the identification by Bredius is adopted and amplified. According to the notation, the second son-in-law of Van Goyen, Jacques de Claeuw, who was a specialist in still lifes, is depicted as well.[15] The conclusions of Bredius and Hofstede de Groot appear to have been formulated too hastily, and for two reasons. First, Jacques de Claeuw was a middle-aged man around 1660, and therefore cannot be the lad with the silver tray. Second, though Jan van Goyen did have three daughters, one of them had already died in 1632.[16]

Staring apparently suspected that there was something wrong, and in his book *De Hollanders thuis* (The Dutch at home), he believed he could recognize in the music-making ladies the widow of Van Goyen and her two daughters, Grietje (who was married to Jan Steen) and Maria (the wife of Jacques de Claeuw), both still living in 1660.[17] But in 1660 the mother-in-law of Jan Steen, Anna van Raelst, was in her sixties, and she therefore cannot be the woman sitting in the middle, as Staring thought. It is possible that Jan Steen's eldest son, Thaddeus, then about ten years old, was the model for the young lad who offers the woman an oyster with lemon.[18] It is therefore not appropriate to call this painting *The Van Goyen Family*. In this case, at any rate, Staring's book has a misleading title. His assertion that Jan van Goyen could never have had the use of such a resplendent interior has often been repeated, along with all the accompanying misconceptions.[19]

Only Willem Martin, who succeeded Bredius as director of the Mauritshuis, sensed the essence of this painting, although he, too, spoke of the family of the landscape painter. He recounted once more that Van Goyen died in poverty, and that this scene

must therefore have been intended ironically. More enlightening, however, was the comment: 'But did not everyone of that time who had any self-respect have himself depicted in surroundings that were not usually his due, with columns and great curtains, or at any rate, in the background, a spacious park with a statue or at least one fountain? [This was] a fashion that continued on in photography, when even our servants were immortalized in parks and pleasure grounds that they would and could never have set foot in' (in translation).[20] Certainly Steen did not depict an actual interior. May we assume that Martin saw a correspondence with the *Portrait of Jacoba Maria van Wassenaer or of Bernardina Margriet van Raesfeld* (The Hague, Mauritshuis) [3] of 1660?[21] The parallel is in any case striking. Just as the little girl is portrayed in fantastic surroundings, loaded with symbolism, so Steen created a double portrait of himself with his deceased father-in-law in an interior that has purely symbolic meaning. He even placed explicatory texts at the left and right. The symmetrical structure of the decor in these two compositions and the strange, deliberately unreal and inconsistent proportions of the figures relative to each other are at all events so similar that they vouch for the autograph status of the painting in Kansas City, as well as for the same time of origin – that is, around 1660.[22]

In the foreground we see references to the pleasant aspects of life: drink, love, and music. At the left, a black boy sets out a bottle of wine in a large marble cooling vat. Such exotic servants in portraits were usually intended as a sign of prosperity.[23] In the kitchen a meal is being prepared, and, in the center, the woman with the music book is being offered an oyster and a half-peeled lemon on a dish. This action itself refers to the temptations of love, as Jan Steen has repeatedly shown us.[24] But Jan Steen was not alone in referring to the meaning of this mollusk. In a painting of 1665 by Eglon van der Neer, a woman holds a plate with three oysters and a lemon and appears to be undecided whether or not to partake of them (Vaduz, collection of the

3
Jan Steen
Portrait of Jacoba Maria van Wassenaer or of Bernardina Margriet van Raesfeld
Canvas, 107.4 x 81.4 cm (42¼ x 32 in.)
On a board at the lower left: *JSteen. 1660*
(JS in ligature)
The Hague, Mauritshuis, inv. no. 166

Princes of Liechtenstein).[25] Because of the universally known aphrodisiac powers of oysters, this scene is erotically charged. For this reason, as in the painting by Steen, one may consider the lemon (golden on the outside, bitter on the inside) as a fruit associated with love (see cat. no. 6).[26] The woman with the music book is accompanied by a long-legged beauty at a clavichord and a girl with a lute. The clavichord has a fantastic base with putti on dolfins and a flute-playing faun. Steen brings home his message with two inscriptions: *DEO GLORIA* (Glory to God) is a universal sentiment, and *MUSICA PELLIT CURAS* (Music drives away care) is a reference to the healing powers of music, an efficacious remedy for melancholy.[27]

Thus, the foreground gives us a happy rendition of the saying 'Wine, Women, and Song.' The theme is more or less repeated in the images on the large linen cupboard: at the left a blindfolded Bacchus, the god of wine; in the middle Venus with Amor, the duo of love; and at the right once more Amor, who is carving his bow. We have approached the core of the story, which the painter turned into the visual center point, namely the chimney above Jan Steen and Jan van Goyen. It shows the opposite side of the coin. In a closely related composition of 1661, Steen also used the mantelpiece as the frame for his message, which may literally be read as '*Soo gewonne / Soo verteert*' (Easy come / Easy go) (Rotterdam, Museum Boymans-van Beuningen) [4].[28] In this scene, the mantelpiece has been taken in all its details from a French print, which demonstrates once more to what degree these interiors were assembled and not painted after real life.[29] The painting on the chimney in the Kansas City canvas has been interpreted as an episode from the life of Alexander the Great.[30] Here we may see how in 326 BC. King Poros from the Punjab, seated on an elephant, engaged in heroic combat with Alexander, in which the latter's horse Bucephalus will die and Poros will be vanquished.[31] This image of futile heroism was seen to be related to Van Goyen's fatal financial adventures. Perhaps it is indeed a kind of homage by Steen to his deceased father-in-law, who, just

like himself, was an enormously productive artist who nevertheless never had any money to spare. Finally, the laureated skull on the mantelpiece lets us know that Death will always win the battle in the end. Perhaps unnecessarily, the painter wrote below: *Discite mori* (Man, learn to die).[32]

1 See Provenance; *Martin 1954*, p. 84, note 19: 'Coll. Hengel'; *Keyszelitz 1956*, p. 58, note 1: 'Slg. Hengel'; *Braun 1980*, p. 170, no. B-110: 'in de collectie van Henri Heugel in Parijs, aan wie het in 1959 nog behoorde' (NB: H. Heugel had passed away in 1916).

2 *Larousse*, vol. V, p. 5259

3 HdG-MS, ad no. 398

4 *Auction Paris 1898*

5 *Brussels 1882*, p. 92, no. 233

6 *Bredius 1882*, p. 183

7 *Koller / Melia*, pp. 169-170

8 *Auction Paris 1889*, p. 5

9 *Auction Paris 1889*, p. 18, no. 11

10 *Bredius 1882*, pp. 183-184

11 Inv. no. 893; *Gudlaugsson 1956*, p. 251 and fig.; *Gudlaugsson 1960*, pp. 104-105, no. 93 and fig.; *Ten Doesschate Chu 1987*, pp. 94-95, no. 21 and fig.

12 *Hollstein*, vol. XIV, p. 75, no. 1 and fig.

13 HdG 860; *Van Thiel et al. 1976*, p. 521, no. A 383 and fig.; for self-portraits by Steen, see *Braun 1980*, pp. 8-9

14 *The Hague 1958-1959*, no. 42: '1665-1667'; *Kansas City 1973*, p. 116: 'About 1670'; *De Vries 1977*, p. 55

15 HdG-MS, ad no. 398

16 *Beck 1972-1973*, vol. I, pp. 25-27, nos. 22-25; *Bredius 1927*, p. 79, did not yet know the information about Catharina Steen.

17 *Staring 1956*, p. 92

18 *Beck 1972-1973*, vol. I, pp. 23-27, nos. 9 and 26

19 *Staring 1956*, p. 92; *Keyszelitz 1956*, pp. 58-61; *The Hague 1958-1959*, no. 41 and fig.; *Kansas City 1973*, p. 116; see also *De Vries 1977*, p. 19 and fig.

20 *Martin 1954*, p. 14

21 HdG 330; *Broos 1987*, pp. 350-354, no. 58 and fig.

22 *Braun 1980*, p. 170, no. B-110, has seriously doubted the autograph status of this painting, which *Sutton 1986*, p. 181, judged to be unfounded (NB: Braun did not understand that the allegorical message was reinforced precisely because of Steen's deviation from reality).

23 *Otte 1987*, p. 7

24 *Broos 1987*, pp. 348-349

25 Inv. no. 475; *Ten Doesschate Chu 1987*, pp. 182-183, no. 65 and fig.

26 *Henkel / Schöne 1967*, kols. 238-239; *De Jongh et al. 1982*, p. 95, took the so often displayed but so rarely explained half-peeled lemon for a demonstration of the virtuosity of the painter.

27 See *Bandmann 1960*

28 HdG 854; *Braun 1980*, pp. 38 and 105, no. 143 and fig.

29 *Lunsingh Scheurleer 1935*, pp. 262-263, figs. 1-2

30 *Staring 1956*, p. 92

31 *Mann / Heuss 1962*, pp. 429-430; it is not known if Steen utilized a visual source for this.

32 The interpretation of *Keyszelitz 1956*, pp. 58-61, is seriously marred by a faulty point of departure (he considered it a group portrait) and the fact that he did not know that Van Goyen's portrait was painted posthumously.

BB

4
Jan Steen
'*Easy Come / Easy Go*'
Canvas, 79 x 104 cm (31⅛ x 41 in.)
On the mantelpiece, beneath the saying: *16 J Steen 61*
(JS in ligature)
Rotterdam, Museum Boymans-van Beuningen,
inv. no. 2527

Leyden 1626 – Leyden 1679

Canvas, 102.5 x 142.5 cm (40⅜ x 56⅛ in.)
Lower left: *JSteen. 1663* (JS in ligature)
Washington, D.C., National Gallery of Art, Widener Collection, inv. no. 1942.9.81

This superb painting of 1663 by Jan Steen was consecutively in three famous private collections in the Netherlands, England, and America: the Bisschop collection in Rotterdam, the Hope collection in London, and the Widener collection in Philadelphia. On a portrait of 1753 by Aert Schouman, the brothers Jan (1680-1771) and Pieter Bisschop (ca. 1690-1758) are engaged in a discussion about art with Olivier Hope (1731-1783) (Blair Castle, Perthshire, collection of the Duke of Atholl) [**1**].[1] We see here three bachelors, united in their love of art. Jan Bisschop and his younger brother Pieter ran a notions shop in a small house in the Kromme Hang (Crooked Bend) in Rotterdam. Theirs was both a retail and wholesale business, and they accumulated enough money to establish an extensive art collection. Their house was soon filled to bursting with art objects – not just paintings, but all sorts of rarities, books, and prints. They showed a marked preference for the work of the Dutch *fijnschilders*.[2] In 1743 they bought a dignified residence on the Leuvehaven for their collection, which they set up as a museum. They themselves continued to live above their store. A part of the Bisschop Museum has now been reconstructed in the Schielandshuis in Rotterdam.[3] The collection of paintings was described in a catalogue published by Gerard Hoet in 1752. In it Steen's painting was described as: 'A merry Company with Dancing and eating

Provenance
Auction The Hague, 1737 (*f* 140)
Collection Jan and Pieter Bisschop, Rotterdam, 1737(?)-1771
Collection Adrian and John Hope, Amsterdam, 1771-1781 (bought after the death of Jan Bisschop)
Collection John Hope, Amsterdam, 1771-1784
Heirs Hope (Hoop), Bosbeek, Heemstede, 1784-1794
Collection Henry Hope, London, 1794-1811
Collection Henry Philip Hope, London, 1811-1839 (temporarily collection Thomas Hope of Deepdene, London, 1819-1831)
Collection Henry Thomas Hope, London, 1839-1862
Collection Adèle Bichat, widow of H.T. Hope, London, 1862-1884
Collection Henry Francis Hope Pelham-Clinton-Hope, London, 1884-1898 (on loan from 1891 to 1898 to the South Kensington Museum)
Dealer Colnaghi & Wertheimer, London, 1898-1901
Dealer Agnew, London, 1901
Collection Peter A.B. Widener, Lynnewood Hall, Philadelphia, 1901-1915 (bought from Agnew's)
Collection Joseph E. Widener, Lynnewood Hall, Philadelphia, 1915-1942
National Gallery of Art, Washington, 1942 (gift of Widener)

Bibliography
Hoet 1752-1770, vol. II, p. 530, vol. III, p. 11, no. 7
Rotterdam 1771, p. 10
London 1824, p. 172, no. 7 or 9 (1818)
Smith 1829-1842, vol. IV, p. 50, no. 150
Waagen 1837-1839, vol. II, p. 334, no. 3
London 1849, p. 11, no. 84
Waagen 1854, vol. II, p. 118
Van Westrheene 1856, pp. 119-120, no. 89
London 1866, p. 9, no. 33
London 1881, p. 27, no. 124
Ashbourne 1885-1900, p. 165
Wertheimer 1891 / 1898, fig. XXV
HdG 655 (vol. I [1907], p. 159, no. 655)
HdG-MS, no. 655
Valentiner 1909, pp. XXVII and 126-127, no. 126 and fig.
Breck 1910, p. 44
Valentiner 1910, pp. 15 and 427, no. 126 and fig.
Wiersum 1910, p. 171, no. 7
Graves 1913-1915, vol. III, p. 1254, no. 138 (1818), p. 1256, no. 84 (1849), p. 1257, no. 33 (1866)
Hofstede de Groot / Valentiner 1913-1916, vol. I, n.p. 'Introduction' and 'Jan Steen' and fig.
Elkins Park 1923 / 1931, p. 220 and fig.
Valentiner 1925, n.p., 'Foreword' and no. 26
Washburn Freund 1925, p. 463
Trautscholdt 1937, p. 513, no. 655
Waldmann 1938, pp. 336-338
Martin 1954, p. 79, no. 1663/655
The Hague 1958-1959, no. 18
Washington 1959, p. 53, no. 677 and fig.
Baird 1960, pp. 28-29 and fig.
Bille 1961, vol. I, p. 105
Constable 1964, p. 117
Washington 1965, p. 124, no. 677
Washington 1968, p. 111, no. 677 and fig.
Reynolds / Malone 1971, p. 71
Buist 1974, p. 492
De Vries 1977, pp. 53-54 and 130, note 91 and p. 162, no. 97

1
Aert Schouman
The Collectors Jan and Pieter Bisschop with Olivier Hope
Panel, 35.5 x 43.1 cm (14 x 17 in.)
Lower left: *A. Schouman 1753*
Blair Atholl, Blair Castle, collection of the Duke of Atholl

Niemeijer 1978, p. 187
Braun 1980, pp. 83 and 110-111, no. 180 and fig., no. 181
Niemeijer 1981, pp. 166 and 197, no. 216
Berlin / London / Philadelphia 1984, pp. 294-295 and fig. 2
Walker 1984, pp. 290-291, no. 379 and fig.
Washington 1985, p. 381, no. 1942.9.81 and fig.
Sutton 1986, p. 309 and fig. 461

figures; by *Jan Steen*, h.[igh] 3 f.[eet] 3 i.[inches], br.[oad] 4 f.[eet] 6 and a half i.[nches]' (in translation).[4] The painting appears to have been bought in 1737 at an anonymous auction in The Hague for 140 guilders (perhaps by the Bisschop brothers).[5] The house on the Leuvehaven attracted many curious foreigners. The Pole Mniszech reported on his visit of around 1766, when he encountered the eighty-six-year-old Jan Bisschop wearing a dressing gown as well as a wig and hat, and in a grouchy mood. Amid the abundance of masterpieces, Mniszech took no particular notice of the piece by Jan Steen.[6]

Jan Bisschop's friend Olivier Hope was an adventurer and something of the black sheep in a family of Rotterdam ship-owners of English origin. His father, Isaac Hope, had earned his fortune from, among other things, transports that took thousands of British immigrants to America.[7] Olivier shared his interest in art with the much older Bisschop brothers, who, as faithful members of the Baptist church, were his fellow believers. Also Baptist were both of Olivier's uncles, who gained world renown in Amsterdam with their banking firm Thomas & Adrian Hope. In 1771 these Amsterdam Hopes, of whom only Thomas had descendants, 'inherited' the Bisschop collection. That is to say, the son of Thomas Hope, John Hope, and his aging bachelor uncle Adrian acquired the collection for 65,000 guilders, while

this sum of money went to the Baptist congregation of Rotterdam.[8] Adrian Hope (1709-1781) provided the money, and his nephew looked after the collection.

In 1762 John Hope (1737-1784), as the only son of Thomas, was taken into the firm, which was subsequently called Hope & Co.[9] In 1764 he married the daughter of the Rotterdam burgomaster, Philippina Barbara van der Hoeven (1738-1790).[10] After the death of his father in 1779 and his uncle Adrian in 1781, John was the sole heir of the Bisschop collection, which he steadily expanded. In the latter year, Sir Joshua Reynolds visited 'The Cabinet of Mr. Hope' and described the painting by Steen as: 'Merry making, two of the figures dancing.'[11] John Hope also bought several houses in Amsterdam and The Hague, as well as some country estates. In 1784 he acquired Bosbeek House near Heemstede, in which he intended to keep his collection of paintings. However, John Hope died at the age of forty-nine, before the renovations were completed. The paintings were inherited by his children, and in 1785 the widow, who was also their guardian, had an inventory drawn up. In it, the painting by Jan Steen was mentioned as intended for Bosbeek House: 'A merry Company or peasant Wedding dancing & playing in front of an Inn, with a great number of spectators. 39 x 55. D.' (in translation).[12] In 1794 the three Hope sons arrived at a division of the inheritance. In that same year the Netherlands were threatened by French invasion, and the Orangeist Hopes decided to take refuge in England. 'The nucleus of the old Bisschop collection left the country, never more to return,' ascertained Niemeijer (in translation) in his impressive reconstruction of the Bisschop and Hope collections.[13]

Initiallly the Hope Cabinet found refuge in the house of Henry Hope (1736-1811) in Harley Street, near Cavendish Square in London.[14] In 1811 Henry Philip Hope (1774-1839) became the owner of the paintings, but being a bachelor who lived by turns in Holland and London, he asked his brother Thomas Hope of Deepdene (1769-1831) [2] to accept responsibility for the care of the collection.[15] In 1819 Thomas had a gallery that was specifically intended for the paintings added to his house in Duchess Street (Portland Place).[16] After the death of the three brothers, Thomas (in 1831), Adrian Elias (in 1834), and Henry Philip (in 1839), Thomas's eldest son Henry Thomas Hope (1808-1862) inherited the London family residence and collection. From 1811 to 1851 the collection (including Jan Steen's *Dancing Couple at an Inn*) was in Duchess Street, where, according to Watkin, the Hope biographer, it rivaled that of the Prince Regent in size and quality.[17] During his study journey

2
Sir William Beechy
Portrait of Thomas Hope (1769-1831)
Canvas, 221.6 x 168.9 cm (87¼ x 66½ in.)
Signature unknown (ca. 1798-1799)
London, National Portrait Gallery, inv. no. 4574

Jan Steen Dancing Couple at an Inn

of 1837-1838 through England, the historian Waagen saw the paintings in Duchess Street, where he noted that Steen's painting was 'rich in humorous ideas, and full of life.'[18]

However, Henry Thomas left the property in Duchess Street and moved in 1851 to a new residence in Piccadilly.[19] A year before his death in 1862, his daughter and only child, Henrietta Adela, married the Duke of Newcastle. The widow of Henry Thomas, the Frenchwoman Adèle Bichat, lived until 1884, when she left the paintings to Henrietta's second son. Lord Henry Francis Hope Pelham-Clinton-Hope became the last English owner of Jan Steen's *Dancing Couple at an Inn*.[20] From 1891 to 1898 the greater portion of the paintings from the Hope collection was to be seen in the South Kensington Museum in London. A catalogue claimed that the ancestors had bought most of the pieces in Amsterdam in the seventeenth century, 'direct from the easels of the masters.'[21] The provenance from the Bisschop collection was totally forgotten and replaced with a misleading legend. In 1898 a judge of the High Court was required to grant permission to sell the collection. The eighty-three paintings then fell into the hands of the dealers Colnaghi & Wertheimer in New Bond Street for 121,550 pounds sterling.[22] The Bisschop-Hope collection was dispersed over the whole globe. In 1901 Peter A.B. Widener (p. 42, fig. 29) bought Jan Steen's *Dancing Couple at an Inn* from the dealer Agnew & Sons.[23] In 1942 the Widener collection became national property (see cat. no. 35).

During the nineteenth century the Hope family regularly lent the painting by Steen for exhibitions at the British Institution and the Royal Academy in London (1818, 1849, 1866, and 1881). The Wideners in their turn also lent it to a couple of major exhibitions, this time in America (New York, 1909; Detroit, 1925).[24] The painting was missing from the great Jan Steen exhibition of 1958-1959 in the Mauritshuis, but an alternate, mirror-image version was shown, which was then still in the possession of the Duchess of Brissac (location unknown)

[3].[25] This painting, which is only just over half the size, is not dated, and is on panel. It was assumed at the time that Steen made the smaller painting before the larger version.[26] But when one compares the illustrations, that is hardly a plausible suggestion. Slight but also substantial differences exist, such as the farmer with the wicker bird cage, who has been left out of the panel painting, and a copse of trees that has been put in his place. The basket that hangs from the ivy in the Washington painting is missing. In addition, a dog is substituted for the bench with the stone jug, a hat lies in the middle of the ground, and the dancing man has his cap in his hand. The man next to the open door grabs the hand of the waitress, whereas in the Widener version he smirkingly feels in his pocket (for money?). The upward-pointed shoe of the man sitting on the ground has also been altered. Especially these latter two changes make the smaller variant the much less witty one. Furthermore, the perspective rendering of the tabletop in this work is a little too clumsy. All in all, it looks as if it was not Jan Steen at work here, but a later copyist. However, certainty on this point is not possible until this copy becomes available for comparison.[27]

The catalogue of that Steen exhibition assumed that we can recognize the painter himself in one of the men behind the table. Steen rather often used models from his immediate surroundings, and it may well be he who strokes his own Grietje van Goyen under the chin. The bearded old man at the head of the table is, in any case, the same as the aged 'new father' in *'The Way You Hear It, Is the Way You Sing It'* (The Hague, Mauritshuis) (see p. 70, fig. 13),[28] in which Jan, Grietje, and their children have also been identified. It is striking that the merry companies of both scenes contain the same number of children: two overgrown boys, two slightly younger children, and a baby. It therefore looks as if in the painting in Washington Jan Steen also employed extras whom he saw around him daily.

The depiction lends itself to several possible interpretations. According to Gudlaugsson, it shows a scene from the popular theater, in which context he thought especially of *The Wedding of Kloris and Roosje*.[29] This piece by Dirck Buysero and Jac. van Rijndorp became popular in the eighteenth century as a postlude to Vondel's *Gijsbrecht van Amstel* and was chosen as a subject by Cornelis Troost and others. It first appeared in print only in 1688.[30] It is therefore improbable that Steen was already informed of its contents in 1663. Moreover, the dancing pair of the painting is not recognizably a bridal couple. It is more likely that Steen translated a Flemish country dance or wedding into contemporary and Dutch guise, on which Troost elaborated

---

3
Jan Steen (copy after)
Dancing Couple at an Inn
Panel, 59 x 37 cm (23¼ x 14⅝ in.)
On the left side of the large stone (not autograph?):
JSteen (after 1663)
Location unknown

in the following century. It so happens that Lyckle de Vries assumed that Steen emulated a composition from the school of Brueghel, which is an attractive train of thought.[31] However, the example (by Pieter Brueghel III?) that he offered might be better replaced by Pieter Aertsen's *Country Inn with Dancing Couple* (Cleveland, Ohio, private collection) [4],[32] a painting which has only recently been rediscovered.

Thus Steen stages a bit of theater – but not a play – with several acquaintances in an amusing ensemble: the men are noisy and insolent, the women smile timidly. In particular, the men in the background do things behind the backs of the remaining guests that are not entirely fit to be seen. Almost unnoticed, the painter presents an admonition along with the guzzling of the older folks. The child behind the seated couple at the right somewhat secretively blows soap bubbles from a small bowl, with which Steen apparently transmitted a moralizing message that was well understood in the seventeenth century. The combination of an exuberantly feasting company with an almost casual reference to the fact that human existence is as fragile as a soap bubble was right up Jan Steen's alley. It is, for instance, at the heart of the painting that has been called *The Life of Man* (The Hague, Mauritshuis).[33] Perhaps other details (such as the broken eggs) are also significant. Sutton assumed that it is 'surely not accidental that the traditionally lascivious bird seller is seen mugging between the dancing couples,' because the figure was intended to refer to 'birding' in the sense of making love.[34] If that is so, the deletion of the bird seller in the copy gains significance; it looks like an expurgated version, and it is therefore certainly not an autograph work.

1 *Niemeijer 1978*, p. 183, pl. v. Jan was baptized in 1699, and Pieter in 1710 – he was presumably eleven years younger, and must therefore have been born around 1690.
2 *Wiersum 1910*, pp. 5-9
3 *Bille 1961*, vol. I, pp. 97-98; *Niemeijer 1978*, pp. 184 and 185, fig. 2
4 *Hoet 1752-1770*, vol. II, p. 530
5 *Hoet 1752-1770*, vol. III, p. 11, no. 7; only Hoet mentions the auction catalogue (see cat. no. 19, note 4).
6 *Van Riemsdijk 1892*, pp. 223-224, note 1; *Bille 1961*, vol. I, pp. 99-100; Gustaf Adolf Sparre (cat. no. 53), too, visited (in 1768) the Bisschop brothers, see *Hasselgren 1974*, pp. 42-43.
7 *Niemeijer 1978*, p. 182
8 *Bille 1961*, vol. II, p. 104; *Niemeijer 1981*, pp. 146-147 and 223, note 42
9 *Buist 1974*, pp. 15-16 and fig.; *Niemeijer 1981*, p. 133
10 *Watkin 1968*, p. 5; *Buist 1974*, pp. 17-18; see also the family tree of the Hopes in *Niemeijer 1981*, p. 131
11 *Reynolds / Malone 1971*, vol. II, p. 77
12 *Niemeijer 1981*, pp. 129 and 197, no. 216
13 *Niemeijer 1981*, p. 168; see also *Van Eijnden / Van der Willigen 1816-1820 / 1976*, vol. II, pp. 413-414
14 *Buist 1974*, p. 492: on 17 December 1795 the paintings were insured for 26,000 pounds; *Niemeijer 1978*, p. 186
15 *Niemeijer 1978*, p. 186; the complicated circumstance surrounding the inheritance are elucidated in *Law / Law 1925*, see *Niemeijer 1978*, p. 189, note 23.
16 *Niemeijer 1978*, p. 186; *Niemeijer 1981*, pp. 168-169
17 *Watkin 1968*, p. 35
18 *Waagen 1854*, vol. II, p. 118
19 *Watkin 1968*, pp. 189-190
20 *Niemeijer 1978*, p. 187; *Watkin 1968*, p. 191
21 *Wertheimer 1891 / 1898*, 'Introduction'
22 Ibidem
23 *Braun 1980*, p. 110, no. 180, stated that he did not know the location of the painting.
24 See Bibliography
25 HdG 585 [is 479]; *The Hague 1958-1959*, no. 18 and fig.; *Braun 1980*, p. 111, no. 181 and fig.
26 *The Hague 1958-1959*, no. 18: 'getekend: JSteen' and '1661-1662.'
27 *Braun 1980*, pp. 110-111, nos. 180-181, called it 'een eerdere versie of een hername' because of the ostensible differences in 'ondergeschikte details.'
28 Inv. no. 742; *Broos 1987*, pp. 355-359, no. 59 and fig.
29 *The Hague 1958-1959*, no. 18
30 *Niemeijer 1973*, pp. 81-88, 246-248, nos. 314 T-318 T, p. 429
31 *De Vries 1977*, p. 130, note 91; *Marlier 1969*, p. 442, fig. 288
32 *Genaille 1983*, pp. 118-119, fig. 6
33 Inv. no. 170; *Hoetink et al. 1985*, p. 444, no. 170 and fig.; *De Jongh 1967*, pp. 81-85 and figs. 70-71
34 *Sutton 1986*, p. 309
BB

4
Pieter Aertsen
Country Inn with Dancing Couple
Panel, 108 x 158 cm (43¹⁄₂ x 62¹⁄₄ in.)
Lower right: AP [with trident] 15 sep 15
Cleveland, Ohio, private collection

Jan Steen Doctor's Visit

Leyden 1626 – Leyden 1679

Panel, 46.3 x 36.8 cm (18¼ x 14½ in.)
Lower right: *JSteen* (js in ligature) (ca. 1663-1665)
Philadelphia, Pa., Philadelphia Museum of Art, John G. Johnson Collection, inv. no. 510

This *Doctor's Visit* by Jan Steen is to be seen in The Hague for the first time since the eighteenth century, when the panel was still part of the Van Heemskerck collection in that city. It has not been back in Holland since the turn of the nineteenth century. In 1792 the painting was bought by Pieter Fouquet, Jr. (1729-1800) (see cat. no. 2, fig. 2 and cat. no. 6, fig. 1), at the Wubbels auction in Amsterdam. Fouquet became well known, or infamous, as the dealer who, in the second half of the eighteenth century, orchestrated the massive export of Dutch masters of the Golden Century, especially to France and England (see cat. nos. 2, 14, 44, and 54).[1]

In 1806 the painting was offered for sale at Christie's in London at an auction of paintings that, according to the praise on the title page of the catalogue, had been acquired abroad: 'These pictures (Genuine Private Property) are the *élite* of whatever has been for many Years procurable in Holland.'[2] The collector was known as 'Mr. Crawford of Rotterdam' and the art dealer and chronicler Buchanan described him as 'a gentleman, who, on account of commercial pursuits, had resided many years in Holland.' There Crawford assembled his collection of just over thirty cabinet pieces, which he moved to London around 1805. However, we learn nothing more from English sources.[3] In 1806, for 63 pounds sterling, Lord Kinnaird became the owner of Steen's *Doctor's Visit*. Charles, the eighth Lord Kinnaird (1780-1826), represented Scotland in the House of Commons and, in May of 1806, married Lady Olivia FitzGerald.[4] Thus he bought the painting a month before his wedding. If it was a gift for his bride, he must have had an unusual sense of humor. For, according to the catalogue of the Crawford auction, it depicted 'The unexpected Return' and showed 'The Jealousy and Indifference of the Husband and Wife.'[5] The doctor dressed in black was apparently thought to be the husband, and the sick young lady his wife!

As we shall see, this interpretation is a good example of the complete failure to understand the meaning of many Dutch genre paintings that was so characteristic of most early non-Dutch collectors and 'connoisseurs.' In 1770 people at least still knew that Jan Steen had depicted himself in this painting: 'Behind her [the 'Little Lady'] stands *Jan Steen* himself, with

Provenance

Collection Jan Henry (Joan Hendrik) van Heemskerck, The Hague, before 1730
Collection Dowager van Heemskerck, The Hague, 1730-1766
Auction Van Heemskerck, The Hague, 1770 (ƒ314 to Cornelis van Heemskerck)
Auction Cornelis van Heemskerck, The Hague, 1783 (ƒ500 to Wubbels)
Collection Jan Wubbels, Amsterdam, 1783-1792
Auction Wubbels, Amsterdam, 1792 (ƒ520 to Pieter Fouquet)
Collection Crawford, Rotterdam, before 1806
Auction Crawford, London, 1806 (£63 to Lord Kinnaird)
Collection Charles Lord Kinnaird, Rossie Priory, Carse of Gowrie, Scotland, 1806-1826(?)
Auction Albert Levy, London, 1876 (£195 to Rutly)
Collection Jean Louis Miéville, London, before 1878-1899
Auction Miéville, London, 1899 (£760 to Agnew)
Collection John G. Johnson, Philadelphia, 1899 (from Agnew & Sons)
Philadelphia Museum of Art, Philadelphia, 1917 (bequest of John G. Johnson)

Bibliography

Auction The Hague 1770, pp. 43-44, no. 109
Auction The Hague 1783, pp. 3-4, no. 2
Auction Amsterdam 1792, p. 51, no. 292
Auction London 1806, p. 5, no. 13
Buchanan 1824, vol. II, p. 183, no. 13
Smith 1829-1842, vol. IV, p. 24, no. 76
Van Westrheene 1856, p. 159, no. 362
Auction London 1876, p. 67, no. 370
London 1878, p. 23, no. 113
Auction London 1899, p. 30, no. 83 and fig.
HdG 172 (vol. I [1907], p. 47, no. 164 and p. 49, no. 172)
HdG-MS 172
Grant 1908, pp. 144-145 and 149 and fig.
Valentiner 1913, p. 101, no. 510 and p. 355 and fig.
Graves 1913-1915, vol. III, p. 1258, no. 113 (1878)
Trautscholdt 1937, p. 511, nos. 164 and 172
McCall / Valentiner 1939, p. 174, no. 358 and pl. 74
Art Digest 1941, p. 28
Philadelphia 1941, p. 38, no. 510
De Groot 1952, p. 51, note 28 and p. 116, note 172
Philadelphia 1953, p. 166, no. 510 and fig.
Philadelphia 1972, p. 81, no. 510 and fig. opp. p. 285
Bedaux 1975, pp. 31, 33, 35 and fig. 18
De Vries 1976, pp. 16 and 76, fig. 44
De Vries 1977, pp. 58-59, 64, 99-100, 131, note 110, p. 148, note 138, p. 164, no. 123
Braun 1980, pp. 9, 132-133, no. 315 and fig.
Butler 1982-1983, pp. 45-47, 49-58 and fig. 5
Sutton 1982-1983, pp. 3, 4 and fig. 1, pp. 7, 21-24 and pl. 5
Berlin / London / Philadelphia 1984, pp. 296-298, no. 105 and fig., pp. 369-370, no. 105, notes 1-16
Sutton 1986, pp. 230-231 and fig. 338
Van Dijck / Koopman 1987, no. 169 and fig.

a Herring in the one, and Leeks or Onions in the other hand, wearing a jolly countenance' (in translation).[6] The painting was auctioned in that year as part of the estate of the Dowager van Heemskerck, Anna Petronella van Schuylenburch (1693-1766), daughter of the Hague burgomaster Willem van Schuylenburch. The auction was held in the house of mourning on the Noordeinde in The Hague, opposite the Oude Hof (Old Court). She had inherited the painting in 1730 from her husband, Jan Henry van Heemskerck, Lord of Achttienhoven, den Bosch, and Eyndschoten (1689-1730), and son of the renowned diplomat Coenraad van Heemskerck (1646-1702), from whom he had taken the title of Count of the Holy Roman Empire.[7] Joan Hendrik (as the auction catalogue called him) is as yet the earliest owner of the painting to be identified from the sources. How long he had owned Steen's *Doctor's Visit* at the time of his death in 1730 is not known. During the greater part of the eighteenth century, the panel remained in the possession of the family in The Hague. Cornelis van Heemskerck, the grandson of Coenraad, bought it back at the auction of his mother's estate.[8] This meant that the painting moved from the Noordeinde in The Hague to the Lange Voorhout. In 1771 Cornelis van Heemskerck built at number 32 one of the most beautiful patrician homes of the court capital. There are still four rooms with decorative paintings from 1773 and 1782 by Hendrik Willem Schweickhardt, and a room with decorations of 1773 by Dirck van der Aa.[9] There, only little more than a stone's throw from the Mauritshuis, the *Doctor's Visit* by Jan Steen hung until 1783, when Cornelis van Heemskerck died a bachelor and his collection came under the hammer.[10]

The subsequent peregrinations of the painting are only partly known. In a copy of the auction catalogue of 1783, the name of a 'baron nagel' is marked next to that of Jan Wubbels. Hofstede de Groot assumed that the buyer was the well-known collector Baron Von Nagel, and that identification has been repeated until recently. However, the painting does not feature in his estate of 1795.[11] Possibly Von Nagel bid on the painting, but it went to Jan Wubbels instead. The latter's collection was auctioned in 1792, and included in it was Jan Steen's *Doctor's Visit*. About the somewhat risqué subject, the auction catalogue of the sale observed: 'the different Characters are unusual[ly well] observed in this piece' (in translation).[12] Jan Wubbels was presumably a not-too-gifted painter of small seascapes, who was also an art dealer and later 'curator of the art cabinet of the old Gentleman *HOPE*' (in translation).[13] He appears to have lined and cleaned all the old master paintings owned by John Hope. The latter, too, was a collector, primarily of Dutch old masters.[14] Thus, chance would have it that Wubbels was in possession of Jan Steen's *Doctor's Visit* just when he was allowed to treat the latter's *Dancing Couple at an Inn* (cat. no. 59) for Hope.

The later locations of this painting, which after the Wubbels auction ended up in England by way of Fouquet and Crawford, are as yet only vaguely known. It was in the collections of Albert Levy and Jean Louis Miéville, which were auctioned in London in 1876 and 1899, respectively. The sources are also silent about these latter collectors. For a longer period the panel probably hung in Scotland, in the country estate Rossie Priory, which the eighth Lord Kinnaird had built in 1807 and where he housed his art collection, including paintings by Gainsborough and Reynolds.[15]

In 1899 the painting by Steen became an American possession for good. John Graver Johnson (1841-1917) bought it in May of 1899 from the dealer Agnew, who had only just purchased it at the Miéville auction in London. Around the turn of the century, the lawyer Johnson made several trips to Europe with his friend Peter A.B. Widener (p. 42, fig. 29), who shared his passion for collecting. It was his aim to build a comprehensive collection, in which all phases of the history of art would be represented. As well, he intended to serve society, and to this end he left his 1,279 paintings to his native city of Philadelphia when he died. From 1923 to 1933 his collection could be seen in his former residence at 510 South Broad Street, after which time the paintings were placed in a separate department of the Philadelphia Museum of Art. Not the museum but the city of Philadelphia itself owns Johnson's collection, and thus Steen's *Doctor's Visit*.[16]

A low point in the appreciation of the painting appears to have been the auction in 1806, when under the previously adduced title of 'The unexpected Return' the scene was explained as a depiction of 'Jealousy and Indifference.' Incredibly, the leer of the figure with the herring were explained as 'the Pleasure of the foolish Servant discovering the Supper prepared.'[17] We now

1
Jan Steen
The Gallant Offer
Canvas on panel, 79 x 64 cm (31⅛ x 25¼ in.)
Bottom right: *JSteen* (JS in ligature) (ca. 1664-1668)
Brussels, Musées royaux des Beaux-Arts,
inv. no. 1717

know that in popular speech the herring was seen as a phallic symbol.[18] Together with the two onions or garlic bulbs in the other hand of our guide (in whom we recognize Jan Steen himself) this naturally forms an image of the male sexual parts. Steen painted this depiction more than once. In a scene with the somewhat veiled name of *The Gallant Offer* (Brussels, Musées royaux des Beaux-Arts) [1],[19] a joker appears who, to the amusement of the ladies, storms into the room, holding up a herring with two onions below it. The reply of one of the 'gentlemen' is an obscene gesture. Did people in pre-Victorian England no longer recognize these witticisms, or were they no longer willing to acknowledge them? However, it is difficult to misconstrue Steen. To heighten the fun of the Philadelphia scene, he added a bed behind the broadly laughing figure, to indicate where the solution of the joke can be found. Of course the girl is sick with desire.

All of the ingredients of the scene by Jan Steen were easily recognizable for a keen observer. The doctor is called in to help but can offer none, for he is characterized as a charlatan, dealing in deceiving the public. Because of his old-fashioned clothing and silly high hat, he looks as if he had just escaped from one of the many theatrical comedies of the time.[20] The quack drew his pseudo-knowledge largely from studying the urine of the patient. Possibly even more popular as a diagnostic technique was the taking of the pulse. From the urine, it was believed, one could read the condition of the liver, and from the beating pulse, that of the heart.[21] In 1920 J.B.F. van Gils once more drew attention to one detail found in many of Steen's doctor paintings. It is the coal pan from which hangs a piece of burning lace or an apron string. According to popular belief, the smoke from a piece of blue ribbon, preferably taken from the pinafore, was an efficacious remedy for fainting, which was known as a specifically ladies' ailment.[22] In this context, the missive that the girl has dropped from her hand can only be a love letter. Like the doctor, the woman who makes music on the virginal is trying to help the lascivious girl, for music could exorcise melancholy. Love sickness and music were often depicted in combination.[23]

In case the visual message was still not clear enough, the artist added a written text, as in his *Doctor's Visit* painted between 1661 and 1663 (Munich, Alte Pinakothek) [2].[24] On the letter held by the sick woman, whose pulse is read by the quack, we read: 'Daar baat geen / medesyn / want het is / min[n]epyn' (No medicine is of help here, for it is love sickness). The only thing that can bring relief from the burning love in this picture is the presence or return of a (or the) lover. No wonder, then, that the lover at the door is hailed with joy. Of course the amazement of the silly doctor in the painting in Philadelphia is due to the sudden improvement in his patient. This makes us laugh because we know what is happening behind his back. It is really incomprehensible that in 1806 people were so blind to what Steen displayed so openly.

1 *Bille 1961*, vol. I, pp. 196-197
2 *Auction London 1806*, title page
3 *Buchanan 1824*, vol. II, pp. 180-181; *Maclaren 1960*, p. 21, no. 820; according to *McCall / Valentiner 1939*, p. 174, no. 358, this Crawford was identical with the writer Quintin Craufurd (1743-1819), but that is an invention.
4 *Auction London 1806*, p. 5, no. 13 (copy RKD); *Buchanan 1824*, vol. II, p. 183, no. 13; DNB, vol. XXXI, p. 189
5 *Auction London 1806*, p. 5, no. 13
6 *Auction The Hague 1770*, pp. 43-44, no. 109
7 NNBW, vol. IX, cols. 333-334; *Elias 1903-1905*, vol. I, pp. 76-77
8 *Auction The Hague 1770*, p. 43
9 *Sluijter 1975*, pp. 147, 151, 153-156, figs. 4, 5, 9, 10, 12-14; *De Regt 1986*, pp. 88-90
10 *Auction The Hague 1783*, p. 3, no. 2
11 *Auction The Hague 1783*, p. 3, no. 2 (copy RKD); HdG 172; L 5286
12 *Auction Amsterdam 1792*, p. 51, no. 292
13 *Van Eijnden / Van der Willigen 1816-1820*, vol. III, p. 414
14 *Niemeijer 1981*, p. 148; *Auction Amsterdam 1792* (together with the work of Jan van der Heyden, David Teniers and Philips Wouwermans, the canvas by Steen was among the most expensive paintings).
15 DNB, vol. XXXI, p. 189
16 *Philadelphia 1953*, pp. v-vi; *Philadelphia 1972*, pp. v-vi; *Sutton 1979*, p. 387; *Art Digest 1941*, pp. 8 and 28
17 *Auction London 1806*, p. 5, no. 13
18 *Bax 1949*, pp. 34-35; *De Jongh 1968-1969*, p. 32; *Bedaux 1975*, p. 35; *Bax 1979*, pp. 218-219
19 HdG 385; *Brussels 1984*, p. 284, no. 1717 and fig.; *Braun 1980*, p. 117, no. 224 and fig.
20 *Gudlaugsson 1945*, pp. 8-23; *Sutton 1982-1983*, p. 24, notes 20-21
21 *Bedaux 1975*, p. 17
22 *Van Gils 1920*, pp. 200-201
23 See *Bandmann 1960*
24 HdG 138; *Munich 1983*, pp. 504-505, no. 158 and fig.; *Braun 1980*, p. 107, no. 154 and fig.
BB

2
Jan Steen
Doctor's Visit
Canvas, 61 x 52.1 cm (24 x 20½ in.)
On the letter: *JSteen* (JS in ligature) (ca. 1661-1663)
Munich, Alte Pinakothek, inv. no. 158

Jan Steen The Wrath of Ahasuerus (not in San Francisco)

Leyden 1626 – Leyden 1679

Canvas, 70 x 92.9 cm (27½ x 36⅝ in.)
Neither signed nor dated (ca. 1668)
Cleveland, Ohio, The Cleveland Museum of Art, inv. no. 64.153

In his discussion of the Jan Steen exhibition in Leyden in 1926, Willem Martin, then the director of the Mauritshuis, called the discovery of a series of hitherto unknown works by the so-called *kluchtschilder* (painter of farce) one of its most important outcomes.[1] One of these paintings was *The Wrath of Ahasuerus*, now in Cleveland, which was then in the Dreesmann collection in Amsterdam. The pre-1900 provenance of this painting is difficult to determine because Steen depicted this biblical story more than once, and the oldest auction catalogues usually do not mention the dimensions of canvases or panels. Nevertheless, is assumed here that this painting circulated for a long time in various Amsterdam collections. It was probably the version in the collection of Willem Six (1662-1733), scion of the well-known patrician dynasty, three times burgomaster of Amsterdam and confirmed bachelor. He left behind an important collection of paintings, with no fewer than eighteen Rembrandts.[2] From the hand of Jan Steen he owned *De Maaltyd* [Meal] *van Hester en Haman*, which may well be identical with the painting in Cleveland.[3] He had probably acquired it 1727 in Amsterdam, where it came under the hammer once more in 1752, at the D. Reus auction, as *De koning* [king] *Asveros, Hester en Haman*.[4] Mention must be made that a painting of this kind was also to be found in a seventeenth-century collection. On 9 December 1684 a *Hester en Haman door* [by] *Jan Steen* was described as part of the estate of Jan de Wijs of Amsterdam. It is certainly highly speculative to propose that this refers to the painting now in Cleveland.[5] Nonetheless, it was identical with a painting that was sold in Amsterdam in 1764. On this occasion it was described as 'a rich Ordinance of eighteen Figures painted strongly and in detail on a Canvas' (in translation), and that is precisely what this painting shows us.[6]

At some unknown time this biblical piece by Jan Steen was bought from the dealer Douwes Brothers by W.J.R. Dreesmann (1885-1954) [1]. He was the director of the Amsterdam drapery business Vroom & Dreesmann and head of the board of various

Provenance

(?) Collection Jan de Wijs, Amsterdam, 1684
(?) Auction Amsterdam, 1727
(?) Auction Willem Six, Amsterdam, 1734 (*f*19.5 to Jan Hendrik Mos)
(?) Auction D. Reus, Amsterdam, 1752
Auction Amsterdam, 1764 (*f*151 to P. Yver)
Dealer Douwes Bros., Amsterdam, before 1926
Collection W.J.R. Dreesmann, Amsterdam, 1926-1954
Museum Dreesmann, Amsterdam, before 1938-1954
Collection heirs Dreesmann, Wassenaar, 1954-1960
Auction Dreesmann, Amsterdam, 1960 (*f*40,000)
Dealer Douwes Bros., Amsterdam, 1960-1962
Dealer G. Cramer, The Hague, 1963
The Cleveland Museum of Art, Cleveland, 1964 (John L. Severance Fund)

Bibliography

Hoet 1752-1770, vol. I, p. 417, no. 124
Auction Amsterdam 1764, p. 6, no. 30
Leyden 1926, p. 21, no. 37
Bredius 1927, pp. 29 and 105, no. 7 and fig. 8
Martin 1927-1928, p. 325
HdG-MS, no. 19A
Amsterdam 1929, p. 40, no. 139
Trautscholdt 1937, p. 511, no. 19A
Amsterdam 1939, p. 51, no. 60f
Heppner 1939-1940, p. 42, note 2 and pl. 4d
Berendsen 1952, p. 44, no. 88 and fig. 50
Birmingham 1952, p. 102 and fig.
Amsterdam 1955, p. 18, no. 59 and fig.
Pigler 1956, vol. I, p. 203
Tel Aviv 1959, no. 106
Auction Amsterdam 1960, p. 6, no. 15 and fig.
WCA, vol. XII (1960), p. 440, no. 4961
Amsterdam 1962, no. 23 and fig.
Florence 1963, p. 304 and fig.
Art Quarterly 1964, pp. 372 and 382 and fig.
Burlington Magazine 1964, p. 303 and pl. 1
Bury 1964, p. 48 and fig.
Tzeutschler Lurie 1965, pp. 94-100 and fig. 9 (and cover)
Cleveland 1966, no. 166 and fig.
Cleveland 1970, p. 125 and fig.
Pigler 1974, vol. I, p. 203
Bader 1976, pp. 128-129, no. 59 and fig.
Kirschenbaum 1977, pp. 48, 50, 66, 70, 78, 80, 88, 98, 119 and no. 19a, pp. 120, 207 and fig. 74
Cleveland 1978, p. 162 and fig.
Braun 1980, p. 129, no. 300 and fig., p. 130, no. 301
Amsterdam / Detroit / Washington 1980-1981, pp. 282-283, no. 85 and fig.
Cleveland 1982, pp. 274-275, no. 121 and fig.
Reitlinger 1982, vol. I, p. 457
Sutton 1986, pp. 64-65 and fig. 90

1
Bep Westendorp-Osieck
Portrait of W.J.R. Dreesmann (1885-1954) (detail)
Chalk drawing, 242 x 398 mm (9½ x 15⅝ in.)
Lower left: *B. Westendorp-Osieck Febr. 1942.*
Amsterdam, Gemeentearchief, Dreesmann collection, inv. no. 36 10-46

cultural institutions. It was on his initiative that the Museum Dreesmann, a now long-defunct and largely forgotten institution, was founded. Dreesmann collected paintings, prints, drawings, and books about the topography and history of Amsterdam (today these materials may be found under the heading of Dreesmann Atlas in the Municipal Archives of Amsterdam), as well as Rembrandt etchings, old master paintings, and works by Jan Toorop. In the late thirties the Dutch state recognized his house at 2 Johannes Vermeerstraat in Amsterdam as a museum, which could be visited under certain conditions.[7] From 1950 on, the former residence was opened to the public, and one could see there an important collection of Vondelliana and, for example, a complete porcelain tea service with views of Amsterdam custom made in China. After the collector passed on, his family decided to liquidate the collection. The property at 2 Johannes Vermeerstraat was auctioned on 23 May 1954: it presently houses the Art-Historical Institute of the University of Amsterdam. For several years the collection remained in the hands of the Dreesmann heirs, but it was finally sold over the course of four days in March 1960 for a total of 4,250,000 guilders.[8] *The Wrath of Ahasuerus* fetched 40,000 guilders.[9]

Four years later The Cleveland Museum of Art was the new owner. The museum was able to buy the painting in 1964 using the fund established by John Long Severance (1863-1936), who had been president of the museum and the most important benefactor of its collection.[10] At that time the advisor for the European department of the museum was Wolfgang Stechow, Professor in the History of Art at Oberlin College. In 1958 he had accompanied the acquisition of Jan Steen's *Merry Company* by the Allen Memorial Art Museum in Oberlin with an article in the museum bulletin.[11] In it he reconstructed the oeuvre of Steen around 1668. It was to be expected that, in 1964, Cleveland was also able to profit from his connoisseurship. *The Wrath of Ahasuerus* is also generally dated to 1668.[12] Kirschenbaum placed it in a group of twenty history pieces, generally with dramatic subjects, of the late Haarlem period, of which three have the date 1667 or 1668.[13] The work was lent to the exhibitions of Dutch history painting (Milwaukee, 1976) and seventeenth-century Dutch history painting (Amsterdam, Detroit, Washington, 1980-1981), and has been chosen for the present exhibition in part because Sutton called it 'one of the finest Dutch history paintings in Cleveland.'[14]

Of the various versions that Steen painted of this subject, one has been lost without a trace [2].[15] It is a repetition of the work in Cleveland with only minor differences. Abraham Bredius knew

it from the collection of Count Potocki in Paris (where Hofstede de Groot had also seen it), and in his monumental monograph of 1927 Bredius compared it to the version that was then with Dreesmann. He thought the latter version more handsome, although Ahasuerus was a bit too much of a ham for his tastes and Esther presumably showed too little expression. He thought her – and also the maid to the left – more beautifully painted than in Count Potocki's version, whereas, according to him, the despair of Haman was more subtly represented in the Dreesmann painting.[16] Whether this variant is an autograph replica or a later copy cannot be determined on the basis of a

▲ **2**
Jan Steen (copy after?)
The Wrath of Ahasuerus
Canvas, 83 x 100 cm (32⅝ x 39⅜ in.)
Neither signed nor dated (after 1668)
Location unknown

► **3**
Jan Steen
The Wrath of Ahasuerus
Canvas, 129 x 167 cm (50¾ x 65¾ in.)
Lower left: *JSteen* (ca. 1668-1670)
Birmingham, The Barber Institute of Fine Arts,
inv. no. B 68

mediocre reproduction. Bredius observed a signature on the piece in Cleveland, but nothing now remains to be seen.[17] Bredius also knew the scene of *The Wrath of Ahasuerus* at the University of Birmingham (The Barber Institute of Fine Arts) [**3**], which he thought the best of the three.[18] This composition is a mirror image of the one in Cleveland, whereas the pose of Esther may be seen as a repetition. This cannot be said of the leaping Ahasuerus, who rolls his eyes frightfully, and Haman, who almost crawls under the table with fear. The peacock pie that tumbles from the table is the focal point of this extremely baroque composition.

It is sometimes assumed that the figures of Ahasuerus in these depictions were borrowed from the famous painting of around 1635 by Rembrandt: *The Feast of Balthasar* (London, National Gallery).[19] Whether or not this is the case, both Rembrandt and Jan Steen appear to have been familiar with Pieter Lastman's *Haman Begging Esther for Mercy* (Warsaw, Muzeum Narodowe) [**4**],[20] which has been called the prototype for an extended series of related history pieces of the seventeenth century.[21] In all instances, the peacock pie on the table reminds us of this example, as does the wildly arm-swinging Ahasuerus. However, more clearly than in Lastman's prototype, the painting in Cleveland incorporates a much earlier visual source, namely the print by Philips Galle after Maarten van Heemskerck [**5**].[22] Relating these images is the central place of the Persian king behind the table at which, to his left and right (respectively the right and left), Esther and Haman are seated. In the background we see vistas through arches and, behind the throne of Ahasuerus, a kind of baldachin in which a glass sphere hangs. Why Steen thought this detail so important that he took it from the print is an intriguing question, which still begs for an explanation.[23]

Steen and many of his fellow painters repeatedly chose the history of Esther as a subject.[24] Because it concerns the Jews who cast off the Persian yoke, it reminded the Dutch of their own revolt against the Spaniards. Both writers and visual artists used the theme. Owing to its surprising moments and intrigues, the story lent itself to all sorts of dramatic treatments. At the Jewish feast of the Purim, the biblical book of Esther was read from a scroll in the synagogue, and Purim plays and costume parties for this feast day arose at a later date. At least three plays with Esther in the main role appeared in Holland before 1655: *Haman. Treurspel* (Haman. Tragedy) by Jacob Revius (Deventer 1630); *Esther, ofte 't Beeldt der Ghehoorsaamheid* (Esther; or, the Picture of Obedience) by Nicolaes Fonteyn (Amsterdam 1638); and *Hester oft Verlossing der Joden* (Esther; or, the Salvation of the

4
Pieter Lastman
Haman Begging Esther for Mercy
Panel, 52 x 78 cm (20½ x 30¾ in.)
Upper middle: *P. Lastman fecit. A 161[?]*
Warsaw, Muzeum Narodowe, inv. no. M.Ob. 558

5
Philips Galle after Maarten van Heemskerck
Haman, Ahasuerus, and Esther
Engraving, 190 x 243 mm (7½ x 9⅝ in.)
Below center: *MHEE.IN.* (MH in ligature)
(ca. 1560-1565)
Amsterdam, Rijksprentenkabinet

Jews) by Johannes Serwouters (Amsterdam 1659).[25] The latter piece particularly was repeatedly reprinted throughout the seventeenth century.[26]

Though in his paintings Jan Steen depicted the world as the proverbial stage, it may well be going too far to propose that he here located the biblical story of Esther in the playhouse of Amsterdam.[27] The decor that Jacob van Campen designed in 1637, known to us from a print by Salomon Saverij [6],[28] was replaced in 1665 with a deeper scene with movable parts.[29] The composition of Steen's biblical piece generally resembles the original stage, with its two rear exits, columns, and curtains, but it may just as well have been taken from the print by Galle [5]. Steen certainly helped himself to reminiscences of the theater. The actors are dressed in stage costumes: Haman especially is got up as an old-fashioned buffoon.[30] The court jester at the right, with his crooked hat and mocking grimace, is a direct reference to the contemporary stage, in which he played a fixed part. The gestures of the principal figures are highly theatrical, and there is no greater contrast imaginable than between this and the almost dignified depictions that De Gelder made of diverse episodes of the book of Esther (see cat. no. 21). One can well imagine that Steen sought above all to convey the atmosphere of the theater. Possibly as he painted there resounded in his ears the dramatic words spoken by the actors in the fifth act of Serwouters's play, when Esther has revealed that Haman wants to destroy the Jews (and therefore herself, the king's wife): 'Ahasuerus: Fie, Haman, curse now openly the hour of thy birth. Haman: Where can I hide? I dare no longer look at the Monarch. Woe is me! I have myself brewed this misfortune. My eminence takes, Oh Gods! a wondrous turn' (in translation).[31]

1 *Martin 1927-1928*, p. 325
2 *De Boer 1948*, pp. 27-29
3 *Auction Amsterdam 1734*, p. 13, no. 125; *Kirschenbaum 1977*, p. 120, no. 20b
4 *Kirschenbaum 1977*, p. 120, nos. 20a and 21; *Hoet 1752-1770*, vol. I, p. 320, no. 16, vol. II, p. 339, no. 24
5 *Bredius 1927*, p. 100
6 *Auction Amsterdam 1764*, p. 6, no. 30
7 *Brugmans / Japikse 1938*, p. 386
8 *Kruizinga / Banning 1966*, p. 140
9 *WCA*, vol. XII (1960), p. 440, no. 4961; *Reitlinger 1982*, vol. I, p. 457
10 *Millikin 1943*, p. 25-26; *Comstock 1943*, pp. 61-62
11 Inv. no. 57.14; HdG 593; *Stechow 1967*, p. 143 and 255, fig. 68; *Braun 1980*, pp. 134-135, no. 325 and fig.; *Stechow 1958*
12 *Tzeutschler Lurie 1965*, p. 94; *Kirschenbaum 1977*, p. 119, no. 19a; *Tzeutschler Lurie in Cleveland 1982*, p. 275
13 *Kirschenbaum 1977*, pp. 49-50
14 *Sutton 1986*, p. 64
15 HdG 19; *Kirschenbaum 1977*, p. 119, no. 19 and fig. 75
16 *Bredius 1927*, p. 29
17 *Bredius 1927*, p. 105, no. 7
18 HdG 18; *Bredius 1927*, p. 29; *Kirschenbaum 1977*, pp. 118-119, no. 18 and fig. 59; *Birmingham 1952*, p. 102 and fig.
19 Inv. no. 6350; *Gerson / Bredius 1969*, pp. 408 and 598, no. 497 and fig.
20 *Brunswick etc. 1988-1990*, pp. 24-27, no. 1 and fig.
21 *Kahr 1966*, p. 228, note 3
22 *Hollstein*, vol. VIII, p. 243, nos. 248-255
23 For a possible parallel in a work by Vermeer, see *De Jongh 1975-1976*, pp. 71-74, figs. 1-3
24 *Pigler 1974*, vol. I, pp. 198-204; *Kirschbaum / Braunfels*, vol. I, cols. 684-687
25 *Van de Waal 1969*, p. 218, note 55
26 *Heppner 1939-1940*, p. 41
27 *Tzeutschler Lurie 1965*, p. 98 and fig. 2
28 *Hollstein*, vol. XXIV, p. 12, no. 15
29 *Gudlaugsson 1951*, p. 181 and fig. 1; *Hummelen 1967*, figs. XXI-XXIV; *Kirschenbaum 1977*, p. 78
30 *Gudlaugsson 1945*, pp. 54-56 and figs. 57-58
31 *Serwouters 1659 / 1698*, p. 49
BB

6

Salomon Saverij
The Stage of the Amsterdam Playhouse
Engraving, 516 x 733 cm (20⅜ x 28⅞ in.)
Below the depiction, among other things: *in 't Iaar 1658*
Amsterdam, Rijksprentenkabinet, F.M. 1779

Amersfoort(?) ca. 1600 – Sicily(?) after 1649

Canvas, 158.7 x 128.5 cm (62½ x 50⅝ in.)
Neither signed nor dated (ca. 1630)
Greenville, N.C., Bob Jones University Collection, inv. no. P.59.172

Even though all sources call him Stom, the practice of writing this artist's surname as Stomer has come to be widely adopted. An untraceable notice recorded that he came from Amersfoort. Possibly his fellow townsman Paulus Bor encouraged him to go to Rome. He lived there in the same house as did Bor, who had returned to his native city in 1626. Before Stomer was in Rome (in 1630), he must have become acquainted in Utrecht with the Caravaggists Ter Brugghen and Honthorst. In 1632 he was in Naples but then moved permanently to Sicily, where he received important commissions from churches and private patrons. Don Antonio Ruffo Duke of Messina, Rembrandt's Maecenas of later years, bought diverse works of Stomer's up to 1649. After that date we hear nothing more of the painter.

Provenance
Collection Schieffelin Crosby, Cold Spring, N.Y.
Dealer Victor D. Spark, New York, before 1941-1959
Wadsworth Atheneum, Hartford, Conn., 1941-1942
(on loan from Victor D. Spark)
Bob Jones University Collection, Greenville, 1959
(purchased from Victor D. Spark)

Bibliography
Pauwels 1953, pp. 164-165, fig. 9
Art Quarterly 1960, pp. 302 and 306, fig. Top 3
Greenville 1962, vol. II, pp. 200 and 290-291, no. 169 and fig.
Hope 1965-1966, p. 161 and fig. 24
Nicolson 1977, p. 241, no. 3
Nicolson 1979, p. 93
Steel 1984, pp. 16 and 128-130, no. 40 and fig.
Sutton 1986, p. 99 and fig. 139

'Matteo Stom fiam[min]go' must have been virtually a stranger in his own land, assuming that he was indeed born in the Northern Netherlands. His relatively extensive oeuvre – which consists largely of biblical pieces – was painted mainly in Italy, where, as of 1630, he found the ecclesiastical patrons who were, at least officially, not to be found in Protestant Holland. The painting *Lot Leaving Sodom*, however, may still have been executed in the Netherlands. It shows a great affinity with the style of the Utrecht Caravaggists. The canvas was on the art market for a long time and was given on loan for a few years to one of the oldest museums in the United States, the Wadsworth Atheneum in Hartford, Connecticut (1941-1942). The collection of the Bob Jones University at Greenville, North Carolina, now constitutes an appropriate environment for this work (p. 97, fig. 15) because this collection concentrates on paintings with biblical scenes or religious figures. This conservative Christian institution describes itself as 'a non-denominational, co-educational, Christian liberal arts university standing without apology for the old-time religion and the absolute authority of the Bible.'[1] The Bob Jones Collection could be assembled relatively quickly at a time when biblical scenes were not greatly in demand with collectors. Until the 1960s, art works of the baroque period – if they were not by Rembrandt or Van Dyck – could still be obtained at favorable prices.[2] In part thanks to the 1980 exhibition *God, Saints, and*

Matthias Stomer Lot Leaving Sodom

Heroes,[3] Dutch religious art of the seventeenth century has only recently come to enjoy much favor. Significantly, for instance, one of the rare biblical history paintings by Karel du Jardin, *Saint Paul Healing the Lame Man from Lystra* (p. 72, fig. 16), fetched more than a million guilders at auction in December 1987, even though it had been appraised at a much lower amount.[4]

In the painting from Greenville, Stomer tells the story of Lot, Abraham's nephew, who flees Sodom, the city that did not number even ten virtuous people among its inhabitants. Two angels had visited Lot, and he was therefore called to explain himself before the people of the town. However, angels struck the Sodomites with blindness, and Lot fled the doomed city. 'And when the morning arose, then the angels hastened Lot, saying, Arise, take thy wife, and thy two daughters, which are here; lest thou be consumed in the iniquity of the city. And while he lingered, the men laid hold upon his hand, and upon the hand of his two daughters; the LORD being merciful unto him; and they brought him forth, and set him without the city' (Genesis 19:15-16).

Lot's flight is usually shown at the moment at which his wife looks back at the burning city and, as punishment, changes into the (now proverbial) pillar of salt (Genesis 19:26).[5] The fresco by Raphael and his collaborators in the Loggia of the Vatican is a good example of this.[6] In Stomer's case, on the contrary, Lot's wife still walks in the procession, which shows that the artist must have known one of Rubens's executions of this biblical episode. We have from the period between 1613 and 1615 three painted versions that are substantially the work of Rubens's shop assistants (in Tokyo, Sarasota, and Miami).[7] Although Stomer may have seen such a shop copy, the more plausible inference is that he used the famous print after Rubens engraved by Lucas Vorsterman in 1620 [**1**].[8] The arrangement of the fleeing group, though in mirror image to the print, is for the most part identical. The procession is preceded by a pointing angel with a flapping cloak, and a blonde daughter of Lot brings up the rear of the cortege and serves as *repoussoir* as well. She carries a basket with beakers and a jug, which signifies that she must be the first-born. It was she, we recall, who contrived the plan to intoxicate her father with wine in order to beget offspring without his knowledge (Genesis 19:31-33). To be sure, Lot allows himself to be carried along with less hubbub than in the print, but with the dog leading the way, our painter makes it clear that he studied the example in detail. Nevertheless, he rendered the depiction in his own formal language.

1
Lucas Vorsterman after Rubens
Lot Leaving Sodom
Engraving, 317 x 382 mm (12½ x 15 in.)
Lower right: *Lucas Vorsterman sculp. et excud. An.º*
1620.
Haarlem, Teylers Museum

Although the painting at Greenville is neither signed nor dated, it is relatively easy to place it in Stomer's oeuvre. Nicolson isolated a group of paintings that were made just before or after the painter arrived in Rome, that is, around 1630.[9] Characteristic of these works is the bright palette with many light blue, rose red, and yellowish gray elements, the muted flesh tints, and drapery passages with contrived folds. Gleaming locks of hair frame the softly rounded faces, as in the *Saint John the Baptist* (Amsterdam, Rijksmuseum).[10] This painting, which was for a long time the only known Stomer in the Dutch public domain,

2
Matthias Stomer
Tobias and the Angel
Canvas, 111 x 125 cm (43¾ x 49¼ in.)
On the block: *M. Stom* (ca. 1630-1632)
The Hague, Museum Bredius, inv. no. 202-1946

was described in 1757, when it was in the princely collection Het Loo, as being 'after the manner of Louis Carats [Lodovico Carracci]' (in translation).[11] The face of Saint John seems to repeat that of the young Tobias in *Tobias and the Angel* (The Hague, Museum Bredius) [2].[12] This is a characteristic early work, as well as being one of the few paintings that feature the authentic signature *M. Stom*.

The angel in the latter work is in turn virtually identical to the angel leading Lot out of Sodom. It is typical of Stomer's work that the painting is full of repetitions. If he was satisfied with a composition, he used it more than once, and he was apparently quite content to repeat the same motif. Thus the head of Lot is of a type that he used repeatedly in paintings with the apostle Peter. For instance, the mussed crop of hair, the raised eyebrows, and the wrinkled forehead appear in identical form in *The Repentant Saint Peter* (Amsterdam, dealer K. & V. Waterman) [3].[13] It is quite possible that the Amersfoort painter may have sought to repeat the physiognomic studies by Hendrick ter Brugghen, as seen, for instance, in the *The Liberation of Saint Peter* (The Hague, Mauritshuis) [4] of 1624.[14]

For want of any documentation, Nicolson sketched the earliest activities of Stomer as a cautious working hypothesis.[15] Since then it has become certain that Stomer's art was rooted in Utrecht, that is, in the oeuvre of Gerard van Honthorst and Hendrick ter Brugghen.[16] That his origins are to be sought in the Northern Netherlands may not be irrefutable, but it has certainly become highly probable. The present painting, too, demonstrates that he knew the work of the Utrecht Caravaggists well. *Lot Leaving Sodom* demarcates, as it were, the moment at which Stomer left his teacher(s) in Utrecht and began his successful Italian career.[17]

1 *Hope 1965-1966*, p. 154; *Steel 1984*, p. 9
2 *Steel 1984*, p. 12
3 *Amsterdam / Detroit / Washington 1980-1981*; *Steel 1984*, p. 13
4 *Wrey 1988*, p. 31 and fig. (auctioned on 11 December 1987 for 613,800 dollars)
5 *DIAL* 71 C 12 4 (The Flight of Lot); 71 C 12 41 (Lot's Wife Looking Back); *Kauffmann 1971*, col. 110; *Pigler 1974*, vol. 11, did not isolate the Flight of Lot as a separate iconographic theme.
6 *Prisco / De Vecchi 1966 / 1979*, pp. 120-121, no. 149 D-4 and fig.
7 *Robinson et al. 1980*, no. 41 and fig., commented in detail on the three versions.
8 *Voorhelm Schneevoogt 1873*, p. 2, no. 9; *Rooses 1886-1892*, vol. 1, pp. 122-125, no. 102 and pl. 28
9 *Nicolson 1977*, p. 241
10 Inv. no. A 216; *Van Thiel et al. 1976*, p. 526, no. A 216 and fig.
11 *Drossaers / Lunsingh Scheurleer 1974-1976*, vol. 11, p. 644, no. 99
12 *Blankert 1978*, pp. 131-132, no. 161 and fig.
13 *Blankert / Slatkes 1986-1987*, pp. 343-344, no. 78 and fig.
14 *Broos 1987*, pp. 89-92, no. 15
15 *Nicolson 1977*, p. 240; compare also *Fokker 1929*, p. 19.
16 On his connections with the Utrecht Caravaggists, see *Pauwels 1953*, pp. 142-143 and 176-184; *Blankert / Slatkes 1986-1987*, pp. 334-336, no. 75.
17 *Nicolson 1977*, pp. 240-241, nos. 1-2, dated the Utrecht period between 1625 and 1629; *Blankert / Slatkes 1986-1987*, p. 334, no. 75, dated the early work in Rome ca. 1628-1633 (there are, however, no pertinent documents).
    BB

4
Hendrick ter Brugghen
The Liberation of Saint Peter
Canvas, 105 x 85 cm (41³/₈ x 33¹/₂ in.)
Upper left: *HTBrugghen / [16]24* (HTB in ligature)
The Hague, Mauritshuis, inv. no. 966

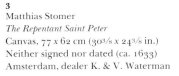

3
Matthias Stomer
The Repentant Saint Peter
Canvas, 77 x 62 cm (30³/₈ x 24³/₈ in.)
Neither signed nor dated (ca. 1633)
Amsterdam, dealer K. & V. Waterman

Brussels 1618 – Goa 1664

Canvas, 37 x 29.2 cm (14½ x 11½ in.). Neither signed nor dated (ca. 1656)
Hartford, Conn., Wadsworth Atheneum, The Ella Gallup Sumner and Mary Catlin Sumner Collection,
inv. no. 1940.198

Michael Sweerts was born in Brussels in 1618, the son of a cloth merchant. Nothing is known about his student years or his career before 1646. Probably from that year on, Sweerts lived in Rome. He moved in the circles of the *Virtuosi del Pantheon*, a strongly religiously inclined brotherhood of artists who adhered to academic, classical ideals in their work. This penchant for classicism is noticeable in Sweerts's depictions of the life of common people. In marked contrast to the work of his direct predecessors, the *Bamboccianti*, is the atmosphere of these paintings, which is never droll but rather melancholic. It is assumed that Sweerts remained in Rome until at least 1654.

In 1656 he received permission from the civic authorities of Brussels to found a drawing school, and he produced a sequence of etchings that could be used for purposes of instruction. Many atelier scenes also date from this period. In 1659 he became a member of the Brussels guild. In 1661 he lived and worked in Amsterdam, where, among other things, he rendered many portraits and paintings with religious subject matter. By then he already had contacts with the French Société des Missions Etrangères. With its founder, Bishop François Pallu, and several others, he traveled by land in late 1661 to Cochin China (South Vietnam) with the aim of establishing a mission school there. However, he was forced to leave the company in Persia on account of his problematic behavior. Nothing is known about the period from 1662 to 1664. According to a notation in the archives of the Société des Missions Etrangères, he died in 1664, in the Portuguese colony of Goa.

'A surprising museum': thus Vitale Bloch (1900-1975) described the Wadsworth Atheneum in Hartford in 1948.[1] Besides being an art critic, Bloch was also a respected collector with a predilection for the so-called minor masters (see cat. no. 57).[2] He therefore admired the acquisitions policy of the museum, which did not emphasize acquiring works of famous masters: 'Here the collecting was not done according to historical principles or a striving after completeness, but the intention was much more to bring together all those artists who in the last twenty or thirty years had made art-historical hearts beat faster' (in translation).[3]

Provenance

Collection Lord Northbourne, Betteshanger Park, near Sandwich, Kent, to 1893(?)
Collection Lord Hastings
Collection Money-Coutts
Dealer Arnold Seligmann, Rey & Co., New York, ca. 1940
Wadsworth Atheneum, The Ella Gallup Sumner and Mary Catlin Sumner Collection, Hartford, 1940

Bibliography

Trautscholdt 1938, p. 349
Austin 1940, pp. 7-8 and fig. p. 7
Hartford 1941, no. 33
Kansas City 1941, no. 58
Bloch 1948, pp. 64-65 and fig. p. 62
Bloch 1950, p. 218
Stechow 1951, pp. 211-212, 214-215, note 23 and fig. 5
Kultzen 1954, vol. I, pp. 151-153, vol. II, p. 303, no. 74
New York etc. 1954-1955, p. 80, no. 80
Bloch 1958, p. 441
Hartford 1958, p. 70 and fig.
Hartford / Sarasota 1958, no. 75
Nicolson 1958, p. 441
Rotterdam 1958, pp. 15, 55-56, no. 48 and fig. on cover
Rome 1958-1959, pp. 13, 52, no. 49, p. 50, fig. 48 and fig. on cover
Comstock 1959, pp. 270-271
Bedó 1962, p. 107 and fig. 2
Bloch 1965, p. 169 and fig. 104
Hefting 1969, no. 161 and fig.
Marlow 1969, p. 749 and fig. 6
Fahy 1973, p. 317 and fig. 7
Haverkamp-Begemann 1978, pp. 13, 194-195, no. 154, pl. 87 and fig. on cover
Zafran 1978, pp. 245-246 and fig. 10
Waddingham 1980, p. 66
Sutton 1986, p. 108 and fig. 153
Kultzen 1987, pp. 214-215 and fig. 12
Milwaukee 1989, p. 102 and fig. 2

Michael Sweerts A Boy with a Hat

As an example of this mode of collecting, Bloch cited the acquisition in 1940 of Michael Sweerts's *A Boy with a Hat*.

During much of the nineteenth century, Sweerts enjoyed only partial recognition as an etcher (see cat. no. 64).[4] His paintings were generally placed under the name of other artists, or under the category of unknown masters. In 1882 it was discovered by accident that the painting *At the Inn* (Munich, Alte Pinakothek), which until then had passed for a Ter Borch, had been sold in the eighteenth century as being by 'cavalier Swartz.'[5] It was quickly realized that this Swartz (or Swarts) was the same person as the etcher Sweerts.

The interest in the rediscovered painter increased after 1907, when Martin published an 'Attempt at a Biography and a Catalogue of His Paintings' (in translation) in the periodical *Oud-Holland*.[6] This important article stimulated further research which, in addition to new biographical data, yielded a considerable expansion of the oeuvre. In 1954 the German art historian R. Kultzen earned his doctorate with a dissertation on the painter.[7] However, the temporary height of the renewed appreciation for Sweerts was the monographic exhibition – largely Kultzen's brain child – that was seen in Rotterdam and Rome in 1958 and 1959.[8] The Wadsworth Atheneum was one of the first American museums to add a work by Sweerts to its collection. Before 1940 only The Detroit Institute of Arts owned a painting by him, *The Painter's Studio*.[9] Only a year after the acquisition of *A Boy with a Hat*, Sweerts also made his entrance in the museum at Oberlin (cat. no. 64), while the Wadsworth Atheneum acquired a second example of his work.[10]

A Boy with a Hat was still missing in the 'catalogue' by Martin. It was first mentioned in 1938 by Eduard Trautscholdt. According to this author, the painting was already known in the eighteenth century as a work by 'cavaliere Swarts,' and came from the collection of Lord Northbourne.[11] To what extent this information is correct cannot be verified because Trautscholdt did not cite his source. He might have meant Walter Charles James Northbourne (1816-1893), who was a trustee of the National Gallery in London from 1871 to his death.[12] The painting later came into the possession of the Hastings family, subsequently to end up in the Money-Coutts collection.[13] Around 1940 it was with the dealer Arthur Seligmann, Rey & Co. in New York.[14]

After its acquisition by the Wadsworth Atheneum, *A Boy with a Hat* became one of Sweerts's most beloved works. The boy graces the covers of the exhibition catalogues of 1958-1959 and of the catalogue of the Wadsworth Atheneum of 1978. Diverse authors expressed their feelings about the painting in lyrical terms such as 'touchingly romantic' (Austin 1940), 'sensitive and introspective' (Bloch 1958), and 'fleeting lyricism of hypersensitive youth' (Waddingham 1980).[15] The appreciation of this painting must be seen in relation to the work of Vermeer. It was regularly compared to the *Girl Wearing a Turban* by Johannes Vermeer in the Mauritshuis, especially in the treatment of color and light.[16] Wolfgang Stechow rightly observed in 1951 that Vermeer stood only at the very beginning of his career when Sweerts left Holland in 1661.[17] That Vermeer's work should have influenced Sweerts's therefore seems improbable.

A large number of heads of children by Sweerts have come down to us. Some of these belong in series of the five senses. The children are then provided with a specific attribute.[18] In other examples these attributes are lacking. In addition to *A Boy with a Hat*, the head of a girl from the Leicester Art Gallery,[19] the portrait of a boy from the Groninger Museum,[20] and that from The Fine Arts Museums of San Francisco [1], among others, belong to this group.[21] Kultzen recently suggested that the children's heads without attributes are of a later date than those with attributes. Within the later group of heads he saw a development from paintings still executed with strong plasticity, to which the girl in the Leicester Art Gallery presumably belongs, to those in which a freer treatment of color and light and a greater individuality of the features, more closely approximating the portrait, would point to an increasing measure of influence from Holland. In *A Boy with a Hat* this influence is presumably already strongly in evidence, culminating in a painting like the head of a girl that is found in a French private collection. Sweerts is thought to have rendered the painting from Hartford in the period between 1658-1659 and 1661.[22]

This argument is open to question. We may ask if Sweerts actually had to live in Amsterdam to fall under the spell of Dutch painting. The distance between Brussels and Amsterdam is not all that great, and the skills of the Dutch painters were well known in the south. Another question could be raised as to the

1
Michael Sweerts
Head of a Boy
Canvas, 39.4 x 34.8 cm (15 1/2 x 13 3/4 in.)
Neither signed nor dated (ca. 1656)
San Francisco, The Fine Arts Museums of San Francisco, inv. no. 66.9

function of the heads of children. It is striking that the type of child that Sweerts presents to us in these heads also occurs frequently in his atelier scenes. The latter are related to Sweerts's attempt to found a drawing academy in Brussels, with the ulterior motive of breathing new life into the declining industry of tapestry weaving of that city. The pupils of the academy would presumably have supplied the cartoons after which tapestries were woven. This academy was a remarkable and daring initiative of Sweerts. It was the first attempt to establish such an institution in the Netherlands. Although Sweerts got cooperation from the Brussels magistrates, his academy only survived for a short time.[23] It is not clear if his atelier scenes populated by throngs of pupils are a reflection of the true situation in that period, or a dream never come true.

In 1656, with a view to instruction in his academy in Brussels, Sweerts rendered a series of separate prints with the title: *Diversae facies / in usum / iuvenum et / aliorum* (Diverse heads for the benefit of youths and others).[24] We do not know the size of the original series, but a dozen sheets have come down to us. It is a series of busts of children, young men, and old men in traditional or exotic dress. They are so-called master's models, which is to say that the types were designed by Sweerts himself, presumably on the basis of his painted oeuvre. Similarly, in 1650, Frederik Bloemaert executed a series of heads designed by his father for Abraham Bloemaert's *Artis Apellae liber*.[25] The idea for such a series came from Italy. In 1616 J. Janssonius incorporated busts rendered after examples from drawing books, such as those of the school of Caracci, in his *Diagraphia, sive ars delineatoria*.[26]

The intention was probably for the pupil to learn to manipulate the models supplied to him, combining the motifs, first in drawings and later on canvas. It was possibly with this in mind that Sweerts painted heads like *A Boy with a Hat*. They form a perfect didactic complement to the series of prints by showing the pupil what might be achieved by way of diligence and practice. In the case of *A Boy with a Hat* this hypothesis appears to be supported when we put the painting next to two prints from the *Diversae facies*, namely *A Boy with a Cap* [**2**][27] and *A Boy with a Buttoned Jacket* [**3**].[28] Whereas the position of torso and head could have been taken over from the former print, the other could have been used for the face and the jacket. This boy recurs in many variations in the atelier scenes by Sweerts, while he also seems to have found his way into similar works by contemporaries, as is evident, for instance, from *The Drawing Lesson* by Jan Steen in The J. Paul Getty Museum in Malibu (p. 107, fig. 2).[29] It is possible that as a type he represents the ideal student of the artist, the virtuoso in the making. His luxuriant head of hair could point to this as well (see cat. no. 64).

The painting *A Boy with a Hat* does not so much belong to Sweerts's Amsterdam period as to the years around 1656, during which he devoted himself to the formation of an academy in Brussels. It may have been used as a demonstration model there. That there is a development from 'plastic' to 'pictorial' to be discerned within the series of painted heads accords well with the idea of such a didactic series.

2
Michael Sweerts
A Boy with a Cap
Etching, 83 x 78 mm (3¼ x 3 in.)
From: *Diversae facies* (Brussels 1656)
Lower left: *MS* (in ligature)
Amsterdam, Rijksprentenkabinet, inv. no. A 18826

3
Michael Sweerts
A Boy with a Buttoned Jacket
Etching, 83 x 78 mm (3¼ x 3 in.)
From: *Diversae facies* (Brussels 1656)
Lower left: *MS* (in ligature)
Amsterdam, Rijksprentenkabinet

1 *Bloch 1948*, p. 61

2 *Rotterdam 1978*, pp. 3-9

3 *Bloch 1948*, p. 61

4 *Nagler*, vol. XVIII (1847), pp. 57-60

5 Inv. no. 854; *Munich 1983*, p. 523 and fig.; *Martin 1907*, p. 133; *Rotterdam 1958*, p. 52, no. 40 and fig. 41

6 *Martin 1907*

7 *Kultzen 1954*

8 *Rotterdam 1958* and *Rome 1958-1959*

9 Inv. no. 217; *Detroit 1982*, pp. 113-115 and fig., also fig. on cover; *Rotterdam 1958*, pp. 37-38, no. 5 and fig. 5

10 Inv. no. 1941.595; *Haverkamp-Begemann 1978*, pp. 13, 57 and pl. 56, pp. 192-194, no. 153 and fig. 42; *Rotterdam 1958*, pp. 45-46, no. 27 and fig. 26

11 *Trautscholdt 1938*, p. 349

12 *Doubleday / De Walden 1936*, pp. 689-690

13 On the Hastings family, see *Townend 1963*. The Money-Coutts collection is mentioned for the first time in *Rotterdam 1958*, p. 56, no. 48, under 'herkomst.'

14 *Rotterdam 1958*, p. 56, no. 48, under 'herkomst'

15 *Austin 1940*, p. 8; *Bloch 1958*, p. 441; *Waddingham 1980*, p. 66

16 Inv. no. 670; see, for instance, *Bloch 1948*, pp. 64-66; *Broos 1987*, pp. 390-394, no. 66 and fig.

17 *Stechow 1951*, p. 215, note 23

18 See *Rotterdam 1958*, p. 57, nos. 50-51 and fig. and pp. 57-58, nos. 52-53 and fig.

19 Inv. no. 201.1975; *Rotterdam 1958*, p. 56, no. 49 and fig. 47; *Kultzen 1987*, p. 214 and fig. 11

20 Inv. no. 1931-123 (from the collection of C. Hofstede de Groot, who donated it to the museum in 1931); *Rotterdam 1958*, pp. 55-56, no. 47 and fig. 48; *Kultzen 1987*, p. 215 and fig. 14

21 *Haverkamp-Begemann 1980*, p. 105 and fig. 7

22 *Kultzen 1987*, pp. 214-217 and fig.

23 *Kultzen 1954*, pp. 226-227, appendix F

24 *Bolten 1979*, pp. 56-57, pp. 140-142

25 *Bolten 1979*, pp. 26-29, pp. 139-140

26 *Bolten 1979*, pp. 67-68

27 *Hollstein*, vol. XXIX, p. 131, no. 13; not in *Illustrated Bartsch*

28 *Hollstein*, vol. XXIX, p. 131, no. 11; *Illustrated Bartsch*, vol. V, p. 384, no. 16 (421) and fig.

29 Inv. no. 83.PB.388; *Malibu 1986*, p. 100 and fig. on cover

JR (with thanks to Edwin Buijsen)

Brussels 1618 – Goa 1664

Canvas, 94.5 cm x 73.4 cm (37¼ x 28⅞ in.)
Neither signed nor dated (ca. 1656)
Oberlin, Ohio, Allen Memorial Art Museum, Oberlin College, R.T. Miller, Jr., Fund, inv. no. 41.77

In 1902 this *Self-Portrait as a Painter* was offered at the auction of the collection of a certain Edward Twopeny in London as a portrait of 'Gerard Torburg [ter Borch],' painted by Sweerts. The same lot included an etching after the painting.[1] This must have been the print in mirror image that Michael Sweerts rendered after his self-portrait and that he signed in full: *Michael Sweerts Eq[ues] Pi[nxit] et fe[cit]* [1].[2] It is not known on what grounds he called himself a knight (Eques), and it is further too bad that he did not date the print, as this could have avoided a great deal of confusion.

In England in 1902, Sweerts was still unknown as a painter. The print, however, had earlier been described in reference works. In 1824 the painter and lexicographer Johann Heinrich Füssli (1741-1825), called Henry Fuseli after 1770, believed that this was a portrait of Gerard ter Borch, painted and subsequently etched by Michael Sweerts: 'Terburg holds the brush in his right hand and the palette in his left' (in translation).[3] In 1843, in his supplement to the catalogue by Adam Bartsch – who had identified the etching as a *Self-Portrait* by Sweerts – Weigel took over this unfounded identification, after which Nagler referred to the conflicting opinions.[4] It is almost superfluous to observe that none of these authors knew the portrait in Oberlin. In Houbraken, the biography of Sweerts is conspicuous by its absence, and Bartsch commenced his introduction to the sixteen etchings by Sweerts with the observation: 'Sweerts is only known for the prints that he engraved' (in translation).[5] Finally, in his pioneering article of 1907 on the artist, Martin published twenty-eight paintings by the Fleming, who also worked in the Netherlands.[6] The rediscovery of this somewhat mysterious painter was

Provenance
Collection William Twopeny, London
Collection Edward Twopeny, Woodstock Castle, Sittingbourne, Kent
Auction Edward Twopeny, London, 1902 (£189 to Buttery)
(?) Dealer Thos. Agnew & Sons, Ltd., London
Collection Washington B. Thomas, Boston, 1902 / 1903-1929
Collection Mr. and Mrs. William Tudor Gardiner, Gardiner, Maine, 1929-1941(?)
Dealer M. Knoedler & Co., New York, 1941
Allen Memorial Art Museum, Oberlin, 1941 (gift of the R.T. Miller, Jr., Fund)

Bibliography
Moes 1897-1895, vol. II, p. 441, no. 7756
Auction London 1902, no. 57
Boston 1903, no. 86
Martin 1907, pp. 136, 138-140 and fig. opp. p. 133, and p. 145, no. 1 and fig.
Wurzbach, vol. II (1910), p. 684
Graves 1918-1921, vol. III, p. 189 (1902)
Trautscholdt 1938, p. 348
Boston 1939, p. 84, no. 129 and pl. 61
Stechow 1949, p. 121
Bloch 1950, p. 218
Stechow 1951, pp. 211-214, note 18 and fig.
Stechow 1952, pp. 64-65 and fig.
Ebbinge Wubben 1953, p. 4, note 3
Kultzen 1954, vol. I, pp. 139-141, 143, vol. II, p. 300, no. 69
Gerson 1958, p. 14
Rotterdam 1958, pp. 25 and 54, no. 43 and fig. 45
Waddingham 1958, p. 71
Rome 1958-1959, pp. 50-51, no. 44 and fig. 43
AMAM Bulletin 1959, p. 78
AMAM Bulletin 1959-A, fig. p. 137
Incisa della Rocchetta 1959, p. 117
Schaar 1959, p. 44
Winkler Prins van de Kunst 1959, vol. III, p. 387
Bedó 1962, p. 107
Kenwood 1962, no. 32
Nicolson 1962, p. 310
Van Hall 1963, p. 323
Bloch 1965, pp. 169-170
Rosenberg / Slive / Ter Kuile 1966, p. 173
Oberlin 1967, pp. 145-146 and fig. 66
Bloch 1968, pp. 24-25 and fig. 25
Kindlers, vol. V (1968), p. 464
Rotterdam 1969, p. 50
Bader 1972, p. 475 and fig. 46
Bader / Stechow 1974, no. 24 and fig.
Apollo 1976, p. 85 and fig.
Waddingham 1976-1977, p. 59, p. 64, note 14
Chiarini 1979, pp. 63-64
Florence 1980, p. 1014, no. A 920
Liedtke 1983, p. 21
Levine 1984, p. 294
Sutton 1986, pp. 210-213 and fig. 305
Kultzen 1987, p. 217

1
Michael Sweerts
Self-Portrait as a Painter
Etching, 210 x 165 mm (8¼ x 6½ in.)
Lower left: *Michael Sweerts Eq. Pi. et fe* (ca. 1656)
Amsterdam, Rijksprentenkabinet

Michael Sweerts Self-Portrait as a Painter (not in San Francisco)

crowned in 1958 and 1959 with exhibitions in Rotterdam and Rome.[7]

In 1902 or 1903, possibly with the mediation of the dealer Thos. Agnew & Sons of London, the portrait of 'Gerard Torburg' came into the possession of Washington Butcher Thomas (1857-1929), an immensely rich sugar manufacturer in Boston.[8] Presumably after his death in 1929, the painting was inherited by Margaret Thomas, who in 1916 had married the future governor of Maine, William Tudor Gardiner (1892-1953).[9] In 1939 it was still in their possession, but in 1941 the Allen Memorial Art Museum was able to acquire it by way of Knoedler & Co.[10] In the meantime Martin had opened his article of 1907 with a reproduction of this painting, which, according to him, should be considered a self-portrait.[11] The writer intuitively dated it to 1656, analogously to Sweerts's *Portrait of a Young Man* (Leningrad, Hermitage),[12] which is dated to that year. The clothing is indeed similar in the large puffed shirtsleeves that bulge through slits in the coat. Bartholomeus van der Helst is dressed just as fashionably in his *Self-Portrait in 1655* (cat. no. 29).

Martin believed that the sitter was between thirty-five and forty years old, and that Sweerts must therefore have been born between 1615 and 1620.[13] However, after archival research suggested that Sweerts was born in 1624, it was generally concluded that the *Self-Portrait as a Painter* must have originated later, between 1658 and 1660, and that it may even have been made in Amsterdam.[14] The stylistic influence of Van der Helst was adduced as an argument. But the twenty-five-year-old artist called 'Michele fiammingo' living in the Via Margutta, mentioned in 1649 in the parish archives of Santa Maria del Popolo in Rome, cannot have been Sweerts, unless the age was specified incorrectly.[15] It has been established beyond a doubt that Michael Sweerts was baptized in Brussels on 29 September 1618.[16] If we assume that the *Self-Portrait as a Painter* in Oberlin does not depict a man of forty or older, then Martin's dating of the portrait around 1656 would appear to be the most plausible.

Wolfgang Stechow (1896-1974) (p. 93, fig. 12), Professor of Art History at Oberlin, on whose advice the painting had been acquired by the museum in 1941, wrote an article ten years later about several portraits by Sweerts. He rightly wondered if it had been proven that the etching (and therefore the painting) really is a self-portrait. According to Stechow, the pose in particular, which springs from an old tradition, points in that direction – although a landscape background is virtually unique with a portrait of an artist.[17] We usually see the painter at work in his studio. Probably Sweerts – who was not a true landscape painter – intended to refer to Italy, in which his art was rooted.

Quite recently a number of portraits by Sweerts have been identified as self-portraits. In 1979 Chiarini pointed to a canvas in the famous collection of artists' self-portraits belonging to Leopoldo de' Medici, which is mentioned in the inventory drawn up after his death in 1675 as being painted by 'Suarz' (Florence, Galleria degli Uffizi) [2].[18] This portrait shows a great similarity to that in Oberlin. Here we see Sweerts, only younger, wearing a dashing velvet beret with a large, dangling, white feather, which gives him the appearance of a bohemian. The figure in diverse scenes by Sweerts showing an artist at work resembles the long-haired painter as we know him from the self-portraits in Florence and Oberlin.[19]

In 1968 a portrait of a man with a pointing index finger turned up in the art trade in Munich. Dr. Alfred Bader of Milwaukee acquired it as a Pieter Franchoys and later compared it in the presence of Wolfgang Stechow with 'his' *Self-Portrait as a Painter* in Oberlin. Thus a new self-portrait by Sweerts was discovered, and Bader revealed in an article what this apparently empty gesture of the sitter signified. During a restoration an overpainted skull had emerged, at which the sitter points emphatically (Milwaukee, collection Dr. Alfred Bader) [3].[20] Therefore this turns out to be a self-portrait with *vanitas* implications. It was presumably painted a little earlier than the one in Oberlin.[21]

A fourth painting, which is actually more a *tronie* (mug) than a true self-portrait by Sweerts, has for a long time been attributed to Barent Fabritius (Cambridge, Mass., Fogg Art Museum) [4].[22] In this work Sweerts holds a long Gouda pipe, and his luxuriant hair is tucked away under a cap. The left side of his face is lit by a dramatic beam of light, and he looks at us from dark eye sockets. There must be some connection with a second etching inscribed *Michael Sweerts Eq[ues] Pi[nxit] et fe[cit]*, for which he once again took himself as a model.[23] Here too he is depicted smoking, and in the company of a boy (an apprentice?). He gives, as it were,

2
Michael Sweerts
Self-Portrait
Canvas, 55 x 43.5 cm (21⅝ x 17⅛ in.)
Neither signed nor dated (ca. 1648-1650)
Florence, Galleria degli Uffizi, inv. no. 1633

the wrong example to generate the right response. This negative exemplum of the smoking artist may pride itself on a modest tradition.[24]

Sweerts has turned each of these four self-portraits into expressive portraits by using an attribute. However, it is an illusion to think that the painter revealed his deepest self. Especially since the Sweerts exhibitions of 1958 and 1959, people have been seeking to analyze the presumably difficult or peculiar character of Sweerts, which manifested itself during his failed journey as a missionary, and which was used to explain why he did not marry and was so fond of painting boys. Waddingham asked himself why Sweerts occupied himself with 'dandies with their effeminate graces,' and Gardenier believed that the 'spiritual and psychological instability of Sweerts [...] may be read from his paintings.'[25] Nicolson later observed, with relief as it were, that in his *Self-Portrait as a Painter*, Sweerts at least does not show himself from his eccentric side, but as 'a self-confident,

well-adjusted bourgeois.'[26] Bader cited this passage and believed that the portrait with a skull in his collection 'corresponds more closely to our vision of the artist.'[27]

It is pointless to attempt to deduce a personality from a seventeenth-century self-portrait. Raupp demonstrated in full what Stechow had already pointed out in a few words: first and foremost artists' portraits follow the laws of a very old tradition.[28] One traditional mode of representation was as a craftsman with palette, brushes, and painter's stick. Famous highpoints of this formula are the self-portraits by Antonio Moro (Florence, Galleria degli Uffizi)[29] of 1558 and that by Rembrandt (London [Kenwood], The Iveagh Bequest),[30] which was made just over a century later. One may imagine that Sweerts knew the print by Hieronymus Wierix with the *Portrait of Pieter Coecke van Aelst* [5],[31] which was published in 1572 by the humanist Domenicus Lampsonius and the printer Hieronymus Cock in a series of famous artists' portraits.[32]

3
Michael Sweerts
Self-Portrait with a Skull
Canvas, 78.7 x 60.3 cm (31 x 23¾ in.)
Neither signed nor dated (ca. 1655)
Milwaukee, Wis., collection Dr. Alfred Bader

4
Michael Sweerts
'Self-Portrait' as a Smoker
Canvas, 66 x 48.3 cm (26¼ x 19 in.)
Neither signed nor dated (ca. 1655)
Cambridge, Mass., Fogg Art Museum, The Harvard
University Art Museums, inv. no. 1941.110

5
Hieronymus Wierix
Portrait of Pieter Coecke van Aelst
Engraving, 265 x 165 mm (10³/₈ x 6¹/₂ in.)
Upper left: *IHW* (1572)
Amsterdam, Rijksprentenkabinet

PETRO COECKE ALOSTANO, PICTORI.

Pictor eras · nec eras tantùm, Petre, pictor · Aloſtum
Qui facis hac Orbi notius arte tuum:
Multa ſed acceſsit multo ars tibi parta labore,
Cuius opus pulchras ædificare domos.
Serlius hanc Italos · tu, Serli deinde bilinguis
Interpres, Belgas, Francigenaſque doces.

Sweerts combined this by-then old-fashioned typology with a new manner of depiction, in which the artist is presented as the ideal virtuoso more than as a craftsman. Anthony van Dyck popularized this type in his renowned *Iconographie*, a collection of eighty portrait etchings that was published in 1645 but conceived almost two decades earlier.[33] He drew his inspiration for this series from older series of prints (such as that by Lampsonius), but also based it on the 1584 treatise on the art of painting by the Italian G.P. Lomazzo.[34]

Raupp has analyzed the *Iconographie* for positions, clothing, gestures, facial types, expressions, and hairstyles. Sweerts's *Self-Portrait as a Painter* meets several general criteria. Because of the close cropping, our full attention is drawn to the figure, which looks imposing owing to the amply cut clothing and the somewhat downward glance at the spectator. The glance is lively and betrays inner activity. The hair is luxuriant – as abundant as the thoughts that spring from the head of the artist. Elegantly formed hands generate respect and point to inner nobility. The overall presentation is one of controlled temperament and inner order and harmony, the so-called *leggiadria*.[35] It is not unthinkable that Sweerts, who called himself 'Eques,' liked to see himself as the ideal artist à la Van Dyck, who could measure up to the greatest artists of all times.[36] After all, artists had also been included in the *Iconographie*, which further consisted of portraits of rulers, politicians, generals, scholars, diplomats, and art lovers.

Finally, one asks oneself which *Self-Portrait* Michael Sweerts donated to the Brussels guild of painters in 1660 to commemorate himself before he left for Amsterdam.[36] This was presumably not a portrait in which he alluded to his own mortality and to his possible vices. It would not surprise us if the gift to his colleagues was the painting under discussion, in which we see him as an old-fashioned craftsman but also as a modern virtuoso.

1 *Auction London 1902*, no. 57
2 *Hollstein*, vol. XXIX (1984), p. 134, no. 19 and fig.
3 *Füssli 1779-1824*, vol. IV, p. 1837
4 B. 416 (vol. IV, p. 416, no. 3); *Weigel 1843*, pp. 224-225, no. B. 3; *Nagler 1858-1878*, vol. XVIII (1843), p. 58, no. 3
5 B., vol. IV, p. 414
6 *Martin 1907*
7 *Rotterdam 1958*; *Rome 1958-1959*
8 *WWWA*, vol. I, pp. 1230-1231
9 *WWWA*, vol. III, p. 312
10 *Boston 1939*, p. 84, no. 3
11 *Martin 1907*, fig. opp. p. 133
12 Inv. no. 3654; *Kuznetsov / Linnik 1982*, nos. 44-45 and fig.
13 *Martin 1907*, p. 136

14 *Stechow 1951*, p. 211

15 *Hoogewerff 1911*, p. 135

16 *Bodart 1970*, p. 421 and note 2

17 *Stechow 1951*, pp. 211 and 214, note 20

18 *Chiarini 1979*, pp. 63-64 and fig. 54; *Florence 1980*, p. 1014, no. A 920 and fig.

19 *Van Hall 1963*, p. 323; (like *Raupp 1984*, p. 230) he wrongly called the portrait in Leningrad (see note 12) a self-portrait.

20 *Bader 1972*, p. 475 and fig. 1; *Bader / Stechow 1974*, no. 24 and fig.; *McTavish 1984*, pp. 58-59, no. 26 and fig.; the overpainting was applied before a copy was made of this portrait (Salt Lake City, private collection; *Bader 1972*, fig. 45)

21 *Milwaukee 1989*, pp. 102-103

22 According to the photograph at the RKD

23 *Hollstein*, vol. XIX, p. 132, no. 16 and fig.; *Illustrated Bartsch*, vol. V, p. 377, no. 2 and fig.

24 *Raupp 1984*, pp. 318-319 and fig. 193; he gave examples by Jan Davidsz de Heem, Jan Miense Molenaer, and Pieter de Grebber; for smoking as a *vanitas* symbol, see *Broos 1987*, pp. 87-88.

25 *Waddingham 1958*, p. 71; *Gardenier 1958*, p. 240

26 *Nicolson 1962*, p. 310

27 *Bader 1972*, p. 475

28 *Raupp 1984*

29 Inv. no. 1637; *Florence 1980*, p. 939, no. A 621 and fig.

30 Inv. no. 57; *Gerson / Bredius 1969*, pp. 29 and 549, no. 34 and fig.

31 *Hollstein*, vol. IV, p. 184, no. 1-23

32 *Puraye 1956*

33 *Mauquoy-Hendrickx 1956*; *Raupp 1984*, pp. 45-164

34 *Lomazzo 1584*; *Raupp 1984*, p. 97

35 *Raupp 1984*, pp. 96-126

36 See also *Raupp 1984*, pp. 78-79; curiously, cat. no. 64 is not found in Raupp's study of the artists' portrait in the seventeenth century.

37 *Wauters 1877*, p. 306; *Schaar 1959*, p. 44

BB & JR

Willem van de Velde the Younger and Cornelis van de Velde (?)

Leyden 1633 – London 1707 and
London ca. 1675 – London 1729

Willem van de Velde the Younger was the son of the painter who went by the same name (1611-1693). He was first taught by his father in Amsterdam, after which he received further training from Simon de Vlieger in Weesp. His earliest dated works are from 1653. The paintings from the beginning of his career show subdued, peaceful scenes with ships on still waters – altogether in the manner of De Vlieger. However, Van de Velde preferred a more lively range of colors than we encounter in the known work of his master. Later on it became his aim to render technically perfect ships, thus arriving at ship portraits. His compositions were largely derived from those of his father and did not undergo any dramatic developments. In 1672, the year of disaster due to the start of the Third English War, both Van de Veldes departed for England, where they entered the service of King Charles II in 1674 at an annual salary of one hundred pounds. The younger Van de Velde was charged with the execution in oils of designs drawn by his father.

After the death of Charles II, they remained in the service of the court of James II, for whom they painted maritime events. They had a studio in the Queen's House in Greenwich until 1691, and then moved to Westminster. Van de Velde must also have been in Amsterdam now and then, because, besides other works, he painted a *View of Amsterdam* in 1686 for the governing body of the port wardens. In his later work, which was largely commissioned, the painter did not always avoid the uninspired repetition of his established formula. He must also have had the assistance of many studio collaborators. His drawings, of which thousands are known, have always retained their individual qualities.

One of his sons, Cornelis van de Velde, a painter like his father, was married in Knightsbridge in 1699 to Bernarda, daughter of the painter Jan van der Hagen. Cornelis's talent was highly praised in contemporary testimony, but the quantity and nature of his oeuvre is still relatively unknown.

65 | An English Man-of-War at Anchor

Canvas, 104.5 x 89 cm (41⅛ x 35 in.)
On the back of the original canvas: *w, v, v* (1707)
Coral Gables, Fla., private collection

Provenance
(?) Collection Edward Augustus Inglefield, London, before 1894
Collection John Frederick Crompton Inglefield, Parwich Hall, Ashbourne, Derbyshire
Dealer J. Hoogsteder, The Hague, 1984
Collection Mr. and Mrs. George M. Kaufman, Norfolk, Va., 1986(?)
Private collection, Coral Gables, Fla. (bought from dealer O. Naumann, New York)

Bibliography
Never before published

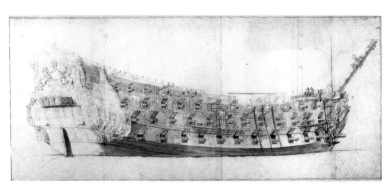

1
Willem van de Velde the Younger
The Ship 'Prince'
Pen and wash drawing on counterproof,
422 x 931 mm (16⅝ x 36⅝ in.)
Neither signed nor dated (ca. 1673)
Rotterdam, Museum Boymans-van Beuningen, inv. no. MB 1866/T-334

This painting has never before been published. It has several surprising aspects in addition to its pictorial quality and outstanding condition. For generations it may possibly have been in the possession of an English family of naval officers, who probably

Willem van de Velde the Younger and Cornelis van de Velde (?) An English Man-of-War at Anchor

treated the canvas with exceptional care. According to an oral tradition the painting has come from the estate of the late John Frederick Crompton-Inglefield of Parwich Hall in Ashbourne (Derbyshire).[1] It is a justified assumption that one of his ancestors acquired the painting, probably as early as the eighteenth century. In 1759, at the age of eleven, John Nicholson Inglefield (1748-1828) joined the English navy. For a long time he served under Commodore Samuel Hood, after whom he named his son Samuel Hood Inglefield. The latter died in China in 1848 at the rank of rear admiral. His son, Sir Edward Augustus Inglefield (1820-1894), enjoyed a brilliant career as commander and, after 1879, as admiral. Sir Edward was also an amateur artist, who exhibited his portraits and watercolors of ships in action at the Royal Academy between 1851 and 1870. We do not know, alas, about any collection of paintings owned by the older Inglefields, or by their descendants.[2]

The painting under discussion represents a large English man-of-war of the type that was built from the 1670s on and that occurs often in the paintings of Willem van de Velde the Younger's English period. It somewhat resembles the ship *Prince*, built in 1670, and converted in 1692 to the *Royal William*. Around 1673 Willem van de Velde made a drawing of the *Prince* (Rotterdam, Museum Boymans-van Beuningen) [1].[3] The details of the ship in the painting do not point to any vessel known by name, for they are not specific enough. The banner above the stern displays the Union flag in the upper-left canton, as had been the custom since the middle of 1707. The front rowboat also carries this latest form of the flag. The banner at the top of the three-master is painted in such a way that it is clearly evident it is the royal standard of Queen Anne, which was carried between 1707 and 1714 [2].[4] The coat of arms on the stern shows the same arms once more, but not in as legible a form. The emphasis on these details would appear to have been the wish of the patron. He naturally wanted to indicate that he agreed wholeheartedly with the renewal of the union between England and Scotland, which had been cemented in 1707. This union meant the beginnings of the United Kingdom.

This same year of 1707 was also the one in which Willem van de Velde the Younger, to whom the painting is attributed, died at the age of seventy-four. To be precise, Willem died on 6 April 1707, and the union commenced on 1 May 1707.[5] This means that the painter can never have seen these flags in use and therefore could not be the one who applied them. Naturally the ensuing question is what else he did not paint on this canvas. For the time being, this question cannot be answered.[6]

During a recent cleaning a twenty-inch-wide monogram of *w, v, v* in letters seven inches high emerged on the back of the original canvas [3]. The way it is written closely resembles the autograph monograms of the younger Van de Velde, though the customary *J* (to distinguish his signature from that of his father) is lacking.[7] Signatures on the backs of paintings are rare, however, and only a few by Willem van de Velde are known, one instance being his last dated work of 1706, *An English Sixth-Rate Firing a Salute* (Greenwich, National Maritime Museum) [4].[8] One suspects that though this painting was certified by the master, it was nevertheless painted after his example by a collaborator.[9] It seems that this unusually large inscription should not be viewed as his signature but as a certificate of his shop, for it is more than probable that toward the end of his life the septuagenarian painter received a substantial amount of assistance from collaborators. David Cordingly, curator of the National Maritime Museum in Greenwich, concluded: 'The greater part of Van de Velde's last years must have been spent in overseeing the work of his studio. There is some confusion regarding the members of the Van de Velde circle in London, but there can be no doubt that there were a large number of marine artists producing versions, variations, and copies of van de Velde's paintings. These included the Younger van de Velde's son William, his [...] son Cornelis van de Velde, Van der Hagen, Isaac Sailmaker, Jacob Knyff and Peter Monamy.'[10]

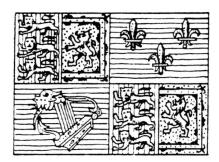

2
The Union flag and the Royal Standard since 1707
From: *Robinson 1974*, vol. I, p. 230

3
Monogram on the back of cat. no. 65

Another example of a signed and dated work from after 1700 is a painting of 1703 that was executed in a more monumental format, *The 'Royal Sovereign' at Anchor* (Greenwich, National Maritime Museum) [**5**].[11] A minute comparison of the rendering of the ships and figures of these late paintings with the work published here might be able to establish if they are by the same hand(s). For now it looks as if the painting was begun by Willem van de Velde the Younger before his death, but that it was subsequently completed and brought up-to-date in reference to the new political situation. That it is not a ship of 1707 which is depicted, but an old-fashioned type, makes it all the more probable that it was initially not intended to be equipped with the symbols of the union.

In view of the unmistakable pictorial power with which this painting is executed, it is assumed here that the best painter of the Van de Velde studio laid the last hand on the composition.[12] This was Willem's son Cornelis, who carried on the studio of his father, but of whose own work very little is known. Only one single *Marine* signed *C v Velde* (London, dealer)[13] is illustrated in the entire art-historical literature. Michael Robinson has for the time being attributed some seven sea pieces to him, of which only one is in a public collection (New York, The Metropolitan Museum of Art).[14] According to one connoisseur who is said to

have seen him at work, there was no better marine painter in London than Cornelis van de Velde. This connoisseur was Jacob Campo Weyerman, who was repeatedly in London for long stays between 1702 and 1709.[15] In 1729 the biographer recalled: 'We were mutually acquainted with this Artist in England [...] he being now the very best Marine painter that we would be Able to name. He has satisfactorily the same manner as his inventive father, as he paints the briny juice of Nereus as translucently as rock crystal; and paints his ships, skies, beaches, and cliffs gloriously and copiously' (in translation).[16]

1 Report by W. van de Watering, dated 27 September 1984 (documentation archives Mauritshuis)
2 *DNB*, vol. XXVIII (1891), pp. 437-438; *Boase 1965*, vol. v, p. 746
3 *Robinson / Weber 1979*, vol. I, p. 117, no. T 334, vol. III, figs. 244-245
4 *Robinson 1974*, vol. I, p. 230 and fig.
5 *London 1982*, p. 8 and *Leadam 1909*, p. 107
6 Michael S. Robinson is not prepared, at this time, to include this painting in his oeuvre catalogue of Willem van de Velde the Younger. He wrote to us: 'he [the painter] has shown the ship with a Dutch stern, the planking going square across the transom instead of coming round in a bend to the stern post in the English fashion' (letter dated 15 February 1990). We thank him for his comments.
7 *Robinson 1958*, vol. I, p. 25, discussed the various kinds of signatures of Willem van de Velde the Younger.
8 *London 1988*, p. 404, no. BHC0908 and fig. c; a painting formerly dated [17]07, no longer shows this date (London, Wallace Collection; HdG 89; *London 1968*, p. 341, no. P 137).
9 *London 1982*, p. 125, no. 135: presumably executed by Peter Monamy (1681-1749) after sketches by Van de Velde.
10 *London 1982*, p. 20
11 *London 1988*, p. 406, no. BHC3614 and fig. b
12 Not an unusual procedure; *Hecht 1989-1990*, p. 114, no. 22, recently discussed an example of this.
13 *Bol 1973*, p. 244 and fig. 249
14 Inv. no. 60.94.2; *Baetjer 1980*, vol. I, p. 127 (attributed to Peter Monamy), vol. II, p. 251 and fig.; in 1982 a seascape was auctioned with a *C V V* monogram (*Auction New York 1982*, no. 147 and fig.); we see the union flag several times in the seven Cornelis van de Velde paintings that Robinson is about to publish.
15 According to A.J.M. Broos in his yet to be published dissertation on *Weyerman 1729-1769*.
16 *Weyerman 1729-1769*, vol. III, p. 386; on Cornelis van de Velde, see *Thieme / Becker*, vol. XXXIV (1926), p. 199; *London 1982*, p. 126, no. 136.
    BB

5
Willem van de Velde the Younger
The 'Royal Sovereign' at Anchor
Canvas, 180.5 x 145 cm (71 x 57 in.)
Lower right(?): *W van Velde J 1703*
Greenwich, National Maritime Museum,
inv. no. 33-41

4
Willem van de Velde the Younger and Peter Monamy(?)
An English Sixth-Rate Firing a Salute
Canvas, 42 x 37 cm (16½ x 14½ in.)
On the back: *W.V.Velde J 1706*
Greenwich, National Maritime Museum,
inv. no. 63-33

Simon Verelst Full Daffodils in a Vase

The Hague 1644 – London 1721

Panel, 43 x 34.5 cm (17 x 13½ in.)
Neither signed nor dated (before 1669?)
Hartford, Conn., Wadsworth Atheneum, inv. no. 1956.782

Simon Verelst descended from a family of artists, of which he was the most talented. His teacher was presumably his father, Pieter Verelst, who painted genre scenes. Simon specialized in the flower still life. In 1663 he was a member of the guild in The Hague; he left from there for England in 1669 with his brother Herman and the latter's son Cornelis. He entered the service of the second Duke of Buckingham, and King Charles II bought several of his still lifes with flowers. He later also enjoyed success as portraitist of the court nobility. There are several anecdotes known about his boundless vanity and conceitedness; near the end of his life things are said to have gone to his head to such an extent that he had to be shut up in a madhouse for a while. Because of a lack of familiarity with his technique, many of his flower still lifes have been abraded, one of the results being that the leaves have turned blue.

Provenance
Dealer Eugene Slatter, London, 1953
Dealer Mortimer Brandt, New York, 1953 (bought from Slatter)
Collection Mrs. Arthur L. Erlanger, New York, 1956
Wadsworth Atheneum, Hartford, 1956 (gift of Mrs. Erlanger)

Bibliography
Illustrated London News 1953, p. 621 and fig.
London 1953, no. 25
Illustrated London News 1957, p. 475 and fig.
WAB 1957, fig. on dust jacket
Haverkamp-Begemann 1978, p. 93, pl. 126 and p. 198, no. 193
Lewis 1979, p. 39, no. 127
Sutton 1986, p. 107
Grimm 1988, p. 248

One will seek in vain in Dutch museums for a work by the Hague painter Simon Verelst, who once caused a furor at the English court. The Rijksmuseum does not have a work by this unjustly forgotten master even in its study collection: for paintings by Verelst one must go mainly to Cambridge (Fitzwilliam Museum) and Oxford (Ashmolean Museum).[1] A flower piece in the Groninger Museum is presently not on view due to lack of space.[2] Only the Museum Bredius in The Hague used to exhibit a splendid *Bouquet in a Glass Vase* [**1**], until this collection had to close its doors to the public.[3] This flower piece is signed and dated 1669, the same year, therefore, that Verelst departed for London with his brother and nephew. On 11 April the newcomer had already been visited by Samuel Pepys, who described a flower painting with enthusiasm: 'the drops of Dew [were] hanging on the leaves, so as I was forced again and again to put my finger to it to feel whether my eyes were deceived or no. He doth ask 70 l[ivres] for it; I had the vanity to bid him 20 l[ivres].'[4] This description could apply to the painting in the Bredius collection, or to a similar work.

Ever since 1953, when the *Full Daffodils in a Vase* was shown for the first time with the dealer Slatter in London, the painting has been attributed to Verelst.[5] It was later bought by the dealer

1
Simon Verelst
Bouquet in a Glass Vase
Canvas, 44 x 35 cm (17⅜ x 13¾ in.)
Lower left: *S. Verelst F. 1669*
The Hague, Museum Bredius, inv. no. 124-1946

Mortimer Brandt in New York and donated to the Wadsworth Atheneum in Hartford in 1956 by Mrs. Arthur L. Erlanger.[6] This institution, founded in 1842 by Daniel Wadsworth (1771-1848), is one of the oldest museums in America and owns the most striking collection of Dutch paintings outside the big cities in the United States. The acquisitions policy of the Wadsworth Atheneum has in fact served many another museum in America as a model.[7] In the 1978 catalogue of the Dutch paintings in Hartford, the preeminent expert in this field, Egbert Haverkamp-Begemann, called the attribution of the painting to Simon Verelst 'fully acceptable,' knowing that he was supported in this by Laurens J. Bol.[8]

What place this still life occupies in the oeuvre of Verelst is difficult to ascertain, though it may be taken for granted that it is out of the ordinary. In 1979 Lewis published a survey of Verelst's work. He arranged the approximately 150 paintings by size, from large to small. This emergency measure was necessary because according to this author – aside from the still life of 1669 – not a single painting carries a date (and at the most twenty pieces have a signature or monogram).[9] It therefore seems like a hopeless task to decide on a chronology for his work.

It is clear, however, that the composition featuring a bunch of flowers in a glass vase standing on a simple stone surface with the sun shining through it was a favorite of Simon Verelst. He concentrated completely on depicting the flowers; the rest of the composition usually seems of secondary importance. Due to its simplicity, the still life with the two full daffodils in Hartford stands alone in the oeuvre of this master, who usually painted much more exuberant compositions. The attribution to Verelst

2
Simon Verelst
Flowers in a Vase
Panel, 26.7 x 22.9 cm (10½ x 9 in.)
Lower center: *s v* (in ligature) (ca. 1670)
London, dealer Richard Green

nevertheless becomes acceptable when, for instance, one compares the painting with an undated flower piece (London, dealer Richard Green) [2][10] that is provided with his monogram. Especially striking are the correspondences of the form of the flower at the upper right and the strongly concentrated fall of light on the bouquet. It is assumed here as a working hypothesis that the Hartford painting preceded all the more elaborate compositions by Verelst, including, therefore, the bouquet in the Museum Bredius. *Full Daffodils in a Vase* could therefore have been painted in The Hague before 1669, when the artist went to try his luck in England.

The panel in Hartford is unique within the oeuvre of Verelst, but certainly outside it as well. Still lifes showing only one flower or type of flower are decidedly the exception. Around 1640 Balthasar van der Ast painted a single tulip in a glass vase (Solingen, Galerie Müllenmeister) [3].[11] This is presumably a portrait of a specially cultivated tulip, which Segal identified with some reservations as the Marcus Aurelius Augustus.[12] The *Tulip in a Kendi Vase* (Rotterdam, Museum Boymans-van Beuningen) [4][13] should also be seen as a portrait, one that Dirck van Delen painted in 1637. This flower has been identified as the precious 'Generael der generaelen van Gouda' (General of generals from Gouda). This General was portrayed in the year that saw an abrupt end to the 'tulip mania' to which this small painting alludes (see cat. no. 3).[14] Nevertheless, the still life in Hartford does not appear to have been conceived with a comparable botanical interest, nor are there symbolic or literary references to be distilled from the secondary motifs – a somewhat stiff butterfly and a dragonfly.[15]

The small panel by Van Delen is remarkable not just because single flowers were rarely painted, but also because it was made by a specialist in church interiors who never again made a flower still life. The uniqueness of a painting may sometimes lend it an extra dimension that makes it even more attractive for the collector. That is true, for instance, of the *Still Life with Stone Jug and Pipes* (cat. no. 12, fig. 1) of 1658 by Pieter van Anraadt. This painting was acquired some time ago by the Mauritshuis in part because it is the only still life by an artist otherwise known as a mediocre portraitist. In addition, the painting is of exceptional quality.[16] Also exceptional is the *Full Daffodils in a Vase* by Simon Verelst, who is an artist too little known not only in the United States but also in the Netherlands. Moreover, it is in all its simplicity an engaging work.

◄ **3**
Balthasar van der Ast
A Tulip in a Glass Vase
Panel, 26.5 x 20 cm (10⅜ x 7⅞ in.)
Lower right: .*B. vander. Ast.* (ca. 1640)
Solingen, Galerie Müllenmeister

► **4**
Dirck van Delen
A Tulip in a Kendi Vase
Panel, 38.5 x 29 cm (15⅛ x 11⅜ in.)
Lower right: *DVDELEN / 1637* (DVD in ligature)
Rotterdam, Museum Boymans-van Beuningen,
inv. no. 2887

1 *Lewis 1979*, pp. 45-46: Index of Owners (past and present)
2 Inv. no. 1919.B.228; *Wright 1980*, p. 468; not in *Lewis 1979*
3 *Blankert 1978*, pp. 140-141, no. 177 and fig.; the museum is due to be reopened
in a property at the Hofvijver in The Hague.
4 *Pepys 1970-1983*, vol. IX, pp. 514-515
5 *London 1952*, no. 25
6 *WAB 1957*, n.p. and fig. cover
7 *Sutton 1986*, p. 103
8 *Haverkamp-Begemann 1978*, p. 198, no. 163 and note 2
9 *Lewis 1979*, pp. 23-41, nos. 1-143 (signatures or monograms on nos. 12, 19, 22,
23, 46, 52, 57, 67, 79, 98, 107, 118, 126, 131, 133, 134, 140, and 142); see also
pp. 43-44, nos. 145-155)
10 *Lewis 1979*, pp. 40-41, no. 140 and fig.
11 *Bol 1960*, p. 72, no. 18 and pl. 37a; *Bakker et al. 1984*, pp. 146-147, no. 15 and
fig.; *Segal 1984*, p. 54
12 *Segal 1982*, p. 39
13 *Meijer 1989*, pp. 72-73, no. 12 and fig.
14 *Segal 1988-1989*, pp. 109 and 235, no. 23 and fig.; see also *Haarlem 1974*
(on 'tulip mania').
15 *Van Boven / Segal 1980*, p. 90 on the daffodil (*narcissus*) in connection with death
and self-love (the story of Narcissus).
16 *Hoetink 1978*, p. 104; see also *Broos 1987*, pp. 20-23, no. 2 and fig.
B B

Delft 1632 – Delft 1675

Canvas, 45 x 39.9 cm (17¾ x 15¾ in.)
On the frame of the still life: *IVMeer* (IVM in ligature) (ca. 1666)
Washington, D.C., National Gallery of Art, inv. no. 1962.10.1

Johannes Vermeer was the son of Reynier Jansz Vermeer, a silk painter from Flanders who had become an art dealer and inn-keeper in Delft. His teacher was probably Leonard Bramer, and in 1653 he became a master in the guild of Saint Luke in Delft. In that year he married Catharina Bolnes, and they had fifteen children, four of whom died young. In 1662 and 1670 he was dean of the guild. Vermeer's oeuvre was quite small, but relatively much of it has been preserved. Thirty-one works, which were made between 1654 and 1675, are now still believed to be from his own hand. Because only three of these are dated, the chronology is problematic. It may well seem odd that not one drawing or print by the artist is known.

Vermeer initially painted history pieces. These show the unmistakable influence of the Utrecht Caravaggists, but also that of identifiable models by Amsterdam history painters such as Jacob van Loo and Erasmus Quellinus. However, Vermeer concentrated on interior scenes, initially summarily indicated rooms with one figure, and later clearly constructed interiors using a tile pattern as departure point, perhaps by analogy with the Delft painters of church interiors. After the fashion of the genre painters of his time, his scenes take place in bourgeois surroundings, in which the figures and the subsidiary features together form a meaningful whole and reveal a symbolic or moralizing content. Thus a letter received refers to love, a sleeping girl to moderation, and a woman weighing gold to transiency. Vermeer further painted two exteriors, which became famous as *The Street* (Amsterdam, Rijksmuseum) and the *View of Delft* (The Hague, Mauritshuis). Vermeer remains most admired for his technique and illusionistic effects.

His earliest works are painted in clear hues that lend clarity and sensual beauty to the forms. The suggestion of tangible reality is very strong. From about 1662 on, the rendering of matter becomes less sharply defined, and the lighting more muted. Vermeer's ability to evoke a poetic atmosphere using purely pictorial means in images taken from daily life has been rarely equaled.

Provenance

Collection Pieter Claesz van Ruijven, Delft, before 1674
Collection Maria de Knuijt, the widow Van Ruijven, Delft, 1674-1681
Collection Magdalena van Ruijven, Abraham and Jacob Dissius, Delft, 1682-1696
Auction Dissius, Amsterdam, 1696 (ƒ63)
Auction Van Buren, The Hague, 1808
Auction Luchtmans, Rotterdam, 1816 (ƒ70)
Collection Kamermans, Rotterdam, 1819
Auction Kamermans, Rotterdam, 1825 (ƒ305 to Lelie)
Auction Reydon et al., Amsterdam, 1827 (to De Robiano)
Collection François-Xavier Count de Robiano, Brussels, 1827-1837
Auction De Robiano, Brussels, 1837 (BF400 to J. Héris acting for De Robiano)
Collection Ludovic Count de Robiano, Brussels, 1837-1887
Collection heirs De Robiano, 1888-1906
Dealer J. & A. LeRoy, Brussels, 1907
Collection J. Pierpont Morgan, New York, 1907-1913
The Metropolitan Museum of Art, 1907-1913(?) (loan from Pierpont Morgan)
Collection J. Pierpont Morgan, Jr., New York, 1913-1939 (on consignment with dealer Knoedler, New York, 1935-1939)
Collection Sir Harry Oakes, Nassau, Bahamas, 1940-1943
Collection Lady Eunice Oakes, Nassau, Bahamas, 1943-1946
Collection Horace Havemeyer, New York, 1946-1956 (bought by way of dealer Knoedler)
Collection Mrs. Horace Havemeyer, New York, 1956-1966
National Gallery of Art, Washington, D.C., 1962 (gift of Harry Waldron Havemeyer and Horace Havemeyer, Jr., in memory of their father, Horace Havemeyer, delivered in 1966)

Bibliography

Hoet 1752-1770, vol. I, p. 36, no. 35
Auction The Hague 1808, p. 264, no. 22
Auction Rotterdam 1816, p. 26, no. 90
Murray 1819-1823, p. 29
Auction Rotterdam 1825, p. 13, no. 70
Auction Amsterdam 1827, p. 6, no. 26
Auction Brussels 1837, p. 78, no. 436
Thoré-Bürger 1866, p. 564, no. 40
Brussels 1873, p. 76, no. 264
Havard 1888, p. 38, no. 43
HdG 36 (vol. I [1907], p. 603, no. 36)
HdG-MS 36
Hofstede de Groot 1907-1930, vol. II, p. 5 and pl. 43
Bulletin MMA 1908, p. 76
Vanzype 1908/1925, pp. 22, 31, 34 and 87
Cortissoz 1909, p. 166
Stephenson 1909, pp. 168 and 172 and fig.
Valentiner 1909, p. 137, no. 136 and fig.
Cox 1909-1910, pp. 246 and 303 and fig.
Breck 1910, pp. 5 and 41
Cicerone 1910, pp. 109-110
Friedländer 1910, p. 98
Plietzsch 1911, p. 118, no. 31 (36)
Hale 1913, p. 240 and fig.

Johannes Vermeer A Girl Writing a Letter

Hausenstein 1924, p. 27 and fig. 22
Chantavoine 1926, pp. 47, 59, 76 and 97 and fig.
De Hévésy 1935, pp. 365-366 and fig.
Van Overbeek 1935, p. 235 and fig. LIII
Rotterdam 1935, p. 37, no. 86a
Martin 1936, vol. I, p. 193
Bremmer 1937, no. 87 and fig.
Hale et al. 1937, p. 101, no. 35 and p. 226
McCall / Valentiner 1939, p. 195, no. 399 and pl. 72
Plietzsch 1939, p. 30 and fig. 31
Studio 1939, p. 53 and fig.
Trivas 1939, p. 139
De Vries 1939, pp. 46-47 and 88, no. 26 and fig. 50
Bodkin / Goldscheider 1940, p. 13 and fig. 35
Comstock 1940, p. 112 and fig.
Frankfurter 1940, p. 9 and fig.
Trautscholdt 1940, p. 268
New York 1941, pp. 18-19, no. 17
Frankfurter 1942, p. 11 and fig.
McCall / Barnouw 1942, pp. 89 and 159, no. 68 and fig.
Rigby / Rigby 1944, p. 13
Blum 1945, p. 179, no. 40
New York 1946, no. 15 and fig.
Hultén 1948, p. 91, no. 35
Van Thienen 1948, p. 42 and fig.
De Vries 1948, p. XIII and fig. 19
Allen 1949, p. 199
Swillens 1950, p. 53, no. 8, pp. 67, 78, 82, 87, 89, 108, 155 and pl. 8
Gowing 1952, p. 134, no. XVIII and fig. 42
Malraux 1952, p. 65, no. XIII and fig.
Bloch 1954 / 1963, p. 35, no. 53 and fig.
Goldscheider 1958, pp. 141-142, no. 20 and fig. 50
Goldscheider 1958-A, pp. 129-130, no. 20 and fig. 50
Descargues 1966, p. 65 and figs. pp. 130 and 134
Gerson 1967, col. 743
Ungaretti / Bianconi 1967, p. 93, no. 28 and fig.
Koningsberger 1968, pp. 154-155 and fig.
New York 1968, p. 298
Sutton 1969, p. 231
Fahy 1973, p. 316 and fig. 6
Canfield 1974, p. 107 and fig. p. 160
Grimme 1974, p. 77, no. 27 and fig. 18
Blankert 1975, pp. 11, 36, 82-84, 109, 153-154, no. 20 and pl. 20
Washington 1975, pp. 362-363, no. 1664 and fig.
De Vries 1976, p. 23 and pl. 23
Wright 1976, pp. 12, 42 and 44, no. 16 and fig.
Menzel 1977, p. 68 and fig. 65
Van Straaten 1977-A, pp. 48-49 and fig. 60
Washington 1977, p. 47 and fig.
Blankert 1978-A, pp. 10, 25, 54, 56, 73 and 164, no. 20 and figs. 20-20a
Slatkes 1981, pp. 70-71 and fig.
Wheelock 1981, pp. 124-127 and pls. 31-32
Reitlinger 1982, vol. I, p. 483
Walker 1984, pp. 300-301, no. 405 and fig.
Ota / Takahashi 1985, no. 22 and fig.
Washington 1985, p. 421 and fig.
Blankert / Montias et al. 1987, pp. 11, 46, 52, 85, 132, pl. 22, pp. 189-190, no. 20
Montias 1987, p. 73
Tokyo 1987, pp. 221-222, no. 86 and fig.
Montias 1989, pp. 191-192, 196, 256, 266 and fig. 44

This *Girl Writing a Letter* was one of the last authentic paintings by Jan Vermeer to move from private property to the public domain.[1] There exists an anecdote about the collector Pierpont Morgan (p. 40, fig. 26) that must concern this painting. The antiquarian G.S. Hellman brought the multimillionaire a canvas and noted to his amazement that 'the great Dutchman's name was strange to the Morgan ear.' He briefly explained something about the painter, his place in the history of art, and the amounts that then passed hands for a Vermeer. 'Morgan gazed at the picture; abruptly asked the price. "One hundred thousand dollars," said the dealer. "I'll take it," snapped Morgan, and the deal was concluded.'[2]

This must have taken place in 1907, when the painting was thought to be a lost work. Hofstede de Groot wrote that it had disappeared after the auction in 1837 of François-Xavier Count de Robiano (1778-1836).[3] It can now be revealed where the painting was in the interim. It is apparent from a note in the archives of the dealer LeRoy in Brussels, made during the De Robiano auction, that the painting was bought for 400 Belgian francs by the dealer Héris 'for the Count de Robiano beaufort' (in translation).[4] This means that the De Robiano family bought the painting back, no doubt through the agency of Count Ludovic (1807-1887), the eldest son of François-Xavier, who was married to Louise-Ida de Beauffort (1810-1892). Until now it has further gone unobserved that in 1873 Ludovic lent the painting to a benefit exhibition in Brussels.[5] Besides, Havard turns out to have known the location of the painting by 1888: 'Belongs to Count L. de Robiano, ex-Senator of Belgium' (in translation),[6] who had died the year before. All later authors thought that this referred to François-Xavier – which could not be right – and believed with Hofstede de Groot that the location remained unknown for three-quarters of a century. Presumably the painting was bequeathed by way of the only daughter of Ludovic de Robiano, Jeanne-Louise (1835-1900), to her husband, Gustave Baron de Senzeille (1824-1906), and sold after his death.[7]

In 1910 the art-historical periodical *Der Cicerone* announced that the painting had fallen into American hands: 'The firm J. & A. Leroy has sold to America a painting by Vermeer of Delft, measuring 37 x 42 cm and depicting a girl writing, wearing a yellow jacket edged with mink, which was until now in the possession of the Robiano family' (in translation).[8] In 1908 Hofstede de Groot saw it in The Metropolitan Museum of Art in New York and noted: 'Is the painting, that has been lost for so long. It is the little woman who looks at the viewer. The owner bought it from an art buyer in the Rue Scribe in Paris; I believe he is named Glauser' (in translation).[9] The latter information was probably a false rumor.

In 1816 François-Xavier de Robiano had become chamberlain to King William I in Brussels, but in 1830 he sided with the patriots in the Belgian Revolt. He was rewarded with the governorship of the province of Antwerp and with honorary positions such as the presidency of the Commission for Fine Arts.[10] During sojourns in Holland, he had also been active as an art buyer. He must have bought the *Girl Writing a Letter* in 1827, at the Reydon auction in Amsterdam,[11] five years after the king had acquired Vermeer's *View of Delft* for 'his' Mauritshuis.[12] Hendrik Reydon (1764-1826) ran a pharmacy in Amsterdam, on the northwest corner of the Leliegracht and the Herengracht.[13] As Hofstede de Groot has established, the painting was sighted at a pair of auctions in Rotterdam in 1816 and 1825.[14] According to Frits Lugt, the auction of 1816 contained paintings from the property of Dr. Luchtmans.[15] Cornelis Jan Luchtmans (1777-1860) was a scion of the well-known Leyden dynasty of municipal and academic publishers. He took his doctorate in medicine in 1800 and subsequently set up practice in Rotterdam. There, in 1816, he had a number of paintings from his possession sold, including the *Girl Writing a Letter*.[16] He had presumably bought the painting in 1808, in The Hague, at the Van Buren auction. The owner up to that point had been Mr. [Master of Jurisprudence] J. van Buren, Bailiff of Noordwijkerhout, Hillegom, Lisse, and Voorhout.[17] Thus we now know quite precisely through whose hands the painting passed since about 1800. The question that still remains is where the painting was in the eighteenth century. The canvas was last seen at the sensational Dissius auction in Delft in 1696, when numerous works by Vermeer came under the hammer.

Jacob Dissius (1653-1695) left a large collection of Vermeers that had come to him from his father-in-law, Pieter van Ruijven, whom Michael Montias has recently identified as the Maecenas of the painter.[18] In 1885 Bredius published the descriptions of nineteen paintings by Vermeer in the inventory of Dissius's property, but was not able to identify these works. He therefore wrote in despair: 'What a treasure! And where has this all gone?' (in translation).[19] The definitive answer to this question was supplied by Montias more than a century later. It appears from the archives that two-thirds of the known oeuvre of Vermeer was in the possession of the wealthy Delft brewer's son Pieter Claesz van Ruijven (1626-1674), who, as early as 1657, acted as Vermeer's financial backer.[20] As a consequence, paintings from

the period between 1657 and 1660 are identified as being in the possession of Van Ruijven, who had them described in a will of 1665 as 'the art of painting.'[21] A little later, his collection was enlarged with the *Girl Writing a Letter*, which Van Ruijven presumably bought directly from the painter.[22] Van Ruijven's widow, Maria de Knuijt, had from 1674 on life interest in the estate, which, after her death in 1681, came into the hands of her daughter Magdalena van Ruijven. When Magdalena died a year later, the document published by Bredius was drawn up. In 1694, by way of her father-in-law Abraham Dissius, the paintings finally ended up with her husband, Jacob Dissius.[23] In 1696, the year after his death, the auction was held in Amsterdam, a catalogue of which has survived. In it, the 'art of painting' by Vermeer, which had in the meantime grown to twenty-one works, is described item by item. The painting of De Robiano and Pierpont Morgan is mentioned in this catalogue as: 'A Young Lady Writing, very well [done] by the same [J. vander Meer van Delft]' (in translation).[24] The archival research by Montias has determined that it was not Jacob Dissius, but his father-in-law, Pieter van Ruijven, who was Vermeer's principal financial backer. Unfortunately this information did not find its way into the recent monograph by Blankert, in which we still find the old misunderstanding that Jacob Dissius was the 'most important customer' of the painter.[25] A little research could have revealed much sooner that Dissius could hardly have been the Maecenas and collector of Vermeer. When Vermeer died, Jacob had just turned twenty-two.[26]

The provenance of this painting may therefore be traced back to Vermeer's studio, and leads by way of auctions in Amsterdam, The Hague, and Rotterdam, to Brussels, and finally to the United States, where, in April 1908, J. Pierpont Morgan lent it to The Metropolitan Museum of Art in New York. John Pierpont Morgan, Sr. (1837-1913) (p. 40, fig. 26) was one of the most legendary collectors of the past century. 'Gigantic in business enterprise and Homeric in the collecting world, his personality alone became a force. There have been other American collectors more sympathetic, more generous, more admirable. But it is probably the Morgan personality, among them all, that will be remembered longest and with greatest contemplation,' wrote Douglas and Elisabeth Rigby in their book *Lock, Stock and Barrel*.[27] Morgan loved to be compared with Lorenzo the Magnificent.[28] 'The Great Pierpont Morgan' died in 1913, and the loan must subsequently have been revoked. In 1935 his son J. Pierpont Morgan, Jr., lent the painting to the Vermeer exhibition in Rotterdam.[29] The Knoedler firm was the mediator in this, and attempts were apparently made to sell the canvas. In 1940 it had a new owner and, at a benefit exhibition for the Red Cross War Fund, Knoedler presented it as an anonymous loan.[30]

The new owner was Sir Harry Oakes (1874-1943) of Nassau, who was Justice of the Peace of the Bahamas.[31] Duveen Brothers exhibited it in 1942 in a show in New York held for the benefit of the Queen Wilhelmina Fund.[32] Sir Harry was murdered by the Mafia during the night of 7 to 8 June 1943 because he had refused to cooperate with the opening of a casino in the Bahamas.[33] His widow, Lady Eunice Oakes, sold the painting in 1946, once again by way of Knoedler's. The canvas was therefore not, as Wright believed in 1976, 'isolated for long in a collection in the Bahamas.'[34] In November 1946, Horace Havemeyer (1886-1956) became the lucky owner. He was the son of the famous collecting couple Henry (1847-1907) and Louisine (1855-1929) Havemeyer, who in 1929 had left their collection of French impressionist paintings to The Metropolitan Museum

1
Johannes Vermeer
Lady with Maidservant
Canvas, 92 x 78.7 cm (36¼ x 31 in.)
Neither signed nor dated (ca. 1666)
New York, The Frick Collection, inv. no. 19.1.126

2
Johannes Vermeer
The Love Letter
Canvas, 44 x 38.5 cm (17⅜ x 15⅛ in.)
To the left of the maidservant: *JVMeer* (JVM in ligature) (ca. 1666)
Amsterdam, Rijksmuseum, inv. no. A 1595

3
Gerard ter Borch
Woman Writing a Letter
Panel, 39 x 29.5 cm (15⅜ x 11⅝ in.)
In the center, on the edge of the table: *GTB* (in ligature) (ca. 1655)
The Hague, Mauritshuis, inv. no. 797

of Art.[35] In 1962 the National Gallery of Art in Washington officially received title to Vermeer's *Girl Writing a Letter*, but the widow Havemeyer and her sons, Horace, Jr. (born 1914), and Harry Waldron Havemeyer (born 1929), retained life interest. In 1966 they decided to exhibit the painting in the museum only for a while, but it has remained there ever since. In 1974 they waived all further claims.[36]

'It is the little woman who looks at the viewer,' wrote Hofstede de Groot, and this fact has given some people the idea that this must be a portrait.[37] However, Jan Vermeer apparently did not wish to exploit his talents working as a portrait painter, though his way of painting was well suited for this. In imitation of Carel van Mander he probably believed that the 'depicting after life' ought to be regarded as a 'side road of art.' In 1678 Van Hoogstraten still did not have much use for portraitists. Both theoreticians considered history painting to be the highest branch of art.[38] The painting in Washington was indeed intended to be something more than a portrait or a record of reality.

Vermeer does appear to have painted the scene using a live model in surroundings that he had himself arranged. The desk set and jewel box on the table, for instance, are also depicted in the *Lady with Maidservant* (New York, Frick Collection) [1].[39] In the Washington version, however, Vermeer has the light falling from the left on the small chest in such a way that the copper tacks reflect the sun. We also see such reflections of light, which are characteristic of Vermeer, on the back of the so-called Spanish chair that repeatedly appears in his compositions.[40] The jacket of yellow satin trimmed with white mink worn by the lady is a familiar item that may well have come from the wardrobe of Catharina Bolnes, Vermeer's spouse.[41] It occurs in the painting in New York and also in *The Love Letter* (Amsterdam, Rijksmuseum) [2].[42] The still life on the wall is undoubtedly a piece from Vermeer's own collection, which, in the will of the painter, was described as 'A [painting] in which [there is] a bass and a skull' (in translation).[43] Since 1951 art historians have been parroting Boström, who incorrectly maintained that this is a still life by Cornelis van der Meulen (instead of one by Baschenis, as had earlier been claimed).[44] The still lifes by Van der Meulen that are known to us date from the late seventies and the eighties (1677, 1681, 1684, 1689), something Böstrom failed to mention.[45]

In 1696 the painting in New York was called 'A Young Lady who is brought a letter by a Maid' (in translation).[46] The Washington painting also clearly treats an activity that was reserved for young ladies, with the maid at the most serving as letter carrier. Writing letters was a fashion that had come from France, and it was especially love letters that flowed from the well-sharpened quills of passionate young ladies or bold gentlemen.[47] The letters in all the paintings by Vermeer in which a lady writes, receives, or reads a letter are intended to be seen as love letters. The context need not explicitly emphasize this. In this instance, it is only the *vanitas* painting with the skull that makes it clear that the woman who looks at us reflectively ought to be aware of the transience of existence and of worldly pleasures. Gerard ter Borch also preferred to omit all-too-obvious references; his *Woman Writing a Letter* (The Hague, Mauritshuis) [3] may have served as Vermeer's example.[48] In this case the letter may safely be assumed to be a love letter.[49] When, in the seventeenth century, a painting was entitled 'A Young Lady Writing, very well [done],' people knew at a glance that it concerned an amorous message.[50] That it is also superbly painted goes without saying.

1 See Provenance; the only work that still remains in private hands (*Blankert / Montias et al. 1987*, pp. 198-199, no. 27 and pl. 27), was stolen in 1986.

2 *Allen 1949*, p. 199; *Canfield 1974*, p. 107

3 *Hofstede de Groot 1907-1930*, vol. II, pp. 5-6; *Thoré-Bürger 1866*, p. 564, no. 40: 'A retrouver.'

4 Index cards LeRoy (RKD), no. 52

5 *Brussels 1873*, p. 76, no. 264

6 *Havard 1888*, p. 38, no. 43; *Noblesse Belge 1897*, p. 2022

7 *Noblesse Belge 1912*, p. 395; this reconstruction is the work of Drs. Marjolein de Boer.

8 *Cicerone 1910*, pp. 109-110

9 Index cards Hofstede de Groot (RKD); this 'discovery' was mentioned in a newspaper report of 6 October 1908 (RKD). In April 1908 the painting was in place in gallery 24, see *Bulletin MMA 1908*, p. 76.

10 *BNB*, vol. XIX (1907), col. 536; *Noblesse Belge 1897*, pp. 2021-2022; on the De Robiano family, see *Goethals 1852*.

11 *Auction Amsterdam 1827*, p. 6, no. 26 (see also no. 27, a work by Vrel then attributed to Vermeer. Thus De Robiano bought two 'Vermeers') there.

12 Inv. no. 92; *Broos 1987*, p. 382-389, no. 65 and fig.

13 Dossier Reydon (Centraal Bureau voor Genealogie, The Hague).

14 HdG 36

15 L 8868

16 *Van der Aa 1852 / 1969*, vol. IV, p. 215

17 *Auction The Hague 1808*, title page and p. 264, no. 22; first mentioned by *Blankert / Montias et al. 1987*, p. 1900.

18 *Montias 1987*, pp. 68-71 (reprinted in *Montias 1989*, pp. 246-262)

19 *Bredius 1885*, p. 222

20 *Blankert / Montias et al. 1987*, p. 210; *Montias 1987*, pp. 69-71; *Montias 1989*, p. 248

21 *Montias 1987*, p. 69; *Montias 1989*, pp. 248 and 323

22 *Montias 1987*, p. 73; *Montias 1989*, p. 256

23 *Montias 1987*, p. 72; *Montias 1989*, pp. 251-255; NB: Initially Abraham and Jacob Dissius had divided the estate of Magdalena among each other by lot.

24 *Hoet 1752-1770*, vol. I, p. 36, no. 35

25 *Blankert / Montias et al. 1987*, p. 155

26 *Montias 1987*, p. 71, note 25; *Wheelock 1977*, p. 439: 'curiously, no evidence of their relationship exists.'

27 *Rigby / Rigby 1944*, p. 282

28 *Rigby / Rigby 1944*, p. 285; see also *Hartford / New York / Fort Worth 1987*, pp. 10-57

29 *Rotterdam 1935*, p. 37, no. 86a

30 *Comstock 1940*, p. 112

31 *Burke's 1963*, p. 1841; according to a note accompanying the photograph in The Hague (RKD), Oskar B. Cintas (Havana) was the owner in 1940.

32 *McCall / Barnouw 1942*, p. 89, no. 68

33 *Highsmith 1976*, p. 853

34 *Wright 1976*, p. 12

35 *Constable 1964*, pp. 76-79

36 Documentation archives National Gallery of Art, Washington; *Weitzenhoffer 1986*, pp. 16-17, provided a genealogical tree of the Havemeyer family.

37 See note 9; *Swillens 1950*, p. 108 and *Wheelock 1981*, p. 124

38 *Van Mander 1604*, fol. 281 recto; *Van Hoogstraten 1678*, p. 87; see also *Broos 1978-1979*, pp. 117-118

39 *Blankert / Montias et al. 1987*, pp. 133 and 190-192, no. 21 and fig.

40 See, for instance, *Swillens 1950*, p. 78

41 *Blankert / Montias et al. 1987*, p. 46; *Montias 1989*, p. 196

42 *Van Thiel et al. 1976*, p. 572, no. A 1595 and fig.; *Blankert / Montias et al. 1987*, pp. 131 and 192-193, no. 22 and fig.

43 *Blankert / Montias et al. 1987*, p. 213: 26 February 1676

44 *Boström 1951*, p. 117

45 Photographs RKD

46 *Hoet 1752-1770*, vol. I, p. 34, no. 7

47 *De Jongh 1971*, pp. 178-179; see also cat. no. 43

48 *Hoetink et al. 1985*, pp. 146-147, no. 14 and p. 342, no. 797 and fig.

49 *Amsterdam 1976*, pp. 36-39, no. 2

50 See note 24

BB

Rotterdam 1600 / 1601 – Weesp 1653

Canvas, 89 x 135 cm (35 x 53 in.)
At the right, on a plank: S DE VLIEGER 1646
Los Angeles, Calif., collection of Mr. and Mrs. Edward William Carter

Simon de Vlieger lived in Rotterdam until 1633 (where he was married in 1627). In 1634 he became a member of the painters' guild in Delft, but four years later he left for Amsterdam, where he was registered as a burgher in 1643. The last four years of his life he lived in Weesp. It is not known who his teacher was, but the early work (after 1624) consists of fantastic shore landscapes with rough seas in the manner of Jan Porcellis.

After 1630 he painted the beach as it could actually be seen along the Dutch coast. The weather is by preference that of a cloudy day in spring or fall with a watery sun behind high cloud banks. From 1650 on he made seascapes with calm waters, which were especially influential for the most important marine painters of the second half of the seventeenth century (Jan van de Cappelle, Hendrick Dubbels, and Willem van de Velde the Younger).

This *View of a Beach*, signed and dated 1646 by Simon de Vlieger, has, as far as we know, only been sold in public twice. The difference in proceeds indicates the tumultuous developments with respect to first-rate paintings in the art market of the last decades. Shortly after World War II the painting was auctioned in London from the estate of a certain T.A. Carlyon, a resident of Southbourne, Bournemouth, who had assembled a very modest collection of Dutch masters. Not one piece went for more than seventy-five pounds, but the canvas by De Vlieger turned out to be an exception. The dealer D. Katz from Dieren bought it for 483 pounds.[1]

Subsequently the painting was with various dealers and in private hands, but the precise facts are not known to us. In 1980 it was once again auctioned in London from the collection of Mrs. M.D. Langlois van den Bergh of Wassenaar.[2] Until then, this beach view by De Vlieger had been a virtually unknown painting, which was only mentioned in passing in the literature and which had never before been illustrated.[3] At that auction of 1980, however, it was recognized as an important masterpiece, for it went for no less than 68,000 pounds, which was more than 140 times the amount that it brought in 1946.[4] In 1981 the dealer Koetser of Geneva sold the canvas to the collector Carter of Los Angeles for an unknown amount.

Provenance
Collection T.A. Carlyon, Bournemouth, before 1946
Auction Carlyon, London, 1946 (£483 to Katz, Dieren)
Dealer A. Kaufmann, London, 1946
Dealer A. Brod, London, 1952
Collection Mrs. M.D. Langlois van den Bergh, Wassenaar, before 1980
Auction London, 1980 (£68,000)
Dealer Koetser, Geneva, 1981
Collection Mr. and Mrs. Edward William Carter, Los Angeles, 1981

Bibliography
Auction London 1946, p. 9, no. 83
Kelch 1971, p. 168, no. 97
Bol 1973, p. 184
Auction London 1980, vol. I, no. 82 and fig.
WCA, vol. XXXII (1980), p. 343
Walsh 1981, pp. 383-384 and pl. VII
Walsh / Schneider 1981-1982, addendum, n.p. and fig.

I
Edward William Carter (born 1911)
Photograph by John Engstead
Los Angeles, The Los Angeles County Museum of Art

Simon de Vlieger View of a Beach

Edward William Carter (born 1911) [1] and his wife showed their collection to the public for the first time in 1981 and 1982 in Los Angeles, Boston, and New York. The De Vlieger could only be included in an addendum to the catalogue.[5] Carter is a successful businessman, who began collecting late in life: he bought his first paintings in 1957. He prefers Dutch paintings of the Golden Age, and though his collection is small in size, it is great in quality. In the seventies he bought from several important European collections which were then being dispersed, such as those of Sidney van den Bergh (see cat. no. 12) and B. de Geus van den Heuvel. 'He was [...] the envy of other collectors and museum curators, who could rarely match his speed and his determination to secure the finest examples,' wrote Walsh in connection with the exhibition of the Carter collection.[6] Carter has announced that he intends to leave his collection to the museum of his hometown, Los Angeles.[7]

The title of the exhibition of 1981 and 1982 had been deliberately chosen: *A Mirror of Nature*. This was done with reference to a passage in *De Hooge Schoole der Schilderkonst* (The Advanced School of the Art of Painting) of 1678 by Van Hoogstraten, who had written: 'For a perfect Painting is like a mirror of Nature, which makes the things that are not, appear to be' (in translation).[8] It so happens that for Carter realism is the most attractive quality of Dutch painting. He loves paintings that are done *naer het leven* (after real life), and not history pieces or genre scenes.[9] His view of art appears to be quite deliberately different from the seventeenth-century vision, according to which invented compositions ought to be more highly appreciated than scenes simply copied from the model, such as landscapes or still lifes. That, in any case, was the theory (see cat. nos. 16 and 56). But, in addition, Carter seeks out unusual works by minor masters (such as cat. no. 12), and he pays particularly close attention to the state of the work of art.[10] In the case of this *View of a Beach* by Simon de Vlieger, the condition is altogether flawless.

The scene shows us a view from the dunes looking down on a beach crowded with people; things are equally busy on the water. Actually, this is more an elaborate 'genre' scene than a landscape, because the people and their activities dominate. De Vlieger did his utmost to come up with amusing details, as if he were recreating a winter scene by Avercamp in a summery variant. On the top of a dune to the left, for instance, a gentleman sits on a red cloak (as he does not want to dirty his pants) looking through a telescope at what is happening on the large three-master, from which a salute is just being fired. To the right of him a fisherman

kisses his wife farewell – or we assume that such is the case – while behind them a man walks onto the beach with rabbits that he has just poached in the dunes, looking for customers. There are enough potential buyers, although most are heading for the fishermen who are bringing their catch on land. Ladies and gentlemen from the city stand somewhat haughtily amid these simple seamen. The fishwife in the foreground sells a large codfish to a man with a broad gray beard. A horseman with two whippets halts his mount next to a vendor who is displaying his wares. At the right a group of porters waits with empty baskets, which have been turned upside down so that the women may sit on them.

The Dutch beach then looked totally different from the way it looks today. Sunbathing and swimming were most unusual. People sometimes waded or enjoyed the fresh air. Depictions of beach amusements are definitely in the minority in the seventeenth century. In 1658 Adriaen van de Velde painted a *View of the Beach at Scheveningen* (Kassel, Staatliche Kunstsammlungen, Gemäldegalerie) [2],[11] in which we see a man who has rolled up his pant legs and who stares pensively over the North Sea. In this scene he symbolizes, as it were, the aura of doing sweet nothing. If De Vlieger made a drawing *naer het leven*, the

3
Simon de Vlieger
Fishermen on the Beach at Noordwijk
Pen and wash drawing, 210 x 377 mm (8¼ x 14⅞ in.)
Neither signed nor dated (ca. 1645-1650)
Vienna, Graphische Sammlung Albertina,
inv. no. 9170

4
Simon de Vlieger
Ten Perspectival Studies
Pen drawing, 320 x 210 mm (12⅝ x 8¼ in.)
Lower left (autograph?): *S. d Vliger 1645*
London, British Museum, inv. no. 1874.8.8.99

activities of the fishmongers on the beach were usually his subject.
To this end he made separate figure studies but also finished
drawings. One example of such a 'realistic' beach view is provided
by the drawing *Fishermen on the Beach at Noordwijk* (Vienna,
Graphische Sammlung Albertina) [**3**].[12]

A close look will reveal correspondences between some figures
in this drawing and in Carter's painting (the man lifting a basket,
for instance). Naturally the painted beach view originated in the
studio, using preparatory studies for an imaginary composition. It is known how the artist proceeded in setting up a
landscape or seascape. In 1645 Simon de Vlieger demonstrated
– presumably to a pupil – how simply an effective composition
can be constructed. He made a facile sketch with ten examples
(London, British Museum) [**4**].[13] Striking in each of the sketches
is the low horizon that was characteristic of the Dutch landscape
in the heyday of seventeenth-century painting. The two upper
drawings indicate how one could depict a diversity of figures –
as in a beach view – in a natural way, with ever smaller figures
receding into the background. In several other drawings he
composed formations of ships with no more than a horizon line
as reference.[14] One can, of course, appreciate the beach view of
1646 as a 'Mirror of Nature,' but only with the knowledge that
reality has been altered to suit the artist.

When the painting turned up in 1946, the depiction was made
to appear more interesting by presenting it as a historic event,

namely, *The Arrival of the Prince of Orange in Vlissingen*.[15] There is,
however, no indication to be found in the painting that what is
happening at sea constitutes the main subject of the whole.
The large three-master is recognizable as a Dutch ship, with the
tricolor at the top and an orange flag above the stern. With some
difficulty the coat of arms of Amsterdam is to be seen on this
stern, with the decussate cross of Saint Andrew and the
emperor's crown above it, and shield bearers to the left and
right. Only recently Jan Kelch has decisively, but without any
foundation, identified this three-master as the *Aemilia* (or *Amalia*)
of Admiral Maarten Harpertsz Tromp.[16] Willem van de Velde
the Younger had drawn this ship (Rotterdam, Museum Boymans-
van Beuningen),[17] the stern of which obviously did not carry the
coat of arms of Amsterdam, but that of Amalia van Solms.[18]

De Vlieger therefore painted neither merely a coastal landscape
nor a typical 'marine' with portraits of ships of the kind his pupil

5
Simon de Vlieger
View of a Beach
Panel, 60.6 x 83.5 cm (23⅞ x 32⅞ in.)
Lower right: S. DE VLIEGER A 1643
The Hague, Mauritshuis, inv. no. 558

Willem van de Velde later often rendered (cat. no. 65). The background, after all, is but a scenic setting for what takes place in the foreground. This genre of the beach view is Simon de Vlieger's own invention, in which he excelled during the forties.[19] There is usually not as much of a hubbub as in Carter's painting, and the activities often take place on one side of the composition. The wide prospect and a range of events characterize some splendid beach views, such as that in the Mauritshuis (The Hague) [**5**],[20] which is dated 1643. Until now it was said to be one of the most important works by Simon de Vlieger, and even 'one of his most sublime paintings' (in translation).[21] It is no exaggeration to state that the canvas in the Carter collection rivals the painting in The Hague.

1 *Auction London 1946*, p. 9, no. 83
2 *Auction London 1980*, vol. 1, no. 82, where the owner is mistakenly called 'Langloh-van den Bergh.'
3 *Kelch 1971*, p. 168, no. 97; *Bol 1973*, p. 184
4 *WCA*, vol. XXXII (1980), p. 343
5 *Walsh / Schneider 1981-1982*, addendum
6 *Walsh 1981*, p. 380
7 *Sutton 1986*, p. 129
8 *Van Hoogstraten 1678*, p. 25, with reference to trompe-l'oeils, such as cat. no. 57.
9 *Walsh 1981*, p. 380; this is therefore not quite what Hoogstraten intended (see the previous note).
10 *Walsh 1981*, p. 382
11 HdG 355; *Haak 1984*, p. 472, fig. 1041
12 *Bernt 1957-1958*, vol. II, no. 653 and fig.
13 *Hind 1915-1931*, vol. IV, p. 100, no. 14 and pl. LIX
14 *Ruurs 1983*, pp. 190-194, figs. 1-11, presented a technical analysis of the drawing.
15 *Auction London 1946*, p. 9, no. 83
16 Communicated in *Walsh / Schneider 1981-1982*, addendum, note 1.
17 Inv. no. MB 1866 / T 216; *Robinson / Weber 1979*, vol. I, p. 91, no. T 216, vol. III, p. 93 and fig.
18 On the *Aemilia* as a theme in the work of De Vlieger, see *Kelch 1971*, pp. 101-105.
19 *Kelch 1971*, pp. 164-170, nos. 85-104, summarized this genre in the work of De Vlieger.
20 *Duparc 1980*, pp. 120-121 and 241, no. 558 and fig.
21 *Bol 1973*, p. 183; *Duparc 1980*, p. 120: 'behoort tot de belangrijkste werken van Simon de Vlieger.'
   BB

Hendrick van Vliet Interior of the Old Church in Delft

Delft 1611 / 1612 – Delft 1675

Canvas, 82.6 x 66 cm (32½ x 26 in.)
On the dark stripe on the base of the front column: *H. van vliet - 1660*
New York, The Metropolitan Museum of Art, inv. no. 1976.23.2

Provenance
Dealer Babcock Galleries, New York
Collection C. Douglas Dillon, Far Hills, N.J., 1975
The Metropolitan Museum of Art, New York, 1975
(gift of Clarence Douglas Dillon)

Bibliography
Baetjer 1980, vol. I, p. 194, no. 1976.23.2, vol. III,
p. 428, no 1976.23.2 and fig.
Liedtke 1982, pp. 10, 64, 65, 67, 107, no. 68, fig. 50
and pl. VII
Liedtke 1982-A, pp. 65-66 and fig. 7
Liedtke 1986, pp. 802 and 804, fig. 27

Hendrick Cornelisz van Vliet learned painting from his uncle, the portrait painter Willem van Vliet, and from Michiel Jansz van Mierevelt. Initially he made primarily portraits, even though he also painted scenes with mythological or historical content. In 1651 and 1652, when he was already forty years old, he applied himself, no doubt inspired by the success that Gerard Houckgeest reaped with it, to 'portraying' church interiors, notably those of the Old and New Church in Delft. His best paintings date from the period between 1652 and 1654, in which he differentiated himself from Houckgeest, and also from Emanuel de Witte, by his clever rendering of the cool and moist atmosphere in these churches.

After De Witte had left for Amsterdam in 1652, Houckgeest had gone to live on his country estate near Bergen op Zoom in 1653, and Carel Fabritius had met with his accidental death in 1654, Van Vliet enjoyed a monopoly in Delft painting architectural and perspectival views. From 1658 on he tried to introduce variety into his interiors with new vantage points, which sometimes led to a forced and distorted perspective. After this period he was inspired again by Houckgeest's work of the early fifties, which he imitated but on which he also made variations.

This painting shows us the interior of the Old Church of Delft seen from the southern aisle in a northwesterly direction. We see the northern transept, which was built from 1512 to 1525 by the brothers Rombout and Anthony Keldermans, as well as the wood-vaulted Onze-Lieve-Vrouwekoor (Choir of Our Lady). After 1536, when the church burned during a city fire, this part was rebuilt. Whereas the New Church was famous because it housed the tomb of the 'father of the fatherland,' William of Orange, who was murdered in 1584, the Old Church could pride itself on the dignified tomb of Piet Hein, which was made by Pieter de Keyser, and a monument to Maarten Harmensz Tromp, by the hand of Jacob van Campen. Both were naval heroes of the Eighty Years' War. However, neither of these sculptures is visible from the viewpoint chosen for Van Vliet's New York painting.

Against the third column at the right we see a splendidly

carved Renaissance pulpit from 1548. In the foreground, next to a detached pew, there is an unfinished grave, from which a spade protrudes, while a broom is placed against the column in the foreground. There are but few visitors in the church, among whom are a young man standing with his back to us and, farther back, a woman with a small child, two gentlemen, and a man and woman. A large number of wooden grave signs are attached to the columns, where we see parts of several Renaissance epitaphs. This painting is a typical example of the direction taken by Van Vliet at the end of the fifties, when he no longer had any competition in Delft. In this period he began to investigate alternatives to the standard 'portraits' of this interior.[1]

The *Interior of the Old Church in Delft* in the Baltimore Museum of Art [1], which is dated 1658, shows how Van Vliet presumably painted the church for the first time from the southern aisle in a northeasterly direction.[2] Here the distance from the painter and spectator to the columns separating the aisles and nave is still great, so that the wooden vaulting of the aisle is visible. Conspicuous is the busy and lively staffage, which strongly reminds us of the way in which Emanuel de Witte populated his interiors. In the painting from The Metropolitan Museum of Art, however, the complement of figures has been reduced to a minimum.

In the *Interior of the Old Church in Delft during a Service* in Vienna (Akademie der bildenden Künste) [2], which, according to the American art historian Walter Liedtke, must date from 1659, we find ourselves much closer to the columns, and hence the wooden vault is no longer visible.[3] The painting in The Metropolitan Museum of Art of 1660 shows the next step, which has us standing very close to the columns, which have now taken on gigantic proportions. They lead us upward in the direction of the Gothic window in the north transept; our attention is drawn to the red in the stained glass windows. In contrast with the two previously mentioned paintings, the human figures here are so tiny that the dimensions indicated have no relationship to the reality of the Old Church. We see an almost systematic investigation into the limits of what effects can be achieved by perspective that is still acceptable. Houckgeest also gave in to such experiments, as may be seen in works such as his *Interior of the New Church in Delft* (The Hague, Mauritshuis) [**3**].[4]

Having depicted the shafts of the columns so prominently in the foreground, Van Vliet could give full expression to one particular aspect of the painting of interiors, the representation of the tangible. In this he was decidedly the superior of both Houckgeest and De Witte. He was not concerned with the reproduction of shafts of light in the church interior but with the rendering of the atmosphere, the cool and clammy character of such an unheated church, with the moisture that appears to attack the plaster on the columns both from the inside and outside, causing the formation of translucent yellow and green patches. The atmosphere of Van Vliet's paintings stands in sharp contrast to the literally and figuratively 'dry' portraits of church interiors of the kind rendered by Pieter Saenredam. As well, the many-sided bases of the columns by Van Vliet here and there clearly betray the signs of wear and tear. This careful rendering applies only to the front plane. Farther back, things quickly become less focused.

Perhaps the uncompleted grave in the foreground and the fork that is formed visually by the shafts of the spade and broom flanking one of the visitors to the church were intended as a memento mori. Unfortunately it is not clear who would have bought such unusual depictions as the *Interior of the Old Church*.

We know little about the later history of this painting other than that C. Douglas Dillon (born 1909) of New Jersey donated it to The Metropolitan Museum of Art in New York in 1975. Dillon had been a trustee of the museum since 1951, of which he was president from 1970 to 1978. He is also a well-known collector of French impressionist paintings, eighteenth-century European porcelain, furniture, and decorative arts, as well as Chinese painting. On the back of the canvas (now relined) there used to be an old sticker saying, *Babcock Galleries, 19 East 49th Street, New York*. Babcock Galleries no longer exist, so that research into the provenance of this *Interior with the Old Church* by Van Vliet regrettably ends there.[5]

1 *Liedtke 1982*, p. 65
2 *Liedtke 1982*, pp. 65 and 106, no. 33 and fig. 47
3 *Liedtke 1982*, pp. 65 and 108, no. 82 and fig. 49; *Jantzen 1910*, p. 173, no. 555, *Poch-Kalous 1968*, p. 189 and fig. p. 132
4 *Hoetink et al. 1985*, p. 381, no. 57 and fig.; see also *Broos 1987*, pp. 218-221 and fig. 2
5 This is all the information about the provenance that Walter Liedtke, curator of The Metropolitan Museum of Art in New York, was able to supply.
    JR

3
Gerard Houckgeest
Interior of the New Church in Delft
Panel, 65.5 x 77.5 cm (27¾ x 30½ in.)
On the base of the front column: *GH 1651*
The Hague, Mauritshuis, inv. no. 57

Amsterdam 1621 – Huis ter Mey (near Utrecht)
1660 / 1661

Canvas, 66.7 x 80 cm (26¼ x 31½ in.)
Upper left: *Gio: Batta: Weenix* (ca. 1650)
Detroit, Mich., The Detroit Institute of Arts, inv. no. 41.57

Jan Baptist Weenix was a pupil of Abraham Bloemaert in Utrecht, and of Nicolaes Moeyaert in Amsterdam. In 1639 he married a daughter of the landscape painter Gillis d'Honde-coeter. In 1642 he left for Italy, where he received many commis-sions, especially from Cardinal Pamphili, who became Pope Innocent x in 1644. He was back in Amsterdam in 1647, settling in Utrecht two years later. Three years before his premature death (at the age of thirty-nine), he occupied a manor house to the north of Utrecht.

Jan Baptist Weenix painted a whole range of subjects: portraits and still lifes and, after his stay abroad, primarily Italian landscapes, especially harbor views. The architecture – ruins or Roman buildings – plays an important role in his compositions, in which much attention is also paid to figures and animals. His coloration is highly refined and variegated, while, especially in the late fifties, he achieved optimal effects with the play of light and dark. He is considered to be one of the best Italianizing landscape painters, and was already much admired in his own time. His son and pupil Jan Weenix continued to build on his successes.

Provenance
Collection Johann Christoph Werther, Amsterdam, before 1791
Auction Werther, Amsterdam, 1792
The Detroit Institute of Arts, Detroit, 1941 (gift of Mrs. John A. Bryant in memory of her husband)

Bibliography
Auction Amsterdam 1792-A, p. 7, no. 39
Stechow 1948, pp. 188, 197, note 13 and fig. 6
Detroit 1949, p. 116 and fig.
Detroit 1960, p. 148 and fig.
Ann Arbor 1964, no. 68 and fig. iv
Blankert 1965, pp. 178-179, no. 99 and fig. 102
Rosenberg / Slive / Ter Kuile 1966, p. 177 and fig. 154 A
Detroit 1967, p. 121
Ginnings 1970, vol. i, p. 38, vol. ii, p. 133, no. 22
Robinson 1974, p. 18
Sullivan 1979, pp. 65 and 66, fig. 3
Berlin / London / Philadelphia 1984, p. 355 and fig. 1
Sutton 1986, p. 86 and fig. 123, p. 228
Sutton 1990, p. 354, fig. 130-3

In 1695 in Amsterdam a painting by Jan Baptist Weenix was assessed at no less than ninety guilders: 'A woman with a child on the lap by J.B. Weenix' (in translation).[1] It is impossible to iden-tify such a reference with an extant work by the painter because the depiction of a mother and child (sometimes the Virgin Mary with Jesus) is quite common in his work. It is astonishing that the painting under discussion was not mentioned in the literature until it was acquired by the museum in Detroit in 1941. Sutton recently called it 'certainly one of the greatest Dutch paintings in the collection.'[2]

Here we are able to announce that the landscape appeared once at an auction, in Amsterdam. In 1792 the collection of a Johann Christoph Werther (ca. 1737-1791), who had come from Germany, was auctioned in that city. He had assembled almost four hundred Dutch masters in his house on the Lauriergracht. The auction catalogue mentioned a canvas by Weenix with the dimensions of 26 x 32 inches, which was probably identical with

Jan Baptist Weenix Mother and Child in an Italian Landscape

the painting in Detroit. The description reads: 'An Italian landscape with ruins; in the foreground a woman with a child at the breast, with further staffage' (in translation).[3]

The Detroit Institute of Arts is one of the first museums in the United States to have taken the collecting of old masters seriously from the very beginning. This was apparent from, among other things, the appointment of Wilhelm (William) Valentiner (1880-1958) [1] as advisor and, beginning in 1924, director of the museum. Valentiner had begun his career in The Hague, with Cornelis Hofstede de Groot, whom he assisted in 1906 and 1907 with the latter's life's work, the reissue of John Smith's catalogue raisonné of the Dutch painters.[4] It is no wonder that during the directorship of Valentiner many Dutch masterpieces were bought or donated thanks to him. The museum in Detroit owed the formation of the collection during his reign largely to contributions by private individuals, which may be called a typically American phenomenon.[5] *Mother and Child in an Italian Landscape* by Jan Baptist Weenix was a gift of Mrs. J.A. Bryant in memory of her husband. John Arthur Bryant (1880-1938) had been president of Bryant & Detwiler, pioneers in reinforced concrete construction. Their most handsome structure is said to be The Detroit Institute of Arts building, a creation of Paul Crêt, which was opened in 1927.[6]

The Art Quarterly, in which the landscape by Weenix was for the first time described and illustrated, was founded in Detroit in 1938 to provide an international forum for the scholarly ambitions of the museum.[7] It is in this periodical that Wolfgang Stechow published his well-known article on Jan Baptist Weenix in 1948. In her 1970 dissertation on the oeuvre of the painter, Rebecca Jean Ginnings rightly referred to his accurate description of the coloration of the painting. 'There is purple, red, blue, brown, and white in the woman, and orange-brown in the child; the flesh tones are rose with cool, white highlights. The dogs are masterpieces in broad gray brushstrokes. The colors in the group of peasants in the middle-ground are skillful echoes of the ones in the main group. The sky is very light; the ground in front, rose-brown with light gray shadows; the rocks, a very light grayish-blue. It is easily one of Weenix' most charming works; imaginative, carefree, just a little awkward in the poses and in composition but disarmingly so, and coloristically superb.'[8]

Weenix signed his painting with the Italian version of his

▲ 2
Jan Baptist Weenix
Mother and Child in an Italian Landscape
Panel, 68.2 x 87.2 cm (26⅞ x 34⅜ in.)
Lower right: *Gio Batta Weenix f. / A° 1658 10 m[aanden] / 20 d[agen] in het huys ter Mey*
The Hague, Mauritshuis, inv. no. 901

▲ 3
Jan Baptist Weenix
The Tinker
Canvas, 57.5 x 67 cm (22⅝ x 26⅜ in.)
On the lantern: *1650 / Gio Batta Weenix*
England, collection Viscount Allandale

◄ 1
Wilhelm Valentiner (1880-1958) in front of
The Detroit Institute of Arts
Photograph: The Detroit Institute of Arts Museum
Archives

Christian name: *Gio[vanni] Batt[ist]a Weenix*. This is how he preferred to sign his work after he had returned from Italy in 1647. In that year he first signed *Gio Batta* to a painting with a mother and child as its subject (in a, for him, rare interior) (New York, private collection).[9] His last known work with the same theme, which repeats the composition in Detroit in a more complicated version, and which is more slickly painted, is found in the Mauritshuis [**2**].[10] It is dated 20 October 1658 and, according to the inscription, was painted *in het huys ter Mey* (in the house Ter Mey). At that time Weenix inhabited an old manor house outside Utrecht.[11] The painting in Detroit must have been made between 1647 and 1658. In view of the relatively loose handling of paint, the work more likely dates from the earlier part of this period. Stechow thought 1649 to be likely, and Blankert decided on a corresponding date.[12] This looks like an acceptable proposition, certainly if one compares the composition and handling of paint with a work dated 1650, *The Tinker* (England, collection Viscount Allandale) [**3**].[13]

There are no known preparatory studies for Weenix's paintings. As a good pupil of Abraham Bloemaert, he nevertheless made figure and animal studies in preparation for his painted compositions.[14] A good example of this is a study sheet with dogs in various positions (Rotterdam, Museum Boymans-

van Beuningen) [**4**].[15] It shows animals that are presumably of the same breed as the dogs that dominate the right foreground of the painting in Detroit. In the case of painters who made frequent use of preparatory studies (such as Bloemaert, cat. no. 8, fig. 2), repetitions of figures in paintings are understandable. The seated woman with the big straw hat appears repeatedly in Weenix's work.[16] The little guy with the bare bottom sitting on her lap is very similar to the Child Jesus in *The Rest on the Flight into Egypt* (Philadelphia Museum of Art) [**5**].[17] This is the first Italianizing history piece that the museum in Philadelphia acquired – in 1984.[18] It is an indication of the generally heightened appreciation in the United States for the Italianizing landscape and Dutch history painting. The exhibitions dedicated to these genres in 1965 (Utrecht) and 1980-1981 (Amsterdam, Detroit, Washington), have contributed to this reappraisal to a considerable degree.[19]

1 *Künstler-Inventare*, vol. IV, p. 1238
2 *Sutton 1986*, p. 86
3 *Auction Amsterdam 1792-A*, p. 7, no. 39; with thanks to Jaap van der Veen for the information concerning Werther.
4 *Agnew 1958*, p. 442
5 Richardson in *Detroit 1960*, p. 8
6 *NCAB*, vol. XXXI, pp. 296-297
7 Richardson in *Detroit 1960*, p. 9
8 *Stechow 1948*, p. 188; *Ginnings 1970*, vol. II, p. 133, no. 22
9 *Berlin / London / Philadelphia 1984*, pp. 338-340, no. 124 and fig.; *Ginnings 1970*, vol. II, p. 116, no. 10
10 *Duparc 1980*, pp. 122-123 and 243, no. 901 and fig.; *Ginnings 1970*, vol. II, p. 186, no. 68
11 *Broos 1987*, p. 397, fig. 1
12 *Stechow 1948*, p. 188; *Blankert 1965*, p. 179, no. 99
13 *Ginnings 1970*, vol. II, p. 180, no. 63; opinions differ on the reading of this last numeral (o or 6): *Waterhouse 1951*, p. 261 (1656); *Blankert 1965*, p. 181 (1650 or 1656); *Haak 1984*, pp. 404-405 and fig. 875 (1650); on the photograph that is reproduced here one clearly reads a 0.
14 *Schatborn 1981-1982*, pp. 69 and 144, no. 99
15 *Gernsheim* 37181
16 Compare, for instance, *Blankert 1965*, pp. 177-179, nos. 98 and 99 and figs. 101-102
17 Not in *Ginnings 1970*; *Sutton 1986*, p. 228, fig. 333; the related piece in Rotterdam (Museum Boymans-van Beuningen, inv. no. 2803; *Jansen / Luijten 1988*, p. 61, no. 26 and fig.) has a more apparent biblical setting.
18 *Sutton 1986*, p. 228; *Sutton 1990*, p. 353, no. 130 and fig.
19 *Blankert 1965* and *Amsterdam / Detroit / Washington 1980-1981*
B B

▲ **4**
Jan Baptist Weenix
Study Sheet with Dogs
Chalk drawing with wash and body color,
317 x 421 mm (12¹⁄₂ x 16⁵⁄₈ in.)
Neither signed nor dated (ca. 1650)
Rotterdam, Museum Boymans-van Beuningen,
inv. no. J.B. Weenix 8

◄ **5**
Jan Baptist Weenix
The Rest on the Flight into Egypt
Canvas, 50.3 x 40.9 cm (19⁷⁄₈ x 16¹⁄₈ in.)
Under Mary's foot: *Gio Batta Weenix f* (ca. 1647-1650)
Philadelphia, Philadelphia Museum of Art,
inv. no. E'1984-1-1

Emanuel de Witte Interior of the Old Church in Amsterdam during a Service

Emanuel de Witte

Alkmaar 1618 – Amsterdam 1692

71 | Interior of the Old Church in Amsterdam during a Service

Canvas, 67.3 x 73.7 cm (26½ x 29 in.)
Neither signed nor dated (ca. 1660-1665)
Coral Gables, Fla., private collection

According to his biographer Houbraken, Emanuel de Witte learned the principles of the *meetkunst* (art of geometry) from his father, who was a schoolmaster in Alkmaar. In 1636 he was registered as a member of the guild of Saint Luke of that city. In 1639 and 1640 he probably lived and worked in Rotterdam, before moving to Delft in 1641. Until shortly before his departure for Amsterdam in 1652, he did history paintings and portraits, but then, undoubtedly inspired by Gerard Houckgeest and Hendrick van Vliet, he turned to church interiors. Within this genre he soon developed his own style, in which he harmoniously combined motifs from his favorite churches, the Old Church and New Church in Delft and the Old Church and New Church in Amsterdam. However, he also painted entirely invented Gothic and Renaissance church interiors, alternately with a Protestant or a Catholic character. The architecture is definitely less dominant in the splendidly lit church interiors by De Witte than in the work of Houckgeest and Van Vliet. Instead, it forms a setting for the many carefully painted and colorful figures with which he furnished his interiors.

De Witte's work was highly appreciated in his time. In 1662 the poet Jan Vos named him along with Rembrandt and Flinck as a painter who brought great fame to Amsterdam. In contrast to this appreciation stood bitter reversals in his private life and, after 1660, great poverty as well. Houbraken, who described De Witte as a highly cultivated but quarrelsome man, claimed he came to his end by drowning after failing to hang himself from an Amsterdam bridge.

According to tradition this painting once belonged to the English painter John Constable (1776-1837). In London in 1838 there was a major auction not only of his work but also of several paintings by old masters that he had collected. Under number seven of the auction catalogue we find: 'De Wytt [...] An Interior of a Cathedral, with numerous figures, a chef d'oeuvre.' It was sold for twenty-eight pounds and seven shillings, but to whom is not known.[1]

If this church interior by De Witte did indeed belong to John Constable, then the latter also knew the particulars of his life.

Provenance
(?) Collection John Constable
(?) Auction John Constable, London, 1838
Collection Francis Gibson, Saffron Walden, 1848-1859
Collection Rt. Hon. Lewis Fry, M.P., Bristol
Collection Dr. Lewis S. Fry, Delafords, Essex (grandson of Lewis Fry), to 1975
Collection children of Lewis S. Fry, 1975
Auction M. Astor, London, 1975 (£16,800)
Auction Lord Congleton, London, 1985 (£129,600)
Private collection, Coral Gables, Fla., 1985

Bibliography
(?) *Auction London 1838*, no. 7
London 1876, p. 26, no. 207
Bredius 1902, p. 9
London 1902, p. 45, no. 172
Jantzen 1910, p. 243, no. 677
London 1929, no. 315
London 1945, p. 18, no. 40
Manke 1963, p. 90, no. 55 and fig. 49
Norwich 1966, p. 19, no. 52
Auction London 1975, p. 34, no. 34 and fig.
WCA, vol. XXVII (1975), p. 322
Mayer, vol. X (1976), p. 1049
Auction London 1985, no. 90 and fig.
Wrey 1985, p. 37 and fig.

For we happen to know that Constable owned an edition of Houbraken.[2] Possibly Constable, who was also a 'lonely genius,' recognized himself in De Witte, but the English painter must have felt especially drawn to De Witte's handling of light and textures. It was observed during a recent restoration that the left half of the painting was overpainted in the early nineteenth century, possibly by Constable himself, who was in the habit of restoring paintings. This overpainting has since been removed. When we compare the current state with the old [1], it looks as if the nineteenth-century restorer wanted to heighten the sense of unity of the architecture by rounding off the composite pier that stands next to a smooth column. The springing of the arch was hidden behind several long banners. The two arched openings of different dimensions behind it have been covered up by a single, lower opening with, above it, a wall with neo-Gothic tracery. A straight partition replaced the organ with Renaissance motifs and its substructure, while, behind it, an entirely new pointed arch was inserted. The round arched window, which is responsible for the beam of light on the wall next to it, was replaced by the shadow of a window with a pointed arch. The fall of light in the left section was substantially adjusted, apparently once again to introduce greater clarity. Not only the painting but also the interior of the church itself was 'restored' along these lines, which apparently conformed more closely to the then current image of how a Gothic church should look. The American collector who bought this painting in 1985, and who wishes to remain anonymous at this exhibition, has had the work returned to its original state.

For more than 125 years the work was in the possession of the descendants of the English banker Francis Gibson. The canvas has been exhibited several times in England. In 1902 Abraham Bredius, who was then director of the Mauritshuis in The Hague, saw it at an exhibition at the Royal Academy in London and reported on it with enthusiasm in *De Nederlandsche Spectator*: '[It] is one of the clearest works by him, with a large number of splendid figures who are listening to a preacher' (in translation).[3] From Bredius on, it was recognized that the work depicts the Old Church in Amsterdam. In her 1963 monograph on De Witte, Ilse Manke pointed out for the first time that the motifs at the left, making up about one third of the painting, are invented.[4] She did not, in this context, think of overpainting, presumably because she knew that De Witte himself often combined existing and fanciful motifs.

The Old Church in Amsterdam came into being through the alteration of a fourteenth-century hall church with choir, of

1
Cat. no. 71, before the restoration of 1985

which the columns and transverse arches are still found in the present nave and west elevation. The present hall choir, with its narrow ambulatory around the main choir, dates from around 1370. The transept came into being through alterations to several of the side chapels that were added after 1385. The plan to turn the church into a larger cross-shaped basilica originated at the beginning of the sixteenth century. It was intended to assure the largest possible spaces, the widest possible roofing, and the widest and highest windows with a minimum of means. Thus arose a somewhat hybrid building, one that has been described as an overgrown village church.[5]

De Witte did not intend to make a topographically correct 'portrait' of the church. One will search in vain on a floor plan for the place in which the painter might have stood to render precisely this part of the interior. Assuming he worked close to where the side organ is located, one would expect a different, more chaotic configuration of the composite piers and smooth columns than is to be seen in this painting. De Witte has isolated a few motifs that together form a clear and characteristic picture of the interior of the Old Church.

We look over the heads of the crowd that has gathered in the church, in the direction of the choir. In the small stained-glass windows above we find portraits of the counts of Holland. In earlier paintings by De Witte, the choir screen lacks a pediment and has a closed center panel. It is not clear how much this is based on imagination. The handsome oak pulpit dates from about 1640. The organ of the choir is shown as it looked after 1658, when it got a large number of new pipes, and shutters painted by Cornelis Brisé.[6]

Emanuel de Witte certainly also painted several accurate depictions of the interior of the Old Church. The oldest signed painting of this type carries the date 1661 (Amsterdams Historisch Museum) [2] and used to hang in the room of the church warden in the Old Church itself. In this canvas we are granted a glance into the transept, in which we again see the organ in question. Noach assumed in 1937 that the functionary of the Old Church who ordered this painting (and whom we presumably see portrayed at the right with his wife and children), tolerated no deviations from the truth.[7]

This brings us back to the crowd of listeners in the church. According to Manke, this type of architectural piece showing the interior of a church during a mass or sermon is an invention of De Witte himself.[8] Heisner compared the interiors by De Witte and pointed to a number of stereotypes among those people present. Several of them often occur together, such as the gravedigger who is being spoken to, a lonesome youth in costly clothing who stands with his back to the spectator, children playing, a mother nursing her child, a mother holding a child's hand, and a sleeping man. According to Heisner, they have a symbolic and moralizing meaning.[9] In comparison with other interiors, however, these types hardly appear in the painting in the American private collection, although, at the left, we do see the sleeping man. According to Heisner, he represents vanity. We must be very careful with labels of this kind.

In the right foreground we see a woman dressed in precious,

2
Emanuel de Witte
Interior of the Old Church in Amsterdam during a Service
Canvas, 98 x 118 cm (38⅝ x 46½ in.)
In the shadow of the bench: *E De Witte Aº 1661*; at the lower right, a second, partly illegible signature: *Je[...]*
and the year *1734*
Amsterdam, Amsterdams Historisch Museum
(on loan from the Foundation 'De Oude Kerk' in Amsterdam), inv. no. 504 (3. 4929)

3
Emanuel de Witte
Interior of the Old Church in Amsterdam during a Service
Canvas, 78.1 x 63.1 cm (30¾ x 24⅞ in.)
Neither signed nor dated (ca. 1660)
London, National Gallery, inv. no. 6402

fur-trimmed clothing. Manke discovered that she also occurs in an interior of the Old Church of about 1660, which is now in the National Gallery in London [3].[10] In this painting we also reencounter the little girl with a cap on her head, who in the American painting stands just in front and to the left of the fashionable woman, and the seated woman and standing man, located to her right. The assumption, however, that this is a portrait group seems to me incorrect.

Rather, it is the group just to the left of center, including the woman holding a child on her lap, that is to be considered a portrait group. The men who look at us from the church pew at the left probably belong to this group as well, as does the man making the rounds with the collection bag. It could be that we are concerned here with the family of a church functionary. A hidden clue to this interpretation could be that all the perspective lines meet in the overly large man with a hat located behind the choir screen [4].

There are more interiors of the Old Church with groups of people who, by dint of the prominent place they occupy, by the fact that they look at the spectator, or by the special lighting that they receive, suggest that we are looking at portraits. In one case this may also be proved. The National Gallery in Cape Town has a church interior of 1678 by De Witte.[11] De Witte portrayed the people depicted in it separately in a group portrait that is now located in the Alte Pinakothek in Munich [5], but that in the nineteenth century was also in the possession of Francis Gibson.[12] It depicts a rich Amsterdam burgher with his wife and child, surrounded by attributes that point to a virtuous marriage. On the back wall of the room we again see a church interior by De Witte, provided with a curtain that has been pulled aside. This probably emphasized the piety of the principals.[13]

Emanuel de Witte's personal preference for the old Gothic churches is quite understandable; their complex spatial composition and fall of light offered many possibilities to the painter. The question is, however, why these rich people did not insist on

5
Emanuel de Witte
Family Portrait
Canvas, 66 x 84 cm (26 x 33 in.)
Lower left: *E. De Witte 1678*
Munich, Alte Pinakothek, inv. no. FV 2

being depicted in one of the new churches of Amsterdam, such as the Western Church or Southern Church, which would have accorded much better with their life-style. An explanation for this may be that Protestant worship in the Old Church could pride itself on a measure of tradition. The Old Church was furthermore one of the places in Amsterdam where iconoclasm had raged at its fiercest. Perhaps it was felt to be chic to belong to just this church, which more than any other stood for the resolve and triumph of Calvinism. Finally, it could be that people preferred the old Gothic churches because the new style was being used in the southern Netherlands for churches for those who adhered to the ideology of the Counter-Reformation.

With his free approach to the interior of the Old Church, Emanuel de Witte satisfied some of the important criteria for the painting of architecture that were written down by Samuel van Hoogstraten several years later, in 1678; one of these was that 'he who would prosper from painting must avoid [too] much architectural decoration' (in translation).[14] Van Hoogstraten urged the architecture painter 'also to put his own ingenuity to work': 'what has been disseminated here and there, although

4
Schematic diagram of perspectival lines
(drawing by J. Roding)

every part may be good,' must be combined to form a new unity. In this pursuit it must have been a great challenge to the painter not to lose sight of the problem of the *maetschiklijkheyt* (interdependent proportions).[15] In this *Interior of the Old Church in Amsterdam during a Service*, which Manke dated to the early sixties, De Witte fully succeeded in this task.

1 *Auction London 1838*, no. 7

2 *Hawes 1963*, appendix

3 *Bredius 1902*, p. 9

4 *Manke 1963*, p. 90, no. 55: 'Die Architekturmotive im linken Bilddrittel sind Phantasie.'

5 *Kunstreisboek voor Nederland 1977*, p. 357

6 *Wijnman et al. 1974*, p. 51

7 *Blankert 1975 / 1979*, p. 365, no. 504 (B. 4929); *Noach 1937*, pp. 116-117, no. 1 and fig.; see also *Jantzen 1910*, pp. 121-122, no. 625

8 *Manke 1963*, p. 16

9 *Heisner 1980*, pp. 107-114

10 *London 1986*, p. 684, no. 6402 and fig.; see also *Manke 1963*, pp. 89-90, no. 53 and fig. 47

11 On loan from J.H. Tresfon, Johannesburg; *Manke 1963*, p. 89, no. 51 and fig. 81

12 *Munich 1983*, pp. 571-572 no. FV 2 and fig.; *Manke 1963*, pp. 79, no. 10 and fig. 83

13 See *De Jongh 1974*, *Eikemeier 1974*, and *Bedaux 1989*, pp. 150, 155, 162 and p. 153, fig. 4

14 *Van Hoogstraten 1678*, p. 127

15 Idem, pp. 127, 191 and 185

JR

Philips Wouwermans Merry and Rowdy Peasants at an Inn (not in San Francisco)

Haarlem 1619 – Haarlem 1668

Canvas, 69.9 x 111.8 cm (27½ x 44 in.)
Lower right, on the shore: *PHILS W* (PHILS in ligature) and on the rowboat: *Ao 1653*
Minneapolis, Minn., The Minneapolis Institute of Arts, inv. no. 81.107

According to his biographer Cornelis de Bie, Philips Wouwermans was a pupil of Frans Hals, but his way of painting and
choice of themes more closely resemble those of Pieter van Laer,
who had returned to Haarlem from Italy in 1638. After the latter's
death in 1642, Wouwermans is supposed to have come into
possession of his atelier effects. In 1640 he became a member of
the Haarlem guild, where he continued to live and work.

Although he died before his fiftieth birthday, he left an
impressive oeuvre that is estimated at more than one thousand
paintings. The horse was his favorite subject, which he represented in simple equestrian pieces or in massive battles, in
elegant hunting parties or in bucolic scenes. The dapple gray
horse is sometimes called his mark in trade. The horse pieces by
Wouwermans were much sought after both during his lifetime
and after his death, with the result that those collections that were
formed early (Dresden, The Hague, Leningrad) are able to
display much of his work.

Although this is one of the rare dated paintings by Philips
Wouwermans and therefore a key piece of his oeuvre, it is also
one of his least-known works. It has attracted little attention in
the literature, which is understandable, as will become apparent,
considering the history of its provenance.[1] A[nn]o 1653, it says
on the rowboat in which two boys are getting undressed to go
swimming. On the shore at the lower right we see his remarkable
monogram, which is formed by the letters of his first name,
PHIL[IP]s, and the W of his surname, written as two superimposed letters v. Wouwermans is also known to have signed his
rather rare drawings, such as *A Horseman with Washerwomen*
(Haarlem, Teylers Museum) [1], in this way.[2] Only in 1981 did
the *Merry and Rowdy Peasants at an Inn* move out of private hands
into public ownership, to the museum in Minneapolis.

The history of this work of art has large gaps. In 1722 it is
mentioned at the auction of 'the universally renowned cabinet' of
'Jacques Meyers' in Rotterdam as 'A Landscape with a big crowd
of farmers enjoying themselves' (in translation).[3] This description of the scene is somewhat superficial, because there is a lot
more going on than that. The negative side of pleasure is also

Provenance

Auction Meijers, Rotterdam, 1722
Collection Duke of Berry, Paris, before 1820
Collection Duchess of Berry, Paris / Naples,
1820-1834
Dealer Christie's, London, 1834
Collection Samuel Woodburn, London, 1834-1853
(bought from Christie's for £500)
Auction Woodburn, London, 1853 (£405 to Norton)
Collection R. Baillie Hamilton, London, 1881, 1883
Dealer Rosenberg & Stiebel, New York, 1954
Collection Mr. and Mrs. Charles B. Sweatt, Wayzata,
Minn., 1954-1977
Collection Mrs. Margaret L. Sweatt, Wayzata, Minn.,
1977-1981
The Minneapolis Institute of Arts, Minneapolis, 1981
(gift of Margaret L. Sweatt)

Bibliography

Auction Rotterdam 1722, p. 11, no. 104
Hoet 1752-1770, vol. I, p. 276, no. 103
Smith 1829-1842, vol. IX, pp. 147-148, no. 28
London 1834, pp. 30-31, no. 60
Auction London 1853, p. 13, no. 79
Bredius 1881, p. 78
London 1881, p. 18, no. 73
HdG 1020 (vol. II [1908], pp. 586-587, no. 1020) and
HdG 1024b (vol. II [1908], pp. 588-589, no. 1024b,
p. 651)
Graves 1913-1915, vol. IV, p. 1714, no. 73 (1881)
Graves 1918-1921, vol. III, p. 349 (1853)
New York etc. 1954-1955, p. 92 and fig.
Whitley 1973, vol. II, p. 272
Keyes 1983, pp. 194-200 and fig. 9
Minneapolis 1986, pp. 62-63 and fig.
Sutton et al. 1987-1988, pp. 530-531 and fig. 3
Lipschultz 1988, p. 98 and fig.

1
Philips Wouwermans
A Horseman with Washerwomen
Chalk drawing with wash, 135 x 190 mm (5⅜ x 7¼ in.)
Upper right: *PHILS. W* (PHILS in ligature)
(ca. 1650-1660)
Haarlem, Teylers Museum, inv. no. P* 34

shown in detail, such as the harmful consequences of excessive drinking. Looking back on the tumult, a man in the right foreground stands relieving himself, while a woman (his wife?) lets a child squat with its pants down. In the center foreground a sloshed farmer is led away by his wife from the fray at his back. A drunkard, who has collapsed among the pigs, empties his stomach, and behind him women and children prevent two hooligans from carving one another up with their knives. At the left, people continue to drink and dance merrily to the sounds of a bagpipe player, while a few men in the company of women of easy virtue have retreated to the steps of a brothel. The young amuse themselves by swimming in the river. In general such depictions were intended to point to the opposite of what was being shown, as is summarized beneath the title print of Bredero's *Boertigh liedt-boeck* (Bucolic songbook) of 1622: 'Who would not be revolted by the farmers' feast and fair? They do nothing there but grub, swill, and puke. They play the viol, jump, and dance. They play the bagpipe and the flute, and before they are parted the knife is drawn' (in translation).[4]

The appreciative words that the biographer Houbraken once wrote about the scenes by Wouwermans, are particularly applicable here: 'He has moreover been able to depict everything so individually and naturally, or in its natural character, [so] that the Figures, no matter how small at times, make clear at the first glance what they are doing. Even in the depiction of exceptional cases, he has observed things that are hardly imaginable save by those who have been present at such instances' (in translation).[5] Houbraken called such scenes 'natural,' which is the seventeenth-century term for realistic. In the seventeenth century, everyday hygiene was a public matter, which the artist gladly recorded.[6] Apparently such realistic touches were later less appreciated, for the fact that the man is urinating against a gate in the foreground is now barely visible. Nevertheless such motifs were part and parcel of Wouwerman's repertoire. Presumably there is a question of a deliberately obliterated passage. Similarly, the most pithy motif of his *White Horse Passing Water* (London, National Gallery) [2-2a],[7] was invisible for a long time due to an overpainting.

The common activities in the foreground are situated in front of an invented panorama that is reminiscent of Italy. Wouwermans never traveled south, but he knew the landscape and the atmosphere from, among other things, the drawings and paintings of Pieter van Laer. After the latter's death in 1642, Wouwermans is even supposed to have taken possession of 'his Trunk with Models, Drawings, and Sketches' and to have availed him-

2
Philips Wouwermans
A White Horse Passing Water
Panel, 31.8 x 26.3 cm (12½ x 10⅜ in.)
Lower left: *PHILS W* (PHILS in ligature)
(ca. 1650-1660)
London, National Gallery, inv. no. 881

▼ **2a**
Detail of fig. 2 before restoration

3
Pieter van Laer
Landscape with Bathers and a Gray Horse
Panel, 55 x 83 cm (21⅝ x 32⅝ in.)
Below, to the right of center: *PVLaer* (PVL in ligature)
(ca. 1640)
Bremen, Kunsthalle, inv. no. 69-1856

self of these so unconscionably that, 'lying on his deathbed,' he had the sheets 'burned before his eyes' out of shame. We again have this account from Houbraken (in translation), who had the story at secondhand from someone who knew Wouwermans well. The biographer repeated the story 'for the same price for which I received it' (meaning 'for what it is worth').[8] This destructive act could therefore also be an exaggeration of the disclosure that Wouwermans borrowed his figures from the sketches by 'Bamboots' (Van Laer), very few of which, one might add, have been preserved. It is a fact that Wouwermans copied Van Laer's figure studies in his paintings.[9] Such borrowing is also in evidence in the painting in Minneapolis. The swimmer pulling his shirt over his head is identical to a figure in Pieter van Laer's painting *Landscape with Bathers and a Gray Horse* (Bremen, Kunsthalle) [3], which was made around 1640.[10] Presumably Wouwermans's figure is based on a drawing by Van Laer, and that is probably true of this landscape as a whole as well. After all, these are wider expanses than Wouwermans could actually have seen in Holland.

After the auction of 1722 in Rotterdam, none of the numerous references to Wouwermans's work in many eighteenth-century collections correspond to the painting in Minneapolis. Only in 1834 did it emerge in London at the famous exhibition sale of the collection of the Duchess of Berry, a tragic heroine of French history. Maria-Carolina of Bourbon (1798-1870) [4] was the daughter of the man who became King Francis I of Both Sicilies, who was chased from Naples by Napoleon's army. In 1816 she married Charles Ferdinand Duke of Berry (1778-1820), who was murdered in 1820. She gave birth to his postumously born son, Henry Duke of Bordeaux, whom she later tried to help to the throne. After the July Revolution of 1830, she left France, stayed for some time in England, and then secretly married an Italian nobleman in Rome. In 1832 she attempted to stir up a revolt in the Vendée, where she stayed, disguised as a farmer, under the name of Petit Pierre. Her hiding place was betrayed, and she was imprisoned in the citadel of Blaye. There she revealed her secret liaison, which was proven by the birth of a daughter. She was therefore released because, on account of this marriage, she was no longer of political importance. In 1833 she returned to Naples, where she continued to call herself Duchess of Berry. The campaign in the Vendée had ruined her, so that an auction of paintings from the family collection became inescapable.[11] Although she died in 1870, biographies of her usually end in 1833.[12]

In February 1834 the paintings from the Berry collection were sent from Paris to London to be sold. They were then said to have come from the collection of the Duke of Berry, the first husband of Maria-Carolina of Bourbon. Exceptionally, the

4
François Gérard
Portrait of the Duchess of Berry and Her Two Children
Canvas, dimensions unknown
Neither signed nor dated (?) (1820)
Versailles, Musée National des Châteaux de
Versailles et de Trianon, inv. no. 4923

auction house owner Christie did not hold a public sale. The one hundred and thirty Flemish and Dutch works were exhibited at his home in King Street and – whenever possible – sold at set prices. Christie even printed a catalogue of the collection.[13] The newspapers also kept track of events. On 14 April the *Morning Chronicle* announced that the exhibition had been visited by 'all the nobility, artists, and patrons of art during the last week.' About ten works had already been sold: 'Messrs Woodburn have bought a landscape (with flooded country) by Wouwerman, £500,-.'[14]

According to this disclosure, the dealership of Woodburn Brothers, which was active at virtually all the auctions held in London during the first half of the nineteenth century, became the new owner. Woodburn himself, however, kept the painting in his private collection, from which it was auctioned after his death in 1853.[15] Samuel Woodburn (1786-1853) was the odd man out among the collectors of his time. For instance, he collected early Italian paintings when these were still rejected in

England as curiosities.[16] He also formed (and later sold) the famous drawing collection of Sir Thomas Lawrence, which included sheets by Raphael and Michelangelo.[17] According to an anecdote, the Marquess of Hertford visited him one day and said: 'Oh, Mr. Woodburn, you are the very man I wish to see: I have a spare one hundred thousand pounds; tell me what to do with it. – Build a picture-gallery, my Lord, and let me fill it for you,' Woodburn is said to have replied.[18] The Dutch King Willem II was one of his best customers. In 1857 the rumor made the rounds that the Woodburn collection would be bought by the National Gallery in London, but that never happened.[19] At a number of auctions in 1853 and afterward the paintings owned by Woodburn were sold and therefore dispersed.[20]

The vicissitudes of this painting by Wouwermans between 1853 and 1954 are virtually unknown. In 1881 the painting was lent to an exhibition at the Royal Academy in London by Robert Baillie-Hamilton (1828-1891), a successful stockbreeder from Berwickshire.[21] The ever-assiduous Abraham Bredius, since 1880 assistant director of the Dutch Museum for History and Art, was in London in 1881 and admired the works by Wouwermans on display there: 'most splendid and of the very highest quality.' He called the painting of 1653 'a true gem; it depicts a landscape with a crowd of figures, a troupe of fairgoers, riders, a ship with bathers, etc., Painted with love' (in translation).[22] Bredius's description is actually also a censored interpretation of the depiction. These were to be for a long time the last words dedicated to this painting by an eyewitness. In his catalogue of 1908 of the works of Wouwermans, Hofstede de Groot was able only to paraphrase the text of 1842 by Smith.[23] He had never seen the painting itself.

When, after a century of oblivion, the *Merry and Rowdy Peasants at an Inn* finally resurfaced at an exhibition in New York, Toledo, and Toronto, the new owners turned out to be Mr. and Mrs. Sweatt of Wayzata, Minnesota.[24] Charles Baxter Sweatt (1894-1977), who was born in Minneapolis, was president of an appliance factory.[25] In 1981, following his death in 1977, his widow donated the painting to the museum of his native city. Thus a striking and virtually unknown work by Philips Wouwermans came to be added to a series of noteworthy Dutch landscapes in Minneapolis (see cat. nos. 24, 32, and 56).[26]

1 See Bibliography; HdG, vol. 11, p. 651, contains a survey of the dated works.
2 *Scholten 1904*, p. 170, no. P* 34; *Van Regteren Altena 1972*, p. 37, no. 79 and fig.
3 *Auction Rotterdam 1722*, p. 11, no. 104
4 *Alpers 1975-1976*, p. 134, fig. 10; for the correct interpretations, see *Miedema 1977*, pp. 213-214.

5 *Houbraken 1718-1721*, vol. II, p. 72

6 *Roding 1986*, pp. 27-28 and fig.

7 HdG 1006; *Maclaren 1960*, p. 466, no. 881

8 *Houbraken 1718-1721*, vol. II, p. 75

9 *Schatborn 1974*, pp. 5-6 and figs. 3-4; see also *Blankert 1968*, pp. 129-130

10 *Blankert 1965*, pp. 94-95, no. 35 and fig.; *Blankert 1968*, p. 126, fig. 14 and p. 130, note 31; *Briganti et al. 1983*, p. 59, dated this painting after 1639.

11 *DBF*, vol. VI, pp. 158-159; *Larousse*, vol. II, p. 1203

12 *Dejean 1913*; *Larousse 1865-1878*, vol. II, p. 611

13 *London 1834*, pp. 30-31, no. 60; according to *Whitley 1973*, vol. II, p. 272, the catalogue was never printed.

14 *Whitley 1973*, vol. II, p. 272

15 *Auction London 1853*, title page

16 *Haskell 1976*, p. 53

17 *Whitley 1973*, vol. II, pp. 276-278; *Lugt 1921*, pp. 483-485, no. 2584; *Turner 1986*, pp. 18-19

18 *Lugt 1921*, p. 484

19 *Brigstocke 1982*, p. 478; *Hinterding / Horsch 1989*, pp. 19-21

20 *Lugt 1921*, pp. 484-485

21 *London 1881*, p. 18, no. 73; *Graves 1913-1915*, p. 1714, no. 73 (1881); *Boase 1965*, vol. IV, p. 231

22 *Bredius 1881*, p. 78

23 *Smith 1829-1842*, vol. IX, pp. 147-148, no. 28; HdG, pp. 586-587, no. 1020 (NB: 'London 1889' should be '1881')

24 *New York etc. 1954-1955*, p. 92

25 *WWWA*, vol. VII, p. 557

26 *Sutton 1986*, p. 157

BB

Joachim Wtewael

Utrecht 1566 – Utrecht 1638

Canvas, 169.5 x 124.8 cm (66¾ x 49⅛ in.)
On stone at left: *JOACHIM. WTEN/ WAEL. FECIT/ 1600*
Kansas City, Mo., The Nelson-Atkins Museum of Art, inv. no. F84-71

Joachim Anthonisz Wtewael was born in Utrecht in 1566 and spent most of his life in his native city. Born into an established middle-class family, he worked first with his father, a glassmaker and engraver, and was later apprenticed to Joos de Beer, with whom Abraham Bloemaert also studied. The young Wtewael then traveled for about six years, visiting Italy and France, spending much of this time in the company of Charles de Bourgneuf de Cuce, the bishop of Saint Malo.

Wtewael had returned to Utrecht by 1592, entering the saddlers' guild in that year. The time spent in Italy proved to be the determining influence on his artistic personality. The Italian mannerist idiom had reached Holland prior to Wtewael's return, popularized in part by Carel van Mander, Cornelius van Haarlem, and Hendrick Goltzius, whose prints circulated the drawings and inventions of the Flemish painter Bartholomeus Spranger. Spranger had also traveled to Italy, was active there between 1565 and 1576, and was among the most influential Flemish painters to exploit the decorative potential of the Italian *maniera*. Thus on his return, Wtewael found the artistic community of Utrecht predisposed to the figural exaggerations he favored as a result of his Italian experience. Wtewael never completely forsook the mannerist aesthetic and vibrant decorative palette he derived from such Italian artists as Parmigianino and Pellegrino Tibaldi.

Provenance

Collection Messrs. Hadfield & Burrowes, by 1785
Auction Hadfield & Burrowes, London, 1785
Dealer Philip Hill, London, by 1807
Auction Hill, London, 1807 (£13.2.6 to Michael Bryan)
Dealer Michael Bryan, London, 1807
Collection Sir Edward Cockburn, Herefordshire, by 1903
Auction Cockburn, London, 1903 (to Hamblin)
(?) Collection Hamblin
Dealer Van der Perre, Paris, 1905
Dealer S.A. l'Antiquaille, Paris, 1937
Dealer P. Graupe, Paris, 1938
Private collection, France, 1938
Auction Monaco, 1984 (to Bruno Meissner)
Dealer Bruno Meissner, Zürich, with dealer Newhouse Galleries, New York, 1984
The Nelson-Atkins Museum of Art, Kansas City, 1984 (museum purchase)

Bibliography

Auction London 1785, p. 11, no. LXXIX, frontispiece
Auction London 1807, p. 7, no. 44
Auction London 1903, p. 30, no. 139
Le Gille 1905, no. 1
Lindeman 1929, pp. 50-53, no. VII, p. 249 and pl. XI
Stechow 1930, pp. 130-131
Lindeman 1947, p. 286
Lowenthal 1975, pp. 77-78, no. A 35, pp. 244-245 and fig.
Auction Monaco 1984, p. 15, no. 3305 and fig.
Connaissance des arts 1984, p. 30 and fig.
Apollo 1985, p. 393 and pl. VI
Foucart 1985, pp. 62-63
Antiques 1986, p. 380 and fig.
Lowenthal 1986, pp. 93-94, no. A 35, pp. 41, 48, 54, 60, and pls. 21-23
Sutton 1986, p. 123, pl. 4 (reversed)
Ward 1987, p. 146, no. 63 and fig.
Kansas City 1988, p. 50, no. 20 and fig.

1
Anonymous after Joachim Wtwael
Saint Sebastian
Engraving, 179 x 114 mm (7 x 4½ in.)
Lower left: *Broadstreet Golden s me Fecit* (1785)
Frontispiece from: *Auction London 1785*
The Hague, Rijksbureau voor Kunsthistorische Documentatie

From sixteenth-century Italy also came the fashion for painting on copper, of which Wtewael was the major Northern exponent.

Local politics, family and business affairs, as well as painting, vied for Wtewael's attention in Utrecht. Married in 1595 to Christina van Halen, he had four children. He took a leading role in both the formation of the independent guild for artists in Utrecht in 1611 and in the peaceful, but unsuccessful, civil revolt in 1610, aimed at limiting the power of the nobility in the city government. The artist also held a seat on the Utrecht town council at different times throughout his life. A successful flax merchant and investor in the East India Company, he became a wealthy man; he also supported several charitable causes.

Together with Bloemaert, Wtewael was the principal Utrecht artist of the seventeenth century working in the mannerist style, which he practiced throughout his career. He seems to have stopped painting during the 1630s and died on 1 August 1638. Although he had several students, none of them rivaled his stature.

One of the most significant Dutch mannerist pictures in America, the Wtewael *Saint Sebastian* only came to this country in 1984, purchased from its joint owners, Bruno Meissner in Zürich and Newhouse Galleries in New York. The known provenance for the work, however, begins in 1785, when it was illustrated by an engraving in the 10 May sale of the 'First Part of the Large Collection of Pictures made by Messrs. Hadfield and Burrowes, during their Tour Through Flanders, France, Germany and Holland' [1].[1] The *Saint Sebastian* apparently had been acquired by Messrs. Hadfield and Burrowes on the Continent some time prior to May 1785.

It is not known who purchased the painting at the sale, but it reappeared on the art market in 1807.[2] In addition to an apt description of the composition of the *Saint Sebastian*, the catalogue entry offers a precise record of the signature and date of the Kansas City picture: JOACHIM / WTEN WAEL / 1600. Although an 'anonymous' sale, various annotated copies of the catalogue note that the owner of these paintings was the London dealer Philip Hill, who had his rooms in Greek Street. The buyer is recorded as Michael Bryan, who purchased the *Saint Sebastian* for thirteen pounds, two shillings, and six pence.

From 1798 to 1804 Bryan (1757-1821) was an important art dealer in London, particularly renowned for his part in negotiating the importation and sale of the Italian paintings from the collection of Philippe Egalité, Duke of Orleans.[3] In addition,

Bryan was a recognized expert on Dutch and Flemish masters, this the result of long periods of residency in the Low Countries. Interestingly, it is frequently noted that Bryan left the art trade in 1804 and moved to Yorkshire; the purchase of the Wtewael falls after this date. Between 1813 and 1816 the first two-volume edition of Bryan's *Biographical and Critical Dictionary of Painters and Engravers* was published;[4] although Wtewael is listed, the *Saint Sebastian* is not. Bryan died in 1821; however, the sale of his collection on 20 June 1821, at Squibb & Son, London, did not include the Kansas City painting.

The subsequent whereabouts of the *Saint Sebastian* is unknown until 1903, when it was sold as the property of Sir Edward C. Cockburn (1834-after 1903), the seventh Baronet of Cockburn of Herefordshire.[5] The work then passed through the hands of a succession of French dealers and spent almost fifty years in an unidentified French private collection, before going to sale at Sotheby's, Monaco, in 1984.[6] The *Saint Sebastian*, purchased there by the dealer Bruno Meissner of Zürich, was acquired from the joint owners Meissner and Newhouse Galleries by Kansas City that same year.

Signed and dated 1600, the *Saint Sebastian* is a masterpiece of the Northern mannerist idiom. The iconography of the martyrdom of Saint Sebastian is familiar to students of Renaissance and baroque art, as it was a favorite theme during this period, in part owing to the fact that Sebastian was seen as a protector against the plague.[7] A centurion in the Praetorian guard of the third-century emperor Diocletian, Sebastian was sentenced to die by the arrows of his own men after it was learned that he had converted to Christianity.[8] The moment traditionally represented in the narrative is after the sentence has been carried out, the saint's body shown pierced with arrows. Wtewael here chooses the moment just before, imbuing the scene with a sense of anticipation and veiled brutality directly opposed to the sensuous beauty of the male form.

Wtewael capitalizes on the expressive potential of the human body, exaggerating musculature and pose to create the curvaceous contours that activate and energize the composition. The upward torque of the saint's nude form is countered by the diagonal stretch – one parallel to the picture plane, the other almost perpendicular to it – of the two captors, who strain to tighten Sebastian's bonds. The glances of the three principal figures also establish directional forces, each pointing in a different direction, fracturing the pictorial unity. This compositional restlessness echoes the emotional tenor of the scene as Sebastian looks imploringly at the putto, who can offer as com-

Joachim Wtewael Saint Sebastian (not in The Hague)

fort only the laurel wreath and palm frond, symbols of the Christian martyr's triumph over death.

Artistically, Wtewael must have been satisfied with this figural motif, because he used it later, this time with a mythological female protagonist. The figure of Andromeda in the drawing of *Perseus and Andromeda* (Vienna, Graphische Sammlung Albertina) copies the pose and undulating contours of the Saint Sebastian [2];[9] and of course the similarity of the two narratives makes Wtewael's reuse of the motif appropriate. Although the drawing is horizontal in format, the compositional elements are almost identical. Similar settings and light / dark patterns are established, before which the human form is displayed. In both instances, the torsion of the human form gives visual expression to the torment not only of the body but also of the spirit.

Lowenthal's dating of the Albertina drawing places it after the *Saint Sebastian* but several years before the 1611 painting of *Perseus and Andromeda* (Paris, Musée du Louvre), in which we see the pose reversed [3].[10] Although still very mannered, the contour of this painted Andromeda is much more lithe than the undulating form of the male figure or of the Andromeda in the drawing. In this characterization of the female form, the Louvre painting perhaps reflects more closely Wtewael's pictorial sources for this figural motif, including the 1593 print by Goltzius representing *Andromeda*.[11] Indeed, the exceedingly androgynous character of Wtewael's Saint Sebastian might in part be explained if the origins of this figure lie in the female form of Andromeda.[12]

The emphasis on the physical beauty of the male form, coupled with the novel iconography, hints that the Wtewael *Saint Sebastian* was not originally intended for a religious context, which the painting's great size might otherwise indicate. Indeed, the prominent placement and careful description of the still life of archery equipment, longbow, crossbow, arrows, and quiver, suggest that the *Saint Sebastian* was designed for a secular context. As Saint Sebastian was the patron saint of the guild of *Sebastiaandoelen,* the municipal militia of archers, it may have been commissioned by them for placement in their guild hall.

2
Joachim Wtewael
Perseus and Andromeda
Pen and brown ink with brown wash and white heightening, 158 x 203 mm (6¼ x 8 in.)
Neither signed nor dated (ca. 1605)
Vienna, Graphische Sammlung Albertina, inv. no. 8133

3
Joachim Wtewael
Perseus and Andromeda
Canvas, 180 x 150 cm (70⅞ x 59 in.)
On rock at left: *Joachim wte / wael fecit / Anno 1611*
Paris, Musée du Louvre, inv. no. R.F. 1982-51 (MN)

1 *Auction London 1785*, p. 11, no. LXXIX, fig. I would like to thank Eliot Rowlands for bringing to my attention the ms. letter from Burton Fredericksen, director of The Provenance Index, The Getty Center for the History of Art and the Humanities, which discusses the earliest provenance of the *Saint Sebastian*.

2 *Auction London 1807*, p. 7, no. 44

3 *Philadelphia / Berlin / London 1984*, pp. 362-363

4 *Bryan 1816 / 1964*

5 *Auction London 1903*, p. 30, no. 139. An annotated catalogue of the sale, in the Resource Collection of The Getty Center for the History of Art and the Humanities, notes 'Hamblin' next to lot 30. This party has not been identified.

6 *Auction Monaco 1984*, p. 15, no. 3305 and fig.

7 Ancient legend told that Apollo's arrows spread the plague. Because Sebastian survived being shot with arrows, he became the focus of a popular cult from the fourteenth century on, throughout periods of outbreaks of the plague.

8 Taken for dead, the body of Sebastian was thrown into the Cloaca Maxima, Rome's main sewer. Rescued and revived by Saint Irene, Sebastian confronted the emperor again and was put to death by the sword.

9 *Lowenthal 1986*, p. 131 and pl. 84

10 *Lowenthal 1975*, p. 287 and fig. D 36; *Lowenthal 1986*, pp. 130-131, no. A 59 and pl. 82

11 *Lowenthal 1986*, p. 131 and fig. 95. Lowenthal discusses at some length the Dutch and Italian pictorial sources for the Andromeda figural type, tracing its origin to Titian's *Perseus and Andromeda* (London, Wallace Collection, inv. no. 11; *Wethey 1975*, vol. III, pp. 169-171, no. 30 and pls. 134-136). The pose had subsequently been adopted for other figures as well, such as Bartholomeus Spranger's *Fortune* (The Dayton Art Institute, inv. no. 62.13; *Dayton 1969*, p. 76, no. 24 and fig.).

12 For a discussion of the homoerotic interpretation of the *Saint Sebastian*, see *Lowenthal 1986*, pp. 93-94.

LFO

Scholarly Apparatus

Compiled by Lynn Federle Orr
with Elise Breall

Exhibitions of Seventeenth-Century Dutch Art in American Museums and Public Galleries: 1888-1991

1888-1889 / Chicago, Ill.
The Art Institute of Chicago *Ehrich Collection: Paintings by Dutch and Flemish Masters*

1890 / Chicago, Ill.
The Art Institute of Chicago *Old Dutch Masters and Other Pictures from the Demidoff Collection*

1892 / Chicago, Ill.
The Art Institute of Chicago *Old Dutch Masters and Other Pictures from the Demidoff Collection*

1892 / Chicago, Ill.
The Art Institute of Chicago *The Rembrandt of Pecq: Abraham Entertaining the Angels*

1909 / New York
The Metropolitan Museum of Art *The Hudson-Fulton Celebration: Loan Exhibition of Paintings by Old Dutch Masters* [exh. cat. by W.R. Valentiner]

1910 / New York
The Metropolitan Museum of Art *Loan Exhibition of Paintings by Old Dutch Masters Held in the Metropolitan Museum of Art in Connection with the Hudson-Fulton Celebration* [exh. cat. by W.R. Valentiner]

1912 / Detroit, Mich.
The Detroit Institute of Arts *Rembrandt Etchings from the Scripps Collection*

1923 / Detroit, Mich.
The Detroit Institute of Arts *Rembrandt Portraits*

1925 / Detroit, Mich.
The Detroit Institute of Arts *Loan Exhibition of Dutch Paintings of the Seventeenth Century* [exh. cat. by W.R. Valentiner]

1929 / Detroit, Mich.
The Detroit Institute of Arts *The Ninth Loan Exhibition: Dutch Genre and Landscape Paintings of the Seventeenth Century* [exh. cat. by W.R. Valentiner]

1930 / Detroit, Mich.
The Detroit Institute of Arts *Rembrandt Etchings*

1930 / Detroit, Mich.
The Detroit Institute of Arts *The Thirteenth Loan Exhibition of Old Masters: Paintings by Rembrandt* [exh. cat. by W.R. Valentiner]

1931 / Detroit, Mich.
The Detroit Institute of Arts *Dutch Paintings of the Seventeenth Century* [exh. cat. by W.R. Valentiner]
Traveled

1935 / Detroit, Mich.
The Detroit Institute of Arts *The Seventeenth Loan Exhibition of Old Masters: An Exhibition of Fifty Paintings by Frans Hals* [exh. cat. by W.R. Valentiner]

1935 / Los Angeles, Calif.
Los Angeles County Museum of History, Science, and Art *Exhibition of Dutch and Flemish Paintings of the Seventeenth Century*

1935 / San Francisco, Calif.
California Palace of the Legion of Honor *Loan Exhibition of Dutch and Flemish Landscapes* [exh. cat.; foreword by T.C. Howe]

1935-1936 / Chicago, Ill.
The Art Institute of Chicago *Paintings, Drawings, and Etchings by Rembrandt and His Circle* [exh. cat.]

1936 / Worcester, Mass.
Worcester Art Museum *Rembrandt and His Circle* [exh. cat.]

1937 / Indianapolis, Ind.
John Herron Art Museum *Dutch Paintings, Etchings, Drawings, Delftware of the Seventeenth Century* [exh. cat.]

1937 / Los Angeles, Calif.
Los Angeles County Museum of History, Science, and Art *Rembrandt Etchings*

1938 / Providence, R.I.
Museum of Art, Rhode Island School of Design *Dutch Painting in the Seventeenth Century* [exh. cat. by W. Stechow]

1939 / Detroit, Mich.
The Detroit Institute of Arts *The Twentieth Loan Exhibition of Old Masters: An Exhibition of Dutch Landscape Paintings* [exh. cat. by E.P. Richardson]

1940 / Detroit, Mich.
The Detroit Institute of Arts *Rembrandt Etchings from the Lessing J. Rosenwald Collection*

1940 / Grand Rapids, Mich.
Art Gallery *Masterpieces of Dutch Art* [exh. cat.]

1941 / Kansas City, Mo.
William Rockhill Nelson Gallery of Art *Seventh Anniversary Exhibition of German, Flemish, and Dutch Painting* [exh. cat.]

1942 / Chicago, Ill.
The Art Institute of Chicago *Paintings by the Great Dutch Masters of the Seventeenth Century* [exh. cat. by G.H. McCall and A.J. Barnouw]

1942 / Detroit, Mich.
The Detroit Institute of Arts *Dutch Architectural Paintings of the Seventeenth Century*

1942 / Los Angeles, Calif.
Los Angeles County Museum of History, Science, and Art *Dutch Paintings*

1944 / Washington, D.C.
National Gallery of Art *Rembrandt: Prints and Drawings*

1946 / Washington, D.C.
National Gallery of Art *The Life of Christ as Depicted in the Etchings of Rembrandt*

1946 / Washington, D.C.
National Gallery of Art *Paintings Looted from Holland, Returned through the Efforts of the United States Armed Forces* [exh. cat. by A.P.A. Vorenkamp]
Traveled to 14 cities throughout the United States

1947 / Los Angeles, Calif.
Los Angeles County Museum of History, Science, and Art *Loan Exhibition of Paintings by Frans Hals and Rembrandt* [exh. cat. by W.R. Valentiner]

1948 / Cambridge, Mass.
Fogg Art Museum, Harvard University *Rembrandt: Paintings and Etchings* [exh. cat.]

1949 / Washington, D.C.
National Gallery of Art *Prints by Adriaen van Ostade*

1950 / Hartford, Conn.
Wadsworth Atheneum *Life in Seventeenth-Century Holland: Views, Vistas, Pastimes, Pantomimes, Portraits, Peep Shows* [exh. cat. by C.C. Cunningham]

1951 / Coral Gables, Fla.
Joe and Emily Lowe Art Gallery, Miami University *Paintings by Dutch Old Masters: Part 11 from the Collection of Walter P. Chrysler, Jr.* [exh. cat. by A. McNab]

1952 / Chicago, Ill.
The Art Institute of Chicago *Dutch Pictures, 1450-1750* [exh. cat.]
Also London, Royal Academy of Arts (1953)

1952 / Corning, N.Y.
Corning Museum of Glass *Glass Vessels in Dutch Painting of the Seventeenth Century*
[exh. cat.]

1952 / Los Angeles, Calif.
Los Angeles County Museum of History, Science, and Art *The J. Paul Getty Collection of Dutch Paintings of the 17th Century*

1954 / New York
The Metropolitan Museum of Art *Dutch Painting: The Golden Age, An Exhibition of Dutch Pictures of the Seventeenth Century, Under the High Patronage of Her Majesty the Queen of the Netherlands* [exh. cat. by T. Rousseau]
Also Toledo, The Toledo Museum of Art; Toronto, Art Gallery of Toronto (1955)

1954 / Pittsburgh, Pa.
Carnegie Institute *Pictures of Everyday Life: Genre Painting in Europe, 1500-1900*
[exh. cat. by G.B. Washburn]

1954 / Washington, D.C.
National Gallery of Art *Drawings and Watercolors by Flemish and Dutch Masters*
[exh. cat.]
Also Baltimore, Md., The Baltimore Museum of Art; Cambridge, Mass., Fogg Art Museum, Harvard University; Cleveland, Ohio, The Cleveland Museum of Art; San Francisco, Calif., M.H. de Young Memorial Museum

1956 / Raleigh, N.C.
North Carolina Museum of Art *Rembrandt and His Pupils*
[exh. cat. by W.R. Valentiner]

1957-1958 / Birmingham, Ala.
The Birmingham Museum of Art *Dutch, Flemish, and German Paintings from the Collection of Walter P. Chrysler, Jr.* [exh. cat.]
Traveled

1958 / Indianapolis, Ind.
John Herron Art Museum *The Young Rembrandt and His Times: Dutch Painting of the First Four Decades of the Seventeenth Century* [exh. cat. by S. Slive]
Also San Diego, Calif., Fine Arts Gallery of San Diego

1958 / Washington, D.C.
National Gallery of Art *Drawings and Prints by Rembrandt*

1958 / Washington, D.C.
National Gallery of Art *Dutch Drawings: Masterpieces of Five Centuries*
[exh. cat. by J.Q. van Regteren Altena]
Also New York, The Pierpont Morgan Library; Minneapolis, Minn., The Minneapolis Institute of Arts; Boston, Mass., Museum of Fine Arts; Cleveland, Ohio, The Cleveland Museum of Art; Chicago, Ill., The Art Institute of Chicago (1959)

1958 / Williamstown, Mass.
Sterling and Francine Clark Art Institute *Dutch and Flemish Masters* [exh. cat.]

1959 / Raleigh, N.C.
North Carolina Museum of Art *In Memory of William R. Valentiner 1880-1958: Masterpieces of Art Representing His Achievements during Fifty Years of Service in American Museums* [exh. cat. by J. Byrnes]

1959 / Washington, D.C.
Smithsonian Institution *Old Master Drawings from the Collection of Sir Bruce Ingram*
[exh. cat. by C. Winter]
Traveled

1960 / Ann Arbor, Mich.
The University of Michigan Museum of Art *Rembrandt Prints*

1960 / New York
The Pierpont Morgan Library *Rembrandt: Drawings from American Collections*
[exh. cat. by J. Rosenberg]
Also Cambridge, Mass., Fogg Art Museum, Harvard University

1961 / Washington, D.C.
National Gallery of Art *Rembrandt Etchings*

1964 / Ann Arbor, Mich.
The University of Michigan Museum of Art *Italy through Dutch Eyes: Dutch Seventeenth-Century Landscape Artists in Italy* [exh. cat. by W. Stechow]

1964 / Providence, R.I.
Museum of Art, Rhode Island School of Design *Northern Baroque Paintings and Drawings from the Collection of Mr. and Mrs. Henry H. Weldon* [exh. cat.]

1965 / Allentown, Pa.
Allentown Art Museum *Seventeenth-Century Painters of Haarlem*
[exh. cat. by R. Hirsch]

1965 / Dayton, Ohio
Dayton Art Institute *Hendrick Terbrugghen in America* [exh. cat. by L.J. Slatkes]
Also Baltimore, The Baltimore Museum of Art (1966)

1965 / Washington, D.C.
National Gallery of Art *Exhibition of 'Portrait of a Man in a Fur-Lined Coat' by Rembrandt, Lent by the Fuller Foundation*

1965 / Washington, D.C.
National Gallery of Art *Exhibition of 'Portrait of the Artist's Son Titus' by Rembrandt, Lent by the Norton Simon Foundation*

1965 / Washington, D.C.
National Gallery of Art *Landscape Prints by Rembrandt and Other Dutch Artists*

1966 / San Francisco, Calif.
California Palace of the Legion of Honor *The Age of Rembrandt: An Exhibition of Dutch Paintings of the Seventeenth Century* [exh. cat. by H. Gerson]
Also Toledo, Ohio, The Toledo Museum of Art; Boston, Mass., Museum of Fine Arts (1967)

1966 / Waltham, Mass.
Poses Institute of Arts, Rose Art Gallery, Brandeis University *Seventeenth-Century Paintings from the Low Countries* [exh. cat. by C. Gilbert]

1966 / Washington, D.C.
National Gallery of Art *Etchings by Rembrandt in the Collections of the National Gallery of Art*

1967 / Kalamazoo, Mich.
Kalamazoo Institute of Arts *Alfred Bader Collection: Seventeenth-Century Dutch and Flemish Painting*

1967 / Kansas City, Mo.
Nelson Gallery of Art and Atkins Museum *Paintings of Seventeenth-Century Dutch Interiors* [exh. cat. by R. Coe]

1968 / Oshkosh, Wis.
Paine Art Center and Arboretum *Dutch Art of the 1600s* [exh. cat. by R.N. Gregg and A. Bader]

1969 / Boston, Mass.
Museum of Fine Arts *Rembrandt: Experimental Etcher* [exh. cat. by E.A. Sayre and F. Staempfle]
Also New York, The Pierpont Morgan Library (1969-1970)

1969 / Chicago, Ill.
The Art Institute of Chicago *Rembrandt after Three Hundred Years*
[exh. cat. by E. Haverkamp-Begemann et al.]
Also Minneapolis, Minn., The Minneapolis Institute of Arts; Detroit, Mich., The Detroit Institute of Arts (1970)

1969 / Hanover, N.H.
Hopkins Center Art Galleries, Dartmouth College *Selections from the Collection of Dutch Drawings of Maida and George Abrams*
Also Wellesley, Mass., Wellesley College Museum, Jewett Art Center; Providence, R.I., Museum of Art, Rhode Island School of Design; Storrs, Conn., Museum of Art, University of Connecticut

1969 / Los Angeles, Calif.
Los Angeles County Museum of Art *Rembrandt Etchings from Local Collections*

1969 / Montreal, Que.
Montreal Museum of Fine Arts *Rembrandt and His Pupils* [exh. cat.]
Also Toronto, Ont., Art Gallery of Ontario

1969 / New York
The Pierpont Morgan Library *Rembrandt Drawings from American Collections*
[exh. cat.]
Also Cambridge, Mass., Fogg Art Museum, Harvard University
1969 / Washington, D.C.
National Gallery of Art *Rembrandt in the National Gallery of Art*
[exh. cat. by E. Haverkamp-Begemann et al.]
1969 / Wellesley, Mass.
Wellesley College Museum, Jewett Art Center *Selections from the Collection of Dutch Drawings of Maida and George Abrams* [exh. cat. by F.W. Robinson]
1970 / Poughkeepsie, N.Y.
Vassar College Art Gallery *Dutch Mannerism: Apogee and Epilogue*
[exh. cat. by W. Stechow]
1972 / Grand Rapids, Mich.
Grand Rapids Art Museum *Landscapes from the Golden Age: An Exhibition of Seventeenth-Century Dutch Paintings* [exh. cat. by W. Turkenburg et al.]
1972 / Huntington, N.Y.
Heckscher Museum *Windows and Doors* [exh. cat. by R.B. Solomon]
1972 / New York
The Pierpont Morgan Library *Dutch Genre Drawings of the Seventeenth Century: A Loan Exhibition from Dutch Museums, Foundations, and Private Collections*
[exh. cat. by P. Schatborn]
Also Toledo, Ohio, The Toledo Museum of Art; Toronto, Ont., Art Gallery of Ontario; Chicago, Ill., The Art Institute of Chicago; Boston, Mass. Museum of Fine Arts (1973)
1972 / Storrs, Conn.
The William Benton Museum of Art, University of Connecticut *Hendrick Goltzius and the Printmakers of Haarlem* [exh. cat.]
1973 / Cleveland, Ohio
Cleveland Museum of Art *Dutch Art and Life in the Seventeenth Century* [exh. cat.]
1973 / New York
The Metropolitan Museum of Art *Abraham Bloemaert, 1564-1651; Prints and Drawings* [exh. cat.]
1973 / New York
The Metropolitan Museum of Art *Dutch Couples: Pair Portraits by Rembrandt and His Contemporaries* [exh. cat. by J. Walsh, Jr.]
Also Cincinnati, Ohio, The Taft Museum
1973 / Princeton, N.J.
The Art Museum, Princeton University *Seventeenth-Century Landscapes: Italian, French, Flemish, Dutch* [exh. cat.]
1973 / Washington, D.C.
National Gallery of Art *Etchings by Rembrandt*
1973 / Williamstown, Mass.
Sterling and Francine Clark Art Institute *Things of This World: A Selection of Dutch Drawings from the Collection of Maida and George Abrams* [exh. cat.]
1974 / Cambridge, Mass.
Fogg Art Museum, Harvard University *Seventeenth-Century Dutch Allegorical Prints* [exh. cat.]
1974 / Milwaukee, Wis.
The University of Wisconsin Art History Galleries *Low-Life in the Lowlands: Seventeenth-Century Dutch and Flemish Genre Painting* [exh. cat. by M. Chepp et al.]
1974 / Sacramento, Calif.
E.B. Crocker Art Gallery *The Pre-Rembrandtists* [exh. cat. by A. Tümpel et al.]
1975 / Detroit, Mich.
Statewide Services of The Detroit Institute of Arts *Heart of a Collection: Six Dutch Masters*
Traveled to 13 venues in Michigan
1975 / New Haven, Conn.
Yale University Art Gallery *Dutch Religious Art of the Seventeenth Century*
[exh. cat. by P.C. Sutton and O. Naumann]

1975 / Saint Petersburg, Fla.
Museum of Fine Arts *Dutch Life in the Golden Century* [exh. cat. by F.W. Robinson]
Also Atlanta, Ga., The High Museum of Art
1976 / Milwaukee, Wis.
Milwaukee Art Center *The Bible through Dutch Eyes: From Genesis through the Apocrypha* [exh. cat. by A. Bader and T. Atkinson]
1976 / New York
The Metropolitan Museum of Art *Tricolour: Seventeenth-Century Dutch, Eighteenth-Century English, and Nineteenth-Century French Drawings from the Robert Lehman Collection* [exh. cat. by G. Szabo]
1976 / Poughkeepsie, N.Y.
Vassar College Art Gallery *Seventeenth-Century Dutch Landscape Drawings and Selected Prints from American Collections* [exh. cat. by C.O. Baer]
1977 / Los Angeles, Calif.
Los Angeles County Museum of Art *Dutch and Flemish Prints from the Permanent Collection*
1977 / Malibu, Calif.
The J. Paul Getty Museum *Etchings of Rembrandt and His Followers: A Selection from the Robert Engel Family Collection* [exh. cat. by B.B. Fredericksen and R.J. Kibiak]
Also Santa Barbara, Calif., Santa Barbara Museum of Art; Corpus Christi, Tex., Art Museum of South Texas; San Jose, Calif., San Jose Museum of Art; Phoenix, Ariz., Phoenix Art Museum; San Diego, Calif., Fine Arts Gallery of San Diego (1978)
1977 / New York
The Pierpont Morgan Library *Rembrandt and His Century: Dutch Drawings of the Seventeenth Century from the Collection of Frits Lugt* [exh. cat.]
Also Paris, Institut Néerlandais (1978)
1977 / Toronto, Ont.
Art Gallery of Ontario *The Dutch Cityscape in the Seventeenth Century and Its Sources* [exh. cat.]
Also Amsterdam, Amsterdams Historisch Museum
1977 / Washington, D.C.
National Gallery of Art *Seventeenth-Century Dutch Drawings from American Collections* [exh. cat. by F.W. Robinson]
Also Denver, Colo., The Denver Art Museum; Fort Worth, Tex., Kimbell Art Museum
1979 / Ithaca, N.Y.
Herbert F. Johnson Museum of Art, Cornell University *Dutch Drawings of the Seventeenth Century from a Collection* [exh. cat. by C.E. Gilbert et al.]
1979 / New York
The Metropolitan Museum of Art *Seventeenth-Century Dutch and Flemish Drawings from the Robert Lehman Collection* [exh. cat. by G. Szabo]
1979 / New York
The Pierpont Morgan Library *William and Mary and Their House* [exh. cat.]
1979 / South Hadley, Mass.
Mount Holyoke College Art Museum *Baroque Paintings in the Low Countries: Selections from the Bader Collection* [exh. cat. by J.L. Varriano]
1979 / Worcester, Mass.
Worcester Art Museum *Seventeenth-Century Dutch Paintings: Raising the Curtain on New England Private Collections* [exh. cat. by J.A. Welu]
1980 / Boston, Mass.
Museum of Fine Arts *Printmaking in the Age of Rembrandt* [exh. cat. by C.S. Ackley and W.W. Robinson]
Also Saint Louis, The Saint Louis Art Museum (1981)
1980 / Cambridge, Mass.
Fogg Art Museum, Harvard University *The Draughtsman at Work: Drawing in the Golden Century of Dutch Art*

1980 / Houston, Tex.
The Blaffer Foundation *A Golden Age of Painting: Dutch, Flemish, German Paintings, Sixteenth and Seventeenth Centuries from the Collection of the Sarah Campbell Blaffer Foundation* [exh. cat.]

1980 / New York
The Pierpont Morgan Library *Rubens and Rembrandt in Their Century: Flemish and Dutch Drawings of the Seventeenth Century from The Pierpont Morgan Library*
[exh. cat. by F. Stampfle]
Also Paris, Institute Néerlandais; Antwerp, Koninklijk Museum voor Schone Kunsten; London, The British Museum (1979)

1980 / Sarasota, Fla.
The John and Mable Ringling Museum of Art *Dutch Seventeenth-Century Portraiture: The Golden Age* [exh. cat. by W.H. Wilson]

1980 / Washington, D.C.
National Gallery of Art *Gods, Saints, and Heroes: Dutch Painting in the Age of Rembrandt* [exh. cat. by A. Blankert et al.]
Also Detroit, Mich., The Detroit Institute of Arts; Amsterdam, Rijksmuseum (1981)

1980 / West Lafayette, Ind.
Union Gallery, Perdue University *Old Students and Old Masters: The School of Rembrandt. Selections from the Bader Collection* [exh. cat. by D. Parrish]

1981 / Los Angeles, Calif.
Los Angeles County Museum of Art *A Mirror of Nature: Dutch Paintings from the Collection of Mr. and Mrs. Edward William Carter* [exh. cat. by J. Walsh, Jr., and C.P. Schneider]
Also Boston, Mass., Museum of Fine Arts; New York, The Metropolitan Museum of Art (1982)

1981 / Williamstown, Mass.
Sterling and Francine Clark Art Institute *Rembrandt Fecit* [exh. cat. by J. Held]

1982 / Austin, Tex.
Archer M. Huntington Art Gallery, The College of Fine Arts, The University of Texas *Seventeenth-Century Dutch Landscape Drawings* [exh. cat.]

1982 / Cambridge, Mass.
Fogg Art Museum, Harvard University *Jacob van Ruisdael* [exh. cat. by S. Slive and H.R. Hoetink]
Also The Hague, Mauritshuis (1981)

1982 / Norfolk, Va.
The Chrysler Museum *The Discovery of the Everyday: Seventeenth-Century Dutch Paintings from the Wolf Collection* [exh. cat.]
Also Providence, R.I., Museum of Art, Rhode Island School of Design; Tampa, Fla., The Tampa Museum

1982 / Notre Dame, Ind.
Snite Museum of Art *Selections of Seventeenth- and Eighteenth-Century Dutch Art from the Collection of Dr. A.C.R. Dreesmann: A Bicentennial Celebration of Relations between the United States and the Netherlands* [exh. cat. by F. Simons]

1982 / Washington, D.C.
National Gallery of Art *Dutch Figure Drawings from the Seventeenth Century*
[exh. cat. by P. Schatborn]
Also Amsterdam, Rijksprentenkabinet (1981)

1982 / Washington, D.C.
National Gallery of Art *Mauritshuis: Dutch Painting of the Golden Age from the Royal Picture Gallery, The Hague* [exh. cat.]
Also Fort Worth, Tex., Kimbell Art Museum; Chicago, Ill., The Art Institute of Chicago; Los Angeles, Calif., Los Angeles County Museum of Art; Toronto, Ont., Art Gallery of Ontario (1983); New York, The Metropolitan Museum of Art (1984)

1982-1983 / San Francisco, Calif.
M.H. de Young Memorial Museum, The Fine Arts Museums of San Francisco *Rembrandt: Selected Prints and Drawings*

1983 / Hamilton, N.Y.
Picker Art Gallery, Colgate University *Dutch Painting in the Age of Rembrandt from The Metropolitan Museum of Art* [exh. cat. by S. Dickey et al.]
Traveled

1983 / Lawrence, Kans.
Spencer Museum of Art, University of Kansas *Dutch Prints of Daily Life: Mirrors of Life or Masks of Morals?* [exh. cat. by L.A. Stone-Ferrier]

1983 / Los Angeles, Calif.
Los Angeles County Museum of Art *Etchings by Rembrandt and His School from the Engel Family Collection* [exh. cat. by E. Feinblatt]

1983 / New Brunswick, N.J.
Jane Voorhees Zimmerli Art Museum, Rutgers, The State University of New Jersey *Haarlem: The Seventeenth Century* [exh. cat. by F.F. Hofrichter et al.]

1983 / New Haven, Conn.
Yale University Art Gallery *Rembrandt in Eighteenth-Century England*
[exh. cat. by C. White et al.]

1983 / Philadelphia, Pa.
Philadelphia Museum of Art *Jan Steen: Comedy and Admonition*
[exh. cat. by P.C. Sutton and M. Butler]

1983 / Washington, D.C.
National Gallery of Art *The Prints of Lucas van Leyden and His Contemporaries*
[exh. cat. by E.S. Jacobowitz and S.L. Stepanek]

1984 / Kingston, Ont.
Agnes Etherington Art Centre, Queen's University *Pictures from the Age of Rembrandt. Selections from the Personal Collection of Dr. and Mrs. Alfred Bader*
[exh. cat. by D. McTavish]

1984 / Philadelphia, Pa.
Philadelphia Museum of Art *Masters of Seventeenth-Century Dutch Genre Painting*
[exh. cat. by P.C. Sutton et al.]
Also Berlin, Gemäldegalerie, Staatliche Museen Preussischer Kulturbesitz; London, Royal Academy of Arts

1985 / Atlanta, Ga.
The High Museum of Art *Masterpieces of the Dutch Golden Age*
[exh. cat. by F.J. Duparc]

1985 / Minneapolis, Minn.
The Minneapolis Institute of Arts *Dutch and Flemish Masters: Paintings from the Vienna Academy of Fine Arts* [exh. cat. by G.S. Keyes and R. Trnek]
Also Houston, Tex., The Museum of Fine Arts; San Diego, Calif., San Diego Museum of Art

1985 / New York
The Metropolitan Museum of Art *Dutch Drawings of the Seventeenth Century in The Metropolitan Museum of Art*

1985/ New York
Minskoff Cultural Center *The Golden Ambiance: Dutch Landscape Painting in the Seventeenth Century* [exh. cat. by W. Liedtke]

1986 / New York
The Drawing Center *The Northern Landscape*
Also London, The Courtauld Institute

1986 / Pittsburgh, Pa.
The Frick Art Museum *Gardens of Earthly Delight: Sixteenth- and Seventeenth-Century Netherlandish Gardens* [exh. cat. by K.J. Hellerstedt]

1986 / Raleigh, N.C.
North Carolina Museum of Art *Dutch Art in the Age of Rembrandt* [exh. cat.]

1986 / Vancouver, B.C.
Vancouver Art Gallery *The Dutch World of Painting* [exh. cat. by G. Schwartz]

1986 / Washington, D.C.
National Gallery of Art *Jacques de Gheyn II: Drawings* [exh. cat.]
Also Rotterdam, Museum Boymans-van Beuningen (1985)

1986-1987 / Raleigh, N.C.
North Carolina Museum of Art *Dutch Art in the Age of Rembrandt* [exh. cat.]

1987 / Boston, Mass.
Museum of Fine Arts *Masters of Seventeenth-Century Dutch Landscape Painting*
[exh. cat. by P.C. Sutton et al.]
Also Amsterdam, Rijksmuseum; Philadelphia, Pa., Philadelphia Museum of Art
(1988)

1987 / Cincinnati, Ohio
The Taft Museum *Skating in the Arts of Seventeenth-Century Holland: An Exhibition Honoring the 1987 World Figure-Skating Championships* [exh. cat. by L.S. Dixon]

1988 / Cambridge, Mass.
Arthur M. Sackler Museum, Harvard University *Landscape in Perspective: Drawings by Rembrandt and His Contemporaries* [exh. cat. by F.J. Duparc]
Also Montreal, Que., Montreal Museum of Fine Arts

1988 / Fort Worth, Tex.
Kimbell Art Museum *A Prosperous Past: The Sumptuous Still Life in the Netherlands, 1600-1700* [exh. cat. by S. Segal]
Also Cambridge, Mass., Fogg Art Museum, Harvard University; Delft, Stedelijk Museum Het Prinsenhof

1988 / Hempstead, N.Y.
Hofstra Museum, Hofstra University *People at Work: Seventeenth-Century Dutch Art*
[exh. cat. by D. Barnes and L. Stone-Ferrier]

1988 / New York
Cooper-Hewitt Museum *Courts and Colonies: The William and Mary Style in Holland, England, and America* [exh. cat. by R. Baarsen et al.]

1988 / New York
The Metropolitan Museum of Art *Dutch and Flemish Paintings from the Hermitage*
[exh. cat.]
Also Chicago, Ill., The Art Institute of Chicago

1988 / New York
National Academy of Design *Dutch and Flemish Paintings from New York Private Collections* [exh. cat. by E. Haverkamp-Begemann & A.J. Adams]

1988-1989 / Kingston, Ont.
Agnes Etherington Art Centre, Queen's University *Telling Images: Images révélatrices*
[exh. cat. by D. McTavish]
Also Hamilton, Ont., Ontario, Art Gallery of Hamilton; Regina, Sask., MacKenzie Art Gallery; Fredericton, N.B., Beaverbrook Art Gallery; Vancouver, B.C., Vancouver Art Gallery (1989-1990); Halifax, N.S., Art Gallery of Nova Scotia; Wolfville, N.S., Acadia University Art Gallery; Winnipeg, Man., Winnipeg Art Gallery (1991)

1989 / Cambridge, Mass.
Arthur M. Sackler Museum, Harvard University *Rembrandt and His School: Drawings from the Museum Boymans-van Beuningen, Rotterdam* [exh. cat. by J. Giltaj]

1989 / Dearborn, Mich.
Mardigan Library, University of Michigan *Impressions of Faith: Rembrandt's Biblical Etchings* [exh. cat. by S. Perlove]

1989 / Milwaukee, Wis.
Milwaukee Art Museum *The Detective's Eye: Investigating the Old Masters*
[exh. cat. by I. Bader and A. Bader]

1989 / Washington, D.C.
National Gallery of Art *Frans Hals* [exh. cat. by S. Slive et al.]
Also London, Royal Academy of Arts; Haarlem, Frans Halsmuseum (1990)

1989 / Washington, D.C.
National Gallery of Art *Still Lifes of the Golden Age: Northern European Paintings from the Heinz Family Collection* [exh. cat. by I. Bergström and A. Wheelock]
Also Boston, Mass., Museum of Fine Arts

1989 / Wausau, Wis.
Leigh Yawkey Woodson Art Museum *Delights for the Senses: Dutch and Flemish Still Life Paintings from Budapest* [exh. cat. by I. Ember and I. Barkoozi]

1990 / Minneapolis, Minn.
The Minneapolis Institute of Arts *Mirror of Empire: Dutch Marine Art of the Seventeenth Century* [exh. cat. by G.S. Keyes]

Also Toledo, Ohio, The Toledo Museum of Art; Los Angeles, Calif., Los Angeles County Museum of Art (1991)

1990 / Montreal, Que.
Montreal Museum of Fine Arts *Italian Recollections: Dutch Paintings in the Golden Age*
[exh. cat. by F.J. Duparc and L.L. Graif]

1990 / Washington, D.C.
National Gallery of Art *Rembrandt's Landscapes: Drawings and Prints*
[exh. cat. by C. Schneider]

1991 / San Francisco, Calif.
The Fine Arts Museums of San Francisco *Great Dutch Paintings in America*
[exh. cat. by B. Broos et al.]
Also The Hague, Mauritshuis (1990)

Bibliography

A. 1926
A., 'Ein Rembrandt von Schweden nach Amerika verkauft,' *Der Cicerone* 18 (1926), pp. 207-208

Van der Aa 1852 / 1869
A.J. van der Aa, *Biographisch woordenboek der Nederlanden* (7 vols.), Amsterdam 1969 (1st edition)

Aachen 1932
Städtisches Suermondt-Museum. Gemälde-Katalog. Amtliche Ausgabe mit 64 Abbildungen, Aachen 1932

Agnew 1958
C. Agnew, 'Obituary W.R. Valentiner,' *The Burlington Magazine* 100 (1958), p. 442

d'Ailly
A.E. d'Ailly, *Zeven eeuwen Amsterdam* (De stad en haar schoonheid in de zeventiende eeuw III), Amsterdam n.d.

Ainsworth / Brealy et al. 1982
M.W. Ainsworth, J. Brealy et al., *Art and Autoradiography: Insights into the Genesis of Paintings by Rembrandt, Van Dyck and Vermeer*, New York 1982

Albach 1979
B. Albach, 'Rembrandt en het toneel,' *De kroniek van het Rembrandthuis* 31 (1979), pp. 2-33

Album studiosorum 1875
Album studiosorum academiae Lugduno Batavae MDLXXV-MDCCCLXXV, The Hague 1875

Alciatus 1542 / 1967
[A. Alciatus], *Emblematum Libellus*, Darmstadt 1967 (1st edition 1542)

Algemeen Handelsblad 1914
'De Steengracht-schilderijen in het Mauritshuis,' *Algemeen Handelsblad* 7 April 1914, 'Avondblad, derde blad,' p. 10

Allen 1943
J.L. Allen, 'The Museum's Rembrandts,' *The Metropolitan Museum of Art Bulletin* 4 (1945-1946), no. 3, pp. 73-77

Allen 1949
F.L. Allen, *The Great Pierpont Morgan*, New York 1949

Allen 1965
F.L. Allen, *The Great Pierpont Morgan*, New York 1965

Allen / Gardner 1954
J.L. Allen & E.E. Gardner, *A Concise Catalogue of the European Paintings in The Metropolitan Museum of Art*, New York 1954

Alpers 1975-1976
S. Alpers, 'Realism as a Comic Mode: Low-Life Painting Seen through Bredero's Eyes,' *Simiolus* 8 (1975-1976), pp. 115-144

AMAM **Bulletin 1953**
'Exhibition of Paintings from College and University Collections. 20 January – 15 February, 1953,' *Allen Memorial Art Museum Bulletin* 10 (1953), pp. 43-70

AMAM **Bulletin 1959**
'Catalogue. Painting,' *Allen Memorial Art Museum Bulletin* 16 (1959), no. 2, pp. 55-84

AMAM **Bulletin 1959-A**
'Foreword,' *Allen Memorial Art Museum Bulletin* 16 (1959), no. 3, pp. 155-288

American Art News 1909
'Kann Pictures Bought by Duveen Bros.,' *American Art News* 7 (1909), 20 September, p. 3

Amour de l'art 1935
'L'Exposition Rembrandt à Amsterdam,' *L'amour de l'art* 16 (1935), pp. 271-274

Ampzing 1628
S. Ampzing, *Beschryvinge ende lof der stad Haerlem in Holland*, Haarlem 1628

Amstelodamum 1935
'Het 50-jarig jubileum van den heer Mensing,' *Amstelodamum. Maandblad* 22 (1935), pp. 104-106

Amsterdam 1810
Prijzen der schilderijen. Van het beroemd kabinet van wylen den hoog edele gestrengen heer Mr. Pieter de Smeth van Alphen. Benevens de namen derzelver koopers, Amsterdam n.d. (1810)

Amsterdam 1863
Cat. *Beschryving der schilderijen, teekeningen, prenten, prentwerken en boeken in het Museum Fodor te Amsterdam*, Amsterdam 1863

Amsterdam 1867
Katalogus der tentoonstelling van schilderijen van oude meesters Amsterdam (Arti et Amicitiae) 1867

Amsterdam 1898
Cat. *Rembrandt. Collection des oeuvres des maîtres réunies, à l'occasion de l'inauguration de S.M. la Reine Wilhelmine* Amsterdam (Stedelijk Museum) 1898

Amsterdam 1900
Catalogus der verzameling schilderijen en familieportretten van de heeren Jhr. P.H. Six van Vromade, Jhr. Dr. J. Six en Jhr. W. Six wegens verbouwing in het Stedelijk Museum van Amsterdam tentoongesteld Amsterdam (Stedelijk Museum) 1900

Amsterdam 1913
Cat. *Tentoonstelling van een zeven-tal schilderijen, afkomstig uit de verzameling-Steengracht en van twee-en-negentig teekeningen door Rembrandt, waaronder vijf-en-zestig, door dr. C. Hofstede de Groot aan den staat geschonken, gehouden in het Stedelijk Museum te Amsterdam, 25 augustus tot 14 september 1913* Amsterdam (Stedelijk Museum) 1913

Amsterdam 1928
Catalogue des nouvelles acquisitions de la collection Goudstikker, Amsterdam 1928

Amsterdam 1929
Catalogus van de tentoonstelling van oude kunst door de vereeniging van handelaren in oude kunst in Nederland Amsterdam (Rijksmuseum) 1929

Amsterdam 1935
Cat. *Rembrandt tentoonstelling ter herdenking van de plechtige opening van het Rijksmuseum op 13 juli 1885* Amsterdam (Rijksmuseum) 1935

Amsterdam 1935-A
Cat. *Bloemstukken van oude meesters* Amsterdam (P. de Boer) 1935

Amsterdam 1936
Catalogus van de tentoonstelling van oude kunst uit het bezit van den internationalen handel Amsterdam (Rijksmuseum) 1936

Amsterdam 1939
Cat. *Tentoonstelling bijbelsche kunst* Amsterdam (Rijksmuseum) 1939

Amsterdam 1955
Cat. *Jubileumtentoonstelling kunsthandel Gebr. Douwes* Amsterdam (Rokin 46) 1955

Amsterdam 1960
Catalogue of Paintings Amsterdam (Rijksmuseum) 1960

Amsterdam 1962
Cat. *Tentoonstelling van oude meesters* Amsterdam (Gebr. Douwes) 1962

Amsterdam 1963
Catalogue of Old Pictures Amsterdam (P. de Boer) 1963

Amsterdam 1976
Cat. *Tot lering en vermaak. Betekenissen van Hollandse genrevoorstellingen uit de zeventiende eeuw* Amsterdam (Rijksmuseum) 1976

Amsterdam 1978
Cat. *Het Vaderlandsch Gevoel* Amsterdam (Rijksmuseum) 1978

Amsterdam 1981
Cat. *Jan van Goyen. 1596-1656. Conquest of Space* Amsterdam (K. & V. Waterman) 1981

Amsterdam / Detroit / Washington 1980-1981
Cat. *God en de goden* Amsterdam (Rijksmuseum) Detroit (The Detroit Institute of Arts) Washington, D.C. (National Gallery of Art) 1980-1981 (English edition: *Gods, Saints and Heroes*)

Amsterdam / Toronto 1977
Cat. *Opkomst en bloei van het Noordnederlandse stadsgezicht / The Dutch Cityscape in the 17th Century and Its Sources* Amsterdam (Amsterdams Historisch Museum) Toronto (Art Gallery of Ontario) 1977

Ann Arbor 1964
Cat. *Italy through Dutch Eyes. Dutch Seventeenth Century Landscape Artists in Italy* Ann Arbor, Mich. (The University of Michigan Museum of Art) 1964

Antiquarian 1931
'Two Important Museum Acquisitions,' *The Antiquarian* 17 (1931), pp. 41 and 54

Antiques 1986
'Museum Accessions,' *Antiques* 129 (1986), February, p. 380

Antwerp 1959
Beschrijvende catalogus. Oude meesters Antwerp (Koninklijk Museum voor Schone Kunsten) 1959

Apollo 1941
'National Gallery of Art Washington,' *Apollo* 33 (1941), January-June, pp. 111-113

Apollo 1966
'Art and Antique Dealer's Fair,' *Apollo* 93 (1966), October, p. 345

Apollo 1971
'Spring Exhibition of Fine Dutch, Flemish and Italian Old Master Paintings,' *Apollo* 98 (1971), April, pp. 74-90 (advertisements)

Apollo 1976
'A Collection for Connoisseurs,' *Apollo* 103 (1976), January, pp. 82-85

Apollo 1976-A
'Allen Memorial Art Museum, Oberlin College, Oberlin, Ohio,' *Apollo* 103 (1976), February, *passim*

Apollo 1978
'Fogg Art Museum, Harvard University,' *Apollo* 107 (1978), May and June, *passim*

Apollo 1985
'A Major Acquisition for Kansas City,' *Apollo* 122 (1985), November, p. 393

Arnhem 1953
Cat. *17de Eeuwse meesters uit Gelders bezit* Arnhem (Gemeentemuseum) 1953

Arnhem 1960-1961
Cat. *Collectie B. de Geus van den Heuvel te Nieuwersluis* Arnhem (Gemeentemuseum) 1960-1961

Von Arps-Aubert 1932
R. von Arps-Aubert, *Die Entwicklung des reinen Tierbildes in der Kunst des Paulus Potter* (diss.), Halle 1932

Art & Antiques 1987
'America's Top 100 Collectors,' *Art & Antiques* (1987), March, pp. 49-69

Art Digest 1931
'New Galleries,' *The Art Digest* 5 (1931), August, p. 17

Art Digest 1931-A
'Ralph H. Booth's Bequest,' *The Art Digest* 5 (1931), August, p. 6

Art Digest 1935
'Chicago Art Institute Will Show Rembrandt with His Pupils' Work,' *The Art Digest* 9 (1935), 1 December, p. 7

Art Digest 1935-A
'50 Paintings by Frans Hals, Owned in America, Shown in Detroit,' *The Art Digest* 9 (1935), 15 January, pp. 5 and 13

Art Digest 1937
'Frans Hals, "Laureate of Laughter," Honored by His Native Haarlem,' *The Art Digest* 11 (1937), 1 June, pp. 5-7

Art Digest 1940
'Famous Widener Collection of Old Masters Given to the Nation,' *The Art Digest* 15 (1940), no. 3, pp. 10-11 and 27

Art Digest 1941
'Famous Johnson Collection Installed in Philadelphia Museum,' *The Art Digest* 16 (1941), 15 November, pp. 8 and 28

Art Digest 1941-A
'Noted Chrysler Collection Shocks and Stimulates the Southland,' *The Art Digest* 16 (1941), pp. 10 and 30

Artis 1985
'Goltzius-Gemälde aufgetaucht,' *Artis* 37 (1985), no. 3, p. 20

Art Journal 1969
'Bartholomeus Breenbergh. 1599-1657. Scene from the Life of Christ, 1634,' *The Art Journal* 28 (1969), no. 4, p. 361

Art News 1921
'John McCormack Pays $150.000 for a Hals, "Portrait of a Man," from Polish Collection,' *American Art News* 20 (1921), 12 November, p. 1

Art News 1928
'America Lends Dutch Paintings to London Show,' *The Art News* 27 (1928), 29 December, pp. 1 and 12-14

Art News 1930
'Rembrandt Sold by Scott and Fowles,' *The Art News* 28 (1930), 12 April, p. 1

Art News 1931
'A Notable Hals Portrait at the Bachstitz Galleries,' *The Art News* 29 (1931), 28 March, p. 4

Art News 1931-A
'Obituary: Ralph H. Booth,' *The Art News* 29 (1931), 11 July, p. 12

Art News 1938
'The Mensing Pictures: A Famous Amsterdam Collection in the Saleroom,' *The Art News* 37 (1938), 1 October, pp. 15 and 19

Art News 1952
'Enriching U.S. Museums: Cleveland,' *The Art News* 51 (1952), November, pp. 32-33

Art News 1952-A
'Virginia's Williams Gift: Paintings plus $3.500.000,' *The Art News* 51 (1952), November, pp. 34-35 and 65-66

Art News 1953
'Obituaries,' *The Art News* 52 (1953), May, p. 7

Art News 1955
'The Auction Season,' *The Art News* 53 (1955), September, p. 14

Art Quarterly 1942
'A Landscape by Meindert Hobbema,' *The Art Quarterly* 5 (1942), pp. 344-347

Art Quarterly 1955
' "Portrait of an Unknown Woman," by Frans Hals in the City Art Museum of St. Louis,' *The Art Quarterly* 18 (1955), pp. 416-417

Art Quarterly 1956
'Accessions of American and Canadian Museums. July – September, 1956,' *The Art Quarterly* 19 (1956), pp. 418-429

Art Quarterly 1957
' "The Cello Player" by Gabriel Metsu in the M.H. de Young Memorial Museum,' *The Art Quarterly* 20 (1957), pp. 332-335

Art Quarterly 1960
'Accessions of American and Canadian Museums. April – June, 1960,' *The Art Quarterly* 33 (1960), pp. 300-310

Art Quarterly 1961
'Accessions of American and Canadian Museums,' *The Art Quarterly* 34 (1961), pp. 197-218

Art Quarterly 1964
'Accessions of American and Canadian Museums. April – June, 1964,' *The Art Quarterly* 37 (1964), pp. 370-392

Art Quarterly 1968
'Accessions of American and Canadian Museums. July – September 1967,' *The Art Quarterly* 41 (1968), pp. 91-109

Art Quarterly 1969
'Recent Accessions of American and Canadian Museums. April – June, 1969,' *The Art Quarterly* 42 (1969), pp. 437-451

Les Arts 1909
'Collection de feu M. Maurice Kann,' *Les Arts* 88 (1909), April, pp. 1-32

Artsmagazine 1971
'New York Galleries,' *Artsmagazine* 45 (1971), pp. 20-71

Ascott 1963
Cat. *The Ascott Collection* Ascott, Buckinghamshire (The National Trust) 1963

Ashbourne 1885-1900
Catalogue of Paintings Forming the Private Collection of P.A.B. Widener, Ashbourne – near Philadelphia. Part II. Early English and Ancient Paintings, Ashbourne 1885-1900

Ashbourne 1895-1900
Catalogue of Paintings Forming the Private Collection of P.A.B. Widener. Part II. Early English and Ancient Paintings, Ashbourne 1895-1900

Atlanta 1985
Cat. *Masterpieces of the Dutch Golden Age* Atlanta, Ga. (High Museum of Art) 1985

Auction Amsterdam 1704
Catalogus van veele curieuse rariteiten [...] bestaande in konstige en uitgevoerde tekeningen, miniaturen en waterverwen [...] nagelaten by wylen Constant Sennepart Amsterdam (J.P. Somer) 1 April 1704 et seq.

Auction Amsterdam 1708
Catalogus van uytmuntende, konstige, curieuse en plaisante schilderyen [...] door een voornaam liefhebber in jaren by een vergadert Amsterdam (J.P. Zomer & J. Magnus) 12 September 1708

Auction Amsterdam 1734
Catalogus van uitmuntende en extra konstige schilderyen [...] Nagelaten by wylen den wel edelen Heer Mr. Willem Six Amsterdam (Schoenmaker, Ten Brink) 12 May 1734

Auction Amsterdam 1738
Catalogus van het zeer befaamde, uitmuntende heerlyk en vorstelyk cabinet Schilderyen [...] nagelaten door zyn Excellentie Ferdinand Grave van Plettenberg en Wittem ... Amsterdam (G. Hol & P. van der Land) 2 April 1738

Auction Amsterdam 1746
Catalogus der uitmuntende schilderyen van N. Verkolje Amsterdam (J. Verkolje) 18 April 1746

Auction Amsterdam 1754
Catalogus van 't uitmuntend kabinet schilderyen, craionnen, teekeningen [...] nagelaten door den heere Jeronimus Tonneman Amsterdam (H. de Leth) 21 October 1754 et seq.

Auction Amsterdam 1763
Catalogus van een uitmuntend kabinet met konstige schilderyen [...] nagelaten door wylen de heer Johannes Verkolje ... Amsterdam (H. de Winter) 24 October 1763

Auction Amsterdam 1764
Catalogus van een fraay kabinet met konstige schilderijen ... Amsterdam (J.A. Jolles & H. de Winter) 23 May 1764

Auction Amsterdam 1765
Catalogus van een fraay kabinet met konstige schilderyen ... Amsterdam (M. van der Linden & H. de Winter) 5 June 1765 et seq.

Auction Amsterdam 1765-A
Catalogus van een zeer ryk en magnifiek cabinet schilderyen van de beroemdste Italiaansche en Nederlandsche meesters. Met veel moeite en kosten byeen verzameld door wylen de heer de N**** Amsterdam (Jan Matthias Cok) 19 June 1765

Auction Amsterdam 1766
Catalogus van een uitmuntend en schoon kabinet konstige, fraaye en playsante schilderyen [...] zynde van 't beroemde kabinet van den heer Braamcamp Amsterdam (J. de Bosch & J.M. Cok) 4 June 1766

Auction Amsterdam 1771
Catalogus van het uitmuntend kabinet schilderyen, tekeningen, prenten, beelden, enz. [...] door geheel Europa beroemd, en in veele jaaren byeenverzameld door den heere Gerret Braamcamp Amsterdam (P. van der Schley et al.) 31 July 1771 et seq.

Auction Amsterdam 1771-A
Pryzen der schilderyen [...] uitmakende het beroemd en uitmuntend kabinet van wylen den heere Gerret Braamcamp ... Amsterdam 1771

Auction Amsterdam 1773
Catalogus van een uitmuntend en overheerlyk kabinet konstige schilderyen [...] nagelaaten door wylen den wel ed. gestrenge heer Mr. Johan van der Marck Aegidz Amsterdam (H. de Winter & J. Yver) 25 August 1773 et seq.

Auction Amsterdam 1774
Catalogus van fraaye schilderyen, door Nederlandsche schilders [...] alles byeen verzameld en nagelaten, door wylen den hoog edelen heere Jan Lucas van der Dussen (3 vols.) Amsterdam (P. van der Schley et al.) 31 October 1774 et seq.

Auction Amsterdam 1792
Catalogus van een fraay kabinet schilderijen Amsterdam (Van der Schley & Ten Kate) 16 July 1792 et seq.

Auction Amsterdam 1792-A
Catalogus van een fraai kabinet van konstige schilderijen [...] nagelaten door wylen den heer Johan Christoph Werther Amsterdam (P. van der Schley et al.) 25-26 April 1792

Auction Amsterdam 1796
Catalogus van een uitmuntende collectie schilderijen, door allerberoemste Nederlandsche meesters [...] Alles naargelaaten door wyle vrouwe Elisabeth Hooft, weduwe den heere Wouter Valckenier Amsterdam (C. Blasius et al.) 31 August 1796 et seq.

Auction Amsterdam 1799
Catalogus van een fraaije verzameling schilderijen, alle door beroemde Nederlandsche meesters [...] by een verzameld en nagelaaten door een der oudste en aanzienlijkste geslagten van Nederland Amsterdam (P. van der Schley et al.) 21 August 1799 et seq.

Auction Amsterdam 1802
Catalogus van een uitmuntend cabinet schilderyen, door beroemde Nederlandsche en andere voorname meesters [...] nagelaten door een kunst-liefhebber uit Friesland ... Amsterdam (P. van der Schley et al.) 29 September 1802

Auction Amsterdam 1810
Catalogus van het kabinet schilderijen, nagelaten door den hoog edelen gestrengen heer Mr Pieter de Smeth van Alphen Amsterdam (P. van der Schley et al.) 1-2 August 1810 (also a French edition)

Auction Amsterdam 1811
Catalogus van eene fraaije verzameling van uitmuntende schilderijen [...] bijeen verzameld door een voornaam liefhebber Amsterdam (Van der Schley et al.) 24 April 1811

Auction Amsterdam 1814
Catalogue d'une collection choisie et précieuse de tableaux [...] ayant appartenue à feu Madame La Douarière Boreel Amsterdam (Van der Schley, De Vries et al.) 23 September 1814

Auction Amsterdam 1822
Catalogus van eene uitmuntende verzameling schilderijen, door de beroemdste Nederlandsche meesters: merendeels uitmakende het kabinet van wijlen den heer S.J. Stinstra van Harlingen Amsterdam (J. de Vries et al.) 22 May 1822

Auction Amsterdam 1827
Catalogus van eene uitgebreide verzameling fraaije schilderijen [...] meerendeels nagelaten door wijlen den heer Hendrik Reydon Amsterdam (J. de Vries et al.) 5-6 April 1827

Auction Amsterdam 1925
Cat. *Tableaux anciens et modernes ...* Amsterdam (A. Mak) 9-11 June 1925

Auction Amsterdam 1926
Cat. *Tableaux anciens, tableaux modernes [...] collections D. Komter, marchand d'art à Amsterdam* Amsterdam (A. Mak) 9 March 1926

Auction Amsterdam 1928
Cat. *50 Tableaux anciens de l'école hollandaise, eaux-fortes et dessins de Rembrandt provenant de la collection-Six* Amsterdam (Mensing, Muller & Cie) 16 October 1928

Auction Amsterdam 1938
Collection de feu M.-Ant. W.M. Mensing d'Amsterdam. Catalogue des tableaux anciens Amsterdam (F. Muller & Cie) 15 November 1938

Auction Amsterdam 1960
Cat. *Collection de feu M. W.J.R. Dreesmann. Tableaux anciens et modernes [...] provenant du musée privé et de la collection particulière* Amsterdam (Muller) 22-25 March 1960

Auction Amsterdam 1976
Sale Catalogue 258. The B. de Geus van den Heuvel Collection Amsterdam (Sotheby Mak van Waay) 26-27 April 1976

Auction Berlin 1916
Cat. *Gemälde des 15. bis 18. Jahrhunderts, die hinterlassenen Sammlungen der Herren Alex Schönlank, Berlin und Carl Franze, Tetschen ...* Berlin (Lepke) 7 November 1916

Auction Berlin 1933
Cat. *Sammlung und Bibliothek eines Berliner Kunstfreundes* Berlin (Internationales Kunst- und Auktions-Haus GMBH) 9 May 1933

Auction Bordeaux 1818
Catalogue d'une collection de jolis tableaux des écoles flammandes et hollandaise Bordeaux (Martin Commissaire-Priseur) 3-4 August 1818

Auction Brussels 1837
Catalogue d'une belle collection de tableaux [...] délaissés par M. le Comte F. de Robiano Brussels (Barbé) 1 May 1837 et seq.

Auction Cologne 1935
Cat. *Westdeutscher Museumbesitz. Sammlung Wesendonk-Von Bissing* Cologne (M. Lempertz) 27 November 1935

Auction Dordrecht 1785
Catalogus van een uitmuntend cabinet konstige en plaisante schilderyen [...] nagelaaten door wylen den wel-edelen heer Johan van der Linden van Slingeland Dordrecht (Yver & Delfos) 22 August 1785

Auction Florence 1880
Catalogue des objets d'art et d'ameublement, tableaux ... Florence (San Donato Palace) 15 March 1880 et seq.

Auction The Hague 1737
Catalogus van een groot en uitmuntend cabinet schilderyen [...] nagelaten door den heer en Mr. Samuel van Huls The Hague ('ten Sterfhuize van den Overledenen') 24-25 April 1737

Auction The Hague 1747
Catalogus van een uitmuntend en overheerlyk cabinet zo van konstige, uytvoerige, als plaisante schilderyen [...] nagelaten door wylen den alom beroemden konst-schilder Jaques de Roore The Hague (Hendrik Verheyden) 4 September 1747

Auction The Hague 1763
Catalogus van een groot en uytmuntent cabinet schilderyen [...] nagelaten door wylen den heere agent Willem Lormier The Hague (A. Franken) 4 July 1763 et seq.

Auction The Hague 1765
Cat. *Nagelaten zo door wylen den Heer President, Burgenmeester, Gerard van Oostrum, te Heusden, et al.* The Hague (Kunst-Confrerie-Kamer) 23 September 1765

Auction The Hague 1770
Catalogus van een uitmuntend en fraai cabinet schilderijen [...] verzameld door wylen den heere Joan Hendrik van Heemskerk [...] laatstelyk nagelaaten door wylen mevrouwe de Douairière Van Heemskerk The Hague ('in 't Noordeinde') 29-30 March 1770

Auction The Hague 1783
Catalogus van een fraaye verzameling van konstige schilderyen [...] nagelaten door den wel ed. geb. heer Mr. Cornelis van Heemskerck The Hague ('in 't Voorhout') 18 November 1783

Auction The Hague 1808
Catalogus eener allerkostbaarste verzameling van boeken [...] en een fraaye party schilderyen [...] verzameld door den wel edelen geboren heer Mr. J. van Buren The Hague (Scheurleer) 7-12 November 1808

Auction The Hague 1850
Catalogue des Tableaux anciens et modernes, de diverses écoles; dessins et statues formant la Galerie de feu sa majesté Guillaume II, ... The Hague ('palais de feu sa majesté') 12 August 1850

Auction Leyden 1768
Catalogus van een zeer fraai kabinetje kunstige schilderijen [...] nagelaten door wylen den wel. ed. gestrengen heer, Pieter Caauw ... Leyden (S. & J. Luchtmans) 24 August 1768

Auction Leyden 1781
Catalogus van een uitmuntend kabinet schilderyen [...] nagelaten door wylen den heere Paulus van Spyk Leyden (N. Reyers & B. Coclers) 23 April 1781

Auction London 1773
A Catalogue of a Superb Collection of Pictures, Consigned from Amsterdam by that Celebrated Collector De Heer Fouquet London (Langford's) 10-11 February 1773

Auction London 1777
A Catalogue of the Noble, Superb, and Truly Capital Collection of Italian, French, Flemish, and Remarkable Highly-Finished Dutch Pictures, of John Astley, Esq. London (Christie & J. Ansell) 2-3 May 1777

Auction London 1785
Descriptive Catalogue of the First Part of the Large Collection of Pictures Made by Messers Hadfield and Burrows London (Greenwood) 16 May 1785

Auction London 1795
A Catalogue of the Capital, Valuable and Genuine Collection of Pictures [...] Late the Property of Noel Desenfans Esq. London (Skinner & Dyke) 24-28 February 1795

Auction London 1803
Catalogue of a Most Truly Superb and Valuable Collection of Italian, French, Flemish & Dutch Pictures [...] The Late Property of a Distiguished Connoisseur, Removed from George Street, Hannover Square London (Edwards) 31 March-1 April 1803

Auction London 1806
A Catalogue of a Small but Exquisite Assemblage of Thirty-Two Cabinet Pictures Recently Acquired from Abroad London (Christie) 26 April 1806

Auction London 1807
Catalogue of a Most Capital and Valuable Collection of Pictures [...] the Property of an Eminent Collector ... London (Christie) 20 June 1807

Auction London 1809
A Catalogue of A Select Collection of Italian, French, Flemish, Dutch, and English Pictures [...] the Genuine and Sole Property of Charles Offley, Esq. ... London (Phillips) 12 May 1809

Auction London 1812
A Catalogue of a Select Collection of Twenty-Two Valuable Paintings [...] The Entire Property of a Gentleman London (Phillips) 25 March 1812

Auction London 1814
A Catalogue of the Distinguished Collection of Valuable Original Pictures, of the First Class of the Italian, Flemish, and Dutch Schools, the Property of A. Delahante, Esq. Returning to Paris London (Phillips) 2 June 1814

Auction London 1815
The Catalogue of a Superb Collection of Truly Valuable Dutch and Flemish Cabinet Pictures ... London (Stanley) 7 June 1815

Auction London 1826
A Catalogue of the Very Noble Collection of Italian, French, Flemish, and Dutch Pictures, of the Right Honourable Admiral Lord Radstock, Deceased London (Christie) 12-13 May 1826

Auction London 1828
A Catalogue of the Genuine Collection Original and Splendid Italian, Dutch and Flemish Paintings, the Entire Property of M.M. Zachery, Esq. ... London (Phillips) 31 May 1828

Auction London 1829
A Catalogue of the Valuable and Very Select Collection of Italian, French, Flemish, and Dutch Pictures. The Genuine Property of the Right Hon. the Earl of Liverpool, Deceased London (Christie) 25 May 1829

Auction London 1838
A Catalogue of the Valuable Finished Works, Studies of John Constable, Esq. R.A. Deceased [...] Also, A Few Pictures by Old and Modern Masters London (Foster and Sons) 15 May 1838 et seq.

Auction London 1849
Catalogue of the Beautiful Collection of Pictures of the Very Highest Class, of William Williams Hope, Esq. London (Christie & Manson) 14 June 1849

Auction London 1850
Catalogue of the Entire and Valuable Collection of Italian, Flemish, Dutch and French Pictures, the Property of the Earl of Ashburnham London (Christie & Manson) 20 July 1850

Auction London 1851
Catalogue of the Very Choice Collection of Pictures, of the Highest Class, the Property of William Theobald, Esq., Deceased London (Christie) 10 May 1851

Auction London 1852
Catalogue of Italian, Flemish and Dutch Pictures [...], Including the Choice Portion of the Well-Known Collection of the Late General Sir John Murray London (Christie, Manson & Woods) 19 June 1852

Auction London 1853
Catalogue of the First and Most Important Portion of the Highly Valuable Collection [...] Formed by Samuel Woodburn, Esq., Deceased London (Christie & Manson) 24 June 1853

Auction London 1856
Catalogue of the Very Choice Collection of Dutch Pictures, of a High Class [...] of Robert Field, Esq., Deceased, Removed from Pyrgo Park, Essex London (Christie) 3-6 June 1856

Auction London 1861
Catalogue of the Very Important and Extensive Collection of Pictures, by Ancient and Modern Masters. The Property of that Distinguished Amateur, Charles Scarisbrick, Esq., Deceased, Removed from Scarisbrick Hall and Wrightington Hall, Lancashire London (Christie, Manson & Woods) 10 May 1861 et seq.

Auction London 1866
Catalogue of the Choice Collection of Pictures, by Old Masters, of John Shaw Phillips, Esq. London (Christie, Manson & Woods) 12 May 1866

Auction London 1875
Catalogue of the Choice Collection of Ancient & Modern Pictures [...] The Very Choice and Well-Known Bredel Collection ... London (Christie, Manson & Woods) 1 May 1875

Auction London 1876
Catalogue of the Collection of Pictures by Old Masters of Albert Levy, Esq. London (Christie, Manson & Woods) 6 April 1876

Auction London 1885
The Bohn Collection. Catalogue of the Very Extensive and Valuable Collection of Pictures, Miniatures etc., Formed during the Last Fifty Years by that Well-Known Amateur Henry G. Bohn, Esq. London (Christie, Manson & Woods) 20 March 1885

Auction London 1894
Catalogue of the Renowned Collection of Pictures by Old Masters, Formed by the Late Adrian Hope, Esq. ... London (Christie, Manson & Woods) 30 June 1894

Auction London 1899
Catalogue of the Highly Important Collection of Ancient and Modern Pictures Formed by Jean Louis Miéville, Esq. London (Christie, Manson & Woods) 29 April 1899

Auction London 1902
A Catalogue of the Pictures, Drawings and Engravings of the Late Edward Twopeny, Esq. ... London (Foster's) 5 March 1902

Auction London 1902-A
Catalogue of Ancient & Modern Pictures. The Property of a Gentleman [...] Removed from a Mansion in Essex London (Christie, Manson & Woods) 7 April 1902

Auction London 1903
Catalogue of the Choice Collection of Pictures and Drawings of the Norwich School of George Holmes, Esq. et al. ... London (Christie, Manson & Woods) 25 April 1903

Auction London 1908
Catalogue of Important Ancient and Modern Pictures and Drawings the Property of a Gentleman in Scotland [...] Different Sources London (Christie, Manson & Woods) 3 July 1908

Auction London 1911
Catalogue of Paintings & Drawings [...] Pictures by Old Masters [...] The Property of a Gentleman London (Christie, Manson & Woods) 9 December 1911

Auction London 1913
Catalogue of Choice Pictures by Old Masters Chiefly of the Dutch School. The Property of A.F. Walter et al. ... London (Christie, Manson & Woods) 20 June 1913

Auction London 1915
Catalogue of Important Pictures by Old Masters of the Dutch School, the Property of the Late Lord Huntingfield ... London (Christie, Manson & Woods) 25 June 1915

Auction London 1919
Catalogue of Pictures by Old Masters. The Property of [...] Miss Virginia Purdy Bacon ... London (Christie, Manson & Woods) 12 December 1919

Auction London 1920
Catalogue of Pictures by Old Masters, the Property of H. de Beaumont Randolph [...] and from Other Sources ... London (Christie, Manson & Woods) 5 March 1920

Auction London 1921
Catalogue of Old Pictures, the Property of Mary, Lady Carbery London (Christie, Manson & Woods) 4 March 1921

Auction London 1923
Catalogue of Important Pictures by Old Masters Removed from Ashridge, Berkhamsted and Sold by Order of the Executors of the Late Rt. Hon. Adelbert Wellington, 3rd Earl Brownlow ... London (Christie, Manson & Woods) 4 and 7 May 1923

Auction London 1923-A
Catalogue of Pictures by Old Masters [...] Part of the Collection of Edward R. Bacon, Esq. ... London (Christie, Manson & Woods) 13 July 1923

Auction London 1925
Catalogue of Ancient and Modern Pictures and Drawings. The Property of a Gentleman London (Christie, Manson & Woods) 27 April 1925

Auction London 1925-A
Catalogue of Pictures by Old Masters [...] the Property of E. Bromley Martin, Old Pictures & Drawings from Various Sources London (Christie, Manson & Woods) 4 December 1925

Auction London 1929
Catalogue of Old Pictures, the Property of H.A. Chestermaster [...] Old Pictures and Drawings from Other Sources London (Christie, Manson & Woods) 8 July 1929

Auction London 1929-A
Catalogue of Ancient and Modern Pictures & Drawings, the Property of the Rt. Hon. Lord Revelstoke, P.C., G.C.V.O. et al. London (Christie, Manson & Woods) 26 July 1929

Auction London 1935
Catalogue of Old Pictures [...] from Various Sources London (Christie, Manson & Woods) 26 July 1935

Auction London 1936
Catalogue of Ancient and Modern Pictures and Drawings, Being the Final Portion of the Important Collection Formed by the Late C.H.T. Hawkins, Esq. ... London (Christie, Manson & Woods) 30 October and 2 November 1936

Auction London 1937
Catalogue of Fine Paintings by Old Masters ... London (Christie, Manson & Woods) 23 June 1937

Auction London 1937-A
The Collection of Pictures by Old Masters [...] the Property of Captain E.N.F. Lloyd London (Christie's) 30 April 1937

Auction London 1938
Cat. *Ancient and Modern Pictures and Drawings, the Property of His Grace the Duke of Norfolk, K.G. ...* London (Christie's) 11 February 1938

Auction London 1946
Catalogue of Pictures by Old Masters ... London (Christie, Manson & Woods) 4 October 1946

Auction London 1948
Catalogue of Important Drawings & Paintings by Old Masters ... London (Sotheby & Co.), 25 February 1948

Auction London 1948-A
Catalogue of the Property of Mrs. Greville Phillips [...] Removed from Friar's House, Hereford London (Christie, Manson & Woods) 13 May 1948

Auction London 1949
Catalogue of Old Pictures, the Properties of [...] Lieut.- Col. R.F.A. Sloane-Stanley, Deceased, Late of 'Hardwicke,' Esplanade, Cowes, Isle of Wight ... London (Christie, Manson & Woods) 25 February 1949

Auction London 1950
Catalogue of Pictures by Old Masters [...] the Properties of Lady Frances Vyvyan ... London (Christie, Manson & Woods) 23 June 1950

Auction London 1954
Catalogue of Pictures by Old Masters ... London (Christie, Manson & Woods) 9 April 1954

Auction London 1956
Catalogue of Old Master Drawings and Paintings ... London (Sotheby & Co.) 25 April 1956

Auction London 1960
Catalogue of Highly Important Netherlandish Pictures from the Collection Formed by the Late Dr. C.J.K. van Aalst, K.B.E. of Huis te Hoevelaken, Holland ... London (Christie, Manson & Woods) 1 April 1960

Auction London 1960-A
Catalogue of Pictures by Old Masters London (Christie, Manson & Woods) 18 March 1960

Auction London 1965
Catalogue of Important Old Master Paintings London (Sotheby & Co.) 8 December 1965

Auction London 1966
Catalogue of Important Pictures by Old Masters London (Christie, Manson & Woods) 1 July 1966

Auction London 1968
Catalogue of Important Pictures by Old Masters London (Christie, Manson & Woods) 21 June 1968

Auction London 1970
Catalogue of Important Old Master Paintings ... London (Sotheby & Co.) 25 November 1970

Auction London 1975
Cat. *Addenda to the Catalogue of Important Old Master Paintings* London (Sotheby & Co.) 9 July 1975

Auction London 1975-A
Cat. *Important Pictures by Old Masters (M. Astor - Children of the Late Lewis S. Fry)* London (Christie's) 11 April 1975

Auction London 1980
Catalogue of Important Old Master Paintings (2 vols.) London (Sotheby's) 10 December 1980

Auction London 1985
Cat. *Important Pictures by Old Masters (Lord Congleton et al. – The Property of a Family Trust)* London (Christie's) 19 April 1985

Auction London 1989
Cat. *Old Master Paintings. First Session* London (Sothebey's) 6 December 1989

Auction Monaco 1984
Tableaux anciens Monaco (Sotheby Parke-Bernet Monaco B.A.) 25 June 1984

Auction Monaco 1985
Natures mortes des XVIIe et XVIIIe siècles. Tableaux anciens Monaco (Sotheby's Monaco S.A.M.) 22 June 1985

Auction Munich 1892
Katalog der reichhaltigen Gemälde-Sammlung alter Meister des Realitätenbesitzers Hernn Heinrich Theodor Hoech Munich (Fleischmann's, Lempertz & Schall) 19 September 1892 et seq.

Auction Munich 1892-A
Katalog der reichhaltigen Gemälde-Sammlung alter Meister des Realitätenbesitzers Hernn Heinrich Theodor Hoech Munich (Fleischmann's, Lempertz & Schall) 19 September 1892 et seq. (illustrated edition)

Auction New York 1910
The Charles T. Yerkes Collection of Very Valuable Paintings New York (The American Art Galleries) 5-8 April 1910

Auction New York 1910-A
Catalogue de Luxe of Ancient and Modern Paintings Belonging to the Estate of the Late Charles T. Yerkes New York (American Art Association) 5-8 April 1910

Auction New York 1941
Cat. *European & American Paintings from the XV Century to the Present ...* New York (Parke-Bernet) 8 May 1941

Auction New York 1948
Cat. *Dutch and Flemish Old Masters and Italian Renaissance Paintings from the Collection of Baron and Baroness Raoul Kuffner de Dioszegh* New York (Parke-Bernet) 18 November 1948

Auction New York 1954
Cat. *Important Paintings Collected by the Late Katherine Deere Butterworth* New York (Parke-Bernet) 20 October 1954

Auction New York 1981
Cat. *Important Paintings by Old Masters. The Properties of The Metropolitan Museum of Art ...* New York (Christie's) 9 January 1981

Auction New York 1982
Cat. *Important Old Master Paintings* New York (Sotheby's) 17 June 1982

Auction New York 1983
Cat. *Important Paintings by Old Masters* New York (Christie, Manson & Woods International) 10 June 1983

Auction New York 1988
Cat. *The Linda and Gerald Guterman Collection* New York (Sotheby's) 14 January 1988

Auction New York 1990
Old Master Paintings New York (Christie's) 4 April 1990

Auction Paris 1772
Catalogue des tableaux qui composent le cabinet de monseigneur Le Duc de Choiseul ... Paris (Hôtel Crozat) 6-10 April 1772

Auction Paris 1773
Catalogue d'une très-belle collection de tableaux [...] assemblés par un artiste (Lebrun peintre) Paris (Rémy) 20-23 December 1773

Auction Paris 1777
Catalogue des tableaux & desseins du cabinet de feu de M. Randon de Boisset [...] par Pierre Rémy Paris (P. Rémy et al.) 27 February 1777

Auction Paris 1780
Catalogue raisonné des tableaux, dessins, estampes [...] qui composoient le cabinet de feu M. Poullain, receveur général des domaines du roi ... Paris (Langlier et al.) 15 March 1780 et seq.

Auction Paris 1784
Catalogue raisonné d'une très-belle collection de tableaux [...] qui composent le cabinet de M. le Comte de Vaudreuil [...] par J.B.P. le Brun Paris (J.B.P. Lebrun et al.) 24 November 1784

Auction Paris 1787
Catalogue d'une précieuse collection de tableaux et d'objets rares et curieux [...] provenant du cabinet de M. le Duc de Ch*** Paris (Lebrun) 10 December 1787

Auction Paris 1793
Catalogue des tableaux précieux des écoles d'Italie, de Flandres, de Hollande et de France [...] le tout provenant du cabinet de feu M. Choiseul-Praslin Paris (A.J. Paillet & L.F.J. Boileau) 18 February 1793

Auction Paris 1793-A
Catalogue des objets précieux. Trouvés après le décès du Citoyen Vincent Donjeux ... Paris (Lebrun, Paillet) 29 April 1793 et seq.

Auction Paris 1794
Catalogue d'une collection très-précieuse de tableaux [...] composant le cabinet du Citoyen Destouches Paris (A.J. Lebrun & P.F. Julliot) 21 March 1794

Auction Paris 1802
Catalogue de tableaux formant une réunion imposante [...] ledit catalogue rédigé par A. Paillet et M. Delaroche Paris (Maison des Divisions Supplémentaires) 19 July 1802 et seq.

Auction Paris 1808
Catalogue d'une réunion précieuse de tableaux [...] ledit catalogue rédigé par A. Paillet et A. Delaroche Paris (Paillet & Delaroche) 14-15 December 1808

Auction Paris 1818
Catalogue d'une collection précieuse et du plus beaux choix de tableaux des trois écoles [...] après le décès de Madame Le Rouge Paris (Laneuville) 27 April 1818 et seq.

Auction Paris 1837
Catalogue des tableaux de l'école hollandaise, flamande et française, provenant de l'ancienne galerie du Palais de l'Elysée Paris (C. Paillet) 4-6 April 1837

Auction Paris 1852
Catalogue d'une précieuse collection de tableaux anciens des maîtres allemands, flamands et hollandais [...] par suite du décès de M. le Général Comte De Turenne, ancien Pair de France, etc. Paris (Reynard & Silvestre) 17-19 May 1852

Auction Paris 1861
Cat. *Collection de Mme James Odier. Tableaux anciens* Paris (Hôtel Drouot) 25 March 1861

Auction Paris 1865
Catalogue des tableaux anciens & modernes [...] qui composent les collections de feu M. le Comte de Pourtalès-Gorgier Paris (C. Pillet & E. Escribe) 27 March 1865 et seq.

Auction Paris 1869
Catalogue de 43 tableaux de maîtres anciens provenant de la collection de M. le Comte Koucheleff Besborodko Paris (Hôtel Drouot) 5 June 1869

Auction Paris 1881
Catalogue des tableaux anciens de toutes les écoles composant la très importante collection de M. le b[ar]on de Beurnonville Paris (Ch. Pillet) 9-16 May 1881

Auction Paris 1881-A
Catalogue de tableaux anciens et modernes, livres d'art formant la collection de feu M. François Nieuwenhuys Paris (Hôtel Drouot) 28 April 1881

Auction Paris 1889
Catalogue de douze tableaux importants [...] provenant de la collection d'Oultremont Paris (Chevalier) 27 July 1889

Auction Paris 1898
Catalogue des tableaux, aquarelles, gouaches et dessins anciens et modernes ... Paris (Chevalier) 20-22 June 1898

Auction Paris 1899
Cat. *Succesion du Duc de Talleyrand, Valençay et Sagan. Tableaux anciens, objets d'art et d'ameublement provenant du chateau de Valençay* Paris (Georges Petit) 29 May-1 June 1899

Auction Paris 1899-A
Catalogue des tableaux anciens des différentes écoles [...] dépendant de la succession du duc de Talleyrand, Valençay et Sagan et provenant des chateaux de Valençay et de Sagan Paris (Georges Petit) 2 December 1899

Auction Paris 1905
Catalogue de tableaux anciens et modernes [...] composant la collection de M. Edwards Paris (Hôtel Drouot) 25 May 1905

Auction Paris 1905-A
Catalogue de tableaux anciens et modernes [...] composant la collection de M. Edwards Paris (Hôtel Drouot) 25 May 1905 (illustrated edition)

Auction Paris 1913
Galerie Steengracht. Tome I. Catalogue des tableaux anciens. Ecole Hollandaise du XVIIe siècle, école Flamande du XVIIe siècle dont la vente aux enchères publiques après décès du Jonkheer H.A. Steengracht van Duivenvoorde ... Paris (Galerie Georges Petit) 9 June 1913

Auction Paris 1919
Catalogue des tableaux modernes [...] tableaux anciens [...] composant la collection L. de M. Paris (Georges Petit) 16-19 June 1919 (illustrated edition)

Auction Paris 1919-A
Catalogue des tableaux modernes [...] tableaux anciens [...] composant la collection L. de M. Paris (Georges Petit) 16-19 June 1919

Auction Paris 1924
Catalogue des tableaux anciens [...] composant la galerie de feu M. A. de Ridder, ayant fait l'objet d'une mésure de séquestre Paris (Galerie Georges Petit) 2 June 1924

Auction Philadelphia 1856
Catalogue of the Extensive and Very Valuable Collection of Original Oil Paintings, of the Late Charles Graff, Esq. Philadelphia (Crissy & Markley) 17 October 1856

Auction Rome 1845
Galerie de feu s.e. le Cardinal Fesch [...] ou catalogue raisonné des tableaux de cette galerie [...] deuxième et troisième parties Rome (Ricci Palace) 17-18 March 1845

Auction Rotterdam 1722
Catalogus van uijtmuntende schilderyen bevonden in het alom vermaarde kabinet van den over leeden heer Jacques Meijers Rotterdam ('ten sterfhuize') 9 September 1722 et seq.

Auction Rotterdam 1816
Catalogue d'une belle collection de tableaux, receuillie avec soin depuis plusieurs années par un amateur à Rotterdam Rotterdam (Muys, Van Leen & Lamme) 20-22 April 1816

Auction Rotterdam 1817
Catalogue d'une très belle collection de tableaux ...
Rotterdam (G. van Leen & A. Lamme) 25 April 1817
Auction Rotterdam 1825
Catalogus eener nette en fraaije verzameling, meerendeeels van oude schilderijen, door beroemde meesters, toebehorende aan den heer J. Kamermans Rotterdam (A. Lamme) 3 October 1825
Auction San Francisco 1984
Cat. *Selected European and American Paintings and Sculpture* San Francisco (Butterfield & Butterfield) 8 November 1984
Auction Stockholm 1935
Aktiebolaget H. Bukowskis konsthandel Stockholm. Katalog nr. 300 Stockholm (H. Bukowski) 11-12 April 1935
Auction Vienna 1872
Catalog der vom vielbekannten Kunstfreunde Herrn Isidor Sachs (gestorben zu Paris während der Schreckenszeit 1871) hinterlassen schönen Gemälde-Sammlung Vienna (Posonyi) 17-18 December 1872
Austin 1940
A.E. Austin, Jr., 'The New Purchases at Hartford,' *The Art News* 39 (1940), 16 November, pp. 7-8
Avondpost 1907
'De collectie Six en het melkmeisje door Jan Vermeer,' *De Avondpost* 30 September 1907, 'tweede blad,' n.p.
De Azeredo Perdigão 1979
J. de Azeredo Perdigão, *Calouste Gulbenkian Collector*, Lisbon n.d. (1979)
B. + number
A. [von] Bartsch, *Le peintre-graveur* (21 vols.), Vienna 1854-1876 (1st edition 1803-1821) (also the numeration from *Bartsch*)
Baard 1981
H.P. Baard, *Frans Hals*, New York 1981
Baas 1985
J. Baas, *Treasures of the Hood Museum of Art, Dartmouth College*, Hanover, N.H. 1985
Bachmann 1966
F. Bachmann, *Die Landschaften des Aert van der Neer*, Neustadt an der Aisch 1966
Bachmann 1972
F. Bachmann, *Aert van der Neer als Zeichner*, Neustadt an der Aisch 1972
Bachmann 1982
F. Bachmann, *Aert van der Neer 1603 / 4-1677*, Bremen 1982
Backlin-Landeman 1967
H. Backlin-Landeman, 'The Art Museum, Princeton University,' *Antiques* 92 (1967), November, pp. 670-678
De Bacourt 1851
A. de Bacourt (ed.), *Correspondance entre le Comte de Mirabeau et le Comte de la Marck, Prince d'Arenberg, pend[ant] les années 1789, 1790 et 1791* (2 vols.), London / Brussels 1851
Bader 1968
A. Bader, cat. *Dutch Art of the 1600s* Oshkosh, Wis. (Paine Art Center) 1968

Bader 1972
A. Bader, 'An Unknown Self-Portrait of Michael Sweerts,' *The Burlington Magazine* 114 (1972), p. 475
Bader 1976
A. Bader, cat. *The Bible through Dutch Eyes. From Genesis through the Apocrypha* Milwaukee, Wis. (Milwaukee Art Centre) 1976
Bader / Stechow 1974
A. Bader & W. Stechow, *Selections from the Bader Collection*, Milwaukee, Wis. 1974
Badt 1961
K. Badt, *Modell und Maler von Jan Vermeer*, Cologne 1961
Baetjer 1980
K. Baetjer, *European Paintings in The Metropolitan Museum of Art by Artists Born in or before 1865* (3 vols.), New York 1980
Baird 1960
T.P. Baird, *Dutch Painting in the National Gallery of Art*, Washington, D.C. 1960
Bakker et al. 1984
N. Bakker, I. Bergström, G. Jansen, S.H. Levie & S. Segal, cat. *Masters of Middelburg* Amsterdam (K. & V. Waterman) 1984
Balfour 1955
S. Balfour, 'Preferably in Pittsburgh. The A.W. Mellon Centennial: 1855-1955,' *Carnegie Magazine* 29 (1955), pp. 86-89
Ballhausen 1923
P.C. Ballhausen, *Der erste englisch-holländische Seekrieg 1652-1654, sowie der schwedisch-holländische Seekrieg 1658-1659*, The Hague 1923
Baltimore 1984
Cat. *The Taste of Maryland. Art Collecting in Maryland, 1800-1934* Baltimore, Md. (Walters Art Gallery) 1984
Bandmann 1960
G. Bandmann, *Melancholie und Musik. Ikonographische Studien*, Cologne / Opladen 1960
Bangel 1914
R. Bangel, 'Eeckhout, Gerbrand van den' in: *Thieme / Becker*, vol. x (1914), pp. 355-357
Banks 1937
M.A. Banks, 'Mr. Rowe, the Director of the Museum,' *Bulletin of the Rhode Island School of Design* 25 (1937), pp. 23-37
Barnes 1988
D. Barnes, cat. *People at Work: Seventeenth-Century Dutch Art* Hempstead, N.Y. (Hofstra Museum) 1988
Barnouw-de Ranitz 1978
L. Barnouw-de Ranitz, 'Abraham Bredius, een biografie' in: *Blankert 1978*, pp. 9-19
Barth 1981
R. Barth, cat. *Rembrandt & seine Zeitgenossen. Handzeichnungen niederländischer und flämischer Meister des 17. Jahrhunderts aus dem Besitz der Kunstsammlungen zu Weimar* Weimar (Kunsthalle) 1981
Bartsch
A. Bartsch, *Catalogue raisonné de toutes les estampes qui forment l'oeuvre de Rembrandt et ceux de ses principaux imitateurs*, Vienna 1797

Basan 1781
[P.F.] Basan (ed.), *Collection de cent-vingt estampes gravées d'après les tableaux & dessins qui composoient le cabinet de M. Poullain, receveur général des domaines du roi, decédé en 1780*, Paris 1781
De Bastide 1766
[J.A] de Bastide, *Le temple des arts ou le cabinet de M. Braamcamp*, Amsterdam 1766
Bathoe 1758
A Catalogue of the Collection of Pictures, &c., Belonging to King James the Second [...] Printed for W. Bathoe, London 1758
Bauch 1929-1930
K. Bauch, 'Ausstellung holländischer Kunst von 1450-1900 in London,' *Zeitschrift für bildende Kunst* 63 (1929-1930), pp. 9-23
Bauch 1959
K. Bauch, 'A Portrait of Rembrandt's Last Period,' *The Burlington Magazine* 101 (1959), pp. 105-106
Bauch 1966
K. Bauch, *Rembrandt. Gemälde*, Berlin 1966
Baudouin 1969
F. Baudouin, 'De "Constkamer" van Cornelis van der Geest, geschilderd door Willem van Haecht,' *Antwerpen. Tijdschrift der stad Antwerpen* 15 (1969), pp. 158-173
Bauman / Liedtke et al. 1990
G. Bauman, W. Liedtke et al., *Flemish Paintings in America*, Antwerp 1990
Bax 1949
D. Bax, *Ontcijfering van Jeroen Bosch*, The Hague 1949
Bax 1979
D. Bax, *Hieronymus Bosch. His Picture-Writing Deciphered*, Rotterdam 1979
Beck 1972-1973
H.U. Beck, *Jan van Goyen. 1596-1656. Ein Oeuvreverzeichnis* (2 vols.), Amsterdam 1972-1973
Beck 1987
H.U. Beck, *Jan van Goyen. 1596-1656. Ein Oeuvreverzeichnis. III (Ergänzungen)*, Doornspijk 1987
Becker 1985
D.P. Becker, cat. *Old Master Drawings at Bowdoin College* Brunswick, Maine (Bowdoin College Museum of Art) 1985
Bedaux 1975
J.B. Bedaux, 'Minnekoorts-, zwangerschaps- en doodsverschijnselen op zeventiende-eeuwse schilderijen,' *Antiek* 10 (1975-1976), pp. 17-42
Bedaux 1989
J.B. Bedaux, 'Fruit and Fertility; Fruit Symbolism in Netherlandish Portraiture of the Sixteenth and Seventeenth Century,' *Simiolus* 19 (1989), pp. 150-168
Bedö 1962
R. Bedö, 'Ein Doppelporträt des Michael Sweerts,' *Acta Historiae Artium* 8 (1962), pp. 107-110
Behrman 1952
S.N. Behrman, *Duveen*, New York 1952
Behrman 1960
S.N. Behrman, *Duveen und die Millionäre. Zur Soziologie des Kunsthandels in Amerika*, Munich 1960

Bell 1899
M. Bell, *Rembrandt van Rijn and His Work*, London 1899

Bender 1987
T. Bender, *New York Intellect*, Baltimore, Md. 1987

Benesch 1928
O. Benesch, *Die Zeichnungen der niederländischen Schulen des XV. und XVI. Jahrhunderts* (Beschreibender Katalog der Handzeichnungen in der Graphischen Sammlung Albertina – II), Vienna 1928

Benesch 1935
O. Benesch, *Rembrandt. Werk und Forschung*, Vienna 1935 (reprint Lucerne 1970)

Benesch 1935-A
O. Benesch, 'Rijn, Rembrandt Harmensz. van' in: *Thieme / Becker*, vol. XXIX (1935), pp. 259-271

Benesch 1973
O. Benesch, *The Drawings of Rembrandt* (6 vols.), London 1973 (1st edition 1954-1957)

Bénézit 1948-1955
E. Bénézit, *Dictionnaire critique et documentaire des peintres, sculpteurs, dessinateurs et graveurs* (8 vols.), n.p. 1948-1955

Benkard 1912
E.A. Benkard, 'Die Sammlung De Ridder. Bemerkungen zur Kunst der Holländer des 17. Jahrhunderts,' *Kunst und Künstler* 10 (1912), pp. 602-609

Berendsen 1952
A. Berendsen, cat. *Prisma der bijbelse kunst* Delft (Stedelijk Museum Het Prinsenhof) 1952

Berenson / Valentiner 1941
B. Berenson & W.R. Valentiner, *Duveen Pictures in Public Collections of America. A Catalogue Raisonné with Three Hundred Illustrations of Paintings by the Great Masters, which Have Passed through the House of Duveen*, New York 1941

Beresford Chancellor 1908
E. Beresford Chancellor, *The Private Palaces of London: Past and Present*, London 1908

Bergen op Zoom etc. 1982
Cat. *Colf. Kolf. Golf. Van middeleeuws volksspel tot moderne sport* Bergen op Zoom (Gemeentemuseum het Markiezenhof) Gent (Saint Pietersabdij) Antwerp (Volkskundemuseum) Amersfoort (Museum Flehite) 1982

Bergström 1947 / 1956
I. Bergström, *Dutch Still-Life Painting in the Seventeenth Century*, London 1956 (1st edition 1947)

Bergström 1983
I. Bergström, ' "Portraits" of Gilt Cups by Pieter Claesz,' *Tableau* 5 (1983), no. 6, pp. 440-445

Bergström / Wheelock 1989
I. Bergström & A.K. Wheelock, cat. *Still Lifes of the Golden Age. Northern European Paintings from the Heinz Family Collection* Washington, D.C. (National Gallery of Art) Boston, Mass. (Museum of Fine Arts) 1989

Berlin 1888
Gemälde-Sammlung von Otto Wesendonck in Berlin (2 vols.), Berlin 1888

Berlin 1925
Cat. *Gemälde alter Meister aus Berliner Besitz* Berlin (Akademie der Künste) 1925

Berlin 1975
Cat. *Katalog der ausgestellten Gemälde des 13.-18. Jahrhunderts* Berlin (Gemäldegalerie Staatliche Museen Preussischer Kulturbesitz) 1975

Berlin / London / Philadelphia 1984
Cat. *Von Frans Hals bis Vermeer. Meisterwerke holländischer Genremalerei* Berlin (Gemäldegalerie Staatliche Museen Preussischer Kulturbesitz) London (Royal Academy of Arts) Philadelphia, Pa. (Philadelphia Museum of Art) 1984

Bernt 1948-1962
W. Bernt, *Die niederländischen Maler des 17. Jahrhunderts* (4 vols.), Munich 1948-1962

Bernt 1957-1958
W. Bernt, *Die niederländischen Zeichner des 17. Jahrhunderts* (2 vols.), Munich 1957-1958

Bernt 1970
W. Bernt, *The Netherlandish Painters of the Seventeenth Century* (3 vols.), London 1970

Bernt 1979-1980
W. Bernt, *Die niederländischen Maler und Zeichner des 17. Jahrhunderts* (5 vols.), Munich 1979-1980

Bierens de Haan 1957
J.A. Bierens de Haan, 'Het huis van een 18e eeuwsen mercator sapiens,' *Amstelodamum. Jaarboek* 49 (1957), pp. 110-128

Bille 1961
C. Bille, *De tempel der kunst of het kabinet van den heer Braamcamp* (2 vols.), Amsterdam 1961

Birmingham 1952
Catalogue of Paintings, Drawings and Miniatures in the Barber Institute of Fine Arts, University of Birmingham, Cambridge 1952

Birmingham etc. 1957-1958
Cat. *An Exhibition of Dutch, Flemish and German Paintings from the Collection of Walter P. Chrysler, Jr.* Birmingham, Ala. (The Birmingham Museum of Art) etc. 1957-1958

Blake-More Godwin 1939
Mrs. Blake-More Godwin, *The Toledo Museum of Art. Founded by Edward Drummond Libbey. Catalogue of European Paintings*, Toledo, Ohio 1939

Blake-More Godwin 1955
Mrs. Blake-More Godwin, 'Toledo Museum of Art, Post-War Additions,' *The Connoisseur* 136 (1955), no. 547, pp. 133-140

Blanc 1857
C. Blanc, *Les trésors de l'art à Manchester*, Paris 1857

Blanc 1857-1858
C. Blanc, *Le trésor de la curiosité tiré des catalogues de vente ...* (5 vols.), Paris 1857-1858

Blanc 1859-1864
C. Blanc, *L'oeuvre complet de Rembrandt* (3 vols.), Paris 1859-1864

Blanc 1860-1863
C. Blanc, *Histoire des peintres de toutes les écoles. Ecole hollandaise* (2 vols.), Paris 1860-1863

Blankert 1965
A. Blankert, cat. *Nederlandse 17e eeuwse Italianiserende landschapschilders* Utrecht (Centraal Museum) 1965

Blankert 1966
A. Blankert, 'Invul-portretten door Caspar en Constantyn Netscher,' *Oud Holland* 81 (1966), pp. 263-269

Blankert 1968
A. Blankert, 'Over Pieter van Laer als dier- en landschapschilder,' *Oud Holland* 83 (1968), pp. 117-134

Blankert 1975
A. Blankert (with contributions by R. Ruurs & W. van de Watering), *Johannes Vermeer van Delft. 1632-1675*, Utrecht / Antwerp 1975

Blankert 1975-1979
A. Blankert, *Amsterdams Historisch Museum. Schilderijen daterend van voor 1800. Voorlopige catalogus*, Amsterdam 1975-1979

Blankert 1976
A. Blankert, *Ferdinand Bol. 1616-1680. Een leerling van Rembrandt* (diss. Utrecht), The Hague 1976

Blankert 1978
A. Blankert, *Museum Bredius. Catalogus van de schilderijen en tekeningen*, The Hague 1978

Blankert 1978-A
A. Blankert, *Vermeer of Delft. Complete Edition of the Paintings*, Oxford 1978

Blankert 1982
A. Blankert, *Ferdinand Bol (1616-1680). Rembrandt's Pupil*, Doornspijk 1982

Blankert et al. 1982
A. Blankert, D. Hensbroek-van der Poel, G. Keyes, R. Krudop & W. van de Watering, *Hendrick Averkamp (1585-1634), Barent Avercamp (1612-1679): Frozen Silence*, Amsterdam 1982

Blankert et al. 1983
A. Blankert, B. Broos, G. Jansen, W. van de Watering & E. van de Wetering, cat. *The Impact of a Genius. Rembrandt, His Pupils and Followers in the Seventeenth Century* Amsterdam (K. & V. Waterman) Groningen (Groninger Museum) 1983

Blankert et al. 1988
A. Blankert, J.M. Montias & G. Aillaud, *Vermeer*, New York 1988

Blankert / Montias et al. 1987
A. Blankert, J.M. Montias, G. Aillaud, R. Ruurs, W.L. van de Watering & P. Resche-Rigon, *Vermeer*, Amsterdam 1987

Blankert / Slatkes 1986-1987
A. Blankert & L. Slatkes, cat. *Nieuw licht op de gouden eeuw. Hendrick ter Brugghen en tijdgenoten* Utrecht (Centraal Museum) Brunswick (Herzog Anton Ulrich-Museum) 1986-1987

Blankert / Slatkes 1986-1987-A
A. Blankert & L. Slatkes, cat. *Holländische Malerei in neuem Licht. Hendrick ter Brugghen und seine Zeitgenossen* Utrecht (Centraal Museum) Brunswick (Herzog Anton Ulrich-Museum) 1986-1987

Blarek 1887

K. Blarek, *Der abgestorbene Adel der Provinz Schlesien und der O. Launitz* (Siebmachers Wappenbuch VI-VIII), Nuremberg 1887

Van Bleysweijck 1667

D. van Bleysweijck, *Beschrijvinge der stadt Delft* (2 vols.), Delft 1667

Bloch 1948

V. Bloch, 'Een verrassend museum,' *Maandblad voor Beeldende Kunst* 24 (1948), pp. 61-66

Bloch 1950

V. Bloch, 'Nederland en Italië,' *Maandblad voor Beeldende Kunst* 26 (1950), pp. 215-219

Bloch 1954 / 1963

V. Bloch, *All the Paintings of Jan Vermeer*, London 1963 (Italian edition)

Bloch 1958

V. Bloch, 'On Michael Sweerts,' *The Burlington Magazine* 100 (1958), pp. 440-441

Bloch 1965

V. Bloch, 'Michael Sweerts und Italien,' *Jahrbuch der Staatliche Sammlungen Baden-Württemberg* 2 (1965), pp. 155-174

Bloch 1968

V. Bloch, *Michael Sweerts* (Suivi de *Sweerts et les Missions Etrangères* par Jean Guennou), The Hague 1968

Bloch 1973

V. Bloch, 'Postskriptum zu Sweerts' in: *Bruyn et al. 1973*, pp. 40-41

Block 1940

M. Block, *Current Biography. Who's News and Why. 1940*, New York 1940

Bloomington 1966

Cat. 25 *Still Life Paintings* Bloomington, Ind. (University Art Museum) 1966

Bloomington 1980

Guide to the Collections: Highlights from the Indiana University Art Museum, Bloomington, Ind. 1988

Blum 1945

A. Blum, *Vermeer et Thoré-Bürger*, Geneva 1945

BNB

Biographie Nationale publiée par l'Académie Royale des sciences, des lettres et des beaux-arts de Belgique (44 vols.), Brussels 1866-1985 / 1986

Boase 1965

F. Boase, *Modern English Biography* (6 vols.), London 1965

Bock / Rosenberg 1930

E. Bock & J. Rosenberg, *Staatliche Museen zu Berlin. Die niederländischen Meister* (2 vols.), Berlin 1930

Bodart 1970

D. Bodart, *Les peintres des Pays-Bas méridionaux et de la principauté de Liège à Rome au XVIIe siècle* (2 vols.), Brussels / Rome 1970

Bode 1871

W. Bode, *Frans Hals und seine Schule*, Leipzig 1871

Bode 1881

W. Bode, 'Berichte und Mittheilungen aus Sammlungen und Museen, über staatliche Kunstpflege und Restaurationen, neue Funde. Die Pflege der alten Kunst in Holland,' *Repertorium für Kunstwissenschaft* 4 (1881), pp. 293-301

Bode 1881-A

W. Bode, 'De behartiging der oude kunst in Holland,' *Nederlandsche Kunstbode* 3 (1881), pp. 297-301

Bode 1883

W. Bode, *Studien zur Geschichte der holländischen Malerei*, Brunswick 1883

Bode 1895

W. Bode, 'Alte Kunstwerke in den Sammlungen der Vereinigten Staaten,' *Zeitschrift für bildende Kunst* 6 (1895), new series, pp. 13-19

Bode 1900

W. Bode, cat. *Die Gemälde-Galerie des Herrn Rudolf Kann in Paris*, Vienna 1900

Bode 1902

W. Bode, 'Die amerikanische Konkurrenz im Kunsthandel und ihre Gefahr für Europa,' *Kunst und Künstler* 1 (1902), pp. 5-12

Bode 1904

W. Bode, 'Die amerikanischen Gemäldesammlungen in ihrer neueren Entwicklung,' *Kunst und Künstler* 2 (1903-1904), pp. 387-389

Bode 1905

W. Bode, 'Rudolf Kann und seine Sammlungen,' *Kunstchronik* 16 (1905), new series, pp. 291-294

Bode 1906

W. Bode, *Rembrandt und seine Zeitgenossen. Charakter-Bilder der grossen Meister der holländischen und vlämischen Malerschule im siebzehnten Jahrhundert*, Leipzig 1906

Bode 1906-A

W. Bode, 'Die amerikanische Gefahr im Kunsthandel,' *Kunst und Künstler* 5 (1906-1907), pp. 3-6

Bode 1907-1908

W. Bode, 'Der Verkauf der Sammlung Rudolf Kann in Paris nach Amerika,' *Die Kunst für Alle* 23 (1907-1908), pp. 16-22

Bode 1909

W. Bode, 'Paris und London unter dem Gestirn der amerikanischen Kaufwut,' *Der Cicerone* 1 (1909), pp. 441-443 and 525

Bode 1910

W. Bode, *Die Gemäldegalerie des Herrn A. de Ridder in seiner Villa zu Schönberg bei Cronberg im Taunus*, Berlin 1910

Bode 1910-A

W. Bode, 'Die Berliner Museen und die amerikanische Konkurrenz,' *Der Cicerone* 2 (1910), pp. 81-84

Bode 1911

W. Bode, 'Jan Vermeer und Pieter de Hooch als Konkurrenten,' *Jahrbuch der königlich preussischen Kunstsammlungen* 32 (1911), pp. 1-2

Bode 1913

W. Bode, *Die Gemäldegalerie des weiland Herrn A. de Ridder in seiner Villa zu Schönberg bei Cronberg im Taunus*, Berlin 1913

Bode 1930

W. Bode, *Mein Leben* (2 vols.), Berlin 1930

Bode / Binder 1914

W. von Bode & M.J. Binder, *Frans Hals. Sein Leben und seine Werke* (2 vols.), Berlin 1914

Bode / Hofstede de Groot 1897-1905

W. Bode & C. Hofstede de Groot, *Rembrandt. Beschreibendes Verzeichnis seiner Gemälde* (8 vols.), Paris 1897-1905

Bodkin / Goldscheider 1940

T. Bodkin & L. Goldscheider, *The Paintings of Jan Vermeer*, Oxford / New York 1940

De Boer 1913

J. de Boer, 'Stichting Rembrandthuis. Tentoonstelling van teekeningen van Rembrandt uit de verzameling J.P. Heseltine, die in Nederland zijn gebleven,' *Onze Kunst* 24 (1913), pp. 95-96

De Boer 1948

M.G. de Boer, 'Vergeten leden van een bekend geslacht,' *Amstelodamum. Jaarboek* 42 (1948), pp. 10-34

De Boer / Leistra 1990

M.M. de Boer & J. Leistra, *Bredius en het Mauritshuis*, The Hague 1990 (in preparation)

Börsch-Supan 1964

H. Börsch-Supan, *Die Gemälde in Jagdschloss Grunewald*, Berlin 1964

Du Bois 1916-1917

G. Pène du Bois, 'Famous American Collections. The Collection of Mr. Michael Friedsam,' *Arts and Decoration* 7 (1916-1917), pp. 397-402

Bol 1955

L.J. Bol, 'Een Middelburgse Brueghel-groep. III. In Bosschaerts spoor. 1. Balthasar van der Ast,' *Oud Holland* 70 (1955), pp. 138-154

Bol 1960

L.J. Bol, *The Bosschaert Dynasty. Painters of Flowers and Fruit*, Leigh-on-Sea 1960

Bol 1966

L.J. Bol, 'Twee Braziliaanse schildpadden. Albert Eckhout (ca. 1610-1666),' *Openbaar Kunstbezit* 10 (1966), pp. 57a-b

Bol 1969

L.J. Bol, *Holländische Maler des 17.Jahrhunderts nahe den grossen Meister. Landschaften und Stilleben*, Brunswick 1969

Bol 1973

L.J. Bol, *Die holländische Marinemalerei des 17. Jahrhunderts*, Brunswick 1973

Bol 1981

L.J. Bol, 'Goede onbekenden. VII. Schilders van het vroege Nederlandse bloemstuk met kleingedierte als bijwerk,' *Tableau* 3 (1981), no. 4, pp. 578-586

Bolten 1979

J. Bolten, *Het Noord- en Zuidnederlandse tekenboek. 1600-1750* (diss. Amsterdam), Ter Aar 1979

Bolten / Bolten-Rempt 1978
J. Bolten & H. Bolten-Rempt, *The Hidden Rembrandt*, Oxford 1978

Van den Boogaart 1982
E. van den Boogaart, 'Europeanen en niet-Europeanen in zestiende eeuws Nederlands perspectief,' *De Gids* 145 (1982), pp. 2-25

Borenius 1928
T. Borenius, 'A Loan Exhibition in New York,' *Apollo* 7 (1928), pp. 212-215

Borenius 1929
T. Borenius, 'Die holländische Ausstellung in London,' *Pantheon* 3 (1929), pp. 57-64

Boston 1892
Cat. *Exhibition Illustrating the Technical Means of the Reproductive Arts from the XV. Century to the Present Time with Special Reference to the Photo-Mechanical Processes* Boston, Mass. (Museum of Fine Arts) 1892

Boston 1903
Cat. *Old Masters* Boston, Mass. (Copley Society) 1903

Boston 1939
Cat. *Art in New England. Paintings, Drawings, Prints from Private Collections in New England* Boston, Mass. (Museum of Fine Arts) 1939

Boston 1945
Cat. *A Thousand Years of Landscape East and West (Paintings, Drawings, Prints)* Boston, Mass. (Museum of Fine Arts) 1945

Boston 1972
Cat. *The Rathbone Years: Masterpieces Acquired for the Museum of Fine Arts, Boston 1955-1972 and for the Saint Louis Art Museum 1940-1955* Boston, Mass. (Museum of Fine Arts) 1972

Boström 1951
K. Boström, 'Jan Vermeer van Delft en Cornelis van der Meulen,' *Oud Holland* 66 (1951), pp. 117-122

Boswell 1921
P. Boswell, 'Notes from the New York Galleries,' *Art and Archeology* 12 (1921), pp. 277-278

Van Boven / Segal 1980
M. van Boven & S. Segal, *Gerard & Cornelis van Spaendonck. Twee Brabantse bloemenschilders in Parijs*, Maarssen 1980

Bowen 1958
W.W. Bowen, *A Pioneer Museum in the Wilderness, the Dartmouth College Museum*, Hanover, N.H. 1958

Bowron 1983
E.P. Bowron, *The North Carolina Museum of Art. Introduction to the Collections*, Raleigh, N.C. 1983

Brandt 1687
G. Brandt, *Het leven en bedryf van den heere Michiel de Ruiter*, Amsterdam 1687

Brandus 1928
E. Brandus, 'La collection des tableaux anciens de M. Jules S. Bache, à New-York,' *La renaissance* (1928), May, pp. 181-198

Brant 1494
S. Brant, *Das Narrenschiff*, Basel 1494

Brant 1570
S. Brant, *Das Narrenschiff*, London 1570

Braun 1966
H. Braun, *Gerard und Willem van Honthorst*, Göttingen 1966

Braun 1979-1980
K. Braun, *Alle tot nu toe bekende schilderijen van Rubens* (2 vols.), Rotterdam 1979-1980

Braun 1980
K. Braun, *Alle tot nu toe bekende schilderijen van Jan Steen*, Rotterdam 1980

Braun / Lecaldano 1976
K. Braun & P. Lecaldano, *Alle tot nu toe bekende schilderijen van Rembrandt*, Rotterdam / Milan 1976

Brayer 1979
B. Brayer, 'George Eastman, Collector' in: *The George Eastman Collection, Memorial Art Gallery of the University of Rochester*, Rochester, N.Y. 1979, pp. 2-6

Breck 1910
J. Breck, 'Hollandsche kunst op de Hudson-Fulton tentoonstelling te New-York,' *Onze Kunst* 9 (1910), vol. XVII, pp. 5-12 and 41-47

Breck 1910-A
J. Breck, 'L'art hollandais à l'exposition Hudson-Fulton à New-York,' *L'art flamand et hollandais* 13 (1910), pp. 48-61

Breckenridge 1955
J.D. Breckenridge, cat. *A Handbook of Dutch and Flemish Paintings in the William Andrews Clark Collection* Washington, D.C. (The Corcoran Gallery of Art) 1955

Bredius 1881
A. Bredius, 'De wintertentoonstelling van oude schilderijen in de zalen der Royal Academy te Londen, 1881,' *Nederlandsche Kunstbode* 3 (1881), pp. 67-69, 76-78 and 100-102

Bredius 1882
A. Bredius, 'De tentoonstelling te Brussel,' *De Nederlandsche Spectator* (1882), pp. 182-184

Bredius 1885
A. Bredius, 'Iets over Johannes Vermeer ("De Delftsche Vermeer"),' *Oud Holland* 3 (1885), pp. 217-222

Bredius 1892
A. Bredius, 'De schilder Johannes van de Cappelle,' *Oud Holland* 10 (1892), pp. 26-40

Bredius 1893
A. Bredius, 'De portretten van Joris de Caullery,' *Oud Holland* 11 (1893), pp. 127-128

Bredius 1897
A. Bredius, 'Onbekende Rembrandts in Polen, Galicie en Rusland,' *De Nederlandsche Spectator* (1897), pp. 197-199

Bredius 1901
A. Bredius, 'Kunstveilingen te London,' *De Nederlandsche Spectator* (1901), pp. 143-144

Bredius 1902
A. Bredius, 'De verzameling Rudolph Kann te Parijs,' *Woord en Beeld* 7 (1902), pp. 26-35

Bredius 1902-A
A. Bredius, 'De "Old Masters" in The Royal Academy te Londen,' *De Nederlandsche Spectator* (1902), nos. 11-14, p. 9

Bredius 9-18-1907
A. Bredius, 'De "beschouwingen" van Frits Lugt over den aankoop van een deel der Six-Collectie,' *Het Vaderland* 18 September 1907, 'Eerste avondblad,' n.p.

Bredius 9-23-1907
A. Bredius, 'De Collectie-Six,' *Het Vaderland* 23 September 1907, 'Eerste avondblad,' n.p.

Bredius 10-1-1907
A. Bredius, 'Schilderijen-aankoop voor het Rijk,' *Het Vaderland* 1 October 1907, 'Eerste avondblad,' n.p.

Bredius 10-2-1907
A. Bredius, 'De Heer Mensing over Pierpont Morgan, en nog iets over de Collectie-Six,' *Het Vaderland* 2 October 1907, 'Eerste avondblad,' n.p.

Bredius 1912
A. Bredius, 'De nalatenschap van Jan van der Heyden's weduwe,' *Oud Holland* 30 (1912), pp. 129-151

Bredius 11-12-1913
A. Bredius, 'Holland in Amerika,' *Nieuwe Rotterdamsche Courant* 12 November 1913, 'Avondblad,' p. B1

Bredius 12-8-1913
A. Bredius, '[untitled],' *Nieuwe Rotterdamsche Courant* 8 December 1913, 'Avondblad,' p. B1

Bredius 12-9-1913
A. Bredius, 'Te New York,' *Nieuwe Rotterdamsche Courant* 9 December 1913, 'Avondblad,' p. A1

Bredius 12-19-1913
A. Bredius, 'Dr. Bredius in Amerika,' *Nieuwe Rotterdamsche Courant* 19 December 1913, 'Avondblad,' p. B1

Bredius 12-20-1913
A. Bredius, 'Dr. Bredius in Amerika,' *Nieuwe Rotterdamsche Courant* 20 December 1913, 'Avondblad,' p. B1

Bredius 1914
A. Bredius, 'Bijdragen tot de levensgeschiedenis van Hendrick Goltzius,' *Oud Holland* 32 (1914), pp. 137-146

Bredius 1-5-1914
A. Bredius, 'Dr. Bredius in Amerika,' *Nieuwe Rotterdamsche Courant* 5 January 1914, 'Avondblad,' p. B1

Bredius 1-21-1914
A. Bredius, 'Dr. Bredius in Amerika,' *Nieuwe Rotterdamsche Courant* 21 January 1914, 'Avondblad,' p. B1

Bredius 2-18-1914
A. Bredius, 'Dr. Bredius in Amerika,' *Nieuwe Rotterdamsche Courant* 18 February 1914, 'Avondblad,' p. B1

Bredius 2-19-1914
A. Bredius, 'Dr. Bredius in Amerika,' *Nieuwe Rotterdamsche Courant* 19 February 1914, 'Avondblad,' p. B1
Bredius 2-20-1914
A. Bredius, 'Dr. Bredius in Amerika,' *Nieuwe Rotterdamsche Courant* 20 February 1914, 'Avondblad,' p. B1
Bredius 1923
A. Bredius, 'Self-Portraits by Ferdinand Bol,' *The Burlington Magazine* 42 (1923), pp. 72-82
Bredius 1927
A. Bredius, *Jan Steen*, Amsterdam 1927
Bredius 1935
A. Bredius, *Rembrandt. Schilderijen. 630 afbeeldingen*, Utrecht / Vienna 1935
Bredius / Veth 1887
A. Bredius & G.H. Veth, 'Poulus Lesire,' *Oud Holland* 5 (1887), pp. 45-51
Breesnee 1948-1949
G.H.C. Breesnee, 'De Haagse kunstverzamelaars Adriaan Leonard van Heteren en Willem Lormier en hun voorgeslacht,' *Die Haghe Jaarboek* (1948-1949), pp. 118-138
Brejon de Lavergnée et al. 1979
A. Brejon de Lavergnée, J. Foucart & N. Reynaud, *Catalogue sommaire illustré des peintures du Musée du Louvre. 1. Ecoles flamande et hollandaise*, Paris 1979
Bremmer 1937
H.P. Bremmer, 'Vermeer,' *Beeldende Kunst* 23 (1937), March, no. 87
Brenninkmeyer-De Rooij / Broos et al. 1988
B. Brenninkmeyer-De Rooij, B. Broos, E. de Heer & B. Slot, cat. *Paintings from England. William III and the Royal Collections* The Hague (Mauritshuis) 1988
Brière-Misme 1927
C. Brière-Misme, 'Tableaux inédits ou peu connus de Pieter de Hooch,' *Gazette des Beaux-Arts* 69 (1927), 5th series, vol. XV, pp. 361-380; vol. XVI, pp. 51-79 and 258-286
Briganti et al. 1983
G. Briganti, L. Trezzani & L. Laureati, *The Bamboccianti. The Painters of Everyday Life in Seventeenth Century Rome*, Rome 1983
Brigstocke 1982
H. Brigstocke, *William Buchanan and the 19th Century Art Trade: 100 Letters to His Agents in London and Italy*, n.p. (London) 1982
Brion / Heimann 1956
M. Brion & H. Heimann, *The Bible in Art. Miniatures, Paintings, Drawings and Sculptures Inspired by the Old Testament*, London 1956
Brochhagen 1958
E. Brochhagen, *Karel Dujardin. Ein Beitrag zum Italianismus in Holland im 17. Jahrhundert* (diss.), Cologne 1958
Brockwell 1910
M.W. Brockwell, 'Bray, Jan de' in: *Thieme / Becker*, vol. IV (1910), p. 555

Brockwell 1918
M. Brockwell, 'The Johnson Collection in Philadelphia,' *The Connoisseur* 50 (1918), pp. 143-145
Brockwell 1920
M.W. Brockwell, *A Catalogue of Paintings in the Collection of Mr. and Mrs. Charles P. Taft at Cincinnati, Ohio*, New York 1920
Brom 1957
G. Brom, *Schilderkunst en literatuur in de 16e en 17e eeuw*, Utrecht / Antwerp 1957
Brooks 1985
V.F. Brooks, 'Danaë Discovered in Wrong Part of Town,' *Artnews* (1985), February, p. 19
Broos 1971
B.P.J. Broos, 'De caers uut, de schaemschoe uut. Een vergeten erotisch symbool,' *Vrij Nederland* 31 (1971), 24 April, p. 25
Broos 1972
B.P.J. Broos 'Rembrandt. verandert. En over-geschildert,' *De kroniek van het Rembrandthuis* 26 (1972), pp. 137-152
Broos 1974
B.P.J. Broos, 'Rembrandt's Portrait of a Pole and His Horse,' *Simiolus* 7 (1974), pp. 193-218
Broos 1975-1976
B.P.J. Broos, 'Rembrandt and Lastman's *Coriolanus*: the History Piece in 17th-Century Theory and Practice,' *Simiolus* 8 (1975-1976), pp. 199-228
Broos 1977
B.P.J. Broos, *Index to the Formal Sources of Rembrandt's Art*, Maarssen 1977
Broos 1977-A
B.P.J. Broos, *Rembrandt-Studies* (diss.), Utrecht 1977
Broos 1977-B
B. Broos, 'De totale uitverkoop van het werk van Aelbert Cuyp,' *Vrij Nederland* 38 (1977), 24 December, p. 45
Broos 1978-1979
B.P.J. Broos, ' "A Monument to Hals" [Review of *Slive 1970-1974*],' *Simiolus* 10 (1978-1979), pp. 115-123
Broos 1981
B.P.J. Broos, *Rembrandt en tekenaars uit zijn omgeving* (Oude tekeningen in het bezit van de Gemeentemusea van Amsterdam waaronder de collectie Fodor – III), Amsterdam 1981
Broos 1981-1982
B.P.J. Broos, '[Review of *Strauss / Van der Meulen 1979*],' *Simiolus* 12 (1981-1982), pp. 245-262
Broos 1984
B.P.J. Broos, ' "Notitie der Teekeningen van Sybrand Feitama:" de boekhouding van drie generaties verzamelaars van oude Nederlandse tekenkunst,' *Oud Holland* 98 (1984), pp. 13-36
Broos 1985-1986
B. Broos, cat. *Rembrandt en zijn voorbeelden / and His Sources* Amsterdam (Rembrandthuis) 1985-1986
Broos 1986
B. Broos, cat. *De Rembrandt à Vermeer. Les peintres hollandais au Mauritshuis de La Haye* Paris (Grand Palais) 1986

Broos 1987
B. Broos, *Meesterwerken in het Mauritshuis*, The Hague 1987
Broos 1988
B. Broos, *Mauritshuis 's-Gravenhage. Mauritshuis The Hague. Gids van het Koninklijk Kabinet van Schilderijen. Guide to the Royal Cabinet of Paintings*, The Hague 1988
Broos 1988-A
B. Broos, 'Abraham Bloemaert en de Vader van de Schilderkunst,' *Nederlands Kunsthistorisch Jaarboek* 38 (1987), pp. 62-72
Broulhiet 1938
G. Broulhiet, *Meindert Hobbema (1638-1709)*, Paris 1938
Brown 1976
C. Brown, cat. *Art in Seventeenth Century Holland* London (National Gallery) 1976
Brown 1979
C. Brown, 'Jan Lievens at Brunswick,' *The Burlington Magazine* 121 (1979), pp. 741-746
Brown 1981
C. Brown, cat. *Scholars of Nature. The Collecting of Dutch Paintings in Britain 1610-1857* Hull, Que. (Ferens Art Gallery) 1981
Brown 1983
C. Brown, 'Jan Lievens in Leiden and London,' *The Burlington Magazine* 125 (1983), pp. 663-671
Brown 1984
C. Brown, *Scenes of Everyday Life: Dutch Genre Paintings of the Seventeenth Century*, London 1984
Brown 1986
C. Brown, cat. *Dutch Landscape. The Early Years. Haarlem and Amsterdam 1590-1650* London (National Gallery) 1986
Brown 1986-A
C. Brown, ' "Mercury and Argus" by Carel Fabritius: A Newly Discovered Painting,' *The Burlington Magazine* 128 (1986), pp. 797-798
Brown 1988
C. Brown, '[Review of *Sutton et al. 1987-1988*],' *Simiolus* 18 (1988), pp. 76-81
Brugmans / Japikse 1938
H. Brugmans, N. Japikse et al., *Persoonlijkheden in het koninkrijk der Nederlanden in woord en beeld. Nederlanders en hun werk*, Amsterdam 1938
De Brune 1636
J. de Brune, *Nieuwe wyn in oude le'er-zacken*, Middelburg 1636
Brunswick 1979
Cat. *Jan Lievens. Ein Maler im Schatten Rembrandts* Brunswick (Herzog Anton Ulrich-Museum) 1979
Brunswick 1987
Hendrick ter Brugghen und die Nachfolger Caravaggios in Holland: Beiträge eines Symposions ..., Brunswick 1987

Brunswick etc. 1988-1990
Cat. *Europäische Malerei des Barock aus dem Nationalmuseum in Warschau* Brunswick (Herzog Anton Ulrich-Museum) Utrecht (Centraal Museum) Cologne (Wallraf-Richartz Museum) Munich (Alte Pinakothek) 1988-1990

Brusse 1926
M.J. Brusse, *Knoeierijen in den schilderijenhandel*, Rotterdam 1926

Brussels 1833
Catalogue et description des tableaux qui forment la collection de S.A.S. le Prince Auguste d'Arenberg, Brussels 1833

Brussels 1873
Cat. *Exposition de tableaux et dessins d'anciens maîtres organisée par la société néerlandaise de bienfaisance à Bruxelles* Brussels (Musées Royaux) 1873

Brussels 1882
Cat. *Exposition néerlandaise de beaux-arts organisée au bénéfice de la société néerlandaise de bienfaisance à Bruxelles*, Brussels 1882

Brussels 1935
Cat. *Cinq siècles d'art. Tome 1: Peintures* Brussels (Exposition universelle et internationale) 1935

Brussels 1971
Cat. *Rembrandt en zijn tijd* Brussels (Paleis voor Schone Kunsten) 1971

Brussels 1984
Koninklijke Musea voor Schone Kunsten van België. Departement Oude Kunst. Inventariscatalogus van de oude schilderkunst, Brussels 1984

Bruyn 1984
J. Bruyn, '[Review of *Sumowski 1983*],' *Oud Holland* 98 (1984), pp. 146-162

Bruyn 1987-1988
J. Bruyn, 'Toward a Scriptural Reading of Seventeenth-Century Dutch Landscape Paintings' in: *Sutton et al. 1987-1988*, pp. 84-103

Bruyn et al. 1973
J. Bruyn, J.A. Emmens, E. de Jongh et al., *Album Amicorum J.G. van Gelder*, The Hague 1963

Bruyn et al. 1982
J. Bruyn, B. Haak, S.H. Levie, P.J.J. van Thiel & E. van de Wetering, *A Corpus of Rembrandt Paintings. I. 1625-1631*, The Hague / Boston, Mass. / London 1982

Bruyn et al. 1986
J. Bruyn, B. Haak, S.H. Levie, P.J.J. van Thiel & E. van de Wetering, *A Corpus of Rembrandt Paintings. II. 1631-1634*, Dordrecht / Boston, Mass. / Lancaster 1986

Bruyn et al. 1989
J. Bruyn, B. Haak, S.H. Levie et al., *A Corpus of Rembrandt Paintings. III. 1635-1642*, Dordrecht / Boston, Mass. / London 1989

De Bruyn Kops 1965
C.J. de Bruyn Kops, 'Vergeten zelfportretten van Govert Flinck en Bartholomeus van der Helst,' *Bulletin van het Rijksmuseum* 13 (1965), pp. 20-29

De Bruyn Kops 1965-A
C.J. de Bruyn Kops, 'Kanttekeningen bij het nieuw verworven landschap van Aelbert Cuyp en enige bijzonderheden over de waardering en export van zijn werk in het verleden,' *Bulletin van het Rijksmuseum* 13 (1965), pp. 162-176

Bryan 1816 / 1964
G.C. Williamson (ed.), *Bryan's Dictionary of Painters and Engravers* (2 vols.), Washington, D.C. 1964 (1st edition 1816)

Buchanan 1824
W. Buchanan, *Memoirs of Painting with a Chronological History of the Importation of Pictures by the Great Masters into England since the French Revolution* (2 vols.), London 1824

Buffalo 1942
Cat. *Souvenir of a Small Exhibition of European Paintings of the Fifteenth, Sixteenth, Seventeenth, and Eighteenth Centuries* Buffalo, N.Y. (Albright Art Gallery) 1942

Buist 1974
M.G. Buist, *At spes non fracta. Hope & Co. 1770-1815. Merchant Bankers and Diplomats at Work* (diss. Groningen), The Hague 1974

Bulletin AIC 1915
'The Wirt Walker Gallery,' *Bulletin of The Art Institute of Chicago* 9 (1915), pp. 80-81

Bulletin Detroit 1954-1955
'Recent Acquisitions. Jan Both,' *Bulletin of The Detroit Institute of Arts* 34 (1954-1955), pp. 10-11

Bulletin Detroit 1954-1955-A
'Accessions January 1, 1954 to December 31, 1954,' *Bulletin of The Detroit Institute of Arts* 34 (1954-1955), pp. 53-54

Bulletin MMA 1908
'Recent Loans,' *Bulletin of the Metropolitan Museum of Art* 3 (1908), no. 4, p. 76

Burchfield 1952
L.H. Burchfield, '"The Music Party" by de Hooch,' *The Bulletin of The Cleveland Museum of Art* 39 (1952), no. 6, pp. 118 and 121-123

Burda 1969
C. Burda, *Das Trompe-l'oeil in der holländischen Malerei des 17. Jahrhunderts* (diss.), Munich 1969

Burger-Wegener 1976
C. Burger-Wegener, *Johannes Lingelbach 1622-1674* (diss. Berlin), Munich 1976

Burke 1968
J.S. Burke, Jr., *The First Century. A History of B. Altman and Co.*, New York 1968

Burke 1976
J.D. Burke, *Jan Both: Paintings, Drawings and Prints*, New York / London 1976

Burke 1980
J.D. Burke, 'Dutch Paintings,' *The Saint Louis Art Museum Bulletin* 15 (1980), no. 4, pp. 5-24

Burke 1981
M.R. Burke, cat. *Handbook of the Collection, Bowdoin College Museum of Art*, Brunswick, Maine 1981

Burke's 1963
P. Townend (ed.), *Burke's Genealogical and Heraldic History of the Peerage, Baronetage and Knightage*, London 1963

Burlington Magazine 1911
'Rembrandt's Mill,' *The Burlington Magazine* 19 (1911), pp. 3-4

Burlington Magazine 1937
'A National Gallery for America,' *The Burlington Magazine* 70 (1937), pp. 142-143

Burlington Magazine 1957
'Notable Works of Art Now on the Market,' *The Burlington Magazine* 99 (1957), supplement, n.p. (after p. 220)

Burlington Magazine 1964
'Notable Works of Art Now on the Market,' *The Burlington Magazine* 106 (1964), supplement, n.p. (after p. 303)

Burlington Magazine 1969
'Notable Works of Art Now on the Market,' *The Burlington Magazine* 111 (1969), supplement, n.p. (after p. 411)

Burman Becker 1869
J.G. Burman Becker, *Notices sur la famille Verkolje*, Copenhagen 1869

Burnet 1850
J. Burnet, *A Treatise in Four Parts, Consisting of an Essay on the Education of the Eye with Reference to Painting, and Practical Hints on Composition, Chiaroscuro, and Colour*, London 1850

Burnet 1859
J. Burnet, *Rembrandt and His Works, Comprising a Short Account of His Life*, London 1859

Burroughs 1907
B. B[urroughs], 'A Recent Loan,' *Bulletin of the Metropolitan Museum of Art* 2 (1907), pp. 23 and 140-141

Burroughs 1925
B. Burroughs, 'The Collis P. Huntington Bequest,' *Bulletin of the Metropolitan Museum of Art* 20 (1925), no. 5, pp. 134-135

Burroughs 1925-A
B. Burroughs, 'The Collis P. Huntington Collection Comes to the Museum,' *Bulletin of the Metropolitan Museum of Art* 20 (1925), no. 6, pp. 142-143

Burroughs 1926
B. Burroughs, *The Metropolitan Museum of Art. Catalogue of Paintings*, New York 1926

Burroughs 1931
B. Burroughs, *The Metropolitan Museum of Art. Catalogue of Paintings*, New York 1931

Burroughs / Wehle 1932
B. Burroughs & H.B. Wehle, 'The Michael Friedsam Collection,' *Bulletin of the Metropolitan Museum of Art* 27 (1932), no. 11, pp. 5-52

Burt 1977
N. Burt, *Palaces for the People: A Social History of the American Art Museum*, Boston, Mass. 1977

Bury 1964
A. Bury, 'In the Galleries,' *The Connoisseur* 157 (1964), September, pp. 48-49

Butler 1982-1983
M.H. Butler, 'Appendix: An Investigation of the Technique and Materials Used by Jan Steen,' *Bulletin Philadelphia Museum of Art* 78 (1982-1983), pp. 44-61

Butlin / Joll 1977
M. Butlin & E. Joll, *The Paintings of J.M.W. Turner* (2 vols.), New Haven / London 1977

Butterfield et al. 1762-1784
L.H. Butterfield, M. Friedlander, M.J. Kline (eds.), *The Book of Abigail and John: Selected Letters of the Adams Family 1762-1784*, Cambridge, Mass. 1975

Caffin 1909
C.H. Caffin, *The Story of Dutch Painting*, New York 1909

Cambridge 1931
Handbook, Fogg Art Museum, Harvard University, Cambridge, Mass. 1931

Cambridge 1989
Cat. *Treasures from the Fitzwilliam: 'The Increase of Learning and other Great Objects of that Noble Foundation'* Cambridge (Fitzwilliam Museum) 1989

Canfield 1974
C. Canfield, *The Incredible Pierpont Morgan. Financier and Art Collector*, London 1974

Cannons 1923
H.G.T. Cannons, *Art Prices Current 1922-1923*, London 1923

Carasso-Kok / Levy-van Halm et al. 1988
M. Carasso-Kok, J. Levy-van Halm et al., *Schutters in Holland. Kracht en zenuwen van de stad*, Zwolle / Haarlem 1988

Carter 1976
M.N. Carter, 'The Chrysler Museum: Clouded by Controversy,' *Artnews* (1976), February, pp. 56-62

Cary 1910
E.L. Cary, 'Some Masters of Portraiture,' *Putnam's Magazine* 7 (1910), pp. 525-535

Catalani 1968
C. Catalani, *Het bed. 5000 Jaar waken en slapen*, Bussum 1968

Catroux 1924
R.C. Catroux, 'La galerie A. de Ridder,' *L'amour de l'art* 5 (1924), pp. 126-130

Cats 1625
J. Cats, *Houwelick*, Middelburg 1625

Cats 1712
Alle de wercken van den heere Jacob Cats (2 vols.), Amsterdam 1712

Catton Rich 1969
D. Catton Rich, *Worcester Art Museum. The Seventy-Third Annual Report of the Trustees and Officers*, Worcester, Mass. 1969

Cave 1978-1984
K. Cave, *The Diary of Joseph Farington* (16 vols.), New Haven, Conn. / London 1978-1984

Chanin 1954
A.L. Chanin, 'The Unerring Taste of Stephen Clark,' *Art Digest* (1954), January, pp. 13-14

Chantavoine 1926
J. Chantavoine, *Vermeer de Delft* (Les grandes artistes), Paris 1926

Chapman 1858
J.G. Chapman, *The American Drawing Book: Manual for the Amateur, and Basis for the Professional Artist ...*, New York 1858

Chetham 1969
C. Chetham, 'The Smith College Museum of Art,' *Antiques* 96 (1969), no. 5, pp. 768-775

Chetham 1970
C. Chetham, *Nineteenth- and Twentieth-Century Paintings from the Collection of the Smith College Museum of Art*, Northampton, Mass. 1970

Chetham et al. 1986
C. Chetham, D.F. Grose, A.H. Sievers (eds.), *A Guide to the Collections: Smith College Museum of Art*, Northampton, Mass. 1986

Chiarini 1979
M. Chiarini, 'L'autoritratto di Michael Sweerts già nella collezione del cardinale Leopoldo di Medici,' *Paragone* 30 (1979), no. 355, pp. 62-65

Chicago 1888
Cat. *Ehrich Collection: Paintings by Dutch and Flemish Masters* Chicago, Ill. (The Art Institute of Chicago) 1888

Chicago 1934
Catalogue of a Century of Progress. Exhibition of Paintings and Sculpture 1934 Chicago, Ill. (The Art Institute of Chicago) 1934

Chicago 1935-1936
Cat. *Loan Exhibition of Paintings, Drawings and Etchings by Rembrandt and His Circle* Chicago, Ill. (The Art Institute of Chicago) 1935-1936

Chicago 1961
Paintings in The Art Institute in Chicago. A Catalogue of the Picture Collection, Chicago, Ill. 1961

Chicago 1961-A
Cat. *Sobriety and Elegance in the Baroque: An Exhibition of Portraits from the University of Notre Dame Collection, Presented by the Renaissance Society at the University of Chicago*, Chicago, Ill. 1961

Chicago / Minneapolis / Detroit 1969-1970
Cat. *Rembrandt after Three Hundred Years. An Exhibition of Rembrandt and His Followers* Chicago, Ill. (The Art Institute of Chicago) Minneapolis, Minn. (The Minneapolis Institute of Arts) Detroit, Mich. (The Detroit Institute of Arts) 1969-1970

Chilvers / Farr 1988
I. Chilvers & D. Farr (eds.), *The Oxford Dictionary of Art*, Oxford 1988

Christison 1972
M.B. Christison, 'Herman Charles Krannert, 1888-1972,' *Art Journal* 31 (1972), p. 487

Chronique des arts 1919
'Collection L. de M. [Lebeuf de Montgermont], *La chronique des arts et de la curiosité* (1917), pp. 219-220

Chronique des arts 1962
'Etats-Unis,' *La chronique des arts* (1962), no. 1117, pp. 18-48

Chronique des arts 1972
'Etats-Unis,' *La chronique des arts* (1972), no. 1237, pp. 66-124

Chronique des arts 1977
'Principales acquisitions des musées en 1975,' *La chronique des arts* (1977), no. 1298, pp. 1-87

Chronique des arts 1978
'Etats-Unis,' *La chronique des arts* (1978), no. 1316, pp. 15-19

Chronique des arts 1986
'Autres acquisitions ou dons récents,' *La chronique des arts* (1986), no. 1406, pp. 58-62

Cicerone 1910
'Kleine Nachrichten,' *Der Cicerone* 2 (1910), pp. 109-110

Cincinnati 1939
Catalogue of the Taft Museum, Cincinnati, Ohio 1939

Cincinnati 1945
Taft Museum Catalogue, Cincinnati, Ohio n.d. (1945)

Cincinnati 1973-1974
Cat. *Dutch Couples. Rembrandt and His Contemporaries* Cincinnati, Ohio (The Taft Museum) 1973-1974

Clark 1954
E. Clark, *History of the National Academy of Design 1825-1953*, New York 1954

Clark 1982
H.N.B. Clark, 'A Fresh Look at the Art of Francis W. Edmonds: Dutch Sources and American Meanings,' *The American Art Journal* 14 (1982), no. 2, pp. 73-94

Clark 1982-A
H.N.B. Clark, 'A Taste for the Netherlands: The Impact of Seventeenth-Century Dutch and Flemish Genre Painting on American Art 1800-1860,' *The American Art Journal* 14 (1982), no. 3, pp. 23-38

Clark 1982-B
H.N.B. Clark, *The Impact of Seventeenth-Century Dutch and Flemish Genre Painting on American Genre Painting, 1800-1865* (diss.), Delaware, Md. 1982

Clark 1987
H.N.B. Clark, 'The Legacy of the Low Countries: The Influence of Dutch and Flemish Art on 19th-Century American Paintings,' *Art and Auction* 10 (1987), pp. 146-151

Clark 1988
H.N.B. Clark, cat. *Francis W. Edmonds, American Master in the Dutch Tradition* Fort Worth, Tex. (Amon Carter Museum) 1988

Cleveland 1936
Catalogue of the Twentieth Anniversary Exhibition of the Cleveland Museum of Art. The Official Art Exhibit of the Great Lakes Exposition Cleveland, Ohio (The Cleveland Museum of Art) 1936

Cleveland 1952
Paintings in The Cleveland Museum of Art (Picture Book IV), Cleveland, Ohio 1952

Cleveland 1958
Cat. *In Memoriam Leonard C. Hanna, Jr.* Cleveland, Ohio (The Cleveland Museum of Art) 1958
Cleveland 1958-A
The Cleveland Museum of Art Handbook, Cleveland, Ohio 1958
Cleveland 1966
Cat. *Selected Works* Cleveland, Ohio (The Cleveland Museum of Art) n.d. (1966)
Cleveland 1970
Handbook of The Cleveland Museum of Art / 1969, Cleveland, Ohio 1970
Cleveland 1978
Handbook of The Cleveland Museum of Art, Cleveland, Ohio 1978
Cleveland 1982
European Paintings of the 16th, 17th, and 18th Centuries. The Cleveland Museum of Art. Catalogue of Paintings. Part Three, Cleveland, Ohio 1982
Coben / Ratner 1983
S. Coben & L. Ratner (eds.), *The Development of American Culture*, New York 1983
Cohen 1910
W. Cohen, 'Die Sammlung Wesendonk,' *Zeitschrift für bildende Kunst* 21 (1910), new series, pp. 58-67
Cohen 1914
W. Cohen, *Katalog der Gemäldegalerie vorwiegend Sammlung Wesendonk* Bonn (Provinzial-Museum in Bonn) 1914
Cohen 1963
A.A. Cohen, cat. *The Hebrew Bible in Christian, Jewish and Muslim Art* New York (The Jewish Museum) 1963
Cohn 1986
M.B. Cohn, *Francis Calley Gray and Art Collecting in America*, Cambridge, Mass. 1986
Collins Baker 1920
C.H. Collins Baker, *Catalogue of the Petworth Collection of Pictures in the Possession of Lord Leconfield*, London 1920
Collins Baker 1925
C.H. Collins Baker, *Masters of Painting. Pieter de Hooch*, London 1925
Comfort 1867
G.F. Comfort, 'Esthetics in Collegiate Education,' *The Methodist Quarterly Review* (1867), October, pp. 21-23
Complete Peerage
G.E.C., G.F. White, R.S. Lea et al., *The Complete Peerage or a History of the House of Lords and All Its Members from the Earliest Times* (13 vols.), London 1910-1940
Comstock 1937
H. Comstock, 'The Connoisseur in America. Paintings by Hals Sent to Haarlem,' *The Connoisseur* 100 (1937), vol. II, pp. 87-88
Comstock 1940
H. Comstock, 'The Connoisseur in America. Loan Exhibition for War Relief,' *The Connoisseur* (1940), September, pp. 112-114

Comstock 1943
H. Comstock, 'The Connoisseur in America,' *The Connoisseur* 111 (1943), March, pp. 57-63
Comstock 1946
H. Comstock, 'The Widener Collection at the National Gallery of Art, Washington,' *The Connoisseur* (1946), December, pp. 129-137
Comstock 1948
H. Comstock, 'Gifts from the Booth Collection,' *The Connoisseur* 122 (1948), September, p. 40
Comstock 1956
H. Comstock, 'The Connoisseur in America. Late Portraits by Hals,' *The Connoisseur* 138 (1956), vol. III, pp. 278-279
Comstock 1956-A
H. Comstock, 'The Connoisseur in America. Rembrandts in the Oakes Collection,' *The Connoisseur* 138 (1956), vol. III, pp. 73-74
Comstock 1959
H. Comstock, 'The Connoisseur in America,' *The Connoisseur* 142 (1959), pp. 270-273
Comstock 1962
H. Comstock, 'The Clark Bequest,' *The Connoisseur* 149 (1962), vol. III, p. 132
Connaissance des arts 1984
'Gould et cinq jours de Monte-Carlo,' *Connaissance des arts* (1984), September, no. 391, p. 30
Connoisseur 1911
'Current Art Notes: Rembrandt's Mill,' *The Connoisseur* 29 (1911), January-April, pp. 267-269
Connoisseur 1966
'Important Paintings by Old Masters,' *The Connoisseur* 162 (1966), June, p. XCII
Connoisseur 1971
'Spring Exhibition of Fine Dutch, Flemish and Italian Old Master Paintings,' *The Connoisseur* 176 (1971), April, pp. 32-48 (advertisements)
Constable 1950
W.G. Constable, 'Department of Paintings,' *Museum of Fine Arts, Boston, Seventy-Fifth Annual Report for the Year 1950*, Boston, Mass. 1950, pp. 35-41
Constable 1964
W.G. Constable, *Art Collecting in the United States of America. An Outline of a History*, London etc. 1964
Conway 1887
W.M. Conway, *Early Flemish Artists*, London 1887
Conway 1905
M. Conway, 'Sir William van Horne's Collection at Montreal,' *The Connoisseur* 12 (1905), July, pp. 135-142
Cook 1899
H.F. Cook, 'Correspondence d'Angleterre: L'exposition Rembrandt à Londres,' *Gazette des Beaux-Arts* 41 (1899), vol. XXI, pp. 248-257
Coral Gables 1951
Cat. *Dutch Old Masters* Coral Gables, Fla. (The University of Miami Art Gallery) 1951

Corning 1952
Cat. *Glass Vessels in Dutch Painting of the Seventeenth Century*, Corning, N.Y. (The Corning Museum of Glass) 1952
Coronet 1939
'Four Paintings of the Dutch School,' *Coronet* (1939), February, pp. 11-14
Cortissoz 1909
R. Cortissoz, 'Old Dutch Masters,' *Bulletin of the Metropolitan Museum of Art* 4 (1909), no. 10, pp. 162-167
Cosentino 1974
A.J. Cosentino, 'Charles Bird King: An Appreciation,' *American Art Journal* 6 (1974), pp. 54-71
Cosentino 1977
A.J. Cosentino, cat. *The Paintings of Charles Bird King* Washington, D.C. (National Collection of Fine Arts) 1977
Cox 1909-1910
K. Cox, 'Art in America. Dutch Pictures in the Hudson-Fulton Exhibition,' *The Burlington Magazine* 16 (1909-1910), pp. 178-184, 245-246 and 302-306
Craven 1980
W. Craven, 'Luman Reed, Patron: His Collection and Gallery,' *The American Art Journal* 12 (1980), no. 2, pp. 40-59
Crawford 1953
W.R. Crawford (ed.), *The Cultural Migration: The European Scholar in America*, Philadelphia, Pa. 1953
Czobor 1956
A. Czobor, 'Über ein unbekanntes Bild des Hendrick Terbrugghen,' *Oud Holland* (1956), pp. 229-232
Czobor 1969
A. Czobor, *Rembrandt and His Circle*, Budapest 1969
DAB
Dictionary of American Biography (29 vols., index, and 7 vols. supplement), New York 1928-1981
Daniëls 1976-1977
G.L.M. Daniëls, 'Doe heb ick uyt verkooren ...,' *Antiek* 11 (1976-1977), pp. 329-341
Van Dantzig 1937
M.M. van Dantzig, *Frans Hals. Echt of onecht*, Amsterdam 1937
Dattenberg 1967
H. Dattenberg, *Niederrheinansichten holländischer Künstler des 17. Jahrhunderts*, Düsseldorf 1967
Dayton 1948
Cat. *Old Masters from Midwestern Museums* Dayton, Ohio (The Dayton Art Institute) 1948
Dayton 1969
Cat. *Fifty Treasures of The Dayton Art Institute* Dayton, Ohio (The Dayton Art Institute) 1969
Dayton 1976
'A Selected Checklist of the Collection of The Dayton Art Institute,' *The Dayton Art Institute Bulletin* 34 (1976), no. 2, *passim*

Dayton / Baltimore 1965-1966
Cat. *Hendrick Terbrugghen in America* Dayton, Ohio
(The Dayton Art Institute) Baltimore, Md. (Baltimore
Museum of Art) 1965-1966

DBF
Dictionnaire de Biographie Française (16 vols.), Paris
1933-1985

Debrett's 1980
P. Montague-Smith (ed.), *Debrett's Peerage and
Baronetage*, London 1980

Debrunner 1979
H.W. Debrunner, *Presence and Prestige: Africans in
Europe. A History of Africans in Europe before 1918*,
Basel 1979

Decamps 1872
L. Decamps, 'Un musée transatlantique,' *Gazette des
Beaux-Arts* 4 (1872), 2nd series, vol. v, pp. 33-40 and
434-437

Dejean 1913
E. Dejean, *La Duchesse de Berry et les monarchies
européennes (août 1830-décembre 1833)*, Paris 1913

Delbanco 1928
G. Delbanco, *Der Maler Abraham Bloemaert (1564-
1651)*, Strasbourg 1928

Delft 1952-1953
Cat. *Kersttentoonstelling* Delft (Museum Het
Prinsenhof) 1952-1953

Delft 1956
Cat. *Er was eens ...* Delft (Museum Het Prinsenhof)
1956

Delft 1962
Cat. *Meesterwerken uit Delft* Delft (Museum Het
Prinsenhof) 1962

Delft / Antwerp 1964-1965
Cat. *De schilder in zijn wereld. Van Jan van Eijk tot Van
Gogh en Ensor* Delft (Stedelijk Museum Het
Prinsenhof) Antwerp (Koninklijk Museum voor
Schone Kunsten) 1964-1965

Delftsche Courant 1910
'Een nieuwe Delftsche Vermeer,' *Delftsche Courant*
6 December 1910, 'Tweede blad,' n.p.

Derham 1988
A. Derham, 'Blue-and-White at a Price,' *Apollo* 128
(1988), December, pp. 406-407

Descamps 1753-1765
J.B. Descamps, *La vie des peintres flamands et hollandais
...* (4 vols.), Paris 1753-1765

Descargues 1966
P. Descargues, *Vermeer*, Geneva 1966

Descargues 1967
P. Descargues, *The Hermitage*, London 1967 (2nd
edition)

Desenfans 1786
[N.J.] Desenfans, *A Catalogue of that Truly Superb, and
Well-Known Collection of Pictures of the Roman, Venetian,
Spanish, French, Flemish, Dutch and English Schools ...*
London (late the Royal Academy, 125 Pall Mall) 1786

Desenfans 1802
N. Desenfans, *A Descriptive Catalogue [...] of Some
Pictures [...] Purchased for His Majesty the Late King of
Poland [...] Vol. 1*, London 1802

Detroit 1929
Cat. *The Ninth Loan Exhibition. Dutch Genre and
Landscape Paintings of the Seventeenth Century* Detroit,
Mich. (The Detroit Institute of Arts) 1929

Detroit 1939
Cat. *Loan Exhibition of Dutch Landscape Paintings* Detroit,
Mich. (The Detroit Institute of Arts) 1939

Detroit 1949
Cat. *Masterpieces of Painting and Sculpture from The Detroit
Institute of Arts*, Detroit, Mich. 1949

Detroit 1960
Treasures from The Detroit Institute of Arts, Detroit,
Mich. 1960

Detroit 1967
*Paintings in The Detroit Institute of Arts. A Checklist of the
Paintings Acquired before January, 1967*, Detroit, Mich.
1967

Deys 1981
H.P. Deys, *Achter Berg en Rijn. Over boeren, burgers en
buitenlui in Rhenen*, Rhenen 1981

Dezarrois 1912
A. Dezarrois, 'Un tableau retrouvé. La "Danaé"
d'Henri Goltzius,' *La revue de l'art ancien et moderne* 32
(1912), vol. II, pp. 219-222

DIAL
Decimal Index of the Art of the Low Countries (RKD), The
Hague 1958

Dickey et al. 1983
S. Dickey, S.D. Kuretsky & D.F. Mosby, cat. *Dutch
Painting in the Age of Rembrandt from The Metropolitan
Museum of Art* Hamilton, N.Y. (The Picker Art
Gallery) Rochester, N.Y. (The Memorial Art Gallery)
Amarillo, Tex. (Amarillo Art Center) 1983

Dieren 1937
Cat. *Tentoonstelling van belangrijke 16e en 17e eeuwsche
Hollandsche schilderijen* Dieren (Firma D. Katz) 1937

Van Dijck / Koopman 1987
L. van Dijck & T. Koopman, *Het klavecimbel in de
Nederlandse kunst tot 1800. The Harpsichord in Dutch Art
before 1800*, Zutphen 1987

Dillis 1839
[Dillis], *Catalogue des tableaux de la Pinacothèque Royale à
Munich*, Munich 1839

Dingeldein 1969
W.H. Dingeldein, *Singraven. Beelden uit verleden en
heden van een Twentse havezate*, Enschede 1969

Dingeldein / Döhmann 1934
W.H. Dingeldein & K. Döhmann, *Singraven. De
geschiedenis van een Twentsche havezate* (4 vols.),
Brussels 1934

Dittrich 1976-1977
C. Dittrich, 'Unbekannte Zeichnungen des Abraham
Bloemaert,' *Jahrbuch der Staatlichen Kunstsammlungen
Dresden* (1976-1977), pp. 89-102

Dixon 1987
L.S. Dixon, cat. *Skating in the Arts of Seventeenth-
Century Holland* Cincinnati, Ohio (The Taft Museum)
1987

DNB
Dictionary of National Biography (63 vols., 3 vols.
supplement, index, and errata), London 1885-1904

Dobrzycka 1966
A. Dobrzycka, *Jan van Goyen, 1596-1656*, Poznan
1966

Dodgson 1903-1911
C. Dodgson, *Catalogue of Early German and Flemish
Woodcuts Preserved in the Department of Prints and
Drawings in the British Museum* (2 vols.), London
1903-1911

Ten Doesschate Chu 1974
P. ten Doesschate Chu, *French Realism and the Dutch
Masters*, Utrecht 1974

Ten Doesschate Chu 1987
P. ten Doesschate Chu & P.H. Boerlin, cat. *Im Lichte
Hollands. Holländische Malerei des 17. Jahrhunderts aus
den Sammlungen des Fürsten von Liechtenstein und aus
Schweizer Besitz* Basel (Kunstmuseum) 1987

Ten Doesschate Chu 1987-A
P. ten Doesschate Chu, 'Nineteenth-Century Visitors
to the Frans Hals Museum' in: *Weisberg / Dixon 1987*,
pp. 111-144

Dolders 1985
A. Dolders, 'Some Remarks on Lairesse's *Groot
Schilderboek*,' *Simiolus* 15 (1985), pp. 197-220

Dordrecht 1977-1978
Cat. *Aelbert Cuyp en zijn familie. Schilders te Dordrecht*
Dordrecht (Dordrechts Museum) 1977-1978

Doubleday / De Walden 1936
'Northbourne of Betteshanger and of Jarrow Grange'
in: H.A. Doubleday & H. de Walden (eds.), *The
Complete Peerage*, vol. IX (1936), pp. 689-691

Dresden 1979
*Gemäldegalerie alte Meister Dresden. Katalog der
ausgestellten Werke*, Dresden 1979

Drossaers / Lunsingh Scheurleer 1974-1976
S.W.A. Drossaers & Th.H. Lunsingh Scheurleer,
*Inventarissen van de inboedels in de verblijven van de
Oranjes en daarmede gelijk te stellen stukken. 1567-1795*
(3 vols.), The Hague 1974-1976

Dudok van Heel 1975
S.A.C. Dudok van Heel, 'Honderdvijftig advertenties
van kunstverkopingen uit veertig jaargangen van de
Amsterdamsche Courant. 1672-1711,' *Amstelodamum.
Jaarboek* 67 (1975), pp. 149-173

Dudok van Heel 1977
S.A.C. Dudok van Heel, 'Ruim honderd advertenties
van kunstverkopingen uit de Amsterdamsche
Courant 1712-1725,' *Amstelodamum. Jaarboek* 69
(1977), pp. 107-122

Dülberg 1930
F. Dülberg, *Frans Hals, ein Leben und ein Werk*,
Stuttgart 1930

Düsseldorf 1904
Cat. *Kunsthistorische Ausstellung* Düsseldorf
(Kunstakademie) 1904
Dumont-Wilden
L. Dumont-Wilden, *La collection Michel van Gelder.
Au Château Zeecrabbe Uccle*, n.p. (Brussels) n.d.
Dunlap 1834
W. Dunlap, *History of the Rise and Progress of the Arts of
Design in the United States*, New York 1834
Duparc 1975
F.J. Duparc, *Een eeuw strijd voor Nederlands cultureel
erfgoed*, The Hague 1975
Duparc 1980
F.J. Duparc, *Mauritshuis. Hollandse schilderkunst.
Landschappen 17de eeuw*, The Hague 1980
Durand-Gréville 1887
E. Durand-Gréville, 'La Peinture aux Etats-Unis,'
Gazette des Beaux-Arts 29 (1887), 2nd series, vol. XXVI,
pp. 68-75 and 220-225
Durantini 1979 / 1983
M.F. Durantini, *The Child in Seventeenth-Century Dutch
Painting*, Ann Arbor, Mich. 1983 (1st edition 1979)
Durden-Smith / Desimone 1984
J. Durden-Smith & D. Desimone, 'Art Town U.S.A.
How Williamstown Came to Have the Most Art per
Capita of Any American Community,' *Connoisseur*
(1984), July, pp. 86-91
Dutuit 1885
E. Dutuit, *Tableaux et dessins de Rembrandt. Catalogue
historique et descriptif*, Paris 1885
Duyvené de Wit-Klinkhamer 1966
Th.M. Duyvené de Wit-Klinkhamer, 'Een vermaarde
zilveren beker,' *Nederlands Kunsthistorisch Jaarboek* 17
(1966), pp. 79-103
Ebbinge Wubben 1953
J.C. Ebbinge Wubben, 'Een Romeins straattafereel
door Michael Sweerts,' *Bulletin Museum Boymans
Rotterdam* 4 (1953), pp. 3-8
Eckardt 1971
G. Eckardt, *Selbstbildnisse niederländischer Maler des 17.
Jahrhunderts*, Berlin 1971
Edel 1956
L. Edel (ed.), *Henry James, The American Essays*, New
York 1956
Edel 1974
L. Edel, 'Henry James as an Art Critic,' *American Art
Journal* 6 (1974), pp. 5-14
Edel 1985
L. Edel, *Henry James, A Life*, New York 1985
Edinburgh 1986
'A New Landscape by Koninck,' *The National Gallery of
Scotland News* (1986), March-April, p. 1
Edinburgh 1986-A
'Recent Museum Acquisitions in Edinburgh,' *The
Burlington Magazine* 128 (1986), pp. 632-637
Edwards 1986
L.M. Edwards et al., cat. *Domestic Bliss: Family Life in
American Painting, 1840-1910* Yonkers, N.Y. (The
Hudson River Museum) **1986**

Van Eeghen 1958
I.H. v[an] E[eghen], 'Amsterdamse kunst-
verzamelingen omstreeks 1875,' *Amstelodamum.
Maandblad* 45 (1958), pp. 226-228
Van Eeghen 1960
I.H. van E[eghen], 'Het poppenhuis van Petronella
de la Court huisvrouw van Adam Oortmans,'
Amstelodamum. Maandblad 47 (1960), pp.159-198
Van Eeghen 1973
I.H. van Eeghen, 'De nakomelingen van Jan van der
Heyden,' *Amstelodamum. Maandblad* 60 (1973),
pp. 128-134
Van Eeghen 1973-A
I.H. van E[eghen], 'De groepsportretten in de familie
Van Loon,' *Amstelodamum. Maandblad* 60 (1973),
pp. 121-127
Van Eeghen 1983
I.H. van Eeghen, 'De familie Trip en het
Trippenhuis' in: *Meischke / Reeser et al. 1983*,
pp. 27-125
Van Eijnden / Van der Willigen 1816-1820 / 1976
R. van Eijnden & A. van Willigen, *Geschiedenis der
vaderlandsche schilderkunst* (4 vols.), Amsterdam 1976
(1st edition Haarlem 1816-1820)
Eikemeier 1974
P. Eikemeier, 'Das Familienbildnis des Emanuel de
Witte in der Alte Pinakothek,' *Pantheon* 32 (1974),
pp. 255-302
Eisendrath 1956
W.N. Eisendrath, 'Portrait of a Woman by Frans
Hals,' *Bulletin of the City Art Museum of St. Louis* 16
(1956), pp. 18-21
Eisler 1969
C. Eisler, '*Kunstgeschichte* American Style: A Study in
Migration' in: *Fleming / Bailyn 1969*, pp. 544-629
Eisler 1977
C. Eisler, *Paintings from the Samuel H. Kress Collection.
European Schools Excluding Italian*, Oxford 1977
Ekkart 1979
R.E.O. Ekkart, 'Bredius, Abraham' in: *Biografisch
Woordenboek van Nederland*, vol. I, The Hague 1979,
pp. 89-90
Ekkart 1979-A
R.E.O. Ekkart, 'Hofstede de Groot, Cornelis' in:
Biografisch Woordenboek van Nederland, vol. I, The
Hague 1979, pp. 248-249
Ekkart 1985
R.E.O. Ekkart, 'Martin, Wilhelm' in: *Biografisch
Woordenboek van Nederland*, vol. II, The Hague 1985,
pp. 378-380
Ekkart 1989
R.E.O. Ekkart, 'Veth, Jan Pieter' in: *Biografisch
Woordenboek van Nederland*, vol. III, The Hague 1989,
pp. 621-622
Elias 1903-1905 / 1963
J.E. Elias, *De vroedschap van Amsterdam. 1578-1795*
(2 vols.), Amsterdam 1963 (1st edition 1903-1905)
Elias 1916-1930
J.E. Elias, *Schetsen uit de geschiedenis van ons zeewezen*
(6 vols.), The Hague 1916-1930

Elkins 1887-1900
Cat. *Catalogue of Paintings in the Private Collection of
W.L. Elkins. Part II. Early English and Old Masters*,
n.p. 1887-1900
Elkins Park 1923 / 1931
Cat. *Paintings in the Collection of Joseph Widener at
Lynnewood Hall, Elkins Park, Pennsylvania*, Elkins Park,
Pa. 1923 (2nd edition 1931)
Emerson 1961
G. Emerson, 'The Kress Collection. A Gift to the
Nation,' *National Geographic Magazine* (1961),
December, pp. 823-865
Emmens 1968
J.A. Emmens, *Rembrandt en de regels van de kunst*,
Utrecht 1968
Emmens 1981
J.A. Emmens, *Kunsthistorische opstellen* (Verzameld
werk III-IV), Amsterdam 1981
Engelson 1966
L. Engelson, *The Influence of Dutch Landscape Painting
on the American Landscape Tradition* (diss.), New York
1966 (unpublished)
Enschede 1980
Cat. *Oost-Nederland model. Landschappen, stads- en
dorpsgezichten. 17de-19de eeuw* Enschede (Rijks-
museum Twenthe) 1980
Erftemeijer 1986
J. Erftemeijer, 'Danae en de gouden regen: een regen
van interpretaties,' *Hermeneus* 58 (1986), pp. 286-294
Errera 1920-1921
J. Errera, *Répertoire des peintures datés* (2 vols.),
Brussels / Paris 1920-1921
Ertz 1979
K. Ertz, *Jan Brueghel der Ältere (1568-1625)*, Cologne
1979
Evans 1969
B.H. Evans, *Fifty Treasures of The Dayton Art Institute*,
Dayton, Ohio 1969
EWA
Encyclopedia of World Art (15 vols.), New York /
Toronto / London 1959-1968
Faberman / Wight 1988
H. Faberman & K. Wight, *Illustrated Catalogue of
European and American Painting and Sculpture. The
University of Michigan Museum of Art*, Ann Arbor,
Mich. 1988
Fahy 1973
E. Fahy, 'Johannes Vermeer' in: *Fahy / Watson 1973*,
pp. 309-321
Fahy / Watson 1973
E. Fahy & F.B.J. Watson, cat. *The Wrightsman
Collection, v: Paintings, Drawings, Sculpture* New York
(The Metropolitan Museum of Art) 1973
Faison 1958
S.L. Faison, Jr., *A Guide to the Art Museums of New
England*, New York 1958
Faison 1964
S. L. Faison, *Art Tours & Detours in New York State*,
New York 1964

Faison 1968
S.L. Faison, Jr., 'Baroque and Nineteenth-Century Paintings,' *Apollo* (1968), December, pp. 466-477

Faison 1979
S.L. Faison, *Handbook of the Collection, Williams College Museum of Art*, Williamstown, Mass. 1979

La Farge / Jacacci 1907
J. La Farge & A.F. Jacacci (eds.), *Noteworthy Paintings in American Private Collections*, New York 1907

Farington 1922-1928
J. Farington (ed. J. Grieg), *The Farington Diary* (8 vols.), London 1922-1928

Feinblatt 1949
E. Feinblatt, 'Note on Paintings by Bartholomeus Breenbergh,' *The Art Quarterly* 12 (1949), pp. 266-271

Filedt Kok 1972
J.P. Filedt Kok, *Rembrandt Etchings & Drawings in the Rembrandt House. A Catalogue*, Maarssen 1972

Finley 1973
D.E. Finley, *A Standard of Excellence. Andrew W. Mellon Founds the National Gallery of Art at Washington*, Washington D.C. 1973

Finley / Walker 1949
D.E. Finley & J. Walker, cat. *Paintings and Sculpture from the Mellon Collection* Washington, D.C. (National Gallery of Art) 1949

Fischer 1972
P. Fischer, 'Music in Paintings of the Low Countries in the 16th and 17th Centuries. Musik auf niederländischen Gemälden im 16. und 17. Jahrhundert,' *Sonorum Speculum* 50-51 (1972), pp. 3-128

Flanigan 1986
J.M. Flanigan, cat. *American Furniture from the Kaufman Collection* Washington, D.C. (National Gallery of Art) 1987

Fleming / Bailyn 1969
D. Fleming & B. Bailyn (eds.), *The Intellectual Migration: Europe and America, 1930-1960*, Cambridge, Mass. 1969

Floerke 1906
H. Floerke, *Das Leben der niederländischen und deutschen Maler* (2 vols.), Munich / Leipzig 1906

Florence 1963
Cat. *Mostra mercato internazionale dell' antiquariato* Florence (Palazzo Strozzi) 1963

Florence 1980
Gli Uffizi. Catalogo Generale, Florence 1980

Fock 1976
C.W. Fock, 'De schilderijengalerij van Prins Willem V op het Buitenhof te Den Haag (1),' *Antiek* 11 (1976), no. 2, pp. 113-137

Fokker 1929
T.H. Fokker, 'Nederlandsche schilders in Zuid-Italië,' *Oud Holland* 46 (1929), pp. 1-24

Fort Worth 1987
In Pursuit of Quality. The Kimbell Art Museum. An Illustrated History of the Art and Architecture, Fort Worth, Tex. / New York 1987

Foshay / Mills 1983
E.M. Foshay & S. Mills, cat. *All Seasons in Every Light. Nineteenth Century American Landscapes from the Collection of Elias Lyman Magoon* Poughkeepsie, N.Y. (Vassar College Art Gallery) 1983

Von Fossen 1969
D.R. von Fossen, *The Paintings of Aert de Gelder* (diss.), Cambridge, Mass. 1969

Foucart 1981
J. Foucart, 'Du Palais-Royal au Louvre: Le *Jupiter et Danaé* de Joachim Wtewael,' *La revue du Louvre et des musées de France* 31 (1981), pp. 114-124

Foucart 1985
J. Foucart, 'Manières du Nord,' *Connaissance des arts* (1985), April, no. 398, pp. 60-69

Foucart-Borville 1970
J.-P. Foucart-Borville, 'Un tableau reconstitué au Musée d'Amiens. Le Repas d'Esther d'Aert de Gelder,' *La revue du Louvre et des musées de France* 20 (1970), pp. 209-220

Fowler / Cornforth 1974
J. Fowler & J. Cornforth, *English Decoration in the 18th Century*, Princeton, N.J. 1974

Fowles 1976
E. Fowles, *Memories of Duveen Brothers*, London 1976

Franits 1989
W.E.J. Franits, *'The vertues which ought to be in a complete woman': Domesticity in Seventeenth-Century Dutch Art* (diss.), Ann Arbor, Mich. 1989

Frankfurter 1933
A.M. Frankfurter, 'The Paintings in the William Rockhill Nelson Gallery of Art,' *The Art News* 32 (1933), 9 December, pp. 29-30

Frankfurter 1937
A.M. Frankfurter, 'Celebrating the Return of Hals. New York Sees the Loans to Haarlem,' *The Art News* 36 (1937), 13 November, pp. 12 and 24-25

Frankfurter 1937-A
A.M. Frankfurter, 'A Frans Hals Festival in Haarlem,' *The Art News* 36 (1937), 17 July, pp. 9-10 and 25

Frankfurter 1940
A.M. Frankfurter, 'Allied Art for Allied Aid. Important French, British, Dutch and Flemish Works in the Red Cross Benefit,' *The Art News* 39 (1940), 15 June, pp. 8-9 and 17

Frankfurter 1942
A.M. Frankfurter, 'Proving the Dutch Masters Great,' *The Art News* 41 (1942), 15-31 October, pp. 11 and 35

Frankfurter 1948
A.M. Frankfurter, 'Booth: Hand-picking the Renaissance,' *The Art News* 47 (1948), pp. 15 and 52-53

Fredericksen 1972
B.B. Fredericksen, *Catalogue of the Paintings in The J. Paul Getty Museum*, Malibu, Calif. 1972

Fredericksen 1988
B.B. Fredericksen, *Masterpieces of Painting in The J. Paul Getty Museum*, Malibu, Calif. 1988

Frederiks 1913
J.W. Frederiks, 'Ons comptabiliteitsstelsel en museumaankoopen,' *Nieuwe Rotterdamsche Courant* 21 May 1913, 'Avondblad,' p. B1

Freise 1908
K. F[reise], 'Das Schicksal der Sammlung Six,' *Kunstchronik* 19 (1908), new series, pp. 46-48

Friedländer 1910
[M.J.] Friedländer, 'Die Ausstellung holländischer Bilder im Metropolitan Museum zu New York 1909,' *Repertorium für Kunstwissenschaft* 33 (1910), pp. 95-99

Friedländer 1913
M.J. F[riedländer], 'Amsterdam. Auktion von Rembrandt-Zeichnungen der Heseltine-Sammlung,' *Kunst und Künstler* 11 (1912-1913), pp. 529-530

Friedländer 1913-A
M.J. F[riedländer], 'Am 9 Juli ...,' *Kunst und Künstler* 11 (1912-1913), p. 530

Fromentin 1876
F. Fromentin, *Les maîtres d'autrefois, Belgique – Hollande*, Paris 1876

Fromentin 1876 / 1976
E. Fromentin, *De meesters van weleer*, Rotterdam 1976 (1st edition 1876)

Fuchs 1973
R.H. Fuchs, 'Rembrandt en Italiaanse kunst: opmerkingen over een verhouding' in: O. von Simson & J. Kelch (eds.), *Neue Beiträge zur Rembrandt-Forschung*, Berlin 1973, pp. 75-82

Füssli 1779-1824
[J.R. Füssli], *Allgemeines Künstlerlexikon* (6 vols.), Zürich 1779-1824

Gabeau 1904
A. Gabeau, 'La galerie de tableaux du Duc de Choiseul,' *Réunion des Sociétés des Beaux-Arts* 28 (1904), pp. 232-271

Gaedertz 1869
T. Gaedertz, *Adrian van Ostade. Sein Leben und seine Kunst*, Lübeck 1869

Galichon 1868
E. Galichon, 'La Galerie de San Donato,' *Gazette des Beaux-Arts* 24 (1868), 1st series, vol. XXIV, pp. 404-408

Garas 1973
K. Garas, *The Budapest Gallery. Paintings in the Museum of Fine Arts*, Budapest 1973

Gardenier 1958
J. Gardenier, 'Michael Sweerts,' *Kroniek van Kunst en Kultuur* 18 (1958), pp. 238-244

Gaskell 1982
I. Gaskell, 'Gerrit Dou, His Patrons and the Art of Painting,' *The Oxford Art Journal* 5 (1982), no. 1, pp. 15-23

Geelhaar 1978
C. Geelhaar, 'Looking at Pictures with David Hockney. An Interview,' *Pantheon* 36 (1978), pp. 230-239

Van Gelder
H.E. van Gelder, *W.C. Heda, A. van Beyeren, W. Kalf* (Palet Serie), Amsterdam n.d.

De Gelder 1921
J.J. de Gelder, *Bartholomeus van der Helst*, Rotterdam 1921

Van Gelder 1948-1949
J.G. van Gelder, 'De schilders van de Oranjezaal,' *Nederlands Kunsthistorisch Jaarboek* 2 (1948-1949), pp. 118-164

Van Gelder 1950
J.G. van Gelder, *Catalogue of the Collection of Dutch and Flemish Still-Life Pictures Bequeated by Daisy Linda Ward* Oxford (Ashmolean Museum) 1950

Van Gelder 1957
H.E. van Gelder, *Ikonografie van Constantijn Huygens en de zijnen*, The Hague 1957

Van Gelder / Emmens 1958
J.G. van Gelder & J.A. Emmens, *De Schilderkunst van Jan Vermeer*, Utrecht 1958

Van Gelder / Gerson 1931
H.E. van Gelder & H. Gerson, *Levensbericht van Dr. C. Hofstede de Groot*, Leyden 1931

Van Gelder / Jost 1972
J.G. van Gelder & I. Jost, 'Doorzagen op Cuyp,' *Nederlands Kunsthistorisch Jaarboek* 23 (1972), pp. 223-239

Genaille 1983
R. Genaille, 'A propos d'un tableau retrouvé de Pieter Aertsen, L'Intérieur Paysan avec Danseurs,' *Jaarboek van het Koninklijk Museum voor Schone Kunsten Antwerpen* (1983), pp. 105-127

Genealogie Boreel
Genealogie van het geslacht Boreel, n.p., n.d.

Genealogisches Taschenbuch
Genealogisches Taschenbuch (documentation Hoge Raad van Adel, The Hague)

Geneva 1974
Cat. *De Genève à l'Ermitage. Les collections de François Tronchin* Geneva (Musée d'art et d'histoire) 1974

Gent 1960
Cat. *Bloem en tuin in de Vlaamse kunst* Gent (Museum voor Schone Kunsten) 1960

Gerdts 1981
W.H. Gerdts, *Painters of the Humble Truth. Masterpieces of American Still Life 1801-1939*, Columbia, Ohio / London 1981

Gerdts / Burke 1971
W. Gerdts & R. Burke, *American Still-Life Painting*, New York / Washington / London 1971

Gernsheim
W. Gernsheim, *Corpus Photographicum of Drawings*

Gersaint 1748
E.F. Gersaint, *Catalogue raisonné des bijoux, porcelaines [...] tableaux, desseins, estampes [...] provenans de la succesion de M. Angran, Vicomte de Fonspertuis* Paris (P. Prault & J. Barrois) 4 March 1748 et seq.

Gerson 1930
H. Gerson, 'Metsu' in: *Thieme / Becker*, vol. XXIV (1930), pp. 439-441

Gerson 1936
H. Gerson, *Philips Koninck. Ein Beitrag zur Erforschung der holländischen Malerei des XVII. Jahrhunderts*, Berlin 1936

Gerson 1942
H. Gerson, *Ausbreitung und Nachwirkung der holländischen Malerei des 17. Jahrhunderts. De expansie der 17e-eeuwse Hollandsche schilderkunst*, Haarlem 1942

Gerson 1950
H. Gerson, *Van Geertgen tot Frans Hals* (De schoonheid van ons land VIII; De Nederlandse schilderkunt I), Amsterdam 1950

Gerson 1953
H. Gerson, 'Dutch Landscape,' *The Burlington Magazine* 95 (1953), pp. 47-52

Gerson 1958
H. Gerson, 'Michael Sweerts en tijdgenoten. Tentoonstelling in het Museum Boymans,' *Het Vaderland* 15 November 1958, pp. 13-14

Gerson 1966
H. Gerson, 'Hooch, Pieter de' in: *Kindlers*, vol. III (1966), pp. 308-312

Gerson 1967
H. Gerson, 'Vermeer' in: *EWA*, vol. XIV (1967), cols. 739-746

Gerson 1968
H. Gerson, *Rembrandt Paintings*, Amsterdam 1968

Gerson 1973
H. Gerson, 'A Monograph on Hals,' *The Burlington Magazine* 115 (1973), pp. 170-174

Gerson 1980
H. Gerson, *Philips Koninck. Ein Beitrag zur Erforschung der holländischen Malerei des XVII. Jahrhunderts*, Berlin 1980 (reprint *Gerson 1936*)

Gerson / Bredius 1969
H. Gerson, *Rembrandt. The Complete Edition of the Paintings. By A. Bredius*, London 1969

Geselschap 1970
J.E.J. Geselschap, 'Werd Adriaan van der Spelt vermoord?,' *Oud Holland* 85 (1970), pp. 186-189

Getty Museum Journal 1985
'Acquisitions / 1985,' *The J. Paul Getty Museum Journal* 14 (1985), pp. 175-286

GGT
Gothaisches Genealogisches Taschenbuch der Adligen Häuser, Gotha 1900-1942

Gibson 1928
W. Gibson, 'The Six Sale at Amsterdam,' *Apollo* 8 (1928), pp. 239-243

Gibson 1929
W. Gibson, 'The Dutch Exhibition at Burlington House,' *Apollo* 9 (1929), pp. 1-12 and 81-94

Gilbert 1966
C. Gilbert, *Seventeenth-Century Paintings from the Low Countries* Waltham, Mass. (Rose Art Museum, Brandeis University) 1966

Le Gille 1905
Le Gille (1905), September, no. 1

Gilman 1937
R. Gilman, 'Mr. Rowe, the Director of the School,' *Bulletin of the Rhode Island School of Design* 25 (1937), pp. 18-20

Van Gils 1920
J.B.F. van Gils, 'Een detail op de doktersschilderijen van Jan Steen,' *Oud Holland* 38 (1920), pp. 200-201

Giltay 1980
J. Giltay, 'De tekeningen van Jacob van Ruisdael,' *Oud Holland* 94 (1980), pp. 141-208

Giltay et al. 1988
J. Giltay, J. Bruyn & G. Jansen, cat. *Een gloeiend palet. Schilderijen van Rembrandt en zijn school* Rotterdam (Museum Boymans-van Beuningen) 1988

Ginnings 1970
R.J. Ginnings, *The Art of Jan Baptist Weenix and Jan Weenix* (diss.) (2 vols.), Delaware, Md. 1970

Glasgow 1973
Cat. *Glasgow's University's Pictures. A Selection of Paintings, Drawings, Prints, and Other Works from the Hunterian Museum, University of Glasgow* Glasgow (Hunterian Museum) 1973

Göcke / Jung / Spass 1913
T. Göcke, W. Jung & W. Spass, *Die Kunstdenkmäler des Kreises Weststernberg* (Die Kunstdenkmäler der Provinz Brandenburg VI / III), Berlin 1913

Goedde 1989
L.O. Goedde, *Tempest and Shipwreck in Dutch and Flemish Art. Convention, Rhetoric, and Interpretation*, London 1989

Goethals 1852
F.V. Goethals, *Dictionnaire généalogique et héraldique des familles nobles du royaume de Belge. Tome Quatrième*, Brussels 1852

Göthe 1895
G. Göthe, *Tafvelsamlingen på Wanås*, Stockholm 1895

Goheen 1988
E.R. Goheen, *The Collection of The Nelson-Atkins Museum*, New York 1988

Goldscheider 1958
L. Goldscheider, *De schilderijen van Vermeer. Complete editie*, London 1958

Goldscheider 1958-A
L. Goldscheider, *Johannes Vermeer. The Paintings. Complete Edition*, London 1958

Goodwood House 1877
Catalogue of Pictures at Goodwood, n.p. 1877

Van Gool 1750-1751
J. van Gool, *De nieuwe schouburg der Nederlantsche kunstschilders en schilderessen* (2 vols.), The Hague 1750-1751

Goris / Held 1947
J.A. Goris & J.S. Held, *Rubens in America*, New York 1947

Gorter 1867
S. Gorter, 'Eene tentoonstelling van oude kunst. Nalezing en nabetrachting,' *De Gids* 30 (1867), 3rd series, vol. V, pp. 453-493

De Gou 1922
J.B. de Gou, 'Overheid en Kunst. Naar aanleiding van de overname der collectie-Six,' *Opgang* 2 (1922), pp. 236-240

Goudappel / Snapper 1979
H. Goudappel & F. Snapper, 'Het Leidse schoutambt 1564-1795,' *Jaarboekje voor geschiedenis en oudheidkunde van Leiden en omstreken* 71 (1979), pp. 31-58

Gower 1875
R. Gower, *Handbook to the Art Galleries Public and Private of Belgium and Holland*, London 1875

Gower 1875-A
R. Gower, *A Pocket Guide to the Public and Private Galleries of Holland and Belgium*, London 1875

Gowing 1951
L. Gowing, 'Light on Baburen and Vermeer,' *The Burlington Magazine* 93 (1951), pp. 169-170

Gowing 1952
L. Gowing, *Vermeer*, London 1952

Gowing 1984
L. Gowing, 'Domestic Harmonies in Dutch Painting,' *Antique Collector* 55 (1984), October, pp. 58-63

Von Graevenitz 1973
A.-M. von Graevenitz, *Das niederländische Ohrmuschel-Ornament: Phänomen und Entwicklung dargestellt an den Werken und Entwürfen der Goldschmiedefamilien van Vianen und Lutma* (diss. Amsterdam), Bamberg 1973

Granberg 1884
O. Granberg, 'Drei unbekannte Gemälde von Rembrandt,' *Zeitschrift für bildende Kunst* 19 (1884), pp. 30-32

Granberg 1885
O. Granberg, *Sveriges Privata Tafvelsamlingar*, Stockholm 1885

Granberg 1886
O. Granberg, *Catalogue raisonné de tableaux anciens inconnus jusqu'ici dans les collections privées de la Suède*, Stockholm 1886

Granberg 1911
O. Granberg, *Inventaire général des trésors d'art, peintures & sculptures, principalement de maîtres étrangers (non scandinaves) en Suède* (4 vols.), Stockholm 1911

Grand Rapids 1940
Cat. *Masterpieces of Dutch Art. Exhibition Manual* Grand Rapids, Mich. (Art Gallery) 1940

Grant 1908
J.K. Grant, 'Mr. John G. Johnson's Collection of Pictures in Philadelphia,' *The Connoisseur* 21 (1908), May-August, pp. 3-11 and 143-151; 22 (1908), September-December, pp. 3-9 and 141-152

Gratama 1943 / 1946
G.D. Gratama, *Frans Hals*, The Hague 1946 (1st edition 1943)

Graves 1913-1915
A. Graves, *A Century of Loan Exhibitions. 1813-1912* (5 vols.), London 1913-1915

Graves 1918-1921
A. Graves, *Art Sales. From Early in the Eighteenth Century to Early in the Twentieth Century* (3 vols.), London 1918-1921

Green 1971
S.M. Green, 'English Origins of New England Painting,' in: *Quimby 1971*, pp. 15-69

Greenville
A Brief Guide to the Bob Jones Art Gallery and Museum, Greenville, South Carolina, Greenville, S.C. n.d.

Greenville 1962
The Bob Jones Collection of Religious Paintings (2 vols.), Greenville, S.C. 1962

Greenville 1968
Supplement to the Catalogue of the Art Collection, Bob Jones University: Paintings Acquired, 1963-1968, Greenville, S.C. 1968

Grijzenhout / Van Tuyll van Serooskerken 1989
F. Grijzenhout & C. van Tuyll van Serooskerken, cat. *Edele eenvoud. Neo-classicisme in Nederland 1765-1800* Haarlem (Frans Halsmuseum / Teylers Museum) 1989

Grimm 1971
C. Grimm, 'Frans Hals und seine Schule,' *Münchner Jahrbuch der bildenden Künste* 22 (1971), pp. 147-178

Grimm 1972
C. Grimm, *Frans Hals. Entwicklung, Werkanalyse, Gesamtkatalog*, Berlin 1972

Grimm 1988
C. Grimm, *Stilleben. Die niederländischen und deutschen Meister*, Stuttgart / Zürich 1988

Grimm / Montagni 1974
C. Grimm & E.C. Montagni, *L'opera completa di Frans Hals*, Milan 1974

Grimme 1974
E.G. Grimme, *Jan Vermeer van Delft*, Cologne 1974

Grisebach 1974
L. Grisebach, *Willem Kalf, 1619-1693*, Berlin 1974

Groen 1987
K. Groen, 'Het loof is wat na den blauwen treckende', *Kunstschrift. Openbaar Kunstbezit* 31 (1987), pp. 106-111

De Groot 1952
C.W. de Groot, *Jan Steen. Beeld en woord*, Utrecht / Nijmegen 1952

Gudlaugsson 1945
S.J. Gudlaugsson, *De komedianten bij Jan Steen en zijn tijdgenooten*, The Hague 1945 (English edition Soest 1975)

Gudlaugsson 1951
S.J. Gudlaugsson, 'Jacob van Campens Amsterdamse schouwburg door Hans Jeurriaensz van Baden uitgebeeld,' *Oud Holland* 66 (1951), pp. 179-183

Gudlaugsson 1959
S.J. Gudlaugsson, *Geraert Ter Borch*, The Hague 1959

Gudlaugsson 1960
S.J. Gudlaugsson, *Katalog der Gemälde Gerard ter Borchs sowie biographisches Material*, The Hague 1960

Gudlaugsson 1964
S.J. Gudlaugsson, 'Bray, Jan de' in: *Kindlers*, vol. 1 (1964), pp. 518-519

Gudlaugsson 1968
S. Gudlaugsson, 'Kanttekeningen bij de ontwikkeling van Metsu,' *Oud Holland* 83 (1968), pp. 13-44

Guillaud / Guillaud 1986
J. & M. Guillaud, *Rembrandt. The Human Form and Spirit*, Paris / New York 1986

GWP
Grote Winkler Prins. Encyclopedie in twintig delen, Amsterdam / Brussels 1966-1975

H. 1928
H., 'Veilingen,' *Maandblad voor Beeldende Kunsten* 5 (1928), pp. 353-355

Haak 1968
B. Haak, *Rembrandt: zijn leven, zijn werk, zijn tijd*, Amsterdam n.d. (1968)

Haak 1984
B. Haak, *Hollandse schilders in de Gouden Eeuw*, n.p. (Amsterdam) 1984

Haarlem 1911
Verslag van den toestand van het Gemeentelijk Museum te Haarlem, over het jaar 1911

Haarlem 1937
Cat. *Frans Hals tentoonstelling ter gelegenheid van het 75-jarig bestaan van het Gemeentelijk Museum te Haarlem op 30 juni 1937* Haarlem (Frans Halsmuseum) 1937

Haarlem 1962
Cat. *Frans Hals. Tentoonstelling ter gelegenheid van het honderdjarig bestaan van het Gemeentemuseum te Haarlem. 1862-1962* Haarlem (Frans Halsmuseum) 1962

Haarlem 1974
Cat. *Tulpomania* Haarlem (Frans Halsmuseum) 1974

Haarlem 1986
Cat. *Op zoek naar de Gouden Eeuw* Haarlem (Frans Halsmuseum) 1986

Hagens 1979
H. Hagens, *Molens, mulders, meesters. Negen eeuwen watermolens in de Gelderse Achterhoek, Salland en Twente*, Almelo 1979

The Hague 1754
Catalogus van schilderyen van den heer agent Willem Lormier in 's Gravenhage, n.p., n.d. (The Hague 1754)

The Hague 1881
Catalogus der Tentoonstelling van schilderijen van oude meesters te 's Gravenhage ten behoeve van watersnoodlijdenden The Hague (Gothisch Paleis) 1881

The Hague 1897
Beknopte catalogus der schilderijen en beeldhouwwerken van het Koninklijk Kabinet van Schilderijen (Mauritshuis) te 's-Gravenhage, The Hague 1897

The Hague 1900
Cat. *Geschiedkundige tentoonstelling van het Nederlandsche zeewezen te 's Gravenhage*, The Hague 1900

The Hague 1910
Beknopte catalogus der schilderijen en beeldhouwwerken in het Koninklijk Kabinet van Schilderijen (Mauritshuis) te 's-Gravenhage, The Hague 1910 (1st edition 1891, also English, French and German editions)

The Hague 1954
Beknopte catalogus der schilderijen en beeldhouwwerken The Hague (Mauritshuis) 1954

The Hague 1958-1959
Cat. *Jan Steen* The Hague (Mauritshuis) 1958-1959
The Hague 1966
Cat. *In het licht van Vermeer. Jubileumtentoonstelling Mauritshuis 1816-1966. Vijf eeuwen schilderkunst* The Hague (Mauritshuis) 1966
The Hague 1974
Cat. *Gerard Ter Borch. Zwolle 1617. Deventer 1681* The Hague (Mauritshuis) 1974
The Hague 1981-1982
Cat. *Jacob van Ruisdael 1628/29-1682* The Hague (Mauritshuis) 1981-1982
The Hague 1982
Cat. *Terugzien in bewondering. A Collectors' Choice* The Hague (Mauritshuis) 1982
The Hague 1985
Cat. *Victor de Stuers. Referendaris zonder vrees of blaam* The Hague (Koninklijke Bibliotheek) 1985
Hahr 1910
A. Hahr, *Svenska slott och herresäten*, Stockholm 1910
Hale 1913
P.L. Hale, *Jan Vermeer of Delft*, Boston, Mass. 1913
Hale et al. 1937
P.L. Hale, F.W. Coburn & R.T. Hale, *Vermeer*, London 1937
Van Hall 1963
H. van Hall, *Portretten van Nederlandse beeldende kunstenaars. Portraits of Dutch Painters and Other Artists of the Low Countries. Specimen of an Iconography*, Amsterdam 1963
Hamburg 1966
Katalog der alten Meister der Hamburger Kunsthalle, Hamburg 1966 (5th edition)
Hannema 1943
F. Hannema, *Gerard Terborch*, Amsterdam 1943
Harck 1888
F. Harck, 'Aus amerikanischen Galerien,' *Repertorium für Kunstwissenschaft* 11 (1888), pp. 72-81
Harms Tiepen 1913
[C. Harms Tiepen], 'Holland waakt!,' *Holland. Geïllustreerd Maandschrift* 1 (1913), nos. 3-4, pp. 121-125
Harms Tiepen 1913-A
[C.] Harms Tiepen, 'Bij Dr. A. Bredius,' *Holland. Geïllustreerd Maandschrift* 1 (1913), no. 7, pp. 35-47
Harris 1976
J.C. Harris, cat. *Collegiate Collections 1776-1876* South Hadley, Mass. (Mount Holyoke College) 1976
Hartford 1941
Cat. *The Ella Gallup Sumner and Mary Catlin Sumner Fund, Recent Acquisitions* Hartford, Conn. (Wadsworth Atheneum) 1941
Hartford 1948
Cat. *The Life of Christ* Hartford, Conn. (Wadsworth Atheneum) 1948
Hartford 1950-1951
Cat. *Life in Seventeenth-Century Holland* Hartford, Conn. (Wadsworth Atheneum) 1950-1951
Hartford 1958
Wadsworth Atheneum Handbook, Hartford, Conn. 1958

Hartford 1964
Cat. *Let There Be Light* Hartford, Conn. (Wadsworth Atheneum) 1964
Hartford / New York / Fort Worth 1987
Cat. *J. Pierpont Morgan, Collector. European Decorative Arts from the Wadsworth Atheneum* Hartford, Conn. (Wadsworth Atheneum) New York (The Pierpont Morgan Library) Fort Worth, Tex. (The Kimbell Art Museum) 1987
Harvey 1928
G. Harvey, *Henry Clay Frick, The Man*, New York 1928
Harwood 1988
L.B. Harwood, *Adam Pynacker (c. 1620-1673)*, Doornspijk 1988
Haskell 1970
F. Haskell, 'The Benjamin Altman Bequest,' *Metropolitan Museum Journal* 3 (1970), pp. 259-280
Haskell 1976
F. Haskell, *Rediscoveries in Art. Some Aspects of Taste, Fashion and Collecting in England and France*, London 1976
Hasselgren 1974
I. Hasselgren, *Konstsamlaren Gustaf Adolf Sparre. 1746-1794. Hans studiersa, våning och konstsamling i Göteborg*, Göteborg 1974
Hasselgren 1988
I. Hasselgr[é]en, 'Konstsamlaren Gustaf Adolf Sparre och Sparreska våningen i Göteborg,' *Konsthistorisk tidskrift* 57 (1988), no. 3-4, pp. 141-145
Van Hasselt 1977-1978
C. van Hasselt, cat. *Rembrandt et ses contemporains. Dessins hollandais du dix-septième siècle* New York (The Pierpont Morgan Library) Paris (Institut Néerlandais) 1977-1978
Hausenstein 1924
W. Hausenstein, *Vermeer van Delft* (Das Bild. Atlanten der Kunst x), Munich 1924
Havard 1879-1881
H. Havard, *L'art et les artistes hollandais* (3 vols.), Paris 1879-1881
Havard 1885
H. Havard, *The Dutch School of Paintings*, London 1885
Havard 1888
H. Havard, *Van der Meer de Delft* (Les artistes célèbres), Paris 1888
Haverkamp-Begemann 1969
E. Haverkamp-Begemann, 'Rembrandt und seine Schule,' *Kunstchronik* 22 (1969), pp. 281-289
Haverkamp-Begemann 1973
E. Haverkamp-Begemann, '[Review of *Wagner 1971*],' *The Burlington Magazine* 115 (1973), pp. 401-402
Haverkamp-Begemann 1978
E. Haverkamp-Begemann, *Wadsworth Atheneum Paintings. Catalogue 1. The Netherlands and the German-Speaking Countries. Fifteenth–Nineteenth Centuries* Hartford, Conn. (Wadsworth Atheneum) 1978

Haverkamp-Begemann 1978-A
E. Haverkamp-Begemann, et al., cat. *The William A. Clark Collection* Washington, D.C. (The Corcoran Gallery of Art) 1978
Haverkamp-Begemann 1980
E. Haverkamp-Begemann, 'Dutch and Flemish Masters of the Seventeenth Century,' *Apollo* 111 (1980), March, pp. 202-211
Haverkamp-Begemann / Adams 1988
E. Haverkamp-Begemann & A. Jensen Adams, cat. *Dutch and Flemish Paintings from New York Private Collections* New York (National Academy of Design) 1988
Haverkamp-Begemann / Logan 1970
E. Haverkamp-Begemann & A.-M. Logan, cat. *European Drawings and Watercolors in the Yale University Art Gallery 1500-1900* (2 vols.), New Haven, Conn. / London 1970
Hawcroft 1967
F.W. Hawcroft, cat. *A Loan Exhibition of English Drawings from the Whitworth Art Gallery, University of Manchester* London (Colnaghi) 1967
Hawes 1963
L. Hawes, Jr., *John Constable's Writings on Art*, Ann Arbor / London 1963
Hawthorne 1941
N. Hawthorne (ed. Randall Stewart), *The English Notebooks*, New York / Oxford 1941
HdG
C. Hofstede de Groot, *Beschreibendes und kritisches Verzeichnis der Werke der hervorragendsten holländischen Maler des XVII. Jahrhunderts* (10 vols.), Esslingen a.N. / Paris 1907-1928
HdG-MS
Typescript supplement of HdG (Ms. RKD)
Hecht 1986
P. Hecht, 'The Debate on Symbol and Meaning in Dutch Seventeenth-Century Art: An Appeal to Common Sense,' *Simiolus* 16 (1986), pp. 173-188
Hecht 1989-1990
P. Hecht, cat. *De Hollandse fijnschilders. Van Gerard Dou tot Adriaen van der Werff* Amsterdam (Rijksmuseum) 1989-1990
Hecht / Luijten 1986
P. Hecht & G. Luijten, 'Nederland verzamelt oude meesters: tien jaar aankopen en achtergronden,' *Kunstschrift. Openbaar Kunstbezit* 30 (1986), pp. 190-217
Hefting 1969
V. Hefting, *Kinderportretten*, Rotterdam 1969
Heijbroek 1983
J.F. Heijbroek, 'De Vereniging Rembrandt en het Rijksmuseum,' *Bulletin van het Rijksmuseum* 31 (1983), pp. 153-194
Heil 1930
W. Heil, 'Die Rembrandt-Ausstellung in Detroit,' *Pantheon* 6 (1930), pp. 380-383

Heisner 1980
B. Heisner, 'Mortality and Faith: the Figural Motifs within Emanuel de Witte's Dutch Church Interiors,' *Studies in Iconography* 6 (1980), pp. 107-114

Held 1981-A
J. Held, cat. *Rembrandt Fecit* Williamstown, Mass. (Sterling and Francine Clark Art Institute) 1981

Held 1982
J. Held, *Rubens and His Circle*, Princeton, N.J. 1982

Held 1983
J.S. Held, *Rembrandt-Studiën*, Leipzig 1983

Hellens 1911
F. Hellens, *Gérard Terborch*, Brussels 1911

Hellerstedt 1986
K. J. Hellerstedt, cat. *Gardens of Earthly Delight. Sixteenth- and Seventeenth-Century Netherlandish Gardens* Pittsburgh, Pa. (The Frick Art Museum) 1986

Hellerstedt 1988
K.J. Hellerstedt, *Clayton: The Pittsburgh Home of Henry Clay Frick, Art and Furnishings* Pittsburgh, Pa. (The Frick Art Museum) 1988

Hendy 1974
P. Hendy, *European and American Paintings in the Isabella Stewart Gardner Museum*, Boston, Mass. 1974

Henkel / Schöne 1967
A. Henkel & A. Schöne, *Emblemata. Handbuch zur Sinnbildkunst des XVI. und XVII. Jahrhunderts*, Stuttgart 1967

Hennus 1936
M.F. Hennus, 'Tentoonstelling oude kunst uit het bezit van den internationalen handel,' *Maandblad voor Beeldende Kunsten* 13 (1936), pp. 219-253

Heppner 1939-1940
A. Heppner, 'The Popular Theatre of the Rederijkers in the Work of Jan Steen and His Contemporaries,' *Journal of the Warburg and Courtauld Institutes* 3 (1939-1940), pp. 22-48

De Hévésy 1935
A. de Hévésy, '[Review of *Rotterdam 1935*],' *Le bulletin de l'art, ancien et moderne* 68 (1935), pp. 363-366

Herrmann 1980
G. Herrmann, *Selected Paintings at the Norton Simon Foundation*, Pasadena, Calif. 1980

Hibbard 1980
H. Hibbard, *The Metropolitan Museum of Art, New York*, London / Boston, Mass. 1980

Highsmith 1976
P. Highsmith, 'The Trouble with Sir Harry,' *Times Literary Supplement* (1976), 9 July, pp. 853

Hijmersma 1983
H.J. Hijmersma, *100 Jaar Vereniging Rembrandt. Een eeuw particulier kunstbehoud in Nederland*, n.p. 1983

Hijszeler / Wassenbergh-Clarijs 1972 / 1984
F.R. Hijszeler & P. Wassenbergh-Clarijs, *Singraven, een havezate in Twente* (Nederlandse Kastelen Stichting XIII), n.p. 1984 (1st edition 1972)

Hind 1915-1931
A.M. Hind, *Catalogue of Drawings by Dutch and Flemish Artists [...] in the British Museum* (4 vols.), London 1915-1931

Hinterding / Horsch 1989
E. Hinterding & F. Horsch, '"A Small but Choice Collection": The Art Gallery of King Willem II of the Netherlands (1792-1849)'; 'A Note on Willem II's Collection of Drawings'; 'Reconstruction of the Collection of Old Master Paintings of King Willem II,' *Simiolus* 19 (1989), nos. 1-2, pp. 5-45, 46-54 and 55-122

Hirschmann 1915
O. Hirschmann, 'Zwei Gemälde von Hendrick Goltzius,' *Oud Holland* 33 (1915), pp. 129-131

Hirschmann 1916
O. Hirschmann, *Hendrick Goltzius als Maler 1600-1617* (Quellenstudien zur holländischen Kunstgeschichte IX), The Hague 1916

Hirschmann 1921
O. Hirschmann, 'Goltzius (Goltz, Golzius, Goltius), Hendrick' in: *Thieme / Becker*, vol. XIV (1921), pp. 349-353

Hirth / Muther 1888
G. Hirth & R. Muther, *Der Cicerone in der Königl. Älteren Pinakothek zu Munich*, Munich 1888

Hiss / Fansler 1934
P. Hiss & R. Fansler, *Research in Fine Arts in the Colleges and Universities of the United States* New York (The Carnegie Corporation) 1934

Hoeber 1909-1910
A. Hoeber, 'Some Pictures from the Collection of Mr. and Mrs. Charles P. Taft,' *The International Studio* 39 (1909-1910), pp. LXXI-LXXIV

Hoet 1752-1770
G. Hoet, *Catalogus of naamlyst van schilderyen, met derzelver pryzen* (3 vols.), The Hague 1752-1770

Hoetink 1974
H.R. Hoetink, 'Koninklijk Kabinet van Schilderijen "Mauritshuis"' in: *Nederlandse Rijksmusea in 1972*, The Hague 1974, pp. 210-219

Hoetink 1978
H.R. Hoetink, 'Beschouwingen naar aanleiding van een unicum' in: *Boymans bijdragen. Opstellen van medewerkers en oud-medewerkers van het Museum Boymans-van Beuningen voor J.C. Ebbinge Wubben*, Rotterdam 1978, pp. 104-109

Hoetink 1979
H.R. Hoetink, 'Koninklijk Kabinet van Schilderijen "Mauritshuis"' in: *Nederlandse Rijksmusea in 1977*, The Hague 1979, pp. 191-194

Hoetink et al. 1985
H.R. Hoetink, N.C. Sluijter-Seijffert et al., cat. *The Royal Picture Gallery Mauritshuis* (Art Treasures of Holland I), Amsterdam / New York 1985

Hoffmann 1958
E. Hoffmann, 'New York,' *The Burlington Magazine* 100 (1958), pp. 453-454

Hofrichter 1983
F.F. Hofrichter, cat. *Haarlem: The Seventeenth Century* New Brunswick, N.J. (The Jane Voorhees Zimmerli Art Museum) 1983

Hofrichter 1983-A
F.F. Hofrichter, 'Haarlem the Seventeenth Century at Rutgers University,' *Tableau* 5 (1982-1983), pp. 270-274

Hofstede de Groot 1892
C. Hofstede de Groot, 'Proeve eener kritische beschrijving van het werk van Pieter de Hooch,' *Oud Holland* 10 (1892) pp. 178-191

Hofstede de Groot 1892-A
C. Hofstede de Groot, 'Berichten en mededeelingen,' *De Nederlandsche Spectator* (1892), pp. 296 and 304

Hofstede de Groot 1906
C. Hofstede de Groot, *Die Urkunden über Rembrandt (1575-1721)* (Quellenstudien zur holländischen Kunstgeschichte III), The Hague 1906

Hofstede de Groot 1907-1930
C. Hofstede de Groot, *Jan Vermeer van Delft en Carel Fabritius. Photogravures naar al hunne bekende schilderijen met biographischen en beschrijvenden tekst* (3 vols.), Amsterdam n.d. (1907-1930)

Hofstede de Groot 1910
C. Hofstede de Groot, 'Schoone kunsten op de staatsbegrooting,' *Nieuwe Rotterdamsche Courant* 15 December 1910, 'Avondblad,' p. B1

Hofstede de Groot 1913
C. Hofstede de Groot, 'Benjamin Altman †,' *Nieuwe Rotterdamsche Courant* 10 October 1913, 'Avondblad,' p. B1

Hofstede de Groot 1922
C. Hofstede de Groot, 'Hals, Frans' in: *Thieme / Becker*, vol. XV (1922), pp. 531-534

Hofstede de Groot 1923
C. Hofstede de Groot, 'Self-Portraits by Ferdinand Bol,' *The Burlington Magazine* 43 (1923), pp. 22-28

Hofstede de Groot 4-17-1925
C. Hofstede de Groot, 'Een groote daad van Abraham Bredius,' *Nieuwe Rotterdamsche Courant* 17 April 1925, 'Avondblad,' p. B1

Hofstede de Groot 12-21-1925
C. Hofstede de Groot, 'Bredius' uitlatingen over kunstexpertises,' *Nieuwe Rotterdamsche Courant* 21 December 1925, 'Avondblad,' p. C1

Hofstede de Groot 1928
C. Hofstede de Groot, 'Winsten in den Kunsthandel,' *Nieuwe Rotterdamsche Courant* 1 December 1928, 'Avondblad,' p. B1

Hofstede de Groot / Valentiner 1913-1916
C. Hofstede de Groot & W.R. Valentiner, *Pictures in the Collection of P.A.B. Widener at Lynnewood Hall, Elkins Park, Pennsylvania* (3 vols.), Philadelphia, Pa. 1913-1916

Hollstein
F.W.H. Hollstein, *Dutch and Flemish Etchings, Engravings and Woodcuts. Ca. 1450-1700* (23 vols.), Amsterdam 1949-1988

Holmes 1907-1908
C.J. Holmes, 'From the Kann Collection, I – Pictures of the Dutch and Flemish Schools,' *The Burlington Magazine* 12 (1907-1908), pp. 197-205

Von Holst 1939
N. von Holst, 'Sammlertum und Kunstgutwanderung in Ostdeutschland und den benachbarten Ländern bis 1800,' *Jahrbuch der preussischen Kunstsammlungen* 60 (1939), pp. 111-126

't Hooft 1900
C.G. 't Hooft, 'De collectie Six,' *De Kroniek* 6 (1900), pp. 243-244 and 250-251

't Hooft 1912
C.G. 't Hooft, *Amsterdamsche stadsgezichten van Jan van der Heyden*, Amsterdam 1912

Hoogewerff 1911
G.J. Hoogewerff, 'Nadere gegevens over Michiel Sweerts,' *Oud Holland* 29 (1911), pp. 134-138

Hoogewerff 1916
G.J. Hoogewerff, 'Michiel Sweerts te Rome,' *Oud Holland* 34 (1916), pp. 109-110

Hoogewerff 1940
G.J. Hoogewerff, 'Karel Dujardin's schilderijen met gewijde voorstellingen,' *Mededeelingen van het Nederlandsch Historisch Instituut te Rome* (1940), 2nd series, vol. X, pp. 107-121

Hoogewerff / Van Regteren Altena 1928
G.J. Hoogewerff & J.Q. van Regteren Altena, *Arnoldus Buchelius 'Res Pictoriae'. Aanteekeningen over kunstenaars en kunstwerken 1583-1639*, The Hague 1928

Van Hoogstraten 1678
S. van Hoogstraten, *Inleyding tot de hooge schoole der schilderkonst ...*, Rotterdam 1678

Hoover 1981
C. Hoover, 'The Influence of David Wilkie's Prints on the Genre Paintings of William Sidney Mount,' *American Art Journal* 13 (1981), pp. 4-33

Hope 1771-1778
[J. Hope], 'Cabinet schilderyen' (Ms. RKD, added to *Hope 1785*), n.p. (1771-1778)

Hope 1785
Catalogus van het cabinet & andere rariteiten (Ms. RKD, for Dowager Hope, 20 April 1785)

Hope 1965-1966
H.R. Hope, 'The Bob Jones University Collection of Religious Art,' *The Art Journal* 25 (1965-1966), pp. 154-162

Hope 1970-1971
H.R. Hope, 'The Indiana University Art Museum,' *The Art Journal* 30 (1970-1971), pp. 170-177

Hope 1973-1974
H.R. H[ope], 'Midwestern University Paintings Exhibition,' *The Art Journal* 33 (1973-1974), pp. 264-272

Hôtel Drouot 1924
Gazette de l'Hôtel Drouot 33 (1924), 3 June

Houbraken 1718-1721
A. Houbraken, *De groote schouburgh der Nederlantsche konstschilders en schilderessen ...* (3 vols.), Amsterdam 1718-1721

Houston 1958
Cat. *The Human Image* Houston, Tex. (The Museum of Fine Arts of Houston) 1958

Huebner 1928
F.M.H[uebner], 'Die Versteigerung der Sammlung Six in Amsterdam,' *Der Cicerone* 20 (1928), pp. 713-714

Hultén 1948
K.G. Hultén, 'Zu Vermeers Atelierbild,' *Konsthistorisk tidskrift* 17 (1948), pp. 90-98

Van Hulzen 1981
A. van Hulzen, 'Pellecussenpoort moest waarschuwen bij gevaar,' *Utrechts Nieuwsblad* 21 November 1981, p. 2

Hummelen 1967
W.M.H. Hummelen, 'Inrichting en gebruik van het toneel in de Amsterdamse schouwburg van 1637,' *Verhandelingen der Koninklijke Nederlandse Akademie van Wetenschappen. Adeling Letterkunde* (1967), new series, vol. LXXIII, no. 3

Hunnewell 1986
R.W. Hunnewell, *Gerrit Dou's Self Portraits and Depictions of the Artist* (diss. Boston 1983), Ann Arbor, Mich. 1986

Hussey 1926
C. Hussey, *Petworth House Sussex. The Seat of Lord Leconfield*, London 1926

Hymans 1884-1885
H. Hymans, *Le livre des peintres de Carel van Mander* (2 vols.), Paris 1884-1885

Illustrated Bartsch
W.L. Straus (ed.), *The Illustrated Bartsch* (several vols.), New York 1979 –

Illustrated London News 1935
'Two of Six Paintings Sold from the J.P. Morgan Collection ...,' *The Illustrated London News* (1935), 9 February, p. 194

Illustrated London News 1953
'Peasant and Burgher, Landscape and Flowers: Dutch and Flemish Art in a London Exhibition,' *The Illustrated London News* (1953), 18 April, p. 621

Illustrated London News 1957
'Royal Gifts to the Guildford Cathedral Sale; Drawings in London; Paintings in the U.S.,' *The Illustrated London News* (1957), 21 September, p. 475

Incisa della Rocchetta 1959
G. Incisa della Rocchetta, 'La mostra di Michael Sweerts a Roma,' *Arte antica e moderna* 5 (1959), pp. 115-118

Indianapolis 1937
Cat. *Dutch Paintings, Etchings, Drawings, Delftware of the Seventeenth Century* Indianapolis, Ind. (John Herron Art Museum) 1937

Indianapolis / San Diego 1958
Cat. *The Young Rembrandt and His Times* Indianapolis, Ind. (John Herron Art Museum) San Diego, Calif. (The Fine Arts Gallery) 1958

Ingersoll 1971
R.S. Ingersoll, 'William L. Elkins and His Descendants,' *Bulletin Philadelphia Museum of Art* 66 (1971), no. 305, pp. 5-13

Isarlov 1936
G. Isarlov, 'Rembrandt et son entourage,' *La renaissance* (1936), July-September, pp. 3-50

Jaarverslag Rembrandt 1912
Jaarverslag over 1912. Vereeniging Rembrandt, n.p. 1913

Jaarverslag Rembrandt 1913
Jaarverslag over 1913. Vereeniging Rembrandt, n.p. 1914

Jackson 1978
Cat. *With a Little Help from Our Friends* Jackson, Miss. (Mississippi Museum) 1978

Jacquemart 1864
A. Jacquemart, 'La galerie Pourtalès. I. Objets d'art et de curiosité,' *Gazette des Beaux-Arts* 17 (1864), 1st series, vol. XVII, pp. 377-397

Jaffé 1972
M. Jaffé, 'The Flemish and Dutch Schools,' *Apollo* 96 (1972), December, pp. 504-513

Jaffe 1975
I. Jaffe, *John Trumbull, Patriot-Artist of the American Revolution*, Boston 1975

James 1872 / 1956
H. James, 'The Metropolitan Museum's "1871 Purchase"' in: *Sweeney 1956*, pp. 52-66

James 1875 / 1986
H. James, *Roderick Hudson*, Harmondsworth 1986 (1st edition 1875)

James 1878 / 1985
H. James, *The Europeans*, Harmondsworth 1985 (1st edition 1878)

James 1879
H. James, *Hawthorne*, New York 1879

James 1903 / 1960
H. James, *The Ambassadors*, Cambridge, Mass. 1960 (1st edition New York 1903)

James 1909 / 1956
H. James, 'An American Art Scholar: Charles Eliot Norton' in: *Edel 1956*, pp. 118-128

Jameson 1842
Mrs. Jameson, *A Handbook to the Public Galleries of Art in and near London. With Catalogue of the Pictures ...* (2 vols.), London 1842

Jameson 1844
Mrs. Jameson, *Companion to the Most Celebrated Private Galleries of Art in London ...*, London 1844

Janse 1966
J.A. Janse, *In geuren en kleuren. Een geschiedenis van de Hollandse bolgewassen*, Utrecht 1966

Jansen et al. 1988
G. Jansen, S. van Heugten, A. Chong & J. Hoes, cat. *Meesterlijk vee. Nederlandse veeschilders 1600-1900* Dordrecht (Dordrechts Museum) Leeuwarden (Fries Museum) 1988

Jansen / Luijten 1988
G. Jansen & G. Luijten, cat. *Italianisanten en bamboccianten. Het italianiserende landschap en genre door Nederlandse kunstenaars uit de zeventiende eeuw* Rotterdam (Museum Boymans-van Beuningen) 1988

Janson 1952
H.W. Janson, *Apes and Ape Lore in the Middle Ages and the Renaissance*, London 1952

Janson 1986
A.F. Janson, *Great Paintings from the John and Mable Ringling Museum of Art*, New York 1986

Jantzen 1910
H. Jantzen, *Das niederländische Architekturbild*, Leipzig 1910

Jarves 1869
J.J. Jarves, *Art Thoughts*, New York 1869

Jervis 1854
Lady Jervis White Jervis (ed.), *Painting and Celebrated Painters, Ancient and Modern, Including Historical and Critical Notices of the Schools of Italy, Spain, France, Germany, and the Netherlands*, vol. II, London 1854

Johnson 1975
M.M. Johnson, 'Abraham van Beyeren's "Still Life,"' *Bulletin Krannert Art Museum* 1 (1975), pp. 10-26

Johnson 1983
D.J. Johnson, *Old Master Drawings from the Museum of Art, Rhode Island School of Design*, Providence, R.I. 1983

De Jonge 1947
C.H. de Jonge, *Oud-Nederlandsche majolica en Delftsch aardewerk* (2 vols.), Amsterdam 1947

De Jongh 1764
J. de Jongh, *Het leven der [...] schilders [...] beschreven door Karel van Mander* (2 vols.), Amsterdam 1764

De Jongh 1967
E. de Jongh, 'Austerity and Extravagance in the Golden Age,' *Apollo* (1967), July, pp. 16-25

De Jongh 1967-A
E. de Jongh, *Zinne- en minnebeelden in de schilderkunst van de zeventiende eeuw*, n.p. 1967

De Jongh 1968-1969
E. de Jongh, 'Erotica in vogelperspectief. De dubbelzinnigheid van een reeks 17de eeuwse genrevoorstellingen,' *Simiolus* 3 (1968-1969), pp. 22-74

De Jongh 1969
E. de Jongh, 'The Spur of Wit: Rembrandt's Response to an Italian Challenge,' *Delta* 12 (1969), no. 2, pp. 49-67

De Jongh 1971
E. de Jongh, 'Realisme en schijnrealisme in de Hollandse schilderkunst van de zeventiende eeuw' in: *Brussels 1971*, pp. 143-194

De Jongh 1974
E. de Jongh, 'Grape Symbolism in Paintings of the 16th and 17th Centuries,' *Simiolus* 7 (1974), pp. 166-191

De Jongh 1975
E. de Jongh, '[Review of *Grimm 1972* and *Slive 1970-1974*],' *The Art Bulletin* 57 (1975), pp. 583-587

De Jongh 1975-1976
E. de Jongh, 'Pearls of Virtue and Pearls of Vice,' *Simiolus* 8 (1975-1976), pp. 69-97

De Jongh 1986
E. de Jongh, cat. *Portretten van echt en trouw. Huwelijk en gezin in de Nederlandse kunst van de zeventiende eeuw* Haarlem (Frans Halsmuseum) 1986

De Jongh et al. 1982
E. de Jongh, T. van Leeuwen, A. Gasten & H. Sayles, cat. *Still-Life in the Age of Rembrandt* Auckland (City Art Gallery) etc. 1982

De Jongh / Vinken 1961
E. de Jongh & P.J. Vinken, 'Frans Hals als voortzetter van een emblematische traditie. Bij het huwelijksportret van Isaac Massa en Beatrix van der Laen,' *Oud Holland* 76 (1961), pp. 117-152

Jonker 1977
M. Jonker, 'Cornelis Apostool (1762-1844), cultureel ambtenaar,' *Bulletin van het Rijksmuseum* 25 (1977), pp. 97-112

Josi 1821
C. Josi, *Collection d'imitations de dessins d'après les principaux maîtres hollandais et flamands, commencée par C. Ploos van Amstel*, London 1821

Jowell 1974
F.S. Jowell, 'Thoré-Bürger and the Revival of Frans Hals,' *The Art Bulletin* 56 (1974), pp. 101-117

Judson 1959
J.R. Judson, *Gerrit van Honthorst: A Discussion of His Position in Dutch Art*, The Hague 1959

Judson 1961
J.R. Judson, '[Review of *Nicolson 1958*],' *The Art Bulletin* 43 (1961), pp. 341-348

Judson 1963
J.R. Judson, 'A New Insight into Cornelis Ketel's Method of Portraiture,' *Master Drawings* 1 (1963), no. 4, pp. 38-41

Jürss 1982
L. Jürss, *100 Jahre Staatliches Museum Schwerin 1882-1992. Holländische und Flämische Malerei des 17. Jahrhunderts. Bestandskatalog I*, Schwerin 1982

Junius 1641
F. Junius, *De schilderkunst der oude*, Middelburg 1641 (1st edition *De pictura veterum*, Amsterdam 1637)

Kahr 1966
M. Kahr, 'Rembrandt's Esther. A Painting and an Etching Newly Interpreted and Dated,' *Oud Holland* 81 (1966), pp. 228-244

Kahr 1978
M.M. Kahr, *Dutch Painting in the Seventeenth Century*, New York 1978

Kalamazoo 1967
Cat. *The Alfred Bader Collection: 17th Century Dutch and Flemish Painting* Kalamazoo, Mich. (Kalamazoo Institute of Arts) 1967

Kan 1946
A.H. Kan, *De jeugd van Constantijn Huygens door hem zelf beschreven*, Rotterdam / Antwerp 1946

Kansas City 1933
Handbook of the William Rockhill Nelson Gallery of Art, Kansas City, Mo. 1933

Kansas City 1941
The William Rockhill Nelson Collection, Kansas City, Mo. n.d. (1941)

Kansas City 1941-A
Cat. *Seventh Anniversary Exhibition of German, Flemish and Dutch Painting* Kansas City, Mo. (William Rockhill Nelson Gallery of Art) 1941

Kansas City 1955
The William Rockhill Nelson Collection. Housed in the William Rockhill Nelson Gallery and Mary Atkins Museum of Fine Arts, Kansas City, Mo. 1955 (3rd edition)

Kansas City 1959
Handbook of the Collections in the William Rockhill Nelson Gallery of Art and Mary Atkins Museum of Fine Art, Kansas City, Mo. 1959 (4th edition)

Kansas City 1967-1968
Cat. *Paintings of 17th-Century Dutch Interiors* Kansas City, Mo. (The Nelson Gallery of Art and Atkins Museum) 1967-1968

Kansas City 1973
Handbook of the Collections in the William Rockhill Nelson Gallery of Art and Mary Atkins Museum of Fine Arts. Volume 1: Art of the Occident, Kansas City, Mo. 1973

Kansas City 1988
The Collections of The Nelson-Atkins Museum of Art, Kansas City, Mo. / New York 1988

Karlsruhe 1960
Holländische Meister aus der Staatlichen Kunsthalle Karlsruhe, Karlsruhe 1960

Kauffmann 1971
C.M. Kauffmann, 'Lot' in: *Kirschbaum / Braunfels*, vol. III (1971), cols. 107-112

Kauffmann 1973
A. Kauffmann, 'Die Stiftung Sammlung E.G. Bührle' in: *Zürich 1973*, pp. 29-30

Kauffmann 1982
C.M. Kauffmann, *Catalogue of Paintings in the Wellington Museum*, London 1982

Keersmaekers 1957
A.A. Keersmaekers, *De dichter Guilliam van Nieuwelandt en de Senecaans-classieke traditie in de zuidelijke Nederlanden* (Koninklijke Vlaamse Academie voor Taal- en Letterkunde VI, no. 80), Gent 1957

Kelch 1971
J. Kelch, *Studien zu Simon de Vlieger als Marinemaler* (diss.), Berlin 1971

Kelch / Becker 1984
J. Kelch & I. Becker, cat. *Holländische Malerei aus Berliner Privatbesitz* Berlin (Gemäldegalerie Staatliche Museen Preussischer Kulturbesitz) 1984

Kenwood 1962
Cat. *An American University Collection* Kenwood (London County Council) 1962

Kettlewell 1981
J. Kettlewell, *The Hyde Collection Catalogue*, Glen Falls, N.Y. 1981

Keyes 1982
G.S. Keyes, 'Hendrick Avercamp and the Winter Landscape' in: *Blankert et al. 1982*, pp. 37-55

Keyes 1983
G.S. Keyes, 'Paintings of the Northern Schools,' *Apollo* 107 (1983), March, pp. 194-200

Keyes 1984
G.S. Keyes, *Esaias van den Velde 1587-1630*, Doornspijk 1984

Keyes 1986
G. Keyes, 'Department of Paintings' in: *Minneapolis 1986*, pp. 56-64

Keyszelitz 1956
R. Keyszelitz, *Der 'clavis interpretandi' in der holländischen Malerei des 17. Jahrhunderts* (diss.), Munich 1956

KHI-U
Kunsthistorisch Instituut der Rijksuniversiteit, Utrecht

Der Kinderen-Besier 1950
J.H. der Kinderen-Besier, *Spelevaart der mode. De kledij onzer voorouders in de zeventiende eeuw*, Amsterdam 1950

Kindlers
G. Bazin, H. Gerson, L. Gowing et al., *Kindlers Malerei Lexikon* (6 vols.), Zürich 1964-1971

Kirschbaum / Braunfels
E. Kirschbaum & W. Braunfels et al., *Lexikon der christlichen Ikonographie* (8 vols.), Rome etc. 1968-1976

Kirschenbaum 1977
B.D. Kirschenbaum, *The Religious and Historical Paintings of Jan Steen*, New York / Montclair, N.Y. 1977

Van Kleffens 1980
E.N. van Kleffens, *Belevenissen I. 1894-1940*, Alphen aan de Rijn 1980

Klessmann 1981
R. Klessmann, 'Ad tragoedias, non ad vitam' in: *Ars auro prior. Studia Ioanni Bialostocki sexagenario dicata*, Warsaw 1981, pp. 367-372

Klessmann 1983
R. Klessmann, *Herzog Anton Ulrich-Museum Braunschweig. Die holländischen Gemälde. Kritisches Verzeichnis mit 485 Abbildungen*, Brunswick 1983

Klessmann et al. 1978
R. Klessmann, W.J. Müller & K. Renger, cat. *Die Sprache der Bilder. Realität und Bedeutung in der niederländischen Malerei des 17. Jahrhunderts* Brunswick (Herzog Anton Ulrich-Museum) 1978

Knuttel 1935
G. Knuttel Wzn, cat. *Gemeentemuseum 's Gravenhage. Catalogus van de schilderijen, aquarellen en teekeningen*, The Hague 1935

Knuttel 1956
G. Knuttel, *Rembrandt. De meester en zijn werk*, Amsterdam 1956

Koller / Melia
F. Koller & S. Melia (eds.), *Armorial général de Belgique*, Brussels n.d.

Koningsberger 1968
H. Koningsberger, *De wereld van Vermeer. 1632-1675*, Amsterdam 1968

Konst- en Letterbode 1810
'Pryzen van eenige der voornaamste schilderstukken uit het verkochte beroemde kabinet van wylen den heer De Smeth van Alphen,' *Algemeene Konst- en Letterbode* (1810), vol. II, pp. 90-92

Korf 1981
D. Korf, *Nederlandse majolica*, Haarlem 1981

Koskoff 1978
D.E. Koskoff, *The Mellons*, New York 1978

Kramm 1857-1864
C. Kramm, *De leven en werken der Hollandsche en Vlaamsche kunstschilders, beeldhouwers, graveurs en bouwmeesters* (6 vols.), Amsterdam 1857-1864

Kren 1980
T. Kren, 'Chi non vuol Baccho: Roeland van Laer's Burlesque Painting about Dutch Artists in Rome,' *Simiolus* 11 (1980), pp. 63-80

Kris / Kurz 1934
E. Kris & O. Kurz, *Die Legende vom Künstler. Ein geschichtlicher Versuch*, Vienna 1934

Kronig 1911
J.O. Kronig, 'Een tijdelijke aanwinst van 't Gemeentelijk Museum te Haarlem,' *Kunst en Kunstleven* 1 (1911), pp. 137-138

Kruizinga / Banning 1966
J.H. Kruizinga & J.A. Banning, *Amsterdam van A tot Z*, Amsterdam 1966

De Kruyter 1976
S.W. de Kruyter, 'Jacobus Heyblocq's *album amicorum* in the Koninklijke Bibliotheek at The Hague,' *Quaerendo* 6 (1976), pp. 109-153

Künstler-Inventare
A. Bredius, *Künstler-Inventare* (6 vols., addendum, index), The Hague 1915-1922

Ter Kuile 1985
O. ter Kuile, *Seventeenth-Century North Netherlandish Still Lifes* (Catalogue of Paintings by Artists Born before 1870 – VI) The Hague (Rijksdienst Beeldende Kunst) 1985

Kulik 1960
J. Kulik, 'De Haagse Sint Sebastiaansdoelen,' *Vereniging 'Die Haghe.' Jaarboek* (1960), pp. 27-42

Kultzen 1954
R. Kultzen, *Michael Sweerts (1624-1664)* (diss.) (2 vols.), Hamburg 1954 (unpublished)

Kultzen 1983
R. Kultzen, 'Französische Anklänge im Werk von Michael Sweerts' in: *Essays in Northern European Art Presented to Egbert Haverkamp-Begemann on His Sixtieth Birthday*, Doornspijk 1983, pp. 127-133

Kultzen 1987
R. Kultzen, 'Michael Sweerts als Bildnismaler,' *Wiener Jahrbuch für Kunstgeschichte* 40 (1987), pp. 209-380

Kunstreisboek voor Nederland 1977
Kunstreisboek voor Nederland (compiled by the Rijksdienst voor Monumentenzorg in Zeist), Amsterdam / Antwerp 1977

Kuznetsov / Linnik 1982
Y. Kuznetsov & I. Linnik, *Dutch Painting in Soviet Museums*, Amsterdam / Leningrad 1982

Kyzer 1883
R.J. Kyzer, *Het ontstaan der Vereeniging Rembrandt*, Amsterdam 1883

L. + number
F. Lugt, *Répertoire des catalogues de ventes publiques* (4 vols.), The Hague 1938-1986

De Lairesse 1707
G. de Lairesse, *Groot Schilderboek ...* (2 vols.), Amsterdam 1707

De Lairesse 1707 / 1740
G. de Lairesse, *Groot Schilderboek ...* (2 vols.), Haarlem 1740 (1st edition 1707)

Lammers 1989
A. Lammers, *Uncle Sam en Jan Salie. Hoe Nederland Amerika ontdekte*, Amsterdam 1989

Lane 1939
J.W. Lane, 'Thirty-Three Masterpieces in a Modern Collection. Mr. Stephen C. Clark's Paintings by American and European Masters,' *The Art News Annual* (1939), pp. 131-134, 137-152 and 158-160

Laren 1958
Cat. *Kunstbezit rondom Laren. 13de-20ste Eeuw* Laren (Singer Museum) 1958

Laren 1959
Cat. *Kunstschatten. Twee Nederlandse collecties schilderijen uit de vijftiende tot en met de zeventiende eeuw en een collectie oud aardewerk* Laren (Singer Museum) 1959

Larousse
Grand dictionnaire encyclopédique Larousse (10 vols.), Paris 1982-1985

Larousse 1865-1878
P. Larousse, *Grand dictionnaire universel* (15 vols. and 2 vols. supplement), Paris 1865-1878

Larsen 1988
E. Larsen, *The Paintings of Anthony van Dyck*, Freren 1988

Laskin / Pantazzi 1987
M. Laskin & M. Pantazzi, *Catalogue of The National Gallery of Canada, Ottawa. European and American Painting, Sculpture and Decorative Arts* (2 vols.), Ottawa 1987

Laurentius / Niemeijer / Ploos van Amstel 1980
Th. Laurentius, J.W. Niemeijer & G. Ploos van Amstel, *Cornelis Ploos van Amstel. 1726-1798. Kunstverzamelaar en prentuitgever*, Assen 1980

Lauts 1966
J. Lauts, *Katalog alte Meister bis 1800* (2 vols.) Karlsruhe (Staatliche Kunsthalle) 1966

Lavin 1983
M.A. Lavin, *The Eye of the Tiger: The Founding and Development of the Department of Art and Archaeology, 1883-1923, Princeton University*, Princeton, N.J. 1983

Law / Law 1925
H.W. Law & I. Law, *The Book of the Beresford Hopes*, London 1925

Leadam 1909
I.S. Leadam, *The History of England from the Accession of Anne to the Death of George II (1702-1760)*, London etc. 1909

Leader 1980
B.K. Leader, 'The Boston School and Vermeer,' *Arts Magazine* 55 (1980), pp. 172-176

De Leeuw / Sillevis / Dumas 1983
R. de Leeuw, J. Sillevis & C. Dumas, cat. *De Haagse School. Hollandse meesters van de 19de eeuw* Paris (Grand Palais) London (Royal Academy of Arts) The Hague (Haags Gemeentemuseum) 1983

De Lempicka-Foxhall / Phillips 1987
K. de Lempicka-Foxhall & C. Phillips, *Passion by Design. The Art and Times of Tamara de Lempicka*, New York 1987

Leningrad 1838
Livret de la Galerie Impériale de l'Ermitage de Saint-Pétersbourg ..., Leningrad [Saint Petersburg] 1838

Leningrad 1885
Ermitage impérial. Catalogue de la galerie des tableaux. Second volume. Ecoles néerlandaises et école allemande, Leningrad [Saint Petersburg] 1885 (3rd edition)

Van Lennep 1959
F.J.E. van Lennep, 'Amsterdammers in 's-Graveland,' *Amstelodamum. Jaarboek* 51 (1959), pp. 93-169

Lettieri 1980
D. Lettieri, 'Text, Narrative and Tradition: Scenes from *Esther* by Aert de Gelder,' *The J. Paul Getty Museum Journal* 8 (1980), pp. 69-86

Levallet 1925
Levallet, 'Notes inédites sur la collection De Choiseul,' *Bulletin de la Société de l'Histoire de l'Art Français* (1925), pp. 201-211

Levey
L.S. Levey, *The Jules S. Bache Collection* (Ms. documentation archives The Metropolitan Museum of Art, New York)

Levine 1984
D.A. Levine, *The Art of the Bamboccianti* (diss.) (2 vols.), Princeton, N.J. 1984

Lewis 1979
F. Lewis, *Simon Pietersz Verelst. 1644-1721*, Leigh-on-Sea 1979

Leyden 1926
Cat. *Jan Steen tentoonstelling* Leyden (Stedelijk Museum De Lakenhal) 1926

Leyden 1965
Cat. *17de eeuwse meesters uit Nederlands particulier bezit. Oude meesters uit de collectie van de Heer en Mevrouw Sidney J. van den Bergh-Bendix* Leyden (Stedelijk Museum De Lakenhal) 1965

Leyden 1966
Cat. *Gabriel Metsu* Leyden (Stedelijk Museum De Lakenhal) 1966

Leyden 1970
Cat. *IJdelheid der ijdelheden. Hollandse vanitas-voorstellingen uit de zeventiende eeuw* Leyden (Stedelijk Museum De Lakenhal) 1970

Liedtke 1976
W. Liedtke, 'Faith in Perspective; The Dutch Church Interior,' *The Connoisseur* 193 (1976), October, pp. 127-133

Liedtke 1979
W.A. Liedtke, 'Hendrik van Vliet and the Delft School,' *Museum News. Toledo Museum of Art* 21 (1979), no. 2, pp. 41-52

Liedtke 1982
W.A. Liedtke, *Architectural Painting in Delft*, Doornspijk 1982

Liedtke 1982-A
W.A. Liedtke, 'Cornelis de Man as a Painter of Church Interiors,' *Tableau* 5 (1982), no. 1, pp. 62-66

Liedtke 1983
W.A. Liedtke, '"Clothing the Naked" by Michiel Sweerts,' *Apollo* 117 (1983), January, pp. 21-23

Liedtke 1984
W. Liedtke, cat. *Flemish Paintings in The Metropolitan Museum of Art* (2 vols.), New York 1984

Liedtke 1986
W.A. Liedtke, 'De Witte and Houckgeest: Two New Paintings from Their Years in Delft,' *The Burlington Magazine* 128 (1986), pp. 802-805

Liedtke 1989
W. Liedtke, 'Reconstructing Rembrandt: Portraits from the Early Years in Amsterdam (1631-1634),' *Apollo* 129 (1989), May, pp. 323-331

Liège 1939
Cat. *Rétrospective d'art. Peinture, sculpture, tapisserie, gravure, art japonais. Grande saison internationale de l'eau*, Liège 1939

Lilienfeld 1913
K. Lilienfeld, 'Die Sammlung Steengracht zu ihrer bevorstehenden Auflösung,' *Der Cicerone* 5 (1913), pp. 327-333

Lilienfeld 1914
K. Lilienfeld, *Arent de Gelder. Sein Leben und seine Kunst*, The Hague 1914

Lindeman 1928
C.M.A.A. Lindeman, *De oorsprong, ontwikkeling en beteekenis van het Romanisme in de Nederlandsche schilderkunst* (diss.), Utrecht 1928

Lindeman 1929
C.M.A.A. Lindeman, *Joachim Anthonisz Wtewael*, Utrecht 1929

Lindeman 1947
C. Lindeman, 'Wtewael' in: *Thieme / Becker*, vol. XXXVI (1947), pp. 285-286

Lipschultz 1988
S. Lipschultz, *Selected Works: The Minneapolis Institute of Arts*, Minneapolis, Minn. 1988

Lisbon 1982
Museu Calouste Gulbenkian. Catálogo, Lisbon 1982

Lomazzo 1584
G.P. Lomazzo, *Trattato dell' arte de la pittura [...] Diviso in sette libri ...*, Milan 1584

London 1815
Cat. *British Institution for Promoting the Fine Arts in the United Kingdom ...* London (British Institution) 1815

London 1824
An Account of all the Pictures Exhibited in the Rooms of the British Institution, from 1813 to 1823, Belonging to the Nobility and Gentry of England: with Remarks, Critical and Explanatory, London 1824

London 1829
Cat. *British Institution for Promoting the Fine Arts in the United Kingdom* London (British Institution) 1829

London 1834
A Catalogue of the Matchless Collection of Dutch and Flemish Pictures of His Late Royal Highness the Duke de Berri which Formed the Celebrated Cabinet of l'Elysée Bourbon and Now Exhibited for Sale by Private Contract London (Christie, Manson & Woods) 17 April 1834

London 1838
Catalogue of Pictures by Italian, Spanish, Flemish, Dutch and French Masters ... London (British Institution) 1838

London 1849
Cat. *British Institution for Promoting the Fine Arts in the United Kingdom* London (British Institution) 1849

London 1850
Catalogue of Pictures by Italian, Spanish, Flemish, Dutch, French and English Masters with which the Proprietors Have Favoured the Institution London (British Institution) 1850

London 1850-A
Cat. *British Institution for Promoting the Fine Arts in the United Kingdom* London (British Institution) 1850

London 1863
Cat. *British Institution for Promoting the Fine Arts in the United Kingdom* London (British Institution) 1863

London 1866
Cat. *British Institution for Promoting the Fine Arts in the United Kingdom* London (British Institution) 1866

London 1866-A
Catalogue of the Choice of Pictures by Old Masters of John Shaw Phillips, Esq., Removed from Culham House, Oxon London (Christie, Manson & Woods) 12 May 1866

London 1867
Cat. *British Institution for Promoting the Fine Arts in the United Kingdom* London (British Institution) 1867

London 1871
A Selection of Permanent Facsimiles of the Drawings in the Albertina Collection at Vienna, Reproduced by A. Braun, Dornach, London 1871

London 1876
Cat. *Exhibition of Works by the Old Masters and by Deceased Masters of the British School (Winter Exhibition)* London (Royal Academy of Arts) 1876

London 1878
Cat. *Exhibition of Works by the Old Masters, and by Deceased Masters of the British School ...* London (Royal Academy of Arts) 1878

London 1880
Cat. *Exhibition of Works by Old Masters and by Deceased Masters of the British School ...* London (Royal Academy of Arts) 1880

London 1881
Cat. *Exhibition of Works by the Old Masters, and by Deceased Masters of the British School ...* London (Royal Academy of Arts) 1881

London 1884
Cat. *Exhibition of Works by the Old Masters and by Deceased Masters of the British School ...* London (Royal Academy of Arts) 1884

London 1887
Cat. *Exhibition of Works by the Old Masters ...* London (Royal Academy of Arts) 1887

London 1888
A Handbook for Travellers in Surrey, Hampshire, and the Isle of Wight, London 1888

London 1892
Descriptive Catalogue of the Loan Collection of Pictures ... London (Guildhall) 1892

London 1899
Cat. *Exhibition of Works by Rembrandt* London (Royal Academy of Arts) 1899

London 1902
Cat. *Exhibition of Works by the Old Masters Including a Special Collection of Paintings and Drawings by Claude (Winter Exhibition)* London (Royal Academy of Arts, Burlington House) 1902

London 1906
Cat. *The Annual Exhibition on Behalf of the Artists' General Benevolent Institution* London (T. Agnew & Sons) 1906

London 1928
Cat. *Exhibition of Art Treasures 1928* London (The Grafton Galleries) 1928

London 1929
Cat. *Exhibition of Dutch Art. 1450-1900* London (Royal Academy of Arts) 1929

London 1929-A
Dutch Art. An Illustrated Souvenir of the Exhibition of Dutch Art at Burlington House, London, London 1929

London 1930
Commemorative Catalogue of the Exhibition of Dutch Art Held in the Galleries of the Royal Academy, Burlington House, London, January-March 1929, Oxford / London 1930

London 1938
Cat. *Ancient and Modern Pictures and Drawings, the Property of His Grace the Duke of Norfolk, K.G. ...* London (Christie) 11 February 1938

London 1945
Cat. *Masterpieces of Dutch Painting in the Seventeenth Century. Loan Exhibition under the Auspices of the Anglo-Netherlandish Society* London (Eugene Slatter) 1945

London 1945-A
Cat. *Seventeenth-Century Dutch Paintings* London (Arts Council) 1945

London 1946-1947
Catalogue of the Exhibition of the King's Pictures London (Royal Academy of Arts) 1946-1947

London 1952-1953
Cat. *Dutch Pictures 1450-1750* London (Royal Academy of Arts) 1952-1953

London 1953
Cat. *Exhibition of Dutch and Flemish Masters* London (Eugene Slatter Gallery) 1953

London 1955
Cat. *Major Mills. Hillborough* London (The Courtauld Institute) 1955 (typescript copy, RKD)

London 1957
Cat. *The Ernest Cook Bequest to the Nation. A Selection from more than 150 Pictures and Works of Art* London (National Art-Collections Fund) 1957

London 1961
Cat. *Forgeries and Deceptive Copies* London (British Museum) 1961

London 1962
Cat. *Primitives to Picasso. An Exhibition from Municipal and University Collections in Great Britain* London (Royal Academy of Arts) 1962

London 1965
The Iveagh Bequest. Catalogue of Paintings, London, Kenwood 1965 (3rd edition)

London 1968
Wallace Collection Catalogues. Pictures and Drawings, London 1968 (16th edition)

London 1973
The National Gallery. Illustrated General Catalogue, London 1973

London 1982
Cat. *The Art of the Van de Veldes. Paintings and Drawings by the Great Dutch Marine Artists and Their English Followers* London, Greenwich (National Maritime Museum) 1982

London 1986
National Gallery. Illustrated General Catalogue, London 1986

London 1988-A
Concise Catalogue of Oil Paintings in the National Maritime Museum, London 1988

Longhi 1934
R. Longhi, 'Zu Michiel Sweerts,' *Oud Holland* 51 (1934), pp. 271-277

Van Loon 1723-1731
G. van Loon, *Beschryvinghe der Nederlandsche historipenningen ...* (4 vols.), The Hague 1723-1731

Los Angeles 1933
Five Centuries of European Painting. Catalogue Los Angeles, Calif. (Los Angeles Museum) 1933

Los Angeles 1947
Cat. *Loan Exhibition of Paintings by Frans Hals. Rembrandt* Los Angeles, Calif. (Los Angeles County Museum) 1947

Los Angeles 1949
Handlist of Paintings in the Elisabeth Holmes Fisher Gallery, Los Angeles, Calif. 1949

Louisville 1973
J.B. Speed Art Museum Handbook, Louisville, Ky. 1973

Lowenthal 1974
A.W. Lowenthal, 'Wtewael's *Moses* and Dutch Mannerism,' *Studies in the History of Art* 6 (1974), pp. 124-141

Lowenthal 1975
A.W. Lowenthal, *The Paintings of Joachim Anthonisz. Wtewael (1566-1638)* (diss. Columbia University) (2 vols.), Ann Arbor, Mich. 1975

Lowenthal 1986
A. Lowenthal, *Joachim Wtewael and Dutch Mannerism*, Doornspijk 1986

Lugt 1907
F. Lugt, *Is de aankoop door het Rijk van een deel der Six-collectie aan te bevelen? Beschouwingen*, n.p. (Amsterdam) 1907

Lugt 1907-A
F. Lugt, *Is de aankoop door het Rijk van een deel der Six-collectie aan te bevelen? Beschouwingen*, n.p. (Amsterdam) 1907 (2nd edition)

Lugt 10-2-1907
F. Lugt, 'De Collectie-Six,' *Het Vaderland* 2 October 1907, 'Eerste avondblad,' n.p.

Lugt 1918
F. Lugt, 'De kunstverzamelaar August Janssen †,' *De Amsterdammer. Weekblad voor Nederland* 20 April 1918, p. 7

Lugt 1921
F. Lugt, *Les marques de collections de dessins & d'estampes* (and supplement), Amsterdam 1921

Lugt 1929
F. Lugt, *Musée du Louvre. Inventaire général des dessins des écoles du nord. Ecole hollandaise* (2 vols.), Paris 1929

Luiken 1708
J. Luiken, *Beschouwing der wereld, bestaande in honderd konstige figuren*, Amsterdam 1708

Lunsingh Scheurleer 1935
T.H. Lunsingh Scheurleer, 'De schoorsteen-ontwerpen van I. Barbet en hun invloed in Nederland,' *Oud Holland* 52 (1935), pp. 261-266

Luthy 1979
H.A. Luthy, 'The E.G. Bührle Foundation,' *Apollo* (1979) October, pp. 324-327

Maastricht 1990
Cat. *The European Fine Art Fair 1990. Handbook* Maastricht (Maastricht Exhibition and Congress Centre) 1990

Maclaren 1960
N. Maclaren, *National Gallery Catalogues. The Dutch School*, London 1960

MacKay 1989
M. MacKay, 'Victorian and Thriving,' *New York Times Magazine* (1989), 23 April, pp. 47-50

Madrid 1921
Catalogo de pintoros holandeses dibujos, escultera, litografia y arte aplicado, llevados por la comisión del consejo para les artes representativas de la comisión holandesa en el extranjero, Madrid 1921

Madrid 1980
Guia ilustrada. Pintura Extranjera. Museo del Prado, Cuenca 1980

Madsen 1907
K. Madsen, 'Une visite chez Dou et une note sur Rembrandt,' *Bulletin [...] Nederlandschen Oudheidkundigen Bond* 8 (1907), pp. 228-230

Magazine of Art 1936
'Rembrandt and His Circle, Chicago,' *The American Magazine of Art* 29 (1936), no. 1, pp. 49-50

Malibu 1986
The J. Paul Getty Museum. Handbook of the Collections, Malibu, Calif. 1986

Malraux 1952
A. Malraux (ed.), *Vermeer de Delft*, n.p. 1952

Manchester 1857
Catalogue of the Art Treasures of the United Kingdom. Collected at Manchester in 1857 Manchester (Museum of Ornamental Art) 1857

Manchester 1979
The Currier Gallery of Art. Handbook of the Collection, Manchester, N.H. 1979

Van Mander 1604
C. van Mander, *Het Schilder-Boeck ...*, Haarlem 1604

Van Mander 1604-A
C. van Mander, *Wtlegghingh op den Metamorphosis Pub. Ovidy Nasonis ...*, Haarlem 1604 (bound with *Van Mander 1604*)

Manke 1963
I. Manke, *Emanuel de Witte*, Amsterdam 1963

Mann / Heuss 1962
G. Mann & A. Heuss, *Propyläen Weltgeschichte. Dritte Band. Griechenland. Die hellenistische Welt*, Berlin / Frankfurt / Vienna 1962

Mantz 1865
P. Mantz, 'La Galerie Pourtalès. IV. Les peintures espagnoles, allemandes, hollandaises, flamandes et françaises,' *Gazette des Beaux-Arts* 18 (1865), 1st series, vol. XIX, pp. 97-117

Van der Marel 1964
A. van der Marel, 'De kunstschilders de Bray en hun familie,' *De Nederlandsche Leeuw* 81 (1964), cols. 6-26

Marguillier 1904
A. Marguillier, 'L'exposition des maîtres anciens à Düsseldorf,' *Gazette des Beaux-Arts* 46 (1904), 3rd series, vol. XXXII, pp. 271-285

Marius 1907
G.H. Marius, 'De Delftsche Vermeer,' *Het Vaderland* 7 October 1907, 'Eerste avondblad,' n.p.

Marlier 1969
G. Marlier (posthumous, revised and annotated by Jacqueline Folie), *Pierre Brueghel le Jeune*, Brussels 1969

Marlow 1969
P.O. Marlow, 'The Paintings at the Wadsworth Atheneum,' *Antiques* 96 (1969), pp. 745-753

Martin 1901
W. Martin, *Het leven en de werken van Gerrit Dou beschouwd in verband met het schildersleven van zijn tijd* (diss.), Leyden 1901

Martin 1902
W. Martin, *Gerard Dou*, London 1902

Martin 1907
W. Martin, 'Michiel Sweerts als schilder. Proeve van een biografie en een catalogus van zijn schilderijen,' *Oud Holland* 24 (1907), pp. 18-156

Martin 1908
W. Martin, ''s Rijks Aankoop uit de Six-collectie,' *Bulletin [...] Nederlandschen Oudheidkundigen Bond* 1 (1908), 2nd series, pp. 5-9

Martin 1909
W. Martin, 'Iets over Amerikaansche schilderijverzamelingen,' *Elsevier's Geïllustreerd Maandschrift* 19 (1909), vol. XXXVII, pp. 73-87

Martin 1911
W. Martin, *Gérard Dou. Sa vie et son oeuvre. Etude sur la peinture hollandaise et les marchands aux dix-septième siècle*, Paris 1911

Martin 1911-A
W. Martin, 'Ausstellung alt-holländischer Bilder in Pariser Privatbesitz II,' *Monatshefte für Kunstwissenschaft* 4 (1911), pp. 502-508

Martin 1911-B
W. Martin, 'De tentoonstelling van oud-Hollandsche schilderijen te Parijs,' *Elsevier's Geïllustreerd Maandschrift* 21 (1911), vol. XLII, pp. 161-175, 241-254

Martin 1913
W. Martin, *Gerard Dou. Des Meisters Gemälde* (Klassiker der Kunst XXIV), Stuttgart / Berlin 1913

Martin 1914
W. Martin ''s Rijks aanwinsten uit de verzameling Steengracht,' *Bulletin [...] Nederlandschen Oudheidkundigen Bond* 7 (1914), 2nd series, pp. 8-18

Martin 1916
W. Martin, 'Nog een Sweerts,' *Oud Holland* 34 (1916), pp. 181-182

Martin 1918
W. Martin, *Alt-holländische Bilder*, Berlin 1918

Martin 1925
W. Martin, 'Oud-Hollandsche schilderijen in den vreemde,' *Haagsch Maandblad* 4 (1925), vol. II, pp. 474-483

Martin 1927-1928
W. Martin, 'Neues über Jan Steen,' *Zeitschrift für bildende Kunst* 61 (1927-1928), pp. 325-341

Martin 1929
W. Martin, 'Die holländische Ausstellung in Londen,' *Der Kunstwanderer* 10 (1928-1929), pp. 199-202 and 299-303

Martin 1929-A
W. Martin, 'Last Words on the Dutch Exhibition,' *The Connoisseur* 83 (1929), pp. 131-142

Martin 1935
W. Martin, *De Hollandsche schilderkunst in de zeventiende eeuw. Frans Hals en zijn tijd*, Amsterdam 1935

Martin 1936
W. Martin, *De Hollandsche schilderkunst in de zeventiende eeuw. Rembrandt en zijn tijd*, Amsterdam 1936

Martin 1946
W. Martin, 'Abraham Bredius 1855-1946 in memoriam,' *Maandblad voor Beeldende Kunsten* 22 (1946), pp. 71-74

Martin 1954
W. Martin, *Jan Steen*, Amsterdam 1954

Maser 1962
E.A. Maser, 'The Samuel H. Kress Study Collection Program. The List of the Samuel H. Kress Study Collections at American Colleges and Universities,' *The Art Journal* 21 (1962), no. 3, pp. 177-178 and 180-190

Mauquoy-Hendrickx 1956
M. Mauquoy-Hendrickx, *L'iconographie d'Antoine van Dyck. Catalogue raisonné* (2 vols.), Brussels 1956

Mayer
E. Mayer, *International Auction Records* (24 vols.), Zürich 1967-1989

Mayer-Meintschel 1986
A. Mayer-Meintschel, 'Vermeers Kupplerin,' *Jahrbuch der Staatlichen Kunstsammlungen Dresden* (1986), p. 8

McCall 1942
G.H. McCall, *Paintings by the Great Dutch Masters of the Seventeenth Century* New York (Duveen Galleries) 1942

McCall / Barnouw 1942
G.H. McCall & A.J. Barnouw, cat. *Paintings by the Great Dutch Masters of the Seventeenth Century. Loan Exhibition in Aid of the Queen Wilhelmina Fund and the American Women's Voluntary Services* New York (Duveen Galleries) 1942

McCall / Valentiner 1939
G.H. McCall & W.R. Valentiner, *Catalogue of European Paintings and Sculpture from 1300-1800* New York (World Fair) 1939

McCoy 1962
J.W. McCoy, 'A Self-Portrait by Bol,' *The Dayton Art Institute Bulletin* 20 (1962), p. 2

McNeil Kettering 1983
A. McNeil Kettering, *The Dutch Arcadia. Pastoral Art and Its Audience in the Golden Age*, Montclair, N.J. 1983

McNeil Kettering 1988
A. McNeil Kettering, *Drawings from the Ter Borch Studio Estate* (Catalogue of the Dutch and Flemish Drawings in the Rijksprentenkabinet V) (2 vols.), The Hague 1988

McLanathan 1968
R. McLanathan, *The American Tradition in the Arts*, New York 1968

McTavish 1984
D. McTavish, cat. *Pictures from the Age of Rembrandt. Selections from the Personal Collection of Dr. & Mrs. Alfred Bader* Kingston, Ont. (Agnes Etherington Art Centre, Queen's University) 1984

Meijer 1989
F.G. Meijer, cat. *Stillevens uit de Gouden Eeuw. Still Life Paintings from the Golden Age* Rotterdam (Museum Boymans-van Beuningen) 1989

Meis 1981
R. Meis, *Zakhorloges. Van halshorloge tot tourbillon. Vormgeving en techniek*, Haarlem / Antwerp 1981

Meischke / Reeser et al. 1983
R. Meischke & H.E. Reeser et al., *Het Trippenhuis te Amsterdam*, Amsterdam / Oxford / New York 1983

Meldrum 1923
D.S. Meldrum, *Rembrandt's Paintings with an Essay on His Life and Work*, New York n.d. (1923)

Mellaart 1923
J.H.J. Mellaart, 'Self-Portraits by Ferdinand Bol,'
The Burlington Magazine 43 (1923), pp. 153-158

Mensing 9-21-1907
A.W. Mensing, 'De Collectie-Six,' *Het Vaderland*
21 September 1907, 'Tweede avondblad,' p. B

Mensing 9-30-1907
A.W. Mensing, 'Het aanbod van de familie Six van
Vromade,' *Het Vaderland* 30 September 1907,
'Tweede avondblad,' p. B

Mensing 10-30-1907
A.W. Mensing, 'Collectie-Six,' *Het Vaderland*
3 October 1907, 'Tweede avondblad,' p. B

Menzel 1977
G.W. Menzel, *Vermeer*, Leipzig 1977

Mesnil 1908
J. Mesnil, 'De verspreide verzameling van Rudolf
Kann,' *Onze Kunst* 7 (1908), vol. XIII, p. 121-124

Mesnil 1913
J. Mesnil, 'Veiling der verzameling Steengracht, in de
Galerie Georges Petit te Parijs,' *Onze Kunst* 12 (1913),
vol. XXIV, pp. 66-68

Metcalf 1988
P.C. Metcalf (ed.), cat. *Ogden Codman and the
Decoration of Houses* Boston, Mass. (Boston Atheneum)
1988

Meyer 1988
R.K. Meyer, 'The Tafts of Pike Street,' *Apollo* (1988),
December, pp. 389-393 and 452

De Meyere 1988
J. de Meyere, *Utrecht op schilderijen*, Utrecht 1988

Miami 1984
Cat. *In Quest for Excellence. Civic Pride, Patronage,
Connoisseurship* Miami, Fla. (Center for the Fine Arts)
1984

Michel 1890
E. Michel, *Hobbema et les paysagistes de son temps en
Hollande*, Paris 1890

Michel 1893
E. Michel, *Rembrandt. Sa vie, ses oeuvres et son temps*,
Paris 1893

Michel 1901
E. Michel, 'La Galerie de M. Rodolphe Kann,' *Gazette
des Beaux-Arts* 43 (1901), 3rd period, vol. XXV,
pp. 385-400 and 493-506

Middelburgsche Courant 9-23-1907
Torenwachter, 'Van den Haagschen Toren,' *De
Middelburgsche Courant* 23 September 1907, n.p.

Middelburgsche Courant 9-30-1907
Torenwachter, 'Schilderijen-aankoop door het Rijk,'
De Middelburgsche Courant 30 September 1907, n.p.

Middelburgsche Courant 10-5-1907
Torenwachter, 'Van den Haagschen Toren,' *De
Middelburgsche Courant* 5 October 1907, n.p.

Middelburgsche Courant 11-9-1907
'Tweede kamer: Aankoop collectie Six,' *De
Middelburgsche Courant* 9 November 1907, n.p.

Miedema 1977
H. Miedema, 'Realism and Comic Mode: the Peasant,'
Simiolus 9 (1977), pp. 205-219

Van Mieris / Van Alphen 1762-1784
F. van Mieris & D. van Alphen, *Beschryving der stad
Leyden* (3 vols.), Leyden 1762-1784

Miller 1962
D.C. Miller, cat. *Seventeenth- and Eighteenth-Century
Painting from the University of Notre Dame* Champaign-
Urbana, Ill. (Krannert Art Museum, University of
Illinois) 1962

Miller 1966
L.B. Miller, *Patrons and Patriotism: The Encouragement
of the Fine Arts in the United States 1790-1860*, Chicago,
Ill. 1966

Miller 1985
D. Miller, *Jan Victors (1619-76)* (diss. Maryland)
(2 vols.), n.p. 1985

Milliken 1936
W.M. Milliken, 'Superb Art Display Marks Cleveland
Museum's 20th Anniversary,' *The Art Digest* 10 (1936),
1 July, pp. 5-14 and 22

Milliken 1936-A
W.M. Milliken, 'World Art at Cleveland,' *The
American Magazine of Art* 29 (1936), pp. 428-439

Milliken 1943
W.M. Milliken, 'Mr. Severance's Gifts to the
Museum,' *The Bulletin of The Cleveland Museum of Art*
33 (1943), pp. 25-26

Milman 1984
M. Milman, *Das Trompe-l'oeil*, Geneva 1984

Milnes Gaskell 1977
T. Milnes Gaskell, 'Documentary Silver-Gilt Ewer' in:
John Herbert (ed.), *Christie's. Review of the Season
1977*, London 1977, pp. 170-171

Milwaukee 1976
Cat. *The Bible through Dutch Eyes: From Genesis through
the Apocrypha* Milwaukee, Wis. (Milwaukee Art
Center) 1976

Milwaukee 1989
Cat. *The Detective's Eye Investigating the Old Masters*
Milwaukee, Wis. (Milwaukee Art Museum) 1989

Minneapolis 1955
'Fortieth Anniversary Exhibition,' *The Minneapolis
Institute of Arts Bulletin* 44 (1955), no. 1, pp. 3-7

Minneapolis 1963
European Paintings in The Minneapolis Institute of Arts,
Minneapolis 1963

Minneapolis 1970
*A Guide to the Galleries of The Minneapolis Institute of
Arts*, Minneapolis, Minn. 1970

Minneapolis 1970-A
*European Paintings from The Minneapolis Institute of
Arts*, New York / Washington, D.C. / London 1970

Minneapolis 1986
*The Art of Collecting. Acquisitions at The Minneapolis
Institute of Arts 1980-1985*, Minneapolis, Minn. 1986

Minneapolis etc. 1968
Cat. *Loan Exhibition. Selections from the Drawing
Collection of David Daniels* Minneapolis, Minn. (The
Minneapolis Institute of Arts) Chicago, Ill. (The Art
Institute of Chicago) Kansas City, Mo. (The Nelson-
Atkins Museum of Art) Cambridge, Mass. (Fogg Art
Museum) 1968

Mireur 1901-1912
H. Mireur, *Dictionnaire des ventes d'art faites en France et
à l'étranger pendant les XVIIIme & XIXme siècle* (7 vols.),
Paris 1901-1912

De Mirimonde 1967
A.P. de Mirimonde, 'La musique dans les allégories
de l'amour. II. Eros,' *Gazette des Beaux-Arts* 109 (1967),
6th series, vol. LXIX, pp. 319-341

Mitchell 1973
P. Mitchell, *European Flower Painters*, London 1973

Moes 1897-1905
E.W. Moes, *Iconographia Batavia. Beredeneerde lijst van
geschilderde en gebeeldhouwde portretten van Noord-
nederlanders in vorige eeuwen* (2 vols.), Amsterdam
1897-1905

Moes 1909
E.W. Moes, *Frans Hals, sa vie et son oeuvre*, Brussels
1909

Ter Molen 1979
J.R. ter Molen, 'Adam van Vianen's Silverware in
Relation to Seventeenth-Century Dutch Painting,'
Apollo (1979), December, pp. 482-489

Ter Molen 1984
J.R. ter Molen, *Van Vianen, een Utrechtse familie van
zilversmeden met een internationale faam* (diss. Leyden)
(2 vols.), n.p. (Leiderdorp) 1984

Von Moltke 1938-1939
J.W. von Moltke, 'Jan de Bray,' *Marburger Jahrbuch für
Kunstwissenschaft* 11-12 (1938-1939), pp. 421-523

Von Moltke 1939
J.W. von Moltke, *Dutch and Flemish Old Masters in the
Collection of Dr. C.J.K. van Aalst, Huis-te-Hoevelaken,
Holland*, n.p. 1939

Mongan 1965-1966
A. Mongan, cat. *Memorial Exhibition: Works of Art from
the Collection of Paul J. Sachs, Given and Bequeathed to
the Fogg Art Museum* Cambridge, Mass. (Fogg Art
Museum) 1965-1966

Mongan / Mongan 1969
A. & E. Mongan, cat. *European Paintings in the Timken
Art Gallery* San Diego, Calif. (Timken Art Gallery)
1969

Monod 1923
F. Monod, 'La Galerie Altman au Metropolitan
Museum de New-York,' *Gazette des Beaux-Arts* 65
(1923), 5th series, vol. VIII, pp. 179-198 and 297-312

De Montenay 1571 / 1973
G. de Montenay, *Emblemes, ov devises chrestiennes*,
Menston 1973 (1st edition Lyon 1571)

Montias 1987
J.M. Montias, 'Vermeer's Clients and Patrons,' *The Art
Bulletin* 69 (1987), no. 1, pp. 68-76

Montias 1989
M. Montias, *Vermeer and His Milieu. A Web of Social History*, Princeton, N.Y. 1989

Montreal 1944
Cat. *Loan Exhibition of Great Paintings. Five Centuries of Dutch Art. Exposition de tableaux célèbres. Cinq siècles d'art hollandais* Montreal (Art Association of Montreal) 1944

Montreal / Toronto 1969
Cat. *Rembrandt and His Pupils. A Loan Exhibition of Paintings Commemorating the 300th Anniversary of Rembrandt* Montreal (The Montreal Museum of Fine Arts) Toronto (Art Gallery of Ontario) 1969

Moore 1985
J. Moore, 'Putnam Sisters,' *Reader* 14 (1985), 31 January, pp. 1-10, 12-21

Moore 1988
A.W. Moore, *Dutch and Flemish Painting in Norfolk. A History of Taste and Influence, Fashion and Collecting*, London 1988

Moormann / Uitterhoeve 1987
E.M. Moormann & W. Uitterhoeve, *Van Achilles tot Zeus. Thema's uit de klassieke mythologie in literatuur, muziek, beeldende kunst en theater*, Nijmegen 1987

Mooz 1973
R.P. Mooz, 'Colonial Art' in: *Wilmerding 1973*, pp. 25-79

Moreno 1982
I.L. Moreno, 'Vermeer's *The Concert*: A Study in Harmony and Contrasts,' *The Rutgers Art Review* 3 (1982), pp. 51-57

Mortimer 1985
K.A. Mortimer, *HUAM: A Guide to the Collections*, New York 1985

Morton 1961
F. Morton, *The Rothschilds. A Family Portrait*, London 1961

Moscow 1961
Katalog Kartinnoi Galerei Moscow (Pushkin Museum of Fine Arts) 1961

Motley 1852
J.L. Motley, *The Rise of the Dutch Republic. A History* (3 vols.), New York 1852

Münster / Baden Baden 1979-1980
Cat. *Stilleben in Europa* Münster (Westfälisches Landesmuseum für Kunst und Kulturgeschichte) Baden Baden (Staatliche Kunsthalle) 1979-1980

Mumford 1931
L. Mumford, *The Brown Decades. A Study of the Arts in America, 1865-1895*, New York 1931

Munich 1836
Catalogue des tableaux de la pinacothèque royale à Munich, Munich n.d. (1836)

Munich 1889
Cat. *Permanente Gemälde-Ausstellung alter und moderner Meister und Kunsthandlung von A. Rupprecht's Nachfolger* (vol. 1) Munich (Briennerstrasse 8) 1889

Munich 1904
Katalog der Gemälde-Sammlung der Kgl. Älteren Pinakothek in München, Munich 1904

Munich 1913
Katalog der Kgl. Älteren Pinakothek. Amtliche Ausgabe, Munich 1913 (12th edition)

Munich 1920
Katalog der Älteren Pinakothek zu München. Amtliche Ausgabe, Munich 1920 (13th edition)

Munich 1925
Katalog der Älteren Pinakothek zu München. Amtliche Ausgabe, Munich 1925 (15th edition)

Munich 1930
Katalog der Älteren Pinakothek zu München. Amtliche Ausgabe, Munich 1930 (17th edition)

Munich 1962
Cat. *Meister der Manierismus. Gemälde. Hand-zeichnungen. Druckgraphik* Munich (Galerie Wolfgang Gurlitt) 1962

Munich 1966
Cat. *11. Deutsche Kunst- und Antiquitäten-Messe* Munich (Haus der Kunst) 1966

Munich 1983
Bayerische Staatsgemäldesammlungen. Alte Pinakothek München. Erläuterungen zu den ausgestellten Gemälden, Munich 1983

Munro 1954
E.C. Munro, 'To Honor the Metropolitan,' *The Art News* 52 (1954), no. 9, pp. 36 and 85

Munrow 1976
D. Munrow, *Instruments of the Middle Ages and Renaissance*, London 1976

Murphy 1985
A. Murphy, *Summary Catalogue of the European Paintings*, Boston, Mass. 1985

Murphy 1985-A
A.R. Murphy, *European Paintings in the Museum of Fine Arts, Boston: An Illustrated Summary Catalogue*, Boston, Mass. 1985

Murray 1819-1823
[J. Murray], *Tour in Holland in the Year MDCCCXIX*, London n.d. (1819-1823)

Murray 1980
P. Murray, *Dulwich Picture Gallery. A Catalogue*, London 1980

Museum News 1954
'The Music Lesson. Gerard Ter Borch,' *Museum News. The Toledo Museum of Art* (1954), no. 156

Myers 1955
B.S. Myers (ed.), *The Encyclopedia of Painting*, New York 1955

Nagler
G.K. Nagler, *Neues allgemeines Künstler-Lexikon* (22 vols.), Munich 1835-1852

Nagler 1858-1878
G.K. Nagler, *Die Monogrammisten ...* (5 vols.), Munich 1858-1878

Naumann 1981
O. Naumann, *Frans van Mieris the Elder (1635-1681)* (2 vols.), Doornspijk 1981

NCAB
National Cyclopedia of American Biography, New York (documentation The Fine Arts Museums of San Francisco)

Near 1985
P. Near, 'European Paintings and Drawings: The Williams Collection and Fund,' *Apollo* (1985), December, pp. 440-451

Netscher 1918
F. Netscher, 'A. Preyer,' *De Hollandsche Revue* 23 (1918), pp. 325-331 and 382-391

Neumann 1902 / 1905
C. Neumann, *Rembrandt*, Berlin 1902 (2nd edition Berlin / Stuttgart 1905)

Neumeyer 1955
A. Neumeyer, 'The Samuel H. Kress Collection of The M.H. de Young Museum in San Francisco,' *The Art Quarterly* 18 (1955), pp. 272-282

New Haven 1931
Handbook. A Description of the Gallery of Fine Arts and the Collections. School of Fine Arts, Yale University, New Haven, Conn. 1931

New Haven 1956
Cat. *Pictures Collected by Yale Alumni* New Haven, Conn. (Yale University Gallery) 1956

New York 1904
Catalogue of Paintings and Sculpture in the Collection of Charles T. Yerkes, Esq. 1, New York 1904

New York 1925
Cat. *Loan Exhibition of Dutch Masters of the Seventeenth Century* New York (Knoedler & Co.) 1925

New York 1928
Cat. *A Loan Exhibition of Twelve Masterpieces of Painting* New York (Knoedler & Co.) 1928

New York 1928-A
Cat. *Handbook of the Benjamin Altman Collection* New York (The Metropolitan Museum of Art) 1928 (2nd edition)

New York 1929
A Catalogue of Paintings in the Collection of Jules S. Bache, New York 1937

New York 1933
Recent Social Trends in the United States, New York 1933

New York 1937
Cat. *Paintings by Frans Hals* New York (Schaeffer Galleries) 1937

New York 1937-A
A Catalogue of Paintings in the Bache Collection, New York 1937

New York 1938
Cat. *Masters of Portraiture Lent by Several Collectors* New York (The Century Club) 1938

New York 1941
Cat. *Loan Exhibition in Honor of Royal Cortissoz and His 50 Years of Criticism in the New York Herald Tribune* New York (Knoedler & Co.) 1941

New York 1944
The Metropolitan Museum of Art. Dutch Paintings. A Picture Book, New York 1944

New York 1946
Cat. *Loan Exhibition. 24 Masterpieces* New York (Knoedler & Co.) 1946
New York 1950
Cat. *Rembrandt* New York (Wildenstein & Co.) 1950
New York 1954
Cat. *A Benefit Exhibition of Paintings. A Collectors Taste. Selections from the Collection of Mr. and Mrs. Stephen C. Clark* New York (Knoedler & Co.) 1954
New York 1954-A
Cat. *Loan Exhibition. Magic of Flowers in Painting for the Benefit of The Lenox Hill Neighborhood Association* New York (Wildenstein) 1954
New York 1958
Cat. *Fifty Masterpieces* New York (Wildenstein Galleries) 1958
New York 1958-A
Cat. *The H.O. Havemeyer Collection* New York (The Metropolitan Museum of Art) 1958
New York 1959
Cat. *Masterpieces of The Corcoran Gallery of Art* New York (Wildenstein) 1959
New York 1961
Cat. *Schaeffer Galleries. Twenty-Fifth Anniversary 1936-1961* New York (Schaeffer Galleries) 1961
New York 1965
Cat. *Still Life Painters: Pieter Aertsen (1508-1575) to Georges Braque (1882-1963)* New York (Finch College Museum of Art) 1965
New York 1968
The Frick Collection. An Illustrated Catalogue. Vol. 1. Paintings. American, British, Dutch, Flemish and German, New York 1968
New York 1973
Cat. *Abraham Bloemaert. 1564-1651. Prints and Drawings* New York (The Metropolitan Museum of Art) 1973
New York 1973-A
Cat. *Dutch Couples. Pair Portraits by Rembrandt and His Contemporaries* New York (The Metropolitan Museum of Art) 1973
New York 1975
Cat. *The Metropolitan Museum of Art. Notable Acquisitions 1965-1975* New York (The Metropolitan Museum of Art) 1975
New York 1985
Cat. *Landscape Painting in Rome, 1595-1675* New York (Richard L. Feigen & Co.) 1985
New York 1987
Cat. *The American Paradise: The World of the Hudson River School* New York (The Metropolitan Museum of Art) 1987
New York etc. 1954-1955
Cat. *Dutch Painting in the Golden Age. An Exhibition of Dutch Pictures of the Seventeenth Century* New York (The Metropolitan Museum of Art) Toledo, Ohio (The Toledo Museum of Art) Toronto (The Art Gallery of Ontario) 1954-1955

New York etc. 1973-1975
Cat. *Paintings from Midwestern University Collections. Seventeenth–Twentieth Centuries* New York (Wildenstein & Co.) Columbus, Ohio (Ohio State University) 1973-1975
New York / Palm Beach 1957
Cat. *Paintings and Sculpture from The Minneapolis Institute of Arts. A Loan Exhibition* New York (The Knoedler Galleries) Palm Beach, Fla. (The Society of the Four Arts) 1957
Nichols 1985
L.W. Nichols, 'Onsterfelijkheid in smetteloos naakt,' *Kunstschrift. Openbaar Kunstbezit* 29 (1985), pp. 154-161
Nicolle 1908
M. Nicolle, 'La Collection Rodolphe Kann,' *La revue de l'art* 23 (1908), vol. I, pp. 197-204
Nicolson 1952
B. Nicolson, 'Caravaggio and the Netherlands,' *The Burlington Magazine* 94 (1952), pp. 247-252
Nicolson 1956
B. Nicolson, 'The Rijksmuseum "Incredulity" and Terbrugghen's Chronology,' *The Burlington Magazine* 98 (1956), pp. 103-110
Nicolson 1958
B. Nicolson, 'Further Notes on the Sweerts Exhibition,' *The Burlington Magazine* 100 (1958), p. 441
Nicolson 1958-A
B. Nicolson, *Hendrick Terbrugghen*, London 1958
Nicolson 1958-B
B. Nicolson, 'Terbrugghen's *Old Man Writing*,' *Smith College Museum of Art Bulletin* (1958), no. 38, pp. 52-57
Nicolson 1960
B. Nicolson, 'Second Thoughts about Terbrugghen,' *The Burlington Magazine* 102 (1960), pp. 465-473
Nicolson 1962
B. N[icolson], 'Current and Forthcoming Exhibitions,' *The Burlington Magazine* 104 (1962), pp. 310-313
Nicolson 1962-A
B. Nicolson, 'A Postscript to Baburen,' *The Burlington Magazine* 104 (1962), pp. 539-543
Nicolson 1977
B. Nicolson, 'Stomer Brought Up-to-Date,' *The Burlington Magazine* 119 (1977), pp. 230-245
Nicolson 1979
B. Nicolson, *The International Caravaggesque Movement*, Oxford 1979
Niemeijer 1973
J.W. Niemeijer, *Cornelis Troost. 1696-1750*, Assen 1973
Niemeijer 1978
J.W. Niemeijer, 'A Conversation Piece by Aert Schouman and the Founders of the Hope Collection,' *Apollo* (1978), September, pp. 182-189
Niemeijer 1981
J.W. Niemeijer, 'De kunstverzameling van John Hope (1737-1784),' *Nederlands Kunsthistorisch Jaarboek* 32 (1981), pp. 127-232

Nienhuis 1976
H.S. Nienhuis, *Catalogus schilderijen – aquarellen en etsen. Verzameling B. de Geus van den Heuvel Nieuwersluis*, Amsterdam 1976
Van Nierop 1936
L. van Nierop, 'Het dagboek van Jacob Bicker Raye,' *Amstelodamum. Jaarboek* 33 (1936), pp. 172-242
Van Nieulant 1624
W. van Nieulant, *Aegyptica ofte Aegyptische tragoedie ...*, Antwerp 1624
Nieuwenhuys 1834
C.J. Nieuwenhuys, *A Review of the Lives and Works of Some of the Most Eminent Painters: with Remarks on the Opinions and Statements of Former Writers*, London 1834
Nieuwe Courant 1914
'De Steengracht-schilderijen in het Mauritshuis,' *De Nieuwe Courant* 8 April 1914, 'Eerste bijblad van het avondblad,' n.p.
Nieuws van den Dag 1913
'Een Rembrandt heroverd,' *Het Nieuws van den Dag* 1 November 1913 (Knipselboek 1885-1927, p. 40, documentation archives Mauritshuis, The Hague)
Nihom-Nijstad 1983
S. Nihom-Nijstad, cat. *Reflets du siècle d'or. Tableaux hollandais du dix-septième siècle* Paris (Institut Néerlandais) 1983
Nijland 10-6-1907
H. Nijland, 'Collectie Six,' *Het Vaderland* 6 October 1907, 'Ochtendblad,' n.p.
Nijland 10-11-1907
H. Nijland, 'De Collectie-Six,' *Het Vaderland* 11 October 1907, 'Tweede avondblad,' p. B
Nimmons 1923
G.C. Nimmons, *The Need of Art Training in College and Its Application in After Life* (United States Bureau of Education, Higher Education Circular, no. 27), n.p. October 1923
Noach 1937
A. Noach, *Het materiaal tot de geschiedenis der Oude Kerk te Amsterdam*, Amsterdam 1937
NNBW
Nieuw Nederlandsch Biografisch Woordenboek (10 vols. and register), Amsterdam 1974 (1st edition Leyden 1911-1937)
Noblesse Belge 1897
'De Robiano' in: *La Noblesse Belge. Annuaire de 1897* (1897), pp. 2021-2023
Noblesse Belge 1912
'De Robiano' in: *La Noblesse Belge. Annuaire de 1912* (1912), pp. 394-396
Noë 1954
H. Noë, *Carel van Mander en Italië. Beschouwingen en notities naar aanleiding van zijn 'Leven der dees-tijtsche doorluchtighe Italiaensche schilders,'* The Hague 1954
Norfolk 1982
Cat. *The Discovery of the Everyday: Seventeenth Century Dutch Paintings from the Wolf Collection* Norfolk, Va. (The Chrysler Museum) 1982

Northampton 1986
A Guide to the Collections. Smith College Museum of Art, Northampton, Mass. 1986

Norwich 1966
Cat. *Dutch Paintings from East Anglia. Loan Exhibition* Norwich (Norwich Castle Museum) 1966

Notre Dame 1967
Handbook of the Collections. Art Gallery, University of Notre Dame, Notre Dame, Ind. 1967

Notulenboek Rembrandt
Notulenboeken van het Dagelijks Bestuur van de Vereniging Rembrandt (Secretarial Office of the Rembrandt Society, The Hague)

NRC 7-8-1905
'Schilderijendiefstal,' *Nieuwe Rotterdamsche Courant* 8 July 1905, 'Eerste blad,' p. C

NRC 7-30-1905
'De gestolen Frans Hals terug,' *Nieuwe Rotterdamsche Courant* 30 July 1905, 'Eerste blad,' p. B2, 'Tweede blad,' p. 2

NRC 9-26-1907
'De Collectie-Six,' *Nieuwe Rotterdamsche Courant* 26 September 1907, 'Eerste blad,' p. B3

NRC 27-9-1907
'Six en Pacca,' *Nieuwe Rotterdamsche Courant* 27 September 1907, 'Eerste blad,' p. B2

NRC 10-21-1909
'Hollandsche kunst naar Amerika (Particuliere correspondentie),' *Nieuwe Rotterdamsche Courant* 21 October 1909, 'Ochtendblad,' p. A1

NRC 10-26-1909
'Leuk,' *Nieuwe Rotterdamsche Courant* 26 October 1909, 'Avondblad,' p. A1

NRC 11-4-1909
'Indrukken uit Amerika. Een onderhoud met Dr. C. Hofstede de Groot,' *Nieuwe Rotterdamsche Courant* 4 November 1909, 'Avondblad,' p. A1

NRC 6-9-1913
'Het einde van de Steengracht-verzameling,' *Nieuwe Rotterdamsche Courant* 9 June 1913, 'Avondblad,' p. B1

NRC 6-10-1913
'De veiling Steengracht'; 'Veiling Steengracht'; 'De veiling Steengracht en de Vereeniging Rembrandt,' *Nieuwe Rotterdamsche Courant* 10 June 1913, 'Avondblad,' p. B1

NRC 1915
'P.A.B. Widener †,' *Nieuwe Rotterdamsche Courant* 13 November 1915, 'Avondblad,' p. B1

Nuremberg 1893
Katalog der im Germanischen Museum befindlichen Gemälde, Nuremberg 1893

Nuremberg 1909
Katalog der Gemälde-Sammlung des germanischen Nationalmuseums in Nürnberg, Nuremberg 1909

Ny Illustrerad Tidning 1892
'Rembrandts tafla,' *Ny Illustrerad Tidning* 28 (1892), no. 38, p. 311

NYT 1945
'John McCormack, Noted Tenor, Dies,' *The New York Times* 17 September 1945, pp. 21 and 23

NYT 1966
'A Lady Writing,' *The New York Times* 14 May 1966

Oberhuber 1979
K. Oberhuber (ed.), cat. *Old Master Drawings. Selections from the Charles A. Loeser Bequest* Cambridge, Mass. (Fogg Art Museum) 1979

Oberhuber / Robinson 1984
K. Oberhuber & W. Robinson (eds.), cat. *Master Drawings and Watercolors, the Hofer Collection* Cambridge, Mass. (Fogg Art Museum) 1984

Oberlin 1967
Catalogue of European and American Paintings and Sculpture in the Allen Memorial Art Museum, Oberlin, Ohio 1967

O'Brien 1986
M.C. O'Brien, cat. *In Support of Liberty: European Paintings at the 1883 Pedestal Fund Art Loan Exhibition* Southampton, N.Y. (The Parrish Art Museum) 1986

ÖBL
Österreichisches Biographisches Lexikon 1815-1950 (9 vols.), Vienna 1957-1988

Van Oerle 1975
H.A. van Oerle, *Leiden binnen en buiten de stadsvesten* (2 vols.), Leyden 1975

Ohl Godwin 1953
M. Ohl Godwin, *Master Works in the Toledo Museum of Art Founded by Edward Drummond Libbey*, Toledo, Ohio 1953

Olson 1986
S. Olson, *John Singer Sargent: His Portrait*, New York 1986

Onze Kunst 1928
'Amsterdam. Verzameling Six,' *Onze Kunst* 24 (1928), pp. 231-232

Ormond 1970
R. Ormond, *John Singer Sargent*, New York 1970

Oslo 1959
Cat. *Fra Rembrandt til Vermeer* Oslo (Nasjonalgalleriet) 1959

Oswald 1938
A. Oswald, 'Paultons, Romsey, Hampshire,' *Country Life* 84 (1938), 17 September, pp. 276-281

Ota / Takahashi 1985
H. Ota & T. Takahashi, *Vermeer*, n.p. 1985

Otte 1987
M. Otte, ' "Somtijts een Moor." De neger als bijfiguur op Nederlandse portretten in de zeventiende en achttiende eeuw,' *Kunstlicht* 8 (1987), no. 3, pp. 6-10

Van Overbeek 1935
J.M.C. van Overbeek, 'Jan Vermeer en zijn Delftsche omgeving. Naar aanleiding van de tentoonstelling in het nieuwe Boymansmuseum,' *Elsevier's Geïllustreerd Maandschrift* 45 (1935), pp. 231-238

Oxford 1920
University of Oxford, Ashmolean Museum. Summary Guide, Oxford 1920 (3rd edition)

Pach 1940
W. Pach, cat. *Masterpieces of Art. Catalogue of European & American Paintings, 1500-1900* New York (New York's World Fair) 1940

Palmer / Holton 1934
A.M. Palmer & G. Holton, *College Instruction in Art* (Association of American Colleges), New York 1934

Panofsky 1933
E. Panofsky, 'Der gefesselte Eros (Zur Genealogie von Rembrandts Danae),' *Oud Holland* 50 (1933), pp. 193-217

Panofsky 1955
E. Panofsky, *Meaning in the Visual Arts*, Garden City, N.Y. 1955

Pantheon 1928
'Kunstliteratur. Amerika,' *Pantheon* 8 (1928), pp. 296-271

Pantheon 1935
'Rundschau,' *Pantheon* 15 (1935), pp. 146-150

Paris 1892
Cat. *Cent chefs-d'oeuvre des écoles françaises et étrangères* (deuxième exposition) Paris (Galerie Georges Petit) 1892

Paris 1898
Illustrated Catalogue of 300 Paintings by Old Masters Paris (Sedelmeyer Gallery) 1898

Paris 1911
Cat. *Exposition des grands et petits maîtres hollandais du XVIIe siècle* Paris (Jeu de Paume) 1911

Paris 1921
Exposition hollandaise. Tableaux, aquarelles et dessins anciens et modernes Paris (Orangerie des Tuileries) 1921

Paris 1950
Cat. *Le paysage hollandais au XVIIe siècle* Paris (Orangerie des Tuileries) 1950

Paris 1952
Cat. *La nature morte de l'antiquité à nos jours* Paris (Orangerie des Tuileries) 1952

Paris 1970-1971
Cat. *Le siècle de Rembrandt. Tableaux hollandais des collections publiques françaises* Paris (Musée du Petit Palais) 1970-1971

Paris 1989
Les donateurs du Louvre Paris (Réunion des musées nationaux) 1989

Parks 1957
R.O. Parks, 'Smith College Museum. Recent Acquisitions,' *College Art Journal* 17 (1957), no. 1, Fall, pp. 73-75

Parrish 1980
D. Parrish, cat. *Old Students and Old Masters: The School of Rembrandt. Selections from the Bader Collection* West Lafayette, Ind. (Union Gallery, Purdue University) 1980

Parthey 1863-1864
G. Parthey, *Deutscher Bildersaal. Verzeichnis der in Deutschland vorhandenen Oelbilder verstorbener Maler aller Schulen. In alphabetischer Folge zusammengestellt* (2 vols.), Berlin 1863-1864

Passavant 1833
J.D. Passavant, *Kunstreise durch England und Belgien nebst einem Bericht über den Bau des Domthurms zu Frankfurt am Main*, Frankfurt am Main 1833

Pauly 1964-1975
Der kleine Pauly. Lexikon der Antike ... (5 vols.), Stuttgart 1964-1975

De Pauw-de Veen 1969
L. de Pauw-de Veen, *De begrippen 'schilder,' 'schilderij' en 'schilderen' in de zeventiende eeuw*, Brussels 1969

Pauwels 1953
H. Pauwels, 'De schilder Matthias Stomer,' *Gentse bijdragen tot de kunstgeschiedenis* 14 (1953), pp. 139-192

Pavière 1962
S.H. Pavière, *A Dictionary of Flower, Fruit, and Still Life Painters. Vol. 1. 15th-17th Centuries*, Amsterdam 1962

Van Peer 1968
A.J.J.M. van Peer, 'Jan Vermeer van Delft: drie archiefvondsten,' *Oud Holland* 83 (1968), pp. 220-224

Peeters / Fleurbaay 1989
J. Peeters & E. Fleurbaay, '16de en 17de-eeuwse topografische voorstellingen en het standpunt van de kunstenaar,' *Bulletin [...] Nederlandschen Oudheidkundigen Bond* 88 (1989), no. 5, pp. 30-41

Pelinck 1953
E. Pelinck, 'Paulus van Spijk en zijn verzameling,' *Jaarboekje voor geschiedenis en oudheidkunde van Leiden en omstreken* 45 (1953), pp. 120-123

Pels 1681
A. Pels, *Gebruik èn misbruik des tooneels*, Amsterdam 1681

Pepys 1970-1983
R. Latham & W. Matthews (eds.), *The Diary of Samuel Pepys* (10 vols. and index), London 1970-1983

Perkins / Gavin 1980
R.F. Perkins, Jr. & W.J. Gavin III, *The Boston Atheneum, Art Exhibition Index 1827-1874*, Boston, Mass. 1980

Perlove 1989
S. Perlove, cat. *Impressions of Faith: Rembrandt's Biblical Etchings* Dearborn, Mich. (Mardigan Library, University of Michigan) 1989

Pers 1662
D.P. Pers, *Bellerophon, of lust tot wysheyt: Door sinne-beelden leerlijck vertoont ...*, Amsterdam 1662

Pevsner 1963
N. Pevsner, *Wiltshire* (The Buildings of England XXVI), Harmondsworth 1963

Pevsner 1969
N. Pevsner, *Lancashire. 2. The Rural North*, Harmondsworth 1969

Philadelphia 1941
John G. Johnson Collection. Catalogue of Paintings, Philadelphia, Pa. 1941

Philadelphia 1953
Johnson Collection. Two Hundred and Eighty-Eight Reproductions. Italian, Dutch, Flemish, German, Spanish, French, English & 19th Century Paintings, Philadelphia, Pa. 1953

Philadelphia 1965
Check List of Paintings in the Philadelphia Museum of Art, Philadelphia, Pa. 1965

Philadelphia 1972
John G. Johnson Collection. Catalogue of Flemish and Dutch Paintings, Philadelphia, Pa. 1972

Philadelphia / Berlin / London 1984
P. Sutton et al., cat. *Masters of Seventeenth-Century Dutch Genre Painting* Philadelphia, Pa. (Philadelphia Museum of Art) Berlin (Gemäldegalerie, Staatliche Museen Preussischer Kulturbesitz) London (Royal Academy of Arts) 1984

Pigler 1955
A. Pigler, 'Gruppenbildnisse mit historisch verkleideten Figuren und ein Hauptwerk des Joannes van Noordt,' *Acta Historiae Artium Academiae Scientiarum Hungaricae* 2 (1955), pp. 169-187

Pigler 1956
A. Pigler, *Barockthemen* (2 vols.), Budapest 1956

Pigler 1968
A. Pigler, *Katalog der Galerie alter Meister* (2 vols.) Budapest (Szépmüvészeti Múzeum) 1968

Pigler 1974
A. Pigler, *Barockthemen* (3 vols.), Budapest 1974

Plietzsch 1911
E. Plietzsch, *Vermeer van Delft*, Leipzig 1911

Plietzsch 1914
E. Plietzsch, 'Dujardin (Du Jardin, Du Gardijn), Karel' in: *Thieme / Becker*, vol. X (1914), pp. 102-104

Plietzsch 1936
E. Plietzsch, 'Gabriel Metsu,' *Pantheon* 18 (1936), January, pp. 1-13

Plietzsch 1939
E. Plietzsch, *Vermeer van Delft*, Munich 1939

Plietzsch 1944
E. Plietzsch, *Gerard ter Borch*, Vienna 1944

Plietzsch 1960
E. Plietzsch, *Holländische und flämische Maler des XVII. Jahrh.*, Leipzig 1960

Ploos van Amstel 1771
C. Ploos van Amstel, 'Berigt [...] aan de beminnaaren der schilderkunst,' *Nieuwe Vaderlandsche Letteroefeningen* (1771), vol. V / II, pp. 139-147

Poch-Kalous 1968
M. Poch-Kalous, *Die Gemäldegalerie der Akademie der bildenden Künste in Wien*, Vienna 1968

Poirters 1646 / 1714
A. Poirters, *Het masker van de wereldt afgetrocken*, Antwerp 1714 (1st edition 1646)

Polesden Lacey 1964
Polesden Lacey. The National Trust, Plaistow 1964

Pope-Hennessy 1984
J. Pope-Hennessy, *The Jack and Belle Linsky Collection in The Metropolitan Museum of Art*, New York 1984

Popovitch 1967
O. Popovitch, *Catalogue des peintures du Musée des Beaux Arts de Rouen*, Paris 1967

Porkay 1963
M. Porkay, *Die Abenteuer zweier unechter Rembrandts*, Munich 1963

Potterton 1986
H. Potterton, *Dutch Seventeenth- and Eighteenth-Century Paintings in the National Gallery of Ireland. A Complete Catalogue*, Dublin 1986

Poughkeepsie 1967
Cat. *Selections from the Permanent Collection* Poughkeepsie, N.Y. (Vassar College Art Gallery) 1967

Poughkeepsie 1983
Vassar College Art Gallery. Paintings 1300-1900. A Complete Illustrated List of Works in the Art Gallery's Collection, Poughkeepsie, N.Y. 1983

Prague 1971
Cat. *Sbìrka starého umeni* Prague (Národní Galerie) 1971

Praz 1971
M. Praz, *Conversation Pieces: A Survey of the Informal Group Portrait in Europe and America*, London 1971

Preyer 1909
D.C. Preyer, *The Art of the Metropolitan Museum of New York*, Boston, Mass. 1909

Princeton 1986
Selections from the Art Museum, Princeton University, Princeton, N.J. 1986

Prisco / De Vecchi 1966 / 1979
M. Prisco & P. de Vecchi, *L'opera completa di Raffaello* Milan 1979 (1st edition 1966)

Providence 1956
Cat. *Treasures in the Museum of Art* Providence, R.I. (Rhode Island School of Design) 1956

Puraye 1956
J. Puraye, *Dominique Lampson. Les effigies des peintres célèbres des Pays-Bas*, n.p. 1956

Van Puyvelde 1929
L. van Puyvelde, 'Hollandsche kunst te Londen,' *Onze Kunst* 25 (1929), pp. 151-169

Van Puyvelde 1941
L. van Puyvelde, 'The Taste of John G. Johnson, Collector,' *The Art News* 40 (1941), November, pp. 15-20 and 36

Van Puyvelde 1944
L. van Puyvelde, *The Dutch Drawings in the Collection of His Majesty the King at Windsor Castle*, London / New York 1944

Quakers mondstopper 1659
[*De Quakers mondstopper ...*] *Wert in Druck vijtgegeven tot respect en reputatie van den manhafften capitejn Joris de Caulerii*, Copenhagen n.d. (1659)

Quimby 1971
I. Quimby (ed.), *American Painting to 1776. A Reappraisal* (Winterthur Conference Report 1971), Charlottesville, Va. 1971

Ten Raa / De Bas 1911-1950
F.J.G. ten Raa & F. de Bas, *Het staatsche leger. 1568-1795* (7 vols.), Breda 1911-1950

Rademaker 1725
A. Rademaker, *Kabinet van Nederlandsche outheden en gezichten ...*, Amsterdam 1725

Raleigh 1959
Cat. *Masterpieces of Art* Raleigh, N.C. (North Carolina Museum of Art) 1959

Raleigh 1983
Cat. *Introduction to the Collections* Raleigh, N.C. (North Carolina Museum of Art) 1983

Raleigh 1986-1987
Cat. *Dutch Art in the Age of Rembrandt* Raleigh, N.C. (North Carolina Museum of Art) 1986-1987

Raupp 1978
H.-J. Raupp, 'Musik im Atelier. Darstellungen musizierender Künstler in der niederländischen Malerei des 17. Jahrhunderts,' *Oud Holland* 92 (1978), pp. 106-129

Raupp 1984
H.-J. Raupp, *Untersuchungen zu Künstlerbildnis und Künstlerdarstellung in den Niederlanden im 17. Jahrhundert* (Studien zur Kunstgeschichte xxv), Hildesheim / Zürich / New York 1984

Réau 1955-1959
L. Réau, *Iconographie de l'art chrétien* (3 vols.), Paris 1955-1959

Recueil Choiseul 1771
Recueil d'estampes gravées d'après les tableaux du cabinet de Monseigneur le Duc de Choiseul, Paris 1771

Redford 1888
G. Redford, *Art Sales. A History of Sales of Pictures and Other Works of Art ...* (2 vols.), London 1888

Redmond 1981
E. Redmond, 'The Codman Collection of Pictures,' *Old-Time New England* 71 (1981), pp. 103-114

De Regt 1986
E. de Regt, *Monumenten in Den Haag*, The Hague 1986

Van Regteren Altena 1959
I.Q. van Regteren Altena, 'Over Michael Sweerts als portrettist,' *Oud Holland* 74 (1959), pp. 222-224

Van Regteren Altena 1972
I.Q. van Regteren Altena, cat. *Cent dessins du Musée Teyler Haarlem* Paris (Musée du Louvre) 1972

Reinewald 1987
C. Reinewald, 'Musea en Galeries in Amerika. Het Getty Museum: een Romeinse villa aan de Pacific Coast,' *Tableau* 9 (1987), no. 4, pp. 64-66

Reiss 1975
S. Reiss, *Aelbert Cuyp*, London 1975

Reiss 1978
S. Reiss, 'The Old Guardhouse by Aelbert Cuyp,' *The Burlington Magazine* 120 (1978), pp. 87-89

Reitlinger 1982
G. Reitlinger, *The Economics of Taste. The Rise and Fall of Picture Prices 1760-1960* (3 vols.), New York 1982

Renckens / Duyvetter 1959
B.J.A. Renckens & J. Duyvetter, 'De vrouw van Gabriel Metsu, Isabella de Wolff, geboortig van Enkhuizen,' *Oud Holland* 74 (1959), pp. 179-182

Rendell Head 1879
P. Rendell Head, *Van Dyck*, London 1879

Residentie Bode 1910
De Residentie Bode 3 January 1910 (Knipselboek 1885-1927, p. 56, documentation archives Mauritshuis, Den Haag)

Reuterswärd 1956
P. Reuterswärd, 'Tavelförhänget. Kring ett motiv i holländskt 1600-talsmåleri,' *Konsthistorisk tidskrift* 25 (1956), pp. 97-113

Reuterswärd 1980
P. Reuterswärd, 'Om realismen i holländsk bildtradition,' *Konsthistorisk tidskrift* 49 (1980), pp. 1-16

Reynolds / Malone 1971
J. Reynolds, *The Works. Edited by Edmond Malone (1797)* (2 vols.), Hildesheim / New York 1971

Reznicek 1961
E.K.J. Reznicek, *Die Zeichnungen von Hendrick Goltzius* (2 vols.), Utrecht 1961

Reznicek 1986
E.K.J. Reznicek, 'Hendrick Goltzius and His Conception of Landscape' in: *Brown 1986*, pp. 57-62

Reznicek-Buriks 1956
E.J. Reznicek-Buriks, 'Enkele maniëristische tekeningen uit de verzameling De Grez,' *Oud Holland* 71 (1956), pp. 165-170

Rich 1935
D.C. Rich, 'Rembrandt Remains,' *Parnassus* 7 (1935), October, pp. 2-5

Rich 1953
D.C. Rich, 'In a Minor Key,' *The Art Institute of Chicago Quarterly* 47 (1953), no. 2, pp. 30-34

Richardson 1937
E.P. Richardson, 'Hals. An Important Showing,' *Parnassus* 9 (1937), pp. 4-7

Richmond 1961
Cat. *Treasures in America* Richmond, Va. (The Virginia Museum of Fine Arts) 1961

Richmond 1966
European Art in the Virginia Museum of Fine Arts. A Catalogue, Richmond, Va. 1966

Richter 1894
J.P. Richter, 'Versteigerung der Adrian Hope-Sammlung in Londen,' *Repertorium für Kunstwissenschaft* 17 (1894), pp. 331-333

Van Riemsdijk 1892
B.W.F. van Riemsdijk, 'Schilderijen-kabinetten in de xviiie eeuw,' *Oud Holland* 10 (1892), pp. 219-228

Van Riemsdijk 1900
B.W.F. van Riemsdijk, 'De collectie-Six,' *Eigen Haard* (1900), pp. 440-443

Rifkin 1969
B.A. Rifkin, 'Rembrandt and His Circle. Part 3,' *Art News* 68 (1969), November, pp. 30-33 and 89-91

Rigby / Rigby 1944
D. & E. Rigby, *Lock, Stock and Barrel. The Story of Collecting*, Philadelphia, Pa. / New York / London 1944

Van Rijckevorsel 1932
J.L.A.A.M. van Rijckevorsel, *Rembrandt en de traditie* (diss. Nijmegen), Rotterdam 1932

Ripa / Pers 1644
C. Ripa (ed. D.P. Pers), *Iconologia of uytbeeldingen des verstands ...*, Amsterdam 1644

Ritchie 1966
A.C. Ritchie, *The Visual Arts in Higher Education: A Study Prepared for the College Art Association of America, under a Grant from the Ford Foundation*, New Haven, Conn. 1966

RKD
Rijksbureau voor Kunsthistorische Documentatie, The Hague

Roberts 1897
W. Roberts, *Memorials of Christie's. A Record of Art Sales from 1766 to 1896* (2 vols.), London 1897

Roberts 1907
W. Roberts, *Pictures in the Collection of J. Pierpont Morgan at Prince's Gate & Dover House, London*, London 1907

Roberts 1909
W. Roberts, ' "The King of the Belgians," Collection of Old Masters,' *The Connoisseur* 24 (1909), August, pp. 203-210

Robinson 1958
M.S. Robinson, *Van de Velde Drawings. A Catalogue of Drawings in the National Maritime Museum by the Elder and the Younger Willem van de Velde*, Cambridge 1958

Robinson 1969
F.W. Robinson, 'The Banquet of Antony and Cleopatra,' *The Currier Gallery of Art Bulletin* (1969), October-December, n.p.

Robinson 1969-A
F.W. Robinson, cat. *Selections from the Collection of Dutch Drawings of Maida & George Abrams. A Loan Exhibition* Wellesley, Mass. (Wellesley College Museum) 1969

Robinson 1970
F.W. Robinson, 'The Banquet of Anthony and Cleopatra by Jan de Bray,' *Apollo* (1970), October, pp. 284-285

Robinson 1974
F.W. Robinson, *Gabriel Metsu (1629-1667). A Study of His Place in Dutch Genre Painting of the Golden Age*, New York 1974

Robinson 1974-A
M.S. Robinson, *Van de Velde Drawings. A Catalogue of Drawings in the National Maritime Museum Made by the Elder and the Younger Willem van de Velde. Volume 11*, Cambridge 1974

Robinson 1982
F.W. Robinson, cat. *The Discovery of the Everyday: Seventeenth-Century Dutch Paintings from the Wolf Collection* Norfolk, Va. (The Chrysler Museum, Norfolk Museum of Art) Providence, R.I. (Rhode Island School of Design) Tampa, Fla. (The Tampa Museum) 1982

Robinson 1984
W. Robinson, 'The Sacrifice of Isaac: An Unpublished Painting by Nicolaes Maes,' *The Burlington Magazine* 126 (1984), pp. 540-544

Robinson 1985
F.W. Robinson, *Gabriel Metsu: The Letter* San Diego, Calif. (Timken Art Gallery) 1985

Robinson et al. 1980
F.W. Robinson, W.H. Wilson & L. Silver, *Catalogue of the Flemish and Dutch Paintings 1400-1900* Sarasota, Fla. (The John and Mable Ringling Museum of Art) 1980

Robinson / Weber 1979
M.S. Robinson & R.E.J. Weber, *The Willem van de Velde Drawings in the Boymans-van Beuningen Museum Rotterdam* (3 vols.), Rotterdam 1979

Roding 1986
J. Roding, *Schoon en net. Hygiëne in woning en stad*, The Hague 1986

Roemer Visscher 1614
A. Roemers, *Roemer Visschers Zinnepoppen. Alle verziert met rijmen, en sommighe met proze, door zijn dochter Anna Roemers*, Amsterdam 1614

Roemer Visscher / Brummel 1614 / 1949
L. Brummel, *Sinnepoppen van Roemer Visscher*, The Hague 1949 (1st edition 1614)

Röthlisberger 1967
M. Röthlisberger, 'Abraham Bloemaert' in: *Vienna 1967*, pp. 15-26

Roethlisberger 1969
M. Roethlisberger, *Bartholomäus Breenbergh. Handzeichnungen*, Berlin 1969

Roethlisberger 1981
M. Roethlisberger, *Bartholomeus Breenbergh. The Paintings*, Berlin / New York 1981

Roland Holst 1907
R.N. R[oland] H[olst], 'De collectie-Six,' *Het Volk* 5 October 1907, 'Eerste blad,' n.p.

Rome 1956-1957
Cat. *Le XVIIe siècle européen. Réalisme classicisme baroque* Rome (Palazzo degli Esposizioni) 1956-1957

Rome 1958-1959
Cat. *Michael Sweerts e i bamboccianti* Rome (Palazzo Venezia) 1958-1959

Rooses 1886-1892
M. Rooses, *L'oeuvre de P.P. Rubens* (5 vols.), Antwerp 1886-1892

Rosenberg 1897
A. Rosenberg, *Terborch und Jan Steen*, Bielefeld / Leipzig 1897

Rosenberg 1928
J. Rosenberg, *Jacob van Ruisdael*, Berlin 1928

Rosenberg 1982
P. Rosenberg, cat., *France in the Golden Age: Seventeenth-Century French Paintings in American Collections* New York (The Metropolitan Museum of Art) Paris (Grand Palais) Chicago, Ill. (The Art Institute of Chicago) 1982

Rosenberg / Slive / Ter Kuile 1966
J. Rosenberg, S. Slive & E.H. ter Kuile, *Dutch Art and Architecture. 1600-1800*, Harmondsworth 1966

Rosenblum 1955
R. Rosenblum, 'The Kress Collection: Past and Future,' *The Art Digest* (1955), March, pp. 16 and 23

Rotgans / Strengholt 1708 / 1968
L. Rotgans (introduction and annotations by L. Strengholt), *Boerekermis*, Gorinchem 1968 (1st edition Amsterdam 1708)

Rotterdam 1771
Kabinet van schilderijen, berustende, onder den heere Jan Bisschop, te Rotterdam, Rotterdam 1771

Rotterdam 1935
Cat. *Vermeer. Oorsprong en invloed. Fabritius, De Hooch, De Witte* Rotterdam (Museum Boymans) 1935

Rotterdam 1938
Cat. *Meesterwerken uit vier eeuwen 1400-1800* Rotterdam (Museum Boymans) 1938

Rotterdam 1938-1939
Catalogus schilderijen, teekeningen en beeldhouwwerken uit particuliere Nederlandsche verzamelingen Rotterdam (Museum Boymans) 1938-1939

Rotterdam 1955
Cat. *Kunstschatten uit Nederlandse verzamelingen* Rotterdam (Museum Boymans) 1955

Rotterdam 1958
Cat. *Michael Sweerts en tijdgenoten* Rotterdam (Museum Boymans) 1958

Rotterdam 1962
Catalogus schilderijen tot 1800 Rotterdam (Museum Boymans-van Beuningen) 1962

Rotterdam 1969
Cat. *Portretten van kunstenaars 1500-1800* Rotterdam (Museum Boymans-van Beuningen) 1969

Rotterdam 1972
Cat. *Old Paintings 1400-1900. Illustrations* Rotterdam (Museum Boymans-van Beuningen) 1972

Rotterdam 1978
Cat. *Legaat Vitale Bloch* Rotterdam (Museum Boymans-van Beuningen) 1978

Rotterdam 1986-1987
Cat. *In het spoor van de Liefde. Japans-Nederlandse ontmoetingen sinds 1600* Rotterdam (Museum voor Volkenkunde) 1986-1987

Rotterdamsch Nieuwsblad 1905
'De portret-koop,' *Rotterdamsch Nieuwsblad* 14 July 1905, 'Derde blad,' n.p.

Rouchès 1924
G. Rouchès, 'La collection De Ridder,' *L'Illustration* (1924), 31 May, pp. 525-530

Rowe 1921
L.E. Rowe, 'A Painting by Aert de Gelder,' *Bulletin of the Rhode Island School of Design* 9 (1921), pp. 38-40

Roy 1972
R. Roy, *Studien zu Gerbrand van den Eeckhout* (diss.), Vienna 1972

De Rudder 1914
A. de Rudder, *Pieter de Hooch et son oeuvre*, Brussels / Paris 1914

Rumpf 1794
J.D.F. Rumpf, *Beschreibung der aeussern und inneren Merkwurdigkeiten der koeniglichen Schlosser in Berlin, Charlottenberg, Schoenhausen, in und bey Potsdam*, Berlin 1794

Russell 1989
W.M.J. Russell et al., *De regelen der kunst. Drie opstellen over de verhouding tussen kunst en recht*, Amsterdam 1989

Rutledge 1949
A.W. Rutledge, 'Robert Gilmor, Jr., Baltimore Collector,' *Journal of the Walters Art Gallery* 12 (1949), pp. 18-39

Ruurs 1983
R. Ruurs, ' "Even If It Is Not Architecture": Perspective Drawings by Simon de Vlieger and Willem van de Velde de Younger,' *Simiolus* 13 (1983), pp. 189-200

Van Ryn 1887
G. van Ryn, 'Arent van Buchel's Res Pictoriae. Aanteekeningen betreffende kunst en kunstenaars,' *Oud Holland* 5 (1887), pp. 143-154

Saarinnen 1968
A.B. Saarinen, *The Proud Professors*, New York 1968

Salerno 1977-1978
L. Salerno, *Landscape Painters of the Seventeenth Century in Rome / Pittori di Paesaggio del Seicento a Roma* (3 vols.), Rome 1977-1978

Samuels 1979
E. Samuels, *Bernard Berenson: The Making of a Connoisseur*, Cambridge, Mass. 1979

Samuels 1987
E. Samuels, *Bernard Berenson: The Making of a Legend*, Cambridge, Mass. 1987

Sandrart 1675
J. von Sandrart, ... *Teutsche Academie der Edlen Bau-, Bild- und Mahlerey-Künste* (2 vols.), Nuremberg 1675

San Francisco 1939
Cat. *Masterworks of Five Centuries* San Francisco, Calif. (Golden Gate International Exposition) 1939

San Francisco 1966
European Works of Art in the M.H. de Young Memorial Museum, Berkeley, Calif. 1966

San Francisco 1987
The Fine Arts Museums of San Francisco. Selected Works, San Francisco, Calif. 1987

San Francisco Chronicle 1964
'Museum Patron. Roscoe F. Oakes Is Dead at 92,' *The San Francisco Chronicle* 8 January 1964, p. 26

San Francisco / Toledo / Boston 1966-1967
Cat. *The Age of Rembrandt* San Francisco, Calif. (California Palace of the Legion of Honor) Toledo, Ohio (The Toledo Museum of Art) Boston, Mass. (Museum of Fine Arts) 1966-1967

Sarasota 1976
Catalogue of the Italian Paintings before 1800 Sarasota, Fla. (The John and Mable Ringling Museum of Art) 1976

Sarasota / Hartford 1958
Cat. *A. Everett Austin, Jr.: A Director's Taste and Achievement* Sarasota, Fla. (John and Mable Ringling Museum of Art) Hartford, Conn. (Wadsworth Atheneum) 1958

Schaar 1958
E. Schaar, *Studien zu Nicolaes Berchem* (diss. Hamburg), Cologne 1958

Schaar 1959
E. Schaar, 'Michael Sweerts e i bamboccianti. Ausstellung im Palazzo Venezia in Rom,' *Kunstchronik* 12 (1959), pp. 41-49

Schaefer 1986
S. Schaefer, 'Paintings,' *Apollo* (1986), November, pp. 410-413

Schaefer / Fusco / Wiens 1987
S. Schaefer, P. Fusco & P.-T. Wiens, *European Painting and Sculpture in the Los Angeles County Museum of Art. An Illustrated Summary Catalogue*, Los Angeles, Calif. 1987

Schama 1987
S. Schama, *The Embarrassment of Riches*, New York 1987

Schapelhouman / Schatborn 1987
M. Schapelhouman & P. Schatborn, cat. *Land & water. Hollandse tekeningen uit de 17de eeuw in het Rijksprentenkabinet / Dutch Drawings from the 17th Century in the Rijksmuseum Print Room* Amsterdam (Rijksprentenkabinet) 1987

Schatborn 1974
P. Schatborn, 'Figuurstudies van Nicolaes Berchem,' *Bulletin van het Rijksmuseum* 22 (1974), pp. 3-16

Schatborn 1981-1982
P. Schatborn, cat. *Figuurstudies. Nederlandse tekeningen uit de 17de eeuw* Amsterdam (Rijksprentenkabinet) Washington, D.C. (National Gallery of Art) 1981-1982

Schatborn 1985
P. Schatborn, *Tekeningen van / Drawings by Rembrandt, zijn onbekende leerlingen en navolgers / His Anonymous Pupils and Followers* (Catalogue of the Dutch and Flemish Drawings in the Rijksprentenkabinet, Rijksmuseum, Amsterdam – IV), The Hague 1985

Schatborn / Ornstein-van Slooten 1988-1989
P. Schatborn & E. Ornstein-van Slooten, cat. *Jan Lievens. Prenten & tekeningen. Prints & Drawings* Amsterdam (Rembrandthuis) 1988-1989

Scheen 1970
P.A. Scheen, *Lexicon Nederlandse beeldende kunstenaars 1750-1950*, vol. II, The Hague 1970

Schiedam 1952-1953
Cat. *Schilderijen der Nederlandse- en Franse school uit de verzameling B. de Geus van den Heuvel, Amsterdam. Tweede gedeelte* Schiedam (Stedelijk Museum) 1952-1953

Von Schleinitz 1898-1899
O. van Schleinitz, 'Die Rembrandt-Ausstellung in der Royal-Academy in London,' *Kunstchronik* 10 (1898-1899), new series, cols. 193-197

Schlesinger 1983
A.M. Schlesinger (ed.), *The Almanac of American History*, New York 1983

Schlie 1882
F. Schlie, cat. *Beschreibendes Verzeichnis der Werke älterer Meister in der Grossherzoglichen Gemälde-Gallerie zu Schwerin*, Schwerin 1882

Schloss 1982
C.S. Schloss, *Travel, Trade, and Temptation. The Dutch Italianate Harbor Scene, 1640-1680*, Ann Arbor, Mich. 1982

Schmidt 1981
W. Schmidt, *Studien zur Landschaftskunst Jacob van Ruisdaels. Frühwerke und Wanderjahre* (Studien zur Kunstgeschichte XV), Hildesheim / New York 1981

Schmidt Degener 1908
F. Schmidt Degener, 'Een laatste bezoek aan de verzameling Rodolphe Kann,' *De Gids* 26 (1908), 4th series, vol. I, pp. 343-353

Schmidt Degener 1913
F. S[chmidt] D[egener], 'De verzameling Steengracht,' *Nieuwe Rotterdamse Courant* 18 May 1913, 'Ochtend-blad,' p. A1

Schnackenburg 1981
B. Schnackenburg, *Adriaen van Ostade. Isack van Ostade. Zeichnungen und Aquarelle. Gesamtdarstellung mit Werkkatalogen* (2 vols.), Hamburg 1981

Schneede 1968
U.M. Schneede, 'Gabriel Metsu und der holländische Realismus,' *Oud Holland* 83 (1968), pp. 45-61

Schneider 1919
H. Schneider, 'Der Maler Johan van Swieten,' *Oud Holland* 37 (1919), pp. 223-230

Schneider 1989
N. Schneider, *Stilleben. Realität und Symbolik der Dinge*, Cologne 1989

Schneider / Ekkart 1973
H. Schneider (supplement by R.E.O. Ekkart), *Jan Lievens. Sein Leben und seine Werke*, Amsterdam 1973 (1st edition 1932)

Scholten 1904
H.J. Scholten, *Musée Teyler à Haarlem. Catalogue raisonné des dessins des écoles française et hollandaise*, Haarlem 1904

Schotel 1871
G.D.J. Schotel, *Geschiedenis der rederijkers in Nederland* (2 vols.), Rotterdam 1871

Schotel / Rogge
G.D.J. Schotel (revised by H.C. Rogge), *Het oud-Hollandsch huisgezin der zeventiende eeuw*, Leyden n.d. (2nd edition)

Schrevelius 1648
T. Schreveli[us], *Harlemias, ofte, om beter te seggen, de eerste stichtinghe der stadt Haerlem*, Haarlem 1648

Schröder 1971
T. Schröder, *Jacques Callot. Das gesamte Werk. Handzeichnungen. Druckgraphik* (2 vols.), Munich 1971

Schulte Nordholt 1982
J.W. Schulte Nordholt, *The Dutch Republic and American Independence*, Chapel Hill, N.C. / London 1982 (also a Dutch edition, Baarn 1979)

Schulz 1974
W. Schulz, cat. *Die holländische Landschaftszeichnung 1600-1740* Berlin (Kupferstichkabinett) 1974

Schulz 1982
W. Schulz, *Herman Saftleven 1609-1685. Leben und Werke. Mit einem kritischen Katalog der Gemälde und Zeichnungen*, Berlin / New York 1982

Schulze 1977
F. Schulze, 'A Consistently Discriminating Connoisseurship,' *The Art News* 76 (1977), no. 4, pp. 64-67

Schwartz 1984
G. Schwartz, *Rembrandt. Zijn leven, zijn schilderijen*, Maarssen 1984

Schwartz / Bok 1989
G. Schwartz & M.J. Bok, *Pieter Saenredam. De schilder in zijn tijd*, Maarssen / The Hague 1989

Schweizerisches Geschlechterbuch 1936
'Pourtalès-Gorgier' in: *Schweizerisches Geschlechterbuch. Almanach généalogique suisse*, vol. VI (1936), pp. 529-533

Scott 1987
M.A. Scott, *Dutch, Flemish, and German Paintings in the Cincinnati Art Museum. Fifteenth through Eighteenth Centuries*, Cincinnati, Ohio 1987

Seattle 1962
Catalogue. Masterpieces of Art Seattle, Wash. (Fine Arts Pavilion, Seattle World's Fair) 1962

Segal 1982
S. Segal, cat. *Een bloemrijk verleden. Overzicht van de Noord- en Zuidnederlandse bloemschilderkunst, 1600-heden* Amsterdam (P. de Boer) Den Bosch (Noordbrabants Museum) 1982

Segal 1983
S. Segal, cat. *A Fruitful Past. A Survey of the Fruit Still Lifes of the Northern and Southern Netherlands from Brueghel till Van Gogh* Amsterdam (P. de Boer) Brunswick (Herzog Anton Ulrich-Museum) 1983

Segal 1984
S. Segal, 'Still-Life Painting in Middelburg' in: *Bakker et al. 1984*, pp. 25-95

Segal 1987
S. Segal, 'Exotische bollen als statussymbool,' *Kunstschrift. Openbaar Kunstbezit* 31 (1987), pp. 88-97

Segal 1988-1989
S. Segal, cat. *A Prosperous Past. The Sumptuous Still Life in the Netherlands 1600-1700* Delft (Stedelijk Museum Het Prinsenhof) Cambridge, Mass. (Fogg Art Museum) Fort Worth, Tex. (The Kimbell Art Museum) 1988-1989

Von Seidlitz 1911
W. von Seidlitz, 'Rembrandts Mühle,' *Kunst und Künstler* 9 (1911), pp. 550-552

Seligman 1961
G. Seligman, *Merchants of Art: 1880-1960. Eighty Years of Professional Collecting*, New York 1961

Serwouters 1659 / 1698
J. Serwouters, *Hester oft Verlossing der Jooden*, Amsterdam 1698 (1st edition 1659)

Seymour et al. 1961
C. Seymour, J. Walker & J. Emerson, *Art Treasures for America. An Anthology of Paintings & Sculptures in the Samuel H. Kress Collection*, London 1961

Sharp 1905
E.A. Sharp, *Rembrandt*, New York n.d. (1905)

Sherrill 1976
S.B. Sherrill, 'Oriental Carpets in Seventeenth- and Eighteenth-Century America,' *Antiques* 109 (1976), pp. 142-167

Von Sick 1930
I. von Sick, *Nicolaes Berchem, ein Vorläufer des Rokoko*, Berlin 1930

Simon 1930
K.E. Simon, *Jacob van Ruisdael. Eine Darstellung seiner Entwicklung*, Berlin 1930

Simons 1982
F. Simons, cat. *On Loan from Holland: A Dutch Treat. Selections of XVII and XVIII Century Dutch Art from the Collection of Dr. A.C.R. Dreesmann* Notre Dame, Ind. (Snite Museum of Art) 1982

Simpson 1988
C. Simpson, *The Artful Partners. The Secret Association of Bernard Berenson and Joseph Duveen*, London / Sydney / Wellington 1988

Singer 1937 / 1967
H.W. Singer, *Neuer Bildniskatalog* (4 vols.), Stuttgart / Liechtenstein 1967 (1st edition Leipzig 1937)

Siple 1933
W.H. Siple, 'The Taft Museum,' *Bulletin of the Cincinnati Art Museum* 4 (1933), pp. 2-21

Siple 1937
E.S. Siple, 'Paintings from American Collections Now on Loan in the Frans Hals Museum at Haarlem,' *The Burlington Magazine* 71 (1937), pp. 90-93

Six 1908
J. Six, 'De techniek van Vermeer in "Een Meyd die melk uytgiet",' *Bulletin [...] Nederlandschen Oudheidkundigen Bond* 1 (1908), 2nd series, pp. 1-5

Six 1919
J. Six, 'Bevestigde overlevering,' *Oud Holland* 37 (1919), pp. 80-86

Slatkes 1965
L.J. Slatkes, *Dirck van Baburen, ca. 1595-1624. A Dutch Painter in Utrecht and Rome*, Utrecht 1965

Slatkes 1970
L.J. Slatkes, 'Dutch Mannerism,' *The Art Quarterly* 33 (1970), pp. 420-440

Slatkes 1981
L.J. Slatkes, *Vermeer and His Contemporaries*, New York 1981

Slive 1953
S. Slive, *Rembrandt and His Critics. 1630-1730*, The Hague 1953

Slive 1964
S. Slive, 'Frans Hals Reconsidered,' *Art News Annual* 29 (1964), pp. 50-81 and 154

Slive 1970-1974
S. Slive, *Frans Hals* (3 vols.), London 1970-1974

Slive 1974
S. Slive et al., cat. *European Paintings in the Collection of the Worcester Art Museum* (2 vols.) Worcester, Mass. (Worcester Art Museum) 1974

Slive 1974-1975
S. Slive, 'Address in Honor of Wolfgang Stechow,' *Bulletin of the Allen Memorial Art Museum* 32 (1974-1975), no. 3, pp. 87-93

Slive et al. 1989
S. Slive et al., *Frans Hals* Washington, D.C. (National Gallery of Art) London (Royal Academy of Arts) Haarlem (Frans Halsmuseum) 1989-1990

Slive / Hoetink 1981-1982
S. Slive & H.R. Hoetink, cat. *Jacob van Ruisdael* The Hague (Mauritshuis) Cambridge, Mass. (Fogg Art Museum) 1981-1982

Sluijter 1975
E.J. Sluijter, 'Hendrik Willem Schweickhardt (1746-1797); een Haagse schilder in de tweede helft van de achttiende eeuw,' *Oud Holland* 89 (1975), pp. 142-212

Sluijter 1986
E.J. Sluijter, *De 'heydensche fabulen' in de Noordnederlandse schilderkunst circa 1590-1670* (diss. Leyden), The Hague 1986

Sluijter et al. 1988
E.J. Sluijter, M. Enklaar & P. Nieuwenhuizen, cat. *Leidse fijnschilders. Van Gerrit Dou tot Frans van Mieris de Jonge. 1630-1760* Leyden (Stedelijk Museum De Lakenhal) 1988

Smith 1829-1842
J. Smith, *A Catalogue Raisonné of the Works of the Most Eminent Dutch, Flemish, and French Painters ....* (8 vols. and supplement), London 1829-1842

Smith 1912
E.B. Smith, *The Study of the History of Art in the Colleges and Universities of the United States*, Princeton, N.J. 1912

Smith 1978
D.R. Smith, *The Dutch Double and Pair Portrait: Studies in the Imagery of Marriage in the Seventeenth Century* (diss. Columbia), Ann Arbor, Mich. / London 1978

Smith 1982
D.R. Smith, *Masks of Wedlock. Seventeenth-Century Dutch Marriage Portraiture*, Ann Arbor, Mich. 1982

Smith 1982-A
D.R. Smith, 'Rembrandt's Early Double Portraits and the Dutch Conversation Piece,' *The Art Bulletin* 64 (1982), pp. 259-288

Smith 1982-B
J.S. Smith, *Elsie de Wolfe. A Life in the High Style*, New York 1982

Smith 1986
D.R. Smith, 'Courtesy and Its Discontents: Frans Hals's *Portrait of Isaac Massa and Beatrix van der Laen*,' *Oud Holland* 100 (1986), pp. 2-34

Snoep-Reitsma 1973
E. Snoep-Reitsma, 'Chardin and the Bourgeois Ideals of His Time,' *Nederlands Kunsthistorisch Jaarboek* 24 (1973), pp. 147-243

Snow 1979
E.A. Snow, *A Study of Vermeer*, Berkeley, Calif. 1979

Somof 1895
A. Somof, *Ermitage impérial. Catalogue de la galerie des tableaux. Second volume. Ecoles néerlandaises et école allemande*, Leningrad [Saint Petersburg] 1895

Somof 1901
A. Somof, *Ermitage impérial. Catalogue de la galerie des tableaux. Deuxième partie. Ecoles néerlandaises et école allemande*, Leningrad [Saint Petersburg] 1901

Spear 1971
R.E. Spear, cat. *Caravaggio and His Followers* Cleveland, Ohio (The Cleveland Museum of Art) 1971

Spectator 1877
'Berichten en mededeelingen,' *De Nederlandsche Spectator* (1877), 25 August, p. 265

Spectator 1877-A
'Berichten en mededeelingen,' *De Nederlandsche Spectator* (1877), 10 November, pp. 353-355

Spectator 1878
'Berichten en mededeelingen,' *De Nederlandsche Spectator* (1878), 2 March, p. 65

Spectator 1881
'Berichten en mededeelingen,' *De Nederlandsche Spectator* (1881), 28 May, pp. 185-187

Spectator 1881-A
'Op de auctie Beurnonville,' *De Nederlandsche Spectator* (1881), 28 May, p. 187

Spencer 1971
J.R. Spencer, 'University Museum. Accidental Past, Purposeful Future?,' *Art in America* 59 (1971), July, pp. 84-90

Spielmann 1910
M.H. Spielmann, 'The Yerkes Collection,' *The Art Journal* (1910), pp. 110-114

Spierdijk 1973
C. Spierdijk, *Horloges en horlogemakers*, Amsterdam 1973

Spriggs 1967
A.I. Spriggs, 'Oriental Porcelain in Western Paintings. 1450-1700' in: *Translations of the Oriental Ceramic Society. 1964-1965. 1965-1966*, London 1967, pp. 73-86

Springer 1910-1912
J. Springer, *Die Radierungen des Hercules Seghers*, Berlin 1910-1912

Spruyt 1829
C. Spruyt, *Lithographies d'après les principaux tableaux de la collection de S.A. Monseigneur le Prince Auguste d'Arenberg avec le catalogue descriptif*, Brussels 1829

Staring 1925
A. Staring, 'Een Schotsch verzamelaar en de Nederlandsche kunst,' *Oud Holland* 42 (1925), pp. 96-108

Staring 1953
A. Staring, 'Een Leidsch verzamelaar en zijn lijfschilder,' *Jaarboekje voor geschiedenis en oudheidkunde van Leiden en omstreken* 45 (1953), pp. 114-123

Staring 1956
A. Staring, *De Hollanders thuis*, The Hague 1956

Stebbins / Sutton 1986
T.E. Stebbins, Jr., & P.C. Sutton, cat. *Masterpiece Paintings from the Museum of Fine Arts, Boston*, Boston, Mass. / New York 1986

Stechow 1930
W. Stechow, '[Review of *Lindeman 1929*],' *Zeitschrift für bildende Kunst* 63 (1930), pp. 130-131

Stechow 1938
W. Stechow, *Salomon van Ruysdael*, Berlin 1938

Stechow 1938-A
W. Stechow, 'Die "Pellekussenpoort" bei Utrecht auf Bildern von J. van Goyen und S. van Ruysdael,' *Oud Holland* 55 (1938), pp. 202-208

Stechow 1938-B
W. Stechow, cat. *Dutch Painting in the Seventeenth Century* Providence, R.I. (Rhode Island School of Design) 1938

Stechow 1941
W. Stechow, '[Review of *Trivas 1941*],' *College Art Journal* 1 (1941), pp. 113-115

Stechow 1942
W. Stechow, 'On College Museums,' *The Art Journal* 2 (1942), November, pp. 21-23

Stechow 1948
W. Stechow, 'Jan Baptist Weenix,' *The Art Quarterly* 11 (1948), pp. 181-198

Stechow 1949
W. Stechow, 'Die Sammlung des Oberlin College in Oberlin, Ohio,' *Phoebus* 2 (1949), no. 3, pp. 116-122

Stechow 1951
W. Stechow, 'Some Portraits by Michael Sweerts,' *The Art Quarterly* 14 (1951), pp. 206-215

Stechow 1952
W. Stechow, 'A Self-Portrait by Michael Sweerts,' *Allen Memorial Art Museum Bulletin* 9 (1952), no. 2, pp. 64-65

Stechow 1958
W. Stechow, 'Jan Steen's Merry Company,' *Allen Memorial Art Museum Bulletin* 15 (1958), no. 3, pp. 90-100

Stechow 1960
W. Stechow, 'Landscape Paintings in Dutch Seventeenth-Century Interiors,' *Nederlands Kunsthistorisch Jaarboek* 2 (1960), pp. 165-184

Stechow 1966
W. Stechow, *Dutch Landscape Painting of the Seventeenth Century*, London 1966

Stechow 1967
W. Stechow, *Catalogue of European and American Paintings and Sculpture in the Allen Memorial Art Museum*, Oberlin, Ohio 1967

Stechow 1970
W. Stechow, cat. *Dutch Mannerism. Apogee and Epilogue* Poughkeepsie, N.Y. (Vassar College Art Gallery) 1970

Stechow 1974
W. Stechow, *Selections from the Bader Collection*, Milwaukee, Wis. 1974

Stechow 1975
W. Stechow, *Salomon van Ruysdael. Eine Einführung in seine Kunst*, Berlin 1975

Stechow 1976
W. Stechow, *Catalogue of Drawings and Watercolors in the Allen Memorial Art Museum, Oberlin College*, Oberlin, Ohio 1976

Steel 1984
D.H. Steel, Jr., cat. *Baroque Paintings from the Bob Jones University Collection* Raleigh, N.C. (North Carolina Museum of Art) New York (Colnaghi) 1984

Steenhoff 1899-1901
W. Steenhoff, 'Collectie Six,' *Bulletin [...] Nederlandschen Oudheidkundigen Bond* 1 (1899-1900), pp. 205-211 and 2 (1900-1901), pp. 22-31

Steenhoff 1908
W. Steenhoff, 'De collectie Six en de aanwinst eruit door het Rijksmuseum,' *Onze Kunst* 7 (1908), vol. XIII, pp. 205-219

Steenhoff 1913
W. Steenhoff, 'Een daad van de Vereeniging Rembrandt,' *De Amsterdammer. Weekblad voor Nederland* (1913), 31 August, p. 7

Steland-Stief 1962-1963
A.C. Steland-Stief, *Jan Asselyn* (diss.) (2 vols.), Freiburg im Breisgau 1962-1963

Steland-Stief 1964
A.C. Steland-Stief, 'Jan Asselyn und Willem Schellinks,' *Oud Holland* 79 (1964), pp. 99-109

Steland-Stief 1970
A.C. Steland-Stief, 'Drei Winterlandschaften des Italianisten Jan Asselyn und ihre Auswirkungen,' *Kunst in Hessen und am Mittelrhein* 10 (1970), pp. 59-65

Steland-Stief 1971
A.C. Steland-Stief, *Jan Asselyn, nach 1610 bis 1652* Amsterdam 1971

Stephens 1895
F.G. Stephens, 'Mr. Yerkes' Collection at Chicago: "The Old Masters,"' *Magazine of Art* 18 (1895), pp. 96-101 and 140-147

Stephenson 1909
B.P. Stephenson, 'Great Dutch Artists,' *Bulletin of The Metropolitan Museum of Art* 4 (1909), no. 10, pp. 167-173

Sterne 1980
M. Sterne, *The Passionate Eye. The Life of William R. Valentiner*, Detroit 1980

Stheeman 1929
A. Stheeman, 'Over enkele oude meesters op de Londensche tentoonstelling van Hollandsche kunst. Een leeken-indruk,' *Elsevier's Geïllustreerd Maandschrift* 39 (1929), vol. LXXVIII, pp. 145-153, 234-245 and 300-311

St. John Brooks 1954
E. St. John Brooks, *Sir Hans Sloane. The Great Collector and His Circle*, London 1954

Stockholm 1893
Katalog öfver utställningen af äldre Mästares taflor ur Svenska privatsamlinger Stockholm (I Konstföreningens F.D. Lokal) 1893

Stockholm 1952
Cat. *Äldre nordiska målningar och skulpturer* Stockholm (Nationalmuseum) 1952

Stone-Ferrier 1983-1984
L. Stone-Ferrier, cat. *Dutch Prints of Daily Life: Mirrors of Life or Masks of Morals?* Lawrence, Kans. (Spencer Museum of Art) 1983-1984

Stott 1986
A. Stott, *American Painters Who Worked in the Netherlands, 1880-1914* (diss.), Boston, Mass. 1986

Van Straaten 1977
E. van Straaten, *Koud tot op het bot. De verbeelding van de winter in de zestiende en zeventiende eeuw in de Nederlanden*, The Hague 1977

Van Straaten 1977-A
E. van Straaten, *Johannes Vermeer. 1632-1675. Een Delfts schilder en de cultuur van zijn tijd*, The Hague 1977

Strahan 1879
E. Strahan [Earl Shinn], *The Art Treasures of America* (3 vols.), Philadelphia, Pa. 1879

Strauss / van der Meulen 1979
W. Strauss & M. van der Meulen, *The Rembrandt Documents*, New York 1979

Struyck-van der Loeff 1987
L. Struyck-van der Loeff, 'Op zoek naar de originele kleuren van Van Aelst,' *Kunstschrift. Openbaar Kunstbezit* 31 (1987), pp. 112-114

Studio 1939
'Masterpieces of Painting at the New York World's Fair,' *The Studio* 118 (1939), pp. 43-57

De Stuers 1873 / 1975
V. de Stuers, *Holland op zijn smalst*, Bussum 1975 (1st edition 1873)

De Stuers 1881
V. de Stuers, 'De tentoonstelling van oude schilderijen te 's Gravenhage,' *Nederlandsche Kunstbode* 3 (1881), pp. 92-94

Van Stuwe 1913
J.R. van Stuwe Hzn., 'Hollandsche schilderijen naar Amerika,' *De Nieuwe Gids* 28 (1913), October, pp. 529-539

Suida 1949
E. Suida, *Catalogue of Paintings in the John & Mable Ringling Museum of Art*, Sarasota, Fla. 1949

Suida 1955
W. Suida, cat. *The Samuel H. Kress Collection* San Francisco, Calif. (M.H. de Young Memorial Museum) 1955

Sullivan 1974
S.A. Sullivan, 'A Banquet Piece with Vanitas Implications,' *Bulletin of The Cleveland Museum of Art* 61 (1974), pp. 271-281

Sullivan 1979
S.A. Sullivan, 'Jan Baptist Weenix: *Still Life with a Dead Swan*,' *Bulletin of The Detroit Institute of Arts* 57 (1979), no. 2, pp. 65-71

Sullivan 1980
S.A. Sullivan, 'Rembrandt's *Self-Portrait with a Dead Bittern*,' *The Art Bulletin* 62 (1980), pp. 236-243

Sullivan 1984
S.A. Sullivan, *The Dutch Gamepiece*, Totowa, N.J. /
Montclair, N.J. 1984
Sumowski 1957-1958
W. Sumowski, 'Nachträge zum Rembrandtjahr 1956,'
*Wissenschaftliche Zeitschrift der Humboldt-Universität zu
Berlin. Gesellschafts- und sprachwissenschaftliche Reihe*
7 (1957-1958), pp. 223-278
Sumowski 1961
W. Sumowski, *Bemerkungen zu Otto Beneschs Corpus der
Rembrandtzeichnungen II*, Bad Pyrmont 1961
Sumowski 1962
W. Sumowski, 'Gerbrand van den Eeckhout als
Zeichner,' *Oud Holland* 77 (1962), pp. 11-39
Sumowski 1965
W. Sumowski, 'Notizen zu Zeichnungen von F. Bol'
in: *Festschrift Dr. h.c. Eduard Trautscholdt zum siebzigsten
Geburtstag am 13. Januar 1963*, Hamburg 1965,
pp. 119-124
Sumowski 1973
W. Sumowski, 'Kritische Bemerkungen zur neuesten
Gemäldekritik' in: O. von Simson & J. Kelch (eds.),
Neue Beiträge zur Rembrandt-Forschung, Berlin 1973,
pp. 91-108
Sumowski 1979-1985
W. Sumowski, *Drawings of the Rembrandt School*
(9 vols.), New York 1979-1985
Sumowski 1983
W. Sumowski, *Gemälde der Rembrandt-Schüler. I.
J.A. Backer – A. van Dijck*, Landau 1983
Sumowski 1983-A
W. Sumowski, *Gemälde der Rembrandt-Schüler. II.
G. van den Eeckhout – I. de Joudreville*, Landau 1983
Sumowski 1983-B
W. Sumowski, *Gemälde der Rembrandt-Schüler. III.
B. Keil – J. Ovens*, Landau 1983
Sutton 1969
P. Sutton, 'Pleasure for the Aesthete,' *Apollo* (1969),
September, pp. 230-239
Sutton 1977
P. Sutton, cat. *Treasures from the Rochester Memorial Art
Gallery of the University of Rochester* New York
(Wildenstein Galleries) 1977
Sutton 1979
P. Sutton, 'A Lawyer from Philadelphia,' *Apollo*
(1979), May, pp. 123-393
Sutton 1980
P.C. Sutton, *Pieter de Hooch. Complete Edition*, Oxford
1980
Sutton 1982-1983
P.C. Sutton, 'The Life and Art of Jan Steen,' *Bulletin.
Philadelphia Museum of Art* 78 (1982-1983), pp. 3-43
Sutton 1986
P.C. Sutton, *A Guide to Dutch Art in America*, Grand
Rapids, Mich. / Kampen 1986
Sutton 1990
P.C. Sutton, *Northern European Paintings in the
Philadelphia Museum of Art: From the Sixteenth through
the Nineteenth Century*, Maarssen 1990

Sutton et al. 1987-1988
P.C. Sutton et al., cat. *Masters of 17th-Century Dutch
Landscape Painting* Amsterdam (Rijksmuseum)
Boston, Mass. (Museum of Fine Arts) Philadelphia,
Pa. (Philadelphia Museum of Art) 1987-1988
Sweeney 1956
J.L. Sweeney (ed.), *The Painter's Eye. Notes and Essays
on the Pictorial Arts by Henry James*, London 1956
Swillens 1935
P.T.A. Swillens, *Pieter Janszoon Saenredam, schilder van
Haarlem 1597-1665*, Amsterdam 1935 (reprint 1970)
Swillens 1949
P.T.A. Swillens, 'Een schilderij van Willem
Schellinks,' *Kunsthistorische mededelingen van het
Rijksbureau voor Kunsthistorische Documentatie* 4 (1949),
pp. 19-21
Swillens 1950
P.T.A. Swillens, *Johannes Vermeer. Painter of Delft.
1632-1675*, Utrecht / Brussels 1950
Szabo 1975
G. Szabo, *The Robert Lehman Collection. A Guide*, New
York 1975
Tableau 1982
'Remarkable Monograph on Frans van Mieris the
Elder,' *Tableau* 4 (1982), no. 4, p. 387
Taine 1871
H. Taine, *Art in the Netherlands*, New York 1871
Taylor 1957
F.H. Taylor, *Pierpont Morgan as a Collector and Patron,
1837-1913*, New York 1957
Taylor 1979
J.C. Taylor, *The Fine Arts in America*, Chicago /
London 1979
Tel Aviv 1959
Cat. *Holland's Golden Age. Paintings, Drawings, Silver of
the XVIIth Century Lent by Dutch Museums and Private
Collections* Tel Aviv (Helena Rubinstein Pavilion) 1959
Van Thiel 1961
P.J. van Thiel, 'Frans Hals' portret van de Leidse
rederijkersnar Pieter Cornelisz. van der Morsch, alias
Piero (1543-1628),' *Oud Holland* 75 (1961), pp. 153-
172
Van Thiel 1967-1968
P.J.J. van Thiel, 'Marriage Symbolism in a Musical
Party by Jan Miense Molenaer,' *Simiolus* 2 (1967-
1968), pp. 90-99
Van Thiel 1983
P. v[an] Th[iel], 'Johannes Vermeer. De liefdesbrief,'
Bulletin van het Rijksmuseum 31 (1983), pp. 197-199
Van Thiel et al. 1976
P.J.J. van Thiel et al., *Alle schilderijen van het
Rijksmuseum*, Amsterdam / Haarlem 1976
Van Thiel / De Bruyn Kops 1984
P.J.J. van Thiel & C.J. de Bruyn Kops, cat. *Prijst de
lijst. De Hollandse schilderijlijst in de zeventiende eeuw*
Amsterdam (Rijksmuseum) 1984
Thieme / Becker
U. Thieme & F. Becker, *Allgemeines Lexikon der
bildenden Künstler von der Antike bis zur Gegenwart*
(37 vols.), Leipzig 1907-1950

Van Thienen 1945
F. van Thienen, *Pieter de Hoogh* (Palet Serie),
Amsterdam n.d. (1945)
Van Thienen 1948
F. van Thienen, *Vermeer* (Palet Serie), Amsterdam
n.d. (1948)
Thies 1869
L.J. Thies, *Catalogue of the Collection of Engravings
Bequeathed to Harvard College by Francis Calley Gray*,
Cambridge, Mass. 1869
Thompson 1989
D.D. Thompson, 'Frans Hals and American Art,'
Antiques 136 (1989), pp. 1170-1183
Thoré-Bürger 1857
W. Bürger, *Trésors d'art exposés à Manchester en 1857 et
provenant des collections royales, des collections publiques et
des collections particulières de la Grande Bretagne*, Paris
1857
Thoré-Bürger 1858-1860
W. Bürger, *Musées de la Hollande* (2 vols.), Paris 1858-
1860
Thoré-Bürger 1859
W. Bürger, *Galerie d'Arenberg à Bruxelles*, Brussels
1859
Thoré-Bürger 1865
W. Bürger, *Trésors d'art en Angleterre*, Paris 1865
Thoré-Bürger 1866
W. Bürger, 'Van der Meer de Delft,' *Gazette des Beaux-
Arts* 21 (1866), 1st series, vol. XXI, pp. 297-330, 458-
470 and 542-575
Thornton 1974
P. Thornton, 'Back-Stools and Chaises à Demoiselles,'
Connoisseur 185 (1974), pp. 99-105
Thornton 1978
P. Thornton, *Seventeenth-Century Interior Decoration in
England, France and Holland*, New Haven, Conn. /
London 1978
Thwing 1906
C.W. Thwing, *A History of Higher Education in America*,
New York 1906
Tillema 1982
J.A.C. Tillema, *Victor de Stuers, ideeën van een
individualist*, Assen 1982
Tintner 1986
A.R. Tintner, *The Museum World of Henry James*, Ann
Arbor, Mich. 1986
T.L.H. 1935
T.L.H., 'Masterpieces from the Morgan Collection
Sold,' *Apollo* (1935), pp. 166-167
Tocqueville / Heffner 1956
A. de Tocqueville (ed. D. Heffner), *Democracy in
America*, New York 1956 (1st editions 1835 and 1840)
Tokyo 1987
Cat. *Space in European Art* Tokyo (National Museum
of Western Art) 1987
Tokyo / Kyoto 1968-1969
Cat. *The Age of Rembrandt. Dutch Paintings and
Drawings of the 17th Century* Tokyo (National Museum
of Western Art) Kyoto (Kyoto City Art Museum)
1968-1969

Toledo 1976
The Toledo Museum of Art. European Paintings, Toledo, Ohio 1976

Toledo 1976-A
The Toledo Museum of Art. A Guide to the Collections, Toledo, Ohio 1976

Tomkiewicz 1950
W. Tomkiewicz, *Catalogue of Paintings Removed from Poland by the German Occupation Authorities during the Years 1939-1945*, Warsaw 1950

Tomkins 1973
C. Tomkins, *Merchants and Masterpieces. The Story of The Metropolitan Museum of Art*, New York 1973

Tonks / Rindge 1939
O.S. Tonks & A. Rindge, *Vassar College Art Gallery Catalogue*, Poughkeepsie, N.Y. 1939

Toronto 1926
Catalogue of Inaugural Exhibition Toronto (Art Gallery of Toronto) 1926

Toronto 1936
Catalogue of Exhibitions. Sixteenth and Seventeenth Century Paintings by European Masters. Paintings by Nineteenth Century French Artists Toronto (Toronto Arts Club) 1936

Townsend / Howard 1919
J.B. Townsend & W.S. Howard, *Memorial Catalogue of Paintings by Old and Modern Masters Collected by Edward R. Bacon*, New York 1919

Traudenius 1662
D. Traudenius, *Tyd-zifter, dat is, kort bericht of onderwys van de onderscheidinge en afdeelinge des tydts [...] met een rymbundel*, Amsterdam 1662

Trautscholdt 1937
E. Trautscholdt, 'Steen, Jan' in: *Thieme / Becker*, vol. XXXI (1937), pp. 509-515

Trautscholdt 1938
E. Trautscholdt, 'Sweerts (Suerz), Michiel' in: *Thieme / Becker*, vol. XXXII (1938), pp. 348-350

Trautscholdt 1940
E. Trautscholdt, 'Vermeer, Johannes (Jo[a]nnis)' in: *Thieme / Becker*, vol. XXXIV (1940), pp. 265-275

Trivas 1939
N.S. Trivas, 'Oude kunst op de New Yorksche Wereldtentoonstelling,' *Elsevier's Geïllustreerd Maandschrift* 49 (1939), vol. XCVIII, pp. 136-141

Tuckerman 1867
H.T. Tuckerman, *Book of the Artists. Biographical Critical Sketches of American Artists...*, New York 1867

Tümpel 1974
A. Tümpel, 'Claes Cornelisz. Moeyaert,' *Oud Holland* 88 (1974), pp. 1-163

Tümpel 1986
C. Tümpel, *Rembrandt*, Antwerp 1986

Tuinman 1726
C. Tuinman, *De Nederduitsche spreekwoorden* (2 vols.), Middelburg 1726

Turner 1983
E.H. Turner, *The Ackland Art Museum. A Handbook*, Chapel Hill, N.C. 1983

Turner 1986
N. Turner, cat. *Florentine Drawings of the Sixteenth Century* London (British Museum) 1986

Tzeutschler Lurie 1965
A. Tzeutschler Lurie, 'Esther, Ahasuerus and Haman,' *The Bulletin of The Cleveland Museum of Art* 52 (1965), pp. 94-100

Tzeutschler Lurie 1979
A. Tzeutschler Lurie, 'The Weeping Heraclitus by Hendrick Terbrugghen in The Cleveland Museum of Art,' *The Burlington Magazine* 121 (1979), pp. 279-287

Ungaretti / Bianconi 1967
G. Ungaretti & P. Bianconi, *L'opera completa di Vermeer*, Milan 1967

Utica / Rochester 1963
Cat. *Masters of Landscape: East and West* Utica, N.Y. (Museum of Art) Rochester, N.Y. (The Rochester Memorial Art Gallery) 1963

Utrecht 1952
Cat. *Caravaggio en de Nederlanden* Utrecht (Centraal Museum) 1952

Utrecht 1961
Cat. *Catalogue raisonné of the works by Pieter Jansz Saenredam* Utrecht (Centraal Museum) 1961

Utrechtsche Courant 1903
'Een mooie daad,' *Utrechtsche Courant* 16 March 1903 (Knipselboek 1885-1927, p. 40, documentation archives Mauritshuis, The Hague)

Valentiner 1909
W.R. Valentiner, cat. *The Hudson-Fulton Celebration. Catalogue of an Exhibition Held in The Metropolitan Museum of Art. Volume 1* New York (The Metropolitan Museum of Art) 1909

Valentiner 1909-A
W.R. Valentiner, *Rembrandt. Des Meisters Gemälde* (Klassiker der Kunst II), Stuttgart / Berlin 1909 (3rd edition)

Valentiner 1909-B
W.R. Valentiner, *Catalogue of a Collection of Paintings by Dutch Masters of the Seventeenth Century*, New York 1909

Valentiner 1910
W.R. Valentiner, 'Die Ausstellung holländischer Gemälde in New York,' *Monatshefte für Kunstwissenschaft* (1910), pp. 5-12

Valentiner 1910-A
W.R. Valentiner, *Catalogue of a Loan Exhibition of Paintings by Old Dutch Masters Held at The Metropolitan Museum of Art in Connection with the Hudson-Fulton Celebration, September-November MCMX* New York (The Metropolitan Museum of Art) 1910

Valentiner 1913
W.R. Valentiner, *Catalogue of a Collection of Paintings and some Art Objects. Vol. II. Flemish and Dutch Paintings*, Philadelphia 1913

Valentiner 1913-1914 / 1972
W.R. Valentiner, *John G. Johnson Collection. Catalogue of Flemish and Dutch Paintings*, Philadelphia, Pa. 1972 (1st edition 1913-1914)

Valentiner 1914
W.R. Valentiner, *The Art of the Low Countries*, Garden City, N.Y. 1914

Valentiner 1918-1919
W.R. Valentiner, 'Amerikanische Privatsammlungen,' *Kunst und Künstler* 18 (1918-1919), pp. 347-370

Valentiner 1921
W. Valentiner, *Rembrandt. Wiedergefundene Gemälde (1910-1920)*, Berlin / Leipzig 1921

Valentiner 1924
W.R. Valentiner, *Nicolaes Maes*, Stuttgart / Berlin / Leipzig 1924

Valentiner 1925
W.R. Valentiner, cat. *Loan Exhibition of Dutch Paintings of the Seventeenth Century* Detroit, Mich. (The Detroit Institute of Arts) 1925

Valentiner 1927
W.R. Valentiner, 'Pieter de Hooch,' *Art in America* 15 (1927), pp. 45-64 and 66-77

Valentiner 1929
W.R. Valentiner, *Pieter de Hooch. Des Meisters Gemälde in 180 Abbildungen mit einem Anhang über die Genremaler um Pieter de Hooch und die Kunst Hendrik van der Burchs* (Klassiker der Kunst XXXV), Stuttgart / Berlin / Leipzig 1929

Valentiner 1930
W.R. Valentiner, cat. *The Thirteenth Loan Exhibition of Old Masters. Paintings by Rembrandt* Detroit, Mich. (The Detroit Institute of Arts) 1930

Valentiner 1930-A
W.R. Valentiner, 'Important Rembrandts in American Collections,' *The Art News* 28 (1930), 26 April, pp. 3-4

Valentiner 1930-B
W.R. Valentiner, *Das unbekannte Meisterwerk in öffentlichen und privaten Sammlungen*, Berlin 1930

Valentiner 1931
W.R. Valentiner, *Rembrandt Paintings in America*, New York 1931

Valentiner 1935
W.R. Valentiner, cat. *An Exhibition of Fifty Paintings by Frans Hals* Detroit, Mich. (The Detroit Institute of Arts) 1935

Valentiner 1935-A
W.R. Valentiner, 'Great Hals Exhibition Opens in Detroit,' *The Art News* (1935), January, pp. 1, 4 and 11

Valentiner 1935-B
W.R. Valentiner, 'New Additions to the Work of Frans Hals,' *Art in America* 23 (1935), June, pp. 84-103

Valentiner 1936
W.R. Valentiner, *Frans Hals Paintings in America*, Westport, Conn. 1936

Valentiner 1939
W.R. Valentiner, 'Foreword' in: *Von Moltke 1939*, pp. IX-XVI

Valentiner 1956
W.R. Valentiner, cat. *Rembrandt and His Pupils. A Loan Exhibition* Raleigh, N.C. (The North Carolina Museum of Art) 1956

Valentiner 1956-A
W.R. Valentiner, *Catalogue of Paintings. Including Three Sets of Tapestries* Raleigh, N.C. (The North Carolina Museum of Art) 1956

Valentiner / Voll 1923
W.R. Valentiner & K. Voll, *Hals. Des Meisters Gemälde* (Klassiker der Kunst XXVIII), Stuttgart / Berlin / Leipzig 1923 (2nd edition)

Vanderbilt 1959
K. Vanderbilt, *Charles Eliot Norton. Apostle of Culture in a Democracy*, Cambridge, Mass. 1959

Vanzype 1908 / 1925
G. Vanzype, *Vermeer de Delft*, Brussels 1908 (2nd edition 1925)

Varriano 1979
J.L. Varriano, cat. *Baroque Paintings in the Low Countries: Selections from the Bader Collection* South Hadley, Mass. (Mount Holyoke College Museum of Art) 1979

Vasseur 1987
D.H. Vasseur, 'Portrait of a Young Man,' *Dayton Medicine* 43 (1987), p. 279

Van de Velde 1975
C. van de Velde, *Frans Floris (1519 / 20-1570). Leven en werken*, Brussels 1975

Vergara 1985
L. Vergara, 'New York. Roman Landscapes at Feigen,' *The Burlington Magazine* 127 (1985), pp. 405-406

Vermeulen 1914
F. Vermeulen, 'De schilderijen uit de verzameling Steengracht in het Mauritshuis,' *Eigen Haard* 40 (1914), pp. 438-444

De Vesme / Massar 1971
A. de Vesme & P.D. Massar, *Stefano della Bella* (2 vols.), New York 1971

Veth 1884
J. Veth, 'Aelbert Cuyp,' *Oud Holland* 2 (1884), pp. 256-290

Veth 1906
J. Veth, *Rembrandt's leven en kunst*, Amsterdam 1906

Veth 1908
J. Veth, 'De rijksaankoop van schilderijen uit de kollektie-Six,' *De Gids* 26 (1908), 4th series, vol. I, pp. 187-193

Veth 1910
J. Veth, 'Oud-Hollandsche schilderijen in de Vereenigde Staten' in: *Beelden en groepen*, Amsterdam (1910), pp. 83-90

Veth 1911
J. Veth, 'Oud-Hollandsche schilderijen te Parijs. I,' *Nieuwe Rotterdamsche Courant* 24 May 1911, 'Avondblad,' p. B1

Veth 1911-A
J. Veth, 'Oud-Hollandsche schilderijen te Parijs. II,' *Nieuwe Rotterdamsche Courant* 26 May 1911, 'Avondblad,' p. B1

Veth 1914
J. Veth, 'Rembrandts Lucretia (1914),' *Beelden en groepen*, Amsterdam (1914), pp. 116-126

Veth 1938
C. Veth, 'Meesterwerken uit vier eeuwen,' *Maandblad voor Beeldende Kunsten* 15 (1938), pp. 194-204

Veth / Van Regteren Altena 1941
J. Veth & I.Q. van Regteren Altena, *Rembrandts leven en kunst*, Amsterdam 1941

Vey 1973
H. Vey, 'Niederländische Meister des 16. und 17. Jahrhunderts' in: *Zürich 1973*, pp. 350-368

Veysey 1965
L.R. Veysey, *The Emergence of the American University*, Chicago, Ill. / London 1965

Vienna 1967
Cat. *Gemälde bedeutender niederländischer Meister des 17. Jahrhunderts* Vienna (Galerie Friederike Pallamar) 1967

Vinken / De Jongh 1963
P.J. Vinken & E. de Jongh, 'De boosaardigheid van Hals' regenten en regentessen,' *Oud Holland* 78 (1963), pp. 1-26

Voll 1905
K. Voll, *Die Meisterwerke der Kgl. Älteren Pinakothek zu München*, London / Munich / New York 1905

Voorhelm Schneevoogt 1873
C.G. Voorhelm Schneevoogt, *Catalogue des estampes gravées d'après P.P. Rubens ...*, Haarlem 1873

Vorenkamp 1933
A.P.A. Vorenkamp, *Bijdrage tot de geschiedenis van het Hollandsch stilleven in de zeventiende eeuw* (diss.), Leyden 1933

Vorenkamp 1938
A.P.A. Vorenkamp, 'Masterpieces of Dutch Paintings: An Important Exhibition at the Providence Museum,' *The Art News* 37 (1938), 10 December, pp. 8-12

Vorsterman van Oijen 1885-1890
A.A. Vorsterman van Oijen, *Stam- en wapenboek van aanzienlijke Nederlandsche familiën met genealogische en heraldische aanteekeningen* (3 vols.), Groningen 1885-1890

Vosmaer 1868
C. Vosmaer, *Rembrandt Harmens van Rijn. Sa vie et ses oeuvres*, The Hague 1868

Vosmaer 1877
C. Vosmaer, *Rembrandt. Sa vie et ses oeuvres*, The Hague 1877

De Vries 1939
A.B. de Vries, *Jan Vermeer van Delft*, Amsterdam 1939

De Vries 1948
A.B. de Vries, *Jan Vermeer van Delft*, Basel 1948

De Vries 1964
A.B. de Vries, 'Old Masters in the collection of Mr. & Mrs. Sidney van den Bergh,' *Apollo* (1964), July, pp. 352-359

De Vries 1968
A.B. de Vries, *Verzameling Sidney J. van den Bergh*, Wassenaar 1968

De Vries 1976
A.B. de Vries, *Vermeer*, New York / Toronto 1976

De Vries 1976-A
L. de Vries, *Jan Steen. De schilderende Uilenspiegel*, Weert 1976

De Vries 1977
L. de Vries, *Jan Steen 'de kluchtschilder'* (diss.), Groningen 1977

De Vries 1984
L. de Vries, *Jan van der Heyden*, Amsterdam 1984

Vroom 1945
N.R.A. Vroom, *De schilders van het monochrome banketje*, Amsterdam 1945

Waagen 1837-1839
G.F. Waagen, *Kunstwerke und Künstler in England und Paris* (3 vols.), Berlin 1837-1839

Waagen 1838
G.F. Waagen, *Works of Art in England* (2 vols.), London 1838

Waagen 1843-1845
G.F. Waagen, *Kunstwerke und Künstler in Deutschland* (2 vols.), Leipzig 1843-1845

Waagen 1854
[G.F.] Waagen, *Treasures of Art in Great Britain: Being an Account of the Chief Collections of Paintings, Drawings, Sculptures, Illuminated Mss., &c.&c.* (3 vols. and supplement), London 1854

Waagen 1864
G.F. Waagen, *Die Gemäldesammlung in der kaiserlichen Ermitage zu St. Petersburg nebst Bemerkungen über andere dortige Kunstsammlungen*, Munich 1864

Waagen 1870
G.F. Waagen, *Die Gemäldesammlung in der kaiserlichen Ermitage zu St. Petersburg nebst Bemerkungen über andere dortige Kunstsammlungen*, Leningrad [Saint Petersburg] 1870

Van de Waal 1952
H. van de Waal, *Drie eeuwen vaderlandsche geschied-uitbeelding. 1500-1800. Een iconologische studie* (2 vols.), The Hague 1952

Van de Waal 1969
H. van de Waal, 'Rembrandt and the Feast of Purim,' *Oud Holland* 84 (1969), pp. 199-223

Van de Waal 1969-A
H. van de Waal, 'Rembrandt at Vondel's Tragedy Gijsbreght van Aemstel' in: *Miscellanea I.Q. van Regteren Altena. 16 / V / 1969*, Amsterdam 1969, pp. 145-149

WAB 1957
'Simon Verelst – Still Life,' *Wadsworth Atheneum Bulletin* (1957), Summer, n.p.

WAB 1962
'Annual Report 1961,' *Wadsworth Atheneum Bulletin* (1962), 5th series, no. 10

Waddingham 1958
M.R. Waddingham, 'The Sweerts' Exhibition in Rotterdam,' *Paragone* 9 (1958), pp. 67-73

Waddingham 1976-1977
M.R. Waddingham, 'Michael Sweerts, *Boy Copying the Head of a Roman Emperor*,' *The Minneapolis Institute of Arts Bulletin* 63 (1976-1977), pp. 57-65

Waddingham 1980
M.R. Waddingham, 'Additions to the Oeuvre of Michael Sweerts,' *The J. Paul Getty Museum Journal* 8 (1980), pp. 63-68

Waddingham 1986
M.R. Waddingham, 'Two Enigmatic Portraits by Michael Sweerts,' *Apollo* 124 (1986), August, pp. 95-97

Waetzoldt 1924
W. Waetzoldt, *Deutsche Kunsthistoriker. Zweiter Band. Von Passavant bis Justi*, Leipzig 1924

Wagner 1971
H. Wagner, *Jan van der Heyden. 1637-1712*, Amsterdam / Haarlem 1971

Waldmann 1910
E. Waldmann, 'De Tentoonstelling van Hollandsche 17de-eeuwsche kunst te New-York,' *Kunstkroniek* (1910), pp. 150-153, 167-169 and 184-187

Waldmann 1938
E. Waldmann, 'Die Sammlung Widener,' *Pantheon* 22 (1938), pp. 334-343

Walker 1948
J. Walker, 'Introduction' in: *Washington 1948*, pp. VII-X

Walker 1963
J. Walker, *National Gallery of Art, Washington, D.C.*, New York 1963

Walker 1969
J. Walker, *Self-Portrait with Donors. Confessions of an Art Collector*, Boston, Mass. 1969

Walker 1973
J. Walker, *Self-Portrait with Donors. Confessions of an Art Collector*, Boston, Mass. / Toronto 1973

Walker 1976
J. Walker, *National Gallery of Art*, New York 1976

Walker 1980
J. Walker (ed.), *The Armand Hammer Collection. Five Centuries of Masterpieces*, New York 1980

Walker 1984
J. Walker, *National Gallery of Art, Washington*, New York 1984

Walker 1985
J. Walker, *National Gallery of Art, Washington*, New York n.d. (1985)

Van de Wall 1936
C. van de Wall, *Carel van Mander. Dutch and Flemish Painters. Translation from the Schilderboeck*, New York 1936

Walsh 1973
J. Walsh, 'Vermeer,' *The Metropolitan Museum of Art Bulletin* 31 (1973), n.p.

Walsh 1974
J. Walsh, 'New Dutch Paintings at The Metropolitan Museum,' *Apollo* (1974), May, pp. 340-349

Walsh 1976
J. Walsh, Jr., 'Obituary for Wolfgang Stechow,' *The Burlington Magazine* 118 (1976), pp. 855-856

Walsh 1981
J. Walsh, ' "A Mirror of Nature": The Carter Collection of Dutch Paintings,' *Apollo* 112 (1981), December, pp. 380-389

Walsh 1986
J. Walsh, 'Paintings,' *The J. Paul Getty Museum Journal* 14 (1986), pp. 211-224

Walsh / Schneider 1979
J. Walsh, Jr., & C.P. Schneider, 'Little-Known Dutch Paintings in the Museum of Fine Arts, Boston,' *Apollo* 110 (1979), December, pp. 498-506

Walsh / Schneider 1981-1982
J. Walsh & C.P. Schneider, cat. *A Mirror of Nature. Dutch Paintings from the Collection of Mr. and Mrs. Edward William Carter* Los Angeles, Calif. (Los Angeles County Museum of Art) Boston, Mass. (Museum of Fine Arts) New York (The Metropolitan Museum of Art) 1981-1982

Walton 1909-1910
W. Walton, 'Exhibition in New York of Paintings from the Collection of Mr. and Mrs. Charles P. Taft,' *The Burlington Magazine* 16 (1909-1910), p. 368

Wang 1975
A. Wang, *Der 'Miles Christianus' im 16. und 17. Jahrhundert und seine mittelalterliche Tradition*, Frankfurt 1975

Ward 1987
R. Ward (ed.), *A Bountiful Decade. Selected Acquisitions 1977-1987. The Nelson-Atkins Museum of Art*, Kansas City, Mo. 1987

Washburn Freund 1925
F.E. Washburn Freund, 'Eine Ausstellung niederländischer Malerei in Detroit,' *Der Cicerone* 17 (1925), pp. 460-464

Washburn Freund 1929
F.E. Washburn Freund, 'Die Ausstellung altholländischer Malerei in Detroit,' *Der Cicerone* 21 (1929), pp. 704-707

Washington 1932
Cat. *Illustrated Handbook of the W.A. Clark Collection* Washington, D.C. (The Corcoran Gallery of Art) 1932

Washington 1941
National Gallery of Art. Preliminary Catalogue of Paintings and Sculptures, Washington, D.C. 1941

Washington 1948
Cat. *Paintings and Sculpture from the Widener Collection* Washington, D.C. (National Gallery of Art) 1948

Washington 1959
Cat. *Paintings and Sculptures from the Widener Collection* Washington, D.C. (National Gallery of Art) 1959

Washington 1961-1962
Cat. *Exhibition of Art Treasures for America from the Samuel H. Kress Collection* Washington, D.C. (National Gallery of Art) 1961-1962

Washington 1965
Summary Catalogue of European Paintings and Sculpture Washington, D.C. (National Gallery of Art) 1965

Washington 1968
European Paintings and Sculpture. Illustrations Washington, D.C. (National Gallery of Art) 1968

Washington 1969
Cat. *Rembrandt in the National Gallery of Art* Washington, D.C. (National Gallery of Art) 1969

Washington 1975
European Paintings. An Illustrated Summary Catalogue Washington, D.C. (National Gallery of Art) 1975

Washington 1977
1976 Annual Report Washington, D.C. (National Gallery of Art) 1977

Washington 1985
European Paintings. An Illustrated Catalogue Washington, D.C. (National Gallery of Art) 1985

Washington 1989
Cat. *Still Lifes of the Golden Age: Northern European Paintings from the Heinz Family Collection* Washington, D.C. (National Gallery of Art) 1989

Waterhouse 1951
E.K. Waterhouse, 'Exhibitions of Old Masters at Newcastle, York and Perth,' *The Burlington Magazine* 93 (1951), pp. 261-265

Waterhouse 1967
E. Waterhouse, *The James A. de Rothschild Collection at Waddesdon Manor. Paintings*, Fribourg 1967

Van de Watering 1981
W.L. van de Watering, 'Jan van Goyen in Dutch Public Collections' in: *Amsterdam 1981*, pp. 29-43

Van de Watering 1982
W. van de Watering, cat. *Terugzien in bewondering. A Collector's Choice* The Hague (Mauritshuis) 1982

Waterschoot 1983
W. Waterschoot, *Ter liefde der Const. Uit het Schilder-Boeck (1604) van Karel van Mander*, Leyden 1983

Watkin 1968
D. Watkin, *Thomas Hope (1769-1831) and the Neo-Classical Idea*, London 1968

Watson 1963
F.J.B. Watson, *The Choiseul Box*, London 1963

Wauters 1877
A. Wauters, 'Essai historique sur les tapissiers de haute et de basse-lice de Bruxelles. VII-VIII,' *Bulletin des commissions royales d'art et d'archéologie* 17 (1877), pp. 253-335

Wauters 1885
A.L. Wauters, *The Flemish School of Painting*, London 1885

WCA
F.A. van Braam (ed.), *World Collector's Annuary* (37 vols.), n.p. 1946-1985 / 1987

Wehle 1925
H.B. Wehle, 'Notes on Paintings in the Huntington Collection,' *Bulletin of the Metropolitan Museum of Art* 20 (1925), no. 7, pp. 178-180

Wehle 1944
H.B. Wehle, 'A Fashionable Portrait by Rembrandt,' *The Metropolitan Museum of Art Bulletin* 2 (1943-1944), no. 6, pp. 177-180

Wehle et al. 1930
H.B. Wehle et al., 'The Exhibition of the H.O. Havemeyer Collection,' *Bulletin of the Metropolitan Museum of Art* 25 (1930), pp. 54-76

Weigel 1843
R. Weigel, *Suppléments au Peintre-Graveur de Adam Bartsch*, Leipzig 1843

Von Weiner 1923
P.P. von Weiner, *Meisterwerke der Gemäldesammlung in der Eremitage zu Petrograd*, Munich 1923

Weisberg / Dixon 1987
G.P. Weisberg & L. S. Dixon, *The Documented Image. Visions in Art History*, Syracuse 1987

Weisner 1964
U. Weisner, 'Die Gemälde des Moyses van Uyttenbroeck', *Oud Holland* 79 (1964) pp. 189-228

Weitzenhoffer 1986
F. Weitzenhoffer, *The Havemeyers. Impressionism Comes to America*, New York 1986

Welcker 1933
C.J. Welcker, *Hendrick Avercamp (1585-1634), bijgenaamd 'De Stomme van Campen' en Barent Avercamp (1612-1679) 'Schilders tot Campen,'* Zwolle 1933

Welcker / Hensbroek-van der Poel 1979
C.J. Welcker & D. Hensbroek-van der Poel, *Hendrick Avercamp (1585-1634), bijgenaamd 'De Stomme van Campen' en Barent Avercamp (1612-1679) 'Schilders tot Campen,'* Zwolle 1979

Weltkunst 1938
'Ein holländisches Versteigerungsereignis,' *Die Weltkunst* 12 (1938), no. 47, 20 November, pp. 1-2 and 4

Welu 1975
J. Welu, ' "Card Players and Merrymakers," A Moral Lesson,' *Worcester Art Museum Bulletin* 4 (1975), new series, no. 3, May, pp. 8-16

Welu 1979
J.A. Welu, cat. *17th-Century Dutch Paintings. Raising the Curtain on New England Private Collections* Worcester, Mass. (Worcester Art Museum) 1979

Wertheimer 1891 / 1898
A. Wertheimer, *The Hope Collection of Pictures of the Dutch and Flemish Schools with Descriptions Reprinted from the Catalogue Published in 1891 by the Science and Art Department of the South Kensington Museum*, London 1898 (1st edition 1891)

West 1979
R.V. West, 'The Crockers and Their Collection: A Brief History' in: *Crocker Art Museum. Handbook of Paintings*, Sacramento, Calif. 1979, pp. 7-12

Westmacott 1824
C.M. Westmacott, *British Galleries of Painting and Sculpture, Comprising a General Historical and Critical Catalogue, with Seperate Notices of Every Work of Fine Art in the Principal Collections*, London 1824

Van Westrheene 1856
T. van Westrheene, *Jan Steen. Etude sur l'art en Hollande*, The Hague 1856

Van Westrheene 1867
T. van Westrheene, *Paulus Potter. Sa vie et ses oeuvres*, The Hague 1867

Van Westrheene 1868
T. van Westrheene, 'De tentoonstelling van schilderijen van oude meesters te Amsterdam,' *Kunstkroniek* 9 (1868), new series, pp. 41-43

Van de Wetering 1983
E. van de Wetering, 'Isaac Jouderville, a Pupil of Rembrandt' in: *Blankert et al. 1983*, pp. 59-69

Van de Wetering 1986
E. van de Wetering, *Studies in the Workshop Practice of the Early Rembrandt* (diss.), Amsterdam 1986

Wethey 1975
H.E. Wethey, *The Paintings of Titian* (3 vols.), London 1975

Weyerman 1729-1769
J.C. Weyerman, *De levens-beschryvingen der Nederlandsche konst-schilders en konst-schilderessen* (4 vols.), The Hague / Dordrecht 1729-1769

Wheelock 1977
A. Wheelock, '[Review of *Blankert 1975*],' *The Art Bulletin* 59 (1977), pp. 439-441

Wheelock 1977-A
A.K. Wheelock, 'De geschiedenis en bekoring van "De Molen",' *De kroniek van het Rembrandthuis* 29 (1977), pp. 20-32

Wheelock 1981
A.K. Wheelock, Jr., *Jan Vermeer*, New York 1981

Wheelock 1984
A. Wheelock, Jr., *Dutch Painting in the National Gallery of Art*, Washington 1984

Wheelock 1988
A.K. Wheelock, Jr., *Jan Vermeer*, New York 1988

White 1853
R.G. White, *Companion to the Bryan Gallery of Christian Art*, New York 1853

White 1959
C. White, 'Dutch and Flemish Paintings at Waddesdon Manor,' *Gazette des Beaux-Arts* 101 (1959), 6th series, vol. LIV, pp. 67-74

White 1982
C. White, *The Dutch Pictures in the Collection of Her Majesty the Queen*, Cambridge etc. 1982

Whitehill 1970
W.M. Whitehill, *Museum of Fine Arts, Boston. A Centennial History* (2 vols.), Cambridge, Mass. 1970

Whitley 1973
W.T. Whitley, *Art in England* (2 vols.), New York 1973

Wiegand 1971
W. Wiegand, *Ruisdael-Studien. Ein Versuch zur Ikonologie der Landschaftsmalerei* (diss.), Hamburg 1971

Wiersum 1910
E. Wiersum, 'Het schilderijen-kabinet van Jan Bisschop te Rotterdam,' *Oud Holland* 28 (1910), pp. 161-186

Wiersum 1910-A
E. Wiersum, 'Jan Bisschop,' *Rotterdamsch Jaarboekje* 8 (1910), pp. 50-74 (offprint at the RKD, pp. 2-25)

Van den Wijngaert 1940
F. van den Wijngaert, *Inventaris der Rubeniaansche prentkunst*, Antwerp 1940

Wijnman et al. 1974
H.F. Wijnman, E. Werkman, J.H. van den Hoek Ostende et al., *Historische gids van Amsterdam*, Amsterdam 1974

Wilenski 1929
R.H. Wilenski, *An Introduction to Dutch Art*, London 1929

Williams 1980
R. Williams, *Russian Art and American Money 1900-1940*, Cambridge, Mass. 1980

Williamstown 1973
Cat. *Things of This World: A Selection of Dutch Drawings from the Collection of Maida and George Abrams* Williamstown, Mass. (Sterling and Francine Clark Art Institute) 1973

Wilmer 1980
C.C.S. Wilmer, *Utrecht getekend. Vier eeuwen tekeningen en aquarellen uit de topografische atlas van het Gemeentearchief*, The Hague 1980

Wilmerding 1973
J. Wilmerding (ed.), *The Genius of American Painting*, London / New York 1973

Wilmerding 1976
J. Wilmerding, *American Art* (Pelican History of Art), New York 1976

Wilson 1930
R. Wilson, 'In Memoriam,' *Bulletin of the Cincinnati Art Museum* 1 (1930), pp. 26-27

Wilson 1980-1981
W.H. Wilson, cat. *Dutch Seventeenth Century Portraiture. The Golden Age* Sarasota, Fla. (The John and Mable Ringling Museum of Art) 1980-1981

Winchester 1959
A. Winchester, 'The Man behind the Association,' *Antiques* (1959), p. 170

Winkelman 1942
B.F. Winkelman, *John G. Johnson, Lawyer and Art Collector*, Philadelphia, Pa. 1942

Winkler Prins van de Kunst 1959
W.R. Juynboll & V. Denis (eds.),'*Winkler Prins van de Kunst. Encyclopedie van de architectuur, beeldende kunst, kunstnijverheid* (3 vols.), Amsterdam / Brussels 1959

Winnipeg 1952
Cat. *Treasures of Dutch Old Masters. Landscape, Portraits, Still Life, Interiors and Genre of the 17th Century* Winnipeg, Ont. (Winnipeg Art Gallery Association) 1952

Winter 1958
C. Winter, *The Fitzwilliam Museum: An Illustrated Survey*, Cambridge 1958

Wishnevsky 1967
R. Wishnevsky, *Studien zum 'portrait historié' in den Niederlanden* (diss.), Munich 1967

Wittmann 1966
O. Wittmann, *A Guide to the Collections. The Toledo Museum of Art*, Toledo, Ohio 1966

Wittmann 1967
O. Wittmann, 'The Golden Age in the Netherlands,' *Apollo* 86 (1967), pp. 466-477

Wittmann 1976
O. Wittmann, 'Treasures for Toledo,' *The Toledo Museum of Art. Museum News* 19 (1976), pp. 43-82

Wittmann 1976-A
O. Wittmann, 'Introduction' in: *Toledo 1976*, pp. 9-13

Woodward 1985
C.M. Woodward, 'Acquisition, Preservation and Education: a History of the Museum' in: *A Handbook of the Museum of Art, Rhode Island School of Design*, Providence, R.I. 1985, pp. 11-60

Worcester 1936
Cat. *Rembrandt and His Circle. A Loan Exhibition of Paintings, Drawings and Etchings* Worcester, Mass. (Worcester Art Museum) 1936

Worcester 1974
European Paintings in the Collection of the Worcester Art Museum (2 vols.), Worcester, Mass. 1974

Wrangel 1909
N. Wrangel, *Les chefs-d'oeuvre de la galerie de tableaux de l'Ermitage impérial à St-Pétersbourg*, London / Munich / New York n.d. (1909)

Wrey 1985
M. Wrey, *Christie's. Review of the Season 1985*, Oxford 1985

Wrey 1988
M. Wrey, *Christie's. Review of the Season 1988*, Oxford 1988

Wright 1976
C. Wright, *Vermeer*, London 1976

Wright 1980
C. Wright, *Paintings in Dutch Museums. An Index of Oil Paintings in Public Collections in the Netherlands by Artists Born before 1870*, Amsterdam 1980

Wright 1981
C. Wright, *A Golden Age of Painting. Dutch, Flemish, German Paintings, Sixteenth-Seventeenth Centuries from the Collection of The Sarah Campbell Blaffer Foundation*, San Antonio, Tex. 1981

Wright 1982
C. Wright, *Rembrandt: Self-Portraits*, London 1982

Wurfbain 1976-1977
M.L. Wurfbain, cat. *Geschildert tot Leyden anno 1626* Leyden (Stedelijk Museum De Lakenhal) 1976-1977

Wurfbain 1980
M.L. Wurfbain, 'Portret van Cuniera van der Cocq, Frans van Mieris de Oude, 1635-1681,' *Vereniging Rembrandt. Nationaal Fonds Kunstbehoud. Verslag* (1980), pp. 55-56

Wurzbach
A. von Wurzbach, *Niederländisches Künstler-Lexikon* (3 vols.), Vienna / Leipzig 1906-1911

Wurzbach 1886
A. von Wurzbach, *Rembrandt-Galerie*, Stuttgart 1886

WWA
Who's Who in America (2 vols.), Wilmette, Ill. 1988-1989

WWA-A
Who's Who in America (documentation The Fine Arts Museums of San Francisco)

WWAA
Who's Who in American Art 1980, New York / London 1980

WWWA
Who Was Who in America (10 vols. and index), Chicago / Wilmette, Ill. 1943-1989

Zafran 1976
E. Zafran, 'Jan Victors and the Bible,' *The Israel Museum News* 12 (1976) pp. 92-120

Zafran 1978
E. Zafran, 'The Northern School at Hartford,' *Apollo* (1978), October, pp. 242-247

Zafran 1981
E. Zafran, 'Unfamiliar Aspects of Dutch Art,' *Apollo* 113 (1981), May, pp. 328-329

Zantkuijl 1975
H.J. Zantkuijl, *Bouwen in Amsterdam. Het woonhuis in de stad*, Amsterdam 1975

Zürich 1958
Cat. *Sammlung Emil G. Bührle. Festschrift zu Ehren von Emil G. Bührle zur Eröffnung des Kunsthaus-Neubaus und Katalog der Sammlung Emil G. Bührle* Zürich (Kunsthaus) 1958

Zürich 1973
Stiftung Sammlung Emil G. Bührle. Foundation collection Emil G. Bührle. Foundation Emil G. Bührle Collection, Zürich / Munich 1973

Zwartendijk 1929
J. Zwartendijk, 'Wijzigingen in onzen smaak. Naar aanleiding van de tentoonstelling van Hollandsche kunst, te Londen gehouden,' *Elsevier's Geïllustreerd Maandschrift* 39 (1929), vol. LXXVII, pp. 385-393

Index

Compiled by Marjolein de Boer,
Ben Broos, Sophie Hazenberg,
Peter van der Ploeg, and Els Vlieger

Index of personal names (artists, dealers, collectors, etc.), institutions, and locations of works of art. Museums, archives, and libraries are arranged under place. An *italic* page number (after the name of an artist or the person portrayed) refers to an illustration; see also Photo Credits.

Photo Credits

Amherst, Mass.
Amherst College Archives: Kuretsky, fig. 4
Amsterdam
Amsterdams Historisch Museum: cat. no. 47, figs. 1 and 4; cat. no. 48, fig. 3; cat. no. 71, fig. 2
Collection Van Regteren Altena: cat. no. 27, fig. 2
Gemeentearchief, collection Dreesmann: cat. no. 61, fig. 1
Koninklijk Oudheidkundig Genootschap: cat. no. 31, fig. 2
Dealer Gebr. Douwes Fine Art: see London
Dealer K. & V. Waterman: cat. no. 53, fig. 1; cat. no. 62, fig. 3
Rembrandthuis: cat. no. 19, fig. 2
Rijksmuseum: Buijsen, fig. 8; cat. no. 2, figs. 2 and 5; cat. no. 3, fig. 5; cat. no. 6, fig. 1; cat. no. 11, fig. 2; cat. no. 15, fig. 2; cat. no. 16, fig. 1; cat. no. 19, fig. 1; cat. nos. 25-26, fig. 4; cat. no. 29, fig. 3; cat. no. 30, fig. 5; cat. no. 35, fig. 2; cat. no. 39, fig. 4; cat. no. 45, figs. 2 and 4; cat. no. 46, fig. 3; cat. no. 48, fig. 4; cat. no. 53, fig. 7; cat. no. 56, fig. 2; cat. no. 57, fig. 2; cat. no. 58, fig. 2; cat. no. 67, fig. 2
Rijksmuseum Nederlands Scheepvaart Museum: cat. no. 50, fig. 4
Rijksprentenkabinet: Buijsen, fig. 4; cat. no. 2, fig. 4; cat. no. 3, fig. 6; cat. no. 8, fig. 5; cat. no. 9, figs. 2 and 3; cat. no. 11, fig. 5; cat. no. 13, figs. 3 and 5; cat. no. 14, fig. 4; cat. no. 17, fig. 4; cat. no. 18, fig. 4; cat. no. 21, fig. 1; cat. no. 23, fig. 1; cat. no. 24, fig. 1; cat. no. 27, fig. 2; cat. no. 29, fig. 2; cat. no. 39, figs. 3 and 4; cat. no. 45, fig. 3; cat. no. 46, fig. 4; cat. no. 57, fig. 6; cat. no. 58, fig. 1; cat. no. 61, figs. 5 and 6; cat. no. 63, figs. 2 and 3; cat. no. 64, figs. 1 and 5
Stichting Lichtbeelden Instituut, Rijksakademie van Beeldende Kunsten: cat. no. 6, fig. 2
Stichting Museum van Loon: cat. no. 45, fig. 1
Antwerp
Koninklijk Museum voor Schone Kunsten: cat. no. 56, fig. 3
Museum Plantin Moretus en Prentenkabinet: cat. no. 43, fig. 6
Arlington, Va.
Private collection: cat. no. 46
Baltimore, Md.
Baltimore Museum of Art: cat. no. 69, fig. 1
Berlin
Jagdschloss Grunewald: cat. no. 57, fig. 7
Nationalgalerie: Introduction, fig. 3
Staatliche Museen, Gemäldegalerie: cat. no. 14, fig. 2
Birmingham
The Barber Institute of Fine Arts: cat. no. 61, fig. 3
Blair Atholl
Blair Castle, collection Duke of Atholl: cat. no. 59, fig. 1
Bloomington, Ind.
Indiana University Art Museum: Kuretsky, fig. 17
Den Bosch
Noordbrabants Museum: cat. no. 30, fig. 4
Boston, Mass.
Collection George and Maida Abrams: Sutton, figs. 13 and 14
Isabella Stewart Gardner Museum: Liedtke, fig. 23; cat. no. 5, fig. 1
Medical Library in the Francis A. Countway Library of Medicine: Liedtke, fig. 2
Museum of Fine Arts: Liedtke, fig. 7; cat. no. 5; Sutton, fig. 1
Private collection: Sutton, fig. 20
Bremen
Kunsthalle: cat. no. 72, fig. 3

Brunswick
Herzog Anton Ulrich-Museum: cat. no. 18, fig. 3; cat. no. 39, fig. 1
Brunswick, Maine
Bowdoin College Museum of Art: Kuretsky, figs. 3 and 7
Brussels
Musées royaux des beaux-arts: cat. no. 60, fig. 1
Budapest
Szépművészeti Múzeum: cat. no. 21, fig. 3
Burlington, Vt.
The Robert Hull Fleming Museum, University of Vermont: Kuretsky, fig. 13
Cambridge, Mass.
Harvard University Art Museums: Kuretsky, fig. 10; cat. no. 30; cat. no. 64
Harvard University, The Houghton Library: Kuretsky, fig. 11
Champaign-Urbana, Ill.
Krannert Art Museum, University of Illinois: Kuretsky, fig. 14; cat. no. 7
Chantilly
Musée Condé: cat. no. 54, fig. 5
Chicago
The Art Institute of Chicago: cat. no. 57
Cincinnati, Ohio
Cincinnati Art Museum: cat. no. 10, fig. 5
The Taft Museum: Liedtke, fig. 33; cat. no. 51 and fig. 1
Cleveland, Ohio
The Cleveland Museum of Art: cat. no. 7, fig. 2; cat. no. 15, fig. 1; cat. no. 36; cat. no. 61
Collinsburgh
Collection Dowager Crawford and Balcarres: cat. no. 55, fig. 5
Cooperstown, N.Y.
New York State Historical Association: Liedtke, fig. 13
Copenhagen
Kongelige Bibliotek: cat. no. 50, fig. 5
Coral Gables, Fla.
Private collection: cat. no. 65; cat. no. 71
Darmstadt
Hessisches Landesmuseum: cat. no. 39, fig. 2
Dayton, Ohio
The Dayton Art Institute: cat. no. 9
Detroit, Mich.
The Detroit Institute of Arts: cat. no. 11; cat. no. 37, fig. 1; cat. no. 70
Dordrecht
Dordrechts Museum: cat. no. 9, fig. 6
Dresden
Staatliche Kunstsammlungen, Gemäldegalerie: cat. no. 6, fig. 4; cat. no. 13, fig. 6; cat. no. 16, fig. 2; cat. no. 21, fig. 2
Dublin
National Gallery of Ireland: cat. no. 22, fig. 1; cat. no. 54, fig. 2
Edinburgh
National Gallery of Scotland: cat. no. 38, fig. 2
Florence
Galleria degli Uffizi: cat. no. 64, fig. 2
Florida
Private collection: Sutton, figs. 12 and 17

The Metropolitan Museum of Art: Liedtke, figs. 1, 4, 6, 11, 16, 19, 21, 26, and 35; Buijsen, figs. 1 and 14; cat. no. 8; cat. no. 19; cat. no. 51, fig. 2; cat. no. 52; cat. no. 69

Private collection: cat. no. 9; cat. no. 37

The Pierpont Morgan Library: cat. no. 55, fig. 3

UPI / Bettman Archive: Liedtke, fig. 38

Norfolk, Va.

Collection Mr. and Mrs. George M. Kaufman: Sutton, fig. 6; cat. no. 31; cat. no. 39

Northampton, Mass.

Smith College Museum of Art: Kuretsky, fig. 9; cat. no. 15

Nottingham

City Art Museum: cat. no. 48, fig. 2

Nuremberg

Germanisches Nationalmuseum: cat. no. 16, fig. 3

Oberlin, Ohio

Allen Memorial Art Museum, Oberlin College: cat. no. 64

Oldenburg

Landesbibliothek: cat. no. 22, fig. 2

Oxford

Ashmolean Museum: cat. no. 1, figs. 1 and 4; cat. no. 3, fig. 4; cat. no. 7, fig. 3

Ottawa, Ont.

National Gallery of Canada: cat. no. 32, fig. 3

Paris

Bibliothèque Nationale: cat. no. 47, fig. 2

Collection heirs Edmond Baron de Rothschild: cat. no. 34, fig. 1

Collection heirs Robert Baron de Rothschild: cat. no. 51, figs. 3 and 4

Collection Stephan Higgons: cat. no. 22, fig. 4

Fondation Custodia: cat. no. 38, fig. 3

Musée du Louvre: cat. no. 8, fig. 4; cat. no. 32, fig. 2; cat. no. 73, fig. 3

Pasadena, Calif.

Norton Simon Museum, The Norton Simon Foundation: Sutton, fig. 3

Pennsylvania

Heinz Family Collection: Sutton, fig. 8

Philadelphia, Pa.

The Pennsylvania Academy of the Fine Arts: Liedtke, fig. 10

Philadelphia Museum of Art: Liedtke, fig. 9; cat. no. 41; cat. no. 49; cat. no. 60; cat. no. 70, fig. 5

Pittsburgh, Pa.

Frick Art Museum: Liedtke, fig. 25

Polesden Lacey

Polesden Lacey (The National Trust): cat. no. 35, fig. 3

Poughkeepsie, N.Y.

Vassar College Art Gallery: Kuretsky, fig. 8; cat. no. 16

Vassar College Library: Kuretsky, fig. 6

Prague

Národní Galeri: cat. no. 18, fig. 6

Princeton, N.J.

The Art Museum, Princeton University: Kuretsky, fig. 2; cat. no. 13, fig. 2

Collection Mrs. Piasecka Johnson: Buijsen, fig. 16

Providence, R.I.

Museum of Art, Rhode Island School of Design: Kuretsky, fig. 1; cat. no. 21

Raleigh, N.C.

North Carolina Museum of Art: cat. no. 55

Richmond, Va.

Virginia Museum of Fine Arts: cat. no. 36, fig. 3; cat. no. 45

Rotterdam

Historisch Museum, Stichting Atlas van Stolk: cat. no. 30, fig. 6

Museum Boymans-van Beuningen: cat. no. 2, fig. 6; cat. no. 18, fig. 2; cat. no. 36, fig. 1; cat. no. 43, fig. 5c; cat. no. 58, fig. 4; cat. no. 65, fig. 1; cat. no. 66, fig. 4; cat. no. 70, fig. 4

Saint Louis, Mo.

The Saint Louis Art Museum: cat. no. 28; cat. no. 33 and fig. 1

San Diego, Calif.

Timken Art Gallery, Putnam Foundation: cat. no. 42

San Francisco, Calif.

The Fine Arts Museums of San Francisco: cat. no. 1; cat. no. 34; cat. no. 43 and fig. 5a; cat. no. 50; cat. no. 63, fig. 1

Sarah Ferris Cowles 1941 Trust: cat. no. 4

Santa Monica, Calif.

The Resource Collections of the Getty Center for the History of Art and the Humanities: cat. no. 33, figs. 3, 4, and 5

Sarasota, Fla.

The John and Mable Ringling Museum of Art: cat. no. 40 and fig. 1; cat. no. 48

Schwerin

Staatliches Museum: cat. no. 2, fig. 3; cat. no. 6, fig. 5; cat. no. 18, fig. 3

Solingen

Galerie Müllenmeister: cat. no. 66, fig. 3

Southampton, N.Y.

Parrish Art Museum: Liedtke, fig. 20

Stockholm

Nationalmuseum: cat. no. 6, fig. 6

Sussex

Petworth House (The National Trust): cat. no. 52, fig. 1

Toledo, Ohio

The Toledo Museum of Art: cat. no. 10; cat. no. 29

Toronto, Ont.

Art Gallery of Ontario: cat. no. 15, fig. 4

Utrecht

Centraal Museum: cat. no. 32, fig. 2

Gemeentearchief: cat. no. 24, figs. 3, 4, 5, and 6

Kunsthistorisch Instituut: cat. no. 22, fig. 3; cat. no. 39, fig. 5; cat. no. 52, figs. 2 and 4; cat. no. 70, fig. 3

Versailles

Musée National du Château de Versailles et des Trianons: cat. no. 72, fig. 4

Vienna

Akademie der bildenden Künste: cat. no. 69, fig. 2

Graphische Sammlung Albertina: cat. no. 8, fig. 2; cat. no. 14, fig. 5; cat. no. 40, fig. 3; cat. no. 68, fig. 3; cat. no. 73, fig. 2

Waddesdon

Waddesdon Manor (The National Trust): cat. no. 10, fig. 4; cat. no. 17, fig. 2

Warsaw

Muzeum Narodowe: cat. no. 61, fig. 4

Washington, D.C.

The Corcoran Gallery of Art: Liedtke, figs. 8 and 12; cat. no. 23

National Gallery of Art: Liedtke, figs. 17, 29, and 30; Buijsen, fig. 12; Introduction, fig. 1; cat. no. 17; cat. no. 35; cat. no. 47; cat. no. 53 and fig. 6; cat. no. 59; cat. no. 67

National Museum of American Art, Smithsonian Institution: Liedtke, fig. 15

Weimar

Schlossmuseum: cat. no. 8, fig. 3

West Coast

Private collection: Sutton, figs. 18 and 19

Windsor Castle

Collection Her Majesty the Queen: cat. no. 9, fig. 5

Worcester, Mass.

Worcester Art Museum: Liedtke, figs. 3 and 5; cat. no. 2; cat. no. 54, fig. 4

Zwolle

Rijksarchief in de Provincie Overijssel: cat. no. 32, fig. 5

ISBN 90 6630 253 4 (paperback)
ISBN 90 6630 244 5 (hard cover)

Design
Hans Bockting / Toula Antonakos, UNA, Amsterdam

Typesetting and printing
Waanders Printers, Zwolle
Text set in Baskerville 8.6 / 12 point on Linotronic

Lithography
Litho Twente International, Enschede

Binding
De Ruiter, Zwolle

Cover
Johannes Vermeer, *A Girl Writing a Letter* (detail), cat. no. 67,
National Gallery of Art, Washington, D.C.
Willem and Cornelis(?) van de Velde, *An English Man-of-War* at Anchor
(detail), cat. no. 65, private collection, Coral Gables, Fla.
Rembrandt, *Portrait of Joris de Caulerij* (detail), cat. no. 50,
The Fine Arts Museums of San Francisco, Calif.

Frontispiece
Matthias Stomer, *Lot Leaving Sodom* (detail), cat. no. 62,
Bob Jones University Collection, Greenville, N.C.